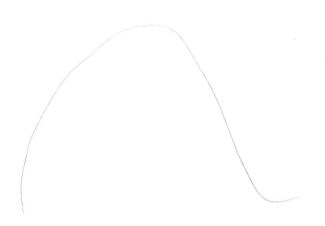

MANAGING
HUMAN RESOURCES

Through Strategic Partnerships 9e

Susan E. Jackson
Rutgers University

Randall S. Schuler
Rutgers University

THOMSON
★
SOUTH-WESTERN

Australia · Canada · Mexico · Singapore · Spain · United Kingdom · United States

THOMSON
™
SOUTH-WESTERN

Managing Human Resources Through Strategic Partnerships, Ninth Edition
Susan E. Jackson and Randall W. Schuler

VP/Editorial Director:
Jack W. Calhoun

VP/Editor-in-Chief:
Dave Shaut

Senior Publisher:
Melissa S. Acuña

Acquisitions Editor:
Joe Sabatino

Developmental Editor:
Mardell Toomey

Marketing Manager:
Jaquelyn Carrillo

Production Editor:
Chris Sears

Manager of Technology, Editorial:
Karen Schaffer

Technology Project Editor:
Kristen Meere

Web Coordinator:
Scott Cook

Manufacturing Coordinator:
Diane Lohman

Production House:
Buuji, Inc.

Printer:
Quebecor World
Versailles, KY

Art Director:
Anne Marie Rekow

Internal Designer:
Jen2 Design

Cover Designer:
Anne Marie Rekow

Cover Images:
© Photodisc

Photo Manager:
Deanna Ettinger

Library of Congress Control Number:
2004113136

For more information about our products,
contact us at:
Thomson Learning Academic Resource
Center
1-800-423-0563

Thomson Higher Education
5191 Natorp Boulevard
Mason, OH 45040
USA

Asia (including India)
Thomson Learning
5 Shenton Way
#01-01 UIC Building
Singapore 068808

Australia/New Zealand
Thomson Learning Australia
102 Dodds Street
Southbank, Victoria 3006
Australia

Canada
Thomson Nelson
1120 Birchmount Road
Toronto, Ontario
M1K 5G4
Canada

Latin America
Thomson Learning
Seneca, 53
Colonia Polanco
11560 Mexico
D.F. Mexico

UK/Europe/Middle East/Africa
Thomson Learning
High Holborn House
50/51 Bedford Row
London WC1R 4LR
United Kingdom

Spain (including Portugal)
Thomson Paraninfo
Calle Magallanes, 25
28015 Madrid, Spain

brief contents

contents

chapter 2

Understanding the External
and Organizational Environments   39

chapter 3

Ensuring Fair Treatment and Legal Compliance   81

chapter 4

HR Planning for Alignment and Change   127

chapter 5

Using Job Analysis and Competency Modeling   173

chapter 6

Recruiting and Retaining Qualified Employees 215

chapter 7

Selecting Employees to Fit the Job and the Organization   261

chapter 8

Training and Developing a Competitive Workforce   309

chapter 9

Developing an Approach to Total Compensation   361

chapter 10

Measuring Performance and Providing Feedback   407

chapter 11

Using Performance-Based Pay to Enhance Motivation

chapter 12

Providing Benefits and Services   501

chapter 13

Promoting Workplace Safety and Health   539

chapter 14

Understanding Unionization and Collective Bargaining

577

Managers from the very largest multinational firms to the smallest domestic firms claim that managing people effectively is vital to success in today's highly competitive marketplace. "The relationships we have with our people and the culture of our company is our most sustainable competitive advantage," says Howard Schultz, chair of Starbucks. According to Mike Eskew, CEO of UPS, "Our business model is based largely on driving efficiencies and economies of scale while encouraging our people."

Managing Human Resources Through Strategic Partnerships, Ninth Edition, offers a detailed picture of how successful companies manage human resources in order to compete effectively in a dynamic, global environment. Because organizations differ from each other in so many ways—including their locations, competitive strategies, products and services, and corporate cultures—we use many different companies to illustrate how businesses are addressing the challenge of managing human resources effectively. Examples of companies in many different industries include Southwest Airlines, Continental, Lincoln Electric, IBM, Cisco, SAS Institute, Bayer, MetLife, Starbucks, GE, Levi Strauss, Mayo Clinic, Cirque du Soleil, Cendant Mortgage, UPS, Dell, Toyota, Coca-Cola, Disney, Weyerhaeuser, FedEx, The Ritz-Carlton, Owens Corning, and many, many others. By combining a respect for established principles of human resource management with a willingness to experiment and try new approaches, these companies succeed year after year.

THE STRATEGIC PARTNERSHIPS PERSPECTIVE FOR MANAGING HUMAN RESOURCES

The task of managing human resources includes all the activities that organizations use to affect the behaviors of all the people who work for them. Because the behaviors of employees influence profitability, customer satisfaction, and a variety of other important indicators of organizational effectiveness, managing human resources is a key strategic challenge. To explain how organizations meet this challenge, this book uses the "strategic partnerships" perspective.

The strategic partnerships perspective is summarized in Exhibit 1.3 on page 14. At the center of the exhibit are human resource management (HRM) activities, including both the formal policies of the organization and the actual daily practices that people experience. Most chapters in this book focus on describing specific HRM activities, such as recruitment, training, performance management, compensation, and so on. Together, these activities form the organization's human resource management system. An effective system supports the organization's efforts to satisfy its key stakeholders. Not all HRM systems are alike, however. As Exhibit 1.3 shows, each organization's approach to managing human resources is characteristic of the particular organization and the external environment in which that organization operates.

ALIGNING HRM PRACTICES WITH THE EXTERNAL AND ORGANIZATIONAL ENVIRONMENTS

If you have worked in more than one organization, you know from experience that there are many different approaches to managing human resources. Some employers are highly selective in whom they hire, while others seem to hire anyone who walks in the door. Some provide extensive training to employees, while others let new hires sink or swim. Some pay well and offer large bonuses; others don't. Many of these differences in how organizations manage people are due to differences in the environments of organizations. Rapid changes in technologies, as well as economic, political, and social conditions, mean that few organizations can effectively compete today by just using the old tried-and-true approaches of yesterday. Nor can they simply copy other organizations. As the best organizations realize, continuous change requires continuous learning.

Increasingly, the great companies—the "Most Admired" and the "Best Companies to Work For"—manage their human resources based upon an understanding of the company and its environment. In order to recruit the right people with the right competencies and keep these people motivated to do their best work, managers and HR professionals alike need to understand the demands and nature of the business. A computer company that competes by continually offering innovative new products and services is likely to manage people differently than a retailer that competes by offering low-cost goods, or a manufacturer that competes by offering the best quality possible. Furthermore, each of these companies may adopt a different approach during good economic times than when the economy is not performing well. Managing human resources with this understanding of the nature of the organizational and external environments is central to managing human resources strategically.

SATISFYING MULTIPLE STAKEHOLDERS

Ultimately, an organization is effective only if it satisfies its major stakeholders. Effective organizations recognize that there's more to "success" than just a good bottom line (profits). The best companies balance their concerns over short-term, bottom-line results with the recognition that long-term success requires satisfying a variety of stakeholders. In addition to satisfying the demands of shareholders, the best organizations also address the concerns of employees and their families, customers, members of the local communities, government regulators, unions, public interest groups, and other organizations that they do business with—suppliers, distributors, alliance partners, and so on. These various stakeholders care deeply about how businesses conduct themselves, and in particular, how they treat their employees.

Throughout this textbook, we consider how different approaches to managing human resources can influence the way stakeholders view an organization—for better or for worse. Although it's not always possible to satisfy all stakeholders equally well, effective organizations make a habit of analyzing the available alternatives from multiple perspectives and seeking solutions that meet as many concerns as possible. The approach of developing human resource management policies and practices that are responsive to the concerns of an organization's key stakeholders is central to the strategic partnerships perspective adopted throughout this book.

THE HR TRIAD: MANAGERS, EMPLOYEES, AND HR PROFESSIONALS

Given the importance of addressing the concerns of many stakeholders, it is not surprising that another quality shared by successful companies is their recognition that managing human resources is everyone's responsibility. Naturally, HR professionals carry much of the responsibility for ensuring that the organization is applying the best knowledge available and conforming to legal requirements. But day in and day out, line managers and the employees themselves carry most of the responsibility for managing human resources. Managers translate the formal policies of the organization into daily practice. Employees, in turn, may be asked to participate in many HR practices, such as interviewing potential new hires, assisting with training, providing feedback on the performance of colleagues, suggesting improvements, and so on. This view—that managing human resources is a shared responsibility—is highlighted throughout this book in a feature called "The HR Triad." Within each chapter, it details the roles and responsibilities of HR professionals, managers, and employees.

FOUR SPECIAL CHALLENGES

As organizations strive to manage employees effectively, they face many challenges. Of these, we pay special attention to four that companies are currently struggling to understand and resolve:

- managing teams,
- managing diversity,
- managing globalization, and
- managing change.

Managing Teams.   Many managers now believe that improving the teamwork processes in their organization is essential for ensuring their organizations' success. Using team-based organizational structures, employers hope to achieve outcomes that could not be achieved by individuals working in isolation. But the payoff from teams isn't automatic. To create and orchestrate teams, people need to be selected, appraised, compensated, and trained in ways that reflect the unique relationships that develop between employees who work together. Examples of how organizations use HR practices to maximize team effectiveness are highlighted in the "Managing Teams" feature.

Managing Diversity.   Just as organizations have come to realize the benefits of teamwork, they have also discovered that the people who were being put into teams are more diverse than ever before. Today, organizations are finding that diversity management practices must be sensitive to issues of gender, ethnicity, personality, nationality, religion, sexual orientation, marital and family status, age, and various other unifying life experiences. The "Managing Diversity" feature in this book describes how effective organizations use HR practices to leverage employee diversity and create competitive advantage.

Managing Globalization. Throughout the 21st century, technological advances in transportation and communications will continue to support the growth of international commerce. As firms evolve from domestic to global, they face several challenges related to managing human resources. One challenge is learning how to manage people in different countries effectively. Differences in employment laws, labor market conditions, and national cultures mean that companies cannot assume that HR practices that work in the United States will be equally effective in other countries. Another challenge is to learn how to help employees around the world work together. Although detailed treatment of the issues raised by globalization is beyond the scope of this book, the "Managing Globalization" feature provides a glimpse of how some companies are addressing these challenges.

Managing Change. In most organizations, the current approach to managing people reflects both tradition and some new experimentation. A never-ending stream of new technologies makes possible new approaches to recruiting and training employees—not to mention the possibility of a virtual organization. Merging with another firm, spinning off a business unit, and flattening the hierarchical structure all involve changing who does what and how. A dynamic, changing environment means that even the most successful organizations can't rest on prior successes. Almost always, changes in business practices mean changes in HR practices, and examples of this are provided throughout this book in the "Managing Change" feature.

ORGANIZATION OF THIS BOOK

The many topics discussed in this book are organized according to the strategic partnerships perspective illustrated in Exhibit 1.3. We begin by discussing the "big picture," then we discuss each of the HR activities listed at the center of the exhibit, and finally we wrap up with a discussion of the HR profession.

THE BIG PICTURE

Chapter 1 describes each component of the strategic partnerships perspective shown in Exhibit 1.3. This important chapter provides an orientation for thinking about why it is so important—and difficult—for organizations to develop effective HR policies and practices. Then Chapters 2 and 3 describe in more detail the external and organizational environments, including globalization, the changing labor market, new technologies, restructuring due to mergers and acquisitions, and employment laws and regulations. In these chapters we also describe the organizational environment, focusing on competitive strategies, internal structures, corporate cultures and employees' views of what constitutes fair employment practices. As these chapters make clear, managing human resources effectively starts at the top of the organization with leaders who understand the importance of people and are committed to addressing the needs of their employees.

Specific HR Activities

Having described the environment that shapes how companies manage their human resources, we then turn to descriptions of the specific HR policies and practices that organizations use to manage their workforces. An effective HRM system requires planning and coordination as well as continual evaluation and readjustment. Chapter 4 describes how strategic planning and HR planning together can be used to align HR practices with conditions in the global and organizational environments. HR planning also serves to align the various HR activities with each other. Chapter 5 describes how job analysis and competency modeling can be used to develop an understanding of the work and the competencies employees need in order to maximize their performance in current jobs as well as their longer-term success.

To get work done, organizations need to attract people to apply for jobs and retain those who do their jobs well. Chapter 6 describes how companies recruit applicants to apply for job openings and some of the ways they can reduce unwanted turnover. After applicants have applied for a position, but before they are made a job offer, the process of selection occurs. As described in Chapter 7, employers want to select employees who will be able and willing to learn new tasks and continually adapt to changing conditions. They also want employees who fit well with the organizational culture.

With rapid changes in job requirements, existing employees must be both willing and able to develop new competencies, become proficient in new jobs, and even change their occupations. Chapter 8 describes training and development practices that enable employees to develop themselves and remain employable despite rapid changes in the world of work.

Employees work in exchange for compensation, whether monetary or otherwise. A total compensation package typically includes base wages or salary, some form of incentive pay, and various types of benefits. Chapter 9 describes how organizations design the total compensation package. To ensure that employees perform satisfactorily and receive appropriate compensation, performance must be measured and employees must receive usable feedback and the support needed to identify and correct performance deficiencies. When appropriate performance standards, measures, and feedback are provided, capable employees become a high-performance workforce. Chapter 10 describes principles for performance measurement and feedback and sets the stage for a discussion of using rewards to further motivate employees. Then Chapter 11 describes the use of incentives, bonuses, and other forms of rewards that employers offer to motivate employees to perform at their peak.

The best companies often become targets for recruitment by competitors. Offering innovative benefits packages and employee services that address a wide array of employees' concerns is one tactic for warding off such poaching, as described in Chapter 12. In addition to the benefits that employers offer voluntarily, Chapter 12 describes benefits required by law.

Chapter 13 focuses on what employers can do to ensure that the workplace is safe and that employees are healthy. Exposure to toxic chemicals and dangerous equipment remains a concern in some work environments, but more often air quality and ergonomic concerns top the agenda. Increasing concern about violence in the workplace is another unfortunate development described in Chapter 13.

Chapter 14 addresses the current state of unionization and collective bargaining. Because unions have maintained their strength in many other countries, they play a vital role in companies that strive to be globally competitive and profitable.

THE HR PROFESSION

The design and implementation of effective HRM systems requires substantial expertise. Although line managers from all areas of an organization must also be involved in the process, professional HR knowledge is essential. Appendix A specifically addresses readers who wish to pursue a career in human resource management, working either as an HR staff member within an organization or as an external consultant. It covers the competencies you will need to succeed in this field, and the professional and ethical standards that exist as described by the Society for Human Resource Management, the largest professional organization in the United States for HR professionals. It also provides details about the salaries, bonuses, and incentives for HR professionals in a variety of HR positions.

FEATURES OF THIS EDITION

We have already referred to a few features that appear throughout this book, but others have yet to be mentioned. Following are descriptions of all the special features that we use to reinforce key ideas and bring the topic of managing human resources to life.

COMPANY EXAMPLES

As an introduction to each chapter, we provide a brief company example that illustrates the strategic importance of the HR activity to be discussed in the chapter. This opening example and many other company examples are used throughout the chapter to illustrate basic principles and to show how companies use HR activities to gain a competitive advantage. Also in each chapter you will see many examples that illustrate how some of the best and most admired companies manage human resources to deal with the special challenges of today—Managing Teams, Managing Diversity, Managing Globalization, and Managing Change. By the end of each chapter, you will come to know many companies and how they manage their human resources in some detail.

The company examples reinforce two important lessons. First, successful companies follow well-established principles for managing human resources, and second, they also are willing to experiment with new ideas in order to improve upon what is known. Through these examples, we hope to convince readers that managing human resources effectively requires mastering what is known and then having the confidence to venture into the unknown.

THE HR TRIAD

The HR Triad feature summarizes the key points and highlights the role that each member of the triad plays in designing and implementing effective HR policies and practices. It appears near the beginning of each chapter and provides a quick preview of the key topics discussed in the chapter. It also serves to reinforce the need for HR professionals, managers, and all other employees to work together in order to ensure the effectiveness of an organization's HRM system.

MARGIN NOTES

Throughout the chapters, margin notes reinforce and extend key ideas. The *fast facts* offer tidbits of information that may be particularly interesting and useful. The *quotations* illustrate the perspectives of real managers, HR professionals, and other employees. We selected some quotes because the people who spoke them are well-known executives or public figures. Other quotes come from typical employees. These employees may not be well-known, but they know what organizational life is like and are willing to tell it like it is. Although you may not recognize all the names, we think you'll agree that their insights are worth remembering.

TERMS TO REMEMBER

Throughout the chapters, key terms are shown in bold and defined in italic. A complete list of all the key terms described in the chapter is provided at the end of the chapter. The list of key terms makes it easy for you to check whether you recall and understand the key vocabulary associated with the content of the chapter. If you see a term you aren't sure about, you may want to go back and review that section of the chapter again, or ask the instructor to help clarify the meaning for you.

DISCUSSION QUESTIONS

The discussion questions at the end of each chapter seek to determine your understanding of the material found in the chapter. Discussion questions challenge you to think critically about the material and consider its implications for managing human resources. By the time you finish reading and studying all the chapters, you should know a great deal about basic principles for managing human resources, about what particular companies are doing today, and about what companies should be preparing to do as they face the future.

PROJECTS TO EXTEND YOUR LEARNING

To further enrich your understanding, each chapter includes supplemental projects:

- Integration and Application
- Exploring the Internet
- Experiential Activity

Integration and Application.   The Integration and Application project focuses your attention on the human resource management activities used by the two companies portrayed in the end-of-text integrative cases—Lincoln Electric and Southwest Airlines. By comparing and contrasting how these two companies manage their human resources, you will gain a deeper understanding of how the characteristics of an organization and the organization's external environment influence its approach to managing human resources.

Exploring the Internet.   The project called Exploring the Internet directs you to explore several useful Internet resources that can be used to investigate companies, become familiar with relevant professional associations and the services they offer, find out about the products and services offered by HR consultants and vendors, and in many other ways enrich your understanding of managing human resources effectively.

Experiential Activity.   A new feature in this ninth edition, the Experiential Activity at the end of each chapter, asks you to extend your learning about the topics covered in the chapter. Some experiential activities require you to complete a short questionnaire that can be used to gauge your own knowledge and improve your understanding of your own attitudes about current issues. Some activities provide interview questions that you can use to learn more about the perspective of managers and employees in various types of work settings. Some activities provide suggestions for discussions to hold with classmates as a means for learning from them. And some activities require you to develop a personal action plan. In all cases, the goal is to challenge you to grapple with the practical implications of the material covered in the chapter.

END-OF-CHAPTER CASES

A case at the end of each chapter offers challenge and variety. It is up to you to analyze what is going on and suggest improvements. In some instances, discussion questions are presented to guide your thinking; in other instances, you are on your own to determine the issues most relevant to the material in the chapter. Many of the companies in these cases are disguised, but their problems and challenges are real and they are likely to be familiar to many experienced managers.

ENDNOTE CITATIONS

At the end of each chapter, you will find an extensive list of endnotes, which provide full citations to the materials used in preparing the chapter. For anyone wishing to dig deeper into the content of the chapter, the endnotes are an excellent starting point. Included are citations to the latest academic research as well as citations for coverage that has appeared in the public press and relevant Internet addresses.

End-of-Text Integrative Cases

At the end of the textbook we present two longer cases. They describe various human resource activities at Lincoln Electric and Southwest Airlines. By studying each case, you should gain an appreciation for how the many aspects of human resource management described throughout the text work together as a total system. By necessity, any particular chapter focuses on only one small piece of the total HR puzzle. In the real world, the pieces must fit together into a meaningful whole. The end-of-text integrative cases illustrate two very different HRM systems found in two successful organizations. These cases provide rather detailed examples of how two firms are meeting the challenges of managing human resources through strategic partnerships.

Appendices

There are two special appendices. Appendix A describes the HR manager position in detail. This includes information about competencies, salaries, and responsibilities as described earlier. Appendix B presents some elementary statistics that are important in managing human resources effectively.

SUPPORT MATERIALS

We designed a comprehensive set of support materials to guide instructors and students through the many issues involved in managing human resources effectively. Supplementary materials for *Managing Human Resources Through Strategic Partnerships*, Ninth Edition, include the following.

Instructor's Manual with Test Bank

The instructor's manual and test bank were prepared by Jane E. Barnes of Meredith College. The instructor's manual includes recapped learning objectives, chapter overviews, and lecture material that is enhanced with summaries of company vignettes and other special features, including end-of-chapter case notes. Answers to all review and discussion questions are included. Most chapters also include additional experiential and skill-building exercises. The test bank includes approximately 40 multiple-choice questions, 25 true-false questions, and 5 essay questions for each chapter.

ExamView Testing Software

ExamView is a computerized version of the printed test bank that allows instructors to easily create customized tests for their students.

Instructor's Resource CD-ROM (IRCD)

The instructor's resource CD-ROM includes the instructor's manual, test bank, and ExamView electronic test bank (see earlier descriptions) along with a PowerPoint® slide presentation. The PowerPoint slides, prepared by Charlie Cook, University of West Alabama, greatly enhance classroom lectures. The slides are designed to hold student interest and prompt questions that will help students learn.

TEACHING TRANSPARENCY ACETATES

Derived from the most useful exhibits found in the main text, transparencies provide visual support for lectures.

VIDEO PACKAGE

A brand-new video features companies with innovative HR practices, many of which are Optimas Award winners, recognized for their excellence in HR practices. All video content is closely tied to contemporary HR management issues and concepts within the text. A video guide within the instructor's manual provides suggestions for incorporating the video in the classroom.

TEXTBOOK WEBSITE

The URL for the textbook website is http://jackson.swlearning.com. When you adopt *Managing Human Resources Through Strategic Partnerships*, Ninth Edition, you and your students will have access to a rich array of teaching and learning resources that you won't find anywhere else. This outstanding site features chapter-by-chapter online tutorial quizzes, chapter outlines, chapter reviews, chapter-by-chapter Web links, flashcards, and more!

ACKNOWLEDGMENTS

As with the previous editions, many fine individuals were critical to the completion of the final product. They include Paul Buller at Gonzaga University; Paul Adler at the University of Southern California; Hugh Scullion at Strathclyde University in Glasgow, Scotland; Paul Sparrow at Manchester Business School in England; Shimon Dolan at ESADE in Barcelona, Spain; Stuart Youngblood at Texas Christian University; Gary Florkowski at the University of Pittsburgh; Bill Todor at The Ohio State University; Vandra Huber at the University of Washington; John Slocum at Southern Methodist University; Lynn Shore at Georgia State University; Mary Ahmed at Grand Forks; Ed Lawler at the Center for Effective Organizations, University of Southern California; Gerold Frick at Fachhochschule Aalen; Lynda Gratton and Nigel Nicholson at the London Business School; Chris Brewster at the Henley Management College near London; Shaun Tyson at the Cranfield Management School; Michael Poole at the Cardiff Business School; Paul Stonham at the European School of Management, Oxford; Jan Krulis-Randa and Bruno Staffelbach at the University of Zürich; Albert Stähli and Julia Schirbach at the GSBA Zürich; Dennis Briscoe at the University of San Diego; Mark Mendenhall at the University of Tennessee, Chattanooga; Helen De Cieri and Denise Welch of Monash University; Yoram Zeira of Tel Aviv University; Dan Ondrack, the University of Toronto; Moshe Banai, Baruch College; Steve Kobrin, Wharton School; Steve Barnett, York University; Christian Scholz, University of Saarlandes; Pat Joynt, Henley Management College; Reijo Luostarinen, Helsinki School of Economics and Business Administration; Mickey Kavanagh, SUNY, Albany; Wayne Cascio, University of Colorado, Denver; Peter Dowling at the University of Canberra in Australia; Ricky Griffin,

Texas A&M University; Ed van Sluijs at GTIP in The Netherlands; and Dean Barbara Lee, John Burton, Mark Huselid, Jim Sesil, Dave Lepak, Charles Fay, and Paula Caliguiri at Rutgers University.

In their roles of reviewers and evaluators, the following individuals provided many valuable ideas and suggestions for changes and alterations, all of which we very much appreciated:

Wendy Boswell, Texas A&M University

James Browne, University of Southern Colorado

Barbara Cardeli-Arroyo, New York University

Gary Chaison, Clark University

John Cote, Baker College

Hyacinth Ezeamii, Albany State College

Bob Figler, University of Akron

Jenny M. Hoobler, Northern Illinois University

David Hudson, Spalding University

Glenn Johns, Cedarcrest College

Ron Karren, University of Massachusetts

J. N. Kondrasuk, University of Portland

Ken Kovach, University of Maryland at College Park

Mitchell Lambert, CUNY Brooklyn

Preston Lytle, Columbia Union College

Arthur Matthews, Cornell University

Gordon Morse, George Mason University

John Ogilvie, University of Hartford

Janet Oppedisano, Southern Connecticut University

David Ozag, Gettysburg College

Michael Wesson, Texas A&M

Several human resource managers and practicing line managers also contributed in many important ways to this ninth edition, particularly with examples and insights from their work experiences. They include Johan Julin for his extensive comments on Chapter 5, Mark Saxer, Libby Child, Mike Mitchell, Manfred Stania, Tom Kroeger, Doug Bray, Patricia Ryan, Georges Bächthold, Dick Fenton, Esther Craig, Ann Howard, Don Bohl, Bob Kenny, Jack Berry, Robert Joy, Paul Beddia, John Fulkerson, Cal Reynolds, Jon Wendenhof, Michael Losey, Debbie Cohen, Nick Blauweikel, Mike Loomans, Sandy Daemmrich, Jeffery Maynard, Lyle Steele, Rowland Stichweh, Bill Maki, Rick Sabo, Bruce Cable, Gil Fry, Bill Reffett, Jerry Laubenstein, Richard Hagan, Horace Parker, Steve Grossman, Paris Couturiaux, John Guthrie, and Paul Sartori.

The following individuals graciously provided case and exercise materials: George Cooley, Richie Freedman, Ari Ginsberg, Bruce Evans, Mitchell W. Fields, Hugh L. French Jr., Peter Cappelli, Marcia Miceli, Anne Crocker-Hefter, Stuart Youngblood, Ed Lawler, John Slocum, Jeff Lenn, Hrach Bedrosian, Kay Stratton, Bruce Kiene, Martin R. Moser, James W. Thacker, Arthur Sharplin, and Jerry Laubenstein.

The support, encouragement, and assistance of many individuals were vital to the production of this work. They include Elizabeth Douthitt, Stanford University; Ibraiz Tarique, Pace University; Aparna Joshi, University of Illinois; Jane E. Barnes, Meredith College; and Mila Lazarova, Simon Fraser University—all of whom used the eighth edition and offered us their feedback. Also, several people at Thomson Business & Professional Publishing deserve our special thanks for their help and support: Joe Sabatino, Senior Acquisitions Editor; Mardell Toomey, Senior Developmental Editor; Chris Sears, Production Editor; Jacquelyn Carrillo, Marketing Manager; Anne Marie Rekow, Art/Design Coordinator; and Kristen Meere, Media Developmental Editor. We also thank Sara Dovre Wudali, project manager at Buuji, Inc. for her dedication to the production of this edition. Without the professional assistance of all of these people, this book would not have been possible.

We also thank our colleagues who have worked so diligently to prepare the supporting materials that accompany this book: Jane E. Barnes at Meredith College who prepared the instructor's manual and the test bank; and Charlie Cook, University of West Alabama, who prepared the PowerPoint slide presentation.

Finally, we thank the many students who have used prior editions of this book. Their reactions to the book and related course materials, their unique insights into how organizations treat employees, and their suggestions for improvements in prior editions of this book have helped us develop our approach to teaching and to writing *Managing Human Resources Through Strategic Partnerships*.

Susan E. Jackson and Randall S. Schuler
Rutgers University and GSBA Zürich

chapter 1

Managing Human Resources Through Strategic Partnerships

Cisco Systems was founded in 1984 by Leonard Bosack and Sandy Lerner, a husband and wife team who invented a technology to link together separate computer systems at Stanford University. With venture funding from Don Valentine at Sequoia Capital and a new chief executive officer (CEO) in John Morridge, Cisco went public in 1990. By 2001, the company was ranked third on Fortune's list of the "100 Best Companies to Work for in America." It had more than 30,000 employees. Then the market for its products collapsed. The value of its stock decreased almost 80%! The value of the stock options held by many of the employees had been decimated. Cisco laid off 6,000 employees in 2001, yet voluntary turnover was only 8% in an industry that averages 30%. Despite a weak economy, slow sales, and virtually no hiring in 2003, its turnover rate declined to 2% and more than 50,000 applicants applied for jobs. Apparently Cisco is doing something that employees like.

   As part of its approach to managing human resources, Cisco espouses five core values: a dedication to customer success; innovation and learning; openness; teamwork; and doing more with less. These values are continually articulated by CEO John Chambers and reinforced—in the mission statement, human resource

1

(HR) policies and practices, and the company culture. Signaling the importance of customer satisfaction as a core value, Chambers personally reviews up to 15 critical accounts per day and often calls on customers himself. When it comes to openness and teamwork, employees applaud the company for giving them the straight scoop. Says account manager Kim Fisher, who passed up medical school to work for Cisco three and a half years ago, "You have a say in where the company's going and the vision. Where else can you have an impact at 25?" The way jobs are structured and managed reinforces culture and values. At the company's sales offices, no one "owns" a workspace: It is all "hot desks" or "nonterritorial" office space. The HR group ensures that these and other HR policies and practices are aligned with the business strategy and continually reinforced.[1]

THE STRATEGIC IMPORTANCE OF MANAGING HUMAN RESOURCES

"The industrial revolution was about economies of scale. The internet revolution will be about economies of skill and how you empower people."

John Chambers
CEO
Cisco Systems

Leaders such as John Chambers of Cisco Systems see human resources as assets that need to be managed conscientiously and in tune with his organization's needs. Tomorrow's most competitive organizations are working now to ensure they have available tomorrow and a decade from now employees who are eager and able to address key competitive challenges. Increasingly this means attracting and retaining superior talent and stimulating employees to perform at peak levels. When brainpower drives the business, as it does at Cisco Systems, then attracting and keeping great intellectual talent becomes a necessity. When customer service is important to the business, a key challenge is attracting and keeping employees who deliver ever-better service day in and day out even to the most difficult customers. Thus while many factors influence the success of a company, it is very difficult to succeed without managing human resources effectively.

Satisfying Multiple Stakeholders

"Chief executives should heed the interests of various stakeholders including shareholders, customers, suppliers, and the employees."

Sidney Harman
CEO
Harman International

Today, companies and society are saying that the success of an organization is determined by the evaluations of its multiple stakeholders. An organization's approach to managing human resources is central to its ability to satisfy its multiple stakeholders.

Stakeholders *are individuals or groups that have interests, rights, or ownership in an organization and its activities.* Stakeholders who have similar interests and rights are said to belong to the same stakeholder group. Customers, suppliers, employees, society, and other organizations are examples of stakeholders, as illustrated in Exhibit 1.1.

Stakeholders benefit from the organization's successes and can be harmed by its failures and mistakes. Similarly, the organization has an interest in maintaining the general well-being and effectiveness of key stakeholders. If one or more of the stakeholder groups breaks off their relationships with the organization, the organization suffers.

For any particular organization, some stakeholder groups may be relatively more important than others. The most important groups—the primary stakeholders—are those whose concerns the organization must address in order to ensure its own survival.[2] When success is defined as effectively serving the interests of these groups, their needs define a firm's fundamental objectives. These objectives, in turn, drive the organization's approaches to managing employees.

Ex 1.1   Stakeholders and Examples of Their Concerns

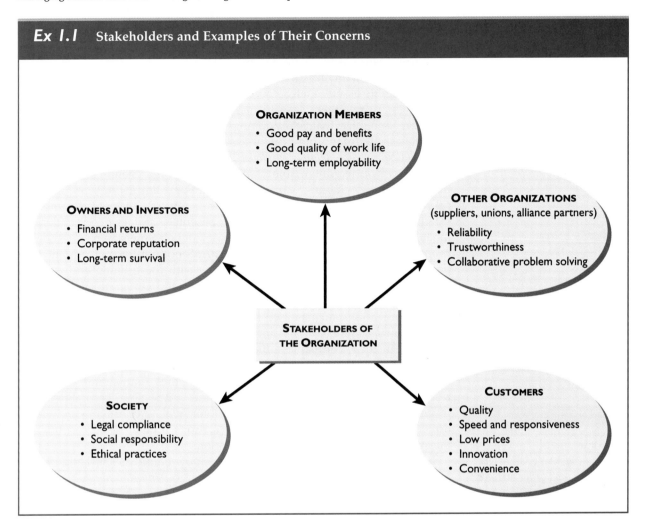

The principle that effective management requires attending to all relevant stakeholders is as true for managing human resources as for other management tasks. Human resource practices cannot be designed solely to meet the concerns of employees. Nor can they be designed by considering only their consequences for the bottom line. Organizations that are the most effective in managing people develop HRM systems that meet the needs of all key stakeholders. In order to develop a stakeholder-friendly approach to managing human resources, it is necessary to understand the concerns of each stakeholder group.

OWNERS AND INVESTORS

Most owners and investors invest their money in companies for financial reasons. At a minimum, owners and shareholders want to preserve their capital for later use, and ideally they want to experience a growth in their capital. To achieve these goals, their capital should be invested primarily in profitable companies.

The job of institutional investors, which is to make money by choosing which companies to investment in, has become increasingly complex as difficult-to-measure assets have become more important. In the old economy, investors focused on measuring tangible assets in order to determine a firm's value. Tangible assets, such as inventory, equipment, real estate, and financial assets are relatively easy to measure. In the new economy, however, investors recognize that many intangible assets can be just as valuable as tangible assets. **Intangible human assets** *include such things as reputation as an employer-of-choice, depth of employee talent and loyalty, and the firm's ability to innovate and change.* Intangible assets affect an organization's bottom line through complex chains of cause-and-effect. For example, suppose a chemical manufacturing firm uses training and a rewards program to improve safety and reduce accidents. As a result, absenteeism goes down and so do medical and insurance costs. Reduced costs and absenteeism result in better productivity—eventually improving the firm's bottom-line performance.[3] In this case, the cause-and-effect chain begins with the training and rewards programs, which have effects on absenteeism and costs, and finally these effects appear on the company's bottom-line financial indicators.

In organizations such as investment banks, consulting firms, and advertising agencies, there is almost nothing there except intangible human assets. Investing in these companies often means hoping that the best employees will continue working at and for the company.[4] As one study of initial public offering (IPO) companies showed, companies that attend to human resource management issues are rewarded with more favorable initial investor reactions as well as longer-term survival.[5] Accountants may have difficulty attaching monetary values to a firm's human resources, but this doesn't stop investors from paying attention.

Because intangible human assets such as how employees feel and behave can be used to predict financial performance,[6] business analysts pay attention to how people are being managed. For 20 years, the staff at *Fortune* magazine have conducted extensive interviews with employees in order to create their annual lists of "Best Companies" to work for.[7] To determine just how important happy workers were for achieving higher shareholder returns, *Fortune*'s research staff conducted one of the earliest efforts to look at this question. They studied the publicly traded firms on their 1987 list of "100 Best Companies to Work for in America." Shareholder returns for these 100 companies were compared to those of the Russell 3000, an index that includes comparable companies. The bottom line? If you invested $1,000 in the Russell 3000 in 1987, you would have had $3,976 in 1997; but if you had invested the same amount in the "100 Best Companies to Work for in America," you would have had $8,188 by 1997—more than twice as much.[8] Research such as this shows that it's possible for organizations to manage employees in ways that satisfy investors as well as employees.

Several other studies have shown that the approaches companies take to managing their human resources can translate into greater profitability, higher annual sales per employee (productivity), higher market value, and higher earnings-per-share growth.[9] Exhibit 1.2 illustrates the results from a study of several hundred companies. A survey was used to measure the companies' HR practices. These responses were then used to create a score of 0 to 100, which represented the extent to which the company's HR practices represented state-of-the-art knowledge. The performance of these companies was measured using financial accounting data. As the graph shows, companies with better HR practices experienced greater increases in market value per employee. That is, firms with the best human resource management systems were rewarded the most by investors.[10]

CUSTOMERS

Like Siebel Systems and many other firms, improving customer satisfaction is a primary means through which HR practices affect success. Creating new products, reducing costs, improving product quality, and improving service quality all are ways to improve customer satisfaction.[11] Whatever approach is used to satisfy customers, success depends on how employees are managed. Human resource executives understand this, and so do chief financial officers (CFOs). In fact, a survey of 200 CFOs revealed that 92% believed managing employees effectively has a great effect on customer satisfaction.[12]

The relationship between HR practices and customer satisfaction is explicit in the ways many companies manage their employees. To meet customers' demands for higher quality, companies such as Weyerhaeuser, Cisco Systems, Siebel Systems, Lincoln Electric, Southwest Airlines, and FedEx maintain an environment conducive to full participation and personal and organizational growth for their employees. When the internal climate of the organization is positive, with employees generally getting along well and

"First is our absolute commitment to 100% customer satisfaction. Instead of going off and engineering products and then trying to sell them, we talk to customers first, find out what they want, and then design the products and services that meet their need."

Tom Siebel
Former CEO
Siebel Systems

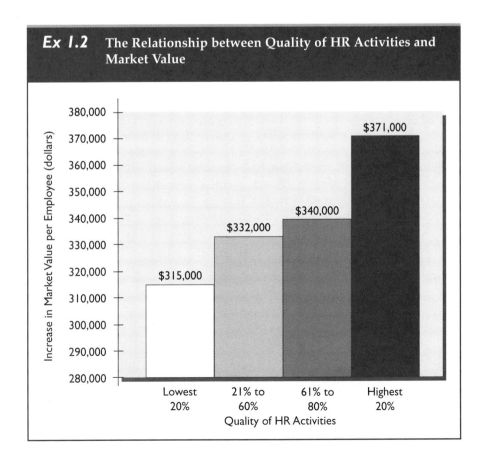

Ex 1.2 **The Relationship between Quality of HR Activities and Market Value**

Increase in Market Value per Employee (dollars)

- Lowest 20%: $315,000
- 21% to 60%: $332,000
- 61% to 80%: $340,000
- Highest 20%: $371,000

Quality of HR Activities

not leaving the company at too rapid a pace, customers report they're more satisfied and intend to return.[13]

Improving customer satisfaction often requires finding ways to improve the company's ability to understand the customer's perspective. For example, through its hiring practices, a company can make sure that the employees in a company are demographically similar to customers. The assumption is that communication improves when employees and customers share similar experiences. Such reasoning led American Express to recruit gay and lesbian financial advisers in order to improve service for gay and lesbian customers. They also sought to improve customer satisfaction among this group by educating financial advisers about the special needs of the gay and lesbian market.[14]

For Saks Fifth Avenue, the luxury retailer, giving customers excellent service means keeping sales employees engaged in their work. Saks conducted an employee survey to measure the importance of employee engagement and found that stores with greater employee engagement also had more satisfied customers. Vice president Jay Redman was convinced by the results of the study, "There absolutely is a correlation between employee engagement and customer engagement. We've seen 20 to 25% improvement in stores with great engagement." To engage employees, managers at Saks Fifth Avenue make a point of asking employees what they need to do their jobs, and following up with initiatives that address employees' concerns. "We've probably done 100 things over three years," explained Redman. As employee engagement went up, Saks saw increases in customer loyalty and sales.[15]

SOCIETY

For organizations such as public schools, nonprofit foundations, and government agencies, the concerns of owners—that is, taxpayers and contributors—often are essentially those of society at large. But for privately owned companies and those whose shares are publicly traded, the concerns of owners—that is, investors—may be quite different from those of society in general.

"We believe that the winning companies of this century will be those that not only increase shareholder value, but increase social and environmental value."

Carly Fiorina
Chair and CEO
Hewlett-Packard

Under free-market capitalism, the primary managerial obligation is to maximize shareholders' profits and their long-term interests. Nobel Prize–winning economist Milton Friedman is probably the best-known advocate of this approach.[16] Friedman argues that using resources in ways that do not clearly maximize investor interests amounts to spending the owners' money without their consent—and is equivalent to stealing. According to Friedman, a manager can judge whether a decision is right or wrong by considering its consequences for the company's economic needs and financial well-being. If it improves the financial bottom line, it's right, but if it detracts from the financial bottom line, it's wrong. Thus, for example, a company would be justified in hiring long-term welfare recipients if an analysis showed that this paid off given that government tax incentives and wage subsidies are available. But it could not justify that action simply by asserting that it's the right thing to do.

The average American rejects the idea that making money is the only role of business. In fact, socially responsible corporations are the more attractive alternative to prospective employees.[17] In other words, the best employers do more than simply obey the letter of the law—they seek to have a positive impact on society.

Legal Compliance. Codes of conduct for some aspects of business behavior take the form of formal laws, and many of these have implications for managing human resources. In addition, businesses are subject to regulation through several federal agencies and various state and city equal employment commissions and civil rights commissions. Finally, multinational corporations (MNCs) must be aware of the employment laws in other countries. By complying with legal regulations, firms establish their legitimacy and gain acceptance and support from the community. Ultimately, they increase their chances for long-term survival.[18] Because they affect virtually all human resource management activities, many different laws, regulations, and court decisions are described throughout this book, beginning with an overview in Chapter 3.

Community Relations. Formal laws and regulations establish relatively clear guidelines for how society expects a company to behave, but effective companies respond to more than simply these formal statements. They understand that the enactment of formal laws and regulations often lags behind public opinion by several years. Long before legislation is agreed to, communities communicate their expectations and attempt to hold organizations accountable for violations of those expectations. In turn, proactive organizations stay attuned to public opinion and use it as one source of information that may shape their own management practices. With heightened public interest in corporate social responsibility, many companies are discovering that they can't avoid having people evaluate how well they perform in this respect.[19]

FAST FACT When Cisco laid off 6,000 employees, it offered a unique severance package. Pink-slipped employees who agreed to work for one year at a local nonprofit organization were paid one-third of their salary plus benefits and stock options, and the right to be first in line for rehiring in the future.

A commitment to community involvement and development can have major implications for managing human resources. Voluntary labor is often a community's biggest need. Organizations that encourage employees to participate as volunteers help communities meet this need. For example, UPS has sponsored its Community Internship Program for nearly 40 years. As part of this four-week program, managers live in poor neighborhoods while working in soup kitchens and women's shelters. Being socially responsive in these and other ways has many implications for managing human resources, including

- the type of employees the company chooses to hire,
- the criteria used to evaluate their performance,
- the scheduling and coordinating of activities within work units, and
- compensation practices associated with paying employees for time spent in the community.

OTHER ORGANIZATIONS

Companies of all types are becoming increasingly interdependent with other organizations. Other organizations that can be considered major stakeholders include suppliers, unions, and alliance partners, among others.

Suppliers. Suppliers provide the resources a company needs to conduct its business. In addition to the capital of owners and investors, the resources needed by most companies include material and equipment, information, and people. Other companies usually supply material and equipment. Suppliers of people might include schools, the professional associations that serve specific occupational groups, state employment agencies, and companies that offer electronic recruiting services.

Unions. Unions may also serve as a supplier of people, but their role is much larger than this. Firms with employees who are represented by a union involve unions in joint discussions on issues such as improving productivity; outsourcing policies; and improving safety, compensation, benefits, and various other conditions of work. In recent years, union leaders and their members have moved away from their traditional adversarial relationship with management to a collaborative, problem-solving relationship. Despite this general trend, work slowdowns and strikes remain as threats to companies in which unions represent the employees. Such work disruptions often reach far beyond the firm itself. When strikes involve transportation or communications workers, the entire country feels their effects.

Alliance Partners. Through cooperative alliances with other firms, a company seeks to achieve goals that are common to all members of the alliance. Some alliances are formed to influence government actions. In New Jersey, for example, leaders from business, government, and labor organizations formed an alliance to address the government's approach to managing the state's transportation infrastructure (including roads, rivers, and rails). Research and development needs are another common reason for alliance formations. International Sematech is an example of a multilateral alliance that supports learning through collaborative research. Through joint participation, 13 semiconductor manufacturers from 7 countries share knowledge and expertise in ways that ultimately influence the entire industry.

Joint ventures represent yet another basis for forming alliances. When a bottle maker learned how to recycle plastic, it recognized the commercial opportunities of the technology. Subsequent discussions with suppliers, customers, and competitors about a collaborative venture eventually helped all the partners realize that the idea would require substantial investment in research and development. Out of this, a collaborative research network was born. Each company paid toward the research at a university and participated in quarterly board meetings. The research output became the venture's property, and all interested parties were assured licensing rights for a nominal fee.

Organizational Members (The Employees)

Organizational members are another key stakeholder group. Unlike the other stakeholders discussed previously, organizational members reside within the organization. Included in this group are *all* of the employees who have hold positions within the organization, including the CEO and top-level executives, other managers and supervisors, professionals and administrative specialists, line employees, part-time employees, and so on. Because they are such a diverse stakeholder group, they have a great variety of con-

"I don't want my tombstone to read, 'He shipped a billion parts of jeans.' I can sleep better at night knowing that the package we put together for our displaced people provided them with far more benefits than what is conventional. [Nevertheless], you have to have a financially viable business or all the words about values can ring hollow."

Robert D. Haas
Chair, Levi Strauss

cerns. Nevertheless, most members of this stakeholder group share concerns about pay and benefits, quality of work life, and employability.

Pay and Benefits. Most organizational members want to be paid well and they want to be paid fairly. For women, the desire to receive equal pay for equal work is among the most important workplace issues, according to a national survey of 40,000 women. Nevertheless, many women as well as men feel that their employers don't live up to this principle. Of nearly equal importance to fair pay is the desire for secure and affordable health insurance, paid sick leave, and assured pension and retirement benefits. Some people may be surprised that child-care issues are considerably less important than these other concerns for the majority of women surveyed.[20] In fact, it is precisely because people's attitudes can be difficult to estimate that progressive companies use surveys to monitor the concerns of organizational members. Human resource policies and practices can then be developed to address the most important concerns.

Quality of Work Life. Besides earning a good living, most employees also want to enjoy a good quality of life while on the job. Starbucks' Howard Schultz grew up knowing his father felt beaten down by his work. At Starbucks, Schultz strives to make sure that workers have self-esteem no matter what the nature of their jobs. Providing generous health insurance benefits for everyone— even part-timers—is part of strategy.[21] Many aspects of human resource management contribute to a good quality of working life, including

FAST FACT Starbucks is one of *Fortune*'s Best Companies to Work For. Each year it receives nearly one million job applications. Its turnover is about 7%.

- training and development to improve employees' skills and knowledge,
- job designs that allow employees to really use their knowledge and skills,
- management practices that give employees responsibility for important decisions,
- selection and promotion systems that ensure fair and equitable treatment,
- safe and healthy physical and psychological environments, and
- work organized around teams.

Such practices increase employee commitment, satisfaction, and feelings of empowerment, which in turn result in greater customer satisfaction.[22] In general, corporate cultures characterized by greater employee involvement and participation generate higher returns on sales and investments in subsequent years.[23]

FAST FACT J. M. Smucker is one of the Best Companies to Work For. It provides 70 hours of training per year to each employee.

Employability. In recent years, the changing economy and its effects on the workplace have introduced tremendous uncertainty, creating feelings of insecurity and anxiety for employees and their families. When IBM restructured its organization in the early 1990s, it terminated more than 100,000 employees. The company had long been known for its policy of job security, so employees were shocked when IBM replaced some of its managers with temporary people hired to finish ongoing projects.

Today, downsizing and layoffs are an accepted part of life in most large companies. Employees are no longer surprised when they occur. Nevertheless, security remains a concern for employees. To address employee's security concerns, companies like IBM now strive to develop a sense of *employment* security, not job security. Employment security increases when employees develop skills and knowledge that they need to be employable should they lose their current job. Feelings of employment security also improve when employers provide outplacement assistance as part of the severance package offered to laid-off workers.

CREATING WIN-WIN SITUATIONS

Clearly, the primary concerns of the stakeholder groups differ somewhat, and conflict among stakeholders is common. But shared interests aren't unusual either. Effective managers determine the interests of their multiple stakeholders and work with them to find a solution that addresses each set of objectives. More and more managers are beginning to understand that a company's human resource practices can either exacerbate apparent conflicts among their multiple stakeholders, or create synergies. Consider what happens during restructuring and downsizing. Decisions to reduce layers of management, sell off a poorly performing division, or outsource work to an overseas location usually are made to improve efficiency and profitability in order to satisfy shareholders. The employees who lose their jobs in the process are victims of the conflict between their need for employment and shareholders' desire for financial gain. However, when the compensation system is used to ensure that employees are owners themselves, managers and other employees may put more effort into finding a solution that minimizes employee displacements while also meeting the organization's financial goals.

In the chapters that follow, we argue that approaches to managing human resources can provide organizations with effective solutions to the challenge of how best to satisfy the objectives of its multiple stakeholders, even when the objectives of different stakeholders seem to conflict. In more cases than not, appropriate HR practices make it possible to create win-win situations. The approach of developing human resource management policies and practices that are responsive to the concerns of an organization's multiple stakeholders is what we mean by *Managing Human Resources through Strategic Partnerships.*

Creating human resource policies and practices to satisfy a company's multiple stakeholders is very challenging to say the least. It takes a great deal of knowledge and the involvement of many employees. This situation is both positive and negative. It is negative because it takes so much time and understanding. It is positive because those few companies that succeed will gain a competitive advantage.

GAINING AND SUSTAINING A COMPETITVE ADVANTAGE

Some firms use their approaches to managing human resources to gain a sustainable competitive advantage. A company has a competitive advantage when all or some of its customers prefer its products and/or services. *If a company's advantage is difficult for competitors to understand and copy, the com-*

pany has a **sustainable competitive advantage.**[24] Firms attempt to gain a sustainable competitive advantage in many ways: Southwest Airlines coordinates all of its operations to ensure that customers get excellent service at the lowest possible price; Wal-Mart Stores uses rapid market intelligence and competitive pricing so that the right products are always available in the right amounts at the lowest price. Starbucks negotiates special supplier arrangements to ensure that they receive the best coffee beans. Management practices such as these can all help a firm gain a competitive advantage. But no strategy can create a sustainable advantage unless the company also has the human resources it needs to successfully implement the strategy.

Next we describe the three conditions an organization must meet in order to gain sustainable competitive advantage through managing human resources effectively.

"The relationship we have with our people and the culture of our company is our most sustainable competitive advantage."

Howard Schultz
Chair and Chief Global Strategist,
Starbucks

EMPLOYEES WHO ARE A SOURCE OF ADDED VALUE

Employees add value by using skills and knowledge to transform the organization's other resources (e.g., raw materials, component parts, equipment, real estate, information, etc.) to produce and deliver products and services that generate profits or other valued forms of return.

Employees who are most closely associated with the activities that generate valued returns usually have the most opportunity to add value. Sometimes referred to as "core" employees, they are closest to the essential work of the organization. In software development firms, programmers are core employees. In pharmaceutical firms, scientists and researchers are core employees. In orchestras, musicians are core employees. In health care institutions, doctors and nurses are core employees.

Core employees can add value to an organization in a variety of ways—through research and new product development, production, problem diagnosis, service delivery, and so on. In most organizations, many other employees working in a staff and managerial jobs support the work of the core employees. They can improve the organization's efficiency by keeping costs low, analyzing the environment to identify new market opportunities, carrying out necessary administrative tasks, and facilitating coordination among core employees.

Regardless of the specific work being done, the objective of effective human resource management is to maximize the value added by all employees. To achieve this objective, the organization must be staffed with the right employees doing the right things at the right time and place and under the right conditions.

EMPLOYEES WHO ARE RARE

To be a source of sustainable competitive advantage, human resources must also be rare. If competitors can easily access the same pool of talent, then that talent provides no advantage against competitors. By being an employer of choice, organizations can gain access to the best available talent. Books, articles, and websites that purport to identify the "best" places to work are especially popular among students graduating from college, who view firms high in the rankings as desirable places to land their first postgraduation job. In other words, "The Best Get the Best," as Cisco, Smucker's, and Southwest

Airlines have learned. Dissatisfied workers who are looking for better employment situations read these lists too. Over time, a good reputation for attracting, developing, and keeping good talent acts like a magnet, drawing the best talent to the firm and keeping it.

When Lincoln Electric Company in Cleveland, Ohio, announced it was planning to hire 200 production workers, it received more than 20,000 responses. When BMW Incorporated announced that it had selected Spartanburg, South Carolina, as the site for its first U.S. production facility, it received more than 25,000 unsolicited requests for employment. Numbers this large make it more feasible for Lincoln Electric and BMW to hire applicants who are two to three times more productive than their counterparts in other manufacturing firms.

A Culture That Can't Be Copied

Getting the best people into the firm is just a first step. Keeping the best people happy and productive is equally important. When done well, business and human resource practices can create a strong company culture that keeps employees happy and productive and is also difficult for other companies to copy. Business and human resource practices that are easy for competitors to copy don't provide sources of sustained competitive advantage. Similarly, a company culture that's easily copied provides little advantage. Southwest Airlines and FedEx are two companies with strong company cultures that contribute to business success and are difficult for competitors to copy. These company cultures are difficult to copy because they have developed over a long period of time and are unique to each company's total approach to doing business.

Southwest Airlines. The customer-oriented culture of Southwest Airlines is unique in an industry known for disruptive strikes and low customer satisfaction. Besides hiring the best people, Southwest Airlines maintains a company culture that keeps employees happy and motivates them to achieve peak performance. Employees at Southwest Airlines understand the company's strategy and do everything possible to achieve outstanding company success. When a gate supervisor was asked what makes Southwest different from other airlines, she said, "We're empowered to make on-the-spot decisions. For example, if a customer misses a flight, it's no sweat. We have the latitude to take care of the problem. There's no need for approvals."

A profit-sharing program is one aspect of Southwest Airlines' approach to managing human resources that keeps employees focused on the company's performance. An incident in Los Angeles illustrates the point: An agent from another airline asked to borrow a stapler. The Southwest agent went over with the stapler, waited for it to be used, and brought it back. The other agent asked, "Do you always follow staplers around?" The Southwest agent replied, "I want to make sure we get it back. It affects our profit sharing." Setting goals and targets for the performance of the company as a whole and never setting separate departmental goals is another approach to managing people that ensures employees all pull together. At Southwest, the philosophy is that everyone should share common goals and that setting up different goals for different areas would be likely to create a schism within the company.[25]

FedEx. Since day one, its basic philosophy of doing business, as stated by Chair, CEO, and President Frederick W. Smith, has been People, Service, and Profit. Its motto is 100% Customer Satisfaction. In a business that relies on individuals delivering packages overnight to customers anywhere, 100% customer satisfaction comes only from managing human resources as if they really matter. The FedEx philosophy of managing people is represented in the following policies:

- achieve no layoffs;
- guarantee fair treatment;
- use surveys to obtain feedback and guide action;
- promote from within;
- share profits; and
- maintain an open-door policy.

Like Southwest Airlines, FedEx has developed a complex and integrated system of human resource practices designed to keep employees focused on the needs of customers and the business. Its system was not simply copied intact from another company, nor did the firm develop it by applying some formula that could guarantee a correct solution. Rather, through a systematic process of analysis over many years, FedEx developed its own unique human resource policies and practices. As a consequence, its company culture is difficult for outsiders to fully understand, and thus it's impossible to copy.[26]

A FRAMEWORK FOR MANAGING HUMAN RESOURCES THROUGH STRATEGIC PARTNERSHIPS

When you hear the words *human resources,* what do you think these words mean? For many readers, "human resources" is just another phrase to describe employees. But in this book, the term means more than this. *Human resources* are all of the people who currently contribute to doing the work of the organization, as well as those people who potentially could contribute in the future, and those who have contributed in the recent past. The best organizations understand that managing human resources effectively involves more than focusing only on current employees—it requires a long-term perspective that is responsive to the concerns of current employees, potential future employees, and recent employees who no longer work for the organization. *Together, past employees, current employees, and potential future employees make up a firm's total* **human resources;** *these human resources are available as potential contributors to the creation and realization of the organization's vision, mission, goals, and objectives.*

Exhibit 1.3 illustrates our overall framework for managing human resources effectively. At the center of the framework are human resource management (HRM) activities—recruitment, selection, compensation, performance measurement, training, and so on. Human resource management activities are important because they partly determine how well a company

> *"At other places managers say that people are their most important resource, but nobody acts on it. At Southwest, they have never lost sight of the fact."*
>
> Alan S. Boyd
> Retired Chair
> Airbus North America

Ex 1.3   A Framework for Managing Human Resources through Strategic Partnerships

EXTERNAL ENVIRONMENT

Local Conditions	National Conditions	Multinational Conditions

Economic Conditions	Political Trends	Industry Dynamics	Labor Markets	Country Cultures	Laws and Regulations	Unionization and Collective Bargaining

ORGANIZATIONAL ENVIRONMENT

Leadership

Strategy
- Vision
- Mission
- Values

Technology

Business Strategy

ACTIVITIES FOR MANAGING HUMAN RESOURCES

Formal Policies and Daily Practices

- Understanding the External and Organizational Environments
- Ensuring Fair Treatment and Legal Compliance
- HR Planning for Alignment and Change
- Job Analysis and Competency Modeling
- Recruitment and Retaining Qualified Employees
- Selecting Employees to Fit the Job and the Organization
- Training and Developing a Competitive Workforce
- Developing an Approach to Total Compensation
- Measuring Performance and Providing Feedback
- Using Performance-based Pay to Enhance Motivation
- Providing Benefits and Services
- Promoting Workplace Safety and Health
- Unionization and Collective Bargaining

STAKEHOLDER OBJECTIVES TO BE SATISFIED

Owners and Investors
- Financial returns
- Corporate reputation
- Long-term survival

Customers
- Quality
- Speed and responsiveness
- Low prices
- Innovation
- Convenience

Society
- Legal compliance
- Social responsibility
- Ethical practices

Other Organizations
- Reliability
- Trustworthiness
- Collaborative problem-solving

Organization Members
- Good pay and benefits
- Good quality of work life
- Long-term employability

THE HR PROFESSION

satisfies the concerns of its multiple stakeholders, as described earlier. These activities do not occur in a vacuum, however. They are shaped by various forces in the external environment and by several organizational factors.

THE IMPORTANCE OF THE EXTERNAL AND ORGANIZATIONAL ENVIRONMENTS

If you have worked for more than one employer, you know from experience that there are many different approaches to managing human resources. Some employers are highly selective in who they hire, while others seem to hire anyone who walks in the door. Some provide extensive training, while others let new hires sink or swim. Some pay well and offer large bonuses; others don't. Many of these differences in how organizations manage people are due to differences in the environments of the organizations.

The External Environment. The external environment affects all organizations, but its effects are not the same for all organizations. Small businesses do not have to comply with the same employment laws that apply to large organizations. Labor market conditions for businesses in high-tech industries can be very different from those in the retail industry. Global businesses face a stronger imperative to respond to differences in country cultures than do most domestic businesses.

Chapter 2 describes in detail several aspects of the external environment that can influence an organization's approach to managing human resources. In addition to the globalization of business, it reviews the important role of economic conditions, political organizations, industry dynamics, labor market conditions, and cultural differences between countries.

Chapter 3 describes U.S. employment laws and regulations, and employees' evolving attitudes about what constitutes fairness. It describes legal definitions of fairness, such as those provided by equal opportunity laws and various other regulations. Chapter 3 provides a foundation for other discussions of fairness and legal considerations that appear in subsequent chapters.

The Organizational Environment. Several characteristics of the organizational environment can also influence human resource management activities. Organizational characteristics often explain why similar companies in the same industry treat employees so differently. Consider the policies and practices for managing people used by two grocery store chains: Wal-Mart and Wegman's.

Wal-Mart's leaders say that people matter, but their approach to managing human resources doesn't always show it. Hourly wages are low, minimal health benefits are offered, annual employee turnover rates are in the range of 50% (which is near the average for this industry), and many employees feel they have little opportunity for advancement. These practices fit Wal-Mart's business strategy of offering goods at the lowest possible price.[27]

Like Wal-Mart, Wegman's is very profitable. But its business strategy is the opposite of Wal-Mart's. Wegman's is an upscale store that offers top-quality foods for which customers pay premium prices. Wegman's vice president of people sums up the company's approach to managing human resources like this: "If we take care of our people, they will take care of our customers." Wegman's sets its pay levels above the competition. It seeks out the best-caliber employees and gives most full- and part-time employees free health coverage. Annual turnover among full-time employees is 6 to 7% (38% for part-timers).[28]

Organizational characteristics that tend to shape the way a company manages its people include the leadership approach of top-level managers and the company's culture, technology, and business strategy. Chapter 4 provides a general description of these elements of an organizational environment, and also gives examples to illustrate how organizations can differ. Subsequently, when we explain the specific HR activities, we provide additional examples that show how aspects of the organizational environment can shape the way human resources are managed.

ACTIVITIES FOR MANAGING HUMAN RESOURCES

Watson Wyatt's Human Capital Index shows that improvements in 30 HR practices are associated with an increase of 30% in market value.

Every organization, from the smallest to the largest, engages in a variety of human resource management activities. **Human resource (HR) activities** *include the formal HR policies developed by the company as well as the actual ways these policies are implemented in the daily practices of supervisors and managers.*

In some organizations, the formal HR policies and daily practices are closely aligned. In many organizations, the formal policies are regarded as statements of expectations and aspirations, but they are not implemented in actual daily practices. Consequently, the actual practices that evolve are not aligned with the formal policies. The more that policies and practices are aligned and the more systematic companies are in creating HR activities to fit the organization and its environment, the more effective the organization is likely to be.[29]

The many human resource policies and practices that companies need to understand and create include:

- HR planning for alignment and change
- Job analysis and competency modeling
- Recruiting and retaining qualified employees
- Selecting employees to fit the job and the organization
- Training and developing a competitive workforce
- Developing an approach to total compensation
- Measuring performance and providing feedback
- Using performance-based pay to enhance motivation
- Providing benefits and services
- Promoting workplace safety and health
- Unionization and collective bargaining

When an organization systematically understands, creates, coordinates, aligns, and integrates all of their policies and practices, it creates a **human resource management (HRM) system.**

HR Planning for Alignment and Change. An effective HRM system requires planning and coordination as well as continual evaluation and readjustment. Chapter 4 describes how strategic planning and HR planning together can be used to align HR practices with conditions in the external and organizational environments.

Human resource planning also serves to align the various HR activities with each other. For example, if a company decides to offer employees a relatively low rate of pay, it can anticipate that employees may not stay for a long time. If the turnover rate is high, then recruitment will always be ongoing. Also, if employees will have short careers with the organization, the company may decide to not invest heavily in training. Throughout this book, we provide you with several examples that illustrate how organizations create alignment among the many specific activities that comprise a total HRM system.

Job Analysis and Competency Modeling. All organizations divide the work to be done into jobs. Jobs comprise a set of task and role responsibilities. Effective HRM systems are grounded in a clear understanding of the way work is allocated among jobs, the competencies needed by employees who work in those jobs, and a long-term view of how these are likely to change in the future. Chapter 5 describes how job analysis and competency modeling can be used to develop an understanding of jobs in the organization and the competencies employees need in order to maximize their performance in those jobs.

Recruiting and Retaining Qualified Employees. To get jobs done, organizations need to attract people to apply for jobs and retain those who do their jobs well. When jobs openings occur, recruitment may involve looking outside the organization for new employees. Alternatively, current employees may be recruited to move from their current jobs to new ones. Regardless of whether recruits come from outside or inside the organization, retaining the best employees is usually desirable. Chapter 6 describes how companies recruit applicants to apply for job openings and some of the ways they can reduce unwanted turnover. An understanding of why excellent employees voluntarily leave reveals the important role of HR practices in retaining the best talent.

Selecting Employees to Fit the Job and the Organization. After applicants have applied for a position, but before they are made a job offer, the process of selection occurs. Selection involves sorting and ranking applicants using a standard set of criteria. As described in Chapter 7, the criteria used to select employees flow from the results of job analysis and competency modeling. Increasingly, employers want to select employees who will be able and willing to learn new tasks and continually adapt to changing conditions. They also want employees who fit well with the organizational culture.

Training and Developing a Competitive Workforce. To ensure that people know what they're supposed to do, employers often provide some instruction and training. Training and retraining are critical issues in the technology-driven information era. With rapid changes in job requirements, existing employees must be both willing and able to develop new competencies, become proficient in new jobs, and even change their occupations. Chapter 8 describes the socialization, training, and development practices that enable employees to develop themselves and remain employable despite rapid changes in the world of work.

Developing an Approach to Total Compensation. Employees work in exchange for compensation, whether monetary or otherwise. A total compensation package typically includes base wages or salaries, some form of incentive pay, as well as various types of benefits. Chapter 9 describes how organizations design the total compensation package. It also describes in detail the process used to set the level of compensation to be offered for specific jobs.

Measuring Performance and Providing Feedback. To ensure that employees perform satisfactorily and receive appropriate recognition, performance must be measured in some way. Employees need fair and clearly stated performance standards. They deserve useable feedback and the support needed to identify and correct performance deficiencies. When appropriate performance standards, measures, and feedback are provided, capable employees become a high-performance workforce. Chapter 10 describes these activities and sets the stage for a discussion about using rewards to further motivate employees.

Using Performance-Based Pay to Motivate Employees. During the past decade, employers have been changing the design of total compensation. An overarching objective has been to increase the extent to which performance is a key driver of the pay that people receive. In the long run, creating a stronger linkage between performance and pay should improve motivation and productivity, which in turn helps to control labor costs. Chapter 11 describes the use of incentives, bonuses, and other forms of rewards that employers offer.

Providing Benefits and Services. As many organizations have discovered, the best companies often become targets for recruitment by competitors. Offering innovative benefits packages and employee services that address a wide array of employees' concerns is one tactic for warding off such poaching, as described in Chapter 10. Such benefits include those with obvious monetary value, such as health insurance, as well as others whose monetary value is more difficult to quantify, such as flexible work arrangements and telecommuting options. In addition to the benefits that employers offer voluntarily, Chapter 12 describes mandatory benefits required by law.

Promoting Workplace Safety and Health. Chapter 13 focuses on what employers can do to ensure that the workplace is safe and that employees are healthy. As jobs in the United States have shifted out of manufacturing, and even manufacturing jobs have become less labor-intensive, issues of workplace safety and health also have changed. Exposure to toxic chemicals and dangerous equipment remains a concern in some work environments, but more often air quality and ergonomic concerns top the agenda. Increasing concern about violence in the workplace is another unfortunate development described in Chapter 13.

Unionization and Collective Bargaining. Chapter 14 addresses the current state of unionization and collective bargaining activity. Although union membership has been shrinking steadily in the United States for many years, firms such as GE, Southwest Airlines, Continental Airlines, AT&T, and the major U.S. auto companies all hold joint discussions with the unions on issues such as productivity gains, the quality of working life, and outsourcing. Because unions have maintained their strength in many other countries, they play a vital role in companies that strive to be globally competitive and profitable.

THE HR TRIAD

Used systematically and correctly, human resource management policies and practices can transform a lackluster company into a star performer. Used without a systematic and informed approach, they create havoc. In some companies, existing approaches to managing human resources reflect chance and happenstance. Instead of analyzing how their HRM systems affect all aspects of the business, some organizations continue to do things the same way year after year. Ask why salespeople in the shoe section are paid on commission and people in toys are not, and you are likely to be told, "That's just the way we've always done it." When companies do change the way they manage people, they may do so for the wrong reason. Why did that small retail food chain just send all its middle managers to off-site wilderness training? "Everybody in the industry's doing it—we can't be the only ones who don't." Why did your insurance company start randomly listening in on calls from customers? "The new telecommunications system we installed last year included it as a no-cost feature, so we decided we should use it."

Whether a company chooses its human resource policies and practices systematically or somewhat haphazardly, those policies and practices can have powerful effects. Ensuring that those effects are *positive* rather than destructive requires the involvement of three key players, who we refer to as the **HR Triad:**

- *HR professionals,*
- *line managers, and*
- *all the other employees who are affected by HRM policies and practices.*

No department can, by itself, effectively manage a company's human resources.[30] That's why there's a saying at Merck that goes like this, "Human resources are too important to be left to the HR department." Companies like Merck, Hallmark Cards, Cisco Systems, Lincoln Electric, and Southwest Airlines have developed approaches to managing people that reflect all three perspectives in the HR Triad. The special expertise of HR professionals is used by, and in cooperation with, the expertise of line managers, other administrative staff, and all first-line employees in every department. So, regardless of whether line managers ever hold formal positions in human resource management, they are held accountable for the task of managing people.

LINE MANAGERS HAVE ALWAYS BEEN RESPONSIBLE

In small businesses, owners must have HR expertise as they build the company from the ground up. Usually, the founder makes all of the hiring and pay decisions when the company is first getting started. In smaller companies, performance appraisals are likely to occur on the spot whenever there seems to be a performance problem. Formal policies may not exist at all! This reality is clearly reflected in the various popular magazines targeted to small-business owners—for example, *Inc., Money, Success,* and *Entrepreneurship.* These publications devote a great deal of space to discussing issues related to managing the people who make up a small company.

Eventually, as a company grows, the owner may contract out some of the administrative aspects related to managing people (e.g., payroll), or delegate some of the responsibilities to a specialist, or both. If the company grows larger, more specialists may be hired—either as permanent staff or on a contract basis to work on special projects, such as designing a new pay system. As with other business activities, these specialists assist the company, but responsibility for the work remains with the company managers.

HR PROFESSIONALS PROVIDE SPECIAL EXPERTISE

Human resource (HR) professionals *are people with substantial specialized and technical knowledge of HR issues, laws, policies, and practices.* The leaders of HR units and the people who work within the department usually are HR professionals, although this isn't always the case. Sometimes organizations fill the top-level HR position with a person who has a history of line experience but no special expertise in the area of HR. According to one survey of 1,200 organizations, this is a growing trend. Line managers who are doing a "tour of duty" in the HR department would be appropriately referred to as HR managers, but they would not be considered HR professionals—at least not until they gained substantial experience and perhaps took a few executive development courses devoted to human resource management.

External experts who serve as HR consultants or vendors for the organization *may* be HR professionals, but don't assume that consultants or vendors are HR professionals just because they offer HR products or services. In addition to a record of substantial HR experience, other things that might indicate that a consultant or vendor has the specialized expertise of a professional include a college-level degree in the field and accreditation from a professional association.

Human resource professionals of all types have many roles and responsibilities. Reflecting on the work she does an HR professional, Janet Brady, vice president of human resources at The Clorox Company, described how challenging her job can be:

> *I serve the board of directors, executive management, general office employees, retirees, production and salespeople across the country, every type of function—and they all view HR slightly differently based on their backgrounds, their needs and their histories. That has told me there isn't a one-size-fits all solution. I've got to listen and ask questions, so that we can ultimately do something that's fair for everybody. HR can be very challenging because what we do can affect people at the most personal level and we can't lose sight of that.*[31]

Exhibit 1.4 describes in more detail the several roles played by HR professionals who work as high-level managers and executives with responsibility for managing an organization's human resource activities.

Ex 1.4	Key Roles for the HR Department and the HR Leader
KEY ROLES	**WHAT IS EXPECTED ON THE JOB**
Business Partner	Shows concern for objectives of all stakeholders Understands the external and organizational environment Assists with strategy formulation and implementation Assists with mergers, acquisitions, and international joint ventures Shows how human resource management activities can affect the bottom line
Consultant	Views line managers and other employees as customers and works as partner to meet their needs Develops HR practices and policies with input from other members of the HR Triad
Innovator	Initiates—does not wait for others to call attention to the need for action Uses e-learning, the Internet, and other newly evolving technologies to improve HR services Continually revises and updates HR policies and practices
Monitor	Ensures employment laws are known and observed Evaluates the effectiveness of the organization's HR policies and practices Coaches and encourages line managers to practice the HR policies as intended Works with line managers and other employees in the HR Triad to revise policies as needed
Change Manager	Is guided by a long-term vision of where the business is headed Understands what talent is needed for executing future strategies Anticipates the concerns of employees and creates solutions to address them

Key HR Competencies. To be effective, HR professionals need many competencies and a great deal of knowledge. Research conducted at the University of Michigan Business School during the past two decades has identified five major types of competencies that HR professionals need in order to be effective. These competencies and their weighted impact on business performance are:

1. Strategic understanding and contribution (43%)
2. Personal credibility (23%)
3. HR delivery (18%)
4. Business acumen (11%)
5. HR technology (5%)[32]

As is true in other professional occupations, there is an examination and certification process available to assess the competencies of HR professionals. The most well-known certification process is conducted by the **Society**

for Human Resource Management (SHRM), *which is a professional association that has several thousand HR professionals as members.* Certification is provided by SHRM for two levels of expertise for HR professionals: PHR and SPHR. The test specifications for PHR and SPHR, along with jobs and compensation levels, are described in Appendix A. The contents of this book provide a good preparation for the PHR and SPHR certification examination programs.

At Weyerhaeuser, each major division, led by its human resources director, is responsible for developing a list of the specific competencies required by members of the HR staff. The HR directors work with their staff to generate a slate of competencies. The HR leaders interview their internal "customers"—in the organization—and also use their own knowledge of what the staff will be doing in their jobs. The corporation is aiming to predict future HR issues so they can describe the future competency requirements for HR staff. The senior HR professionals at Deutsche Bank (DB) went through a similar process to the one used by Weyerhaeuser. In their efforts to help DB become more globally competitive, the HR department realized it had to display more competencies and play more roles.[33]

HR Competencies for Global Firms. The globalization of business is putting HR professionals from around the world in almost daily contact with each other and with line managers representing many different countries and cultures. Coinciding with this globalization of business is the globalization of the HR profession. The World Federation of Personnel Management Associations (WFPMA) links together country- and region-specific professional associations around the world, including SHRM. As a service to its members, the WFPMA investigated the question of how the work of HR professionals is similar and different around the world. Their research helped develop an understanding of global HR competencies. Another study done by Cranfield University for the Chartered Institute for Personnel and Development (CIPD), in England, found that within many countries HR competencies reflect the roles the HR professionals need to play, which are determined in part by the environment.[34] Thus while many HR leaders and departments around the world have many of the same roles and responsibilities, the specifics of what they do reflect the culture, laws, and economy of each country.

Ethical Behavior. Human resource professionals are guided in their work by the **HR profession's code of ethics,** which *states that HR professionals must regard the obligation to implement public objectives and protect the public interest as more important than blind loyalty to an employer's preferences.* More specifically, in daily practice, HR professionals are expected to

- thoroughly understand the problems assigned to them and undertake whatever study and research are required to ensure continuing competence and the best of professional attention;
- maintain a high standard of personal honesty and integrity in every phase of daily practice;
- give thoughtful consideration to the personal interest, welfare, and dignity of all employees who are affected by their prescriptions, recommendations, and actions; and

- make sure that the organizations that represent them maintain a high regard and respect for the public interest and that they never overlook the importance of the personal interests and dignity of employees.[35]

Ex 1.5 Excerpts from the SHRM Code of Ethical and Professional Standards for Human Resource Professionals

PROFESSIONAL RESPONSIBILITY

Core Principle: As HR professionals, we are responsible for adding value to the organizations we serve and contributing to the ethical success of those organizations. We accept professional responsibility for our individual decisions and actions. We are also advocates for the profession by engaging in activities that enhance its credibility and value.

Guidelines

1. Adhere to the highest standards of ethical and professional behavior.
2. Measure the effectiveness of HR in contributing to or achieving organizational goals.
3. Comply with the law.
4. Work consistent with the values of the profession.
5. Strive to achieve the highest levels of service, performance and social responsibility.
6. Advocate for the appropriate use and appreciation of human beings as employees.
7. Advocate openly and within the established forums for debate in order to influence decision-making and results.

PROFESSIONAL DEVELOPMENT

Core Principle: As professionals we must strive to meet the highest standards of competence and commit to strengthen our competencies on a continuous basis.

Guidelines

1. Pursue formal academic opportunities.
2. Commit to continuous learning, skills development and application of new knowledge related to both human resource management and the organizations we serve.
3. Contribute to the body of knowledge, the evolution of the profession and the growth of individuals through teaching, research and dissemination of knowledge.
4. Pursue certification such as CCP, CEBS, PHR, SPHR, etc. where available, or comparable measures of competencies and knowledge.

ETHICAL LEADERSHIP

Core Principle: HR professionals are expected to exhibit individual leadership as a role model for maintaining the highest standards of ethical conduct.

Guidelines

1. Be ethical; act ethically in every professional interaction.
2. Question pending individual and group actions when necessary to ensure that decisions are ethical and are implemented in an ethical manner.
3. Seek expert guidance if ever in doubt about the ethical propriety of a situation.
4. Through teaching and mentoring, champion the development of others as ethical leaders in the profession and in organizations.

(continued)

Ex 1.5   (continued)

FAIRNESS AND JUSTICE

Core Principle: As human resource professionals, we are ethically responsible for promoting and fostering fairness and justice for all employees and their organizations.

Guidelines

1. Respect the uniqueness and intrinsic worth of every individual.
2. Treat people with dignity, respect and compassion to foster a trusting work environment free of harassment, intimidation, and unlawful discrimination.
3. Ensure that everyone has the opportunity to develop their skills and new competencies.
4. Assure an environment of inclusiveness and a commitment to diversity in the organizations we serve.
5. Develop, administer and advocate policies and procedures that foster fair, consistent and equitable treatment for all.
6. Regardless of personal interests, support decisions made by our organizations that are both ethical and legal.
7. Act in a responsible manner and practice sound management in the country(ies) in which the organizations we serve operate.

CONFLICTS OF INTEREST

Core Principle: As HR professionals, we must maintain a high level of trust with our stakeholders. We must protect the interests of our stakeholders as well as our professional integrity and should not engage in activities that create actual, apparent, or potential conflicts of interest.

Guidelines

1. Adhere to and advocate the use of published policies on conflicts of interest within your organization.
2. Refrain from using your position for personal, material or financial gain or the appearance of such.
3. Refrain from giving or seeking preferential treatment in the human resources processes.
4. Prioritize your obligations to identify conflicts of interest or the appearance thereof; when conflicts arise, disclose them to relevant stakeholders.

USE OF INFORMATION

Core Principle: HR professionals consider and protect the rights of individuals, especially in the acquisition and dissemination of information while ensuring truthful communications and facilitating informed decision-making.

Guidelines

1. Acquire and disseminate information through ethical and responsible means.
2. Ensure only appropriate information is used in decisions affecting the employment relationship.
3. Investigate the accuracy and source of information before allowing it to be used in employment related decisions.
4. Maintain current and accurate HR information.
5. Safeguard restricted or confidential information.
6. Take appropriate steps to ensure the accuracy and completeness of all communicated information about HR policies and practices.
7. Take appropriate steps to ensure the accuracy and completeness of all communicated information used in HR-related training.

The SHRM code of ethics is shown in Exhibit 1.5. The SHRM also publishes a manual that HR professionals can use as a guide to developing and instituting an employer's code of ethics for their total workforce.

Ethical organizations have an edge in their ability to hire and retain the best people, and this ensures that the best workforce possible is working to achieve the organization's objectives.[36] Increasingly, HR professionals are becoming involved in managing the ethical issues that arise in the workplace.[37] In a survey conducted by the SHRM and the Commerce Case Clearing House (CCCH), HR professionals agreed that workplace ethics require people to be judged solely on job performance. Ethical human resource management requires managers to eliminate such things as favoritism, friendship, sex bias, race bias, and age bias from promotion and pay decisions (it is, of course, also unlawful to take sex, race, or age into account).[38] For more information on SHRM's code of ethics visit their home page (http://www.shrm.org).

Because HR professionals share responsibility for designing reward systems, they can encourage ethical behavior.[39] A good starting point is to encourage the top-level executives to critically examine practices as such reward systems to ensure that they do not encourage the achievement of organizational goals at almost any cost. Other HR activities that professionals can use to encourage ethical business practices include developing standards and guidelines that employees can consult when they face difficult decisions, and setting up an easy-to-use hot line for reporting behavior that doesn't meet ethical standards.

EMPLOYEES SHARE RESPONSIBILITY

The responsibilities of line managers and HR professionals are especially great; nevertheless, they share responsibility with the third key player in the HR Triad, namely, all the other employees who are affected by HR policies and practices. Regardless of their particular jobs, all employees in an organization share some of the responsibility for effective human resource management. Some employees write their own job descriptions and even design their own jobs. Many employees provide input for the appraisal of their own performance or the performance of their colleagues and supervisors, or both. Many organizations ask employees to participate in annual surveys where they can express their likes and dislikes about the organization's approach to managing people. Perhaps most significant, employees assess their own needs and values and must manage their own careers in accordance with these. Doing so effectively involves understanding many aspects of their employer's human resource management practices. As we move forward, we all need to position ourselves for the future. Learning about how effective organizations are managing human resources is an essential step for getting into position.

To help readers understand the role of the three key players in the HR Triad, each chapter includes a feature titled "The HR Triad." In this chapter, the HR Triad, entitled "The HR Triad: Roles and Responsibilities for Managing Human Resources," describes some of the general roles and responsibilities of the three key players in the Triad. In subsequent chapters, the HR Triad focuses on roles and responsibilities that are relevant to the specific HR activities described in the chapter.

"It's comforting to know that ethical issues are out there and I'm not alone. But it's disheartening to know that they're so commonplace."

Participant
Online ethics bulletin board

The HR Triad

Roles and Responsibilities for Managing Human Resources

LINE MANAGERS	HR PROFESSIONALS	EMPLOYEES
• Work closely with HR professionals and employees to develop HR policies.	• Work closely with line managers and employees to develop HR policies.	• Work closely with line managers and HR professionals to develop and implement HR policies and practices.
• Engage in HR practices consistent with HR policies.	• Help line managers and employees practice HRM consistent with HR policies.	
• Include HR professionals in the formulation and implementation of business strategy and discussions of its HR implications.	• Stay informed of the latest technical principles for managing human resources.	• Accept responsibility for managing their own behavior and careers in organizations.
• On a daily basis, consider the implications of business decisions for managing human resources.	• Develop the skills and competencies needed to support change processes.	• Recognize the need for personal flexibility and adaptability.
• Accept shared responsibility for managing human resources strategically and work to reduce barriers to this objective.	• On a daily basis, consider how well the organization's approaches to managing human resources fit with the current global and organizational environment.	• Be committed to learning and changing continuously throughout one's career.
• Learn about and apply basic accepted principles for managing human resources.	• Be proactive in learning about how leading companies are managing human resources, and what they're learning from their experiences.	• Learn about and apply basic accepted principles for managing human resources for HR activities in which they participate (e.g., selecting team members, appraising supervisors, and training coworkers).
• Seek input from employees and HR professionals in order to improve own competency for managing human resources.	• Work with employees to help them voice their concerns effectively, and serve as their advocate when appropriate.	• Be willing to share ideas that might help the company manage its people better.

LOOKING AHEAD: FOUR SPECIAL CHALLENGES

As organizations strive to manage employees effectively, they face many challenges. In subsequent chapters, we pay attention to four special challenges that companies are currently struggling to understand and utilize:

- managing teams,
- managing diversity,
- managing globalization, and
- managing change.

As you will see, all of the human resource management activities discussed in subsequent chapters can help organizations address these special issues, as well as the ever-present issues of attracting, retaining, motivating, and improving a competitive workforce.

Managing Teams

In a study of U.S. and Canadian companies, half the managers responding believed that improving teamwork processes to focus on customers is the strategic initiative with the greatest potential for ensuring their organizations' success. According to a survey conducted by The Conference Board, innovation and on-time delivery were the two most common reasons for the increasing use of work teams. Exhibit 1.6 lists several other reasons for organizing employees into work teams instead of having them work on small tasks that they can complete alone.[40]

The increasing popularity of team-based organizational structures reflects the belief that teamwork can achieve outcomes that cannot be achieved by the same number of individuals working in isolation. But as many organizations are discovering, the payoff from teams isn't automatic. Although teams offer great potential for increased innovation, quality, and speed, the potential isn't always realized. Even when teams do fulfill their potential in these areas, team members and their organizations may experience unanticipated negative side effects, such as lingering unproductive conflicts and turnover.[41]

Ex 1.6 Why Organizations Use Work Teams	
THE MOST COMMON REASONS FOR HAVING EMPLOYEES WORK IN TEAMS	
TO SATISFY CUSTOMERS	**TO SATISFY EMPLOYEES**
✔ Improve on-time delivery of results	✔ Facilitate management development and career growth
✔ Improve customer relations	✔ Reinforce or expand informal networks in the organization
✔ Facilitate innovation in products and services	✔ Improve employees' understanding of the business
✔ Improve quality	✔ Increase employee ownership, commitment, and motivation
✔ Reduce costs and improve efficiency	

Human resource management practices can make the difference between success and failure for organizations using teams. To create and orchestrate teams, people need to be selected, appraised, compensated, and trained in ways that reflect the unique relationships that develop between employees who work together. Most companies realize that people working in teams should not be managed just the same as people who work more or less independently. Nevertheless, teamwork really is a somewhat new phenomenon in the American workplace, so considerable experimentation in how best to manage teams is still taking place around the country. Some practices now viewed as experimental will undoubtedly become commonplace within the next decade. Examples of how organizations are using human resource practices to maximize team effectiveness are highlighted throughout this book in the "Managing Teams" feature.

MANAGING DIVERSITY

"The burden is on us, not the employee, to change. For many of us, that's a new recognition."

Charles R. Romea
Employee Benefits Director
ConAgra

At about the same time that organizations began to recognize the benefits of teamwork, they discovered that the people who were being put into teams were more diverse than ever before. More and more women are working, for example, resulting in a new gender mix that's nearly balanced instead of being male-dominated. Throughout the 20th century, immigration patterns also changed, resulting in more cultural diversity. In addition, employees differ from each other on a wide variety of values and lifestyles. Thus organizations are finding that diversity management practices must be sensitive to issues of religion, sexual orientation, marital and family status, age, and various other unifying life experiences.[42]

For organizations that are committed to fully utilizing their human resources, having a workforce that is diverse in terms of gender, ethnicity, culture, lifestyle, religion, sexual orientation, age, and many other characteristics requires finding new ways of managing. The increasing diversity of the workforce, combined with changing attitudes about differences that may have been ignored in the past, presents both challenges and opportunities for organizations and their employees. Throughout this book, the "Managing Diversity" feature describes how effective organizations use HR practices to leverage employee diversity and create competitive advantage.

MANAGING GLOBALIZATION

During the past 50 years, technological advances in transportation and communications have spurred the growth of international commerce. As a result, many firms evolved from being purely domestic to becoming truly global. The first step in this evolution was simply to export goods for sale in one or two foreign markets. The next step was to manufacture those goods overseas because it was more efficient than shipping products thousands of miles to markets. Setting up operations close to foreign markets also helped a company better understand its customers. A transnational firm has "headquarters" in several nations, and no single national culture is dominant in the firm.[43]

One of the most difficult challenges for truly global organizations is developing an approach to managing human resources

FAST FACT

In EU countries, newly hired employees are entitled to at least four weeks of vacation in their first year. In France, they get five weeks unless they are between 18 and 21 years old. In the United States, employees typically receive only one week of vacation after their first year on the job.

that works at home as well as abroad.[44] When Lincoln Electric began to globalize, they assumed that their very American approach to managing employees would work just as effectively in other countries as it worked in Cleveland, Ohio. They soon discovered that exporting their approach to managing human resources wouldn't work. In fact, some of their practices were illegal in other countries, just as some practices that are common in other countries may be illegal in the United States. A firm's decisions about which HR practices will be used universally and which will be adapted to reflect local conditions may ultimately determine its success or failure.

Throughout this book, we return repeatedly to issues of how globalization affects organizations' management of their human resources. Although detailed treatment of this topic is beyond the scope of this text, many of the issues that global organizations face are illustrated in the "Managing Globalization" feature. Readers who are particularly interested in cross-cultural and international human resource management should consult the relevant sources referenced throughout the chapters.

MANAGING CHANGE

Current approaches to managing people within any particular company reflect both the past and the process of letting go of the past in order to prepare for the future. As environmental change quickens, more and more companies are concluding that some of the traditional approaches to managing human resources must be modified. A shortage of qualified employees may lead an organization to change its human resources management system in order to attract more job applicants. A never-ending stream of new technologies makes possible new approaches to recruiting—not to mention the possibility of a virtual organization. Changing laws and regulations may threaten old practices or create new opportunities. Merging with another firm, spinning off a business unit, and flattening the hierarchical structure all involve changing who does what and how. A dynamic, changing environment makes innovation and change as important—if not more important—for established organizations as they are for new organizations. Even the most successful organizations can't rest on prior successes. If they become complacent, competitors will woo away employees as well customers.

Regardless of the cause, achieving radical change often requires huge investments in planning and implementing the change.[45] Almost always, changes in business practices mean changes in HR practices. Throughout this text, the "Managing Change" feature describes examples of how organizations use HR practices to manage change.

SUMMARY

Managing human resources is critical to the success of all companies, large and small, regardless of industry. The more effectively a firm manages its human resources, the more successful the firm is going to be.

Organizations define success by how well they serve their stakeholders. Stakeholders include those who have a claim on the resources, services, and products of the companies. The primary stakeholders who shape the typical organization's approach to managing human resources include (but aren't limited to) the shareholders and owners, society, customers, other organizations, and organization members. It is, in part, the existence of these powerful stakeholders that makes managing human resources such a challenging and important task.

Managing human resources involves many policies and practices, which taken together form an organization's human resource management system. Some approaches to managing human resources are more effective than other approaches. Nevertheless, there is no one best way to manage employees. Organizations need to manage human resources to fit the external environment and the organizational environment. Every human resource (HR) activity sends a message to employees. If all these activities send different messages, the employees are likely to respond in rather unpredictable ways. A strategic approach to managing human resources involves systematically and correctly creating HR policies and practices that are consistent with each other and aligned with the environment.

The complexity of managing human resources means that no one person can manage this task alone. Instead, line managers, HR professionals, and all other employees in the organization must work together. These three key players—whom we refer to as the HR Triad—share responsibility for managing human resources in a way that balances the concerns of an organization's primary stakeholders.

Because of the increasing complexity of human resource management, nearly all mid- to large-sized companies employ human resource professionals—as full-time employees, as vendors with long-term contracts, and/or as consultants who work on short-term projects. Regardless of how HR activities are structured, however, companies that are most concerned with HR management seek professionals who have the competencies needed for their work and who are guided by the HR profession's code of ethical conduct.

Looking ahead, organizations face many challenges. Four challenges described throughout the chapters of this book are managing teams, managing diversity, managing globalization, and managing change. By developing effective human resource management policies and practices, the best organizations will be able to meet these challenges with success.

TERMS TO REMEMBER

HR profession's code of ethics
HR triad
Human resource (HR) activities
Human resource management
  (HRM) system
Human resource (HR) professionals

Human resources
Intangible human assets
Society for Human Resource
  Management (SHRM)
Stakeholders
Sustainable competitive advantage

DISCUSSION QUESTIONS

1. What has Cisco Systems been doing that demonstrates the value of managing human resources effectively? Why have employees stayed with Cisco during the tough times?

2. Refer to the list of stakeholders and their objectives in Exhibit 1.1. For each stakeholder group, state at least one *additional* concern that you think may shape how organizations manage human resources. Then, for each stakeholder group, give one specific example of how each stakeholder's concerns could affect a major HR activity (e.g., planning, staffing, appraisal, compensation, or training).

3. Explain the meaning of managing human resources through strategic partnership. Is it realistic to expect organizations to be strategic in managing human resources? What organizational and individual barriers are likely to make it difficult to adopt a strategic approach?

4. Give some examples to illustrate the possible consequences that occur when the daily HR practices of managers are inconsistent with the organization's formal HR policies.

5. Which member of the HR Triad has the most responsibility for ensuring that organizations effectively manage their human resources? Explain your answer.

6. Why are the challenges of managing teams, managing diversity, managing globalization, and managing change so important today? Are these challenges likely to decrease in importance during the next decade? Why or why not?

PROJECTS TO EXTEND YOUR LEARNING

1. *Integration and Application.* Read the two cases at the end of this book entitled "The Lincoln Electric Company" and "Southwest Airlines." Then, using Exhibit 1.1 as a guide, make an illustration that identifies the stakeholders of each company and shows the relative importance of each stakeholder to each company. Here, as in the chapters to follow, you can gather your information from materials in the chapter, the cases at the end of the text, and from other sources including newspapers, magazines, the Internet, and your experience. If you are unable to obtain information you feel is relevant, make assumptions based on your best judgment. Note any major assumptions you make. You'll want to visit the home pages of these two companies often, so be sure to make bookmarks for future use. (Home pages are, respectively, http://www.lincolnelectric.com and http://www.southwest.com.)

2. *Exploring the Internet.*
   a. Find out about this year's "100 Best Companies to Work For in America" (http://www.fortune.com/fortune/bestcompanies)
   b. Visit several professional associations in the United States with members who are experts in managing the human resources area, including

> The Society for Human Resource Management (http://www.shrm.org)
> Human Resource Planning Society (http://www.hrps.org)
> The Human Resources Division of the Academy of Management (http://www.aom.pace.edu)
> WorldatWork (http://www.worldatwork.org)
> Society for Industrial and Organizational Psychology (http://www.siop.org)
> You can find links to associations in other countries at the home page of the World Federation of Personnel Management Associations (http://www.wfpma.com).

    c.   Learn about procedures and requirements for obtaining HR certification from the Human Resource Certification Institute (http://hrci.org).

    d.   Compare the HR code of ethics provided by the Society for Human Resource Management (http://www.shrm.org/ethics/code-of-ethics.asp) with the code of ethics for another profession of interest to you (e.g., physician, accountant, lawyer, psychologist).

    e.   Begin to learn more about the two companies featured in the cases at the end of this book, Lincoln Electric (http://www.lincolnelectric.com) and Southwest Airlines (http://www.southwest.com). You'll want to visit the home pages of these companies often.

3. ***Experiential Activity.*** Locate an HR professional who is willing to be interviewed for about 15 minutes. You can do this by visiting an organization, attending a meeting or conference where there are likely to be HR professionals present, or speaking to a friend or relative who works in the field of HR. Ask the HR professional the following questions. Take notes and be prepared to report what you learn to your classmates.

1. *Questions to ask an HR professional during your individual interview:*
    a.   What are your most important roles and responsibilities?
    b.   Describe the most difficult challenges that you face as an HR professional.
    c.   In your current job, how important are issues of managing teams, managing globalization, managing diversity, and managing change?
    d.   What are the most difficult ethical issues that you face as an HR professional?

2. *Questions to discuss with your classmates:*
> After the interview, meet with several classmates and discuss the following questions:

    a.   What similarities do you see in the comments of the several HR professionals you interviewed?
    b.   How did the answers given by the HR professionals seem to differ? What accounts for the differences in the answers?
    c.   What do you feel is the single biggest challenge in managing human resources effectively?

CASE STUDY

MANAGING HUMAN RESOURCES AT BARDEN BEARINGS

The Barden Bearings Corporation manufactures high-precision ball bearings for machine tools, aircraft instruments and accessories, aircraft engines, computer peripherals, textile spindles, and medical and dental equipment. Currently, it employs about 1,000 people and includes a marketing department and a small corporate staff. It was founded during World War II to manufacture the special bearings needed for the Norden bombsight and has been nonunion since the beginning. Mr. Donald Brush, vice president and general manager of the Precision Bearings Division, gave the following description of his division:

Reporting directly to me is a small staff comprising a manufacturing manager, a quality manager, an engineering manager, a director of manufacturing planning, and a manager of human resources (see Case Exhibit 1). We meet several times a week to discuss current problems, as well as short- and long-range opportunities and needs. On alternate weeks, we augment this group by including the supervisors who report to the senior managers listed in Case Exhibit 1. I might interject here that all supervisors meet with hourly employees on either a weekly or biweekly basis to review specific departmental successes and failures, and to otherwise keep employees informed about the business and to encourage ownership of their jobs. The managers themselves meet on call as the Employee Relations Committee to discuss and recommend approval of a wide range of issues that include the evaluation and audit of hourly and salaried positions, as well as the creation and modification of all divisional personnel policies.

A few words about our Human Resource Department: There are six employees who together

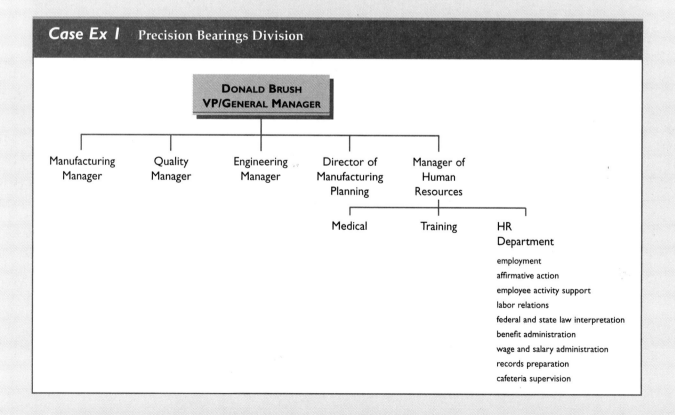

Case Ex 1   Precision Bearings Division

DONALD BRUSH
VP/GENERAL MANAGER

Manufacturing Manager

Quality Manager

Engineering Manager

Director of Manufacturing Planning

Manager of Human Resources

Medical

Training

HR Department

employment
affirmative action
employee activity support
labor relations
federal and state law interpretation
benefit administration
wage and salary administration
records preparation
cafeteria supervision

provide the basic services of employment, affirmative action, employee activity support, labor relations, interpretation of the federal and state laws, benefits administration, wage and salary administration, records preparation and maintenance, cafeteria supervision, and so on. There are, in addition, two people who coordinate our rather extensive training activities.

As currently organized, the Medical Department comes under the supervision of the manager of human resources. Its authorized staff includes a medical director, the manager of employee health and safety (who is an occupational health nurse), a staff nurse, a safety specialist, and a secretary/clerk.

The development and execution of plans and programs, including those of a strategic nature, almost invariably involve the active participation of HR. And that's how we want it to be. On the other hand, the HR Department doesn't run the business. By this I mean they don't hire or fire, promote or demote. They don't write job descriptions or determine salaries or wages. All these things are done by the line managers with the HR Department providing a framework to ensure that all actions are consistent with and appropriate to company goals. You might say that HR is our "Jiminy Cricket"—they're there for advice, consent, and, importantly, as a conscience.

HR Objectives

During the past several months, we have been running into many issues that affect the very essence of our business objectives: growth, profits, survival, and competitiveness. Because the issues involve our human resources, these must be our major focus. Would you please give us your experience, expertise, and suggestions as to how we can solve them? Thanks! The following briefly describes the nature of each of the four HR objectives.

Recruiting and Training New Hourly Employees. The need to recruit and train approximately 125 new hourly workers to respond to a surge in business is very challenging. By midyear, it became evident that we had an opportunity to significantly increase our business. In order to achieve otherwise attainable goals, we need to increase our hourly workforce by a net of about 125

employees (that is, in addition to normal turnover, retirements, etc.) in one year. I have asked HR to test the waters, recognizing that the unemployment in the Danbury labor market for skilled workers has reached an unprecedented low of about 2.6%.

Safety and Occupational Health Improvement. The need to create a heightened awareness by the workforce for safety and occupational health considerations is very important. This is an evolving mission born of a dissatisfaction on our part about "safety as usual." Over the years, Barden employees have assumed that, because we are a metalworking shop, people were just going to get hurt. But we cannot afford to have people get hurt and miss work anymore. Yet, as our workforce ages, the employees seem to get out of shape and become more injury- and illness-prone.

Managing Health Costs of an Aging Workforce. The spiraling health costs of an aging and, sometimes, out-of-shape workforce are very costly. All employers face this. Barden's problem is a little unique in that hourly employees tend to stay with the company and retire from the company. For example, we still have several employees whose careers began with us 45 years ago, shortly after the company was founded. Our average age approaches 45 for employees and their dependent spouses. Generally, our jobs do not require much physical effort, and it's easy to become out of shape. As a consequence, employees get sick, use hospitals, and have accidents.

New Machines and the Development of Qualified Workers. The technological evolution of increasingly complex machinery and related manufacturing equipment, and the development of trained workers to operate and maintain this equipment, are important facts of life. This process is unceasing and requires a good deal of planning for both the short and the long run. For example, what should we do in the next year, or five years out, in order to remain competitive in terms of cost, quality, and service? Buying and rebuilding machines is part of the story. Running them efficiently is quite another. As you know, modern equipment of this sort requires operational people who are not only knowledgeable about the turning or grinding of metals, but also conversant with computerized numerical controls. The employee who sets up and operates a $500,000 machine must be well trained. Yet finding trained people is getting more difficult.

Mr. Brush knows that these HR objectives all reflect the increasing diversity of the workforce. He also knows these issues will be around for a long time. He requests that you provide him with your general ideas and suggestions. He doesn't want details at this time.

CASE QUESTIONS

1. Which of the HR objectives facing Mr. Brush are really the most important to the success

of the business? Prioritize them and justify your list.
2. Now consider this list of objectives from the perspective of employees. Using the employees' perspective, how would you prioritize the list? What are the implications of any differences in the two lists of priorities for Mr. Brush?
3. Choose two objectives. For each, describe the key roles and responsibilities of the HR manager, the line managers, and other employees.

Source: This case was prepared by Randall S. Schuler, who expresses his appreciation for the cooperation of Donald Brush.

ENDNOTES

1 R. Levering and M. Moskowitz, "The 100 Best Companies to Work For," *Fortune* (January 8, 2001): 148–168; R. Levering and M. Moskowitz, "The 100 Best Companies to Work For," *Fortune* (January 12, 2004): 56–78; Adapted from C. A. O'Reilly III and J. Pfeffer, *Hidden Value: How Great Companies Achieve Extraordinary Results with Ordinary People* (Boston: Harvard Business School Press, 2000): 49–77; D. B. Turban and D. M. Cable, "Firm Reputation and Applicant Pool Characteristics," *Journal of Organizational Behavior* 24 (2003): 733–751; S. Bates, "Seven Organizations Win Double Honors as Great Places to Work," http://www.shrm.org/hrnews_published/articles/CMS_005603.asp (September 30, 2003).

2 S. Rosen, J. Simon, J. R. Vincent, W. MacLeod, M. Fox, and D. M. Thea, "AIDS Is Your Business," *Harvard Business Review* (February 2003): 81–87; A. J. Vogl, "Does It Pay to Be Good?" *Across the Board* (January/February 2003): 16–23; D. Robson, "The Green Utility That's in the Black," *Business Week* (March 26, 2001): 108; C. Schmitt, "Corporate Charity: Why It's Slowing," *Business Week* (December 18, 2000): 164–166; O. C. Richard, "Racial Diversity, Business Strategy, and Firm Performance: A Resource-Based View," *Academy of Management Journal* 43 (2000): 164–177; M. B. E. Clarkson, "A Stakeholder Framework for Analyzing and Evaluating Corporate Social Performance," *Academy of Management Review* 20 (1995): 92–117; R. E. Freeman, *Strategic Management: A Stakeholder Approach* (Boston: Pittman/Ballinger, 1994); T. M. Jones, "Instrumental Stakeholder Theory: A Synthesis of Ethics and Economics," *Academy of Management Review* 20 (1995): 404–437.

3 R. S. Kaplan and D. P. Norton, "Measuring the Strategic Readiness of Intangible Assets," *Harvard Business Review* (February 2004): 52–63.

4 N. Wong, "Let Spirit Guide Leadership," *Workforce* (February 2000): 33–36; C. Handy, "A Better Capitalism," *Across the Board* (April 1998): 16–22.

5 T. M. Welbourne and A. O. Andrews, "Predicting the Performance of Initial Public Offerings: Should Human Resource Management Be in the Equation?" *Academy of Management Journal* 39 (1996): 891–919.

6 T. A. Stewart, "Real Assets, Unreal Reporting," *Fortune* (July 6, 1997): 207–208.

7 D. Whitford, "A Human Place to Work," *Fortune* (January 8, 2001): 108–120.

8 B. Schneider, P. J. Hanges, D. B. Smith, and A. N. Salvaggio, "Which Comes First: Employee Attitudes or Organizational Financial and Market Performance?" *Journal of Applied Psychology* 88(5) (2003): 836–851; L. Grant, "Happy Workers, Happy Returns," *Fortune* (January 12, 1998): 81. Also see G. E. Fryzell and J. Wang, "The Fortune Corporation 'Reputation' Index: Reputation for What?" *Journal of Management* 20 (1994): 1–14.

9 J. K. Harter, F. L. Schmidt, and T. L. Hayes, "Business-Unit-Level Relationship between Employee Satisfaction, Employee Engagement, and Business Outcomes: A Meta-Analysis," *Journal of Applied Psychology* 87(2) (2002): 268–279; For descriptions of other studies that show the linkage between managing human resources and organizational effectiveness, see J. Bae and J. Lawler, "Organizational and HRM Strategies in Korea: Impact on Firm Performance in an Emerging Economy," *Academy of Management Journal* 43 (2000): 502–517; B. E. Becker and M. A. Huselid, "High Performance Work Systems and Firm Performance: A Synthesis of Research and Managerial Implications," in G. Ferris (ed.), *Research in Personnel and Human Resources Management* (Greenwich, CT: JAI Press, 1998); and the following articles, which all appeared in the *Academy of Management Journal's* "Special Research Forum on Human Resource Management and Organizational Performance," Vol. 39(4) (August 1996): B. Becker and G. Gerhart, "The Impact of Human Resource Management on Organizational Performance: Progress and Prospects," 779–801; J. E. Delery and D. H. Doty, "Modes of Theorizing in Strategic Human Resource Management: Tests of Universalistic, Contingency, and Configural Performance Predictions," 802–825; M. A. Youndt, S. A. Snell, J. W. Dean, Jr., and D. P. Lepak, "Human Resource Management, Manufacturing Strategy, and Firm Performance," 836–867; R. D. Banker, J. M. Field, R. G. Shroeder, and K. K. Sinha, "Impact of Work Teams on Manufacturing Performance: A Longitudinal Field Study," 867–890.

10 B. Becker and M. Huselid, "Measuring HR?: Benchmarking Is Not the Answer!" *HR Magazine* (December 2003): 57–61; S. Bates, "The Metrics Maze," *HR Magazine* (December 2003): 51–55; Based on data presented in B. E. Becker, M. A. Huselid, and D. Ulrich, *The HR Scorecard: Linking People, Strategy, and Performance* (Boston: Harvard Business School Press, 2001).

11 A. Wilkinson, G. Godfrey, and M. Marchington, "Bouquets, Brickbats and Blinkers: Total Quality Management and Employee Involvement in Practice," *Organization Studies* 18(5) (1997): 799–819.

12   A. Wilkinson, G. Godfrey, and M. Marchington, *Human Capital Management: The CFO's Perspective* (New York: Mercer, 2003).

13   J. W. Johnson, "Linking Employee Perceptions of Service Climate to Customer Satisfaction," *Personnel Psychology* 49 (1996): 831–846.

14   R. Abelson, "Welcome Mat Is Out for Gay Investors," *New York Times* (September 1, 1996): Section 3: 1, 7.

15   S. Bates, "Getting Engaged," *HR Magazine* (February 2004): 44–51.

16   M. A. Friedman, "Friedman Doctrine: The Social Responsibility of Business Is to Increase Its Profits," *New York Times Magazine* (September 13, 1970): 32ff.

17   K. H. Hammonds, W. Zellner, and R. A. Melcher, "Writing a New Social Contract," *Business Week* (March 11, 1997): 60–61.

18   W. R. Scott, "The Adolescence of Institutional Theory," *Administrative Scientific Quarterly* (1987): 493–511; L. G. Zucker, "Institutional Theories of Organization," *Annual Review of Sociology* (1987): 443–464; J. W. Meyer and B. Rowan, "Institutionalized Organizations: Formal Structure as Myth and Ceremony," *American Journal of Sociology* (1977): 340–363.

19   To learn how researchers attempt to measure corporate social performances, see D. Kirkpatrick, "Looking for Profits in Poverty," *Fortune* (February 5, 2001): 175–176; B. M. Ruf, K. Muralidhar, and K. Paul, "The Development of a Systematic, Aggregate Measure of Corporate Social Performance," *Journal of Management* 24 (1998): 119–133.

20   T. Lewin, "Equal Pay for Equal Work Is No. 1 Goal for Women," *New York Times* (September 5, 1997): A20.

21   K. F. Clark, "Leaders of the Pack," *Human Resource Executive* (May 6, 1997): 80–82.

22   E. E. Lawler III, *The Ultimate Advantage: Creating the High Involvement Organization* (San Francisco: Jossey-Bass, 1992); E. E. Lawler III, S. A. Mohrman, and G. E. Ledford, *Employee Involvement in America: An Assessment of Practices and Results* (San Francisco: Jossey-Bass, 1992).

23   E. E. Lawler III et al., *Employee Involvement and Total Quality Management* (San Francisco: Jossey-Bass, 1992); D. R. Denison, *Corporate Culture and Organizational Effectiveness* (New York: John Wiley, 1990).

24   B. Patterson and S. Lindsey, "Mining the Gold: Gain Competitive Advantage through HR Data Analysis," *HR Magazine* (September 2003): 131–136; M. A. Hitt, L. Bierman, K. Shimizu, and R. Kochhar, "Direct and Moderating Effects of Human Capital on Strategy and Performance in Professional Service Firms," *Academy of Management Journal* 44 (2001): 13–28; J. Barney, "Firm Resources and Sustained Competitive Advantage," *Journal of Management* 17(1) (1991): 99–120.

25   D. P. Shuit, "That Sartain Touch," *Workforce Management* (August 2003): 42–45; B. Leonard, "Ready to Soar," *HR Magazine* (January 2001): 52–56; W. Zellner, "Southwest: After Kelleher, More Blue Skies," *Business Week* (April 2, 2001): 45.

26   D. Roth, "My Job at the Container Store," *Fortune* (January 10, 2000): 74–78.

27   D. P. Shuit, "People Problems on Every Aisle," *Workforce Management* (February 2004): 26–34.

28   E. R. Demby, "The Insider: Benefits," *Workforce Management* (February 2004): 57–59.

29   For an example of a study that demonstrates the value of aligning human resources with strategic needs, see B. C. Skaggs and M. Youndt, "Strategic Positioning, Human Capital, and Performance in Service Organizations: A Customer Interaction Approach," *Strategic Management Journal* 25 (2004): 85–99.

30   See all references in Endnote 9.

31   S. Bates, "Business Partners," *HR Magazine* (September 2003): 45–53; University of Michigan Business School, *The New HR Agenda: 2002 Human Resource Competency Study (HRCS)* (Ann Arbor, MI: University of Michigan Business School, May 2003); Society for Human Resource Management, *The Future of the HR Profession: Eight Leading Consulting Firms Share Their Visions for the Future of Human Resources* (Alexandria, VA: Society for Human Resource Management, 2002); L. Davidson, "Survey Results Show HR's Progress," *Workforce* (August 1999): 68–74; J. J. Laaabs, "Painting a Vivid Picture of HR," *Workforce* (October 1998): 26–30.

32   W. Brockbank, *Human Resource Competency Toolkit* (Alexandria, VA: Society for Human Resource Management/University of Michigan/Global Consulting Alliance, 2003).

33   D. Dunn and K. Yamashita, "Microcapitalism and the Megacorporation," *Harvard Business Review* (August 2003): 46–54; C. Dawson, D. Brady, J. Greene, and K. Capell, "Top Global Companies," *BusinessWeek* (July 14, 2003): 58–62; M. Svoboda and S. Schroder, "Transforming Human Resources in the New Economy: Developing the Next Generation of Global HR Managers at Deutsche Bank," *Human Resource Management* (Fall 2001): 261–273.

34   J. Vocino, "On the Rise," *HR Magazine* (November 2003): 74–84; S. J. Wells, "From HR to the Top," *HR Magazine* (June 2003): 46–60; C. Brewster, E. Farndale, and J. van Ommeren, "HR Competencies and Professional Standards," *World of Federation Personnel Management Associations* (June 2000).

35   S. Meisinger, "Strategic Contribution: The Crucial Competency," *HR Magazine* (August 2003): 8; BNA and Society for Human Resource Management, *HR Department Benchmarks and Analysis 2002: Excerpts from the Complete Survey-Based Study of Human Resource Departments* (Washington, DC: BNA, 2002); S. L. Rynes, K. G. Brown, and A. E. Colbert, "Seven Common Misconceptions about Human Resource Practices: Research Findings versus Practitioner Beliefs," *Academy of Management Executive* 16(3) (2002): 92–103; J. Walker and W. Stopper, "Developing Human Resource Leaders," *Human Resource Planning* (1999): 38–44; M. Langbert, "Professors, Managers, and Human Resource Education," *Human Resource Management* 39(1) (Spring 2000): 65–78; F. Shipper and J. Dillard, "A Study of Impending Derailment and Recovery of Middle Managers Across Career Stages," *Human Resource Management* 39(4) (Winter 2000): 331–345.

36   J. Joseph and E. Esen, 2003 *Business Ethics Survey* (Alexandria, VA: Society for Human Resource Management, 2003); J. Schramm, "A Return to Ethics?" *HR Magazine* (July 2003): 144; D. Patel, "Ethics in HR Practices Good for Bottom Line, Research Suggests," *HR News* (July 2001): 14; L. Grensing-Pophal, "Walking the Tightrope," *HR Magazine* (October 1998): 112–119; M. T. Brown, *Working Ethics: Strategies for Decision Making and Organizational Responsibility* (San Francisco: Jossey-Bass, 1990); L. L. Nash, *Good Intentions Aside: A Manager's Guide to Resolving Ethical Problems* (Boston: Harvard Business School Press, 1990); L. T. Hosmer, *The Ethics of Management* (Homewood, IL: Irwin, 1991).

37   R. W. Beatty, J. R. Ewing, and C. G. Tharp, "HR's Role in Corporate Governance: Present and Perspective," *Human Resource Management* 42(3) (Fall 2003): 257–269.

38   S. H. Applebaum, *1991 SHRM/CCCH Survey* (June 26, 1991); M. T. Brown, *Working Ethics: Strategies for Decision Making and Organizational Responsibility* (San Francisco: Jossey-Bass, 1990).

39   "HR Staff Feeling, Seeing Ethics Pressure," *Bulletin to Management* 49(6) (February 12, 1998): 41.

40   H. Axel, "Teaming in the Global Arena," *Across the Board* (February 1997): 56; S. A. Mohrman and A. M. Mohrman, Jr., *Designing and Leading Team-based Organizations: A Workbook for Organizational Self-design* (San Francisco: Jossey-Bass, 1997); R. D. Banker, J. M. Field, R. G. Schroeder, and K. K. Sinha, "Impact of Work Teams on Manufacturing Performance: A Longitudinal Field Study," *Academy of Management Journal* 36 (1996): 867–890.

41 S. E. Jackson, K. E. May, and K. Whitney, "Understanding the Dynamics of Diversity in Decision Making Teams," in R. A. Guzzo and E. Salas (eds.), *Team Effectiveness and Decision Making in Organizations* (San Francisco: Jossey-Bass, 1995); S. E. Jackson and R. N. Ruderman (eds.), *Diversity in Work Teams: Research Paradigms for a Changing Workplace* (Washington, DC: 1995).

42 For a description of the cultural experiences of Latino Americans, see R. Suro, *How Latino Immigration Is Transforming Us* (New York: Knopf, 1998).

43 D. R. Briscoe and R. S. Schuler, *International Human Resource Management*, 2nd ed. (London: Routledge, 2004); N. Adler and S. Bartholomew, "Managing Globally Competent People," *Academy of Management Executive* 6 (1992): 52–65.

44 C. Gomez, "The Influence of Environmental, Organizational, and HRM Factors on Employee Behaviors in Subsidiaries: A Mexican Case Study of Organizational Learning," *Journal of World Business* 39 (2004): 1–11.

45 K. E. Weick and R. E. Quinn, "Organizational Change and Development," *Annual Review of Psychology* 50 (1999): 361–386.

chapter 2

Understanding the External and Organizational Environments

When Bill Zollars was hired as the new CEO of Yellow Freight System, the company had just finished one of its worst years in its 70-year history. This old-economy company had suffered losses of $30 million, two rounds of layoffs, and a major strike by the teamsters.

After the transportation industry was deregulated in the 1980s, new competition had entered the market. Yellow Freight didn't seem to understand the implications of this new competitiveness environment. Zollars was brought in to bring the company out of decline and save it from disaster. After his arrival, Yellow Freight was transformed. Before, the efficient delivery of goods was Yellow's most important objective. As long as a shipment arrived approximately when the customer was told to expect it, Yellow claimed it had done what it had agreed to. Today when customers call, they tell a Yellow employee what services they need, and Yellow does everything possible to meet the customers' needs. Deliveries can be scheduled to arrive in hours, days, or weeks, and customers can specify the desired arrival times. According to Zollars, "We've gone from being a company that thought it was in the trucking business to one that realizes it's in the service business." The vision is to be "the leading provider of guaranteed, time-definite, defect-free, hassle-free transportation for business consumers worldwide."[1]

THE STRATEGIC IMPORTANCE OF UNDERSTANDING THE EXTERNAL AND ORGANIZATIONAL ENVIRONMENTS

For Yellow Freight System, a poor understanding of what changes in the environment meant for the company nearly led to the company's demise. Fortunately, it found a new CEO with the ability to understand the environment and the leadership skills needed to help the company adapt to and thrive in its new environment. Zollars's role in Yellow Freight's turnaround shouldn't be underestimated. He understood that the people doing the work were taking their cues from the behaviors they saw from him and other company leaders. He also realized that the company's employees would ultimately determine whether the company would survive. That's why he took an 18-month road trip to visit hundreds of terminals around the country. Some days he made 10 visits to 10 different locations. For employees who had seldom seen a top-level executive, and certainly never talked to one, it left a big impression. His success also impressed the Board, who has since appointed him chair and CEO of Yellow Corporation. Today, Yellow Corporation is continuing to grow by acquiring competitors like Roadway.

Unfortunately, not all CEOs share Zollars's enlightened view of employees. As Exhibit 2.1 shows, many leaders view people as a cost rather than valuable assets.[2] As you read this chapter, think about how a CEO's view of employees is likely to affect the way she or he deals with the changing business environment in the United States.

In Chapter 1, we presented our guiding framework for managing human resources, illustrated in Exhibit 1.3. Look again at Exhibit 1.3 and you will see that it highlights the importance of the many elements of an organization's external and organizational environments. Changing industry dynamics and new technologies—elements of the environment that were so important for Yellow Freight—are just two of many environmental conditions that create business threats and opportunities. In this chapter, we briefly describe how these and several other elements of the external and organizational environments can influence human resource management. In subsequent chapters, we elaborate on this discussion by describing how these elements can influence each specific HRM activity.

"HR professionals need to scan the environment everyday—whether by Internet, newspapers, or magazines. Everything has the potential to impact everything we do."

Charles Tharp
HR Consultant

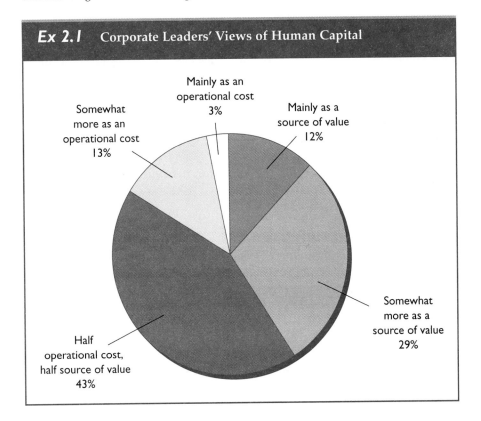

Ex 2.1   Corporate Leaders' Views of Human Capital

Mainly as an operational cost 3%

Somewhat more as an operational cost 13%

Mainly as a source of value 12%

Somewhat more as a source of value 29%

Half operational cost, half source of value 43%

ELEMENTS OF THE ENVIRONMENT

As shown in Exhibit 1.3, organizations can be thought of as existing within an external environment. The organization itself can also be thought of as having an environment in which individual employees are embedded. Notice also that we do not include stakeholders when we refer to elements of the external and organizational environments. Instead, we treat stakeholders as distinct groups of people whom the organization seeks to satisfy.

External Environment.   The **external environment** *encompasses local, national, and multinational conditions that confront an organization.* The specific elements of the external environment described in this chapter are:

- economic conditions,
- the political landscape,
- industry dynamics,
- labor markets, and
- country cultures.

Two other important aspects of the external environment—legal institutions and unions—are discussed later in Chapters 3 and 14, respectively.

While the external environment clearly influences how organizations manage their workforce, it does not fully determine their approach. A more accurate portrayal is to think of the external environment as a set of constraints and opportunities.

Organizational Environment.   The **organizational environment** *refers to conditions within the organization itself.* These are sometimes referred to as the internal environment. Effective organizations seek to create an internal organizational environment that fits the current external environment yet is flexible enough to change as new conditions arise. Because the external environment changes constantly, changes in the organizational environment often are needed.

Organizations are complex systems that include many elements. We will not attempt to describe *all* of these in this chapter. Instead, we focus on a few elements that have particular relevance for managing human resources, namely:

- technology,
- company culture, and
- strategy.

These organizational elements provide an immediate context for managing human resources. As is true of the external environment, components of the organizational environment are highly interdependent.

THE HR TRIAD

Forces in the external environment constantly stimulate companies to reassess elements of the organizational environment. Because the external environment changes continually, companies continually evolve. Ultimately, the success of an organization depends on its ability to adapt and change over time. Managers, HR professionals, and all other employees contribute to the organization's ability to adapt by monitoring the environment, interpreting events that occur in the environment, and making adjustments as needed, as explained in Chapter 4. Specific examples of actions that members of the HR Triad can take to improve a company's chances of success in the context of continual change are summarized in "The HR Triad: Roles and Responsibilities for Understanding the External and Organizational Environments."

Next, we describe several aspects of the external and organizational environments and provide examples of their implications for managing human resources. As you learn more about specific HR activities (e.g., selection, training, compensation), you will also learn more about how a firm's external and organizational environments can influence the effectiveness of specific approaches to managing the workforce.

ECONOMIC GLOBALIZATION

Depending on your perspective, you may believe the United States is either too open to foreign competition or not open enough. Regardless of one's perspective, it's clear that the size and wealth of the U.S. market make it a desirable target for foreign competitors. In comparison with other markets of similar size, it has remained relatively open regardless of which political party is in power. An open market means that U.S. domestic firms face fierce foreign competition from foreign firms selling to U.S. customers. Imports of

FAST FACT

You can learn about the 500 companies included in the *Fortune* Global 500 by visiting http://www.fortune.com/global500.

Roles and Responsibilities for Understanding the External and Organizational Environments

LINE MANAGERS	HR PROFESSIONALS	EMPLOYEES
UNDERSTANDING THE EXTERNAL ENVIRONMENT		
• Stay informed about economic and political conditions and their possible implications for the organization.	• Stay informed about economic and political conditions and their possible implications for the organization.	• Stay informed about economic and political conditions and their possible implications for the organization.
• Investigate potential new markets for products and services. Encourage discussion of the potential implications that you learn.	• Investigate foreign labor market qualifications and conditions. Encourage discussion of the potential implications that you learn.	• Develop a basic understanding of how global conditions are likely to affect your organization and career.
• Develop an understanding of the culture of selected countries of likely importance to the business.	• Educate the organization about the new issues to be addressed as the organization expands beyond domestic borders.	• Develop an understanding of at least one culture other than your own.
	• Provide resources for managers and other employees to learn about cultural differences and to develop skills in cross-cultural interaction.	• Develop an understanding of the unique aspects of your own culture and how people from other cultures view it.
ALIGNING THE ORGANIZATIONAL ENVIRONMENT: TECHNOLOGY, CULTURE, AND STRATEGY		
• Investigate new technologies to learn how they can be used to gain competitive advantage.	• Learn to use advanced HRIM technologies and apply them to gain competitive advantage.	• Take responsibility for continuously developing skills needed to use new technologies.
• Advocate and support the use of new HRIM technology as appropriate.	• Advocate and support the use of new HRIM technology as appropriate.	• Develop ideas for how HRIM technology can be used in your own work area.
• Understand, communicate, and behave in line with the vision, mission, and values.	• Align HR policies and practices with the vision, mission, and values.	• Focus efforts on contributing to the mission; behave consistently with the values.
• Recognize elements of the company's desired culture and set a positive example through your own behavior.	• Develop HR practices that send a clear and consistent message about the desired company culture.	• Seek to understand the company culture and its implications for your own behavior.
• Assist HR professionals in determining the competencies and behaviors needed to implement the firm's strategy, and encourage these behaviors among employees.	• With line managers, determine the behaviors need to implement the firm's strategy and develop policies and practices to support the needed behaviors.	• Learn which behaviors are needed to implement the firm's strategy; develop the skills needed for strategy implementation; assist other employees with needed behaviors and skills.

shoes, textiles, and electronics continue to increase, even as the intense pressure they create for domestic producers threatens to put them out of business. Less than 10 years ago, U.S. companies dominated the office copier business here and abroad. Today their share of the domestic market is less than 50%.

COMPETING ON COST VERSUS COMPETING ON KNOWLEDGE

Finding it difficult to compete in their established areas of expertise, some U.S. manufacturers are surviving by diversifying their products and services in order complete in industries where cost pressures are less severe. The 150-year Menasha Corporation, which makes containers and packaging, diversified into logistics and information technology in order to increase their profitability. One of their new products is a label with an embedded computer chip that uses radio frequencies to transmit data about the package being shipped. To develop this new product, Menasha leveraged their knowledge about logistics to develop a technology they were using in their factories.

Malden Mills, the textile company that makes Polartec, is also counting on its knowledge resources. Located in Massachusetts, its factory employees can't compete with the low-cost labor in other countries. Instead, it needs to leverage research capabilities to develop new products and production methods. As these and other factories evolve, low-skilled jobs will be replaced by jobs requiring much higher skills. Employers and employees alike will be required to adapt accordingly.[3]

WORLDWIDE OPERATIONS

"I think probably the biggest impact to employee relations and to the HR field is this concept of globalization."

Harry Newman
IBM

Just as many foreign firms are expanding into the United States, many American companies are expanding to serve a global market that's growing at a much faster pace. In industries such as computers, machinery, autos, and chemicals, foreign sales account for between one-third and two-thirds of a typical U.S. company's total sales. For service firms, expanding into global markets often means setting up operations in those markets. Examples of U.S. service firms that generate substantial sales in other countries include Hilton Hotels, FedEx, EDS, and IBM. At Hewlett-Packard, providing service to a global market meant creating worldwide sales and marketing groups so that multinational clients could get all their worldwide needs met at a single source.[4]

When Harry Newman was the director of employee relations at IBM, he saw clearly how these changes are shaping human resource management practices. "It [globalization] is rapidly accelerating," he observed, "and it means shifting a lot of jobs, opening a lot of locations in places we had never dreamt of before, going where there's low-cost labor, low-cost competition, shifting jobs offshore." Seeing the long-term implications for employment in the United States, some observers predict that unions will regain their strength in this country if workers begin to fight to keep jobs at home.

Whether globalization is ultimately good or bad for employees is a matter of considerable debate.[5] One thing that no one disputes, however, is that it is changing the way companies manage their human resources. These changes, in turn, will have significant implications for employees, owners and investors, customers, and the community. Exactly how each group of stakeholders in affected will depend on a variety of factors, one of which is how governmental and nongovernmental agencies choose to regulate business activity, as we discuss next.

REGIONAL TRADE ZONES

Trade relations often are strongest among countries that are geographically close to each other. Besides shared trade, countries within geographic regions often share similar languages, cultures, and environmental concerns. Thus, the development of regional cooperation seems only natural as a strategy for survival amidst global competition. By forming regional trade zones, smaller countries can reap the benefits of economies of scale in consumer markets and gain easier access to a larger labor pool.

Many attempts at regionalism have not yet succeeded—for example, in Africa and Latin America. Others, such as the Association of Southeast Asian Nations (ASEAN), have been effective in promoting greater cooperation but do not yet have formal, binding treaties or agreements. The North American Free Trade Agreement (NAFTA) and the European Union (EU) are examples of regionalism that has succeeded to the point of creating free-trade zones and permanently changing the competitive landscape.

North American Free Trade Agreement. In 1993, the Canadian Parliament, the U.S. Congress, and the Mexican Congress each approved a historic agreement designed to allow for eventual free trade among these three countries— the **North American Free Trade Agreement (NAFTA).** The NAFTA immediately removed all tariffs for some classes of goods (e.g., computers, telecommunications, and aerospace and medical equipment) as well as for all new services. Tariffs for other goods and services were decreased gradually over subsequent years. Now, nearly all tariffs have been eliminated.

Following the passage of NAFTA, dozens of major U.S. manufacturing companies set up factories along the U.S.–Mexico border in plants referred to as **maquiladoras.** In many cases, low-skilled, low-paying jobs moved from the U.S. side of the border to the Mexican side, where wages are substantially lower. Predictably, unemployment levels in U.S. border towns went up, often to levels that were two and three times higher than the national average. What was perhaps less predictable was that average wages in the area also rose, on both sides of the border. Wages for maquiladora workers remain much lower than they would be in the United States, but their average wage is five times Mexico's minimum wage.[6]

Wage differences between Canada and the United States have quite different consequences. Typically, employees who hold lower-level jobs are paid more in Canada than in the United States. In contrast, Canadian professionals and managers typically earn one-third less than their U.S. counterparts. Feeling underpaid, some Canadian managers and professionals seek employment across the border. As more Canadian professionals and managers seek employment in the United States, Canadian companies face the possibility of a "brain drain."

Nearly a decade after NAFTA took effect, observers disagree about whether the economic benefits of NAFTA outweigh its negative social consequences. The supporters seem to be in the majority, however, and talks

"The [economic] dominance of the U.S. is already over. What is emerging is a world economy of blocs represented by NAFTA, the European Union, and ASEAN."

Peter Drucker
Management Guru

about expanding NAFTA to cover the entire Western Hemisphere have begun. As of 2004, the Central American Free Trade Agreement (CAFTA) established free trade between the United States, El Salvador, Guatemala, Honduras, Nicaragua, and Costa Rica.

European Union.   The **European Union (EU)** *describes itself as "an institutional framework for the construction of a united Europe."* The EU developed out of a desire to reduce conflict in the region and prevent another devastating event like World War II. Similar to NAFTA, the EU has a primary goal of creating a single market through the removal of trade barriers, such as tariffs. Prior to the establishment of the euro (€), which most EU countries have adopted, each EU country had its own currency. Through monetary union and the trade agreements that the EU can make with other countries, EU members expect to reduce costs associated with currency conversions and increase economic stability within the region.

In addition, the EU establishes free movement of people across its members' borders, creating a more mobile workforce. Directives of the EU also address numerous other issues relevant to employment. For example, EU policies provide employees with considerable privacy protection; compared to U.S. regulations, they make it much more difficult for employers to use personal data about employees and to engage in electronic monitoring of employees. Policies of the EU also provide protection from several forms of discrimination, require employers to conduct wage audits to ensure fair pay, and give employees the right to access the wage audit results if they suspect they are victims of pay discrimination. These and a variety of other employment directives seek to create fair and uniform employment conditions throughout EU member countries.[7]

Association of Southeast Asian Nations.   The **Association of Southeast Asian Nations** (ASEAN) *states that it strives to "accelerate the economic growth, social progress, and cultural development in the regions through joint endeavors in the spirit of equality and partnership in order to strengthen the foundation for a prosperous and peaceful community of Southeast Asian nations."* When ASEAN was established in 1967, intrapartner trade among its 10 members accounted for less than 15% of the region's total trade. Since then it has more than doubled.

Historically, labor and employment issues have not been central to ASEAN's concerns, but this seems to be changing. At a meeting in 2003, several specific policy areas related to employment were identified for future discussion, including: creating a framework for labor labor laws and regulations, wages, productivity improvement, and harmony of industrial relations with technological and economic integration. As it develops new policies in these areas, ASEAN is calling on its neighbors (e.g., China, Japan, Republic of Korea) for advice and guidance, which will promote further integration of employment policies throughout the region.[8]

THE POLITICAL LANDSCAPE

The globalization of business operations is unfolding against a complex and changing political landscape. As government administrations come and go, businesses must constantly analyze the implications of their philosophies and policies. Trade policies and military conflicts can have enormous consequences, obviously. Also important among the many aspects of the political landscape are international nongovernmental organizations, which often include labor issues among their concerns.

Members of nongovernmental organizations generally have no official authority to impose rules of business conduct. The force of their appeals to business is determined by the support they receive in the social realm. Among the most influential of such organizations are the International Labor Organization (ILO), Social Accountability International (SAI), and the World Trade Organization (WTO).

INTERNATIONAL LABOR ORGANIZATION

The **International Labor Organization (ILO)** *is housed within the United Nations and its mandate is to promote "social justice and internationally recognized human and labor rights."* Representatives within the ILO include workers, employers, and governments. Together, these stakeholders formulate international labor standards regarding the right to organize, collective bargaining, forced labor, equality of opportunity and treatment, safety and health, and an array of other working conditions.

SOCIAL ACCOUNTABILITY INTERNATIONAL

Social Accountability International (SAI) *promotes socially responsible approaches to conducting business and administers a certification process called Social Accountability 8000.* Companies that wish to be considered for SA 8000 certification volunteer to undergo an intensive audit and to permit additional scheduled and unscheduled inspections. To obtain certification, the company must satisfy standards in the areas of child labor, forced labor, health and safety, collective bargaining, discrimination, disciplinary action, working hours, and compensation.

WORLD TRADE ORGANIZATION

With 146 member countries, the **World Trade Organization (WTO)** *is the most inclusive international trade organization, and it is the only global body able to enforce its decisions through its own court.* Established in 1995, the WTO promotes harmonization through the agreements it negotiates among member countries. For example, the WTO requires that taxes and tariffs applied to imported goods and services must be applied equally to their domestic equivalents, unless a concession is negotiated and approved. Based on the most-favored-nation principle, businesses operating in WTO countries know that concessions offered to one WTO member country will automatically apply to all other WTO members. The WTO also promotes global harmonization of trade policies by establishing cooperative relationships with other international trade organizations, including three major regional ones: NAFTA, the EU, and ASEAN.

INDUSTRY DYNAMICS

Economic and political events often have different implications for different industries. Changes in national policies regarding tariffs or wages may be viewed as favorable for one industry and unfavorable for another. An overall trend in the direction of increasing productivity at the national level can mask the fact that some industries are enjoying substantial gains while other industries may actually be declining.

Industry boundaries are both fuzzy and unstable, so the question "What industry are we in?" isn't always easy to answer. Nevertheless, companies within the same industry—those that offer similar products and services—typically experience similar patterns of growth. They may also share a common industry culture. Generally, companies within the same industry are a firm's most significant competitors. They are also their most likely partners in strategic alliances, and their most likely targets for mergers and acquisitions. In addition, companies within the same industry tend to draw upon the same labor pool for people working in the technical areas that define the industry. Thus common approaches to managing human resources tend to evolve within industries.

INDUSTRY LIFE CYCLES

Like people and the organizations they work in, industries have life cycles. Companies within the same industry may experience these life cycles in tandem. An **industry life cycle** *can be thought of as a series of stages that create certain similarities in the issues industry members face and the solutions they adopt.* When there are many opportunities for growth (e.g., because of strong demand or government deregulation), many firms can thrive within the industry. Eventually, however, competition is likely to intensify, and eventually growth of the industry levels off or even contracts.[9]

Nascent.   During the nascent stage of an industry's life cycle, firms are competing to establish a distinctive reputation and to create customer loyalty. Because the industry isn't yet well established, there is a great deal of risk associated with this stage of an industry's life cycle. Simply surviving is the primary concern. A major HR challenge is finding highly qualified employees who accept the high risk of working in an industry that is not yet well established and can see the opportunities that lie ahead.

Rapid Growth.   Companies that survive the early phase of an industry's creation usually enjoy a period of rapid growth. Now acquiring new talent and retaining employees become more central. Competition for talent intensifies among firms within the growing industry, and job-hopping becomes more common as employees seek the best deal. Unless staffing can be maintained at adequate levels, opportunities for growth may be missed.

Mature.   In most industries, the rate of growth eventually slows and the industry moves into a mature stage. Now there are a few large firms all striving to become more efficient while also improving the quality of their products. Employers begin to seek every way possible to reduce labor costs. One common approach is to shrink the size of the firm's so-called "core" workforce, and then hire contingent employees. Often referred to as "free agents," contingent employees work on an as-needed basis. This staffing approach can reduce costs associated with paying for benefits such as medical insurance and vacation time. The number of contingent workers has been increasing in recent years, as shown in Exhibit 2.2.[10]

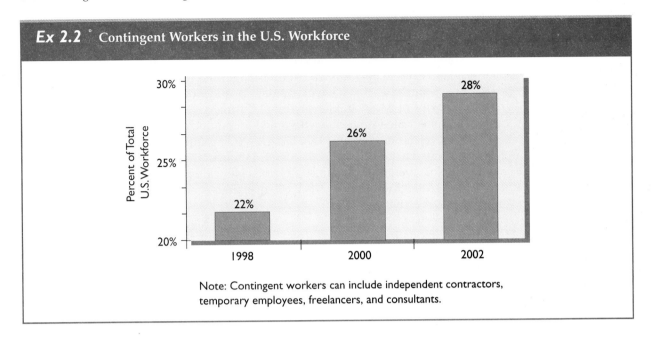

Ex 2.2 · Contingent Workers in the U.S. Workforce

Note: Contingent workers can include independent contractors, temporary employees, freelancers, and consultants.

For employees, working on a contingent basis may have some advantages—such as more flexibility to take time off, and often better hourly pay. But these advantages may be gained at the cost of less health care coverage and less employment security.

Decline and Renewal. Finally, an industry may go into decline as its products and services become obsolete. During this stage, companies in the industry may go through repeated downsizings before they eventually go out of business. For employees who have spent many years in the industry, being laid off means the beginning of long-term unemployment. If their skills are not easily transferred to other industries, laid-off employees may have to accept lower-paying jobs while they develop the new skills needed in growing industries.

MERGERS AND ACQUISITIONS

Companies today need to be fast growing, efficient, profitable, flexible, adaptable, future-ready, and dominant in market position. Without these qualities, it is virtually impossible to be competitive in today's global economy. In order to compete in this environment, many firms evolve and grow by mergers or acquisitions (M&As).

In the computer and biotech industries, a major objective of M&As is gaining access to the skills and talents of people employed by another company. Any technology or pharmaceutical discovery that a company owns will quickly become outdated. But if the people who created that technology or drug stay and remain energized, they're likely to create new products that will continue to succeed in the marketplace.

HR Issues in M&As. Mergers and acquisitions unfold through many stages. At each stage, success requires effectively managing specific human resource issues. Through experience, some companies have learned that M&As are more successful when human resource issues are addressed early and often. Exhibit 2.3 describes the stages of M&A implementation, the key HR issues to be addressed at each stage, and related HR activities.[11]

Companies that have made many acquisitions usually recognize the complexity of M&A implementation. To manage the process, they may have sophisticated procedures designed to minimize the problems that can arise. Novell is one company that has grown by acquiring other companies. Novell wanted to ensure that its executives thought through all of the key HR issues before merging companies. To assist Novell's executives, the HR staff developed the Merger Book. Its 2,000 questions serve as a road map for Novell's M&A activities.[12]

Reasons for M&A Failures.　With the importance of and need for mergers and acquisitions growing, and the base of experience expanding, it may seem reasonable to also assume that success is more likely to occur than failure in these types of combinations. Indeed, the opposite is true. Most M&As in the United States fail to achieve their financial objectives, as measured by share value, return on investment, and profitability. In Europe, a study of deals valued at $500 million or more showed that 50% destroyed share-

---

Ex 2.3　Key HR Issues and Activities in the Implementation of M&As

HR Issues	Key HR Activities
Stage 1—Precombination	
• Identifying reasons for the M&A • Forming M&A team/leader • Searching for potential partners • Selecting a partner • Planning for managing the process • Planning to learn from the process	• Participate in preselection assessment of target firm • Assist in conducting thorough due diligence assessment • Participate in planning for combination • Assist in developing HR practices that support rapid learning and knowledge transfer
Stage 2—Combination	
• Selecting the integration manager(s) • Designing/implementing transition teams • Creating the new structure/strategies/leadership • Retaining key employees • Managing the change process • Communicating to and involving stakeholders • Developing new policies and practices	• Assist in recruiting and selecting integration manager(s) • Assist with transition team design and staffing • Develop retention strategies and communicate to top talent • Assist in deciding who goes • Facilitate establishment of a new culture • Provide assistance to ensure implementation of HR policies and practices
Stage 3—Solidification and Assessment	
• Solidifying leadership and staffing • Assessing the new strategies and structures • Assessing the new culture • Assessing the concerns of stakeholders • Revising as needed • Learning from the process	• Participate in establishing criteria and procedures for assessing staff effectiveness • Monitor the new culture and recommend approaches to strengthen it • Participate in stakeholder satisfaction • Assist in developing and implementing plans for continuous adjustment and learning

holder value, 30% had minimal impact, and only 17% created shareholder returns.[13]

Mergers and acquisitions fail for a variety of reasons. Among the reasons most often cited are culture clashes, incompatibility, and loss of key talent—all human resource issues.[14] Plans that look logical on paper often fall apart when managers try to implement them. People, it seems, get in the way. Clashes between company cultures can be so severe that the financial benefits of a merger can't be realized. This is what happened at DaimlerChrysler. From the day it was first announced, many outsiders believed that the culture differences between Daimler and Chrysler would create major problems. The quintessential values and attitudes of each company's host country were reflected in everything—from product design to manufacturing, marketing, and approaches to managing human resources. Top executives in the new firm seemed to believe that the two company cultures could simply be put in a blender and poured out as a new synergistic company. Either top management at Daimler and Chrysler did not fully realize the implication of cultural differences, or they chose to focus on operational and business synergies while simply hoping that cultural differences would resolve themselves. DaimlerChrysler struggled with its integration process for several years after the merger. Throughout it all, the company's problems were chronicled by the business press and often made headline news.[15]

LABOR MARKETS

Just as firms must compete for customers, so must they compete for employees. Employees can be sought in the domestic labor market only, or employers can broaden their horizons to include the entire global labor market[16]

U.S. LABOR MARKET

Slow Growth.   With a population of more than 290 million today, projections indicate that the U.S. population will continue to grow, reaching 383 million by 2050. Despite this change, the rate of growth in the working population—the domestic labor market—is expected to slow each year between now and 2020. Exhibit 2.4 illustrates this trend.[17] The biggest reason for the slowing growth in the size of the workforce is the impending retirement of Baby Boomers (those born between 1946 and 1961). Another reason is that much of the growth during the last 30 years was due to the influx of women workers. Now that so many women are already working, their entry into the workforce is no longer a source of labor market growth.

FAST FACT

At 63%, the portion people aged 55 to 64 who are active members of the labor force is the highest since World War II.

Skills Shortage.   The slow growth of the labor market means that in many industries employers cannot find workers with the needed skills. After installing millions of dollars worth of computers in its Burlington, Vermont, factories, the IBM Corporation discovered that it had to teach high school algebra to thousands of workers before they could run the computers. Labor shortages are even more severe for so-called new economy and high-tech jobs. Projections indicate that the fastest job growth during this decade will be in computer-related jobs, as shown in Exhibit 2.5.[18] Given that enroll-

"The U.S. is now No. 3 in the world and quickly falling behind No. 1 [India] and No. 2 [China] in terms of computer science graduates."

Steven A. Balmer
CEO
Microsoft

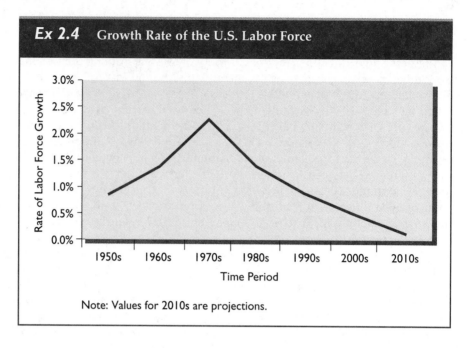

Ex 2.4 Growth Rate of the U.S. Labor Force

Note: Values for 2010s are projections.

Ex 2.5 Fastest-Growing Occupations

OCCUPATION	EMPLOYMENT (IN THOUSANDS)		
	2000	2010	CHANGE (%)
Computer software engineers, applications	380	760	100%
Computer support specialists	506	996	97%
Computer software engineers, systems software	317	601	90%
Network and computer systems administrators	229	416	82%
Network systems and data communications analysts	119	211	77%
Desktop publishers	38	63	67%
Database administrators	106	176	66%
Personal and home care aides	414	672	62%
Computer systems analysts	431	689	60%
Medical assistants	329	516	57%

ments in college science and engineering programs have been dropping steadily during the past two decades, it is clear that the people to fill these jobs will not come from the U.S. workforce alone.[19]

The construction industry provides another example of the looming skills shortages that can be expected during the next decade. A recent search by the Construction Industry Institute revealed that there are too few project engineers available in the industry's talent pipeline, given the projected number of engineers who are likely to be retiring in the near future. For the industry, the talent shortage may limit the level of growth that is possible. For individual firms, the rapid retirement of experienced engineers combined with too few replacements may mean that valuable knowledge gained through years of experience is lost.

The Construction Industry Institute's research has several implications for managing human resources in that industry. One implication is that employers in the industry should be proactive in recruiting students into the field, for example, by partnering with local universities. Another implication suggested by the Institute's research is that the traditional demographics of this workforce (predominantly male and mostly Caucasian) are likely to change, which will require the industry to learn to manage diversity effectively. A third predictable implication of this talent shortage is that compensation costs will increase, putting more pressure on firms to find new ways to maintain their current levels of profitability.[20]

Competition.   When people and skills are in short supply, competition among employers heats up as they seek to attract and retain the human resources they need. In Des Moines, Iowa, 68% of children under six years of age have no stay-at-home parent. For the Principal Financial Group, Des Moines' largest employer, this means that there is no untapped labor pool to draw on as the firm grows. According to the firm's vice president of HR, "The goal then becomes to make jobs attractive enough to keep those spouses in the workforce and keep our turnover as low as possible." Even during the recent recession, this was a key concern for Principal Financial. And how does the company make itself attractive? Among the benefits they offer are these:

- Free financial counseling
- Free parking (which is quite valuable in a downtown location)
- Lactation centers for new mothers
- A Muslim prayer room
- Subsidized Weight Watchers programs
- On-site childbirth classes
- Elevated skyways that connect the building to a nearby school, so employees can easily visit it during the workday
- Daddy Boot Camp (where dads-to-be learn to care for their newborns)
- A state-of-the-art athletic facility, which offers tai chi, Pilates, spinning, volleyball, and more![21]

Immigrants.   In recent years, foreign-born workers have constituted nearly half of the net labor force increase. These workers are less likely to be employed in professional specialty occupations and are overrepresented in occupations that do not require a high school education.[22] In New York City, immigrants from numerous countries work together to produce pianos for Steinway & Sons. Steinway pianos are still crafted mostly by hand using traditional methods. As U.S. immigration patterns have changed, so have the faces of Steinway's employees. For generations after it was founded in 1853, Steinway hired mostly immigrants from Germany, Austria, Italy, and Ireland. By the 1980s, the immigrants they hired were mostly from Haiti and the Dominican Republic. During the 1990s, they began hiring refugees from

"At the height of the conflict [in Yugoslavia], we had fund-raising going on on one floor of the factory, and clothing and food collection going on on another floor for the opposite sides, and we still made pianos every day."

Michael A. Anesta
Personnel Director
Steinway & Sons

the war in Yugoslavia—from Croatia, Serbia, and Bosnia. While their relatives at home fought against each other in war, these immigrants worked side-by-side making Steinways.[23]

GLOBAL LABOR MARKET

Currently there are more than 6 billion people on this planet. Projections indicate that the labor force in developing nations alone will expand by about 700 million people by the year 2010. To get a sense of where in the world people live, study the figures presented in Exhibit 2.6.[24]

When employers make decisions about where to place their operations, and where to locate their workers, they begin by considering where people live, but they also consider many other factors, including costs, skills, and health issues.

Labor Costs. It is well known that the lower cost of labor in other counties is one reason that U.S. employees have moved some operations offshore. When IBM disclosed that it was shifting 3,000 U.S. jobs overseas in 2003, the influence of labor costs were apparent: In the United States, it cost $56.00/hour to employ a programmer with three to five years of experience. In China, it cost only $12.60/hour. (Both figures include salary and benefits.)[25] More details about the relative cost of labor in several counties can be seen in Exhibit 2.7.[26]

Where the Skills Are. The high cost of U.S. labor is certainly one reason many U.S. jobs have been relocated to other countries. But, as some people are surprised to learn, the lack of skilled labor in the domestic labor market is another factor that has led U.S. companies to look elsewhere for their employees. Consider the data shown in Exhibit 2.8, which shows the math and science scores of 8th graders in several countries.[27] Increasingly, well-educated, entry-level workers can be found in developing countries. Furthermore, educational gains are being made more rapidly in developing countries. In 1970, less than 25% of all college students were in developing countries; today, the figure has risen to about 50%. For U.S. companies that

---

Ex 2.6 Selected Characteristics of the World Population

If the world's population were shrunk to a village of 100 people but the existing ratios remained the same, the population breakdown would be as shown below:

	1990	EST. 2025
Asians	57	61
Europeans	21	9
North and South Americans	14	13
Africans	8	17
Nonwhite	70	80
White	30	20

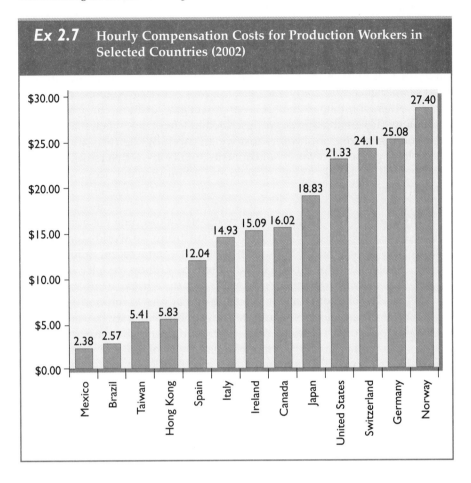

Ex 2.7 Hourly Compensation Costs for Production Workers in Selected Countries (2002)

Ex 2.8 A Sampling of Test Scores for Eighth Graders around the World

MATH		SCIENCE	
604	Singapore	569	Chinese Taipei
585	Chinese Taipei	568	Singapore
582	Hong Kong SAR	550	Japan
579	Japan	540	Australia
534	Slovak Republic	538	England
531	Canada	535	Slovak Republic
526	Russian Federation	533	Canada
525	Australia	530	Hong Kong SAR
502	United States	529	Russian Federation
496	England	515	United States
466	Israel	468	Israel

require high skill levels in areas such as science and engineering, adopting an international approach is no longer questioned.

India is a particularly desirable labor market for U.S. employers due to the prevalence of English language skills and various technical skills. The successes experienced by companies like GE and American Express have convinced other companies that it is an excellent location for information technology (IT)–enabled jobs. As described in Chapter 4, when planning for their staffing needs, employers must weigh carefully the costs and benefits of employing labor in a variety of countries to fill jobs as diverse as customer service, medical transcription, finance and accounting services, and media publications.

Health Issues.   According to a recent report by the United Nations, more people have now died from HIV/AIDS than from the world's other large catastrophes, including the bubonic plague and a more recent influenza epidemic, which both killed about 20 million people. In several African countries (including South Africa, Zimbabwe, and Zambia), one in five working-age adults is infected with HIV. Epidemiologists warn that India and China may be on the verge of similar disease rates. For employers who are evaluating whether to rely on these populations as part of their future workforce, the cost of AIDS may outweigh any other benefits. The costs to employers of sick employees include the following:

FAST FACT

In Zambia, an estimated 66% of manager mortality is attributable to HIV/AIDS.

- Medical care for affected employees
- Benefits payments, to employees and their families
- Higher recruitment and training costs, due to loss of severely ill and dying workers
- Higher insurance premiums throughout the region
- Accidents due to ill workers and inexperienced replacements
- Increased litigation over benefits and other issues
- Lower productivity due to workers who are ill while at work, absenteeism, unpredictable job vacancies, and loss of experienced workers
- Depressed morale
- Costs associated with employer-sponsored prevention programs
- More management time must be devoted to dealing with health issues[28]

Unless this epidemic is brought under control, it threatens to choke economic development in regions of the world that would otherwise be expected to grow rapidly during the 21st century. The role to be played by employers in the region is now under debate, but gradually it is likely that a consensus will be reached that employers must adopt a code of behavior that ensures humane and economically sustainable HR practices.[29]

COUNTRY CULTURES

Entire volumes have been devoted to describing differences in country cultures around the world and the space here isn't nearly sufficient to summarize this work. Nevertheless, it is important to recognize that managing in a global environment requires developing new approaches to managing people.[30]

Cultural differences have many far-reaching consequences for managing organizations. As described in the feature "Managing Globalization: Mercedes-Benz Sets Up in Alabama," cultural differences often show up in how companies are managed.[31] Cultural differences in how work is designed, employees' expectations for how they will be treated, and even management styles must all be bridged as a company expands beyond its borders.

Differences among country cultures can be significant even when comparing cultures that we may think of as similar (e.g., because they share the same language). For example, compared with those in the United States, companies in Australia place much less emphasis on merit, and they tend to adopt a more top-down approach with a command-and-control management style.[32] In Japan, the country culture and values go hand-in-hand with HR practices that adopt a long-term perspective. Employees typically expect to stay at the same firm for many years. Even in difficult economic times, Japanese firms are less likely to use large-scale layoffs as a means of reducing costs. Employees, in turn, often feel more loyalty toward their employ-

Managing Globalization

Mercedes-Benz Sets Up in Alabama

Mercedes-Benz is one of the world's most widely recognized brands. It stands for quality and luxury. Some people are surprised to learn that Mercedes-Benz manufactures some of its automobiles in Vance, Alabama. That's where Mercedes-Benz U.S. International (MBUSI) is located, and it's where the award-winning M-Class SUV was born. A team of executives and workers who came from three countries—Germany, the United States, and Japan—created the facility.

Each country has its own approach to designing and building automobiles. In Germany, engineers are highly trained experts who develop their skills by working as an apprentice to a *Meister* (a master in the profession). Workers accept the authority of the Meister and don't expect to be treated as equals to the Meister. Once they learn the skills they need, they expect to carry out their tasks without close supervision. This is a sign that they are respected and can be trusted to do a good job. Strong norms exist concerning the importance of producing automobiles of superior quality. In traditional U.S. automobile plants, managers control workers through division of labor and narrow spans of control. Henry Ford's assembly-line approach still dominates many production plants. At the Jeep plant in Ohio, relationships between managers and subordinates are relatively informal. People are quite direct in saying

what they think. Americans tend to be driven to get things done, and they are more willing to begin production before working through every problem. In Japan, strong norms concerning the importance of quality are similar to those in Germany. However, quality is achieved using a system of team-based production and continuous improvement. Employees are generalists rather than specialists and it is important to reach consensus. At MBUSI, elements of all three cultures have been blended together. How did they do it?

The creation of MBUSI began with U.S. executives spending 18 months in Germany, where they worked with German engineers to design the plant. When the Vance plant was built, German engineers spent two years there helping to train the Americans. Following the Japanese model, multidisciplinary teams are used to manage the operation. Each team is autonomous and self-managing. They are held accountable for meeting quality standards, controlling costs, and meeting production schedules. Relationships between managers and their subordinates are egalitarian and open. Apparently the new hybrid organizational culture is a success. Demand for the M-Class SUV is stronger than expected, and customers seem to be delighted with it.

ers.[33] Managers working in a culture that they don't understand are likely to make poor decisions about how to staff their organizations and motivate employees.[34]

DIMENSIONS OF COUNTRY CULTURES

Geert Hofstede developed the best-known framework for comparing and contrasting country cultures, based on research conducted at IBM several decades ago. Hofstede's work continues to serve as a foundation for describing cultural differences, but in recent years more complex frameworks have been developed. In this section, we use results from the Global Leadership and Organizational Behavior Effectiveness (GLOBE) research project to describe cultural differences. The GLOBE is a team of 150 researchers who have collected data on cultural values from 18,000 managers in 62 countries. The GLOBE results indicate that cultural comparisons are best described using the dimensions shown in Exhibit 2.9. Examples of countries that are high and low on each dimension are also shown in Exhibit 2.9.[35]

CONSEQUENCES OF COUNTRY CULTURES

Associated with differences in country cultures are differences in the HR practices that employers are likely to adopt.[36] As one example, U.S. employers make much more use of incentive pay compared to employers in many European countries. Of course, culture also shapes how employees relate to work. Compared to many other cultures, Americans tend to view work as more central to their lives and they are more willing to make personal sacrifices in order to perform well on the job.[37]

United States employers cannot simply impose their domestic HR practices on employees around the world and expect them to be effective. For example, one study found that workers in the United States, Mexico, and Poland responded well to HR practices that empowered them to make work-related decisions, but employees in India responded negatively to empowerment. On the other hand, employees in all of these countries responded well to HR practices that support continuous improvement.[38] Using data from 18 countries, another study showed that European and Asian work units had better financial performance when HR practices in the units were congruent with the country culture.[39]

For companies with little experience beyond their domestic borders, cultural differences may be more disruptive than anticipated. Even experienced executives are surprised by the powerful impact of cultural differences, as the DaimlerChrysler example revealed. Some of that firm's managers said that differing management philosophies and organizational cultures caused the problems—not differences in the American and German cultures. But separating organizational and country cultures from each other is difficult, if not impossible. Organizational cultures almost always develop within a country context; they reflect and incorporate local values and practices. It's true that organizations within a country are likely to have different organizational cultures. Nevertheless, it is also true that, on average, predictable differences can be found when comparing organizations in different countries. The key challenge in a global environment is finding a balance that respects local differences while enabling global success.

Ex 2.9 Dimensions for Comparing National Cultures

CULTURAL DIMENSION	SAMPLE COUNTRIES	SAMPLE COUNTRIES
Behaviors That Society Encourages and Rewards	**Low-Scoring Countries or Regions**	**High-Scoring Countries or Regions**
Assertiveness Toughness, confrontation, competitiveness (vs. modesty, tenderness)	Sweden Switzerland Kuwait	Spain United States Greece
Future Orientation Planning, investing in future, delaying gratification	Russia Argentina Poland	Netherlands Switzerland Singapore
Gender Differentiation Males and females expected to behave differently and be treated differently (vs. accepting gender neutral behavior)	Hungary Poland Slovenia	South Korea Egypt Morocco
Uncertainty Avoidance Orderliness, consistency, following formal procedures and laws	Russia Hungary Bolivia	Germany (former West) Sweden Switzerland
Power Distance Recognizing and showing respect for people and groups with greater authority, prestige, status, material possessions than oneself	Denmark Netherlands South African (blacks)	Thailand Argentina Morocco
Institutional Collectivism Participating in legislative, economic, and political processes (vs. personal autonomy). Behaviors that support the collective good are encouraged through formal institutions, taxes, etc.	Greece Hungary Germany (former East)	Japan South Korea Sweden
In-Group Collectivism Taking pride in one's membership in smaller groups such as family, circle of close friends, employer	Denmark Sweden New Zealand	China India Iran
Performance Orientation Performance improvements and excellence, acceptance of feedback	Russia Argentina Greece	New Zealand Hong Kong Singapore
Humane Orientation Being fair, generous, altruistic, kind toward others	Germany (former West) Spain France	Malaysia Ireland Philippines

TECHNOLOGIES

Technology *refers to the process of making and using tools and equipment plus the knowledge used in this process.* Technology has been evolving for thousands of years. In early civilization, the available technology was limited to simple tools—hammers, levels, pulleys, shovels, picks, spears—and related knowledge about how to use them.

The rate of technological evolution greatly accelerated after reliable technology was created for generating power. The steam engine, introduced in the late 1700s, was a revolutionary technology. By powering ships and trains, it greatly expanded the speed and reach of trade and commerce. By powering machines such as the "spinning jenny," it lowered production costs, lowered prices, and in doing so expanded markets for the goods produced. The expanding demand required more workers, more machines, and a larger scale of production, and soon another fundamentally new technology evolved—the factory.

Factories and Mass Production Technologies

With the factory system came myriad new challenges related to managing human resources. The first challenge was recruitment. People had to be convinced to leave their farms or small workshops and move near the factory—usually in a large city and often far away. Once recruited to the factory, people had to be convinced to accept the authority of factory owners and their agents, and they had to accept standardized procedures for doing their work. Workers who had enjoyed personal autonomy and felt pride in their work were now asked to accept work that was routine and depersonalized. Factory owners, in turn, had to address the issue of skills. Most laborers had little education. They were unable to read instruction sheets or manuals. They knew little about planning large-scale production processes or managing other workers. Their skills simply didn't match those needed in the factory.[40]

Computer Technologies

More recently, computers have revolutionized how people work and how they are managed. Employees who work in factories have robots as coworkers. At the New Balance Athletic Shoe Inc. factory in Maine, skilled employees use sophisticated computer technology to produce shoes similar to those that most competitors are producing overseas using low-tech workers. A computer runs 20 sewing machine heads at once. A camera-guided automated stitcher sews six times faster than a person. A shoe that takes three hours to produce in China can be made in 24 minutes in Maine. Finding workers to operate their high-tech factories is just one of the challenges New Balance faces. Another is keeping labor costs at the factory low enough to make it competitive with the alternative means of production—low-wage workers in China who use traditional sewing equipment. By managing their human resources effectively, New Balance can continue operating in Maine to produce shoes for its American market.[41]

For U.S. workers who don't work in factories, information technology (IT) is more relevant to their daily lives than robotics. As customers, we often must negotiate an electronic menu before speaking with a person. When we do speak with a customer service employee, it is likely to be someone working in a call center, and the call center might be located anywhere in the world. The same technologies make it possible for accountants in India to process U.S. tax returns for Ernst & Young. Technology also makes it possible for physicians around the country to simultaneously view an X-ray and discuss its implications. In Bangalore, India, radiologists now analyze CT scans and chest X-rays for American physicians. By making such innovations possible, IT promises to improve patient care and customer service while reducing their costs at the same time.[42]

Sophisticated technologies are central to implementing Yellow Freight's new customer-focused strategy. Customers—who are located throughout the United States, Canada, Mexico, and Puerto Rico—can place their orders online, track shipments, and review their accounts. Dockworkers and drivers can communicate instantly with each other and easily access schedule and delivery information using wireless, mobile data terminals. A sophisticated information system also allows sales representatives to instantly learn about a customer's company, the type of loading dock it has, and who needs to sign for deliveries, among other things. Of course, changing to this high-tech approach has required tremendous change from managers and employees. Managers had to learn to support a more empowered workforce. Employees had to learn to use the new technologies and completely change the way they work with customers. Now they see that the company's success requires that they understand how the business works. Their weekly company newsletter provides honest assessments of how Yellow is performing and explains important trends in the industry.

VIRTUAL WORKFORCE

Perhaps the most dramatic consequence of the IT revolution is that it makes it possible for an organization to employ a virtual workforce, with employees located all over the world. Members of the **virtual workforce** *perform their jobs anywhere and anytime, often on an as-needed basis.* By eliminating the need for office space for employees who telecommute, IBM reduced its real estate expenses by about 50% per office site. Hewlett-Packard reported that it doubled revenue per salesperson after adopting virtual work arrangements.[43]

Of course, the benefits of a virtual workforce are not won without overcoming significant challenges. Employees working under such arrangements may feel isolated and detached from their employer. If their actions are closely monitored electronically, their morale may suffer. If they have not been properly trained in the use of IT, their insensitive electronic interactions with others may create misunderstandings or resentment among coworkers or even clients. As we discuss in subsequent chapters, a variety of human resource activities can be used to address these challenges and enable organizations and their employees alike to enjoy the benefits of a virtual workforce.

"Our economic future is wedded to technological change, and most of the jobs of the future are still ours to invent."

Robert Reich
Professor, Brandeis University
Former Secretary of Labor

FAST FACT

On any given day, about 40% of IBM's employees telecommute from home or on the road.

HUMAN RESOURCE INFORMATION MANAGEMENT

Just as technology is revolutionizing jobs and organizations, it is revolutionizing human resource management, too. One change that every job applicant knows about is web-based recruitment. According to one recent poll, 88% of employers now post job openings on the Internet, and almost all large employers now accept electronic applications. Technology is also changing the daily lives of employees long after they are initially recruited.[44]

New technologies also change the way employees are managed. *When computer technologies are used to gather, analyze, and distribute information about the people in an organization, the resulting system is referred to as a* **human resource information management (HRIM)** system (also referred to as HRIS, for human resource information system). Low-level HRIM systems merely allow employees to access general information (e.g., policies, procedures, company events) using a company intranet. A sophisticated HRIM architecture allows employees and managers to enter performance data, display and analyze it for trends over time, and use the data as input for both the employee's personal development plan and the organization's longer-term workforce and succession planning.

The HRIM systems make it easier to communicate a company's values and strategy to all employees, regardless of their location. They also make it easier for firms to design and implement HR policies and practices that are common across different cultures. Dow Chemical's HRIM system facilitates the worldwide coordination among its employees. Managers working from any workstation in the company can get information about employees working anywhere in the company. Conversely, employees around the world can access:

- information about the performance expectations and competencies required for all types of jobs in the company;
- personal development plans and tools for managing their own development;
- descriptions of job openings and employment opportunities everywhere in the company; and
- compensation information—including benefits—for all job families on a country-by-country basis.

Employees are expected to take a proactive approach to managing their careers. If they are interested in possibly changing jobs, they can keep informed of the 3,000 or so jobs that become available in a typical year. If they are considering an international move, they can study the compensation and benefits likely to be available to them before deciding which country to target and prepare themselves accordingly. Managers, in turn, serve as coaches and mentors to employees, while also being more proactive in identifying potential internal hires for open positions.

COMPANY CULTURE

A **company culture** *is the unique pattern of shared assumptions, values, and norms that shape the socialization activities, language, symbols, and ceremonies of people in the organization.* Assumptions, values, and norms form the base of a culture, but they can't be observed directly. They can only be inferred from a culture's more visible elements—its socialization activities, language, symbols, and ceremonies.

Like personality, a company's culture affects in predictable ways how people behave when no one is telling them what to do. As the best CEOs understand, human resource practices contribute to the development of a strong company culture when they are aligned with and supports a firm's strategic direction. This is illustrated in the feature, "Managing Change: Alberto-Culver's Culture Gets a Makeover."[45]

"We have a killer culture. People work hard and play hard. They are here because they want to change the world."

Jerry Yang
Cofounder and Chief Yahoo
Yahoo!

LEADERSHIP

Effective leadership ensures that people are generally working to achieve the same results. By formulating a vision, mission, and values, company leaders convey answers to questions such as, "Where are we going?" and "Why are we going there?" Together, an organization's vision, mission, and values create a framework that points people in one direction. They state the firm's aspirations for what it would like to be, though few organizations fully live up to these expectations.

Leaders also shape the culture by how they treat employees. At The Container Store, the founders support the culture by sending handwritten notes to employees and personally offering their praise for work that is well done.

Human resource professionals help organizations build strong cultures by developing HR practices to ensure that everyone behaves in ways that are

Managing Change

Alberto-Culver's Culture Gets a Makeover

Alberto-Culver Company may be best known for its VO5 hair care products, but the company also manufactures and markets many other personal care, specialty grocery, and household products worldwide. When Carol Lavin Bernick and her husband took over the leadership roles in the company founded by her parents, the company needed a makeover. Sales were flat, margins were slipping, and the competitive environment was getting tougher due to the emergence of power retailers (such as Wal-Mart). Bernick believed the best way to change the company's performance was to change its culture.

Like other companies, most of their employees understood little about how the company made money or how their jobs affected sales and profits. To change this, the company named 70 growth development leaders (GDLs) and charged them with creating cultural change. Each GDL mentors about a dozen people. As mentors, GDLs help employees understand how their work is related to achieving company goals, participate in performance reviews, and make sure employees understand and take advantage of the company's family-friendly benefits. The GDLs also meet with the CEO every six weeks or so. They bring their people's questions to the meeting and work with the top management team to develop solutions. Four years after the GDLs were established, the company introduced an award to recognize those who were most successful. A year later, two other change initiatives were introduced: A formal statement of the company's cultural values was published and new employee performance measures were developed.

To assess whether the changes are working, Bernick examines the effects on sales and pretax profits. The company also conducts annual employee surveys to assess its progress in changing the corporate culture. "I'm a firm believer that you change what you measure," says Carol Lavin Bernick. Her analyses have convinced her that the cultural changes made in the past several years are responsible for the large increases in sales and pretax profits that have accumulated during that time.

consistent with the corporate vision, mission, and values. In their first year on the job, full-time employees at The Container Store attend more than 200 hours of training to learn about the company's philosophy, its culture, and its products. At Adobe Systems in San Jose, California, the company culture is preserved by recruiting and selecting new hires who share the same values. Adobe also weaves the values into the company's reward and recognition programs. Each year, six Adobe employees receive the Founders Award, to honor them for upholding the company's core values of integrity, respect, innovation, leadership, operational excellence, customer focus, and community involvement.[46]

VISION

A **vision** *is top management's view of the kind of company it is trying to create. It can be thought of as a best-case scenario of where the company will be in the future.*[47] In a study of more than 300 chief executives, when asked to write down their vision statement, all but one were able to do so.[48] At the 58,000-employee Weyerhaeuser lumber and paper company, the vision is to be The Best Forest Products Company in the World. At American Express, the vision is "to become the world's most respected service brand." Southwest Airlines' vision is "to be the airline of choice." The vision of The Ritz-Carlton states, "We want to be the world's No. 1 hospitality provider." The success of each company in pursuit of its vision rests in part upon employees: For Southwest to be the airline of choice, employees (i.e., associates) have to be treated well enough to satisfy their customers.

MISSION

A **mission statement** *defines a company's business and provides a clear view of what the company is trying to accomplish for its customers.* A mission statement is more specific than the vision. It provides more guidance for developing plans that can be implemented to fulfill the vision. Often the mission statement addresses issues that more directly reflect the interests of the organization's different stakeholders, including employees. For Merck Pharmaceuticals, the mission is to

- Provide society with superior products and services—innovations that improve the quality of life and satisfy customer needs
- Provide employees with meaningful work and advancement opportunities
- Provide investors with a superior rate of return

Bill Gates, founder and chair of Microsoft, believes a company's mission is ultimately what inspires employees to do their best at work. According to Gates, "When people come to work, it's important that they be connected to a dream." When Gates founded Microsoft, the mission was "A computer on every desk in every home." By 2003, that mission had been largely accomplished—at least in developed countries, so the company developed a new mission: "To enable people and businesses throughout the world to realize their full potential."[49]

VALUES

Values *are the strong enduring beliefs and tenets that the company holds dear— they help to define the company and differentiate it from other companies.* Value statements have a direct impact on managing human resources because they state how employees are expected to behave—toward each other, toward customers, toward suppliers, and toward the community. As shown in Exhibit 2.10, Progressive Casualty Insurance states very clearly what their values mean for the way employees should be treated and how they should behave.[50]

At UPS, "sustainable development" is an important value. The value of sustainable development does not just mean protecting the physical environment. It also means being a socially responsible partner with local communities all around the world. And it means making decisions with a long-term view—for the next quarter-century instead of the next quarter. How does this value influence the company's approach to managing human resources? Actually, it has many consequences, of which these are just a few:

- Having citizens of the local community run the "Brown" company in each country, instead of using expatriates to run the local businesses
- Investing about $300 million annually in global training programs
- Including the Senior Vice President for Human Resources as a member of the Board of Directors[51]

Timberland also values its community partnerships. Planning analyst Anthony Gow knows that Timberland's actions are consistent with their values. As a way of contributing, Timberland allows employees to take off up to 40 hours of paid leave for community service. Gow was granted a six-month sabbatical to help a local food pantry.[52]

Ex 2.10 **Excerpts from the Corporate Values Statement at Progressive Casualty Insurance**

OUR VALUES

- Integrity . . . revere honesty and adhere to high ethical standards, report promptly and completely, encourage disclosing bad news, and welcome disagreement.

- Golden Rule . . . respect all people, value the differences among them and deal with them in the way we want to be dealt with. This requires that we know ourselves and try to understand others.

- Objectives . . . strive to communicate clearly Progressive's ambitious objectives and our people's personal and team objectives. We evaluate performance against all of these objectives.

- Excellence . . . strive constantly to improve in order to meet and exceed the highest expectations of our customers, shareholders and people. . . . base rewards on the results and promotion on ability.

- Profit . . . The opportunity to earn a profit is how the competitive free-enterprise system motivates investment to enhance human health and happiness. . . . We value all people's well-being and strive to give back to our communities.

Company Subcultures

A **company subculture** *exists when assumptions, values, and norms are shared by some—but not all—organizational members*. It's not unusual to find several subcultures within a single organization.

Company subcultures occur for a variety of reasons. Organizational subcultures are common in international firms, where country and company cultures combine to create distinct subcultures. After a merger or acquisition, subcultures are likely to exist as the two established organizations come together to form a new one. Subcultures may also emerge among employees working in different divisions or occupations, and among employees from different demographic groups, as Exhibit 2.11 illustrates.[53] Of course, not all members of each generation are exactly alike. Also, people of different ages share many experiences and values. Nevertheless, age-based subcultures are found in many societies around the world.

Managers have many different views about whether subcultures are "good" or "bad" for business. Sometimes organizational subcultures coexist peacefully within an overall organizational culture; at other times subcultures are a major source of continuing conflict.[54]

Benefits. Some managers believe that the presence of distinct subcultures can be beneficial. Disney CEO Michael Eisner expressed a similar view: "We believe in diversity because the more diverse you are as an organization, the more diverse are the opinions that get expressed. That will make us more creative."[55] At Ford Motor Company, the rationale for valuing the perspectives present in different subcultures focuses on customers. According to Mary Ellen Heyde, director of Ford's lifestyle vehicles, "If you have a diverse workforce, then you know that the customer's point of view will always be represented." The design and marketing teams for Ford's Windstar minivan, which is bought mostly by women, included many women. Their involvement in the project accounts for features such as the "sleeping baby mode" for overhead lights.[56]

Challenges. The presence of subcultures sometimes creates problems for employees and employers. After an acquisition, employees in the acquired firm may now be expected to give up the culture of their old company and

Ex 2.11 Generations Present in the U.S. Workforce		
When They Were Born	**Label Used**	**Characteristics**
1945 or before	Traditionalists	Prize loyalty. Prefer top-down management approach. Information should be provided on a need-to-know basis.
1946–1964	Baby Boomers	Optimistic and idealistic. Achieve success by challenging authority and creating open lines of communication.
1965–1980	Generation Xers	More skeptical than other generations. Often distrust institutions and prize individualism. Value work-life balance.
1981 or after	Millennials	Approach work with realization that they will change employers many times and may also change the type of work they do.

adopt the culture of the company that acquired then. Suddenly, the old ways of doing things are unacceptable. Often, managers in the acquired firm feel that their level of status and influence has been reduced.

Like employees of an acquired firm, members of demographic minority groups often feel that their subculture is not valued as highly as the culture of the majority group. Consider the experience of Eula Adams, who was the first African American to become a partner at Touche (which is now Deloitte). When Adams began working at Touche in the 1970s, none of the 800 partners was African American. "The loneliness, especially in the early days," he remembers.[57] Despite the early challenges, Adams was very successful and eventually became a partner in the firm. *Fortune* magazine included him on its list of "The Most Powerful Black Executives in America."

In general, research shows that employees who are part of a minority subculture often perceive that a glass ceiling exists, which limits their career opportunities.[58] Clashes between ethnic cultures may be one reason why a recent survey conducted by the National Society of Black Engineers found that 71% of black engineers were considering leaving their companies. Surprisingly, even employees who work for companies that have been recognized as "America's Best Companies for Minorities" often feel dominated and undervalued by members of the majority.[59] Worries about possible cultural clashes also play a role in the decisions gay and lesbian employees make about whether to be open about their sexual orientation.[60]

To reduce the negative consequences of clashes between subcultures, many organizations are in the process of transforming themselves into multicultural organizations. A **multicultural organization** *has a workforce representing the full mix of cultures found in the population at large, along with a commitment to utilize fully these human resources.* Multicultural organizations strive to permit many subcultures to coexist while ensuring that no one subculture dominates the others. In Chapter 4, we describe how U.S. firms are beginning to address the challenge of managing the diverse subcultures that often are present in organizations.

BUSINESS STRATEGIES

A **business strategy** *is a set of integrated and coordinated commitments and actions intended to achieve stated business goals.* Like a vision, mission, and values, a business strategy serves as a guide for action, but it is much more closely linked to the nature of the company's business.[61] When well-chosen business strategies are implemented well, they generate profits and improve the firm's competitiveness.

Business strategies influence the types of employees who must be recruited to work at the company, the behaviors needed from those employees, the conditions in which employees are expected to work, and so on. At ExxonMobil and many other companies, managers articulate the implications of their strategy using a strategy map. A **strategy map** *shows the cause-and-effect relationships that ultimately determine firm performance.*[62] Mobil's managers created a strategy map to understand the causes of return on capital—an important financial indicator of their success. Their strategy map helped them see that three human resource management practices could help improve their return on capital. They realized they needed to (a) help employees develop expertise in several key functional areas, (b) develop everyone's leadership skills, and (c) develop an integrated view of the company among all employees. Achieving these HR objectives would contribute to operational excellence, which in turn would improve Mobil's ability to satisfy its customers (dealers) and establish win-win relationships with them. Through win-win relationships with dealers, ExxonMobil would improve both the performance of the dealers and their own performance, which would ultimately generate more available capital.[63]

To fully describe a business strategy can be complicated—especially if the organization is large and complex. Throughout this book, when we discuss business strategies, we usually are interested in how human resource practices can be used to implement the competitive strategy of a specific business. A **competitive strategy** *describes how a particular business or business unit competes against direct rivals who offer the same products and services.* The competitive strategy states how the business will attract and retain customers— what value will the business offer that its competitors will find difficult to match? Large corporations develop different competitive strategies for each business unit. Time Warner has competitive strategies for America Online, Warner Brothers Studios, HBO, and its various other lines of business. Most small and medium-sized businesses have one competitive strategy for the entire company.

TOTAL QUALITY

One way to differentiate one's products and services from those of others is to offer outstanding quality. Delivering total quality depends on all parts of the organization working together. Increasingly, these efforts are guided by feedback from customers, because quality is in the eyes (and ears and hands and taste buds!) of customers.

Firms that compete on quality adopt practices such as Total Quality Management (TQM) and Six Sigma to ensure that their products and services meet the highest possible quality standards. Many firms pursuing total quality rely heavily on employee empowerment.[64] Empowering workers is critical to getting employees involved and committed to finding ways to continuously improve the quality of products and services. Empowered employees have the autonomy and responsibility to make key decisions about how work gets done, without seeking approval from their supervisors.

Mabe is a company that cares deeply about the quality of its products. Mabe manufactures refrigerators, ranges, heating elements, and compressors for companies such as GE, which then sell those products to consumers. Numerous HR practices help to ensure Mabe's success in satisfying the quality standards set by GE and others. For example, Mabe invests heavily in training. At least 6% of an employee's working hours are spent in training. Thus, at its plants in Mexico, the average employee receives about three weeks of training. Training programs teach employees how to set production objectives and how to assume responsibility for six-sigma-level quality. Training also teaches employees the skills they need to work in self-managed teams, where they are responsible for measuring defects, reducing the amount of scrap, and maintaining their equipment. These training efforts are successful because the employees Mabe hires have been carefully selected—

they all have the reading and math skills as well as the attitudes that are needed in this empowered factory setting.[65]

Low Cost

Competing on the basis of cost is another common competitive strategy. A firm pursuing a cost leadership strategy seeks to generate a high volume of sales to make up for the low margin associated with each sale. Efficient production systems, tight cost monitoring and controls, low investment in research and development (R&D), and a minimal sales force are characteristic of this strategy.

Human resource management practices also must support the goal of maximizing efficiency. This usually implies keeping labor costs low. To succeed in keeping labor costs as low as possible, the company may need employees who will accept part-time and shift work, perform repetitive behaviors efficiently and accept the boredom this often engenders, work in a no-frills facility, and accept minimal fringe benefits.

Customer Service

As most companies within an industry learn to produce excellent-quality products and reduce their costs, the basis for competing may change. For many industries, providing excellent customer service has become increasingly important as a basis for differentiating themselves from their competitors.

Sabre is an example of a company that competes by offering excellent service to customers all over the world. You may have never heard of Sabre, but if you ever booked a reservation through Travelocity.com, you've done business with them. Sabre's North American division relies heavily on multidisciplinary virtual teams, each with about eight members located all over the continent. The challenges that these virtual teams face and Sabre's solutions to them are described in the feature "Managing Teams: Sabre's Virtual Teams."[66]

Innovation

Companies that pursue an innovation strategy and compete by developing new products often need highly educated employees from specific fields (e.g., engineering or biochemistry). Once hired, these employees must be managed in ways that encourage experimentation and risk taking. Teamwork is usually important for innovation, and frequent failures are to be expected. Because highly skilled employees are so important to the success of firms that compete through innovation, HR practices are designed to attract and retain the very best talent. Addressing the needs of employees takes priority over cost considerations.

Innovation is central to IBM's strategy. Before Sam Palmisano became CEO of IBM in 2002, Big Blue (as the company is known) spent 10 years pulling itself back from the brink. A firm that revolutionized computing earlier in the 20th century seemed to have lost its way as that century came to a close. Now the firm is striving to become the one-stop provider of on-

Managing Teams

Sabre's Virtual Teams

Sabre, the company that invented electronic commerce for the travel industry, processes more than 400 million travel bookings annually—that's 40% of the world's travel reservations. Sabre's customers include companies such as Travelocity.com. Account executives sell the reservation system, field service technicians install it, training representatives teach customers how to use it, and so on. Members of the team occasionally work alongside each other at a location, but most of the time they work in isolation. A whole team meets face-to-face only once per year. To coordinate their activities, teams use e-mail, telephones, videoconferencing, and web-based conferencing. Interviews with members of Sabre's virtual teams revealed that they encountered some unique challenges. The following chart describes these challenges and shows the HR actions that Sabre has used to address them.

Challenges	HR Actions
Building Trust: Team members are often strangers with few opportunities for personal bonding.	*Establish Norms for Reliable Performance:* Team members developed trust when they responded rapidly to each other's communications and agreed to norms for how to communicate.
Creating Synergy: Because team members do not see each other often, it's difficult to clarify roles and spot problems before they become serious.	*Team Building and Team Training:* Before a team's launch, members receive classroom training to help them develop a team mission and values statement, set objectives, clarify roles, and build relationships. They also complete 15 CD-ROM training modules.
Feeling Isolated: In face-to-face teams, people share personal stories and family pictures, take breaks together, celebrate birthdays, and so on. When such social activities don't occur, people feel detached and isolated.	*Member Selection:* Sabre uses interviews to identify people who may not enjoy virtual teamwork, provides realist previews, and allows candidates to opt out of isolating positions if they become dissatisfied.
Balancing Technical Skills and Communication Competencies: At first, Sabre believed technical skills were almost all that mattered. They soon realized that communication competencies were much more important than they had thought.	*Member Selection:* Sabre assesses communication and teamwork competencies before hiring virtual team members. Team members and managers use teleconferencing to conduct panel interviews and assess a candidate's fit with the team.
Performance Management: Sabre discovered that traditional methods of measuring and rewarding performance didn't work when managers seldom saw the people they were managing.	*Using Multiple Performance Measures:* Sabre invested in developing new measures of team effectiveness, including customer satisfaction ratings, electronic monitoring of team discussions, and 360-degree performance assessments.

demand e-business computing. The radical new strategy of the firm assumes that companies will no longer own and house their own computing systems. Instead, they will purchase computing power directly from a provider in a way that's similar to what we now do with electrical power. Only about 10% of the technology needed for this strategy to succeed is actually available today. The rest still has to be invented. To rev up IBM's ability to innovate, Palmisano restructured the business around teams in charge of operations, strategy, and technology. Made up of people from all levels of the company, he believed these teams would be the engines of creativity at IBM. To motivate the teamwork needed for innovation, Palmisano asked the Board to cut his own bonus and set the money aside as a pool to be shared based on team performance.[67]

SUMMARY

Managing people effectively is a critical task for organizations that strive to achieve excellence and remain competitive. The external environment is complex and dynamic, creating a constant flow of new opportunities and challenges for organizations and the people who work there. Economic conditions, the political landscape, industry dynamics, labor markets, and country cultures are key elements of the external environment. Continuous change in the external environment means that adjustments often are needed in the organizational environment. Key elements of the organizational environment include the technology, the company culture, and business strategies. For a firm to gain competitive advantage, all of these elements must be aligned internally and also be well suited to the conditions in the external environment.

The intensity of competition is one reason many U.S. companies become involved in international activities. International competition is not shaped by economic conditions alone. Political events and regional trade alliances also play important roles. Shortages of skilled labor at home and the wealth of talent and skills elsewhere in the world further contribute to globalization. Employing a global labor force is made possible, in part, by information technologies. Many types of skilled jobs can be performed anywhere in the world—no longer is it necessary for office work to be performed at a centrally located office. Besides making new forms of organizing work possible, technology is changing various human resource management activities. The HRIM systems often shift HR tasks to line managers and their employees and out of the hands of specialized HR staff.

As an organization evolves, it develops a distinctive company culture. A strong culture provides clear guidelines for how people in the organization should behave. When matched with the organization's objectives and the concerns of multiple stakeholders, a strong company culture can enhance organizational performance as well as individual performance and satisfaction. Leadership sets the stage for managing human resources by providing a broad set of guidelines that help people make choices and direct their energies. The organization's vision, mission, and values convey to employees answers to questions such as: Where are we going? Why are we going there? And how will we get there? While a company's vision statement may seem very general to outsiders, if formulated with the deliberation and input of many employees, it can take on great meaning, especially for the company's approach to managing human resources. In addition, company values often suggest how employees are to be treated and what is expected from them in return.

Business strategies describe more specifically how the firm seeks to create value for customers and gain an advantage over competitors. Because a firm's strategy can have many implications for the competencies and behaviors needed from employees, it should tailor its approach to managing people to fit its specific strategy. Systems for selecting and socializing new employees, managing performance, and providing rewards and recognition should all support the behaviors needed to innovate, deliver high-quality goods and services, continuously increase efficiency and reduce costs, and/or spur innovation, as called for by the strategy.

Human resource planning, alignment, and change management practices are central to the task of creating an organization that can respond effectively to a changing environment. As described in Chapter 4, effective planning requires collaboration and coordination between line managers and HR professionals. When change is called for, other employees will also need to become directly involved. Working together, members of the HR Triad can identify the key business issues a company faces and develop specific HR practices to address those issues.

TERMS TO REMEMBER

Association of Southeast Asian
  Nations (ASEAN)
Business strategy
Company culture
Company subculture
Competitive strategy
European Union (EU)
External environment
Human resource information
  management (HRIM)
Industry life cycle
International Labor Organization
  (ILO)
Maquiladoras

Mission statement
Multicultural organization
North American Free Trade
  Agreement (NAFTA)
Organizational environment
Social Accountability International
  (SAI)
Strategy map
Technology
Values
Virtual workforce
Vision
World Trade Organization (WTO)

DISCUSSION QUESTIONS

1. Globalization has many implications for business. It also has implications for employees. From your perspective, what are the three most significant implications of globalization for employees of U.S. companies?

2. Imagine that you work at a local bank in a mid-level management position. You learn on the evening news that your company has agreed to a merger with a competitor. The rationale given for the merger is, "There are many synergies that a merger will allow us to exploit. This merger is about becoming more efficient—this is the way of the future for our industry." Assume this statement is true. Describe three significant HR issues for the new organization.

3. Think about the most recent technological developments. What are the likely implications of these developments for employers during the next 10 years? For employees?

4. Some people argue that organizations can develop their own strong company culture, and that doing so will make differences in country

cultures irrelevant to effectively managing human resources. Do you agree? Explain your opinion.

5. Describe how a powerful and clear statement of an organization's vision, mission, and values can be helpful to employees of the organization.

PROJECTS TO EXTEND YOUR LEARNING

1. *Integration and Application.*   Review the cases of Southwest Airlines and Lincoln Electric at the end of this book.

   a. Describe the relevance of the following environmental forces for Lincoln Electric's approach to managing human resources:
      - Global economic conditions
      - The country culture of the United States
      - The competitive strategy of Lincoln Electric

   b. Describe the relevance of the following possible events for Southwest Airlines' approach to managing human resources:
      - The unemployment rate declines, putting more pressure on wages.
      - A tax law change makes it more difficult for business travelers to treat airfare as a deductible expense.
      - A new agreement creates a regional trade zone that covers all of the Americas, and business travel throughout the region skyrockets.

2. *Exploring the Internet.*

   a. Read the code of conduct that students helped develop to ensure that goods bearing university labels were produced under fair labor conditions (http://www.workrights.org).
   b. Read the trade provisions created by NAFTA (http://www.mac .doc.gov/nafta).
   c. Find out how the European Union's official institutions make and enforce policies (http://europa.eu.int).
   d. Go to the website of the International Labor Organization (http://www.ilo.org) for information about labor force characteristics in different countries. You may also find the country descriptions provided by the CIA useful (http://www.odci .gov/cia/publications/factbook).
   e. Find out what you can learn about economic conditions and trends by visiting the Bureau of Economic Analysis (http:// www.bea.gov).
   f. Learn more about the domestic labor market from the Bureau of Labor Statistics (http://bls.gov) and the Census Bureau (http:// www.census.gov).
   g. Learn about recent developments in HRIM technology from the International Association for Human Resource Information Management (http://www.ihrim.org).

3. *Experiential Activity: Generational Similarities and Differences.*   Professor Warren Bennis had a hunch that people who

grew up during different eras are motivated by different things. To find out if he was right, he conducted in-depth interviews with 25 "geezers" and 18 "geeks." The geezers were all 70 or older, and the geeks were all 35 or younger. Regardless of their ages, all of the people interviewed were accomplished leaders in their fields. But these two groups had very different experiences earlier in their lives.

Geezers.   The geezers were Traditionalists. They had experienced the Great Depression and World War II. These events shaped the way they viewed the world and what was important to them. As children and young adults, they worried about their own security and how to satisfy their basic needs. For many of them, success meant making money and earning a steady paycheck. A successful career meant getting ahead in terms of increasing salary and rank. When they were young, geezers expected to work hard and "pay their dues" so that eventually they would get ahead. Some were entrepreneurs, of course, who built their own companies. For them, a primary motivation seemed to be gaining control over their own work lives. Balancing career and family was a matter people didn't talk about—at least not openly. Most of the geezers grew up in homes where fathers worked in an organization and the mothers managed the family and home.

Geeks.   The geeks were mostly from Generation X. In the families of their childhoods, it was much more common for both parents to earn income outside the home. Also much more common were divorce, second marriages, and blended families. As the geeks entered adulthood, the economic possibilities available to many seemed almost endless. Furthermore, they saw no reason why family life should have to suffer in order to realize those economic possibilities. Both men and women could have it all—a great job and a fulfilling family life. When asked what motivated them in their careers, the geeks sought to make a difference in the world. They were concerned with their own identities, they wanted to develop themselves as individuals, and they wanted to maintain a healthy balance between work and other aspects of life.

Although most of the geezers interviewed by Bennis were over 70 years old, they were still employed and actively involved in their jobs. They may be a bit older than your typical manager, but they are not so different from many CEOs of large U.S. companies. In these same companies, the middle- and lower-level managers are more similar to the geeks.[67]

Activities

1. Talk to at least two people from these different generations. Ask them whether they agree or disagree with the descriptions of their generations. Also ask them to describe other generational similarities or differences that they have observed.

2. Next, talk to at least two Baby Boomers—people born between 1946 and 1964. Ask them to describe how their generation is similar or different to that of the Geezers interviewed by Bennis.

3. Finally, talk to at least two people who are between the ages of 18 and 25. People from this generation are often called Millenials. Ask them to compare their generation to older generations and have them describe generational similarities or differences that they have observed.

4. Share this information with your classmates. As a class, discuss the similarities and differences that really seem to exist, based on the interviews conducted by everyone.

5. Given the generational differences that have been identified (by you, your classmates, and Professor Bennis), what are the implications for the types of company cultures that geeks and geezers are likely to prefer? How can organizations that want a strong company culture manage to achieve this when their employees have different perspectives about what a "good" company culture is like?

CASE STUDY

LEVI STRAUSS & COMPANY

In 1872, Levi Strauss received a letter from Jacob Davis. A Nevada tailor, who had been buying bolts of fabric from Strauss's dry goods company, Davis wrote to explain how he used metal rivets to strengthen the construction of the overalls he made. Because Davis couldn't afford to file for a patent, he invited Strauss to become a partner. Strauss knew a good idea when he saw it, and the two were granted the patent in 1873.

Today, Levi Strauss & Company is still privately owned, and the company's approach to ethical management is as familiar to business leaders as its jeans are to teenagers. Its mission statement begins, "The mission of Levi Strauss & Co. is to sustain responsible commercial success as a global marketing company of branded apparel." Its Aspiration Statement goes on to say, "We all want a company people can be proud of, . . ." which includes "leadership that epitomizes the stated standards of ethical behavior."

At Levi Strauss, ethical leadership extends well beyond company walls, to its dealings with some 500 cutting, sewing, and finishing contractors in more than 50 countries. Despite cultural differences in what is viewed as ethical or as common business practices, the company seeks business partners "who aspire as individuals and in the conduct of all their businesses" to ethical standards compatible with those of Levi Strauss. In addition to legal compliance, the company will do business only with partners who share a commitment to the environment and conduct their business consistent with its own Environmental Philosophy and Guiding Principles. In the area of employment, partners must pay prevailing wage rates, require less than a 60-hour week, not use workers under age 14 and not younger than the compulsory age to be in school, not use prison labor, and not use corporal punishment or other forms of coercion. Levi Strauss regularly conducts contractor evaluations to ensure compliance. It helps companies develop ethical solutions when noncompliance is discovered.

Closer to home, Levi Strauss actively promotes ethical business practices through activities such as membership in Business for Social Responsibility —an alliance of companies that share their successful strategies and practices through educational programs and materials. The company's domestic employment policies also are known for being ahead of the times. For example, during the 1950s, they were pioneers in integrating factories in the South. In the 1990s, they were among the first companies to offer insurance benefits to their employees' unmarried domestic partners. Through this and other policies, the company has taken a strong

Case Ex 1   Social Audit Criteria Considered by Levi Strauss & Company

STAKEHOLDER GROUP	EXAMPLES OF CRITERIA CONSIDERED WHEN ASSESSING PERFORMANCE
Owners and Investors	Financial soundness Consistency in meeting shareholder expectations Sustained profitability Average return on assets over five-year period Timely and accurate disclosure of financial information Corporate reputation and image
Customers	Product/service quality, innovativeness, and availability Responsible management of defective or harmful products/services Safety records for products/services Pricing policies and practices Honest, accurate, and responsible advertising
Organization Members	Nondiscriminatory, merit-based hiring and promotion Diversity of the workforce Wage and salary levels and equitable distribution Availability of training and development Workplace safety and privacy
Community	Environmental issues Environmental sensitivity in packaging and product design Recycling efforts and use of recycled materials Pollution prevention Global application of environmental standards Community involvement Percentage of profits designated for cash contributions Innovation and creativity in philanthropic efforts Product donations Availability of facilities and other assets for community use Support for employee volunteer efforts

stance in favor of the diversity that employees bring to the workplace. That said, Levi's has fallen on hard times and has had to reduce its worldwide workforce. It also has ceased production of jeans in North America.

To assess how well the company adheres to its values, the company conducts a social audit. Some of the criteria they evaluate the company against are shown in Case Exhibit 1.[68]

To learn more about the company's current activities, visit the home page at http://www.levistrauss.com/.

CASE QUESTIONS

1. Knowing that its managers are willing to trade off some economic efficiency in order

to operate according to their collective view of what is "ethical," would you buy shares of stock in this company? Why or why not?

2. Managers at Levi Strauss believe that they run an ethical company, but some critics view their liberal employment and benefits policies as immoral. These critics object to the policies because they're inconsistent with the critics' religious views. Analyze the pros and cons of an organizational culture that includes socially liberal employment policies that are viewed by some members of society (including potential employees and potential customers) as immoral.

3. Suppose you are looking for a new job. You have two offers for similar positions—one at Nike and one at Levi Strauss. Both

organizations have indicated that they would like you to work for a year in one of their offshore production plants somewhere in southeast Asia. The two salary offers are very similar, and in both companies you would be eligible for an annual bonus. The bonus would be based largely on the productivity of the production plant where you will be located. Which offer would you accept? Explain why.

4. In recent years, Levi's has not performed well financially. Sales began declining in 1996, and since then the company has closed more than 50 plants worldwide. Employment has gone from a peak of 37,000 employees to fewer than 10,000. There is no longer any jean production in North America. Do you think the company was living up to its vision when it laid off so many workers and contracted work to suppliers in 50 countries outside the United States?

ENDNOTES

1 Adapted from C. Sulter, "On the Road Again," *Fast Company* (January 2002): 58.

2 Source: Mercer HR Consulting, http://www.mercerHR.com; "Cost-Cutting Shifts the Terrain," *Workforce Management* (December 2003): 86.

3 S. Diesenhouse, "To Save Factories, Owners Diversify," *New York Times* (November 30, 2003): BU5.

4 More details about trends in offshoring can be found in J. Schramm, "Offshoring: SHRM Research Report," *Workplace Visions* 2 (2004): 1–8.

5 R. Miller and P. Engardio, "The Job Drain: Is It China's Fault?" *Business Week* (October 13, 2003): 32–35.

6 G. Smith and C. Lindblad, "A Tale of What Free Trade Can and Cannot Do," *Business Week* (December 22, 2003): 66–72; T. Stundza, "Trade Approaches $600 Billion," *Purchasing* (March 9, 2000): 70; see also http://www.mac.doc.gov/nafta/ (July 2, 2000).

7 J. Schramm, "Does Europe Matter?" *Workplace Visions* (January 2004): 1–7.

8 Based on information provided at the ASEAN home page, http://www.aseansec.org/home.htm (January 20, 2004).

9 K. Lucenko, "Strategies for Growth," *Across the Board* (September 2000): 63; I. M. Jawahar and G. L. McLaughlin, "Toward a Descriptive Stakeholder Theory: An Organizational Life Cycle Approach," *Academy of Management Review* 26 (2001): 397–414.

10 American Staffing Association, http://www.staffingtoday.net; "An Army of Surplus Labor," *Workforce Management* (December 2003): 96.

11 Source: R. S. Schuler and S. E. Jackson, "HR Issues in Mergers and Acquisitions," *European Management Journal* (June 2001): 59–73.

12 D. Anfuso, "Novell Idea: A Map for Mergers," *Personnel Journal* (March 1994): 48–55; "Doing Mergers by the Book Aids Growth," *Personnel Journal* (January 1994): 59.

13 J. Bower, "Not All M & A's Are Alike—and That Matters," *Harvard Business Review* (March 2001): 93–101; A. Charman, "Global Mergers and Acquisitions: The Human Resource Challenge," *International Focus* (Alexandria, VA: Society for Human Resource Management, 1999).

14 For a full discussion of reasons for failure, see M. A. Hitt, R. D. Ireland, and R. E. Hoskisson, *Strategic Management: Competitiveness and Globalization* (Cincinnati, OH: South-Western, 2001); see also R. S. Schuler, S. E. Jackson, and Y. Luo, *Managing Human Resources in Cross-Border Alliances* (London: Routledge, 2004).

15 A. Taylor, "Bumpy Roads for Global Auto Makers," *Fortune* (December 18, 2000): 18; A. Blanco, "When a Merger Turns Messy," *Business Week* (July 17, 2000): 90–93; F. Gibney Jr., "Daimler-Benz and Chrysler Merge to DaimlerChrysler," *Time* (May 24, 1999); C. Tierney, "Defiant Daimler," *Business Week* (August 7, 2000): 89–93; B. Vlasic and B. A. Stertz, "Taken for a Ride," *Business Week* (June 5, 2000): 84–89; "Daimler to Adopt Aspects of Chrysler Culture, Stallkamp Says," http://www.geocities.com/MotorCity/Downs/9323/dc.htm.

16 For a detailed discussion of labor market trends and their implications for human resource management, see D. Patel, *Workplace Forecast: A Strategic Outlook 2002-2003* (Alexandria, VA: SHRM Research, July 2002). For a historical review of changes in the U.S labor market, see M. Toossi, "A Century of Change: The U.S. Labor Force, 1950–2050," *Monthly Labor Review* (May 2002): 15–28.

17 A. Bernstein, "Too Many Workers? Not for Long," *Business Week* (May 2002): 126–130; D. Patel, *Workplace Forecast: A Strategic Outlook 2002-2003* (Alexandria, VA: SHRM Research, July 2002); D. Patel, "Globalization," *Workplace Visions* 5 (2002): 1–8; for a contrarian's point of view, see A. Overbolt, "The Labor-Shortage Myth," *Fast Company* (August 2004): 23–24.

18 "Data Bank Annual 2003: Labor Markets," *Workforce Management* (December 2003): 92–99; based on data from the Bureau of Labor Statistics, http://www.bls.gov/emp.

19 For a detailed analysis of labor shortages, see R. Herman, T. Olivo, and J. Gioia, *Impending Crisis: Too Many Jobs, Too Few People* (Winchester, VA: Oakhill Press, 2003).

20 G. E. Gibson, Jr., A. Davis-Blake, K. E. Dickson, and B. Mentel, "Workforce Demographics among Project Engineering Professionals—Crisis Ahead?" *Journal of Management in Engineering* (October 2003): 173–182.

21 A. Overholt, "The Hippest City in the USA?: Des Moines," *Fast Company* (October 2003): 96–98.

22 A. T. Mosisa, "The Role of Foreign-Born Workers in the U.S. Economy," *Monthly Labor Review* (May 2002): 3–14.

23 J. Barron, "88 Keys, Many Languages, One Proud Name: Workers at Steinway Reflect the Changing Face of New York," *New York Times* (October 6, 2003): B1.

24 "Earth Population Breakdown," *ACA News* (July/August 1996): 17.

25 W. M. Bulkeley, "IBM Data Give Rare Look at Sensitive 'Offshoring' Plans," *CNN Money*, http://money.cnn.com/services/tickerheadlines/for5/200401190053DOIWJONESONLINE (January 19, 2004).

26 "Slow Growth Shapes Policies," *Workforce Management* (December 2003): 136. Chart based on data from the Bureau of Labor Statistics.

27 National Center for Education Statistics, *Trends in International Mathematics and Science Study, 1999*, http://nces.ed.gov/timss/results.asp (February 12, 2004). Also see A. M. Konrad and J. R. Deckop, "Human Resource Management Trends in the United States: Challenges in the Midst of Prosperity," *International Journal of Manpower* (August 2001).

28 S. Rosen, J. Simon, J. R. Vincent, W. McLeod, M. Fox, and D. M. Thea, "AIDS Is Your Business," *Harvard Business Review* (February 2003): 80–87.

29 For detailed discussions of the HR issues faced by employers in Africa, including HIV/AIDS, see K. Kamoche, Y. Debrah, F. Horwitz, and G. N. Muuka, *Managing Human Resources in Africa* (London: Routledge, 2004).

30 See D. R. Briscoe and R. S. Schuler, *International Human Resource Management: Policy and Practice in Global Enterprises,* 2nd ed. (London: Routledge, 2004), for a recent discussion.

31 G. Apfelthaler, H. J. Muller, and R. R. Rehder, "Corporate Global Culture as a Competitive Advantage: Learning from Germany and Japan in Alabama and Austria," *Journal of World Business* 37 (2002): 108–118.

32 B. Kabanoff and J. P. Daly, "Values Espoused by Australian and U.S. Organizations," *Applied Psychology: An International Review* 49(2) (2000): 284–314.

33 C. L. Ahmadjian and P. Robinson, "Safety in Numbers: Downsizing and the Deinstitutionalization of Permanent Employment in Japan," *ASQ* (December 2001): 623–654.

34 R. Tung and V. Worm, "East Meets West: Northern European Expatriates in China," *Business and the Contemporary World* 9 (1997): 137–148; and N. Rogovsky and R. S. Schuler, "Managing Human Resources Across Cultures," *Business and the Contemporary World* 9 (1997): 63–75.

35 M. Javidan and R. J. House, "Cultural Acumen for the Global Manager: Lessons from Project GLOBE," *Organizational Dynamics* 29(4) (2001): 289–305; R. J. House, P. J. Hanges, M. Javidan, P. W. Dorfman, and V. Gupta, *Culture, Leadership, and Organizations: The GLOBE Study of 62 Societies* (Thousand Oaks, CA: Sage, 2004).

36 Z. Aycan, R. Kanungo, M. Mendonca, K. Yu, J. Deller, G. Stahl, A. Kurshid, "Impact of Culture on Human Resource Management Practices: A 10-Country Comparison," *Applied Psychology: An International Review* 49 (2000): 192–221. For detailed descriptions of these differences, see P. R. Sparrow, C. Brewster, and H. Harris, *Globalizing Human Resource Management* (London: Routledge, 2004); P. Budhwar, *Managing Human Resources in Asia-Pacific* (London: Routledge, 2004); H. H. Larsen and W. Mayrhofer, *Managing Human Resources in Europe* (London: Routledge, in press); M. Elvira and A. Dávila, *Managing Human Resources in Latin America* (London: Routledge, 2005).

37 E. F. Stone-Romero, D. L. Stone, and E. Salas, "The Influence of Culture on Role Conceptions and Role Behavior in Organizations," *Applied Psychology: An International Review* 52(3) (2003): 328–362; R. W. Brislin and E. S. Kim, "Cultural Diversity in People's Understanding and Uses of Time," *Applied Psychology: An International Review* 52(3) (2003): 363–382.

38 C. Robert, T. M. Probst, J. J. Martoccio, F. Glasgow, and J. J. Lawler, "Empowerment and Continuous Improvement in the United States, Mexico, Poland, and India: Predicting Fit on the Basis of Dimensions of Power Distance and Individualism," *Journal of Applied Psychology* 85 (2000): 643–658.

39 K. L. Newman and S. D. Nollen, "Culture and Congruence: The Fit Between Management Practices and National Culture," *Journal of International Business Studies* (1996): 753–776.

40 D. A. Wren, *The Evolution of Management Thought* (New York: John Wiley, 1994).

41 A. Berstein, "Low-skilled Jobs: Do They Have to Move?" *Business Week* (February 26, 2001): 94.

42 N. D. Schwartz, "Down and Out in White-Collar America," *Fortune* (June 23, 2003): 79–83; R. B. Reich, "High-Tech Jobs Are Going Abroad! But That's Okay," http://Washingtonpost.com (November 2, 2003).

43 W. F. Cascio, "Managing a Virtual Workplace," *Academy of Management Executive* 14(3) (2000): 81–90; see also A. J. Walker, "Visions of the Future: The Workforce of the Future," *IHRM Journal* (October–December 2000): 8–12.

44 "Digital Dilemmas: A Survey of the Internet Society," *The Economist* (January 25, 2003): 2–26; S. M. Bruyere, W. E. Erickson, and J. Schramm, "Disability in a Technology-Driven Workplace," *Workplace Visions* 5 (2003): 1–8.

45 C. L. Bernick, "When Your Culture Needs a Makeover," *Harvard Business Review* (June 2001): 53–64.

46 P. Babcock, "Is Your Company Two-faced?" *HR Magazine* (January 2004): 43–52.

47 J. F. Budd Jr., "A Vision of a Mission," *Across the Board* (July/August 2001): 8.

48 L. Larwood, C. M. Falbe, M. P. Kriger, and P. Miesing, "Structure and Meaning of Organizational Vision," *Academy of Management Journal* 39 (1995): 740–769.

49 B. Schlender, "Ballmer Unbound," *Fortune* (January 26, 2004): 117–124.

50 "Our Values," Progressive Casualty Insurance Company, http://www.progressive.com/progressive/values.asp (January 8, 2004).

51 L. Soupata, "Integration Versus Extraction Mentality: Sustainable Development on a Global Scale," speech given on June 4, 2003, accessed at http://www.pressroom.ups.com/execforum/speeches/speech/text/0,1403,481,00.html.

52 R. Levering and M. Moskowitz, "The 100 Best Companies to Work For," *Fortune* (January 12, 2004): 57–78.

53 L. C. Lancaster and D. Stillman, *When Generations Collide* (New York: Harper Business, 2002); T. Gutner, "A Balancing Act for Gen X Women," *Business Week* (January 21, 2002): 82; W. G. Bennis and R. J. Thomas, *Geeks and Geezers: How Era, Values and Defining Moments Shape Leaders* (Boston: Harvard Business School Press, 2002); C. Loughlin and J. Barling, "Young Workers' Work Values, Attitudes, and Behaviors," *Journal of Occupational and Organizational Psychology* 74 (2001): 543–558.

54 B. Burlingham, "What's Your Culture Worth?" *Inc.* (September 2001): 133; B. Burlingham, *A Stake in the Outcome* (New York: Doubleday, 2002).

55 S. Wetlaufer, "Common Sense and Conflict: An Interview with Disney's Michael Eisner," *Harvard Business Review* (January–February 2000): 113–124.

56 "UI: Mary Ellen Heyde," *Fast Company* (April 2000): 112.

57 C. Daniels, "The Most Powerful Black Executives in America," *Fortune* (July 22, 2002): 60–80.

58 S. Foley, D. L. Kidder, and G. N. Powell, "The Perceived Glass Ceiling and Just Perceptions: An Investigation of Hispanic Law Associates," *Journal of Management* 28 (2002): 471–496.

59   S. H. Mehta, "What Minorities Really Want," *Fortune* (July 10, 2000): 181–186; E. LaBlanc, L. Vanderkam, and K. Vella-Zarb, "America's Best 50 Companies for Minorities," *Fortune* (July 10, 2000): 190–200.

60   K. H. Griffeth and M. R. Hebl, "The Disclosure Dilemma for Gay Men and Lesbians: 'Coming Out' at Work," *Journal of Applied Psychology* 87 (2002): 1191–1199.

61   This definition is adapted from the one provided by M. A. Hitt, R. D. Ireland, and R. E. Hoskisson, *Strategic Management: Competitiveness and Globalization* (Cincinnati, OH: South-Western, 2001): 144.

62   R. S. Kaplan and D. P. Norton, *Strategy Maps: Converting Intangible Assets into Tangible Outcomes* (Boston: Harvard Business School Press, 2004).

63   R. S. Kaplan and D. P. Norton, "Having Trouble with Your Strategy? Then Map It," *Harvard Business Review* (September–October 2000): 167–176; B. E. Becker, M. A. Huselid, and D. Ulrich, *The HR Scorecard: Linking People, Strategy and Performance* (Boston: Harvard Business School Press, 2001).

64   R. Forrester, "Empowerment: Rejuvenating a Potent Idea," *Academy of Management Executive* 14(3) (2000): 67–73.

65   Adapted from H. W. Lane, M. B. Brechu, and D. T. A. Wesley, "Mabe's President Luis Berrondo Avalos on Teams and Industry Competitive-ness," *Academy of Management Executive* 13(3) (1999): 8–10, and http://www.mabe.com.mx (January 2003); also see N. Athanassiou, W. F. Crittenden, L. M. Kelly, and P. Marquez, "Founder Centrality Effects on the Mexican Family Top Management's Group. Firm Culture, Strategic Vision and Goals, and Firm Performance," *Journal of World Business* 37 (2002): 139–150.

66   B. L. Kirkman, B. Rosen, C. B. Gibson, P. E. Tesluk, and S. O. McPherson, "Five Challenges to Virtual Team Success: Lessons from Sabre, Inc.," *Academy of Management Executive* 16(3) (2002): 67–79; for more suggestions about leading virtual teams, see the entire issue of *Organizational Dynamics* 31(4) (2003), which is devoted to this topic.

67   S. E. Ante, "The New Blue," *Business Week* (March 17, 2003): 80–88; S. E. Ante and I. Sager, "IBM's New Boss," *Business Week* (February 11, 2002), accessed at http://www.businessweek.com/magazine/content/02 _06/b3769001.htm (April 25, 2003).

68   W. Zellner, "Lessons from a Faded Levi Strauss," *Business Week* (December 15, 2003): 44; K. Schoenberger, "Tough Jeans, a Soft Heart and Frayed Earnings," *New York Times* (June 25, 2000): Section 3: 1, 12, 13; J. Makower, *Beyond the Bottom Line: Putting Social Responsibility to Work for Your Business and the World* (New York: Simon & Schuster, 1994).

chapter 3

Ensuring Fair Treatment and Legal Compliance

Tom Coughlin, chief of Wal-Mart's U.S. stores, found himself explaining in court how he tried to encourage store managers to bring more women and minorities up to higher levels in the company: "I've rearranged rooms by ethnicity and gender to try to drive home that we're not all recognizing what our opportunities are relative to finding people in the organization that better represent both the gender and race issue." Apparently, this approach to managing workforce diversity—dubbed "managing by musical chairs" by one reporter—did not work. Coughlin was in court that day because a female employee named Stephanie Odle had filed a complaint with the Equal Employment Opportunity Commission (EEOC), and that complaint eventually led to a class action lawsuit against Wal-Mart. Odle's original complaint claimed that she was fired for protesting how she was treated *when she asked for a raise. Odle was an assistant manager at the time. One day she learned that her pay was $10,000 less than that of a male assistant manager. When she inquired about the pay difference, she was told that her coworker was paid more because he had "a wife and kids to support." Odle, who was a single mother, protested. She was told to submit a household budget to support her request for a pay raise, which she did. The result? She was granted a pay raise of $40/week. At the time, Odle didn't know that throughout Wal-Mart, female assistant managers earned $16,402 less than male assistant managers, on average.*

It turns out that Stepanie Odle wasn't the only woman who felt mistreated. Within two years, testimony from at least 100 other Wal-Mart employees in California was used as the basis for a class action lawsuit, referred to as Dukes vs. Wal-Mart. *To date, it is the largest discrimination case in history. One issue is pay: The plaintiffs claim that women are paid less than men in every job category. Another issue is promotions: Whereas 66% of hourly employees are women, only 14% of store managers are women.*

Wal-Mart is the nation's largest employer, and its executives admit that it has some work to do to improve how its managers treat employees. As one spokeswoman put it, "When you have one million people working for you, there are always going to be a couple of knuckleheads who do dumb things."[1]

THE STRATEGIC IMPORTANCE OF FAIRNESS AND LEGAL COMPLIANCE

In an idealized capitalistic economic system, managers on behalf of share-holders seek to maximize profits free of noneconomic external constraints—that is, without constraints other than those imposed by consumers and competitors. In the real world, however, effective businesses address the concerns of many stakeholders, including society and employees. They take a proactive stance in their relationship toward society and employees, going beyond codified laws and regulations in order to live up to society's ethical principles. At the other extreme, some companies allow managers and other employees to flagrantly violate existing laws and regulations. Dillard's department store provides an example of the abuses found in some companies. When that company was sued for racial discrimination, police officers who worked off-duty as security guards for Dillard's testified that they were instructed to follow black customers and alert the store to the presence of black shoppers. After losing the case, which was brought by a black human resources manager who had been searched by a security guard at an upscale suburban store, Dillard issued no apologies and appealed the verdict. Meanwhile, the mayor asked the city's pension managers to ensure that the city didn't own any Dillard's stock.[2] As Dillard learned, fairness is a topic that concerns society in general as well as members of the workforce.

SOCIETY AND THE LAW

The concept of fairness has many connotations, so ensuring fair treatment can be a major challenge. Society's view of what constitutes fair treatment of employees is in constant flux. Practices that were considered fair at the beginning of the 20th century had become illegal by the middle of the 20th century. Similarly, practices considered fair today may no longer be legal in five or ten years.

Affirmative action laws and practices illustrate how society's views about fairness change over time. They are built on the basic premise that organizations should actively recruit job applicants to build a workforce that reflects the demographics of the qualified local labor force. During the past three decades, affirmative action practices have become common and relatively well accepted in many organizations. But recently, they have become quite controversial. In 2003, the affirmative action practices built into the University of Michigan's student admissions procedures were challenged in a case heard by the U.S. Supreme Court. Like many employers, the University of Michigan argued that it was appropriate to take into account their desire for a culturally diverse student body when making admissions decisions. Two white applicants who were denied admission sued. The white applicants argued that it was illegal for the University of Michigan to take into account their ethnic background.

The University of Michigan case dealt with affirmative action in education, not employment. Nevertheless, employers followed the case closely. Similar affirmative action practices are quite common in business, but this case suggested that society's acceptance of these policies might be waning. When affirmative action regulations were first introduced in the 1970s, many employers resisted them. But by 2003, such practices were widely accepted and employers were not ready to dismantle them. In fact, 30 prominent companies—including Microsoft, General Motors, Steelcase, and Bank One—publicly wrote in support of the university. In their brief, they explained that having a culturally diverse workforce is essential to business success because diversity "facilitates unique and creative approaches to problem solving" and makes it possible for their organizations to "appeal to a variety of consumers." Furthermore, employers need educated workers. If universities do not provide education to a diverse group of students today, then the future success of these businesses would be in jeopardy. In deciding the case, the Supreme Court agreed with the logic presented by these companies. Their ruling permits the University of Michigan to continue to strive toward creating a student body that is culturally diverse. At the same time, the Supreme Court made it clear that universities should not simply give points to nonwhite students. Admissions officers should consider each student's entire record and use a holistic approach when deciding whom to accept. Subsequently, the Michigan ruling has been cited as a precedent that supports the use of similar affirmative action programs used by employers.[3]

As the example of affirmative action shows, companies must continually adjust to society's changing attitudes about fairness. To make matters more complicated, companies operating internationally must be responsive to the different views of fairness held within multiple societies.

Legal institutions provide one channel for the labor force to use in communicating their fairness concerns to employers. In the United States, the legal system helps define and interpret the meaning of fair treatment within employment settings. Through elected government representatives, members of the labor force initiate and ultimately create federal and state laws. Through their tax payments, employees pay for the operations of a vast array of government agencies and courts, which are responsible for interpreting and enforcing the laws. Thus, employment laws should be thought of not only as legal constraints; but also as sources of information about the issues that potential employees are likely to be thinking about as they decide whether to join or leave an organization. Simply complying with legal laws and regulations is seldom enough to ensure that employees feel they are fairly treated, however.

CONCERNS OF THE LABOR FORCE

People believe that fairness is a desirable social condition: We want to be treated fairly, and we want others to view us as being fair.[4] Companies that rank high as the best places to work generally emphasize fairness as part of their corporate culture. Fairness creates the feeling of trust that's needed to "hold a good workplace together."[5]

Members of the labor force communicate their fairness concerns to employers in many ways. As free agents, they communicate their concerns to employers directly. When deciding where to work, a potential employee evaluates whether a company pays a fair wage, whether it offers desirable benefits, whether the corporate culture is appealing, and so on. When making these evaluations, perceptions of what is "fair," "desirable," and "appealing" reflect the applicant's fairness concerns. The free agency of job applicants, combined with the diversity of the U.S. labor force, means that companies must consider a broad array of labor force concerns in order to attract and hire the best talent.

Once hired, employees continue to express their concerns about fairness and evaluate whether their employer is addressing those concerns. Employees may voice their concerns informally and indirectly through daily conversations at work. If they feel unfairly treated, they may "vote with their feet" and seek employment elsewhere.[6] Or, like Kim Miller, who says she complained more than a dozen times about her treatment at Wal-Mart, they may eventually file a lawsuit.[7] To avoid such departures and surface problems before they become severe, many companies offer formal channels of expression, such as employee surveys and employee grievance systems. Union members voice their concerns directly when they collectively bargain with employers over working conditions and compensation.

CUSTOMERS WIN WHEN EMPLOYERS TREAT EMPLOYEES FAIRLY

"Treat people fairly and give them an environment that they can work in and trust. If you do that, you can take care of your business objectives and your employees and everybody can win."

Joe Lee
CEO and Chair
Darden Restaurants

Clearly, treating employees fairly is good for employees. Fairness also is something society generally values. It turns out that fairness is also good for business. When employees are treated fairly, they treat customers better. As one hotel chain discovered, employees who feel mistreated at work can drive away customers. The hotel chain discovered this after agreeing to participate in a large research project. Nearly 9,000 employees at 111 different locations completed surveys about their fairness perceptions. For example, employees indicated whether the employer showed concern for their rights, whether they could appeal management decisions, whether employees' concerns were listened to, and so on. Customer satisfaction data were available from 84 of the locations. Analysis of these data showed that customer satisfaction ratings were higher in locations where employees felt they were treated more fairly. Both the formal procedures followed by managers and the way individual supervisors treated employees proved to be important.[8]

In this chapter, we first explain how employees evaluate whether they are treated fairly and how this affects their behavior at work. Then we describe workplace policies and practices that support fair treatment of employees. As you will see, some approaches to managing workplace fairness mirror the procedures used in U.S. courts. Finally, this chapter concludes with an overview of the legal rights and responsibilities of employers and employees.

THE HR TRIAD

Fairness and legal compliance are complex issues that implicate all three members of the HR Triad, as shown in the feature "The HR Triad: Roles and Responsibilities to Ensure Fair Treatment and Legal Compliance." Human resource professionals, with the assistance of legal experts, share responsibility for enforcing the legal responsibilities of employers and protecting the legal rights of employees. They may participate in policy development, monitor HR actions and their consequences, provide training, and serve as mediators when conflicts arise. Managers carry out their responsibility for ensuring fairness and legal compliance through daily interactions with employees. Besides treating job applicants and employees fairly and legally, they help set a tone that communicates what behaviors the company endorses and tolerates. Managers play a key role in determining whether the workplace is a hostile or welcoming place for members of a diverse workforce. Finally, all employees share responsibility for reporting illegal workplace behaviors, respecting the property rights of employers, and safeguarding the company's intellectual capital.

WHAT FAIRNESS MEANS TO EMPLOYEES

Imagine that you are the employees involved in the following two situations. How do you feel? And what will you do?

A Missed Promotion. Michelle Chang graduated with her master's of business administration (MBA) five years ago. Since then, she has worked for a large financial services company as an industry analyst. Her performance reviews have always been positive. She and her peers assumed she was on the company's informal fast track. But recently, she has begun to wonder. After the manager of her unit left last month for a better opportunity at another firm, Michelle applied for the job. She didn't get the promotion. To her surprise, the person chosen to be the new boss for her unit was Jim Johnson, a 20-year veteran of the firm who was transferred from another unit. After three weeks at his new job, it has become obvious that Jim's previous experiences have not provided him with the knowledge he needs. Michelle feels that the company's decision to give Jim the job is a signal that her future may not be as bright as everyone thought. Perhaps it's time to look into possibilities at other companies.

An Unexpected Layoff. Bill Markham works for the same firm as Michelle and Jim. He has been with the organization about seven years, coming there after working for twelve years at a large computer company and for eight years as an independent consultant. As manager of the Information Services Department, he has been responsible for managing all the company's computer specialists. Last week, the firm unexpectedly disclosed plans for a major reor-

"I worked there longer than most people are married these days and I never got a promotion."

Kim Miller
Greeter
Wal-Mart

The HR Triad

Roles and Responsibilities to Ensure Fair Treatment and Legal Compliance

LINE MANAGERS	HR PROFESSIONALS	EMPLOYEES
• Proactively seek to understand and respond to employees' fairness concerns.	• Encourage managers to use societal views of fairness to guide behavior rather than adopting a narrow legalistic model.	• Accept and fulfill responsibilities to behave fairly toward your colleagues and employer.
• Stay informed about laws and regulations protecting employees' rights and behave in accordance with them.	• Stay up-to-date about new legal developments in employment law; consult with legal experts as needed.	• Be informed about laws and regulations protecting employees' rights and behave in accordance with them.
• Establish and review policies to ensure fair treatment of employees in collaboration with HR professionals.	• Develop and help implement policies that support fair and ethical behavior by everyone in the organization.	• Work with HR professionals in establishing procedures for dealing fairly with workplace issues.
• Learn the steps involved in the organization's grievance procedures and follow them.	• Administer grievance procedures and participate in alternative dispute resolution activities.	• Report discriminatory or other illegal behavior among subordinates, colleagues, or superiors to an HR professional.
• Intervene if you observe discriminatory or other illegal or unethical behavior among subordinates, colleagues, or superiors.	• Help keep employer and employee rights and responsibilities in balance.	• Help educate employees from other cultures about U.S. employment law; learn about employment laws in other countries.

ganization of Information Services. To "improve efficiency," the company has decided to decentralize several staff activities. In the new structure, the activities of Information Services will be carried out by generalists who will work within each of the firm's several divisions. Of course, everyone knows that the words improve efficiency are a code, meaning the size of the Information Services staff will be reduced. Bill was not worried when he heard the announcement; he expected to be assigned to the largest division and had already begun discussing the idea of a major move with his family. He was shocked when he learned that he was going to be let go. He appreciated the firm's offer to pay for outplacement counseling, but he wondered whether he should accept its decision as final. As a 50-something white male, he imagined that finding a new job would be pretty tough. Maybe he should put up a fight.

How much do Michelle and Bill trust their employer? Has each person been treated fairly? What other information might you want to obtain before deciding whether this company is treating employees fairly?

Since the mid-1970s, social and organizational scientists have conducted numerous studies designed to improve our understanding of concepts such as fairness and justice. This research has shown that people's perceptions of fairness reflect at least three features of the situations in which they find themselves: the actual *outcomes*, the *procedures* used in arriving at these outcomes, and the *interactions* the employees have with their managers. These features are referred to as distributive justice, procedural justice, and interactional justice, respectively.[9]

DISTRIBUTIVE JUSTICE

When employees believe that the outcomes they experience are fair in comparison to the outcomes of others, they feel a sense of **distributive justice.** Is pay distributed fairly among people from the top to the bottom of the organization? Are performance evaluations distributed fairly among good and poor performers? Are promotions distributed fairly? Many women who worked for Wal-Mart didn't think so. They could see that the outcomes (pay, promotions, training opportunities) received by women were generally less that what men received. In other words, these outcomes seemed to be distributed according to one's gender, and not based purely on merit.

Generally, people see pay as fair when they believe that the distribution of pay across a group corresponds to the relative value of the work being done by each person. Similarly, when the relative sizes of raises correspond to the relative performance levels of people in the unit, people tend to accept the system as fair. Not surprisingly, people prefer favorable outcomes for themselves. In the cases of Michelle and Bill, a promotion is better than no promotion and a transfer is better than being let go. Nevertheless, we do not necessarily feel that we have been treated unfairly when we do not get the best possible outcome.

Perceptions of fairness hinge on how our own outcomes compare with the outcomes of other people, taking into account our own situation and the situations of others. In evaluating the fairness of her situation, for example, Michelle compares her outcome with Jim's. If Michelle felt that the outcomes she and Jim experienced reflected their relative qualifications, then Michelle probably would accept the situation as fair even though she didn't get promoted. Furthermore, Michelle and Jim's coworkers use similar heuristics in evaluating their employer. When Michelle's coworkers see that she has been unfairly treated, they not only feel bad about what happened to Michelle, but they also may conclude that their employer generally treats employees unfairly.[10]

Employees in the United States typically experience distributive justice under conditions of equity, or merit-based decision making.[11] Employees from other countries and cultures may see things quite differently, however. American culture is individualistic, whereas many other cultures are more collectivistic. In collectivistic cultures—like many of those found throughout Asia—concern for social cohesion is greater than in the United States. Going along with a perspective that focuses more on groups, people from collectivistic cultures value *equality* of treatment and treatment based on *need*, and they allocate rewards accordingly.[12] From a collectivistic perspective, Michelle might be viewed as having been treated fairly because she was treated the same as her coworkers (equally), and perhaps Jim needed the job more than did Michelle.

PROCEDURAL JUSTICE

Perceptions of justice depend on more than the relative distribution of outcomes. Also important to perceived fairness are beliefs about the entire process used to determine outcomes. The term **procedural justice** *refers to perceptions about fairness in the process used to make decisions.* For example, Michelle and Bill might wonder *how* their company made its decisions in their situations. Research suggests that in the U.S. culture, employees consider a formal procedure to be fair if it meets the conditions shown in Exhibit 3.1.[13]

When employees believe their employer is concerned with ensuring procedural justice, they are more productive and less likely to be absent.[14] They also may be more trusting of their managers. According to one study, fair HR practices give employees confidence that they will be treated well by their employer. They feel they can trust their managers even if they experience some conflict. As a result, employees are more willing to "go the extra mile" for the company.[15]

Ex 3.1   **Conditions to Be Met in Order for Employees to Perceive Formal Procedures as Fair**

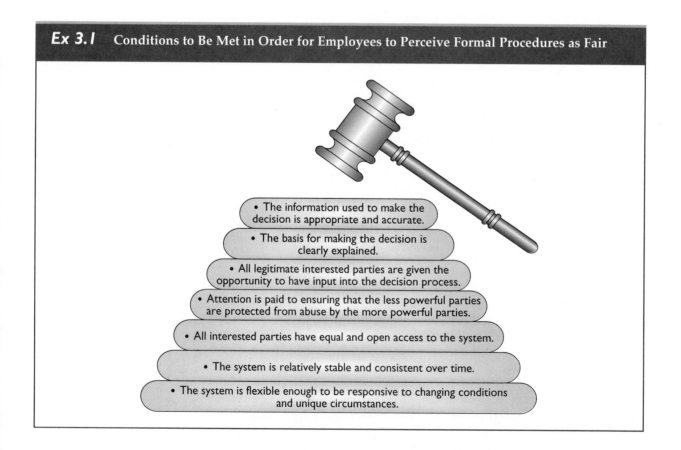

- The information used to make the decision is appropriate and accurate.
- The basis for making the decision is clearly explained.
- All legitimate interested parties are given the opportunity to have input into the decision process.
- Attention is paid to ensuring that the less powerful parties are protected from abuse by the more powerful parties.
- All interested parties have equal and open access to the system.
- The system is relatively stable and consistent over time.
- The system is flexible enough to be responsive to changing conditions and unique circumstances.

INTERACTIONAL JUSTICE

The formal system is only one aspect of the procedures to which employees react. Employees also take into account how they personally are treated in their interactions with the managers who carry out the formal procedures. Perceptions of **interactional justice** *reflect employees' feelings about whether managers are sensitive to their situations and treat them politely and respectfully as well as whether employees feel they are given sufficient and timely information about the procedures.*[16] Employees respond more favorably when they feel they have been given a full and reasonable account of what happened.[17]

REACTIONS TO UNJUST TREATMENT

Consider again the situation of Michelle and the actions she might take. If you were Michelle, you would probably consider actions that fall into one of the following categories:

A. Exit the organization and put the incident behind you;
B. Stay and simply accept the situation as something you must tolerate;
C. Stay but engage in negative behaviors that help you restore your sense of fairness (e.g., shorten your hours a bit; stop attending unnecessary meetings and functions);
D. Voice your concern to people inside the organization (e.g., discuss the situation with your colleagues; talk about it with a mentor; talk to someone in the employee relations office); or
E. Voice your concern to external authorities (e.g., explore possible legal action; talk to the press).[18]

Quit? For high performers like Michelle, choice A, quitting, may be the best alternative. From the organization's perspective, however, having Michelle leave and perhaps join the competition may be the least desirable alternative. From society's perspective, turnover caused by feelings of injustice is undesirable because it tends to reduce productivity.

Stay and Accept the Situation? Alternative B would be better for Michelle's employer, but it's probably not very common because few people easily shrug off injustices suffered at the hands of their employers. Instead, their outlook sours. Employees who stay in situations that they believe are unfair lose confidence in the competence of management and feel they cannot trust management.[19] Employees who feel unfairly treated also report feeling more distressed, dissatisfied, and uncommitted to both their employers and the goals their employers set for them.[20]

Seek Revenge? Feelings of injustice affect behavior, not just attitudes, even for employees who decide not to quit because of unfair treatment. Therefore, reactions that fall into categories C and E are possible. Employees attempt to maintain a sense of balance in their relationship with employers. If a legal issue is involved, employees may seek legal solutions. Often, however, feelings of unfairness arise in response to perfectly legal management behavior. This was illustrated quite dramatically in a company that temporarily cut employees' pay. The company was a large manufacturer of aerospace and automotive parts.

Owing to the loss of two contracts, temporary pay cuts were required at two of the company's three plants. Everyone at the two plants took a 15% pay cut for 10 weeks, including management. The situation created a natural opportunity for the company and a researcher to learn more about how best to implement pay cuts, so a small experiment was conducted. In one plant, the company tried to convey how much it regretted the pay cuts, explained that the pay cuts would eliminate the need for layoffs, and assured employees that no favoritism would occur. At a full meeting with the employees, top management spent an hour answering employees' questions. At the second plant involved, the pay cut was announced at a brief 15-minute meeting with no apology and very little explanation. The third plant was used as a control group. Employees' reactions were assessed in terms of theft rates, turnover, and responses to a survey.

At both the plants taking pay cuts, theft rates went up during the weeks the cuts were in effect and then went back down again when full pay was restored, particularly at the plant where the inadequate explanation was given. Turnover in this plant also soared, from 5% to 23%. Survey results confirmed that employees at this plant didn't understand how their pay cut was determined and felt they had been treated unfairly.[21] As this company found out, people are sensitive to changes that disturb their sense of equity, and will seek ways to rebalance the scales if they're tipped.[22] Perhaps that is why employee thefts cost U.S. employers $40 billion annually.

Talk to Others in the Organization? The way companies manage fairness can greatly influence how employees react.[23] When employers inspire feelings of loyalty in employees, employees are likely to use informal communication channels to voice their concerns.[24] Wal-Mart employees have a reputation for being loyal to the company, so it is not surprising that Stephanie Odle first talked to people inside the company about her concerns. As this example illustrates, such informal discussions do not always resolve employees' concerns. In those situations, managing fairness effectively involves using formal organizational systems to deal with conflicts and disputes. By fully explaining *how* decisions are made and by offering employees opportunities to *voice* their concerns and have their questions answered (choice D), employers can minimize negative employee reactions. In well-managed companies, employees' feelings of dissatisfaction are intentionally surfaced and used to stimulate positive changes that actually benefit both employees and employers. Unfortunately, Wal-Mart didn't have a system in place to ensure that Stephanie's concerns were voiced and addressed.

Complain to External Authorities? Employees who feel they have been treated unfairly can seek redress through the legal system. Like Stephanie Odle, they can file a complaint with the EEOC. Or they can hire a lawyer to pursue their case. Either way, research shows that perceptions of distributive and procedural injustice are likely to result in a lawsuit.[25] Depending on their circumstances, employees may sue their employer claiming unfair discrimination, wrongful termination, failure to comply with laws regulating pay, and so on. If they win, employees who bring such lawsuits may be reinstated in their old jobs, given promotions, given payments to cover lost compensation, and so on. Regardless of whether the employee wins or loses, litigating and settling such lawsuits can end up costing employers millions of dollars as well as immeasurable reputational loss in the eyes of the public.

MANAGING TO ENSURE FAIR TREATMENT

Because employees' perceptions of fairness can have such far-reaching consequences, employers use a variety of policies and practices to ensure fairness. Various laws and regulations mandate some, while others are voluntary. Issues of fairness and legal compliance pervade almost every area of human resource management. In Chapters 5 and 6, for example, you will learn about laws governing staffing procedures and the means that employers can use to ensure that job applicants are treated fairly. In Chapters 9, 10, and 12 you will learn about laws governing compensation and practices that improve employees' perceptions of pay fairness. In those and other chapters, the laws, policies, and practices that are especially important to the activities will be described in more detail.

This chapter sets the stage for discussions in subsequent chapters by describing some of the most sweeping legislation and the agencies that enforce it. We also describe proactive management practices that can reduce the likelihood of lawsuits being filed. As you read about these, keep in mind that good policies are not enough. Inevitably, employees sometimes feel that a decision or procedure is unfair. Sensitive supervisors and managers who acknowledge these situations and express their concern can minimize the disruptive effects of the situations. As simple as it seems, apologies reduce anger.

LEGAL MEANS TO ENSURE FAIR TREATMENT

United States companies must act in accordance with several different types of laws, including constitutional laws, statutory laws, administrative regulations, executive orders, and common law rules. Laws are simply society's values and standards that are enforceable in the courts. The legal environment communicates society's concerns through state and federal laws, regulations, and court decisions. In general, the legal system is designed to encourage socially responsible behavior.[26] That is, it considers the outcomes of all parties concerned and attempts to impose decisions and remedies that balance the perspectives of employees, employers, and other stakeholders.[27]

As society's concerns change, so do employees' legal rights. At one time, U.S. employers could legally discriminate against women and minorities in hiring and promotions. As a consensus developed that such discriminatory practices were unethical, laws such as the Civil Rights Act were passed to stop the practices and ensure equal employment opportunities for all citizens. In addition, the federal government issued regulations requiring government agencies and federal contractors to work at correcting the effects of past discrimination.

Today, society's views concerning gay, lesbian, bisexual, and transgender (GLBT) employees are in flux, and so are employers' legal responsibilities. In 2000, only 51% of the largest 500 U.S. employers had policies that prohibited discrimination based on sexual orientation. By 2004, 95% of the largest employers had such policies. Likewise, the portion of large companies offering domestic partner benefits to unmarried employees jumped from 25% in 2000 to 70% in 2004.[28]

To understand how the legal environment affects the way companies manage human resources, it's necessary to understand several major employment laws and regulations that are promulgated and enforced by our legal system.[29]

U.S. CONSTITUTION

In countries that have one, the constitution is the fundamental law of the land. The U.S. Constitution is the oldest written constitution still in force in the world. It defines the structure and limits of the federal government and allocates power among the federal government and the states. Within the legal framework established by the Constitution have flourished numerous other state and federal laws (called "statutes"), regulations, and court decisions that further define the legal contours of the relationship between an employer and its employees.

TITLE VII OF THE CIVIL RIGHTS ACT

FAST FACT

Citizens of the United States employed elsewhere by a firm that's controlled or owned by an American parent are protected by Title VII of the Civil Rights Act, the Age Discrimination in Employment Act (ADEA), and the Americans with Disabilities Act (ADA).

One especially important federal employment law has been Title VII of the Civil Rights Act. It was originally enacted in 1964, and later revised in 1978 and 1991. The 1991 law reinforced the intent of the Civil Rights Acts of 1964 but states more specifically how cases brought under the act should proceed.[30] Today, **Title VII of the Civil Rights Act** *prohibits discrimination by employers, employment agencies, and unions on the basis of race, color, religion, sex, national origin, or pregnancy.*

Title VII is one of several key statutory laws that affect the employment relationship. Several other important federal laws are summarized in Exhibit 3.2. We cannot fully discuss all of these laws here, but you should familiarize yourself with them in preparation for future chapters, where they are referred to again.

STATE LAWS

As already noted, state laws must be consistent with federal law, but this does not mean that state and federal laws must be the same. Three important differences between state and federal laws are common. First, state laws often cover companies that are not covered by federal laws. For example, federal employment laws such as Title VII often apply only to businesses with fifteen or more employees, but similar state laws often apply to even smaller businesses. Second, state laws often offer greater protection to employees than do federal laws. For example, although several states and the District of Columbia prohibit discrimination on the basis of sexual orientation, at this time no federal law prevents such discrimination.[31]

FAST FACT

As of 2004, 36 states allowed the firing of an employee because of sexual orientation; 14 states and the District of Columbia banned it.

Family leave laws provide another example of how state laws may offer greater protection to employees than federal laws do. The federal Family and Medical Leave Act requires employers to provide time off for family

Ex 3.2 Major Federal Employment Laws and Regulations

ACT	JURISDICTION	BASIC PROVISIONS
National Labor Relations Act (Wagner Act, 1935)	Most nonmanagerial employees in private industry	Provides right to organize; provides for collective bargaining; requires employers to bargain; unions must represent all members equally
Fair Labor Standards Act (FLSA; 1938)	Most nonmanagerial employees in private industry	Establishes a minimum wage; controls hours through premium pay for overtime; controls working hours for children
Equal Pay Act (1963)	Most employers	Prohibits unequal pay for males and females with equal skill, effort, and responsibility working under similar working conditions
Title VII of the Civil Rights Act (1964; 1991)	Employers with 15 or more employees; employment agencies; unions	Prevents discrimination on the basis of race, color, religion, sex, or national origin; establishes EEOC; provides reinstatement, back pay, compensatory and punitive damages; permits jury trials
Executive Order 11246 (1965)	Federal contractors with large contracts and 50 or more employees	Prevents discrimination on the basis of race, color, religion, sex, or national origin; establishes Office of Federal Contract Compliance (OFCC)
Age Discrimination in Employment Act (ADEA; 1967)	Employers with more than 20 employees	Prevents discrimination against persons age 40 and over, and states compulsory retirement for some employees
Occupational Safety and Health Act (OSHA; 1970)	Most employers involved in interstate commerce	Assures as far as possible, safe and healthy working conditions and the preservation of our human resources
Rehabilitation Act (1973)	Government contractors and federal agencies	Prevents discrimination against persons with physical and mental disabilities
Employee Retirement Income Security Act (ERISA; 1974)	Most employers with pension plans	Protects employees covered by a pension plan from losses and benefits due to mismanagement, job changes, plant closings, and bankruptcies
Pregnancy Discrimination Act (1978)	Employers with 15 or more employees	Identifies pregnancy as a disability and entitles the woman to the same benefits as any other disability
Worker Adjustment and Retraining Notification Act (WARN; 1988)	Employers with more than 100 employees	Requires 60 days' notice of plant or office closing or substantial layoffs
Americans with Disabilities Act (ADA; 1990)	Employers with 15 or more employees	Prohibits discrimination against individuals with disabilities
Family and Medical Leave Act (1993)	Employers with 50 or more employees	Allows workers to take up to 12 weeks' unpaid leave for childbirth, adoption, or illness of employee or a close family member
Sarbanes-Oxley Act (2002)	Most publicly-held companies	Imposes strict rules intended to reduce wrong-doing in public by corporations and strengthens the protections for employees who report wrong-doing.

care, but does not require employers to pay employees while they are on leave. California was the first state to require paid leave. Eligible workers in California receive half pay for six weeks while they tend to a newborn, move a parent to a nursing home, or in other ways care for family members. Unlike the federal law, which applies only to employers with 50 or more workers, California's leave plan—called Family Temporary Disability Insurance—applies to all employers regardless of size.[32]

The third difference between state and federal laws is that state laws often anticipate federal laws and, in this sense, tell us what to expect in the future at the federal level. For example, New York had adopted a fair employment law in 1945 and about half the states had adopted similar laws by the time the Civil Rights Act of 1964 was passed at the federal level. Florida, Maine, and the District of Columbia had each adopted family leave legislation before the federal Family and Medical Leave Act of 1993 (FMLA) was enacted. Massachusetts's first minimum wage legislation in 1912 was a predecessor of the federal Fair Labor Standards Act of 1938 (FLSA).

Administrative Regulations

| FAST FACT |
| In most states, employees have up to 300 days after an alleged discriminatory event to file a charge with the EEOC. |

At both the federal and state levels, the legislative and executive branches of government can delegate authority for rule making and enforcement to an administrative agency. In carrying out their duties, administrative agencies make rules (often called standards or guidelines), conduct investigations, make judgments about guilt, and impose sanctions. In practice, this means these federal agencies have the responsibility and authority to prosecute companies they believe are violating the law. In other words, administrative regulations explain how the agency will put legislation into practice.

Three administrative agencies of particular importance for managing human resources are:

- the Equal Employment Opportunity Commission (EEOC),
- the Occupational Safety and Health Administration (OSHA), and
- the National Labor Relations Board (NLRB).

| FAST FACT |
| Since 1980, staffing at the EEOC has shrunk 17% while complaints have increased 50%. |

EEOC. The **Equal Employment Opportunity Commission (EEOC)** *administers Title VII of the Civil Rights Act as well as the Equal Pay Act of 1963 and the Age Discrimination in Employment Act of 1967.* For each of these acts, the EEOC has produced regulations that inform employers of how the agency will assess whether or not a legal violation has occurred.

As you read subsequent chapters, you will see that EEOC regulations have implications for nearly every area of HR activity—recruitment, selection, training, pay, performance measurement, termination, and so forth. The EEOC is one of the most influential agencies responsible for enforcing employment laws.

As an enforcer of laws, the EEOC can prosecute employers who break the law. Each year, the EEOC receives approximately 85,000 complaints annually from employees. Exhibit 3.3 shows the types of discrimination charges filed in a recent year.[33]

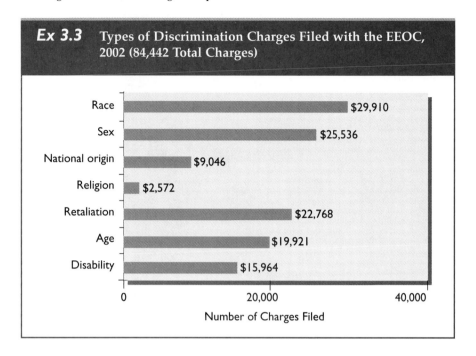

Ex 3.3 Types of Discrimination Charges Filed with the EEOC, 2002 (84,442 Total Charges)

- Race: $29,910
- Sex: $25,536
- National origin: $9,046
- Religion: $2,572
- Retaliation: $22,768
- Age: $19,921
- Disability: $15,964

Number of Charges Filed

Large monetary settlements often occur when the EEOC files a class action suit against an employer. In a **class action lawsuit,** *a group of similar employees (i.e., a "class") asserts that all members of the employee class suffered due to an employer's unfair policies and practices.* As Exhibit 3.4 shows, the monetary benefits that the EEOC won for employees grew substantially during the 1990s.

OSHA. The **Occupational Safety and Health Administration (OSHA)** *administers the Occupational Safety and Health Act.* As described in Chapter 13, OSHA conducts safety and health inspections, investigates accidents and alleged hazardous conditions, issues citations for violations, levies fines, collects mandatory reports prepared by employers, and compiles statistics on work injuries and illnesses.

NLRB. The **National Labor Relations Board (NLRB)** *administers the National Labor Relations Act.* The NLRB's responsibilities include protecting the rights of employees to engage in group actions for the purpose of influencing their work conditions. As described in Chapter 15, the NLRB focuses much of its attention on group activities related to union organizing and collective bargaining. This is not the NLRB's only area of jurisdiction, however. In recent years, for example, the NLRB has become involved in several cases concerning nonunion employees who protested their company's actions using their company's e-mail system. As discussed in Chapter 9, the National Labor Relations Act also provides for a fair minimum wage, establishes employees' right to overtime pay, and constrains working hours for children.

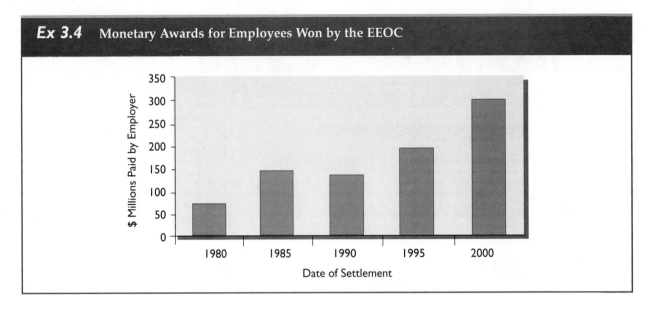

Ex 3.4   Monetary Awards for Employees Won by the EEOC

Executive Orders

United States presidents shape the legal environment by approving and vetoing bills passed by Congress and by influencing how vigorously administrative agencies carry out their duties and responsibilities. In addition, the president can create law by issuing an executive order. An **executive order** *specifies rules and conditions for government business and for doing business with the government.*

Approximately 70,000 companies are federal government contractors.

FAST FACT

In the area of employment, the actions of government contractors (organizations that do work for the federal government) are most affected by Executive Order 11246, issued in 1965 by President Lyndon B. Johnson. Like Title VII, Executive Order 11246 prohibits discrimination on the basis of race, color, religion, or national origin. It applies to federal agencies and to federal contractors and subcontractors. In 1966, Executive Order 11375 was issued to prohibit discrimination based on sex by these employers.

Whereas Executive Orders 11246 and 11375 parallel federal law that applies to all employers, Executive Order 11478, issued in 1969, has no parallel in federal statutory law. Executive Order 11478 requires that employment policies of the federal government be based on merit. Although most employees agree that merit-based employment policies are a good idea, there is no federal law that *requires* businesses to make merit-based employment decisions.

Common Law Rules

Common law rules *are rules made by judges as they resolve disputes between parties.* The U.S. system of common law is rooted in English common law, which was established after the Normans conquered England in 1066. To help unify the country, William the Conqueror established the King's Court. Its purpose was to develop a common set of rules and apply them uniformly throughout the kingdom. Decisions were based on the opinions of judges and legal precedents. Judges used **legal precedents** *when they referred back to important decisions that were made in the past and used these as the basis for making a decision in a new case.* When new types of disputes arose, judges created new law to resolve them. This system is still in effect today in England.

Unlike English judges, U.S. judges do not make laws; they only interpret and apply them. But their interpretations continue in the tradition of setting precedent to decide new cases. The use of precedent to decide cases helps employers anticipate how the courts might rule should they find themselves involved in a similar case. When interpreting the implications of court decisions, keep in mind that rulings made by the Supreme Court carry the most weight because many of the decisions made by federal and state courts are subject to review by the Supreme Court.

SETTLING DISPUTES

Even the best companies occasionally experience disputes over the treatment of employees. In the most extreme cases, such disputes may end up in court, where they are eventually resolved by a legal decision or through a legal settlement. More often, however, disputes are resolved through alternative dispute resolution procedures before they reach a court.

USING THE COURTS TO SETTLE DISPUTES

For employment law cases that are resolved by a court decision, two common remedies to violations are monetary damages and settlement agreements.

Monetary Damages. If the court determines that an employee's legal right has been violated and that this has resulted in injury, the employer may be required to pay monetary damages to the plaintiff. Compensatory monetary damages are intended to help victims retrieve what they have lost (e.g., back pay and attorneys' fees). Punitive monetary damages are intended specifically to punish wrongdoers and deter future wrongdoing.

Settlement Agreements. When lawsuits are resolved by a **settlement agreement,** *the defendant (employer) usually does not admit to wrongdoing; nevertheless, it may agree to pay money to the plaintiff or plaintiffs.* For example, when Coca-Cola settled the racial discrimination lawsuit brought against it on behalf of African American employees, it denied any wrongdoing. At the same time, it agreed to pay an average of $40,000 to each of the company's 2000 black employees, set aside $59 million for a fund to cover claims of emotional distress, and set aside nearly $67 million to be used to correct past pay disparities and eliminate pay disparities in the future.[34] As is common in settlement agreements, Coca-Cola did more than agree to pay money to the plaintiffs. They also agreed to make significant changes in their HR management policies and practices, as directed by the court.

Texaco is another example of a company that agreed to change its management practices as part of a settlement agreement. In 1990, in the process of its normal monitoring activities, the Department of Labor found that Texaco was deficient in its minority representation, and in 1995, the EEOC issued a similar finding. Although the company's employment numbers indicated it had been making some progress in terms of hiring a more diverse workforce, promotion and pay rates lagged behind those of other companies in the industry. Eventually, the EEOC took Texaco to court. As part of the lawsuit settlement, Texaco agreed to implement broad-reaching diversity management initiatives. The specific goals and action steps are described in the feature "Managing Change: Texaco's Plan for a Cultural Shift".[35]

COMPANY GRIEVANCE PROCEDURES

Grievance procedures *(also referred to as complaint resolution procedures) encourage employees to voice their concerns to the company instead of the courts, and they encourage employees to seek constructive resolutions without litigation.* In unionized settings, the presence of such procedures had already become nearly universal by 1950.[36] Almost all public and private unionized employees are covered by contracts that specify formal written grievance procedures.[37] More than half of America's largest corporations also have some type of formal complaint resolution system.[38] The growing popularity of formal complaint resolution is consistent with managers' beliefs that employees have a right to fair treatment.[39] At many companies, employees who feel they have been unfairly treated can ask to have a management decision reviewed by a board or panel of their peers. This approach can be particularly helpful in environments where employees lack the representation and negotiating power of a union.[40] At Coors, an appeal process gives employees a voice in how they're treated, which may result in employees being more willing to continue working at Coors even if they have some complaints.[41]

For many years, employees of Coors Brewing Company relied on their union to deal management on issues of fairness. But after a failed strike against the company, employees voted to decertify the union. This left employees without protection from what they saw as the "potential abuses of management."

Employees were afraid that management would take control from them and give them no recourse in such matters as employee discipline. To their way of thinking, "if management wants to get us out of here, they'll do it and do it without a fair hearing." Representatives for the workers told Bill Coors, who was head of the company, "Our employees are frightened because they've had this union here that was taking care of our needs and making sure that discipline was meted out fairly. Now we don't have that and we've got to either find a way to provide it or ultimately the employees will bring in another union." To address these concerns, the HR department set up a peer review system designed to give employees a chance to air their complaints and have their peers take part in evaluating whether their complaints were legitimate. Coors' peer review system works like this:

Step 1. An employee who's unsatisfied with the application of a company policy—but not the policy itself—may file an appeal with the employee relations representative within seven working days. The employee relations representative then sets up an appeal board by randomly selecting two members of management and three employees from the same job category as the appellant.

Texaco's Plan for a Cultural Shift

The seriousness of Texaco's problems became public in 1996, when secretly recorded conversations revealed that senior executives used racial epithets and plotted to destroy documents demanded by the courts in a discrimination case. Other evidence presented during the case revealed that it was common for supervisors to refer to members of racial subgroups in derogatory terms. Many employees did nothing to protest such treatment for fear of losing their jobs, while others quit. Eventually, some took their evidence to court.

As part of their lawsuit settlement, Texaco agreed to pay $140 million—at the time, it was the largest settlement ever for a case of racial discrimination. An outline of the massive cultural change effort that the company agreed to initiate follows.

Components of Texaco's Cultural Change Initiatives

Recruiting and Hiring

- Ask search firms to identify wider arrays of candidates
- Enhance the interviewing, selection, and hiring skills of managers
- Expand college recruitment at historically minority colleges

Identifying and Developing Talent

- Form a partnership with INROADS, a nationwide internship program that targets minority students for management careers
- Establish a mentoring process

- Refine the company's global succession planning system to improve identification of talent
- Improve the selection and development of managers and leaders to help ensure that they're capable of maximizing team performance

Ensuring Fair Treatment

- Conduct extensive diversity training
- Implement an alternative dispute resolution process
- Include women and minorities on all HR committees throughout the company

Holding Managers Accountable

- Link managers' compensation to their success in creating "openness and inclusion in the workplace"
- Implement 360-degree feedback for all managers and supervisors
- Redesign the company's employee attitude survey and begin using it annually to monitor employee attitudes

Improving Relationships with External Stakeholders

- Broaden the company's base of vendors and suppliers to incorporate more minority- and women-owned businesses
- Increase banking, investment, and insurance business with minority- and women-owned firms
- Add more independent, minority retailers and increase the number of minority managers in company-owned gas stations and Xpress Lube outlets

Step 2. A hearing is held, orchestrated by the employee relations representative. At the hearing, the supervisor describes the circumstances and the employee explains why the supervisor's action was unfair. Board members may ask questions of both parties during the proceedings and request testimony from witnesses.

Step 3. When board members have all the information they need, they privately discuss the case. They decide by majority vote whether to uphold the action, reduce the severity, or overturn the action completely. The board's decision is final. The employee relations representative notifies the supervisor and the employee of the decision through a brief, written summary, signed by all the board members. In the past decade, the board has overturned a supervisor's actions for about 10% of the appeals.[42]

As is true of most administrative systems, the specific details of a grievance procedure policy are not as important as the way the policy is carried out on a daily basis. When they work well, grievance procedures not only help lower the legal costs associated with resolving disputes in the courts, but they also increase employee loyalty and commitment.[43]

MEDIATION AND ARBITRATION

When disputes cannot be resolved through a company's internal process, a second step may be taken before resorting to the courts. Because the courts are a slow, expensive, and difficult way to resolve serious disputes, a growing number of businesses are using alternative dispute resolution when employees make charges of unfair treatment.

Alternative dispute resolution (ADR) *involves making an agreement to forego litigation and instead resolve disputes by either internal or external mediation or arbitration.* Working out a dispute before it reaches litigation can promote goodwill between management and employees and reduce the adverse publicity often associated with legal disputes.[44] It can also reduce legal costs to both employers and society. Mediation and arbitration are the two most common forms of alternative dispute resolution.

> **FAST FACT**
>
> When the EEOC uses mediation to dissolve disputes, resolution takes 96 days on average—half the time needed when charges are not mediated.

Mediation. In **mediation,** *all concerned parties present their case to a third-party neutral-the mediator.* Mediators may be appointed by a judge, selected by the parties or their representatives, or be recommended by agencies such as the EEOC. Often, the disputing parties are required to prepare a confidential written statement of their case and a statement the resolutions they would find acceptable. Each side then presents its arguments in a private meeting with the mediator. Like a diplomat shuttling between warring parties, the mediator's role is to help the parties understand each other's views and to help each party understand the strengths and weaknesses in its own case. During these meetings, the ultimate goal is to steer the parties toward compromise and construct a fair settlement.[45]

Mediation is the most popular form of ADR, partly because its format is less formal, more flexible, and less public than those of other proceedings. Parties to a civil dispute may be ordered into mediation by the court, or they may volunteer to submit to the process in an effort to settle the dispute without litigation. The U.S. Postal Service resolved 17,645 informal disputes in the first three years after it began using a new mediation process called Redress. During the same time, formal complaints dropped 30%.

Arbitration. Compared to mediation, **arbitration** *is a more formal process for alternative dispute resolution, yet not so formal that the rules of a court must be followed.* Employees must be permitted to have a representative for their case (usually an attorney), and representatives must present their cases in a formal manner. Typically, decisions are rendered by a panel of arbitrators. Unlike court judges, arbitrators do not need to provide written decisions or use previous cases in rendering their decisions.

The use of arbitration procedures has skyrocketed since the early 1990s. Many employers ask employees to sign contracts upon being hired stating that they'll accept arbitration as a means to settle any potential future discrimination complaint. Usually employees are asked to agree to *binding* arbitration in which the arbitrator's decision is final, subject to a very limited right of appeal. In most cases, employees who sign arbitration agreements give up their right to a court hearing. Because of the requirement that employees sign away their right to pursue other legal action, the legal status of such employment agreements has long been considered controversial.

In 2001, however, much of the controversy about the legal status of arbitration agreements was resolved by a Supreme Court decision. In the case of *Saint Clair Adams v. Circuit City*, the court ruled that Adams could not pursue a complaint of sexual harassment through the California state courts because he had signed an arbitration agreement upon accepting employment at Circuit City.[46]

The Supreme Court's decision in *Saint Clair Adams v. Circuit City* was split 5 to 4. Like the justices, other experts disagree about whether the benefits of arbitration outweigh its potential problems. Exhibit 3.5 summarizes the arguments for and against mandatory arbitration practices.[47] Before signing an arbitration agreement, job applicants should investigate the details of an employer's arbitration process and be sure that they fully understand and are willing to accept the consequences of signing such an agreement.

Ex 3.5	**Weighing the Pros and Cons of Using Mandatory Arbitration to Settle Disputes**

PROS	CONS
Quick dispute resolution	Relinquishment of employees' statutory rights to a trial as a condition of employment
Lower personal, professional, and financial costs for both parties	Availability of "user-friendly" arbitration may stimulate a flood of claims
Reduction in employers' advantage in litigation by outspending and outlasting an employee	May prevent better guidance for future action since courts are better able to provide consistent and clear interpretations of law
More business-related experience and expertise of professional arbitrators	Arbitrators may not be competent or impartial
Reduction in exposure to unpredictable jury awards for emotional distress and punitive damages	Small monetary penalties may reduce their effectiveness as remedies in the case of a wronged employee
Permits disputes to remain private	Confidentiality of the process may reduce its deterrent effect; conversely, confidentiality isn't guaranteed
May improve communication and employee relations	May deter some talented employees from accepting employment

Resolving Disputes Online

The newest approaches to alternative dispute resolution take advantage of web-based technology to prevent, manage, and resolve employment grievances. Online dispute resolution initially evolved to address e-commerce disputes, but the technology has since migrated to employment disputes. Among the pioneers in this area were mediators working for the Federal Mediation and Conciliation Service (FMCS). They began experimenting in 2001 with software that allows parties in a dispute to view a mediator's proposals for resolution, see notes submitted by each party, keep track of open issues, and participate in a chat line.[48] Because this approach to employment dispute resolution in so new, little is known about its effectiveness in comparison to traditional face-to-face approaches.

PROACTIVE APPROACHES TO ENSURING FAIR TREATMENT

A resort by employees to grievance procedures, alternative dispute resolution, or litigation indicates that the organization is not succeeding in the goal of treating all employees in ways that they consider to be fair. Effective means for resolving disputes quickly will always be needed, but many employers realize that these reactive measures alone are not sufficient. Proactive measures that reduce the occurrence of disputes also are needed.

One goal of a proactive approach to fairness is to reduce the need for employees to go to court in order to assert their fairness rights. Perhaps if Wal-Mart had been more proactive in its effort to ensure fair treatment, its employees would not have gone to court. According to one person familiar with the situation, the lawsuit was "the end of a long journey for a lot of people. Many, many people had been complaining for a long time—even some senior executives had acknowledged the absences of women and lamented it for a decade or more."[49] Diversity management initiatives and harassment training are two proactive approaches that might have benefited Wal-Mart and its employees.

Diversity Initiatives

Beginning in about 1990, many companies began to proactively address employees' fairness concerns by initiating a variety of diversity management policies and practices. In most organizations that have them, **diversity management initiatives** *are policies and practices that the organization adopts voluntarily (not because of legal requirements) for the purpose of ensuring that all members of a diverse workforce feel they are treated fairly.* Some diversity management initiatives look very similar to the Texaco plan that was imposed in their court settlement. The difference is that the courts forced Texaco to adopt their plan for diversity management after concluding that many Texaco employees had suffered the consequences of discrimination.

Who Is Covered by Diversity Initiatives? When they first appeared, diversity management initiatives targeted the issues of fairness among women and minority employees. Today, it's increasingly evident that members of many demographic groups sometimes are victims of unfair discrimination. Diversity initiatives generally address the concerns of groups that are protected legally, but they may also address the concerns of some groups that enjoy no legal protections. Federated Department Stores, parent of Macy's and Bloomingdales, provides a typical example. In 1996, their diversity initiatives covered only two employee groups—women and minorities. Today, Federated's diversity initiatives cover more than two dozen employee groups, including seniors, people with disabilities, homosexuals, atheists, the devout, and many others.[50]

Before continuing, test your own diversity knowledge by taking the quiz shown in the feature "Managing Diversity: What's Your Diversity IQ?"

Critics of a broad approach to diversity management argue that all-inclusive diversity initiatives dilute the impact of the organization's efforts. According to this view, a broad approach robs women and ethnic minorities of the resources and attention required to address persistent problems rooted in long histories of systemic sex and race discrimination. Supporters of a broad approach argue that focusing on the concerns of only a few

---

Managing Diversity

What's Your Diversity IQ?

How informed are you about issues of workforce diversity? To get a sense of how well you are able to separate myth from fact, take the diversity knowledge quiz presented here.

Diversity Knowledge Quiz

Instructions: Indicate whether each of the following statements is true (by circling "T") or false (by circling "F"). Correct answers are given on page 121.

1. T F Joy and fear are feelings that can be accurately recognized from facial expressions, regardless of which cultures people are from.

2. T F A person who is older than 65 years and living in one of the world's developing regions (e.g., Southeast Asia, Africa, India) is three times more likely to be working than a person of that age living in a developed region (e.g., United States, Europe, Australia).

3. T F Worldwide, about 50% of women between the ages of 15 and 64 are in the labor force.

4. T F Most Americans with Japanese heritage come from families who have lived in the United States for two or three generations.

5. T F During the past decade, college graduation rates have been declining for men and increasing for women.

6. T F Most people could count on their fingers the number of female and minority CEOs who head one of the 500 largest firms in the United States.

7. T F In America's 10 largest cities, an average of one out of four persons is of Latino origin.

8. T F Compared to other demographic groups, gay men tend to be better educated and hold higher-paying jobs.

9. T F Compared to other employees, people with disabilities have better safety records on the job.

10. T F Mental speed begins to slow down slightly beginning at about age 30, but performance of many complex mental tasks continues to improve steadily as people age.

11. T F As recently as 1970, interracial marriages were illegal in some parts of the United States.

12. T F Almost all Fortune 500 firms indicate that they are implementing initiatives to manage diversity.

13. T F The proportion of companies with at least one woman board director is greater among Fortune 500 companies than among companies ranked 501 through 1,000.

groups ignores the legitimate concerns of many other groups and may also stimulate backlash and feelings of ill-will among some employees. Exhibit 3.6 shows the diversity areas typically covered by corporate initiatives.[51]

A Culture of Inclusion. What has become increasingly apparent is that simply trying to "obey the law" is not a very effective way for employers to ensure they treat employees fairly. A better approach to meeting employees' and society's concerns about fairness is to create a company culture in which all employees respect each other and everyone feels included.

Using diversity initiatives to create a **culture of inclusion,** *employers strive to create a company culture in which everyone feels equally integrated into the larger system.* Members of majority and minority subcultures feel respected; everyone has an equal chance to express views and influence decisions; and everyone has similar access to both formal and informal networks within the organization. When all members of the workforce feel they have equal opportunities and access within the company, they are less likely to feel the need to exercise their right to resort to legal means for ensuring fair treatment.

Respect for all employees is shown when employment decisions are made on the basis of merit rather than personal demographic attributes. At UPS, there is no chief diversity officer or even a committee devoted solely to managing diversity. Yet, UPS is one of *Fortune*'s 50 Best Companies for Minorities to Work For. According to Jovita Carranza, the company's highest-ranking female executive, "[for me] additional responsibility came as part of doing a good job . . . we have a culture of making everyone on the team a success."[52]

Evaluating the Effectiveness of Diversity Initiatives. Diversity initiatives are most likely to be effective when they are developed to meet clear objectives and then monitored to ensure that those objective are met. When

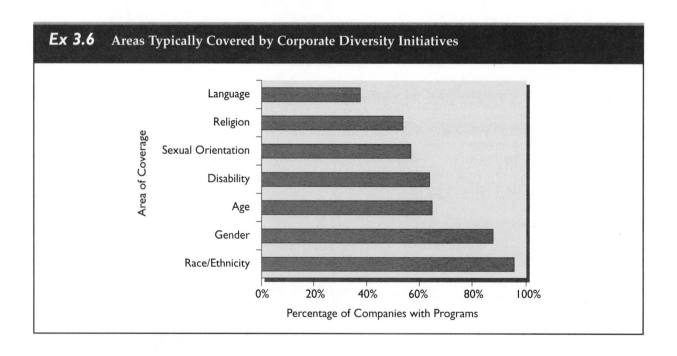

Ex 3.6   **Areas Typically Covered by Corporate Diversity Initiatives**

Montgomery Watson Harza (MWH) launched its first diversity initiative in 1998, the goal was to create a more harmonious and productive workplace through the improvement of individual awareness and group effectiveness. Several senior managers were selected as champions for the initiative and given the goal of helping the organization improve its understanding and appreciation of differences. As part of the diversity initiative, the senior leadership team participated in diversity training sessions; network groups were established for employees with common backgrounds and interests; the quarterly newsletter carried stories describing the contributions made by diversity employees in the company; and numerous courses were offered at MWH's corporate university.

To measure the effectiveness of their diversity initiative, the senior managers at MWH created a balanced scorecard. Some of the items in the scorecard were:

- Number of employees who attended the diversity courses offered by the company
- Number of "diverse" new hires throughout the company
- Number of "diverse" candidates who achieved the level of vice president or above[53]

At many other companies, measures used to assess the effectiveness of diversity initiatives also include:

- Comparing turnover patterns for employees belonging to different demographic groups
- Being named as one of the best companies for women and minorities to work for
- Improving the satisfaction expressed by employees when they respond to attitude surveys
- Reducing complaints, grievances, and lawsuits related to discrimination

HARASSMENT POLICIES

Under EEOC regulations, employers have a duty to maintain a working environment free of harassment based on sex, race, color, religion, national origin, age, or disability.[54] Like diversity management initiatives, policies and practices aimed at reducing the problem of workplace harassment focus on improving relationships among employees from differing demographic groups. Despite this similarity, companies often manage these two issues as if they were separate from each other. One reason behind this separation of the issues is history. Most modern-day diversity initiatives grew out of concerns about inequality in access to jobs and upward career progress. In contrast, the issue of harassment deals simply with the daily interactions among coworkers and the consequences of those interactions for how coworkers *feel*.

What Is Harassment? **Harassment** *refers to conduct that creates a hostile, intimidating, or offensive work environment; unreasonably interferes with the individual's work; or adversely affects the individual's employment opportunities.* Harassing conduct includes such things as racist epithets, raunchy jokes,

FAST FACT

Men's claims account for 13.5% of all sexual harassment charges brought to the EEOC.

"I was repeatedly humiliated and depressed. I am a law-abiding person and I didn't deserve the insults and cruel treatment."

Elisan Khan
Restaurant Employee
Plaza Hotel, New York City

and ethnic slurs. Usually, though not always, the conduct has to be repetitive or systematic. Harassment creates an offensive, hostile, and stressful work environment that prohibits effective performance; often it leads to expensive financial settlements and negative publicity as well. Ultimately, it interferes with the ability of the organization to attract and retain the best talent. Indeed, whole industries can be hurt when the public learns about unfavorable workplace climates.[55]

Following the terrorist attacks on September 11, 2001, many American Muslims were harassed at work. They were called names; graffiti was written in their work areas; and bosses subjected them to questions about their family members. Several Muslims eventually took their cases to court. It may be years before those cases are settled, however.[56]

According to a *Wall Street Journal/NBC* poll, 31% of American women experience workplace harassment. In several cases, the offending behavior has taken the form of inappropriate e-mail or Internet messages.[57] For example, in one well-publicized case, Salomon Smith Barney discharged two managing directors for sharing X-rated material on their office computers. A month earlier, Morgan Stanley settled a lawsuit brought against them by two black employees who charged that they lost out on promotions because they had complained about the distribution of e-mail messages containing racist jokes.[58]

The perpetrators of harassment often feel that people who complain about it are overreacting to coworkers who are just having a little fun and trying to relieve some of the stress that builds up in high-pressure environments. But such explanations carry little weight. The standard for evaluating harassment is whether a "reasonable person" in the same or similar circumstances would find the conduct intimidating, hostile, or abusive. The perspective of the victim—reflecting her or his race, gender, age, place of origin, and so forth—has an important place in the evaluation. This is an expansion of the "reasonable woman" standard articulated in *Ellison v. Brady* (1991). There the court said that "unsolicited love letters and unwanted attention . . . might appear inoffensive to the average man, but might be so offensive to the average woman as to create a hostile working environment." The "average woman" in this case became the "reasonable woman."[59] In 1998, in the case of *Oncale v. Sundown Offshore Service Inc.*, the court further clarified the rules by stating that employers could be held liable for same-sex harassment.[60]

FAST FACT

A recent survey by the U.S. Merit Systems Protection Board revealed that 43% of women in the federal workforce had experienced at least one episode of sexual harassment in the past two years.

Preventing Harassment. The EEOC guidelines clearly state that employers are liable for the acts of those who work for them if they knew or should have known about the conduct and took no immediate, appropriate corrective action. Employers who fail to develop explicit, detailed antiharassment policies and grievance procedures may put themselves at particular risk.

One way to reduce the incidence of harassment is by having and enforcing a "zero tolerance" policy. For a zero tolerance policy to have meaning, companies need clear procedures for dealing with complaints about harassment, effective training to teach employees about what is and isn't acceptable, and strong enforcement. Awareness training programs help employees understand the pain and indignity of harassment. If they're comprehensive and used aggressively, such programs can be highly effective. Being willing to dismiss problem employees is also part of a zero tolerance approach. When Salomon Smith Barney discharged two top executives for their offensive behaviors, it signaled that the firm was serious about adopting a zero tolerance approach to dealing with harassment.

FAST FACT If an outside contractor's employees sexually harass the on-site workers, those workers can sue their employer who hired the outside contractor.

Exhibit 3.7 describes the components that should be part of a sexual harassment policy.[61] Such policies may not eliminate harassment, but they do help communicate the company's expectations and provide a fair means for enforcing appropriate behavior.

Research shows that female employees appreciate it when company leaders make honest efforts to stop harassment. When they know the leaders are sincere, women who experience harassment not only are more likely to report it, but also are more satisfied with the process for resolving their complaints and feel more committed to the organization.[62]

FAIRNESS MUST BE RECIPROCATED

It's easy to emphasize the responsibility of employers to treat employees fairly. Fairness is a two-sided coin, however, and the other side is the responsibility of employees to treat their employers fairly. Unfortunately, employee misconduct is as much a problem as employer misconduct. A National Business Ethics Survey identified the following types of prevalent miscon-

---

Ex 3.7　Preventing Harassment in the Workplace

✔ Clearly Inform Employees of the Rules
- Raise affirmatively the issue of harassment. Acknowledge that it may be present in the organization, and make all employees aware of the company's position on harassment.
- Provide a clear and broad statement defining what constitutes harassment.
- Specify that offenders will be subject to appropriate discipline, up to and including discharge.

✔ Establish Procedures to Detect Harassment and Handle Complaints
- Build in checkpoints designed to detect harassment. For example, review all discharges to ensure that the employee was clearly performing poorly and had been given adequate opportunity to improve.
- Set up a list of names and positions to whom complaints can be made. The list should make it clear that employees who are harassed by supervisors have alternative reporting options.
- State that employees who experience or witness harassment are required to report it.
- Establish procedures for investigating and corroborating a harassment charge.

✔ Provide Protection to Those Involved in Harassment Investigations
- Give the person accused of harassment opportunity to respond immediately after charges are made. Due process must be provided the alleged perpetrator as well as the alleged victim.
- Assure employees that they won't be subjected to retaliation for reporting incidents of harassment.

✔ Provide a Fair System for Discipline and Punishment
- Specify a set of steps in a framework of progressive discipline for perpetrators of harassment. These could be the same steps used by the organization in treating any violation of organizational policies.

duct: lying, withholding needed information, misreporting actual time or hours worked, and abusive or intimidating behavior. A similar survey conducted by the Society for Human Resource Management found that employees are quite aware that such behaviors occur. Although they may not report it, the following figures indicate they see it happen:

- 27% of employees observed stealing or theft;
- 36% of employees observed lying on reports or falsifying records; and
- 45% of employees observed lying to supervisors.[63]

Also troubling are data showing that employees who see misconduct often don't report it. The National Business Ethics Survey found that younger employees are much less likely to report misconduct—only 43% reported it when they saw it. The reasons many younger workers gave for not reporting misconduct was that they believed no corrective action would be taken.[64]

The prevalence of workplace misconduct reflects, and at the same time contributes to, the fraying of trust between employers and employees. Of increasing concern to employers is another violation of trust—leaking or failing to keep secure valuable information about the firm's products, services, competitive strategies, and intellectual property. In many firms, the responsibilities of employees are spelled out in a code of ethics. A **code of ethics** *informs employees that they are expected to conduct business in a way that upholds high standards of integrity.* Typically, a code of ethics communicates that *employees* are expected to:

- Act with personal and professional integrity.
- Understand and comply fully with the letter and spirit of laws and regulations, as well as the firm's rules and policies.
- Safeguard the firm's reputation.
- Preserve the confidentiality of information about clients, colleagues, and the firm.

In exchange, the *company* often agrees to:

- Engage in business activities that are consistent with its reputation for integrity.
- Articulate its standards and rules clearly.
- Provide support in making legal and ethical decisions.
- Refuse to tolerate illegal, unethical, or unprofessional conduct.

Perhaps the best indicator of how fairly employees feel they're being treated is the degree to which they're willing to accept responsibility for behaving fairly in all dealings with their employers.

CHALLENGES FOR THE 21ST CENTURY

Managers will always need to be alert to employees' concerns about fairness. Yet, at particular times in history and in particular organizations or industries, specific fairness issues are especially salient and in need of attention. Today, in addition to the issues of diversity and harassment, two other significant fairness concerns are employment-at-will and privacy. We conclude this chapter by discussing these current fairness issues in a bit more detail.

Employment-at-Will

As the industrial era was beginning, employers managed their businesses under *the assumption that they had the right to terminate employees for any reason, which is known as the* **employment-at-will rule.** This is a common law rule with historical roots in medieval England. In the United States, one Tennessee court explained it as follows:

> *All may dismiss their employee(s) at will, be they many or few, for good cause, for no cause, or even for cause morally wrong without being thereby guilty of legal wrong.* (Payne v. Western & A.R.R Co., 1884)

Counterbalancing the employer's right to dismiss employees is the right of an employee to leave their employer at any time and for any reason.

Limits to Employment-At-Will. The courts still recognize the force of at-will employment. Nevertheless, over the years, there has been a shift in the balance of power between employers and employees. The courts give employers wide latitude, but they also acknowledge that employers should not have absolute autonomy to end a person's employment. Giving employers too much self-government would be harmful to employees and essentially nullify all employee rights.

Since 1884 many laws have been enacted to limit the rights of employers. The Civil Rights Act, the Age Discrimination in Employment Act (ADEA), and the Americans with Disabilities Act (ADA) curtail employers' use of the employment-at-will doctrine by stating that certain personal characteristics cannot be used as justification for employment decisions of any kind, including termination. In addition, the National Labor Relations Act (NLRA) prohibits discharge for union-organizing activities or for asserting rights under a union contract, even if the employee in question had a record of poor performance. Other acceptable and unacceptable reasons for terminating employees are listed in Exhibit 3.8.[65]

Procedural Justice. Most court decisions regarding an employer's right to terminate employees emphasize the value of procedural justice. That is, termination of employment should be the last step in a series of documented steps designed to ensure that an employee understood that performance problems existed and had opportunity to improve. Even though an employer may have the right to discharge an employee, the employer may be required to show evidence indicating that none of the protections against wrongful termination were violated. All evidence and material relevant to each step should be documented and filed. Employers may also terminate an entire workforce in a plant or location, if proper procedures are followed. According to the Worker Adjustment and Retraining Act of 1988 (WARN), employers are required to provide workers with 60 days' notice of a plant or office closing. Employers are also required to offer training programs in order to assist workers in adjusting to new employment conditions elsewhere.

Implied Contracts. Beginning in the 1970s, the courts began applying the doctrine of implied contracts to limit the conditions under which employers could terminate employees. An **implied contract** *refers to employees' beliefs*

Ex 3.8   Acceptable and Unacceptable Reasons to Terminate Employees

ACCEPTABLE REASONS FOR DISMISSAL

- Incompetence in performance that does not respond to training or to accommodation
- Gross or repeated insubordination
- Civil rights violations such as engaging in harassment
- Too many unexcused absences
- Illegal behavior such as theft
- Repeated lateness
- Drug activity on the job
- Verbal abuse
- Physical violence
- Falsification of records
- Drunkenness on the job

UNACCEPTABLE REASONS FOR DISMISSAL

- Blowing the whistle about illegal conduct by employers (e.g., opposing and publicizing employer policies or practices that violate laws such as the antitrust, consumer protection, or environmental protection laws)
- Cooperating in the investigation of a charge against the company
- Reporting Occupational Safety and Health Administration violations
- Filing discrimination charges with the Equal Employment Opportunity Commission or a state or municipal fair employment agency
- Filing unfair labor practice charges with the National Labor Relations Board (NLRB) or a state agency
- Filing a workers' compensation claim
- Engaging in concerted activity to protest wages, working conditions, or safety hazards
- Engaging in union activities, provided there is no violence or unlawful behavior
- Complaining or testifying about violations of equal pay or wage and hour laws
- Complaining or testifying about safety hazards or refusing an assignment because of the belief that it's dangerous

about the agreement that an employer has with employees regarding their conditions of employment. These beliefs may be grounded in verbal assurances made by managers, explanations given during performance appraisal meetings, and many other daily experiences of employees.

When Wayne Pugh was fired by See's Candies in 1973, Pugh filed a lawsuit charging wrongful termination. Pugh argued that an implied contract existed between See's and its employees. Based on his 32 years of experience in the company, Pugh argued that employees expected that they would not be terminated without good cause. The court agreed that See's management practices created such an implied contract in the minds of employees, and that such contracts were just as binding on the employers as a formal policy. Therefore, when See's terminated Pugh at-will, they broke a legally valid contract.[66] Since the Pugh case, many states have passed laws that state the limits of employers' ability to discharge employees.

Explicit Contracts. In an effort to avoid wrongful termination lawsuits based on the doctrine of implied contracts, many employers have become more explicit in stating their policies about termination. An **explicit contract** *is written down and often appears in a policy manual that contains clear language.* Today, most explicit employment contracts state that accepting employment with the company carries no guarantee of security and employees may be terminated at the employer's option. To further protect themselves, many employers require employees to sign agreements in which they waive their rights to sue as a condition for accepting severance packages during layoffs. At Lucent, laid-off employees get no severance pay at all unless they sign such a waiver. For 33-year veteran Kathy Fionte, the decision to sign was one she put off until the last minute. But in the end, she was willing to waive her rights in order to collect 30 weeks of severance pay.[67]

As employers seek to avoid being caught in a flood of litigation, they have turned to explicit contracts that require workers to accept the employer's right to terminate them at will or waive their rights to legal action against an employer. Critics of such practices argue that employees have little choice when they sign such agreements and that they may be giving up too many rights. They argue that employees do not enter into such agreements voluntarily. Instead, they sign under duress when threatened with the loss of an employment opportunity or a large severance package. Because employers wield such power, employees feel they have little choice but to sign away rights that they would otherwise have under current law.

EMPLOYEE PRIVACY

Simply stated, the right to privacy is the right to keep information about ourselves to ourselves. Earlier in our history, Henry Ford faced no resistance from the government when he sent social workers to the homes of employees to investigate their personal habits and family finances. Such invasions of privacy went hand-in-hand with the doctrine of employment-at-will. This changed in 1965, when the U.S. Supreme Court concluded that various guarantees stated in the Constitution (e.g., the Fourth Amendment's protection against illegal search and seizure) have the effect of creating zones of privacy. Since then, new state and federal legislation has begun to address employee privacy rights more explicitly.[68]

Most statutes simply give individuals the right to access and verify the information others already have. The Privacy Act of 1974 was the first major statute to address issues of privacy directly. This act, which applies only to federal agencies (not private employers), gives individuals the right to verify information collected about them and used in selection and employment decisions. It allows individuals to:

- determine which records pertaining to them are collected, used, and maintained;
- review and amend such records;
- prevent unspecified use of such records; and
- pursue civil suit for damages against those intentionally violating the rights specified in the act.

The Privacy Act is consistent with the Freedom of Information Act of 1974, which allows individuals to see all the material a federal agency uses in its decision-making processes.

In contrast to federal employees, private-sector employees are relatively unprotected against employers, who have the ability to access and use information, often without the knowledge or consent of employees or job applicants. Two laws establish exceptions to this generalization. The Fair Credit

"If privacy in America were an animal, it would be on the endangered species list."

Lewis Maltby
President
National Workrights Institute

and Reporting Act of 1970 permits job applicants to know the nature and content of their credit files. The Employee Exposure and Medical Records Regulation of 1980 gives employees the right to access their on-the-job medical records and records that document their exposure to toxic substances.

Concerns about privacy also are addressed by state-level legislation. Several state laws (e.g., in California, Connecticut, Maine, Michigan, Oregon, and Pennsylvania) give employees access to their human resource files and define what information employees are and are not entitled to see, as well as where, when, and under what circumstances employees may view their files.

Issues of privacy continue to be debated. Two topics of continuing discussion are employer access to medical information and employee monitoring.[69]

Access to Medical and Lifestyle Information. Health insurance costs have grown so dramatically since the mid-1980s that many employers now feel pressure to do whatever is necessary to reduce them. One way to lower costs is to employ people who make little use of health care services, because insurance for such employees is less expensive. Information about lifestyles and genetic makeup could help an employer determine who is likely to need extensive and expensive health care.

Some health conditions are clearly protected by the Americans with Disabilities Act (ADA), which states that a medical exam may be given only after a conditional job offer has been made. Then, the offer may be rescinded only if the exam reveals a condition that would prevent the applicant from performing the job and if the condition cannot be accommodated. The ADA does not protect employees against all uses of health-related information, however.[70]

Like insurance companies, employers can predict how much health care a person is likely to need if they have information about factors that put people into high-health-risk categories: Does she smoke? Is he overweight? Does she abuse alcohol? Other drugs? Does he exercise regularly? Does she participate in "extreme" sports? Does he often drive too fast? Employers can penalize, refuse to hire, or even terminate employees because of some conditions associated with high health care costs.

Data about the link between behaviors such as these and a person's use of health care support General Mills' policy of lowering workers' insurance premiums if they lead healthy lives. Insurance costs also help explain why drug testing has quickly gone from a rare to a routine practice: Whereas in 1987, only about 20% of employers conducted drug testing, now more than 90% do so.[71]

Access to Genetic Information. The ADA primarily protects people with disabilities. It does not address directly the question of how employers might use information about genetic makeup. Advances in our understanding of the link between genetics and disease susceptibility raise new concerns about medical privacy. Should a 25-year-old applying for a sales job be required to undergo genetic screening for diseases that may be experienced in middle age? Is it fair to penalize workers with high cholesterol, given that genes as well as diet affect cholesterol levels? Federal legislation that would prohibit employers from using genetic testing for staffing decisions has been proposed but has not yet been passed by Congress.[72]

Employers who seek medical and genetic information usually do so for good reasons. They may be concerned about how to keep health insurance costs as low as possible, which benefits the company's bottom line and may ultimately mean that healthy employees see a bigger paycheck. Or they may be concerned about protecting employees from diseases. Genetic information may be directly relevant to such concerns. But as the list of possible legitimate employer concerns grows, so do the misgivings of those who value their privacy.

Monitoring Communications. Research has shown linkages between watching violent television shows and movies and engaging in violent behavior.[73] With violence in the workplace becoming a major issue in our society, should employers be allowed, perhaps even expected, to attempt to screen out employees whose viewing behaviors suggest they're likely to be violent?[74] Or suppose an employer wants to ensure that employees do not engage in illegal behaviors of various sorts, such as industrial espionage, drug dealing, or insider trading: Does this give the employer the right to listen in on employees' telephone calls?

FAST FACT Internet monitoring software makes it possible for employers to track which websites employees visit, how much time they spend at each site, and the cost to the company of Internet usage not related to company business.

How would you feel if you discovered that your employer, as part of an effort to detect the illegal behavior of another employee, made a videotape of you while you were in the bathroom or locker room, installed a monitoring device to learn what magazines you were reading during your lunch break, and hired undercover agents to pose as employees as a way to keep tabs on workers? This is what the Campbell Soup Company did—before terminating 62 employees.[75] In fact, most major U.S. companies now monitor their employees through e-mail, phone connections, and/or video.

Even when employees acknowledge that employers have a right to prevent certain types of employee behavior, most resent the idea of being too closely monitored. Employers are not likely to discontinue the practice voluntarily, however. Too often their monitoring efforts uncover behavior that is so inappropriate it results in terminating an employee—from spending several hours shopping online or trading stocks to gambling, viewing and distributing pornography, distributing company secrets, and even running a private business.[76] Thus, the challenge is finding approaches to monitoring that employees agree are legitimate and acceptable.[77]

As technology continues to make monitoring both easy and unobtrusive, employers are likely to continue increasing their use of it, absent new legal restrictions. Current regulations make it clear that employers must inform employees before listening in on their personal telephone conversations, but the rapid speed of technological change means that the language of existing laws quickly becomes obsolete. As an example, consider a 1987 Supreme Court ruling that concluded employers generally have no right to go through a purse, briefcase, or piece of luggage brought into the workplace: Would the Court draw the same conclusion now that laptop computers fit inside all of these? The intermingling of work and nonwork both at home and on the employer's property introduces additional complexity and ambiguity. Precedent establishes that employers generally are permitted to gain access to voicemail messages if they have a business purpose for doing so. Does that right hold for employees who work from home but do not have a separate company-paid phone line?[78]

One common approach employers use to cope with the possible negative reactions that employees might have to electronic monitoring is to explicitly ban all nonbusiness and/or personal use of e-mail and the Internet and to inform employees that their use of these will be monitored. But the NLRB has argued that this amounts to banning people from talking about anything other than their work while in their "work area." E-mail has become so ubiquitous that for many employees it's the primary mode of communication with their coworkers. The NLRB's logic in recent years has been that the more computer-intensive the workplace is, the less appropriate it is for employers to enforce highly restrictive e-mail policies.[79] Nevertheless, Congress has failed to pass legislation that obliges companies to inform employees if and how their Internet use is being tracked. Today, only about half of all employers who conduct Internet tracking make a point of telling employees this when they conduct training sessions.[80]

Fairness in the Global Context

Clearly, keeping up with both legal requirements and employee attitudes about various employment practices requires substantial time as well as expertise. Some developing countries have few laws to protect employees' rights. Even if laws exist, enforcement may be lax and citizens may seldom pursue litigation against their employers in court. In some countries, including many in Latin America, nondiscrimination laws are relatively new, and it will take time for employers and their employees to change how they behave. On the other hand, the laws of many countries provide greater protection to employees than do U.S. laws. Laws relevant to almost every imaginable aspect of the employment relationship exist, and they take dozens of different forms in countries around the world.[81]

Work Conditions and Pay. Some manufacturers have struggled to manage their businesses across countries with huge differences in laws and local practices related to work conditions and compensation.[82] Clothing manufacturers with offshore plants in developing countries have learned that it's not just the locals who watch what employers do. People back home are watching too.

Conditions in a shoe manufacturing plant in Donguann, China, illustrate the challenge for global firms of ensuring that all employees are treated fairly. Some 50,000 employees, many of them younger than the Chinese minimum age of 16 for working in factories, were making products for Nike, Adidas, Reebok, LA Gear, Puma, and New Balance. Many were paid less than the Chinese minimum wage of $1.90 per day, with no benefits. They worked under conditions that were typical in the region but are harsh by global standards. Mandatory overtime hours typically amounted to 80 hours per month, or double the amount allowed by Chinese law. Meal breaks lasted only 10 to 15 minutes. At other factories in the area, conditions were even worse. To manage the high turnover rates, some local employers required employees to pay a "deposit" equivalent to two weeks pay. Employees forfeited the deposit if they left before their contracts expired. Other employers confiscated migrant workers' identification papers so that they could not job-hop or even remain in the city.

Public interest groups concerned about human rights and students on many U.S. campuses protested these conditions. At first, the companies shrugged off the protests. But eventually Nike and the others agreed to provide workers worldwide with the protection of various American health and safety standards (e.g., air quality), and to include representatives from labor and human rights groups in a team of independent auditors for monitoring compliance with the standards globally. Extending the protection of U.S. laws to non–U.S. citizens is not legally required, but Nike concluded that going beyond what is legally required is good business practice.[83]

Gradually, workers in other Chinese factories have begun to demand better treatment. Employees at a factory that makes Etch-a-Sketch toys in DaKang, China, protested by refusing to work for two days. Their employer acknowledged his guilt to the *New York Times*, saying, "I know that I need to increase my wages and to comply with the law"; and said he planned to do so in the future. At the time, he was paying less than the law required and forcing employees to put in long overtime hours. It seems likely that the news of how poorly the Etch-a-Sketch workers were being treated resulted in some U.S. customers choosing not to buy Etch-a-Sketch toys for the holidays coming up that December.[84]

Terminations and Layoffs. Globalization creates many challenges for U.S. employers accustomed to using layoffs to adapt to changing business conditions. Most countries have some traditional or legally required practices that come into play in the event of a plant closing or a substantial reduction of the workforce.[85] In general, laws and regulations regarding layoffs and terminations in other countries create more extensive and costlier employer obligations than do laws regarding layoffs in the United States and Canada. In many countries, termination of employment is viewed as a harsh action that's potentially harmful to employees. In fairness to employees, it should occur only for good cause, and employers are held responsible for minimizing its negative consequences.

One obligation employers may have when terminating employees in other countries is payment of cash indemnities in addition to the individual termination payments required by law, collective bargaining agreements, or individual contracts. In Germany and Italy, for example, termination for sexual harassment may not be considered good cause. Consequently, employers who terminate harassers may be required to pay termination indemnities.

In many countries, a company that wishes to close down or curtail operations must develop a "social plan" or its equivalent, typically in concert with unions and other interested stakeholders. The plan may cover continuation of pay, benefit plan coverage, retraining allowances, relocation expenses, and supplementation of statutory unemployment compensation. Frequently, a company planning a partial or total plant closing must present its case to a government agency. In the Netherlands, for example, authorities may deny permission for a substantial workforce reduction unless management is able to demonstrate that the cutback is absolutely necessary for economic reasons and that the company has an approved social plan.

Privacy. Laws and regulations intended to protect employee privacy also vary from country to country. For example, the European Union's **Data Protection Directive** *sets restrictions on which personal information can be collected and stored; it applies to all areas of everyday activity and to all EU member countries.* Each member country decides how to implement the Directive. Failure to comply with the Directive can result in civil penalties (up to $500,000 in Spain) and criminal penalties (up to three years in France).

Details of the Data Protection Directive are described in the feature "Managing Globalization: Privacy in the European Union." Compared to U.S. laws and regulations, the EU is much more restrictive. According to one HR systems manager in a Fortune 500 company, "Most international companies violate the Directive every day, faxing things back and forth or talking about personnel over the phone."[86]

When operating abroad, as when operating at home, complying with legal regulations is one step toward managing fairly. To be truly effective, however, managers need to realize that perceptions of fairness reflect cultural assumptions and values—not just legal realities. Managers who are insensitive to the broader social fabric will find it difficult to anticipate employees' reactions to how they're treated. Unenlightened managers run the risk of triggering negative employee reactions.[87]

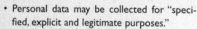

Managing Globalization

Privacy in the European Union

The goals of the European Union's Data Protection Directive are to protect the personal privacy of EU citizens and to standardize privacy regulations across the EU countries. It has four basic provisions, which state that:

- Personal data may be collected for "specified, explicit and legitimate purposes."
- Any person on whom data is kept is to receive information about who is processing that information and for what purposes.
- Any person has the right to access any data that is being kept and to change or delete information that is not correct.
- People who believe their data are being misused have the right to pursue remedies through the court system.

United States companies with operations in the EU must comply with the Directive in those operations. Compliance typically requires that an employer submit a plan to the Data Protection Authority before it collects, processes, or analyzes any employee information. Because the Directive regulates the flow of information, U.S. companies must also be concerned with the law's restrictions on data transfers between EU locations and operations in other countries, including an HR office in a U.S. headquarters location. The Directive forbids companies from sending any data in any form to any country that the EU judges to have inadequate privacy protection laws.

Companies that demonstrate they are in compliance with the Directive can be certified by the U.S. Department of Commerce. To receive such certification, companies must state that they adhere to the following principles:

Notice. Individuals are notified about what information is collected, how it is used, who receives the information, and who to contact with questions or complaints.

Choice. Individuals must be able to refuse to have their data disclosed to third parties or used for purposes other than those for which it was originally collected.

Transfer. Data must be sent only to other organizations that satisfy the certification principles.

Access. Individuals can access their information, and correct or delete inaccurate information.

Security. The organization must take adequate measures to protect the information against loss, destruction, or misuse.

Integrity. The information must be relevant, accurate, complete, and current.

Enforcement: The company must have an acceptable process for complaint resolution.

SUMMARY

Treating employees fairly and legally is a strategic challenge faced by all employers. Failure to meet this challenge can result in litigation, legal penalties and fines, consumer boycotts, employee turnover, reduced numbers of new job applications, lower productivity, and poor service quality, among other negative consequences. Managers and HR professionals may find the question "What is fair?" difficult to answer. Historically, the power to determine workplace conditions rested largely in employers' hands. Gradually, society recognized that this was unfair and a shift in the power balance was needed. Numerous laws now sanction some employer actions because they're clearly unfair to employees. A first step toward ensuring workplace fairness, therefore, is legal compliance. By following the laws, employers should at least be able to protect themselves from losing lawsuits alleging unfair employment practices.

Workplace fairness is more than an issue of legal compliance, however. Individual feelings and perceptions as well as societal norms also come into play. Even legal actions by an employer may be considered unfair by employees. Managing human resources fairly requires an understanding of how employees evaluate fairness.

Managing in ways that meet the principles of distributive and procedural justice is one approach to creating fair employment conditions. Managers also need to understand that the same policy and the same outcome can be perceived as relatively fair or unfair depending on the attitudes they display and the amount of respect they show personally for the concerns of employees. Managing diversity initiatives are one way that organizations can improve perceptions of fairness among members of a diverse workforce. In addition to meeting the legal and fairness challenges that arise in a diverse domestic organization, globalization requires many U.S. employers to address fairness and legal concerns in their operations around the world and across diverse nationalities.

TERMS TO REMEMBER

Alternative dispute resolution (ADR)
Arbitration
Class action lawsuit
Code of ethics
Common law rules
Culture of inclusion
Data Protection Directive
Distributive justice
Diversity management initiatives
Employment-at-will rule
Equal Employment Opportunity Commission (EEOC)
Executive order
Explicit contract

Grievance procedures
Harassment
Implied contract
Interactional justice
Legal precedents
Mediation
National Labor Relations Board (NLRB)
Occupational Safety and Health Administration (OSHA)
Procedural justice
Settlement agreement
Title VII of the Civil Rights Act

DISCUSSION QUESTIONS

1. Describe an example of when you felt you (or someone you know) were treated unfairly. Did the incident occur due to a lack of procedural, distributive, and/or interactional justice?

2. Describe some of the key federal regulatory agencies and the employment laws and regulations that they administer and enforce.

3. Some people feel there are simply too many laws and regulations governing how companies may manage their employees. These people believe everyone would be better off if we let the free-market system work without so much government interference. Other people believe that employees are not sufficiently protected against unfair treatment by employers. They believe employers would treat employees poorly if our laws didn't forbid it. Which position do you most agree with? Explain why.

4. Suppose a coworker harassed you. Would you prefer to resolve it using mediation, arbitration, or through the court system? Would your answer change if the harasser were your boss? Why or why not?

5. Develop counterarguments for the following arguments in support of the employment-at-will doctrine:

   a. If the employee can quit for any reason, the employer can fire for any reason.
   b. Discharged employees are always free to find other employment.
   c. Employers have economic incentives not to discharge employees unjustly; therefore, their power to terminate should not be restricted by laws.

PROJECTS TO EXTEND YOUR LEARNING

1. *Integration and Application.* Review the end-of-text cases before answering the following questions for both Lincoln Electric and Southwest Airlines:

   • What evidence exists to demonstrate that each company manages employees fairly and legally? Are there company practices that you would consider unfair? Which ones, and why?
   • Describe what management appears to expect from employees in each company. What does Lincoln agree to give employees in return? How do the expectations and responsibilities of management relate to the notions of distributive, procedural, and interactional justice?

2. *Exploring the Internet.*

   a. Visit the home page of the EEOC. Learn more about the laws prohibiting discrimination, and also read about the procedures employees should follow to file a claim with the EEOC (http://www.eeoc.gov).
   b. Visit the home page for a field office of the EEOC near you. For example, if you live in Minnesota, you may want to visit the

Minneapolis field office (http://www.eeoc.gov/minneapolis/index.html). Links to local, area, and district EEOC field offices can be found by going to the federal EEOC home page (http://www.eeoc.gov/offices.html).

c. Investigate the services provided by the Federal Mediation and Conciliation Program (http://www.eeoc.gov/mediate/history.html).

d. The Catalyst Award honors innovative approaches with proven results taken by companies to address the recruitment, development, and advancement of all managerial women, including women of color. Learn more about the Catalyst Award and the companies that have been recognized by Catalyst for excellence in managing gender diversity at work (http://www.catalystwomen.org/catalyst_award/overview.htm).

e. Visit the Privacy Rights Clearinghouse for facts and additional resources related to privacy in the workplace (http://www.privacyrights.org).

f. NATLEX is the database of national labor, social security and related legislation maintained by the International Labour Standards Department of the International Labour Organization (ILO). Visit NATLEX and learn more about employment laws around the world (http://www.ilo.org/dyn/natlex).

3. *Experiential Activity.* The following 10 questions might be asked during an employment interview. Some of them are illegal and should never be asked. Employers who ask illegal questions may be subject to legal prosecution for employment discrimination. Place a check mark in the appropriate column to indicate whether you believe the question is legal or illegal. Before taking this quiz, visit the home page of the Equal Employment Opportunity Commission (EEOC) http://eeoc.gov).

		Legal	Illegal
1.	How old are you?	____	____
2.	Have you ever been arrested?	____	____
3.	Do any of your relatives work for this organization?	____	____
4.	Do you have children, and if you do, what kind of child-care arrangements do you have?	____	____
5.	Do you have any handicaps?	____	____
6.	Are you married?	____	____
7.	Where were you born?	____	____
8.	What organizations do you belong to?	____	____
9.	Do you get along well with other men [or women]?	____	____
10.	What languages can you speak and/or write fluently?	____	____

NOTE: Answers appear on the following page.

Answers to Experiential Activity in Projects to Extend Your Learning

The following evaluations provide clarification rather than strict legal interpretation because employment laws and regulations are constantly changing.

1. *How old are you?*

   This question is legal but inadvisable. An applicant's date of birth or age can be asked, but telling the applicant that federal and state laws prohibit age discrimination is essential. Avoid focusing on age, unless an occupation requires extraordinary physical ability or training and a valid age-related rule is in effect.

2. *Have you ever been arrested?*

   This question is illegal unless an inquiry about arrests is justified by the specific nature of the organization—for instance, law enforcement or handling controlled substances. Questions about arrests generally are considered to be suspect because they may tend to disqualify some groups. Convictions should be the basis for rejection of an applicant only if their number, nature, or recent occurrence renders the applicant unsuitable. In that case, the question(s) should be specific. For example: Have you ever been convicted of theft? Have you been convicted within the past year on drug-related charges?

3. *Do any of your relatives work for this organization?*

   This question is legal if the intent is to discover nepotism.

4. *Do you have children, and if you do, what kind of child-care arrangements do you have?*

   Both parts of this question are currently illegal; they should not be asked in any form because the answers would not be job-related. In addition, they might imply gender discrimination.

5. *Do you have any handicaps?*

   This question is illegal as phrased here. An applicant doesn't have to divulge handicaps or health conditions that don't relate reasonably to fitness to perform the job.

6. *Are you married?*

   This question is legal, but may be discriminatory. Marriage has nothing directly to do with job performance.

7. *Where were you born?*

   This question is legal, but it might indicate discrimination on the basis of national origin.

8. *What organizations do you belong to?*

   As stated, this question is legal; it's permissible to ask about organizational membership in a general sense. It's illegal to ask about membership in a specific organization when the name of that organization would indicate the race, color, creed, gender, marital status, religion, or national origin or ancestry of its members.

9. *Do you get along well with other men [or women]?*

   This question is illegal; it seems to perpetuate sexism.

10. *What languages can you speak and/or write fluently?*
     Although this question is legal, it might be perceived as a roundabout
     way of determining an individual's national origin. Asking how a
     particular language was learned isn't permissible.

Answers to the Diversity Quiz on Page 103

Scoring: Count the number of times you circled "T" for true. This is your
total score. The highest score possible is 13—all of the statements are true. If
your score was less than 10, it indicates that you may not have accurate
information about several aspects of cultural diversity. What are some implications of not having accurate knowledge about these facts? What could you
do to improve your knowledge?

CASE STUDY

WHAT'S WRONG WITH WHAT'S RIGHT?

Stuart Campbell, now 35, moved slowly down the front steps of the courthouse and squinted as the last rays of sunlight pierced through downtown Cleveland. It had been a long day in the life of Stuart Campbell, who had spent the entire day in court recalling the details of his past employment with Nako Electronics, a major marketer of audio-tapes in the United States. Nako Electronics had—and still has—a considerable stake in Stuart Campbell. The arbitrator's decision and the award of $500,000 plus interest of $82,083.50 was a bitter pill for Nako to swallow for having terminated their Midwest sales representative.

Stuart had agreed to meet his attorney, Jim Baldwin, for a couple of drinks and to unwind from the courtroom tension. His spirits began to pick up as he maneuvered through the city traffic, but he couldn't help thinking how, within a year's time, his good job had soured.

Five years ago, Stuart Campbell was riding high as the Midwest representative for Nako, covering Ohio, West Virginia, and Pennsylvania. Stuart, a hard worker, contracted with Nako Electronics and then boosted the sluggish sales of Nako audiotapes from less than $300,000 to a $2 million business in about 14 months. In fact, business was going so well for Stuart that he began driving a Mercedes-Benz 450 SEL. But that's when

Mike Hammond, vice president of marketing at Nako Electronics, took notice of Campbell. On one of his visits to Campbell's territory, Hammond commented to Stuart that he really liked his car. Mike remarked that he was making a trip to California soon. "I distinctly remember Mike saying he would like to have a Buick," Stuart testified. "He didn't want anything as fancy as I had, because a new Buick would be adequate and, after all, he wanted me to bear the expense!"

Mike Hammond unfortunately couldn't be in court that day to defend himself; Hammond had died unexpectedly the previous year of a heart attack. During the trial, though, Nako Electronics had to defend a number of allegations made against Mike Hammond. It seems that some of Stuart Campbell's coworkers suffered a similar fate. Not only had Stuart refused to go along with Hammond's car scheme, but he also refused to invest in a cartridge business begun by Hammond, which Stuart believed was phony. Hammond, in fact, had approached all the sales representatives of Nako Electronics to invest in the cartridge company at $1,250 a share, a company for which Hammond and two other associates paid $1 a share for 80% of the stock. Stuart's attorney, Jim Baldwin, made sure that two of Stuart's former fellow sales representatives testified at the court proceedings that they were mysteriously fired after refusing Mike Hammond's demands to invest in his side company.

In the year following Stuart's successful boost in the sales of Nako audiotapes and Hammond's thwarted attempts at commercial shakedown, Nako increased Campbell's sales quota by more than 75%. As Campbell further testified, Nako sabotaged a substantial proportion of his sales by refusing to give his large customers promotional assistance. In the fall of that year, Nako fired Stuart without explanation. Nako argued in court that it didn't need a reason to fire Campbell, and besides, Campbell wasn't meeting his new, increased sales quota. Moreover, the company argued, Mr. Hammond could not defend himself against the charges of Campbell and others.

Stuart rehashed these details many times with his attorney, both during the private arbitrator hearing and during numerous rehearsals for the trial. As he arrived at the restaurant, he hoped he could put these memories behind him. As they talked, Jim summarized the day's proceedings and expressed cautious optimism for the final outcome. "But you know, Stuart," mused Jim, "If you would have kicked in the $10 or $15K that Hammond demanded, you would have outlived him, you'd have a business worth over $4 million in sales today, and we wouldn't be having this drink!"

CASE QUESTIONS

1. Why did the arbitrator award Stuart so much money?

2. Was the arbitrator's decision a just and fair one?

3. Did Nako have to give Stuart a reason for firing him?

4. If Campbell's firing was due to his failure to invest in Hammond's side company, could this be defended in court?

5. Do you think there was anything Stuart could have done, legally, to avoid being fired?

6. How do you think Stuart's former coworkers at Nako would react to what happened to Stuart?

Source: Stuart A. Youngblood, Texas Christian University.

ENDNOTES

1   C. Daniels, "Women vs. Wal-Mart," *Fortune* (July 21, 2003): 79–82; R. Zeilberger, "Is Wal-Mart Unfair to Its Female Employees: And Why They'll Still Work There," *DiversityInc* (December 2003/January 2004): 89–92.

2   L. Louise, "Dillard's Is Meeting with Minorities to Talk of Diversity: Years of Silence End as a Store Chain Acts to Resolve Race-Bias Allegations," *Wall Street Journal* (April 8, 1998): B4.

3   R. O. Crockett, "Memo to the Supreme Court: 'Diversity Is Good for Business,'" *Business Week* (January 27, 2003): 96; J. D. Glater, "Some Companies Back Michigan in Affirmative Action Policy," *New York Times* (January 29, 2003): C1; L. Greenhouse, "Justices Look for Nuance in Race-Preference Case," *New York Times* (April 2, 2003): A1, A15; S. Henderson, "Michigan Diversity Ruling Gets Tested Outside Education," *The Star-Ledger* (December 26, 2003): 25.

4   S. Naumann and N. Bennett, "A Case for Procedural Justice Climate: Development and Test of a Multilevel Model," *Academy of Management Journal* 43 (2000): 881–889; J. Greenberg, "Looking Fair vs. Being Fair: Managing Impressions of Organizational Justice," in B. M. Staw and L. L. Cummings (eds.), *Research in Organizational Behavior*, vol. 12 (Greenwich, CT: JAI Press, 1990): 111–157.

5   M. Konovsky, "Understanding Procedural Justice and Its Impact on Business Organizations," *Journal of Management* 26 (2000): 489–511; W. C. Kim and R. Maugorgne, "Fair Process: Managing in the Knowledge Economy," *Harvard Business Review* (July–August 1997): 65–75.

6   J. C. Morrow, P. C. Morrow, and E. J. Mullen, "Intraorganizational Mobility and Work-Related Attitudes," *Journal of Organizational Behavior* 17 (1996): 363–374.

7   M. Conlin and W. Zellner, "Is Wal-Mart Hostile to Women?" *Business Week* (July 16, 2001): 58–59; see also R. Garonzik, J. Brockner, and P. Siegel, "Identifying International Assignees at Risk for Premature Departure: The Interactive Effect of Outcome Favorability and Procedural Fairness," *Journal of Applied Psychology* 85 (2000): 13–20.

8   T. Simons and Q. Roberson, "Why Managers Should Care about Fairness: The Effects of Aggregate Justice Perceptions on Organizational Outcomes," *Journal of Applied Psychology* 88(3) (2003): 432–443.

9   J. A. Colquitt, D. E. Conlon, M. J. Wesson, C. Porter, and K. Y. Ng, "Justice at the Milennium: A Meta-Analytic Review of 25 Years of Organizational Justice Research," *Journal of Applied Psychology* 86 (2001): 425–445; H. Schroth and P. Shah, "Procedures: Do We Really Want to Know Them? An Examination of the Effects of Procedural Justice on Self-Esteem," *Journal of Applied Psychology* 85 (2000): 462–471; R. Cropanzano (ed.), *Justice in the Workplace: From Theory to Practice* (Mahwah, NJ: LEA, 2000).

10   D. M. Mansour-Cole and S. G. Scott, "Hearing It through the Grapevine: The Influence of Source, Leader-Relations, and Legitimacy on Survivors' Fairness Perceptions," *Personnel Psychology* 51 (1998): 25–53.

11   C. Lee, K. Law, and P. Bobko, "The Importance of Justice Perceptions on Pay Effectiveness: A Two-Year Study of a Skill-Based Pay Plan," *Journal of Management* 25 (1999): 851–873; M. P. Miceli, "Justice and Pay System Satisfaction," in R. Cropanzano, *Justice in the Workplace;* R. L. Heneman, D. B. Greenberger, and S. Strasser, "The Relationship between Pay-for-Performance Perceptions and Pay Satisfaction," *Personnel Psychology* 41 (1988): 745–761; M. P. Miceli et al., "Predictors and Outcomes of Reactions to Pay-for-Performance Plans," *Journal of Applied Psychology* 76 (1991): 508–521.

12   H. C. Triandis, "Cross-Cultural Industrial and Organizational Psychology," in H. C. Triandis, M. D. Dunnette, and L. M. Hough (eds.), *Handbook of Industrial and Organizational Psychology,* vol. 4 (Palo Alto, CA: Consulting Psychologists Press, 1994): 103–172.

13   Cropanzano, *Justice in the Workplace.*

14   J. A. Colquitt, R. A. Noe, and C. L. Jackson, "Justice in Teams: Antecedents and Consequences of Procedural Justice Climate," *Personnel Psychology* 55 (2002): 83–109.

15   M. A. Korsgaard, S. E. Brodt, and E. M. Whitener, "Trust in the Face of Conflict: The Role of Managerial Trustworthy Behavior and Organizational Context," *Journal of Applied Psychology* 87(2) (2002): 312–319.

16   J. A. Colquitt, "On the Dimensionality of Organizational Justice: A Construct Validation of a Measure," *Journal of Applied Psychology* 86 (2001): 386–400.

17   R. J. Bies and J. S. Moag, "Interactional Justice: Communication Criteria for Fairness," in B. L. Sheppard (ed.), *Research on Negotiation in Organizations,* vol. 1 (Greenwich, CT: JAI Press, 1986): 43–55.

18   B. B. Dunford and D. J. Devine, "Employment At-Will and Employee Discharge: A Justice Perspective on Legal Action Following Termination," *Personnel Psychology* 51 (1998): 903–934; C. E. Rusbult et al., "Impact of Exchange Variables on Exit, Voice, Loyalty and Neglect: An Integrative Model of Responses to Declining Job Satisfaction," *Academy of Management Journal* 31 (1998): 599–627; J. Brockner and B. Wiesenfeld, "An Integrative Framework for Explaining Reactions to Decisions: Interactive Effects of Outcomes and Procedures," *Psychological Bulletin* 120 (1996): 189–208; A. Davis-Blake, J. P. Broschak, and E. George, "Happy Together? How Using Nonstandard Workers Affects Exit, Voice, and Loyalty among Standard Workers," *Academy of Management Journal* 46 (2003): 475–485.

19   T. R. Tyler and S. L. Blader, *Cooperation in Groups: Procedural Justice, Social Identity and Behavioral Engagement* (New York: Taylor & Francis, 2000).

20   S. Foley, D. L. Kidder, and G. N. Powell, "The Perceived Glass Ceiling and Justice Perceptions: An Investigation of Hispanic Law Associates," *Journal of Management* 28(4) (2002): 471–496; M. Elovainio, M. Kivimaki, and K. Helkama, "Organizational Justice Evaluations, Job Control land Occupational Strain," *Journal of Applied Psychology* 86 (2001): 418–424; D. B. McFarlin and P. D. Sweeney, "Distributive and Procedural Justice as Predictors of Satisfaction with Personal and Organizational Outcomes," *Academy of Management Journal* 35 (1992): 626–637.

21   D. P. Skarlicki, R. Folger, and P. E. Tesluk, "Personality as a Moderator of the Relationship between Fairness and Retaliation," *Academy of Management Journal* 42 (1999): 100–108; D. P. Skarlicki and R. Folger, "Retaliation in the Workplace: The Roles of Distributive, Procedural and Interactive Justice," *Journal of Applied Psychology* 82 (1997): 434–443; J. Greenberg, "Employee Theft as a Reaction to Underpayment Inequity: The Hidden Cost of Pay Cuts," *Journal of Applied Psychology* 75 (1990): 561–568.

22   See R. B. Freeman and J. L. Medoff, *What Do Unions Do?* (New York: Basic Books, 1984); D. G. Spencer, "Employee Voice and Employee Retention," *Academy of Management Journal* 29 (1986): 488–502; G. E. Fryxell and M. E. Gordon, "Workplace Justice and Job Satisfaction as Predictors of Satisfaction with Union and Management," *Academy of Management Journal* 32 (1989): 851–866.

23   R. H. Moorman, "Relationship between Organizational Justice and Organizational Citizenship Behaviors: Do Fairness Perceptions Influence Employee Citizenship?" *Journal of Applied Psychology* 76(6) (1991): 845–855.

24   J. B. Olson-Buchanan and W. R. Boswell, "The Role of Employee Loyalty and Formality in Voicing Discontent," *Journal of Applied Psychology* 87(6) (2002): 1167–1174.

25   B. M. Goldman, "Toward an Understanding of Employment Discrimination Claiming: An Integration of Organizational Justice and Social Information Processing," *Personnel Psychology* 54 (2001): 361–386; E. A. Lind, J. Greenberg, K. S. Scott, and T. D. Welchans, "The Winding Road from Employee to Complainant: Situational and Psychological Determinants of Wrongful Termination Claims," *Administrative Science Quarterly* 45 (2000): 557–590.

26   This discussion is based mostly on R. E. Ringleb and H. A. Meiners, *Legal Environment of Business* (Cincinnati, OH: South-Western, 2001). Useful overviews also appear in R. D. Arvey and R. H. Faley, *Fairness in Selecting Employees,* 2nd ed. (Reading, MA: Addison-Wesley., 1988); and A. Gutman, *Law and Personnel Practices* (Newbury Park, CA: Sage, 1993).

27   J. Ledvinka, "Government Regulation and Human Resources," in A. Howard (ed.), *The Changing Nature of Work* (San Francisco: Jossey-Bass, 1995).

28   C. Edwards, "Coming Out in Corporate America," *Business Week* (December 15, 2003): 64–72.

29   For a more detailed discussion of relevant federal and state laws and regulations, see B. A. Lee and D. R. Sockell, "Regulation of the HRM Function," in J. B. Mitchell, M. A. Zaidi, and D. Lewin (eds.), *The Human Resource Management Handbook* (Greenwich, CT: JAI Press, 1997): 199–232.

30   H. R. Fox and L. P. Karunaratne, "EEOC Updates on Sexual Discrimination," *The Industrial-Organizational Psychologist* (January 2001): 150–151; McAfee and Taft, *Age Discrimination in the Workplace* (Alexandria, VA: SHRM, 1999); P. E. Varca and P. Pattison, "Evidentiary Standards in Employment Discrimination: A View toward the Future," *Personnel Psychology* 46 (1993): 239.

31   D. Ambrosio, "Sexual Orientation Discrimination," http://www.workforce.com/feature/22/27/56/ (October 28, 2004).

32   G. M. Davis, "The Family and Medical Leave Act: 10 Years Later," *Legal Report* (July–August 2003): 1–8. For a summary of other key areas of developing state legislation, see J. Schramm, "State Public Policy and Its Impact on HR," *Workplace Visions* (3) (2004): 1–8.

33   Source: U.S. Equal Employment Opportunity Commission (http://www.eeoc.gov); "Cost-Cutting Shifts the Terrain," *Workforce Management* (December 2003): 91.

34   L. Lawrence, "Coca-Cola Agrees to Record Discrimination Settlement," *HR News* (January 2001): 1, 4, 8.

35   "Rooting Out Racism," *Business Week Online,* http://www.businessweek.com/reprints/00-02/b3663022.htm; *Texaco Task Force Report on Equality and Fairness Issues: Third Annual Report (2000),* http://www.texaco.com; A. Bryant, "How Much Has Texaco Changed? A Mixed Report Card on Anti-Bias Efforts," *New York Times* (November 2, 1997): 3–1, 3–16, 3–17; V. C. Smith, "Texaco Outlines Comprehensive Initiatives," *Human Resource Executive* (February 1997): 13; and "Texaco's Workforce Diversity Plan," as reprinted in *Workforce* (March 1997): Supplement.

36   "Arbitration Provisions in Union Agreements in 1949," *Monthly Labor Review* 70 (1950): 160–165.

37   See M. E. Gordon and G. E. Fryxell, "The Role of Interpersonal Justice in Organizational Grievance Systems," in Cropanzano, *Justice in the Workplace.*

38   R. Ganzel, "Second-Class Justice?" *Training* (October 1997): 84–96; A. J. Conti, "Alternative Dispute Resolution: A Court-Backed, Mandatory Alternative to Employee Lawsuits," *Fair Employment Practices Guidelines* (October 10, 1997): 1–15; P. Feuille and J. T. Delaney, "The Individual Pursuit of Organizational Justice: Grievance Procedures in Nonunion

Workplaces," *Research in Personnel and Human Resources Management* 10 (1992): 187–232.

39 D. W. Ewing, "Who Wants Employee Rights?" *Harvard Business Review* 49 (November–December 1971): 22–35.

40 K. S. Robinson, "Employees Engaging in Deceptive Behaviors at Alarming Rates," *HR News* (September 2000): 22; R. B. Peterson, "The Union and Nonunion Grievance System," in D. Lewin, O. S. Mitchell, and P. D. Sherer (eds.), *Research Frontiers in Industrial Relations and Human Resources* (Madison, WI: Industrial Relations Research Association, 1992): 131–164.

41 J. B. Olson-Buchanan, "Voicing Discontent: What Happens to the Grievance Filer after the Grievance?" *Journal of Applied Psychology* 18 (1996): 52–63; C. Handy, "A Better Capitalism," *Across the Board* (April 1998): 16–22.

42 D. Anfuso, "Coors Taps Employee Judgment," *Personnel Journal* (February 1994): 56.

43 W. R. Boswell and J. B. Olson-Buchanan, "Experiencing Mistreatment at Work: The Role of Grievance Filing, Nature of Mistreatment, and Employee Withdrawal," *Academy of Management Journal* 47 (2004): 129–139; C. Gopinath and T. Becker, "Communication, Procedural Justice, and Employee Attitudes: Relationships under Conditions of Divestiture," *Journal of Management* 26 (2000): 63–83; M. T. Miklave, "Why 'Jury' Is a Four Letter Word," *Workforce* (March 1998): 56–64; K. Aquino, R. F. Griffeth, D. G. Allen, and P. W. Hom, "Integrating Justice Constructs into the Turnover Process: A Test of a Referent Cognitions Model," *Academy of Management Journal* 40 (1997): 1208–1227; M. Schminke, M. L. Ambrose, and T. W. Noel, "The Effect of Ethical Frameworks on Perceptions of Organizational Justice," *Academy of Management Journal* 40 (1997): 1190–1207; S. P. Schappe, "Bridging the Gap between Procedural Knowledge and Positive Employee Attitudes: Procedural Justice as Keystones," *Group and Organization Management* 21(3) (September 1996): 337–364.

44 V. C. Smith, "Sign of the Times," *Human Resource Executive* (April 1997): 57–63; S. Caudron, "Blow the Whistle on Employment Disputes," *Workforce* (May 1997): 51–57; R. Furchgott, "Opposition Builds to Mandatory Arbitration at Work," *New York Times* (July 20, 1997): F11; "Employee Relations," *HR Reporter* 14(12) (December 1997): 1–12; "NASD Votes to Nix Mandatory Arbitration," *Fair Employment Practices* (August 21, 1997): 99.

45 M. Barrier, "The Mediation Disconnect," *HR Magazine* (May 2003): 54–58; M. M Clark, "EEOC's Efforts to Expand Mediation Gain Momentum," *HR Magazine* (May 2003): 32, 34; P. Salvatore, "Mediation and Arbitration of Employment Law Claims," *Legal Report* (March–April 2001): 7–8; see also R. J. Weinstein, *Mediation in the Workplace: A Guide for Training, Practice, and Administration* (Westport, CT: Quorum Books, 2000).

46 G. Flynn, "High Court Weighs in on Arbitration," *Workforce* (June 2001): 100–101; M. Meece, "The Very Model of Conciliation," *New York Times* (September 6, 2000): C1; D. Casey and B. Lee, "Mandatory Arbitration Clauses in Individual Employment Contracts: Enhancing Fairness and Enforceability," *Employee Relations Law Journal* 25 (Winter 1999): 57–75; G. Glynn, "Mandatory Binding Arbitration—Ensure Your Plan Is Usable," *Workforce* (June 1997): 121–127.

47 M. L. Bickner and C. Feigenbaum, "Developments in Employment Arbitration," *Dispute Resolution Journal* (January 1997): 234–251; S. Caudron, "Blow the Whistle on Employment Disputes," *Workforce* (May 1997): 51–57.

48 B. Sunoo, "Hot Disputes Cool Down in Online Mediation," *Workforce* (January 2001): 48–52.

49 L. Bean, "What Happened to Diversity's Bad Boys? Texaco, Denny's, Coca-Cola," *DiversityInc* (October/November 2003): 111–116.

50 J. Kahn, "Diversity Trumps the Downturn," *Fortune* (July 9, 2001): 114–116.

51 *SHRM Survey Report on the Impact of Diversity Initiatives on the Bottom Line*, http://www.shrm.org/surveys, May 2001; see also T. Kochan,

K. Bezrukova, R. Ely, S. Jackson, A. Joshi, K. Jehn, J. Leonard, D. Levine, and D. Thomas, "The Effects of Diversity on Business Performance: Report of the Diversity Research Network," *Human Resource Management* 42(1) (Spring 2003): 3–21.

52 J. Hickman, C. Tkaczyk, E. Florian, and J. Stemple, "50 Best Companies for Minorities," *Fortune* (July 7, 2003): 103–120.

53 J. P. Johnson, III, "SHRM White Paper: Creating a Diverse Workforce," Society for Human Resource Management, http://www.shrm.org/hrresources/whitepapers_published, December 13, 2003.

54 For a discussion of color discrimination, see P. Mirza, "Where Is Color Discrimination Headed?" *HR Magazine* (December 2003): 64–67. See also G. Maatman, Jr. (ed.), *Worldwide Guide to Termination, Employment Discrimination, and Workplace Harassment Laws* (Chicago: Baker & McKenzie/CCH, 2001); R. Abelson, "If Women Complain, Does Ford Listen?" *New York Times* (January 28, 2001): Section 3: 1, 13; K. Schneider, R. Hitlan, and P. Radhakrishnan, "An Examination of the Nature and Correlates of Ethnic Harassment Experiences in Multiple Contexts," *Journal of Applied Psychology* 85 (2000): 3–12; "EEOC Proposes Harassment Guidelines," *Fair Employment Practices Guidelines* (July 29, 1993): 87.

55 "A Question of Ethics," *Bulletin to Management* (July 9, 1992): 211.

56 K. S. Robinson, "American Muslims Report Discrimination after Sept. 11 Terrorist Attacks," *Society for Human Resource Management* (October 2002): 17; S. Saulny, "Muslim Workers Claim Bias at the Plaza," *New York Times* (October 1, 2003): B3.

57 A. M. Townsend, M. E. Whitman, and R. J. Aalberts, "What's Left of the Communications Decency Act?" *HRM Magazine* (June 1998): 124–127.

58 P. McGeehan, "Two Analysts Leave Salomon in Smut Case," *Wall Street Journal* (March 31, 1998): C1, C25.

59 J. Steinhauer, "If the Boss Is Out of Line, What's the Legal Boundary," *New York Times* (March 27, 1997): D1, D4; "Reasonable Woman Standard Gains Ground," *Fair Employment Practices Guidelines* (June 25, 1993): 4.

60 K. M. Jarin and E. K. Pomfert, "New Rules for Same Sex Harassment," *HRM Magazine* (June 1998): 115–123.

61 W. K. Turner and C. S. Thrutchley, "Employment Law and Practices Training: No Longer the Exception—It's the Rule," *Legal Report* (July–August 2002): 1–8; "Preventing Sexual Harassment: Helpful Advice and Another Reason," *Fair Employment Practices* (February 19, 1998): 21; M. Raphan and M. Heerman, "Eight Steps to Harassment-Proof Your Office," *HR Focus* (August 1997): 11–12; D. E. Terpstra and D. D. Baker, "Outcomes of Federal Court Decisions on Sexual Harassment," *Academy of Management Journal* 35 (1992): 181–190; B. A. Gutek, A. G. Cohen, and A. M. Konrad, "Predicting Social-Sexual Behavior at Work: A Contact Hypothesis," *Academy of Management Journal* 33 (1990): 560–577. For details about how to investigate harassment complaints, see A. Oppenheimer and C. Pratt, "Investigating Workplace Harassment," *HR Magazine* (September 2002): 135–136.

62 L. R. Offermann and A. B. Malamut, "When Leaders Harass: The Impact of Target Perceptions of Organizational Leadership and Climate on Harassment Reporting and Outcomes," *Journal of Applied Psychology* 87(5) (2002): 885–893.

63 K. S. Robinson, "Employees Engaging in Deceptive Behaviors at Alarming Rates," *HR News* (September 2000): 22.

64 M. M. Clark, "Corporate Ethics Programs Make a Difference, but Not the Only Difference," *HR Magazine* (July 2003): 36.

65 M. Conlin, "Revenge of the 'Managers,'" *Business Week* (March 12, 2001): 60–62; L. Guernsey, "The Web: New Ticket to a Pink Slip," *New York Times* (December 16, 1999): G1, 8; M. W. Walsh, "More Than Just a Wrongful Termination," *New York Times* (January 31, 2001): G1; "Policy Guide: What Constitutes 'Good Cause' for Firing?" *Bulletin to Management* 49(3) (January 22, 1998): 24; "How Employers Can Use Employment-at-Will Disclaimers Effectively," *Fair Employment Practices*

Guidelines (November 10, 1997): 6–8; "A Pledge of Job Security Can Alter At-Will Status," *Bulletin to Management* (August 14, 1997); S. A. Youngblood and L. Bierman, "Due Process and Employment-at-Will: A Legal and Behavioral Analysis," in K. M. Rowland and G. R. Ferris (eds.), *Research in Personnel and Human Resources Management* (Greenwich, CT: JAI Press, 1985): 185–230.

66 M. Heller, "A Return to At-Will Employment," *Workforce* (May 2001): 42–46.

67 J. D. Glater, "For Last Paycheck More Workers Cede Their Right to Sue," *New York Times* (February 24, 2001): 1, 4.

68 For detailed information about state and federal privacy laws, see D. Safon and Worklaw Network, *Workplace Privacy: Real Answers and Practical Solutions* (Toronto: Thomson, 2000).

69 For a critique of employer monitoring practices, see F. S. Lane, III, *The Naked Employee* (New York: AMACOM, 2004). See also E. Eddy, D. Stone, E. Stone-Romero, "The Effects of Information Management Policies on Reactions to Human Resource Information Systems: An Integration of Privacy and Procedural Justice Perspectives," *Personnel Psychology* 52 (1999): 335–358; J. Lipson, "HR Struggles with Fine Lines of Workplace Privacy," *HR News* (March 2001): 15, 19; D. Saton and Worklaw Network, *Workplace Privacy: Real Answers and Practical Solutions* (Toronto: Thomson, 2000).

70 For details about the ADA, see J. W. Spechler, *Reasonable Accommodation: Profitable Compliance with the Americans with Disabilities Act* (Delray Beach, FL: St. Lucie Press, 1996).

71 W. L. Holstein, "From Rare to Routine," *New York Times* (November 28, 1993): 3–11.

72 T. Raphael, "Testing Issue Still Unsettled," *Workforce* (June 2001): 19. For more information on the status of genetic testing and to learn about state laws that are applicable, see http://www.genome.gov/.

73 W. Wood, F. Y. Wong, and J. G. Chachere, "Effects of Media Violence on Viewers' Aggression in Unconstrained Social Interaction," *Psychological Bulletin* 109 (1991): 371–383.

74 H. F. Bensimon, "Violence in the Workplace," *Training and Development Journal* (January 1994): 27–32; M. Braverman and O. M. Kurland, "Workplace Violence," *Risk Management* 40 (1993): 76–77; D. J. Peterson and D. Massengill, "The Negligent Hiring Doctrine—A Growing Dilemma for Employers," *Employee Relations Law Journal* 15 (1989–1990): 419–432; *A Post Office Tragedy: The Shooting at Royal Oak*. Report of the Committee on Post Office and Civil Service, United States House of Representatives, 1992.

75 "Video Surveillance Withstands Privacy Challenge," *Bulletin to Management* 48(16) (April 17, 1997): 121; "Secret Video OK'd as Inspection Tool," *Bulletin to Management* (February 12, 1998): 44.

76 "Big Bro Is Eyeing Your E-Mail," *Business Week* (June 4, 2001): 30.

77 J. Lipson, "HR Struggles with Fine Lines of Workplace Privacy," *Inside SHRM* (March 2001): 1, 19; W. S. Hubbartt, *The New Battle over Workplace Privacy* (New York: AMACOM, 1998).

78 L. Guernsey, "The Web: New Ticket to a Pink Slip," *New York Times* (December 16, 1999): G1, 8, 9.

79 J. E. Lyncheski and L. D. Heller, "Cyber Speech Cops," *HR Magazine* (January 2001): 145–150.

80 L. Conley, "The Privacy Arms Race," *Fast Company* (July 2004): 27–28.

81 For an excellent review of how U.S. discrimination laws apply abroad, see W. A. Carmell, *International Focus: Application of U.S. Antidiscrimination Laws to Multinational Employers* (Alexandria, VA: SHRM, 1999).

82 M. Roffer and N. Sanservino, Jr., "Holding Employees' Native Tongues," *HR Magazine* (September 2000): 177–184; R. Thompson, "Federal Anti-Bias Protections Extended to Undocumented Workers," *HR News* (December 1999): 7, 13; D. M. Truxillo and T. Bauer, "Applicant Reactions to Test Score Banding Entry-Level and Promotional Contexts," *Journal of Applied Psychology* 84 (1999): 322–339; V. Dobnik, "Study: Chinese Workers Abused while Making Nike, Reebok Shoes," Associated Press, *Corpus Christi Caller-Times* (September 21, 1997): A8; A. Chan, "Boot Camp at the Shoe Factory," *Washington Post* (November 3, 1996): C1, C4; W. A. Carmell, "Will U.S. Employee Protection Laws Extend Overseas to Non-Citizens?" *International Update* (April 1999): 6.

83 S. Holmes, "The New Nike," *Business Week* (September 20, 2004): 78–86.

84 J. Kahn, "Ruse in Toyland: Chinese Workers' Hidden Woe," *New York Times* (December 7, 2003): 1, 24.

85 D. R. Briscoe and R. S. Schuler, *International Human Resource Management: Policy and Practice in Global Enterprises*, 2nd ed. (London: Routledge, 2004).

86 D. Robb, "Restricting Data Flow," *HR Magazine* (April 2003): 97–99.

87 M. J. Gelfand, M. Higgins, L. H. Nishii, J. L. Raver, A. Dominguez, F. Murakami, S. Yamaguchi, and M. Toyama, "Culture and Egocentric Perceptions of Fairness in Conflict and Negotiation," *Journal of Applied Psychology* 87(5) (2002): 833–845; S. Wasti, M. Bergman, T. Glomb, and F. Drasgow, "Test of the Cross-Cultural Generalizability of a Model of Sexual Harassment," *Journal of Applied Psychology* 85 (2000): 766–778; W. A. Carmell, "U.S. Law Heads Abroad," *International HR Update* (July 1998): 5.

chapter 4

HR Planning for Alignment and Change

With yearly sales of about $20 billion and approximately 57,000 employees in the United States and 17 other countries, Weyerhaeuser Company is one of the largest paper and forest products companies in the world. Through the 1970s, it enjoyed fairly consistent success. In the 1980s, global and domestic competition roared in at the same time that the national economy went into recession, and the housing industry entered a major slump. Overcapacity plagued the paper industry. Suddenly the company's successful strategy of being a large-commodity lumber and paper business was no match against the new, smaller, and speedier competitors who focused more on the customer. Faced with a do-or-die crisis, top management restructured the company into three major divisions: forest products, paper products, and real estate. They also specified the firm's core values, which highlighted the importance of Customers, People, Accountability, Citizenship, and Financial Responsibility.

To live by these values, employees would have to change their behaviors. To support the new behaviors, a new human resource management (HRM) system was needed. Managers were trained to understand the new strategy and its implications for how the new business units would be managed. Performance appraisals and compensation were revised to evaluate and reward environmental responsibility, customer focus, and teamwork.

As business conditions continue to change, Weyerhaeuser's strategy and structure will continue to evolve, and further alignment of its HR policies and practices may be needed. Continuous HR planning will surely accompany the company's continuous process of systematic environmental scanning, strategic business planning, and objective setting.[1]

THE STRATEGIC IMPORTANCE OF HR PLANNING FOR ALIGNMENT AND CHANGE

At Weyerhaeuser, changes in the global environment were a major impetus for strategic change efforts. In order to succeed under new competitive conditions, the company changed its vision, values, structure, strategy, and even its corporate culture. All of these changes had significant implications for the behaviors and competencies needed from people in the organization. To encourage and support the behaviors required in the new organization, many of the company's HR policies and practices had to be changed. Over a period of several years, Weyerhaeuser succeeded in repositioning itself to become a highly successful global competitor. Human resource planning for (re)alignment and change—the focus of this effort—greatly aided the company's strategy for repositioning itself within the industry.

Alignment

Major environmental changes and organizational actions such as those at Weyerhaeuser are being repeated in hundreds of companies in every industry. Environmental changes that provoke major organizational actions include: changing global labor market conditions, new customer demands, increased competition, new regulations, new technologies, growth of the Internet, and fundamental changes in the structure and dynamics in the industry.

Today, events requiring major organizational actions are constant. And regardless of the type of actions an organization undertakes, success almost always requires changes in HR policies and practices. Sometimes a firm's entire HRM system is transformed in order to align the competencies and behavior of employees with strategic business objectives.[2] When HR policies and practices facilitate the behaviors and competencies needed for organizational success, the HRM system, and the needs of organization, the HRM system is in a state of alignment.

Actually, there are two components of alignment, which are sometimes referred to as vertical alignment and horizontal alignment. Human resource planning provides a means for achieving both vertical and horizontal alignment.

Vertical Alignment.   **Vertical alignment** *exists when the HRM system fits with all other elements of the organizational environment—the culture, strategy,* *structure, and so on.* When Dow Chemical restructured its worldwide business, it had to change its compensation practices to align them with the new business. Prior to the restructuring, Dow was organized around countries and regions, and different compensation practices were used throughout the world. Today, Dow has a single system that is used by managers everywhere to make pay decisions. When the annual pay planning begins, HR professionals provide managers with a set of guidelines for pay rates. Managers then develop plans for their units that fall within the guidelines. Managers consistently rate Dow's pay planning process as one of the company's best HR practices.[3]

When Fairchild Semiconductor was created as a spin-off from National Semiconductor, one of its first strategic business objectives was to make a transition from National's data management system to one of its own. It chose an Enterprise Resource Planning (ERP) application from Peoplesoft, and then set about adapting its processes to meet the software's requirements. The first step was to form teams of employees from all over the world to rework the company's business processes in finance, manufacturing, logistics, and human resources. By including HR professionals in these cross-functional teams, Fairchild ensured that new HR policies and practices would be vertically aligned with the business objective. Training was then used to teach employees the new tasks they would be expected to perform, and to explain why these new tasks were important. The company felt that employees would be less likely to take shortcuts to reduce their own workloads if they understood how their own contributions affected other people in the company and the bottom line. To build employees' confidence in their ability to use the new system and to reduce their fears, training sessions provided plenty of time for people to practice using the software and receive feedback. At Fairchild, installing new ERP software was a change that resulted in employees becoming more knowledgeable about the business and more excited about their own roles within the company.[4]

Horizontal Alignment. **Horizontal alignment** *exists when all the HR policies and practices that comprise the HRM system are consistent with each other so that they present a coherent message to employees concerning how employees should behave while at work.* At Weyerhaeuser, horizontal alignment was created by its HR professionals, who had an understanding of the business and who worked in partnership with line managers as new HR policies and practices were developed. Working together, they crafted HR policies and practices that supported and reinforced employee behaviors such as environmental responsibility, customer focus, and teamwork. As explained in Chapter 2, horizontal alignment is necessary in order to provide employees with meaningful direction.

TYPES OF ORGANIZATIONAL CHANGE

Organizations can undergo many types of planned change, which vary in both degree and timing.

Degree of Change. *When organizations make major adjustments in the ways they do business, it usually creates the need for* **radical change.** Adopting a new organizational structure, merging with another organization, or changing from a privately held to a publicly traded company is likely to require radical organizational change.

Radical change is relatively infrequent and generally takes a long time to complete. When managers undertake radical change, they often make huge investments in planning and implementing the change.[5] Radical change touches everyone and everything in the organization. It changes the daily lives of every employee, as well as other key stakeholders, such as customers, suppliers, and alliance partners. The change to a new ERP system usually involves radical change.

In contrast, **incremental change** *is an ongoing process of evolution over time, during which many small changes occur routinely.* Over time, the cumulative effect of many small changes may be to transform the organization totally. Yet, while they are occurring, the changes seem to be just a normal aspect of revising and improving the way that work gets done. Total Quality Management (TQM) is an approach that relies heavily on incremental change. Employees routinely look for ways to improve products and services, and they make suggestions for changes day in and day out. Incremental change is also important in learning organizations. The desire to improve performance continuously in order to stay ahead of competitors is a common reason for smaller organizational changes.[6] Successful organizations are equally adept at making both radical and incremental changes.

Timing of Change.   In addition to the differences in the magnitude of change are differences in the timing of change. **Reactive change** *occurs when an organization is forced to change in response to some event in the external or organizational environment.* New strategic moves made by competitors, new scientific or technological discoveries, and performance problems are common reasons for reactive change. Weyerhaeuser didn't foresee the changes that would shake the paper and lumber industry, so it was forced into reactive change.

Reactive change can be radical or incremental. Weyerhaeuser's reactive change was radical. If an organization adapts to a change in the environment without undergoing a substantial reorientation in its strategy or values, the change is reactive and incremental.

When an unexpected economic recession hit in 2001, it ended one of the biggest economic expansions in U.S. history. As CEO of Seibel Systems, the computer company, Thomas Seibel realized that steering his high-growth company through an economic downturn required him to adopt a new set of short-term strategic business objectives. Seibel's financial planners reacted quickly—they developed a new budget that was more appropriate given the slowing demand for projects. Implementing the budget would require widespread incremental change. One implication of the new budget was that payroll costs had to be reduced. Seibel reduced the workforce by 10% and postponed bonuses. Spending on travel was cut in half. Recruiting costs were cut from $8 million to $1 million. Some employees were reassigned from their other jobs to work as members of sales teams. Everyone focused their energies on closing big contracts. These changes helped Seibel Systems outpace its competitors during a difficult business downturn without requiring any fundamental changes in the company's mission, vision, values, or long-range strategic direction.[7]

Sometimes upcoming events are predictable so managers can foresee that change will be needed to succeed in the future. *When an organization takes action in anticipation of upcoming events or early in the cycle of a new trend, it undergoes* **anticipatory change.** The best-run organizations always look for better ways to do things in order to stay ahead of the competition. Some companies strive to keep their costs low by continually introducing technological improvements. Others stay ahead of their competitors by always raising their standards for customer satisfaction.

Often, anticipatory change is incremental and results from constant tinkering and improvements. Occasionally anticipatory change is radical, however. Visionary leaders within the organization become convinced that major changes are needed even though there is no apparent crisis. Because there is no crisis, the changes can be planned carefully and implemented gradually. Successful companies are adept at all types of change. They understand the need to assess whether HR policies and practices are aligned and how to make adjustments to the HRM system when needed. Increasingly, they are also adept at learning from their experiences so that they can be more effective in making future changes.[8]

> *"The species that survive are not the biggest but the most adaptable."*
>
> Charles Darwin

Learning Organizations

During the past decade, many companies identified organizational learning as an important core competency. A **learning organization** *continually finds new ways to satisfy customers and other stakeholders by skillfully integrating the resources of information, technology, and people to produce and then effectively use new knowledge.* Learning organizations are changing all the time.

As Exhibit 4.1 shows,[9] continuous organizational learning and change has many implications for managing human resources. Together with other elements of the organizational environment (leadership, culture, strategy), HR policies and practices support the behaviors for continuous learning and change. These behaviors include experimentation, learning from others, documenting what is learned, and several others listed in Exhibit 4.1. In learning organizations, the process of HR planning is used to ensure that the HRM system supports these needed behaviors by providing learning opportunities, building learning competencies, and keeping employees motivated and interested in learning.

OVERVIEW OF THE HR PLANNING AND CHANGE PROCESS

In many organizations, the process of business planning begins with a scanning of the external environment and a vision of where the organization needs to be in five (or even ten) years. Once a long-term vision and clear objectives are developed, the management team works backward to understand the near-term implications. Subsequently, the organization may then go through numerous cycles of short-term (e.g., annual) planning as it moves toward its long-term objectives.

Strategic change seldom occurs without a bit of chaos. Indeed, a few organizations seem to thrive on chaos. But most organizations strive to impose some order and keep chaos under control during strategic change by engaging in systematic planning.

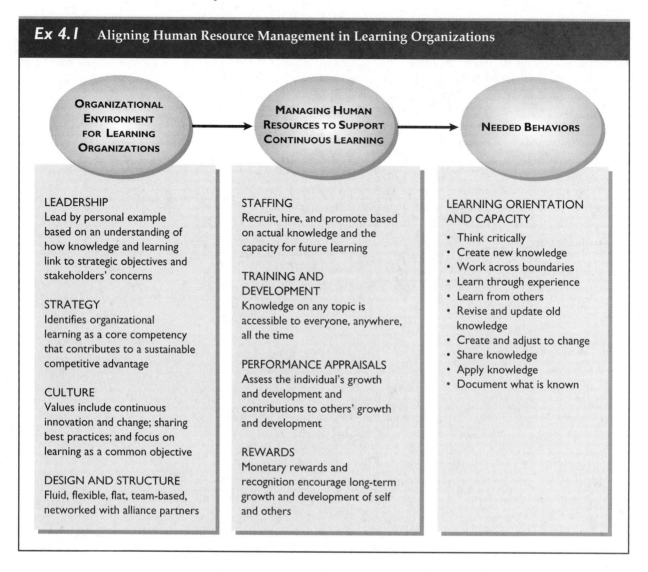

Ex 4.1   Aligning Human Resource Management in Learning Organizations

ORGANIZATIONAL ENVIRONMENT FOR LEARNING ORGANIZATIONS

MANAGING HUMAN RESOURCES TO SUPPORT CONTINUOUS LEARNING

NEEDED BEHAVIORS

LEADERSHIP
Lead by personal example based on an understanding of how knowledge and learning link to strategic objectives and stakeholders' concerns

STRATEGY
Identifies organizational learning as a core competency that contributes to a sustainable competitive advantage

CULTURE
Values include continuous innovation and change; sharing best practices; and focus on learning as a common objective

DESIGN AND STRUCTURE
Fluid, flexible, flat, team-based, networked with alliance partners

STAFFING
Recruit, hire, and promote based on actual knowledge and the capacity for future learning

TRAINING AND DEVELOPMENT
Knowledge on any topic is accessible to everyone, anywhere, all the time

PERFORMANCE APPRAISALS
Assess the individual's growth and development and contributions to others' growth and development

REWARDS
Monetary rewards and recognition encourage long-term growth and development of self and others

LEARNING ORIENTATION AND CAPACITY
- Think critically
- Create new knowledge
- Work across boundaries
- Learn through experience
- Learn from others
- Revise and update old knowledge
- Create and adjust to change
- Share knowledge
- Apply knowledge
- Document what is known

THE ELEMENTS OF HUMAN RESOURCE PLANNING

The term **human resource planning** *refers to the activities associated with (a) scanning and assessing the environment; (b) specifying the objectives to be achieved by HR activities along with the measures to be used to assess the achievement of those objectives; and (c) developing specific plans for HR policies and practices, along with timetables for implementing those plans.* These are the activities highlighted in the shaded box shown on the right side of Exhibit 4.2. The planning process may not always proceed exactly as shown, but regardless of the sequence, these activities are the basic components of a systematic approach to HR planning.[10]

Scanning.   The framework shown in Exhibit 4.2 highlights the importance of systematically and continuously scanning and assessing the external and organizational environments described in Chapter 2, and considering their implications for managing the firm's human resources. This is the first phase of the planning process.

Ex 4.2 Phases in Strategic Business and HR Planning for Alignment and Change

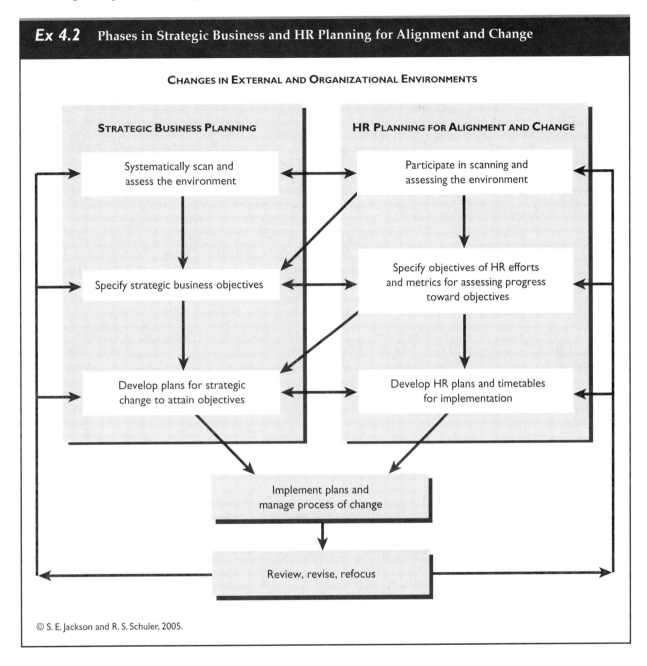

CHANGES IN EXTERNAL AND ORGANIZATIONAL ENVIRONMENTS

STRATEGIC BUSINESS PLANNING

- Systematically scan and assess the environment
- Specify strategic business objectives
- Develop plans for strategic change to attain objectives

HR PLANNING FOR ALIGNMENT AND CHANGE

- Participate in scanning and assessing the environment
- Specify objectives of HR efforts and metrics for assessing progress toward objectives
- Develop HR plans and timetables for implementation

Implement plans and manage process of change

Review, revise, refocus

© S. E. Jackson and R. S. Schuler, 2005.

To illustrate how scanning relates to a specific strategic issue, consider merging with or acquiring another firm. Refer again to Exhibit 2.3 (p. 50), which describes the key HR activities associated with mergers and acquisitions (M&As). As you can see, during the first phase of M&As, one way that HR professionals participate is by scanning the environment to assess potential target firms. Research on integration following mergers and acquisitions shows that the HR implications of M&As should not be treated as an afterthought. By planning for the human side of the integration, merging companies can build trust and prepare people for the changes they are about to undergo.[11]

Objectives and Metrics.   In many companies, changes in the HRM system are stimulated by the company's strategic objective of improving customer satisfaction. A study by The Conference Board found that customer-driven changes were common in the manufacturing and service sectors. Exhibit 4.3 summarizes some of the findings from that study.[12] **HR objectives** *state in quantitative or qualitative terms what is to be achieved with regard to the firm's human resources.* Ideally, if the stated HR objectives are met, the firm will meet its overall strategic objectives. For the objectives listed in Exhibit 4.3, how would *you* measure the organization's progress?

In order to evaluate whether the objectives are being met, organizations need to identify the measures they will use to assess progress. *The measurements that are used to assess progress against HR objectives are often referred to as* **HR metrics.** The list of potential HR objectives and metrics that an organization might use is almost limitless. Each organization must develop its own unique set of HR objectives and metrics to fit its specific situation.

When Sears, the department store, set out to improve customer satisfaction and store revenues, it established an HR objective of increasing employee commitment. Sears had conducted a study to improve its understanding of the factors that lead to customer satisfaction. Using data from all of its stores around the country, it created a cause-and-effect model showing the factors that explained customer satisfaction. Stores with higher employee commitment and lower employee turnover were found to have more satisfied customers. Thus, Sears began using measures of employee attitudes and retention as key HR metrics.[13]

Plans and Timetables.   Once the objectives are clearly specified, HR plans for achieving the objectives can be developed. **HR plans** *can be thought*

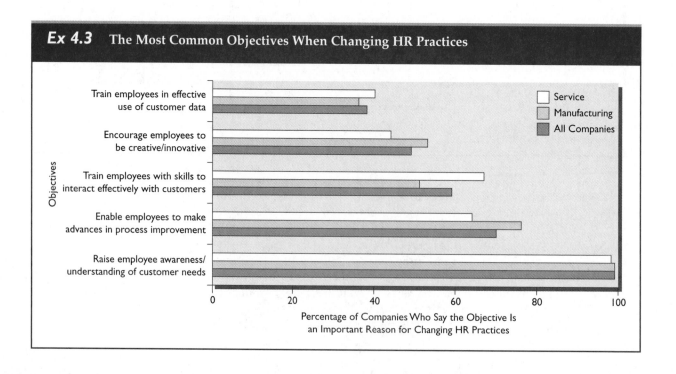

Ex 4.3   **The Most Common Objectives When Changing HR Practices**

Percentage of Companies Who Say the Objective Is an Important Reason for Changing HR Practices

of as blueprints for action; they specific who needs to do what, where, and how; **timetables** *specify when each planned activity will be completed.* At this stage, HR plans need to address two key issues: What procedures will be used to design new HR policies and practices that will be aligned with the new business plans? And, how will the new HR policies and practices be introduced to the workforce? Developing plans and timetables requires close coordination between the HR professionals and the line managers involved in creating business plans. Whatever time frame is adopted, HR planning should parallel the business planning process.[14]

THE HR TRIAD

As Exhibit 4.2 suggests, two members of the HR Triad—line managers and HR professionals—play significant roles and share a great deal of responsibility for the HR planning processes. Working together, their goal is to understand the external environment and work toward ensuring that the organization is capable of being effective in the context of a changing environment. Of course, planning is only the initial phase of organizational alignment and change. Once plans have been developed, implementation can begin. Later in this chapter, the role of employees will become more apparent when we discuss some of the challenges that arise during the implementation phase.

The primary opportunities for collaboration among line managers, HR professionals, and employees during planning, alignment, and change are described in "The HR Triad: Roles and Responsibilities for HR Planning, Alignment, and Change."

ALIGNING BUSINESS PLANNING AND HR PLANNING

Historically, in times of greater environmental stability, human resource planning focused almost exclusively on matching human resource demand with human resource supply. Its primary purpose was ensuring that the right number and type of people were available at the right time and place to serve relatively predictable business needs that resulted from business plans created in relatively stable environmental conditions. If the business was growing at a rate of 10%, for example, top management would continue to add to the workforce by 10%: It worked before, it would work again. Today, because environmental conditions seldom remain stable for long, HR planning is becoming a more integral part of overall business planning. As a consequence, HR planning takes on greater strategic importance.[15]

FAST FACT Since the introduction of its Trac II razor 30 years ago, Gillette has always included a consideration of HR implications when planning to launch new products.

The double-headed arrows in Exhibit 4.2 show that close coordination and collaboration between line managers and HR professionals is desirable during strategic business planning and HR planning. At Weyerhaeuser, close coordination and collaboration helped the company achieve its strategic business objectives during its changes in strategy and structure. As Weyerhaeuser did, managers and HR professionals should systematically consider changes in HR policies and practices in the context of issues related to other tangible and intangible resources, including finances, technology, physical resources, and the firm's current and desired reputation. Unfortunately, this ideal situation is not always realized. In fact, according to

The HR Triad

Roles and Responsibilities for HR Planning, Alignment, and Change

LINE MANAGERS	HR PROFESSIONALS	EMPLOYEEES
• Systematically scan and assess the environment to help establish specific strategic objectives.	• Participate in environmental scanning and assessment to gain an understanding of specific strategic objectives.	• Monitor and seek to understand the environment and its potential implications for the company.
• In early phases of planned change, provide information about the current external and organizational environments and help forecast likely changes.	• Manage HR planning activities, including forecasting of labor needs and supplies, and identification of the HR implications of planned changes.	• Provide input during early phases of planning for change as needed (e.g., by providing opinions for use during organizational assessment and forecasting).
• Share information with and involve HR professionals during development of plans, including development of metrics and timetables for evaluating change.	• Develop detailed HR objectives, plans, metrics, and timetables for strategic change. Facilitate the change process as it unfolds.	• Provide input during the development of HR plans. Approach change with a positive attitude rather than resistance.
• Collaborate in the collection and interpretation of data to assess progress toward strategic and HR objectives.	• Develop, collect, and analyze data to assess progress toward strategic and HR objectives.	• Collaborate in the collection and interpretation of data to assess progress toward strategic and HR objectives.
• Learn about effective change processes and act as a role model for effective learning and change.	• Serve as the facilitator of change; help line managers and other employees develop an enhanced capacity for leading and accepting change.	• Recognize that change is constant and develop a personal capacity for frequent change.
• Communicate constantly with employees concerning planned changes using formal and informal means.	• Work with line managers to develop and disseminate formal communications about planned changes in HR activities; respond promptly and candidly to questions about planned changes in HR activities.	• Take personal responsibility for ensuring own understanding of planned changes and their implications.
• Participate in the process of evaluating and revising change initiatives.	• Assist in conducting evaluations of change initiatives, interpreting the results, and revising plans accordingly.	• Participate in the process of evaluating change and making adjustments as needed.

one recent study, only one out of five firms succeed in establishing a strong link between HR planning and strategic business planning. The results of this study are illustrated in Exhibit 4.4.[16]

In this same study, HR professionals were asked to describe who was involved in their organization's strategic business planning process. Their responses are summarized in Exhibit 4.5.[17] In approximately half of the companies surveyed, members of the senior HR team participated in the devel-

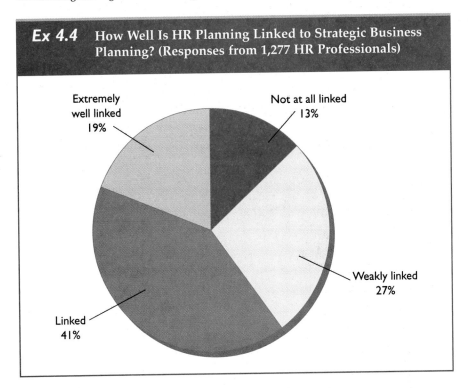

Ex 4.4 How Well Is HR Planning Linked to Strategic Business Planning? (Responses from 1,277 HR Professionals)

Extremely well linked 19%

Not at all linked 13%

Weakly linked 27%

Linked 41%

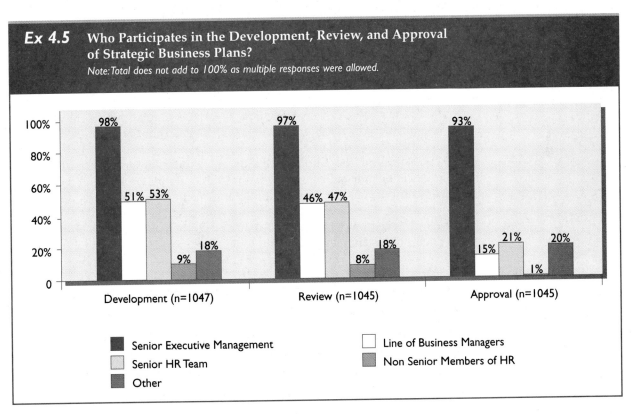

Ex 4.5 Who Participates in the Development, Review, and Approval of Strategic Business Plans?

Note: Total does not add to 100% as multiple responses were allowed.

Development (n=1047): 98%, 51%, 53%, 9%, 18%

Review (n=1045): 97%, 46%, 47%, 8%, 18%

Approval (n=1045): 93%, 15%, 21%, 1%, 20%

- Senior Executive Management
- Senior HR Team
- Other
- Line of Business Managers
- Non Senior Members of HR

opment and review of the strategic business plan. Notice that the involvement of the senior HR team is similar to the involvement of line managers. Not surprisingly, HR professionals and line managers were less often involved in the final approval of the strategic plan. Nevertheless, in one out of five organizations, approval of the plan by the senior HR team was sought.

SCANNING AND ASSESSING THE EXTERNAL AND ORGANIZATIONAL ENVIRONMENTS

The first phase of human resource planning for change involves gathering data to learn about and understand all aspects of the environment. As described in Chapter 2, the external environment includes local, national, and multinational conditions, such as:

- Economic conditions
- Political landscape
- Regional Trade Zone
- Technology
- Industry Dynamics
- Labor Markets
- Country Cultures
- Laws and Regulations
- Unions and Labor Relations

The likely and possible changes in customers' needs and preferences also must be considered.[18] Chapter 2 also described the elements of the internal organizational environment, which include its business strategies and company culture.

During this early phase of HR planning, the expertise of HR professionals is especially relevant for assessing labor market conditions, making predictions about how new employment laws and regulations might affect the organization, alerting managers to relevant trends in union activity and labor relations, and assessing the organizational culture.

Changes in the external and organizational environments often have implications for managing human resources, but their specific implications depend on each company's situation. Consider the age trends depicted in Exhibit 4.6. For some firms, the aging workforce may mean that older workers will experience increasing frustration as they realize that a glut of senior talent means that fewer of them will be able to continue their climb up the corporate ladder. For many firms, like Chevron Texaco, having a glut of workers nearing retirement made downsizing easier—generous buyout packages can be used to encourage voluntary early retirement, eliminating the need for layoffs. For Deloitte, these trends mean that the number of partners over age 50 will double in five years, to make up 25% of the total. Partners are highly paid, and they become vested in the firm's pension plan at age 50. Retirement at age 50 is likely to be financially feasible for most partners. Whereas some companies might welcome mass retirements, they could be disastrous for Deloitte, because partners are a very valuable source of experience and talent. Unless the firm does something to keep these people, they may begin exiting the firm at a very high cost.

Ex 4.6   Changing Age Demographics of the U.S. Population

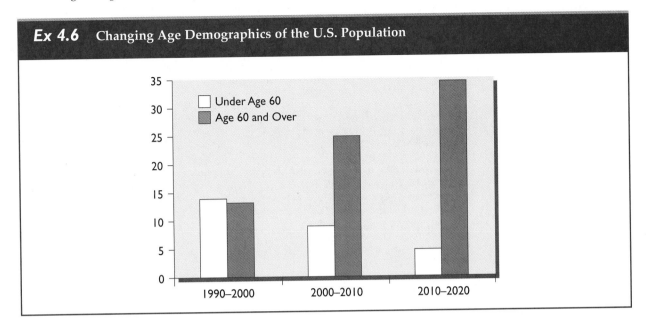

ORGANIZATIONAL ANALYSIS

An assessment of the external and internal environments is often referred to as **organizational analysis.** The aim is to fully understand the current environment before taking action. The idea that organizational analysis should precede action for both human resources and for the company as a whole may seem obvious, but its importance is often underestimated.[19]

When A. G. Lafley took the helm as CEO of Procter & Gamble (P&G), half of the company's top brands were losing market share. A major corporate restructuring had been taking place in recent years, and employees seemed demoralized by its effects. To make things worse, the company's stock price had fallen dramatically. An organizational analysis was the first step to getting things back on track. The organizational analysis of P&G was not limited to addressing HR issues; it turned out, however, that people issues were at the center of many of the company's problems. The feature entitled "Managing Change: Organizational Analysis at Procter & Gamble" describes the company's efforts.[20]

Stengel's team at P&G understood that reviewing a variety of information is the best approach when conducting an organizational analysis. As a marketing expert, he began his analysis using marketing techniques to analyze the concerns of his workforce. In many ways, this activity is similar to some activities used in typical HR methods. Three common HR methods used during organizational analysis are HR forecasts, employees' opinions, and behavioral cause-and-effect models.

HR FORECASTS

HR forecasts *estimate the firm's future human resource needs.* Earlier, in times of greater environmental stability, forecasting human resource needs and planning the steps necessary to meet those needs was largely a numbers game.

"The assets at P&G are what? Our people and our brands."

A. G. Lafley
CEO
Procter & Gamble

Managing Change

Organizational Analysis at Procter & Gamble

Procter & Gamble is a household name in the United States and abroad. With brands such as Crest toothpaste and Pampers diapers, the company is a marketing-driven organization. So when the market share of P&G brands fell, rebuilding the company's marketing strength became a top priority. The job fell to Chief Marketing Officer Jim Stengel. With the help of two marketing professors, Stengel began the change process by conducting an in-depth organizational analysis. After talking with other executives, Stengel concluded that P&G's leaders really didn't understand the problems confronting the company's core talent—its marketers. To develop a clearer picture of the problems, Stengel's team used its own marketing methods to understand employees' concerns.

The marketing professors began by shadowing a cross-section of marketing directors, brand managers, and brand assistants as they went about their work. After people got comfortable with the "shadows," they opened up and began expressing their frustrations. At the same time, the shadows were able to observe the positive behaviors engaged in by employees (e.g., using face-to-face communication for some tasks instead of relying on e-mail). These would later become the basis for new training programs.

After several days of shadowing, the next step was to conduct focus groups. Six to eight market-ing employees met for two to three hours to discuss a variety of issues. In addition, several one-on-one interviews were conducted with marketing managers. The focus groups were confidential, but the interviews with managers were taped. One manager observed that "there is a real need to get back to the basics of people development. No one even understands . . . how to evaluate people anymore." Another recalled, "When I came to P&G 15 years ago, you got your 15 minutes of coaching from your boss every day. We now have nothing. Coaching is a skill we have lost."

Stengel was beginning to get it. To create action plans, he convened a task force headed by the director of human resources for global marketing. The task force understood that a systematic change effort was needed. The company couldn't solve all of its problems with a few new training courses—it would have to rethink its compensation and rewards practices, career paths, and every aspect of its management approach that sent signals to employees about what was important. By 2004, the changes at P&G were having an effect. As one manager from a major competitor put it, "Things are getting tougher for us [the competing company]. P&G has coming roaring back!"

Forecasting efforts focused on (a) developing estimates of how many people with which competencies would be needed, (b) forecasting the likely supply of people and skills, and (c) implementing plans to ensure that the right number and type of people would be available at the right time and place. If the supply of people was expected to exceed the projected needs, downsizing plans might be developed. If the projected needs were greater than the anticipated supply, aggressive recruiting plans might be developed.

FAST FACT

In Los Angeles, 53% of children under 18 years of age are Latino. In San Antonio, the figure is 61%.

In many organizations, quantitative forecasts of future human resource needs continue to be one important ingredient in an organizational analysis. At Chevron Texaco, for example, all operating units must conduct a demographic analysis each year to identify where talent shortages or surpluses are likely to occur. In addition to information about the supply and productivity of employees, data about skills, competencies, educational levels, turnover and absenteeism rates, and attitudes may be used to forecast future human resource needs.

The quality of any forecast depends on the accuracy of information used and the predictability of events. The shorter the time horizon, the more predictable the events and the more accurate the information. For example, organizations are generally able to predict how many graduates they need for the coming year, but they are less able to predict how many they will need for the next five years. And predicting the behavior of new college graduates is easier than predicting the behavior of people at the other end of their employment cycle. You can count on new graduates to be looking for jobs, but at what age should you expect older workers to be thinking about retirement?

Forecasting involves approximations, not absolutes or certainties. A variety of forecasting methods—some simple, some complex—can be used to predict an organization's demand for human resources and the likely supply that will be available to meet the demand. Two commonly used methods are judgmental forecasts and statistical forecasts.

Judgmental Forecasts. **Judgmental forecasts** *rely on the opinions of informed experts (usually managers), who provide their estimates of current and projected productivity levels, market demand, and sales, as well as current staffing levels and mobility information.* One way to arrive at an agreement about what estimates to use is the Delphi technique. At a Delphi meeting, experts take turns at presenting their forecasts and assumptions to the others, who then make revisions in their own forecasts. This collaborative process continues until a viable composite forecast emerges. The composite may represent specific projections or a range of projections, depending on the experts' positions. Although judgmental forecasts rely on less data than those based on statistical methods, they tend to dominate in practice.

Union Pacific, the railroad company, used judgmental forecasting to estimate how many employees it needed to hire in order to meet the demands of its new customer, UPS. United Parcel Service (UPS) provided Union Pacific with fairly accurate predictions concerning how much they would need the railroad to ship for them. But Union Pacific had a difficult time estimating how this new customer's demands would influence the railroad's hiring needs. The problem was that Union Pacific had not anticipated how many of its employees would retire when the Railroad Retirement Board changed the rules to make earlier retirement more attractive to railroad employees. To predict how many people would retire, Union Pacific conducted focus groups, conducted employee surveys, and even hired the Gallup organization to take a poll. Despite these efforts, the railroad was surprised by how many employees chose to retire when the new rules took effect. "We admit we got caught short of people," said Robert Turner, a senior vice president at Union Pacific. The staff shortages soon led to overworked crews. Managers pushed people to work harder and punished those who tried to take time off. Poor labor relations developed, and people who could retire decided it was a good time to do so. Due to Union Pacific's staff shortage, shipments for UPS were delayed, but so were agricultural shipments. Some observers worried that the delays would affect international trade. Meanwhile, to correct the problem, Union Pacific was rushing to hire and train nearly 4,000 new employees and worrying about how they would cope when the holiday shipping season kicked in.[21]

Statistical Forecasts. **Statistical forecasts** *rely heavily on objective data and formal models.* For example, statistical methods might be used to predict labor needs under various conditions of business growth or decline. As another example, statistical forecasting could be used to determine how long it would take to reduce the workforce

"The railroad took a punitive attitude toward people who had already worked to exhaustion. You're threatening people who have already worked too much to get them to go to work more."

James Brunkenhoefer
National Legislative Director
United Transportation Union

by 15% through normal attrition. Fairly accurate statistical forecasts are possible when large amounts of historical data are available for analysis, and when past conditions are similar to those during which the forecast is to apply. Statistical projections often are used to estimate the likely supply of labor in the external labor market, for example. In that case, data about birth rates, typical retirement ages, and educational trends can be used to forecast future labor supplies.

Statistical forecasts also can be used to predict future labor supply and demand given changes in demand for the products and services provided by the organization. Again, making such forecasts is possible only if the organization keeps track of the information needed to make such forecasts. For this example, an organization would need a well-specified model of how changes in demand for products and services translate into changes in the company's operations—and thus changes in the number, types, and locations of employees needed.

Regardless of the method used, forecasts of future labor needs and supplies should be considered rough estimates, at best. Accurate forecasts depend on the ability to predict changing conditions in the external labor market, the impact of new technologies, current employees' future employment competencies, and often both employee attitudes and employee behaviors.

EMPLOYEES' OPINIONS

Employees' opinions are another one of the many sources of information that can be useful when conducting an organizational analysis. Opinions about both problems and potential solutions can be helpful when planning for change.

Employee Surveys. Employee surveys are one method for finding out employees' opinions. The content of the survey depends on the areas of most concern to the organization.

An organization interested in implementing Total Quality Management (TQM) may want to assess the organizational environment to determine whether the company culture is aligned with TQM principles. For this type of assessment, a survey tool for assessing employee's views is available from the National Institute of Standards and Technology. As shown in Exhibit 4.7, the survey asks the organization's leaders to indicate their degree of agreement with statements that describe the culture of effective TQM organizations. Items are grouped into categories that reflect the criteria used to evaluate organizations for the Malcolm Baldrige Award. Analysis of responses to these items can be used when developing plans for creating a strong TQM company culture. Then, after new initiatives have been deployed, the survey can be administered again to assess the success of the organization's change efforts.[22]

FAST FACT

Malcolm Baldrige National Quality Award was created by a public law passed in 1987. It is awarded annually to companies that meet the highest standards for quality and performance excellence.

Yum! restaurant uses an employee survey to assess the state of the organization's culture in order to determine whether any managerial actions are needed to improve it. Items in the employee survey ask people to assess their commitment to the company's core values, which include customer focus, teamwork, recognition, and excellence, among others. The results are

Ex 4.7   Leadership Survey to Assess a Company's Culture for TQM

Following are selected items from a survey tool developed by the National Institute of Standards and Technology. By asking leaders to respond to the survey and analyzing their responses, an organization can assess which aspects of their culture are not fully aligned with TQM principles. Note that the items are grouped into categories. These reflect the criteria used to evaluate organizations for the Malcolm Baldrige Award.

DESCRIPTIVE STATEMENT (SELECTED EXAMPLES)	STRONGLY DISAGREE	DISAGREE	NEITHER AGREE NOR DISAGREE	AGREE	STRONGLY AGREE
1. Leadership					
Our employees know our organizational mission (what we are trying to accomplish)	☐	☐	☐	☐	☐
Our leadership team shares information about the organization	☐	☐	☐	☐	☐
2. Strategic Planning					
As our leadership team plans for the future, we ask our employees for ideas	☐	☐	☐	☐	☐
Our employees know how the parts of our organization's plans will affect them and their work	☐	☐	☐	☐	☐
3. Customer and Market Focus					
Our employees know who their most important customers are	☐	☐	☐	☐	☐
Our employees ask if their customers are satisfied or dissatisfied with their work	☐	☐	☐	☐	☐
4. Measurement, Analysis, and Knowledge Management					
Our employees know how to measure the quality of their work	☐	☐	☐	☐	☐
Our employees know how the measures they use in their work fit into our organization's overall measures of improvement	☐	☐	☐	☐	☐
5. Human Resource Focus					
Our employees can make changes that will improve their work	☐	☐	☐	☐	☐
We encourage and enable our employees to develop their job skills so they can advance in their careers	☐	☐	☐	☐	☐

(continued)

Ex 4.7   (continued)

DESCRIPTIVE STATEMENT (SELECTED EXAMPLES)	STRONGLY DISAGREE	DISAGREE	NEITHER AGREE NOR DISAGREE	AGREE	STRONGLY AGREE
6. Process Management					
Our employees collect information (data) about the quality of their work	☐	☐	☐	☐	☐
Our employees have control over their personal work processes	☐	☐	☐	☐	☐
7. Business Results					
Our employees' customers are satisfied with their work	☐	☐	☐	☐	☐
Our organization has high standards and ethics	☐	☐	☐	☐	☐
Our employees know how well our organization is doing financially	☐	☐	☐	☐	☐
Our organization obeys laws and regulations	☐	☐	☐	☐	☐
Our organization helps our employees help their community	☐	☐	☐	☐	☐
Our employees are satisfied with their jobs	☐	☐	☐	☐	☐

broken out for each functional area and each level. Managers receive the results for their area of responsibility. If the survey results are unsatisfactory, a manager is required to develop an action plan to improve the situation.[23]

Focus Groups.   A focus group brings together a small number of employees to discuss a specific issue during a conversation guided by a trained facilitator. Texas Instruments (TI) used focus groups when it launched an effort to revise its HRM system. Over time, TI had developed a cumbersome set of HR policies that prevented the company from responding quickly to a rapidly changing environment. It set an objective of developing a new HRM system around a small set of "application guidelines." These guidelines would reflect TI's core values. But what were these core values? To find out, the HR staff conducted 30 focus group discussions with employees from all around the world. These conversations revealed three core values that were shared throughout the company: integrity, innovation, and commitment. These values became the foundation of TI's new application guidelines, around which they built a new HRM system.[24]

Involving Employees in Developing Plans.   Another way to ensure employees' views are taken into consideration is by involving employees directly in the development of the HR plans. As described in the feature

Managing Globalization

Building Global Leaders at Unilever BestFoods

Headquartered in Englewood Cliffs, New Jersey, Unilever BestFoods is one of the largest branded food companies in the United States. Its operations are a part of the Unilever company, one of the largest consumer products companies with sales of $50 billion. Its products include Hellmann's mayonnaise, Mazola corn oil, Skippy peanut butter, and Thomas' English muffins. Unilever operates in more than 88 countries and employs more than 275,000 workers. The company's projections are that future growth will come primarily from Africa, Asia, Eastern Europe, the Middle East, and the countries of the former Soviet Union.

When BestFoods learned that more than 80% of purchasing decisions for its products were made by women, they decided it was time to develop and promote more women into senior leadership positions within the company. To begin to address this strategic issue, the CEO worked with the Corporate Strategy Council to convene a week-long Women's Global Leadership Forum. Attended by 55 women from 25 countries, the event was an intensive work session that sought to document women's beliefs about the current situation, identify barriers to advancement, and provide suggestions for an action plan that the company could implement. To inform discussions at the Forum, the company conducted a survey of its 20 corporate officers and of 125 senior executives. The survey results, which were presented by the CEO at his kickoff address to the Forum, documented top management's perceptions of the benefits associated with having more women in leadership positions and also solicited suggestions for what the company could do to increase the number of high-ranking women leaders.

Throughout the week, global teams met to develop recommendations for how the company could begin to create change, which fell into three categories: enhancing career opportunities, increasing women's representation in senior positions, and addressing issues of work/life balance in order to enable women to perform at their highest capabilities. For each category, suggestions were made for implementation at both global and local levels within the company. Within two months, the company's Strategic Council had reviewed and approved the suggestions and launched a companywide change effort based the recommendations received.

"Managing Globalization: Building Global Leaders at Unilever BestFoods," employees' opinions can be more than a source of diagnostic information—they may also form the basis of a plan to address strategic business issues.[25]

In the example of Unilever BestFoods, employees' opinions were the primary method of organizational analysis as well as the basis for a large-scale plan to ensure that the company's top leadership understood and became connected to its key customer base—women around the world.

BEHAVIORAL CAUSE-AND-EFFECT MODELS

As explained in Chapter 1, behavioral cause-and-effect models can be used to provide a more detailed understanding of how employee attitudes and behaviors influence organizational outcomes of interest. When behavioral cause-and-effect models include business outcomes that reflect the perspective of shareholders and investors, they make it easy for managers to see the linkages between how human resources are managed and the firm's success at implementing its strategy. For example, if a pharmaceutical company's strategic business objective is growing revenues, its strategy map would probably show that revenues are determined, in part, by the ability of the firm to develop innovative drugs and marshal them through the regulatory approval process. Developing innovative drugs, in turn, requires managing research and development (R&D) teams effectively. A behavioral cause-and-effect model could be used to understand the attitudes and behaviors that contribute to the success of R&D teams that develop new products and obtain approval for them from the Federal Drug Administration.[26]

Cause-and-effect models can also show direct links between specific HR practices and measures of organizational performance. For example, a study of 61 hospitals in England found that the HR practices used in the hospitals predicted patient mortality rates. Mortality rates were lower in hospitals that relied more on teams and in those with more sophisticated training and more rigorous performance appraisal.[27] Procter & Gamble used employee opinions to construct a behavioral cause-and-effect model as part of its organizational analysis. Based on the qualitative information from its shadowing, focus groups, and interviews (described in the "Managing Change" feature), Stengel's team created an employee survey and used it to gather systematic data from its worldwide marketing workforce of 3,500 people. The survey contained 300 questions and covered 10 major issues. By analyzing the responses, P&G determined three major drivers of business unit effectiveness. The basic cause-and-effect model created by P&G is illustrated in Exhibit 4.8. This cause-and-effect model captures the employees' views about what drives business unit effectiveness.

DETERMINING HR OBJECTIVES AND METRICS

LINKING HR OBJECTIVES TO STRATEGIC BUSINESS OBJECTIVES

Strategic business objectives help focus attention on several important aspects of managing employees, including (a) the number of employees that

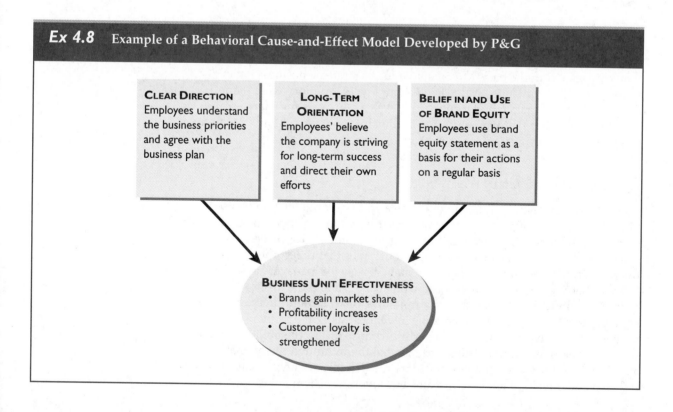

Ex 4.8 Example of a Behavioral Cause-and-Effect Model Developed by P&G

will be needed as a consequence of anticipated growth or decline, (b) new competencies and behaviors that will be required as a consequence of aspiring to provide higher-quality customer service, and (c) higher levels of productivity needed as a consequence of identifying the reduction of operating costs as an objective.

Once the strategic business objectives of a change effort have been specified, the implications for HR become clearer. If strategic business objectives call for involvement in mergers and acquisitions, an HR objective might be developing competencies needed for involvement in "soft" due diligence activities. **Soft due diligence** *describes the activities that firms use to assess the compatibility of potential new partners, taking into consideration the corporate cultures and specific HR policies and practices in the organizations being combined.* If the strategic objectives call for improving the organization's learning capacity, an HR objective might be to help the various businesses learn from each other and derive more synergies from their common membership in the larger corporate entity. If strategic objectives call for implementing a customer service strategy, all HR policies and practices may have to be changed to ensure that employees exhibit the behaviors consistent with customer service.

Successful strategic changes are guided by clear objectives. The strategic business objectives of a major change effort typically flow directly from an analysis of the environment and what the company needs to do in the time period ahead. At Unilever BestFoods, the company's international growth strategy stimulated a discussion about how to ensure the company would have the global leaders it would need to succeed in the future. At P&G, one of the strategic business objectives that drove change efforts was rebuilding market share for its leading brands.

Another example of how the organization's strategic business objectives can set the stage for change is provided by Continental Airlines, described in the feature "Managing Change: Flying High at Continental."[28] When CEO Gordon Bethune took over beleaguered Continental Airlines, he was charged with turning around a losing operation. His battle cry was "From worst to first." Bethune realized early on that achieving the company's strategic objectives would require several changes in the company's HR policies and practices for better HR alignment with the needs of the business. Employees were given specific, companywide goals, and incentives were offered to reward them for achieving the goals. To improve the performance of managers, employees regularly rated their managers on an employee survey. Besides improving the bottom line, the changes resulted in higher pay for employees, while the rates of sick leave, turnover, workers' compensation claims, and on-the-job injuries all went down.

DEVELOPING METRICS TO MATCH THE OBJECTIVES

In order to track the effectiveness of their change efforts, the best organizations develop clear metrics for assessing their progress. Measurement makes assessing improvement possible. The best HR metrics are accepted by managers as legitimate, are relatively easy to use, and have an obvious connection to the stated business and HR objectives. Continental Airlines made sure managers accepted the metrics it used by linking rewards to managers' success in making progress toward goals that were defined using their metrics.

> *"The sequence should be to figure out where you're going before you figure out how to get there."*
>
> William Byham
> CEO
> Development Dimensions International

> **About the changes at Continental Airlines:**
> *"I've been doing this for 20 years and I've never seen a turnaround of a workplace culture as dramatic as this one."*
>
> Robert Levering
> Coauthor of *100 Best Places to Work for in America*

> *"We measure everything around here, except how high the grass grows."*
>
> Dave Sanchez
> Plant Manager
> Ford factory, Kansas City

Managing Change

Flying High at Continental

Before its turnaround, Continental Airlines was on the verge of bankruptcy. That would have been its third time. That's when the company began a complete transformation, which rivaled Cinderella's at the stroke of midnight. Even the vice president of corporate communications admitted that the company had been in serious trouble: "This airline was probably, candidly, one of the least-respected airlines in corporate America. It could *not* get any worse." Two years later, Continental was celebrating its highest pretax profits ever. By 2001, it had fully regained its reputation as one of the better airlines in the United States. (It had not yet matched Southwest Airlines, however.)

Gordon Bethune, CEO during the transformation, initiated the change effort by setting out the following strategic objectives and specific metrics for assessing success:

1. *Fly to win.* The goal was to achieve top-quartile industry profit margins.
2. *Fund the future.* To do so required reducing interest expense by owning more hub real estate.
3. *Make reliability a reality.* Specific goals included ranking among the top airlines on

the four metrics used by the U.S. Department of Transportation (DOT).
4. *Work together.* The goal was to have a company where employees would enjoy working and would be valued for their contributions.

When the specific goals were met, specific rewards followed. For example, one goal was to be ranked in the top five of the DOT on-time performance ratings. For each month the goal was achieved, employees would earn an extra $65. Two months later, Continental was in first place. Goals and rewards were developed for executives, too. For example, employees regularly rated their managers on an employee survey, reporting on how well they communicated, set goals, and treated employees. Executives' bonuses reflected their performance as measured by the survey.

Going forward it appears likely that many of these HR practices will remain in place, with some modification, under the new CEO Larry Kellner. When Gordon Bethune announced this transition in CEOs in early 2004, he called Mr. Kellner a "strong leader with tremendous people, operational marketing and analytical skills."

"Bottom-Line" HR Metrics. One way to gain managers' acceptance of the HR metrics used to track the success of change efforts is to use HR metrics that are similar to other so-called bottom-line measures.[29] A human capital return-on-investment (HC ROI) metric is an example of this approach. One way to calculate such an index would be as follows:

$$HR\ ROI = \frac{Revenue - (Operating\ expense - [Compensation\ cost + Benefit\ cost])}{Compensation\ cost + Benefit\ cost}$$

Another alternative is to calculate a human capital value-added index. This might be done as follows:

$$HR\ Value\ Added = \frac{Revenue - (Operating\ expense - [Compensation\ cost + Benefit\ cost])}{Total\ number\ of\ full\text{-}time\ equivalent\ employees\ (FTEs)}$$

In organizations that are focused on keeping costs low, a simple index of HR Expenses might be appropriate, such as:

$$HR\ Expense\ Ratio = \frac{Total\ of\ all\ HR\ expenses}{Total\ operating\ expenses}$$

Compare the information provided by an expense ratio to the following index, which focuses on revenues. This index might be used by a company who strategy emphasizes the importance of growth:

$$\text{HR Revenue Ratio} = \frac{\text{Total revenue}}{\text{Total number of full-time equivalent employees (FTEs)}}$$

HR metrics such as these are gaining popularity because they provide a simple index for tracking changes in the organization's effectiveness in managing its human capital. Nevertheless, such metrics must be used with caution. Currently, there are no widely accepted accounting rules to guide an organization's efforts to develop sound human capital metrics. Over a period of time, changes in HR metrics such as these can be caused by many factors that have nothing to do with an organization's human resource management effectiveness. Nevertheless, indices such as these may prove helpful as a means of tracking general trends over the course of several years.

HR Metrics for Deutsche Bank. At Deutsche Bank, the concept of risk management is central to the business strategy, and the HR metrics used by the firm reflect this concern. The firm's research established the following HR risk factors that required careful management: employee motivation, adaptability, qualification, and resignations (departures). Within these domains of risk, the company also determined that losing high performers with key areas of the business was the most significant risk. In fact, the cost of losing a key employee was estimated to be 1.5 times the person's annual salary. Deutsche Bank's HR metrics, described in Exhibit 4.9, were designed to help the firm manage these risks.[30]

As managers learn to interpret HR-related measures, they begin to see how their own actions can support or impede progress. Over time, they are likely to appreciate the value of measures that track progress toward achieving HR objectives and other precursors of business success instead of focusing exclusively on financial measures.

FAST FACT Of the *Fortune* Most Admired companies, 40% track progress on retention, career development, and other employee-oriented measures—more than triple the percentage of companies that didn't make the list.

HR Metrics for SunTrust Bank. When SunTrust Bank adopted the OneBank concept as a principle for its new business strategy, the implications for managing human resources were huge. Until then, there were 28 different HR departments serving 1,200 branches spread across 6 southeastern states. One of the objectives for HR was to develop a single, centralized approach for recruiting, evaluating, and hiring new employees. Besides adhering to professional HR standards for effective staffing, the new system would have to meet the needs of all the branch managers in order for it to be accepted and used. To ensure that these objectives were met, HR professionals and branch managers would develop the system together, making sure to incorporate the best practices being used throughout the bank. In order to evaluate the effectiveness of the new staffing system, SunTrust used the met-

Ex 4.9   HR Metrics for Risk Management at Deutsche Bank

HR Objective: Maintain strong employee commitment and minimize turnover of key employees.

Metrics

1. Three times a year, conduct survey of at least 1,000 employees and analyze their responses to survey items that assess:
   - Willingness to stay
   - Attitudes about the labor market
   - Emotional involvement with the organization
   - Early warning signs

2. Focusing on recent hires, assess the extent to which their expectations upon joining the firm have been met, exceeded, or disappointed.

3. Focusing on key leavers, record the reasons for departure, using both managers' judgments and data from exit interviews.

HR Objective: Maintain strong corporate identity by living a set of shared values.

Metrics

Annually conduct a survey of approximately 4,000 employees to assess their attitudes toward the values of
   - Teamwork
   - Trust
   - Innovation
   - Customer focus
   - Performance

Responses are broken out by departments and fed back to managers.

(Based on responses from manager director reports, managers are given suggestions for specific actions they should take to improve employees' attitudes toward the values.)

HR Objective: Maintain status as an employer of choice.

Metrics

At least every three years, conduct a survey of all employees to assess their perceptions of the organization's image, their feelings about their individual job situation, and the corporate culture. Measures include perceptions of:
   - Coordination and integration
   - Strategic direction and intention
   - Organizational learning
   - Recognition
   - Responsibility and empowerment
   - Performance
   - Compensation
   - Leadership

rics shown in Exhibit 4.10. As this exhibit shows, the plans that SunTrust developed and implemented helped speed up the hiring process and also reduced costs.[31]

DEVELOPING HR PLANS AND TIMETABLES

For major actions that involve a great deal of change, the strategic plan for the organization as a whole can be quite complex because it includes plans for all levels and all units involved in the change effort. If an organization is structured along functional departments, then each department develops a strategic plan; if it is organized by region, then plans for each region are developed; and so on.

At P&G, a cross-functional team headed by an HR director planned many of the changes. The changes that would eventually be implemented required a great deal of HR expertise during the planning and design phase, but in

Ex 4.10 **Staffing Metrics Used by SunTrust Bank to Measure the Success of Its New Staffing Practices**

STRATEGIC BUSINESS OBJECTIVE	Develop a OneBank approach to managing all units of SunTrust Bank at all locations	
STRATEGIC HR OBJECTIVE	Develop staffing practices to fit the OneBank strategic objective	
METRICS USED TO EVALUATE THE NEW HR PRACTICES	BEFORE THE CHANGE	ONE YEAR AFTER IMPLEMENTING THE CHANGE
Turnover rate for full-time tellers	47%	34%
Turnover rate for call center employees	43%	28%
Time to fill vacant positions	28 days	19.5 days
Average cost to fill nonexempt positions	$1,125	$983

order for the plan to be implemented effectively, managers had to be committed to the changes and be actively involved in making them happen. Thus, in this example, the human resource component of the strategic plan was fully integrated with the strategic plans of the marketing organization.

Regardless of how the HR plan is structured, its development begins with a full consideration of alternatives. After evaluating the pros and cons associated with each alternative, choices are made about which HR activities and policies will change.

CONSIDERING ALTERNATIVES

After the attack on the World Trade Center and the Pentagon sent the airlines industry into a tailspin in the autumn of 2001, most major airlines soon began announcing plans to cut their workforces by as much as 20%. But Southwest Airlines' Chair Herb Kelleher was determined to do everything possible to avoid layoffs. Instead of cutting costs through layoffs, the company scrapped its growth plans, delayed deliveries of new aircraft, and prepared for possible damage to its stock price. This approach to dealing with the economic downturn was possible in part because the company was debt-free and had $1 billion in cash.

Another company that has avoided layoffs is Pella, the window manufacturer. Even during the Depression, Pella chose to keep employees on the job, washing windows over and over again, instead of resorting to layoffs. In choosing to adopt a "no-layoffs" policy, some companies have decided that the costs associated with maintaining their workforce are justified to avoid the hidden costs associated with layoffs. These costs include:

- Severance payments made to departing employees
- Fees paid to consultants who assist with the downsizing process
- Litigation from aggrieved workers
- Loss of trust in management
- Lack of staff needed to grow when the economy rebounds
- Loss of reputation in the labor market, making future hiring more difficult
- Cynical and paranoid behaviors among layoff survivors
- Declining customer satisfaction resulting from low employee morale[32]

For most strategic business objectives, the list of alternative ways to achieve them can be quite long. The same is true for most HR objectives. For example, some of the alternatives available to employers who face an HR objective of coping with the shortage of skilled workers are listed in Exhibit 4.11.

As Exhibit 4.11 reveals, the available alternatives have both potential advantages and potential disadvantages. Solutions that might work in the short term may create new problems in the long term. Solutions that might work in the long term may do little to address short-term needs. Similarly, different alternatives have different advantages.

Suppose an organization has the goal of reducing labor costs. Following are several alternatives the firm might consider. Under what conditions would each of these be most appropriate?

Ex 4.11   Alternatives for the HR Objective of Coping with Shortages of Skilled Workers

POSSIBLE SOLUTIONS TO A LABOR SHORTAGE	POSSIBLE NEGATIVE CONSEQUENCES
• Raise base wages to attract more applicants	• May attract more applicants, but new applicants may not be any more qualified. Recruiting costs per hire go up as number of applicants to be screened goes up.
• Offer more financial incentives in an effort to motivate employees to boost their productivity	• If productivity increases don't keep up with increased labor costs, margins will shrink unless consumers are willing to pay higher prices.
• Reduce turnover rates to lessen the need for new hires	• May drive up labor costs if wages tend to increase with time at the company. Too little turnover may stifle creativity. Skills obsolescence may become a problem.
• Hire people without the skills needed and train them	• Productivity of new hires is low. Increased supervision of new workers is required, which raises costs. Can be costly, takes time, and workers, once trained, may leave to work for competitors.
• Buy up other companies to acquire their workforce	• The challenge of integrating the acquired company may cause productivity declines in the short term. Success rates for mergers and acquisitions are only about 50%.
• Buy new technologies that reduce the number of people needed	• Major changes in technology require major organizational changes, which take time. New technologies may require even higher levels of skill to operate.
• Utilize foreign labor markets	• The organizational learning curve is steep for domestic firms with no prior international experience. Competition for labor in the global market may be just as stiff as in the domestic market.
• Make business decisions that will reduce the need for more skilled workers	• May be possible, but would probably involve major changes in strategy and even changing the businesses in which the company competes.

Layoffs and RIFs. A recent analysis of the average size of U.S. firms revealed that the average size of companies grew at a fairly steady pace from 1935 until about 1985. After that, average firm size began to decline rapidly. The reasons that led firms to shrink in size are many, but the approach they used was often the same—massive layoffs and reductions in force (RIFs). Layoffs can be used to reduce costs relatively quickly, and thereby achieve a short-term gain in profits. This appears to explain their popularity. Layoffs have been especially common within the manufacturing sector.[33]

Facing the threat of job loss and seeing others lose their jobs can be a traumatic and bitter experience for employees, however.[34] Furthermore, the long-term economic benefits of downsizing are not well established. These are among the reasons why many excellent companies do everything possible to avoid layoffs.[35] Despite their best efforts, however, even the most employee-friendly companies may deal with difficult economic conditions by reducing their workforces.

Reducing Turnover. When large and immediate cost reduction is not necessary, an alternative may be to cut costs by reducing employee turnover. According to a study of over 200 companies, conducted by consulting firm William M. Mercer, turnover costs reach $40,000 per person for 10% of all vacancies when you take into account lost productivity due to the vacancy, search fees, management time used to interview, and training costs. For 30% of all vacancies, the costs range between $10,000 and $40,000.[36] Reducing turnover may be an effective way to reduce costs if a company has a relatively high turnover rate and it is willing to invest in making the changes that would be needed to retain workers longer. But other alternatives also are available for achieving the goal of lowering labor costs, including outsourcing and offshoring.

Outsourcing. In **outsourcing,** *work that had been performed inside the company is contracted out to another company.* For example, a retailer may decide to let IBM manage all its computer operations, and thereby reduce the total number of employees the firm needs to employ. IBM has much greater expertise than retailers when it comes to managing computer operations, so they can do this work more efficiently and with higher quality. For the retailer, the total number of employees needed is reduced by this outsourcing tactic, and the retail managers can focus their energies on what they do best. Jobs may be lost at one company, but they are not lost to the U.S. economy. They are simply shifted to another employer.

 FAST FACT Financial services companies in the United States said they expected to transfer 500,000 jobs—8% of industry employment—to foreign countries between 2003 and 2008.

Offshoring. In **offshoring,** *a company decides to continue to do the work itself, but the work is moved to another country.* Since its founding, Levi Strauss was proud of its American-made jeans, but eventually the pressure to reduce its labor costs grew too great. In order to survive, it decided to close its U.S. plants and move the work to China and other lower-wage countries. In recent years, many U.S. companies have relocated their software design work and call center operations to India, where talent is plentiful and wages are far below those in the United States. Indeed, the use of offshoring has become so widespread that it has begun to raise concerns about the long-term economic prospects of the American workforce.[37]

Still More Alternatives!   The 3M company, based in St. Paul, Minnesota, works hard to keep employees even when its own business units eliminate jobs. Instead of being fired, displaced employees are given first consideration for other job openings within the unit. If no suitable placement can be found, they are put on the Unassigned List, which makes them eligible for jobs in other units. They can stay on the list for six months. During that time, finding employment is the employee's responsibility. The company supports their efforts, however. Before recruiting externally to fill open positions, managers first check the qualifications of people on the Unassigned List. The company also sponsors an optional three-day workshop that covers topics such as outplacement, coping with job loss, resume writing, and interviewing skills. For the first four months that they are on the Unassigned List, employees have the option of taking a severance package and leaving the company. Approximately 50% of the people on the list find other jobs at 3M within the four-month window. When that happens, both employees and the company are winners.[38]

Internal transfers are just one of many alternatives to massive layoffs. Others include:

- Restricting overtime
- Reducing the hours in a standard workweek
- Not renewing contracts for temporary and part-time workers
- Offering temporary leaves
- Job sharing
- Retraining
- Providing seed funds and entrepreneurship training and encouraging employees to start their own businesses
- Transferring staff to other companies (e.g., suppliers, customers)
- Giving early retirement with preferential conditions
- Reducing executive salaries and incentive pay
- Partnering with government agencies and professional societies to find jobs for displaced employees
- Managing an employee buyout of the company[39]

BUILDING A COMPLETE HR PLAN

Addressing strategic business objectives such as the need to reduce costs usually requires multipronged solutions. Thus, a comprehensive HR plan for change is likely to have many components, just as a companywide plan for change has many components. To illustrate what some of the components of an HR plan might be, we briefly describe examples of the HR activities of staffing, training, leadership development, and managing benefits.

Staffing Plans.   The plans for staffing arise out of forecasts about future labor demand and supply. Earlier in this chapter, we described how domestic skilled labor shortages and the age demographics within an organization make staffing a strategic issue. For growing businesses, HR objectives often focus on ensuring that new people are available to support the projected growth. For businesses undergoing global expansion, the HR plan may include developing new approaches to evaluating the ability of new hires and current employees to work in multicultural settings and their effectiveness while working on projects completed by virtual teams.

The strategic objectives for HR in a business undergoing a turnaround might state where to cut staff levels, and by how much. In this situation, the HR objectives should also include maintaining the skill levels, motivation, and performance of employees who remain after staff reductions are completed. When P&G restructured during the late 1990s, the marketing group was downsized. Due to the reduced staff levels, numerous formal and informal training programs fell apart. As a result, those who were still employed (and subsequent new hires) felt they didn't have the competencies needed. Because managing layoffs and the process of downsizing is so important, Chapter 6 provides more details about how to plan for these strategic events.[40]

Talent Management Plans. Forecasting human resource demand and supply is essential for succession planning and the development of replacement charts. The objective of **succession planning** *is to ensure that the organization is prepared to fill key positions when the current incumbents leave, for whatever reason.*[41] For employees, succession planning provides useful information about the direction their career is likely to take if they continue to work in the organization.

Succession planning for CEOs often receives attention in the business press, because staffing for this position is so important to shareholders. Up to a year prior to the CEO's planned retirement, a successor may be named so that there is no uncertainty about the company's plans. Or several possible successors may be identified, with the understanding that their performance will be closely monitored during the next year and used as a basis for making a final decision when the CEO steps down.

Although less public, many organizations conduct similar succession planning for all executive positions, and some also engage in succession planning for all managerial positions. Often, these succession plans involve formal procedures for tracking talent and preparing replacement charts. To keep track of their top talent, many organizations maintain a talent pool. A **talent pool** *refers to a list of employees who have been identified as having high potential for advancement—usually because they are top performers in their current positions.* The employees in a talent pool are the people whom the organization is especially interested in retaining and developing. Ensuring that employees in the talent pool are considered when job openings occur is one tactic for successful long-term staffing of the organization.

A replacement chart is used to keep track of opportunities for people in the talent pool. In a **replacement chart,** *the titles of key jobs in the organization are displayed along with the names of current incumbents.* Also included are the names of current employees who might be used to fill potential vacancies (i.e., the most appropriate employees from the talent pool). Besides serving the career objectives of employees in the talent pool, replacement charts also serve to alert the organization to possible areas of vulnerability, in the event of an unexpected departure.

Identifying a talent pool and maintaining replacement charts are not the only steps that go into effective succession planning. According to a recent study of "best practices" in succession planning, the best companies also include the elements shown in Exhibit 4.12.

Training Plans. At United Stationers, the HR objectives of clarifying managerial accountability and helping employees see how they fit into the

---

Ex 4.12   Best Practices in Succession Planning

- The process is simple, with minimal paperwork.
- Process is decentralized and owned by local managers.
- Information technology makes it easy to give employees feedback.
- The process fits with the corporate culture.
- Employees receive a variety of job assignments early in their careers.
- Bosses are trained to hold good career discussions.
- Bosses are held accountable for ensuring that developmental action plans are implemented.
- One-on-one mentoring and mentoring networks are supported by the company.

---

big picture led to HR plans that emphasized training activities. To help managers perform in their new roles, the HR group developed a leadership framework and offered to train interested managers. (Note that it was up to the managers to decide whether or not to receive training in the leadership framework.) To help employees see how they fit into the picture, HR professionals worked with line managers to develop business awareness training modules for employees. The HR experts made sure the training modules met professional-quality standards, but line managers were responsible for the actual business content and for delivering the training to employees.

At P&G, the need for better skills among marketers was met with a plan to develop a marketing university. Now employees can attend several one-week "colleges" that focus on developing the competencies needed for new job assignments. Also available are refresher courses to help employees improve skills such as interviewing and coaching. Opportunities for learning also are available through newly instituted centers of expertise—networks of employees linked together as a virtual community led by a "master" who organizes learning forums for the group.

Leadership Development Plans.   At Weyerhaeuser, the HR plans for creating strategic change emphasized leadership development activities. Leadership development activities are likely to be important for firms whose strategic objectives include transitioning to a transnational organizational structure.[42] As organizations globalize, meeting the leadership challenge is often a top priority. In addition to answering the question of who will be available for the senior leadership roles, HR plans should provide a means to ensure that the available people have the competencies required to do the work.

Unfortunately, many global firms do not have the leadership talent they need. According to one study of 1,500 executives in 50 global companies, the degree to which the HRM system was aligned with the needs of the global business lagged far behind the degree to which other systems had been developed. For example, on average, these firms generated 40% of their business from other countries, yet only 8% of their top 100 executives were from other countries. Furthermore, only one third of the executives in the study reported having any expatriate experience, and less than 20% spoke a second language. Clearly, to begin developing their talent pool of the future, such firms must develop new practices to encourage and support the development of global leaders.[43] As we describe in Chapters 5 and 8, 3M is one company that has a comprehensive plan for developing the global leaders they need. The analysis conducted by 3M to determine the competencies needed is described in Chapter 5. Then, in Chapter 8, you will learn about the specific HR practices that 3M uses to help managers develop these competencies.

Plans for Changes in Benefits.   For organizations that are growing as well as those that need to reduce costs or downsize, HR plans for creating strategic change often include changes in employee benefits. As described in Chapter 6, offering an attractive benefits package is one way to attract top talent, so growing firms may want to upgrade the benefits they offer. When AT&T set as its objective eliminating 10,000 jobs, the HR staff designed a voluntary retirement incentive program to encourage people to leave voluntarily. Qualified employees were offered more liberal retiree health care benefits, pension incentives, and even financial assistance in making career changes. People who left to start their own businesses were eligible for $10,000 in start-up funds.[44]

TIMETABLES

Change is tough work that often involves making difficult and sometimes painful decisions. If people can put it off, they will. Building in deadlines and scheduling checkpoints is one way to keep the change process moving ahead. The challenge is to set deadlines that are challenging but achievable.

Realistic expectations about how quickly change will occur are important to the long-term success of change efforts. Changes designed to help employees balance their work and nonwork commitments might be effective within only a year or two. More fundamental changes can require much longer. Usually even changes that seem relatively simple occur more slowly than expected. Xerox began changing its culture to be more receptive of diversity more than 30 years ago and continues to do so. It is doubtful that managers anticipated how long this change effort would continue to evolve.

At Weyerhaeuser, the process of change unfolded over a period of 10 years. Continuity in the company's senior management ranks helped facilitated this long-term realignment of the business. From the beginning, top-level managers understood that they were embarking on a long journey that would require patience and persistence. Over the years, they learned from their mistakes, and because most managers stayed at the company, the lessons they learned were retained and used as new challenges arose.

Timelines for Developing Talent.   When a computer manufacturing company that produced leading-edge specialty products for business decided to change its strategy to include the consumer market, it knew it would need managers with a different set of skills. The company estimated it would need five years to build the talent pool. The first year was spent analyzing the environment, developing a model of the skills that would be needed, and developing a strategy for building the talent pool. The initiatives taken during the next four years included

- assessing their current managers to determine who had the skills needed for the new business strategy,
- training managers on the meaning of the new strategy,
- externally recruiting new managers with the needed skills, and
- meeting quarterly with senior executives to keep them informed of progress.

As these planned initiatives were rolled out, it then became clear that changes were needed in most other aspects of the HRM system, including development of a variety of additional training programs and changes in the organizational structure and the compensation system.[45] You will learn more about Weyerhaeuser's leadership development efforts in our discussion of training and development in Chapter 8.

Timelines for Layoffs and Plant Closings.   Often, it is the process of establishing timetables that reveals the full complexity of a change effort. Consider the planning process for layoffs and plant closings. For employers with 100 or more employees, some elements of the HR timetable are specified by the Worker Adjustment and Retraining Act of 1988 (WARN). For plant closings and layoffs covered under the WARN act, employees must describe their planned actions and give at least 60 days' advance notice of those actions to:

- Employees (or their union representatives, if applicable),
- The mayor or other chief elected official of the local government, and
- The top official of the state's dislocated workers program.

The WARN act specifies that these notices be given in writing, but few employers rely only on written notices. Instead, they set timetables for meetings with managers and employees to explain what will happen at each site, when, and how.

Often employees experience shock and confusion when layoffs are first announced. The result is that they retain little of the information presented at the early meetings. Consequently, HR professionals must make plans to follow up with additional meetings. They may also establish hot lines, provide counseling services, and provide other services to assist those who are laid off. Because some employees may react violently, additional security measures may be needed for several months after the announcement. The HR timetable for a layoff or plant closing may also include dates by which:

- decisions will be made about the status of individual employees;
- offers will be made to encourage voluntary employee departures;
- employees must sign a separation agreement;
- meetings will be held to explain the implications for employees' benefits;
- media announcements will be released;
- negotiations with unions will be initiated and completed; and
- service contracts will end for relevant outside vendors (e.g., recruiters, outplacement counselors).[46]

IMPLEMENTING THE HR ACTION PLANS FOR ALIGNMENT: FACILITATING CHANGE

INVOLVING EMPLOYEES

An important role for HR professionals during the planning and implementing of a plan of action is finding ways to involve people throughout the organization. For a change effort to be effective, those who are affected by it must buy into it. The best way to ensure that they do is through early involvement.[47] It seems obvious that employees should be involved when planning change, but often even experienced managers forget this principle. Task forces, focus groups, surveys, hot lines, and informal conversations are just a few of the ways managers can involve employees and other stakeholders in planning change efforts.[48]

FAST FACT To align employees' self-interests with the goals of Mercedes Benz, Georg Bauer offered the security of a new—and probably better—job to anyone bold enough to eliminate his or her own current position.

To involve managers in developing plans for meeting strategic business objectives, Siemens uses its university. Its in-house corporate training gives responsibility for solving real business problems to analysts and engineers from around the world, who work together in "student" teams. Students share their analyses with business units and debate the benefits and costs of their plans.

ESTABLISHING ACCOUNTABILITY

When specifying objectives, it is important to state not only what is to be achieved, but also who is responsible for making the needed changes. If the change is a success, will only managers reap the rewards? If things don't go well, will the lower-level employees be the ones who suffer most? Involvement is likely to be most effective when people also have a stake in the outcomes that result.

Holding people accountable for achieving the objectives of a change can have a variety of implications for human resource management practices. Typically, accountability translates into new approaches to awarding incentive pay and bonuses. Depending on the nature of the strategic objectives, and whether they are qualitatively different from those of the past, new performance measurement systems may be required. Procedures for deciding on future promotions may also be affected. At Unilever BestFoods, for example, the compensation system was changed as part of the HR plan to improve the representation of women in leadership positions. Senior managers were given goals for developing and retaining high-performing women, and incentive pay was linked to success in achieving the goals.

CHANGE HAS ALREADY STARTED

If the people who are responsible for drawing up the blueprint for strategic change efforts have followed the principle of involvement, the implementation stage is actually already well underway by the time the plans have been fully developed. People already have a good grasp of the vision—they had to understand it in order to be involved in the planning process. Although a leadership team may have been responsible for putting the plan together, many details (e.g., goals and timetables) were developed using substantial input from the people who will be expected to implement the plan. If honest two-way communication has occurred throughout the planning process, major obstacles to implementing change have already been identified and removed. If empowered employees have been energized by the challenges identified, some are already experimenting with new approaches to their work. To the extent this is true, problems of resistance—the major barrier to implementing change—will be lessened. Even in the best of circumstances, however, pockets of resistance will be found.

MANAGING RESISTANCE TO CHANGE

Few planned organizational change efforts of any kind proceed smoothly. Most run into some amount of resistance. The various forms that resistance can take include immediate criticism, malicious compliance, sabotage, insincere agreement, silence, deflection, and in-your-face defiance.[49] The reasons for such resistance include fear, misunderstandings, and cynicism.[50]

"They stopped all the projects and withdrew all the ongoing projects. That was when most staff realized that there was something wrong with the company, and then fear started to spread."

(Name withheld)
Bank employee
Describing feelings during a change

Fear.   Some people resist change because they fear that they'll be unable to develop the competencies required to be effective in the new situation. When Mercedes-Benz Credit Corporation set out to restructure its operations in the United States, employees seemed to have good reason to be fearful of the future. Weren't layoffs sure to follow? The company's president, Georg Bauer, knew that fear could be a problem and that it would make getting needed help from employees difficult. "It was absolutely essential to establish a no-fear element in this whole change process," he said. Rather than resist change, he wanted employees to help create a new, more efficient organization by expressing their ideas about where to cut and how to do work differently. Besides empowering employees to make decisions about how to change their work, he offered an incentive to convince employees that even cutting their own jobs wouldn't harm them financially.[51]

"My biggest challenge was to change management. Poor communication will cause a re-org to fail. If people understand and accept the change and the ups and downs that come with it, they will make it work. If they don't accept the change, it will disintegrate on you."

Ken Troyan
Senior Vice President
SunTrust Bank

Misunderstandings.   People resist change when they don't understand its implications. Unless quickly addressed, misunderstandings and lack of trust build resistance. When wide-ranging changes are planned, managers and HR professionals should anticipate that misunderstandings will develop and take steps to minimize them. Top managers must be visible during the change process to spell out clearly the new direction for the organization and what it will mean for everyone involved. Getting employees to discuss their problems openly is crucial to overcoming resistance to change.[52] Senior managers at Weyerhaeuser provided frequent, clear, and precise communications throughout that company's restructuring efforts. The communications helped keep employees informed about what was happening, and why.

At Prudential Insurance, a specially designed game was used to help employees understand the implications of the company's impending change from a mutual association to a public company. Small groups of employees at all levels and in all types of jobs throughout the company were brought together to play the game, which was both informative and fun. Top management was convinced that this approach to informing the workforce about the implications of the change they were about to experience would enable the change process to go smoothly—and it did.

Cynicism.   In some organizations, initiating change efforts is seen simply as something that new managers do to make their mark.[53] Over time, employees see change efforts come and go, much like the seasons of the year, as managers implement one fad after the other. Eventually, cynicism sets in and employees refuse to support yet another change "program." Without employee support, the change efforts fail, which further contributes to cynicism.[54] Cynicism is difficult to combat, once it sets in. Perhaps the best approach is to prevent it from developing by avoiding the temptation to always adopt the latest management fad. Organizations that take a strategic and systematic approach to developing and implement change efforts are less likely to initiate a change effort simply because it is the latest new craze.

SHOWING RESPECT IN DIFFICULT TIMES

Sometimes, employees' fears are justified. When a firm's strategic plan calls for substantial reductions in the size of its workforce, some employees will lose their jobs. When employees must be let go, the process by which jobs are eliminated can make a difference—for those who are terminated as well as for those who remain. Loss of attachment, lack of information, and a perception of apparent managerial capriciousness as the basis for decisions about who will be terminated cause anxiety and an obsession with personal survival.[55]

> **FAST FACT**
> When Cisco dismissed its full-time employees, it offered them 33% of their compensation and the opportunity to be rehired if they agreed to work for a nonprofit organization.

The negative cycle of reactions may not be inevitable. If survivors feel that the process used to decide whom to let go was fair, their productivity and the quality of their job performance may not suffer as much. It's not terminations *per se* that create bitterness—it's the manner in which terminations are handled.

Survivors often express feelings of disgust and anger when their friends and colleagues have been fired. If they believe their own performance is no better than those who have been let go, survivors may feel guilty that they have kept their jobs.[56] Statistics showing that older displaced workers who find new work earn about one-third less than they did in their old job contribute to survivors' angst.[57] Thus, in developing human resource policies, procedures, and practices for effective downsizing and layoffs, even the needs of survivors require attention.

> **FAST FACT**
> Many companies use outplacement firms, such as Lee Hecht Harrison; Manchester; and Challenger, Gray and Christmas, to help ensure that this separation process is done professionally.

As with any major organizational change, the steps of diagnosing the current situation and developing a careful plan to implement change are essential during downsizing. But the process of downsizing isn't just about strategies and plans; it's also about relationships between the people in a company, and it's about personal character. The greatest challenges for companies and their managers are maintaining employee morale and regaining employee trust while the actions of the company seem to say, "You are not valuable."[58]

REVIEW, REVISE, AND REFOCUS

When a company offers a product to the external marketplace, it almost certainly reviews and evaluates the success of that product using objective indicators. Likewise, the success of products and services offered in the company's internal marketplace should be monitored. At this point, the measures developed to track the progress of change efforts come into play. The measures define the criteria for evaluating whether a program or initiative is successful or is in need of revision. For example, if personal self-development is the only goal one hopes to achieve from holding diversity awareness workshops, then asking employees whether the workshop experience was valuable may be the only data that should be collected. However, when large investments are made for the purposes of reducing turnover, attracting new or different employees to the firm, or improving team functioning (or all three), then data relevant to these objectives should be examined.

A human resource information management (HRIM) system facilitates evaluation by allowing for more thorough, rapid, and frequent collection and dissemination of data. Based on what is learned, people can make informed decisions about whether to stay the course as planned, or revisit and perhaps revise the original plan. Overall objectives for the change effort are not likely to be changed at this point, but new goals might be added and timetables might be adjusted.

Change expert John Kotter believes that change can be facilitated by virtually guaranteeing that the review and evaluation process produces some positive results, which can then be used as a cause for celebration. He calls these "short-term wins." The slowness of change can be demotivating. After several months of all-out effort, employees will almost certainly be asked to rededicate themselves for another several months of effort. Without some evidence that the new ways of doing things are paying off, too many people may give up and join the ranks of the resisters. Rather than leave to chance the question of whether there will be anything to celebrate after a year or two of effort, Kotter suggests specifically assigning a few excellent people to the task of creating a short-term win. And when they meet the challenge, be sure to involve everyone in the celebration.[59]

Whether or not the evaluation of progress against goals is accompanied by celebration, pausing to reflect on how the evaluation process is an essential part of any effective change process is valuable. This ensures that the change process will be self-correcting and should prevent most misjudgments made during the planning process from turning into major fiascoes.

SUMMARY

The dynamic external environment often creates the need for organizations to do things differently, requiring new strategies and new strategic objectives. In order to achieve their strategic objectives, organizations may need to focus on a new vision, restructure their operations, expand, downsize, or otherwise transform who they are and what they do. In doing so, they realize all the implications for managing human resources. For example, a new competitive strategy may require new employee behaviors and competencies. This being the case, new HR policies and practices may be needed, such as different selection and training activities. Thus, as the environment changes, organizations also change. The HR activities need to be correctly aligned with these changing conditions.

Human resource planning refers to the systematic efforts of firms and HR professionals to identify and respond to the short- and long-term human resource implications of a company's strategic business objectives created by the changing environment. The several phases of HR planning are depicted linearly in Exhibit 4.2, although change is seldom a linear experience. The HR planning phases include: assessing the global and organizational environment; specifying HR objectives and metrics for change; and developing specific HR plans and timetables. A comprehensive HR plan for strategic change is likely to address a variety of HR activities, including staffing, training, leadership development, and benefits.

Significant change almost always involves unforeseeable sources of resistance and unintended consequences. Although these cannot be avoided, their detrimental effects can be minimized by involving the entire organization in planning for and evaluating the change process. Managers and other employees who will be affected by strategic changes should be involved in developing the plan for change and in monitoring the outcomes of changes made. Monitoring key indicators of success throughout the change process makes it possible for an organization to quickly detect when corrective action is needed, as well as when key milestones have been reached and can be celebrated.

Effective HR planning, aligning, and changing improve the ability of organizations to satisfy customers while also addressing the concerns of other stakeholders. The HR planning, aligning, and changing, in turn, require an understanding of specific HR policies and practices and their impact on employees. By studying the remaining chapters, you will begin to gain the insight and understanding required to design and implement an HRM system that is aligned with and appropriate for an organization's specific strategic objectives and its environment.

TERMS TO REMEMBER

Anticipatory change	Organizational analysis
Horizontal alignment	Outsourcing
HR forecasts	Radical change
HR metrics	Reactive change
HR objectives	Replacement chart
HR plans	Soft due diligence
Human resource planning	Statistical forecasts
Incremental change	Succession planning
Judgmental forecasts	Talent pool
Learning organization	Timetables
Offshoring	Vertical alignment

DISCUSSION QUESTIONS

1. Review Chapter 2, which describes several aspects of the external and internal organizational environments. Which aspects of the external environment will be most likely to stimulate change in the next 10 years? Do you think these changes will be incremental or radical? Explain.

2. Now consider the HR implications of the changes you identified in question 1: Which HR policies and practices are most likely to be affected by these changes (e.g., recruitment, training, performance management, etc.)? Describe the consequences you think are most likely.

3. Deutsche Bank relies heavily on employee surveys to create its HR metrics. What are some advantages and disadvantages of employee surveys as a method for assessing progress toward HR objectives? For each HR objective shown in Exhibit 4.9, describe one HR metric of actual employee behavior that could be used.

4. Is it inevitable that employees will respond to change with feelings of fear? If you believe the answer is yes, state the implications of this for managing strategic change. If you believe the answer is no, describe what managers can do to minimize such feelings during change.

5. A thorough approach to planning for change can take a great deal of time. When time is short, which steps in the planning process can be eliminated most readily? What are the potential risks of skipping these steps? Explain your logic.

6. Throughout your career you will often be expected to lead and facilitate radical change initiatives. What can you personally do now to become better prepared to be an effective change leader and facilitator?

PROJECTS TO EXTEND YOUR LEARNING

1. *Integration and Application.* In recent years, Southwest Airlines has been changing from a regional carrier to a national carrier. Suppose you were assigned to a task force charged with planning for the addition of service into a new hub location in Vermont. Assume the new hub will be open for operation in six months.

   a. Establish a timetable and indicate the major HR objectives that will have to be achieved in the next six months.
   b. Prioritize the top five HR objectives that would be associated with expanding operations into a new state.
   c. For the top five HR objectives, list at least five HR metrics that could be used to measure progress toward meeting them.

2. *Exploring the Internet.*

   a. Learn about assessment tools that can be used during organizational analysis, including:

      • KEYS, a survey published by the Center for Creative Leadership that is designed to assess the organization's climate for creativity (http://www.ccl.org), and
      • an expert system intended to identify strategic misalignments (http://www.ecomerc.com).

   b. Visit the home pages of several professional organizations whose members have special expertise in the area of strategic change, including:

- The Academy of Management's Division of Organizational Change and Development (http://www.aom.pace.edu/odc), and
- The Tavistock Institute (http://www.tavinstitute.org).

3. *Experiential Activity: Choosing Metrics for an Employer of Choice.* Your instructor will assign students to small groups. Before you meet with your group, you need to prepare individually. Your group will be asked to meet for a few minutes to make a final recommendation. Here is the situation:

You just started in your new job at the Farma Pharmaceuticals firm. You are serving on a task force charged with developing HR metrics that can be used to track the firm's progress toward becoming an employer of choice. Members of the task force are all recent hires because Farma Pharmaceuticals believes new hires are in the best position to understand the implications of being an employer of choice. The task force has met several times and now has a list of specific HR metrics that it is considering. Today, the task force is meeting to make its final decision about which HR metrics it will recommend to top management. Exhibit 4.13 (p. 166) lists descriptions of the most-favored metrics. Use the exhibit to indicate your evaluation of these metrics. Rank-order these choices using "1" to indicate the measure you think is best, "2" for the second-best measure, and so on. Be sure to make notes to justify your reasoning so you can explain your rationale to the other members of your task force.

CASE STUDY

ALIGNING HR WITH THE BUSINESS AT SBC

Mike Mitchell left the Bank of Montreal to become vice president of human resources at the North American branch of the Swiss Bank Corporation (SBC) in the autumn of 1993. It was a move up for him in terms of status, responsibility, monetary compensation, and challenge. Of these, it was the challenge that was most intriguing to Mitchell. In his mid-30s, he saw this as perfect time to take a risk in his career. He realized that if he succeeded, he would establish a prototype that could be marketed to other firms. In addition, success could lead to further career opportunities and challenges. While he had a general idea of what he wanted to do and had gotten verbal support from his superiors, the senior vice president of human resources and the president of SBC, North America, the details of exactly what he was going to do and how he was going to do it remained to unfold.

In 1992, the parent company of SBC (a $110 billion universal bank headquartered in Basel, Switzerland) decided it needed a clearer statement of its intentions to focus its energies and resources in light of the growing international competition. Accordingly, it crafted a vision statement to the effect that the bank was going to better serve its customers with high-quality products that met their needs rather than just those of the institution. While the North American operation was relatively autonomous, it was still expected to embrace this vision. The details of its implementation, however, were in local hands. For the human resource side, the hands became those of Mitchell.

While Mitchell had spent some time in human resources at the Bank of Montreal in New York, the bulk of his work experience was as an entrepreneur in Montreal, Canada. It was this experience that

Ex 4.13	**Choosing Metrics for an Employer of Choice**	

RANK	METRIC BEING CONSIDERED YOUR NOTES
☐	Cost per hire (includes advertising, external recruiter fees, employee referral bonuses, candidate travel expenses, and product giveaways)
☐	Number of positions that remain open for ___ days before being filled. Metrics are kept for each of the following times: • 0–50 days • 51–100 days • 101–150 days • 151–200 days • 200+ days Separate metrics are kept for four categories: • Entry level • Mid-level • Executives • Technical and professional
☐	Year-to-date accept/decline ratio. Number of offers accepted divided by number of offers made, averaged across all positions
☐	Intern conversion ratio. Percent of interns who are subsequently hired for full-time positions
☐	Offer acceptance rate. Percent of offers for full-time work that are accepted
☐	Retention ratios. Percent of employees who remain with the company for: • Less than one year • 1–2 years • More than two years
☐	Percent offers not accepted for each of the following reasons: • Pay not competitive • Benefits not competitive • Personal reasons such as family considerations • Aspects of the job or work itself • Unspecified reasons

affected his thinking the most. Thus, when he came to the SBC, his self-image was a businessperson who happened to be working in human resources. It was in part because of this image that his stay at the Bank of Montreal was brief: The idea of human resources was a bit too conservative for his style. Too many of his ideas "just couldn't be done." In interviewing with the top managers at SBC, they warned him of the same general environment.

Thus, he knew change would be slow among the 1,000 employees, including his own department of 10 employees. He knew, however, that he wanted to reposition and "customerize" the HR department at SBC. He also understood the importance of connecting the HR department to the business.

Mitchell identified four major aspects for his program to reposition and customerize the HR department. The four aspects included: gathering information; developing action agendas; implementing those agendas; and then evaluating and revising the agendas.

Gathering Information

To gather information about the current environment, Mitchell asked questions of customers, diagnosed the environment, and consulted with the HR department itself. From the customers, Mitchell learned the nature of the business strategy and how HR currently fit with or helped that strategy. Customers discussed what they were getting from the HR department, what their ideal would be, and how the ideal could best be delivered. Each HR activity, as well as the entire department and the staff, was discussed. From the environment, Mitchell learned what other companies were doing with their HR departments and HR practices. He examined competitors and those in other industries in order to gather ideas for the entire department and for each HR activity. From the HR department, he learned about how they saw themselves in relation to servicing their customers, their knowledge of strategy, how they thought the customers perceived the department, and their desire to improve and change.

Developing Agendas

Making agendas based upon this information was the second aspect of Mitchell's plan. As the HR staff analyzed the information, they were asked to develop plans (agendas) for resolving any discrepancies between what they were currently doing and what their customers wanted. As the staff worked, they began to recognize a need to determine a vision for themselves—to formulate a statement of who they were and how they interacted with the rest of the organization. They also began to examine whether their current ways of operating and the department's current structure were sufficient to move ahead. The need to reorganize became apparent. Once the vision began to take shape and the agendas were developed, the HR department established a game plan to implement their agendas. Approval by top management and the line managers who were immediately affected was seen as critical to successful implementation.

Implementing the Agendas

To begin the implementation phase, the HR staff met with the customers to discuss the agendas. In addition to responding to the specific needs of the line managers, the HR department also had to sell the line managers on other activities. With a new focus that was more strategic and customer-oriented than in the past, the HR department began to develop programs that went beyond the regular administrative activities and services that it had provided to the line managers. Because these services were new, they had to be sold to their customers, at least at first. So in addition to implementing the specifically agreed upon agendas and contracts, this aspect included developing, selling, and implementing new programs.

Evaluating and Revising

Developed along with the agendas were contracts that specified what would be delivered to the customer. The customer was given the right to appraise the work delivered. Based on these appraisals by the customers (line managers), the agendas were evaluated. Revisions and adjustments were then made for continual improvement. In addition to such contracts, the work of the HR department was reviewed internally using such criteria as the reduction in turnover resulting from better selection procedures and an increase in the number of new ideas or innovations resulting from a change in the HR practices to facilitate the innovative strategy of the business.

Implications for the HR Department

There were several implications for the HR department (Mitchell and his staff) in their efforts to reposition and customerize:

- The HR department was reoriented to be strategic and customer-oriented.
- The HR department became a constant gatherer of information from the internal and external environments. By knowing the competition, the business strategy, and the current assets of the company, the HR staff could develop new HR activities, implement new ideas, and work to maintain the company's competitive advantage.

- The HR department identified the level of excellence it wanted to attain. The staff worked to make the department a strategic player while fulfilling their managerial and operational roles.
- HR managers and staff worked closely with the line managers to design systems to gather the needed services and information. They also worked with the line managers to develop contracts by which the HR department would be evaluated by the line managers.
- The HR department was changing so that there was more of a generalist than a specialist orientation. A greater team orientation was also built.
- Things would never be the same. The HR professionals in the department would now be gathering, servicing, evaluating, revising, and most of all listening. And because the business is always changing, the HR department will continue to evolve and change.

IMPLICATIONS FOR THE LINE MANAGERS

There were also several implications in the repositioning and customerization program for the line managers:

- The line managers needed to cooperate with Mitchell and his staff as they gathered information and implemented new ideas and practices. Together, they became partners in the business. The line managers had to accept the new role being played by Mitchell and his HR staff.
- The line managers needed to work closely with the HR staff in developing the action agendas.
- The line managers had to continue working with the HR staff in appraising the success of the HR efforts.

BENEFITS FROM THE PARTNERSHIP

From Mitchell's perspective, several outcomes resulted from the repositioning and customerization program. They include:

- enhancing the quality and responsiveness of the HR department;
- developing the HR department in terms of new jobs (skillwise), providing new excitement, and building commitment to the company's mission, goals, and strategies;

- linking HR with the business and integrating HR with the corporate strategy;
- becoming market- or customer-oriented, with flexibility to respond to and anticipate changes;
- developing criteria by which the behaviors of the HR department can be evaluated and changed;
- gaining an ability to develop and use HR practices to gain competitive advantage;
- developing an awareness of the potential ways different HR practices can be done by constantly monitoring what other successful companies are doing;
- becoming more keenly aware of the internal and external environments;
- providing standard HR products more efficiently;
- developing new products and services;
- developing technology to deliver the new products and services;
- selling new services and products outside the company;
- changing the HR department dramatically and consequently becoming a catalyst for change with the company; and
- becoming a department where everyone wants to work.

CASE QUESTIONS

1. Who were the customers of Mitchell and his HR staff?
2. What did Mitchell have to do so that his staff could do the things necessary to reposition and customerize?
3. Do you think the line managers would cooperate with Mitchell and his staff? What would it take to see that they would cooperate? Why might they resist a partnership with the HR department?
4. Develop a matrix with projects, dates, milestones, and people involved (i.e., HR, line managers, and employees) for Mitchell and his staff.

Source: Prepared by Randall S. Schuler, who expresses his appreciation for the cooperation of Michael Mitchell who moved from SBC to Tiffany and Company. SBC merged with UBS in 1998 (http://ubs.com).

ENDNOTES

1   The authors thank Bill Maki for his descriptions of the Weyerhaueser transformation process.

2   J. Collison and C. Frangos, *Aligning HR with Organization Strategy Survey* (Alexandria, VA: Society for Human Resource Management, 2002); M. Beer and N. Nohria, "Cracking the Code of Change," *Harvard Business Review* (May–June 2000): 133–141; for reviews of the academic literature on managing change, see A. Armenakis and A. Bedeian, "Organizational Change: A Review of Theory and Research in the 1990s," *Journal of Management* 25 (1999): 293–315; K. E. Weick and R. E. Quinn, "Organizational Change and Development," *Annual Review of Psychology* 50 (1999): 361–386.

3   F. Hansen, "Power to the Line People," *Workforce* (June 2003): 70–75.

4   S. F. Gale, "For ERP Success, Create a Culture Change," *Workforce* (September 2002): 80–83.

5   Radical change is also referred to as discontinuous or fundamental change, retrofitting, transformation, and change and reinvention. Incremental change is also referred to as evolutionary change. D. A. Nadler and M. B. Nadler, *Champions of Change: How CEOs and Their Companies Are Mastering the Skills of Radical Change* (San Francisco: Jossey-Bass, 1998); K. E. Weick and R. E. Quinn, "Organizational Change and Development."

6   M. Beer and N. Nohria, *Breaking the Code of Change* (Boston: Harvard Business School Press, 2000); R. A. Johnson, "Antecedents and Outcomes of Corporate Refocusing," *Journal of Management* 22 (1996): 439–483.

7   J. Kerstetter, "Silicon Seer," *Business Week* (August 27, 2001): 112.

8   P. J. Brews and M. R. Hunt, "Learning to Plan and Planning to Learn: Resolving the Planning School/Learning School Debate," *Strategic Management Journal* 20 (1999): 889–913; A. Van De Ven, H. Angle, and M. S. Poole, *Research on the Management Innovation* (Oxford University Press, 2000); Y-T. Cheng and A. H. Van de Ven, "Learning the Innovation Journey: Order Out of Chaos," *Organization Science* 7 (1996): 593–614.

9   Adapted from S. E. Jackson and R. S. Schuler, "Turning Knowledge into Business Advantage," *Financial Times* (January 15, 2001): Mastering Management Supplement. Copyright held by S. E. Jackson and R. S. Schuler. Used with permission.

10   P. J. Robertson, D. R. Roberts, and J. I. Porras, "Dynamics of Planned Change: Assessing Empirical Support for a Theoretical Model," *Academy of Management Journal* 36 (1993): 619–663

11   Corporate Executive Board, *M&A Communications—Toward a Common Culture* (Washington, DC: Corporate Executive Board, December 2002); Corporate Executive Board, *Best Practices in Acquiring Companies* (Washington, DC: Corporate Executive Board, February 2002); J. A. Schmidt, "The Correct Spelling of M&A Begins with HR," *HR Magazine* (June 2001): 102–108; J. Birkinshaw, H. Bresman, and L. Hakanson, "Managing the Post-Acquisition Integration Process: How the Human Integration and Task Integration Processes Interact to Foster Value Creation," *Journal of Management Studies* 37 (2000): 395–425; M. L. Marks and P. H. Mirvis, "Making Mergers and Acquisitions Work: Strategic and Psychological Preparation," *Academy of Management Executive* 15(2) (2000): 80–92.

12   K. Troy, *Change Management: Striving for Customer Value: A Research Report* (New York: Conference Board, 1996).

13   S. P. Kirn, A. J. Rucci, M. A. Huselid, and B. E. Becker, "Strategic Human Resource Management at Sears," *Human Resource Management* 38 (1999): 329–336; A. J. Rucci, S. P. Kirn, and R. T. Quinn, "The Employee-Customer-Profit Chain at Sears," *Harvard Business Review* (January–February 1998): 82–97.

14   Adapted from R. S. Schuler, S. E. Jackson, and J. Storey, "HRM and Its Link with Strategic Management," in J. Storey (ed.), *Human Resource Management: A Critical Text* (London: Blackwell, 2001): 137–159. See also A. Armenakis and A. Bedeian, "Organizational Change: A Review of Theory and Research in the 1990s," *Journal of Management* 25(3) (1999): 293–315; J. W. Walker, "The Ultimate Human Resource Planning: Integrating the Human Resource Function with the Business," in G. R. Ferris (ed.), *Handbook of Human Resource Management* (Oxford, England: Blackwell, 1995); S. E. Jackson and R. S. Schuler, "Human Resource Planning: Challenges for I/O Psychologists," *American Psychologist* (February 1990): 223–239.

15   For example, see M. Baer and M. Frese, "Innovation Is Not Enough: Climates for Initiative and Psychological Safety, Process Innovations, and Firm Performance," *Journal of Organizational Behavior* 24 (2003): 45–68; K. M. B. Gravenhorst, R. A. Werkman, and J. J. Boonstra, "The Change Capacity of Organizations: General Assessment and Five Configurations," *Applied Psychology: An International Review* 52(1) (2003): 83–105.

16   J. Collison and C. Frangos, *Aligning HR with Organizational Strategy Survey* (Alexandria, VA: Society for Human Resource Management, 2003).

17   J. Collison and C. Frangos, *Aligning HR with Organization Strategy Survey* (Alexandria, VA: Society for Human Resource Management, 2002).

18   J. Kirby, "Reinvention with Respect: An Interview with Jim Kelly of UPS," *Harvard Business Review* (November 2001): 116–123; M. Beer and N. Nohria, "Cracking the Code of Change," *Harvard Business Review* (May–June 2000): 133–141.

19   J. Collison and C. Frangos, *Aligning HR with Organization Strategy Survey* (Alexandria, VA: Society for Human Resource Management, 2002); P. J. Brews and M. R. Hunt, "Learning to Plan and Planning to Learn: Resolving the Planning School/Learning School Debate," *Strategic Management Journal* 20 (1999): 889–913; A. Howard and Associates, *Diagnosis for Organizational Change: Methods and Models* (San Francisco: Jossey-Bass, 1994). See also J. Waclawski and A. H. Chruch, *Organizational Development: Data Driven Methods for Change* (San Francisco: Jossey-Bass, 2002).

20   J. R. Stengel, A. L. Dixon, and C. T. Allen, "Listening Begins at Home," *Harvard Business Review* (November 2003): 106–117; Berner, "How A. G. Lafley Is Revolutionizing a Bastion of Corporate Conservatism," *Business Week* (July 7, 2003): 52–63.

21   D. Phillips, "Freight-Car Congestion Is Worrying Union Pacific," *New York Times,* (March 31, 2004): C1, C4.

22   For more information about this survey and the Malcolm Baldrige Award, visit http://www.baldrige.nist.gov/Progress_Leaders.htm.

23   B. Mike and J. W. Slocum Jr., "Slice of Reality: Changing Culture at Pizza Hut and Yum! Brands, Inc.," *Organizational Dynamics* 32(4) (2003): 319–330;

24   T. M. Begley and D. P. Boyd, "Articulating Corporate Values through Human Resource Policies," *Business Horizons* (July–August 2000): 8–12.

25   N. Adler, L. Brody, and J. Osland, "The Women's Global Leadership Forum: Enhancing One Company's Global Leadership Capability," *Human Resource Management* 39(2 & 3) (Summer/Fall 2000): 209–225.

26   R. S. Kaplan and D. P. Norton, *The Strategy-Focused Organization: How Balanced Scorecard Companies Thrive in the New Business Environment* (Boston: Harvard Business Press, 2000); B. E. Becker, M. A. Huselid, and D. Ulrich, *The HR Scorecard: Linking People, Strategy, and Performance* (Boston, MA: Harvard Business School Press, 2001); C. Creelman, "Mark Huselid and the HR Balanced Scorecard," http://www.hr.com/Hrcom/index.cfm/WeeklyMag/, February 20, 2001.

27 M. A. West, C. Borrill, J. Dawson, J. Scully, M. Carter, S. Anelay, M. Patterson, and J. Waring, "The Link between the Management of Employees and Patient Mortality in Acute Hospitals," *International Human Resource Management* 13 (December 2002): 1299–1310.

28 A. Farnham, "Worst Airline?" Forbes (June 11, 2001): 105–115; G. Bethune and S. Huler, *From Worst to First: Behind the Scenes of Continental's Remarkable Comeback* (New York: John Wiley, 1999); M. Maynard, "Chief Executive of Continental to Step Down," *New York Times* (January 17, 2004): E1.

29 For more discussion about HR metrics, see J. Fitz-Enz, *ROI of Human Capital: Measuring the Economic Value of Employee Performance* (New York: AMACOM, 2000), and B. E. Becker, M. A. Huselid, and D. Ulrich, *The HR Scorecard* (Boston: Harvard Business School Press, 2001).

30 H. Fischer and K. D. Mittorp, "How HR Measures Support Risk Management: The Deutsche Bank Example," *Human Resource Management* 41 (2002): 477–490.

31 M. Hammers, "SunTrust Bank Combines 28 Recruiting and Screening Systems into One," *Workforce Management* (November 2003): 59–60.

32 M. Conlin, "Where Layoffs Are a Last Resort," *Business Week* (October 8, 2001): 42.

33 W. M. Baumol, A. S. Blinder, and E. N. Wolff, *Downsizing in America: Reality, Causes, and Consequence* (New York: Russell Sage Foundation, 2003).

34 R. L. Knowdell, E. Branstead, and M. Moravec, *From Downsizing to Recovery—Strategic Transition Options for Organizations and Individuals* (Palo Alto, CA: CPP Books, 1994); G. E. Prussia, A. J. Kinicki, and J. S. Bracker, "Psychological and Behavioral Consequences of Job Loss: A Covariance Structure Analysis Using Weiner's (1985) Attribution Model," *Journal of Applied Psychology* 78 (1993): 382–394; C. R. Leana and D. C. Feldman, *Coping with Job Loss: How Individuals, Organizations, and Communities Respond to Layoffs* (New York: Lexington Books, 1992).

35 E. Zimmerman, "Why Deep Layoffs Hurt Long-Term Recovery," *Workforce* (November 2001): 48–53. A detailed discussion of internal labor markets can be found in L. T. Pinfield and M. F. Berner, "Employment Systems: Toward a Coherent Conceptualization of Internal Labor Markets," *Research in Personnel and Human Resource Management* 12 (1994): 41–78.

36 "Job Turnover Tab," *Business Week* (March 20, 1998): 8.

37 S. E. Ante, "Shifting Work Offshore? Outsourcer Beware," *Businesss Week* (January 12, 2004): 36–37 ; A. Meisler, "Think Globally, Act Rationally," *Workforce Management* (January 2004): 40–45; F. Vogelstein, "Silicon Valley's Hiring! (and Firing)," *Fortune* (June 23, 2003): 86.

38 P. Kiger, "At First USA Bank, Promotions and Job Satisfaction are Up," *Workforce* (March 2001): 54–56; P. Cappelli, "A Market-Driven Approach to Retaining Talent," *Harvard Business Review* (January–February 2001): 103–111; M. Nealy Martinez, "Retention: To Have and To Hold," *HR Magazine* (September 1998): 131–138.

39 "Companies Continue to Increase Staff Size," *HR Magazine* (January 2001): 35–36; "To Cut or Not to Cut," *The Economist* (February 10, 2001): 61–62; S. Kuczynski, "Help! I Shrunk the Company," *HR Magazine* (June 1999): 40–45; T. Mroczkowski and M. Hanaoka, "Effective Rightsizing Strategies in Japan and America: Is There a Convergence of Employment Practices?" *Academy of Management Executive* 11(2) (1997): 57–67; M. London, "Redeployment and Continuous Learning in the 21st Century: Hard Lessons and Positive Examples from the Downsizing Era," *Academy of Management Executive* 10(4) (1992): 67–79; W. N. Davis, III, D. L. Worrell, and J. B. Fox, "Early Retirement Programs and Firm Performance," *Academy of Management Journal* 39(4) (1996): 970–984; R. Maurer, "Alternative to Downsizing," *Solutions* (October 1996): 40–48.

40 P. Cappelli, "Will There Really Be a Labor Shortage?" *Organizational Dynamics* 32(3) (2003): 221–233; P. Cappelli, "Labor Shortage? What Labor Shortage?" *HR Magazine* (October 2003): 12; D. P. Lepak, R.

Takeuchi, and S. A. Snell, "Employment Flexibility and Firm Performance: Examining the Interaction Effects of Employment Mode, Environmental Dynamism, and Technological Intensity," *Journal of Management* 29(5) (2003): 681–703; S. A. Feeney, "Irreplaceable You," *Workforce Management* (August 2003): 36–40; F. Brock, "Who'll Sit at the Boomers' Desks?" *New York Times* (October 12, 2003): 9; M. C. Kernan and P. J. Hanges, "Survivor Reactions to Reorganization: Antecedents and Consequences of Procedural, Interpersonal, and Informational Justice," *Journal of Applied Psychology* 87(5) (2002): 916–928; F. Jossi, "Take the Road Less Travelled," *HR Magazine* (July 2001): 46–51.

41 A. Karaevli and D. T. Hall, "Growing Leaders for Turbulent Times: Is Succession Planning Up to the Challenge?" *Organizational Dynamics* 32(1) (2003): 62–79.

42 A. Karaevli and D. T. Hall, "Growing Leaders for Turbulent Times: Is Succession Planning Up to the Challenge?" *Organizational Dynamics* 32(1) (2003): 62–79; R. M. L. Maznevski and J. DiStefano, "Global Leaders Are Team Players: Developing Global Leaders through Membership on Global Teams," *Human Resource Management* 39(Summer/Fall 2000): 195–208; M. Harvey, M. Novicevic and C. Speier, "An Innovative Global Management Staffing System: A Competency-Based Perspective," *Human Resource Management* 39(4) (Winter 2000): 381–394; Y. Baruch and M. Peiperl, "Career Management Practices: An Empirical Survey and Implications," *Human Resource Management* 39(4) (Winter 2000): 347–366.

43 Adapted from S. L. Davis, "Assessment as Organizational Strategy," in R. Jeanneret and R. Silzer (eds.), *Individual Psychological Assessment: Predicting Behavior in Organizational Settings* (San Francisco: Jossey-Bass, 2001).

44 R. K. Miller, "Going the Distance," *HR Executive*, http://www.hrexecutive.com/weir.htm, February 22, 2001.

45 K. M. B. Gravenhorst, R. A. Werkman, and J. J. Boonstra, "The Change Capacity of Organizations: General Assessment and Five Configurations," *Applied Psychology: An International Review* 52(1) (2003): 83–105; L. Herscovitch and J. P. Meyer, "Commitment to Organizational Change: Extension of a Three-Component Model," *Journal of Applied Psychology* 87(3) (2002): 474–487; C. Campbell-Hunt, "What Have We Learned about Generic Competitive Strategy? A Meta-Analysis," *Strategic Management Journal* 21 (2000): 127–154; D. Pottruck and T. Pearce, "Creating Culture," *Business 2.0* (May 2000): 362–378; R. Silzer, "Shaping Organizational Leadership: The Ripple Effect of Assessment," in R. Jeanneret and R. Silzer (eds.), *Individual Psychological Assessment: Predicting Behavior in Organizational Settings*.

46 P. E. Figge, *Plan Closings—A Practical Guide* (Alexandria, VA: Society for Human Resource Management, 2003); see also W. F. Cascio, "Strategies for Responsible Restructuring," *Academy of Management Executive* 16(3) (2002): 80–91.

47 C. Wanberg and J. Banas, "Predictors and Outcomes of Openness to Changes in a Reorganizing Workplace," *Journal of Applied Psychology* 85(1) (2000): 132–142.

48 R. Pascale, "Change How You Define Leadership and You Change How You Run a Company," *Fast Company* (April–May 1998): 110–120; G. Hamel, "Reinvent Your Company," *Fortune* (June 12, 2000): 99–118.

49 S. Oreg, "Resistance to Change: Developing an Individual Differences Measure," *Journal of Applied Psychology* 88(4) (2003): 680–693; L. Gardenswartz and A. Rowe, "Overcoming Resistance to Your Diversity Initiative," *MOSAICS: SHRM Focuses on Workplace Diversity* 8(4) (October 2002): 3, 5; W. Echikson, "Nestle: An Elephant Dances," *Business Week e.Biz* (December 11, 2000): 44–48; R. Maurer, *Beyond the Wall of Resistance* (Austin, TX: Bard Books, 1996).

50 R. Kanter, "The Ten Deadly Mistakes of Wanna-Dots," *Harvard Business Review* (January 2001): 91–100; J. Kerstetter, "Peoplesoft's Hard Guy," *Business Week* (January 15, 2001): 76–77; K. Skoldberg, "Tales of Change," *Organization Science* 5 (1994): 219–238.

51 T. Petzinger, Jr., "Georg Bauer Put Burden of Downsizing into Employees' Hands," *Wall Street Journal* (May 10, 1996): B1.

52 M. C. Kernan and P. J. Hanges, "Survivor Reactions to Reorganization: Antecedents and Consequences of Procedural, Interpersonal, and Informational Justice," *Journal of Applied Psychology* 87(5) (2002): 916–928; S. Bates, "Middle Managers Anxious to Bolt Firms," *HR Magazine* (October 2003): 12; E. S. Barnes, "Even in a Bad Economy, Hypertherm Just Says No to Pink Slips," *Workforce Management* (July 2003): 96–99; C. Heckscher, *White-Collar Blues* (New York: Basic Books, 1995).

53 Research shows change initiatives are more often undertaken earlier in the careers of executives, and less likely to occur later, for example, see D. Miller and J. Shamsie, "Learning Across the Life Cycle: Experimentation and Performance among the Hollywood Studio Heads," *Strategic Management Journal* 22 (2001): 724–745; M. Baer and M. Frese, "Innovation Is Not Enough: Climates for Initiative and Psychological Safety, Process Innovations, and Firm Performance," *Journal of Organizational Behavior* 24 (2003): 45–68.

54 J. W. Dean Jr., P. Brandes, and R. Dharwadkar, "Organizational Cynicism," *Academy of Management Review* 23(1998): 341–352; A. E. Reichers, J. P. Wanous, and J. T. Austin, "Understanding and Managing Cynicism about Organizational Change," *Academy of Management Executive* 11(1997): 48.

55 E. W. Morrison, "When Employees Feel Betrayed: A Model of How Psychological Contract Violation Develops," *Academy of Management Review* 22 (1997): 226–256; E. M. Mervosh, "Downsizing Dilemma," *Human Resource Executive* (February 1997): 50–53.

56 D. M. Schweiger, J. M. Ivancevich, and F. R. Power, "Executive Actions for Managing Human Resources before and after Acquisition," *Academy of Management Executive* 1(2) (1986): 127–138.

57 G. Koretz, "Downsizing's Painful Effects," *Business Week* (April 13, 1998): 23.

58 H. Axel, *HR Review: Implementing the New Employment Compact* (New York: The Conference Board, 1997).

59 J. P. Kotter, "Leading Change: Why Transformation Efforts Fail," *Harvard Business Review* (March–April 1995): 59–67.

Using Job Analysis and Competency Modeling

Aetna Inc., with almost 28,000 employees, is a leading provider of insurance and financial services. Its lines of business include health care, casualty coverage for commercial and personal property, life insurance, and asset management. After more than 100 years of great success, Aetna's profits started to decline in 1987. This happened partly because the company had a product line that was too large *and too diversified and partly because some of its businesses were unprofitable. Overhead expenses exceeded the industry average in many cases.*

In the early 1990s, then-CEO Ronald E. Compton set about the task of making the company more profitable. Like other large insurers in the industry, such as ITT Corporation, Hartford Fire Insurance Company, and Cigna Corporation, Aetna started eliminating unprofitable lines of business. These included its individual health and reinsurance operations. At the same time, Compton announced that some of the workforce would be laid off. In addition to eliminating people and lines of business, Aetna reengineered many areas of the business and introduced new technologies. Throughout the process, corporate HR staff partnered with managers to implement the new strategy. Human resource professionals, using input from other employees and managers, helped the company reduce more than 7,000 individual job titles to just 200 job titles. In effect, they redesigned jobs to give employees more latitude. The old job classification system delineated specific tasks that employees were supposed to do, which discouraged employees from taking on additional responsibilities. With the new jobs, employees can perform a greater variety of tasks and be rewarded for doing so, without going through a promotion procedure and without having to revise the job description. Aetna used job analysis to redefine the boundaries and content of its jobs.[1]

Job analysis and competency modeling are procedures for systematically understanding the work that gets done in an organization. Among HR practitioners, there is some disagreement about whether job analysis and competency modeling are two different procedures, or just two variations on the same theme.[2] Our view is that competency modeling represents one particular approach to job analysis. In other words, *job analysis* is a broader and more general term, with competency modeling being one approach to job analysis.[3] This chapter describes the competency modeling approach— which currently enjoys great popularity—as well as other more traditional approaches to job analysis.

Regardless of which specific procedures one uses to conduct a job analysis, the results of the job analysis are used to write job descriptions. A **job description** *spells out essential job functions, describes the conditions in which the job is performed, and states special training or certification requirements for the job.* For employees, a job description produced through job analysis serves as a guide to work behavior. For supervisors and managers, a job description serves as a guide to performance evaluation and feedback. Job descriptions also serve as the basic building blocks for designing pay policies and training programs. In other words, job analysis provides the foundation upon which to build virtually all components of the human resource management (HRM) system. It can be used to ensure that an organization's entire system for managing people is internally consistent and appropriate for the organization's context as shown in Exhibit 5.1.

THE STRATEGIC IMPORTANCE OF JOB ANALYSIS AND COMPETENCY MODELING

The strategic importance of job analysis and competency modeling is grounded first and foremost in their usefulness as systematic procedures that provide a rational foundation on which to build a coherent approach to managing human resources. This role for job analysis and competency mod-

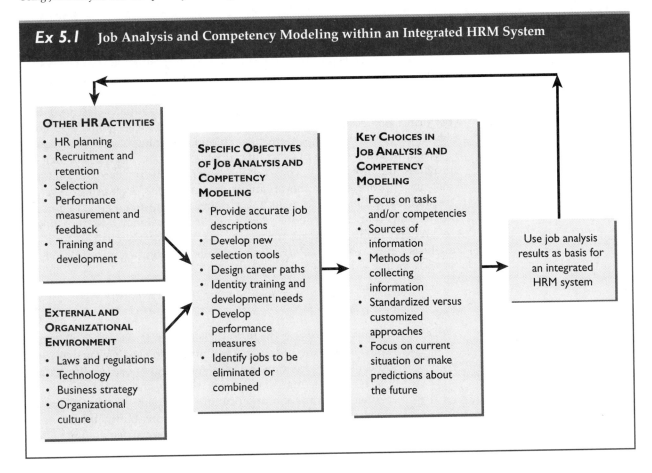

Ex 5.1 Job Analysis and Competency Modeling within an Integrated HRM System

OTHER HR ACTIVITIES

- HR planning
- Recruitment and retention
- Selection
- Performance measurement and feedback
- Training and development

EXTERNAL AND ORGANIZATIONAL ENVIRONMENT

- Laws and regulations
- Technology
- Business strategy
- Organizational culture

SPECIFIC OBJECTIVES OF JOB ANALYSIS AND COMPETENCY MODELING

- Provide accurate job descriptions
- Develop new selection tools
- Design career paths
- Identity training and development needs
- Develop performance measures
- Identify jobs to be eliminated or combined

KEY CHOICES IN JOB ANALYSIS AND COMPETENCY MODELING

- Focus on tasks and/or competencies
- Sources of information
- Methods of collecting information
- Standardized versus customized approaches
- Focus on current situation or make predictions about the future

Use job analysis results as basis for an integrated HRM system

eling becomes especially obvious during periods of strategic change, when jobs in an organization are likely to be suddenly transformed. Legal considerations also contribute to the strategic importance of job analysis. As described in Chapters 1 and 3, compliance with various employment laws and regulations is one of the many objectives of effective organizations.

STRATEGIC CHANGE

As the example of Aetna illustrates, the nature of jobs can change radically when an organization undergoes a strategic change, such as restructuring the organization around key processes. When the nature of the jobs in an organization changes, many aspects of the HRM system are likely to be affected as well. At Aetna, broader jobs and reduced layers of management meant there were fewer opportunities for advancement through promotion. Job analysis helped the HR professionals address this problem by providing a new map of how people could achieve career advancement in the new organizational structure.

For many organizations, the process of restructuring occurs in the context of a merger or acquisition. During a merger or acquisition, job analysis provides a systematic basis for comparing the content of jobs that existed in the separate companies. When the companies are brought together, a key challenge is treating people fairly. For example, if two people are doing essentially the same work, they should be paid essentially the same following the merger. Job analysis provides a means for determining which employees are doing essentially the same work. Job analysis also identifies redundant jobs that might be candidates for elimination. Other uses of job analysis following a merger or acquisition include specifying the competencies needed to perform a job, redesigning jobs to accommodate employees with disabilities, developing measures of job performance, and designing training programs.[4]

Regardless of why an organization undergoes restructuring, job analysis provides the information needed to develop new HR policies and practices that are appropriate for the organization's new jobs. According to recent research by William M. Mercer, Inc., driving strategic change is one of the key reasons that organizations are turning to competency-based job analyses. When a company moves into a new market or a new business area, job analysis can be used to identify the new skills and competencies that will be needed to succeed in the new venture.[5]

Legal Considerations

FAST FACT

Section 14.C.2 of the U.S. Department of Labor's *Uniform Guidelines* states that "there shall be a job analysis which includes an analysis of the important work behaviors required for successful performance."

Because it serves as the basis for selection decisions, performance appraisals, compensation, and training, job analysis has received considerable attention from legal and regulatory bodies. By regularly conducting job analysis studies and documenting the results in formal job descriptions, employers can better protect themselves against claims of unfair treatment. Principles for conducting appropriate job analyses have been articulated in federal regulatory guidelines and several court decisions.[6]

Nondiscrimination. During the past three decades, the courts have clearly indicated that employers should conduct thorough job analyses for all jobs in the organization and use the results of those job analyses as the basis for a variety of personnel decisions. By conducting job analyses and documenting job requirements, employers can reduce the role of stereotypes and uninformed opinions about the skills needed to perform a job. For example, in *Rowe v. General Motors* (1972), the court ruled that to prevent discriminatory practices in promotion decisions, a company should have written objective standards for promotion. In *United States v. City of Chicago* (1978), the court stated that employers should have objective standards for promotion and that these standards should describe the job to which the person is being considered for promotion. These objective standards can be determined through job analysis.[7]

The Americans with Disabilities Act of 1990 (ADA) also draws attention to the importance of job analysis. The ADA makes it unlawful to discriminate against a qualified individual who has a disability. It applies to anyone who has a physical or mental impairment that substantially limits one or more major life activities. A person is considered qualified for a job if she or he can perform the job's "essential functions," although some accommodation may be necessary on the part of the employer. For example, a hearing-impaired employee may be able to perform the essential functions of a proofreading job, provided the employer makes some reasonable accommodations in the procedures used to assign work to the individual. In this example, it would not be legal for the employer to use the employee's hearing disability as a basis for refusing to allow her to work as a proofreader.[8]

Independent Contractors. For purposes of compensation and taxation, the law treats independent contractors (who are only temporary employees) and regular employees quite differently. For regular workers only, employers must withhold and pay Social Security and Medicare taxes and pay for unemployment insurance. None of these are required for contract workers.

FAST FACT

Estimates place the percentage of contract workers at about 20% of the workforce.

Another major difference is that regular workers enjoy the right to certain benefits and overtime pay to which independent contractors are not entitled.

Thoroughly documenting workers' job duties is a good approach to determining whether they qualify as independent contractors or regular employees.[9] During the 1990s, as Microsoft thrived, it hired thousands of workers through local personnel agencies and *treated* them as "temps"—paying them no company benefits and clearly stating that full-time employment in the future was not guaranteed. These temps (who wore orange badges) stayed around so long that they acquired the nickname "permatemps." Eventually, the permatemps filed a class action lawsuit, claiming they had been denied benefits (including the opportunity to purchase company stock) that they were entitled to receive. After eight years of legal battles, the courts ruled in favor of Microsoft's permatemps, agreeing that these employees did not forfeit the rights ordinarily granted to regular employees (who wore blue badges) just because they had signed a waiver stating that they understood their "temporary" status.[10] The court ruled that they should be classified as regular employees and that they were entitled to back pay and the value of stocks they had not received. Microsoft was ordered to reimburse these workers at an estimated cost of $97 million. In addition to the financial costs, Microsoft's image as an employer of choice took a beating in the public press. Today, Microsoft continues to employ several thousand independent contractors, but now the company is much more careful to ensure that these contractors are truly "temporary."[11]

Employers can use job analysis to assess whether a worker who has been classified as an independent contractor should be reclassified and treated as a regular employee. Some of the key questions that a job analysis can clarify are these:

- Does the job description tell the worker *how* to do the job, or indicate that a supervisor will tell the person *how* to do the job? An employer should not tell independent contractors how to do their jobs.
- Does the job description state that the work performed on the job is an essential part of the business? Independent contractors should not be hired to perform essential tasks or services.
- Does the job description state that the worker must do the work him- or herself? An independent contractor should be allowed to hire someone else to do the work.
- Does the job description specify the hours to be worked? An independent contractor should be allowed to determine the hours of work needed to complete the job.
- Does the job description indicate that the worker is expected to work full-time? An independent contractor should not be prevented from doing work for other employers.

- Does the job description specify that the work is to be performed at the company's facilities? An independent contractor chooses where to do the work.[12]

PARTNERSHIP ROLES IN JOB ANALYSIS AND COMPETENCY MODELING

As this chapter describes, the process of conducting a thorough job analysis or competency study can involve many different people. Human resource professionals almost always have primary responsibility for overseeing the process, but they cannot conduct an adequate analysis on their own. The people who work in a job and the people who observe a job being done day in and day out are the experts when it comes to describing the job, so their involvement in job analysis is essential. During the restructuring at Aetna, job analysis required the cooperation of nearly everyone in the organization. The feature "The HR Triad: Partnership Roles in Job Analysis and Competency Modeling" summarizes the major ways that HR professionals, managers, and other employees get involved in job analysis. In the remainder of this chapter, we describe these roles in more detail.

BASIC TERMINOLOGY

In everyday conversations, people often use the word *job* whenever they refer to an employment situation. But when an entire system for managing

The HR Triad

Partnership Roles in Job Analysis and Competency Modeling

LINE MANAGERS	HR PROFESSIONALS	EMPLOYEES
• With knowledge of strategic business plans, work with HR managers to determine whether jobs need to be analyzed or reanalyzed.	• Ensure that job analysis information is up-to-date and that it is used as the foundation for the organization's entire HRM system.	• Help line managers recognize when major changes in a job indicate the need for job analysis or reanalysis.
• Participate in job analysis through interviews and questionnaires.	• Serve as a job analysis expert, or help select an external vendor to conduct job analysis.	• Provide accurate information for the job analysis process.
• Facilitate job incumbents' participation in job analysis.	• Ensure that line managers and employees are aware of legal considerations.	• Use job analysis results for career planning and job choice decisions.
• Understand the relationship among job analysis and other HR practices.	• Prepare and update job descriptions with line managers and employees.	
	• Keep up-to-date on new techniques and changing trends in job analysis.	

human resources depends on understanding the jobs in an organization, more specific terminology is needed. More precise use of several related terms facilitates clear communication.

POSITIONS, JOBS, AND OCCUPATIONS

Human resource professionals use the term **position** *to refer to the activities carried out by any single person.* Each employee holds one position in an organization. The term **job** *refers to positions that are functionally interchangeable in the organization.* In small organizations, each job may have only one position associated with it; no two employees would be expected to do the same thing. An example of this situation would occur if Raol's position is Account Manager and only Raol holds the job of Account Manager.

As organizations grow, the number of positions associated with some jobs increases. A family bakery may eventually hire more people to work as bakers as well as more people to work at the sales counter. The bakery's growth requires adding positions without increasing the number of jobs. If the bakery continues to expand, new jobs may eventually be added. If the bakery adds seating and coffee service for customers, the job of waiter might be added. Additional jobs could also be created through increased specialization. In a small bakery, the job of baker includes baking breads as well as pies and cakes, but as the organization grows, the baker's job is split into two jobs: bread baker and pastry maker.

An **occupation** *refers to a group of jobs that involve similar work and requires similar competencies, training, and credentials.*[13] The U.S. government categorizes jobs into approximately 1,000 occupations, which can be grouped into the categories listed in Exhibit 5.2. Which occupational category do you think the jobs in a bakery fit into?

JOB ANALYSIS

Job analysis *is a systematic process of describing and recording information about job behaviors, activities, and worker specifications.*[14] Typically, the information described and recorded includes the

---

Ex 5.2 Standard Occupational Categories Used by the Federal Government

Architecture and engineering	Education, training, and library	Management
Arts, design, entertainment, sports, and media	Farming, fishing, and forestry	Military
	Food preparation and service	Office and administrative support
Building and grounds cleaning and maintenance	Health care practitioner and technical occupations	Personal care and service
Business and financial operations	Health care support	Production
Community and social services	Installation, maintenance, and repair	Protective services
Computer and mathematical	Legal	Sales and related occupations
Construction and extraction	Life—physical and social science	Transportation and material moving

- purposes of a job;
- major duties or activities required of job holders;
- conditions under which the job is performed; and
- competencies (i.e., skills, knowledge, abilities and other attributes)[15] that enable and enhance performance in the job.

Human resource experts have devoted a great deal of attention to developing systematic job analysis techniques; many different techniques are available. In fact, according to one recent review of the available techniques, there are at least 15 major job analysis approaches.[16]

The focus of a job analysis is one feature that accounts for why there are so many techniques. Most techniques are either task-oriented or worker-oriented. Traditional approaches tend to focus on tasks. **Task-oriented job analysis** *focuses on what the job involves in terms of work activities and outcomes.* Time-and-motion studies are a task-focused method of job analysis, as are most other traditional approaches to job analysis.

Worker-oriented job analysis *focuses on the characteristics of job incumbents that are required to perform the job well.* The objective is to provide a description of the skills, abilities, attitudes, personality characteristics, and so on that lead to successful job performance. Here the question is *who* can do the job. Competency modeling is a worker-focused approach to job analysis.

Each of the available job analysis techniques has certain strengths and weaknesses. Indeed, the reality is that no one technique is perfect. The usefulness of a particular technique often depends on the purpose for conducting the job analysis. For example, if the results of a job analysis will be used to design a new recruitment plan, a worker-oriented approach that identifies needed competencies may be desirable. On the other hand, the results of a task-focused approach may be more useful for designing a job training or employee coaching program. Thus, HR professionals often rely on a combination of job analysis techniques when developing an organization's total HRM system.

"Friendly and caring personality. Competent in handling difficult situations. Able to communicate effectively with people from all parts of the world. Supportive of colleagues. Able to remain calm and efficient under pressure. Self-reliant and independent. Willing to treat everyone as an individual."

From British Airways vacancy announcement

COMPETENCY MODELING

A **competency** *is a measurable pattern of knowledge, skill, abilities, behaviors, and other characteristics that an individual needs to perform work roles or occupational functions successfully.*[17] As already noted, we consider competency modeling to be a specific approach to conducting a job analysis. Although some consultants prefer to use the new language of competency modeling to describe the services they offer, the basic procedures and objectives of competency modeling are firmly grounded in traditional job analysis procedures. What distinguishes the competency modeling approach is that it places much more emphasis on specifying the individual characteristics that are associated with effective performance in a job.

For **competency modeling,** *the objective is to describe the skills, knowledge, abilities, values, interests, and personality of successful employees.* It is similar to worker-oriented job analysis. Ideally, a competency model describes a set of competencies that are necessary for successful job performance and provides behavioral indicators that can be used to assess an individual's proficiency on each competency.[18] Competency models are particularly useful when an organization is developing career paths and developmental or training experiences that enable employees to progress along those career paths.[19]

Job Descriptions

FAST FACT

Southwest Airlines recruiting announcement for the job of flight attendant: Flight Attendants ensure that Customers' safety and comfort come first, and create a memorable experience by providing friendly, enthusiastic, courteous and fun service.

Often, the most immediate use of job analysis and competency modeling results is writing job descriptions that detail what the jobholder is expected to do and the competencies needed for the job. Job descriptions are part of the written contract that governs the employment relationship. Exhibit 5.3 shows an example of a job description. During

---

Ex 5.3 Job Description

Title: Corporate Loan Assistant   Department: Corporate Banking

Date: June 2004   Location: Head Office

Note: *Statements included in this description are intended to reflect, in general, the duties and responsibilities of this classification and are not to be interpreted as being all-inclusive.*

RELATIONSHIPS

Reports to: Corporate Account Officer or Sr. Corporate Account Officer

Subordinate staff: None

Internal customers: Middle and Senior Managers within Corporate Banking

External contacts: Major bank customers

SUMMARY DESCRIPTION

Assist in the administration of commercial accounts to ensure maintenance of profitable bank relationships.

DOMAINS

A. Credit Analysis (Weekly)

   Under the direction of a supervising loan officer, analyze a customer company's history, industry position, present condition, accounting procedures, and debt requirements. Review credit reports, provide summaries of analysis, and recommend courses of action for potential borrowers; review and summarize performance of existing borrowers. Prepare and follow up on credit reports and loan agreement compliance sheets.

B. Operations (Weekly)

   Help customers with banking problems and needs. Give out customer credit information to valid inquirers. Analyze account profitability and compliance with balance arrangements; distribute to customer. Direct loan note department in receiving and disbursing funds and in booking loans. Correct internal errors.

C. Loan Documentation (Weekly)

   Develop required loan documentation. Help customers complete loan documents. Review loan documents immediately after a loan closing for completeness and accuracy.

D. Report/Information System (Weekly)

   Prepare credit reports, describing and analyzing customer relationship and loan commitments; prepare for input into information system. Monitor credit reports for accuracy.

E. Customer/Internal Relations (Weekly)

   Build rapport with customers by becoming familiar with their products, facilities, and industries. Communicate with customers and other banks to obtain loan-related information and answer questions. Prepare reports on customer and prospect contacts and follow up. Write memos on events affecting customers and prospects.

(continued)

Ex 5.3 *(continued)*

F. Assistance to Officers (Monthly)

Assist assigned officers by preparing credit support information, summarizing customer relationships, and accompanying officers on calls or making independent calls. Monitor accounts and review and maintain credit files. Coordinate information flow to banks participating in loans. Respond to customer questions or requests in absence of assigned officer.

G. Assistance to Division (Monthly)

Represent bank at industry activities. Follow industry/area developments. Help division manager plan the division's approach to and prospects for new business. Interview loan assistant applicants. Provide divisional backup in absence of assigned officer.

H. Competencies (Any item with an asterisk will be taught on the job)

Oral communication, including listening and questioning. Intermediate accounting proficiency. Writing. Researching/reading to understand legal financial documents. Organizational/analytical skills. Social skills to represent the bank and strengthen its image. Sales. Knowledge of bank credit policy and services.* Skill to use bank computer system.* Knowledge of bank-related legal terminology. Independent work skills. Work efficiently under pressure. Knowledge of basic corporate finance.

I. Physical Characteristics

See to read fine print and numbers. Hear speaker 20 feet away. Speak to address a group of five. Mobility to tour customer facilities (may include climbing stairs).

J. Other Characteristics

Driver's license. Willing to: work overtime and weekends occasionally; travel out of state every three months/locally weekly; attend activities after work hours; wear clean, neat, businesslike attire.

recruitment, clear job descriptions provide job applicants with realistic information.

Once on the job, employees use their job descriptions to guide their behavior. Well-written job descriptions help employees direct their energies to the most important aspects of the job. Supervisors use job descriptions in evaluating performance and providing feedback. Well-written job descriptions can also guide supervisors in writing references and incumbents in preparing resumes. Typically, a well-written job description includes the elements listed in Exhibit 5.4.[20]

SOURCES OF INFORMATION

Information about a job can be obtained from anyone who has specific information about what the work involves. *The people used as sources of information about specific jobs are often referred to as* **subject matter experts (SMEs).** They can include current job incumbents, supervisors, trained job analysts, and/or customers. Each of these sources sees the job from a different perspective. Associated with each source of information about a job are different advantages and disadvantages.

By using several sources, there is less chance of error in the final result. Some common job analysis errors and the conditions that can cause them are described in Exhibit 5.5.[21] To conduct the most comprehensive job analysis, the best strategy is to include as many different sources as possible.[22]

Ex 5.4	**Elements of a Job Description and What They Should Specify**
ELEMENT	**WHAT SHOULD BE SPECIFIED**
Job title	• Defines a group of positions that are interchangeable (identical) with regard to their significant duties.
Department or division	• Indicates where in the organization the job is located.
Date the job was analyzed	• Indicates when the description was prepared and perhaps whether it should be updated. A job description based on a job analysis conducted prior to any major changes in the job is of little use.
Job summary	• An abstract of the job, often used during recruitment to create job postings or employment announcements and to set the pay levels.
Supervision	• Identifies reporting relationships. If supervision is given, the duties associated with that supervision should be detailed under work performed.
Work performed	• Identifies the duties and underlying tasks that make up a job. A *task* is something that workers perform or an action they take to produce a product or service. A *duty* is a collection of related, recurring tasks. Duties should be ranked in terms of the time spent on them as well as their importance. Specified duties are used to determine whether job accommodations for individuals protected under the Americans with Disabilities Act are reasonable, whether the job is exempt from overtime provisions of the Fair Labor Standards Act, and whether two jobs with different titles should be treated as equal for purposes of compliance with the Equal Pay Act.
Job context	• Describes the physical environment that surrounds the job (e.g., outdoors, in close quarters, in remote areas, in extremely high or low temperatures, exposed to dangerous conditions such as fumes and diseases) as well as the social environment in which work is performed (e.g., teamwork, flexibility, and continuous learning). Increasingly, the degree of change and uncertainty associated with the job, the corporate culture, and elements of the organizational mission or vision statement are specified.

JOB INCUMBENTS

Job incumbents, *the people who are currently doing the job,* have the most direct knowledge about the tasks and competencies associated with a job. Incumbents usually provide input into job analysis by participating in an interview or responding to a questionnaire.

One concern in job analysis is selecting the particular job incumbents to include. If your publishing firm employs 30 copy editors, do you need to obtain information from them all in order to understand the job of a copy editor? Many companies feel that it is inefficient to survey everyone, so they select only a sample. When a sample is used, it must be a representative sample. That is, it should include men and women, members of different ethnic groups and nationalities, younger people as well as older ones, people who work in different divisions or regions, and so on.[23] A representative sample captures the full variety of perspectives among people in the job.

Line managers and incumbents usually agree about whether an incumbent performs specific tasks and duties. However, incumbents tend to see their jobs as requiring greater skill and knowledge than do line managers or outside job analysts. One reason for this difference is that job-specific information is more salient to incumbents who perform the work than it is to outsiders. The difference may also be due to self-enhancement. Because job

"The auto worker is almost a scientist in a technical way. He's required to know so many trades, he's required to know so much."

Joe Lo Galbo
Machinery repairman turned trainer
Ford Motor Company

Ex 5.5 Job Analysis Inaccuracy

SOURCE OF ERROR	POSSIBLE CONSEQUENCES	CONDITIONS LIKELY TO CAUSE ERROR
Low accuracy motivation	Incomplete information about job	Tasks aren't meaningful, the group is large, individuals do not feel accountable.
Impression management	Inflated descriptions of job or competency requirements	Job incumbents feel the job analysis results will be used to evaluate them as individuals.
Demand effects	Inflated agreement and inflated descriptions of job or competency requirements	Supervisors convey their preference for employees to portray their jobs as challenging and/or as more complex than in the past.
Reliance on heuristics and job stereotypes	Incomplete and unreliable task ratings	Too many items on a questionnaire, creating fatigue and loss of ability to differentiate among similar tasks.
Use of extraneous and irrelevant information	Inaccurate ratings, either inflated or deflated	Extraneous information about things such as employees' salaries and tenure levels are known.
Halo	All job tasks are given similar ratings	The rater has insufficient job information available, little personal knowledge of the job, or low motivation.
Leniency and severity	All job tasks are given high (lenient) or low (severe) ratings	Leniency is more likely when it can result in benefits for the raters (e.g., a possible pay raise). Severity may occur if the job analyst thinks it may benefit the organization (e.g., help justify elimination of a job or low wages).

analysis is related to many human resource outcomes—for example, performance appraisal and compensation—incumbents, and to a lesser extent their supervisors, may exaggerate job duties in order to maximize organizational rewards and self-esteem.[24]

Although incumbents may inflate the difficulty of their jobs, there are still good reasons to include them in the job analysis process. First, they're the source of the most current and accurate information about the job. Second, their inclusion allows line managers and incumbents to gain a shared perspective about job expectations. Third, including incumbents can increase perceptions of procedural fairness and reduce resistance to changes that might be introduced on the basis of job analysis results.

SUPERVISORS

FAST FACT

In most convenience stores, 25 inches separate a cashier and customer, 80 inches separate two cashiers, and managers are far from the work floor.

Like incumbents, supervisors (line managers) have direct information about the duties associated with a job. Therefore, they're also considered SMEs. Yet, because they're not currently performing the job, supervisors may find it more difficult to explain all the tasks involved in it. This is especially true of tasks the supervisors cannot observe directly, such as mental tasks or tasks performed out in the field. On the other hand, supervisors who have seen more than one job incumbent perform a job bring a broader perspective to the job analysis process. Supervisors also may be in a better position to describe what tasks should be included in the job, and what tasks could be included if the job is to be redesigned.[25]

TRAINED JOB ANALYSTS

Some methods of job analysis require input from trained job analysts. Supervisors or incumbents can be taught to serve as job analysts, but usually outside consultants or members of the company's HR staff perform this role.

An advantage of enlisting the help of trained job analysts is that they can observe many different incumbents working under different supervisors and in different locations. Trained job analysts also can read through organizational records and technical documentation and provide information culled from these indirect sources. Furthermore, trained experts are more likely to appreciate fully the legal issues associated with conducting job analysis. Nevertheless, like every other source of information, trained job analysts are imperfect. One drawback to using their skills is that, like supervisors, they cannot observe all aspects of a job. They can see the physical aspects, but not the mental and emotional demands. Also, they may rely too much on their own stereotypes about what a job involves, based on the job title, rather than attending to all the available information. Finally, especially in the case of outside consultants, their services may be expensive.

CUSTOMERS

If satisfying customers is a strategic imperative, it seems obvious that customers should also be used as subject matter experts. In actuality, this is seldom done. Collecting information from customers has been considered to be a marketing activity rather than an HR activity. Yet, in some jobs, customers are clearly an excellent source of information about a job. For example, cashiers spend 78% of their time interacting with customers and only 13% of their time interacting with managers.[26] For jobs like these, it seems obvious that using customers as SMEs is likely to become more common as organizations increasingly incorporate the perspectives of customers when designing jobs and assessing employee performance.

METHODS OF COLLECTING INFORMATION

Just as many sources provide information about jobs and the organization as a whole, many methods are used to obtain that information. The three most common ways to collect job and organizational analysis information are: (1) observations; (2) individual and group interviews; and (3) questionnaires.

OBSERVATIONS

Observing workers as they perform their work provides rich information about the tasks involved. Observation may mean simply watching people do their jobs, or it may include video-

FAST FACT

Almost all freight trucks are fitted with electronic engines programmed to control speed and gear-shifting and satellite dishes used to monitor the trucks' exact locations at all times.

taping, audiotaping, and computer monitoring. Physical measurements of activities performed, such as measurements of objects that must be moved and descriptions of how equipment is operated, often require some observation of the job as it is performed. Through observation of a "filler" in the original Ben & Jerry's Homemade ice cream factory, an observer could learn that this job involved two basic tasks. At a time when hand-filled pints of ice cream were unusual in the industry, the filler job at Ben & Jerry's required holding a pint container under a pipe that exuded ice cream and then pulling the pint away at just the moment it was filled. At the same time, the filler moved another container under the pipe. As the second container filled, the other hand was used to print a production code on the bottom of the filled container and slide it along a table to the next workstation. Fillers did this over and over again, all day long.[27]

Observation can be very time-consuming, especially if the work tasks and conditions change depending on the time of day or on a seasonal basis. To be practical, the use of observation generally requires sampling. **Work sampling** *refers to the process of taking instantaneous samples of the work activities of individuals or groups of individuals.* A haphazard work sampling approach—which yields equally haphazard results—is to simply observe the work being performed when it's convenient for the job analyst. Systematic work sampling yields better information. To be systematic, a job analyst can observe the incumbent at predetermined times.[28]

INDIVIDUAL AND GROUP INTERVIEWS

Many jobs include tasks that are difficult to observe. The components of the larger organizational system—the structure, culture, and strategy—also may be difficult to discern through simple observation. A better way to understand some jobs and the organizational context may be to conduct interviews with the various people touched by them. For example, to really understand the job of a software designer who develops customized graphics programs for commercial printers, you might interview job incumbents, their supervisors, members of their product design teams, staff members who write the computer codes to implement their designs, and the customers who ultimately define their objectives. Interviews can be conducted individually, or groups of employees can be interviewed together in a focus group. Individual interviews are useful because there is less chance that social pressures will distort the responses of employees. On the other hand, focus groups are useful because employees tend to stimulate each other to think of more ideas. Again, combining multiple approaches to obtaining information is usually the best solution.

QUESTIONNAIRES

Questionnaires are useful for collecting information from many different people because they're more economical than interviews or observations, especially when they are administered electronically. In recent years, information technology has made collecting and analyzing job analysis ratings much quicker and easier, thus removing a major obstacle to the regular use of job analysis.

Questionnaires may be developed for specific circumstances, or standardized questionnaires may be purchased from external vendors. Standardized questionnaires are more economical. Often an added benefit is that the vendor can provide useful information from a larger database. On the other hand, customized questionnaires usually yield information that is more specific to the particular jobs involved. This feature is especially useful for writing meaningful job descriptions and for developing performance measures.

METHODS ANALYSIS

Methods analysis *focuses on analyzing job elements, which are the smallest identifiable components of a job.* Methods analysis can be used, for example, to assess minute physical movements to determine whether they're efficient and to identify those that cause undue strain. Two types of methods analysis are time-and-motion studies and the human factors approach.

 FAST FACT The family life of Frank and Lillian Gilbreth was the inspiration for the best-selling books titled *Cheaper by the Dozen* and *Belles on Their Toes*, which were written by their son.

TIME-AND-MOTION STUDIES

A **time-and-motion study** *involves identifying and measuring a worker's physical movements when performing tasks and then analyzing the results to determine whether some motions can be eliminated or performed more efficiently.* Time-and-motion studies were popularized at the dawn of the industrial revolution by a team of engineers named Frank and Lillian Gilbreth. The Gilbreths used the newly invented motion camera to study the motions of workers and make recommendations for how their work could be carried out with fewer movements that required less physical effort.

At UPS, methods analysis has helped the company thrive, despite stiff competition. In the business where "a package is a package," UPS has always understood that the way people do their work has direct consequences for the company's profitability. In the 1920s, UPS engineers cut away the sides of UPS trucks to study the drivers. Changes in equipment and procedures were then made to enhance workers' efficiency. Today, the study of workers' behavior on the job continues. In one project, a time-and-motion study was used to discover how drivers naturally carried packages and how they handled money received from customers. Job design experts then determined the best way to carry packages (under the left arm) and how to handle money (place it face-up before folding). Training programs now incorporate this information.

As jobs have become more knowledge-intensive and less labor-intensive, many organizations have shifted away from methods analysis. Nevertheless, it's still used by companies such as UPS and Lincoln Electric that rely heavily on human labor to carry out repetitive and routine tasks accurately and efficiently.

"They do everything through computers. The supervisor says you have to do 20.2 stops an hour and you can only do 15. Next day the supervisor tells you it took you two hours longer than the computer says it should take; it's terrible."

Edward Martin
Package Truck Driver
UPS

HUMAN FACTORS APPROACH

The objective of the **human factors approach** *(also known as ergonomic analysis) is to minimize the amount of stress and fatigue experienced as a result of doing work; the focus is on understanding how job tasks affect physical movements and* *physiological responses.*[29] For example, with an understanding of the biomechanics of the wrist, arm, and shoulder, ergonomic analysis of office jobs can be used to identify sources of unnecessary strain. Office equipment that causes unnecessary strain might then be replaced, workers may be trained to operate the equipment in ways that minimize strain, or other accommodations may be made to safeguard employees' health.

The human factors approach to job analysis and redesign has proved useful in automobile factories, where the physical capabilities of the workforce have changed as this workforce has aged. On average, U.S. autoworkers are now more than a decade older than their counterparts in Japan. This makes it increasingly difficult to achieve productivity gains by using the traditional approach of just speeding up the assembly line. Ergonomic analysis of these jobs has helped U.S. auto companies identify the sources of strain that affect their older workers and has guided the auto industry's efforts to redesign plants and install equipment to ease the strain. Now, overhead conveyor belts tilt auto bodies at angles that make assembly work less physically demanding, and the air guns used to drive screws are designed to reduce the stresses that cause carpal tunnel syndrome. Gyms have been installed, and workers have taken "back classes" to learn how to lift without injuring themselves. More discussion of ergonomics is found in Chapter 13, which covers health and safety.

FAST FACT

Eighty percent of us will sustain a back injury during our lifetime.

GENERIC JOB ANALYSIS

For some situations, generic job analysis results may be sufficient to meet an organization's needs. Generic job analysis results are published by the federal government in the *Dictionary of Occupational Titles (DOT)* and electronically on the Occupational Information Network (O*NET).

DICTIONARY OF OCCUPATIONAL TITLES (DOT)

The U.S. Training and Employment Service developed a method called functional job analysis during the 1950s and 1960s to improve job placement and counseling for workers registering at local state employment offices. To conduct a **functional job analysis (FJA),** *trained observers rate tasks performed in jobs according to the level of functioning required by the job incumbents as they work with data, people, and things.*[30] Sidney A. Fine, the acknowledged father of this technique, first used functional job analysis to analyze the jobs of social workers for the Rehabilitation Service of the U.S. Department of Health. Since then, hundreds of thousands of jobs have been analyzed using FJA.

The U.S. Department of Labor has used FJA as a basis for describing thousands of jobs. Since the 1930s, these results have been made available to the public in the *Dictionary of Occupational Titles (DOT)*. Although the *DOT* is now in the process of being replaced by the O*NET (see next section), it is likely to be many years before all organizations fully replace the HRM systems that have been built around job descriptions found in the *DOT*. An example of a *DOT* job description follows:

FAST FACT

The *DOT* describes 12,000 "different" occupations.

JOB ANALYST alternate title: personnel analyst.

Collects, analyzes, and prepares occupational information to facilitate personnel, administration, and management functions of organization. Consults with management to determine type, scope, and purpose of study. Studies current organizational occupational data and compiles distribution reports, organization and flow charts, and other background information required for study. Observes jobs and interviews workers and supervisory personnel to determine job and worker requirements. Analyzes occupational data, such as physical, mental, and training requirements of jobs and workers and develops written summaries, such as job descriptions, job specifications, and lines of career movement. Utilizes developed occupational data to evaluate or improve methods and techniques for recruiting, selecting, promoting, evaluating, and training workers, and administration of related personnel programs. May specialize in classifying positions according to regulated guidelines to meet job classification requirements of civil service system and be known as Position Classifier.

Occupational Information Network (O*NET)

The U.S. Department of Labor's new job analysis service, which was first released to the public in 1998, is titled the Occupational Information Network (O*NET). Available on the Internet, **O*NET** *provides a comprehensive database system for collecting, organizing, describing, and disseminating data on job characteristics and worker attributes.*[31] O*NET describes jobs using the six content areas shown in Exhibit 5.6.[32]

Perhaps the most innovative aspect of O*NET is that it places information about jobs and the people who fill those jobs into an organizational and economic context. For example, O*NET provides descriptions of the labor market conditions, wages, and the future occupational outlook for the jobs included in it. O*NET also describes the typical organizational context in which a job is likely to be found. Such information is useful to HR professionals interested in projecting future labor supplies and recruitment strategies. It is also useful to high school and college students choosing their future careers.

O*NET is intended to serve as a resource for anyone who seeks to make informed employment decisions. Employers and employees can get facts about occupations and jobs by visiting O*NET's home page and searching the database. For example, a search for information about "actuaries" yielded details about the

- specific tasks actuaries perform,
- work conditions of typical jobs,
- education needed to become an actuary (including recommendations that can be used when selecting college courses),
- examinations and occupational certifications that are required for advancement in the profession,
- average salaries for actuaries at different stages of their careers, and
- typical work values of people in this occupation.

O*NET is an important resource for private and public employers. Suppose you're a line manager in a small business. You want to provide job

Ex 5.6   O*NET Content Model for Describing Jobs

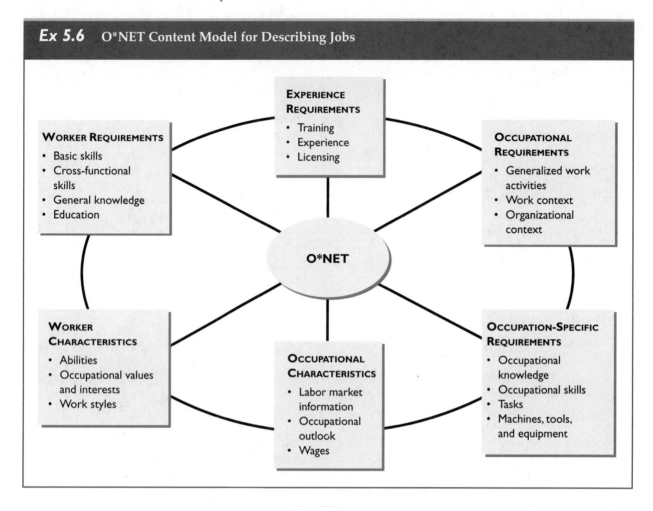

descriptions for all of your employees. How can you do this given your limited resources? O*NET offers one solution. You can find a detailed job description and then adapt it to fit the specific conditions in your company. O*NET can be consulted quickly, and it's essentially free. Furthermore, the job descriptions available through O*NET are based on hundreds of observations.

With a bit of research, you'll soon discover that O*NET is not the only resource of this kind. You can purchase a commercial software product that includes hundreds of job descriptions, ready for you to edit and tailor to your needs. Quick and relatively inexpensive, the software package may be a good alternative to O*NET. But before deciding whether to purchase such commercial software, you need to know whether the procedures used to generate the job descriptions were rigorous. What sources of information were used to generate the job descriptions? Were acceptable job analysis procedures followed in creating the job descriptions, or are the job descriptions just convenient examples? Unless you can be certain that systematic job analysis procedures were applied to very large samples of incumbents in each job of interest to you, O*NET is probably the best solution for this hypothetical small business.

STANDARDIZED JOB ANALYSIS QUESTIONNAIRES

A **standardized job analysis questionnaire** *can be used to collect ratings of behaviors and/or worker characteristics for a wide variety of jobs.* Usually, the ratings are provided by incumbents, supervisors, or HR professionals. The advantage of this approach is that it does not require trained job analysts to observe and rate jobs.

Because the items on standardized questionnaires are intentionally written to be applicable to a wide variety of jobs, they are somewhat general. Consider the job of salesperson in an ice cream parlor. Relevant items from a standardized questionnaire might read "Works in an enclosed area that is cold" and "Chooses among items that differ in terms of color." The value of using such general statements is that they allow you to analyze all types of jobs using the same items. You could use the same questionnaire to analyze the jobs performed by the production workers who make ice cream, the packers who prepare it for shipping, the drivers who deliver it to locations around town, and the salespeople who eventually serve it to customers.

Two of the most widely used standardized job analysis questionnaires are the Position Analysis Questionnaire and the Management Position Description Questionnaire. Both have been used to analyze thousands of different jobs in thousands of different organizations.

Position Analysis Questionnaire

The **Position Analysis Questionnaire (PAQ)** *is a standardized job analysis tool that measures the work behaviors required by a job and relates them to worker characteristics.* It can be used to analyze a wide variety of jobs that involve many different types of tasks, technologies, and duties.

The creator of the PAQ, Ernest J. McCormick, started with two assumptions: (1) a relatively small set of work behaviors are common to all jobs, and (2) all jobs can be described in terms of how much they involve each of these behaviors. Based on these assumptions, he developed a structured questionnaire containing 195 statements that describe worker behaviors. Each statement is rated on scales such as extent of use, importance to the job, and amount of time spent performing the job. The statements are organized into the six divisions shown in Exhibit 5.7.[33]

The PAQ has been used to analyze hundreds of jobs held by thousands of people. The results from many of these job analyses have been centrally stored in a database to allow comparisons between similar jobs in different organizations. The PAQ database also contains information about the relationships between PAQ responses, job aptitudes, and pay rates for the labor market. Thus, the PAQ can be used to decide what selection criteria to use when making hiring decisions, and it can be used to design pay packages. However, the PAQ must be bought from a consulting firm; consequently, direct costs appear to be high. Another potential drawback to using the PAQ is that it requires a postcollege reading comprehension level. Thus, the PAQ shouldn't be given to raters who have lower levels of reading skill or language fluency.[34]

Ex 5.7 The PAQ's Six Divisions for Organizing Work Behaviors

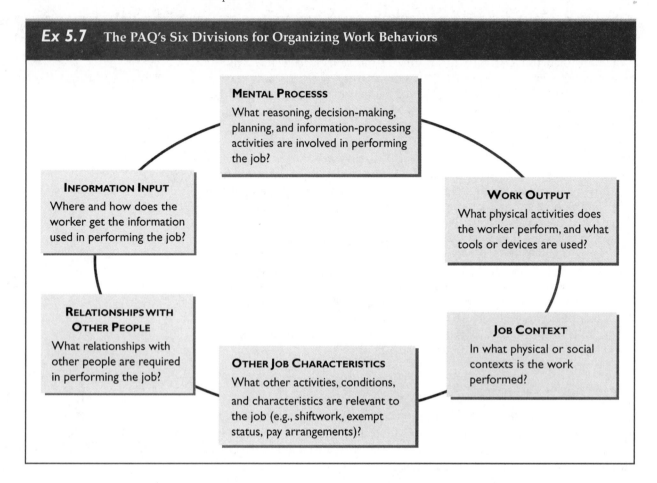

MANAGEMENT POSITION DESCRIPTION QUESTIONNAIRE

The **Management Position Description Questionnaire (MPDQ)** *is a standardized questionnaire containing 197 items related to managers' concerns, responsibilities, demands, restrictions, and miscellaneous characteristics.*[35] These items have been condensed into 13 essential components of managerial jobs, as illustrated in Exhibit 5.8.

The MPDQ is designed for analyzing all managerial positions, so responses are expected to vary by managerial level in any organization and also across different organizations. The MPDQ can be used to develop selection procedures and performance appraisal forms, to determine the training needs of employees moving into managerial jobs, and to design managerial pay systems.

CUSTOMIZED TASK INVENTORIES

Much of the early development work on creating customized job analysis inventories was conducted by the U.S. Air Force and AT&T.

FAST FACT

A **customized task inventory** *is a listing of tasks, work behaviors, or worker characteristics (called items) that has been created specifically for the jobs or group of jobs being analyzed.* The items in the inventory are developed as part of the job analysis process and are unique to the jobs being studied. A customized inventory is

Ex 5.8 Components of Managerial Jobs Assessed by the Managerial Position Description Questionnaire

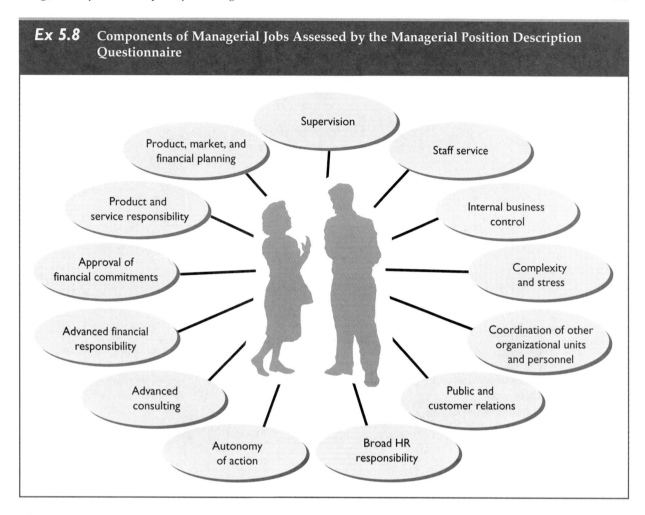

developed from the ground up for each new customer, such as a company, a unit within a company, or a manager.[36] If the job of Human Resource Analyst was analyzed using a customized task inventory, a part of the inventory might look like Exhibit 5.9.

The development of customized task inventories depends heavily on the cooperation of employees. Usually, they must be willing to have their behavior observed, participate in interviews, and respond to lengthy questionnaires. Furthermore, analyzing the results from this method requires complex statistical analysis. Consequently, the use of these instruments is usually limited to organizations that employ many people who work in essentially the same job or occupation (police, firefighters, data entry clerks).

The process of conducting a job analysis using a customized inventory involves using multiple sources of information and multiple methods for collecting information. Usually, observations and interviews are used to learn about the basic activities involved in the jobs being analyzed. Then questionnaires are developed and used to systematically collect more detailed information. In the end, the payoff for this effort is a very detailed

Ex 5.9 Job Analysis Questionnaire for Human Resource Analyst I

WORK BEHAVIORS	A. Is the work behavior performed in the position? 1 = Yes 0 = No	B. Indicate the percentage of time spent performing it. The percentages must total exactly 100.	C. How important is it that this work behavior be performed acceptably? 4 = Critical 3 = Very important 2 = Moderately important 1 = Slightly important 0 = Of no importance	D. Is it necessary that employees new to the position be able to perform this work behavior? 1 = Yes 0 = No
	(circle one)	(fill in)	(circle one)	(circle one)
1. *Counsels employees* on various matters (career opportunities, insurance and retirement options, personal problems relating to employment, etc.) by listening, asking relevant questions, and noting alternative courses of action.	1 0	_____%	4 3 2 1 0	1 0
2. *Disseminates information* (job vacancies and requirements, insurance and retirement programs, merit system rules, etc.) to applicants, employees, and the public verbally through written materials and/or using electronic means.	1 0	_____%	4 3 2 1 0	1 0
3. *Prepares reports* (e.g., management reports, HUD reports) by collecting, organizing, and summarizing statistical data, historical documents, or verbal records, or all three.	1 0	_____%	4 3 2 1 0	1 0
4. *Interviews applicants or employees* in a structured or unstructured manner to investigate applicant or employee complaints, grievances, or adverse action appeal cases and to identify qualified applicants for specific job vacancies.	1 0	_____%	4 3 2 1 0	1 0
5. *Conducts job analyses* by reviewing written records (e.g., job descriptions, class specifications), observing and interviewing job experts, and administering questionnaires.	1 0	_____%	4 3 2 1 0	1 0
		Total = 100%		

understanding of the jobs being analyzed. Exhibit 5.10 illustrates how the job of an administrative assistant was described following a job analysis that used a customized inventory.

DEVELOPING A CUSTOMIZED INVENTORY

The items that appear in a customized job analysis inventory can be generated in a variety of ways. The basic procedures are always the same, how-

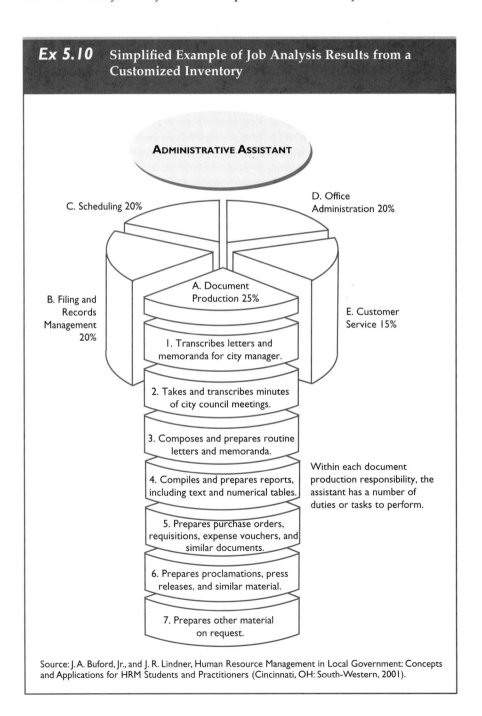

Ex 5.10 Simplified Example of Job Analysis Results from a Customized Inventory

ADMINISTRATIVE ASSISTANT

C. Scheduling 20%

D. Office Administration 20%

B. Filing and Records Management 20%

A. Document Production 25%

E. Customer Service 15%

1. Transcribes letters and memoranda for city manager.

2. Takes and transcribes minutes of city council meetings.

3. Composes and prepares routine letters and memoranda.

4. Compiles and prepares reports, including text and numerical tables.

Within each document production responsibility, the assistant has a number of duties or tasks to perform.

5. Prepares purchase orders, requisitions, expense vouchers, and similar documents.

6. Prepares proclamations, press releases, and similar material.

7. Prepares other material on request.

Source: J. A. Buford, Jr., and J. R. Lindner, Human Resource Management in Local Government: Concepts and Applications for HRM Students and Practitioners (Cincinnati, OH: South-Western, 2001).

ever: First, items are generated for the jobs of interest; then a questionnaire is created and used to collect job ratings.

Generating Items.   Usually, a job analyst begins by observing the job being performed by incumbents and reviewing samples of the materials, forms, and equipment used in the job. Brief, informal interviews may be conducted during this phase, if needed, to clarify observations and identify the purpose of employee activities. This step familiarizes job analysts with various aspects of the job.

During this phase, some job analysts also ask job incumbents and supervisors to describe critical incidents that represent effective or ineffective performance.[37] Those describing the incidents are asked to describe what led up to the incidents, what the consequences of the behavior were, and whether the behavior was under the incumbent's control.

Creating a Questionnaire.   Based on observations, interviews, and reports about critical incidents, the job analyst writes task statements. For example, the librarian's critical incident report was used to create a list of more than 200 task statements like these:

- Handles serious disturbances created by users of the library.
- Represents the library to members of the news media (e.g., reporters).

The items generated from critical incidents are used to create a job analysis questionnaire like the one shown in Exhibit 5.9.

ANALYZING AND INTERPRETING THE DATA

Ratings from the custom-designed questionnaire are arithmetically combined to arrive at a description of the job. Finally, work behaviors included in the job description are screened based on the combined ratings. Each work behavior must meet several minimum criteria in order to be a "qualifying" work behavior that goes into the job description. A "qualifying" work behavior is one performed by the majority of job incumbents.

Exhibit 5.11 shows partial results of work behavior ratings for the job of HR analyst. Item 5 ("Conduct Job Analyses") would be eliminated at this step in the process because it doesn't qualify as being part of the job for most incumbents.

ADVANTAGES AND DISADVANTAGES

A major advantage of customized task inventories is that they generate vivid descriptions of the job. When reading a job description developed with this method, it's easy to picture what the job involves. Rather than generating abstract descriptions that could apply to any job, this method creates specific descriptions that clearly outline the tasks required. This advantage makes it easier to develop training programs for the people who will do the job.[38]

The major disadvantages of customized inventories are the time required to develop the task statements and the complex data analysis required after the ratings have been obtained. For example, one job analysis conducted for an organization with 120 positions (i.e., 120 employees) involved 106,000 task ratings; another job analysis for an organization with 3,600 positions

Ex 5.11   Job Analysis Results for Human Resource Analyst I

		WORK BEHAVIOR RATINGS		
ITEM	WORK BEHAVIOR	PERCENTAGE WHO PERFORM	MEAN PERCENTAGE OF TIME SPENT	MEDIAN IMPORTANCE RATING*
1	Counsels employees	100	5	2
2	Disseminates information	100	20	3
3	Prepares reports	100	33	3
4	Interviews applicants	100	14	2
5	Conducts job analyses	10	8	0

Note: Importance ratings are based on the responses of only SMEs who perform the task.

*Scale for median importance rating:

3 = Critical

2 = Very important

1 = Moderately important

0 = Of slight or no importance

involved 1.8 million ratings. Desktop software, computers, intranets, and even artificial intelligence systems can ease the task of collecting and analyzing data sets like these, so this disadvantage is not as significant as it was just a few years ago.[39] Nevertheless, even large firms often rely on consultants who specialize in this work rather than perform the complex analyses required.

ANALYZING NEEDED COMPETENCIES

Information about required competencies is essential if job analysis results are going to be used to develop procedures for selecting people to perform jobs effectively and to design training programs. Competency information also can be obtained using either a standardized or customized approach.

STANDARDIZED APPROACH

Many consulting firms that perform job analysis collect competency information using fairly standardized procedures.[40] For example, Personnel Decisions Inc. developed a taxonomy of managerial competencies that includes the following basic domains:

- Thinking, which includes analytical agility, creativity, planning, strategy development, and business-specific knowledge;
- Communications, which includes verbal, written, listening, and public speaking skills;
- Inter/intrapersonal, which includes teamwork, influencing, adapatability, and dependability;
- Leadership, which includes supervision, motivation, decisiveness, and work commitment;

- Motivation, which includes driving for results and showing commitment;
- Self-management, which includes acting with integrity, being adaptable, and self-development;
- General operations management, which includes materials management, facilities and security, information management, and international operations; and
- Functional business knowledge, which includes economics, accounting and finance, marketing and sales, and managing human resources.[41]

When a company hires this firm to conduct a job analysis for managerial jobs, the consultants use a fairly standardized process to assess the required levels of competencies for the focal jobs.

Customized Approach

The example analysis questionnaire shown in Exhibit 5.12 illustrates a customized method to assess the competencies needed for a job. The procedure involves asking subject matter experts (usually incumbents and supervisors) to identify all the skills, knowledge, attitudes, values, and so on that they think may be necessary to perform the work. A group interview meeting may be held to create the list of possible competencies to examine. Based on the results of the group interview meeting, a competency rating questionnaire is created and distributed to the SMEs. Respondents rate the competencies along a number of dimensions: (1) whether the competency is required at all; (2) its importance ; (3) whether a new incumbent needs the competency upon entry to the job; and 4) the extent to which the competency distinguishes a highly effective incumbent from an adequate one.

Exhibit 5.13 shows the results of the competency ratings. These results indicate that the organization should ensure that new hires have a good knowledge of HR procedures and good computer skills, as well as some familiarity with relevant laws and ethical standards. To maximize performance, the organization may want to offer additional training in both HR procedures and legal and ethical standards. Investing in computer training for new hires may not pay off as much, however. While computer skills are necessary, they do not contribute much to outstanding performance.

Global Leadership Competencies at 3M

At 3M, two forces put pressure on the organization to invest in conducting a customized competency-based job analysis. As was true at many other companies, the decade of the 1990s brought increased global competition. The fierce competition, in turn, highlighted the need for highly effective leaders who could steer the company through a period of shrinking margins, pressures on pricing, and the ever-present demand for new innovations. This environment highlighted the importance of succession planning as an activity that could promote the company's long-term viability. As described in the feature "Managing Globalization: Modeling Leadership Competencies at 3M," a customized competency model helped this company address this long-term strategic issue.

Ex 5.12 Questionnaire to Identify Competencies Needed for Human Resource Analyst I

COMPETENCIES	1. Is the competency used in the position? 1 = Yes 0 = No	2. How important is this competency to acceptable job performance? 4 = Critical 3 = Very important 2 = Moderately important 1 = Slightly important 0 = Of no importance	3. Is it necessary that employees new to the position possess this competency? 1 = Yes 0 = No	4. To what extent does this distinguish between superior and adequate new employees? 3 = To a great extent 2 = Considerably 1 = Moderately 0 = Not at all
	(circle one)	(circle one)	(circle one)	(circle one)
1. *Knowledge of HR procedures:* Knowledge of the working rules and regulations. Included are policies on overtime, absences, vacations, holidays, sick leave, court leave, selection, promotion, reassignment, disciplinary actions, terminations, grievance procedures, performance appraisals, and so forth, as outlined in relevant manuals.	1 0	4 3 2 1 0	1 0	3 2 1 0
2. *Knowledge of organizational structure:* Knowledge of whom to contact when various situations arise. Included is the knowledge of interrelationships between organizational units, lines of authority, and responsibility within organizational units.	1 0	4 3 2 1 0	1 0	3 2 1 0
3. *Knowledge of laws and ethics:* Knowledge of legal and ethical standards to be maintained in HR work. Included are ethical considerations governing general professional practice (e.g., confidentiality of records) as well as state and federal regulations governing fair employment practices (e.g., EEO legislation and the *Uniform Guidelines on Employee Selection Procedures*).	1 0	4 3 2 1 0	1 0	3 2 1 0
4. *Computer skill:* Skill in the use of a computer. Included is a basic knowledge of the keyboard and of computer terminology.	1 0	4 3 2 1 0	1 0	3 2 1 0

Ex 5.13   Competency Rating Results for Human Resource Analyst I

COMPETENCY RATINGS

ITEM	COMPETENCY	PERCENTAGE WHO USE IT	MEDIAN IMPORTANCE RATING*	PERCENTAGE RATING IT AS NECESSARY AT ENTRY	MEDIAN RATING FOR DISTINGUISHING SUPERIOR EMPLOYEES**
1	Knowledge of HR procedures	100	2.5	70	3.0
2	Knowledge of organizational structure	100	2.0	0	2.0
3	Knowledge of laws and ethics	100	2.0	60	2.5
4	Computer skill	100	2.5	80	0.5

Note: Ratings provided by job incumbents. Results are shown only for SMEs who reported they use the competency.

*Scale for importance ratings:

4 = Critical
3 = Very important
2 = Moderately important
1 = Slightly important
0 = Of no importance

**Scale for extent to which competency distinguishes superior from average employees in the job:

3 = To a great extent
2 = Considerably
1 = Moderately
0 = Slightly or not at all

At 3M, the belief is that the specific desired behaviors and the leadership competencies can be developed. You will learn how 3M does this in Chapter 8, which covers training and development.

CAREER PATHS

The initial results of job analyses are typically many separate and unique job descriptions and employee specifications—as many as there are unique jobs. Often, however, these unique jobs do not differ greatly from each other. That is, employees who perform one job may be able to perform several others. And, increasingly, flexibility is what employers need. This is why many organizations are reducing the number of group titles and creating job descriptions that are broader in scope.[42] By identifying jobs that require similar competencies, a company can help their employees see the logical progression that their careers might take if they stay with the company for a period of years.

Managing Globalization

Modeling Leadership Competencies at 3M

Due to the breadth of businesses and technologies within 3M, it takes years of experience before executives learn to function effectively in the company. Thoughtful succession planning efforts would ensure that the occasional managerial and executive job openings were leveraged as opportunities for leadership development.

Customized Approach. The decision to use a customized approach to developing a leadership competency model for the company fit well with this company's culture. Innovation is a core competence for 3M, and employees are constantly tinkering with products and systems in order to improve them.

Partnership Perspective. The customized approach also served the objective of involving all key players in the process. Human resource professionals worked hand-in-hand with a team of key executives. The process of developing the leadership competency model required getting input from the CEO, from executives who report directly to the CEO, and from representatives in Europe, Asia, Latin America, Canada, and the United States.

    Rather than simply hand the executives an off-the-shelf competency model, the HR professionals held meetings and discussions with the executives to solicit their ideas, craft the language used in describing the competencies, and so on. After all, the leadership competency model would have important implications for the careers of key talent within the company. Involving executives early in the process contributed to the validity of the model and enhanced their acceptance of it.

Strategic Importance. The 12 dimensions of 3M's global leadership competency model reflect the company's corporate values and business strategy. At 3M, the stated values are:

- We satisfy customers with superior quality, value, and service.
- We provide our investors with a fair rate of return through sustained quality growth.
- We respect our social and physical environment.
- We work to make 3M a company employees are proud to be a part of.

These values are apparent in competency dimensions such as "customer orientation," "ethics and integrity," and "developing people."

Behavioral Anchors. Associated with each of 3M's global leadership competencies are specific behaviors that illustrate exemplary levels of competency. Information about the specific behaviors displayed by top-level executives is used by the CEO during his annual review of these executives. Elsewhere in the company, executives and managers refer to the specific behaviors when setting performance expectations, judging performance, and discussing the development needs of their employees. As an example, specific behaviors associated with the competency of "global perspective" include:

- Respects, values, and leverages other customs, cultures, and values.
- Uses global management team to understand and grow the total business.
- Able to leverage the benefits from working in multicultural environments.
- Optimizes and integrates resources on a global basis, including manufacturing, research, and businesses across countries, and functions to increase 3M's growth and profitability.
- Satisfies global customers and markets from anywhere in the world.
- Actively stays current on world economies, trade issues, international market trends, and opportunities.

MANAGING CAREERS

The challenge of providing employees with a satisfying and longer-term career is one that Hovnanian, a large national construction company, faced during the 1990s when a boom in the housing market created a very tight labor market for this industry. The company used job analysis to design a "homebuilding career path." Typically, employees begin their careers working as construction technicians, doing basic carpentry and trade work. As they develop the necessary skills, they can move up to positions that involve greater scope and responsibility. For example, community administrators

"Creating a well-understood path for personal development within our organization enables our Associates to be the best in the business, achieve individual aspirations, and contribute to our strategic business vision."

Ara Hovnanian
President and CEO
K. Hovnanian Companies

become involved in sales and service activities, as well as basic construction work. At higher career levels, the work involves supervising various aspects of the company's building projects. At the highest levels, the work includes activities related to building and sustaining a competitive corporation. Using job analysis, Hovnanian identified a logical progression of jobs that employees could move through if they wanted to advance up the corporate ladder. For all jobs, they pinpointed the skills and knowledge needed to perform the work. Based on this information, they developed training modules and procedures for assessing the competencies of their employees. Finally, the results were used to develop job performance measures that reflected the key responsibilities associated with each job.

Broadbanding

When related jobs are grouped into only a very small set of categories, the term **broadbanding** is used. Broadbanding involves clustering jobs into wide tiers. One use of broadbanding is managing employee career growth—which is what Hovnanian did. Another common reason to engage in broadbanding is to simplify the company's pay system. Flatter and broader pay scales are appropriate for flatter organizational structures, where job descriptions encompass a broad class of jobs rather than specific jobs.[43] Chapter 9 presents a more detailed discussion of how broadbanding is used for pay administration.[44]

MetLife Auto and Home used a modified broadbanding approach to support a new corporate culture that placed less emphasis on rules and more emphasis on flexibility. Their broadbanding approach is described in the feature "Managing Change: Revising Job Analysis to Achieve Business Objectives at Met Life."[45]

TRENDS IN JOB ANALYSIS

At some organizations, such as AT&T and Microsoft, technological changes occur so rapidly that traditional job analysis is all but impossible. And increasingly, job requirements are hard to specify because companies expect employees to do "whatever the customer wants." In these situations, job analysis must be dynamic and fluid. Here, the HR professionals, line managers, and employees all need to value flexibility and adaptability. The fast-paced world of the 21st century poses particularly great challenges for job analysis.

The Decline of Job Analysis?

Decreased job specialization, increased job sharing, and the increased prevalence of work teams are just a few of the reasons why people have begun to question the usefulness of traditional job analysis techniques. Traditional techniques force boundaries to be drawn between jobs and are inconsistent with the trend toward increased sharing of responsibilities across jobs and across levels in the organization.[46]

The apparent inconsistency between the assumptions of traditional job analysis and new approaches to managing employees is so great that it has

Revising Job Analysis to Achieve Business Objectives at Met Life

MetLife Auto and Home was a traditional company with a traditional culture. "We loved job titles and job descriptions," explained Carolyn MacDonald, the Director of Human Resources. "There was a sense of security with our job titles." With 732 job descriptions, there seemed to be more than enough security to go around. But competition was heating up in the insurance industry, and MacDonald sensed the need for change.

After studying what was needed to succeed in the future, MacDonald and her staff concluded that employees should be valued and rewarded based on their individual contributions rather than job titles. Broadbanding seemed to offer one solution. With a broadbanding approach, MacDonald could reduce hundreds of narrowly defined jobs to a few dozen more broadly defined jobs. After several months of research aimed at better understanding both the needs of the organization and employees' concerns, MacDonald and her staff decided to completely eliminate job descriptions and salary ranges. The new approach would give managers the flexibility needed to move employees around in the organization, and it would give employees opportunities to accept new challenges without worrying about whether taking a new position would result in lower pay or status.

A new organizational architecture was designed. Its four key elements are career bands, corporate profiles, functional profiles, and employee development continuums.

Career bands describe the five types of careers followed by most employees: leadership, professional, technical, management, and administrative.

Corporate profiles describe seven areas of competencies that *all* employees should display: knowledge, customer relations, impact/execution, decision making, innovation, communication, and ethics/quality. For each career band, a corporate profile details the responsibilities of people who are moving along that career ladder. For example, for the domain of "innovation," professionals "encourage and foster a learning environment that encompasses a theoretical or scientific area of expertise and its applicability to MetLife Auto and Home." Within this system, no profile is superior to the others, and there are no salary ranges associated with the profiles.

Function profiles describe departmental roles and are used in place of traditional job descriptions. The function profiles describe what is to be achieved and the competencies needed to achieve it. For example, the function of a trainer is to "develop and/or administer programs that will educate claims personnel and enhance the skills necessary to facilitate individual personal and professional development." Performing this function requires knowledge of the company's claims procedures and state regulations, a basic understanding of learning and instructional techniques, effective communication skills, the ability to work independently, as well as several other specified competencies.

Finally, an *employee development continuum* describes how employees can continuously develop their competencies. In this new culture, titles do little more that indicate one's general function. The employees' level of development is what determines their value to the organization, regardless of which career track they're following or which department they work in.

led some HR professionals to raise the question: "Do we need job analysis anymore?" We think the answer to this question is clearly, yes. What seems to be changing, however, is the preference for competency-based approaches to job analysis, over other traditional approaches. As we stated at the beginning of this chapter, job analysis and competency modeling can be valuable tools during strategic change. Also, job analysis is essential to any organization concerned about legal compliance and its ability to defend its employment practices (the legal status of competency modeling is not as well established, however). Clearly, organizations will continue to use job analysis in some form as a foundation upon which to build integrated HRM systems.

While job analysis will not disappear, the procedures used are likely to evolve and change to meet the new needs of organizations. The increasing popularity of competency modeling (instead of task-focused job analysis) is one example of how job analysis is evolving. Part of the appeal of competency modeling seems to be that it is more useful for identifying the "core" competencies and behaviors that are *similar* across all jobs in a department, business unit, or organization. When these are included in employees' job descriptions, competency modeling serves as a tool for defining and communicating a consistent corporate culture.

FROM "MY JOB" TO "MY ROLE"

"The job is just a social artifact. Most societies since the beginning of time have done fine without jobs. In the preindustrial past, people worked very hard, but they did not have jobs."

William Bridges
Author
Job Shift

Traditional job analysis techniques were developed during a time when organizations and jobs were more stable and predictable. People could be hired to do a particular job, and they could expect to do basically the same job in the same way for many months or even years. This arrangement was convenient for management and workers, except when management wanted the workers to change or do something "not in their job descriptions."

Flexibility.   Today's environment requires adaptable organizations and flexible individuals. Organizations focus on how they can get flexibility without worker resistance, while also satisfying workers' needs for comfort. Organizations such as Nissan and Honda hire applicants to work for the company rather than to do a specific job. At Southwest Airlines, HR people like to say that they hire people to do work, not jobs. Thus we are seeing a shift in the employee's attention—from thinking only about doing "my job" to thinking about doing whatever is necessary to accomplish the organization's work.[47] Corresponding to this, some human resource professionals have argued that the term *role analysis* should be used in place of the term *job analysis*.[48] Focusing on roles when conducting job analysis and writing job descriptions is consistent with the philosophy of emphasizing results over procedures, and it works well in organizations that allow employees to use flexible work arrangements, such as telecommuting and flextime, to adapt work requirements to their personal needs.[49]

"The shelf-life of job analysis results is only as long as the duration of the current job configurations."

Karen E. May
Partner
Human Resource Solutions

Teamwork.   This shift from a focus on "the job" to work roles is almost inevitable in organizations where work is organized around teams instead of individuals. In a team environment, the tasks performed by a particular individual may depend on the talents and interests of the other people in the team. The team as a whole is assigned duties and may be held accountable for specific tasks. If the team is self-managed, the team members can organize the team's work in any way they wish. In such situations, asking individuals about their role as a team member may be much more useful than asking them to describe their "individual job."[50]

FUTURE-ORIENTED JOB ANALYSIS AND COMPETENCY MODELING

To address the reality of constant change, both traditional job analysis and competency modeling procedures can be easily modified to provide information about the likely nature of future job tasks and the competencies that employees are likely to need to perform those new tasks. In a **future-**

oriented job analysis, *the emphasis shifts from descriptions of the present to prescriptions about the probable future.*

For example, suppose an organization has decided to downsize. Traditional job analysis could be used to identify all the tasks currently being performed by employees. Then, a future-oriented job analysis could be conducted to focus attention on the question of which tasks the organization *should* continue doing, and which ones they should eliminate or outsource. Thus, in this example, a future-oriented job analysis would be included as part of the organization's strategic planning processes. Following the process of HR planning described in Chapter 4, the results of the future-oriented job analysis would serve as a foundation for developing new HR policies and practices related to hiring, training, performance measurement, pay, and so on.[51]

SUMMARY

The creation and maintenance of effective organizations require a comprehensive understanding of the work that needs to be done and the way that work is structured into jobs. Job analysis and competency modeling provide systematic information about the duties associated with jobs, the behaviors required to fulfill those duties, and the competencies needed by job holders. In turn, this information is helpful for determining hiring criteria, designing training programs, developing measures of performance, creating career paths, and setting pay policies. Thus, job analysis and competency modeling results serve as a basis for linking together all human resource activities and also linking these activities to the needs of the business.

Job analysis can be conducted in a variety of ways. When choosing a method for conducting job analysis, the best choice depends on the intended purpose. Standardized methods make it easy to compare the results for a particular job with the results found for many other similar or dissimilar jobs—including jobs in other organizations. Thus, standardized methods are useful for setting pay schedules and creating career ladders. Compared to standardized approaches, customized job analysis methods provide more job-specific details. Such details are particularly useful for designing training programs and creating performance measurement and feedback systems.

Regardless of the approach, job analysis serves as the foundation for nearly all of the human resource practices described in the chapters ahead. In addition to helping create consistency across the entire HRM system, job analysis can be adapted for use as a strategic planning tool. Future-oriented job analysis is one way to help managers envision how anticipated changes in the business are likely to affect the nature of people's future jobs and the competencies that people will need to perform them.

TERMS TO REMEMBER

Broadbanding
Competency
Competency modeling
Customized task inventory
Functional job analysis (FJA)
Future-oriented job analysis
Human factors approach
Job
Job analysis
Job description
Job incumbents
Management Position Description
  Questionnaire (MPDQ)

Methods analysis
Occupation
O*NET
Position
Position Analysis Questionnaire
  (PAQ)
Standardized job analysis
  questionnaire
Subject matter experts (SMEs)
Task-oriented job analysis
Time-and-motion study
Worker-oriented job analysis
Work sampling

DISCUSSION QUESTIONS

1. Describe how job analysis and competency modeling can be useful
    during times of strategic organizational change (e.g., after a merger,
    prior to downsizing, or during rapid growth).

2. Describe the possible uses of job analysis results. What does it mean
    to say that job analysis serves as a foundation for an organization's
    integrated HRM system?

3. What are the advantages and disadvantages of standardized and cus-
    tomized approaches to job analysis and competency modeling?

4. The courts have recognized task-based job analysis as useful for pre-
    venting unfair discrimination, but some HR professionals worry that
    competency-based approaches are more susceptible to stereotyping
    and bias. From an employee's perspective, would you prefer to have
    a job description and performance appraisal based on a task-oriented
    job analysis or a competency modeling study? Explain why.

PROJECTS TO EXTEND YOUR LEARNING

1. *Integration and Application.* After reviewing the end-of-text cases
    of Lincoln Electric and Southwest Airlines, answer the following
    questions:

    a. Compare the objectives of job analysis in these two cases.
    b. Explain how job analysis can help each organization meet its
        strategic objectives.
    c. For each company, describe the advantages and disadvantages
        of using standardized versus customized job analysis
        techniques.

2. **Exploring the Internet.**

   a. Study the *Uniform Guidelines,* which are available online from the U.S. Department of Labor, to learn more about the legal reasons for conducting a job analysis (http://www.dol.gov/dol/allcfr/Title_41/Part_60-3/toc.htm).

   b. Access an online version of the *Dictionary of Occupational Titles (DOT)* (http://www.oalj.dol.gov/libdot.htm). Then visit the Employment and Training Administration's O*NET services (http://www.doleta.gov/programs/onet). Compare the information provided by the *DOT* to that provided by O*NET.

   c. Job-Analysis. Net provides online assistance for creating a job description. Visit their home page and try creating a job description for a job you have held (http://www.job-analysis.net).

   d. The Society for Industrial and Organizational Psychology has many members who are experts in job analysis and competency modeling. Visit their home page to search for experts and learn about the services they offer (http://www.siop.org).

CASE STUDY

JOB DESCRIPTIONS AT HITEK

Jennifer Hill was excited about joining HITEK Information Services after receiving her bachelor of arts degree. Her job involved examining compensation practices, and her first assignment was to review HITEK's job descriptions. She was to document her work and make recommended changes, which would include reducing more than 600 job descriptions to a manageable number.

BACKGROUND

To its stockholders and the rest of the outside world, HITEK is a highly profitable, highly aggressive company in the computer business. In addition to its numerous government contracts, it provides software and hardware to businesses and individuals. From its inception in the late 1970s, it has maintained its position on the leading edge by remaining flexible and adaptable to the turbulent environment in which it operates. It's a people-intensive organization that relies enormously on its human resources; therefore, it's in HITEK's best interests to establish policies and procedures that nurture productivity and enhance the satisfaction of its employees.

Because the computer industry is growing at an incredible pace, opportunities for placement are abundant, and the competition for high-quality human resources is tremendous. HITEK has grown about 30% in the last three years, and its management knows that, as easily as it attracts new employees, it can lose them. Its turnover rate (14%) is about average for its industry.

HITEK remains relatively small at 1,000 employees, and it prides itself on its "small team company culture." This culture is maintained partly by extensive use of the company's intranet and by the utilization of open office spaces. The relatively flat, lean organizational structure (shown in Case Exhibit 1) and the easy accessibility of all corporate levels also support an open-door policy. All in all, employees enjoy working for HITEK, and management is in touch with the organization's "pulse."

With the notable exception of the HR department, there are few rules at HITEK. In other

Case Ex I   HITEK's Organizational Chart

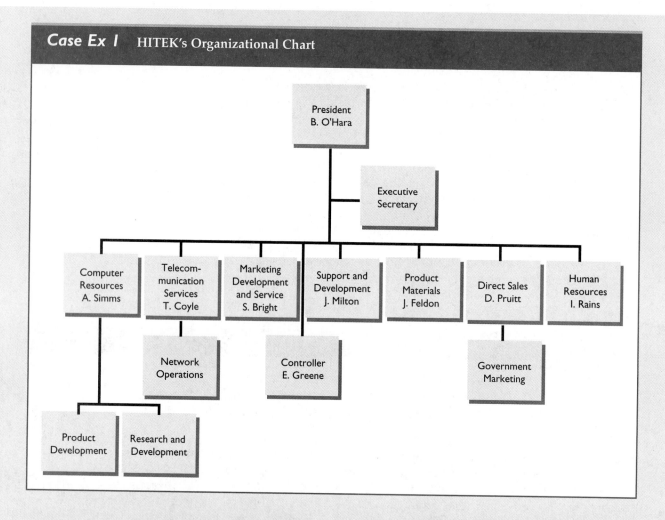

departments, employees at all levels share the work, and positions are redefined to match the specific competencies and the interests of the incumbent so "overqualified" and "overachieving" individuals are often hired but are then promoted rapidly. Nothing is written down; and if newcomers want to know why something is done a certain way, they must ask the person(s) who created the procedure. There is extensive horizontal linkage between departments, perpetuating the blurring of distinctions between departments.

THE HR DEPARTMENT

The HR department stands in stark contrast to the rest of HITEK. About 30 people are employed in the department, including the support staff members, or about one HR employee per 33 HITEK employees. The vice president for human

resources, Isabel Rains, rules the department with an "iron fist." Employees are careful to mold their ideas to match Rains's perspective. When newcomers suggest changes, they're told that "this is the way things have always been done" because "it's our culture." Written rules and standard operating procedures guide all behavior. Department employees know their own job descriptions well, and there is little overlap in employees' duties.

With the exception of one recruiter, all 12 of the incumbents whose positions are represented in Case Exhibit 2 are women. Only half of them have degrees in industrial relations or HRM, and only one-fourth have related experience with another company. Most of them have been promoted from clerical positions. In fact, some employees view the vice president position as a "gift" that was given to Isabel, a former executive secretary, the day after she received her bachelor's degree from a local col-

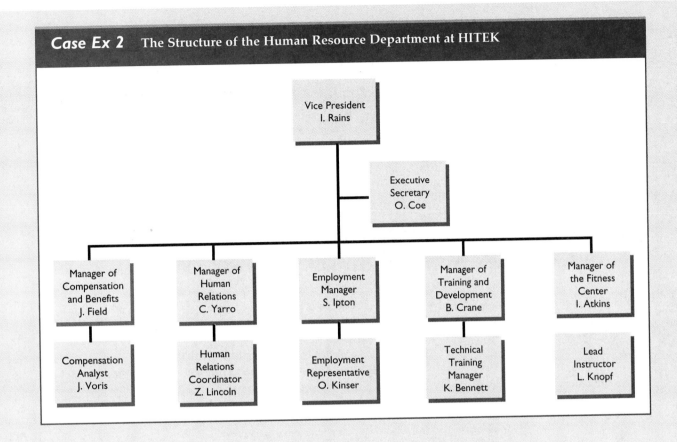

Case Ex 2 The Structure of the Human Resource Department at HITEK

Vice President
I. Rains

Executive
Secretary
O. Coe

Manager of
Compensation
and Benefits
J. Field

Manager of
Human
Relations
C. Yarro

Employment
Manager
S. Ipton

Manager of
Training and
Development
B. Crane

Manager of
the Fitness
Center
I. Atkins

Compensation
Analyst
J. Voris

Human
Relations
Coordinator
Z. Lincoln

Employment
Representative
O. Kinser

Technical
Training
Manager
K. Bennett

Lead
Instructor
L. Knopf

lege. In other departments, it's widely believed that professional degrees and related experience lead to expertise.

One incident that conveyed the department's image to Jennifer Hill occurred during her second week on the job. While preparing a job description with Dave Pruitt, Jennifer explained that she would submit the job description to Janet Voris for final approval. Dave became confused and asked, "But Janet is only a clerical person; why would she be involved?"

JENNIFER HILL'S DUTIES

At HITEK, the pool of job descriptions had grown almost daily as newcomers were hired, but many of the old job descriptions were not discarded, even when obsolete. Other job descriptions needed updating. Jennifer spent some time thinking about how to proceed. She considered the uses of the job descriptions and what steps she would need to take to accomplish all that was expected of her. Support

from within the department was scarce because other employees were busy gathering materials for the annual review of HITEK's hiring, promotion, and development practices conducted by the Equal Employment Opportunity Commission.

After six harried months on the job and much frustration, Jennifer had revised all the descriptions that were still needed (examples of "old" and "new" job descriptions appear in Case Exhibits 3 and 4). She was also beginning to develop some strong opinions about how the HR department functioned at HITEK and what needed to be done to improve its effectiveness and its image. She decided to arrange a confidential lunch with Billy O'Hara, HITEK's president.

CASE QUESTIONS

1. Based on what you know about high-tech companies, what are some likely strategic objectives for HITEK? Given these, what should be the objectives of HITEK's HR

department? Do you think these are the objectives that guide the behaviors of Isabel Rains? Explain.

2. Jobs change frequently at HITEK. What approach to job analysis makes the most sense in such a fast-changing environment? Customized? Standardized? Task-focused? Competency modeling? Evaluate the strengths and weaknesses of the alternative approaches and make recommendations to Jennifer about how to proceed.

3. Is the "new" job description (Case Exhibit 4) better than the "old" one (Case Exhibit 3)? Why or why not? Consider the perspective of employees as well as the perspective of the person supervising this job. Does your answer change depending on the way the job description is being used?

Source: Written by M. P. Miceli, Ohio State University, and Karen Wijta, Macy's.

Case Ex 3 An Old Job Description

ASSOCIATE PROGRAMMER

Basic Objective Perform coding, testing, and documentation of programs, under the supervision of a project leader.

Specific Tasks
- Perform coding, debugging, and testing of a program when given general program specifications.
- Develop documentation of the program.
- Assist in the implementation and training of the users in the usage of the system.
- Report to the manager, management information services as requested.

Job Qualifications Minimum:
- BA/BS degree in relevant field or equivalent experience/knowledge
- Programming knowledge in Java or C++
- Good working knowledge of business and financial applications

Desirable:
- Computer programming experience in a time-sharing environment
- Some training or education in XML, UML, and HTML

Case Ex 4 A New Job Description

ASSOCIATE PROGRAMMER

General Statement of Duties Performs coding, debugging, testing, and documentation of software under the supervision of a technical superior or manager. Involves some use of independent judgment.

Supervision Received Works under close supervision of a technical superior or manager.

Supervision Exercised No supervisory duties required.

Examples of Duties (Any one position may not include all the duties listed, nor do listed examples include all duties that may be found in positions of this class.)

- Confers with analysts, supervisors, and/or representatives of the departments to clarify software intent and programming requirements.
- Performs coding, debugging, and testing of software when given program specifications for a particular task or problem.
- Writes documentation for the program.
- Seeks advice and assistance from supervisor when problems outside the realm of understanding arise.

(continued)

Case Ex 4 *(continued)*

ASSOCIATE PROGRAMMER

- Communicates any program specification deficiencies back to supervisor.
- Reports ideas concerning design and development back to supervisor.
- Assists in the implementation of the system and training of end users.
- Provides some support and assistance to users.
- Develops product knowledge and personal expertise and proficiency in system usage.
- Assumes progressively complex and independent duties as experience permits.
- Performs all duties in accordance with corporate and departmental standards.

Minimum Qualifications

- Education: BA/BS degree in relevant field or equivalent experience/knowledge in computer science, math, or other closely related field.
- Experience: No prior computer programming work experience necessary.
- Knowledge, skills, ability to exercise initiative, and sound judgment.
- Knowledge of a structured language.
- Working knowledge in operating systems.
- Ability to maintain open working relationship with supervisor.
- Logic and problem-solving skills.
- System flowchart development skills.

Desirable Qualifications

- Exposure to Java, C++, and data transfer languages.
- Some training in general accounting practices and controls.
- Effective written and communication skills.

ENDNOTES

1 D. Brady, "Aetna's Painful Recovery," *Business Week* (December 8, 2003): 86–88; J. B. Treaster, "Aetna Is Said to Seek Deal in Health Care," *New York Times* (February 28, 1998): D1; J. B. Treaster, "Aetna Deal for New York Life's Health Unit Is Expected Today," *New York Times* (March 16, 1998): D1; S. Jackson, "Aetna's Brave New World," *Business Week* (March 30, 1998): 180; S. Caudron, "Master the Compensation Maze," *Personnel Journal* (June 1993): 64D; C. Roush, "Aetna's Heavy Ax," *Business Week* (February 14, 1994): 32; "Aetna Life and Casualty Company, Our Vision and Our Values" (internal company document, Hartford, CT, 1994).

2 P. R. Sackett and R. M. Laczo, "Job and Work Analysis," in D. R. Ilgen and R. J. Klimoski (eds.), *Handbook of Psychology: Industrial and Organizational Psychology* (New York: Wiley, 2003): 21–37; J. I. Sanchez and E. L. Levine, "The Analysis of Work in the 20th and 21st Centuries," in N. Anderson, S. S. Ones, H. K. Sinangil, and C. Viswesvaran (eds.), *Handbook of Industrial, Work and Organizational Psychology* (London: Sage, 2001): 70–90.

3 D. Rodriguez, "Developing Competency Models to Promote Integrated Human Resource Practices," *Human Resource Management* 41(3) (Fall 2002): 309–324; see J. Shippmann, R. Ash, M. Batitista, L. Carr, L. Eyde, B. Hesketh, J. F. Kehoe, K. Pearlman, E. Prien, and J. I. Sanchez, "The Practice of Competency Modeling," *Personnel Psychology* 53 (2000): 703–740; S. B. Parry, "The Quest for Competencies," *Training* (July 1996): 48–56.

4 T. R. Athey and M. S. Orth, "Emerging Competency Methods for the Future," *Human Resource Management* 38 (Fall 1999): 215–226.

5 D. Rahbah-Daniels, M. L. Erickson, and A. Dalik, "Here to Stay: Taking Competencies to the Next Level," *World at Work Journal* (First Quarter 2001): 70–77.

6 The essence of the Civil Rights Acts of 1964 and 1991, the Equal Opportunity in Employment Act of 1972, and various court decisions is that employment decisions be made on the basis of whether the individual will be able to perform the job. Chapter 7 expands on the job relatedness of selection procedures.

7 "Objective Employee Appraisals and Discrimination Cases," *Fair Employment Practices* (December 6, 1990): 145–146.

8 M. M. Harris, "Practice Network: ADA and I-O Psychology," *The Industrial-Organizational Psychologist* 36(1) (1998): 33–37; "Job Analyses and Job Descriptions under ADA," *Fair Employment Practices* (April 22, 1993): 45; see also K. Tyler, "Looking for a Few Good Workers?" *HR Magazine* (December 2000): 129; B. D. Sunoo, "Accommodating Workers with Disabilities," *Workforce* (February 2001): 86–93; E. Tahmincioglu, "Job Aides Open Doors for Those Who Can't," *New York Times* (January 24, 2001): G1.

9 N. E. McDermott, "Independent Contractors and Employees: Do You Know One When You See One?" *Legal Report* (November–December, 1999): 1–4.

10 R. Lieber, "The Permatemps Contretemps," *Fast Company* (August 2000): 198–214.

11 J. Myers, "Cast Adrift at Microsoft." *SourceMagazine.com,* http://www.computersourcemag.com/articles, April 2003; D. Richman, "Microsoft 'Permatemps' Win; High Court Refuses Appeal," *Seattle Post-Intelligencer,* http://seattlepi.nwsource.com/business/msft111.shtml, January 11, 2000.

12 S. Bates, "A Tough Target: Employee or Independent Contractor?" *HR Magazine* (June 2001): 69–74.

[13] L. J. Pollack, C. Simons, H. Romero, and D. Hausser, "A Common Language for Classifying and Describing Occupations: The Development, Structure, and Application of the Standard Occupational Classification," *Human Resource Management* 41(3) (Fall 2002): 297–307.

[14] R. J. Harvey, "Job Analysis," in M. D. Dunnette and L. M. Hough (eds.), *Handbook of Industrial Organizational Psychology,* 2nd ed. (Palo Alto, CA: Consulting Psychologists Press, 1991).

[15] Throughout this book, we use the term *competency* to refer to a cluster of related knowledge, skills, abilities, and other personal characteristics and qualities that affect performance on the job.

[16] J. S. Schippmann, *Strategic Job Modeling: Working at the Core of Integrated Human Resources* (Mahwah, NJ: Lawrence Erlbaum, 1999).

[17] D. Rodriguez, "Developing Competency Models to Promote Integrated Human Resource Practices," *Human Resource Management* 41(3) (Fall 2002): 309–324.

[18] P. R. Sackett and R. M. Laczo, "Job and Work Analysis," in D. R. Ilgen and R. J. Klimoski (eds.), *Handbook of Psychology: Industrial and Organizational Psychology* (New York: Wiley, 2003).

[19] For additional information about competency modeling, see J. S. Schippmann and colleagues, "The Practice of Competency Modeling," *Personnel Psychology* 53 (2000): 703–740; D. D. DuBois, "Competency Modeling," in D. G. Langdon, K. S. Whiteside, and M. M. McKenna (eds.), *Intervention Resource Guide: 50 Performance Improvement Tools* (San Francisco: Jossey-Bass, 1999): 106–111.

[20] M. T. Brannick and E. L. Levine, *Job Analysis: Methods, Research, and Applications for Human Resource Management in the New Millennium* (Thousand Oaks, CA: Sage, 2002); Equal Employment Opportunity Commission, "Uniform Guidelines on Employee Selection Procedures," *Federal Register* 43 (1978): 38290–38315; J. Ledvinka and V. G. Scarpello, *Federal Regulation of Personnel and Human Resource Management,* 2nd ed. (Boston: Kent Publishing, 1990).

[21] F. P. Morgenson and M. A. Campion, "Social and Cognitive Sources of Potential Inaccuracy in Job Analysis," *Journal of Applied Psychology* 82 (1998): 627–655.

[22] For a detailed discussion of how to maximize accuracy in job analysis results, see E. C. Dierdorff and M. A. Wilson, "A Meta-Analysis of Job Analysis Reliability," *Journal of Applied Psychology* 88(4) (2003): 635–646; J. I. Sanchez and E. L. Levine, "Accuracy or Consequential Validity: Which Is the Better Standard for Job Analysis Data?" *Journal of Organizational Behavior* 21 (2000): 809–818; F. P. Morgenson and M. A. Campion, "Accuracy in Job Analysis: Toward an Inference Based Model," *Journal of Organizational Behavior* 21 (2000): 819–827; R. J. Harvey and M. A. Wilson, "Yes, Virginia, There Is an Objective Reality in Job Analysis," *Journal of Organizational Behavior* 21 (2000): 829–854.

[23] M. K. Lindell, C. S. Clause, C. J. Brandt, and R. S. Landis, "Relationship between Organizational Context and Job Analysis Task Ratings," *Journal of Applied Psychology* 83 (1998): 769–776; F. J. Landy and J. Vasey, "Job Analysis: The Composition of SME Samples," *Personnel Psychology* 44 (1991): 27–50.

[24] R. D. Arvey, "Sex Bias in Job Evaluation Procedures," *Personnel Psychology* 39 (1986): 315–335; A. P. O'Reilly, "Skill Requirements: Supervisor-Subordinate Conflict," *Personnel Psychology* 26 (Spring 1973): 75–80.

[25] J. I. Sanchez and E. I. Levine, "Accuracy or Consequential Validity: Which Is the Better Standard for Job Analysis Data?" *Journal of Organizational Behavior* 21 (2000): 809–818; J. Shippmann, *Strategic Job Modeling: Working at the Core of Integrated Human Resources* (Mahwah, NJ: Lawrence Erlbaum, 1999).

[26] D. E. Bowen and D. A. Waldman, "Customer-Driven Employee Performance," in D. R. Ilgen and E. D. Pulakos (eds.), *The Changing Nature of Work Performance: Implications for Staffing, Personnel Actions and Development* (San Francisco: Jossey-Bass, 1999).

[27] F. C. Lager, *Ben & Jerry's: The Inside Scoop* (New York: Crown Trade Paperbacks, 1994).

[28] A. W. Mathews, "New Gadgets Trace Truckers' Every Move," *Wall Street Journal* (July 14, 1997): B1, B2.

[29] W. C. Howell, "Human Factors in the Workplace," in M. D. Dunnette and L. M. Hough (eds.), *Handbook of Industrial Organizational Psychology,* vol. 2 (Palo Alto, CA: Consulting Psychologists Press, 1991): 209–270.

[30] For a full description of the FJA as it is practiced today, see S. A. Fine and S. E. Cronshaw, *Functional Job Analysis: A Foundation for Human Resources Management* (Mahwah, NJ: Lawrence Erlbaum, 1999).

[31] Information about O*NET is provided by the Department of Labor at http://www.doleta.gov/programs/onet/. See also N. G. Peterson and associates, "Understanding Work Using the Occupational Information Network (O*NET): Implications for Practice and Research," *Personnel Psychology* 54 (2001): 451–492. For more information on the description of occupations, see L. J. Pollack, C. Simons, H. Romero, and D. Hausser, "A Common Language for Classifying and Describing Occupations: The Development, Structure, and Application of the Standard Occupational Classification," *Human Resource Management* 41(3) (Fall 2002): 297–307.

[32] N. G. Peterson, M. D. Mumford, W. C. Borman, P. R. Jeanneret, and E. A. Fleishman (eds.), *An Occupational Information System for the 21st Century: The Development of O*NET* (Washington, DC: American Psychological Association, 1999).

[33] The PAQ is published by Consulting Psychologists Press. Our description of the PAQ and its development is based on E. J. McCormick, P. R. Jeanneret, and R. C. Mecham, "A Study of Job Characteristics and Job Dimensions as Based on the Position Analysis Questionnaire," *Journal of Applied Psychology* 56 (1972): 347–367; and E. J. McCormick and J. Tiffin, *Industrial Psychology,* 6th ed. (Englewood Cliffs, NJ: Prentice-Hall, 1994).

[34] For additional discussion of the PAQ, see E. T. Cornelius III, A. S. DeNisi, and A. G. Blencoe, "Expert and Naive Raters Using the PAQ: Does It Matter?" *Personnel Psychology* (Autumn 1984): 453–464; E. J. McCormick, A. S. DeNisi, and B. Shaw, "Use of the Position Analysis Questionnaire for Establishing Job Component Validity of Tests," *Journal of Applied Psychology* 64 (1979): 51–56.

[35] W. W. Tornow and P. R. Pinto, "The Development of a Managerial Job Taxonomy: A System for Describing, Classifying, and Evaluating Executive Positions," *Journal of Applied Psychology* 61 (1976): 410–418.

[36] J. I. Sanchez and S. L. Fraser, "On the Choice of Scales for Task Analysis," *Journal of Applied Psychology* 77 (1992): 545–553; M. A. Wilson and R. J. Harvey, "The Value of Relative Time-Spent Ratings in Task-Oriented Job Analysis," *Journal of Business and Psychology* 4 (1990): 453–461.

[37] J. C. Flanagan, "The Critical Incident Technique," *Psychological Bulletin* 51 (1954): 327–358.

[38] I. L. Goldstein, *Training in Organizations: Needs Assessment, Development, and Evaluation* (Pacific Grove, CA: Brooks/Cole, 1993).

[39] R. J. Harvey, "Job Analysis."

[40] E. A. Fleishman and M. D. Mumford, "Ability Requirement Scales" In S. Gael, (ed.), *The Job Analysis Handbook for Business, Industry, and Government,* vol. 2 (New York: John Wiley, 1988).

[41] J. S. Schippman, *Strategic Job Modeling: Working at the Core of Integrated Human Resources;* for more details about PROFILOR, visit the home page of Personnel Decisions Inc., at http://www.pdi-corp.com/offerings/profilor_managers.asp.

[42] Detailed discussions of issues related to creating job families are provided in J. Colhan and G. K. Burger, "Constructing Job Families: An Analysis of Quantitative Techniques Used for Grouping Jobs," *Personnel*

Psychology 48 (1995): 563–586; M. K. Garwood, L. E. Anderson, and B. J. Greengart, "Determining Job Groups: Application of Hierarchical Agglomerative Cluster Analysis in Different Job Analysis Situations," *Personnel Psychology* (1991): 743–762; J. C. Hogan, "Structure of Physical Performance in Occupational Tasks," *Journal of Applied Psychology* 76 (1991): 495–507.

43   ACA/Hewitt Associates, *Life with Broadbands* (Phoenix, AZ: American Compensation Association, 1998); K. S. Abosch, "Confronting Six Myths of Broadbanding," *ACA Journal* (Autumn 1998): 28–35.

44   For other examples of using broadbanding, see M. Enos and G. Limoges, "Broadbanding: Is That Your Company's Final Answer?" *World at Work Journal* (Fourth Quarter 2000): 61–68.

45   L. Sierra, "The Next Generation of Broadbanding: Insurance Company Overhauls Hierarchy with CareerBanding," *ACA News* (February 1998): 21–24; see also D. Gilbert and K. S. Abosch, *Improving Organizational Effectiveness through Broadbanding* (Scottsdale, AZ: American Compensation Association, 1996).

46   R. B. Morgan and J. E. Smith, *Staffing the New Workplace: Selecting and Promoting Quality Improvement* (Milwaukee: ASQC Quality Press,

1996); K. P. Carson and G. L. Stewart, "Job Analysis and the Sociotechnical Approach to Quality: A Critical Examination," *Journal of Quality Management* 1 (1996): 49–64.

47   R. Lieber, "The Permatemps Contretemps," *Fast Company* (August 2000): 198–214; W. Bridges, *Job Shift: How to Prosper in a Workplace without Jobs* (Reading, MA: Addison-Wesley, 1995).

48   C. Joinson, "Refocusing Job Descriptions," *HR Magazine* (January 2001): 67–72; J. I. Sanchez, "From Documentation to Innovation: Reshaping Job Analysis to Meet Emerging Business Needs," *Human Resource Management Review* 4(1) (1994): 51–74.

49   N. B. Kurland and T. D. Egan, "Telecommuting: Justice and Control in the Virtual Organization," *Organizational Science* 10 (1999): 500–513.

50   For a discussion of how to analyze the work of teams, see S. A. Mohrman, S. G. Cohen, and A. M. Mohrman, Jr., *Designing Team-Based Organizations: New Forms for Knowledge Work* (San Francisco: Jossey-Bass, 1995).

51   D. Rahbar-Daniels, M. L. Erickson, and A. Dalik, "Here to Stay: Taking Competencies to the Next Level," *World at Work Journal* (First Quarter 2001): 70–77.

chapter 6

Recruiting and Retaining Qualified Employees

SAS Institute is the largest private software company in the world. It has about 10,000 employees and revenues exceeding $1.5 billion. Headquartered in Cary, North Carolina, it is always highly ranked on the Fortune list of "100 Best Companies to Work For." According to Jim Goodnight, CEO of SAS Institute, "attracting and retaining the best people is crucial to our success."

Surprisingly, SAS Institute was a late adopter of automated online recruiting. Jeff Chambers, Director of Human Resources, acknowledged that this was an activity "that we don't do as progressively as other companies."

The company was slow to adopt new recruiting technologies because the technology wasn't necessary. Turnover averages between 3 and 5% annually, and there are plenty of applicants for each job opening. SAS employees provide a continuing source of leads for potential hires—about 20% of the total last year. A very informal recruiting method worked well, according to Chambers: "A lot of our people will recommend friends, neighbors, and family members because they think we are such a good place to work. We have been known as an employer of choice for a long time." Even without online recruiting, the company received 20,000 applications for 200 job openings.

As a software company, SAS looks to its internal staff to enhance its present system. "Our philosophy has been that we build our own rather than go out and find somebody else, and in that respect, I think we have been underutilizing the potential of the Web," Chambers acknowledges. "We have never had the ability to interface with potential applicants online. We just let them apply without having to send in a resume."

Under the new system, SAS describes its current needs and accepts electronic resumes from people who may have some interest in working at the company. It no longer requires candidates to apply solely for open positions. Instead, people can simply let the company know that they may be interested at some point if there is a potential opportunity to advance. Information about both current employees and potential future employees will be kept in a database that records their competencies. The database makes it possible to scan for critical job skills and keep track of people—something SAS had never done before. SAS is now able to prequalify candidates and to give managers a better range of choices sooner.[1]

THE STRATEGIC IMPORTANCE OF RECRUITING AND RETAINING TALENTED EMPLOYEES

> *"The biggest challenge facing the travel industry is recruiting the best and brightest for our industry."*
>
> Gary Sain
> Chair
> Association of Travel Marketing Executives

Recruitment *involves searching for and obtaining qualified applicants for the organization to consider when filling job openings.* It is the first step in the hiring process. Recruitment stops short of selecting among applicants to decide which individuals should be hired. Research conducted by Ernst & Young shows that the stock purchasing decisions of institutional investors take into account a company's ability to attract talented people. At SAS and many other companies, getting good people into the organization is so important that the chairperson gets personally involved in the firm's recruiting and selection. SAS managers devote time and attention to recruiting because they know it's vital to the company's long-term business success.

We also discuss the issue of retention in this chapter. **Retention** *activities refer to everything an employer does to encourage qualified and productive employees to continue working for the organization.* The objective of retention activities is to reduce unwanted voluntary turnover by people the organization would like to keep in its workforce. Together, effective recruitment and retention attracts individuals to the organization *and* also increases the chance of retaining the individuals once they are hired.

Strategic Choices

Effective approaches to recruiting and retaining qualified employees grow out of the strategic planning process described in Chapter 4. Recruiting efforts should be consistent with the organization's strategy, vision, and values. Consequently, recruiting activities vary across companies, even in the same industry (e.g., insurance). Exhibit 6.1 illustrates how different strategic business objectives can result in different HR implications for recruitment and retention.

Ex 6.1	Examples of How Strategic Business Objectives Create HR Implications for Recruitment and Retention
STRATEGIC OBJECTIVE	**EXAMPLES OF IMPLICATIONS FOR RECRUITMENT AND RETENTION OBJECTIVES**
Increase Market Share by Offering Lowest-Cost Service	• Important to retain current talent as company grows. • Need to predict rate of growth and translate changes in market share to increases needed in size of workforce. • Continuously improve efficiency of recruitment practices needed to keep costs down. • Low-cost strategy puts pressure on compensation and benefits costs, so need to be creative in finding low-cost ways to attract and retain talent.
Increase Return on Investment by Offering Innovative Products and Maintaining High Margins	• Recruiting practices need to focus on attracting highly qualified applicants at the cutting edge of their fields. • Best talent not likely to be looking for jobs, so need to go to them (not wait for them to come to us). • Excellent retention strategy for top talent needed, as workforce will be an attractive pool that other companies will try to raid. Knowledge retention is key strategic concern, also.
Respond to Declining Industry Trends by Diversifying into New Businesses	• May need to develop and implement layoff plans, creating the challenge of how to attract new talent and retain best talent at the same time. • Recruiting efforts for new business areas should include plan for lateral transfers from declining business areas, to minimize need for layoffs. • For new businesses, HR will need to develop strategies for recruiting key talent in those industries.

Questions to be addressed during strategic HR planning might include:

- How many new hires do we need in the near term and three to five years from now?
- Do we want to recruit people who are motivated to stay with the company for a long time, or are we looking for a short-term commitment?
- Are we prepared to pay top dollar, or should we look for people who will be attracted to our company despite the modest compensation we offer?
- Are we interested in finding people who are different from our current employees to bring in new perspectives, or is it important to find people who will fit well in our culture and help maintain the status quo?
- What competencies do we need from our employees, and how rapidly will these change?

Strategic discussions focus on the general needs of the organization. Once those needs are understood, the focus turns to defining the needs of specific units or departments and the requirements for specific positions. At this stage, job analysis results become relevant. As described in Chapter 5, job analysis yields answers to questions such as:

- What are the characteristics of the ideal recruit?
- Which competencies must people have when they first enter the organization, and how important is it that new hires be eager to learn new competencies?
- What career opportunities can we discuss with applicants?

At GE Medical Systems, the strategic business planning process links recruiting plans directly to product development plans. When developing new products, managers draw up a "multigenerational product plan" *and* a "multigenerational staffing plan." These clarify the skills that will be needed as a product moves through three iterations of development. Suppose a plan is being developed for a CT scanner that will complete 1-second scans in its first generation, 3/4-second scans in the second generation, and $\frac{1}{2}$-second scans in the third generation. Along with the product development plan, a recruiting plan would be developed to ensure that enough computer programmers would be available to work on each generation of the product's life cycle. The recruiting plan would specify the number of "absolute algorithm" experts needed to write code for each product generation.

Reducing Expenses and Improving Productivity

Today, concerns about recruiting and retaining talented employees are salient for many employers. Even as many companies continue to downsize, finding the talent that's needed remains a concern. The combination of strong competitive business pressures and tight labor market conditions for the most talented employees means that employers must find a way to keep costs under control and at the same time ensure that the organization has the workforce it needs to grow, diversify into new areas of business, expand internationally, and so on.

At JPS Health Network in Fort Worth, Texas, a shortage of nurses was hampering the health center's ability to deliver high-quality patient care. Ineffective recruiting meant that 17% of nursing jobs were vacant. If a nurse resigned, it usually it took about six or seven weeks to hire a new nurse. As it set out to redesign its recruiting process, JPS started with three goals:

- reduce the vacancy rate to below 12%, which was the average for the local area,
- shorten the time needed to fill vacancies, and
- improve the quality of applicants who applied for open positions.

To achieve these goals, they upgraded their existing online recruiting efforts. An internal study of recruiting problems found that most nurses who applied for jobs at JPS had visited the organization's website but then applied using the traditional paper-and-pencil approach. A study of the websites of competing hospitals suggested many ways to improve: They added more pictures to convey the organization's culture and show what the work environment was like; they made it easier for nurses to apply online; and they made it possible for applicants to contact the hiring managers directly with any questions they had about the open positions. Managers also saw improvements. Completed applications were sent immediately to both the nurse recruiter and the hiring manager, so no one was lost in the shuffle. To shorten processing time, the nurse recruiter conducted telephone interviews to screen applicants instead of arranging on-site interviews.

How successful were JPS's change efforts? Consider these results:

- applications increased by more than 60%,
- time needed to fill vacancies was reduced to about 2.5 weeks,
- the vacancy rate dropped to 7.6%, and
- advertising costs went down 31%.

Although more difficult to measure, JPS believes that their patients and the doctors who care for them also benefited from these changes. With fewer vacancies and a reduced workload, the quality of work life for JPS's nursing staff also improved.[2]

The Value of Retaining the Best Employees

Recruiting people to meet the organization's human resource needs is only half the battle in the war for talent. The other half is keeping these people. Organizations that keep their employee turnover rates lower gain an advantage against their competitors by reducing overall labor costs and improving productivity.

The true cost of turnover includes easy-to-quantify, out-of-pocket expenses and intangible opportunity costs associated with lost productivity. As Exhibit 6.2 shows, the out-of-pocket expenses associated with hiring an employee are substantial.[3] But these out-of-pocket costs are just a portion of the total costs. A study of the costs associated with turnover in supermarkets included the expenses associated with filling the empty positions created by turnover as well as the costs created by inexperienced employees, such as errors in making change, paperwork mistakes, and damaged products. For professional work, turnover hurts productivity because projects are lost when employees who were favored by a client leave. Staffing shortages also hurt firms that rely heavily on professionals because they cannot bid on projects that they cannot staff. Other costs associated with turnover include lower morale among overworked employees who must pick up the extra

"The productivity of a sales rep selling very sophisticated products like software continues to rise for as long as three years."

Warren C. Culpepper
CEO
Culpepper & Associates

Ex 6.2 Hiring Costs

Average Cost Per Hire for Industries with the Largest Number of New Hires.

All-Industry Average			$4,165
Banks	$4,770	Manufacturing, durable goods	$2,757
Computer and data services	$3,986	Manufacturing, nondurable goods	$3,548
Computer software	$7,471	Media, Internet, publishing, radio, TV	$4,773
Consulting	$6,639	Pharmaceutical and biotech	$11,262
Entertainment, recreation	$4,051	Retail	$2,379
Financial services	$5,046	Telecommunications	$4,905
Health care, hospitals	$4,358	Transportation, package and freight	$2,112
Hospitality	$2,309	Utilities, electric and gas	$6,406
Insurance	$4,337		

Note: Based on a survey of 1,302 organizations.

work created when a colleague leaves, lost knowledge that only the depart-ing employee has, and the business contacts that the departing employee may have been able to use to build the business.

For some organizations, high turnover creates more serious problems than merely increasing costs; it threatens the firm's strategic competitive-ness. At Schering-Plough, high turnover apparently contributed to the firm's repeated failure to meet governmental manufacturing standards for its pre-scription drugs. The quality of the company's manufacturing process was so unreliable that the Food and Drug Administration would not grant approval for one new allergy drug until the manufacturing problem was fixed. The company also ordered several large recalls of products after discovering they had been contaminated during the manufacturing process. What was caus-ing these problems? According to an auditor's report, "excessive turnover, shortage and pharmaceutical inexperience of supervisors [had] resulted in inadequate training and oversight of subordinates and manufacturing oper-ations."[4] In this example, the costs of turnover included significant damage to the firm's reputation and brand image.

Addressing Societal Concerns through Legal Compliance

Obtaining a pool of qualified applicants is the primary objective of recruit-ing, but legal compliance is very important, too. As described later in this chapter, legal compliance requires careful record keeping. Managers some-times deride such record keeping as a bureaucratic nuisance, but keeping track of recruiting activities and results is essential for documenting legal compliance. Furthermore, these same records can be used to evaluate the effectiveness of the organization's recruiting efforts. A study of 3,200 employers in Atlanta, Boston, and Los Angeles supports this view. The results indicated that employers who actively engaged in affirmative action efforts, which require extensive recording keeping, were also more likely to carefully evaluate performance and provide training to new hires. Furthermore, the study indicated that effective *recruitment*—not preferential selection—was the key to the success.[5]

The HR Triad

Several of the ways that employees and managers can be involved in recruit-ing and retaining employees are summarized in "The HR Triad: Roles and Responsibilities for Recruiting and Retaining Employees."

HR Professionals.   HR professionals usually take the lead in designing a systematic and integrated approach to recruiting and retaining employees. When Designer Blinds was experiencing production problems, they turned to the HR manager for a solution. The production problems were putting the company at risk, and the high turnover among employees was the source of problem. Without a stable and experienced workforce in the factory, orders were going unfilled and quality suffered. Deb Franklin embarked on an all-out campaign to improve the company's recruiting and to retain its new hires. Her efforts included increased community outreach, better orientation for new hires, and training of managers.

The HR Triad

Roles and Responsibilities for Recruiting and Retaining Employees

LINE MANAGERS	HUMAN RESOURCE PROFESSIONALS	EMPLOYEES
• Work with HR staff to develop recruiting objectives and plans that meet the organization's strategic needs and address employees' concerns.	• Work with line managers to develop recruiting objectives and plans that meet the organization's strategic needs and address employees' concerns.	• Openly discuss your short-term and long-term goals in order to facilitate the development of recruiting plans that address your concerns.
• Develop an understanding of the linkages that exist between recruiting activities, other aspects of the HRM system, and longer-term employee retention.	• Design recruitment and retention activities that contribute to the development of an integrated, internally consistent HRM system.	• When searching for work, consider all aspects of the HRM system before making a decision about where to work.
• Help disseminate information about open positions to all potentially qualified internal candidates.	• Develop recruiting plans that meet legal guidelines and generate a diverse pool of qualified internal and external candidates.	• Participate in recruiting efforts such as referring others to the company and answering questions about what it is like to work there.
• Stay informed of labor market trends in order to anticipate the implications for recruiting and retaining talent.	• Evaluate recruiting outcomes and be innovative in developing practices to ensure a sufficient number of qualified applicants.	• Use knowledge of competitors' recruiting approaches to help your employer develop innovative and more effective practices.
• Understand and abide by relevant legal regulations.	• Provide training as needed to line managers and employees involved in recruitment activities.	• Work with HR professionals and line managers in the organization's efforts to effectively manage workforce diversity.
• Facilitate retention efforts by being supportive of employees and facilitating their development.	• Monitor retention patterns to diagnose potential problems. Use exit interviews, employee surveys, etc. to identify needed improvements.	• Seek out information about openings within the company and actively pursue those that fit your personal career objectives.

Line Managers. As Deb Franklin understood, line managers can help promote the company and make it attractive to employees, or they can be the cause of high turnover. Managers often are less directly involved in the early recruiting stages, and they usually become more actively involved as the selection process gets underway. Then, once employees are onboard, the manager plays a key role in determining whether good employees stay with the company or leave for something better. As a result of Designer Blinds' new recruiting efforts, the company began hiring many more members of Omaha's Sudanese and Hispanic populations. To ensure that these employees felt welcome, managers were trained to improve their understanding of these cultures. To improve the quality of the company's management skills, the company began a formal management development program to teach leadership skills. Managers also began attending weekly meetings to learn about issues such as attitudes and sexual harassment.[6]

Other Employees.   The initial recruiting experience—when an employee is first considered for a position in the organization—is an employee's first exposure to the organization's recruiting activities, but it is not the last one. Employees again become involved in recruiting activities as they help (or hinder) their employers' efforts to attract others to the company. And, when employees eventually consider applying for other jobs in the organization, they again become actively involved in recruiting activities. At this point, employees learn how the organization handles recruiting within its own workforce. These later experiences with the organization's recruiting activities may be especially important in determining whether talented employees are retained.

At Cisco Systems, the active involvement of employees is essential to the company's recruiting efforts. Employees participate in focus groups designed to brainstorm ideas about where to find qualified applicants. The folks Cisco wants to hire aren't spending their time looking through want ads. They are more likely to be found attending local art festivals and garden shows. So Cisco recruiters go to those events and work the crowds. When an interested prospect is identified, Cisco pairs the person with a current employee who has similar interests and skills—a "friend." Friends help screen out unsuitable applicants and serve as advocates to convince the best applicants to accept Cisco's job offers.[7]

RECRUITING AND RETAINING WITHIN AN INTEGRATED HRM SYSTEM

Organizations differ greatly in their efforts to recruit and retain top talent, and job applicants vary greatly in how attracted they are to job openings in different organizations. To understand a particular organization's approach to recruiting and retaining employees, it helps to consider how these activities are shaped by other aspects of the HRM system as well as forces in the external and organizational environments.

LINKS TO OTHER HR ACTIVITIES

This chapter focuses on recruiting as if it were a somewhat discreet aspect of managing human resources, but it is important to recognize that this is not the case. In a fully integrated, strategically aligned system for managing human resources, recruiting activities are developed with a full appreciation for how they may affect other parts of the system, and how other parts of the system may affect recruiting activities.

Recruiting activities should be firmly grounded in the strategic planning process, as described in Chapter 4. Effective planning minimizes unexpected labor shortages created by managerial actions such as excessive layoffs and failing to develop succession plans. The results of job analysis and competency modeling activities provide direction to recruiting activities by identifying the types of talent that are needed by the company, and thus suggesting which populations should be targeted during recruiting (e.g., high school graduates, college graduates, experienced managers). In this chapter, we discuss how an applicant's decision about whether to accept a job offer is affected by the company's compensation plan, benefits, work arrangements, and approach to career development. All of these come into play as applicants consider whether to accept a job offer. For applicants, it is clear that the effectiveness of world-class recruiting practices will be limited if other HR practices are not world-class also.

For managers, the connections between recruiting activities and other aspects of the HRM system become apparent, with experience. Inexperienced managers often focus on speed when evaluating the effectiveness of the organization's recruiting activities. They want jobs filled quickly and with as little effort as possible. Experienced managers recognize that, while speed is important, the quality of people hired is ultimately more important. If the hiring process does not succeed in getting qualified employees, managers will then need to provide more training to new employees or they will soon be looking for more replacements. Similarly, if qualified people are found and convinced to accept job offers, they will be productive and stay only as long as the organization addresses their desire for rewards, work flexibility, career advancement, and so on. In other words, recruiting activities work in concert with the entire HRM system to determine the flow of people through jobs.

Exhibit 6.3 illustrates the relationship between recruiting activities and other aspects of the HRM system, and also summarizes the many sources of potential job applicants and the methods organizations can use to reach them.

EXTERNAL ENVIRONMENT

Also shown in Exhibit 6.3 are several aspects of the external and organizational environments that influence recruitment and retention. The most significant forces in the external environment influencing the recruitment and retention of employees are the labor market, technology, and legal trends.

FAST FACT The number of electrical engineering graduates from U.S. universities has declined by 50% since 1987.

Labor Markets. Clearly, labor market conditions and competitive pressures can be powerful determinants of the resources companies invest to attract and retain top talent. During the high-tech boom of the 1990s, employers spared no expense to recruit talented programmers. By 2004, demand for programmers had cooled off, the average starting salaries for computer programmers were declining, and employers were flooded with applicants.[8] Things are different in the biotech industry, which is still booming. Almost all biotech firms anticipate hiring additional employees during the next several years. To attract the talent it needs, Biogen and other industry leaders promote an open and friendly workplace where new ideas are welcome. By keeping excellent talent in the company, they hope to attract the best new talent. Thus, they also offer employee stock options, a generous personal leave policy, and a six-week sabbatical after six years on the job.

Technology. As illustrated by the opening example of SAS Institute, new technologies also influence the design and implementation of a company's recruiting activities. You may be surprised to learn, however, that few people actually get jobs from electronic job boards. Today, applicants can learn

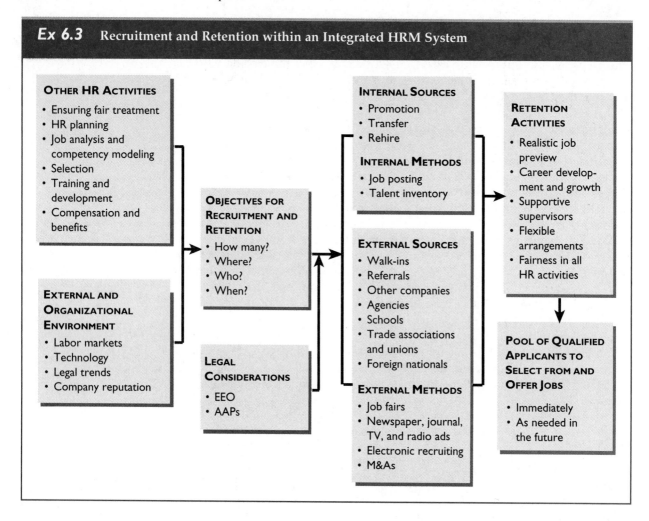

Ex 6.3   Recruitment and Retention within an Integrated HRM System

OTHER HR ACTIVITIES
- Ensuring fair treatment
- HR planning
- Job analysis and competency modeling
- Selection
- Training and development
- Compensation and benefits

EXTERNAL AND ORGANIZATIONAL ENVIRONMENT
- Labor markets
- Technology
- Legal trends
- Company reputation

OBJECTIVES FOR RECRUITMENT AND RETENTION
- How many?
- Where?
- Who?
- When?

LEGAL CONSIDERATIONS
- EEO
- AAPs

INTERNAL SOURCES
- Promotion
- Transfer
- Rehire

INTERNAL METHODS
- Job posting
- Talent inventory

EXTERNAL SOURCES
- Walk-ins
- Referrals
- Other companies
- Agencies
- Schools
- Trade associations and unions
- Foreign nationals

EXTERNAL METHODS
- Job fairs
- Newspaper, journal, TV, and radio ads
- Electronic recruiting
- M&As

RETENTION ACTIVITIES
- Realistic job preview
- Career development and growth
- Supportive supervisors
- Flexible arrangements
- Fairness in all HR activities

POOL OF QUALIFIED APPLICANTS TO SELECT FROM AND OFFER JOBS
- Immediately
- As needed in the future

about job openings in most large companies by visiting the company website or using job boards. According to a recent study by Forrester Research, in 2003 only 4% of job hunters found employment through online job boards, while 23% found work through help-wanted ads.

Even though few applicants get jobs from job boards at present, electronic recruiting remains a significant trend. Increasingly, employers are encouraging applicants to apply online through their company websites because it reduces recruiting costs. When Citigroup studied the cost of electronic recruiting, they found that the average cost per hire was in the range of $300–$400 dollars—similar to the cost of employee referrals and about one-tenth of the cost for employment agencies. When a global publishing company adopted electronic recruiting, they found that it reduced their recruiting and hiring costs by 50%. The savings were due to improved efficiency in several areas. For example, the electronic system was able to screen applicants to assess their basic qualifications, which reduced the amount of time that hiring managers spent interviewing candidates. By using less of the managers' time, the company saved money. Also, the electronic system automated the interview scheduling process. Instead of paying a staff member to call applicants to arrange an interview, applicants scheduled their own interviews using the company's website. The improved efficiency that resulted from the use of an electronic recruiting process yielded an estimated return on investment of $6 for every $1 invested in the new system.[9]

Legal Trends.   As described later in this chapter, a dynamic and changing legal environment is another important factor that organizations must take into account. In particular, recent courts decisions have caused some employers to wonder whether long-established affirmative action recruiting efforts might suddenly be under legal attack.

Company Reputation.   This chapter also discusses the important consequences that an organization's reputation has on recruiting activities. SAS Institute is an example of a company that enjoys a reputation for being an unusually great place to work. Because of that reputation, SAS has an easier time attracting applicants. Once an offer is extended, SAS's reputation also increases the likelihood that the best applicants will accept an offer of employment.

RECRUITING METHODS AND SOURCES

Once the recruiting objectives are specified and job analysis results have been considered, specific recruiting activities can be planned and implemented. In designing recruiting activities, two central issues to address are the methods to use and the sources to target.

 FAST FACT The U.S. Postal Service, which is the largest U.S. employer, starts recruiting in August for the 40,000+ temporary workers it needs to handle the holiday mail in December.

Employers inform potential applicants about employment opportunities using a variety of methods. They place ads, post notices on the company bulletin board, accept applications from people who simply walk into their recruiting offices, and so on. Different sources of applicants can be reached using different methods of recruiting. *The company's current employees are one source of applicants; they are called the* **internal labor market.** Posting announcements in a company newsletter is a good way to recruit applicants who are already employees of the company. Usually, current employees apply for positions that offer higher pay or more interesting work. *Another source of potential applicants are people who don't work for the organization; they are called the* **external labor market.** Holding job fairs and placing ads in local newspapers or trade publications are common methods used to reach those in the external labor market.

Many studies have considered whether recruiting from these different sources results in different employee outcomes (e.g., performance, turnover, loyalty, and job satisfaction). If different sources of applicants were found to have different outcomes, companies could target their recruiting efforts to the most appropriate sources, given their strategic needs. Overall, however, research has shown no clear differences in the employment experiences of new employees recruited from different sources.[10]

Instead of targeting one source of applicants, most employers recruit from multiple sources using multiple methods. This approach helps the organization generate a large applicant pool. In addition, recruiting from multiple sources is a good way to increase the diversity of the applicant pool. Following we describe the most common methods used for recruiting applicants from internal and external labor markets.

INTERNAL LABOR MARKET

Especially when labor shortages are constantly in the news, a natural tendency may be to assume that recruiting efforts should focus on finding *new* employees to hire. But wise employers understand the value of looking first for candidates inside the organization. Cisco Systems and the SAS Institute both place a high value on recruiting from their internal labor markets. For jobs other than those at entry level, current employees should be considered a primary source of applicants for any job opening.

Having expressed their interest in a position, internal applicants typically go through the recruitment process in much the same way as external applicants, becoming candidates for promotions, transfers or development activities. Employers should be particularly careful to manage how internal candidates experience recruiting activities. If they have negative experiences when they apply for jobs within the organization, it may trigger them to look outside the organization for other opportunities.

Internal applicants for job vacancies can be located using several methods. Some (e.g., the grapevine and job postings) assume that potential applicants should take most of the responsibility for learning about opening positions and applying for those they find interesting. Others (e.g., using talent inventories) place more responsibility on the HR staff and line managers.

Job Postings.   **Job postings** *prominently display current job openings to all employees in an organization.* They are usually found on bulletin boards (cork as well as electronic). Other than word-of-mouth, job postings are the most commonly used method for generating a pool of internal applicants. Job postings usually provide complete job descriptions. A well-constructed job description communicates competencies needed as well as organizational goals and objectives. By also including information about compensation and performance standards, job postings send signals to employees about what is valued. Astute employees realize that observing postings over time yields information about turnover rates in various departments, as well as information about the competencies that are most in demand.

Job postings can reduce turnover by communicating to employees that they don't have to go elsewhere in order to find opportunities for advancement and development. Posting jobs also creates an open recruitment process, which helps to provide equal opportunity for advancement to all employees. Job posting has many advantages, but it's not foolproof. If hiring decisions are already made when postings appear, the system will soon lose credibility. Managers who merely go through the motions of posting jobs generate ill will and cynicism.

FAST FACT

Adecco, the giant staffing agency, sets up Job Shop Kiosks in shopping malls so that companies can post job openings.

Talent Inventories.   A **talent inventory** *is a database that contains information about the pool of current employees.* Almost every organization has a reservoir of qualified employees that it can tap when recruiting to fill open positions. Like savings accounts, these reservoirs of internal talent contain easily accessed resources that can be "withdrawn" as needed. In addition, the future value of the organization's reservoir pool can be enhanced through investments in selection procedures, training programs, and retention efforts.

Some organizations identify high-potential employees to create talent pools and replacement charts to use for leadership succession planning, as described in Chapter 4. Similarly, some organizations have a systematic method for keeping track of the entire reservoir of talent at all levels and in all positions, and for ensuring that it's used wisely. Rather than relying on employees to identify appropriate openings in the organization, proactive employers such as the SAS Institute maintain a talent inventory to systematically monitor their internal talent and facilitate the process of matching internal applicants to suitable opportunities. By being proactive, employers can ensure that they consider *all* internal candidates with the necessary qualifications, regardless of whether taking the open position would involve a promotion, transfer, or temporary job rotation.

FAST FACT At Hallmark, 90% of management positions are filled internally.

Talent inventories usually include employees' names, prior jobs and experiences, performance and compensation histories, and demonstrated competencies. The employees' work-related interests, geographic preferences, and career goals also should be included. With an up-to-date talent inventory to consult, there is no need to rely on employees to nominate themselves for job openings. Instead, qualified potential applicants can be identified and encouraged to apply when jobs become available. Citibank uses its talent inventory to identify suitable positions for staff members who wish to transfer or who are seeking another job because of technological displacement or reorganization. With this system, Citibank makes sure it considers suitable internal candidates before recruiting begins outside the organization.

Regardless of how an employee becomes an applicant, recruitment activities can result in three types of career moves within the organization: promotions, transfers, and development activities. Of course, a negative decision could also lead an internal applicant to look for a job with another employer, so it is so important to manage internal applicants with this in mind.

Despite recent corporate staff cutbacks, research by Accenture Consulting showed that 68% of business leaders believe that retaining talent is far more important than acquiring new blood.

Promotions. A promotion generally involves moving into a position that's recognized as having higher status—and often, higher pay. Understandably, current employees often feel they should be given priority as applicants for jobs that represent opportunities for promotion. When this doesn't happen, it creates dissatisfaction.

Transfers. A transfer involves moving into a position that's of similar status, often with no increase in pay. Chapter 5 explained that many organizations have replaced the traditional system of jobs that are organized into clear status hierarchies with job families and broadbanding. Under these new arrangements, taking a new position within the company often involves a lateral job transfer rather than a promotion. After several transfers, employees develop a broader perspective and can better understand how the entire organization functions as a system. Because lateral transfers play such an important role in the long-term development of employees, they represent valuable opportunities for employees. Thus, it is important that the company's recruitment procedures alert employees to such opportunities when they arise.

"All the things that make you an employer of choice are the same things that make you a successful company."

Derek Smart
Personnel Director
Nuclear Electric PLC

Development Activities.   When internal candidates are considered for a job opening, being turned down can be a big disappointment. The applicant may feel embarrassed about being evaluated negatively, and demotivated by the implied negative feedback. Astute managers are alert to these possible negative consequences and take the time to help their employees turn the experience into something more positive. This is often an excellent time to discuss the employee's long-term career goals and evaluate possible development activities that might increase the likelihood of a future promotion. Detailed discussions of career planning and development activities are described in Chapter 8 of this book.

Pros and Cons of Internal Recruitment.   There are several potential benefits associated with recruiting applicants who are eligible for promotions and transfers. Compared to external recruitment, internal recruitment can reduce labor costs because outside recruits tend to receive higher salaries. The organization may also pay a one-time signing bonus to external recruits.

In addition to reducing monetary costs, internal recruiting is valued by employees. Recruiting externally can reduce employee morale and diminish employees' willingness to maximize their productivity in order to be eligible for future career opportunities. Gaining a reputation for excellent employee development is one of the best ways to become an "employer of choice."[11]

When Mirage Resorts launched its lavish Bellagio resort, it needed 9,600 new employees. The organization screened 84,000 applications and interviewed 27,000 finalists in 12 weeks and never used a single sheet of paper to do it.

FAST FACT

Counterbalancing these advantages of internal recruitment are several disadvantages. If internal recruitment is used in place of external recruitment, the most qualified candidates may never be considered. Other disadvantages include infighting between candidates vying for a position, and inbreeding. Inbreeding exists when someone who is familiar with the organization has come to accept its ways of doing things. Such people are less likely to come up with creative and innovative ideas for improvement.

EXTERNAL LABOR MARKET

Rapidly growing organizations and those that require large numbers of highly skilled professionals and managers seldom can meet their labor needs without recruiting from the external labor market. Internal recruitment simply can't produce the numbers of people needed to sustain continued growth. During one of its growth spurts, for example, Cisco Systems was taking on about 1,000 new hires each quarter, which amounted to nearly 10% of the total job growth in Silicon Valley. Later, when there was a downturn in the industry, Cisco switched its philosophy to emphasize internal recruitment and promotion-from-within.

Warmer metropolitan areas attract job seekers far more than seasonal areas, according to the Department of Labor.

FAST FACT

Even when companies are not growing, or are shrinking, they may not be able to generate large numbers of internal applicants with the competencies needed under changing business conditions. If internal candidates would require training in order to be qualified, it may be cheaper, easier, and quicker to go outside the firm and hire people who already have the competencies needed.

Methods for recruiting from the external labor market include walk-ins; electronic recruiting; employee referrals; use of private search firms, public agencies, and school placement services; and staffing with foreign nationals. Regardless of how external applicants are recruited, the goal should be to attract *qualified* applicants—not just a large number of applicants.[12]

Walk-in Applicants.   Some individuals become applicants by simply walking into an organization's employment office and declaring they are interested in working for the organization. They may be motivated by an advertisement indicating that the company is recruiting, or they may simply have a good impression of the organization and want to explore the possibility of working there. Before the Internet explosion, walk-ins were especially prevalent for clerical and service jobs; managerial, professional, and sales applicants were seldom walk-ins.[13] New technology is quickly changing that. Now, applicants for almost any type of job can "walk in" to an organization through its electronic, cyberspace doors.

> *"We found [that] the types of people we get from walk-ins and newspaper ads turned over 2.5 times faster than referrals from employees."*
>
> Walter Kalinowski
> Executive Director of HR
> Petro Stopping Centers

Holding an open house is an excellent way to attract walk-in applicants. An open house can serve to introduce the organization to the community and attract individuals who might not otherwise become applicants. Such events give the firm a chance to look at potential applicants in a fairly informal setting.

Electronic and Other Media.   Virtually every company now has a website that applicants (internal and external to the company), as well as customers, can go to and learn about the company. Many of these sites have specific information about job postings, required competencies, career progression programs, mentoring, diversity initiatives, and benefits. Increasingly, company websites accept—even encourage—electronic applications.

 FAST FACT A study of *Fortune* 500 companies found that recruiting online cut the average hiring time from 43 to 37 days.

The best company websites enable applicants to select themselves out of the application process if the descriptions provided are not appropriate for them. Well-designed websites (e.g., those that are playful or aesthetically appealing) also may increase an applicant's desire to apply for jobs at the company.[14]

One major benefit of electronic recruiting is that it easily reaches a wide range of applicants. Before JPS Health Network improved their website, they recruited applicants mostly from the local area. After the website was redesigned to enhance recruiting for nursing vacancies, JPS hired nurses from Alabama, Arizona, California, Hawaii, Florida, New York, Okalahoma, Pennsylvania, and Utah. Because JPS attracted a wider pool of applicants, they were able to hire nurses who were more experienced and better qualified.

Web-based recruiting is not a panacea, however. According to a recent study of business school graduates who were looking for jobs, poorly designed electronic recruiting causes frustration and turns some applicants off to the company. Exhibit 6.4 describes some of the most common problems encountered by electronic applicants. How many of these problems would you put up with before deciding not to submit a job application?[15]

Employee Referrals.   **Employee referrals** *occur when current employees inform their acquaintances about openings and encourage them to apply.*

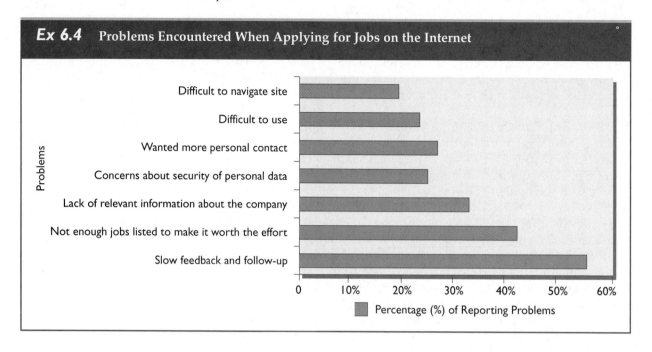

Ex 6.4   Problems Encountered When Applying for Jobs on the Internet

FAST FACT

Forty-one percent of new hires at the Container Store, a top-ranked "Best Company to Work For," come from employee referrals.

Companies such as New York Life Insurance facilitate employee referrals by supporting online alumni networks. Other companies make it easy for their employees to send electronic job announcements to their friends. When labor shortages are severe, some companies offer rewards to employees who refer qualified applicants. The financial incentives may be linked to a recruit's completion of an application, acceptance of employment, or completion of work for a specified time period.

Compared with other external recruiting methods, employee referrals result in the highest one-year survival rates for most occupations. Employees provide a balanced view of organizational life, and the people they refer generally have more information available to them so a better decision is likely. In addition, employees tend to recruit applicants who are similar to them in interests and motivations. Since employees are already adjusted to the organizational culture, this matching process increases the likelihood that applicants also will fit into the environment.[16]

The referral approach seems to be good for applicants as well as employees. At Citibank, referral applications present more appropriate resumes, are more likely to apply under favorable market conditions, perform better in interviews, and are more likely to get hired.[17] A potential disadvantage of referrals is that employees tend to refer others who are similar in age, gender, ethnicity, and religion. If relied on too heavily, this recruiting approach may be detrimental to equal employment opportunity goals.

Employment Agencies and Search Firms.   Public and private employment agencies are good sources of temporary employees and permanent employees. American public employment agencies operate under the umbrella of the U.S. Training and Employment Service; it sets national policies and oversees the operations of state employment agencies, which have branch offices in many cities. State employment agencies offer counseling, testing, and placement services to everyone and provide special services to military veterans, members of some minority groups, colleges, and technical and professional people. Their services are supported by employer contributions to state unemployment funds. The *Social Security Act* provides that, in general, workers who have been laid off from a job must register with the state employment agency in order to be eligible for unemployment benefits. Thus, most state agencies have long rosters of potential applicants.

Private employment agencies—sometimes called headhunter, placement, or search firms—serve professional, managerial, and unskilled job applicants. Agencies dealing with unskilled applicants often provide job candidates whom employers would have a difficult time finding otherwise. Many employers looking for unskilled workers do not have the resources to do their own recruiting or have only temporary or seasonal demands for these workers.

Search firms such as Korn/Ferry, Spencer Stuart, and Heidrick & Struggles play a major role in recruiting professional and managerial candidates. The executive recruiting industry grew at a phenomenal pace during the 1990s, when the economy boomed. Predictably, it is going through a period of consolidation now, with the larger players buying out their smaller competitors.

Executive search firms can be an expensive recruitment method for the employer, who may have to pay fees as high as one-third of the first year's total salary and bonus package for a job that's filled. More troublesome are the hidden costs of using search firms. A search firm generally cannot approach executives it has recently placed, and it may have agreements with its clients that limit its ability to approach the clients' employees. This restricts the pool of applicants considered by a search firm and runs counter to the objective of creating a large pool of qualified applicants. In addition, search firms typically present employers with very few possible candidates to consider. They prescreen heavily before letting the employer and applicant meet. This protects applicants' privacy and saves the employer time. But it also places a great deal of weight on the judgment of the search firm. Because search firms have much less information about the needs of the organization, compared to managers, search firms are more likely to err by rejecting a candidate who would do well. To minimize such costs, close monitoring of the search firm's activities is necessary. In spite of these drawbacks, headhunter firms are doing well, especially when it comes to helping talented people who work in troubled companies find new positions. Exhibit 6.5 offers suggestions for how to select a search firm when one is needed.[18]

School Placement Services and Trade Associations. Schools are important sources of recruits for most organizations, although their importance varies depending on the type of applicant sought. If an organization is recruiting managerial, technical, or professional applicants, then colleges and universities are the most important source. These institutions become less important when an organization is seeking production, service, office, and clerical employees.

For some jobs, the recruiting process begins in the high schools even though the hiring process doesn't kick in until college graduation. Gannett, owner of *Detroit News, Asheville Citizen-Times,* and 80 other newspapers, targets high school students who show even a glimmer of interest in journal-

"I get calls from headhunters and such, offering bigger salaries, signing bonuses, and such. But the excitement of what I'm doing here is equal to a 30% pay raise."

Jorgen Wedel
Executive Vice President
Gillette

Ex 6.5   Tips for Selecting an Executive Search Firm

- Learn about the search industry; be sure to understand its weaknesses.
- Investigate the firm's "completion" rate. Some firms fill the positions they are hired for more than 90% of the time. Others fill the positions less than 70% of the time.
- Be sure you know how many restrictions the firm is under. If a firm you want to use is obligated to not recruit from a long list of clients, you may need to hire more than one firm.
- Determine the ratio of "lions" (the partners who often are essential to arranging a meeting and closing a deal) to "squirrels" (researchers and recruiters who help put together a list of possibilities). Be sure you meet the squirrels before hiring the lions.
- Understand and carefully consider the fee structure. Most fee structures are designed to benefit the search firm making few performance commitments to clients. Negotiate a flat fee rather than a fee based on the new hire's compensation and insist on a refundable retainer.
- Understand the search process used by the firm and evaluate how likely it is that the process will yield candidates who meet your recruitment objectives.

FAST FACT

To guard against trivial assignments being given to student interns, who may then get turned off, JP Morgan Chase requires supervisors to describe intern projects to the HR staffers who oversee recruiting.

ism. Editors speak with the students, talking up the glamorous aspects of a career in journalism. In addition to sponsoring workshops for the staff working on high school newspapers, Gannett's editors offer to critique the papers and invite students into their newsrooms to give them exposure to the excitement. For college students, working as an intern provides additional experience. These and other efforts help Gannett compete effectively for college graduates despite the fact that the publishing industry pays much less than many others.[19]

Many trade and professional associations also provide recruiting opportunities. Often jobs can be announced through their newsletters and/or through links to the association's website. Annual trade conferences provide a more personal forum where employers and potential job applicants can meet. Communities and schools have adopted this idea and now bring together large numbers of employers and job seekers at job fairs. *At a* **job fair,** *usually several employers are present to provide information about employment opportunities at their company.* The setting is often somewhat informal. The public is invited to attend to gather information and ask questions.

FAST FACT

Costa Rica requires high school students to take English; its workforce includes 12,000 engineering students; and its per-capita computer usage rate is higher than that of the United States and Canada.

Foreign Nationals. In some professions—such as chemical engineering, software engineering, and others that involve high-tech skills—labor shortages cause employers to recruit foreign nationals. Foreign nationals may be employed in operations in the United States or abroad. When they work abroad, they serve as **host-country nationals** (*persons working in their own country, not the country of the parent company*) or **third-country nationals** (*persons working in a country that's neither their own nor that of the parent company*).

Increasingly U.S. companies are using host-country nationals to fill newly created jobs that have been "offshored" from the United States to substantially reduce their labor costs. Software programmers in India or Bulgaria or Romania may work at wage levels that are 50–75% less than their U.S. counterparts.[20]

Under the Immigration Reform and Control Act of 1986, the Immigration Act of 1990, and the American Competitiveness in the Twenty-First Century Act of 2000, it's unlawful for employers to hire foreign nationals to work in the United States unless they are authorized to do so. Those hired must be paid the prevailing wage. For professional-level workers, employers typically spend an additional $100,000 to $200,000 in relocation costs.

One way for a foreign worker to enter the U.S. labor market is by obtaining an H1-B visa. A quicker alternative for foreign employees working abroad in U.S. companies is to obtain an L-1 intracompany transferee visa. Such visas are not subject to annual quotas. Another advantage of an L-1 intracompany transferee visa is that it's easier for transferees to bring along family members. TN NAFTA visas are another alternative, but only Canadian and Mexican citizens can obtain these visas. With appropriate documents in hand, newly hired Canadian and Mexican workers can obtain TN NAFTA visas at the border as they enter the United States to begin work.[21]

Recruiting foreign employees to work in the United States is a useful approach to dealing with labor shortages, but it involves some extra administrative work and planning. Several of the activities associated with recruiting foreign workers are summarized in the feature "Managing Globalization: Employing Foreign Workers."

Recruiting foreign nationals successfully requires making an extra effort to understand other cultures from which applicants are sought. For example, whereas U.S. applicants can be expected to recognize the names of many large companies, the names of those companies may be very unfamiliar to applicants outside the United States; or even if the name is recognizable, applicants may have little information about what it would be like to work in a particular U.S. city. Many French students recognize Coca-Cola's brand

FAST FACT Over the next five years, financial services firms expect to transfer 500,000 jobs overseas.

FAST FACT About 550,000 Americans work for Japanese companies located in the United States.

Managing Globalization

Employing Foreign Workers

Complying with federal regulations and facilitating the successful relocation of foreign workers are two responsibilities that must be accepted by employers of foreign workers. Specific activities include the following.

✔ Publicize job openings in foreign labor markets using methods that are culturally appropriate to the location (as well as legally acceptable in the United States).

✔ Document domestic recruiting efforts and their lack of success, in order to meet Department of Labor regulations governing employment of foreign workers.

✔ Monitor salary and benefits of foreign and domestic workers to ensure that foreign workers are treated equally to domestic workers, as required by H1-B visa regulations.

✔ Monitor the percentage of employees holding various types of visas to ensure that legal limits are not exceeded within the company.

✔ Provide relocation support to foreign employees, including assistance with immigration, travel, permanent residence applications, visa renewals, bank accounts, credit cards, drivers' licenses, and so on.

✔ Develop and provide training and acculturation programs for both domestic and foreign employees.

✔ Develop a long-term strategy or how to handle visa expirations.

✔ Assist foreign employees with the process of repatriation into their home country at the end of their employment assignment.

name, but few are likely to have a clear image of what it would be like to work in their Atlanta headquarters.

The job searching approaches used in other countries are another factor to consider when recruiting outside the United States. In Japan, for example, a tradition of long-term employment security means that many excellent potential applicants have had little need to hone their job seeking skills. Also, they may be less likely than U.S. applicants to use the Internet for job hunting, and thus miss job opportunities posted there.[22]

Acquisitions and Mergers.   In contrast with other external methods, hiring new employees by acquiring the firm they work for is a recruiting approach that can facilitate the immediate implementation of an organization's strategic plan. When an organization acquires a company with skilled employees, this ready talent may enable the organization to pursue a business plan—such as entering a new product line—that would otherwise be unfeasible. However, the need to displace employees and to integrate a large number of them rather quickly into a new organization means that the human resource planning and selection process becomes more critical than ever.

Even when a company doesn't acquire a company, merger and acquisition (M&A) activity can provide a good source of applicants. After Thomas Weisel's former employer was acquired by NationsBank, Weisel realized he needed a change. He left NationsBank to start up a new investment bank. Many of the first staff members were former employees from Montgomery, where Weisel worked previously. Because of possible competitive concerns, Weisel had to cut a deal with NationsBank in order to take his colleagues along on his new venture. To fill out the staff, which grew to 800 people in just two years, Weisel recruited many other people in the wake of major M&As in the industry. When word was out that a firm was about to be acquired, Weisel or others in the firm quickly approached the best talent and invited them to consider joining the firm. With a compelling business plan and Weisel's track record of success in the industry, they were able to persuade much of the industry's top talent to join them.[23]

CONTINGENT WORKERS, REHIRES, AND RECALLS

To cope with unexpected or temporary fluctuations in their staffing needs, companies often hire contingent workers. When fluctuating demand is more predictable (e.g., due to seasonal patterns that affect the industry), rehires and recalls can be used as a strategic approach to maintaining the workforce flexibility that's required.

Contingent Workers.   **Contingent workers** *are people hired with no implicit or explicit contract for long-term employment, including "free agents," independent contractors, and temporary workers.* Usually, employers hire contingent workers from the external labor market. The Internet has proved to be a useful tool for recruiting and job searching within this corner of the labor market.

Contingent workers understand that they'll be frequently entering into and exiting from employment relationships. The temporary assignments generally last 3 to 12 months. Therefore, even when they are working on temporary assignments, they nurture their connections to a wide range of possible future employers. In effect, contingent workers must continually maintain their status as a member of the applicant pool in order to ensure their continued employment.[24]

Some contingent workers are recruited directly, but many are recruited indirectly by using the services of temporary help agencies such as Manpower. As more and more companies find it preferable to hire temporary workers, temporary help agencies have experienced a boom. Organizations are using temporary help agencies more than ever because some hard-to-get skills are available nowhere else. This is especially true for small companies that aren't highly visible or can't spend time recruiting. Getting short-term employees without an extensive search is an obvious advantage of temporary help agencies. Agencies serve both temporary workers and employers by helping establish rates of pay, contract terms, standardized billing, and other arrangements.[25]

FAST FACT

Manpower is the world's largest temporary services firm. Based in Milwaukee, it has 3,700 franchises and independent offices in 59 countries. About 50% of revenues come from overseas.

Recalls and Rehires. Many employers recruit workers for temporary employment as part of a planned strategy. Rehiring and recalling are particularly beneficial to organizations that have seasonal fluctuations in the demand for workers, such as department stores, canneries, construction companies, and ski resorts. Each summer and fall during the apple harvest, canneries in eastern Washington state recall large numbers of employees—some of whom have been on the payroll for more than 20 years. Mail-order companies like L. L. Bean continually bring back a large share of their laid-off workforces between September and December, the busiest months of the year.

Recalls and rehires also occur in organizations coping with unexpected staffing problems created by downsizing. A survey of large U.S. companies conducted by the American Management Association found that more than half of the respondents who had downsized said they had lost so many talented people that their ability to compete had been severely damaged. When this happens, many downsized companies end up rehiring as temporary employees the people they just laid off. Indeed, an estimated 17% of contingent employees were previously regularly employed by the same company that now employs them on an as-needed basis; at some companies, as many as 80% of contingent workers were previously working as regular employees.[26]

Advantages and Disadvantages. Rehiring former or laid-off employees is a relatively inexpensive and effective method of recruiting. The organization already has information about the performance, attendance, and safety records of these employees. Rehires are already familiar with job responsibilities, so they need less time to settle in—*unless* the job has changed substantially while they were away.

The growing reliance on contingent employment is often considered a negative trend for employees, however. Contingent workers lead uncertain lives, and they almost never receive benefits. Nevertheless, some employees prefer contingent arrangements because it allows them to work on a schedule of their own choosing. Highly skilled temporary workers often are paid more on an hourly basis than are permanent employees doing similar work. Temporary employment also provides a way to preview different jobs and work in a variety of organizations. For employees, temporary work is a good way to learn about possible new careers. Good temporary employees often receive permanent job offers. Contingent employment also serves the needs of core employees because it facilitates implementation of temporary leave policies.

Recalls, rehires, and contingent employees have some unique disadvantages, however. The commitment of rehires who would have preferred to keep their steady, full-time jobs may be low. Permanent employees who know they are being paid less per hour than comparable temporary hires may feel resentful. For these and other reasons, conflict between permanent and temporary employees is common. L.L. Bean is very aware of these possible disadvantages and realizes that relying on rehires would backfire if all employees weren't fully committed to providing high-quality service. To prevent this, it works very hard to recruit employees who prefer seasonal employment, and then seeks to establish positive employment relationships.

> **FAST FACT**
>
> SAS Institute and Lincoln Electric believe that by not laying off workers, their workers will be more loyal and more productive.

RECRUITING FROM THE APPLICANT'S PERSPECTIVE

Regardless of who the applicants are or how they became applicants for positions, events that occur during recruitment can determine whether they accept or reject an organization's employment offer. Recruiting activities should create positive experiences for all applicants—even those who aren't offered positions. If the firm's recruitment methods promote a favorable image of the company, rejected applicants may try again in the future and encourage their friends to view the company as an employer of choice. In other words, recruitment addresses current labor needs while also anticipating future labor needs.

For organizations to effectively attract *and* retain potentially qualified candidates, they need to understand the behaviors and preferences of the diverse workforce. What do candidates consider when searching for, and choosing, a new job? How do candidates differ in their job search activities? Where do they get their information regarding job availability, and what do they react to the most?

Building a Corporate Reputation

> *"We're one of the few companies where employees identify themselves by the company name—here you're not just an IBM employee—you're an IBMer."*
>
> Randy MacDonald
> HR Senior VP
> IBM

For many applicants, the reputation of the organization they work for is an important consideration. Generally, people prefer to work for an organization that they can be proud of. By the time a job opening needs to be filled, it may already be too late to begin convincing potential applicants that a particular company is a good place to work, however. Research shows that applicants' images of potential employers are shaped by recent publicity and the company's own advertising.[27] Organizations with more positive corporate reputations attract more, and somewhat more qualified, applicants.[28]

Planning.   Building a reputation takes time and requires a long-term planning horizon. Chik-fil-A is proud of the achievements of its employees and makes sure local newspapers communicate that message. Since 1975, this restaurant chain has awarded employees with scholarships worth more than $13 million—and local newspapers cover the stories. Chik-fil-A also informs newspapers when employees earn big incentive rewards—like the "Symbol of Success," which includes the keys to a new automobile. CIGNA Insurance uses a similar strategy to build the company's reputation as a good employer. CIGNA rewards top achievers by making them members of the President's Club. Of those who make the club, 99% get their picture published in their local newspaper.[29]

Risks.   With all the talk about becoming an employer of choice, it's worth pointing out that organizations should think carefully about whether to mount a public campaign to raise public awareness. Unless a company really is a great place to work, employers should not claim that it is. And if managers aren't ready to make significant investments in order to become a great place to work, the company is better off not jumping on this bandwagon. After Merrill Lynch made *Working Woman's* list of best companies in 2000, a group of female stockbrokers started a writing campaign to have the company removed from the list. They also hired an airplane to fly banners at sporting events, informing spectators that the group had sued the company for sex discrimination.

When Martin McGinn announced that Mellon Financial was undertaking an employer-of-choice campaign, his customers warned him that he might be in worse shape if he tried and failed, suggesting that it might be better to not even try. Consider the exposure such a campaign creates. In order to be considered for the "best company" lists, employees must be polled and the company must participate in benchmarking studies to determine whether the pay-and-benefits structure falls below the competition. The exercise revealed that Mellon was underpaying employees relative to the competition. Thousands of employees had to be given raises, which cost the company several million dollars.

> *"There are considerable risks in presenting myself as an employer of choice."*
>
> Martin McGinn
> Chair and CEO
> Mellon Financial Corp.

Making It Easy to Apply

From the applicant's perspective, making it easy to apply for a job is a good way to increase the number of applications received. User-friendly online application software that accepts applicants' resumes is one way to make it easy. Allstate Insurance makes it easy for independent contractors to apply by using software that instantly conducts the initial screening process and gives immediate feedback to the applicant. Successful applicants are told on the spot that an interview will be scheduled as the next step. There is literally no waiting required for the applicant to learn whether the company is a good prospect. JPMorgan/Chase went one step further. They made it *fun* to apply online by creating a job-hunting game that helps applicants match their interests to alternative jobs in the company.[30]

FAST FACT For drivers, FedEx relies heavily on owner-operators employed as independent contractors. They can learn all about the contract terms, submit resumes online, and get online assistance for running their business more efficiently.

Making a Good Personal Impression

To develop an understanding of how job applicants view recruiting practices, one team of researchers decided to conduct intensive, open-ended interviews with a few job hunters. The researchers asked placement directors from four colleges of a large university to identify job seekers who were as different from each other as possible in terms of sex, race, grade point average, and so on. Forty-one job seekers were interviewed early in the recruiting season and again near the end, eight to ten weeks later. The results showed that job seekers' early perceptions of how well they fit a job were affected most by job and company characteristics, then by contacts with recruiters, and then by contacts with other people in the company besides recruiters.

In many instances, recruiters made jobs that initially appeared unattractive seem attractive. Positive impressions were created by the status of recruiters and whether recruiters made applicants feel "specially" treated. On the other hand, almost all job seekers reported that some recruiters or recruiting practices or both created poor impressions and made some jobs seem less attractive. Timing was especially important here, with slow or late decisions being a major reason for negative impressions. Another interesting finding was that the best applicants were more likely than weaker applicants to interpret recruiting practices as indications of what the employing organization was like rather than assuming the practices were just a poor reflection on the particular recruiter involved. In other words, a poor recruiter had the most negative impact on the best applicants.[31]

At Dell Computer, applicants feel special because so many people are involved, as described in the feature "Managing Teams: At Dell, Everyone's a Recruiter."[32]

Effective recruiters show sincere interest in applicants, and, in return, applicants show more interest in the job.[33] Training recruiters is one way to improve the impressions they leave with applicants. Training programs should teach recruiters to spend less time talking about topics that are irrelevant to the job, be receptive to questions from applicants, not be overly aggressive in trying to "sell" the job, and in general convey a professional image of the organization.[34] Recruiters also need to understand the jobs to be filled. This appears to be especially true when recruiting highly skilled professionals. At Chiron, a bio-pharmaceutical firm, recruiters regularly sit in on the business meetings in order to learn about the company and issues in the industry. The goal is to make sure that recruiters can relate to the concerns of job applicants.[35]

> *"I was impressed that these women executives would take the time out to interview me, a mid-level person. I was delighted to find people that embrace the same values I embrace."*
>
> Teri Robinson
> Vice President
> Darden Restaurants

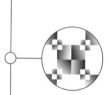

Managing Teams

At Dell, Everyone's a Recruiter

The job of the head of staffing for Dell Computer is to hire world-class people. Regardless of how many new recruits are needed, the company never lowers its standards for quality. Dell wants to hire only the best, and to do so it uses the best recruiters—its own employees, including the CEO when necessary. Besides getting referrals from employees, Dell's recruiting managers use a "leads team." Like a SWAT team, its job is to act quickly and aggressively to tackle hiring problems—such as an unexpected vacancy in a key position. Acting almost like spies, the "leads team" studies newspapers, the Web, trade journals, and anything else they can think of to come up with the names of people who might consider a job change. Dips in stock prices, mergers, or plans for downsizing all provide clues. When good people are found, they often visit the company headquarters in Austin, Texas, before making a final decision. At this point, Dell may involve other people from the community to help. When a recruit wanted to know about the ice-hockey opportunities for his son, a Junior Olympian, Dell had the local youth league president meet with the candidate to provide the information. That was somewhat unusual. More typical would be involving realtors, medical experts, school administrators, and/or religious leaders, depending on candidates' particular concerns. For a company that depends on the talent of its employees for success, all this effort is worth it.

Giving Applicants the Information They Need

Recruiters and the recruiting process help create a good (or bad) impression, but other things matter too. *Most job seekers make trade-offs between different job and organizational attributes; that is, they adopt a* **compensatory approach.**[36] Especially for younger applicants, deciding whether to accept an employment offer may be entangled with choosing an occupation. Economic issues, including the realities of the labor market, have some impact on what applicants pay attention to. Individual needs, interests, and abilities also play a role, as do sociological factors such as one's prior exposure to the occupation through parents and relatives.[37] Contrary to what many people believe, however, the differences between what attracts men and women to jobs are quite small.[38]

It is often assumed that the attractiveness of an offer depends in part on what other offers the applicant is considering. This line of thinking follows from the image of a job seeker who invests a great deal of time and effort to generate as many options as possible and then simultaneously evaluates them. In reality, except for new college graduates, job seekers have only a hazy notion of their options.[39] The objective of most job seekers is to find an acceptable, rather than ideal, job. They usually evaluate opportunities sequentially. If an offer meets minimum criteria, it's accepted; if it doesn't, the sequential search process continues. In other words, alternative offers are less important than past experiences and beliefs about what can realistically be expected. In general, however, applicants usually evaluate the organization, the job, and various elements of the company's HRM system.[40]

The Organization.   When applicants consider whether to pursue a job opening, important organization characteristics include its size, location, general reputation and management ethics as presented in the media, attitudes toward the product, and whether the company is hiring new managers and at the same time laying some people off. Applicants differ considerably on the specific information to which they attend. In general, however, applicants judge whether the organization's values match their own.[41] Savvy recruiters understand the importance of this issue and make an effort to inform applicants about the company as well as the job.

The Job.   Presumably, most applicants seek jobs that fit the skills they have to offer. In addition, important job characteristics include the status of the functional area the job is in as well as the nature of the work itself.[42] In their efforts to attract a large pool of applicants, many employers oversell their virtues and cover over their flaws. Just as applicants work to create the best possible impression,[43] so do employers. Some recruiters tell job applicants only about the positive aspects of a job. This tactic follows from a desire to increase offer acceptances. In the short run, this tactic may work,[44] but in the longer term, it's counterproductive.

FAST FACT

When JigZaw Inc. places job ads, they include the phrase "people interested in flextime are encouraged to apply."

HR Practices.   As described in Chapter 12, benefits and flexible work arrangements often are among the most important considerations. Men and women alike prefer companies that offer more flexibility and opportunities to learn quickly.[45] With the exception of workers under age 30, almost everyone agrees that benefits such as health insurance are among the most important factors to consider. For those at the bottom of the earnings scale, job security is one of the most important concerns.[46] Many people also take into consideration the opportunities for growth, development, and future promotions.

Honesty Pays (Saves).   Accepting a job offer can have far-reaching implications for a person's life—it can influence where a person lives, how much stress a person experiences commuting to work, where a person's children attend school, where a partner works, income levels, and so on. Viewed in this light, persuading a person to take a job becomes a big responsibility.

Tell All.   Clearly, the only ethical approach is to engage in an honest exchange of information with job applicants. In fact, recent research shows that applicants appreciate the concern shown by employers who provide negative as well as positive information.[47] **Realistic job previews** *occur when the organization is careful to describe both the positive and negative aspects of a job and organization.* Research shows that using realistic job previews actually increases the number of eventual recruits. In addition, recruits who receive both types of information are more committed and slightly less likely to quit once they accept the job.[48]

Employees share in the responsibility of acquiring a realistic job preview. In order to make sure they know what they are getting into, applicants should ask questions until they get detailed answers about things such as the expected results, the timetable available to achieve the results, and the resources available to employees.[49]

Use Multiple Sources of Information.   Realistic job previews take many forms, including advertisements, formal job descriptions, film or video presentations, and samples of the actual work. A study involving several large companies found that potential applicants are attracted to companies that provide more information in their ads. When ads tell about the company, the job, and the job benefits, job seekers are more likely to follow up and apply for the job.[50] Another study found that applicants who obtained information through both formal and informal means had more knowledge about the job than those who relied on only one type of information.[51] In general, more information is better, and informal means of communicating about the job often produce more accurate perceptions.[52]

REJECTING WITH TACT

When Mirage Resorts received 84,000 applications for 9,600 job openings, they had to tell thousands of applicants they wouldn't be hired. Southwest Airlines sends the same message to thousands of applicants year after year. If rejected candidates feel angry, they may never again purchase services from the organization. If recruiting procedures are viewed as unfair, too lengthy, or too impersonal, rejected candidates may share their dissatisfaction with friends and associates. For "high-demand" organizations, rejecting with tact is an extremely important step in the total recruitment process.

Most applicants receive the news of their rejection in written form. Whether it's a traditional letter or an e-mail message, the same basic principles apply. To leave a positive impression, a rejection letter should include statements that are friendly, a personalized and correct salutation and address, and a summary of the applicant's job qualifications. Including statements about the size and excellence of the application pool can reduce disappointment and increase perceptions of fairness. Applicants also appreciate timely rejection notices. A recruitment and selection timetable should be specified for applicants, and the organization should meet its self-imposed deadlines.

EQUAL OPPORTUNITY AND NONDISCRIMINATION

Legal considerations play a critical role in the recruiting and hiring processes of most companies in the United States. As described in Chapter 3, U.S. employment laws prohibit discrimination in recruiting.

EEO-1 REPORTS

One method the federal government uses to track compliance with nondiscrimination laws is requiring most employers with more than 100 employees to file annually an Employer Information Report (EEO-1). Each year, about 45,000 employers file EEO-1 reports. Briefly, an **EEO-1 report** gives an accounting of the composition of the workforce using four factors: job family (9 categories), sex (2 categories), race/ethnicity (8 categories), and employment status (5 categories). The reports are confidential, but the Equal Employment Opportunity Commission (EEOC) uses them to investigate reports of employment discrimination.

For organizations that use an electronic applicant tracking system, the record keeping required for EEO-1 reports is quick and easy. An electronic **applicant tracking system** *collects and stores the needed information automatically using a standard format that lists the job content and skill requirements (based on a job description).* Most tracking systems also capture data from applicants (e.g., from resumes) and provide for reports to be entered based on interviews and other selection procedures. In addition to tracking the number and qualifications of applicants, an applicant tracking system makes it easy for employers to track the demographic characteristics of applicants who learned about job openings from different sources (e.g., a job fair, job boards, recruitment agencies). Note, however, that it is important for tracking systems to store demographic information about applicants separately from information about qualifications, as it is illegal to use most demographic information as a basis for hiring decisions.

Besides being convenient, electronic applicant tracking systems can help employers evaluate their recruiting practices against strategic objectives. They make it easy to generate reports of many types, which can be used to assess the speed of recruiting procedures, the number and quality of applicants from different sources, the diversity of applicants attracted using various methods, and so on.[53]

AFFIRMATIVE ACTION PROGRAMS

The U.S. employment laws most directly relevant to recruitment are those describing affirmative action programs. **Affirmative action programs**

(AAPs) *are intended to ensure proportional representation or parity, or to correct underutilization of qualified members of protected groups in an organization's relevant labor market.* Title VII of the Civil Rights Act of 1964 identifies the following as protected groups: women, African Americans, Hispanics, Native Americans, Asian Americans, and Pacific Islander Americans.

Some AAPs are required because the company is a federal contractor. Others are adopted as part of a consent degree. Many AAPs are simply voluntary efforts intended to guard against intentional or unintentional discrimination. Regardless of why an AAP is developed, regulatory guidelines and subsequent Supreme Court decisions make it clear that AAPs must not include strong preferential treatment or strict quotas. Instead, they should emphasize recruiting activities that increase the representation of protected groups and employment practices that eliminate bias.

Approximately 65,000 companies are federal contractors.

FAST FACT

Federal Contractors.   If a company has a federal contract greater than $50,000 and has 50 or more employees, it's referred to as a federal contractor. Executive Order 11246, which became effective in 1965, requires federal contractors to

1. have and abide by an equal employment policy;
2. analyze their workforces to assess possible underutilization of women and ethnic minorities; and
3. when underutilization is revealed, develop a plan of action to eliminate it and make a good faith effort to implement the plan.

In addition to protecting members of the groups identified in Title VII, federal contractors are required to take affirmative action to employ and advance qualified individuals with disabilities (section 503 of the Rehabilitation Act of 1973). The rules further provide that employers with 50 or more employees who hold federal contracts totaling more than $50,000 must prepare written AAPs for disabled workers in each of their establishments (e.g., in each plant or field office).

Federal contractors are required to file written affirmative action plans with the **Office of Federal Contract Compliance Programs (OFCCP),** *which is charged with overseeing the employment practices of federal contracts and enforcing relevant federal regulations.* The Department of Labor specifies the required components of the written plans:

1. **Utilization analysis.** The analysis *determines the number of minorities and women employed in different jobs within an organization.* Under the current regulations, this requirement can be met with a one-page organizational profile.
2. **Availability analysis.** This *measures how many members of minorities and women are available to work in the relevant labor market of an organization.* The **relevant labor market** *is generally defined as the geographic area from which come a substantial majority of job applicants and employees. If an organization employs proportionately fewer members of protected groups than are available, a state of* **underutilization** exists.
3. **Goals and timetables. Goals and timetables** *specify how the organization plans to correct any underutilization of protected groups.* Because goals and timetables become the organization's commitment to equal employment, they must be realistic and attainable. When a

protected group is found to be underutilized, the timetable for addressing the problem is likely to stretch over several years.

These plans are intended to reduce discriminatory practices among employers who receive federal funds.

Several studies indicate that for federal contractors, representation of black males and black females has grown rapidly.[54] A review of the status of women and minorities in these firms suggests that AAPs may not eliminate discrimination, however. In summarizing their findings, an OFCCP official concluded, "In nearly every review we do, we're finding inequities in the compensation for women and minorities compared to white men."[55]

Consent Decrees.   Employers that are not federal contractors may nevertheless be subject to a government-regulated affirmative action plan. A federal court may require an AAP if it finds evidence of past discrimination in a suit brought against the organization through the EEOC. The evidence that leads to such conclusions often comes from a utilization analysis conducted by the EEOC. A **consent decree** *is a legally enforced court ruling that specifies the affirmative action steps an organization must take to remedy the effects of past discrimination.*

Since the 1960s, hundreds of consent degrees have put AAPs into place. Their effectiveness to date is difficult to judge, however. Women and minorities have made some progress in their employment status. Whether progress would have been faster or slower in the absence of the consent decrees is impossible to know. When *Fortune* put together its list of the "50 Best Companies for Asians, Blacks, and Hispanics," the vast majority of the 50 companies selected had aggressive EEOC recruiting plans in place.[56] Some programs were put in place years before in response to consent decrees, while others were likely developed to avoid lawsuits or minimize the damages that would be caused by a lawsuit. One thing *is* clear, however: Perceptions of unfair discrimination persist even among African Americans who are generally optimistic about their futures.[57]

Voluntary Affirmative Action.   Despite recent court decisions suggesting that employers may face legal challenges to affirmative action efforts, many U.S employers take a proactive approach to recruiting a diverse pool of applicants. IBM is just one example of many that could be described. Its approach is explained in the feature "Managing Diversity: IBM's Project View."[58]

Designing AAPs.   The content of a voluntary AAP depends on the organization and the extent to which various groups are underrepresented. It may also depend on the company's strategic business objectives.

The EEOC publishes guidelines for organizations that wish to establish voluntary AAPs, and it offers an annual Exemplary Voluntary Efforts Award to recognize companies with the best voluntary programs. Winning the award appears to have value beyond simply good public relations. A study of firms that have won this award showed that investors bid up the stock prices of the winning companies after the award was announced. By comparison, stock prices fell following announcements of discrimination settlements.[59]

Managing Diversity

IBM's Project View

An IBM motto is, "None of us is as strong as all of us." In a company that values teamwork, it's important that all employees feel that their employer meets their personal needs and the needs of their communities. IBM's commitment to workforce diversity is one way that the company satisfies the needs of all employees. Project view is one program that supports the company's diverse workforce.

Project View was started nearly 20 years ago as a way to bring candidates in for summer positions. Today, it is a core element of IBM's recruiting strategy for regular full-time hires. Project View is a series of multiday events that bring underrepresented minority students who have hardware, software, and business backgrounds to the company for an extended visit during which they see the facilities, obtain information, and participate in interviews. For example, each year, a three-day Native American Project View event is held in the Southwest to recruit qualified applicants from some of this country's 32 tribal colleges. As another example, in 2003, IBM held a two-day People with Disabilities Project View.

Line managers who have available job openings along with HR professionals cohost Project View events. The company's extensive network of relationships with colleges and universities is also central to the event's success. Managers from all over the organization come to the Project View recruiting events. During the two or three days of the event, managers have plenty of opportunity to talk with talented college students who will soon be entering the job market and identify those who have the skills and geographic preferences that fit anticipated job openings. Project View also provides an opportunity for recruits to learn about IBM's other diversity-friendly HR practices. For example, Leadership Development for Asia Pacifics (LEAP) is a five-day program designed to promote the professional development of high-potential employees of Asian Pacific heritage, and IBM has 15 Hispanic/Latin diversity groups. Thus, Project View is just one element of IBM's total strategy for recruiting and retaining a diverse workforce.

Legal Risks of AAPs. Despite research that documents the benefits of AAPs, mandatory and voluntary AAPs have come under increasing political attack. It's unclear how long they'll remain legal.[60] In Chapter 3, we described the recent Supreme Court case over the University of Michigan's affirmative action plans for admitting students to that institution. In that case, an institution that thought it was being socially responsible by taking affirmative actions learned that the Supreme Court would not allow affirmative actions that explicitly took race and ethnicity into account.

A recent case illustrates how the trend of questioning the legality of AAPs influences employment decisions:[61] By the 1990s when this case was first heard, many large broadcasters had developed affirmative action plans based on guidelines published by the Federal Communications Commission (FCC). Those guidelines essentially stated that, as a condition for keeping their license, broadcast companies must make good faith efforts to recruit and hire minorities. However, in 1998, a court ruled that those guidelines were not enforceable. In response, the FCC issued new rules. The revised FCC rules for broadcasters set out initiatives to recruit more minorities and women through activities such as career fairs and internships. Broadcasters were required to undertake four such initiatives. Alternatively, they could develop their own outreach efforts. But if those efforts yielded "few or no applications from women or minorities," the FCC promised to investigate. In explaining the FCC's position, William Kennard stated, "We're at a time when there is a troubling disconnect between images people see on TV and the reality of our multicultural society." But the revised rules were challenged too. The case eventually was heard again in a federal appeals court, which handed down its decision in 2001. The decision, which supported the lower court, stated, "The rule does put official pressure upon broadcasters to recruit minority candidates, thus creating a race-based classification that is not narrowly tailored to support a compelling governmental interest and is therefore unconstitutional." The decision was handed down on the same day that the government released a report showing that the number of television stations owned by minorities had dipped to the lowest level in at least a decade. Kennard, the first black chair of the FCC, described the court's decision as "outrageous." A new FCC chair, Michael Powell, took over the job shortly after the appeals court made its ruling. Powell stated that he believed there was insufficient evidence to show a connection between diversity in employment and diversity in the content offered by broadcasters.

Public Opinion. Views about affirmative action vary greatly within the United States. For example, many business leaders supported the University of Michigan's affirmative action efforts for increasing the diversity of its student body. Several of the nation's largest employers—including Microsoft, Bank One, General Motors, Steelcase, and two dozen others—prepared a formal statement of their opinion and sent it to the U.S. Court of Appeals. Their statement, called an *amicus brief,* argued that campus diversity was essential to developing the type of workforce that employers need. Diversity was good for business, the CEOs argued. Unless colleges educated a diverse workforce, their companies would not be able to benefit from the advantages that diversity can bring.

> *"A diverse college environment is a much better setting for preparing graduates for life in business."*
>
> James P. Hackett
> CEO
> Steelcase, Inc.

Unlike these CEOs, many people oppose affirmative action efforts. Even if they agree that it is unfair to discriminate, opponents of affirmative action argue that preferential treatment often backfires, causing harm to the intended beneficiaries of AAPs. Consistent with this argument, studies have shown that affirmative action hires are *perceived* as being less competent than equally qualified employees not hired under an AAP.[62] Nevertheless, minority applicants tend to be more attracted to firms that advertise the importance of diversity than to those that don't.[63]

According to numerous opinion polls, Americans strongly support efforts designed to ensure equal opportunity and eliminate bias, and they oppose practices that they believe involve giving any group preferential treatment.[64] Research also shows that affirmative action efforts are more acceptable when merit is emphasized as being central to the decision-making process.[65] Furthermore, people who have recently experienced workplace discrimination tend to have more favorable views of affirmative action practices.[66]

Exhibit 6.6 summarizes some of the arguments made for and against affirmative action activities.

BREAKING THE GLASS CEILING

Regardless of why organizations develop AAPs, their presence often stimulates people to think more systematically about their recruiting efforts. Until recently, the disciplined approach associated with AAPs—that is, defining the relevant labor market and tracking how recruiting efforts affect both who is offered a position and who accepts job offers—was used only for lower-level positions and external recruitment efforts. In recent years, however,

Ex 6.6   Two Sides of the Affirmative Action Debate

ARGUMENTS SUPPORTING AFFIRMATIVE ACTION

- Historical inequities in the treatment of members of protected groups cannot be corrected unless affirmative efforts are made to bring these groups up to parity.
- Affirmative action efforts that are appropriately designed and implemented do not result in reverse discrimination.
- They increase the diversity of the applicant pool; they do not involve lowering standards for making hiring decisions.
- Affirmative action efforts benefit society as a whole by ensuring that the country's human resources are not squandered. Without such efforts, significant portions of the population will be caught in a vicious cycle of low economic achievement.
- Some groups may have to suffer temporary reverse discrimination due to affirmative action efforts, but the greater good that such efforts serve justify this.

ARGUMENTS AGAINST AFFIRMATIVE ACTION

- Affirmative action efforts inadvertently harm those who are intended to be the beneficiaries by lowering their self-esteem and causing others to view them as less qualified.
- Affirmative action efforts result in reverse discrimination.
- Any efforts to help one group necessarily mean discrimination occurs against the groups that do not receive such help.
- By classifying employees into protected and unprotected groups, affirmative action efforts create polarization and separation between men and women and between majority and minority ethnic groups. Pitting groups against each other leads to greater racism and prejudice.
- Affirmative action efforts create innocent victims. The males and nonminorities who experience reverse discrimination today are not the same individuals who are responsible for the historical events that resulted in present-day inequities.

similar approaches to monitoring recruiting efforts have been used to evaluate promotion patterns, which reflect internal recruiting processes.

Many companies found that a decade or two of affirmative action recruiting at lower levels meant that by the late 1980s, plenty of women were in the pipeline for higher-level positions. Yet, women still seem to be trapped below a glass ceiling. Based on its intensive study of nine large corporations, the Department of Labor concluded that the recruiting methods typically used to hire managerial talent contributed to the problem of the glass ceiling.[67] Exhibit 6.7 summarizes how several common recruiting practices can contribute to this problem. The challenge for companies is to balance their desire to recruit the best available talent with their desire to break the glass ceiling.

Colgate's approach is one way to overcome this problem. For Colgate-Palmolive, focusing the firm's recruitment efforts on women seemed like a

FAST FACT

Two-thirds of women professionals say they desire top-level positions, and more than half say they'll move to another company if they are passed over for them.

Ex 6.7 Recruiting Practices That May Create a Glass Ceiling

Reliance on Networking—Word-of-Mouth: Middle- and upper-level positions often are filled through word-of-mouth referrals. Corporate executives may learn of individuals, interview them casually at luncheons or dinners, and make them an offer, without a formal recruitment process. People not in the executive network experience diminished opportunities.

Reliance on Networking—Employee Referrals: In some companies, elaborate employee referral systems are in place. If employees in the company do not represent the full diversity of the labor force, the pool of applicants created by their referrals also will not reflect this diversity.

Executive Search Firms: Employers are responsible for obtaining a diverse pool of applicants. Companies may not make executive recruitment firms aware of their equal employment and affirmative action obligations and objectives, or they may not use success in this area in deciding which search firm to hire.

Job Postings: Some companies post job notices for lower-level jobs, but not for mid- to upper-level jobs. At the higher levels, employees learn about openings only through their informal networks. Informal communications tend to flow more intensely among people who are demographically similar, which means that members of many protected groups are less likely to hear about openings for higher-level positions.

Recruiting Venues: Recruiting often occurs at conferences for trade and professional associations and interviews often are scheduled to take place in a hotel room. A study by the Wellesley College Center for Research on Women found that holding job interviews in hotel rooms can be intimidating for many women and reduces the possibility of finding qualified women applicants.

reasonable solution. When one of the four regional vice presidents stepped down, Colgate's CEO decided he wanted to fill the position with a woman. According to CEO Reuben Mark, the company "wanted the best person we could possibly get, but that person had to be a woman." Colgate hired Lois Juliber in 1988 and put her in charge of its Far East and Canadian Operations. A decade later, she was promoted to Executive Vice President and put in charge of North America and Europe, which constitute half of the company's worldwide operations. The appointment was widely viewed as a signal that she was being considered as a top contender for the CEO position.[68]

Other companies use other approaches. Many have developed management intern programs aimed at recruiting recent minority and female college graduates, as well as sponsoring scholarships for minorities and women in disciplines related to the company's business. Some companies have tried to remedy problems related to the glass ceiling with better use of search firms and other forms of recruitment, record keeping, and internal monitoring. All of these can bolster the use of merit-based information and reduce reliance on informal social networks, which are known to have powerful consequences for who gets considered and hired for open positions.[69] Other approaches include awareness training for top executives and cultural audits, which can be used to identify obstacles or barriers that hinder individuals from meeting their career goals.[70]

> *"If you stick to hiring the best and brightest, diversity will take care of itself. That's not to say that people don't have to be trained to develop a comfort level. That's what we're working on."*
>
> Archyne Woodward
> Diversity Coordinator
> The Chubb Corporation

REDUCING RECRUITING BY RETAINING EMPLOYEES

For some organizations, rapid growth is the primary reason that new employees must be recruited. But the need to replace workers who leave is a far more common force driving most recruiting activities. Turnover, not growth, creates most recruitment pressures.

FAST FACT

When Ernst & Young learned that women were much more likely than men to leave this firm to work elsewhere, they created an Office of Retention.

Understanding the Reasons for Turnover

Some turnover is unavoidable. People retire or move for non–job-related reasons. As described in Chapter 4, turnover due to the upcoming retirement of Baby Boomers is expected to have major implications for future recruiting activities. Furthermore, not all turnover is bad. Research suggests that too little turnover can actually harm firm performance.[71] Sometimes organizations encourage employees to leave. The objective may be to shrink the size of the workforce overall, or simply to help unproductive workers realize that they may be better off finding alternative employment. But the lion's share of turnover—that caused by dissatisfied employees—is not desirable and may be avoidable.

FAST FACT

In the fast-food industry, the annual turnover of hourly workers averages 140%.

Exhibit 6.8 shows some of the known causes of voluntary turnover, based on hundreds of research studies conducted over many years.[72] The exhibit illustrates the most common causes of turnover, but each organization is unique. In some organizations, job dissatisfaction may be a big problem, while in other companies, poor pay might be a greater concern to employees. In order to reduce turnover, each organization should diagnose the reasons that good talent voluntarily decides to look elsewhere for employment.

In order to understand the reasons behind their own employees' decisions to seek other employment, some organizations conduct exit surveys. About

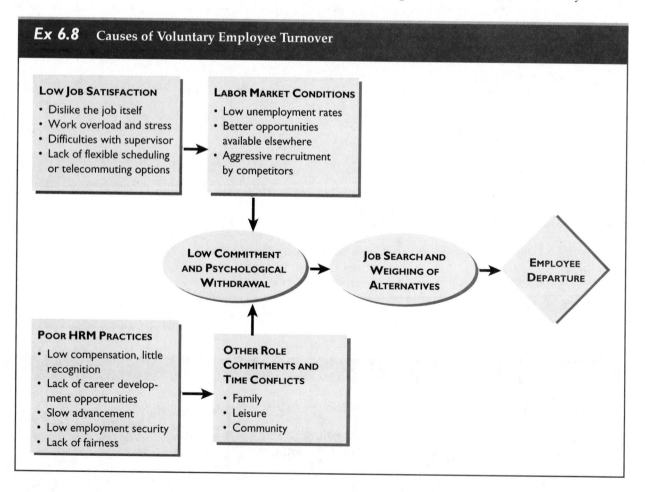

Ex 6.8   Causes of Voluntary Employee Turnover

the time employees leave the organization, they are asked several questions that usually focus on assessing the employees' satisfaction with things such as benefits, work conditions, career advancement and development, supervision, and pay. Such information may be gathered using an interview, a paper-and-pencil survey, or an online survey. Regardless of the method used, the information gathered will not be useful to the employer unless the employee is quite candid.

IMPROVING THE HRM SYSTEM

From Exhibit 6.8, it's easy to see that many causes of turnover are under the employer's control. By improving their HR practices, often employers can make changes that will reduce the rate at which the best employees leave. Examples of such HR practices include electronic monitoring and travel schedules that require extended time away from home. Employers also may be able to offer better pay and benefits, as well as provide more training and improve the quality of supervision.

According to a recent study of people of color aged 21–30 who had recently quit their jobs, poor work relationships with supervisors and peers was a common reason for their leaving. People of color aren't the only ones who leave for this reason, of course. In fact, a study of 25 years of Gallup interviews with more than a million employees found that employees' relationships with their supervisors were a major determinant of whether or not they stayed in a job. Among the things that more effective managers do are taking the time to understand their employees' interests and concerns, providing regular and honest feedback, discussing employees' career plans, and providing suggestions for career development. Through improved selection and performance management practices, employers can improve the supportive behaviors that managers and supervisors use, which can reduce turnover caused by poor supervision. And, with sufficient effort, employers can remove the glass ceilings that prevent otherwise qualified applicants from being promoted.[73]

By understanding the reasons for turnover among its employees and by implementing HR practices that address employees' concerns, the accounting firm of Plante & Moran has been successful in keeping its turnover rate down to just 1.4%. Their approach to minimizing turnover is described in the feature "Managing Diversity: Plante & Moran's People-Friendly Culture."[74]

MANAGING LAYOFFS

Layoffs are typically a short-term solution to difficult economic conditions or an expected decline in the company's business. During business downturns, companies may lay off 5, 10, or even 15% of their employees within a matter of weeks. Often sooner than they expected, companies that have conducted layoffs find that they need to rehire these same people. According to one large study, approximately 25% of the companies that had trimmed their workforces were rehiring people the next year—either for their former jobs or for new permanent jobs.

Managers use layoffs as a quick method of cost cutting, but the approach often backfires. In the longer term, layoffs create problems because the overall trend is that the size of the labor force is growing very slowly.[75] Therefore,

Managing Diversity

Plante & Moran's People-Friendly Culture

If you walked into a Plante & Moran office on a Saturday morning in early April, you might expect to find harried CPAs hunched over their desks and focused only on getting through the brutal realities of the income tax season. In fact, what you are more likely to find are CPAs working alongside a roomful of their tots and toddlers. Plante & Moran is the eleventh largest accounting firm in the country, but it is number one when it comes to keeping its employees satisfied. If an accountant decides to leave, the company estimates that it costs $75,000 to get a replacement—or about one year's salary. By keeping its accountants satisfied, Plante & Moran not only reduces these expenses, but also retains its most talented employees and improves its productivity.

The family-friendly culture at Plante & Moran is part of what makes this company attractive to the growing number of women entering the accounting profession, but the appeal of the company is much broader. Cofounder Frank Moran was a phi-

losophy major before he became an accountant. His personal philosophy was that professionals should be allowed considerable autonomy in doing their work. Instead of working set hours, he believed employees should come and go as needed to serve the needs of clients. At the same time, he understood that serving clients could put tremendous pressure on family life. His company's culture reflects his view that work should allow employees to meet the needs of their clients without sacrificing their personal needs or the needs of family members. Besides child-friendly work sites, other HR practices that keep accountants at this firm include generous vacations, a sabbatical leave program for partners, six months of parental leave for both mothers and fathers, performance evaluations that emphasize results rather than face time, and a breakfast club that ensures that the firm's five managing partners get to know all 1,200 of its employees.

---

as soon as business conditions improve, employers who have conducted layoffs quickly find that they must compete even harder to find new workers. Furthermore, investors often view layoffs as an indication of mismanagement. A four-year study of companies that conducted layoffs found that companies with no layoffs or only small reductions in the workforce (less than 3%) posted share price gains of 9%. During the same time, companies that laid off 3–9% of their workforces showed no gains, and those that cut 10% or more had prices plunge by 38%.[76]

Avoiding Layoffs.   Facing the threat of job loss and seeing others lose their jobs can be a traumatic and bitter experience. This is one reason why many excellent companies do everything possible to avoid layoffs. As described in Chapter 4, there are many alternatives to layoffs. Firms that wish to avoid layoffs can reduce the hours in a standard work week, encourage job sharing, and even arrange for staff members to transfer to other companies. By using practices such as these to avoid layoffs, employers and their employees both reap the benefits. These benefits include maintaining the trust employees feel toward management, building a positive reputation in the labor market, and minimizing disruptions in customer service.[77]

At The Vanguard Group—a money management and mutual fund company—there is no policy statement that guarantees employees that layoffs will never happen, but the company behaves as if they have such a policy. With 10,000 employees, the economic pressures that hit their industry put pressure on Vanguard's bottom line. The company responded by redeploy-

"Our value system is what draws people to our organization. We don't cut people when things get tough and then go off on a hiring splurge six months later."

Kathleen Gubanich
Managing Director of Human Resources
The Vanguard Group

ing people to wherever they could be most useful. This approach fits with their basic hiring philosophy, which Kathleen Gubanich, Managing Director of HR, describes this way: "When we hire somebody, we don't hire them for a position. We hire them for a career."[78]

Assisting Displaced Employees. When downsizing is unavoidable, some companies act as if they have little responsibility to the employees who are downsized. After all, downsizing has become an accepted business practice in America,[79] so shouldn't employees be prepared for it to happen to them? Wise managers understand that layoffs have many consequences. Profits may improve, at least in the short term, but these come at a longer-term cost. As shown in Exhibit 6.9, among the survivors, morale and loyalty often plunge. Some of the best employees may look elsewhere for employment and resign rather than live in fear of what's to come.[80]

To reduce some of the negative consequences of layoffs, the 3M company, based in St. Paul, Minnesota, works hard to keep employees even when its own business units eliminate jobs. Instead of firing people, 3M gives displaced employees first consideration for other job openings within the unit. If no suitable placement can be found, the employee is put on an "unassigned list" and becomes eligible for jobs in other units. A displaced employee can stay on the list for six months. During that time, finding employment is the employee's responsibility, but the company continues to support the employee's effort to find work within 3M. Before recruiting externally to fill open positions, managers first check the qualifications of people on the unassigned list. The company also sponsors an optional three-day workshop that covers topics such as outplacement, coping with job loss,

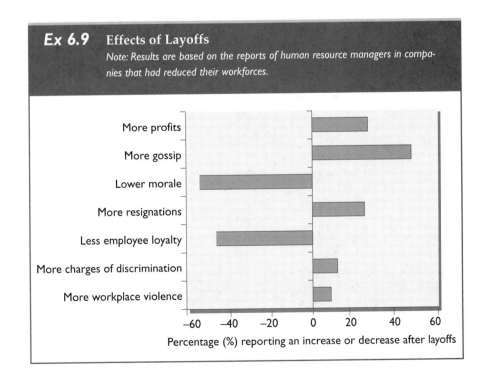

Ex 6.9   Effects of Layoffs

Note: Results are based on the reports of human resource managers in companies that had reduced their workforces.

More profits

More gossip

Lower morale

More resignations

Less employee loyalty

More charges of discrimination

More workplace violence

−60   −40   −20   0   20   40   60

Percentage (%) reporting an increase or decrease after layoffs resume writing, and interviewing skills. For the first four months that they are on the unassigned list, employees have the option of taking a severance package and leaving the company. Approximately 50% of the people on the list find other jobs at 3M within the four-month window. When that happens, both the employees and the company are winners.[81]

Companies like 3M and Pella understand that the conditions that cause current employees to stay committed to an organization also make the organization more attractive to new applicants. Conversely, if employees are leaving a company because they are dissatisfied with how they are treated, that company will have a more difficult time recruiting new employees when they are needed. In general, attracting and retaining the best employees involves nothing less than doing an excellent job in all aspects of managing human resources. This may be more difficult than it sounds, however. Learning about what other companies do can be helpful. But the reality is that every company is likely to face at least a few unique challenges.

SUMMARY

Organizations are dynamic, and the need to attract and retain the right people is perpetual. Two important HR activities that guide effective recruitment and retention are the strategic planning process and job analysis. Planning establishes close linkages between longer-term strategic objectives and activities that address issues related to recruitment and retention. Job analysis enables the organization to convey information accurately (via job descriptions and job specifications) to applicants so that individuals and organizations are well matched. Selection is another activity that should be closely aligned with recruitment, as described in the next chapter. Selection decisions are constrained by the size and quality of the applicant pool, which is created through recruitment and retention activities.

Recruiting involves internal and external searches. For both internal and external recruiting, organizations weigh the costs and benefits of methods in order to choose the most effective ones. The choice of recruitment methods and the implementation of a recruiting plan should take into account the perspective of applicants, as well as the needs of the organization.

Recruiting activities take place within a dynamic legal environment. While the objectives of nondiscrimination legislation are clear, the means that society finds acceptable for creating equal employment opportunities are under debate. Sharply different opinions prevail concerning the best ways to use and design affirmative action programs. It is increasingly difficult for employers to simply "follow the law" when recruiting; they must consider the strategic and social objectives to be achieved, and they must design recruitment strategies to meet those objectives.

For applicants, the process of searching for employment is fundamentally a search for information. Applicants deserve to be given accurate and complete information so they can make the best possible employment decisions. Employers also benefit from this approach, as it reduces posthire dissatisfaction, which in turn can result in early departures.

Retaining employees is one way to reduce the need for extensive recruiting and its associated costs. The development of an effective human resource management system requires understanding the causes of voluntary turnover. Avoiding layoffs also serves to reduce the need for recruiting. Many alternatives to massive layoffs can be used to reduce labor costs while at the same time avoiding the many hidden costs and negative consequences associated with the business practice of downsizing.

TERMS TO REMEMBER

Affirmative action programs (AAPs)
Applicant tracking system
Availability analysis
Compensatory approach
Consent decree
Contingent workers
EEO-1 report
Employee referrals
External labor market
Goals and timetables
Host-country nationals
Internal labor market

Job fair
Job postings
Office of Federal Contract
  Compliance Programs (OFCCP)
Realistic job preview
Recruitment
Relevant labor market
Retention
Talent inventory
Third-country nationals
Underutilization
Utilization analysis

DISCUSSION QUESTIONS

1. How can use of the Internet enable companies like SAS to improve the effectiveness of their recruiting activities? What are the possible disadvantages of Internet recruiting?

2. Review Chapter 4, and then describe the recruiting and retention implications that might follow from a strategic business objective of offering low-cost products to a broad consumer market. Compare these implications to those that might follow from a strategic objective of offering innovative business services to owners of small businesses.

3. What information should be contained in a realistic job preview by a firm seeking to attract the best MBA students? Does your answer depend on the type of industry? The geographic location of the job? On whether it involves an overseas assignment?

4. Do you think firms such as Colgate-Palmolive, American Express, and General Mills should address the glass-ceiling problem by explicitly stating that they want to fill a specific managerial position with a woman? Explain your opinion.

PROJECTS TO EXTEND YOUR LEARNING

1. *Integration and Application.*   After reviewing the two end-of-text cases about Lincoln Electric and Southwest Airlines, answer the following questions:

   a. Which company do you think needs to be most concerned about recruiting? Why?

   b. What should be the objectives of each company's recruiting efforts? Relate the recruiting objectives to each company's strategic objectives.

   c. Which company is likely to have the most difficult time creating a large pool of qualified applicants? Explain your reasoning.

   d. For each company, describe the practices that are most likely to influence employee turnover. Does low turnover contribute to the success of these companies? Explain.

2. *Exploring the Internet.*

   a. Evaluate the possible advantages of aggressively recruiting from the growing ranks of "seniors" by learning more about this population and their work habits. Information is available from:
   American Association of Retired Persons (AARP), http://www .aarp.org
   Senior Community Service Employment Program, http://www .doleta.gov/seniors
   Senior Job Bank, http://www.seniorjobbank.org

   b. Evaluate the possible advantages of aggressively recruiting people with disabilities. Learn more about the Able to Work consortium and read about best practices related to the employment of people with disabilities at http://www.disabilityinfo.gov.

   c. Learn about the services of executive search firms and employment agencies by visiting the company home pages of:
   Adecco, http://www.addecco.com
   Manpower, http://www.manpower.com
   Korn Ferry Future Step, http://www.kornferry.com
   Spencer Stuart, http://www.spencerstuart.com
   Lee Hecht Harrison, http://www.Lhh.com

   d. Learn more about affirmative action plans from the Office of Federal Contract Compliance Programs (OFCCP) at http:// www.dol.gov/elaws/ofccp.htm.

   e. Learn more about the glass ceiling and what companies are doing to reduce its negative consequences by visiting Catalyst at http://www.catalystwomen.org.

3. *Experiential Activity.*   As noted in this chapter, hundreds of studies have been conducted to improve our understanding of why employees choose to leave their employment. You may be surprised to learn that we know much less about the consequences of voluntary turnover than we do about its causes. To improve your understanding of the consequences of turnover for employers and employees, inter-

view four people who are currently employed or were employed until recently. All four people should be familiar with a particular industry (e.g., if you are interested in retailing, select four people with experience in the retail industry). The four interviews can be conducted with class members, family members, coworkers, or anyone else you choose.

Your goal in conducting the four interviews is to generate a list of all the ways turnover affects employers and employees within a particular industry. Working individually or in small teams, prepare a brief presentation that summarizes all the consequences of turnover (both positive and negative) that you identify during the interviews. Use a template like the following one to organize your results.

THE CONSEQUENCES OF TURNOVER		
Type of Industry: _____		
Backgrounds of People Interviewed (e.g., job title, years of experience in the industry, company)		
1. _____ 3. _____		
2. _____ 4. _____		
AFFECTED STAKEHOLDERS	**CONSEQUENCES OF VOLUNTARY EMPLOYEE TURNOVER**	
	POSITIVE	**NEGATIVE**
Customers		
Owners and investors		
Departing employee (DE)		
DE's direct supervisor		
DE's coworkers		
DE's subordinates		
HR professionals		
Other:		
Other:		

CASE STUDY

DOWNSIZING: ANATHEMA TO CORPORATE LOYALTY?

Jim Daniels was unprepared for the dilemma facing Defense Systems, Inc. (DSI). Jim, vice president of human resources for DSI, joined the company one year ago when he was pirated away from one of the company's major competitors. DSI manufactures electronic components used in weapons supplied to the Air Force and many other firms. In addition, DSI makes semiconductors used in many of the weapons systems as well as in personal computers and automotive computers.

When Jim joined DSI, a major drive to build up the staff in engineering was undertaken in anticipation of a major upturn in the semiconductor market. Unfortunately, industry analysts' projections were optimistic, and the semiconductor market failed to pick up. DSI recently completed an aggressive hiring policy at the major universities around the United States, wherein the company had selected 1,000 engineers who were among the cream of the crop with an average GPA of 3.4. Without a pickup in business, however, DSI is confronted with some fairly unpleasant alternatives.

From one point of view, potential cutbacks at DSI fit the overall pattern of cutbacks, restructuring, and downsizing facing many major U.S. companies. The motives among firms who have trimmed their workforces vary—some to please Wall Street and the stockholders, others to keep pace with foreign competitors or to shrink an unwieldy organizational structure. To Jim, DSI layoffs or terminations would be poor alternatives to dealing with a turbulent environment.

The major problem, as Jim sees it, is to preserve as many jobs as possible until business picks up. To terminate the new hires would irreparably harm DSI's future recruitment efforts. On the other hand, underemploying these talented recruits for very long would be bound to lead to major dissatisfaction. Although terminations would improve the balance sheet in the short run, Jim worried about the impact of such a move on corporate loyalty, a fragile and rare commodity at other major firms that have had to cut their white-collar workforce.

Jim is scheduled to meet with the executive committee of DSI in three days to discuss the overstaffing problems and to generate alternatives. In preparation for this meeting, Jim is trying to draw on his experience with his past employer to generate some ideas. A number of differences between DSI and Jim's old employer, though, make comparisons difficult. For one, DSI does not employ nearly the number of temporaries or student interns as did his old employer. Nor does DSI rely on subcontractors to produce parts needed in its assembly operation. Because of extra capacity, DSI can currently produce 50% of the parts it purchases, whereas Jim's ex-employer could produce only 5%.

Another major difference is the degree of training provided by DSI. At Jim's old employer, each employee could expect a minimum of 40 hours of additional training a year; at DSI, however, training consists of about 10 hours per year, much of it orientation training.

Jim wondered whether there might be some additional ways to remove slack from the system and at the same time preserve as many jobs as possible. For example, overtime hours are still paid to quite a few technicians. Would the engineers be willing to assume some of these duties in the interim until business picked up? Some older employees have accumulated several weeks of unused vacation. Could employees be encouraged to take unpaid leaves of absence? Perhaps early retirement incentives could be offered to make room for some of the bright young engineers. DSI also has 14 other geographic locations, some in need of additional workers. Could a recruiting plan for internal transfers address this problem?

As Jim thinks about these options, one thing is clear: He needs to organize and prioritize these ideas concisely if he is to be prepared for his upcoming meeting.

CASE QUESTIONS

1. Why is Jim sensitive to DSI's recruitment efforts?

2. What are some potential problems for the current class of engineers recruited at DSI?

3. How could the use of temporaries, student interns, or subcontractors potentially help DSI?

4. Evaluate Jim's alternatives for reducing DSI's labor surplus. What do you recommend? Why?

ENDNOTES

1 B. Turchin, "SAS Profile—Going Its Own Way," http://www.Software BusinessOnline.com (January/February 2004); G. C. Rappleye, Jr., "How High Is Humanizing Human Resources?" *Workforce* (March 2001); and http://www.sas.com (March 2001).

2 A. Lowe, "Click Here for Nursing Jobs," *HR Magazine* (May 2004): 101–103.

3 Sources: http://www.staffing.org; and "An Army of Surplus Labor," *Workforce Management* (December 2003): 98.

4 M. Petersen, "Faults Found at a Schering Plant," *New York Times* (March 2, 2001): C3.

5 "Does Hiring Minorities Hurt?" *Business Week* (September 14, 1998): 26.

6 M. Hammers, "Almost Curtains," *Workforce Management* (August 2003): 54–55.

7 A. Fisher, "Surviving the Market Turmoil," *Fortune* (April 2, 2001): 98–106; P. Nakache, "Cisco's Recruiting Edge," *Fortune* (September 29, 1997): 275–276.

8 National Association of Colleges and Employers, "No Real Money on the Table," *Workforce Management* (December 2003): 107.

9 P. Buckley, K. Minette, D. Joy, and J. Michaels, "The Use of an Automated Employment Recruiting and Screening System for Temporary Professional Employees: A Case Study," *Human Resource Management Journal* 43 (2004): 233–241.

10 For detailed reviews of research that addresses this and other aspects of recruiting, see S. Rynes and D. Cable, "Recruiting Research in the 21st Century: Moving to a Higher Level," in W. C. Borman, D. R. Ilgen, and R. J. Klimoski (eds.), *Handbook of Psychology, vol. 12: Industrial and Organizational Psychology* (Hoboken, NJ: John Wiley, 2003); J. A. Breaugh and M. Starke, "Research on Employee Recruitment: So Many Studies, So Many Remaining Questions," *Journal of Management* 26(3) (2000): 405–434; A. E. Barber, *Recruiting Employees: Individual and Organizational Perspectives* (Thousand Oaks, CA: Sage, 1998).

11 J. Reingold, "For the Class of 2000, the Sellers' Market Intensifies," *Business Week* (May 8, 2000): 54; H. Axel, *HR Executive Review: Competing as an Employer of Choice* (New York: The Conference Board, 1996).

12 K. D. Carlson, M. L. Connerley, and R. L. Mecham III, "Recruitment Evaluation: The Case for Assessing the Quality of Applicants Attracted," *Personnel Psychology* 55 (2002): 461–4690.

13 C. Joinson, "Capturing Turnover Costs," *HR Magazine* (July 2000): 107–119; B. Davidson, "The Importance of Cost Per Hire," *Workforce* (January 2001): 32–34. For information about sources in recruiting sales-people, see S. L. Martin and N. S. Raju, "Determining Cutoff Scores That Optimize Utility: A Recognition of Recruiting Costs," *Journal of Applied Psychology* 77 (1992): 15–23.

14 R. T. Cober, D. J. Brown, L. M. Keeping, and P. E. Levy, "Recruitment on the Net: Do Organizational Web Site Characteristics Influence Applicant Attraction?" *Journal of Management* 30 (2004): 6236–6246.

15 For suggestions about how to avoid such problems, see I. Kotlyar, "If Recruitment Means Building Trust, Where Does Technology Fit In?" *Canadian HR Reporter* (October 7, 2002): 21–24.

16 A. Van Vianen, "Person-Organization Fit: The Match Between Newcomers' and Recruiters' Preferences for Organizational Cultures," *Personnel Psychology* 53 (2000): 113–149; T. A. Judge and D. M. Cable, "Applicant Personality, Organizational Culture, and Organizational Attraction," *Personnel Psychology* 50 (1997): 359–394; A. M. Saks and B. E. Ashforth, "A Longitudinal Investigation of the Relationships Between Job Information Sources, Applicant Perceptions of Fit, and Work Outcomes," *Personnel Psychology* 50 (1997): 395–426; R. W. Griffeth, P. W. Hom, L. S. Fink, and D. J. Cohen, "Comparative Tests of Multiple Models of Recruiting Sources Effects," *Journal of Management* 23 (1997): 19–36.

17 R. M. Fernandez and N. Weinberg, "Sifting and Sorting: Personal Contacts and Hiring in a Retail Bank," *American Sociological Review* 17 (December 1997): 883–902.

18 M. N. Martinez, "Get Job Seekers to Come to You," *HR Magazine* (August 2000): 45–51; C. McCreary, "Get the Most Out of Search Firms," *Workforce* (Supplement) (August 1997): 28–30.

19 R. S. Johnson, "The 50 Best Companies for Asians, Blacks and Hispanics," *Fortune* (August 3, 1998): 94–122.

20 S. Baker and M. Kripalani, "Will Outsourcing Hurt America's Supremacy?" *BusinessWeek* (March 1, 2004): 84–94; D. Kirkpatrick, "Rage against Off-Shoring Is Off Target," *Fortune* (February 23, 2004): 66; A. B. Fisher, "Think Globally, Save Your Job Locally," *Fortune* (February 23, 2004): 60.

21 L. West and W. Bogumil, "Foreign Knowledge Workers as a Strategic Staffing Option," *Academy of Management Executive* 14(4) (2000): 71–84.

22 S. Overman, "Recruiting in China," *HR Magazine* (March 2001): 87–93; J. L. Laabs, "Recruiting in the Global Village," *Workforce* (April 1998): 30–33.

23 G. Anders, "Talent Bank," *Fast Company* (May–June 2000): 93–97.

24 L. Lawrence, "Microsoft 'Permatemp' Settlement Seen as Warning to Employers," *HR News* (February 2001): 8; see C. von Hippel, S. L. Mangum, D. B. Greenberger, R. L. Heneman, and J. D. Skoglind, "Temporary Employment: Can Organizations and Employees Both Win?" *Academy of Management Executive* 11(1) (1997): 93–104.

25 P. Cappelli, "Making the Most of On-Line Recruiting," *Harvard Business Review* (March 2001): 139–146.

26 N. E. McDermott, "Independent Contractors and Employees: Do You Know One When You See One?" *Legal Report* (November–December 1999): 1–4; D. G. Albrecht, "Reaching New Heights: Today's Contract Workers Are Highly Promotable," *Workforce* (April 1998): 42–48.

27 C. J. Collins and C. K. Stevens, "The Relationship between Early Recruitment-Related Activities and the Application Decisions of New Labor-Market Entrants: A Brand Equity Approach to Recruitment," *Journal of Applied Psychology* 87(6) (2002): 1121–1133.

28 D. B. Turban and D. M. Cable, "Firm Reputation and Applicant Pool Characteristics," *Journal of Organizational Behavior* 24 (2003): 733–751.

29 J. Juergens, "Read All About It," *HR Magazine* (October 2000): 142–150.

30 B. Parus, "The Sky's the Limit in Online Recruiting," *Workspan* (January 2001): 54–56; P. Cappelli, "Making the Most of On-Line Recruiting," *Harvard Business Review* (March 2001): 139–146.

31 S. D. Maurer, V. Howe, and T. W. Lee, "Organizational Recruiting as Marketing Management: An Interdisciplinary Study of Engineering Graduates," *Personnel Psychology* 45 (1992): 807–833.

32 C. Salter, "Andy Esparza Knows What Success Sounds Like," *Fast Company* (December 1999): 218–222.

33 D. B. Turban and T. W. Dougherty, "Influences of Campus Recruiting Applicant Attraction to Firms," *Academy of Management Journal* 35 (1992): 739–765.

34 C. K. Stevens, "Antecedents of Interview Interactions, Interview Ratings, and Applicants' Reactions," *Personnel Psychology* 51 (1998): 54–85.

35 P. J. Kiger, "Search and Employ," *Workforce* (June 2003): 656–658.

36 R. D. Bretz, Jr., J. W. Boudreau, and T. A. Judge, "Job Search Behavior of Employed Managers," *Personnel Psychology* 47 (1994): 275–301.

37 K. G. Wheeler and T. M. Mahoney, "The Expectancy Model in the Analysis of Occupational Preference and Occupational Choice," *Journal of Vocational Behavior* 19 (1981): 113–122.

38 A. M. Konrad, J. E. Ritchie, Jr., P. Lieb, and E. Corrigall, "Sex Differences and Similarities in Job Attribute Preferences: A Meta-Analysis," *Psychological Bulletin* 126(4) (2000): 593–641.

39 D. P. Schwab, S. L. Rynes, and R. A. Aldag, "Theories and Research on Job Search and Choice," in K. Rowland and G. Ferris (eds.), *Research in Personnel and Human Resource Management,* vol. 5 (Greenwich, CT: JAI Press, 1987): 129–166.

40 S. D. Maurer, V. Howe, and T. W. Lee, "Organizational Recruiting as Marketing Management," *Personnel Psychology* 45 (1992): 807–833.

41 W. R. Boswell, M. V. Roehling, M. A. LePine, and L. M. Moynihan, "Individual Job-Choice Decisions and the Impact of Job Attributes and Recruitment Practices: A Longitudinal Field Study," *Human Resource Management* 42(1) (Spring 2003): 23–37; B. R. Dineen, S. R. Ash, and R. A. Noe, "A Web of Applicant Attraction: Person-Organization Fit in the Context of Web-Based Recruitment," *Journal of Applied Psychology* 87(4) (2002): 723–734; V. Corwin, T. B. Lawrence, and P. J. Frost, "Five Strategies of Successful Part-Time Work," *Harvard Business Review* (July–August 2001): 121–127.

42 A. E. Barber, M. J. Wesson, Q. Roberson, and M. S. Taylor, "A Tale of Two Job Markets: Organizational Size and Its Effects on Hiring Practices and Job Search Behavior," *Personnel Psychology* 52 (1999): 841–867; E. Chambers, M. Foulon, H. Handfield-Jones, S. Hankin, and E. Michaels, "The War for Talent," *The McKinsey Quarterly* 3 (1998): 44–57.

43 C. K. Stevens and A. L. Kristof, "Making the Right Impression: A Field Study of Applicant Impression Management During Job Interview," *Journal of Applied Psychology* 80 (1995): 587–606.

44 R. D. Bretz, Jr., and T. A. Judge, "Realistic Job Previews: A Test of the Adverse Self-Selection Hypothesis," *Journal of Applied Psychology* 83 (1998): 230–337.

45 R. C. Barnett and D. T. Hall, "How to Use Reduced Hours to Win the War for Talent," *Organizational Dynamics* 29(3) (2001): 192–210; S. F. Gate, "Formalized Flextime: The Perk That Brings Productivity," *Workforce* (February 2001): 39–42; S. Branch, "MBAs: What They Really Want," *Fortune* (March 16, 1998): 167; N. Munk, "Organization Man," *Fortune* (March 16, 1998): 63–74; T. A. Stewart, "Gray Flannel Suit?" *Fortune* (March 16, 1998): 76–82.

46 M. W. Walsh, "Money Isn't Everything," *New York Times* (January 30, 2001): G10.

47 P. W. Hom, R. W. Griffeth, L. Palich, and J. S. Bracker, "Revisiting Met Expectations as a Reason Why Realistic Job Previews Work," *Personnel Psychology* 52 (1999): 97–112; P. W. Hom, R. W. Griffeth, L. E. Palich, and J. S. Bracker, "An Exploratory Investigation into Theoretical Mechanisms Underlying Realistic Job Previews," *Personnel Psychology* 51 (1998): 421–451.

48 J. P. Wanous et al., "The Effects of Met Expectations on Newcomer Attitudes and Behaviors: A Review and Meta-Analysis," *Journal of Applied Psychology* 77 (1992): 288–297; J. M. Phillips, "Effects of Realistic Job Previews on Multiple Organizational Outcomes: A Meta-Analysis," *Academy of Management Journal* (1999): 156–172.

49 J. Useem, "Welcome to the New Company," *Fortune* (January 10, 2000): 62–70; A. Fischer, "Don't Blow Your New Job," *Fortune* (June 22, 1998): 159–162.

50 R. D. Gatewood, M. A. Gowan, and G. J. Lautenschlager, "Corporate Image, Recruitment Image, and Initial Choice Decisions," *Academy of Management Journal* 36 (1993): 414–427.

51 C. R. Williams, C. E. Labig, Jr., and T. H. Stone, "Recruitment Sources and Posthire Outcomes for Job Applicants and New Hires: A Test of Two Hypotheses," *Journal of Applied Psychology* 78 (1993): 163–172.

52 A. M. Saks, "A Psychological Process Investigation for the Effects of Recruitment Source and Organization Information on Job Survival," *Journal of Organizational Behavior* 15 (1994): 225–244.

53 W. Dickmeyer, "The Basics of Applicant Tracking Systems," *Workforce* (January 2001): 33; W. Dickmeyer, "Applicant Tracking Reports Make Data Meaningful," *Workforce* (February 2001): 65–67. For a discussion of likely changes that may be needed in HRIS software due to changes in EEO-1 forms, see F. Jossi, "Reporting Race," *HR Magazine* (September 2000): 87–94.

54 J. S. Leonard, "The Impact of Affirmative Action Regulation on Employment," *Journal of Economic Perspectives* 3 (1990): 47–63.

55 L. Micco, "Wilcher Describes Changes Under Way at OFCCP," *HR News* (April 1998): 6.

56 R. S. Johnson, "The 50 Best Companies for Asians, Blacks and Hispanics," *Fortune* (August 3, 1998): 94–122.

57 N. Munk, "Hello Corporate America," *Fortune* (June 6, 1998): 136–146.

58 IBM provided this information, which is also described in the company's various recruiting materials.

59 P. M. Wright, S. R. Ferris, J. S. Hiller, and M. Kroll, "Competitiveness Through Management of Diversity: Effects of Stock Price Valuation," *Academy of Management Journal* 38 (1995): 272–286.

60 For a detailed discussion of some possible implications of recent court decisions, see J. A. Segal, "Diversity: Direct or Disguised?" *HR Magazine* (October 2003): 123–132.

61 S. A. Holmes, "Broadcasters Vow to Keep Affirmative Action," *New York Times* (July 30, 1998): A12; S. Labaton, "Court Rules Agency Erred on Mandate for Minorities," *New York Times* (January 1, 2001): A16.

62 M. E. Heilman and V. B. Alcott, "What I Think You Think of Me: Women's Reactions to Being Viewed as Beneficiaries of Preferential Selection," *Journal of Applied Psychology* 86 (2001): 574–582; M. E. Heilman, C. J. Block, and P. Stathatos, "The Affirmative Action Stigma of Incompetence: Effects of Performance Information Ambiguity," *Academy of Management Journal* 40 (1997): 603–625.

63 D. R. Avery, "Reactions to Diversity in Recruitment Advertising—Are Differences Black and White?" *Journal of Applied Psychology* 88(4) (2003): 672–679.

64 For a full review of this and other research on affirmative action, see D. A. Kravitz, D. A. Harrison, M. E. Turner, E. L. Levine, W. Chaves, M. T. Brannick, D. L. Denning, C. J. Russell, and M. A. Conrad, *Affirmative Action: A Review of Psychological and Behavioral Research* (Bowling Green, OH: Society for Industrial and Organizational Psychology, 1997).

65 D. A. Kravitz and S. L. Klineberg, "Reactions to Two Versions of Affirmative Action among Whites, Blacks, and Hispanics," *Journal of Applied Psychology* 85 (2000): 597–611.

66 J. E. Slaughter, E. F. Sinar, and P. D. Bachiochi, "Black Applicants' Reactions to Affirmative Action Plans: Effects of Plan Content and Previous Experience with Discrimination," *Journal of Applied Psychology* 87(2) (2002): 333–344.

67 U.S. Department of Labor, *A Report on the Glass Ceiling Initiative* (Washington, DC, 1991).

68 T. Parker-Pope, "Colgate Puts Lois Juliber in Line for Top," *Wall Street Journal* (January 20, 1997): B5.

69 To learn more about how social networks influence the hiring of top-level managers, see I. O. Williamson and D. M. Cable, "Organizational

Hiring Patterns, Interfirm Network Ties, and Interorganizational Imitation," *Academy of Management Journal* 46(3) (2003): 349–358.

70 Chicago Area Partnerships, *Pathways and Progress: Corporate Best Practices to Shatter the Glass Ceiling* (Chicago: Chicago Area Partnerships, 1996).

71 A. C. Glebbeek and E. H. Bax, "Is High Turnover Really Harmful? An Empirical Test Using Company Records," *Academy of Management Journal* 47 (2004): 2772–2786.

72 Hundreds of studies have examined the reasons for voluntary employee turnover. A detailed discussion is beyond the scope of this chapter. Interested readers can begin to learn more by consulting: C. P. Maertz, Jr., and R. W. Griffeth, "Eight Motivational Forces and Voluntary Turnover: A Theoretical Synthesis with Implications for Research," *Journal of Management* 30 (2004): 676–683; R. W. Griffeth, P. W. Hom, and S. Gaertner, "A Meta-Analysis of Analysis of Antecedents and Correlates of Employee Turnover: Update, Moderator Tests, and Research Implications for the Next Millennium," *Journal of Management* 26(3) (2000): 463–488. Recent studies include C. P. Maertz, Jr., and M. A. Campion, "Profiles in Quitting: Integrating Process and Content Turnover Theory," *Academy of Management Journal* 47 (2004): 566–582; D. G. Allen, L. M. Shore, and R. W. Griffeth, "The Role of Perceived Organizational Support and Supportive Human Resource Practices in the Turnover Process," *Journal of Management* 29(1) (2003): 991–1018; J. D. Kammeyer-Mueller and C. R. Wanberg, "Unwrapping the Organizational Entry Process: Disentangling Multiple Antecedents and Their Pathways to Adjustment," *Journal of Applied Psychology* 88(5) (2003): 779–794.

73 Families and Work Institute, "Retaining Talent," *Fortune* (September 29, 2003): 45; J. D. Dawson, J. E. Delery, G. D. Jenkins, Jr., and N. Gupta, "An Organizational-Level Analysis of Voluntary and Involuntary Turnover," *Academy of Management Journal* 41 (1998): 511–525.

74 J. McGriger, "Balance and Balance Sheets," *Fast Company* (May 2004): 96–97.

75 A. Bernstein, "Too Many Workers? Not for Long," *Business Week* (May 2002): 126–130.

76 D. Rigby, "Look Before You Lay Off," *Harvard Business Review* (April 2002): 20–21.

77 M. Conlin, "Where Layoffs Are a Last Resort," *Business Week* (October 8, 2001): 42.

78 "Keeping the Crew," *Human Resource Executive* (January 2004): 8–12.

79 W. J. Baumol, A. S. Blinder, and E. N. Wolff, *Downsizing in America: Reality, Causes, and Consequences* (New York: Russell Sage Foundation, 2003).

80 E. Zimmerman, "Why Deep Layoffs Hurt Long-Term Recovery," *Workforce* (November 2001): 48–53; for a more detailed discussion, see K. P. DeMeuse and M. L. Marks (eds.), *Resizing the Organization: Managing Layoffs, Divestitures, and Closings* (San Francisco: Jossey-Bass, 2002).

81 P. Cappelli, "A Market-Driven Approach to Retaining Talent," *Harvard Business Review* (January–February 2001): 103–111; M. Nealy Martinez, "Retention: To Have and To Hold," *HR Magazine* (September 1998): 131–138.

chapter 7

Selecting Employees to Fit the Job and the Organization

In the restaurant business, employee turnover can be a big problem. It averages about 200% per year across the industry for hourly employees. Across the 700 Outback Steakhouses, turnover for hourly employees is only about 50%. Many employees have been with the company for six or more years, and 95% of the company's managers were promoted internally from hourly staff jobs.

President Paul Avery believes that the company's low turnover is due to the procedures it uses to select new employees. In its first two years of existence, when the company was small, Outback hired solely on the basis of interviews. As the company grew, it became more important to control turnover costs and hire people who fit the image that the company wanted to be known for. The strategy was to get employees who would indulge customers a bit more than they would expect from a chain restaurant. According to Avery, Outback's culture calls for people who are "fun, spirited, gregarious and team players." When selecting new hires,

Outback uses a personality test to find people who are adaptable, highly social, and meticulous. Avery knows that the personality test is better than interviews at identifying candidates with the appropriate personality. Outback keeps data about the test scores of all of its employees. The company analyzes these data to set the cutoff scores used when hiring new staff members. Applicants who fall below specified cutoff scores on important traits are dropped from consideration, even if they have a great resume and do well when interviewed. Managers conduct the interviews, asking a series of behavioral questions. For example, one question might be, "What would you do if a customer asked for a side dish we don't have on the menu?" Because almost all managers began working as waiters, they are good judges of how likely it is that an applicant will treat customers well.[1]

THE STRATEGIC IMPORTANCE OF SELECTION

Selection *is the process of obtaining and using information about job applicants in order to determine who should be hired for long- or short-term positions.* It begins with an assessment of the requirements to be met by the new hire, including the technical aspects of a job and the more-difficult-to-quantify organizational needs. Applicants are then assessed to determine their competencies, preferences, interests, and personality.

More than 90% of FedEx managers started in nonmanagement jobs.

FAST FACT

Typically, the objective of selection is to predict the likely future performance of applicants—in the job that is open, as well as other jobs that the new hire might hold at the company in the future. The decision about when to promote or transfer a current employee—and in which job—is a selection decision. When a special task force is created and a manager decides whom to recommend or appoint, the manager makes a selection decision. In organizations with mentoring programs, participating mentors make selection decisions when they decide whom to mentor, if anyone. When managers develop replacement charts and succession plans (as described in Chapter 4), they make selection decisions.

Done well, selection practices ensure that employees are (1) capable of high productivity, (2) motivated to stay with the organization for as long as the organization wants to employ them, (3) able to engage in behaviors that result in customer satisfaction, and (4) capable of implementing the strategy of the company.

"No strategy, however well designed, will work unless you have the right people, with the right skills and behaviors, in the right roles, motivated in the right way and supported by the right leaders."

Chris Matthews
CEO, Hay Group

In order for the objectives of selection to be met, selection practices need to do more than assess the technical capabilities of applicants; they must also assess whether the organization is likely to satisfy the applicants' preferences and keep them motivated over the long term.[2] Paul Avery knows that bad hires can damage a company's reputation with customers and hurt business. He describes bad hires as a cancer in the system that affects the entire organization.

SELECTION AND STRATEGY IMPLEMENTATION

Although there is little rigorous research to show it, many executives think it is obvious that different business strategies demand different types of people to implement them effectively. It follows that selection practices contribute to (or detract from) an organization's strategic capabilities. The selection of top executives, key expatriate managers, and lower-level employees all drive firm performance.

Executives. The entrepreneur who starts up a company in the garage and grows it into a successful firm is not always able to manage the larger organization very well. Managers who excel when the strategy calls for innovation may fail when cost-cutting pressures intensify. The competencies needed by managers in a firm that is growing through the acquisition of many smaller firms are likely to be different from those needed by managers in a firm that slowly grows organically from within. Thus, when selection decisions involve staffing positions at the top of an organization or at the top of a business unit, making the right selection may be critical to the success or failure of the business.

Other Employees. The strategic importance of people who fill key roles is apparent, but other selection decisions are no less important. Hiring a scientist who invents or discovers a new product may be worth millions or even billions of dollars to a company. Conversely, hiring a person who engages in fraud or illegal activity may end up costing the companies millions. At Lincoln Electric, the selection of production workers is so important that new hires are put on probation for six months, after which time coworkers decide whether they can stay. At Southwest Airlines, it's important to hire employees with a fun-loving attitude who work well in a team-oriented culture.

THE ECONOMIC UTILITY OF EFFECTIVE SELECTION

The **economic utility** *of a selection procedure refers to the net monetary value associated with using it.* In general, economic utility is a function of the costs incurred to design and use the selection practices and the value of outcomes gained by doing so. Thus, economic utility is essentially a measure of return on investment (ROI).

Value. When the job being filled is CEO, the value of making a good selection decision can be in the millions, even billions, of dollars. Some of the economic gains are returned to the CEO as compensation, but usually most of the gains are returned to shareholders, employees, and the government.

Clearly, the potential value of a good CEO selection decision is the exception. The economic value of any single selection decision is usually not so large. Nevertheless, it is important to realize that the potential to reap large economic gains from effective selection is not limited to selecting people for a few key positions. By making good decisions when hiring people at lower levels in the organization, smaller gains for each decision accumulate across large numbers of people. In large organizations, the accumulated benefits of making thousands of good selections decisions add up quickly. Effective selection also minimizes the risk of harm and the costs of lawsuits brought by victims of criminal, violent, or negligent acts perpetrated by employees who shouldn't have been hired or kept in their jobs.

'The single greatest return on investment comes from the people you hire, yet most companies spend more time evaluating a $10,000 copy machine than they spend evaluating potential employees."

Charlie Wonderlic
President
Wonderlic, Inc.

Cost. The cost of selection decisions includes the value of all the time and resources used to collect information about job applicants. Gleaning information from resumes and brief screening interviews costs relatively little; conducting multiple interviews, conducting background investigations, and paying for medical exams usually costs a great deal. Time used by highly paid employees in the organization (e.g., the CEO) costs more than the time used by those who are paid less (e.g., a product manager). The goal is not to simply reduce these costs. Expensive means of acquiring information may be worthwhile if they enable the organization to make better decisions *and* if substantial consequences are attached to making better decisions. Generally, more expensive procedures may be justified when

- tenure in the job is expected to be relatively long, so return on the investment accrues for several years;
- incremental increases in performance reap large rewards for the organization, so getting someone who performs better is worth a lot; and/or
- the procedure used is very effective in assessing which applicants will perform best.

Expensive procedures might not be justified if

- progressively higher tax bites are associated with increased profits;
- labor costs are variable and rise with productivity gains; and/or
- labor markets are tight, which makes it less likely that the best candidates, once identified, can be enticed to take the position.[3]

Each of these conditions reduces the value to be gained by selecting better employees.

In the past 20 years, numerous studies have demonstrated that well-designed selection practices pay off handsomely.[4] The value of using several selection techniques in combination was demonstrated in a study of 201 companies from several industries. Companies reported their use of practices such as conducting validation studies, using structured interviews, and administering cognitive tests. The researchers showed that companies that used these practices had higher levels of annual profit, profit growth, and overall performance. The relationship between use of these practices and bottom-line performance was especially strong in the service and financial sectors.[5]

Calculating Utility. Calculating the economic value of any HR practice is extremely difficult. On the one hand, it is fairly easy to add up all the costs of interviewing, administering and scoring tests, conducting background checks, and so on. On the other hand, it is very difficult to put dollar values on all the potentially important positive and negative consequences of a selection decision.

Exhibit 7.1 summarizes several of the consequences that result from making correct versus incorrect selection decisions. To be accurate, estimates of economic utility should attach dollar values to all of these consequences. In reality, however, the formulas used typically take into account only the costs and benefits that are easily quantified. Thus, most estimates of economic utility probably underestimate the true value of the procedure being evaluated.[6]

Ex 7.1 The Consequences of Correct and Incorrect Selection Decisions

	Do Not Offer Applicant the Open Position	Offer Applicant the Open Position
High Performance	• Applicant and employer continue to pay costs of continued searching, unnecessarily. • Applicant may decide to accept alternative job that's less well suited to his or her competencies and interests. • Applicants may remain unemployed unnecessarily and forgo rewards they could have earned. • Applicant may file discrimination lawsuit. • Employees may be required to carry an overload until job is filled. • Customers' expectations may not be met while employer is understaffed. **Reject a Qualified Candidate (Incorrect decision)**	• Employee performs well. • Employee receives rewards associated with good performance. • Employee enjoys work. • Peers benefit from employee's good performance and high morale. • Managers achieve their objectives. • Customers receive products and services that meet their expectations. **Accept a Qualified Candidate (Correct decision)**
How Employee Does/Would Perform	• Applicant continues to look for more suitable work. • Employer continues to search for more suitable employee. • Applicant may decide to get more training. • Employer may decide to offer more training so that more applicants can be accepted. • Customers do not suffer from the mistakes of a poor performer. • Employees may continue to carry an overload while search continues, but they do not suffer from the errors produced by an ineffective peer. **Reject an Unqualified Candidate (Correct decision)**	• Employee performs poorly. • Employee loses self-esteem due to poor performance, and forgoes the rewards associated with good performance. • Peers suffer consequences of poorly performing employee. • Customers' expectations aren't met due to employee's poor performance. • Managers fail to meet their objectives. • Injuries, accidents, and other serious problems may occur due to employee's poor job performance. • Employee eventually must find new job, creating additional costs associated with turnover. **Accept an Unqualified Candidate (Incorrect decision)**
Low Performance		

EMPLOYER'S SELECTION DECISION

THE HR TRIAD

Job applicants are one of the key partners in the selection process. Effective selection practices recognize and respect the applicant's concerns and sensitivities. In addition, they actively involve line managers, HR professionals and other employees, as summarized in the feature "HR Triad: Roles and Responsibilities for Selecting Employees."

The HR Triad

Roles and Responsibilities in Selecting Applicants

LINE MANAGERS	HR PROFESSIONALS	EMPLOYEES
• Identify staffing needs through articulating business strategies, and strategic business issues and objectives.	• Coordinate the administrative aspects of the selection process.	• May participate as applicants for internal transfers, promotions, etc.
• Help HR professionals identify appropriate criteria for evaluating the performance of new hires and new placements.	• Develop a selection process that fits the organizational environment and yields reliable and valid results that job applicants accept as fair.	• May participate by identifying appropriate criteria for evaluating performance.
• Help HR professionals develop selection tools.	• Participate in the selection, monitoring, and evaluation of external vendors that provide selection services.	• May interview candidates to work in the team or work unit.
• Coordinate selection process with applicants and HR professionals.	• Schedule applicant interviews with managers and other employees.	• May be involved in selecting new group members.
• Interview applicants. May administer and score some selection tests. May make final hiring decision.	• Provide education and training to everyone involved in the selection process.	• Attend training programs for employees involved in selection processes.
• Understand and comply with relevant legal regulations; provide accurate information to other organizations when they conduct reference checks.	• Monitor selection outcomes and keep complete and accurate records for possible use in defending the organization against lawsuits.	• When considering whether to accept a new position, accept responsibility for self-selecting into jobs that fit you and out of jobs that you aren't likely to perform well.
• Facilitate the organization's accommodation to the ADA.	• Articulate and oversee organizational compliance with the ADA.	• Inform managers of any disabilities requiring accommodation.

"I'd rather interview 50 people and not hire anyone than hire the wrong person."

Jeff Bezos
CEO
Amazon.com

Line Managers. To achieve its strategic objectives, selection must be aligned with the external environment, as well as the organizational environment. The involvement of line managers helps to ensure alignment. Achieving alignment is one reason that Outback Steakhouse has two managers interview an applicant before making a hiring decision. During strategic planning, line managers identify the jobs to be filled, and perhaps the jobs to be eliminated. Line managers also participate in the job analysis and competency modeling activities used to identify the behaviors needed from employees. Eventually managers evaluate employee performance, and these evaluations serve as a basis for promotions, transfers, and dismissals. In many companies, immediate supervisors have almost total control over these selection decisions.

Line managers from other units also play a role. Whether acting as formal mentors or informal sponsors, managers in other units can help to ensure that their protégé's strengths get noticed. They can also withhold information about poor performance of an employee in their unit, in order to increase the likelihood of that person being moved to another unit. Managers who control selection decisions should accept responsibility for making these decisions wisely.

HR Professionals. In very small organizations, there may be no HR professionals involved in selection decisions. But as small organizations experience rapid growth, they often turn to HR professionals to assist with selection processes. In large organizations, human resource professionals usually gather detailed information about applicants and arrange interviews between job applicants and line managers. They may also administer standardized tests to assess the applicants' competencies and select the most qualified applicants for managers to interview. As detailed in Exhibit 7.2, centralization of some aspects of selection benefits both the organization and the applicants.

Multibusiness companies often have several human resource departments, with each serving the unique needs of its own business. The decentralization is intended to produce a closer congruence between HR activities such as selection and the strategy and culture of each business unit. Decentralization does have potential disadvantages, however. If each division or unit operates independently, each is likely to select only from among its own employees and not from the whole workforce. Decentralization may also mean that each unit relies on its own performance appraisal systems, so even if candidates from other divisions become internal applicants, they may be difficult to evaluate. This reality is magnified in global firms: Regions of the world may become virtually unrelated to each other, and the human resources of one region may be completely off limits to the others.

Fundamentally, the role of a company's HR professionals is helping ensure that the best candidates available are identified and placed into open positions. Besides ensuring that selection decisions are based only on relevant information, HR professionals should continually evaluate the effectiveness of the practices in use and look for ways to improve.

"Peers need an opportunity to weigh in on a candidate. They need a chance to ask whether they want to split the pie with a particular individual."

Eric Smolenski
Personnel Manager
Worthington Industries

Ex 7.2 **How Centralizing Selection and Placement Activities Can Benefit Job Applicants and Employers**

BENEFITS FOR APPLICANTS	BENEFITS FOR EMPLOYERS
✔ **Convenient:** Applicants go to only one place to apply for all jobs in the company.	✔ **Efficient:** The company can consider each applicant for a variety of jobs, which is efficient.
✔ **Good Match to Job:** Specialists trained in staffing techniques do hiring, so the selection decisions are often better, resulting in personal success.	✔ **Effective:** Specialists trained in staffing techniques do hiring, so the selection decisions are often better, resulting in better business performance.
✔ **Fair:** People who know about the many legal regulations relevant to selection handle a major part of the hiring process, which improves legal compliance.	✔ **Consistent:** Common selection standards are used throughout the company, making it easier to maintain a workforce of consistent quality, which facilitates employee mobility between business units.

Other Employees. As organizations rely more and more on teamwork, they are likely to involve more and more employees in selecting new coworkers. Coworkers often help determine how well an applicant is likely to fit into the company's culture. At Rosenbluth International, a travel-management company in Philadelphia, applicants for managerial jobs might be asked to play a game of softball with the company team or help repair a broken fence. The objective isn't to test the applicant's skill at softball or fence mending—it's to learn whether the applicant is able and willing to be nice.

Involving employees in the selection process is generally a good idea and is a practice that seems to be growing. When employees are involved in the selection of new team members, they seem to become more committed to making sure the new hires succeed. As employees become more involved in this important decision process, it's essential that they understand the process and receive training about how to make appropriate decisions. Just as managers can be influenced by many factors other than an applicant's ability to perform well, so too are employees susceptible to making decisions for the wrong reasons.

Selection within an Integrated HRM System

Exhibit 7.3 shows how selection practices fit within an integrated HRM system. Clearly, one of the most important activities in this system that must take place prior to making a selection decision is recruitment. Unless the organization attracts a pool of qualified applicants, there is little need to invest time and energy in making a selection decision.

The proportion of applicants from the initial pool in relation to the number who are eventually hired is called the **selection ratio.** The lower the selection ratio, the more opportunity there is for an employer to find a few applicants who are outstanding compared to the others. If an employer must hire nearly every person who walks in the door, it does not make sense to invest time and money to assess how well each person will perform. In general, effective recruitment practices contribute to low selection ratios because they increase the number of job applications received from potentially qualified job seekers. The more favorable the selection ratio, the more chance the employer has of selecting employees who will contribute to the success of the organization. Job analysis is another HR practice that is closely aligned with selection practices. The important role of job analysis is described in detail later in this chapter. Finally, it is worth noting that selection practices should be aligned with an organization's training and development practices. If extensive training will be provided, the selection process may focus on identifying applicants who are likely to learn quickly and succeed after exposure to training.

The feature "Managing Change: Selecting Employees for a New Plant" illustrates some of these interrelationships between selection practices and other aspects of the HRM system.[7]

Exhibit 7.3 also shows the many types of selection decisions made in organizations and the methods that can be used to make these decisions. When choosing among the many available methods, employers consider a variety issues, including: the reliability, validity, and economic utility of the available methods; their potential discriminatory effects; and the reactions that applicants are likely to have toward each method.

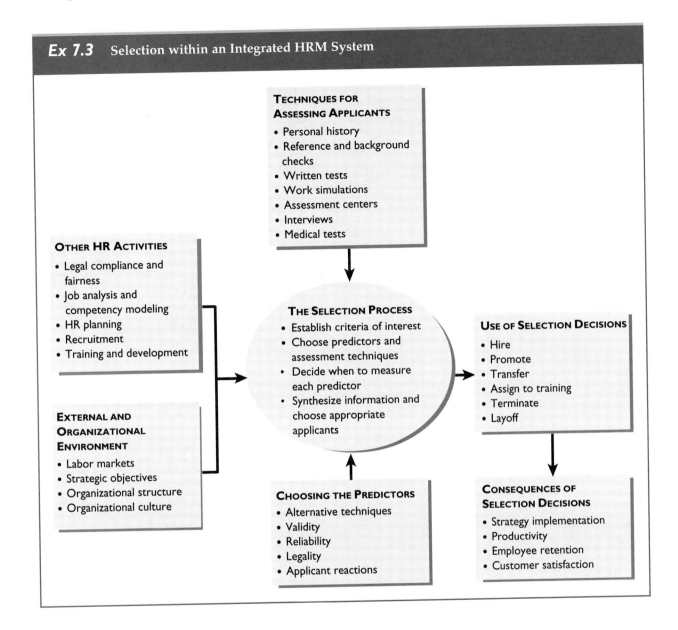

Ex 7.3   Selection within an Integrated HRM System

TECHNIQUES FOR ASSESSING APPLICANTS

- Personal history
- Reference and background checks
- Written tests
- Work simulations
- Assessment centers
- Interviews
- Medical tests

OTHER HR ACTIVITIES

- Legal compliance and fairness
- Job analysis and competency modeling
- HR planning
- Recruitment
- Training and development

EXTERNAL AND ORGANIZATIONAL ENVIRONMENT

- Labor markets
- Strategic objectives
- Organizational structure
- Organizational culture

THE SELECTION PROCESS

- Establish criteria of interest
- Choose predictors and assessment techniques
- Decide when to measure each predictor
- Synthesize information and choose appropriate applicants

USE OF SELECTION DECISIONS

- Hire
- Promote
- Transfer
- Assign to training
- Terminate
- Layoff

CHOOSING THE PREDICTORS

- Alternative techniques
- Validity
- Reliability
- Legality
- Applicant reactions

CONSEQUENCES OF SELECTION DECISIONS

- Strategy implementation
- Productivity
- Employee retention
- Customer satisfaction

OVERVIEW OF THE SELECTION PROCESS

The selection process generally involves the following basic steps:

1. Establish the criteria of interest.
2. Choose predictors and assessment techniques.
3. Decide when to measure each predictor.
4. Synthesize the information collected and make the selection decision.

Selection does not end when the organization makes its decision about whom it wishes to put into an open position. The candidate also makes a decision about whether to accept the new position and under what conditions. As the person enters the new position, accommodation, socialization,

Managing Change

Selecting Employees for a New Plant

Cirent, a computer chip manufacturer, was originally created as a joint venture between Lucent Technologies and Cirrus Logic. When Cirent built a new $600 million clean room in Orlando, Florida, it needed to fill many new jobs, and often those jobs required the skills of trained technicians. Cirent's job analysis for the new jobs indicated that the technicians would need expertise in robotics, pneumatics, vacuum technology, silicon processing, as well as interpersonal communications, writing, and teaching. Of course, they also would need to continuously learn and adapt to change.

To assess applicants for these qualifications, Cirent developed a selection procedure that included written tests to assess knowledge and cognitive ability, as well as interviews to assess interpersonal and communication skills. But Cirent encountered a problem: They could not find the skills they needed in the local labor market. There simply weren't enough people who had these skills. To address this problem, Cirent developed a training curriculum. For the short term, the company offered a serious of courses to newly hired employees, giving them time off from their jobs to attend classes. But their longer-term objective was to develop a larger pool of local labor from which they could select to hire trained technicians. Toward that end, they collaborated with a local community college. Cirent helped the college design the curriculum for an associate degree program that would give technicians the skills Cirent needed.

and training activities may all be involved. As time passes, both the organization and the new job incumbent will reevaluate their decisions.

ESTABLISH THE CRITERIA OF INTEREST

The outcomes that selection decisions are intended to predict are referred to as **criteria.** As described in Chapter 5, job analysis results provide descriptions of the specific tasks involved in a job. Predicting who will perform these tasks well is the goal of selection. Understanding what comprises effective performance also requires knowledge of the company's culture, values, business strategy, and structure. As described in Chapter 4, this information can be determined by conducting an organizational analysis. Ideally, all selection decisions are guided by rigorous job and organizational analyses.

Often, the primary criteria of interest are job performance and organizational citizenship. For a corporate loan assistant, speed and accuracy in documenting decisions would probably be important job performance criteria, and willingness to help out colleagues during times of work overload would be an example of good organizational citizenship. Increasingly, employers also consider other criteria. As described in Chapter 6, organizations seeking to lower their voluntary turnover rates may use the selection process as one tool for achieving that objective. In such situations, turnover is a criterion for selection. Employers also are looking for employees who will adapt quickly in an organization that is continually changing.[8] Companies like W. L. Gore, the makers of Gore-tex, and Patagonia, which makes sports apparel, seek to hire people who will fit into the corporate culture and embrace the philosophy of the organization.

"When people are not successful, more times than not it's because of the inability to work effectively within the culture as much as it is a lack of technical skills."

Jackie Brinton
(no job title—
no one at the company has one)
W. L. Gore & Associates

CHOOSE PREDICTORS AND ASSESSMENT TECHNIQUES

When making selection decisions, employers are making predictions about how people will perform in the future, how long they are likely to stay, whether they will be good organizational citizens, and so on. This is why *the various pieces of information used to make selection are referred to as* **predictors.** Generally, organizations assess skill, ability, knowledge, personality, and behavioral styles and use these as predictors—that is, they use competencies as predictors.[9]

When a job involves a great deal of teamwork, personality and interpersonal skills may be useful predictors.[10] To select people to work in their theme parks, Walt Disney's employees judge the personalities of applicants and assess their ability to fit into the Disney culture. The Disney approach is described in the feature "Managing Teams: Selecting the Walt Disney Cast."[11]

Assessment Techniques. For each predictor of interest—each competency, personality characteristic, and so forth—many different techniques can be used to assess applicants. Information can be obtained using application forms, resumes, reference checks, written tests, interviews, physical examinations, and other measurement approaches. Thus, an important step in designing a selection practice is choosing how to measure the predictors of interest. Exhibit 7.4 illustrates how a company might use several different techniques to capture all the information it wishes to use in selecting a corporate loan assistant (refer to Chapter 5 for information about what is

> *"We are a grow-from-within organization. When we hire somebody, we don't hire them for a position. We hire them for a career. We look not only at the position they're in today, but the position they could be in 5, 10, or 20 years down the road."*
>
> Kathleen C. Gubanich
> **Managing Director of Human Resources**
> **The Vanguard Group**

Managing Teams

Selecting the Walt Disney Cast

The next time you visit Walt Disney World in Florida or Disneyland in California, consider the complexity of finding more than 25,000 people needed to fill more than 1,000 types of jobs that make the entertainment complexes so effective. With over 50 million visitors to Disney World and Disneyland yearly, the company is a major player in the entertainment business.

The managers and employees of the Walt Disney Company view themselves as members of a team whose job is to produce a very large show. This is reflected in the way they speak of themselves, their activities, and the process of selecting new members. Eager applicants to the firm are cast for a role, rather than hired for a job. Rather than being employees, applicants who join the firm become cast members in a major entertainment production. A casting director interviews applicants.

For hourly jobs, a casting director spends about 10 minutes interviewing every applicant. The interviewer's (casting director's) major objective is to evaluate the applicant's ability to adapt to the firm's very strong culture. Does the applicant understand and accept the fact that Disney has strict grooming requirements (no facial hair for men, little makeup for women)? Is the applicant willing to work on holidays—even ones that almost everyone else will have off? After the first screening, the remaining applicants are assessed as they interact with each other and judged as to how well they might fit with the show. Current employees who are experts in their roles participate in this entire process: They assess applicants' behaviors and attitudes while also providing firsthand information about the role the successful applicant will have in the production.

Once people join the firm, they become cast members whose inputs and talents are highly valued by the Walt Disney Company. The company fills 60 to 80% of its managerial positions by promoting existing cast members. In addition, the firm draws on suggested referrals from current cast members for help in hiring the 1,500 to 2,000 temporary employees required during particularly busy periods—Easter, Christmas, and summers.

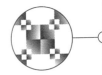

Ex 7.4 Possible Assessment Techniques for Several Competencies

CORPORATE LOAN ASSISTANT

Code	Competencies	Used to Rank?	ASSESSMENT TECHNIQUES							
			SAF	WKT	WS	PCD	SPI	DMI	BI/REF	PAF
MA	1. Communication	Yes	X				X	X	X	X
MQ	2. Math		X		X					
MQ	3. Writing		X							X
MQ	4. Reading		X		X					X
MQ	5. Researching		X							
MQ	6. Organizing	Yes	X							X
MQ	7. Listening	Yes	X				X			X
MQ	8. Social skills		X				X			X
MQ	9. Sales	Yes								X
MQ	10. Interpreting	Yes					X			
WT	11. Bank policy									
WT	12. Bank services	Yes	X	X				X		X
MT	13. Computer				X					

MQ = Is a minimum qualification

MT = May be acquired through training or on the job (desirable); preference may be given to those who possess this competency

MA = Can be accommodated within reason

WT = Will be acquired through training or on the job; not evaluated in the selection process

SAF = Supplemental Application Form

WKT = Written Knowledge Test

WS = Work Sample

PCD = Physical Capability Demonstration

SPI = Structured Panel Interview

DMI = Departmental Manager Interview

BI/REF = Background Investigation/Reference Check

PAF = Performance Appraisal Form (internal hires only)

involved in this job). We describe several of these techniques in more detail later in the chapter.

Establish Validity. A great deal of information often *can* be gathered and used to evaluate candidates; whether that information *should* be gathered and used depends on the likelihood that it will lead to better selection decisions. Put simply, information that predicts the criteria of concern should be used, and information that doesn't predict these outcomes should be avoided. The term **validity** *refers to the usefulness of information for predicting job applicants' job and organizational outcomes.*

High validity is present when low predictor scores translate into low scores on the specified criteria and high predictor scores translate into high scores on the criteria. For most predictors, validity depends on what you want to predict. A personality test that assesses gregariousness might be valid for predicting performance as a fundraiser for the city ballet company, but it's probably useless for predicting performance as a highway landscape designer.

How can you be sure that a given measure is valid for the situation of interest? Three basic strategies are used to ascertain whether inferences based on predictor scores will be valid:

- content validation,
- criterion-related validation, and
- validity generalization.

All these strategies begin with job and organizational analyses. Then, the three strategies diverge. (For more detailed information on these strategies, consult Appendix B at the end of this book.)

Content validation *involves using job analysis results to build a rational argument for why a predictor should be useful.* In the simplest case, an expert consults the results of a competency modeling study and makes judgments about which predictors are likely to be associated with the competencies identified as important. Suppose competency modeling reveals that senior managers should be able to effectively manage relationships with the firm's strategic partners—suppliers, customer, members of an alliance network, and so on. From this, the job analyst might conclude that it would be logical to assess applicants' amount of past experience in managing such relationships. This basic content validation strategy can be substantially improved by involving a wider range of people in judging whether a predictor is likely to be useful. Although such judgments are necessarily subjective, one's confidence is increased when several experts agree that a particular predictor is likely to be useful. When an organization is creating new jobs and experiencing major organizational change, a content validation strategy may be the only feasible validation approach.

FAST FACT

Winner of Hertz's "Business Travel Agent of the Year" Award, Rosenbluth International hires employees on the basis of "niceness" and pursues a policy of putting customers second, after employees.

Criterion-related validation uses statistical data to establish a relationship between predictor scores and outcome criteria. It involves assessing people on the predictor and also assessing actual outcomes, such as performance in the job. If a ballet company wanted to decide whether gregarious people are better fundraisers, it could ask all its current fundraisers to take a personality test (predictor). Then it could correlate the fundraisers' scores on gregariousness with their performance as fundraisers (criteria). If gregariousness and fundraising performance were correlated, criterion-related validity would be established.

Criterion-related validity replaces judgments about which predictors are most useful with quantitative analyses that demonstrate the predictive usefulness of criteria. CapOne, a credit card and financial services firm, used criterion-related validity to establish the usefulness of the online tests it uses to select call center reps. After choosing the test to be given and developing the online technology that would be used, the company had their current call center reps take the tests. Then they developed statistical models to show that the test results were correlated with the performance of reps currently in the job. In this example, the criteria used included sales rates and dollars collected per hour. The predictors included scores on math tests and scores on a simulated over-the-phone interaction, among other things.[12]

Validity generalization assumes that the results of criterion-related validity studies conducted in other companies can be generalized to the situation in your company. This is a relatively new approach that has been gaining acceptance during the past decade and may continue to gain popularity in the 21st century.[13] To illustrate, suppose you are the HR professional at the ballet company referred to earlier. You know that 10 other institutions of the cultural arts have already shown that gregarious people tend to be more successful fundraisers. Even if the correlation between this personality characteristic and fundraising performance was not strong in all those organizations, and even if the type of fundraising was quite different, you might nevertheless conclude that gregariousness is likely to be a valid predictor of fundraising success for your ballet company. If you accept this conclusion, then your company should evaluate gregariousness and use it as a criterion for selecting people whose roles include fundraising.[14]

Validity generalization analyses have been conducted for a large number of applicant characteristics that an employer might assess during the selection process. The results indicate that each of the techniques described in this chapter *can* be effective predictors of performance across a variety of jobs.[15] Exhibit 7.5 shows the results of validity generalization estimates for several commonly used selection procedures.[16] Note that these estimates describe the average relationship between the selection procedure and performance in a variety of different jobs.

Each validation strategy has advantages and disadvantages. The criterion-related strategy has the advantage of documenting empirically that a predictor is correlated with the criteria of interest in a particular job in a par-

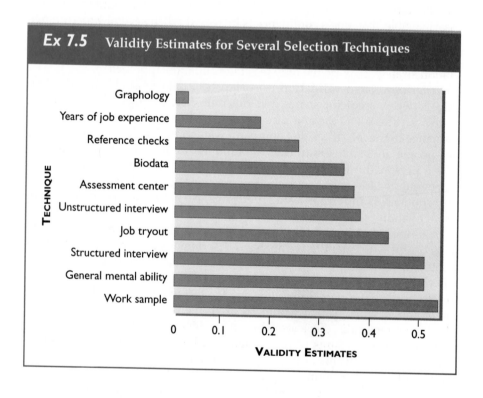

Ex 7.5   Validity Estimates for Several Selection Techniques

ticular organization. CapOne can be very sure that its new automated selection tests will help the company select better call center reps. However, this strategy can be costly and is not applicable for jobs that have only a few incumbents (e.g., CEO). The content validation strategy is more feasible, but it also depends more on subjective judgment. Finally, validity generalization is a low-cost strategy, but you won't know whether results from other organizations will hold in your organization until after you make a selection decision. Furthermore, whereas the legal credibility of the other strategies is well established, validity generalization has not been sufficiently tested in the courts. Ultimately, employers must weigh the costs and benefits of each approach to establishing the validity of the predictors to be used in making selection decisions.

Choose Reliable Predictors. Each bit of information contributes to the final selection decision, so the quality of information used determines the quality of the final outcome. One aspect of information quality that's especially important is reliability. The **reliability** *of a predictor (e.g., an interview, a mathematical reasoning test, or a work simulation) is the degree to which it yields dependable, consistent results.* Unreliable predictors produce different results depending on the circumstances. Different circumstances could include having different people administer and score the measure (e.g., having several different interviewers screen applicants), or administering the measure while different events are occurring (e.g., giving a mathematical reasoning test in August versus during the week immediately after everyone files their tax returns). When purchasing a test of any sort, information about reliability should be requested. Reputable test developers will be able to demonstrate that they have performed and documented all the steps needed to create a reliable and valid test.[17]

Recognizing that selection measures are not always reliable, some organizations use a scoring approach that takes this into account. Known as **test-score banding,** the approach groups applicants into clusters of people who all are considered to be equally qualified for a job, despite small differences in their scores. This approach is similar to assigning grades (A, A-, B+, B, etc.) to clusters of students who have slightly different scores on their class assignments. To select among applicants within a band, the employer can then use secondary criteria, such as ethnicity or gender, to "break the tie."[18]

DECIDE WHEN TO MEASURE EACH PREDICTOR

Often, selection decisions progress through several steps, with each progression to a new step based on some information about how the candidate scored in the prior step. Because more people go through the earlier steps, employers generally try to use less expensive procedures early in the process. This reduces the costs of selection because fewer applicants go through the more expensive stages of the process. Clearly, each piece of information used throughout this process has the potential to determine the final outcome. Perhaps less clearly, information used early in the process is, in effect, weighted the most heavily—applicants who fail to do well early in the process fail by default on all the later steps.

"You can't spend too much time or effort on hiring smart. The alternative is to manage tough, which is far more time-consuming."

Pierre Mornell
Independent Consultant

Synthesize Information to Choose Appropriate Candidates

Closely related to the sequencing of steps in the selection process is the decision about how to combine all the information gathered. A large amount of information of many types—some of it easily quantified and some of it very "soft"—may be available for a large number of applicants. To complicate things further, some applicants might be considered simultaneously for more than one job opening. Combining and synthesizing all available information to yield a yes-or-no decision for each possible applicant-job match can be a fairly complex task. Alternative approaches to combining and synthesizing information might lead to very different final decisions, so this step takes on great significance for both applicants and the organization. When multiple predictors are used, the information can be combined in three ways.

Multiple Hurdles. In the **multiple-hurdles approach,** *an applicant must exceed fixed levels of proficiency on all the predictors in order to be accepted.* A higher-than-necessary score on one predictor doesn't compensate for a low score on another predictor. This approach assumes that some skills or competencies are essential, so if an applicant does not have the needed level of competency, the person simply cannot be successful on the job.

Compensatory. For jobs that do not have absolute requirements, the compensatory approach is commonly used. With the **compensatory approach,** *a high score on one predictor can compensate for a low score on another predictor.* For example, the excellent math skills of an applicant for the job of corporate loan officer may compensate for the person's weak sales skills. With a compensatory approach, no selection decisions are made until the completion of the entire process. Then, a composite index that considers performance on all predictors is developed.

Combined. Many organizations combine the multiple-hurdles and compensatory approaches. With the **combined approach,** *the employer first screens out everyone who does meet one or more specific requirements, and then uses a compensatory approach in comparing the applicants who have passed the required hurdle.* Kinko's, the copy shop, uses a combined approach. The first hurdle assesses basic experience and availability using a short screening test, which is completed by calling a toll-free number and answering some simple questions using automated procedures. Applicants who pass this hurdle enter a second phase when they are asked questions designed to assess their fit with Kinko's culture and business strategy. This is also done using automated telephone technology. Applicants who make it past the second hurdle (about 50%) are invited for interviews. The results of interviews and other selection information are then combined into a composite score that determines the final selection decision.[19]

Companies that are trying to enhance their competitiveness by improving quality seem to agree that the employees at the front line are key to improving and delivering quality. Thus, they devote considerable time and effort to selecting front-line production workers. In high-quality manufacturing environments, work is organized around teams, so selecting people who can be effective as team players is essential. The same is true in many service organizations, where employees work in teams that serve specific customers. To assess these competencies, some organizations use very sophisticated selection procedures, like the one shown Exhibit 7.6. In this exhibit, each box represents one step in a series of multiple hurdles. A compensatory approach is used to combine the information within each step and decide whether to involve the applicant in the next step.

TECHNIQUES FOR ASSESSING JOB APPLICANTS

Clearly, employers have many techniques available to them for making selection decisions. Next we describe some of the most commonly used techniques in more detail.

FAST FACT

Automated, online testing of applicants has quickly become popular due to its convenience and low cost. But verifying who actually takes an online test remains difficult.

PERSONAL HISTORY ASSESSMENTS

Premised on the assumption that past behavior is a good predictor of future performance, personal history assessments seek information about the applicant's background. Application blanks and biodata tests are two commonly used methods of assessing personal histories.

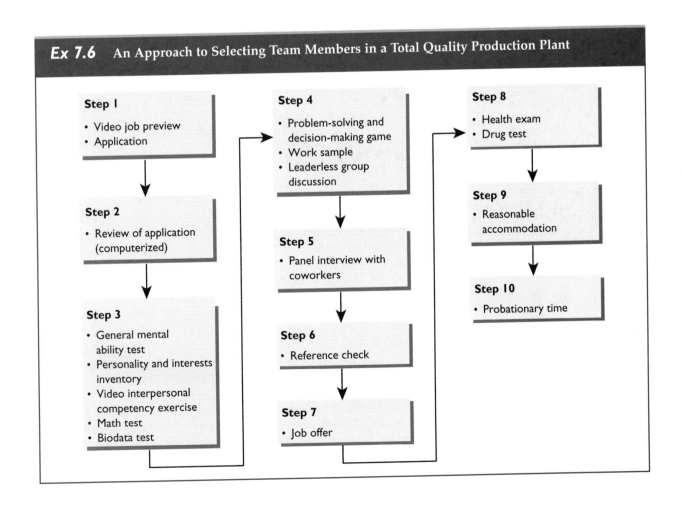

Ex 7.6 **An Approach to Selecting Team Members in a Total Quality Production Plant**

Step 1
- Video job preview
- Application

Step 2
- Review of application (computerized)

Step 3
- General mental ability test
- Personality and interests inventory
- Video interpersonal competency exercise
- Math test
- Biodata test

Step 4
- Problem-solving and decision-making game
- Work sample
- Leaderless group discussion

Step 5
- Panel interview with coworkers

Step 6
- Reference check

Step 7
- Job offer

Step 8
- Health exam
- Drug test

Step 9
- Reasonable accommodation

Step 10
- Probationary time

Application Blank. An **application blank** *is usually a short form that asks applicants to provide basic information about educational achievements and work experience.* It is often the first hurdle applicants must clear. Both educational and experience requirements may be useful in selecting individuals for high-level, complex jobs that cannot be easily learned.[20] Application blanks may also request the applicant's willingness to work split shifts, work on weekends, or work alone. If the job does require split-shift work, items that inquire about shift preferences tend to be good predictors of turnover.[21]

Biodata Test. A **biodata test** asks autobiographical questions related to such subjects as extracurricular activities (e.g., "Over the past five years, how much have you enjoyed outdoor recreation?"), family experiences as a child, and recent and current work activities (e.g., "How long were you employed in your most recent job?"). Responses to these questions are empirically keyed based on research that usually involves hundreds of respondents.[22] Biodata information alone can be quite effective as a predictor of overall performance, and it can also be effective when used in combination with an interview, a general mental ability test, or a personality test.[23] Besides overall performance, other criteria that biodata can predict include turnover, customer service, coping with stress, learning rate, teamwork, and promotability.[24] The validity of these tests is a major reason why they tend to be used in the insurance industry.[25]

FAST FACT

Biodata tests are used in less than 10% of selection decisions.

Despite their validity, biodata tests do have a downside: Applicants often react to them as being unfair and invasive.[26] The major reason for this reaction is that some items do not appear to be job-related. Another downside is that these tests often are quite long—they often include 200–300 items. Finally, experts must design these tests to ensure that they do not include items that are not legally permitted.

REFERENCE CHECKS AND BACKGROUND VERIFICATION

FAST FACT

Within the first year of operation, the Transportation Security Administration discovered that it had inadvertently hired 1,208 airport security screeners with criminal backgrounds.

The information obtained from application blanks, interviews, and biodata tests has proved to be useful in a variety of settings. But increasingly, employers question the accuracy of background information supplied by applicants. ADP Screening and Selection Services performs millions of background checks. Their experience is that about 40% of applicants lie about their work histories and educational backgrounds, and about 20% present false credentials and licenses. Nationwide, an estimated 30% of job applicants make material misrepresentations on their resumes.[27] Distortions vary from a wrong starting date for a prior job to inflated college grades to actual lies involving degrees, types of jobs, and former employers. The most common distortions relate to length of employment and previous salary. Exhibit 7.7 shows that the problem is widespread across a number of different industries.

The large numbers of job applicants who falsify their qualifications and misrepresent their past are one reason employers have stepped up efforts to check references thoroughly. Another reason is that employers have a legal duty to not hire an unfit individual who poses a threat of harm to others. If an employer hires someone who injures others and the employer did not

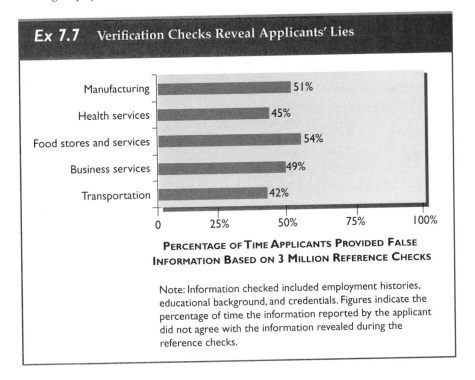

Ex 7.7 Verification Checks Reveal Applicants' Lies

Manufacturing — 51%
Health services — 45%
Food stores and services — 54%
Business services — 49%
Transportation — 42%

PERCENTAGE OF TIME APPLICANTS PROVIDED FALSE INFORMATION BASED ON 3 MILLION REFERENCE CHECKS

Note: Information checked included employment histories, educational background, and credentials. Figures indicate the percentage of time the information reported by the applicant did not agree with the information revealed during the reference checks.

make an adequate effort to discover relevant facts about that applicant, the employer may be found guilty of negligent hiring. Finally, a third reason to check references and conduct background checks is to avoid bad publicity. It can be embarrassing when a company's top executives are found to have lied about their credentials, like Ron Zarrella did. After he was hired as CEO of Bausch and Lomb, the company discovered Zarrella did not posses the MBA he said he had earned. A simple phone call could have determined that fact and prevented the negative image the company suffered when the press later disclosed it.

Instead of relying on unstructured reference letters, which are seldom negative, some organizations hire outside investigators to verify references. Other employers personally contact prior employers to get reference information firsthand.[28] Unfortunately, the potential for defamation-of-character suits has made getting information from past employers more and more difficult. Reference checks of an applicant's prior employment record aren't an infringement on privacy if the information provided relates specifically to work behavior and to the reasons for leaving a previous job. Nevertheless, to avoid possible lawsuits, many employers strictly limit the type of information they provide about former employees.[29]

FAST FACT American Eagle hired M. P. Hillis as a pilot without checking his job reference. When his plane crashed four years later, killing him and 14 others, an investigation revealed a record of poor performance at his previous employer.

WRITTEN TESTS

Due to the widespread use of computer testing technology, the term "written test" is becoming outdated. Nevertheless, it continues to be used to describe tests that originally involved traditional paper-and-pencil testing measures. The most common types of written tests measure ability, personality, and knowledge.

Ability. **Ability tests** *measure the potential of an individual to perform, given the opportunity.* Widely used in the United States and Europe since the turn of the 20th century, numerous studies document the usefulness of such tests for a wide variety of jobs.[30] The number of distinct abilities of potential relevance to job performance is debatable, but generally they fall into three broad groupings: psychomotor (perceptual speed and accuracy); physical (e.g., manual dexterity, physical strength); and cognitive (e.g., verbal, quantitative).[31] Bank tellers need motor skills to operate a computer and finger dexterity to manipulate currency. Performance in jobs such as wine taster, coffee bean selector, and piano tuner may depend on the acuity of a person's senses, such as vision and hearing. Firefighters need physical strength to perform their jobs effectively.

Approximately 30% of employers use tests of cognitive abilities when selecting employees. Cognitive abilities include verbal comprehension, mathematical fluency, logical reasoning, memory, and many others. These abilities predict performance in many jobs. Nevertheless, many employers shy away from using cognitive ability tests because minority applicants often receive lower scores on such tests compared to white applicants. When deciding whether to use cognitive ability tests, employers must weigh their value in predicting job performance against the fact that they are very likely to screen out more members of some ethnic minority groups.[32]

Knowledge. **Knowledge tests** *assess what a person knows at the time of taking the test.* There is no attempt to assess the applicant's future potential—that is, a knowledge test can inform employers about what applicants know now, but not whether they are likely to learn more or learn quickly in the future. Knowledge tests can be useful for jobs that require specialized or technical knowledge that takes a long time to acquire. For example, selection practices for hiring and promoting law enforcement officers usually include a test for knowledge about laws and the appropriate means for enforcing laws.

> **FAST FACT**
>
> It has been estimated that 20% of skills and knowledge possessed by employees working in technological fields becomes obsolete every 12 to 18 months.

Personality. **Personality tests** *assess the unique blend of characteristics that define an individual and determine her or his pattern of interactions with the environment.* A variety of psychological assessment tools can be used to measure personality, but written tests are the most common.[33]

Most people believe that personality plays an important role in job success or failure, but for many years U.S. employers shied away from measuring it largely because research indicated that personality seldom predicted performance. But this early conclusion may have been inaccurate. Recent advances in the academic community's understanding of the nature of personality suggest that employers may have abandoned personality measures too early. The most significant advance has been the realization that most aspects of personality can be captured using only a few basic dimensions. Often referred to as the Big Five, these are

> **FAST FACT**
>
> During its CEO hunt, Hewlett-Packard put Carly Fiorina and other finalists through a two-hour, 900-question personality test.

- Extraversion (sociable, talkative, assertive)
- Agreeableness (good-natured, cooperative, trusting)
- Conscientiousness (responsible, dependable, persistent, achievement-oriented)

- Emotional stability (not being overly tense, insecure, or nervous)
- Openness to experience (imaginative, artistically sensitive, intellectual)[34]

In general, conscientious people perform better, and this seems to hold true even more in managerial jobs characterized by high levels of autonomy. Not surprisingly, extraversion is somewhat predictive of performance in jobs that involve social interaction, such as sales and management, but these linkages are actually not very strong.[35]

Personal integrity (honesty) is another personality characteristic that's attracting a lot of attention among employers. Employee theft is often cited as a primary reason for small-business failures, with some estimates suggesting it's the cause of up to 30% of all failures and bankruptcies. In retailing, inventory shrinkage (unexplained losses in cash, tools, merchandise, and supplies) is a major problem, requiring companies to invest large amounts in security systems. In a survey of 9,000 employees by the Justice Department, one-third admitted to stealing from their employers. White-collar crime involving millions of dollars regularly makes the news. Problems of this scope and magnitude help to explain why employers administer millions of integrity tests annually.[36]

WORK SIMULATIONS

Work simulations *(also referred to as work samples) require applicants to perform activities similar to those required on the job under structured "testing" conditions.* For example, applicants for the job of retail associate at a department store might be asked to watch a videotape that shows a typical customer and then role-play how they would handle the situation. Interactive video assessments of conflict resolution skills can be used to predict the performance of managers.[37]

 FAST FACT When hiring managers for its stores in China, McDonald's requires potential management candidates to work in a restaurant for three days before making a final selection decision.

Work simulations are very difficult to fake. They tend to be more valid than almost all other types of selection devices, and they are the least likely to result in unfair discrimination. Unfortunately, they're usually expensive to develop so they're only cost-effective when large numbers of applicants are to be examined. The total price of work simulations is lower if they're placed at the end of a selection process, when the number of applicants tested is smaller.

ASSESSMENT CENTERS

Assessment centers *evaluate how well applicants or current employees might perform in a managerial or higher-level position.* Some organizations use assessment centers only for developmental purposes. That is, they assess employees' strengths and weaknesses and then provide feedback to employees for use in creating their personal career development plans. When used only for developmental purposes, no selection decision is involved. When an assessment center is used for selection purposes, the objective is to rank-order applicants and choose the best for placement in a new job.

FAST FACT Assessments Centers were developed in the 1950s at AT&T under the direction of Doug Bray. By the time he retired, about 200,000 AT&T employees had been assessed.

Assessment centers usually involve six to twelve attendees, although they can involve more. Customarily, they're conducted off the premises for one to three days. Usually managers from throughout the organization are trained to assess the employees or job applicants. Increasingly, team members who will work with new hires also assess the participants.[38] Assessment centers can be particularly effective for selecting team-oriented candidates, and their use grows each year.[39]

At a typical assessment center, candidates are evaluated using a wide range of techniques. One activity, the in-basket exercise, presents applicants with a variety of situations and problems that they must prioritize and decide how to respond. To simulate a typical day, the in-basket exercise may be performed under time pressure. Business games are another way to simulate organizational situations. Business games are living cases that require individuals to play assigned roles, make decisions, and deal with the consequences of those decisions. Usually, business games involve several people and several rounds of "play," which unfold over several hours or days.

In a leaderless group discussion, a group of individuals is asked to discuss a topic for a given period of time. For example, participants might each be asked to make a five-minute oral presentation about the qualifications of a candidate for promotion and to defend their nomination in a group discussion with several other participants. Participants may be rated on their selling ability, oral communication skill, self-confidence, energy level, interpersonal competency, aggressiveness, and tolerance for stress.

Assessment centers appear to work because they reflect the actual job environment and measure performance on multiple job dimensions. Although they are expensive to operate, the cost seems to be justified. The annual productivity gains that are realized by selecting managers through assessment centers average well above the administrative costs.[40] In addition, assessment centers appear to be nondiscriminatory and valid across cultures.[41]

> *"Teams spend a lot of energy on the hiring process, and they want the new person to succeed."*
>
> Deborah Harrington-Mackin
> President
> New Directions Corporate
> Consulting Group

FAST FACT

The United Nations uses assessment centers to select managers for its operations all around the world.

INTERVIEWS

The job interview is the most widely used procedure for determining who gets a job offer. Interviews that follow sound procedures can be quite useful. Poorly conducted interviews may yield very little useful information, and may even damage the organization's image.

Candidates for flight attendant jobs at Southwest Airlines are first interviewed by a panel of representatives from the People Department and the Inflight Department. Before the selection process is finished, they also have one-on-one interviews with a recruiter, a supervisor from the hiring department, and a peer. Southwest Airlines' interview process was developed in collaboration with a consulting firm that specializes in designing sound selection practices. Thus, the procedures at Southwest Airlines adhere to the basic principles of good interview design: structured questions, focus on behavior, systematic scoring, multiple interviewers, and interviewer training.[42]

Structure. In an **unstructured job interview,** *the interviewer merely prepares a list of possible topics to cover and, depending on how the conversation proceeds, asks or does not ask questions about them.* Although this provides for flexibility, the resulting digressions, discontinuity, and lack of focus may be frustrating to the interviewer and interviewee. Unstructured interviews provide unreliable results and generally have low validity.

In a **structured job interview,** *all the applicants are asked the same questions in the same order.* Usually, the interviewer has a prepared guide that suggests which types of answers are considered good or poor. Although structuring the interview restricts the topics that can be covered, it ensures that the same information is collected on all candidates.[43] In a semistructured job interview, the same questions are asked of all candidates and responses are recorded, but the interviewer also asks follow-up questions to probe specific areas in depth. In general, structured and semistructured interviews are more valid than unstructured interviews.[44] Structured interviews also appear to be less likely to unfairly discriminate against members of ethnic minority groups.[45]

Focus on Behavior.

Behavioral job interviews *use a structured or semistructured approach to asking questions that focus on behavior.* There are two basic approaches to asking behavioral questions.[46] One popular approach is to ask the candidate to describe specific instances of past behavior that reflect a competency for which the employer is looking. The assumption behind this approach is that past behavior is the best predictor of future behavior—an assumption that is well supported by research.

CORE is a consulting firm that specializes in the design and implementation of human resource systems. When designing interview questions for clients to use in their selection process, CORE writes questions that focus the interview on job-related past behavior. Based on job analyses conducted in many different companies, CORE has identified relationship building as one of several important competencies required of managers. Exhibit 7.8 (p. 284) lists some of the types of questions CORE designs to assess an applicant's competency in the area of relationship building.[47]

An alternative approach to conducting behavioral interviews is to pose hypothetical situations that might arise on the job. Interviewees are then asked to describe or role-play what they would do. This approach assumes that behavior on the job can be predicted by an applicant's intentions—this assumption is also supported by research. Questions that ask about behavioral intentions are more appropriate when applicants do not have experience in a job like the one they have applied for. For example, newly promoted managers usually face a variety of new situations associated with coaching, providing performance feedback, discipline, dismissals, and so on.

Systematic Scoring.

Job interviews vary in the degree to which results are scored. At one extreme, an interviewer merely listens to responses, forms an impression, and makes a decision. Alternatively, raters may use a detailed scoring key to score the response to each question. Systematic scoring procedures improve the reliability and validity of interviews because all applicants are evaluated against the same criteria, regardless of who conducts the interview.

Multiple Interviewers.

Typically, interviewers meet with applicants one person at a time. This is true around the world, as shown in Exhibit 7.9

Ex 7.8   Examples of Questions to Use in a Structured Interview

COMPETENCY BEING ASSESSED: RELATIONSHIP BUILDING

Interview Questions Designed to Focus on Behavioral Descriptions

1. Sketch out two or three key strengths you have in dealing with people. Can you illustrate the first strength with a recent example? [Repeat same probes for other strengths.]

   Probes: • When did this example take place?
   • What possible negative outcomes were avoided by the way you handled this incident?
   • How often has this situation arisen?
   • What happened the next time this came up?

2. Tell me about a time when you effectively used your people skills to solve a customer problem.

   Probes: • When did this take place?
   • What did the customer say?
   • What did you say in response?
   • How did the customer react?
   • Was the customer satisfied?

3. Maintaining a network of personal contacts helps a manager keep on top of developments. Describe some of your most useful personal contacts.

   Probes: • Tell me about a time when a personal contact helped you solve a problem or avoid a major blunder.
   • How did you develop the contact in the first place?
   • What did you do to obtain the useful information from your contact?
   • When was the next time this contact was useful?
   • What was the situation at that time?
   • How often in the past six months have personal contacts been useful to you?

"A candidate may be able to fool one interviewer, but he or she isn't likely to fool three people at once."

Antonio Fulk
HR Specialist
Rohr Inc.

(p. 285).[48] But one-on-one meetings are time-consuming, and the interviewer's impressions vary, depending on what was discussed. These problems can be overcome by using a panel interview, in which several individuals (typically two, three, or four) simultaneously interview one applicant. Because all interviewers hear the same responses, panel interviews produce more consistent results. They may also be less susceptible to the biases and prejudices of the interviewers, especially if panel members come from diverse backgrounds.[49] If applicants are to be interviewed by more than one person anyway, panel interviewing can be efficient, reliable, and cost-effective.[50]

Trained Interviewers. Left on their own, interviewers tend to form their impressions based on whatever information is most important or most salient. One interviewer might reject an applicant for being "too aggressive," while another might choose the applicant as being appropriately "assertive." In fact, an interviewer's recommendations about whether to hire an applicant are strongly influenced by how much the interviewer likes the applicant and by the applicant's physical attractiveness.[51] Consequently, interviewers

Ex 7.9   **Comparison of Practices Used in Selected Countries (Part A)**

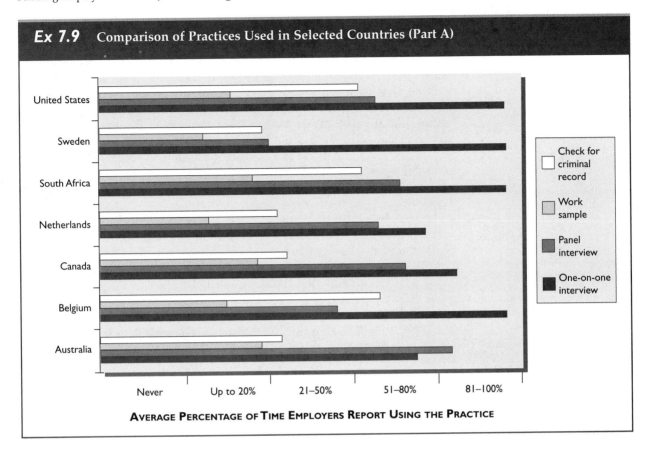

AVERAGE PERCENTAGE OF TIME EMPLOYERS REPORT USING THE PRACTICE

must be trained to use job-relevant information and to apply it consistently across applicants.[52] According to a recent study of 1,302 large organizations, about two-thirds offer formal interview training to hiring managers.[53]

MEDICAL TESTS

Although not all organizations require medical tests, these are being given in increasing numbers. Three types of medical tests that employers sometimes use when making selection decisions are general health examinations, genetic screening, and drug tests.

General Health Examinations. Since the enactment in 1990 of the Americans with Disabilities Act (ADA), general health examinations may be given only after a job offer has been made.[54] Before the offer is made, employers may only describe the job's functions and ask if the applicant is capable of performing the job. Prior to making an initial job offer, which may be contingent on the results of a medical exam, it is illegal to inquire about any disabilities. If a medical exam subsequently determines that the person is not able to perform the job for medical reasons, the employer may then revoke the job offer. In other words, disabilities may be used in making selection decisions only when they are job-related.

FAST FACT

Able to Work is a strategic alliance among a consortium of 22 companies that are working to develop assistive technologies to enable people with disabilities better see a computer screen, hear a telephone call, talk to others when they lack speech, and do word processing when they cannot type.

After Ozark Airlines refused to hire Gary Frey due to a nonfunctioning left ear, the Office of Federal Contract Compliance Programs (OFCCP) sued the airlines on Frey's behalf. Ozark acknowledged that Frey was capable of performing the required job duties. Their defense for not hiring him claimed that the decision was justified because he did not prove that he could do the job without endangering himself and others. The court ruled in favor of Frey, stating that it was Ozark's duty to show that Frey's condition would be a source of danger; Frey did not have to prove that the disability was not a source of endangerment. In this landmark decision, the court also stated that a disabled person is "qualified for employment if he [or she] is capable of performing a particular job with reasonable accommodation to his [or her] handicap" (*OFCCP v. Ozark Airlines*).

Many jobs—including police officer, firefighter, electrical power plant worker, telephone line worker, steel mill laborer, paramedic, maintenance worker, and numerous mechanical jobs—require particular physical, sensory, perceptual, and psychomotor abilities. When job analysis documents that these are needed to perform a job (something Ozark Airlines did not have), employers may be justified in not hiring applicants without the required abilities. The exception is when the employer could make "reasonable accommodations" that would enable the applicant to perform the job despite the disability.[55] Even when accommodation is possible, however, the courts have made it clear that employers are not obligated to hire a person with a disability over a more qualified nondisabled applicant.[56]

> **FAST FACT**
>
> The ADA provides protection only for physical or mental impairments that substantially limit one or more major life activities.

Genetic Testing and Screening. Each year, hundreds of thousands of job-related illnesses and deaths occur. The recent completion of a map of the human genome provides hope for reducing this number substantially. It creates almost endless possibilities for the development of medical tests to assess a person's genetically determined risks of experiencing various medical problems. For example, genetic testing and screening can identify individuals who are hypersensitive to harmful pollutants in the workplace. Once identified, these individuals can be screened out of chemically dangerous jobs and placed in positions in which environmental toxins do not present specific hazards.

Genetic testing and screening are not prohibited by the ADA or other federal legislation. However, numerous state laws do restrict their use in employment, particularly in hiring and termination decisions.

> **FAST FACT**
>
> A survey by the American Management Association found that 61% of companies administer drug tests to job applicants.

Drug and Alcohol Testing. When employers first introduced drug and alcohol testing in the 1980s, the practice was very controversial, but today this practice is common in the United States. In fact, preemployment drug and alcohol testing is mandatory for federal jobs that are safety-sensitive, such as truck drivers, airline pilots, and railroad workers. Drug and alcohol abuse costs U.S. industry more than $100 billion annually, which helps explain why more than 15 million applicants and employees are tested for drugs annually. As shown in Exhibit 7.10, the percentage of applicants who test positive for some drugs is quite high, despite the fact that people usually know in advance that they will be subjected to the tests.[57]

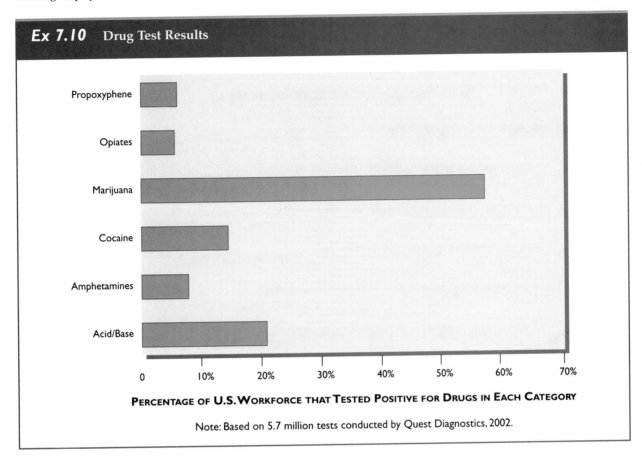

Ex 7.10 Drug Test Results

PERCENTAGE OF U.S. WORKFORCE THAT TESTED POSITIVE FOR DRUGS IN EACH CATEGORY

Note: Based on 5.7 million tests conducted by Quest Diagnostics, 2002.

A recent study of the selection practices used around the world revealed that some of the selection techniques commonly used in the United States are also used in many other countries (e.g., drug testing and medical exams). On the other hand, the popularity of other techniques varies between countries. Exhibit 7.11 illustrates some of the country differences identified by this study.[58]

THE PERSPECTIVE OF APPLICANTS

Applicants almost always care deeply about the outcomes of selection decisions and can have strong reactions to their experiences as they go through the selection process. Applicants' reactions influence their decisions about whether to pursue job opportunities in a company. For applicants already employed in the organization, such as those seeking a promotion, reactions to selection practices can influence their decisions about whether to remain with the company, and perhaps even their levels of work motivation.[59] Equally important, these early experiences serve as an organization's first steps in a socialization process that will continue for several months after an applicant is eventually hired.[60]

"I want to stay in this job a long time, so I'm actually glad they care enough to determine if I'm a good match."

Thuy Pham
Data Analyst
Kelly Blue Book

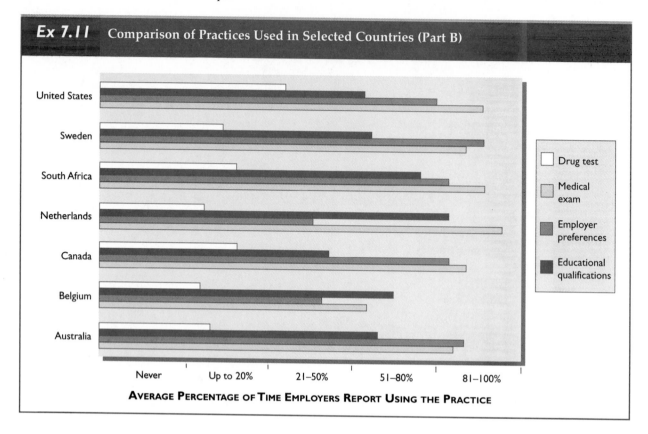

Ex 7.11 Comparison of Practices Used in Selected Countries (Part B)

AVERAGE PERCENTAGE OF TIME EMPLOYERS REPORT USING THE PRACTICE

At the heart of applicants' concerns is the desire to be treated fairly. Applicants judge fairness by the content of the measures used to select people, the administration of the process, and the results of the process.

FAIR CONTENT?

Applicants prefer a process that involves them in activities that have obvious relevance to the available job. Work simulations usually seem more relevant to applicants than written tests and handwriting analysis, for example. Perhaps for this reason, applicants view work simulations as more fair.[61] Applicants react negatively to poorly conducted interviews. Offensive or discriminatory questions obviously send negative messages, but so do questions that appear to be superficial or not clearly related to the job.[62]

PSE&G, a public utility company, wants to be sure its employees know what type of content to expect when they apply for a job in the company. The company has prepared a detailed manual that describes the various types of tests used in the company. The manual describes specific jobs and provides sample items that might appear on tests used to select people for those jobs. Meter readers, for example, must be able to work with figures quickly and accurately. The manual provides an example of a test question that could be used to test this ability. The manual also provides helpful advice on preparing a professional-looking resume and conducting oneself professionally during interviews.

FAIR PROCESS?

Applicants also attend to the process: Did the company tell them what it was evaluating and why? Did it provide feedback about how they scored? Did it appear to respect their desire for confidentiality? Did the company representatives behave professionally and appear to take the task seriously? Was the company respectful of their time and need for information about their chances for a positive outcome? Did it seem to treat all candidates equally, or did it treat some more favorably than others? Did the process appear to recognize the potential for applicants to misrepresent themselves and include steps to ensure that honesty was not penalized? Effective selection includes managing these and many other aspects of the process.[63]

Applicants who apply for jobs at Advanced Financial Systems (AFS) can tell that the company takes selection decisions as seriously as the applicants do. As described in the feature "Managing Teams: Hiring at Advanced Financial Solutions," the process is designed to make sure that the company and the candidate *both* have all the information they need to make the right decision. By communicating intensively during recruitment and selection, AFS avoids hiring people who will not work out as long-term employees.[64]

For job applicants with disabilities, getting information in advance about what the selection process will involve can be critical to their success or failure. A woman who uses a specially adapted keyboard to do computer work described her experience with one job interview like this: She arrived at the company for the interview they scheduled. Unexpectedly, she was asked to take a typing test. Because she did not have her adapted keyboard, she performed poorly. "I failed the typing test miserably," she recalled. "I didn't know I would have to take a typing test. If I had, I would have brought my keyboard." Using it, she could type 40 words per minute, which was fast enough to have passed the employer's selection test.[65]

> *"You cannot expect to delight your customers unless you as an employer delight your employees."*
>
> Carla Paonessa
> Partner
> Accenture Consulting

Managing Teams

Hiring at Advanced Financial Solutions

Located in Oklahoma City, Advanced Financial Solutions (AFS) must compete with the glamour of cities like New York, San Francisco, Boston, and even Paris, Brussels, and Tokyo when hiring software technicians. CEO Gary Nelson knows that keeping the people he hires is important to the firm's success, and he's proud of his record low turnover, which averages only about 1%. How does he make sure that the professionals he hires will like Oklahoma City and their new jobs well enough to stay put? By investing heavily in recruiting and selecting new employees.

Early in the process, applicants participate in lengthy telephone interviews, and detailed reference checks are conducted. Then, when the company thinks it has found a good candidate, he or she is invited to spend one week visiting the company. Spouses also are encouraged to visit. Prospective employees visit all departments and meet everyone from the CEO to the support staff. Spouses are shown around the town, and company volunteers make an effort to answer their questions about life in Oklahoma City: How are the schools? What religious organizations are there? How good are the sports facilities? And so on. No job offers are made until applicants complete their one-week visit. The cost of this approach, which is about $7,500 per hire, is worth it, according to Nelson, who says, "You can't put a price tag on [the] aggravation and grief" caused by hiring the wrong person.

RESULTS OF THE SELECTION DECISION

The content and administrative features of many selection procedures are visible primarily to applicants, but the results are visible to a broader array of people. Selection decisions are usually known by the acquaintances and coworkers of applicants who tell stories about the process, the new coworkers of successful applicants, the managers inside an organization who participated in the process, and people who served as references for applicants. Based on who is selected and who is rejected, all these constituencies form opinions about whether a company uses fair procedures and makes wise choices about who to hire or promote.

The news media also may evaluate the results of an organization's selection procedures. In reporting on companies that made its list of the 50 best places for minorities to work, *Fortune* applauded the fact that 60% of Marriott's new hires were minorities. It also observed that senior management had a different complexion, stating: "Heady minority representation in the workplace has not yet shown gains in the executive ranks." The news story stimulated the company to set a three-year objective of doubling representation of women and minorities in the senior management ranks.[66]

LEGAL CONSIDERATIONS IN SELECTION

Like all HR practices, selection practices must be designed with legal regulations and social norms clearly in mind.[67] These can vary greatly from one country to the next, from state to state within the United States, and from year to year. For example, California prohibits discrimination against people who have a genetic tendency toward disease.[68] Thirteen states have laws prohibiting employers from using information about home ownership. A dozen states prohibit the use of questions that probe into whether an applicant "resides with parents or relatives."[69]

LAWS AND REGULATIONS THAT PROHIBIT DISCRIMINATION

As described in Chapter 3, numerous acts and executive orders prohibit employers from discriminating against employees and job applicants on the basis of various personal characteristics (see Exhibit 3.2 on page 93 to review these laws). Recall that Title VII of the Civil Rights Act and Executive Order 11246 prohibit discrimination on the basis of race, color, religion, sex, or national origin. The Age Discrimination in Employment Act prohibits age discrimination. And the Rehabilitation Act and the Americans with Disabilities Act prohibit discrimination against persons with disabilities.

FEDERAL GUIDELINES AND PROFESSIONAL STANDARDS

Several federal guidelines and documents explain how to develop and use selection tools and how to determine whether a selection procedure discriminates unfairly.

Federal Guidelines. The *Uniform Guidelines on Employee Selection Procedures in 1978* is generally considered the most complete and useful legal document relevant to selection practices. It provides many specific do's and don'ts as well as questions and answers regarding hiring and promotion. The Equal Employment Opportunity Commission (EEOC) also has published many guidelines relevant to selection, including *The Guidelines on Discrimination because of National Origin* and *The Guidelines on Discrimination because of Religion.* To determine how to comply with the Americans with Disabilities Act, employers can refer to the EEOC's *Technical Assistance Manual on Employment Provisions.*

Professional Standards. Selection processes are monitored by the American Psychological Association (APA), which includes among its members many experts in testing and individual assessment. The APA publishes *Standards for Education and Psychological Tests,* which is updated regularly to reflect changes in scientific knowledge as well as changing legal conditions. Another useful set of professional standards is the *Principles for the Validation and Use of Personnel Selection Procedures,* published by the Society for Industrial-Organizational Psychology (SIOP).[70]

DETECTING UNFAIR DISCRIMINATION

In a typical discrimination lawsuit, a person alleges discrimination due to unlawful employment practices. The person may first go to the Equal Employment Opportunity Commission (EEOC) office. The EEOC may seek out the facts of the case from both sides and attempt to facilitate a resolution. Failing a resolution, the person may continue the case and file a suit. In the first phase of the suit, the person filing it (the plaintiff) must establish a prima facie case of discrimination by showing disparate treatment or adverse impact.

FAST FACT At Southwest Airlines, 33% of corporate officers are women—at least twice the level of its airline competitors and more than most companies in other industries.

Disparate Treatment. **Disparate treatment** *is a legal term used to describe illegal discrimination against an individual.* A prima facie case of disparate treatment exists when an individual can demonstrate that

- the individual belongs to a protected group;
- the individual applied for a job for which the employer was seeking applicants; and
- despite being qualified, the individual was rejected; and
- after the individual's rejection, the employer kept looking for people with the applicant's qualifications.

Demonstrating a case of disparate treatment can be difficult. One reason is that discrimination can be subtle. Unless someone makes a very blatant statement during the selection process (e.g., "I don't think women can do this job"), the applicant may never realize that a decision was made on the basis of personal characteristics.[71] Also, most of the decision processes aren't visible to applicants. Rejected applicants, especially external ones, seldom know how other applicants performed or even who was eventually hired. For these reasons, the law provides another means for establishing a case of illegal discrimination—demonstrating adverse impact.

Adverse Impact. **Adverse impact** *(or disparate impact) is a legal term used to refer to discrimination against an entire protected group.* Statistics that reflect the consequences of a large number of hiring decisions made by an employer are used to show adverse impact. Based on the statistics, a judgment is made concerning whether the employer *appears* to have discriminated against members of a protected subgroup. If the statistics show that selection practices resulted in adverse impact against a protected group, then the burden is on the employer to prove that the selection techniques used assessed job-related predictors.

Showing adverse impact generally requires the involvement of the EEOC, which has authority to audit the EEO-1 reports that employers file. As described in Chapter 6, employers file EEO-1 forms with the EEOC to report the demographic characteristics of job applicants—their sex, race, religion, and so on. Without access to such information, it would be nearly impossible for an individual to show that an employer's selection practices have had an adverse impact.[72] The two most common approaches to assessing adverse impact are making comparisons to labor market data and the 80% rule.[73]

Labor Market Comparisons. Comparing the representation of a group in an organization's workforce to the representation of that group in the relevant labor market is one way to document adverse impact. Selection practices have had an adverse impact if an employer's workforce does not reflect parity with the composition of the relevant labor market. For example, if the relevant labor market for a job is 50% male and 50% female, the people an employer hires for that job also should be approximately evenly split on gender. The key to this approach is determining the relevant labor market. The approach preferred by the EEOC is to identify where potentially qualified applicants reside and to consider this population as the relevant labor market. Employers may be able to successfully defend themselves against discrimination claims if they can show that the proportions of protected group members in their workforce mirror the proportions in the relevant labor market.

The 80% Rule. The **80% rule** *(also called the four-fifths rule) evaluates adverse impact by comparing the representation of a group in the applicant pool to the representation of that group among those who have been hired, fired, promoted, transferred, or demoted. The Uniform Guidelines* state that adverse impact is demonstrated when the selection rate "for any racial, ethnic, or sex subgroup is less than four-fifths or 80% of the highest selection rate for any group." The rule applies to *each part* of the selection process as well as to the process as a *whole (Connecticut v. Teal*, 1982). So, if the hiring process contains multiple tests, the 80% rule should be used to evaluate the discriminatory effects of each one.

As an example, consider the use of a physical ability test for selecting firefighters. The test assesses whether an applicant can drag a 220-pound weight a distance of 100 feet in 3 minutes or less. Does this test have adverse impact against women? Using the 80% rule, you would compare the percentage female applicants who passed the test to the percentage of male applicants who passed the test. Suppose 2 out 20 female applicants passed the test and 30 out of 100 male applicants passed the test. The 80% rule compares these pass rates as follows:

.10 (pass rate for females)/.30 (pass rate for males) = .33 (relative success of females compared to males)

In this example, the pass rate for females is only 33% of the pass rate for males. So, according to the 80% rule, this test has adverse impact against women.

One way the firefighters could deal with this apparent problem would be to change the way they score the test. For example, they could make it easier to pass the test by allowing more time, by using a lighter weight, and/or by shortening the distance involved. Suppose they made some changes, and the next time the test was given, 7 out of 10 females passed and 80 out of 100 males passed. Using the 80% rule, the pass rate for females compared to males would now be

.70 (pass rate for females)/.80 (pass rate for males) = .88 (relative success of females compared to males)

Using the new test, the employer could successfully argue that the test does not unfairly discriminate against women because, according to the 80% rule, the pass rates for females is sufficiently similar to the pass rate for males.

DEFENDING DISCRIMINATORY PRACTICES

Once a prima facie case of disparate treatment or disparate impact has been established, the employer is given the opportunity to defend itself. An organization accused of illegal discrimination may be able to successfully defend its employment practices by showing that the demonstrated discrimination is legally justified. Discriminatory employment practices can be acceptable if they're used on the basis of

- job-relatedness,
- business necessity,
- bona fide occupational qualifications,
- bona fide seniority systems, and
- voluntary affirmative action programs.

Job-Relatedness. To demonstrate **job-relatedness,** *the company must show that the information used in selection decisions is related to success on the job.* Job-relatedness can be demonstrated using any of the methods for establishing validity that were described earlier in this chapter.

Business Necessity. Showing the job-relatedness of a selection practice isn't always possible. The law recognizes this and allows companies to defend their selection practices in other ways. To defend a procedure that is discriminatory on the basis of **business necessity,** *an employer they must show that the selection decision was based on a factor that is essential to the safe operation of the business.* The courts and the language of the Civil Rights Act of 1991 define job necessity in very narrow terms. For example, employers cannot argue that

FAST FACT A "no-beard" employment policy may discriminate against African American men who have a predisposition to *pseudofolliculitis barbae* unless the policy is job-related and consistent with business necessity.

business necessity exists because customers prefer employees from certain demographic groups or because not hiring members of certain groups reduces the cost of doing business.

Bona Fide Occupational Qualifications. To use the defense of a **bona fide occupational qualification (BFOQ),** *the employer must show that the discriminatory practice is "reasonably necessary to the normal operation of that particular business or enterprise."* The BFOQ defense is sometimes used to justify hiring based on sex or religion. For example, sex is considered a BFOQ for jobs such as restroom attendants, and religion is considered a BFOQ for some jobs in religious institutions.

Bona Fide Seniority Systems. A **bona fide seniority system** *is one that a company establishes and maintains without the intent to discriminate illegally.* When a bona fide seniority system is in place, decisions regarding promotions, job assignments, and layoffs can be made on the basis of seniority. For many occupations, women and members of ethnic minority groups are more likely to be recent hires, so often using seniority results in adverse impact. Nevertheless, using seniority as a basis for selection decisions may be legal.

Voluntary Affirmative Action Programs. As described in Chapter 6, the legal and social status of voluntary affirmative action programs is currently a topic of much discussion. Nevertheless, past court decisions have held that voluntary affirmative action programs can be a defense against illegal (reverse) discrimination. Voluntary affirmative action programs are legally defensible if they are

- remedial in purpose,
- limited in duration,
- restricted in effect,
- flexible in implementation, and
- minimal in harm to innocent parties.

Legal Considerations for Global Selection

By enacting the Civil Rights Act of 1991, Congress affirmed its policy that American civil rights laws cover U.S. citizens employed outside the country by American multinationals. Sometimes this puts American employers in the position of having to violate local practices in order to comply with American law. The United States also holds foreign companies operating within the United States accountable for adhering to U.S. employment laws. There are some exceptions to this general rule, however. For example, a treaty between the United States and Japan permits companies of either country to prefer their own citizens for executive positions in subsidiaries based in the other country. Japanese firms usually select parent-country (i.e., Japanese) executives to run their American subsidiaries, and they provide few opportunities for promotion to the top management slots for their American managers.[74] United States employees often consider this practice to be discrimination based on national origin. But according to the ruling in *Fortino v. Quasar Co.,* Title VII of the Civil Rights Act was preempted by a subsequent trade treaty. As these examples illustrate, managing human resources effectively in a global organization is not as simple as following the advice offered by one sage: "When in Rome, do as the Romans do."

GLOBAL SELECTION CHOICES

When an organization's strategic plans call for expanding into the global market, the selection of international employees becomes a key determinant of success. The globalization strategy will require operating facilities overseas. The plan may call for building new facilities or acquiring existing operations. Either way, decisions about how to staff the facilities will be among the first strategic choices made. Three choices are: send a parent-country national (PCN) or expatriate, hire a host-country national (HCN), or hire a third-country national (TCN). United States companies have generally favored sending expatriates, but it is common knowledge that U.S. expatriates often do not perform well in such assignments and are very costly for the company. The pros and cons of selecting these three types of individuals are listed in Exhibit 7.12.[75]

An organization's decision to fill a job by hiring an expatriate, HCN, or TCN is likely to reflect a judgment about how difficult it will be to find an

FAST FACT

Worldwide, multinational companies employ about 45 million workers. By 2010, that number could double.

Ex 7.12   Selecting Managers: Pros and Cons of PCNs, HCNs, and TCNs

PARENT-COUNTRY NATIONALS (PCNs)

Advantages	Disadvantages
• Organizational control and coordination is maintained and facilitated.	• The promotional opportunities of HCNs are limited.
• Promising managers are given international experience.	• Adaptation to the host country may take a long time.
• PCNs are the best people for the job.	• PCNs may impose an inappropriate headquarters style.
• The subsidiary will likely comply with the company objectives, policies, and so forth.	• Compensation for PCNs and HCNs may differ.

HOST-COUNTRY NATIONALS (HCNs)

Advantages	Disadvantages
• Language and other barriers are eliminated.	• Control and coordination of headquarters may be impeded.
• Hiring costs are reduced, and no work permit is required.	• HCNs have limited career opportunities outside the subsidiary.
• Continuity of management improves, since HCNs stay longer in positions.	• Hiring HCNs limits opportunities for PCNs to gain overseas experience.
• Government policy may dictate the hiring of HCNs.	• Hiring HCNs could encourage a federation of national rather than global units.
• Morale among HCNs may improve as they see the career potentials.	

THIRD-COUNTRY NATIONALS (TCNs)

Advantages	Disadvantages
• Salary and benefit requirements may be lower than for PCNs.	• Transfers must consider possible national animosities.
• TCNs may be better informed than PCNs about the host-country environment.	• The host government may resent the hiring of TCNs.
	• TCNs may not want to return to their own countries after assignment.

expatriate who is qualified versus finding other talent. This judgment takes into consideration both the nature of the job and the qualifications of people in the two talent pools (at home and abroad). Expatriate managers, for example, must be able to carry out daily activities with the concerns of the parent company clearly in focus, while also responding to the host country's societal concerns and a local culture that's often quite different from their home culture. In addition, expatriate managers typically operate in a culture with a different language—a major obstacle for many of them. Because it is so difficult to find expatriates with the competencies needed to be successful in foreign assignments, many companies prefer to rely on the local labor market.

For expatriate managers to succeed, they need the competencies required to perform their specific job as well as those needed to effectively manage many types of relationships, including those with:

- their coworkers;
- their families;
- the host government;
- their home government;
- the local clients, customers, and business partners; and
- the company's headquarters.

Assessing how well applicants are likely to manage these relationships is necessary regardless of where the applicants are found.[76] However, the selection procedures used may differ depending on whether they are used to assess U.S. applicants or applicants from the local labor market. Expatriates and TCNs are usually selected using U.S practices, while host-country nationals (HCNs) are usually selected using host-country practices.[77]

When making hiring decisions in various parts of the world, Cirque du Soleil must understand the legal constraints as well as the cultural factors that apply in each country. The feature "Managing Globalization: Hiring Is No Laughing Matter for Cirque du Soleil" describes this challenge.[78]

A strategic decision to expand globally sets in place a chain of decision making concerning how to staff the new facilities. Eventually, a selection process will unfold and people will be hired for the key positions. If the selection process results in qualified people being hired, the company improves its chances of successfully implementing the new strategy. Poor selection decisions, on the other hand, may end up costing the company millions of dollars.

FAST FACT

The top six destinations for expatriates are the United States, China, the United Kingdom, Germany, Singapore, and Japan.

Managing Globalization

Hiring Is No Laughing Matter for Cirque du Soleil

Remember the last time you sat under the big top, watching clowns entertain and acrobats tumble across the floor? Perhaps you've even seen a performance of Cirque du Soleil—one of the most unique acts in the world. With corporate headquarters in Montreal and offices in Las Vegas, Nevada, and Amsterdam, Holland, Cirque du Soleil is an international entertainment company that employs more than 1,200 people representing 17 nationalities and speaking at least 13 different languages. Its main products include a permanent show that runs in Las Vegas and several touring shows that run in countries around the world.

In this business, people are clearly the company's most important asset. Success is possible only with careful planning, recruitment, and selection. For its tours, Cirque relies heavily on temporary staff (temps) hired in each city—people who work as ushers, ticket sellers and takers, and security personnel. For a year of tours, that adds up to some 1,800 temps. Although Cirque employs them for only a few days, good temps are essential to the company's reputation because they have the most direct personal contact with customers. To be hired, applicants must conduct themselves well during an interview designed to assess attitude, experience, and skills. For positions in the touring groups, the selection process is more intensive. Throughout these selection processes, the company must ensure that it adheres to all local labor laws. Ideally, Cirque will also be sensitive enough to local conditions to be able to avoid practices that, although legal, are considered undesirable within local cultures.

SUMMARY

Through selection procedures, organizations strive to fill job openings with the most appropriate people. By the same token, job applicants strive to obtain jobs that are appropriate to their personal objectives. Effective selection practices result in the assignment of individuals to jobs (and even career paths) that match the individuals' technical competencies, personalities, behavioral styles, and preferences.

In order to achieve an effective match between individuals and job situations, organizations need to obtain information about the applicant and clearly communicate information about the job and the work setting. Few organizations, if any, rely on a single predictor when making selection decisions. Typically, employers gather several types of information using a variety of methods. The information obtained may be considered sequentially, using the multiple-hurdles approach, or a compensatory approach to decision making may be followed. Regardless of the approach, managing human resources effectively requires the use of predictors that are valid and nondiscriminatory.

Building on the results of job analysis and competency modeling, employers can develop valid selection practices that enable them to make job offers to those applicants who are most likely to perform well in the jobs, be good corporate citizens, and not leave the organization prematurely. Application forms, interviews, written and physical tests, work samples, and assessment centers are among the selection techniques that organizations use for selection purposes. Managers, HR professionals, and the future colleagues of a new hire may all be involved in using these techniques to assess job applicants.

An extensive framework of U.S. legal regulations, court decisions, and guidelines provides U.S. organizations with advice for how to conduct the selection process in a manner that enhances the performance of the work-force while avoiding unfair discrimination. As companies expand abroad, however, they must attend to the legal and cultural conditions that shape selection practices in other countries. At home as well as abroad, effective selection procedures result in hiring the best person for a specific position in a particular organization. Doing so provides benefits to all the organization's important stakeholders.

TERMS TO REMEMBER

Ability test
Adverse impact
Application blank
Assessment centers
Behavioral job interviews
Biodata test
Bona fide occupational qualification (BFOQ)
Bona fide seniority system
Business necessity
Combined approach
Compensatory approach
Content validation
Criteria
Criterion-related validation
Disparate treatment

Economic utility
80% rule
Job-relatedness
Knowledge test
Multiple-hurdles approach
Personality tests
Predictors
Reliability
Selection
Selection ratio
Structured job interview
Test-score banding
Unstructured job interview
Validity
Validity generalization
Work simulations

DISCUSSION QUESTIONS

1. A frequent diagnosis of an observed performance problem in an organization is, "This person was a selection mistake." What are the short- and long-term consequences of so-called selection mistakes? If possible, relate this question to your own experiences with organizations.

2. Successful selection decisions are dependent on other human resource activities. Identify these activities, and explain their relationships to selection practices.

3. Given all the weaknesses identified with unstructured interviews, why do they remain so popular?

4. What are the costs and benefits to employers of being responsive to the applicant's perspective throughout the selection process? Are the concerns of applicants who are eventually accepted different from those of applicants who are eventually rejected? Explain.

5. Should employers be allowed to use the results of genetic tests in their selection decisions? Why or why not?

6. Some people feel the government should not get involved in regulating business practices. To what extent do you think legal regulations affecting selection practices hinder or facilitate running an effective company?

PROJECTS TO EXTEND YOUR LEARNING

1. *Integration and Application.* Review the end-of-text cases of Lincoln Electric and Southwest Airlines. Describe, evaluate, and compare the selection and placement procedures used at these two companies. In preparing your answer, consider the following issues:

   a. the objectives of selection and placement;
   b. the criteria used;
   c. the techniques used to assess the competencies and other characteristics of individual candidates;
   d. the apparent effectiveness of the selection process; and
   e. the roles and responsibilities of managers, HR professionals, and other employees.

2. *Exploring the Internet.*

   a. Assess the potential usefulness of having a third-party vendor conduct reference checks at
      http://www.verifiedcredentials.com,
      http://www.amsnj.com/investigative.htm,
      http://www.pichicago.com/, and
      http://www.accesschecks.com/employmentpackage.htm.
   b. Read about an organization for professionals that provides assessment centers at http://www.assessmentcenters.org.
   c. Take a popular test for assessing personality style at
      http://www.advisorteam.com/ or http://www.psychtests.com.
   d. Find out everything you ever wanted to know about the Federal Civil Service Exam, which is taken by most applicants for federal jobs, at http://www.federaljobs.net/exams.htm.
   e. Get advice about how to handle yourself well during job interviews at http://www.job-interview.net.
   f. Learn more about genetic testing and screening at http://www.osha.gov/ (search for key words "genetic testing") as well as drug testing at http://www.drugtesting.com/.htm and http://www.drugfreeworkplace.gov.
   g. Find out how to file a discrimination charge and what it takes to prove a case of discrimination at http://www.eeoc.gov.

3. *Experiential Activities.*

   a. **Behavioral Job Interview.** You are responsible for interviewing candidates for an entry-level job. Your employer has provided you with very little information about how to proceed. You know that the job does not require a great deal of skill, but it is important to select someone who will fit the company culture. Following is a list of questions you have used in the past during similar interviews. After reading this chapter, you realize that these questions need to be reworded to focus more on behavior. Rewrite each question to show two alternatives to what is listed. First rewrite the questions to ask the interviewees about their behavior in the past. Then rewrite the questions to ask the interviewees how they would be likely to behave in a specific situation. Use situations that would be relevant for the available job, which is assistant animal keeper at the Cleveland Zoo. The job involves cleaning cages in the bird and small animal exhibits and putting out food for the birds and animals.

WRITING BEHAVIORALLY FOCUSED QUESTIONS		
OLD VERSION	NEW QUESTION, FOCUSING ON PAST BEHAVIOR IN OTHER JOBS	NEW QUESTION, FOCUSING ON FUTURE BEHAVIOR IN THIS JOB
1. Are you an introvert or an extrovert?		
2. How important is it to follow the rules?		
3. Do you believe that a person should have fun at work?		
4. How important is a sense of humor at work?		
5. What values are important to you at work?		
6. Describe your problem-solving style.		

After you have completed rewriting the interview questions, list the pros and cons associated with each version.

	ADVANTAGES	DISADVANTAGES
OLD VERSION	1. 2. 3.	1. 2. 3.
New Questions, Focusing on Past Behavior in Other Jobs	1. 2. 3.	1. 2. 3.
New Questions, Focusing on Future Behavior in This Job	1. 2. 3.	1. 2. 3.

b. **Application Blanks.** What information can employers request on job application forms? Check "DO" or "DON'T" in the chart to indicate which topics are acceptable to ask about in a job application, and which are not. (Answers appear later in this chapter.)

Do	Don't	Item
		1. Marital status
		2. Number of children
		3. Skills to do the job
		4. A woman's maiden name
		5. Age of applicant
		6. Driver's license
		7. Religious affiliation
		8. Birthplace of applicant
		9. Club memberships
		10. Whether applicant plans to have children
		11. Preferred hours of work
		12. Whether applicant has disabilities
		13. Other names applicant has used
		14. Arrest record
		15. Applicant's height and weight
		16. Nature of military discharge
		17. Friends or relatives employed by the firm
		18. Clergy members as references
		19. Credit questions
		20. Whether applicant is willing to travel

CASE STUDY

SELECTING PATIENT ESCORTS

City Hospital is located in the heart of a large midwestern city. It is one of five major hospitals in the area and has recently built a small addition for treating well-known patients such as professional football players, top company executives, and singing stars. Visiting or local celebrities always choose City Hospital if they need treatment.

City Hospital has about 1,200 hospital beds and employs 4,500 individuals, including about 40 patient escorts. The job of patient escort is a rather simple one, requiring only minimal training and no special physical talents. When patients need to be

moved from one location to another, patient escorts are summoned to assist in the move. If the move is only a short distance, however, a nurse or orderly can move the patient. Of particular importance is the fact that patient escorts almost always take patients who are being discharged from their hospital room to the front door of the hospital. A wheelchair is always used, even if the patient is able to walk unassisted. Thus, the typical procedure is for the nurse to call for a patient escort, and then the escort gets a wheelchair, goes to the patient's room, assists the patient into the wheelchair, picks up the patient's belongings, wheels the patient down to the hospital's front door or to a car in the parking lot, and returns to the workstation.

The job of patient escort is critical to the hospital, since the escort is always the last hospital representative the patient sees, and hence has a considerable influence on the patient's perception of the hospital. Of the approximately 40 escorts, about three-fourths are men, and one-fourth are women. Most are high school graduates in their early twenties. Some, particularly those on the early morning shift, are attending college at night and working for the hospital to earn money to pay college expenses. Four of the escorts are older women who previously served as hospital volunteers and then decided to become full-time employees instead. Turnover among patient escorts is quite high and has averaged 25% in recent years. In addition, upward mobility in the hospital is quite good; and as a result, another 25% of the escorts typically transfer to other jobs in the hospital each year. Thus, about half of the patient escorts need to be replaced annually.

The hospital follows a standard procedure when hiring patient escorts. When a vacancy occurs, the Personnel Department reviews the file of applications of individuals who have applied for the patient escort job. Usually the file contains at least 20 applications because the pay for the job is good, the work easy, and few skills are required. The top two or three applicants are asked to come to the hospital for interviews. Typically, the applicants are interviewed first by Personnel and then by the patient escort supervisor. The majority of those interviewed know some other employees of the hospital, so the only reference check is a call to these employees. Before being hired, applicants are required to take physical exams given by hospital doctors.

Every new escort attends an orientation program the first day on the job. This is conducted by a member of the hospital's Personnel Department. The program consists of a complete tour of the hospital; a review of all the hospital's personnel policies, including a description of its promotion, compensation, and disciplinary policies; and a presentation of the hospital's mission and philosophy. During this orientation session, employees are told that the hospital's image in the community is of major importance and that all employees should strive to maintain and enhance this image by their conduct. After orientation, all patient escorts receive on-the-job training by their immediate supervisor.

During the last two-year period, the hospital has experienced a number of problems with patient escorts that have had an adverse effect on the hospital's image. Several patients have complained to the hospital administration that they have been treated rudely, or in some cases roughly, by one or more patient escorts. Some complained that they had been ordered around or scolded by an escort during the discharge process. Others stated that the escort had been careless when wheeling them out of the hospital to their cars. One person, in fact, reported that an escort had carelessly tipped him over. All escorts are required to wear identification tags, but patients usually can't remember the escort's name when complaining to the hospital. Additionally, the hospital usually has difficulty determining which escort served which patient because escorts often trade patients. Finally, even when the hospital can identify the offending escort, the employee can easily deny any wrongdoing. Such an employee often counters that patients are generally irritable as a result of their illness and hence are prone to complain at even the slightest provocation.

At the hospital administrator's request, the Personnel Manager asked the Chief Supervisor of Patient Escorts, the head of the Staffing Section within the Personnel Department, and the Assistant Personnel Director to meet with her to review the entire procedure used to select patient escorts. It was hoped that a new procedure could be devised that would eliminate the hiring of rude, insulting, or careless patient escorts.

During the meeting, a number of suggestions were made about how the selection procedure might be improved. Criticisms of the present system were also voiced. The Chief Supervisor of Patient Escorts argued that the problem with the hospital's present system is that the application blank is void of any really useful information. He stated that the questions that really give insights into the employee's personality are no longer on the application blank. He suggested that applicants be asked about their hobbies, outside activities, and their personal likes and dislikes on the application blank. He also suggested that each applicant be asked to submit three letters of recommendation from people who know the applicant well. He wanted these letters to focus on the prospective employee's personality, particularly the applicant's ability to remain friendly and polite at all times.

The Assistant Personnel Director contended that the hospital's interviewing procedure should be modified. He observed that, during the typical interview, little attempt is made to determine how the applicant reacts under stress. He suggested that if applicants were asked four or five stress-producing questions, the hospital might be in a better position to judge their ability to work with irritable patients.

The head of the Staffing Section noted that patient escorts require little mental or physical talent and agreed that the crucial attribute escorts need is the ability to always be courteous and polite. He wondered whether an "attitude" test could be developed that would measure the applicant's predisposition toward being friendly. He suggested that a job analysis could be done on the patient escort position to determine those attitudes that are critical to being a successful patient escort. When the job analysis was complete, questions could be developed that would measure these crit-

ical attributes. The test questions could be given to the hospital's present patient escorts to determine whether the test accurately distinguishes the best from the worst escorts. The head of the Staffing Section realized that many of the questions might need to be eliminated or changed, and if the test appeared to show promise, it would probably need to be revalidated in order to meet government requirements. He felt, however, that a well-designed test might be worth the effort and should at least be considered.

The meeting ended with all four participants agreeing that the suggestion of trying to develop an "attitude test" was probably the most promising. The Assistant Personnel Director and Chief Supervisor of Patient Escorts stated that they would conduct a thorough job analysis covering the patient escort position and develop a list of attitudes that are critical to its success. A second meeting would then be scheduled to prepare the actual test questions.

Source: S. M. Nkomo, M. D. Fottler, and R. B. McAffee, *Applications in Human Resource Management: Cases, Exercises, and Skill Builders* (Mason, OH: South-Western, 2005). Reprinted with permission.

Answers to Experiential Activity: b. Application Blanks

In most situations, it's probably fine to ask questions 3, 6 (when driving is required on the job), 11, and 20 (if job requires travel). Question 12 can be asked in this way, "Is there any condition you have that might make it impossible for you to perform 'essential job functions' even with some accommodation?" Here, however, it is better if the applicant volunteers this information. If you do need to ask about disabilities, it's probably better to do so after a decision to hire has been made. Forget about asking about the rest of the topics.

ENDNOTES

1   S. F. Gale, "Three Companies Cut Turnover with Tests," *Workforce* (April 2002): 66–69.

2   For detailed reviews, see D. Bartram, "Assessment in Organizations," *Applied Psychology: An International Review* 53 (2004): 237–259; I. T. Robertson and M. Smith, "Personnel Selection," *Journal of Occupational and Organizational Psychology* 74 (2002): 441–472; N. Schmitt and D. Chan, *Personnel Selection: A Theoretical Approach* (Thousand Oaks, CA: Sage, 1998).

3   B. Roberts, "Crunching the Numbers," *HR Magazine* (October 2003): 63–68.

4   T. Murphy and S. Zandvakili, "Data- and Metrics-Driven Approach to Human Resource Practices: Using Customers, Employees, and

Financial Metrics," *Human Resource Management* 39(1) (Spring 2000): 93–105.

5   D. E. Terpstra and E. J. Rozell, "The Relationship of Staffing Practices to Organizational Level Measures of Performance," *Personnel Psychology* 46 (1993): 27–48.

6   For detailed discussions of utility analysis, see W. R. Cascio, *Costing Human Resources: The Financial Impact of Behavior in Organizations* (Cincinnati, OH: South-Western, 2000); E. F. Cabrera and N. S. Raju, "Utility Analysis: Current Trends and Future Directions," *International Journal of Selection and Assessment* 9 (2001): 92–102.

7   For detailed discussions of selection processes, see N. Anderson, F. Lievens, K. van Dam, and A. M. Ryan, "Future Perspectives on Employee

Selection: Key Directions for Future Research and Practice," *Applied Psychology: An International Review* 53 (2004): 501; K. Pearlman and M. F. Barney, "Selection for a Changing Workforce," in J. F. Kehoe (ed.), *Managing Selection in Changing Organizations: Human Resource Strategies* (San Francisco: Jossey-Bass, 2000): 3–72.

8 M. M. Lombard and R. W. Eichinger, "High Potentials as High Learners," *Human Resource Management* (Winter 2000): 321–329; H. G. Heneman, III, and T. A. Judge, *Staffing Organizations* (New York: McGraw-Hill/Irwin, 2002).

9 A. J. Vinchur, J. S. Schippmann, F. S. Switzer, III, and P. L. Roth, "A Meta-Analytic Review of Predictors of Job Performance for Salespeople," *Journal of Applied Psychology* 83 (1998): 586–597; D. E. Bowen and D. A. Waldman, "Customer-Driven Employee Performance," in D. R. Ilgen and E. D. Pulakos (eds.), *The Changing Nature of Performance* (San Francisco: Jossey-Bass, 1999): 154–191; R. T. Hogan and R. J. Blake, "Vocational Interests: Matching Self-Concept with the Work Environment," in K. R. Murphy (ed.), *Individual Differences and Behavior in Organizations* (San Francisco: Jossey-Bass, 1996): 89–144.

10 R. G. Jones, M. J. Stevens, and D. L. Fischer, "Selection in Team Contexts," in J. F. Kehoe (ed.), *Managing Selection in Changing Organizations: Human Resource Strategies* (San Francisco: Jossey-Bass, 2000): 210–241; G. Neuman and J. Wright, "Team Effectiveness: Beyond Skills and Cognitive Ability," *Journal of Applied Psychology* 84(3) (1999): 376–389; M. Stevens and M. A. Campion, "Staffing Work Teams: Development and Validation of a Selection Test for Teamwork Settings," *Journal of Management* 25 (1999): 207–228.

11 R. Grover and E. Schine, "At Disney, Grumpy Isn't Just a Dwarf," *Business Week* (February 24, 1997): 38; R. Grover, "Michael Eisner Defends the Kingdom," *Business Week* (August 4, 1997): 73–75; V. C. Smith, "Spreading the Magic," *Human Resource Executive* (December 1996): 28–31.

12 J. Romeo, "Answering the Call," *HR Magazine* (October 2003): 81–84; G. Nicholson, "Automated Assessments for Better Hires," *Workforce* (December 2000): 102–109.

13 K. R. Murphy, *Validity Generalization: A Critical Review* (Mahwah, NJ: Lawrence Erlbaum, 2003).

14 For a discussion of validity generalization and other related approaches, see C. C. Hoffman and S. M. McPhail, "Exploring Options for Supporting Test Use in Situations Precluding Local Validation," *Personnel Psychology* 51 (1998): 987–1003.

15 See F. L. Schmidt and J. E. Hunter, "The Validity and Utility of Selection Methods in Personnel Psychology: Practical and Theoretical Implications of 85 Years of Research Findings," *Psychological Bulletin* 124 (1998): 262–274.

16 Based on data presented in B. O'Leary, M. L. Lindholm, R. A. Whitforc, and S. F. Freeman, "Selecting the Best and Brightest: Leveraging Human Capital," *Human Resource Management* (Fall 2002): 325–340, and F. L. Schmidt and J. E. Hunter, "The Validity and Utility of Selection Methods in Personnel Psychology."

17 C. Boutelle, "New Principles Encourage Greater Accountability for Test Users and Developers," *Industrial-Organizational Psychologist* 41(3) (2004): 20–21.

18 H. Aguinis, *Test-Score Banding in Human Resource Selection* (Westport, CT: Praeger, 2004).

19 S. Hays, "Kinko's Dials into Automated Applicant Screening," *Workforce* (November 1999): 71–73.

20 D. G. Lawrence et al., "Design and Use of Weighted Application Blanks," *Personnel Administrator* (March 1982): 53–57, 101.

21 C. J. Russell et al., "Predictive Validity of Biodata Items Generated from Retrospective Life Experience Essays," *Journal of Applied Psychology* 75(5) (1990): 569–580; H. R. Rothstein et al., "Biographical Data in Employment Selection: Can Validities Be Made Generalizable?" *Journal of Applied Psychology* 75(2) (1990): 175–184.

22 M. Dean, C. J. Russell, and P. Muchinsky, "Life Experiences and Performance Prediction: Toward a Theory of Biodata," *Research in Personnel and Human Resource Management* 17 (1999): 245–281; G. Stokes, M. D. Mumford, and W. Owens (eds.), *Biodata Handbook: Theory, Research, and Use of Biographical Information for Selection and Performance Prediction* (Palo Alto, CA: Consulting Psychologists Press, 1994).

23 P. J. Taylor and B. Small, "Asking Applicants What They Would Do versus What They Did Do: A Meta-Analytic Comparison of Situational and Past Behavior Employment Interview Questions," *Journal of Occupational and Organizational Psychology* 75 (2002): 277–294; M. D. Mumford, D. P. Costanza, M. S. Connelly, and J. E. Johnson, "Item Generation Procedures and Background Data Scales: Implications for Construct and Criterion-Related Validity," *Personnel Psychology* 49 (1996): 361–398; A. T. Dalessio and T. A. Silverhart, "Combining Biodata Test and Interview Information: Predicting Decisions and Performance Criteria," *Personnel Psychology* 47 (1994): 303–319.

24 F. A. Mael and B. E. Ashforth, "Loyal from Day One: Biodata, Organizational Identification, and Turnover among Newcomers," *Personnel Psychology* 48 (1995): 309–333; R. D. Gatewood and H. S. Field, *Human Resource Selection* (Orlando: Harcourt Brace, 1994).

25 M. McManus and M. Kelly, "Personality Measures and Biodata: Evidence Regarding Their Incremental Predictive Value in the Life Insurance Industry," *Personnel Psychology* 52 (1999): 137–148; K. Carlson, S. Scullen, F. L. Schmidt, H. R. Rothstein, and F. Erwin, "Generalized Biographical Data Validity Can Be Achieved Without Multi-Organizational Development and Keying," *Personnel Psychology* 52 (1999): 731–755.

26 R. Folger and R. Cropanzano, *Organizational Justice and Human Resource Management* (Thousand Oaks, CA: Sage, 1998); F. A. Mael, M. Connerley, and R. A. Morath, "None of Your Business: Parameters of Biodata Invasiveness," *Personnel Psychology* 49 (1996): 613–650.

27 P. Babcock, "Spotting Lies," *HR Magazine* (October 2003): 46–52.

28 For a good discussion of the benefits and risks associated with using outside vendors to conduct background checks, see C. Garvey, "Outsourcing Background Checks," *HR Magazine* (March 2001): 95–104.

29 T. B. Stivarius, J. Skonberg, R. Fliegel, R. Blumberg, R. Jones, and K. Mones, "Background Checks: Four Steps to Basic Compliance in a Multistate Environment," *Legal Report* (March–April 2003): 1–8; M. A. Nusbaum, "When a Reference Is a Tool for Snooping," *New York Times* (October 19, 2003): 12; S. Romero and M. Richtel, "Second Chance," *New York Times* (March 5, 2001): C1; L. Walley and M. Smith, *Deception in Selection* (New York: John Wiley, 1998); E. A. Robinson, "Beware—Job Seekers Have No Secrets," *Fortune* (December 29, 1997): 285; "Positive Reference Leads to Claim of Negligence," *Fair Employment Practices Guidelines*, No. 430 (April 25, 1997): 1; "Supreme Court Decision Possible Setback to Employee Reference," *Human Resource Executive* (April 1997): 8.

30 J. F. Salgado, N. Anderson, S. Moscoso, C. Bertua, F. D. Fruyt, and J. P. Rolland, "A Meta-Analytic Study of General Mental Ability Validity for Different Occupations in the European Community," *Journal of Applied Psychology* 88(6) (2003): 1068–1081; T. M. Holly, "A Hire Standard," *HR Magazine* (July 2003): 109–112; M. A. Nusbaum, "When a Reference Is a Tool for Snooping," *New York Times* (October 19, 2003): 12; E. Zimmerman, "Getting to Know You Is as Easy as A, B, C or D," *New York Times* (November 30, 2003): 8; F. L. Schmidt and J. E. Hunter, "The Validity and Utility of Selection Methods in Personnel Psychology: Practical and Theoretical Implications of 85 Years of Research Findings," *Psychological Bulletin* 124 (1998): 262–274.

31 E. A. Fleishman and M. K. Quaintance, *Taxonomies of Human Performance* (New York: Academic Press, 1984).

32 R. L. Roth, C. Bevier, P. Bobko, F. S. Switzer III, and P. Taylor, "Ethnic Group Differences in Cognitive Ability in Employment and Educational Settings: A Meta-Analysis," *Personnel Psychology* 54 (2001): 297–330; N. Schmitt, C. S. Clause, and E. D. Pulakos, "Subgroup Differences Associated with Different Measures of Some Common Job-Relevant Constructs," in C. R. Cooper and I. T. Roberson (eds.), *International*

Review of Industrial/Organizational Psychology, vol. 11 (1996): 115–140. For a discussion of some alternatives to cognitive ability testing, see S. Zedeck and I. L. Goldstein, "The Relationship between I/O Psychology and Public Policy: A Commentary," in J. F. Kehoe (ed.), *Managing Selection in Changing Organizations: Human Resource Strategies* (San Francisco: Jossey-Bass, 2000): 371–396.

33 S. Greengard, "Gimme Attitude," http://www.workforce.com/section/06/feature/23/47/86/index.html, July 15, 2003; R. T. Hogan, J. C. Hogan, and B. W. Roberts, "Personality Measurement and Employment Decisions," *American Psychologist* 51 (1996): 469–477; R. T. Hogan, "Personality and Personality Measurement," in Dunnette and Hough (eds.), *Handbook of Industrial and Organizational Psychology* (1991): 873–890.

34 J. M. Collins and D. H. Gleaves, "Race, Job Applicants, and the Five-Factor Model of Personality: Implications for Black Psychology, Industrial/Organizational Psychology, and the Five-Factor Theory," *Journal of Applied Psychology* 83 (1998): 531–544; R. R. McCrae and P. T. Costa, Jr., "Personality Trait Structure as a Human Universal," *American Psychologist* 52 (1997): 509–535; L. M. Hough and R. J. Schneider, "Personality Traits, Taxonomies, and Applications in Organizations," in K. R. Murphy (ed.), *Individual Differences and Behavior in Organizations* (San Francisco: Jossey-Bass, 1996): 31–88.

35 T. A. Judge, D. Heller, and M. K. Mount, "Five-Factor Model of Personality and Job Satisfaction: A Meta-Analysis," *Journal of Applied Psychology* 87 (2002): 53–541; P. Caligiuri, "The Big Five Personality Characteristics as Predictors of Expatriate's Desire to Terminate the Assignment and Supervisor-Rated Performance," *Personnel Psychology* 53 (2000): 67–88; G. Hurtz and J. Donovan, "Personality and Job Performance: The Big Five Revisited," *Journal of Applied Psychology* 85 (2000): 869–879; T. A. Judge, C. A. Higgins, C. Thiresen, and M. Barrick, "The Big Five Personality Traits, General Mental Ability, and Career Success Across the Life Span," *Personnel Psychology* 52 (1999): 621–652.

36 K. R. Murphy, *Honesty in the Workplace* (Pacific Grove, CA: Brooks/Cole, 1993); D. S. Ones, C. Viswesvaran, and F. L. Schmidt, "Comprehensive Meta-Analysis of Integrity Test Validities: Findings and Implications for Personnel Selection and Theories of Job Performance," *Journal of Applied Psychology* 78 (1993): 679–703; W. J. Camara and D. L. Schneider, "Integrity Tests: Facts and Unresolved Issues," *American Psychologist* 49 (1994): 112–119; J. M. Collins and F. L. Schmidt, "Personality, Integrity, and White Collar Crime: A Construct Validity Study," *Personnel Psychology* 46 (1993): 295–311.

37 J. B. Olson-Buchanan, F. Drasgow, P. J. Moberg, A. D. Mead, P. A. Keenan, and M. A. Donovan, "Interactive Video Assessment of Conflict Resolution Skills," *Personnel Psychology* 51 (1998): 1–24; J. A. Weekley and C. Jones, "Video-Based Situational Testing," *Personnel Psychology* 50 (1997): 25–49.

38 N. J. Kolk, M. P. Born, and H. V. D. Flier, "The Transparent Assessment Center: The Effects of Revealing Dimension to Candidates," *Applied Psychology: An International Review* 52 (2003): 648–668; M. Damitz, D. Manzey, M. Kleinmann, and K. Severin, "Assessment Center for Pilot Selection: Construct and Criterion Validity and the Impact of Assessor Type," *Applied Psychology: An International Review* 52 (2003): 193–212; D. J. Woehr and W. Arthur, Jr., "The Construct-Related Validity of Assessment Center Ratings: A Review and Meta-Analysis of the Role of Methodological Factors," *Journal of Management* 29 (2003): 231–258.

39 J. N. Zall, "Assessment Centre Methods," in P. J. D. Drenth, H. Thierry, and C. J. DeWolff (eds.), *Handbook of Work and Organizational Psychology, vol. 3: Personnel Psychology* (Basingstoke, UK: Taylor & Francis, 1998); D. Briscoe, "Assessment Centers: Cross-Cultural and Cross-National Issues," *Journal of Social Behavior and Personality* 12 (1997): 261–270; A. C. Spychalski, M. A. Quinnones, B. A. Gaugler, and K. Pohley, "A Survey of Assessment Center Practices in Organizations in the United States," *Personnel Psychology* 50 (1997): 71–90.

40 L. M. Donahue, D. M. Truxillo, J. M. Cornwell, and M. J. Gerrity, "Assessment Center Construct Validity and Behavioral Checklists," *Journal of Social Behavior and Personality* 12(5) (1997): 85–108; B. B. Gaugler et al., "Meta-Analysis of Assessment Center Validity," *Journal of Applied Psychology* 72 (1987): 493–511.

41 D. R. Briscoe, "Assessment Centers: Cross-Cultural and Cross-National Issues," *Journal of Social Behavior and Personality* (Special Issue) (1997): 261–270; C. C. Hoffman and G. C. Thornton, III, "Examining Selection Utility Where Competing Predictors Differ in Adverse Impact," *Personnel Psychology* 50 (1997): 455–470.

42 R. A. Posthuma, F. P. Morgeson, and M. A. Campion, "Beyond Employment Interview Validity: A Comprehensive Narrative Review of Recent Research and Trends over Time," *Personnel Psychology* 55 (2002): 1–81; B. P. Sunoo, "How Fun Flies at Southwest Airlines," *Personnel Journal* (June 1995): 62–71. For a detailed discussion of employment interviews, see R. W. Eder and M. M. Harris (eds.), *The Employment Interview Handbook* (Thousand Oaks, CA: Sage, 1999).

43 J. Burnett and S. J. Motowidlo, "Relations Between Different Sources of Information in the Structured Selection Interview," *Personnel Psychology* 51 (1998): 963–983; CCH Incorporated, "20 Factors to Determine Worker Status," *Workforce Extra* (November 1999): 1–2; J. Cortina, N. Goldstein, S. Payne, H. Davidson, and S. Gilliland, "The Incremental Validity of Interview Scores Above Cognitive Ability and Conscientiousness Scores," *Personnel Psychology* 53 (2000): 325–351.

44 A. C. Poe, "Graduate Work: Behavioral Interviewing Can Tell You If an Applicant Just out of College Has Traits Needed for the Job," *HR Magazine* (October 2003): 95–100; R. W. Eder and M. M. Harris, *The Employment Interview Handbook* (London: Sage, 2000); E. D. Pulakos and N. Schmitt, "Experience-Based and Situational Interview Questions: Studies of Validity," *Personnel Psychology* 48 (1995): 289–308; M. A. Campion, D. K. Palmer, and J. E. Campion, "A Review of Structure in the Selection Interview," *Personnel Psychology* 50 (1997): 655–702; M. A. McDaniel et al., "The Validity of Employment Interviews: A Comprehensive Review and Meta-Analysis," *Journal of Applied Psychology* 79 (1994): 599–616; S. J. Motowidlo et al., "Studies of the Structured Behavioral Interview," *Journal of Applied Psychology* 77 (1992): 571–587.

45 J. M. Sacco, C. R. Scheu, A. M. Ryan, and N. Schmitt, "An Investigation of Race and Sex Similarity Effects in Interviews: A Multilevel Approach to Relational Demography," *Journal of Applied Psychology* 88 (2003): 852–865; D. S. Ones and N. Anderson, "Gender and Ethnic Group Differences on Personality Scales in Selection: Some British Data," *Journal of Occupational and Organizational Psychology* 75 (2002): 255–276; A. I. Huffcutt and P. L. Roth, "Racial Group Difference in Employment Interview Evaluations," *Journal of Applied Psychology* 83 (1998): 179–189.

46 P. J. Taylor and B. Small, "Asking Applicants What They Would Do versus What They Did Do: A Meta-Analytic Comparison of Situational and Past Behavior Employment Interview Questions," *Journal of Occupational and Organizational Psychology* 75 (2002): 277–294. For more discussion of these, see G. P. Latham, "The Situational Interview," in R. W. Eder and M. M. Harris (eds.), *The Employment Interview Handbook* (Thousand Oaks, CA: Sage, 1999): 159–178; S. J. Motowidlo, "Asking About Past Behavior Versus Hypothetical Behavior," in R. W. Eder and M. M. Harris (eds.), *The Employment Interview Handbook* (Thousand Oaks, CA: Sage, 1999): 179–190.

47 L. Fogli and K. Whitney, "Assessing and Changing Managers for New Organizational Roles," in R. Jeanneret and R. Silzer (eds.), *Individual Psychological Assessment: Predicting Behavior in Organizational Settings* (San Francisco: Jossey-Bass, 1998).

48 G. Nyfield and H. Baron, "Cultural Context in Adapting Selection Practices Across Borders," in J. F. Kehoe (ed.), *Managing Selection in Changing Organizations: Human Resource Strategies* (San Francisco: Jossey-Bass, 2000): 242–268; A. M. Ryan, L. McFarland, H. Baron, and R. Page, "An International Look at Selection Practices: Nation and Culture as Explanations for Variability in Practice," *Personnel Psychology* 52 (1999): 359–391.

49 T. Lin, G. H. Dobbins, and J. L. Farh, "A Field Study of Race and Age Similarity Effects on Interview Ratings in Conventional and Situational Interviews," *Journal of Applied Psychology* 77 (1992): 363–371; see also A. J. Prewett-Livingston, H. S. Field, J. G. Veres, III, and P. M. Lewis, "Effects of Interview Ratings in a Situational Panel Interview," *Journal of Applied Psychology* (1996): 178–186.

50 E. D. Pulakos, N. Schmitt, D. Whitney, and M. Smith, "Individual Differences in Interviewer Ratings: The Impact of Standardization, Consensus Discussion, and Sampling Error on the Validity of a Structured Interview," *Personnel Psychology* 49 (1996): 85–102.

51 D. M. Cable and T. A. Judge, "Interviewers' Perceptions of Person-Organization Fit and Organizational Selection Decisions," *Journal of Applied Psychology* 82 (1997): 546–561; C. M. Marlowe, S. Schneider, and C. E. Nelson, "Gender and Attractiveness Biases in Hiring Decisions: Are More Experienced Managers Less Biased?" *Journal of Applied Psychology* 81 (1996): 11–21.

52 C. K. Stevens, "Antecedents of Interview Interactions, Interviewers' Ratings, and Applicants' Reactions," *Personnel Psychology* 51 (1998): 55–85.

53 Data collected by Staffing.org, Inc.

54 "EEOC Issues Final Guidance for Medical Examinations under ADA," *Fair Employment Practices Guidelines* (January 25, 1996): 5; "Past Accommodations Do Not Always Determine the Future," *Fair Employment Practices Guidelines*, No. 436 (July 25, 1997): 1; A. Bryant, "Seeing What Really Matters," *New York Times* (December 24, 1997): D1, D4; R. R. Faden and N. E. Kass, "Genetic Screening Technology: Ethical Issues in Access to Tests by Employers and Health Insurance Companies," *Journal of Social Issues* 49 (1993): 75–88.

55 S. Sonnenberg, "Can HR Legally Ask the Questions That Applicants with Disabilities Want to Be Asked?" *Workforce* (August 2002): 42–44. For a detailed discussion of providing accommodation for people with disabilities, see W. J. Campbell and M. E. Reilly, "Accommodations for Persons with Disabilities," in J. F. Kehoe (ed.), *Managing Selection in Changing Organizations: Human Resource Strategies* (San Francisco: Jossey-Bass, 2000): 319–367.

56 F. P. Alvarez, "Disability Management Law Grows Up: Examining the Supreme Court's Recent ADA and FMLA Rulings," *Legal Report* (September–October 2002): 1–8; D. D. Hatch and J. E. Hall, "Disabled Must Compete on Equal Basis," *Workforce* (2000): 109.

57 A. Meisler, "Negative Results," *Workforce Management* (October 2003): 35–40.

58 G. Nyfield and H. Baron, "Cultural Context in Adapting Selection Practices Across Borders," in J. F. Kehoe (ed.), *Managing Selection in Changing Organizations: Human Resource Strategies* (San Francisco: Jossey-Bass, 2000): 242–268; A. M. Ryan, L. McFarland, H. Baron, and R. Page, "An International Look at Selection Practices: Nation and Culture as Explanations for Variability in Practice," *Personnel Psychology* 52 (1999): 359–391.

59 D. S. Chapman, K. L. Uggerslev, and J. Webster, "Applicant Reactions to Face-to-Face and Technology-Mediated Interviews: A Field Investigation," *Journal of Applied Psychology* 88 (2003): 944–953; C. J. Collins and C. K. Stevens, "The Relationship between Early Recruitment-Related Activities and the Application Decisions of New Labor-Market Entrants: A Brand Equity Approach to Recruitment," *Journal of Applied Psychology* 87 (2002): 1121–1133; D. M. Truxillo, T. N. Bauer, M. A. Campion, and M. E. Paronto, "Selection Fairness Information and Applicant Reactions: A Longitudinal Field Study," *Journal of Applied Psychology* 87 (2002): 1020–1031; A. M. Ryan and R. Ployhart, "Applicants' Perceptions of Selection Procedures and Decisions: A Critical Review and Agenda for the Future," *Journal of Management* 26(3) (2000): 565–606.

60 R. Ployhart, A. M. Ryan, and M. A. Bennett, "Explanations for Selection Decisions: Applicants' Reactions to Informational and Sensitivity Features of Explanations," *Journal of Applied Psychology* 84(1) (1999): 87–106.

61 T. Bauer, D. M. Truxillo, R. Sanchez, J. Craig, P. Ferrara, and M. A. Campion, "Applicant Reactions to Selection: Development of the Selection Procedural Justice Scale," *Personnel Psychology* 54 (2001): 387–420; D. Chan, N. Schmitt, J. M. Sacco, and R. P. DeShon, "Understanding Pretest and Posttest Reaction to Cognitive Ability and Personality Tests," *Journal of Applied Psychology* 83 (1998): 471–485.

62 D. Chan, "Racial Subgroup Difference in Predictive Validity Perceptions on Personality and Cognitive Ability Tests," *Journal of Applied Psychology* 82 (1997): 311–320; D. Chan, N. Schmitt, R. P. DeShon, C. S. Clause, and K. Delbridge, "Reactions to Cognitive Ability Tests: The Relationships between Race, Test Performance, Face Validity Perceptions, and Test-Taking Motivation," *Journal of Applied Psychology* 82 (1997): 300–310.

63 S. F. Gale, "Putting Job Candidates to the Test," *Workforce Management* (2004): 91; see Rynes, "Who's Selecting Whom?"

64 J. S. MacNeil, "Hey, Look Us Over," *Growth* (October 2002): 146.

65 A. Rodriguez and F. Prezant, "Better Interviews for People with Disabilities," *Workforce* (August 2002): 38–42.

66 R. Thompson, "Marriott HR Exec Speaks about Successes, Challenges of His Job," *HR News* (December 1999): 1–2, 37.

67 W. F. Cascio, "Reconciling Economic and Social Objectives in Personnel Selection: Impact of Alternative Decision Rules," *New Approaches to Employee Management: Fairness in Employee Selection* 1 (1992): 61–86; M. E. Baehr et al., "Proactively Balancing the Validity and Legal Compliance of Personal Background Measures in Personnel Management," *Journal of Business and Psychology* 8 (Spring 1994): 345–354; S. E. Maxwell and R. D. Arvey, "The Search for Predictors with High Validity and Low Adverse Impact: Compatible or Incompatible Goals?" *Journal of Applied Psychology* 78 (1993): 433–437.

68 L. Micco, "California Bans Employment Bias Based on Genetic Testing," *HR News* (August 1998): 13.

69 For an excellent discussion of legal issues, see J. C. Sharf and D. P. Jones, "Employment Risk Management," in J. F. Kehoe (ed.), *Managing Selection in Changing Organizations: Human Resource Strategies* (San Francisco: Jossey-Bass, 2000): 271–318.

70 Society for Industrial and Organizational Psychology, *Principles for the Validation and Use of Personnel Selection Procedures*, 4th ed. (Bowling Green, OH: Society for Industrial and Organizational Psychology, 2003).

71 To learn more about how subtle discrimination can limit opportunities for women to develop their international competencies, see K. Tyler, "Don't Fence Her In," *HR Magazine* (March 2001): 70–77; [Research Report] *Passport to Opportunity: U.S. Women in Global Business* (New York: Catalyst, 2000).

72 For discussions about how the design of selection procedures can affect adverse impact, see R. P. DeShon, M. R. Smith, D. Chan, and N. Schmitt, "Can Racial Difference in Cognitive Test Performance Be Reduced by Presenting Problems in a Social Context?" *Journal of Applied Psychology* 83 (1998): 438–451; K. Hattrup, J. Rock, and C. Scalia, "The Effects of Varying Conceptualizations of Job Performance on Adverse Impact, Minority Hiring, and Predicted Performance," *Journal of Applied Psychology* 82 (1997): 656–664; P. R. Sackett and J. E. Ellington, "The Effects of Forming Multi-Predictor Composites on Group Differences and Adverse Impact," *Personnel Psychology* 50 (1997): 707–722.

73 For other methods, see S. B. Morris and R. E. Lobsenz, "Significance Tests and Confidence Intervals for Adverse Impact Ratios," *Personnel Psychology* 53 (2000): 89–111.

74 R. Kopp, *The Rice Paper Ceiling: Breaking Through Japanese Corporate Culture* (New York: Stone Bridge Press, 1994).

75 D. R. Briscoe and R. S. Schuler, *International Human Resource Management*, 2nd ed. (London: Routledge, 2004).

76 C. Daily, S. Certo, and D. R. Dalton, "International Experience in the Executive Suite: The Path to Prosperity?" *Strategic Management Journal* 21 (2000): 515–523; M. Dalton, C. Ernst, J. Deal, and J. Leslie, *Success for the New Global Leader* (Greensboro, NC: Center for Creative Leadership, 2002).

77 To learn more about how culture affects hiring practices, see A. M. Ryan, L. McFarland, H. Baron, and R. Page, "An International Look at

Selection Practices: Nation and Culture as Explanations for Variability in Practice," *Personnel Psychology* 52 (1999): 359–391; H. Scullion and M. Linehan, *Global Staffing* (London: Routledge, 2005).

78 C. Hall, "Ringmasters Turn a Circus into an Empire," *Dallas Morning News* (February 8, 1998): H1–H2; G. Flynn, "Acrobats, Aerialists, and HR: The Big Top Needs Big HR," *Workforce* (August 1997): 38–45. Table

adapted from L. B. Pincus and J. A. Belohlav, "Legal Issues in Multinational Business Strategy: To Play the Game You Have to Know the Rules," *Academy of Management Executive* 10(3) (1996): 52–62; J. P. Begin, *Dynamic Human Resource Systems: Cross-National Comparisons* (New York: de Gruyter, 1997); R. Orzechowski and B. Berret, "Setting Up Shop in Vietnam," *Global Workforce* (May 1998): 24–27.

chapter 8

Training and Developing a Competitive Workforce

Based in Webster, New York, Trident Precision Manufacturing fabricates sheet metal for customers such as Xerox, Kodak, and IBM. A decade ago, Trident's managers didn't care who they hired so long as they were breathing and could do the job. The approach clearly wasn't working. Far too many products came off the line with major defects that required them to be redone completely. Changes in the way new employees were selected could contribute to improved performance, but only somewhat. The company wasn't prepared to fire everyone and start over from scratch. Besides being more selective in their hiring, they needed to improve the performance of current employees. They set as their goal to have every employee complete a 25-hour training course devoted to quality improvement. In addition to basic problem-solving and communication skills, employees learned to read blueprints and solve problems using trigonometry. During the past decade, Trident has spent 4.7% of its payroll costs on training—more than three times as much as the industry average. Their investment in training has brought handsome returns. In one year, employees typically make over 2,000 process improvement suggestions, of which about 98% are implemented. Defects have dropped from 3% to .007%. Turnover has dropped from 41% to 3.5%, creating enormous savings due to reduced recruitment and selection costs. And recent employee surveys show that over 90% of employees are satisfied with their work.[1]

STRATEGIC IMPORTANCE OF TRAINING AND DEVELOPMENT

> "At Toyota, we have a really tough time finding good people. Training is important."
>
> Jim Wiseman
> President of External Affairs
> Toyota Motor Manufacturing North America

The best competitors use training and development practices to improve the ability of the workforce to implement their business strategy. In the case of Trident, the strategy called for excellent quality at a low cost. Adopting a Total Quality Management (TQM) philosophy, in turn, required investing in training in order to ensure operational success. Often, changes in company strategy mean that senior managers need to adopt new leadership behavior and acquire new business knowledge. This was illustrated with the example of Weyerhaeuser, described in Chapter 4.

Improving the competence of the workforce is one way that training and development can create a competitive advantage, but it is not the only way. Training and development activities also contribute to organizational success in less direct ways. For example, they can provide shared experiences that promote understanding among employees with many different histories and so help speed the development of organizational cohesiveness and employee commitment. Training and development activities also are a means for employers to address employees' needs. By offering training and development opportunities, employers help employees develop their own personal competitive advantage and ensure their long-term employability.[2]

IMPROVING RECRUITMENT AND RETENTION

In a recent survey, senior executives said that the top HR issues facing their companies are:

- Leadership development
- Motivational pay
- Training and development of their workforce

FAST FACT

Chapter 6 described in detail the strategic importance of being able to attract and retain qualified employees. You may recall from that discussion that one common source of employee dissatisfaction is the lack of career advancement opportunities that some employers provide. For most employees, making a significant career move involves taking a job that requires competencies not needed in their current job. How can employees acquire these competencies? One way is by seeking out educational opportunities on their own—for example, by attending classes at night or on weekends. But a more appealing way for most people is through participation in training and development activities offered by their employer. Many people seek out employers who provide training and development activities that facilitate career advancement. When they receive such opportunities, employees are likely to feel more committed to the organization and are less likely to leave. Offering job training to help employees whose jobs are lost to offshoring or outsourcing is also a means by which to create feelings of loyalty among employees.

Improving Competitiveness

United States corporations spend an estimated $60 billion annually on formal employee training and development programs that use an estimated 1.5 billion hours of time for the more than 56 million employees who participate.[3] Often, large investments in training and development are justified by a belief that training and development will enhance the organization's ability to compete effectively. Trident's 25-hour course in quality is an example of a focused training effort that improved the company's long-term competitiveness.

In highly competitive industries, training for immediate performance improvement is particularly important to organizations with stagnant or declining rates of productivity or customer satisfaction. Training for performance improvement is also important to organizations that are rapidly incorporating new technologies and, consequently, increasing the likelihood of employee obsolescence.

Increasing Productivity. When a Finnish mining and metals conglomerate bought the American Brass Factory in Buffalo, New York, company officials believed that development activities for plant employees would eventually improve the plant's productivity. The plant is one of the largest copper and brass rolling mills in the United States, making everything from buttons to ammunition shell casings to cell phone components. Until a few years ago, the blue-collar workforce understood little about their industry or how world economic conditions affected their daily lives. Many were openly hostile toward the new foreign owners. In a long-term effort to change attitudes and improve productivity, the company began an unusual educational effort. Instructors from a local university taught about the impact of technology on the workplace, the dynamics of international competition, manufacturing costs in developing economies, how to read income statements, and the factors that influence the pricing of commodities. During the first year of the development effort, courses were offered around-the-clock so employees on all three shifts could attend. Subsequently, the plant has offered the courses every three years. In addition, management holds quarterly meetings for all 850 employees. Topics for discussion include: (1) plant operations; (2) market conditions; and (3) investments in equipment. According to Outokumpu president, Warren Bartel, the effects of the education show. "The questions—about pricing, competition, and customers—get better every year," he says.[4]

In a given year, nearly 50% of Hilton's hotel reservation staff will leave. The figure is close to 150% at its largest call centers. Each newly hired person needs to be trained.

Improving Service. Sometimes it takes a lot of feedback from customers before a company realizes the need for training. This was the situation at Quebecor World. Over a period of several years, it had been following a strategy of offering excellent quality at a low price, while growing through a series of acquisitions.

But competition in the printing industry was tough, and eventually Quebecor realized that high-quality work at a low price wasn't enough. Customers wanted more.

Based in Montreal, Quebecor World is the world's largest printing company, with 160 plants in 40 countries. Back in 1998, it was losing hundreds of thousands of dollars annually due to poor customer service. Following a year-long assessment of company needs, improved customer service was identified as a top strategic priority. To remedy this and other problems, Quebecor World University was formed. Initially, the firm's customer service and account reps were trained in account management skills, how to better understand customers' needs, and how to create a team-based customer-oriented culture. The complete program included three 3-day sessions, spaced out over several weeks. To drive home the strategic importance of the training program, a senior manager or president from one of the nine business divisions was present to kick off each session, explaining the company's goals and expectations. At the end of the training, senior managers returned to listen to the participants present what they had learned and to discuss how they intended to apply it back on the job.[5]

"At UPS we use many tools to develop our leaders. In fact, we spend more than $300 million dollars a year on training and education programs for employees."

Cal Darden
Senior VP of U.S. Operations
UPS

Implementing New Technology. New technologies account for much of the enhanced levels of productivity achieved in recent years. But new technology seldom can be introduced without also providing training in how to use it. When Hilton Hotels adopted a new reservation system called HILSTAR, it had to train 5,000 reservation agents around the world how to use it. Seeing an opportunity, Hilton folded several other training components into the program it developed to train employees using the new technology. These included professional service skills, safety training required by OSHA, and the company's harassment-free workplace guidelines.[6]

When Health Partners installed a major upgrade to its data processing system, employees needed to upgrade their skills in order to use it. The feature "Managing Change: High-Return Training at Health Partners" describes how that organization attacked their training needs.[7]

TRAINING FOR CUSTOMERS

Increasingly, training activities are crossing organizational boundaries. Besides training their own workforce, many organizations help their customers train and develop *their* workforces. Siemens USA—one of the world's leading manufacturers of high-technology equipment—conducts a variety of training programs to meet the special needs of customers and their markets. On-the-job training for customers ensures that all the capabilities of the company's technologically advanced systems are fully utilized, and all their benefits are fully realized.

When Chesterton, a company that makes sealing devices, developed a training program for its sales force, it never intended to offer it to customers. But the course proved to be very effective within the company, even among

High-Return Training at Health Partners

Health Partners is a nonprofit organization that administers Medicare and Medicaid coverage for patients in the Philadelphia area. Like other nonprofit organizations, keeping down costs is a daily challenge—and training costs are no exception. Nevertheless, when the company spent $3 million building and installing a new data processing system, it knew it would need to invest in training employees to use it. So it also invested tens of thousands of dollars to hire outside training consultants to prepare the workforce for the change.

Unfortunately, due to unexpected delays in the installation of the system, the training occurred long before the system was ready. By the time it was up and running, employees had already forgotten most of what they had been taught. Employees became frustrated because they could no longer deal with customers' questions efficiently. Naturally, customers were frustrated, too. Health Partners needed to bring employees up to speed quickly. An effective, low-cost training program that wouldn't dangerously disrupt the company's business was needed. If the training sessions took employees away from their desks for long stretches of time, that would just make matters worse.

This time the HR department took responsibility for the training. That alone cut the training costs by half. In order to have enough trainers, HR convinced employees who had performed well in the prior round of training to serve as part-time instructors and support staff. The original training program was redesigned into numerous 45-minute sessions that could easily be scheduled into any workday. Employees were encouraged to retake sessions as many times as they needed in order to develop a sense of mastery. Besides technical training, employees were taught about the longer-term benefits that would be realized once they all could use the new technology. Discussions about the inevitable stresses that accompany major change were also included. Soon employees were speeding through the program, and customer complaints dropped to nearly none.

managers who initially thought it was unnecessary. Before long, Chesterton realized the training could also benefit customers by educating them on the uses and operation of their new equipment. Chesterton doesn't give the training away, however; they prefer using it to generate additional revenue.[8]

LEARNING ORGANIZATIONS AND KNOWLEDGE MANAGEMENT

As described in Chapter 4, in recent years, some companies have elevated the importance of learning and related activities, recognizing them as potential sources of sustained competitive advantage. Organizations that strive to make learning an activity that occurs in many ways every day throughout all parts of the organization have been referred to as learning organizations.

To support their learning agenda, companies such as Xerox, Booz Allen and Hamilton Consulting, General Electric, JPMorganChase, and many others have adopted various types of knowledge management technology. Knowledge management is about making sure that knowledge from employees, teams, and units within an organization is captured, remembered, stored, and shared with others—which is the essence of a learning organization.

Knowledge management technologies provide software that makes it possible for people to share knowledge electronically. The systems, which usually operate on the organization's intranet, can capture and distribute "soft" knowledge as well as quantitative data. For example, employees might enter narrative information about their successes and failures during a project. Later, people working on similar projects can read these entries and learn from the experiences of others. Typically, knowledge management software organizes the stored knowledge and provides a means to search and retrieve it using key words that reflect the everyday language and jargon used in a specific organization. To help ensure that a company's knowledge management technology is fully integrated with other learning activities, many learning organizations have created a position titled Chief Learning Officer or Chief Knowledge Officer.

For knowledge management technology to facilitate learning, employees must be willing to share their knowledge and experiences; and they must be willing to use the ideas and knowledge of others. Neither of these is automatic. As is true for all of the training and development opportunities employers provide, a variety of other practices should be used to encourage, support, and reward the learning process. Managers may need to reward employees for sharing their knowledge so that others can benefit. They also may need to reward employees for using information and knowledge that are in a common stored database, the knowledge management library.[9]

Mergers and Acquisitions

Following mergers and acquisitions, training that focuses on helping employees understand the new culture is probably the most common. But promoting cultural harmony need not be the only objective of postmerger training. Retaining key talent is another objective that postmerger training may serve.

When Gates Energy Products purchased a battery division from GE, the company's managers worried about how difficult it might be to integrate the plant into their existing company culture. According to Robin Kane, an HR manager at Gates, "the GE management philosophy was very strong, and deeply embedded in each manager, through extensive training and leadership classes at GE's corporate university." At Gates, on the other hand, managers had received only informal training. This caused Gates managers to worry that the experienced GE managers would abandon the division, choosing instead to seek other employment within GE. Retaining the managerial talent was a key strategic issue that Gates needed to address in order for their acquisition to pay off. Kane attacked the problem by developing a training program that emphasized the need for trust and teamwork among managers in the merged facilities. Gates wanted GE managers to see that their expertise was needed and appreciated. The company also wanted to convince these managers that they could continue to grow and develop if they remained with Gates. The training seemed to work. Turnover was low among the managers who participated, and their feedback indicated that they learned just as much from the Gates training as they had at GE.[10]

TRAINING AND DEVELOPMENT PRACTICES WITHIN THE INTEGRATED HRM SYSTEM

The activities of training, developing, and socializing employees are so closely related that it is difficult, and perhaps impossible, to make a clear distinction among them. Instead, the entire system of activities usually is referred to simply as "training and development" (T&D). In general, an organization's training and development practices are its *intentional* efforts to improve current and future performance by helping employees acquire the skills, knowledge, and attitudes required of a competitive workforce.[11]

TRAINING, DEVELOPMENT, AND SOCIALIZATION

Usually, **training** *has as its main objective improving performance in the near term and in a specific job by increasing employees' competencies.* Most training for job knowledge and skills is completed in a matter of hours or days.

Depending on an organization's recruitment and selection practices, new hires may have insufficient skills and require training before being placed in a job. For current employees, technological changes, loss of current jobs, and job redesign may create the need for new job skills. Another reason that employees may need new skills or knowledge is because they have been transferred or promoted. And in some cases, employees may need training to "freshen up" on skills that aren't used very much, for example, those used in emergences.

In comparison to the near-term focus of most training efforts, **development** *refers to activities intended to improve competencies over a longer period of time in anticipation of the organization's future needs.* Development activities may improve performance in one's current job, but that is not typically the main objective. In fact, a common approach to development is giving people "stretch" assignments. When employees are given stretch assignments, often the expectation is that performance may not be optimal, but a great deal of valuable learning will occur that should prove useful in the future. For this reason, development activities often are referred to as "career development" and/or "leadership development."

Upon entry into a new job or a new organization, all employees initially need to "learn the ropes." **Socialization** *has the major objective of teaching employees about the organization's history, culture, and management practices.* Through socialization, new employees learn how things are done in the new environment, including things that are not written down in any policy or procedures manual.[12] Intentional efforts to socialize employees usually occur near the time of initial hiring, but merger and acquisition activity in the firm or other major changes may stimulate socialization efforts at other times as well.

LINKS TO OTHER HR ACTIVITIES

The objectives of specific training and development activities vary greatly, as will become apparent in this chapter. The differing objectives, in turn, often determine which other aspects of the HRM system should be more tightly integrated with a particular training and development activity. When the objective of training is improving job performance, the training should be designed using job analysis information about what is required to do the work. If the objective is developing employees for future promotion and advancement, the activities should be aligned with the selection criteria used when hiring people into those higher-level positions. If the objective of training is to create a culture change, it may be appropriate to link performance evaluations and rewards to completion of the training.

"Fulfilling the grow-from-within policy involves a substantial commitment to training. About 60% of Vanguard's 250-strong HR staff is involved in training activities."

Kathleen C. Gubanich
Managing Director of HR
The Vanguard Group

"When people walk in the door, they want to know: What do you expect out of me? What's in this deal for me? What do I have to do to get ahead?"

Fred Smith
Founder and CEO
FedEx

Exhibit 8.1 provides a general overview of training and development activities, and the relationships they have to other HR activities. Because there are so many possible objectives of training and development, all the other areas of HR activities are shown in the exhibit. Here we comment on just a few of the many possible linkages.

Legal Compliance. For some jobs in some industries, federal regulations require employers to provide training. The Occupational Safety and Health Administration (OSHA), the Food and Drug Administration (FDA), and the Federal Aviation Administration (FAA) are examples of agencies that monitor and enforce training requirements. In many other industries, such as financial services and real estate, employees must have a license or be certified to hold particular jobs. When licenses and certification are required, employers may provide the needed training as part of their staffing strategy. In many professions, periodic training is required in order to update the knowledge acquired earlier.

Recent Supreme Court rulings are expected to spur employers to provide training even when it is not required. These decisions established that an employer may not be held liable for discriminatory behavior by its employ-

FAST FACT

Seventy percent of Delta Airline's customer service workforces get annual required FAA training via the Internet.

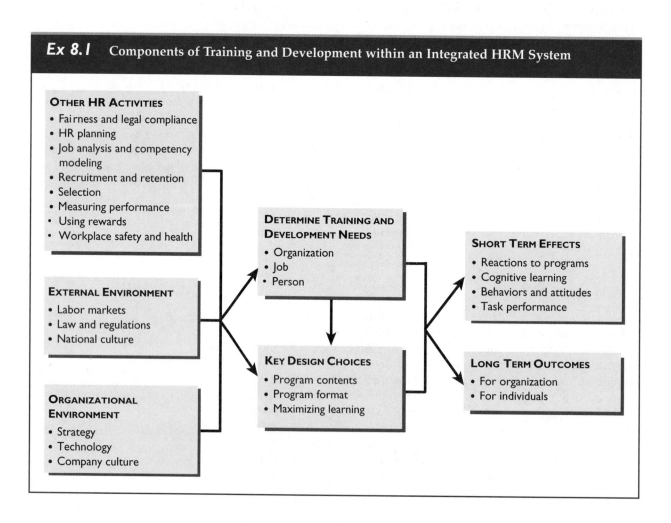

Ex 8.1   Components of Training and Development within an Integrated HRM System

ees if it can show that (a) it acted reasonably to prevent the behavior, and (b) the victim acted unreasonably by not using the company's available procedures for preventing harm. Companies that can prove they offered training to inform employees of their policies and procedures should be able to provide the evidence they need to defend themselves. Exhibit 8.2 summarizes several principles that employers should follow to meet the court's standards for appropriate antidiscrimination training.[13]

Job Analysis, Competency Modeling, and HR Planning. Together, job analysis and competency modeling establish the tasks performed in a job and the competencies required to perform the job well. Such information should serve as the foundation for the design of training programs aimed at improving job performance. Competency models, along with HR planning, also can guide the design of development activities. For many companies, the impending wave of retirements among Baby Boomers has created anxiety about whether the next generation will be ready to fill the high-level jobs that Baby Boomers will soon vacate. With an understanding of the competencies that will be needed by future leaders, companies can begin now to

---

Ex 8.2 Antidiscrimination Training Principles

The following principles are based on statements in several court rulings. These principles represent the suggestions of an informed legal expert. They are not formal regulatory guidelines.

WHAT ARE THE OBJECTIVES?
- ✔ Inform employees of their rights, duties, and responsibilities regarding nondiscriminatory behavior.
- ✔ Create a sense of accountability and shared responsibility for creating a harassment-free workplace.

WHO IS TO BE TRAINED?
- ✔ All employees should be trained, with additional training for supervisors to ensure they understand their duties and responsibilities.

WHEN DOES TRAINING OCCUR?
- ✔ Antidiscrimination training should be offered upon hiring and periodically (e.g., annually) thereafter. Additional training may be appropriate if a complaint is filed.

WHAT IS THE COURSE CONTENT?
- ✔ Communicate the company policy, which should include a statement prohibiting all forms of harassment, disciplinary action, procedures for reporting incidents of harassment, safeguards to prevent retaliation against those who report such incidents, and assurance of confidentiality.
- ✔ The legal meaning of harassment should be explained, and employees should be taught which behaviors constitute harassment. Practical examples should be discussed.
- ✔ The negative consequences of workplace discrimination and harassment should be explained. In addition to legal issues, explain the negative effects on morale and productivity.
- ✔ Supervisors should receive additional training. It should inform them of their duties and explain that the standards for their behavior are more stringent. Disrespectful behavior by rank-and-file employees may not be unlawful, while the same behavior by a supervisor is clearly illegal.

WHAT TO DOCUMENT?
- ✔ In order to provide protection against a lawsuit, keep records of all of the previous information. It may also be useful for employees to sign a document acknowledging that they completed the training.

develop the large pools of managerial and executive talent they will soon need.

For Hovnanian Enterprises, one of the nation's largest homebuilders, rapid growth is driving the need for leadership development. Their succession plan identifies candidates for top-level positions about two years in advance of when an opening is expected. When a candidate for future promotion has been identified, a committee evaluates the candidate's competency profile to determine which technical or managerial skills the candidate needs to improve. Working with an HR professional, the candidate then develops a personal plan of action. For the next one to two years, candidates are expected to spend 10–20% of their work time in personal development activities. So far, the success rate is 100% for candidates who have completed the development program and been promoted. That success rate is twice the success rate for external hires placed into similar positions.[14]

Recruitment and Selection. Disney begins the socialization process during recruitment as a way to discourage applicants who may not fit the corporate culture.[15] To be sure everyone knows what to expect, one of the first steps in the hiring process involves showing applicants a video that details dress codes and rules of grooming and discipline. Like Disney, Procter and Gamble (P&G) also begins socializing employees during recruitment and selection. Applicants meet with an elite cadre of line managers who have been trained in interviewing skills. When interviewing applicants for entry-level positions in brand management, the managers know how to ask appropriate questions that yield information about competencies such as the "ability to turn out high volumes of excellent work." Through the interviewers' questions, applicants begin to learn about the organization's culture. After successfully completing at least two interviews and a test of general knowledge, applicants are flown to P&G headquarters in Cincinnati, Ohio, where they endure a day-long series of interviews. These interviews are two-way communications that continue the socialization process at the same time that selection decisions are being made. If applicants pass the extensive screening process, they then confront a series of rigorous job experiences calculated to induce humility and openness to new ways of doing things. Typically, this phase of socialization involves long hours of work in a pressure-cooker environment. Throughout this phase, new employees learn transcendent company values and organizational folklore, including the importance of product quality and stories about the dedication and commitment of employees long since retired. Intense socialization such as this increases employees' commitment to the success of the company. Commitment, in turn, translates into a greater willingness to work long hours, less absenteeism, and lower turnover rates.

LINKS TO BUSINESS STRATEGY

As is true for other elements of an HRM system, training and development activities that support the business strategy are especially worthwhile investments. Consider how training can support the strategic objectives that typically drive a company to adopt and install Enterprise Resource Planning (ERP) software. The ERP software is designed to be an enterprisewide solution to all the information technology needs a company might have. It can pull together information about the company's financial performance, customer relations, human resources, manufacturing, distribution, and so on. Usually, it is extremely costly, and it can be difficult to implement well.

Changing to an ERP system involves more than having employees learn a new software program. They often must also learn to do a variety of new administrative tasks. For example, salespeople may be asked to record information about the source of all new customers and the reasons for customers canceling their orders. The information doesn't help the salesperson directly, but marketing uses it to assess the productivity of advertising campaigns. When managers decide to purchase ERP software, they may think they are just making a change in the company's IT system. But that's a mistake. As Fairchild Semiconductor learned, installing ERP software is a radical change that can affect the organizational design, the tasks people do, and the way employees feel about their employers.[16]

Fairchild Semiconductor was created as a spin-off from National Semiconductor. After its birth, one of its first goals was to transition from National's data management system to one of its own. It chose an ERP application from Peoplesoft, and then set about adapting its processes to meet the software's requirements. The first step was to form teams of employees from all over the world to rework the company's business processes in finance, manufacturing, logistics, and human resources. The goal was to replace all the customized business processes throughout the company with "plain vanilla" processes that fit the generic software system. Once new processes were designed, extensive training was needed before and after the rollout of the new system. Besides teaching employees the new tasks they would be expected to perform, the training sessions explained why these new tasks were important. The goal was to ensure that employees understood how their own work was related to the overall business processes. The company felt that employees would be less likely to take shortcuts to reduce their own workloads if they understood how their contributions affected both other people in the company and the bottom line. To build employees' confidence in their ability to use the new system, and to reduce their fears, training sessions provided plenty of time for people to practice using the software and receive feedback. At Fairchild, installing new ERP software and training employees to use it was a change that resulted in employees becoming more knowledgeable about the business and more excited about their own roles within the company.

EVALUATING TRAINING AND DEVELOPMENT

Because training and development programs have many different objectives, many different measures can be used to evaluate their effectiveness.[17] The major components that can be included in the evaluation of training and development activities are shown in Exhibit 8.3.

Exhibit 8.3 divides the many possible measures of T&D effectiveness into two broad categories: short-term effects and long-term outcomes. Usually, employers offer training and development in hopes of reaping the long-term outcomes. When it comes to evaluating the effectiveness of their efforts, however, they usually assess only short-term effects. Furthermore, evalua-

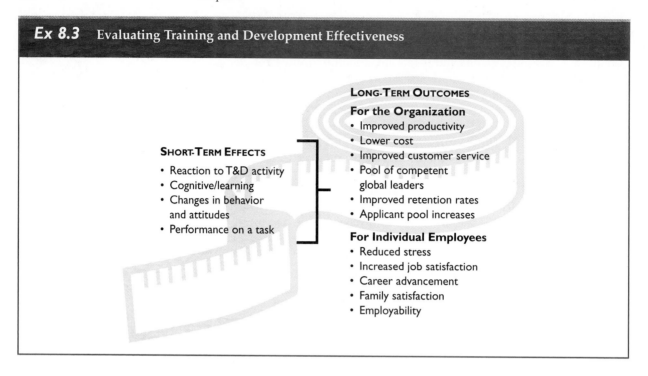

Ex 8.3   Evaluating Training and Development Effectiveness

SHORT-TERM EFFECTS
- Reaction to T&D activity
- Cognitive/learning
- Changes in behavior and attitudes
- Performance on a task

LONG-TERM OUTCOMES

For the Organization
- Improved productivity
- Lower cost
- Improved customer service
- Pool of competent global leaders
- Improved retention rates
- Applicant pool increases

For Individual Employees
- Reduced stress
- Increased job satisfaction
- Career advancement
- Family satisfaction
- Employability

tions usually focus on achievement of the organization's objectives and pay less attention to the objectives of individual employees.

The most frequently used approach to evaluation involves assessing employees' reactions to the training. Although positive reactions to training are desirable, they may have little relationship to other important outcomes. If the objective is to assess cognitive learning, then paper-and-pencil tests can be used. Testing for knowledge acquisition may indicate that cognitive learning has occurred, but it will not reveal whether learning has been transferred to the job. To assess whether behavior or performance has changed, the evaluation should include output measures or performance evaluations.

When Bill Lovejoy, the general manager of the Service Parts Operations (SPO) division of General Motors, decided that his division's employees were not performing at their highest levels of productivity potential, he hired a consulting firm to provide training and offer personal coaching. As an experiment, the coaching was provided to managers in only one location. A year later, the company assessed the effectiveness of the training and coaching intervention by comparing that location to others in the company on several measures:

1. scheduling attainment;
2. quality (errors per order line);
3. productivity (lines shipped per hour);
4. health and safety (recordable injuries per 200,000 hours worked); and
5. absenteeism.

The overall conclusion was that the training and coaching program accounted for about 30% of the improved business performance of that location. It was regarded as a success and has since been expanded to the other facilities within the SPO division.

THE HR TRIAD

Training and development activities can be very expensive, requiring both time and money. Much of the expense is due to employees taking time off from work to participate. Perhaps the most important role of top-level executives is recognizing the value of training investments, and supporting these activities. As organizations begin to embrace a philosophy of continuous learning and improvement, more active participation in the design and delivery of the organization's training system by all stakeholders is seen as both desirable and necessary. For example, at Health Partners, HR professionals sit in on meetings held throughout the company so they can anticipate training needs that are likely to arise. Their training goal is to be prepared to deliver programs within a week or two from the time a manager makes a request. After several successful training initiatives like the one described earlier in this chapter, managers at Health Partners have learned to rely on the in-house training function. Health Partners also believes in the power of

FAST FACT Container Store employees spend an average of 162 hours a year in training—more than four weeks, total.

using its own employees as trainers whenever possible. The HR staff is constantly on the lookout for quick learners who can be "recruited" to serve as volunteer instructors. Employees at Health Partners respond well to having coworkers as instructors. Communication seems to be easier because everyone has the same daily frustrations and challenges. And when a question comes up outside of training sessions, it's easy to catch an instructor in the hallway or at lunch to get advice. Although volunteer instructors don't get paid extra, they often find that teaching brings intrinsic satisfaction. The feature "The HR Triad: Roles and Responsibilities in Training and Development" shows some of the training activities engaged in by line managers, the HR professionals, and other employees.

MANAGERS

Besides providing the financial resources and time needed for training and development, managers can improve the effectiveness of their organization's efforts by participating as trainers, coaches, and mentors. Without top management involvement and commitment, the major focus of an organization is likely to be on other activities. This is particularly true in organizations that focus on short-term goals and getting immediate results; this situation allows too little time to wait for the benefits of training and development. Top

FAST FACT According to a five-year study of 20,000 managers in 40 organizations, continuous personal and professional development is a key characteristic of executives who make a positive difference in their organizations.

managers at UPS, Dell, GE, Toyota, Gillette, Ritz-Carlton, Hilton, the Four Seasons, and PepsiCo began to emphasize training and development at the same time they recognized that they had to develop their people and businesses in order to be effective.[18]

EMPLOYEES

The effectiveness of an organization's training system requires the support and cooperation of all employees in the system—top management's support alone isn't sufficient.

Although most employees aren't actively involved in designing and delivering training systems, most organizations depend heavily on employ-

The HR Triad

Roles and Responsibilities in Training and Development

LINE MANAGERS	HR PROFESSIONALS	EMPLOYEES
• Cooperate with HR professionals in identifying the implications of business plans for training and development.	• Identify training and development needs in cooperation with line managers.	• Seek to understand the objectives of training and development opportunities and accept responsibility for lifelong learning.
• Work with employees to determine their individual training and development needs.	• Assist employees in identifying their individual training and development needs.	• Identify your own training and development needs with HR professionals and line managers.
• Participate in the delivery of training and development programs.	• Communicate with employees regarding training and development opportunities and the consequences of participating in them.	• Consider employment opportunities that will contribute to your own personal development and long-term employability.
• Support employees' participation in training and development opportunities and reinforce the transfer of newly learned behaviors to the job.	• Develop and administer training and development activities.	• Actively participate in training and development opportunities.
• Do much of the on-the-job socialization and training.	• Train the line managers and employees in how to socialize; train and develop employees.	• Assist with the socialization, training, and development of coworkers.
• Participate in efforts to assess the effectiveness of training and development activities.	• Evaluate the effectiveness of training and development activities.	• Participate in efforts to assess the effectiveness of training and development activities.

ees' seeking opportunities to use the available system to their advantage. Research indicates that training and development opportunities are more likely to be used by employees who acknowledge their own needs for improvement and have developed a specific career plan.[19]

Although formal training programs often are mandatory, some may be offered to employees on a voluntary basis. Companies also sponsor informal events designed to provide opportunities for employees to meet other people in the company, develop informal networks and support groups, and even establish mentoring relationships. Career-planning workshops, tuition reimbursement for job-related coursework, and support for attending professional conferences also may be offered. By participating in such activities, employees facilitate their own socialization into the organization, and potentially reap longer-term benefits such as greater income and job satisfaction, and a better sense of personal identity.[20]

HR PROFESSIONALS

HR professionals usually are heavily involved in the design of the training and development system and the delivery of formal training programs. As this chapter explains, a vast array of training techniques is available to employers, and new technologies continually increase the possibilities. Human resource professionals take responsibility for identifying the objectives to be achieved through training and development and then choosing or designing training and development activities that are appropriate, given the objectives. In the best organizations, HR professionals also ensure that investments in training and development result in the desired outcomes.

DETERMINING TRAINING AND DEVELOPMENT NEEDS

Most often training is offered on the basis of need—to rectify skill deficiencies, to provide employees with job-specific competencies, to prepare employees for future roles they may be given, and so on.[21] Sometimes, however, employees receive training and development for reasons other than need. In some organizations, attendance at an executive training program serves as a reward for past performance. In other organizations, participation in training programs is a ritual that signals to newly promoted employees as well as to members of their former work groups that a change in status has occurred (e.g., a rank-and-file employee is now a manager).

Although training and development can serve these and other purposes, a formal needs assessment is a vital part of a training system.[22] The four primary components of the needs assessment process are shown in Exhibit 8.4.[23]

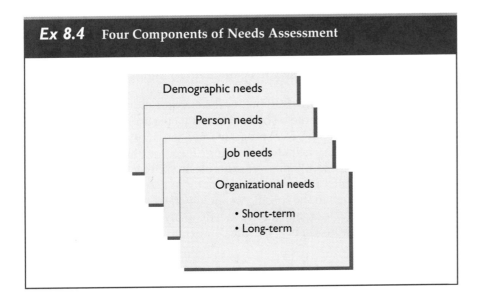

Ex 8.4 **Four Components of Needs Assessment**

Demographic needs

Person needs

Job needs

Organizational needs

• Short-term
• Long-term

ORGANIZATIONAL NEEDS ANALYSIS

Organizational needs analysis *begins with an assessment of the short- and long-term strategy and strategic business objectives of the company.* This step is essentially the same as the organizational assessment, described in Chapter 4, except that the focus is specifically on identifying the implications for future training and development activities.

Goals. The organizational needs analysis should produce a clear statement of the goals to be achieved by the organization's training and development activities. At USA Bank, the results of an employee survey led the company to conclude that they needed to improve their career development activities. The survey, which was conducted following a merger, revealed that employees felt pessimistic about their future prospects at the company. The company's Opportunity Knocks program was subsequently developed to respond to the concerns employees had expressed.[24]

Climate for Training. An organizational needs analysis may also include an assessment of the organization's current climate for training. A supportive training climate improves the chances that employees will successfully transfer what they learn from training programs to the job. Some indicators of a supportive training climate are:

- Incentives are offered to encourage employees to participate in T&D activities.
- Managers make it easy for those who report directly to them to attend T&D programs.
- Employees encourage each other to practice newly learned skills, and do not ridicule each other.
- Employees who successfully use their new competencies are recognized and rewarded with special assignments and promotions.
- There are no hidden punishments for participating in T&D (e.g., T&D activities are not scheduled to conflict with other important events; participation doesn't limit access to overtime pay).
- Managers and others who are effective providers of T&D are recognized and rewarded.

These conditions are most likely to be found in learning organizations.[25]

Resources and Constraints. Finally, the organizational needs analysis should identify the available resources and any constraints that need to be considered when designing T&D programs and activities. Can employees be taken off their jobs to participate in training? If so, for how long? Will training needs differ across locations—for example, in different states or different countries? If computer-based technology is to be used to deliver T&D, do employees have access to the specific technology they will need? By addressing such questions, an organizational needs analysis can help ensure that T&D activities are practical in a specific context.

JOB NEEDS ANALYSIS

A **job** (or **task**) **needs analysis** *identifies the specific skills, knowledge, and behavior needed to perform the tasks required by present or future jobs.* A thorough job analysis with competency modeling, discussed in Chapter 5, provides the information required for job needs analysis. If training is to be provided for existing jobs, traditional job analysis and competency modeling are appropriate. If training and development is intended to address future needs, future-oriented job analysis and competency modeling should be used for the needs analysis.

Before Gillette could introduce its triple-blade razor to the public, it needed to introduce its employees to the new machines that they would be using to produce the razor. The process of conducting the organizational and job needs analysis began approximately a year before the razor hit the shelves. The HR director assembled a cross-functional team with representatives from HR, manufacturing, and engineering. Their charge was to identify the skilled-labor requirements for mechanics and operators and assess the current workforce against these requirements. The exercise provided a picture of the skills that would be needed to operate sophisticated control systems, automated parts handling systems, pneumatics, and hydraulics. It also alerted the company to the increased level of team competencies that would be required by the new manufacturing system. Based on the experiences of many companies, Exhibit 8.5 profiles the competencies needed for employees in a team-oriented, total-quality, modern manufacturing plant.[26] Within the year, Gillette employees had completed some 20,000 hours of required training—enough to guarantee a successful launch of the company's new product.[27]

PERSON NEEDS ANALYSIS

After information about the job has been collected, the analysis shifts to the person. A **person needs analysis** *identifies gaps between a person's current competencies and those identified as necessary or desirable.* Person needs analysis can be either broad or narrow in scope. The broader approach compares actual performance with the minimum acceptable standards of performance and can be used to determine training needs for the current job. The narrower approach compares an evaluation of employee proficiency on each required skill dimension with the proficiency level required for each skill. This approach is useful for identifying development needs for future jobs that will require a specific competency. Whether the focus is on performance of the job as a whole or on particular skill dimensions, several different approaches can be used to identify the training needs of individuals.[28]

Output Measures. Performance data (e.g., productivity, accidents, and customer complaints), as well as performance appraisal ratings, can provide evidence of performance deficiencies. Person needs analysis can also consist of work sample and job knowledge tests that measure performance capability and knowledge. Major advantages of such measures are that

- they can be selected according to their strategic importance,
- they often are easily quantified, and
- when they show improvements, the value of training investments is readily apparent.

A major disadvantage is that such indicators reflect the past and may not be useful for anticipating future needs.

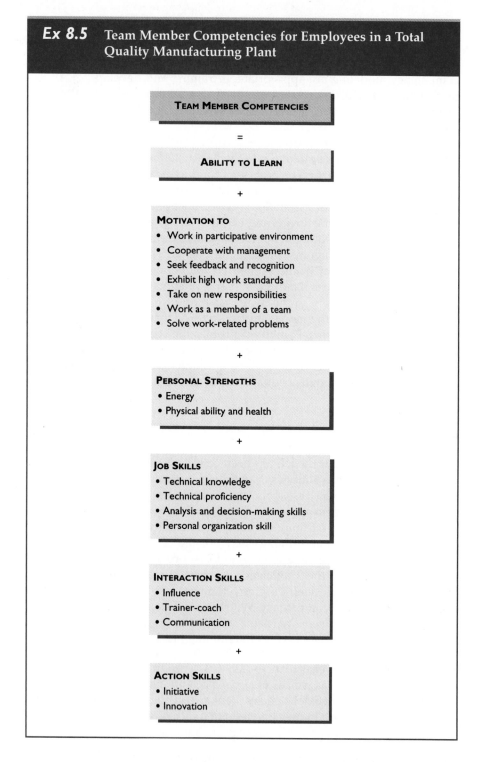

Ex 8.5   Team Member Competencies for Employees in a Total Quality Manufacturing Plant

TEAM MEMBER COMPETENCIES

=

ABILITY TO LEARN

+

MOTIVATION TO
- Work in participative environment
- Cooperate with management
- Seek feedback and recognition
- Exhibit high work standards
- Take on new responsibilities
- Work as a member of a team
- Solve work-related problems

+

PERSONAL STRENGTHS
- Energy
- Physical ability and health

+

JOB SKILLS
- Technical knowledge
- Technical proficiency
- Analysis and decision-making skills
- Personal organization skill

+

INTERACTION SKILLS
- Influence
- Trainer-coach
- Communication

+

ACTION SKILLS
- Initiative
- Innovation

Self-Assessed Training Needs. The self-assessment of training needs is growing in popularity. At Motorola, for example, top managers require employees and their supervisors to identify the business needs for both the department and the business, as well as the skill needs and deficiencies of the individuals. Many major U.S. firms allow managers to nominate themselves to attend short-term or company-sponsored training or education programs. Self-assessment can be as informal as posting a list of company-sponsored courses and asking who wants to attend, or as formal as conducting surveys regarding training needs.

Surveys and worksheets are convenient tools for self-assessment.[29] At Colgate-Palmolive, high-potential employees are expected to conduct a self-assessment and use it to develop a career plan.[30] The components of this development activity are shown in Exhibit 8.6.

Career Planning Discussions. To assist employees in identifying their strengths and weaknesses, some companies make sure that managers hold career planning discussions with employees. At Eli Lily, "high potentials" discuss their strengths and weaknesses with their managers. Prior to the conversation, the managers hold conversations with other executives to get their input. The managers then communicate the key points raised in those discussions. Afterward, the employees prepare a career plan and review it with their managers.[31]

Attitude Surveys. Attitude surveys completed by a supervisor's subordinates and/or customers can provide information about the training needs of the supervisor. A supervisor who receives relatively low scores regarding fairness in the treatment of subordinates may need training in that area. Similarly, if the customers of a particular unit seem to be more dissatisfied

> *"People instinctively want to learn."*
>
> Kent C. Nelson
> Former Chair and Chief Executive Officer
> UPS

Ex 8.6 Components of a Tool Kit for Individual Development

I. OVERVIEW OF THE INDIVIDUAL DEVELOPMENT PROCESS

- Assess individual competencies and values
- Define personal strengths, development needs, and options for career growth
- Identify developmental actions
- Craft individual development plan
- Meet with manager to decide a course of action (based on preceding analysis)
- Accept the challenge of implementing the plan

II. WORKSHEETS FOR INDIVIDUAL ASSESSMENT

- Competency assessment worksheet: assesses strengths and weaknesses for a specified set of competencies
- Personal values survey: assesses preferences for types of work environments, work relationships, work tasks, lifestyle needs, and personal needs
- Development activities chart: describes on-the-job and off-the-job learning opportunities that can be used to develop key competencies
- Global training grid: lists all formal training programs offered by the company and explains how each relates to key competencies
- Individual development plan: developed by the employee, this describes specific development goals and a course of action to be taken to achieve the goals

III. DEFINING AND UNDERSTANDING GLOBAL COMPETENCIES

- This section of the tool kit is like a dictionary. It lists all the competencies considered to be important for various types of jobs throughout the company and describes the meaning of each competency. This section serves as a reference guide and encourages people across the company to use a common set of terms when discussing competencies and career development issues.

than the customers of other units, training may be needed in that unit. Thus, customer surveys can serve a dual role: providing information to management about service and pinpointing employee deficiencies.

DEMOGRAPHIC NEEDS ANALYSIS

The objective of a **demographic needs analysis** *is to determine the training needs of specific populations of workers.* A demographic needs analysis also can be used to assess whether all employees are given equal access to growth experiences and developmental challenges, which are known to be useful on-the-job methods for promoting skill development. For example, one large study of managers compared the developmental career experiences of men and women. In general, men were more likely to have been assigned to jobs that presented difficult task-related challenges (e.g., operation start-ups and "fix-it" assignments). Women were more likely to have been assigned to jobs that presented challenges caused by obstacles to performance (e.g., a difficult boss or a lack of support from top management).[32] If a company finds demographic differences such as these, it might conclude that an intervention is needed to ensure that men and women have equal access to valuable developmental challenges—and equal exposure to debilitating obstacles. Such demographic differences may also suggest the need for diversity training.[33]

SETTING UP A TRAINING AND DEVELOPMENT SYSTEM

Successful implementation of training and development depends on offering the right programs under the right conditions. Before moving to a discussion of issues to consider when designing programs, we consider first the importance of creating the right conditions.

CREATE THE RIGHT CONDITIONS

"You have to hit the executives over the head at the very beginning of an education program and somehow cause failure. Get them to realize they don't know how to do it and confront them with feedback that says, 'You're not as good as you think you are.'"

Jim Moore
Director of Workforce Planning and Development
Sun Microsystems

To guide the design of training and development systems, Personnel Decisions International (PDI), a large and successful HR consulting firm, developed a simple framework with five components. By attending to each of these components, organizations can ensure that the right conditions are in place. Both the design of the T&D activities and a consideration of how T&D activities are integrated into the HRM system contribute to ensuring that these components are in place.[34]

The five components identified by PDI are as follows:

- **Insight:** People need to know what it is they need to learn. Employees gain insight into what they need by participating in person needs analysis and receiving feedback about their current skills and competencies.
- **Motivation:** People need to be motivated by internal or external means, to put in the required effort. Some employees may be eager to learn simply for the sake of learning, but most are likely to be more motivated when they believe that participation in training and development activities will lead to positive benefits. Thus, motivation to participate can be increased by integrating training and development activities with other facets of the HRM system (e.g.,

performance measurement, promotions, incentives, and rewards), as described previously.[35]

Even when explicit rewards are not directly tied to participation in training and development activities, motivation can be enhanced by clearly communicating that participation is valued by the organization. One way to send the message is by involving everyone—including top-level managers. When everyone has been targeted as needing training, as is often the case with major corporate change efforts, top managers often participate first, and other employee groups are scheduled in hierarchical sequence.

- **New skills and knowledge:** People must be shown how to acquire the needed competencies. The design and content of the training and development activities themselves address this issue. Alternatives to consider when developing the content are described in detail later in this chapter.

- **Real-world practice:** Programs that engage participants in activities that are realistic improve the likelihood that they will apply their learning. Similarly, when at their jobs, employees should have the opportunity to practice what is learned. The program design can ensure that training and development activities are realistic, but as already noted, managers and coworkers share responsibility for encouraging people to practice applying their new competencies while on the job. The discussion in this chapter about choosing a learning format illustrates the advantages of some formats for providing real-world experience.

- **Accountability:** Of course, the responsibility for applying new learning is not carried by managers and peers alone. All employees need to feel personally accountable for using what they have learned. The most direct approach to holding employees accountable is to include assessments of improvement as part of the performance appraisal process. However, less formal approaches to providing feedback also can be effective.

DECIDE WHO PROVIDES

Another key question to be addressed when setting up training and development activities is: Who provides the required guidance? Training and development activities may be provided by any of several people, including

FAST FACT

Many line managers spend up to 50% of their time giving and clarifying instructions to new employees.

- supervisors and other managers;
- a coworker;
- an internal or external subject matter expert; and
- the employee.

The person or people selected to teach often depends on where the program is held and what skills or competencies are taught. A member of the HR staff usually handles basic orientation sessions. Literacy and technical competencies are usually taught by the immediate job supervisor or a coworker, although technical competencies may also be taught by internal or external subject matter experts. Interpersonal, conceptual, and integrative competencies for management are often taught by training specialists, university professors, or consultants.

Supervisors and Other Managers. In many organizations, on-the-job training is the only form of training offered. In these circumstances, supervisors almost always are the providers of whatever training employees receive. For development activities that involve mentoring, supervisors and managers are appropriate also, as they are in the best position to assess their employees' career needs.[36] Furthermore, because of their position in the organization, supervisors and managers are accessible to employees and have control over the employees' work assignments, which facilitates their effectiveness.[37] Supervisors and managers may also be effective as trainers in off-the-job programs.

Coworkers. When Disney trains new hires, the company's message is delivered by some of the best "cast" members in the company. Dressed in full costume, they show through example how to create happiness—the most important aspect of their role. After the initial training session, new cast members are paired with experienced employees for 16 to 38 hours of "paired-training," which is essentially one-on-one coaching. As the Disney example illustrates, coworkers can be very effective trainers. Often, coworkers are more knowledgeable about the work than anyone else.

Coworkers also play an important role in many management development programs. For management development programs, it is common to bring together employees from different parts of the organization for several days of training. Participants in such programs often report that the most valuable learning occurs through conversations with their colleagues. Furthermore, exposure to the perspectives of colleagues working around the world helps employees develop more sophisticated "mental maps" of how business is conducted in different locations. ExxonMobil's Global Leadership Workshop takes advantage of this phenomenon. Twice a year, about 30 participants from around the world participate in the workshop. IBM uses a similar model for its eight-day global leadership training program.[38]

Clearly, coworkers can be valuable providers of training. Nevertheless, their effectiveness as trainers or mentors should not be assumed. A concern with relying on coworkers as trainers is that they may not be able to instruct others. They may also teach others their own shortcuts rather than correct procedures. If coworkers are to be trainers, they should receive instruction on how to train and should be given sufficient time on the job to work with trainees.

Experts. Subject matter experts may not be familiar with procedures in a specific organizational culture. As a result, they may be respected for their expertise but mistrusted because they aren't members of the work group. Still, if no one in the immediate work environment possesses the knowledge needed, or if large numbers of individuals need to be trained, the only option may be to hire experts. Experts who are expressive when delivering training and well organized are especially effective.[39]

Employee. Self-paced instruction is also an option. With the growing popularity of computer-based training, self-paced instruction is becoming more common. Trainees benefit from this method by learning at a speed that maximizes retention. However, if they aren't given incentives to complete the instruction in a specified period of time, they may place it on the back burner.

DEVELOPING PROGRAM CONTENT

A training or development program must have content congruent with its learning objectives. Three types of learning objectives are cognitive knowledge, skill-based outcomes, and affective outcomes.[40]

FAST FACT

The Beck Group provides employees with a laptop and/or an Internet connection. Ford Motor does the same.

COGNITIVE KNOWLEDGE

Cognitive knowledge includes the information people have available (what they know), the way they organize this information, and their strategies for using this information. Of these, what people know is by far the primary type of cognitive knowledge that most organizations try to address through training systems.

Company Policies and Practices. **Orientation programs** *brief new employees on benefit programs and options, advise them of rules and regulations, and explain the policies and practices of the organization.* Typically, orientation programs inform new employees about equal employment opportunity practices, safety regulations, work times, coffee breaks, the structure and history of the organization, and perhaps the products or services of the organization. The feature "Managing Teams: Service at Ritz-Carlton Hotel" shows how orientation and subsequent job-specific training helps that company realize its strategic vision.[41]

FAST FACT

The Ritz-Carlton Hotel Company's pervasive training approach is based on its rallying phrase "We Are Ladies and Gentlemen Serving Ladies and Gentlemen."

Managing Teams

Service at Ritz-Carlton Hotel

Employees who work for the Ritz-Carlton Hotel Company are proud of the fact that the company is a two-time winner of the Baldrige National Quality Award. These awards and the excellent customer service they represent did not happen by accident; they arose out of the Ritz-Carlton's excellent staffing practices. First, the company knows what types of people perform well in each job, and it is careful to hire only the right people. Orientation comes next. This is the first step in creating a team of employees who all share the same vision and goals. During orientation, the company infuses new employees with the company's "soul," according to Horst Schultz, the former COO, president, and vice chair. Schultz would begin orientation by explaining that every employee is essential to the company's success. If the employees don't make checking into the hotel a pleasure, keep the rooms clean, and respond to

guests' every need, the company will suffer. In comparison, if Schultz didn't show up one day for work, it would make very little difference.

After the general orientation program, Ritz-Carlton provides the employees with more specific training that reflects their individual jobs. This training is designed and delivered by the five best employees in each job category. Working together, those who are best at doing each job develop a set of principles that everyone in that job needs to understand to perform it well. And the training never stops. For the first ten minutes of each day, all employees participate together in the "line-up," which is used to remind all team members that they should strive to live by the company's values throughout their workday. By constantly reminding employees what the company strives to achieve, it teaches them habits that will serve the guests and the company well.

Basic Knowledge and the Three Rs. Increasingly, organizations are concerned about cognitive knowledge of a more basic nature: the three Rs (reading, writing, and arithmetic). Training programs designed to correct basic skill deficiencies in grammar, mathematics, safety, reading, listening, and writing are still necessary in today's organization. In particular, Total Quality Management (TQM) requires basic math and statistical knowledge that many high school graduates haven't mastered. Statistical tools are fundamental to W. Edwards Deming's approach to quality, which is continuous improvement by the numbers.

The Big Picture. Employees striving for or currently in managerial positions may need knowledge about the organizational structure, the organization's products and services, the organization's business strategies, and changing conditions in the environment. Much of this type of knowledge is learned through standard job assignments as well as through temporary developmental learning experiences, such as serving on a task force or taking an overseas assignment. Adapting to complex and changing environments is often a responsibility for top and middle managers, and conceptual training helps such employees make new associations.

Skills

Whereas cognitive knowledge is essentially inside the head, skills are evident in behaviors. Skill-based learning generally involves practicing desired behaviors, such as those that demonstrate technical and motor skills or language skills.

Technical. Owing to rapid changes in technology and the nature of jobs, as well as the implementation of automated office, industrial, and managerial systems, technological updating and skill building have become a major thrust in training.[42]

> *"Certification for a maid? Absolutely. 'Room attendants,' as we call them, have a most important job in our organization."*
>
> Debra Phillips
> Training manager and quality adviser for the Ritz-Carlton, New York

Six Sigma. Six Sigma is a management process that is used for high-impact improvement efforts. It is grounded in systematic measurement and statistical analysis, and requires that employees use several specific problem-solving skills. Six Sigma was invented at Motorola in the 1980s, and since then it has become a centerpiece of the management systems in companies like GE, Dupont, Ford, Allied Signal, and Dow. When a company decides to adopt Six Sigma, seniors leaders typically are the first to go through the training. After they understand the system, they set goals and often agree to a new compensation package that links their pay to the goals. Next, the entire workforce must be trained in statistical process control techniques. Often a few employees are trained first, and then they serve as trainers for the others. In many companies, employees are awarded the status of "black belts" for achieving high levels of proficiency in Six Sigma techniques.[43]

Interpersonal. Skills in communication, conducting performance appraisals, team building, leadership, and negotiation are increasingly in demand. The development of interpersonal skills is essential for lower- and middle-level managers as well as for employees who have direct contact with the public (e.g., sales associates). Can you describe your experiences with salespeople? What is a good salesperson like? What is a bad one like? Chances are, good interpersonal skills are what made the difference.

When PricewaterhouseCoopers (PwC) chooses partners to promote to the top leadership positions, it looks for people who are able to overcome barriers, hold up under pressure, and forge connections with clients from all around the world. To help them identify professionals with these skills, PwC assesses the performance of its partners while taking part in a management development program called the Ulysses Program. The Ulysses Program sends partners to developing countries to work for eight weeks assisting local communities with business development. PwC believes that partners who have the skills needed to succeed in the difficult conditions they face are more likely to succeed as leaders within PwC.[44]

Language. The need for training in basic language skills is growing as U.S. employers hire increasing numbers of recent immigrants. For employers who hire large numbers of immigrants, providing language training is an effective way to reduce errors and improve job performance, while at the same time enhancing employee loyalty. Bob Chinn's Crabhouse in Wheeling, Illinois, offers English as a Second Language (ESL) training as a way to maximize customer satisfaction. About half of the 350 employees at this restaurant didn't speak fluent English. Most of these employees work in the "back" of the establishment as cooks, food preparation staff, bus persons, and dishwashers. Lack of English fluency often meant mistakes in preparing food orders and lack of responsiveness to customers who made requests to bus persons that should have been directed to the wait staff. To improve their English, now employees can take classes twice a week, beginning at 7:00 A.M. (a time chosen based on employees' preferences!). Part of the training is funded by the Welfare to Work Partnership, a nationwide program that supports efforts to improve work/life skills. In this case, the English classes help employees cope with life outside of work as well as improving their job performance. With improved English skills, they find it easier to apply for drivers' licenses, attend PTA meetings, and be effective members of their communities. The training also seems to have enhanced employee loyalty. Since the ESL training began, annual turnover has dropped to 38%—much lower than 100% turnover rate that had been considered normal in the past.[45]

At Casa Rio, a restaurant on the River Walk in San Antonio, Texas, English-speaking managers take Spanish language training classes so they can communicate more easily with their staff. Afternoon classes are held twice a week, and benefits were almost immediate. After a few classes, the general manager began speaking in Spanish to the staff, and they seemed to love it. By making an effort to learn Spanish, he showed his respect for the staff and established stronger personal bonds with them. Eventually, the company plans to conduct all of its retirement planning and health insurance seminars in both English and Spanish.[46]

> *"Our staff was excited we were taking the time to learn their language."*
>
> Patricia Hutcherson
> Executive Vice President and Chief Financial Officer
> Casa Rio Mexican Foods

AFFECTIVE OUTCOMES

When the desired result of socialization, training, or developmental experiences is a change in motivation, attitudes, or values (or all three), the learning objectives of interest are affective outcomes. The Disney company's orientation and training programs are clearly intended to influence the affect of cast members. They learn about the key Disney "product"—happiness—and their roles in helping to provide it.[47]

The objectives of building team spirit and socializing employees into the corporate culture aren't the only affective outcomes of a training system. In fact, training activities often are designed in part to develop employees' feelings of mastery and self-confidence. For example, mentoring programs not only provide information but also provide the feedback and supportive encouragement that give employees confidence in their ability to take on new tasks and make decisions that might otherwise seem too risky. Self-confidence enhances task performance. This is a point not lost on athletes, their coaches, or sportscasters—nor, apparently, is it lost on the many companies now providing wilderness training. Although the evidence is sparse, testimonials and some research indicate that participating in outdoor group adventures boosts self-confidence.[48]

Training programs designed to enhance employees' emotional intelligence are another example of efforts that target affective outcomes. **Emotional intelligence** *involves recognizing and regulating emotions in ourselves and in others. It includes self-awareness, self-management, social awareness, and relationship management.* One objective of emotional intelligence training is to teach people techniques to deal with emotions in the workplace. For example, people who work in customer service jobs may benefit from training that teaches them to keep their emotions in check when dealing with customers who are upset and angry. For people in many other jobs that create stress, emotional intelligence training can help lower the experience of stress and may contribute to overall improvements in health.[49]

CHOOSING THE PROGRAM FORMAT

Many different formats can be used for training and development activities. Three general categories of formats are on-the-job, on-site but not on-the-job, and off-site. Choices about format may be constrained by the type of learning that's to occur—cognitive, skill-based, or affective—as well as by cost and time considerations. Exhibit 8.7 summarizes the advantages and disadvantages of several learning formats.

E-LEARNING

In 2004, companies spent approximately $23 billion on online corporate (e-learning) education, up from $6.3 billion in 2001.

FAST FACT

Note that the three major categories of training and development formats do not depend on using a specific type of technology. Before the computer, film, and communications industries began to merge, the technology used was often what most clearly distinguished one training format from another. Today, however, *technology makes it possible to combine many formats and deliver them as an integrated learning system that combines, for example, computer-based quizzes, video, interactive simulations, and so on. When such technologies are used for training and development, they often are referred to as* **e-learning.**[50]

One major advantage of e-learning systems is their potential for speeding up communications within large corporations.[51] At A. T. Kearney, a global management consulting firm, e-learning was an obvious solution to their training needs. With employees scattered across 30 countries and 60 offices,

Ex 8.7 Advantages and Disadvantages of Several Learning Formats

TYPE OF PROGRAM	ADVANTAGES	DISADVANTAGES
On the Job e-learning and video tele-conferencing	• Bring employees together from many locations • Speed up communications • May reduce costs • May be done on or off the job	• Start-up and equipment costs are high • Require adaptation to a new learning format
Apprenticeship training	• Does not interfere with real job performance • Provides extensive training	• Takes a long time • Is expensive • May not be related to job
Internships and assistantships	• Facilitate transfer of learning • Give exposure to real job	• Are not really full jobs • Provide vicarious learning
Job rotation	• Gives exposure to many jobs • Allows real learning	• Involves no sense of full responsibility • Provides too short a stay in a job
Supervisory assistance and mentoring	• Is often informal • Is integrated into job • Is expensive	• Means effectiveness rests with the supervisor • May not be done by all supervisors
On-Site, but Not On the Job Corporate universities	• Tailored to company needs • Support company vision and culture	• Can be costly • Require skilled management
Programmed instruction on an intranet or the Internet	• Reduces travel costs • Can be just-in-time • Provides for individualized learning and feedback • Provides for fast learning	• Not appropriate for some skills • Is time-consuming to develop • Is cost-effective only for large groups • Often no support to assist when trainee faces learning problems
Interactive videos	• Convey consistent information to employees in diverse locations	• Costly to develop • Do not provide for individual feedback
Off the Job Formal courses	• Are inexpensive for many • Do not interfere with job	• Require verbal skills • Inhibit transfer of learning
Simulation	• Helps transfer of learning • Creates lifelike situations	• Cannot always duplicate real situations exactly • Costly to develop
Assessment centers and board games	• Provide a realistic job preview • Create lifelike situations	• Costly to develop • Take time to administer
Role-playing	• Is good for interpersonal skills • Gives insights into others	• Cannot create real situations exactly; is still playing
Sensitivity training	• Is good for self-awareness • Gives insights into others	• May not transfer to job • May not relate to job
Wilderness trips	• Can build teams • Can build self-esteem	• Costly to administer • Physically challenging

the time and money needed to keep consultants abreast of the latest developments were quite high. An analysis showed that the company could develop and deliver e-learning for about half of what traditional classroom training was costing them. A year after implementing web-based training, the company had saved about $20 million in training costs.[52]

On the Job

On-the-job training (OJT) *occurs when employees learn their jobs under direct supervision.* Trainees learn by observing experienced employees and by working with the actual materials, personnel, or machinery (or all three) that constitute the job. An experienced employee trainer is expected to provide a favorable role model and to take time from regular job responsibilities to provide job-related instruction and guidance. Assuming the trainer works in the same area, the trainee receives immediate feedback about performance

One advantage of OJT is that transfer of training is high. Because trainees learn job skills in the environment in which they will actually work, they readily apply these skills on the job. However, on-site training is appropriate only when a small number of individuals need to be trained and when the consequence of error is low. Also, the quality of the training hinges on the skill of the manager or lead employee conducting it. OJT is most likely to be effective when it is designed carefully and treated as a formal process for managing workforce performance.[53]

Apprenticeships, Internships, and Assistantships. A method for minimizing the disadvantages of on-the-job training is combining it with off-the-job training. Apprenticeship training, internships, and assistantships are based on this combination.

Apprenticeship training is mandatory for admission to many skilled trades, such as plumbing, electronics, and carpentry. These programs are formally defined by the U.S. Department of Labor's Bureau of Apprenticeship and Training and involve a written agreement "providing for not less than 4,000 hours of reasonably continuous employment . . . and supplemented by a recommended minimum of 144 hours per year of related classroom instruction." The Equal Employment Opportunity Commission (EEOC) allows the 48,000 skilled trade (apprenticeship) training programs in the United States to exclude individuals aged 40 to 70 because these programs are part of the educational system aimed at youth.[54]

Somewhat less formalized and extensive are internship and assistantship programs. Internships are often part of an agreement between schools and colleges, and local organizations. As with apprenticeship training, individuals earn while they learn. Usually the pay rate is lower than that paid to full-time employees or master crafts workers, however. Internships also provide a realistic preview of the job and the organizational conditions in which an employee is likely to work. Assistantships involve full-time employment and expose an individual to a wide range of jobs. However, because the individual only assists other workers, the learning experience is often vicarious. Assistantship programs that combine job or position rotation with active mentoring and career management avoid this problem.

Job Experiences. When development is the objective, employers may put people into jobs in order to facilitate their learning and development. **Job rotation programs** *rotate employees through jobs at a similar level of difficulty in order to train them in a variety of jobs and decision-making situations.* Job rotation programs often are useful for helping employees see the bigger picture, but usually employees aren't in a single job long enough to learn very much, and they may not be motivated to work hard since they know they will move on in the near future.

The philosophy of having employees learn while doing also underlies the use of developmental job assignments. **Developmental job assignments** *are those that place employee in jobs that present difficult new challenges and hurdles.* The assumption is that employees develop new competencies by learning to deal with the new challenges. Components of a developmental job assignment include:

- Unfamiliar responsibilities
- Responsibility for creating change (e.g., to start something new, fix a problem, deal with problem employees)
- High levels of responsibility (e.g., high-stakes and high-visibility assignments; jobs involving many stakeholders, products, or units)
- Boundary spanning requirements (e.g., working with important stakeholders outside the organization)
- Dealing with diversity (working with people from multiple cultures or demographic backgrounds)[55]

Supervisory Assistance and Mentoring. Often the most informal program of training and development is supervisory assistance or mentoring. Supervisory assistance is a regular part of the supervisor's job. It includes day-to-day coaching, counseling, and monitoring of workers on how to do the job and how to get along in the organization. The effectiveness of these techniques depends in part on whether the supervisor creates feelings of mutual confidence, provides opportunities for growth, and effectively delegates tasks.

With **mentoring** *an established employee guides the development of a less-experienced worker, or protégé.* Mentoring can increase employees' competencies, achievement, and understanding of the organization.[56] At AT&T, protégés are usually chosen from among high-potential employees in middle- or entry-level management. Each executive is encouraged to select two people to mentor, and must decide how to develop the relationships. Usually, executives counsel their protégés on how to advance and network in the company, and they sometimes offer personal advice. At some companies, finding enough mentors to provide such advice is getting more difficult. As companies downsize and flatten their management structures, they find that the middle managers who once served as mentors are either no longer with the company or are too busy to spend their time mentoring others. Yet another challenge for mentoring programs is that the best mentor for a particular employee may be located in another state or even another country. To solve this problem, some companies are moving to electronic mentoring, which relies heavily on telephone calls and meetings over the Internet.[57]

Coaching. For high-level executives and other employees who hold visible and somewhat unique jobs, traditional forms of on-the-job training are impractical. Yet, these employees often need to develop new competencies in order to be fully effective. In recent years, more and more executives have turned to personal coaches to address their training needs. **Personal coaches** *typically observe the employee in action and later provide feedback and guidance for how to improve their interaction skills in the future.* Most coaches also encourage their "trainees" to discuss difficult situations as they arise and to work through alternative scenarios for dealing with those situations. Although coaching is rapidly growing in popularity, it's a relatively new technique, and few guidelines are available to evaluate whether a potential coaching relationship is likely to succeed.[58] Nevertheless, the evidence of its effectiveness is beginning to accumulate. An effective coaching program appears to help managers change themselves and, in the process, change their organizations.[59]

ON-SITE BUT NOT ON-THE-JOB

Training at the work site but not on the job is appropriate for required after-hours programs and for programs in which contact needs to be maintained with work units but OJT would be too distracting or harmful. It's also appropriate for voluntary after-hours programs and for programs that update employees' competencies while allowing them to attend to their regular duties.

For example, when a major Northeast grocery store chain switched to computerized scanners, it faced the problem of training thousands of checkers spread out across three states. The cost of training them off-site was prohibitive. Yet management also was fearful about training employees on the job, lest their ineptitude offend customers. To solve the problem, the grocery chain developed a mobile training van that included a vestibule model of the latest scanning equipment. Checkers were trained on-site but off the job in the mobile unit. Once the basic skill of scanning was mastered, employees returned to the store, and the trainer remained on-site as a resource person. According to one store manager, the program was effective because employees could be trained rapidly and efficiently, yet no customers were lost owing to checker errors or slowness.

Corporate Universities and Executive Education Programs. A growing trend in the United States is the development of corporate universities that offer programs tailored to the needs of the company. Corporate universities focus on the education of employees and sometimes customers. McDonald's Hamburger University, begun in 1961, is among the oldest corporate universities. Started in a basement, the center now trains more than 2,500 students annually in the fine details of restaurant and franchise operations. General Electric, an advocate of training and development for years, has an up-to-date facility in Croton-on-Hudson, New York, that it uses for divisional and group training. Corporate universities have been developed by such diverse firms as 3M, Ford, General Motors, Motorola, United Airlines, Boeing, Kodak, Dell, and Harley-Davidson.[60] In fact, research suggests that 65% of all major firms offer some form of executive education. Today, many corporate colleges offer degrees, and hundreds of corporations offer courses leading to degrees. While not always the case, the executive programs at companies may be under the direction of the chief learning officer.

Interactive Video Training. **Interactive video training (IVT)** *programs present a short video and narrative presentation and then require the trainee to respond to it.* This sequence—packaged program, learner response, and more programmed instruction—provides for individualized learning. FedEx has a pay-for-knowledge program that is based on interactive video training and job knowledge testing for its 35,000 customer-contact employees. Before couriers ever deliver a package, they receive at least three weeks of training. Because FedEx is constantly making changes or additions to its products and services, it also must continually update its training programs. Employees at hundreds of FedEx locations around the United States can readily access a 25-disk training curriculum that covers topics such as customer etiquette and defensive driving. Customer-contact employees take a job knowledge test every six months; the company pays each employee for four hours of study and preparation time and for two hours of test-taking time. The knowledge required to do well on the test is so job-related that performance on the test essentially reflects performance on the job. As an incentive for employees to get serious about doing well on the test, the company links their compensation to performance on the test. Employees who excel in applying their knowledge to job performance become eligible for additional proficiency pay.

OFF THE JOB

When the consequence of error is high, it's usually more appropriate to conduct training off the job. Most airline passengers would readily agree that it's preferable to train pilots in flight simulators rather than have them apprentice in the cockpit of a plane. Similarly, it's usually useful to have a bus driver practice on an obstacle course before taking to the roads with a load of schoolchildren.

Off-the-job training is also appropriate when complex competencies need to be mastered or when employees need to focus on specific interpersonal competencies that might not be apparent in the normal work environment. It's difficult to build a cohesive management work team when members of the team are constantly interrupted by telephone calls and subordinate inquiries. Team building is more likely to occur during a retreat, when team members have time to focus on establishing relationships.

FAST FACT UPS encourages executives to work in their communities on projects such as soup kitchens and housing projects as team-building exercises and contributions to social responsibility.

One disadvantage is that the costs of off-the-job training are high. Another cause for concern is that knowledge learned off the job may not transfer to the workplace. The issue of **transfer**—*whether employees can readily apply the knowledge and skills learned during training to their work*—is one of the most important to consider when choosing a format. Research has shown that the more dissimilar the training environment is to the actual work environment, the less likely trainees will be to apply what they learn to their jobs. For example, the transfer-of-knowledge problem is minimal when trainees work with machines that are comparable to the ones in their actual work environment. However, it may be difficult to apply teamwork compe-

FAST FACT The construction and real estate firm Beck Group reimburses workers $4,500 a year for outside courses.

tencies learned during a wilderness survival program to a management job in a large service organization.[61]

Formal Courses. Formal courses can be directed either by the trainee—using programmed instruction, computer-assisted instruction, reading, and correspondence courses—or by others, as in formal classroom courses and lectures. Although many training programs use the lecture method because it efficiently and simultaneously conveys large amounts of information to large groups of people, it does have several drawbacks. Perhaps most importantly, except for cognitive knowledge and conceptual principles, the transfer of learning to the actual job is probably limited. Also, the lecture method does not permit individualized training based on individual differences in ability, interests, and personality.

FAST FACT

Boeing provides training for airline pilots in its flight simulators in St. Louis. Southwest provides this training in Dallas.

Simulation. **Simulations** *present situations that are similar to actual job conditions and allow trainees to practice how to behave in those situations.*[62] All airlines use flight simulators for pilot training. Because the simulated environment isn't real, it's generally less hectic and safer than the actual environment; as a consequence, trainees may have trouble adjusting from the training environment to the actual environment.

The arguments for using a simulated environment are compelling: It reduces the possibility of customer dissatisfaction that can result from on-the-job training; it can reduce the frustration of the trainee; and it may save the organization a great deal of money because of fewer training accidents. Not all organizations, even in the same industry, accept these arguments. Some banks, for example, train their tellers on the job, whereas others train them in a simulated bank environment.

Assessment Centers. Just as they are popular in managerial selection, assessment centers (described in Chapter 7) are an increasingly popular simulation technique for developing managers. Certain aspects of the assessment center, such as management games and in-basket exercises, are excellent for training.[63] When these are used for training purposes, however, it is essential that instructors help participants analyze what happened and what should have happened. The opportunity for improvement may be drastically reduced if the trainees are left to decide what to transfer from the games or exercises to the job.

Business Board Games. Companies are finding that it pays if all employees know how the company makes money, the difference between revenue and profit, and how much profit the company makes on each sale. In order to facilitate this learning, companies such as Prudential and Sears use board games, similar in form and shape to *Monopoly*, that reveal the workings of the company. Employees actually play these games, and as they do, they learn about the company and how the company runs the business and makes a profit or loss.

Role-Playing and Sensitivity Training. Whereas simulation exercises may be useful for developing conceptual and problem-solving skills, two other types of training are used for developing human relation or process skills. Role-playing and sensitivity training develop managers' interpersonal insights—awareness of self and of others—for changing attitudes and for practicing human relation skills, such as leading or interviewing.

Role-playing generally focuses on understanding and managing relationships rather than facts. The essence of role-playing is to create a realistic situation, as in the case discussion method, and then have the trainees assume the parts of specific personalities in the situation. When trainees "get into" the role, the result is a greater sensitivity to the feelings and insights presented by the role.

In sensitivity training, individuals in an unstructured group exchange thoughts and feelings on the "here and now" rather than the "there and then." Although being in a sensitivity group often gives individuals insight into how and why they and others feel and act the way they do, critics claim that these results may not be beneficial because they are not directly transferable to the job.

FAST FACT

Karla Corcoran resigned from her position as the U.S. Postal Service Inspector General after she was accused of wasting public money on $1 million-per-year training retreats at which employees dressed up in costumes and participated in mock trials.

Wilderness Trips and Outdoor Training. To increase employees' feelings about the here and now and raise their self-esteem, organizations sometimes use programs that involve physical feats of strength, endurance, and cooperation. These can be implemented on wilderness trips to the woods or mountains or water. Siemens, for example, dropped 60 managers from around the world onto the shores of Lake Starnberger, south of Munich, and gave them the task of building rafts using only logs, steel drums, pontoons, and rope. Among the rules for the exercise: No talking. The objective was to teach managers the importance of knowledge sharing. Back on the job, managers could earn bonuses for contributing their knowledge to ShareNet—the company's knowledge management software.[64]

FAST FACT

Organizations such as Outward Bound and the Pecos River Learning Center have been offering wilderness trips and other forms of outdoor activities such as rock climbing and rope courses since the late 1970s.

Whereas firms such as Siemens use some variation of outdoor experiences in their management training with success, many others question the degree of transfer to the job that these experiences offer. Firms using outdoor experiences recognize this concern and thus articulate the link between the competencies developed in the experiences and the competencies needed by the managers on the job. At its retreat for managers, Wells Fargo uses activities specifically designed to improve teamwork skills. The firm's CFO feels the expense is justified, explaining that the managers are "very high-powered, very capable, very technically skilled, and very competitive. And they are very individualistic in their approach to work." What he wants is to get them to "see the power of acting more like a team." His view is that activities like walking a narrow plank blindfolded and crossing a river on a jerry-rigged bridge can build the sense of teamwork that Wells Fargo needs.[65]

MAXIMIZING LEARNING

Even when a training technique is appropriate, learning may not take place if the experience isn't structured appropriately. Thus, when designing a training or development program, it is important to take time to set the stage for learning, create conditions that will maximize learning during the training or development program, and provide conditions that will maintain performance in the longer term.

"If, when holding a gun to an employee's head, he or she will perform, the problem isn't a training problem."

Alice Pescuric
Vice President
DDI

SETTING THE STAGE FOR LEARNING

Before launching a training program, trainers or managers need to consider how information will be presented. In addition, they must consider the beliefs of trainees regarding task-specific competencies.[66]

Clear Instructions. Employees must know what is expected in order to perform as desired. Clear instructions establish appropriate behavioral expectations. Training expectations should be stated in specific terms. The conditions under which performance is or isn't expected should be identified, along with the behavior to be demonstrated.

To set the stage for desired performance, it's also useful to specify upfront what the reward will be for performing as desired. Trainees are more likely to be motivated if they know that successful performance can lead to positive reinforcement (e.g., promotion, pay raise, or recognition) or can block the administration of negative reinforcement (e.g., supervisory criticism or firing).[67]

Behavioral Modeling. Even when instructions are clear, the desired behavior still may not occur if the trainee does not know how to perform it. This problem can be overcome through **behavioral modeling,** *which involves having a role model provide a visual demonstration of the desired behavior that the trainee then attempts to imitate.* The important thing is to show employees what needs to be done before asking them to do it. Thus, role models should show not only how to achieve desired outcomes but also how to overcome performance obstacles.

INCREASING LEARNING DURING TRAINING

Although employees should be responsible for their own learning, organizations can do much to facilitate this.

Active Participation. Individuals perform better if they're actively involved in the learning process. Organizational help in this area can range from encouraging active participation in classroom discussions to establishing a set of programs to assist managers in a major strategic change. The important point is to hook the individual on learning. Through active participation, individuals stay more alert and are more likely to feel confident.

Mastery. If individuals dwell on their personal deficiencies relative to the task, potential difficulties may seem more formidable than they really are. When training experiences fail to validate fears about failure, trainees are less likely to feel threatened and more likely to develop a sense of mastery.[68] To facilitate mastery, trainers should arrange the subject matter so that trainees experience success. Whereas this may be easy when tasks are simple, it can be quite difficult when tasks are complex. Solutions include segmenting tasks, shaping behavior, and setting proximal goals.

Task segmentation involves breaking a complex task into smaller or simpler components. For some jobs (e.g., laboratory technician), the components (e.g., drawing blood, culturing a specimen, and running a blood chemistry machine) can be taught individually and in any order. For other jobs (e.g., engineer, chauffeur, and interviewer), segments must be taught sequentially because task B builds on task A and task C builds on task B.[69]

Shaping includes rewarding closer and closer approximations to desired behavior. For example, when managers are learning how to conduct a selection interview, they can be reinforced for making eye contact and for developing situational questions.

The setting of proximal, or intermediary, goals also increases mastery perceptions. Consider a software developer with an overall objective of developing a new word processing package. Proximal goals might include meeting a project specifications deadline, developing algorithms for fonts by a set deadline, developing an algorithm for formatting paragraphs, and so on. These proximal goals all lead to the attainment of the distal, or overall, objective.[70]

Feedback. For individuals to master new concepts and acquire new competencies, they must receive accurate diagnostic feedback about their performance. Feedback can be provided by a supervisor, coworkers, customers, computers, or the individual performing the task. It must be specific, timely, based on behavior and not personality, and practical. If a performance discrepancy exists, the feedback should be diagnostic and include instructions or modeling of how to perform better.[71] The topic of providing performance feedback is discussed in more detail in Chapter 10, where the focus is on performance evaluation. When studying that chapter, keep in mind that feedback is an important element of training and development.[72]

Practice. The goal of skill training is to ensure that desired behavior occurs not just one time but consistently. This is most likely to occur when trainees are able to practice and internalize standards of performance. Even mental practice appears to help improve performance.[73] Practicing the wrong behaviors is detrimental, however; therefore, employees should be given specific feedback about what they are doing wrong in order to ensure that they practice only the correct behaviors.

For some jobs, tasks must be overlearned. When a task is overlearned, the trainee does not have to think consciously about behavior before responding. For example, if a plane is losing altitude rapidly, a pilot must know immediately how to respond. The pilot has no time to think about what should be done. The emergency routine must be second nature and internalized.

MAINTAINING PERFORMANCE AFTER TRAINING

Following employees' exposure to socialization training and development experiences, the environment needs to support the transfer of new behaviors to the job and their maintenance over time. The use of goals and reinforcers can improve performance following training.

Specific Goals. Without goals that are specific and measurable, people have little basis for judging how they're doing.[74] Specific goals for subsequent performance should be challenging but not so difficult as to be perceived as impossible. They also shouldn't be set too early in the learning process. The development of a specific action plan is one approach to setting goals that relates what has been learned to the job in the near future.

Reinforcers. Learning new behaviors is difficult and threatening. To ensure that trainees continue to demonstrate the skills they have learned, behavior must be reinforced. **Reinforcement** *refers to a consequence that follows behavior.* It can be positive (e.g., praise and financial rewards) or negative (e.g., "If you perform as desired, I will quit screaming at you"), but the consequence must be contingent on performance. Often supervisors and coworkers can be taught to reinforce desired changes. If a supervisor or coworker responds positively to a positive change in behavior, the frequency with which the new behavior will be displayed is likely to increase.

> **FAST FACT**
>
> The average Trident employee receives special recognition 10 times per year for behaviors that fit the culture.

Self-Reinforcement. Because it isn't always possible for significant others to reinforce an individual worker, a long-term objective should be to teach employees how to set their own goals and administer their own reinforcement. When people create self-incentives for their efforts, they're capable of making self-satisfaction contingent on their own performance. The challenge here is to ensure that personal goals are congruent with organizational goals, which leads to self-management.

TEAM TRAINING AND DEVELOPMENT

> *"Tomorrow's leader will be a team player who will seek to decentralize leadership and work towards creating an entire organization of leaders. This is a pattern the survey found to be true across all industries and geographic borders."*
>
> Windle Priem
> CEO and President
> Korn/Ferry International

Management often rushes to form work teams without considering how the behaviors needed for effective teamwork differ from those needed for effective individual contributions. Team members may receive little or no training to ensure that they can perform the required tasks and achieve the goals set. NASA takes the opposite approach. Perhaps more than any other organization, NASA understands that training comes before effective teamwork. Before astronauts are sent into space to live in a community that relies heavily on teamwork for survival, NASA has them working together every day for a year or two in order to become a team. They share office space, spend countless hours together in flight simulators, and rehearse everything from stowing their flight suits to troubleshooting malfunctions. Formal training in procedures is part of the experience, but it isn't everything. NASA realizes that teamwork training also involves helping teammates get to know each other and develop confidence in each other.

Most organizations can't afford to give team members a year or two of training before teams begin working on their tasks. They look for quicker ways to achieve the same objectives that NASA has for its training program. Three main goals of most team training programs are to develop team cohesiveness, effective teamwork procedures, and work team leaders. For some teams, such as airline flight crews, team members may also need specialized training to ensure that they respond appropriately to rare and unexpected events, such as equipment failure, when lives are at risk.[75] Organizations that invest resources to train teams can increase both team and organizational effectiveness.[76]

TRAINING TO DEVELOP TEAM COHESIVENESS

To develop team cohesiveness, many organizations use experientially based, adventure training. Evart Glass Plant, a division of Chrysler Group, involved its entire 250-person staff in such training as a way to prepare its employees for working in self-managed work teams. Union members and managers trained side-by-side during employees' normal work hours. A hi-lo driver (similar to a forklift operator), a maintenance person, a shift supervisor, and a receptionist found themselves working together as a team throughout their training. After each activity, trainers led a discussion about the experience to identify the lesson to be learned from it. Exhibit 8.8 describes a few of the activities and associated lessons from the company's specially designed one-day program.

Was the team training at the Evart plant effective? Surveys and personal interviews were conducted to assess employees' reactions, and the results were positive. Employees commented that people now were going out of their way to help others and felt that people were doing a better job of seeking out opinions from employees at all levels. Employees also got to know each other. Explained one engineer, "Personally, I hadn't been on third shift very long and found there were three people on that shift that I had the wrong opinion of. I saw they were real go-getters and they stayed positive throughout the experience; I was surprised." Overall, the training helped break down personal walls that people had built around themselves and helped them see the benefits of being a contributing member of a team.[77]

TRAINING IN TEAM PROCEDURES

Experiential training is an effective way to develop cohesiveness, but used alone it isn't likely to result in optimal work team effectiveness. Work teams can also benefit from more formal training.

Work teams of all types are being empowered to perform tasks that previously weren't employees' responsibility. The greater the degree of self-

---

Ex 8.8 **Examples of Team Training Activities Used at the Evart Glass Plant**

CHALLENGING ACTIVITY	TEAMWORK LESSON
Juggle several objects simultaneously (e.g., tennis balls, hackey sacs, and koosh balls) as a team.	Although everyone has a different role, each person touches and affects the outcome.
Find the path hidden in a carpet maze and move each member through it in a limited amount of time.	Teams must find and use each individual's hidden strengths (e.g., a good memory and the ability to move quickly). Doing so allows the team as a whole to succeed.
Balance 14 nails on the head of a nail that has been pounded into a supporting block of wood, creating a free-standing structure without supports.	Things that may seem impossible can be achieved when people work together.
Draw a vehicle that represents the training teams and signify which part of the vehicle each member represents.	Each member has different strengths, and bringing these strengths together leads to task success.

management, the more the team has authority, responsibility, and general decision-making discretion for tasks. The more self-managing a team is, the more important it is for team members to receive training.

At BP Norge, team members were taught about the characteristics of self-managed teams and provided with information about how such teams have been used in other organizations. This formal training was in addition to more experiential activities, such as role-playing and sensitivity discussions, as described in the feature "Managing Teams: Cultural Change at BP Norge."[78] For self-managed work teams, formal training may also include company-specific procedures for obtaining resources, cost accounting, progress reports, and team evaluations.

Training for Team Leaders

New team leaders often misunderstand their role. Good team leaders are receptive to member contributions and don't reject or promote ideas because of their own personal views. Good team leaders summarize information, stimulate discussion, create awareness of problems, and detect when the team is ready to resolve differences and agree to a unified solution. Training in how to support disagreement and manage meetings is especially useful for new work team leaders.

Managing Teams

Cultural Change at BP Norge

When the Norwegian arm of British Petroleum (BP Norge) decided that it needed to dismantle its hierarchy and move toward becoming a network of collaborators, it decided to restructure the organization around self-managing teams. The company believed that if employees were willing to assume leadership and work across functions, they could speed up decision making, reduce costs and cycle times, and increase innovation. Despite the strong business argument supporting a change to teamwork, the organization found that pushing the change was difficult.

Nine months of frustration led management to conclude that a systematic training initiative was needed to educate the organization and support the development of new teamwork competencies. The first phase of training focused on changing old thought patterns and helping people understand the link between BP Norge's business strategy and the need for self-managed teams. Because employees had been through many change efforts in the past, they had become skeptical and resistant. To convince them that more change was needed, a team of American and Norwegian facilitators conducted two-day workshops, which were attended by a mix of people from all levels and functional specialties. Oil-rig workers and senior managers sat side-by-side, as did Norwegians and Americans—even if they couldn't speak each other's language.

Prior to the workshop, everyone completed a prework assignment. First, they watched a video that explained self-managed teams and showed how other organizations had used them successfully. They also interviewed a few colleagues to find out what they thought about self-managed teams. At the workshop, discussion focused on understanding the process through which teamwork develops. Participants were taught that denial about the need for change and resistance to it are natural reactions, but they were also encouraged to share their concerns with each other and seek answers to their questions. Throughout the two-day workshops, participants also used role-plays to begin practicing the behaviors that they would need in their new team environment. These behaviors included taking risks, communicating about their feelings, and teaching others as well as learning from others.

- **Supporting disagreement.** A skillful work-team leader can create an atmosphere for disagreement that stimulates innovative solutions while minimizing the risk of bad feelings. Disagreement can be managed if the leader is receptive to differences within the team, delays the making of decisions, and separates idea generation from idea evaluation. This last technique reduces the likelihood that an alternative solution will be identified with one individual rather than the team. The absence of disagreement on a work team may be as destructive to its proper functioning as too much disagreement. The use of decision-making aids, such as brainstorming, the nominal group technique, devil's advocacy, and dialectical inquiry, creates productive controversy and can result in better-quality decisions that are fully accepted by members of the team. Training team leaders to use these simple techniques is a good first step toward stimulating constructive controversy within teams.[79]
- **Managing meetings.** People who resist teamwork often point to time wasted in meetings as a big source of dissatisfaction. True, teams do need to meet, one way or another, but team meetings should never be a waste of time. Training team leaders in the tactics of running meetings can make meetings more efficient. In addition, training can help team leaders learn how to strike a proper balance between permissiveness and control. Rushing through a team session can prevent full discussion of the problem, lead to negative feelings, and poor solutions. However, unless the leader keeps the discussion moving, members will become bored and inattentive. Unfortunately, some leaders feel that pushing for an early solution is necessary because of time constraints. Such a move ends discussion before the team has had a chance to work through a problem effectively.

CROSS-CULTURAL TRAINING

The objectives of **cross-cultural training** *may be to prepare people from several cultures to work together or to prepare a person for living in another culture.*[80] Within the United States, the first objective—training people from different cultures to work together—is often the aim of diversity training initiatives. The second objective—preparing a person for living in another culture—is likely to be the aim of training programs for expatriates and their families. Finally, many global firms need managers who are effective when working in a multinational context, regardless of whether they are located in their home country or abroad. We consider each of these special topics next.

DIVERSITY TRAINING FOR EMPLOYEES IN THE UNITED STATES

As the importance of learning to manage workforce diversity became more salient to U.S. employers, many companies looked to cross-cultural training programs as a solution. Their thinking was that diversity can be disruptive to the organization and create dissatisfaction among employees if people from different cultural backgrounds do not understand each other's cultures. The hope was that diversity training programs would improve cross-cultural understanding. Suddenly, thousands of consulting firms were offering diversity training.[81]

Cultural Awareness Training. Many diversity training programs seek to raise cultural awareness among participants. Typically, these programs are designed to teach the participants about how their own culture differs from the cultures of other employees with whom they work. In this context, "culture" is used to refer very broadly to the social group to which a person belongs. Ethnic background is one aspect of culture, but so are one's age, socioeconomic status, religion, and so on. Cultural awareness training also teaches people to understand how the stereotypes they hold about various groups can influence the way they treat people—often in subtle ways that they may not be conscious of. The main objective of this type of diversity training is increasing people's knowledge about their own and other cultures.

A typical cultural awareness program is conducted over the course of one or two days. Among the activities are information sharing intended to educate employees about the array of differences present in the workplace. Some organizations supplement formal training sessions with informal learning opportunities such as Black History Month or Gay and Lesbian Pride Week, using the time to focus on a group's history and cultural traditions. The hope is that raising awareness about differences will lead to attitudinal and behavior changes. Although there is scant research on the effectiveness of such awareness programs, the general consensus is that awareness programs *alone* do little to create positive change.

Building Competencies. Another approach to diversity training focuses more specifically on developing the behavioral competencies needed to work effectively in organizations characterized by diversity. Training designed to develop the interpersonal competencies that are needed in diverse workplaces often includes role-playing and practice sessions. The interpersonal behaviors taught include showing respect and treating people as equals. Videos of leaderless group discussions also may be used to help point out inappropriate behaviors that people may engage in and not be aware of. Changing behaviors and developing interpersonal skills can improve the climate within diverse workplaces.

Supplementing Diversity Training. As companies quickly learned, diversity training alone cannot create fundamental changes in how effectively organizations manage diversity. As already discussed in earlier chapters, the issue of diversity should be considered during succession planning and when developing recruitment and selection practices. In addition, efforts may be needed to ensure that members of minority groups are included on advisory boards and as members of committees involved in compensation decisions. Tying compensation and other rewards to success in meeting goals for recruiting, hiring, developing, and promoting people from diverse backgrounds has been shown to improve the success of diversity training and development interventions.[82] Thus, throughout this book, we continually return to the topic of diversity and its implications for HR practices.

CROSS-CULTURAL TRAINING IN THE INTERNATIONAL CONTEXT

Few things seem certain, but one thing is clear: "Globalization" will continue to be an inescapable buzzword. Businesses will operate in an ever more interconnected world. As shown in Exhibit 8.9, the opportunities for training and development activities in global companies are many. The different groups who can benefit from training include headquarters staff, global managers, expatriates, members of expatriates' families, and members of work teams that include people from different nationalities. The times at which training and development activities can be offered include prior to the departure of expatriates, during international assignments, and upon the return of expatriates.

Clearly, a full discussion of how organizations address all these training and development needs is not feasible here. Instead, we discuss only two widely used training and development activities: (1) cross-cultural training for expatriates and inpatriates; and (2) global leadership development.

CROSS-CULTURAL TRAINING FOR EXPATRIATES AND INPATRIATES

Expatriates. Cross-cultural training for expatriates, and perhaps for members of their families, usually takes the form of a three- to five-day immersion course in the assigned country's values, customs, and traditions. Some debate exists about whether cross-cultural training is more effective if it is offered before departure or after arrival in the host country, but many companies have adopted the predeparture model.[83]

FAST FACT

The typical cost of an international expatriate assignment ranges from $400,000 to $2.5 million.

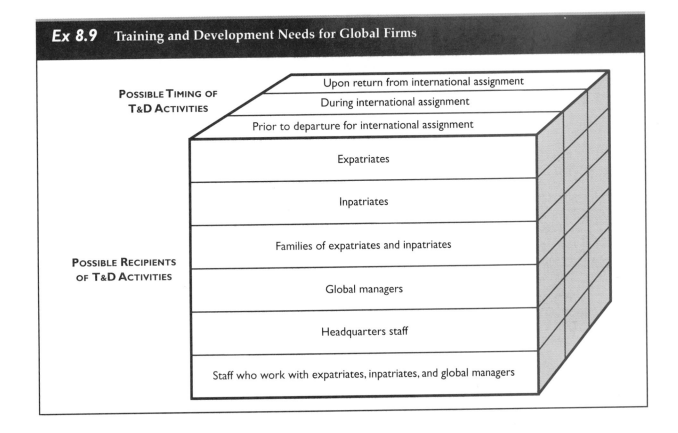

Ex 8.9   Training and Development Needs for Global Firms

POSSIBLE TIMING OF T&D ACTIVITIES
- Upon return from international assignment
- During international assignment
- Prior to departure for international assignment

POSSIBLE RECIPIENTS OF T&D ACTIVITIES
- Expatriates
- Inpatriates
- Families of expatriates and inpatriates
- Global managers
- Headquarters staff
- Staff who work with expatriates, inpatriates, and global managers

A typical three-day cross-cultural program might cover details about what everyday life in the country is like, typical practices that are important to doing business in the country, the role of women in the foreign culture, and a discussion of the culture shock and stress that executives and their families are likely to experience. Such training can improve the work performance of expatriates and reduce the culture shock experienced by their families.

One available tool for cross-cultural training is called a **culture-general assimilator,** which *is a tool that develops self-awareness about one's own culture and prepares people for interaction with other cultures.*[84] Using scenarios that illustrate how culture influences perceptions and behaviors, it teaches people to be more understanding of cultural differences of many types, including approaches to work and to time and space, views about the importance of groups versus individuals, class and status hierarchies, language, and rituals and superstitions, among other things. Because the culture-general assimilator does not teach about a specific culture, it may not be sufficient to completely prepare expatriates for assignments abroad. Nevertheless, this form of general training can prepare people to be alert to the effects of culture so that they can learn about other cultures more quickly. For employees who travel to many different countries within a relatively short time, learning general skills for coping in other cultural environments may be more practical than attempting to learn the specific behaviors, languages, and values of each culture.

Inpatriates. Increasingly, U.S. companies also are recognizing the need for cross-cultural training for their inpatriates, or "in-pats." Inpatriates are employees from other countries who are assigned to work in the United States. They often find relocating to the United States particularly difficult, partly because so few Americans speak another language. The challenge of being an inpatriate in a U.S. company is also partly due to the fact that U.S. employers are less likely to offer cross-cultural training to inpatriates. Like expatriates, inpatriates and their families need accurate information about the local culture (as well as general assistance with the process of relocation).[85]

Global Leadership Training and Development

"Leadership development is about helping people grow, and if I can get people as individuals growing, then I've got a company that grows."

James McNerney, CEO
3M

The leadership in companies today needs to have global competencies. Global leaders face a difficult challenge: They need to manage operations in several different countries simultaneously. Global leadership competency is especially important in global organizations that are structured around products rather than geographic regions. Many companies use expatriate assignments as developmental experiences intended to help managers develop the skills and mind-set needed by global leaders, but success as an expatriate does not guarantee success as a global leader. Additional development is likely to be helpful.

As described in Chapter 5, 3M has been very systematic in developing global leaders. They have done this through specifying global leadership competencies and developmental activities that can develop them.[86] These are described in the feature "Managing Globalization: 3M's Global Leadership Competencies."[87]

Managing Globalization

3M's Global Leadership Competencies

The foundation of many HR practices at 3M is their global leadership competency model. It specifies the major competencies required for success as a leader in this global corporation, which are as follows.

Fundamental Leadership Competencies
New employees should possess these when hired and refine them through experience in successive managerial assignments.

- Ethics and integrity
- Intellectual capacity
- Maturity and judgment

Essential Leadership Competencies
These competencies are developed through experience leading a function or department, and set the stage for more complex executive positions.

- Customer orientation
- Developing people
- Inspiring others
- Business health and results

Visionary Leadership Competencies
These competencies develop as executives take on responsibilities that require them to operate beyond the boundaries of a particular organizational unit, and are used extensively in higher-level positions.

- Global perspective
- Vision and strategy
- Nurturing innovation
- Building alliances
- Organizational agility

SUMMARY

Rapidly changing technology, foreign competition, and changes in organizational strategy and strategic business objectives are putting pressure on organizations to train and develop employees for competitive advantage. This requires careful attention to needs assessment, program development and implementation, and evaluation. Four types of needs analysis—organizational, job, person, and demographic—are designed to diagnose systematically the short- and long-term human resource needs of an organization. When actual performance and desired performance differ, training is needed.

Setting up training and development activities involves deciding who will be trained, who will train, where the training will occur, and what methods will be used. Cost considerations, as well as the types of competencies to be acquired and the format of the training, affect the selection of appropriate methods. Training and development for teams and for global leaders are two especially important types of training that many organizations have been implementing recently.

Regardless of the method chosen, the content of training and development activities should be designed to maximize learning. Principles to consider include clear instructions, proper role models, active participation, feedback, and practice. These should be viewed in relationship to the trainees' self-efficacy or competency beliefs. It is also important to examine the work environment to ensure that new behaviors will be reinforced rather than punished.

TERMS TO REMEMBER

Behavioral modeling
Cross-cultural training
Culture-general assimilator
Demographic needs analysis
Development
Developmental job assignments
E-learning
Emotional intelligence
Interactive video training (IVT)
Job needs analysis
Job rotation programs

Mentoring
On-the-job training (OJT)
Organizational needs analysis
Orientation programs
Personal coaches
Person needs analysis
Reinforcement
Simulations
Socialization
Training
Transfer

DISCUSSION QUESTIONS

1. Describe how Trident's training is likely to be related to other HR activities in the company.

2. What is the role of training and development in learning organizations? Do you think a pharmaceutical company could effectively manage knowledge without having well-developed T&D activities?

3. An auto dealer has hired you to help improve the performance of its sales and service staff. Your first task is to conduct a needs analysis for the organization. Describe what you will do. Then, provide examples of possible training and development activities that could be used to influence the knowledge, behavior, and attitudes of the staff.

4. Consider the various training and development formats described in this chapter. Which three do you think would be most effective for maintaining the skills of IT engineers? Which three do you think would be least effective? Explain your rationale.

5. Imagine your organization—a publishing company—has decided to hire an external vendor to provide diversity training. You want to begin by having the vendor conduct the training for just a small portion of the employees in order to study and assess the training's effectiveness. Describe a plan for evaluating the effectiveness of the diversity training offered by the vendor. What measures will you use, and how will you design the evaluation study?

6. Discuss the strategic role of training and development activities in companies with international operations and markets.

PROJECTS TO EXTEND YOUR LEARNING

1. *Integration and Application.* After reviewing the two end-of-text cases, answer the following questions by comparing and contrasting the training and development activities of Southwest and Lincoln Electric.

    a. For which company is training and development more important?
    b. Describe how the training and development activities in both companies are related to other HR activities.

2. *Exploring the Internet.*

    a. Read about the role of training in ensuring safety and health at work by visiting the Web page of the Occupational Safety and Health Administration at http://www.osha.gov.
    b. Customers of Siemens can receive training from the company. Learn more about the training Siemens offers to its customers at http://siemens.com (see "Training for Customers").
    c. The American Society for Training and Development is an association of T&D professionals. Visit their website (http://www .astd.org/astd) to learn about the resources available through this organization.
    d. Learn more about corporate universities by visiting the Corporate University Xchange at http://www.corpu.com.
    e. The Center for Creative Leadership works with companies to design custom training and development programs. They also offer many standardized leadership development programs for individuals. Learn more about this organization and the research they have done on leadership development at http://www.ccl.org/CCLCommerce/index.aspx.
    f. Find out more about the wilderness training offered by Outward Bound at http://www.outwardbound.org.
    g. Discover resources for expatriate training:
        The Training Registry, http://www.trainingregistry.com
        Global View, http://www.globalview.org
        IOR Global Services, http://www.iorworld.com
        Grovewell.com, http://www.grovewell.com
    h. Learn more about team building and training at http://www.accel-team.com.

3. *Experiential Activity.* Training and development activities are most effective when the people participating in them understand how they can benefit from the experience. What types of training and development activities would be helpful to you? Use the following Personal Development Plan form to list activities that would help you develop specific knowledge, skills, and insights.

PERSONAL DEVELOPMENT PLAN

INSTRUCTIONS

A. *Setting Objectives.* After reviewing this chapter, list five learning objectives that you could benefit from achieving during the next year. Consider cognitive knowledge you need to acquire, technical and interpersonal skills from which you could benefit, and new attitudes that would be helpful for you to develop. List these five learning objectives, being as specific as possible:

1.

2.

3.

4.

5.

B. *Choosing Methods.* For each objective, consider the alternative types of training and development methods that might be available (e.g., e-learning, business games, wilderness training). Several possible methods are listed in the chart that follows, but you may add others if you wish. For each of your five learning objectives, evaluate how effective you think each alternative method would likely be. Use this simple rating system to record your evaluations:

1	2	3	4
Not at all effective	Not sure	May be somewhat useful	Quite effective

METHODS	LIKELY EFFECTIVENESS (1, 2, 3, OR 4)				
	OBJ. 1	OBJ. 2	OBJ. 3	OBJ. 4	OBJ. 5
E-learning					
On-the-job training (OJT)					
Apprenticeship or internship					
Job rotation program					
Mentoring					
Personal coaching					
Corporate university program					
Executive education program at local university					
Interactive video training (IVT)					
Simulation					
Sensitivity training					
Wilderness training					

C. *Developing a Specific Action Plan.* Choose three objectives that are important to you. For each objective, state what you will do to develop yourself. Keep in mind that a useful plan must be feasible. Consider the potential value of the actions you listed and their feasibility for you. Are you willing to make a commitment to carry out any of these actions in the next 12 months?

MY ACTION PLAN		
OBJECTIVE	**ACTIONS**	**TARGET DATE FOR COMPLETION**
1.	a.	
	b.	
	c.	
2.	a.	
	b.	
	c.	
3.	a.	
	b.	
	c.	

CASE STUDY

SEEING THE FOREST AND THE TREES

The face of domestic and global competition that the leaders of the Forest Products Company (FPC) and its parent, the Weyerhaeuser Corporation, saw as they surveyed an industry on its knees in the early 1980s was a far different face from the one Weyerhaeuser and its subsidiaries had successfully competed against for so long. They knew how to compete—and win—against a large-firm, commodity lumber business. But that business was in its death throes, and what was emerging from the ashes presented an entirely new set of challenges, one that would require a radical change in Weyerhaeuser's strategy. The new competitors weren't the old monolithic organizations but were instead small mills—lean and mean, and configured so their products could be tailored to customer demand and their product lines could change rapidly if the need arose. They were nonunion, owner-operated, and entrepreneurial; and in this configuration, they were running the lowest-cost, most market-oriented operation around.

Going out of business was not an alternative anyone cared to think about, but if things didn't change, it would be a definite possibility. Charley Bingham, CEO of the Forest Products Company, knew that something had to be done—and sooner, not later. He gathered his top dozen managers, and together they decided that a massive reorganization was called for, accompanied by a radical change in strategy. According to Bingham, the change in strategy went something like this:

"Approximately 80% of our sales dollars in 1982 represented products sold as commodities. By

1995, we resolved that we must reverse the proportions."

The massive reorganization at FPC mirrored that occurring at its parent company. The Weyerhaeuser Corporation decided to drastically decentralize. The three operating units, of which FPC was one, were given free reign on how to do their business. Given this scenario, Bingham and his team decided they needed to create an organization capable of acting and responding just like their competitors. Thus, they created 200 profit centers with each center being largely responsible for its own bottom line.

This restructuring soon proved to be only a first step in the right direction. The ability of FPC to implement its new strategy was being undermined by low morale, which was pervasive. In addition, many middle managers, those needed to actually carry out the change, were pessimistic about the possibility of sustained future success. Silently, they even questioned their own ability to operate the profit centers.

With insights from Horace Parker, director of executive development at FPC, the rest of the top team came to realize that there would have to be a total transformation of the organization: The cor-

porate culture, knowledge base, skill levels, style of leadership, and team orientation would all have to change, for all employees. With 18,000 employees across the United States, Parker wasn't sure where to start. The others said they would help, but Horace had to tell them what to do. Horace, of course, is waiting to hear what you have to tell him.

CASE QUESTIONS

1. Where does Horace start? What programs does he put in place to deal with the needs of corporate culture, knowledge, skills, leadership, and team orientation?

2. How does he go about developing the programs that he needs to put in place? Does he do it by himself? Can he buy off-the-shelf programs?

3. What time frame does Horace need to implement the programs to make the change successful? If he deals only with executive development programs, does he need to be concerned with programs for middle managers and below? How does he do this?

Source: Randall S. Schuler, Rutgers University

ENDNOTES

1   J. L. Laabs, "Financial Impact: Quality Drives Trident's Success," *Workforce* (February 1998): 44–49.

2   "Four Employers Score with Programs to Develop, Retain Skilled Workforces," *BNA Bulletin to Management* (October 14, 1999): 321; for an extended discussion of the strategic importance of training and development, see S. Tannenbaum, "A Strategic View of Training and Learning, in K. Kraiger (ed.), *Creating, Implementing and Managing Effective Training and Development: State-of-the-Art Lessons for Practice* (San Francisco: Jossey-Bass, 2002): 10–52.

3   "SHRM—BNA Survey No. 63: Human Resource Activities, Budgets & Staffs, 1997–1998," *Bulletin to Management* (June 18, 1998): 2; "High-Technology Firms Lead the Way in Training," *Bulletin to Management* (February 5, 1998): 376; "1997 Industry Report," *Training* (October 1998): 33–65. Also see the ASTD 2003 State of the Industry Report at http://www.astd.org/astd.

4   W. Royal, "A Factory's Crash Course in Economics Pays Off," *New York Times* (April 15, 2001): C9.

5   J. K. Laabs, "Serving Up a New Level of Customer Service at Quebecor," *Workforce* (March 2001): 40–42; S. Caudron, "Training and the ROI of Fun," *Workforce* (December 2000): 34–39.

6   M. Kirk, "No Reservation," *Human Resource Executive* (June 18, 1999): 69–73.

7   P. Kiger, "Health Partners Delivers Training That Works," *Workforce* (November 2002): 60–64.

8   E. Zimmerman, "Better Training Is Just a Click Away," *Workforce* (January 2001): 36–42.

9   S. E. Jackson, M. Hitt, and A. S. DeNisi (eds.), *Managing Knowledge for Sustained Competitive Advantage* (San Francisco: Jossey-Bass/Pfeiffer, 2003); S. E. Jackson and R. S. Schuler, "Turning Knowledge into Business," *Financial Times* (Mastering Management Supplement) (January 2001): 3; S. Greengard, "Will Your Culture Support KM?" *Workforce* (October 1998): 93–94; S. Greengard, "How to Make KM a Reality," *Workforce* (October 1998): 90–91; "In the Know," *Human Resource Executive* (February 1997): 31; E. Raimy, "Knowledge Movers," *Human Resource Executive* (February 1997): 32–37; S. Greengard, "Storing, Shaping and Sharing Collective Wisdom," *Workforce* (October 1998): 82–88.

10   L. Rubis, "Manager Training Helped Company Digest Big Bite," *HR Magazine* (December 2000): 61–62.

11   For detailed discussions of training, see K. Kraiger, "Perspectives on Training and Development," in W. C. Borman, D. R. Ilgen, and R. J. Klimoski (eds.), *Handbook of Psychology: Industrial and Organizational Psychology* (New York: Wiley, 2003): 71–192; K. Kraiger (ed.), *Creating, Implementing and Managing Effective Training and Development: State-of-the-Art Lessons for Practice* (San Francisco: Jossey-Bass, 2002); L. Braid, D. Griffin, and J. Henderson, "Time and Space: Reframing the Training and Development Agenda," *Human Resource Management* 42(1) (Spring

2003): 39–52; and I. L. Goldstein and J. K. Ford, *Training in Organizations* (Belmont, CA: Wadsworth, 2002). For detailed discussions of leadership development, see B. J. Avolio, *Full Leadership Development* (Thousand Oaks, CA: Sage, 1999), and C. D. McCauley, R. S. Moxley, and E. Van Velsor (eds.), *Handbook of Leadership Development* (San Francisco: Jossey-Bass, 1998).

12 R. R. Ritti, *The Ropes to Skip and the Ropes to Know: Studies in Organizational Behavior,* 5th ed. (Columbus, OH: Grid Publishing, 1997).

13 M. Johnson, "Use Anti-Harassment Training to Shelter Yourself from Suits," *HR Magazine* (October 1999): 77–81.

14 S. J. Wells, "Who's Next?" *HR Magazine* (November 2003): 45–50.

15 See D. P. Shuit, "Magic for Sale," *Workforce Management* (September 2004): 35–40.

16 S. F. Gale, "For ERP Success, Create a Culture Change," *Workforce* (September 2002): 78–83.

17 W. Arthur Jr., W. Bennett Jr., P. S. Edens, and S. T. Bell, "Effectiveness of Training in Organizations: A Meta-Analysis of Design and Evaluation Features," *Journal of Applied Psychology* 88(2) (2003): 234–245; J. S. Callahan, D. S. Kiker, and T. Cross, "Does Method Matter? A Meta-Analysis of the Effects of Training Method on Older Learner Trainer Performance," *Journal of Management* 29(5) (2003): 663–680.

18 S. Hays, "HR Strategies Help Push New Razor to Number One," *Workforce* (February 1999): 92–93; Industry Report 1998, "Who Gets Trained? Where the Money Goes," *Training* (October 1998): 55–67.

19 T. J. Maurer and B. A. Tarulli, "Investigation of Perceived Environment, Perceived Outcome, and Person Variables in Relationship to Voluntary Development Activity by Employees," *Journal of Applied Psychology* 79 (1994): 3–14. See also L. A. Hill, *Becoming a Manager: Mastery of a New Identity* (Cambridge, MA: Harvard Business School Press, 1992); T. A. Scandura, "Dysfunctional Mentoring Relationships and Outcomes," *Journal of Management* 24 (1998): 449–467.

20 G. T. Chao et al., "Organizational Socialization: Its Content and Consequences," *Journal of Applied Psychology* 79 (1994): 730–743; E. W. Morrison, "Newcomer Information Seeking: Exploring Types, Modes, Sources, and Outcomes," *Academy of Management Journal* 36 (1993): 557–589; C. Ostroff and S. W. J. Kozlowski, "Organizational Socialization as a Learning Process: The Role of Information Acquisition," *Personnel Psychology* 45 (1992): 849–874.

21 T. A. Stewart, "Brain Power: Who Owns It . . . How They Profit from It," *Fortune* (March 17, 1997): 105–110.

22 R. Zemke, "How to Do a Needs Assessment When You Think You Don't Have Time," *Training* (March 1998): 38–44; "Lifelong Learning and the Skills Shortage: Policy Guide," *Bulletin to Management* (November 27, 1997): 384; "Technology and Training: A Dynamic Duo," *Bulletin to Management* 48(10) (March 6, 1997): 80; L. Saari et al., "A Survey of Management Training and Education Practices in U.S. Companies," *Personnel Psychology* 41 (1988): 731–745.

23 Adapted from I. L. Goldstein, *Training: Program Development and Evaluation* (Monterey, CA: Brooks/Cole, 1986): 8; for a more fully elaborated description of needs analysis, see I. L. Goldstein and J. K. Ford, *Training in Organizations,* 4th ed. (Belmont, CA: Wadsworth, 2002).

24 P. J. Kiger, "At USA Bank, Promotions and Job Satisfaction Are Up," *Workforce* (March 2001): 54–55.

25 For more information about diagnosing the learning climate, see S. I. Tannenbaum, "Enhancing Continuous Learning: Diagnostic Findings from Multiple Companies," *Human Resource Management* 36 (1997): 437–452.

26 Douglas Bray, Chair, Emeritus, Development Dimensions International, Pittsburgh, Pennsylvania, personal communication.

27 S. Hays, "HR Strategies Help Push New Razor to Number One," *Workforce* (February 1999): 92–93; B. Calandra, "Razor Sharp," *Human Resource Executive* (June 4, 1999): 22–25.

28 T. J. Maurer, E. M. Weiss, and F. G. Barberite, "A Model of Involvement in Work-Related Learning and Development Activity: The Effects of Individual, Situational, Motivational, and Age Variables," *Journal of Applied Psychology* 88(4) (2003): 707–724; for more discussion of the advantages and disadvantages of basic assessment techniques, see I. L. Goldstein, "Training in Work Organizations," *Handbook of Industrial and Organizational Psychology* 2 (1991): 507–620.

29 Modified from J. K. Ford and R. A. Noe, "Self-Assessed Training Needs: The Effects of Attitudes toward Training, Managerial Level and Function," *Personnel Psychology* 40 (1987): 39–53.

30 J. Conner and C. A. Smith, "Developing the Next Generation of Leaders: A New Strategy for Leadership Development at Colgate-Palmolive," in E. M. Mone and M. London (eds.), *HR to the Rescue: Case Studies of HR Solutions to Business Challenges* (Houston, TX: Gulf, 1998).

31 W. Byham, "Bench Strength," *Across the Board* (February 2000): 35–41.

32 R. Neil Olson and E. A. Sexton, "Gender Differences in the Returns to and the Acquisition of On-the-Job Training," *Industrial Relations* 35 (January 1996): 59; S. G. Baugh, M. J. Lankau, and A. Terri, "An Investigation of the Effects of Protégé Gender on Responses to Mentoring," *Journal of Vocational Behavior* 49 (1996): 309–323; P. J. Ohlott, M. N. Ruderman, and C. D. McCauley, "Gender Differences in Managers' Developmental Job Experiences," *Academy of Management Journal* 37 (1994): 46–67.

33 D. Brady, "Crashing GE's Glass Ceiling," *Business Week* (July 28, 2003): 76–77; G. H. Harel, S. S. Tzafrir, and Y. Baruch, "Achieving Organizational Effectiveness through Promotion of Women into Managerial Positions: HRM Practice Focus," *International Journal of Human Resource Management* 14(2) (March 2003): 247–263; Staff, "Delta Air Will Give School Grant to Train Minorities as Pilots," *Wall Street Journal* (January 10, 2001): A6.

34 D. B. Sloan, "Identifying and Developing High Potential Talent: A Succession Management Methodology," *Industrial-Organizational Psychologist* (2000): 80–90.

35 J. Colquitt, J. LePine, and R. Noe, "Toward an Integrative Theory of Training Motivation: A Meta-Analytic Path Analysis of 20 Years of Research," *Journal of Applied Psychology* 85(5) (2000): 678–707.

36 See, for example, B. Ragins and J. Cotton, "Mentor Functions and Outcomes: A Comparison of Men and Women in Formal and Informal Mentoring Relationships," *Journal of Applied Psychology* 84(4) (1999): 529–550.

37 See the Special Issue of *Harvard Business Review,* "Inside the Mind of the Leader," January 2004; D. B. Neary, "Creating a Company-Wide, On-Line, Performance Management System: A Case Study at TRW Inc.," *Human Resource Management* 41(4) (Winter 2002): 491–498; C. H. Deutsch, "An Apparent Heir at Xerox," *New York Times* (June 1, 2003): 2.

38 J. Black and H. Gregersen, "High Impact Training: Forging Leaders for the Global Frontier," *Human Resource Management* 39(2 & 3) (Summer/Fall 2000): 173–184.

39 A. J. Towler and R. L. Dipboye, "Effects of Trainer Expressiveness, Organization, and Trainee Goal Orientation on Training Outcomes," *Journal of Applied Psychology* 86 (2001): 664–673.

40 R. J. Sternberg and E. L. Grigorenko, "Are Cognitive Styles Still in Style?" *American Psychologist* 52 (July 1997): 700–712; K. Kraiger, J. K. Ford, and E. Salas, "Application of Cognitive, Skill-Based, and Affective Theories of Learning Outcomes to New Methods of Training Evaluation," *Journal of Applied Psychology* 78 (1993): 311–328.

41 C. Lachnit, "Hire Right: Do It the Ritz Way," *Workforce* (April 2002): 16.

42 J. Strandberg, "Training for a Technology Upgrade," *Training* (November 1997): 36–38.

43 L. Heuring, "Six Sigma in Sight," *HR Magazine* (March 2004): 76–80.

44 J. Hempel and S. Porges, "It Takes a Village—and a Consultant," *Business Week* (September 2004): 76–77.

45 B. Leonard, "Taking HR to the Next Level," *HR Magazine* (July 2003): 57–63. See also S. Kugel, "Foreign Workers Assessing What a New Bill Will Mean," *New York Times* (February 24, 2004): 4.

46 K. Tyler, "I Say Potato, You Say Patata," *HR Magazine* (January 2004): 85–87.

47 L. Rubis, "Show and Tell," *HR Magazine* (April 1998): 110–117.

48 H. W. Marsh, G. E. Richards, and J. Barnes, "Multidimensional Self-Concepts: The Effects of Participation in an Outward Bound Program," *Journal of Personality and Social Psychology* 50 (1986): 195–204; H. W. Marsh, G. E. Richards, and J. Barnes, "A Long-Term Follow-up of the Effects of Participation in an Outward Bound Program," *Personality and Social Psychology Bulletin* 12 (1987): 465–492.

49 See the Special Issue of *Harvard Business Review,* January 2004; J. Laabs, "Emotional Intelligence at Work," *Workforce* (July 1999): 68–71; D. Goleman, *Working with Emotional Intelligence* (New York: Bantam Books, 1998); C. Cherniss and D. Goleman (eds.), *The Emotionally Intelligent Workplace* (San Francisco: Jossey-Bass, 2001).

50 J. Mullich, "A Second Act for E-Learning," *Workforce Management* (February 2004): 51–55; S. Overman, "Dow, Hewlett-Packard Put E-Learning to Work to Save Time and Money," *HR Magazine* (February 2004): 32.

51 S. F. Gale, "Making E-Learning More than 'Pixie Dust,'" *Workforce* (March 2003): 58–62. Also based on research by the American Society for Training and Development, as presented in M. Jones, "Use Your Head When Identifying Skills Gaps," *Workforce* (March 2000): 118–122.

52 P. Harris, "ROI of E-Learning: Closing In," *TD* (February 2003): 31–35.

53 For a full discussion of the conditions required for effective OJT, see I. L. Goldstein and K. J. Ford, *Training in Organizations,* 4th ed. (Belmont, CA: Wadsworth, 2002); see also J. D. Facteau, G. H. Dobbins, J. E. A. Russell, R. T. Ladd, and J. D. Kudisch, "The Influence of General Perceptions of the Training Environment on Pretraining Motivation and Perceived Training Transfer," *Journal of Management* 21 (1995): 1–25; P. J. Ohlott, C. D. McCauley, and M. N. Ruderman, *Developmental Challenge Profile: Learning from Job Experiences* (Greensboro, NC: Center for Creative Leadership, March 1993).

54 "Delta Air Will Give School Grant to Train Minorities as Pilots," *Wall Street Journal* (January 10, 2001): A6; D. Stamps, "Will School-to-Work, Work?" *Training* (June 1996): 72–81.

55 C. McCauley, *The Job Challenge Profile: Participant Workbook* (San Francisco: Jossey-Bass, 1999).

56 A. Murrell, F. Crosby, and R. Ely, *Mentoring Dilemmas: Developmental Relationships within Multicultural Organizations* (Mahway, NJ: LEA, 1999); M. Higgins and K. E. Kram, "Reconceptualizing Mentoring at Work: A Developmental Network Perspective," *Academy of Management Executive* 25(2) (2001): 264–288; S. L. Willis and S. S. Dubin (eds.), *Maintaining Professional Competence: Approaches to Career Enhancement, Vitality and Success throughout a Work Life* (San Francisco: Jossey-Bass, 1990); J. A. Schneer and F. Reitman, "Effects of Employment Gaps on the Careers of M.B.A.'s: More Damaging for Men than for Women?" *Academy of Management Journal* 33 (1990): 391–406; J. H. Greenhaus, S. Parasuraman, and W. M. Wormley, "Effects of Race on Organizational Experiences, Job Performance Evaluations and Career Outcomes," *Academy of Management Journal* 33 (1990): 64–86.

57 S. Overman, "Mentors without Borders," *HR Magazine* (March 2004): 83–86.

58 C. H. Deutsch, "A New Kind of Whistle-Blower: Company Refines Principles of Coaching and Teamwork," *New York Times* (May 7, 1999): C1; B. Filipczak, "The Executive Coach: Helper or Healer?" *Training* (March 1998): 30–36.

59 S. R. Davis, J. H. Lucas, and D. R. Marcotte, "GM Links Better Leaders to Better Business," *Workforce* (April 1998): 62–68.

60 C. L. Cole, "Boeing U.," *Workforce* (October 2000): 62–68; T. Stewart, "See Jack. See Jack Run," *Fortune* (December 27, 1999): 284–290; J. Spiegel Arthur, "Virtual U.," *Human Resource Executive* (March 19, 1998): 44–46.

61 E. F. Holton III and T. T. Baldwin (eds.), *Improving Learning Transfer* (San Francisco: Jossey-Bass, 2003); for a detailed list of conditions that support transfer, see L. Burke and T. T. Baldwin, "Workforce Training Transfer: A Study of the Effect of Relapse Prevention Training and Transfer Climate," *Human Resource Management* 38 (3) (Fall 1999): 227–242.

62 R. Becker, "Taking the Misery out of Experiential Training," *Training* (February 1998): 78–88; M. Hequet, "Games That Teach," *Training* (July 1995): 53–58; T. A. Stewart, "The Dance Steps Get Trickier All the Time," *Fortune* (May 26, 1997): 157–160; G. C. Thornton III and J. N. Cleveland, "Developing Managerial Talent through Simulation," *American Psychologist* (February 1990): 190–199; W. M. Bulkeley, "The World of Work Is a Keystroke Away for Students in Computer-Simulated Jobs," *Wall Street Journal* (May 7, 1996): B1, B2.

63 For an excellent description of the many uses and issues of assessment centers, see the entire special issue, R. E. Riggio and B. T. Mayes (eds.), "Assessment Centers: Research and Applications," *Journal of Social Behavior and Personality* 12 (1997): 1–331; also see the references in Chapter 8.

64 P. Schinzler, "Sharing the Wealth," *Business Week e-Biz* (March 2001): 36–40.

65 D. P. Shuit, "Sound the Retreat," *Workforce Management* (September 2003): 39–48.

66 For a review of related research, see J. A. Cannon-Bowers, L. Rhodenizer, E. Salas, and C. Bowers, "A Framework for Understanding Pre-Practice Conditions and Their Impact on Learning," *Personnel Psychology* 51 (1998): 291–310.

67 M. A. Quinones, "Pretraining Context Effects: Training Assignment as Feedback," *Journal of Applied Psychology* 80 (1995): 226–238; V. L. Huber, "A Comparison of Goal Setting and Pay as Learning Incentives," *Psychological Reports* 56 (1985): 223–235; V. L. Huber, "Interplay between Goal Setting and Promises of Pay-for-Performance on Individual and Group Performance: An Operant Interpretation," *Journal of Organizational Behavior Management* 7 (1986): 45–64.

68 G. May and W. Kahnweiler, "The Effect of a Mastery Practice Design on Learning and Transfer in Behavior Modeling Training," *Personnel Psychology* 53 (2000): 353–373.

69 Huber, "Interplay between Goal Setting and Promises of Pay-for-Performance"; J. D. Eyring, D. Steele Johnson, and D. J. Francis, "A Cross-Level Units-of-Analysis Approach to Individual Differences in Skill Acquisition," *Journal of Applied Psychology* 78 (1993): 805–814; P. C. Earley, "Self or Group? Cultural Effects of Training on Self-Efficacy and Performance," *Administrative Science Quarterly* 39 (1994): 89–117.

70 B. Ragins and J. Cotton, "Mentor Functions and Outcomes: A Comparison of Men and Women in Formal and Informal Mentoring Relationships," *Journal of Applied Psychology* 84(4) (1999): 529–550; V. L. Huber, G. P. Latham, and E. A. Locke, "The Management of Impressions through Goal Setting," in R. A. Giacalone and P. Rosenfield (eds.), *Impression Management in the Organization* (Hillsdale, NJ: Erlbaum, 1989).

71 P. Hogan, M. Hakel, and P. Decker, "Effects of Trainee-Generated vs. Trainer-Provided Rule Codes on Generalization in Behavioral Modeling Training," *Journal of Applied Psychology* 71 (1986): 469–473.

72 W. W. Tornow and M. London, "Maximizing the Value of 360-Degree Feedback: A Process for Successful Individual and Organizational

Development," *Center for Creative Leadership* (March 1998); D. E. Coates, "Don't Tie 360 Feedback to Pay," *Training* (September 1998): 68–78.

73 J. E. Driskell, C. Copper, and A. Moran, "Does Mental Practice Enhance Performance?" *Journal of Applied Psychology*, 79 (1994): 481–492.

74 J. F. Brett and D. VandeWalle, "Goal Orientation and Goal Content as Predictors of Performance in a Training Program," *Journal of Applied Psychology* 84(6) (1999): 863–873; C. Frayne and G. P. Latham, "The Application of Social Learning Theory to Employee Self-Management of Attendance," *Journal of Applied Psychology* 72 (1987): 387–392.

75 See M. J. Waller, "The Timing of Adaptive Group Responses to Nonroutine Events. *Academy of Management Journal* 42 (1999): 127–137.

76 A. P. J. Ellis, J. R. Hollenbeck, D. R. Ilgen, C. O. L. H. Porter, B. J. West, and Henry Moon, "Team Learning: Collectively Connecting the Dots," *Journal of Applied Psychology* 88(5) (2003): 821–835; B. L. Kirkman, B. Rosen, C. B. Gibson, P. E. Tesluk, and S. O. McPherson, "Five Challenges to Virtual Team Success: Lessons from Sabre, Inc.," *Academy of Management Executive* 16(3) (2002): 67–79; E. E. Salas, C. S. Brown, and J. A. Cannon-Bowers, "What We Know About Designing and Delivering Team Training: Tips and Guidelines," in K. Kraiger (ed.), *Creating, Implementing and Managing Effective Training and Development: State-of-the-Art Lessons for Practice* (San Francisco: Jossey-Bass, 2002): 234–262; Salas, J. A. Cannon-Bowers, and E. Eden, *Improving Teamwork in Organizations: Applications of Resource Management and Training* (Englewood Cliffs, N.J.: Lawrence Erlbaum, 2001); R. A. Guzzo and M. W. Dickson, "Teams in Organizations: Recent Research on Performance and Effectiveness," *Annual Review of Psychology* 47 (1996): 307–308; J. Cannon-Bowers, S. A. Tannebaum, E. Salas, and C. Volpe, "Defining Competencies and Establishing Team Training Requirements," *Team Effectiveness and Decision Making* (2000): 333–380.

77 H Campbell, "Adventures in Teamland: Experiential Training Makes the Lesson Fun," *Personnel Journal* (May 1996): 56–62; see also J. P. Meyer, "Four Territories of Experience: A Developmental Action Inquiry Approach to Outdoor-Adventure Experiential Learning," *Academy of Management Learning and Education* 2(4) (2003): 352–363.

78 V. U. Druskat and J. V. Wheeler, "Managing from the Boundary: The Effective Leadership of Self-Managing Work Teams," *Academy of Management Journal* 46(4) (2003): 435–457; M. Moravec, O. J. Johannessen, and T. A. Hjelmas, "Thumbs Up for Self-Managed Teams," *Management Review* (July/August 1997); S. E. Prokesch, "Unleashing the Power of Learning: An Interview with British Petroleum's John Browne," *Harvard Business Review* (September–October 1997); M. Moravec, O. J. Johannessen, and T. A. Hjelmas, "We Have Seen the Future and It Is Self-Managed," *PM Network* (September 1997): 20–22.

79 J. W. Dean, Jr., and M. P. Sharfman, "Does Decision Process Matter? A Study of Strategic Decision Making Effectiveness," *Academy of Management Journal* 39 (1996): 368–396; P. W. Mulvey, J. F. Viega, and P. M. Elsass, "When Teammates Raise a White Flag," *Academy of Management Executive* 10 (1996): 40–49; R. L. Priem, D. A. Harrison, and N. K. Muir,

"Structured Conflict and Consensus Outcomes in Group Decision Making," *Journal of Management* 21 (1995): 691–710.

80 For a review of research on cross-cultural training, see D. P. S. Bhawuk and R. W. Brislin, "Cross-Cultural Training: A Review," *Applied Psychology: An International Review* 49 (2000): 162–191.

81 For reviews, see D. Chrobot-Mason and M. A. Quinones, "Training for a Diverse Workforce," in K. Kraiger (ed.), *Creating, Implementing and Managing Effective Training and Development: State-of-the-Art Lessons for Practice* (San Francisco: Jossey-Bass, 2002): 117–159; S. E. Jackson and A. Joshi, "Research on Domestic and International Diversity in Organizations: A Merger That Works?" in *International Handbook of Work and Organizational Psychology*, vol. 2 (Thousand Oaks, CA: Sage, 2001); see also T. F. Pettigrew, "Intergroup Contact Theory," *Annual Review of Psychology* 49 (1998): 65–85.

82 S. L. Rynes and B. A. Rosen, "A Field Survey of Factors Affecting the Adoption and Perceived Success of Diversity Training," *Personnel Psychology* 48 (1995): 247–270.

83 D. R. Briscore and R. S. Schuler, *International Human Resource Management: Policy and Practice in Global Enterprises*, 2nd ed. (London: Routledge, 2004); J. S. Black (ed.), *Globalizing People through International Assignments* (Reading, MA: Addison-Wesley, 1999).

84 K. Cushner and R. W. Brislin (eds.), *Improving Intercultural Interactions: Models for Cross-Cultural Training Programs* (Thousand Oaks, CA: Sage, 1997).

85 C. Lachmitt, "Low-Cost Tips for Successful Inpatriation," *Workforce* (August 2000): 42–47.

86 D. A. Ready and J. A. Conger, "Why Leadership-Development Efforts Fail," *MIT Sloan Management Review* (Spring 2003): 83–88; I. F. Kesner, "Leadership Development: Perk or Priority?" *Harvard Business Review* (May 2003): 29–38; R. Larsson, K. R. Brousseau, M. J. Driver, M. Holmqvist, and V. Tranovskaya, "International Growth through Cooperation: Brand-Driven Strategies, Leadership, and Career Development in Sweden," *Academy of Management Executive* 17(1) (2003): 7–24; K. Beavan, T. Lockhart, and K. Michaelson, "Leadership Development on the Job," in *2003 Handbook of Business Strategy* (New York: Thomson Media, 2002); D. B. Neary and D. A. O'Grady, "The Role of Training in Developing Global Leaders: A Case Study at TRW, Inc.," *Human Resource Management* (Summer/Fall 2000): 185–193. For extensive views on leadership development, see the Special Issue of *Harvard Business Review* entitled "Inside the Mind of the Leader," January 2004.

87 For a detailed discussion of the 3M leadership competency model, see M. Alldredge and K. Nilan, "3M's Leadership Competency Model: An Internally Developed Solution," *Human Resource Management* 39(2 & 3) (Summer/Fall 2000): 133–145; see also M. Dalton, C. Ernst, J. Deal, and J. Leslie, *Success for the New Global Managers* (San Francisco: Jossey-Bass, 2003).

chapter 9

Developing an Approach to Total Compensation

When the Kellogg Company acquired Keebler Company in 2000, it was obvious that there would have to be some changes made in how people were paid. Keebler used enterprise software provided by the SAP Company to manage compensation and Kellogg used a homegrown enterprise system that allowed for a decentralized, market-based approach. Kellogg's system was designed to put as much information as possible into the hands of the managers and empower them to decide how to pay their direct reports. After the acquisition, the IT department would only provide support to departments using SAP-compatible software. Departments were given one year to adapt, and HR was no exception. In choosing new software, Kellogg gave priority to finding a system that could support their existing compensation system, which was designed to offer competitive pay and give managers maximum control over pay decisions for their direct reports. Kellogg eventually chose TotalComp to manage the monetary compensation for 6,000 of its salaried workers. Now compensation decisions are made and implemented like this: When managers decide on pay raises, they input their performance ratings of employees into the system, using the company's intranet. The system provides managers with data (generated by HR professionals) about the job's market rate and estimates of how difficult the person would be to replace given current labor market conditions. The system also specifies budgetary constraints. Managers make their initial pay recommendations, but before these are communicated to employees, HR professionals analyze them to determine whether there is any evidence of bias against women and minority employees. If problems are discovered, HR works with the manager to correct them. The recommendations are then analyzed against budget considerations. When all concerns have been satisfied, managers inform employees about their pay for the coming year.[1]

THE STRATEGIC IMPORTANCE OF TOTAL COMPENSATION

Like many other aspects of an organization's approach to managing human resources, total compensation can facilitate (or interfere with) achieving many different strategic objectives. Three objectives of particular importance are: (1) attracting and retaining the talent required for a sustainable competitive advantage, (2) focusing the energy of employees on implementing the organization's particular competitive strategy, and (3) improving productivity. By paying close attention to what their competitors are paying employees and monitoring the fairness of pay practices, Kellogg strives to pay wages and salaries that attract good employees and keep them satisfied. The company's centralized budgeting approach keeps labor costs under control. Together, these practices support the company's long-term objective of improving productivity.

ATTRACTING AND RETAINING TALENT

"To the extent that auto insurance is a commodity, our biggest differentiator is our people. We want the best people at every level of the company, and we pay at the top of the market."

Peter B. Lewis
Chair
Progressive Corporation

In conjunction with an organization's recruitment and selection efforts, a total compensation system provides pay that is sufficient to attract the right people at the right time for the right jobs and keep them motivated to perform those jobs to the best of their ability. Unless the total compensation program is perceived as internally fair and externally competitive, good employees are likely to leave.[2]

Pay fairness *refers to what people believe they deserve to be paid in relation to what others deserve to be paid.* People tend to determine what they and others deserve to be paid by comparing what they give to the organization with what they get out of the organization. If they regard the exchange as fair or equitable, they're likely to be satisfied. If they see it as unfair, they're likely to be dissatisfied.[3]

When assessing whether their pay is fair, employees often make judgments about whether their pay is equitable. They compare the ratio of their inputs and outcomes to the ratios of others doing similar work. *Inputs* are what an employee gives to the job (e.g., time, effort, education). *Outcomes* are what people get out of doing the job (e.g., the feelings of meaningfulness, promotions, pay).[4] An example of equity comparison is presented in Exhibit 9.1. It's a simple dollars-per-hour example to illustrate how the ratios work.

Ex 9.1   Comparisons That Influence Equity Perceptions

	Ratio Comparison	Perception
Equity	$\dfrac{\$50}{5 \text{ hrs. work}} = \dfrac{\$100}{10 \text{ hrs. work}} = \$10/\text{hr.}$ $\dfrac{\text{Outcomes (self)}}{\text{Inputs (self)}} = \dfrac{\text{Outcomes (other)}}{\text{Inputs (other)}}$	"I'm being treated fairly."
Inequity	$\left[\dfrac{\$50}{5 \text{ hrs. work}} = \$10/\text{hr.}\right] < \left[\dfrac{\$100}{5 \text{ hrs. work}} = \$20/\text{hr.}\right]$ $\dfrac{\text{Outcomes (self)}}{\text{Inputs (self)}} < \dfrac{\text{Outcomes (other)}}{\text{Inputs (other)}}$	"I'm getting less than I deserve for my efforts."
Inequity	$\left[\dfrac{\$50}{5 \text{ hrs. work}} = \$10/\text{hr.}\right] > \left[\dfrac{\$25}{5 \text{ hrs. work}} = \$5/\text{hr.}\right]$ $\dfrac{\text{Outcomes (self)}}{\text{Inputs (self)}} > \dfrac{\text{Outcomes (other)}}{\text{Inputs (other)}}$	"I'm getting more than I deserve."

In reality the ratios can be quite complex, involving all the elements of total compensation.

As a result of equity perceptions, an employee or even a team will feel fairly rewarded, underrewarded, or overrewarded. Feelings of being overrewarded are probably rare, but when they occur they have beneficial consequences for employers. Overrewarded employees tend to perform better in their jobs and are better members of the organization than employees who haven't been so well rewarded.[5] More typical are situations that result in employees feeling underrewarded.

High performers who feel that their pay is too low may leave the organization. As a result, the company loses their productive talents. If dissatisfied employees stay, they may react by withholding effort in order to restrict output or lower quality. Feelings of inequity often cause frustration, which may lead people to behave in hostile and aggressive ways. A store clerk may be hostile to customers. A factory worker may deliberately sabotage equipment. Unfortunately, such hostility can even lead to such drastic reactions as killing former colleagues and managers.[6]

Most employers understand the importance of pay fairness. But even when employers think they have succeeded in designing "fair" systems, employees may perceive inequities. Three culprits that detract from perceptions of fairness are low pay, pay secrecy, and executive compensation practices.

Low Pay.   When choosing where to work, job applicants consider many aspects of the total pay package: Some focus on the predictable, guaranteed level of pay; others focus on the maximum potential pay; still others focus on the less tangible aspects of total compensation.[7] Once hired, employees continue to evaluate these aspects of their pay, although perhaps with less vigilance. Regardless of what employees attend to when evaluating their pay, they will be dissatisfied if they judge the company's total pay policy to be less generous than that offered by competitors. Employees who are compensated above or on par with the market average are more likely to feel fairly paid than those who are paid below the going rate.

In the past, the issue of external equity—fairness relative to the external market—was typically framed as a simple question: "Should we pay at the market average—or above or below the market?" When a basic salary and a few benefits were what almost everyone received, this simple view made sense. In today's highly competitive environment, however, external equity has become more complex because companies creatively mix several forms of pay. For example, to support a high-volume strategy, sales representatives at one company may receive a low base salary ($30,000) with a high bonus potential ($60,000). They enjoy no job security and receive minimal benefits and services. Employees who focus on the base salary and benefits will perceive this as unfairly low pay. Another company may couple a higher base salary ($65,000) with merit pay increases averaging around 5%. Job security is good and the benefits offered are world-class. Employees who focus on the maximum direct monetary compensation and place little value on the generous benefits package will view this pay as being unfairly low. In the worst circumstances, they may attempt to even things out by stealing from the employer. A Kinko's employee described a typical scenario: "We rip them off anyway all the time. But we don't rip them off for money that I know of. Except for that one guy who got arrested—who was actually taking money. The way people steal is just constantly making posters for their kids and doing all that kind of stuff. It feels like a fringe benefit. Because it is a low-paying kind of endless job. So people do it all the time."[8]

Pay Secrecy. Perceived inequities sometimes occur because employees have inaccurate and/or incomplete information. Although it is illegal for employers to forbid employee discussions of pay,[9] keeping pay secret is the norm in many U.S. organizations.[10] According to organizational etiquette, asking others their salaries is generally considered gauche. In a study at DuPont, all employees were asked if the company should disclose more payroll information so that everyone would know everyone else's pay. Only 18% voted for an open pay system. Managers often favor pay secrecy, too. It makes their lives easier. Without knowledge of pay differentials, employees are less likely to confront supervisors about inequitable pay, so managers don't have to justify their actions.

Not all organizations keep pay a secret, however. At Whole Foods, a grocery retailer, employees are welcome to peruse a notebook that lists every employee's total annual compensation. The company acknowledges that not all employees like the system. According to the company's vice president of human resources, the policy of openness made some employees so uncomfortable that they left, while others decided against taking a job offer.[11] Nevertheless, Whole Foods believes it is easier to engender feelings of trust and fairness by being open about pay decisions rather than hiding behind a curtain of secrecy.

Short of full disclosure about pay, employers can minimize misperceptions by involving employees in pay system design. As discussed in Chapter

"Compensation remains a sacred cow. Business owners still worry about how their workers will react when they find out someone else in the same job makes more than they do."

Kevin Ruble
Managing Director
TranSolution

3, involving employees in decisions promotes acceptance of the decisions and establishes a sense of procedural justice.

A more radical approach to keeping employees satisfied is letting them set their own pay. This may sound far-fetched, but it is not as unusual as it may seem. Romac Industries, a pipe fitting plant, began using this approach more than 20 years ago. Employees request pay raises by completing a form that includes information about their current pay level, previous raise, requested raise, and reasons for thinking a raise is deserved. The requests are posted, along with photographs of the employees, for several working days. Then employees vote, and the majority rules.[12]

Executive Compensation.   During the past decade, employees at the middle and lower levels of organizations have watched the pay of those at the top rise rapidly at a time when increases in their own pay have been relatively modest. Moreover, the gap between those at the top and everyone else has been steadily increasing.[13] During the past 20 years, CEOs have seen their pay increase 514%, or 12 times the rate of inflation. During the same period, the federal minimum wage has increased only 36% and median household income has increased 43%. Even the stock market didn't keep pace with the rapid rise in CEO pay. On average, CEOs in the largest U.S. companies are paid $531 for every $1 paid to the average hourly employee.[14]

How do workers feel about such disparities? Based on activity at the AFL-CIO's website devoted to this topic, many are angry and resentful. Here are examples of how some employees have reacted to data about CEO pay:

"No raise for us little guys for three years while the management all got bonuses and 15% raises. Do you think they will still get the same quality work from the lower ranks?"

"I was laid off from a small but successful software company in the early '90s at the height of the recession. And over 200 [out of 1,000] other employees were also laid off [because] the company didn't want to post a losing quarter that would affect the stock price. The top five executives of the company each received a bonus that was more than my annual salary. Am I resentful? You bet."

"My personal rule is that if the exec is known to receive over one million a year—I will boycott their products, period."

Do workers also boycott these companies as potential places to work? Are they more likely to leave such organizations when other employment opportunities present themselves? The extent to which such feelings translate into decisions about where to work is unknown, but it seems likely that at least some members of the workforce would prefer to decline a job offer from a firm known to have large pay disparities. As the demand for labor strengthens, others may choose to leave their current employers and move to more egalitarian companies.[15]

Implementing the Business Strategy

Do you regard a smile and a "Thank you for shopping" from the cashier of the local store as examples of quality customer-oriented service? Many peo-

"We trust our employees to make decisions about everything else. Why not about their own compensation?"

Roger Sant
Chair Emeritus
AES Corporation

FAST FACT   The number of days a typical CEO has to work to earn an amount equal to a typical employee's yearly salary is 1.5.

ple do and are willing to pay more for the goods in stores that have sales-people who engage in these behaviors. As we have seen, selection practices, socialization, and training help ensure that employees are *able* to engage in courteous, friendly behaviors. Compensation systems provide the supporting structure that *motivates* employees to display these behaviors even under the most trying circumstances.

An effective compensation system enhances employees' feelings of satisfaction while at the same time encouraging the behaviors needed to implement the business strategy.[16] The role of compensation in implementing competitive strategies becomes especially clear when a company changes its strategy and when it acquires or merges with another company.

Changes in Strategy. Employers like General Electric, Motorola, Sears, and IBM have discovered that a compensation system can encourage employees to embrace organizational change. Instead of handing out automatic annual pay increases based on job title and seniority—a common practice in the old economy—these companies reward teamwork, measurable quality improvements, and the acquisition of new skills.

A decade ago, IBM began a major strategic change. Instead of designing systems and then trying to sell them, the new strategy called for designing customized systems and providing more business services. Once the new strategy was announced, the challenge was to find a way for employees to connect to this strategy. Day in and day out, what exactly were the implications of the new strategy for employees? Realizing that employees needed an answer to this question, IBM made significant changes in the design, administration, and communication of several aspects of its HRM system. The objectives were to:

> *"Total rewards are a collection of difficult, interrelated questions about a basic, fundamental way of managing a business and the people who create value."*
>
> Andrew Richter
> Director of Compensation
> IBM

a. Attract and retain the best talent
b. Change the culture and motivate the desired behaviors needed to implement the new strategy
c. Manage costs

One major change was to use skills or competencies as a partial basis for determining employees' base pay and their annual pay increases. IBM's new strategy required new skills. The new compensation system encouraged employees to develop those new skills, and rewarded them for doing so. Business success would also influence one's pay. This was a big change for employees who had grown accustomed to automatic salary increases. These changes were costly for IBM. Compensation as a percent of revenue grew tremendously. "It's a huge business decision and you have to work very tightly with the other areas to keep a handle on it," explained Andrew Richter, a director of compensation at IBM. But the cost increases were considered necessary as the company evolved into a knowledge-intensive service provider.[17]

Changing Structures. When P&G restructured in 1997, it began to shift away from 20 years of managing based on regional locations. For Procter & Gamble, the shift to a single global program for managing all expatriates was consistent with their globalization strategy. That year, it launched its Worldwide Expatriate System (WES), which is a global package of compensation, benefits, and relocation and related services. P&G now has one global policy that governs how all expatriates are treated. It has one pay sheet, one housing policy, one set of relocation premiums, and a single process for administering expatriates. The new system is administered from a central shared services unit located in Cincinnati and replaces a complex array of policies and practices that were previously under the control of regional directors. With the new approach, members of P&G's global workforce know that the company's expatriates are treated the same all around the world.[18]

Mergers and Acquisitions. When companies combine, their cultures often clash. Because compensation systems are so closely linked to company cultures, mergers and acquisitions almost always provoke changes in the compensation system of one or both of the companies involved. Differences in pension plans, health insurance coverage, paid vacations, and collective bargaining agreements all need to be managed.

As Exhibit 9.2 illustrates, four basic approaches can be taken when deciding how to merge the compensation plans of two firms: retain the separate plans; blend together some elements of each plan; create a totally new plan; or impose the system used by one company onto the entire new company.[19] If the intent is to operate the businesses as separate holdings within a corporate portfolio, then keeping the separate plans may be appropriate. Leaving the separate plans intact also makes sense as a short-term strategy if the long-term strategy involves selling off significant portions of the business. If the merging companies have similar strategies and cultures, then blending may be effective. When a merger or acquisition is the beginning of a major strategic shift for both companies, it may be appropriate to create a completely new system. Kellogg chose to impose its compensation practices (but not its software) onto the Keebler business because they had been specifically designed to support Kellogg's business strategy, which did not change after the Keebler acquisition.

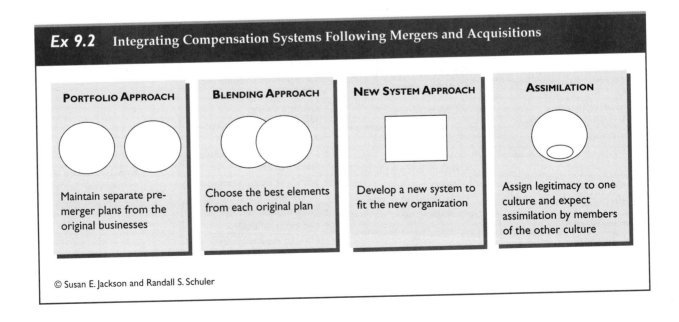

Ex 9.2   Integrating Compensation Systems Following Mergers and Acquisitions

PORTFOLIO APPROACH

Maintain separate pre-merger plans from the original businesses

BLENDING APPROACH

Choose the best elements from each original plan

NEW SYSTEM APPROACH

Develop a new system to fit the new organization

ASSIMILATION

Assign legitimacy to one culture and expect assimilation by members of the other culture

© Susan E. Jackson and Randall S. Schuler

Productivity Improvement.   Compensation practices influence productivity in numerous ways.[20] For example, compensation practices that link employees' pay to the company's financial performance can help focus employees' attention on finding new ways to reduce costs and increase revenues. At Lincoln Electric, production workers have an incentive system that rewards them for the number of products they assemble. As much as 40% of an employee's annual compensation reflects the quantity and quality of the employee's individual work.[21] When people are offered incentive pay, they may or may not work harder. But if the incentive plan is designed well, they will work smarter. Effective compensation practices motivate employees to spend their energy on those activities that are most important to the firm's success.

TOTAL COMPENSATION WITHIN THE INTEGRATED HRM SYSTEM

Exhibit 9.3 summarizes the major choices to be made when designing the total compensation system and shows how these fit within the total HRM

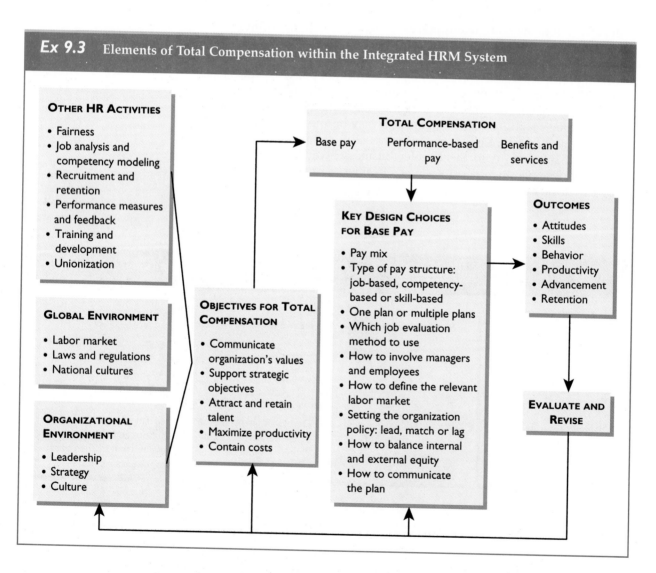

Ex 9.3   Elements of Total Compensation within the Integrated HRM System

system. This chapter explains how organizations development their overall compensation policy and the procedures typically used to set wages and salaries. Chapter 11 discusses the use of performance-based pay in organizations. Chapter 12 discusses the legally mandated and voluntary indirect compensation offered by employers that is commonly referred to as employee "benefits."

As the feature about Kellogg illustrated, companies are eager to link their compensation practices with their business needs and values. However, the description of Kellogg focused on managing only one element of that company's total compensation system—namely, direct monetary pay. At Kellogg and other companies, the **total compensation system** *includes a mix of both monetary and nonmonetary compensation; furthermore, monetary compensation includes money that is paid directly to employees as well as the value of additional benefits paid for by employers.*

FAST FACT

Labor costs account for two-thirds of the average company's expenses.

MONETARY AND NONMONETARY COMPENSATION

Monetary compensation *includes direct payments such as salary, wages, and bonuses, and indirect payments such as payments to cover the costs of private and public insurance plans.* **Nonmonetary compensation** *includes many forms of social and psychological rewards—recognition and respect from others, enjoyment from doing the job itself, opportunities for self development, and so on.* Clearly, both monetary and nonmonetary forms of compensation are important to most employees. Kathleen C. Gubanich, Managing Director of Human Resources at The Vanguard Group, put it this way: "People always want to be paid at a competitive rate. You always have to be clear that you'll be very competitive on pay and benefits. But at the end of the day, people come to and leave organizations not because of money. They stay because of a culture and a career opportunity. Because of the people they work with."[22] Nevertheless, people differ in the value they attach to these different types of compensation.[23]

Some differences in attitudes about pay appear to be due to societal values. Consider the findings shown in Exhibit 9.4. Notice that a majority opinion prevails within some countries: Most people in Mexico appear to value extra time over extra money. Most people in Russia appear to value extra

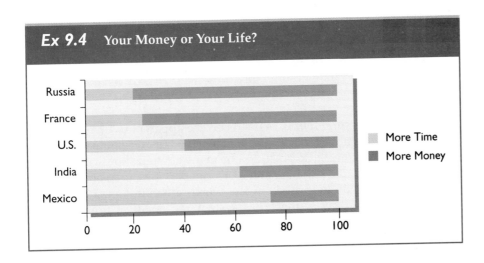

Ex 9.4   Your Money or Your Life?

money over extra time. In the United States, however, attitudes are more mixed. Although most people prefer more money, a large percentage of people would prefer having more time.[24]

OTHER HRM PRACTICES

The many elements of a total compensation system mean that significant effort is needed to ensure all of the elements are aligned with each other. It can be a challenge to design a system that achieves an appropriate balance between rewards based on individual, team, and organizational performance, for example. Added to the challenge of designing a total compensation system that is internally consistent is the challenge of designing a compensation system that is well integrated with other aspects of the total HRM system.

Recruitment and Retention.   As noted in Chapter 6, the monetary and nonmonetary compensation that an organization offers partly determines the number and quality of job applications received during recruitment. Once the best applicants have been selected, their decisions about whether to join the organization are likely to be influenced by the specific salary and bonus offers they receive.

Compensation practices also influence employees' decisions about whether to stay with their employers. At Cendant Mobility, a provider of global relocation services, employee turnover was above 30% annually before it introduced its Flexible Work Options (FWO) program. With FWO, employees are offered daily start- and end-work times, consolidated 4-day workweeks, and several combinations of on- and off-work days. Cendant Mobility also offers wellness programs, on-site flu shots, and educational programs on topics such as elder care and how to quit smoking. By introducing these new forms of nonmonetary compensation, the company reduced turnover to 9% and saved $8.6 million in recruitment and hiring costs.[25]

> **FAST FACT**
>
> Wal-Mart estimates that it costs $2,500 per worker to test, interview, and train a new hire.

Training and Development.   It should be apparent that applicants attach value to the training and development opportunities (e.g., tuition reimbursements, management development programs) offered by employers. While benefits such as tuition reimbursements can easily be quantified in monetary terms, many benefits related to development opportunities are a form of nonmonetary compensation. Compensation is linked to training and development in other ways as well. For example, employers who provide training to develop the skills they need can generally pay less to new hires compared to employers who hire only those who already have the needed skills.

Performance Measurement.   As will become apparent in Chapter 11, the effective use of incentive pay requires that it be tied to excellent performance measurement and feedback practices. In many organizations, poor alignment between the pay system and performance measurement result in employees feeling unmotivated. In the worst situations, poor alignment between these elements of the HRM system can result in unscrupulous, unethical, and illegal employee behaviors.

Developing an Approach to Total Compensation

THE EXTERNAL ENVIRONMENT

Perhaps more than any other aspect of the HRM system, compensation practices must be responsive to the external environment. Of particular importance are conditions in the external labor market. Especially when talent is scarce relative to demand, employers must devise a compensation system that enables them to attract and retain the people they need at a cost they can afford. Industry conditions also influence compensation practices. Of course, legal considerations and union contracts must also be taken into account, especially when setting base pay rates and when designing the benefits.

Labor Market Conditions. Labor market conditions affect the overall level of pay offered and the pay mix. The term **pay level** *refers to how a firm's overall monetary pay compares to that of other firms.* Is the value of the total pay package above what most others are offering, at about the same as the market, or below the market? Typically, the organizations of most interest for market comparison purposes are those competing for the same talent. If a company's pay level is too low, qualified labor won't work for the company. Thus, shortages in the labor market provide qualified workers the opportunity to negotiate better terms of employment.

Under conditions of low unemployment, demand for labor drives labor prices up. Then even burger flippers and java servers may be paid as much as 30 to 40% above the minimum wage.[26] High prices, in turn, attract more entrants to the market—if there are any left to enter! If employees' wage demands are too high, however, employers may react by hiring fewer people.[27] High wage demands push employers to seek alternatives. Introducing new technology that reduces the need for labor is one alternative. Raising prices for products and services is another, as is simply accepting smaller profit margins.[28]

Moving work abroad is another way employers respond to high compensation costs. As a reminder of the differing hourly compensation costs for production workers in several countries, refer back to Exhibit 2.7 in Chapter 2 (page 55).[29] When moving jobs abroad, wage levels, taxes, and productivity all need to be considered. In Germany, for example, the cost of labor and related taxes has been rising. In response, some German companies have moved production out of the country—including to the United States. Arend Oetker, an owner of a food company named Schwartau, explained his company's investment in Switzerland this way: "I am a German, and I want to keep employment here as much as possible. But the more the labor costs rise and the more that taxes rise, the more difficult it is to remain in Germany. No one can be astonished that unemployment is high."[30] The procedures employers use to estimate the labor prices of competitors are described later in this chapter, as are other issues related to decisions about how to set base pay levels.

The **pay mix** *in an organization's compensation system refers to the way compensation is distributed among all elements of total pay, including monetary versus nonmonetary elements.* Over the past several years, compensation systems have included relatively greater variety. Today, competitive pressures to keep costs down and improve productivity are causing many employers to keep wages and salaries low and link pay increases to gains in productivity. With a well-designed variable pay component, a company's labor costs do not increase unless the company can afford it.

Companies differ greatly in terms of the mix of pay components they offer employees. Furthermore, many companies offer a different mix to different groups of employees. This is illustrated in Exhibit 9.5, which shows the pay mixes found in the United States.[31]

Industry Conditions.   Among the many influences on an organization's compensation system is the life cycle stage of the industry. Compensation systems tend to differ for industries at different points in the life cycle. This point is illustrated in Exhibit 9.6.[32]

During an industry start-up phase, attracting key contributors and facilitating innovation are the key HR issues for companies. Risk is high, sales growth is slow, and earnings are low, so a company in that industry stage may offer base salary and benefits that are below the market. Counterbalancing these are broad-based short- and long-term incentives, designed to stimulate innovation and its associated rewards.[33]

During the growth stage, sales grow rapidly, with moderate increases in earnings. Key HR issues are recruitment and training to develop the human capital. Bonuses may be offered for innovation and sales growth, and stock options may be offered to encourage employees to think about the long-term growth of the company. For the entire high-tech industry, these dynamics were readily observable during the latter half of the 1990s.[34]

Industry life cycles have received wide attention as a heuristic device for designing compensation systems, but the concept has critics. More than one set of compensation policies may be appropriate for any given stage in the cycle. Furthermore, organizations often have more than one product, each at a different stage of development. This complexity may make it impossible to cleanly classify a firm and its compensation mix according to a particular cycle of development.[35]

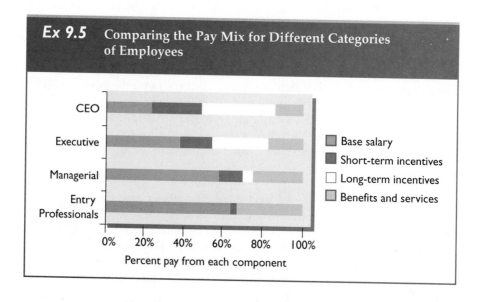

Ex 9.5   **Comparing the Pay Mix for Different Categories of Employees**

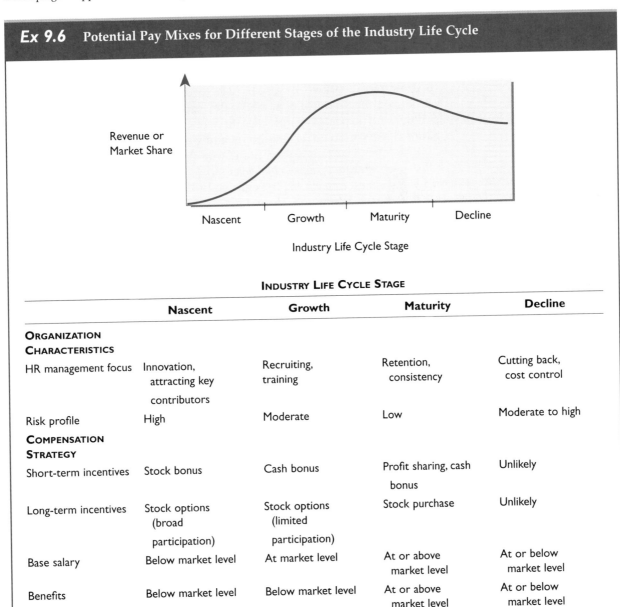

Ex 9.6 Potential Pay Mixes for Different Stages of the Industry Life Cycle

	INDUSTRY LIFE CYCLE STAGE			
	Nascent	**Growth**	**Maturity**	**Decline**
ORGANIZATION CHARACTERISTICS				
HR management focus	Innovation, attracting key contributors	Recruiting, training	Retention, consistency	Cutting back, cost control
Risk profile	High	Moderate	Low	Moderate to high
COMPENSATION STRATEGY				
Short-term incentives	Stock bonus	Cash bonus	Profit sharing, cash bonus	Unlikely
Long-term incentives	Stock options (broad participation)	Stock options (limited participation)	Stock purchase	Unlikely
Base salary	Below market level	At market level	At or above market level	At or below market level
Benefits	Below market level	Below market level	At or above market level	At or below market level

LEGAL CONSTRAINTS AND SOCIAL CONSIDERATIONS

Like other aspects of managing human resources, compensation activities are shaped by a plethora of laws and regulations, covering topics such as taxation, nondiscrimination, fair wages, a minimum wage, the protection of children, hardship pay for employees who work unusually long hours, and income security through pension and welfare benefits. A sociological analysis of all congressional bills introduced from 1951 to 1990 revealed that different visions of work and family have been dominant at different periods, reflecting the changing concerns of the labor market.[36] During the middle of the 20th century, barriers between work and family were considered normal and even desirable. Today, legislation such as the Family and Medical Leave

"It never dawned on me that there was a law against reaching a private agreement with someone over work."

Restaurant Owner
Wage Law Violator

Act encourages employers to remove such barriers and actively support employees' simultaneous involvement in the spheres of work and family.[37]

Significant changes in our view of what is the normal workweek have occurred, as well. A standard workweek now consists of five 8-hour days. In 1840, a typical workweek was six 13-hour days. In 1913, when Henry Ford introduced the 8-hour day at a $5-a-day minimum wage, most of his competitors still expected employees to work 60 hours a week. Eventually, national legislation governing hours and wages was passed.

The **Fair Labor Standards Act (FLSA)** *sets minimum wages, maximum hours, child labor standards, and overtime pay provisions for most employees.* First enacted in 1938, the FLSA (sometimes called the Wage and Hour Law) set the minimum wage at $0.25 an hour. In 2004, it was $5.35 an hour. Not every employee is guaranteed the minimum wage, however. Employers are allowed to pay lower wages to

> **FAST FACT**
>
> The worst industries for wage violations are eating and drinking establishments, apparel manufacturers, and heavy construction.

- learners in semiskilled occupations,
- apprentices in skilled occupations,
- messengers in firms engaged primarily in delivering letters and messages,
- handicapped persons working in sheltered workshops,
- students in certain establishments, and
- employees who receive more than $30 a month in tips (up to 40% of the minimum requirement may be covered by tips).[38]

To prevent abuses regarding children, the act prohibits minors under the age of 18 from working in hazardous occupations. For nonhazardous positions, the minimum age ranges from 14 to 16, depending on the type of work to be performed and whether the employer is the child's parent.[39] The number of hours per week minors are permitted to work ranges between 14 and 18.

The FLSA also establishes who is to be paid overtime for work and who is not. *Wage earners who are covered by the FLSA are called* **nonexempt employees.** These employees must be paid time-and-a-half for all work exceeding 40 hours a week. For nonexempt employees, essentially all work-related activities required by the employer must be compensated at the hourly rate or as overtime.[40] Furthermore, compensation must be in the form of direct pay. Employers may not use a barter system. If a restaurant owner asks employees to come in on their days off and help spruce up their workplace, it's not legal to compensate them by giving them a free pizza-and-beer party instead of overtime pay. Employers can't get around this requirement simply by claiming the work wasn't required. If an employer *permits* someone to work, they're obligated to pay for that work.[41]

> **FAST FACT**
>
> For employees who have "on-call" duty, the general rule is they do not have to be paid for the time they spend waiting if they can use that time the way they want to.

When the department store Sears Roebuck & Company implemented a new Six Sigma strategy, it sought to improve its efficiency by requiring product repair workers to obtain their daily assignments at 7:15 A.M. using a handheld computer. But the official start-time for their days was 8:00 A.M. The new practice allowed product repair workers to complete 16% more repairs at no cost to Sears. In a class action lawsuit that is not yet settled, employees claimed they should have been paid for 45 minutes overtime each day. Given what you know about the FLSA, who do you think is likely to prevail in this case—the product repair workers or their employer?[42]

Exempt employees *are not covered by the overtime and minimum wage provisions of the FLSA.* Executives, managers, professionals, administrators, and many other employees who are paid on a salary basis are exempt employees. To be considered exempt, salaried employees must be paid a fixed, predetermined salary, regardless of the precise number of hours they work in a given week. In addition, they must meet certain criteria regarding the content of their work. Managerial job content, for example, includes:

- undertaking management duties;
- directing the work of two or more employees;
- controlling or greatly influencing hiring, firing, and promotion decisions; and
- exercising discretion.

Professionals who do work that requires a college-level or postgraduate degree in a field of *specialized* study are exempt when the content of their work involves

a. doing work requiring knowledge acquired through specialized, prolonged training;
b. exercising discretion or judgment; and
c. doing work that is primarily intellectual and nonroutine.[43]

Job title alone is not a sufficient basis for treating these jobs as exempt. A comprehensive job analysis is necessary to document the activities required for exempt jobs.

In 2004 the criteria under which jobs are classified as being exempt were revised to recognize that more jobs are "jobs with responsibility." Under the new regulations, more jobs will be classified as exempt, and fewer workers will be eligible for overtime pay. The type of workers who are most likely to be adversely affected by the new regulations are low-level salaried workers who also have college degrees (e.g., a sous-chef) and some supervisory responsibility. Under the old rules, many such workers were more likely to be eligible for overtime pay. Under the new rules, they are likely to be classified as exempt.[44]

Failure to correctly classify employees as exempt or nonexempt can result in costly lawsuits. When 1,300 store managers joined together in a lawsuit against Radio Shack, they claimed that their jobs did not meet the criteria for exempt status and that, therefore, the company acted illegally when it denied them overtime pay. For Radio Shack, the cost of settling the lawsuit was $299 million. When 1,500 engineers claimed that Pacific Bell had illegally denied them overtime pay, the company spent $35 million to settle the claim.[45]

Living Wage Laws.   In addition to federal and state minimum wage laws, some employers are subject to so-called living wage laws. The city of Baltimore passed the first comprehensive living wage law in 1994. Although these laws affect only about 1% of all employees, they reflect a widespread social concern about the need to ensure that low-wage employees earn enough to live at a reasonable level of comfort. More than 80 jurisdictions have living wage laws that require some employers (e.g., those who have contracts with the local government) to pay minimum wages above federal and state levels. Some jurisdictions also specify higher minimum rates for workers who do not receive benefits. The objective of these laws is to bring the minimum wage paid to employees to a level that better reflects the actual cost of living in an area.[46]

Equal Pay Act. In 1963, the Fair Labor Standards Act was amended to include the Equal Pay Act. The **Equal Pay Act** *prohibits an employer from discriminating "between employees on the basis of sex by paying wages to employees . . . at a rate less than the rate at which he pays wages to employees of the opposite sex . . . for equal work on jobs the performance of which requires equal skill, effort and responsibility, and which are performed under similar working conditions."* For monitoring purposes, employers submit compensation data when they file EEO-1 reports (described in Chapter 6).

To establish a *prima facie* case of wage discrimination, the plaintiff needs to show that a disparity in pay exists for males and females performing substantially equal, but not necessarily identical, jobs. Four conditions can be used to legally defend unequal pay for equal work: the existence and use of a seniority system, a merit system, a system that measures earnings or quality of production, or a system based on any additional characteristic other than gender. If the employer can show the existence of one or more of these exceptions, a pay differential for males and females in similar jobs may be justified.

Boeing has been aware of pay disparities between its male and female employees for at least a decade. As described in the feature "Managing Diversity: Boeing's Nose Dive," many women at the company believe that Boeing has treated them unfairly by paying them less than men doing similar work.[47]

Pay Equity (Comparable Worth) Policies. **Pay equity policies** (sometimes referred to as comparable worth policies) *are a means of eliminating race, ethnicity, and gender as wage determinants within job categories and between job categories.* The principle of pay equity or comparable worth uses a more rigorous standard of fairness than what is required by the Equal Pay Act. Under this principle, the logic of "equal pay for equal work" is extended to "equal pay for comparable work." Comparable work may be very different in content and still be of equal value.

Many businesses pay women and men of color less than white males due to wage structures that retain historical biases and inconsistencies that are, in fact, discriminatory. To prevent such discrimination, several state and local governments have passed pay equity legislation. Similar federal legislation has been discussed by the U.S. Congress, but has not yet passed.[48]

Conducting a comprehensive audit of all aspects of a total compensation system is the first step in implementing a pay equity policy. The audit scrutinizes each pay element for possible evidence of pay inequities that are based on gender and/or ethnicity. Pay equity audits go beyond asking whether men and women in the same jobs are paid the same and whether whites and people of color in the same job are paid the same. They consider

FAST FACT

Between 1995 and 2000, the gap in pay for full-time male and female managers increased as follows for each dollar earned (male managers always earned more):

21¢ in arts and entertainment

13¢ in communications

8¢ in finance, insurance, and real estate

4¢ in retail trade

Managing Diversity

Boeing's Nose Dive

In 1998, the Department of Labor's audit of Boeing's pay data showed that men were paid more than women working in the same jobs. The lawsuit that followed was brought on behalf of the 28,000 women who may have been hurt by discriminatory pay practices. The lawsuit had not been settled at the time of this writing, but estimates of the potential cost of a settlement exceed $1 billion. Boeing maintains that it is innocent of any wrongdoing, but news reports tell a different story. According to one report, Boeing documents reveal that the company had been aware of pay disparities for several years. In the 1990s, the company began to allocate $10 million per year to address the disparities, although their analysis indicated that they needed to allocate $30 million annually to resolve the problem. In 1999, the OFCCP settled a claim against Boeing for $4.5 million. At the time, some insiders had estimated

the company's liability might be as much as $125 million. In a court testimony, one HR professional from the company acknowledged that she knew Boeing paid women less than men for the same work, but she did not realize the magnitude of the problem. In other testimony, Boeing's compensation manager testified that he had created a "stealth" compensation plan in an effort to minimize the company's legal risk. The plan was designed to gradually eliminate gender-based pay disparities in a way that would be hidden from the managers who made salary decisions, and from employees who would receive the pay adjustments. Given the potential cost of addressing their compensation problems, it is not surprising that Boeing attempted to keep its problems hidden. In the long run, they may have been better off being more both open with their employees and more aggressive in promoting pay fairness.

whether women and people of color earn approximately what men and whites earn, even if they work in jobs with different content. If occupational segregation has resulted in women and people of color working in lower-paying jobs, the audit would raise the question of whether those jobs really are of less value to the organization. If the jobs require similar education, experience, and competencies, then the pay differences may be due to historical patterns of pay discrimination rather than differences in the true worth of the lower-paid jobs.

When a pay equity audit uncovers apparently discriminatory pay practices, a plan should be developed to correct the problems. The cost of pay equity adjustments usually has been between 2 and 5% of payroll. Following the lead of public employers, many private-sector businesses incorporate pay equity analyses in their annual budget proposals.

The Organization Environment

The organizational environment also plays a role in shaping the design of a total compensation system. Strategy, size, and corporate culture all combine to shape each organization's specific approach to compensation.

Strategy. As we have already explained, an organization's strategic objectives often have important implications for the design of its compensation system. You have read how Kellogg designed its compensation practices to support the company's strategic objectives, and how IBM's strategic change affected that company's pay plan. The detailed description of Lincoln Electric's compensation system, described in the case at the end of this book, provides another example. Additional examples of how business strategies influence the design of a total compensation system will be provided in this chapter as well as in Chapters 11 and 12.

Size. Small organizations typically offer less direct compensation than larger organizations. Exhibit 9.7 illustrates how the pay of engineers in influenced by company size. Similar patterns can be found for most other types of jobs.[49] Despite the fact that employees in small organizations generally earn lower wages and salaries, employees working in smaller organizations typically report being more satisfied. Presumably, employees in smaller organizations are happier because they receive better nonmonetary compensation.

Corporate Culture. The culture of the company and the preferences of top management also have a significant impact on many aspects of a company's total compensation. A comparison of Wal-Mart's Sam's Club and Costco, a major competitor, illustrates the point. Both companies seek to offer goods at very low cost. But the two companies have very different approaches to the way they manage employees as they strive to implement a similar business strategy. As Exhibit 9.8 shows, Costco offers relatively generous compensation in order to motivate and retain good workers. Wal-Mart pays workers much less and accepts in return a much higher rate of employee turnover. Given the wages shown in Exhibit 9.8, it is easy to understand why turnover rates are so much higher at Wal-Mart. But many people might be surprised to learn that Costco's labor costs as a percentage of sales are actually lower than Wal-Mart's. As a consequence, Costco is also more profitable.[50]

"Paying your employees well is not only the right thing to do, it makes for good business."

James D. Sinegal
CEO
Costco

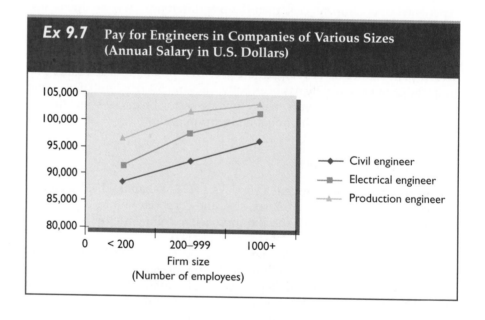

Ex 9.7   Pay for Engineers in Companies of Various Sizes (Annual Salary in U.S. Dollars)

Ex 9.8 Comparison of Compensation at Costco and Wal-Mart

	COSTCO	WAL-MART
PAY ELEMENTS		
• Average hourly wage	$15.97	$11.52 (excluding 25% of work force that are part-timers)
• Annual health costs per worker	$15,735	$3,500
• Annual retirement cost per worker	$1,330	$747
RESULTS		
• Annual employee turnover	6%	21%
• Sales per square foot	$795	$516
• Profits per employee	$13,647	$11,039

THE HR TRIAD

Effective compensation systems align the needs and characteristics of the organization with the motivation and behaviors of employees, and ultimately address the concerns of both. The coordinated efforts of HR professionals, managers, and all other employees are needed to design and implement an effective compensation system. The roles and responsibilities of managers, employees, and HR professionals are summarized in "The HR Triad: Roles and Responsibilities for Total Compensation."

HR PROFESSIONALS

The many roles and responsibilities of HR professionals will become apparent in this and other chapters as we describe the details of total compensation. In general, however, HR professionals take primary responsibility for ensuring the legality and fairness of compensation practices. They also take the lead on a variety of technical aspects of compensation practices, and they coordinate the involvement of managers and employees. Finally, HR professionals should ensure that the compensation system is communicated and understood by everyone who is affected it.

The HR Triad

Roles and Responsibilities for Total Compensation

LINE MANAGERS	HR PROFESSIONALS	EMPLOYEES
• Attend training programs and stay current on legal issues relevant to pay practices.	• Ensure all policies and practices are consistent with legal requirements.	• Take responsibility for understanding the total compensation system.
• Work with HR professionals to ensure alignment of pay system with strategic business objectives.	• With line managers, ensure alignment of pay system with strategic business objectives.	• May participate in designing new pay systems as your employer's strategic objectives change.
• Work with employees to ensure pay system satisfies and motivates them.	• Assess employees' preferences and reactions to pay systematically and regularly.	• Participate in surveys designed to assess pay preferences and pay satisfaction.
• Participate in designing and conducting job evaluations.	• Design processes for job evaluation to involve line managers and job incumbents (employees).	• May participate in conducting job evaluation of own job.
• Communicate pay system principles and abide by them.	• Work with line managers to communicate pay system.	• May provide input into pay decisions for others.
• Fairly administer all components of compensation.	• Work closely with line managers to finalize pay decisions.	• May register complaints about fairness of pay.

MANAGERS

Managers often participate in the design of the compensation system, and they always participate in implementing it. At Kellogg, line managers and HR professionals work hand-in-hand to ensure that pay decisions reflect the supervising managers' performance evaluations of their employees while also respecting budgetary concerns and avoiding unintentional discrimination. To fully understand a compensation system, managers need to know more than just how much the people they supervise are paid. They should also understand how base pay rates are established (explained later in this chapter), the rationale for any incentives that are part of the total pay package (see Chapter 11), and details of the benefits and services offered to employees (see Chapter 12).

According to one recent study, the gap between what managers should know about compensation and what they actually know is significant. Some of the findings from the study are summarized in Exhibit 9.9. The managers may not be to blame for this knowledge gap. The study also found that only about 1 out of 6 employers provided any training at all to teach managers about the company's compensation plan. When training was provided, the most common topics were minimum wage laws and details about pay rates for new hires.

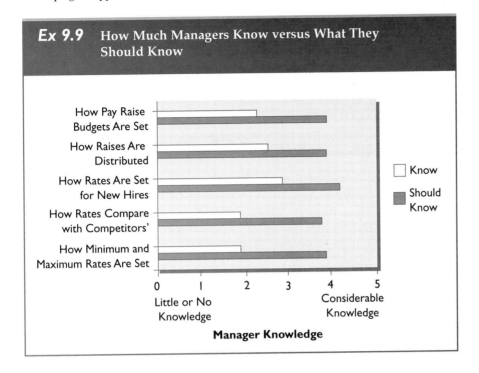

Ex 9.9 How Much Managers Know versus What They Should Know

EMPLOYEES

Given that managers often do not understand the compensation system, it is no surprise that most other employees are in the dark too. Results from two recent surveys indicated that only about 1 out of 3 employees understand how their pay is determined. The research also showed that employee satisfaction was substantially higher among employees who felt they understood the company's pay system.[51]

If designed and implemented well, compensation policies and practices encourage and reward desired employee behaviors while at the same time treating employees fairly. To achieve these goals, many companies actively involve employees in the design of new compensation systems. Employee participation is especially important as a means for ensuring that the diverse needs of all employees are met. Involving employees at all organizational levels and in all job types takes longer, but the investment seems to pay off. Several studies show that plans designed by a task force that includes employees produce both higher satisfaction and better performance.[52]

PAY STRUCTURES FOR BASE SALARY AND WAGE RATES

The remainder of this chapter describes the procedures that organizations typically use to establish a structure that governs the salaries and wages earned by employees. The **pay structure** *combines job evaluation information and information about market pay rates in order to establish a policy that governs the base pay received by employees.* **Base pay** *refers to the wage or salary an employee receives, exclusive of any incentive pay or benefits.*

We begin by describing job evaluation procedures that are used to establish the relative organizational value of jobs—that is, how much is each job worth relative to other jobs in the organization. Next, we describe procedures used to assess the market pay rates for jobs—that is, what do other employers typically pay to people holding similar jobs. Finally, we describe how information about the organizational value of jobs and the market prices typically paid for similar work are used to develop the organization's internal pay structure.

ESTABLISHING THE INTERNAL VALUE OF JOBS

In most organizations, the primary determinant of one's base pay is the job one holds. The value of a job may be based on many factors, including the level of knowledge required, the responsibilities associated with the job or the competencies required for the job. In general, jobs that are more important to the organization are worth more and so employees in those jobs receive higher pay. Internal worth reflects a job's importance or its contribution to the overall attainment of organizational objectives.

OBJECTIVES OF JOB EVALUATION

Job evaluation *is a procedure for establishing the relative internal worth of jobs.* By design, job evaluation focuses internally and does not take into account market forces or individual performance. Job evaluation is closely related to job analysis, but they are not identical. As explained in Chapter 5, job analysis provides a description of job content: what tasks are performed, what are the responsibilities of the job, and what competencies are required? Obtaining this information is an essential prior step to job evaluation. Job evaluation then asks, "What is the relative *value* of jobs with various contents and responsibilities involving the use of various competencies?" By tying wages and salaries to job evaluation results, employers seek to create perceptions of **internal equity**—*that is, employees should feel that they are paid fairly compared to others in the same organization, given the contributions that they and others make to the organization.*

As with any administrative procedure, job evaluation invites give and take. Consensus building is often required among stakeholders (the job holders, managers, HR professionals, union officials) to resolve conflicts that inevitably arise about the relative worth of jobs. The use of group judgments throughout the job evaluation process helps ensure that these conflicts are addressed, producing a compensation system that is congruent with organizational values and strategic objectives and not based solely on external market valuations of worth.[53]

The three major approaches to establishing the value of jobs are: ranking, job classification, and the point factor rating method. Each of these conventional job evaluation methods focuses on the job as the unit of interest. In a **job-based pay structure,** *the pay people receive is determined primarily by the job they hold.* Some methods evaluate the whole job, whereas others evaluate components of jobs using compensable factors.

In recent years, more and more organizations have adopted competency-based and skill-based approaches to designing their pay structures. These alternative methods are also discussed briefly in this chapter.

Job Ranking Method

The simplest approach to job evaluation is the **job ranking method,** *which involves simply placing jobs into a rank order according to the perceived overall value or importance of the job.* The job ranking method is convenient when only a few jobs need to be evaluated and when one person is familiar with them all. As the number of jobs increases, it becomes less likely that one person will know them all well enough to rank-order them. As the number of jobs to be ranked increases, detailed job analysis information becomes more important and input is more likely to be sought from several members of a committee.

Job Classification Method

The **job classification method** *is similar to the job ranking method, except that it first groups jobs into a smaller set of classifications based on the job descriptions, and then ranks the jobs that are found within each classification.* Jobs classified as being similar are usually referred to as being in the same pay grade.

After the grades are established, they can be rank-ordered. Jobs within the same grade are assigned the same value. Classification rules specify the kinds and levels of responsibilities assigned to jobs in each grade, the difficulty of the work performed, and the required employee qualifications. The description of a grade is general enough that several jobs can be slotted into the grade. A small company might have only two pay grades—one for managerial employees and another for everyone else. As the company grows and become more complex, it is likely to increase the number of pay grades it uses. For example, it might have one grade for all managerial jobs, one for professionals doing technical work, one for service providers, and one for all other support staff.

An advantage of the job classification method is that it can be applied to a large number and a wide variety of jobs. As the number and variety of jobs increase, however, the classification process becomes more subjective. This is particularly true when employees work at several locations and in jobs that have the same title but not the same job content. In such cases, it's difficult to attend to the true content of each job, so job evaluators tend to rely on the job title for making a job classification.[54] Employees in these jobs may be more attuned than their managers to differences in the contents of jobs with similar titles, which is a good reason to involve them in the job classification process.

Point Factor Rating Method

As Exhibit 9.10 shows, the most widely used method of job evaluation is the point factor rating method.[55] The **point factor rating method** *uses a sophisticated system of points to assign values to jobs.* When you read about this method, it may appear to be a very objective approach to valuing jobs, but like other job evaluation plans, the point factor rating method involves subjective judgments. Bias or subjectivity can enter at each of the first four steps in the process, which are:

a. selecting compensable factors to use in rating jobs,
b. assigning weights to the compensable factors,
c. defining factor degrees, and
d. establishing the degree of each factor present in a job.

Only the fifth and final step, which involves calculating the final point values, is truly objective.

STEP 1: Select Compensable Factors

Compensable factors *are the dimensions of work that an organization chooses to use when establishing the relative value of jobs.* When selecting compensable factors, employers can choose either to use a standardized off-the-shelf system or they may develop their own customized set of factors. Regardless of their specific approach, the objective for employers is to ensure that the jobs that receive the highest values involve tasks and responsibilities that the organization considers most important.

Standardized Factors. *The most widely used standardized point factor rating method is the* **Hay Guide Chart-Profile,** which was developed by a consulting company now called the Hay Group. The Hay approach has been particularly popular for evaluating executive, managerial, and professional positions, but it's also widely used for technical, clerical, and manufacturing positions.

The original Hay Guide Chart-Profile method relies on three primary compensable factors: problem solving, know-how, and accountability. Point values are determined for each job, using the three factors. According to the Hay Group, a major advantage of this system has been its wide acceptance and usage. Because organizations worldwide use the system, Hay can provide clients with comparative pay data by industry or locale. Another advantage of the system is that it has been legally challenged and found acceptable by the courts.

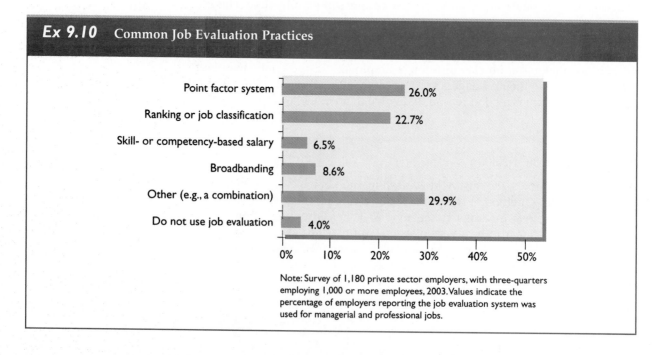

Ex 9.10   Common Job Evaluation Practices

Practice	Percentage
Point factor system	26.0%
Ranking or job classification	22.7%
Skill- or competency-based salary	6.5%
Broadbanding	8.6%
Other (e.g., a combination)	29.9%
Do not use job evaluation	4.0%

Note: Survey of 1,180 private sector employers, with three-quarters employing 1,000 or more employees, 2003. Values indicate the percentage of employers reporting the job evaluation system was used for managerial and professional jobs.

The Hay Guide Chart-Profile Method, like any standardized system, may not reflect a particular organization's true values, however. Thus, each organization needs to consider whether the factors of problem solving, know-how, and accountability are truly congruent with the organization's values. In recognition of the idea that different companies are likely to value different aspects of a job, Hay also works with companies to create tailored point systems that fit specific organizations. The feature "Managing Change: Bayer's New Pay System" describes why that firm switched from the standard Hay system to a custom-designed approach.

Custom-Designed Factors.   In the example of Bayer, selecting new compensable factors to use when setting base pay rates was a key strategic decision. Bayer selected new compensable factors to use in valuing jobs in an effort to improve the alignment of their pay system with their strategic objectives. To replace the standard factors from the original Hay methods, they chose the following compensable factors and defined them:

Improvement Opportunity | How much opportunity is there for people in this job to improve performance?

Contribution | How strong are the requirements for people in this job to achieve results?

Capability | What are the total proficiencies and competencies required in the job? Three categories were considered:
- Expertise and complexity
- Leadership and integration
- Relationship-building skills

Managing Change

Bayer's New Pay System

Bayer Corporation is a Pittsburgh-based subsidiary of the German firm named Bayer Group AG.[56] Today Bayer Group is one corporation with four major businesses, but back in 1991, it was three separate operating companies: a chemical producer called Mobay Chemical Corp.; a healthcare organization called Miles, Inc.; and an imaging company called Agfa. Prior to the merger of the three companies, jobs at Mobay had been relatively unstructured. Miles and Agfa had each used the Hay Guide-Chart Profile Method. But after the merger, managers grew dissatisfied because they felt the old system didn't reflect the new business values in the merged companies. The old system was oriented toward functional and hierarchical values. People often felt that jobs were valued according to the degrees and credentials required for the job rather than their contribution and the way those degrees and credentials were used.

Another problem with the old system was that responsibility was assessed according to the size of one's budget and one's staff.

The Job Advisory Committee had to make a choice: They had to choose a completely new method for evaluating jobs *or* revise the content in the old Hay Guide-Charts. They chose the latter alternative. The new job evaluation system used the following dimensions: Improvement Opportunity; Contribution; and Capability. There is one pay system that values all work using the same dimensions, regardless of whether that work involves health care, chemicals, or imaging technology. This new job evaluation system is used throughout the Bayer Group. Having a single system helps managers and employees alike because it facilitates easy cross-business transfers and promotions.[57]

STEP 2: Assign Factor Weights

Regardless of whether standard or customized factors are used, the next step in valuing jobs involves assigning relative weights to the factors. The weights enable the system to allocate more points to factors that are most important to the company's success. For example, Bayer may wish to give more weight to jobs in which people can make a greater contribution to the firm's performance, while giving less weight to the competencies needed to perform a job. Thus they might assign the weights of 50, 25, and 25 to the three factors listed above. These weights are reflected in the point system. A consequence of this decision might be that key sales jobs with few educational requirements would be assigned more points than some corporate staff positions that require formal degrees and certification.

To further illustrate the use of points and weights, consider the point system presented in Exhibit 9.11. It has six compensable factors. The total maximum number of points that can be assigned to a job using this system is 1,000, and the minimum is 225. Factor weights are built into the points, which makes the system easier for managers to use. The maximum points assigned to the factors can easily be translated into weights, however. To

---

Ex 9.11	**Example of a Compensable Factor and Related Degree Statements**

PART A: SAMPLE POINT EVALUATION SYSTEM

COMPENSABLE FACTOR	FIRST DEGREE	SECOND DEGREE	THIRD DEGREE	FOURTH DEGREE	FIFTH DEGREE
1. Job knowledge	50	100	150	200	NA
2. Problem solving	50	100	150	205	260
3. Impact	60	120	180	240	NA
4. Working conditions	10	30	50	NA	NA
5. Supervision needed	25	50	75	100	NA
6. Supervision given	30	60	90	120	150

Note: NA = Not Applicable, which means that this degree level is not used for the relevant compensable factor.

PART B: EXAMPLE OF A COMPENSABLE FACTOR AND RELATED DEGREE STATEMENTS

PROBLEM SOLVING

This factor examines the types of problems dealt with in your job. Indicate the one level that is most representative of most of your job responsibilities.

Degree 1: Actions are performed in a set order according to written or verbal instructions. Problems are referred to a supervisor.

Degree 2: Routine problems are solved and various choices are made regarding the order in which the work is performed, within standard practices. Information may be obtained from various sources.

Degree 3: Various problems are solved that require general knowledge of company policies and procedures applicable within own area of responsibility. Decisions are made based on a choice from established alternatives. Actions are expected to be within standards and established procedures.

Degree 4: Analytical judgment, initiative, or innovation is required in dealing with complex problems or situations. Evaluation is not easy because there is little precedent or information may be incomplete.

Degree 5: Complex tasks involving new or constantly changing problems or situations are planned, delegated, coordinated, or implemented, or any combination of these. Tasks involve the development of new technologies, programs, or projects. Actions are limited only by company policies and budgets.

obtain the factor weights, simply divide the maximum points for each factor by the total points possible (1,000). This yields the following weights for factors 1 to 6, respectively: 20%, 26%, 24%, 5%, 10%, and 15%.

STEP 3: Define Factor Degrees

Once factors are chosen and weighted, the next step is to construct scales reflecting the different degrees within each factor. Exhibit 9.11 also shows descriptions for five degrees of problem solving. Notice that each degree is anchored by a description of the typical tasks and behaviors associated with that degree.

STEP 4: Establish the Degree of Each Factor Present in Each Job

Steps 1 through 3 focused on designing the point system to be used to establish the value of jobs. In step 4, the point system is put to use. Each job is evaluated using the organization's point system.

Typically, a compensation committee is chosen to assess the degree of each factor present in each job. The committee usually includes managers, union officials (if appropriate), and workers from various job families. Committee members must be trained in the use of the job evaluation process. They begin by evaluating each job independently. Each committee member determines the degree level for each factor for each job, based on job descriptions and other job analysis information. Then, committee members usually discuss their evaluations, and debate continues until consensus is reached. At the end of the process, each job has been assigned degree values for each compensable factor.

STEP 5: Calculate Job Values

The final step in using the point factor rating method is to add up the points for each job. Software programs used for job evaluation usually do this automatically.

COMPETENCY-BASED JOB EVALUATION

As Chapter 5 explained, when organizations analyze jobs, they can focus on the tasks and responsibilities required to do the job, and/or they can emphasize the competencies required for people to perform the job. For a variety of reasons, many organizations have been moving to competency-based HR systems. The compensation plan is one aspect of the HR system that may reflect this shift. **Competency-based job evaluation** *keeps the focus on the job, but the emphasis is on the competencies needed to perform the job rather than the job duties.* The alterations Bayer made to the Hay point system involved a partial shift toward the competency-based job evaluation method for assigning points to jobs. In Bayer's new system, points assigned for Improvement Opportunity and Contribution reflect job activities. The points assigned for Capability reflect competencies.

GlaxoSmithKline began shifting to a competency-based organization in the mid-1990s. The first unit to make the change was Pharm Tech—a small unit that employed about 400 scientists and support staff in the United States and the United Kingdom. Like many organizations, Pharm Tech had just replaced its old functional structure with process-driven teams. In the old culture, career advancement meant moving up the hierarchy within one's functional area. In the new organization, career advancement was conceptualized as moving through four stages. To move through the four stages, employees needed to progress through jobs that required increasing levels of seven key competencies. These seven competencies, identified as central to Pharm Tech's business strategy and culture, are

- innovation,
- teamwork,
- communication,
- use of resources,
- decision making/perspective,
- customer satisfaction, and
- technical ability.

At career stage 1, the work being performed requires relatively low levels of these competencies. At career stage 2, higher levels of competencies are required by the work, and so on. By categorizing jobs according to their fit with these four career stages, Pharm Tech structured its jobs into four broad competency bands. Salaries were tied to these four bands.[58]

Companies often adopt competency-based salary bands because they promote individual development and growth through lateral moves in the organization. Growth through lateral moves is consistent with flatter, team-based structures. This approach does have some drawbacks, however. According to a study by Hewitt and Associates, an HR consulting firm, broad salary bands may meet stiff cultural resistance in many countries. In Brazil, for example, status symbols and titles that differentiate people according to their status are highly valued forms of recognition. Similarly, in India, work often is organized hierarchically. Promotions up through the hierarchy are a major form of reward and recognition for employee loyalty. People typically expect promotions every three or four years. In Singapore, people depend heavily on clear structures and rules as guides to behavior. In contrast, competency-based broadbanding was developed to promote flexibility. It eschews rigid rules, and thus may be more difficult for people in places like Singapore to understand and accept.[59]

Within the United States, the corporate cultures of many organizations reflect some of these same cultural values—they're still hierarchical, bureaucratic, and rule-driven. When companies with such corporate cultures attempt to introduce broad competency-based salary bands, the effort may ultimately fail.[60]

SINGLE PLAN VERSUS MULTIPLE PLANS

Traditionally, organizations have used different job evaluation plans for different job families (e.g., clerical, skilled craft, and professional). This approach assumes that the work content of jobs in different families is too diverse to be captured by one plan. For example, manufacturing jobs may vary in terms of working conditions and physical effort, so these factors should be used in setting pay for those jobs. Professional jobs usually vary in terms of technical skills and knowledge, but not working conditions and physical effort. Thus, pay for professional jobs should be based on the degree of skill and knowledge required. Proponents of multiple plans contend that these differences require the use of different job evaluation systems for different job families.

From a strategic perspective, using multiple systems is incongruent with the objective of communicating a coherent message about what the organization values. If the strategy is to focus on customers, it may be logical to use potential for affecting customers as a variable to determine the relative worth of *all* jobs within the company. If the strategy is to provide excellent quality products, it may be logical to assess the degree to which *all* jobs contribute to the quality of products produced.

Also, the use of a single system for valuing all jobs has been proposed as a partial solution to the problem of sex-based inequities. Proponents of pay equity assert that only if jobs are evaluated using the same criteria can the relative value of all jobs be fairly determined. When separate plans are used, it is much easier to discriminate against specific families of jobs (e.g., clerical versus skilled) because direct comparisons of segregated jobs can be avoided.

Developing a firm-specific job evaluation system with universal variables selected in accordance with the company's strategy and culture is clearly more difficult than adopting off-the-shelf job evaluation systems developed for specific occupational groups. Nevertheless, companies such as Cisco and Hewlett-Packard have concluded that the extra effort of developing a tailored system pays off. These companies use a core set of factors to evaluate all jobs, and they supplement this with another set of factors that are unique to particular occupational groups.

SKILL-BASED PAY

As just described, competency-based job evaluation systems begin to shift the focus of pay systems toward the competencies of employees. Skill-based pay is an even more radical approach to paying people according to their competencies. **Skill-based pay** *rewards employees for the range, depth, and types of skills they're capable of using, regardless of whether the job they currently hold requires the use of those skills.* This is a very different philosophy from the conventional job-based approaches. It moves the compensation of workers toward the approaches used to evaluate many types of professionals.[61]

FAST FACT Skill-based pay is more likely to be used for manufacturing jobs; it's seldom used for service jobs.

Companies using skill-based pay determine people's pay by measuring their competencies directly. With skill-based pay, the question asked is *not*, "What level of competency is required to perform your job?" The relevant question becomes, "At what competency level *can* an employee perform?"

Skill-based pay is premised on the assumption that a person who can do more different tasks or who knows more is of greater value and should be paid according to capabilities, not according to job assignment. With skill-based pay, pay goes up only after the worker demonstrates an ability to perform specific competencies at specific levels of difficulty. For a machine operator, the relevant skills might include an assembly task, a material handling and inventory task, and maintenance tasks. Supervisors might demonstrate increasing skills and knowledge in job domains such as budget planning and analysis, employee performance management, and developing client relationships.[62]

Skill-based pay creates an environment that facilitates worker rotation. This may reduce absenteeism and may ease job assignment pressures for management. Because workers are motivated to learn higher-level skills, they will likely be paid more than the job evaluation rate of the specific jobs to which they're assigned. However, overall labor costs may be lower owing to enhanced workforce flexibility and productivity.[63]

USING EXTERNAL MARKET RATES TO SET PAY LEVELS

An effective compensation system must take into account the realities of the external labor market. Allowing people to negotiate their pay is one way to do this. But even when managers negotiate pay with people they are trying to hire or retain, they usually do so within a system that imposes some constraints. These constraints are defined by the pay structure. **External equity** *exists when employees feel they are being paid fairly relative to what people in similar jobs (or with similar competencies) are paid by other employers.* Achieving external equity involves three more steps:

    a.   determining external market rates,
    b.   establishing the market pay policy, and
    c.   setting the organization pay policy.

Conduct Survey to Assess External Market Rates

A **compensation survey** *is used by employers to obtain data about market pay rates.* Compensation surveys are usually conducted by consulting firms, which sell the results to employers. This removes from employers the need to ask each other about their pay rates. To make use of data from a compensation survey, an organization needs to identify the relevant market and select appropriate benchmarks.

Relevant Labor Market. Using survey data requires defining the relevant labor market.[64] (Recall that in Chapter 6, we discussed the concept of relevant labor and its role in recruitment.) When establishing pay policies, three variables are commonly used to define the relevant labor market: the occupation or skill required, the geographic location (the distance from which applicants would be willing to relocate or commute), and the other employers competing for labor. The relevant geographic labor market for a vice president of sales for Microsoft Corporation may be the entire United States. The relevant geographic labor market for an accounts receivable clerk may be the Greater Seattle area. In global companies, the relevant labor market for some jobs is the entire world.

    Exhibit 9.12 shows how the costs of labor vary with the United States. For the job shown, the median pay in the United States is $30,000. In San Francisco, California, this job is paid $36,750, while in Little Rock, Arkansas, this job is paid $25,500.

> **FAST FACT**
>
> The cost of living in San Francisco is 31% higher than the national average.

Industry differences also may become evident in definitions of the relevant labor market. If industry-specific knowledge and experience is important, an employer may consider the relevant labor market to be defined by other employers in the same industry. Exhibit 9.13 illustrates industry effects on the total cash compensation for selected jobs.[65]

Benchmark Jobs. In order to interpret market survey data, benchmark jobs must be identified. Traditionally, **benchmark jobs** *are jobs commonly*

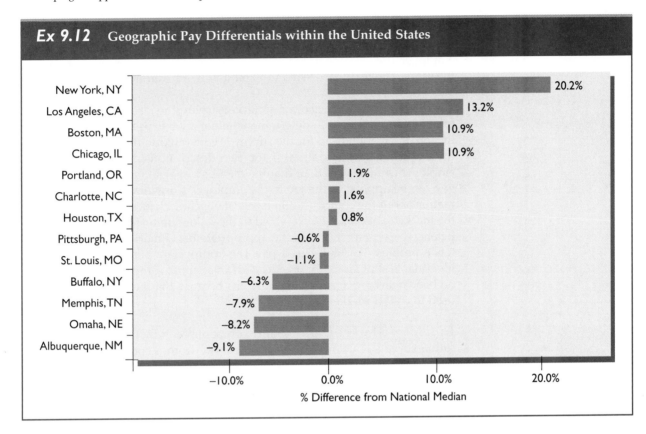

Ex 9.12 Geographic Pay Differentials within the United States

New York, NY	20.2%
Los Angeles, CA	13.2%
Boston, MA	10.9%
Chicago, IL	10.9%
Portland, OR	1.9%
Charlotte, NC	1.6%
Houston, TX	0.8%
Pittsburgh, PA	−0.6%
St. Louis, MO	−1.1%
Buffalo, NY	−6.3%
Memphis, TN	−7.9%
Omaha, NE	−8.2%
Albuquerque, NM	−9.1%

% Difference from National Median

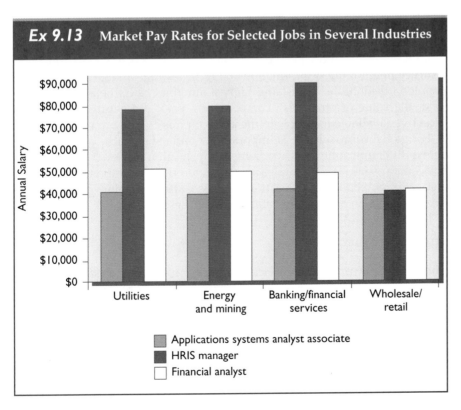

Ex 9.13 Market Pay Rates for Selected Jobs in Several Industries

Applications systems analyst associate
HRIS manager
Financial analyst

found across a range of organizations and they involve essentially the same work and responsibilities regardless of the company. In other words, regardless of the employer, the job description of a benchmark job should sound pretty much the same. The three jobs listed in Exhibit 9.13, for example, could be used as benchmark jobs.

When data are collected for a market survey, the jobs in the survey have brief job descriptions. To determine whether a job is useful as a benchmark, the job description used for the survey is compared to the job description in the employer's organization. If the two descriptions are very similar, the employer can feel confident that the market wage data provided by the survey can be applied to the job in the employer's organization. Market information about the compensation levels of benchmark jobs is used to establish the market pay policy, as explained in the following text. (Note that for competency-based pay systems, the appropriate benchmarks would be competency profiles. For skill-based pay, the appropriate benchmarks would be identifiable skill levels. In practice, however, most companies must still rely on benchmarking against common jobs because that is the method usually used to collect market wage data.)[66]

Obtaining Market Data.   Some companies conduct their own compensation surveys, but most purchase a survey from a consulting firm or use labor market data from government sources. Regardless of who conducts the survey, the process is the same: Employers participating in the survey provide compensation information for selected jobs.

Surveys often focus on specific occupational groups. For example, suppose a survey focused on sales and marketing personnel. In that case, the survey might contain brief descriptions of 100 different jobs (e.g., top marketing manager, sales trainee, account specialist). Employers are asked to identify jobs that exist in their organization and provide detailed information about the way those jobs are compensated. For sales and marketing jobs, a survey might request information about the average annual salary paid to people in the job, the lowest and highest amounts paid, the average bonus paid, the value of other cash compensation paid, the nature of long-term incentives available to people in the jobs, commission pay, and so on.

For global companies, it is important to understand how pay rates vary across different countries. Thus, some compensation surveys focus on country comparisons. For example, an employer with operations throughout Asia can purchase compensation survey data describing pay rates for dozens of jobs in each of several Asian countries.

Establish the Market Pay Policy

The **market pay policy** *is established by plotting pay rates against the evaluation points that the company assigned to the benchmark jobs.* A regression line is calculated to describe the relationship between the evaluation points and market pay rates. Exhibit 9.14 illustrates a market pay policy.

The benchmark jobs in Exhibit 9.14 are labeled Job A, Job B, Job C, and so forth. The points assigned to the jobs are shown on the horizontal axis. Job E was assigned approximately 290 job evaluation points; Job B was assigned 750 job evaluation points; and so on. The average market wage for the benchmark jobs is shown on the vertical axis. For Job E, the average market wage is $35,000. For Job B, it's $73,000. The pay policy for the external mar-

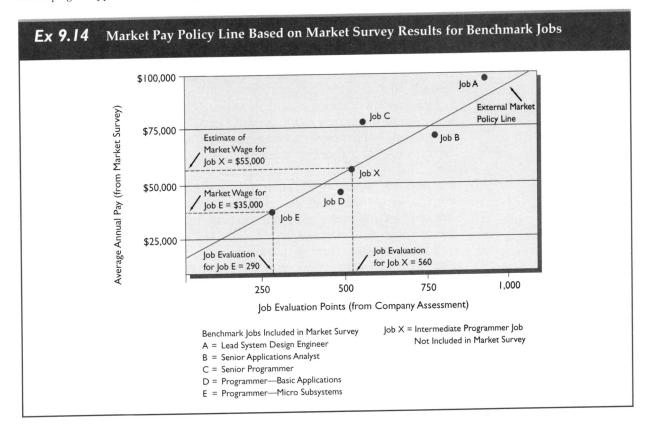

Ex 9.14   Market Pay Policy Line Based on Market Survey Results for Benchmark Jobs

Benchmark Jobs Included in Market Survey
A = Lead System Design Engineer
B = Senior Applications Analyst
C = Senior Programmer
D = Programmer—Basic Applications
E = Programmer—Micro Subsystems

Job X = Intermediate Programmer Job
Not Included in Market Survey

ket is defined by the best-fitting line relating job evaluation points to average market pay. Typically, regression analysis is used to establish the best-fitting line.

Why does an organization need to calculate the external market's policy line? Because market data aren't available for all jobs in the organization. In Exhibit 9.14, Job X represents a job that exists in the organization. But market pay data were not available for Job X because no similar job was included in the market survey. The market policy line makes it possible to assign a dollar value to Job X without knowing its market value.

SET THE ORGANIZATION PAY POLICY

The **organization pay policy** *specifies the pay rates that will be used for the jobs in a particular organization.* If the company wants simply to match the market, it may set its organization pay policy line equal to the line for the external market. Alternatively, the company may choose to pay somewhat above the market or somewhat below the market. The choice of an organization pay policy is influenced by the pay rates of major competitors, the firm's profits or losses, surpluses or shortages of qualified workers, the stage of the firm's development, the role of performance-based pay, the strength of union demands, the organizational culture, and so forth.[67]

A **lead policy** *indicates that the organization intends to pay somewhat above the market rate.* Paying more than other employers maximizes the company's ability to attract and retain quality employees and helps to minimize employee pay dissatisfaction. A lead policy signals that the firm values employees as a source

FAST FACT

The Container Store hires fewer people and pays them two to three times the industry average, which induces fierce employee loyalty and results in high retention rates.

of competitive advantage. A concern is whether the additional pay attracts and retains *the best*—or merely *the most*—applicants. It is also uncertain how much a firm needs to lead others to gain a distinct competitive advantage. Finally, the pay rates of other firms tend to escalate and eventually match the leader's rates.

By far the most common policy is to match the competition. A **match policy** *sets the organization's policy line at the middle of the market.* A match policy does not give an employer a competitive advantage, but it does ensure that the firm isn't at a disadvantage. When Sears restructured its pay system, they discovered from market survey data that past decisions about pay had resulted in an unintended organizational policy of paying above the market. For the company, a lead policy was too costly, so the new system was designed to gradually lower the company's internal pay line in order to more closely match the market.

It is also possible to adopt a **lag policy,** *where the organization intentionally pays below the market.* However, a lag policy may hinder a firm's ability to attract potential employees unless other variables—such as job security, benefits, locale, and job content—compensate for the low base pay.

Exhibit 9.15 shows the pay policies reported by companies that participated in a recent salary survey conducted by the Hay Group. Note that the results shown reflect the pay policies for total cash payments as well as base salary alone.

DESIGNING THE INTERNAL PAY STRUCTURE

When the organization pay policy is set, a pay structure can be developed. This process differs somewhat depending on whether the internal pay structure is job-based, competency-based, or skill-based.

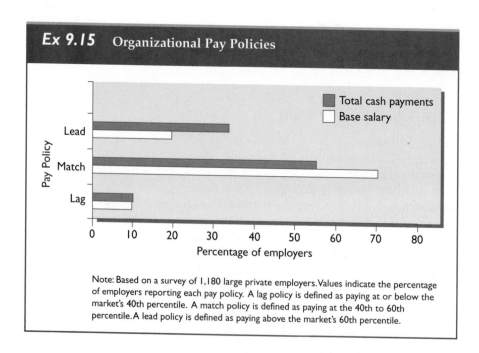

Ex 9.15   Organizational Pay Policies

Note: Based on a survey of 1,180 large private employers. Values indicate the percentage of employers reporting each pay policy. A lag policy is defined as paying at or below the market's 40th percentile. A match policy is defined as paying at the 40th to 60th percentile. A lead policy is defined as paying above the market's 60th percentile.

Developing an Approach to Total Compensation

JOB-BASED PAY GRADES AND RANGES

Exhibit 9.16 shows a conventional job-based pay structure. The boxes are associated with a spread of job evaluation points (the job grade) and a range of pay (the minimum and maximum that can be earned). Usually, several different jobs are covered by one box. The jobs covered by each box have similar evaluation points, but they may have very dissimilar content. The boxes that make up the structure may be the same size or may vary in width and height, but generally they ascend from left to right. This reflects the association of higher pay levels (shown on the vertical axis) with more valued jobs (shown on the horizontal axis).

In establishing pay ranges, the organization pay line generally serves as the midpoint. Maximums and minimums are generally set at a percentage above and below that amount. The difference between the two is the pay range. Some common ranges above and below the pay grade midpoint include:

Nonexempt	
Laborers and tradespeople	Up to 25%
Clerical, technical, and paraprofessional workers	15–50%
Exempt	
First-level managers and professionals	30–50%
Middle and senior managers	40–100%

For the firm depicted in Exhibit 9.16, six equal-interval pay grades were established, each with a width of 100 points. Each grade has a pay range of $1,000. For pay grade II, the range goes from $2,250 (minimum) to $3,250 (maximum) a month; the midpoint is $2,750 a month. Notice that the maximum annual pay for these jobs is less than $60,000, which suggests that the plan does not cover higher-level professionals or executives.

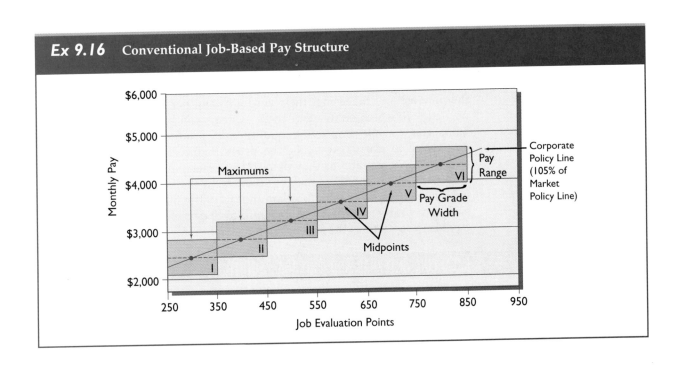

Ex 9.16   Conventional Job-Based Pay Structure

In traditional, hierarchical organizations, there are many different pay grades and each grade has a narrow range (or band). When broadbanding is used, there are fewer pay grades, and each grade has a broader range (or band). Thus, with broadbanding, there is a bigger range between the minimum and maximum pay. Also, there is a bigger difference between the midpoint of a grade and the next higher grade. As a consequence, when employees move from one grade to the next, the promotions have a bigger impact on their pay. However, such promotions occur less often.

COMPETENCY-BASED PAY STRUCTURE

Competency-based pay structures look very similar to job-based pay structures. That is, there are pay grades and ranges established, and these ascend upward along a continuum. The major difference in these systems is that the points on the horizontal axis are assigned to levels of competencies—not jobs. At the lower end of the scale would be jobs that require competencies that are of relatively less value to the organization. At the higher end of the scale would be jobs that require competencies that are more valuable to the organization. In other words, the key difference between competency-based and job-based models is not how points are used—the difference is in how points are assigned to jobs.

SKILL-BASED PAY STRUCTURE

With skill-based pay, increases in pay are associated with increases in skills. Employees are paid for their skills, regardless of the jobs they hold. Thus, the structure of a skill-based system really is fundamentally different from a job-based or competency-based system. The starting assumption is that base pay is more or less equal for everyone covered by the pay system regardless of the job assignment. However, additional pay can be earned by increasing one's skills. Thus, two people working side-by-side in the same job may be paid at different hourly rates simply because one person has more skills. The additional skills may not be needed to perform that job, but they are nevertheless valuable to the organization, so the employee is paid for them.

Approximately 85% of skill-based pay systems are designed to encourage employees to develop the breadth (rather than the depth) of their skills, in the interest of increasing their flexibility to perform different jobs as needed.[68] Research shows that these systems can be effective in lowering labor costs, while improving quality and productivity.[69] To encourage employees to learn new skills, the pay structure is designed to increase employees' wage rates as they demonstrate each new skill. For example, in an automobile plant, there may be 20 different skills that factory employees need in order to be able to move around the entire plant as needed. For each skill, a pay raise is earned when an employee demonstrates proficiency. The pay structure defines the size of the pay increase for each added skill.

BALANCING INTERNAL AND EXTERNAL EQUITY

External and internal data as well as a firm's compensation strategy all influence how firms value and pay for the work of employees. Every organization must find an appropriate approach. Often, the process of setting a pay policy requires that trade-offs be made between paying based strictly on the importance of a job to a particular employer and paying rates that reflect the external market value of a job. For example, study Exhibit 9.14 again, focusing on the job of senior programmer (Job C). The organization's job evaluation system assessed the value of this job at about 570 points, so it should be paid about $60,000. But the market pays more than $75,000 to senior programmers who do similar work. If this organization pays less than the market rate, it may have difficulty attracting and retaining excellent senior programmers. But if it pays the market rate, the organization will be spending more than it judges this job to be worth given how it contributes to the organization's objectives. Sometimes differences between market rates and job evaluation results can be resolved by reviewing the basic decisions associated with evaluating and pricing particular jobs. Sometimes survey data can be ignored or benchmark jobs can be changed or jobs can simply be reevaluated. In cases where the disparities persist, professional judgment is required to resolve them.

Pay Differentials

One way the discrepancy between internal and external equity can be resolved is to establish temporary market differentials. Consider the dilemma confronting a television broadcast company. The broadcast firm conducted a job evaluation study and collected market data for key positions. The job evaluation positioned the job of a broadcast engineer technician in pay grade VI. When designing the pay structure, the pay range for this grade had been set well below the average rate of pay in the external market. The discrepancy persisted even following a check of the job evaluation and wage survey data. Because engineers with broadcast experience are difficult to find, company executives considered reassigning the job to a higher pay grade (they had done this in the past). Although this would provide a "quick fix," the long-term consequences—particularly if other employees found out about the reclassification—could be disastrous, threatening the validity of the entire compensation system. To preserve the integrity of the system while meeting market demands, engineering jobs were left in the appropriate grades and a market differential was paid to employees in these jobs. As long as the external market rate of pay was higher than the station's policy line, engineers would receive the 10% market differential; when the labor market imbalance corrected itself, the differential would be eliminated.

Shift work is another common example of using pay differentials. Although people working different shifts may perform the same job, it is generally more difficult to hire people for shifts that fall outside the standard workday. Consequently, employers pay a shift differential to people who work during less desirable times.

COMMUNICATING THE PAY STRUCTURE

Employers invest enormous resources in designing pay plans that they believe will help attract, retain, and motivate their employees. When a decision is made to revise the organization's compensation system (e.g., to change from a traditional system to broadbanding or competency-based pay), it is not uncommon for the change process to require up to a year of planning. In order for a compensation system to achieve its objectives, employees must understand the system. If employees don't fully understand how their pay is determined, they will not be motivated by the way their pay is structured.[70]

An effective approach to communication helps employees understand how market rates are determined and used to establish their pay and helps them see how the structure of the plan addresses the issue of internal equity. Effective communications also educate employees about what the firm values in terms of tasks, competencies, and skills, and shows them how these values are reflected in the design of the pay system (e.g., in the way points are assigned to jobs).

When Allstate's board decided to restructure executive pay packages, they paid a great deal of attention to explaining the bases for the new packages. Allstate Insurance Company was established in 1931 by Sears, Roebuck and Company. Sixty years later, Sears spun it off to pursue a more focused strategy. When Allstate went public, an outside board of directors was established. Evaluating executive pay packages was among its first tasks. The board commissioned a study of key executives to learn how they perceived their pay and their views about how pay should be determined. The study concluded that Allstate needed a new, simpler plan that linked pay directly to Allstate's business results. When the new pay plan was ready, experts were brought in to develop a communication strategy. The key elements in the communication strategy were: involving employees, focusing on the big picture, and following up.

Involve Employees

Rather than rely on external communications experts to get the message out about their new pay plan, Allstate's consultants collaborated with a team of Allstate managers who had not been involved in developing the pay plan and who represented a variety of specialty areas. Before devising its formal communication strategy, team members began by making sure they understood the new pay plan themselves. "We ripped [the plan] apart, we took the staples out of it—we literally ripped it apart, not figuratively—and stuck the pages up on the walls. . . . We tried to understand the plan and draw it on the board," explained one of the communication experts.

Focus on the Big Picture

Once the team members were sure that they understood the new pay plan, the principle that proved most important as they developed the formal communication strategy was "Keep It Simple." Rather than overwhelm people with all the details, the communicators emphasized the link between achieving business objectives and the pay that the executives would receive. To ensure that the executives could see "the big picture," the written material included a foldout page showing how all the pieces of the package fit together. To give personal meaning to the package, each executive received an individualized statement that showed the maximum amounts that he or she could earn if individual and group targets were achieved.

Follow Up

The final step in the communication strategy was to conduct another survey of the executives affected by the new pay plan. A survey conducted after the new package was explained revealed that 85% of the executives felt that they now had a better understanding than before of their annual incentive pay, their stock options, and the total pay package.[71]

COMPENSATION IN THE CONTEXT OF GLOBALIZATION

As the environment for business becomes more global, international compensation becomes a more significant element of total compensation. When developing international compensation policies, the basic objectives are the same as in a domestic context. The policy should be consistent and fair in its treatment of all employees. It should help attract and retain personnel in the areas where the company has the greatest needs and opportunities. It should motivate employees to take international assignments and perform well.

FAST FACT

The cost of posting an expatriate can be anywhere from three to seven times the expatriate's home base salary.

Balancing internal and external equity is especially challenging for firms operating in multiple countries.[72] For parent-country (U.S.) expatriates, the most widely used philosophy is "keeping the expatriate whole"—that is, offering compensation that allows expatriates to maintain a lifestyle that is comparable to their home country experience. A basic assumption behind this philosophy is that foreign assignees shouldn't suffer a material loss owing to their transfer.

To achieve the objective of keeping the expatriate whole, many companies use the balance sheet approach to figure out what expatriates should be paid. The **balance sheet approach** *provides a level of net spendable income in the new destination that is similar to that received in the previous (usually home) location.*[73] The objective is to equalize the purchasing power—not the compensation in dollars—of employees at comparable position levels living overseas and in the home country, and to provide incentives to offset qualitative differences between assignment locations.[74] Exhibit 9.17 shows the five major categories of expenses that employers typically consider when determining expatriate pay.

Ex 9.17   Expenses Incurred by Expatriates and Often Paid by Employers

Goods and Services	Items such as food, personal care, clothing, household furnishings, recreation, transportation, and medical care.
Housing	The major costs associated with the employees' principal residences.
Income Taxes	Payments to federal and local governments for personal income taxes. For U.S. employees, tax liabilities usually increase when they go abroad, so most U.S. employers adopt a tax equalization policy for assignment-related income.
Reserve	Contributions to savings, payments for benefits, pension contributions, investments, education expenses, Social Security taxes, and so forth.
Shipment and Storage	The major costs associated with shipping and storing personal and household effects.

SUMMARY

Organizations develop strategic compensation in a cost-conscious, competitive business environment that demands high quality and a continuous flow of new products. A total compensation system that is responsive to the external environment, consistent with the organization's business strategy, and perceived as fair by employees improves the organization's ability to compete successfully.

A total compensation system includes many components. Some of the compensation employees receive is monetary, while other forms of compensation are nonmonetary. Monetary compensation includes both direct forms of payment, such as wages and salaries, and indirect forms, such as insurance and other benefits.

For most employees, the majority of compensation received is paid as base pay. When designing the base pay component of a compensation system, employers can choose from many alternatives. Three basic choices are job-based, competency-based, and skill-based pay. The job-based and competency-based approaches are grounded in job evaluation. Job evaluation involves a systematic assessment of the value of jobs in the organization. It is intended to establish internal equity. Ranking and job classification methods evaluate the whole job and rely heavily on intuitive judgments about job worth. The point factor rating method imposes a more rigorous analysis and is the most widely used. To increase employees' acceptance and understanding of pay systems, it is helpful to involve them in the job evaluation process.

To establish actual wage rates, organizations use market surveys, which provide information about what other organizations pay their employees in specific jobs. Market pay rates are used as guides when creating an organization's internal pay policy. The organization may choose a policy that leads, matches, or lags behind the pay offered by competitors.

Organizations operating beyond domestic borders face additional challenges when designing their compensation systems. The basic objectives to be achieved by compensation remain essentially the same, but achieving them usually requires a more complex pay system. Ultimately, as is true for domestic companies, multinational corporations face the daunting challenge of designing and implementing a total compensation system that balances the concerns of employees with those of all stakeholders, including investors, customers, and the many societies in which they do business.

Source: S. M. Nkomo, M. D. Fottler, and R. B. McAfee, Applications in Human Resource Management : Cases, Exercises, and Skill Builders (Mason, OH: South-Western, 2005). Reprinted with permission.

TERMS TO REMEMBER

Balance sheet approach	Equal Pay Act
Base pay	Exempt employees
Benchmark jobs	External equity
Compensable factors	Fair Labor Standards Act (FLSA)
Compensation survey	Hay Guide Chart-Profile
Competency-based job evaluation	Internal equity

Job-based pay structure	Nonmonetary compensation
Job classification method	Organization pay policy
Job evaluation	Pay equity policies
Job ranking method	Pay fairness
Lag policy	Pay level
Lead policy	Pay mix
Market pay policy	Pay structure
Match policy	Point factor rating method
Monetary compensation	Skill-based pay
Nonexempt employees	Total compensation system

DISCUSSION QUESTIONS

1. Explain how an organization's total compensation system can help the organization be effective or prevent it from being effective.

2. How and why do the objectives of total compensation vary across organizations?

3. What are the elements of total compensation, and which ones are most important to you personally?

4. Describe the purpose of job evaluation. What are the advantages and disadvantages of using a simple ranking method? What are the advantages and disadvantages of using a customized job evaluation point system?

5. List the possible negative consequences that organizations are likely to experience if employees do not understand the compensation system.

PROJECTS TO EXTEND YOUR LEARNING

1. *Integration and Application.* After reviewing the end-of-text cases, compare and contrast Lincoln Electric and Southwest Airlines on the following:

   a. The objectives of their total compensation systems
   b. The role of compensation in achieving competitive advantage
   c. The pay mix and employee's reactions to the pay mix

   Which compensation system would you prefer? Explain why.

2. *Exploring the Internet*

   a. The World at Work is an association of compensation professionals. Learn more about the resources available through this organization and current issues of interest to their members at http://www.worldatwork.org.

   b. Learn more about pay equity, comparable worth, and exempt/nonexempt status from
      (1) the Ontario Pay Equity Commission, http://www.gov.on.ca/lab/pec,
      (2) the state of Minnesota's Department of Employee Relations, http://www.doer.state.mn.us,

(3) the Capital Research Center,
http://www.capitalresearch.org, and

(4) the U.S. Department of Labor, http://www.dol.gov/esa/
regs/compliance/whd/fairpay/main.htm.

(5) Find out about the AFL-CIO's position on executive pay
practices at http://www.aflcio.org/corporateamerica/
paywatch.

(6) Learn about pay levels in the United States and discover
what other compensation information is available from the
Bureau of Labor Statistics at http://www.bls.gov; learn
about the federal government job classification at http://
www.opm.gov.

(7) Read more about the Hay Guide-Chart Profile Method by
visiting the Hay Group at http://www.haygroup.com.

3. *Experiential Activity.* As domestic companies begin to expand
overseas, they face many new challenges. Among these is deciding
how to compensate the people who fill top-level management positions in the global operations. Two basic alternatives are (a) pay managers by matching the compensation of local executives in the
non-U.S. locations, or (b) pay managers by matching the compensation of their U.S. counterparts. What are the pros and cons of each
alternative? What HR objectives might best be achieved by each
approach?

Choose one approach to this strategic issue. Assume your company
adopted this approach a year ago when it opened a new facility in
France. Now it is time to evaluate whether the approach that was
selected was the right choice. You have been put in charge of the evaluation project. Your first task is to develop a list of interview questions to ask all of the company's expatriates. There are a total of 50
expatriates working in 6 countries outside the United States. In addition, you have been asked to prepare a list of questions to ask the
managers to whom the expatriates report. Prepare these two lists of
questions to share with other members of your class. Be ready to
explain the logic that guided you as you developed the two lists.

CASE STUDY

THE OVERPAID BANK TELLERS

The State Bank is located in a southwestern town of
about 50,000 people. It is one of four banks in the
area and has the reputation of being the most progressive. Russell Duncan has been the president of
the bank for 15 years. Before coming to State Bank,
Duncan worked for a large Detroit bank for 10
years. Duncan has implemented a number of

changes that have earned him a great deal of
respect and admiration from both bank employees
and townspeople alike. For example, in response to
a growing number of Spanish-speaking people in
the area, he hired Latinos and placed them in critical bank positions. He organized and staffed the
city's only agricultural loan center to meet the

needs of the area's farmers. In addition, he established the state's first "uniline" system for handling customers waiting in line for a teller.

Perhaps more than anything else, Duncan is known for establishing progressive personnel practices. He strongly believes that the bank's employees are its most important asset and continually searches for ways to increase both employee satisfaction and productivity. He feels that all employees should strive to continually improve their skills and abilities, and hence, he cross-trains employees and sends many of them to courses and conferences sponsored by banking groups such as the American Institute of Banking.

With regard to employee compensation, Duncan firmly believes that employees should be paid according to their contribution to organizational success. Hence, 10 years ago, he implemented a results-based pay system under which employees could earn raises from 0 to 12% each year, depending on their job performance. Raises are typically determined by the bank's HR Committee during February and are granted to employees on March 1 of each year. In addition to granting employees merit raises, six years ago the bank also began giving cost-of-living raises. Duncan had been opposed to this idea originally but saw no alternative to it.

One February, another bank in town conducted a wage survey to determine the average compensation of bank employees in the city. The management of the State Bank received a copy of the wage survey and was surprised to learn that its 23 tellers, as a group, were being paid an average of $22 per week more than were tellers at other banks. The survey also showed that employees holding other positions in the bank (e.g., branch managers, loan officers, and file clerks) were being paid wages similar to those paid by other banks.

After receiving the report, the HR Committee of the bank met to determine what should be done regarding the tellers' raises. They knew that none of the tellers had been told how much their raises would be but that they were all expecting both merit and cost-of-living raises. They also realized that, if other employees learned that the tellers were being overpaid, friction could develop and morale might suffer. They knew that it was costing the bank more than $26,000 extra to pay the tellers. Finally, they knew that as a group the bank's tellers were highly competent, and they did not want to lose any of them.

Source: S. M. Nkomo, M. D. Fottler, and R. B. McAffee, *Applications in Human Resource Management: Cases, Exercises, and Skill Builders* (Mason, OH: South-Western, 2005). Reprinted with permission.

ENDNOTES

1 B. Roberts, "Crunching the Numbers," *HR Magazine* (October 2003): 63–68.

2 B. Grow, "A Day's Pay for a Day's Work—Maybe," *Business Week* (December 8, 2003): 100–103; J. Schramm, "Employee Satisfaction," *Workplace Visions* 4 (2003): 1–8; Y. Zhang, N. Rajagopalan, and D. Datta, "Executive Characteristics, Compensation Systems, and Firm Performance," *The Nature of Organizational Leadership* (2001): 270–301; D. C. O. Trevor, B. Gerhart, and J. W. Boudreau, "Voluntary Turnover and Job Performance: Curvilinearity and the Moderating Influences of Salary Growth on Promotions," *Journal of Applied Psychology* 82 (1997): 44–61.

3 S. Werner and D. Ones, "The Determinants of Perceived Pay Inequities: The Effects of Comparison, Other Characteristics and Pay-System Communication," *Journal of Applied Social Psychology* 20 (2000): 1300–1329; K. Klaus, "Share and Share," *ACA News* (April 2000): 22–28; S. Werner and D. Ones, "The Determinants of Perceived Pay Inequities: The Effects of Comparison, Other Characteristics and Pay-System Communication," *Journal of Applied Social Psychology* 20 (2000): 1300–1329; L. A. Witt and L. G. Nye, "Gender and the Relationship between Perceived Fairness of Pay or Promotion and Job Satisfaction," *Journal of Applied Psychology* 77 (1992): 910–917.

4 J. S. Adams, "Toward an Understanding of Equity," *Journal of Abnormal and Social Psychology* 67 (1963): 422–436.

5 A. S. Tsui, J. L. Pearce, L. W. Porter, and A. M. Tripoli, "Alternative Approaches to the Employee–Organization Relationship: Does Investment in Employees Pay Off?" *Academy of Management Journal* 40 (1997): 1089–1121.

6 K. Aquino, R. W. Griffeth, D. G. Allen, and P. W. Hom, "Integrating Justice Constructs into the Turnover Process: A Test of a Referent Cognitions Model," *Academy of Management Journal* 40 (1997): 1208–1227; R. E. Kidwell, Jr., and N. Bennett, "Employee Propensity to Withhold Effort: A Conceptual Model to Intersect Three Avenues of Research," *Academy of Management Review* 18 (1993): 429–456; J. Schaubroeck, D. R. May, and F. W. Brown, "Procedural Justice Explanations and Employee Reactions to Economic Hardship: A Field Experiment," *Journal of Applied Psychology* 79 (1994): 455–161; J. Greenberg, "Employee Theft as a Reaction to Underpayment Inequity: The Hidden Costs of Pay Cuts," *Journal of Applied Psychology* 75 (1990): 561–568.

7 D. Kadlec, "Where Did My Raise Go?" *Time* (May 26, 2003): 44–54; I. Polyak, "Money Talks, but Is Anyone Listening?" *Workforce Management* (August 2003): 26.

8 "Doing Whatever It Takes," *Across the Board* (March/April 2001): 56–61.

9 B. S. Murphy, W. E. Barlow, and D. D. Hatch, "Manager's Newsfront," *Personnel Journal* (December 1992): 22.

10 I. Polyak, "Money Talks, but Is Anyone Listening?" *Workforce Management* (August 2003): 26.

11 A. Markels, "Blank Check," *Wall Street Journal* (April 9, 1998): R11.

12 M. Zippo, "Roundup," *Personnel* (September–October 1980): 43–45.

13 T. Gutner, "How to Shrink the Pay Gap," *Business Week* (June 24, 2002): 151; B. Grow, "A Day's Pay for a Day's Work—Maybe," *Business Week* (December 8, 2003): 100–103; C. Loomis, "This Stuff Is Wrong," *Fortune* (June 25, 2001): 73–84; L. Lavelle, "For Female CEOs It's Stingy at the Top," *Business Week* (April 23, 2001): 70–71; M. Arndt, "From Milestone to Millstone?" *Business Week* (March 20, 2000): 120–122; B. R. Ellig, "CEO Pay," *World at Work Journal* (Third Quarter 2000): 71–78; A. Tang, "Women's Earnings: What a Difference a Degree Makes," *New York Times* (February 23, 2000): G1; H. L. Tosi, S. Werner, J. R. Katz, and L. R. Gomez-Mejia, "How Much Does Performance Matter? A Meta-Analysis of CEO Pay," *Journal of Management* 26(2) (2000): 301–339; R. Veilyath, "Top Management Compensation and Shareholder Returns: Unraveling Different Models of the Relationship," *Journal of Management Studies* 36 (1000): 123–143; J. K. Galbraith, *Created Unequal: The Crisis in American Pay* (New York: Free Press, 1998); J. M. Schlesinger, "Wages for Low-Paid Workers Rose in 1997," *Wall Street Journal* (March 28, 1998): A2; L. R. Gomez-Mejia, "Executive Compensation: A Reassessment and a Future Research Agenda," *Research in Personnel and Human Resource Management* 12 (1994): 161–222.

14 G. Morgenson, "Market Watch: Explaining (or Not) Why the Boss Is Paid So Much," *New York Times* (January 25, 2004): D1; A. Bernstein, "Back on the Edge," *Business Week* (April 23, 2001): 42–43; "Runaway CEO Pay: What's Happening and What You Can Do About It," *AFL-CIO Paywatch,* http://www.aflcio.org/paywatch/ (July 10, 2001).

15 For detailed discussions of the relationship between executive pay and firm performance, see H. Barkema and L. R. Gomez-Mejia, "Managerial Compensation and Firm Performance: A General Research Framework," *Academy of Management Journal* 41(2) (1998): 135–145; Y. Zhang, N. Rajagopalan, and D. Datta, "Executive Characteristics, Compensation Systems, and Firm Performance," *The Nature of Organizational Leadership* (2001): 270–301.

16 For a discussion of designing pay to fit a multinational strategy, see J. Burg, I. Sisovick, and D. Brock, "Aligning Performance and Rewards Practices in Multinational Subsidiaries," *World at Work Journal* (Third Quarter 2000): 64–70.

17 R. K. Platt, "The Big Picture at Big Blue: Total Rewards at IBM," *Workspan* (August 2000): 27; W. Fox, "Staying a Step Ahead of the Competition with Outstanding Total Compensation," *ACA News* (October 1998): 20–22.

18 L. Clague, "Outsourcing/Insourcing: Organizing and Managing the Expatriate Function," in C. Reynolds (ed.), *Guide to Global Compensation and Benefits,* 2nd ed. (San Diego, CA: Harcourt, 2001): 693–726.

19 R. S. Schuler, S. E. Jackson, and Y. Luo, *Managing Human Resources in Cross-Border Alliances* (London: Routledge, 2004).

20 P. E. Platten and D. A. Hofrichter, "The Compensation Lag," *Across The Board* (May 1996): 27–31; L. M. Kahn and P. D. Sherer, "Contingent Pay and Managerial Performance," *Industrial and Labor Relations Review* 43 (1990): 107S–120S; M. L. Weitzman and D. L. Kruse, "Profit Sharing and Productivity," in A. S. Blinder (ed.), *Paying for Productivity* (Washington, DC: Brookings Institute, 1990); R. A. Guzzo, R. D. Jette, and R. A. Katzell, "The Effects of Psychologically Based Intervention Programs on Worker Productivity: A Meta-Analysis," *Personnel Psychology* 38 (1985): 275–291.

21 D. Greising, "Fast Eddie's Future Bank," *Business Week* (March 23, 1998): 74–77.

22 R. F. Stolz, "Keeping the Crew," *Human Resource Executive* (December 2003): 8–12.

23 J. Schramm, "Employee Satisfaction," *Workplace Visions* 4 (2003): 1–8; L. C. Lancaster and D. Stillman, *When Generations Collide* (New York: HarperBusiness, 2002); P. W. Mulvey, J. E. Ledford, Jr., and P. V. LaBlanc, "Rewards of Work: How They Drive Retention and Satisfaction," *World at Work Journal* (October, 2000): 6–18.

24 "The Big Picture: Your Money or Your Life," *Business Week* (May 26, 2003): 18.

25 E. Zimmerman, "The Joy of Flex," *Workforce Management* (March 2004): 38–40.

26 J. Handel, "Job Value: Employees Are in the Driver's Seat," *Workspan* (June 2000): 29–32L; Mannsnerus, "As Law Scramble for New Talent, The New Talent Reaps the Rewards," *New York Times* (January 30, 2001): 4; J. J. Laabs, "What Goes Down When Minimum Wages Go Up," *Workforce* (August 1998): 54–58.

27 V. Infante, "The Future of the Minimum Wage?" *Workforce* (March 2001): 29; "Myth and the Minimum Wage," *Business Week* (October 12, 1998): 6.

28 "The High Cost of Low Prices," *Business Week* (December 6, 2003): 168; J. M. Brett and L. K. Stroh, "Jumping Ship: Who Benefits from an External Labor Market Career Strategy?" *Journal of Applied Psychology* 82 (1997): 331–341; J. Laabs, "What Goes Down When Minimum Wages Go Up," B. S. Klaas and J. M. McClendon, "To Lead, Lag, or Match: Estimating the Financial Impact of Pay Level Policies," *Personnel Psychology* 49 (1996).

29 E. L. Andrews, "Germans Cut Labor Costs with a Harsh Export: Jobs," *New York Times International* (March 21, 1998): A3.

30 E. L. Andrews, "Germans Cut Labor Costs with a Harsh Export: Jobs."

31 M. A. Thompson, "Border Crossing: Canadian Talent Heading South," *ACA News* (May 2001): 33–37.

32 See D. B. Balkin and L. R. Gomez-Mejia, "Compensation Systems in High Technology Companies," in D. B. Balkin and L. R. Gomez-Mejia (eds.), *New Perspectives in Compensation* (Englewood Cliffs, NJ: Prentice-Hall, 1987): 269–277.

33 M. Wanderer, "Dot-comp: A 'Traditional' Pay Plan with a Cutting Edge," *World at Work Journal* (Fourth Quarter 2000): 15–24.

34 D. B. Balkin and L. R. Gomez-Mejia, "Entrepreneurial Compensation," in R. S. Schuler, S. A. Youngblood, and V. L. Huber (eds.), *Readings in Personnel and Human Resource Management:* 14–23.

35 G. T. Milkovich, "A Strategic Perspective on Compensation Management," in K. Rowland and G. Ferris (eds.), *Research in Personnel and Human Resources Management:* 263–288.

36 P. Burstein, R. M. Bricher, and R. L. Einwohner, "Policy Alternatives and Political Change: Work, Family, and Gender on the Congressional Agenda," *American Sociological Review* 60 (1995): 67–83.

37 V. Peckham, "The Value of Being a Child-Friendly Company," *Solutions* (October 1996): 28–29; S. J. Boyd, "Will Compensatory Time Become Law?" *ACA News* (May 1997): 18–19.

38 R. Kuttner, "So Much for the Minimum-Wage Scare," *Business Week* (July 21, 1997): 19; "Crackdown on Child Labor Violations," *Fair Employment Practices Guidelines* 299 (June 6, 1990).

39 R. Dooley, "What Does It Mean to Have a 'Salaried Nonexempt' Employee?" *HR Magazine* (October 2003): 37; "Youth Employment: Child Labor Limitations Reviewed," *Bulletin to Management* (May 19, 1994): 153.

40 M. M. Clark, "Preparations Suggested for Final Overtime Regs," *HR Magazine* (February 2004): 25–26.

41 G. Flynn, "Pizza as Pay? Compensation Gets Too Creative," *Workforce* (August 1998): 91–96.

42 E. Tahmincioglu, "More, More, More," *Workforce Management* (May 2004): 41–43.

43 M. Conlin, "Revenge of the 'Managers,'" *Business Week* (March 12, 2001): 60–61; C. Hirschman, "Paying for Waiting," *HR Magazine* (August 1999): 98–105; "White-Collar Exemptions under FLSA," *Bulletin to*

Management: Datagraph (February 13, 1992): 44–45; "Ask the Experts— Questions and Answers on Classifying White-Collar Employees as Exempt from Overtime Regulations," *Fair Employment Practices Guidelines* (April 10, 1994): 8.

44 L.A. Schreter, "Developing a 'Clock-Work' State of Mind: Avoid 'Off-the-Clock' Work Claims by Non-Exempt Employees," *Legal Report* (July–August, 2004): 1–4; S. Greenhouse, "Controversial Overtime Rules Take Effect," *New York Times* (August 23, 2004): A11; S. Greenhouse, "Labor Dept. Revises Plans to Cut Overtime Eligibility," *New York Times* (April 21, 2004); M. M. Clark, "Preparations Suggested for Final Overtime Regs," *HR Magazine* (February 2004): 25–26; A. Bernstein, "Too Stingy with the Overtime," *Business Week* (December 22, 2003): 81; Y. Armendariz, "Time Is Money, Overtime May Not Be," *New York Times* (February 8, 2004): D1, D5; "DOL Issues Proposal for Changing FLSA Overtime Exemption Requirements," *HR Magazine* (May 2003): 25, 38; A. Bernstein, "Too Stingy with the Overtime: The Labor Dept.'s New Eligibility Rules Would Exclude Millions," *Business Week* (December 22, 2003): 81; see "Record Settlement under Fair Labor Standards Act," *Bulletin to Management* (August 12, 1993): 249.

45 A. Weintraub, "Revenge of the Overworked Nerds," *Business Week* (December 8, 2003): 41.

46 C. Hirchman, "Paying Up," *HR Magazine* (July 2000): 35–41; S. Brull, "What's So Bad About a Living Wage," *Business Week* (September 4, 2000): 68–70.

47 S. Holmes, "A New Black Eye for Boeing?" *Business Week* (April 26, 2004): 90–92; S. Holmes and M. France, "Coverup at Boeing?" *Business Week* (June 28, 2004): 84–90.

48 T. Gutner, "How to Shrink the Pay Gap," *Business Week* (June 2002): 151.

49 "No Real Money on the Table," *Workforce Management* (December 2004): 111.

50 S. Holmes and W. Zellner, "The Costco Way," *Business Week* (April 12, 2004): 76–77.

51 L. Grensing-Pophal, "Communication Pays Off," *HR Magazine* (May 2003): 77–80.

52 J. D. Shaw, N. Gupta, and J. E. Delery, "Pay Dispersion and Workforce Performance: Moderating Effects of Incentives and Interdependence," *Strategic Management Journal* 23 (2002): 491–512; P. L. Gilles, "Enhancing the Participatory Process of Compensation Design," *ACA News* (May 1998): 27–29.

53 J. Koechel, "Free Agent Syndrome Fueling Turnover Frenzy," *Workspan* (January 2001): 6–8; C. O. Trevor and M. Graham, "Deriving the Market Wage," *World at Work Journal* (Fourth Quarter 2000): 69–76; P. Cappelli and W. F. Cascio, "Why Some Jobs Command Wage Premiums: A Test of Career Tournament and Internal Labor Market Hypotheses," *Academy of Management Journal* 34 (1991): 848–868.

54 R. Sneigar, "The Comparability of Job Evaluation Methods in Supplying Approximately Similar Classifications in Rating One Job Series," *Personnel Psychology* (Summer 1983): 371–380.

55 "No Real Money on the Table," *Workforce Management* (December 2003): 116.

56 For an extensive description of Bayer see http://www.bayer.com.

57 Bayer is an international, research-based group active in CROP sciences, materials science, health care, and chemicals. It is composed of four business groups, represented in virtually every country of the world. Visit their website for a full description of their business groups, values, relation to the environment, and job and career opportunities. Materials for this feature are based upon company documents and *Annual Reports* from 1995 to 2004.

58 J. A. Green and R. W. Keuch, "Contribution-Driven Competency-Based Pay," *ACA Journal* (Autumn 1997): 62–71.

59 K. S. Abosch and B. L. Hmurovic, "A Traveler's Guide to Global Broadbanding," *ACA Journal* (Summer 1998): 38–46.

60 B. Parus, "Broadbanding Highly Effective, Survey Shows," *ACA News* (July/August 1998): 40–41; see also M. Enos and G. Limoges, "Broadbanding: Is That Your Company's Final Answer?" *World at Work Journal* (Fourth Quarter 2000): 61–68.

61 N. Gupta et al., "Survey-Based Prescriptions for Skill-Based Pay," *ACA Journal* (Fall 1992): 48–58; M. Rowland, "It's What You Can Do That Counts," *New York Times* (June 6, 1993): F17; M. Rowland, "For Each New Skill, More Money," *New York Times* (June 13, 1993): F16.

62 G. J. Ledford, "Three Case Studies on Skill-Based Pay: An Overview," *Compensation and Benefits Review* (April 1990): 11–23.

63 D. Brown, "The Third Way," *World at Work Journal* (Second Quarter 2000): 15–25; S. Fournier, "Keeping Line Managers in the Know," *ACA News* (March 2000): 46–48; B. Murray and B. Gerhart, "An Empirical Analysis of a Skill-Based Pay Program and Plan Performance Outcomes," *Academy of Management Journal* 41 (1998): 68–78; Ledford, "Three Case Studies on Skill-Based Pay."

64 J. Domat-Connell, "Labor Market Definition and Salary Survey Selection: A New Look at the Foundation of Compensation Program Design," *Compensation and Benefits Review* (March–April 1994): 38–46.

65 E. R. Schultz, D. Van de Voort, and T. G. Nocerino, "Industry and Occupational Influences on Compensation," in C. H. Fay, M. A. Thompson, and D. Knight, *The Executive Handbook on Compensation* (New York: Free Press, 2001): 607–623.

66 K. Lemaire, "Competency-based Pay: A Practitioner's Guide," in C. H. Fay, M. A. Thompson, and D. Knight, *The Executive Handbook on Compensation* (New York: Free Press, 2001): 486–495.

67 Ledford, Tyler, and Dixey, "Skill-Based Pay Case Number Three."

68 N. Gupta and J. D. Shaw, "Successful Skill-Based Pay Plans," in C. H. Fay, M. A. Thompson, and D. Knight, *The Executive Handbook on Compensation* (New York: Free Press, 2001): 513–526.

69 B. Murray and B. Gerhart, "An Empirical Analysis of a Skill-Based Pay Program and Plant Performance Outcomes," *Academy of Management Journal* 41 (1998): 68–78.

70 S. Werner and D. S. Ones, "The Determinants of Perceived Pay Inequities: The Effects of Comparison, Other Characteristics and Pay-System Communication," *Journal of Applied Social Psychology* 20 (2000): 1300–1329; S. Werner and D. Ones, "The Determinants of Perceived Pay Inequities: The Effects of Comparison, Other Characteristics and Pay-System Communication," *Journal of Applied Social Psychology* 20 (2000): 1300–1329.

71 A. M. Healey, "Grabbing Attention for Total Compensation Plans," *ACA News* (October 1996): 11–13.

72 The topic of international compensation is much too complex to address here. For detailed discussions of the issues involved, see C. Reynolds, *Guide to Global Compensation and Benefits,* 2nd ed. (New York: Harcourt, 2001).

73 Adapted from D. R. Briscoe and R. S. Schuler, *International Human Resource Management: Policy and Practice in Global Enterprises,* 2nd ed. (London: Routledge, 2004); W. A. Carmell, "Application of U.S. Antidiscrimination Laws to Multinational Employers," *Legal Report* (July–August 2001): 1–8.

74 D. R. Briscoe and R. S. Schuler, *International Human Resource Management,* 2nd ed. (London, UK: Routledge, 2004); J. Burg, I. Sisovick, and D. Brock, "Aligning Performance and Rewards Practices in Multinational Subsidiaries," *World at Work Journal* (Third Quarter 2000): 64–70; V. Infante, "Three Ways to Design International Pay: Headquarters, Home Country, Host Country," *Workforce* (January 2001): 22–24; V. Frazee, "Is the Balance Sheet Right for Your Expats?" *Global Workforce* (September 1998): 19–26; C. Reynolds, *Compensating Globally Mobile Employees: Approaches to Developing Expatriate Pay Strategies for the Evolving International Corporation* (Scottsdale, AZ: American Compensation Association, 1995).

chapter 10

Measuring Performance and Providing Feedback

TRW is a global business with nearly 100,000 employees worldwide working in four major businesses—automotive, aeronautical systems, space and electronics, and information systems. In 2001, responding to declining business conditions, management sought to revitalize the company by instituting numerous change initiatives. One initiative was targeted at creating a companywide performance appraisal and career development system. Instead of several paper-based systems that were unique to each business unit, top management wanted a single, integrated approach that communicated the behaviors needed for the company's profitability. These behaviors included creating trust, energizing people, embracing change, building teamwork, and being customer-oriented. The global design team, which operated as a virtual team, recognized that an online system would be the best solution. However, because not all employees had access to the company's e-mail hub, a parallel paper-based system was also needed. Within three months, a new four-page form had been created.

Besides evaluating performance against specific goals, managers rated their subordinates' performances against the key behaviors using a four-point scale. For each point on the scale, a paragraph explained what that rating meant. For example, the highest rating was:

Far Exceeds Expectations: *Organizational contributions and excellent work are widely recognized. Performance consistently exceeds all defined expectations, producing important and impactful results through superior planning, execution, and creativity. Employee consistently demonstrated the rated TRW behaviors and/or initiatives at higher levels than expected.*

And the lowest possible rating was:

Needs Improvement: *Performance falls below expectations on one or more critical position competencies, objectives, or tasks. While some responsibilities may be executed in a generally satisfactory manner, improvement is required for performance to become fully competent. Demonstration of the TRW behaviors and/or initiatives is inconsistent or at lower levels than expected.*

In another section, managers described the subordinates' performance goals and professional development activities for the upcoming year. The subordinates' perspectives were also recorded. Subordinates described their strengths and areas they felt they could improve. They also assessed their own future potential and possible future positions. A year after implementing the new system, the company reported that managers and subordinates alike found the new system to be both much more efficient and more effective in achieving a uniform and complete evaluation process.[1]

For companies like TRW, Lincoln Electric, Cendant Mortgage, FedEx, Con-Way, Continental, and Southwest Airlines, this is the difference between being just okay and being the leader in the industry. A **performance management system** *is a formal, structured process used to measure, evaluate, and influence employees' job-related attitudes, behaviors, and performance results.*[2] Performance management systems help to *direct* and *motivate* employees to maximize the effort they exert on behalf of the organization.

Two components of performance management systems are: (a) performance measurement and feedback for individuals and teams, which are the focus of this chapter, and (b) the rewards component of total compensation, which will be explained in Chapter 11. As illustrated by the TRW example, performance measurement and feedback direct the attention of employees

FAST FACT

Two separate surveys of HR professionals revealed that fewer than 10% were "very satisfied" with their company's performance management system.

toward the most important tasks and behaviors. They inform employees about what's valued and provide information about whether the employees' behaviors and results meet the expectations of managers, colleagues, and customers. Performance measurement and feedback are essential to the effective use of incentives and rewards. The elements of performance management and its relationship to other aspects of the HRM system are shown in Exhibit 10.1.

Performance appraisal is a central component of most performance management systems. **Performance appraisal** *involves evaluating performance based on the judgments and opinions of subordinates, peers, supervisors, other managers, and even employees themselves.* It is perhaps the most common approach to performance measurement, but it is not the only approach. Performance management systems also use objective performance measures such as sales figures, error rates, speed of response, and so on. For jobs that involve direct

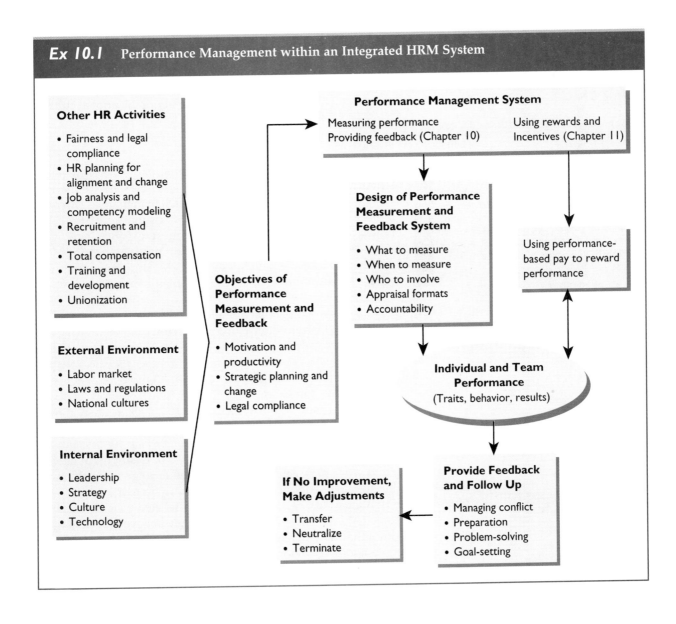

Ex 10.1 Performance Management within an Integrated HRM System

Other HR Activities
- Fairness and legal compliance
- HR planning for alignment and change
- Job analysis and competency modeling
- Recruitment and retention
- Total compensation
- Training and development
- Unionization

External Environment
- Labor market
- Laws and regulations
- National cultures

Internal Environment
- Leadership
- Strategy
- Culture
- Technology

Objectives of Performance Measurement and Feedback
- Motivation and productivity
- Strategic planning and change
- Legal compliance

Performance Management System

Measuring performance
Providing feedback (Chapter 10)

Using rewards and Incentives (Chapter 11)

Design of Performance Measurement and Feedback System
- What to measure
- When to measure
- Who to involve
- Appraisal formats
- Accountability

Using performance-based pay to reward performance

Individual and Team Performance
(Traits, behavior, results)

If No Improvement, Make Adjustments
- Transfer
- Neutralize
- Terminate

Provide Feedback and Follow Up
- Managing conflict
- Preparation
- Problem-solving
- Goal-setting

contact with customers, customer satisfaction data are often used as measures of performance.

Regardless of how performance is measured, its usefulness requires that employees accept it as fair and use performance feedback to guide them in the future. When everything is going well, providing feedback is easy. Everyone wants to give and get feedback that says, "You do not need to change." But today's competitive environment does not usually accept the status quo. Instead, it mandates improvement. In other words, the feedback often says, "We want you to do better." Effective performance management systems result in positive employee reactions to feedback even when the feedback is not positive.[3]

THE STRATEGIC IMPORTANCE OF MEASURING PERFORMANCE AND PROVIDING FEEDBACK

Performance measurement and feedback serve many purposes in organizations. Together, effective measurement and feedback enhance employee motivation and productivity, facilitate strategic planning and change, and ensure legal compliance and fair treatment. To be effective in achieving these outcomes, the performance measurement and feedback process must be aligned with the organization's business strategy and organizational culture.

ENHANCING MOTIVATION AND PRODUCTIVITY

Chapter 8 described how formal training and several developmental activities can be used to improve the knowledge and skills that employees need to perform well in their jobs. There the emphasis was on improving performance by increasing the capabilities of employees. But even the most capable employees won't perform well unless they are motivated to do so. Performance management systems address the issue of motivating employees in order to ensure that their capabilities are fully utilized.

FAST FACT

It is estimated that if companies could get 3.7% more work out of each employee, the equivalent of 18 more minutes of work during each 8-hour shift, the gross domestic product (GDP) in the United States would swell by $355 billion, which is twice the GDP of Greece.

Clearly, motivation is a complex phenomenon, with many factors coming into play. Exhibit 10.2 illustrates some of these factors. Notice that in this model, **motivation** *has two elements: decisions about which behaviors to engage in are one element, and decisions about how much effort to expend are a second element.* Usually, effective job performance requires that employees engage in the appropriate behaviors and exert relatively high levels of effort.[4]

The foundation of the model shown in Exhibit 10.2 is expectancy theory. **Expectancy theory** *states that people choose their behaviors and effort levels after considering whether their behaviors and effort will improve their performance and lead to desired consequences (e.g., recognition and rewards).* Examples of choices that are related to work performance include whether to go to work or call in sick, whether to leave work at the official quitting time or stay late, and whether to exert a great deal of effort or work at a relaxed pace. Expectancy states that people tend to choose behaviors that they believe will help them achieve outcomes that they personally value (e.g., a promotion or job security), and people avoid behaviors that they believe will lead to outcomes they view as undesirable (e.g., a demotion or criticism).

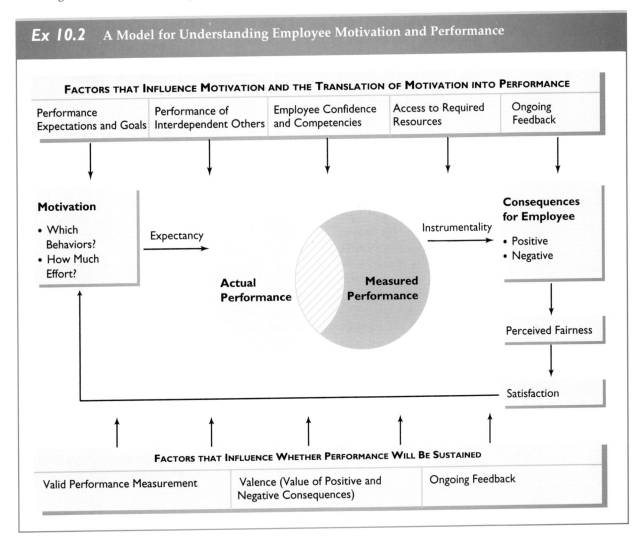

Ex 10.2 A Model for Understanding Employee Motivation and Performance

FACTORS THAT INFLUENCE MOTIVATION AND THE TRANSLATION OF MOTIVATION INTO PERFORMANCE

| Performance Expectations and Goals | Performance of Interdependent Others | Employee Confidence and Competencies | Access to Required Resources | Ongoing Feedback |

Motivation
- Which Behaviors?
- How Much Effort?

Expectancy

Actual Performance

Measured Performance

Instrumentality

Consequences for Employee
- Positive
- Negative

Perceived Fairness

Satisfaction

FACTORS THAT INFLUENCE WHETHER PERFORMANCE WILL BE SUSTAINED

| Valid Performance Measurement | Valence (Value of Positive and Negative Consequences) | Ongoing Feedback |

An employee's motivation to perform well is determined by how he or she responds to three key questions: the expectancy question, the instrumentality question, and the valence question. As you will see, many aspects of an organization's human resource management system can influence how employees answer these questions.

Expectancy. The **expectancy** *question is: If I make an effort, will I be able to perform as intended?* In order for employees to be motivated to expend effort, they must expect that their efforts will translate into performance. Employees are more likely to expect that their efforts will lead to performance if they are confident in their own skills and abilities.[5] Effective selection and training help employees feel confident in their ability to perform. Over time, feedback about performance also can improve employees' confidence in their ability to perform. In addition, the quality of an organization's performance measures is relevant to the expectancy question.

Even when employees know that they can improve their performance, their motivation may remain low if the organization uses inadequate per-

"In the beginning, you're the lowest paid and you're trying hard to get raises. But no matter what I did, nobody reviewed my work and I never got noticed. After awhile, I stopped being so concerned about performance."

John Ranson
Employee
Aerospace industry

formance measures. In Exhibit 10.2, the degree of overlap between "actual" and "measured" performance reflects the adequacy of the organization's performance measure. In an organization where performance measures do a good job of assessing actual performance, the two circles would be completely overlapping. In most organizations, the two circles do not overlap completely. Some aspects of actual performance do not get measured adequately. In addition, biases and inaccuracies on the part of the people who assess an employee's performance can mean that the performance measures reflect irrelevant information, such as whether a person is well-liked by the boss.

Instrumentality. The **instrumentality** *question is: What consequences, if any, will follow from my decision to perform?* The issue here is whether performance is of any instrumental usefulness. An HRM system that uses performance as a basis for incentive pay, decisions about promotions, opportunities for personal development, discipline, and so forth should result in employees believing that desirable consequences await those who perform well, and *only* those who perform well. When important consequences are influenced by factors other than performance (e.g., seniority, personal relationships, and favoritism), employees may feel that performance is of little consequence.

Medi-Health Outsourcing is a fast-growing, young company that helps hospitals and other health care organizations manage patient records and documents for inclusion in national databases. For founders Paula and Ron Lawlor, highly motivated employees are essential to a growing company, which may add as many as 60 or 70 new hospitals to its roster each year. At Medi-Health, employees are held accountable for performance results and rewarded for achieving them. For example, if your job is to code documents for entry into a database, you might be given the goal of abstracting 100 records per week with 95% accuracy. If you meet the goal on Thursday, you can take the rest of the week off.[6]

Valence. The **valence** *question is: How much do I value the consequences associated with the intended behavior?* Even when employees believe that good performers experience different consequences than poor performers, they may not be motivated to put in the required effort. Valences are personal; the same outcome may have a high valence for one person and a low valence for another. Medi-Health strives hard to make sure employees value the rewards they receive from working at the company. The company's employee-friendly approach allows employees to work from home or from the beach, arrange their weekly schedules around their personal needs, and even take three months off without worrying about losing their jobs. When it comes to keeping good performers satisfied, the Medi-Health philosophy is pretty much that "anything goes."

Satisfaction. The model shown in Exhibit 10.2 suggests that an employee's satisfaction is determined by perceptions of whether the rewards received for performance are fair. Satisfied employees are more likely to continue to feel motivated. Dissatisfied employees exert less effort, which results in declining performance and a general downward spiral to ineffectiveness.[7]

"Sometimes I think we baby the heck out of them. But when you ask them to do something, you just don't hear a lot of complaining."

Chuck Hammond
Manager
Medi-Health Outsourcing

It follows from this model of motivation that a company's prospects for attaining peak performance at the individual, team, and organizational levels depend on a performance management system that includes monitoring performance *and* giving employees useful feedback as quickly as possible on how well they're doing.

STRATEGIC PLANNING, ALIGNMENT, AND CHANGE

Besides motivating employees to perform at peak levels, performance measures provide valuable information for use in strategic planning and organizational change. The performance of executives and their management teams is almost synonymous with the performance of the business. If the performance measures used to evaluate executives are designed appropriately, they illuminate the strategic shortcomings and suggest when realignment and change are needed.

FAST FACT

Percentage of companies that view the performance management process as strategic to business:

  Currently: 18%

  Desired: 88%

Detecting Problems. The role of performance management in detecting strategic shortcomings in the business unit is perhaps most easily illustrated by considering performance management for CEOs. Responsibility for evaluating a company's CEO rests with the Board of Directors. The Board is expected to engage the CEO in strategic planning to identify strategic business objectives, set goals, and identify the means for achieving these objectives and goals. The Board also monitors the CEO's progress toward achieving organizational goals and is responsible for staying alert to significant performance problems.

Performance assessments of employees at lower levels in the organization can also be useful for detecting organizational shortcomings. At Pepsi-Cola International, for example, performance information pointed to a deficiency in corporate training. To address the deficiency, the firm established an umbrella organization to deliver training programs around the world. The detection of performance deficiencies also led to a program that brings non-U.S. citizens to the United States for 18 months of training in the domestic Pepsi system.[8]

Evaluating Change. As described in Chapter 4, the process of strategic planning, alignment, and change involves first identifying objectives, and subsequently assessing results against those objectives. Not *all* organizational change efforts target performance improvement as an objective—for example, some change efforts are intended to attract more talent to the organization, others are intended to increase employee satisfaction, and so on. Nevertheless, improving organizational performance, and therefore the performance of at least some of the organization's employees, is the most common objective behind large-scale change efforts. Consequently, employee performance measures should be a key component of a plan for evaluating the success of a change initiative. If human resource issues aren't fully addressed during strategic planning, the performance management system evolves in isolation from strategic initiatives—rather than in anticipation of them.

Ensuring Legal Compliance

In almost all organizations, performance information partly determines pay, promotions, terminations, transfers, and other types of key decisions that affect the well-being of employees and the productivity of a company. Society has a vested interest in ensuring that employers use high-quality information for these important decisions, and their interests are reflected in various laws and regulations. The basic principles for ensuring the legality of a performance management system are similar to those for selection systems. In both cases, the measures used to assess employees should be nondiscriminatory, job-related, and used fairly.

Nondiscriminatory. Numerous laws, regulations, and court decisions provide guidance to employers regarding how to collect and use performance information. Particularly relevant are the Civil Rights Acts of 1964 and 1991, the Americans with Disabilities Act of 1990, and the Age Discrimination in Employment Act of 1967. Each of these emphasize the importance of protecting employees against negative consequences in the workplace that may be caused by unfair discrimination and the use of inappropriate information when making employment decisions.

Job-Related. In general, the legal system makes it clear that employers will be better able to successfully defend any legally contested employment decisions if they can show that their actions were based on valid measures of employee performance. A valid performance measure accurately reflects all aspects of the job, and nothing else. In Exhibit 10.2, a valid performance measure would be indicated by a high degree of overlap between the two circles. *If the performance measure does not assess all of the behaviors and results that are important and relevant to the job, it is* **deficient**. *If the performance measure assesses anything that is unimportant or irrelevant to the job, it is* **contaminated.** Deficient and contaminated measures are quite common in organizations and are among the biggest reasons for employees' complaints about performance measurement.

Valid performance measures are based on job analysis results, which identify the key areas of performance expected in a job. The importance of using job analysis as the basis for developing performance measures was established in *Brito v. Zia Company* (1973). The Zia Company measured performance using the overall judgments and opinions of supervisors. When making their subjective judgments, supervisors were not asked to assess how well each employee performed on specific components of the job—they simply made a global evaluation. These judgments were then used to make decisions about which employees to lay off during a downsizing. When the company conducted its layoffs, a disproportionate number of employees of a protected group lost their jobs because of low scores on the performance measure. The court found that Zia Company was in violation of Title VII because there was no way to be sure that supervisors' evaluations were based on job-related information.

A condensed set of recommended actions for developing and implementing legally defensible performance measurement is detailed in Exhibit 10.3.[9] All of these recommendations are consistent with the objective of developing a performance management system that supports the business strategy and objectives. They also are consistent with creating a system that employees perceive as fair and just.

Fairness. Following the guidelines in Exhibit 10.3 requires careful record keeping and may limit a manager's freedom to make unilateral evaluations. Nevertheless, research indicates that managers respond favorably to the introduction of procedurally just performance management systems. A major advantage for managers is that procedurally fair performance management systems improve relationships between managers and their direct reports.[10] As described in Chapter 3, employees certainly echo the importance of procedural justice. The development and use of alternative dispute resolution mechanisms also attest to this importance. As Chapter 14 describes, unions can be attractive to employees when managers fail to be fair.

THE HR TRIAD

Performance management systems often fall short of achieving strategic objectives. One reason for this is the ambiguity around who owns responsibility for managing the process. Does performance management fall in the domain of human resource departments or line departments? But debates about who is responsible miss the point. Line managers, HR professionals, and employees all need to work together to ensure that appraisals are effective and fair to everyone concerned, as described in the feature "The HR Triad: Roles and Responsibilities for Measuring Performance and Providing Feedback."

Ex 10.3   **Prescriptions for Legally Defensible Appraisal and Feedback**

1. Job analysis to identify important duties and tasks should precede development of a performance appraisal system.

2. The performance appraisal system should be standardized and formal.

3. Specific performance standards should be communicated to employees in advance of the appraisal period.

4. Objective and uncontaminated data should be used whenever possible.

5. Ratings on traits such as dependability, drive, or attitude should be avoided or operationalized in behavioral terms.

6. Employees should be evaluated on specific work dimensions rather than on a single global or overall measure.

7. If work behaviors rather than outcomes are to be evaluated, evaluators should have ample opportunity to observe ratee performance.

8. To increase the reliability of ratings, more than one independent evaluator should perform appraisals whenever possible.

9. Behavioral documentation should be prepared for extreme ratings.

10. Employees should be given an opportuniy to review their appraisals.

11. A formal system of appeal should be available for appraisal disagreements.

12. Raters should be trained to prevent discrimination and to evaluate performance consistently.

13. Appraisals should be frequent, offered at least annually.

The HR Triad

Roles and Responsibilities for Measuring Performance and Providing Feedback

LINE MANAGERS	HR PROFESSIONALS	EMPLOYEES
• Work with HR professionals and employees to develop valid performance measures that meet legal guidelines.	• Work with line managers, providing job analysis data to use in developing valid and legal performance measures.	• Work with line managers and HR professionals to set performance expectations.
• Develop an understanding of how common appraisal rating errors can be avoided.	• Train everyone who completes performance appraisals (e.g., peers, subordinates, and supervisors) how to avoid appraisal rating errors.	• Candidly appraise the work of other employees (boss, peers, etc.).
• Measure employee performance conscientiously and keep accurate records.	• Coordinate the administrative aspects of performance measurement and feedback.	• Participate in self-appraisal.
• Give constructive and honest feedback to employees.	• Train line managers to give and receive feedback.	• Seek and accept constructive and honest feedback.
• Seek and accept constructive feedback about own performance.	• May train self-managing teams to give feedback.	• Learn to give constructive and honest feedback to others.
• Use performance information for decision making.	• Monitor managerial decisions to ensure they're performance-based.	• Develop accurate understanding of performance expectations and criteria.
• Diagnose individual and team performance deficiencies.	• May train self-managing teams to diagnose performance deficiencies.	• Learn to diagnose causes of performance deficiencies for self and team.
• Work with employees to develop performance improvement strategies.	• Ensure managers and employees are aware of all possible ways to deal with performance deficiencies.	• Work with managers to develop performance improvement strategies.
• Provide resources/remove constraints as needed for improvement.	• Provide personal assistance to employees if requested. Develop and administer appeals process.	• Develop goal-setting and self-management skills.

MANAGERS

Usually, managers are responsible for the measuring performance of their subordinates, communicating performance evaluations to their subordinates, and helping their subordinates improve in the future. Regardless of how performance is measured, managers are expected to review performance results with their employees and explain any consequences that may follow (e.g., pay raises, disciplinary action, training). Performance measurement isn't an end to be achieved. Rather, it's a means for moving into a more productive future. For performance evaluations to be useful, employees must *act* on them. Thus, one of a manager's major responsibilities is ensuring that employees accept the feedback they receive and use it as a basis for improving in the future.

EMPLOYEES

The primary performance management responsibilities of employees are seeking honest feedback and using it to improve their performance. Prior to discussions about their performance, employees often are asked to participate by first providing their own assessment of their performance. In addition, all employees—even those with no managerial responsibilities—share responsibility for evaluating the performance of others and providing them with feedback.

Con-Way Transportation Services is a subsidiary of CNF, the giant shipping company. It's a company in which teams are prevalent. Every three months, teams conduct a Team Improvement Review. Before a team improvement meeting, members rate each other on 31 dimensions. To ensure that the feedback environment is "safe," these meetings usually take place with no managers present. In their place is a facilitator who helps the team manage the delicate process of providing feedback that improves rather than destroys team functioning. To begin the process of assessing performance, each team member lists a few of his or her strengths and weaknesses on a sheet of paper. The sheets are then passed around the group. Team members write comments indicating whether they agree or disagree with the items in the list and make suggestions for how and where to focus improvement efforts. The process encourages people to be honest with themselves, and at the same time, it creates a network of support for self-initiated change.[11]

HR PROFESSIONALS

The responsibilities of HR professionals include ensuring that the organization's performance management practices are aligned with the internal organizational contexts, reflect state-of-the-art knowledge, and meet legal standards. HR professionals also help ensure that well-designed practices are implemented appropriately. The role of HR professionals in designing performance management practices is similar to their role in designing other aspects of the HRM systems, as discussed in prior chapters. Rather than reviewing those responsibilities here, we provide a few comments about the role of HR professionals in the implementation of a performance management system.

Support for Managers. Organizations are not always successful in using performance measurement and feedback strategically, and one reason is that line managers do not fully understand and appreciate the basic principles. Most managers spend far more time acquiring technical competencies (e.g., in the areas of accounting, marketing, and operations management) for entry into an organization than they do learning to manage human resources. Yet, skillfully managing the performance of others is necessary for managers to

"Managers are solely responsible for evaluating their employees. No specific, company-side evaluation forms are used for salespeople and managers. Rather, each manager designs his or her own evaluation system."

Mary Kim Stuart
HR Manager
Nordstrom's

achieve their corporate mandate to get things done through other people. The best managers know how to accurately assess performance and have the skills needed to provide feedback in ways that guide and motivate employee improvement. HR professionals can help by teaching managers about the objectives of the organization's performance management system and helping them develop the skills they need to implement it.

Accountability of Managers. A common roadblock to effective performance measurement and feedback is that managers fail to see a payoff. Most organizations offer no obvious incentives for managers to do a good job of measuring employee performance and providing useful feedback to employees. Many managers so dislike these activities that they try to avoid the process entirely.[12] As expectancy theory makes clear, this situation is not optimal! One solution to this problem is to measure how well managers perform this important aspect of their job, and provide them with feedback about how to improve. HR professionals can help ensure that managers are held accountable for effective performance measurement and feedback by including this aspect of managers' jobs in the performance reviews of managers.

"Part of being an 'Employer of Choice' is treating our associates like valued members of the company. Giving them honest and specific feedback about their performance is a major way to do this."

Paris Couturiaux
Senior VP, Human Resources
Cendant Mortgage

Support for Employees. Through their influence on the design of an organization's performance measurement and feedback system, HR professionals provide indirect support to employees. Human resource professionals also can provide direct support to employees. When employees feel their performance evaluations are unfair, HR professionals can assist them in using the organization's appeal process (described in Chapter 3). In many organizations, HR professionals are available to talk to employees about performance problems and provide informal assistance. If necessary, they can recommend other sources of professional assistance. For example, they can help employees find appropriate training opportunities, and they can help employees understand the organization's Employee Assistance Program (EAP). As described in Chapters 12 and 13, EAPs were originally created to battle alcoholism, and some employees still think that EAPs are only relevant for people with alcohol-related problems. But in fact, most EAPs also assist employees with family, financial, and legal problems—all of which can cause unsatisfactory work performance.

As this chapter reveals, developing an effective performance management system requires involvement and buy-in from everyone affected by the system. Achieving this ideal takes time and determination. But for companies like Cendant Mortgage and others who want to be seen as "employers of choice," there is little doubt that investing the effort required contributes to the company's success.

WHAT TO MEASURE

Performance **criteria** *are the dimensions against which the performance of an incumbent, a team, or a work unit is evaluated.* They are the performance expectations that individuals and teams strive for in order to achieve the organization's strategy. If jobs have been designed well, with attention paid to how job demands relate to strategic business needs, then conducting a job analysis should ensure that performance measures reflect strategic concerns. The performance criteria should capture performance on specific tasks and the employee's performance as an organizational citizen.[13] Examples of organizational citizenship (sometimes referred to as contextual performance) include

- volunteering to carry out task activities that are not formally a part of the job;
- persisting with extra enthusiasm or effort when necessary to complete task activities successfully;
- helping others;
- following organizational rules and procedures even when doing so is inconvenient; and
- endorsing, supporting, and defending organizational objectives.[14]

FAST FACT

Employees who perform well on specific job tasks also tend to be good organizational citizens.

When measuring task performance and organizational citizenship, organizations can use three types of performance criteria: personal traits, behaviors, and objective results.

PERSONAL TRAITS

Trait-based criteria *focus on personal characteristics, such as loyalty, dependability, communication ability, and leadership.* Criteria such as these address what a person is, not what a person does or accomplishes on the job. For jobs that involve work that's difficult to observe, trait-based performance measures may be the easiest to use. Unfortunately, they may not be reliable indicators of actual job performance. To one manager, "dependability" may mean showing up to work on time every day; to another manager, it may mean staying late when the boss requests it; to a third manager, it may mean coming to work and not using sick days even when really sick.

Performance evaluations should not depend on who is making the judgment. They should reflect what the employee does, regardless of who is evaluating them. Because trait-based measures of performance are often unreliable, the courts have penalized employers who rely on them when making employment decisions.[15]

Do the position of the courts and the importance of meritocracy in U.S. culture mean that difficult-to-measure personal qualities should not be evaluated as part of the performance appraisal process? Can employers still build corporate cultures around having the right kinds of people as defined by personal qualities that extend beyond job skills? The answer is that personal qualities can be assessed if the measure focuses on employee behaviors.

BEHAVIORS

Behavioral criteria *focus on how work is performed.* Behavioral criteria are particularly important for jobs that involve interpersonal contact. Customer service jobs and managerial jobs are examples that show how behavioral criteria can be used to measure performance.

"The average person puts only 25% of his energy and ability into his work. The world takes off its hat to those who put in more than 50% of their capacity, and stands on its head for those few and far between souls who devote 100%."

Andrew Carnegie

Customer Service. Having friendly cashiers is critical to Au Bon Pain's customers and to the store's image. But Au Bon Pain doesn't use store managers' judgments of employees' friendliness to measure this critical aspect of performance. Instead, it measures behaviors. To assess friendliness, the company generated a list of specific behaviors that employees should engage in. These are behaviors that convey a "friendly" image to most customers. To assess friendliness, the store hires mystery shoppers to buy meals and fill out behavior-based appraisals.

Managing Diversity. As organizations desire to create cultures in which diversity is valued and respected, behavioral criteria are proving useful for monitoring whether managers are investing sufficient energy in the development of employees from diverse backgrounds. Imagine how difficult it would be to evaluate whether a manager achieved a trait-based criterion such as "Values the diversity of subordinates." A trait-based criterion like this provides little guidance to the manager about what actually to *do.* It would be equally difficult for the manager's superior to interpret. (Subordinates, on the other hand, may be quite willing to express their opinions!) For the purpose of performance management, more effective criteria would be *specific* behaviors. For example, one company uses the following items to assess behaviors that managers should be exhibiting in order to manage diversity effectively in their business units:

- Are you a member of a diversity focus group?
- Has your unit formed a diversity focus group?
- Has anyone in your unit filed complaints of discrimination or harassment during the past 12 months?

When combined with performance feedback, behavioral measures are particularly useful for employee development. With behaviors clearly identified, an employee is more likely to exhibit the acts that lead to peak performance. The behaviors identified by TRW included creating trust, energizing people, embracing change, building teamwork, and being customer-oriented. TRW believes that when managers exhibit these behaviors, company success will follow.

Objective Results

Results criteria *focus on what was accomplished or produced rather than on how it was accomplished or produced.* Results criteria may be appropriate if the company does not care how results are achieved, but they are not appropriate for every job. Results criteria are often criticized for missing critical aspects of the job that are difficult to quantify. For example, the number of cases handled annually by a lawyer can easily be counted, but this result does not indicate the quality of legal counsel, the difficulty of the cases, how the cases were resolved, or whether a lawyer helped established any important new legal principles.

Another criticism of results criteria is that they can create unexpected problems by encouraging a results-at-all-costs mentality among employees. A collection agency used the total dollars collected by agents as its sole measure of performance. Large sums of money were collected, but the agency ended up being sued because agents used threats and punitive measures to amass collections.

MULTIPLE CRITERIA

For most jobs, performing well requires performing many tasks well using many different competencies, and job descriptions usually reflect this reality. Just as a job description describes all aspects of the job, performance measures should capture all aspects of the job. For some aspects of the job, trait-based measures may be appropriate. For other duties, behavioral measures or results may be best.

FAST FACT Lincoln Electric's performance measures assess productivity, quality, cooperation, attendance, and creativity.

Some researchers have argued that a limited set of performance domains can be used to capture all aspects of nearly any job. A taxonomy that can be used to describe all the important elements of performance in most organizations is shown in Exhibit 10.4. Notice that this taxonomy includes aspects

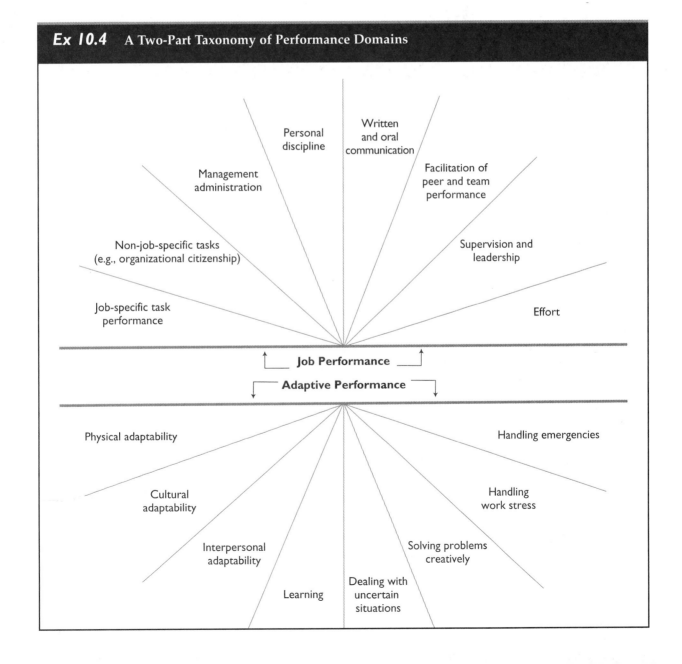

Ex 10.4   A Two-Part Taxonomy of Performance Domains

Personal discipline

Written and oral communication

Management administration

Facilitation of peer and team performance

Non-job-specific tasks (e.g., organizational citizenship)

Supervision and leadership

Job-specific task performance

Effort

Job Performance

Adaptive Performance

Physical adaptability

Handling emergencies

Cultural adaptability

Handling work stress

Interpersonal adaptability

Solving problems creatively

Learning

Dealing with uncertain situations

of the job itself (top half) as well as criteria that reflect how well an employee responds to stress and adapts to new work conditions.[16] The elements in the bottom of Exhibit 10.4 reflect the fact that many jobs and organizations are in a state of constant flux and need employees to be able to adapt and change accordingly.

WEIGHTING THE CRITERIA

For jobs involving multiple performance criteria, another question must be asked: "How should these separate aspects of performance be combined into a composite score that facilitates comparisons of incumbents?" One way is to weight all the criteria equally. If some criteria are much more important than others, then weights should be assigned to reflect these differences. The simplest approach to assigning weights is to use job analysis information—such as ratings of task frequency and importance.

TIMING

"We told employees, 'You have a right to feedback and you can ask for it [any time].'"

Jeff Chambers
HR Director
SAS

The timing of performance measurement *should* reflect strategic considerations. But often the timing of performance measurement and feedback is driven by convenience and tradition. The three most common approaches to timing performance measurement and feedback are focal-point, anniversary, and natural time span.

FOCAL-POINT APPROACH

With the **focal-point approach,** *performance measurement for all employees occurs at approximately the same time.* Many organizations conduct formal review sessions at regular intervals, such as every quarter, every six months, or annually.

Standardization. The major advantage of this system is that supervisors find it easier to make direct comparisons among employees. They consider everyone at once and get a sense of how their performances compare during the same time period. Similarly, top management can compare the performances of different strategic business units to assess how well they're meeting corporate objectives. Such comparative information is particularly important if performance information is used for compensation decisions. At Lincoln Electric, performance measures determine the bonuses of employees, and bonuses are paid out every six months. Prior to distributing the bonus money, line managers spend up to two weeks evaluating the performance of each subordinate. The HR department spends several weeks before this making sure the line managers have all the data they need—including attendance records, productivity figures, and information about the quality of products produced by each employee.

Workload. The focal-point approach creates a tremendous workload for a concentrated period of time, which can be burdensome. The burden can be reduced in two ways: first, by having clear criteria against which to evaluate performance, and second, by ensuring that subordinates share with their supervisors the responsibility for documenting accomplishments relative to performance standards.

Performance Cycles. Another concern about the focal-point approach is that it may create artificial productivity cycles that reflect merely the timing of performance measurement and feedback. Suppose a department store measures performance once each year in July. As part of the process, managers assess the customer responsiveness of each salesperson. Knowing they will be evaluated soon, sales employees are likely to be quite friendly in June. During August and the next several months, they may be less friendly. After all, by next July, their manager is not very likely to remember how they behaved many months ago—in fact, they will even have a new manager by then! Another example might be a law firm that measures performance each year at the end of November: Employees' billable hours may begin to peak in the weeks immediately preceding the appraisal as everyone tries to increase their total billable hours. Then, after the review cycle is over, billable hours may drop below normal as everyone takes time to recover from the frenzy. This problem also occurs when performance is measured subjectively. Knowing that their manager will soon be evaluating their performances, the employees in a unit may all put in extra effort to perform their best. Following the review, employees may reason that their performance at this time will not be remembered by the time the next review cycle begins, causing them to put in less effort for awhile.

Anniversary Approach

The **anniversary approach** *distributes the task of reviewing performance and providing feedback across the year.* Often, an employee's performance review is timed to when they joined the organization. As in the focal-point system, employees may receive reviews every six or twelve months. Assuming the organization hires throughout the year, this approach spreads out the workload, making it less overwhelming for supervisors. However, the anniversary model typically does not tie individual or team performance to the overall performance of the organization, and thus compromises the strategic benefits of the appraisal process. The anniversary model may also make it more difficult for managers to directly compare the performance of one subordinate to others. This is particularly likely if managers must use a forced distribution or "curve." Early in the year, managers tend to be lenient, because they prefer to avoid giving negative evaluations. If the system is set up to permit a fixed percentage of high, medium, and low ratings, then managers who begin the year lenient must balance out the distribution by giving lower ratings later in the year.

Natural Time Span of the Job

Some experts argue that a better timing rule is to schedule reviews to correspond to the natural time span of the job. If performance is assessed too soon in the natural time span, it cannot be reasonably measured due to lack of information. If performance is measured too late, motivation and performance may suffer because the feedback comes too late to be of any use.

> *"Doing annual reviews is like dieting only on your birthday and wondering why you're not losing weight."*
>
> Anne Saunier
> Principal
> Sibson & Co.

Feedback that comes too late is particularly detrimental to a poor performer, who will likely not know how to improve performance until it's too late. In the case of some simple jobs, the time span may be only a few minutes; in the case of a senior-level management job, the appropriate time period may be as long as several years. In an advertising agency, account executives receive evaluation feedback after each presentation.

For teams working on projects, good times for performance measurement and feedback are once about midway through the project and again at the end of the project.[17] At the midway point, team members are open to suggestions for improvement because they have a good understanding of the team's strengths and weaknesses, yet there remains enough time to make changes that may improve the team's performance. After the project ends is the best time to measure performance against deadlines, budget constraints, and other project goals.

PARTICIPANTS IN PERFORMANCE MEASUREMENT AND FEEDBACK

"With 360-degree feedback, we capture input from people with whom the employee works on a regular basis. We call it their 'knowledge network.' The person who receives the evaluation views it as very accurate."

Ann J. Ewen
President
TEAMS, Inc.

It should be apparent by now that there are many sources of performance data, including organizational records, supervisors, employees themselves, peers or team members, subordinates, and customers. Organizational records generally provide objective indicators of performance. All of the other sources—people—provide subjective judgments. Each sources has some advantages and disadvantages.

When determining who to involve when measuring performance, employers need to consider the amount and type of contact each source has with the person being evaluated. Team members, customers, and subordinates see different facets of an individual's task behavior than do supervisors.[18] A customer is more likely to observe the behavior of a sale's representative—for instance, greeting the customer or closing the sale—than is a first-level supervisor. No one—not even the employee—has complete information. To compensate for the disadvantages of gathering data from any single source, most large organizations involve multiple participants when measuring performance and providing feedback.

SUPERVISORS

Many companies assume that supervisors know more than anyone else about how well subordinates perform their jobs, so they give supervisors all the responsibility for measuring performance and providing feedback. Supervisors do produce more reliable performance judgments than other sources, perhaps because they have knowledge about several aspects of employees' performance.[19] Nevertheless, involving other people helps ensure that all aspects of performance are measured and that different perspectives are considered. Employees view this as more fair, which creates greater openness and enhances the quality of the superior-subordinate relationship.

SELF-APPRAISAL

When employees assess their own performance, they conduct a self-appraisal. The use of self-appraisal gained popularity as a component of management by objectives, often referred to as MBO. Management by objectives, described more in the next section, combines the assessment of past performance with goal setting for the future. Subordinates who participate in the evaluation process become more involved and committed to the goals. Subordinate participation also clarifies employees' roles and may reduce role ambiguity and conflict.[20]

FAST FACT

In *Byrd v. Ronayne*, an employer successfully defended the decision to fire an attorney using the attorney's candid self-evaluation that acknowledged performance deficiencies.

Inflation. Self-appraisals increase employees' satisfaction with the appraisal process[21] and are effective tools for self-development, personal growth, and goal commitment. However, self-appraisals are subject to systematic biases and distortions. Self-ratings often are more lenient than those obtained from supervisors. Also, self-appraisals often reveal blind spots—areas of poor performance that the employee is unaware of. High-performing employees appear to have fewer such blind spots than do low-performing employees.[22] Providing extensive performance feedback, building a culture of trust, and including some objective performance data are ways to reduce the problem of leniency in self-appraisals.[23]

Cultural Differences. For global firms, and even domestic firms with culturally diverse workforces, self-appraisals raise another concern—do employees from different cultures approach self-appraisal differently? The tendency to project a positive self-image to others is common in Western culture, which stresses individual achievement, self-sufficiency, and self-respect. In contrast, collectivistic cultures encourage interpersonal harmony, interdependence, solidarity, and group cohesiveness. In the interest of interpersonal harmony, people do not draw attention to their individual achievements.

Are workers in collectivistic cultures more modest than their American counterparts when it comes to rating their own job performance? To find out, an international team of researchers examined the performance ratings of more than 900 pairs of supervisors and their subordinates. The ratings of people working in Taiwan were compared with those of American supervisors. When Taiwanese workers evaluated their own job performance and their own desire to work, they gave themselves lower ratings than did their supervisors. Their ratings were also lower than the ones American workers gave themselves. Consistent with the notion that collectivist cultures value the wisdom that comes with aging, younger Taiwanese workers gave themselves lower ratings than did older Taiwanese workers. The researchers concluded that the use of self-ratings by multinational firms may create bias against employees from collectivist cultures. Besides giving themselves lower ratings, employees from collectivist cultures may be reluctant to engage in self-promotion, which may be necessary for informing supervisors about accomplishments. As a result, supervisors may give these employees ratings that are lower than what's deserved. Unintended discrimination, unfair treatment, lower morale, and ineffective use of the best talent may be consequences of using self-appraisals in a culturally diverse workforce.[24]

PEERS

In team-based organizations, peer involvement in performance management is growing. Research shows that appraisals by peers are useful predictors of future performance.[25] It also shows that the appraisals of peers and subordinates tend to be consistent with each other.[26]

Jamestown Advanced Products Incorporated, a small metal fabrication firm, relies on peers to help manage a variety of performance problems. One problem that came up was tardiness. One person's late arrival disrupted everyone else's schedule, reduced team performance, and consequently lowered financial bonuses. Traditionally, a tardy employee lost some wages but remained eligible for the quarterly performance bonus. Team members thought this was unfair. To increase fairness, the team was encouraged to set performance standards for its members and identify consequences for low performers. The team batted around the issue of how much lateness or absenteeism it could tolerate and how punitive it should be until it reached agreement: Employees could be tardy (defined as one minute late) or absent without notice no more than five times a quarter. Beyond that, they would lose their entire bonus.

SUBORDINATES

Few subordinates have information about all dimensions of their supervisor's performance, but most have access to information about supervisor-subordinate interactions. Organizations such as Johnson & Johnson and Sears have been surveying employees for their opinions about managers for years. *When such surveys are used to evaluate the performance of specific managers, the process is called* **upward appraisal.**

FAST FACT

In a survey of executives of the nation's 1,000 largest companies, 60% said employees should be allowed to participate in a formal review of the boss.

General Mills uses upward appraisal, and even the CEO is included in the process. CEO Steve Sanger understands that he can be a powerful example for the rest of the company's employees. "Just last year, my team told me that I needed to do a better job of coaching my direct reports," he explained. "I have been working on being a better coach for the past year or so. I just reviewed my feedback [for this year and last year]. I'm still not doing as well as I want, but I am doing a lot better." Sanger is proud of the improvement in his coaching, and he also is proud that he got high scores on "effectively responds to feedback."[27]

Anonymity. One drawback to upward feedback is that subordinates don't always evaluate performance objectively or honestly, especially if their ratings are not anonymous.[28] To protect anonymity, evaluations need to be made by several subordinates, and someone other than the supervisor should average the subordinates' ratings.

Usefulness. For managers who do not already perform well, upward appraisal can be quite useful. One study followed managers over a period of five years in order to track changes in performance following upward appraisal and feedback. The results showed that managers who initially performed poorly significantly improved after receiving the results of upward appraisals. The greatest improvements occurred for managers who met with their direct reports to discuss their own performance results.[29] Other research shows that even managers who already perform well benefit from upward feedback. Overall, managers who are confident in their own abilities seem to be the ones who are most able to accept negative feedback and use it to improve their own performance.[30] Finally, research shows that upward feedback is most effective when it is accompanied by specific suggestions about *how* to improve.[31]

CUSTOMERS

At a medical clinic in Billings, Montana, patients routinely rate desk attendants and nursing personnel on behaviors such as courtesy, promptness, and quality of care. Domino's Pizza hires mystery customers who order pizzas and then evaluate the performance of the telephone operator and delivery person. The owner of a carpeting firm uses a customer checklist to monitor the on-site performance of carpet installers. When customers are used as appraisers, it is difficult for employees to discount the results because usually employers obtain the impressions of *many* customers. Nevertheless, a potential difficulty in using real customers is getting a fair sampling of customer experiences. Customers who have had particularly bad experiences may be more likely to complete a questionnaire, for example.

FAST FACT To encourage participation in its customer performance appraisal process, Xerox Business Services plants a tree for each customer who returns a completed form.

360-DEGREE APPRAISALS

When evaluations from supervisors, subordinates, peers, and employees themselves are all used, they are referred to as **360-degree appraisals.** In contrast to the traditional approach, where a single person—usually a supervisor—rates employee performance, 360-degree systems collect performance information from a set of colleagues and internal customers who form a circle around the employee. Many employers have adopted 360-degree appraisal and feedback systems.[32]

Multiple-source evaluations are perceived as being more fair than single-source approaches. The evaluation process produces more valid results because it involves a group of people who interact with the employee in many different ways. For the same reason, the process should be less susceptible to gender and ethnicity biases than are single-source evaluations.[33]

Because the practice is relatively new, little research exists to guide organizations in developing the most appropriate 360-degree practices. However, the limited evidence that's available does suggest that the raters' identities should remain anonymous, when possible. Also, it appears that this technique works best when the full circle is represented—not just one portion of it (e.g., including only subordinates or only peers). In most other

FAST FACT Otis Elevator's Worldwide Engineering Group conducts 360-degree appraisals on their intranet. Although the employees are engineers, they were overwhelmed at first by too much information that they didn't know how to interpret.

respects, the principles for developing an effective appraisal system are essentially the same for single-source and multiple-source assessments.[34]

PERFORMANCE APPRAISAL FORMATS

When performance is measured using performance appraisals (in contrast to objective measures), a format of some sort is provided for appraisers to use. Appraisals may be recorded on paper or electronically. Either way, the appraisal format provides a structure for raters to use when making and recording their judgments.

Norm-Referenced Formats

For many human resource decisions, employees must be compared to each other directly. Special recognition cannot be given without knowing: Who is the best performer in the group? Layoffs should not be conducted without knowing: Who are the weakest performers we can let go, given that we have to cut our workforce? For these types of decisions, norm-referenced formats are appropriate. With a **norm-referenced format,** *the rater is forced to evaluate the individual or team and make comparisons to others.* The two most commonly used norm-referenced formats are straight ranking and forced distribution.

Straight Ranking. In **straight ranking,** *the appraiser lists the focal employees (or teams of employees) in order, from best to worst, usually on the basis of overall performance.* As the number of employees to be ranked increases, straight ranking becomes increasingly difficult. A problem with straight ranking is that ties usually are not allowed. Although no two subordinates perform exactly alike, many supervisors believe that some incumbents perform so similarly that making performance distinctions between them is not appropriate.

Forced Distribution. With the **forced distribution method,** *the appraiser distributes employees across several categories of performance following a set rule about the distribution of ratings that are permitted.* A typical rule specifies five categories of performance and forces most of the evaluations to fall near the middle, as illustrated in the following chart.

Lowest Performers	Next Lowest	Middle	Next Highest	Highest Performers
10%	20%	40%	20%	10%
(5 employees)	(10 employees)	(20 employees)	(10 employees)	(5 employees)

The forced distribution method creates problems for evaluators who believe that the pattern of performances from people being evaluated does not conform to the fixed percentages. Nevertheless, this method seems to be gaining popularity. According to one recent estimate, it is now used in one out of five Fortune 500 companies.[35]

ABSOLUTE STANDARDS FORMATS

With the absolute standards format, appraisers assess performance in relation to specified criteria and do not make direct comparisons among employees. Three widely used formats using absolute standards are graphic rating scales, behaviorally anchored rating scales, and behavioral observation scales.

Graphic Rating Scales. Introduced in the 1920s, graphic rating scales were touted as useful because direct output measures were not needed and the rater was free to make as fine a judgment as desired. The primary advantage of the graphic rating scale format is its simplicity. Exhibit 10.5 shows several graphic rating scales that might be used to assess the quan-

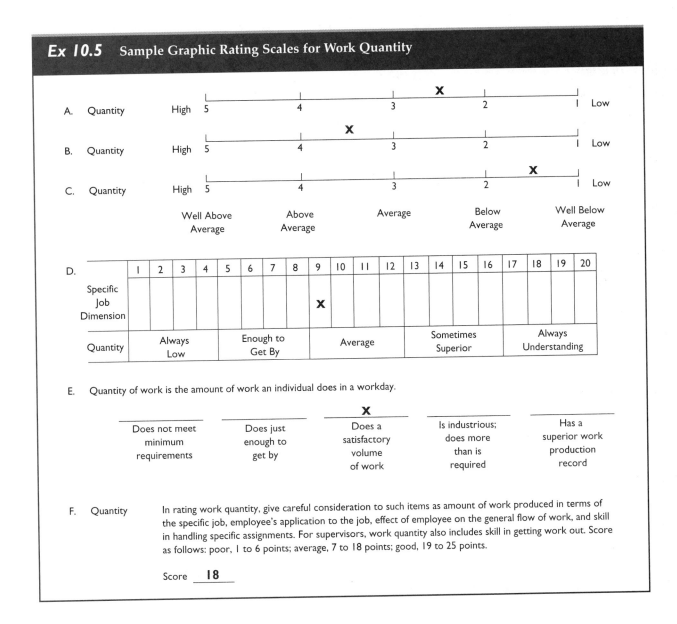

Ex 10.5   Sample Graphic Rating Scales for Work Quantity

tity of work a person completed. In this exhibit, scales A to C require the rater to define the dimension. This obviously leads to different interpretations by different raters. Scales D and E do a better job of defining work quantity, but they still provide latitude for disagreement. Scale F provides the most extensive definition of work quantity, but the rater must consider more than one aspect of quantity. In addition, scale F provides anchors for only three general groups of scale values, although 25 discrete scale values can be used. As these examples illustrate, the major disadvantage of graphic rating scales is their lack of clarity and definition. Even when raters are trained, they still might not define the performance dimensions in the same way. At TRW, four-point rating scales provide very specific descriptions of what each level of performance means on each of the five behavioral criteria described earlier.

Behaviorally Anchored Rating Scales.

Dissatisfaction with graphic rating scales led to the development of formats that include more specific behavioral criteria. **Behaviorally anchored rating scales (BARS)** *provide appraisers with specific examples of the behaviors that go along with each value that can be assigned to an employee's performance.* The behavioral descriptions are intended to ensure that appraisers all use similar interpretations when assigning performance scores.

The development of a BARS performance measure involves collecting descriptions of incidents that illustrate very competent, average, and incompetent work behaviors. These performance descriptions must be obtained in advance—often as part of a job analysis. Exhibit 10.6 shows a behaviorally anchored rating scale for the performance dimension of "transacting loans." A higher scale value means better performance.

Like any format, the BARS format has limitations. Scales can be difficult and time-consuming to develop. This means they are more difficult to modify as jobs change and performance expectations shift. From a cost-benefit perspective, the development of behavioral formats should be restricted to jobs that have many incumbents or for which the job *processes* (versus results) are critical to job success. In the service sector, success often depends on *how* work is performed, so it is worthwhile to invest in the effort required to develop clear behavioral standards.

For raters, problems occur when the incidents shown on the form don't correspond to any behavior the rater has observed, or when the rater has observed the employee displaying behaviors associated with both high and low performance. For example, a corporate loan assistant could prepare follow-up documentation in a timely manner and also receive complaints from loan applicants about rudeness and inappropriate questioning. In such situations, it is difficult to decide whether to give a high or low rating.[36]

Behavioral Observation Scales.

Behavioral observation scales (BOS) *ask appraisers to report how frequently employees engage in specific behaviors.* As with BARS, the behaviors listed are developed using job analysis information. Because of the way points are assigned to behaviors, adding up all the ratings yields an overall measure of performance (items that describe inef-

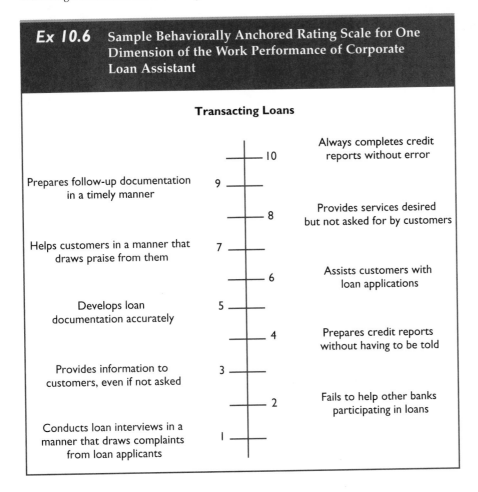

Ex 10.6 Sample Behaviorally Anchored Rating Scale for One Dimension of the Work Performance of Corporate Loan Assistant

Transacting Loans

- 10 — Always completes credit reports without error
- Prepares follow-up documentation in a timely manner — 9
- 8 — Provides services desired but not asked for by customers
- Helps customers in a manner that draws praise from them — 7
- 6 — Assists customers with loan applications
- Develops loan documentation accurately — 5
- 4 — Prepares credit reports without having to be told
- Provides information to customers, even if not asked — 3
- 2 — Fails to help other banks participating in loans
- Conducts loan interviews in a manner that draws complaints from loan applicants — 1

fective performance are reverse-scored). Exhibit 10.7 illustrates the BOS format.[37]

BOS is just as expensive and time-consuming as BARS to develop, but raters find it easier to use. Unfortunately, however, raters often don't have sufficient time or ability to accurately assess the frequency with which behaviors are observed.

RESULTS-BASED FORMATS

For some jobs, or some aspects of a job, the results achieved are more important than the behaviors that led to those results. In such cases, it may be most appropriate to measure actual results. Results-based formats focus on job products as the primary criteria. As is true for the norm-referenced and absolute standards approaches, job analysis should guide the choice of results selected for measurement. Two widely used results-based formats are management by objectives and the direct index approach.

Direct Index Approach. The **direct index approach** *measures performance using objective, impersonal criteria, such as productivity, absenteeism, and turnover.* At Busch's Inc., a retail grocer in

FAST FACT

L. L. Bean sold his first pair of hunting boots in 1912. Ninety of his first 1,000 pairs fell apart and were returned!

Ex 10.7 — Sample Behavioral Observation Scale Items for a Maintenance Mechanic

In completing this form, circle
0– if you have no knowledge of the employee's behavior
1– if the employee has engaged in the behavior 0 to 64 percent of the time
2– if the employee has engaged in the behavior 65 to 74 percent of the time
3– if the employee has engaged in the behavior 75 to 84 percent of the time
4– if the employee has engaged in the behavior 85 to 94 percent of the time
5– if the employee has engaged in the behavior 95 to 100 percent of the time

Customer Relations

	Behavior Frequency					
1. Swears in front of customers (e.g, operators and vendors) (R)	0	1	2	3	4	5
2. Blames customers for malfunction (R)	0	1	2	3	4	5
3. Refers to customers by name or asks for their names when first introduced	0	1	2	3	4	5
4. Asks operators to demonstrate what they were doing at the time of the malfunction	0	1	2	3	4	5

Teamwork

1. Exhibits rude behavior that coworkers complain about (R)	0	1	2	3	4	5
2. Verbally shares technical knowledge with other technicians	0	1	2	3	4	5
3. As needed, consults fellow workers for their ideas on ways to solve specific problems	0	1	2	3	4	5
4. Given an incomplete assignment, leaves a clear, written tie-in for the next day shift to use	0	1	2	3	4	5
5. Works his or her share of overtime						

Planning

1. Estimates repair time accurately	0	1	2	3	4	5
2. Completes assigned jobs on time	0	1	2	3	4	5
3. Is able to set job priorities on a daily or weekly basis	0	1	2	3	4	5
4. Even when the job is not yet complete, cleans up area at the end of the shift	0	1	2	3	4	5
5. Identifies problems or potential problems that may affect repair success or completion time						

Planned Maintenance Repairs

1. Executes planned maintenance repair, requiring no follow-up	0	1	2	3	4	5
2. Adjusts equipment according to predetermined tolerance levels; commits no errors	0	1	2	3	4	5
3. Replaces components when necessary rather than when convenient or easy	0	1	2	3	4	5
4. Takes more time than allotted to complete a planned maintenance repair (R)	0	1	2	3	4	5

Note: "R" denotes item is reverse-scored (5 = 1, 4 = 2, 3 = 3, 2 = 4, 1 = 5, 0 = 0)

Michigan, managers are evaluated on the store's sales figures, profit margins, cost of supplies, employee turnover, and payroll expenses.

One advantage of the direct index approach is that it provides clear, unambiguous direction to employees regarding desired job results. Another advantage is that extraneous factors—for example, prior performance, salary, and personal characteristics like gender—are less likely to bias the results. On the other hand, important job behaviors may be ignored. This problem can be overcome by supplementing the direct indexes with other formats. For example, at Busch's Inc., the direct index approach is combined with graphic ratings scales that assess follow-through, merchandizing execution, creative problem solving, leadership, training and development of subordinates, and use of computers.[38]

Management by Objectives. **Management by Objectives (MBO)** *begins with the establishment of goals or objectives for the upcoming performance period; performance is then measured against the goals or objectives that were set. In some* organizations, superiors and subordinates work together to establish goals; in others, superiors establish goals for work groups or individuals; in still others, in organizations with self-managed work teams, teams may set their own goals. Exhibit 10.8 illustrates goals set by a graphic artist.[39]

Goals should be challenging, but not so difficult that employees don't believe they can be achieved. Easy goals don't give employees any reason to exert extra effort. If goals are too difficult, however, employees will reject them as impossible and won't even bother trying to achieve them.[40]

Once goals are established, the next step is to develop a strategy for goal attainment. Clearly delineating how a goal is to be attained reduces ambiguity and makes goal attainment more likely. Strategy development includes outlining the steps necessary to attain each objective, as well as any constraints that may block attainment of the objective.

At the conclusion of the performance period, actual performance is evaluated relative to the preestablished goals or objectives. During the feedback session, the reasons goals were not attained or were exceeded should be explored. This step helps determine training needs and development potential. The final step is to set new goals and possibly new strategies.

For an MBO system to be effective, managers must be committed to the process. Goals should cascade from the top down, which helps employees see how their efforts link back to the broader strategic business objectives and vision of the company. At NCCI, goal setting and management by objectives are credited with helping motivate employees and align their performance with the organization's strategic business objectives. This is described further in "Managing Change: NCCI's Goals Improve Performance."[41]

"A company needs clear, elevating goals that people at all levels of the organization can understand and relate to. Whether a person is a CEO or a forklift operator in Detroit, they need to understand how what they do for their eight hours at work relates to that clear, elevating vision."

Tony Rucci
Ex. VP and Chief Administrative Officer
Cardinal Health

Ex 10.8 Performance Goals and Subgoals for a Graphic Artist

PROJECT: LOGO DEVELOPMENT FOR CASPER COUNTY PARK SYSTEM

1. Meet all agreed-on deadlines.
2. Keep costs within the agreed-on budget.
3. Bill final hours within plus or minus 10 percent of the agreed-on budget.
4. Achieve supervisor's criteria for logo development. Subgoals include:
   a. Reproduces well in various sizes and in three dimensions
   b. Can be used in one color, line art, and halftone versions
   c. Has a strong identity
   d. Uses type in a unique manner
   e. Has high-quality art
5. Meet client's criteria for logo. Subgoals include:
   a. Conveys desired public image
   b. Message is clear
   c. Logo is easily recognizable
   d. Typeface matches the personality of the park system
6. Strive to exceed client expectations. Indicators that this goal is met include:
   a. Logo design wins an award
   b. Customers express excitement about using the logo
   c. Public learns to recognize the logo without text within one year

Managing Change

NCCI's Goals Improve Performance

Located in Boca Raton, Florida, NCCI is a non-profit consortium that employs 1,200 people. The organization provides workplace injury data to its customers, which include insurance companies, insurance brokers, and state officials in 40 states. When annual employee turnover reached 26% and customers began to express concerns about the service they were receiving, NCCI developed a new approach to motivating employees. Under the new system, employees meet with their managers twice a year to develop performance objectives for the next 12 months. In June, the meeting focuses on specific goals that the employee is to achieve. A billing analyst might have a goal of completing 100% of invoices on time. A marketing manager might have a goal of completing a project by a specific date and within a certain budget. How well an employee's goals are met determines her or his salary increase for the next year. In December, another goal-setting meeting is held, but this time the focus is on the employee's extra contributions to the organization. As Lisa Jarrot, a manager in the finance division puts it, "This is more an above-and-beyond sort of thing. Say that one of the corporate goals is to streamline performance to improve the bottom line. The billing

analyst's objective might be to seek efficiencies in the billing process to improve cycle time." How well an employee does in contributing to this "above-and-beyond" type of goal is used to determine the employee's annual bonus. Jarrot is convinced that the new system is more motivating for employees. "I'm in better control of my own destiny," she says. "There are more opportunities to show improvement and there's more certainty that if I do my job well, I'm going to be rewarded for it."

Besides motivating employees, the system is designed to align the efforts of employees with the organization's business objectives. The board and senior management set the corporate objectives. Then each department identifies what it will contribute to help meet those objectives and finds ways to measure those contributions. Each individual's goals are then linked directly to the department's goals. At NCCI, this approach to motivating employees helped reduce turnover—especially among the most experienced employees. It also helped improve efficiency and productivity and helped NCCI achieve a positive cash flow, thus making it possible for NCCI to give its customers price breaks worth $11 million.

THE RATING PROCESS

Clearly, employers can take many different approaches to measuring performance—some are objective, but most involve some subjectivity. Some use identical standards for all employees, while others allow managers to take into account individual circumstances when assessing performance. None is perfect and all cause some employees to feel uneasy about the problems of bias and inaccuracy.

The quality of performance judgments depends, in part, on the information processing capabilities or strategies of the person making the evaluation.[42] The evaluator first attends to and recognizes relevant information. The information is stored—first in short-term memory and then in long-term memory—until a performance judgment needs to be made. Finally, before the evaluation is recorded officially, it may be revised depending on reactions of the incumbent or higher-level managers, the goals the rater hopes to achieve through the appraisal process, and even organizational norms.[43] The fallibility of managers combines with this process to create numerous types of errors.[44]

Rating Errors

When criteria aren't clearly specified and no incentives are associated with rating accuracy, a variety of errors occur during the rating process. These rater errors, which are described in Exhibit 10.9, can affect all stages of the process, but their effects are most clearly seen at the final stage, after ratings have actually been recorded.[45]

Improving Rater Accuracy

Even the best performance management system may not be effective when so many extraneous errors impinge on the performance appraisal process. Fortunately, several strategies can be used to minimize appraisal errors and improve rater accuracy, including: making the rating scale format precise, providing memory aids and rater training, rewarding timely appraisals, and using multiple raters.

Rating Scale Format. Performance ratings tend to be more accurate when the performance criteria and the rating scales are precise. When the correct elements are in place, evaluators are more accurate in their ratings and more confident about their ratings. Features of a rating scale include:

> *"We had 'rater error.' We had the 'contrast effect.' We had the 'halo effect.' But the biggest problem was that the feedback wasn't leading to changes in behavior."*
>
> Chris Oster
> Director of Organizational Development
> General Motors

Ex 10.9 Common Performance Rating Errors	
Halo and Horn	A tendency to think of an employee as more or less good or bad is carried over into specific performance ratings. Or stereotypes based on the employee's sex, race, or age affect performance ratings. In either case, the rater doesn't make meaningful distinctions when evaluating specific dimensions of performance. All dimensions of performance are rated either low (horn) or high (halo).
Leniency	All employees are rated higher than they should be rated. This happens when managers aren't penalized for giving high ratings to everyone, when rewards aren't part of a fixed and limited pot, and when dimensional ratings aren't required.
Strictness	All employees are rated lower than they should be. Inexperienced raters who are unfamiliar with environmental constraints on performance, raters with low self-esteem, and raters who have themselves received a low rating are most likely to rate strictly. Rater training that includes a reversal of supervisor-incumbent roles and confidence building can reduce this error.
Central Tendency	All employees are rated as average, when performance actually varies. Raters with large spans of control and little opportunity to observe behavior are likely to use this "play-it-safe" strategy. A forced distribution format requiring that most employees be rated average also may create this error.
Primacy	As a cognitive shortcut, raters may use initial information to categorize a person as either a good or a bad performer. Information that supports the initial judgment is amassed, and unconfirming information is ignored.
Recency	A rater may ignore employee performance until the appraisal date draws near. When the rater searches for cues about performance, recent behaviors or results are most salient, so recent events receive more weight than they should.
Contrast Effects	When compared with weak employees, an average employee will appear outstanding; when evaluated against outstanding employees, an average employee will be perceived as a low performer.

- Each performance dimension addresses a single job activity, rather than a group of activities.
- Each performance dimension is rated separately, and the scores are then summed to determine the overall rating.
- Ambiguous terms like *average* are not used because different raters have various reactions to them.[46]

Provide Memory Aids. Everyone involved in making appraisals should regularly record behaviors or results—good or bad—that relate to an employee's or work group's performance. Reviewing these records at the time of the performance appraisal helps ensure that the rater uses all available and relevant information. Consulting a behavioral diary or a critical incident file before rating reduces recency and primacy errors, yielding more accurate measures of performance. Electronic diary-keeping software makes this task easier than ever.[47]

Provide Rater Training. Rating accuracy can also be improved through training that focuses on improving the observation skills of raters. Frame-of-reference training is one of the most useful approaches.[48] A comprehensive frame-of-reference training program might include the following steps:

1. The raters are given a job description and instructed to identify appropriate criteria for evaluating the job.
2. When agreement is reached, the raters view a video of an employee performing the job.
3. Independently, the raters evaluate the video performance, using the organization's appraisal system.
4. The raters' evaluations are compared with each other and with those of job experts.
5. With a trainer as a facilitator, the raters present the rationales for their ratings and challenge the rationales of other raters.
6. The trainer helps the raters reach a consensus regarding the value of specific job behaviors and overall performance.
7. A new video is shown, followed by independent ratings.
8. The process continues until consensus is achieved.[49]

Reward Accurate and Timely Appraisals. One cause of rating inaccuracy is a lack of rater motivation. Without rewards, raters may find it easier to give high ratings than to give accurate ratings.[50] A straightforward strategy for increasing rater motivation is to base salary increases, promotions, and assignments to key positions partly on performance as a rater. Ratings done in a timely and fair manner (as measured by employee attitude surveys) should be rewarded.

Use Multiple Raters. Often, the ratee believes that the rater is solely responsible for a poor evaluation and any subsequent loss of rewards; the rater may also believe this. Research suggests that this negative effect can be minimized by relying on the judgments of multiple raters.[51] The diffusion of responsibility frees each rater to evaluate more accurately. Furthermore, employees are less likely to shrug off negative information when multiple raters were involved.[52] Multiple raters acting as a group that must come to a consensus may be especially effective in producing accurate ratings, because discussion among members of the group helps overcome the various errors and biases of individuals.[53]

PROVIDING FEEDBACK

Performance management is an ongoing process, punctuated by formal performance measurement and formal feedback sessions intended to improve future performance.[54] In feedback sessions, supervisors and subordinates meet to exchange information, including evaluations of performance and ideas for how to improve.[55] Many managers feel uncomfortable providing feedback to employees, in part because the process often stimulates conflict. Understanding the sources of conflict associated with performance feedback is the first step in providing feedback successfully.

FAST FACT

Park View Medical Center in Pueblo, Colorado, doesn't believe in forms. It has an appraisal called the Annual Piece of Paper (APOP), but its only purpose is to document that a conversation focused on performance took place.

DIFFERING PERSPECTIVES

Organizations need to evaluate employees and make employment decisions. Employees need to know how their performance is evaluated in order to know where they stand in the organization and what rewards they are likely to receive. Supervisors and their subordinates are both interested in honest discussion about performance. Both tend to feel more comfortable discussing positive performance rather than negative performance. Nevertheless, both parties should recognize that performance discussions are most productive when they yield concrete suggestions for how to improve future performance. Ideally, a conversation about how to improve in the future follows naturally from a discussion of how well things have gone in the past. But this discussion becomes difficult when employees and their managers have different perspectives about the causes of past performance.

Low-performance situations accentuate a natural tendency that we all share, which is to account for performance in a self-serving manner. To protect our egos, we attribute our own poor performance to external circumstances—a difficult task, unclear instructions, lack of necessary equipment, and other situations that often implicate the supervisor. Supervisors also wish to protect their egos, so they may deny responsibility for the subordinate's poor performance and instead attribute problems to the employee's own deficiencies. These self-serving attributions can make it difficult for supervisors and their employees to come to agreement about how to improve poor performance.

Self-serving attributions may also dampen the expected effects of positive appraisals. When we perform well, the natural tendency is to take full credit for our performance. We use positive evidence to reinforce our high opinion of ourselves, discounting the role external forces may have played. The self-interested perspective of managers, however, leads them to view our success as due to such things as chance or luck and the support we received from the manager and other employees.[56] Add to this our general feeling that we are better-than-average performers, and the scene is set for a potentially dysfunctional cycle: Employees believe they perform well and deserve credit for having done so; their supervisors often evaluate their performance less favorably, and these evaluations are perceived as unfair. When supervisors do recognize good performance, employees may perceive the recognition as merely what they deserved, leaving supervisors to wonder why their subordinates aren't more grateful.

The attributions for performance that supervisors and subordinates make influences the strategies they develop for performance improvement.[57] If the employee is viewed as responsible for performance problems, strategies aimed at changing the subordinate (e.g., retraining) will seem more appropriate. If performance is attributed to external circumstances, strategies that modify the environment, such as changing the job design or providing more rewards, are more likely.

TIMING

The delivery of performance feedback needs to be well-timed. In general, immediate feedback is most useful. Feedback also should involve only as much information as the receiver can use. Providing continuous feedback is the best way to avoid information overload and maximize the value of the feedback given.[58] At Synygy, performance reviews occur once every quarter for all employees. For some managers, the each review cycle consumes as much as a week of time. Yet the company feels strongly that the gains from frequent feedback make this a worthwhile investment of their resources. A recent college graduate who joined the company agreed that quarterly reviews were very helpful to him. "You don't lose a year of your time focusing on the wrong things before you get some guidance," he explained. The company also benefits by spotting the occasional problem employee very early. The extensive documentation that accumulates as a natural part of frequent reviews also puts the company on firm legal ground should they decide to fire someone.[59]

PREPARATION

"Schedule an appointment and have a meeting. Don't give important feedback in the hallway."

Rick Maurer
Consultant

To signal that performance matters, feedback sessions need to be scheduled in advance. In setting up the session, the manager and employee should reach agreement regarding the purpose and content of their discussion. Will the subordinate provide feedback to the supervisor, or will the discussion be one-way? Will the subordinate be asked to provide a self-assessment, or will they discuss only the supervisor's perspective? Will the discussion be restricted to evaluating past performance or to mapping out a strategy for future performance, or will both topics be discussed? By discussing these issues before the actual interview, both participants have time to prepare.

CONTENT OF THE DISCUSSION

The most useful feedback sessions focus on solving problems and planning the future. Problem solving involves diagnosing the causes of performance. Planning for the future involves agreeing to address problems that were revealed in the diagnosis and setting goals. The effort pays off when employees get feedback they find useful and feel motivated to improve.[60]

Diagnosis. The objective of diagnosis is to understand the factors that affect an employee's performance. Diagnosis is particularly important for employees who have not performed as well as required, but it also can be useful even for employees who have performed well. Usually, even the best performers experience roadblocks that, if removed, would allow them to do even better.

The model of motivation shown in Exhibit 10.2 (p. 411) suggests a number of factors that can impede performance. To determine whether any of these are causing problems for an employee, the manager and employee together can consider questions such as those listed in Exhibit 10.10. Sharing perceptions and identifying solutions should be the focus. This type of discussion is difficult for most supervisors, so prior training in problem solving and in giving and receiving feedback should be provided.

Removing Roadblocks. Based on what is learned from the diagnostic process, both the supervisor and subordinate should agree to an action plan.

Ex 10.10   Sample Checklist for Diagnosing the Causes of Performance Deficiencies

Check the determinants of performance or behavior that apply to the situation you are analyzing.

	Yes	No
I. Confidence and Competencies		
A. Does the employee have the competencies needed to perform as expected?	___	___
B. Has the employee performed as expected before?	___	___
C. Does the employee believe he or she has the competencies needed to perform as desired?	___	___
D. Does the employee have the interest to perform as desired?	___	___
II. Goals for the Employee		
A. Were the goals communicated to the employee?	___	___
B. Are the goals specific?	___	___
C. Are the goals difficult but attainable?	___	___
III. Certainty for the Employee		
A. Has desired performance been clearly specified?	___	___
B. Have rewards or consequences for good or bad performance been specified?	___	___
C. Is the employee clear about her or his level of authority?	___	___
IV. Feedback to the Employee		
A. Does the employee know when he or she has performed correctly or incorrectly?	___	___
B. Is the feedback diagnostic so that the employee can perform better in the future?	___	___
C. Is there a delay between performance and the receipt of the feedback?	___	___
D. Can performance feedback be easily interpreted?	___	___
V. Consequences to the Employee		
A. Is performing as expected punishing?	___	___
B. Is not performing poorly more rewarding than performing well?	___	___
C. Does performing as desired matter?	___	___
D. Are there positive consequences for performing as desired?	___	___
VI. Access to Resources		
A. Can the employee mobilize the resources to get the job done?	___	___
B. Does the employee have the tools and equipment to perform as desired?	___	___
C. Is performance under the control of the employee?	___	___

The specific content of the plan depends on both organizational needs and information from the diagnosis. In general, the action plan for the supervisor should address problems such as lack of resources, providing additional information and training, and improving ongoing communications and feedback. The action plan for the subordinate should address behavioral changes that may be needed, career development activities, as well as specific performance goals.

FOLLOW-UP

Follow-up is essential to ensuring that agreements reached during the feedback session are fulfilled. Supervisors should verify that subordinates know what is expected and realize the consequences of good or poor performance. Follow-up can be as simple as a pat on the back or a compliment ("That was nice work, George"), or as tangible as a note placed in the employee's file.[61] Almost everyone appreciates recognition for good performance. Employees with serious performance problems may require constant monitoring and even the use of punishment.

Positive reinforcement *involves the use of positive rewards to increase the occurrence of the desired performance.* Positive reinforcement focuses on the job behavior that leads to desired results, rather than on the results directly. It uses rewards rather than punishment or the threat of punishment to influence that behavior, and is generally a very effective method for creating behavioral changes.[62]

When behavioral problems persist, formal disciplinary action is needed. When used appropriately, **punishment** *decreases the frequency of undesirable behavior.* Punishments can include material consequences, such as a cut in pay, a disciplinary layoff without pay, a demotion, or, ultimately, termination. Punishment is frequently used by organizations because it can achieve relatively immediate results. Besides alerting the marginal employee to the fact that his or her low performance is unacceptable, punishment has vicarious power. When one person is punished, it signals other employees regarding expected performance and behavioral conduct. When the punishment an employee receives is viewed as appropriate by other employees, it may increase their motivation, morale, and performance.

Punishment can also have undesirable side effects. An employee reprimanded for low performance may become defensive and angry toward the supervisor and the organization. As many news reports attest, this anger may result in sabotage (destroying equipment, passing trade secrets) or retaliation (shooting the supervisor). Another concern is that control of the undesirable behavior becomes contingent on the presence of the punishing agent. When the manager isn't present, the behavior is likely to be displayed.

WHEN NOTHING ELSE WORKS

Helping employees improve their work performance is a tough job. It's easy to get frustrated and wonder if we are just spinning our wheels. Even when we want our efforts to work, they sometimes don't. Still, when we conclude that "nothing works," we are really saying that it's no longer worth our time and energy to help the employee improve. This conclusion shouldn't be made in haste, because the organization has already invested a great deal of

> *"There are two things people want more than sex and money—recognition and praise."*
>
> Mary Kay Ash
> Founder
> Mary Kay Cosmetics

time and money in the selection and training of its employees. Nevertheless, some situations require drastic steps, such as when

- performance actually gets worse;
- the problem behavior changes a little, but not enough;
- the problem behavior doesn't change; and/or
- drastic changes in behavior occur immediately, but improvements don't last.

If, after repeated warnings and counseling, performance doesn't improve, the supervisor may need to transfer, neutralize, or terminate the employee.

Transfer. Sometimes, an employee is just not well matched to his or her job. If the employee has useful skills and abilities, it may be beneficial to transfer her or him to another job. Transferring is appropriate if the employee's performance deficiency would have little or no effect in the new position. The concern is that a job must be available for which the employee is qualified.

Neutralize. Neutralizing a problem employee involves restructuring the job in such a way that areas of needed improvement have as little effect as possible. Because group morale may suffer when an ineffective employee is given special treatment, neutralizing should be avoided whenever possible. However, temporary neutralizing may be practical and even benevolent for a valued employee who is close to retiring or suffering unusual personal distress due to illness or family problems.[63]

Terminate. Termination is generally warranted for dishonesty, habitual absenteeism, substance abuse, insubordination including flat refusals to do certain things requested, unethical behavior, and consistently low productivity that can't be corrected through training. Termination, even for legitimate reasons, is unpleasant. In addition to the administrative hassles and required documentation, supervisors often feel guilty. The thought of sitting down with an employee and delivering the bad news makes most supervisors anxious, so they put off firing and justify the delay by saying that they won't be able to find a "better" replacement. Still, when one considers the consequences of errors, drunkenness, unethical behavior, or being under the influence of drugs on the job, it is unwise to avoid firing some problem employees. To ensure that employees are not terminated unfairly, an appeal process and dispute resolution procedures should be used prior to terminating employees.

FAST FACT Dow Chemical, Xerox, and *The New York Times* have fired employees for inappropriate use of the Internet.

PERFORMANCE-DRIVEN CULTURES

Through performance measurement and feedback, organizations seek to maximize the effectiveness of their employees. As competitive pressures intensify, businesses are placing increasing demands on employees. To determine how well employees are meeting the demands, many employers are paying greater attention to performance measurement. Increasingly, promotions, raises, and other financial rewards go only to employees who excel in performing all aspects of their jobs. Some companies regularly dismiss their lowest-performing employees (e.g., bottom 10%) simply as a matter of practice. Many people consider this approach to performance management unjust, but Jack Welch, former CEO and Chair of GE, made it a central feature of his company's performance management system. Even in companies where the lowest performers are not regularly terminated, increasingly everyone is expected to welcome feedback that points out how they can do better. In performance-driven cultures, performance measurement and feedback are central elements of the HRM system—they're not merely annual exercises in which everyone goes through the motions and then carries on as they did before.

Performance-driven cultures share a common focus on monitoring and improving performance, but there are many different ways to go about these tasks. Often, the details of how a performance-driven culture goes about these tasks reflect the philosophies of the company's CEO and/or founder. The examples of Dell Computer and Setpoint illustrate how two companies keep employees focused on performance.

Dell Inc.

Dell Inc., the computer company, has a performance-driven culture. Founder and CEO Michael Dell still thinks of his company as the underdog—always in a fight for survival. With 40,000 employees and annual sales of $40 billion, the company seems to be thriving. Nevertheless, Dell always strives for improvement. Some of his core principles for managing performance are described in Exhibit 10.11.

Dell himself lives by these principles. By nature, Dell seems to be quiet and introverted. To many employees at Dell, even those in the top management ranks, Dell can seem aloof and emotionally detached. Recognizing that perceptions like these may cause some of his top talent to defect the company, Dell set out to change his behavior (some would say he tried to change his personality). The first step was to make a speech to his top team acknowledging that he needed to change. The speech was videotaped, and eventually every manager in the company saw it. Consistent with his own principles for managing the performance of others, he expected his management team to be direct and tell him when his behavior failed to live up to his aspiration of being more emotionally engaged. To remind him of which behaviors he needed to monitor, he used props on his desk. For example, a toy bulldozer reminded Dell to involve others in making key decisions instead of just pushing through his own ideas. By openly acknowledging his own faults and working to improve his own personal style, Michael Dell serves as a powerful example of what Dell expects from all of his employees.[64]

Setpoint

If you like roller coasters, chances are you have enjoyed a product that was manufactured by Setpoint, which is in the business of producing amusement park entertainment. The Super Saturator at Paramount Carowinds park is one of their latest creations. Imagine taking a roller coaster ride and having people take aim at you with water shooters. You would get soaked as your roller car plunged through a forest of shooting water, but you would laugh

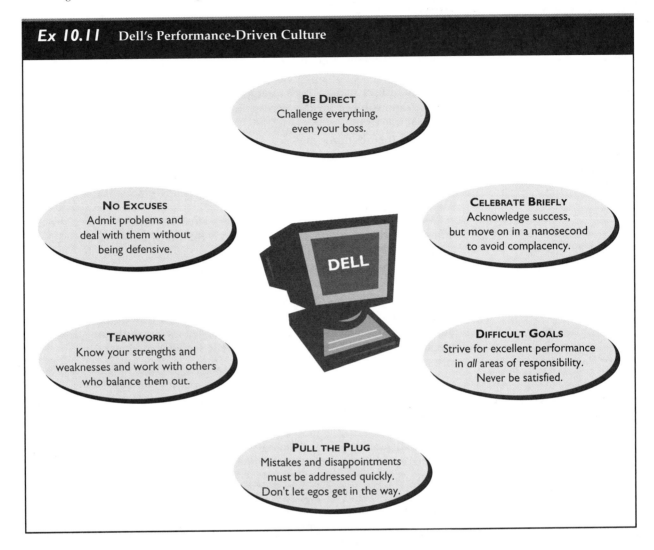

Ex 10.11   Dell's Performance-Driven Culture

BE DIRECT
Challenge everything,
even your boss.

NO EXCUSES
Admit problems and
deal with them without
being defensive.

CELEBRATE BRIEFLY
Acknowledge success,
but move on in a nanosecond
to avoid complacency.

DELL

TEAMWORK
Know your strengths and
weaknesses and work with others
who balance them out.

DIFFICULT GOALS
Strive for excellent performance
in *all* areas of responsibility.
Never be satisfied.

PULL THE PLUG
Mistakes and disappointments
must be addressed quickly.
Don't let egos get in the way.

and scream throughout the entire ride. Creating experiences like these is the mission of Setpoint.

For Setpoint's employees, having fun at work is as important as creating fun for others. And at this company, having fun goes hand-in-hand with a focus on performance. Setpoint's CEO, Joe Knight, has managed to create a culture that aligns the way employees think about their work with Setpoint's strategic objectives. Setpoint's culture embraces employee involvement. It uses an open-book approach to management. Regardless of their specific jobs, employees receive financial training and are expected to participate in enhancing the firm's financial performance. During its first few years, Setpoint's practice was to distribute financial spreadsheets to employees on a monthly basis. But now the numbers are displayed on "the board." By studying the board, anyone can figure out what stage a project is at and its financial success. For each project, employees can track operating expenses and gross profits per hour. And because everyone understands how the company makes money, they can interpret the figures to understand how their projects are doing compared to other projects.

Every Monday morning, the board is the focus of a company "huddle"—projects are reviewed and tactics are discussed to ensure that goals are met. In most companies, understanding and monitoring the performance measures and project management plans detailed on the board would be the responsibility of managers. At Setpoint, everyone who works on a project shares responsibility for its success. Employees understand both their own personal role in the project, and how the performance of everyone involved influences their bottom-line success. One visitor described the atmosphere at Setpoint like this: "I talked to several of them and I just couldn't get over the positive attitude they had and their understanding of the business. That openness—we started with it [but] you lose that feeling over time. We want to get it back. It's something to strive for."

Of course, "the board" hasn't been responsible for all the positive attitudes this visitor observed; they are also a reflection of a history of people working together and helping each other out through tough times. In addition, employees have fun together outside of work. About half are dirt-bike fanatics who go riding together and show off their antics by posting photos of themselves in the shop. At Setpoint, the scoreboard that has been the focus of so much employee attention symbolizes the open and trusting relationships that managers and other employees share. At the same time, the board and the huddles that take place around it strengthen the company's performance-driven culture.[65]

SUMMARY

Human variability is a fact of life, especially organizational life. Much of human resource management involves attending to this variability. This chapter and the next discuss how organizations manage performance variability and use that variability as the basis for making employment decisions.

The strategic use of performance management seeks to direct and motivate employees to invest effort that contributes to the achievement of business objectives. Employees tend to do what is expected and what they believe is valued by "the system" (i.e., the performance management system). When firms use performance measures that reflect concerns about teamwork and customer satisfaction, they're more likely to get teamwork and customer satisfaction from their employees. Performance measurement informs people about how well they are doing and where they stand. Feedback provides specific information and direction to individuals so that they can improve their performance.

Performance appraisal and feedback are linked to many other human resource activities. The importance of using job analysis results to develop job-related performance criteria can't be emphasized too much. Performance results can be used to guide strategic planning and monitor organizational change efforts. They also provide diagnostic information about training needs and the effectiveness of the organization's selection practices. Finally, performance measurement and feedback are central elements of a performance management system that includes using incentives and performance-based pay.

Despite well-laid plans for a performance management system, human resource professionals are often frustrated by the failure of line managers to measure performance appropriately and provide their employees with constructive and supportive feedback. A number of obstacles contribute to resistance from managers: They may not have sufficient opportunities to observe their subordinates' performance; they may not have clearly specified performance standards to use when making judgments; as human judges, they may realize they are prone to errors and be concerned about how these errors get translated into consequences for their subordinates' lives; and they may view the entire process of performance measurement and feedback as a conflict-filled activity to be avoided. Training managers to avoid these pitfalls is one approach that can help managers improve their skills in assessing performance and giving feedback. Developing a performance-driven culture is another approach. In performance-driven cultures, paying attention to performance is everyone's responsibility, and improving performance is an objective for everyone. Building performance measurement and feedback into the way everyone approaches their work, day in and day out, reduces the stigma attached to discussions about how to improve and also reduces the anxieties that often accompany performance feedback discussions.

TERMS TO REMEMBER

Anniversary approach
Behavioral criteria
Behaviorally anchored rating scales (BARS)
Behavioral observation scales (BOS)
Contaminated
Criteria
Deficient
Direct index approach
Expectancy
Expectancy theory
Focal-point approach
Forced distribution method
Instrumentality

Management by Objectives (MBOs)
Motivation
Norm-referenced format
Performance appraisal
Performance management system
Positive reinforcement
Punishment
Results criteria
Self-appraisal
Straight ranking
360-degree appraisals
Trait-based criteria
Upward appraisal
Valence

DISCUSSION QUESTIONS

1. What are the advantages and disadvantages of TRW's approach to performance measurement and feedback?

2. Why is job analysis essential for the development of performance measures?

3. What are the advantages and disadvantages of 360-degree appraisals?

4. Explain how poorly designed performance measures can contribute to performance deficiencies. Can well-designed measures contribute to improving performance? Explain.

5. Assume you are supervising employees who fall into one of three categories: (1) effective performers who have lots of potential for advancement; (2) effective performers who are happy to stay where they are and who lack motivation or ability, or both, for advancement; and (3) ineffective performers. You've assessed their performance, and now it's time to have a feedback session. What are your objectives for each of these three discussions? Explain how your discussions will be similar and how they will be different.

PROJECTS TO EXTEND YOUR LEARNING

1. *Integration and Application.* Review the cases of Lincoln Electric and Southwest Airlines at the end of the text.

    a. Compare Lincoln Electric and Southwest Airlines with respect to the major purposes of performance measurement and feedback. Which organization seems more concerned with traits? With behavior? With results? What uses does performance measurement serve in these two companies?
    b. For Lincoln Electric, how well do the performance criteria fit the company's strategic objectives? Identify potential sources of deficiency and contamination in the company's performance measures.
    c. Compare the sources of performance information used at Lincoln Electric and Southwest Airlines. Would you recommend that these organizations use 360-degree appraisals? Why or why not?

2. *Exploring the Internet.*

    a. Visit websites that provide resources for learning more about issues in performance measurement and feedback:
    Zigon Performance Group, http://www.zigonperf.com
    HR Guide, http://www.hr-guide.com
    b. Learn more out about Employee Assistance Programs:
    http://www.eap-sap.com/eap
    http://www.annclarkassociates.com
    http://www.farwestfamilyservices.com
    c. Visit the website of the American Arbitration Association to learn more about issues related to employee terminations, http://www.adr.org.

3. *Experiential Activity: Here's Looking at You*

    Develop a plan to change your own behavior and performance by taking the following steps. You may choose to focus on behavior related to your life at work, at school, or at home. Most important is that you focus on something fairly specific.

    Step 1. Choose a behavior that you really would like to change (e.g., walking more and driving less). Briefly, I want to change this behavior:

_____

_____

_____

Step 2. State a specific short-term goal for changing the behavior (e.g., within six months, I'll increase the number of times I walk to work from one to five times per week):

_____

_____

_____

Step 3. Develop a procedure for monitoring the behavior (e.g., I'll make a chart and tape it to my bathroom mirror):

_____

_____

_____

Step 4. Create a plan to reward yourself for making progress toward your goal (e.g., each day I walk, I'll put $5 in a special reward fund, to be spent at the end of each month. Each day I drive, I'll remove $6):

_____

_____

_____

Step 5. Consider the obstacles you are likely to face as you attempt to implement your plan. Consider your own attitudes and motivations as well as the behavior of others, time constraints, resources, and so on. To what extent do these obstacles interfere with your "expectancy" and "instrumentality" beliefs? Is there anything else you can add to your plan to strengthen your expectancy and instrumentality beliefs regarding this behavior change, and increase your motivation to change? List three additional things you can do to strengthen your expectancy and/or instrumentality beliefs:

_____

_____

_____

Step 6. Now, try to implement your plan. Keep a diary of your experience and use it to write an essay describing what this experience has taught you about performance measurement and feedback.

CASE STUDY

360-DEGREE APPRAISALS

In Durham, North Carolina, 170 GE employees work in nine teams to produce the GE90 jet engines that Boeing installs in its long-range 777 aircraft. Each team "owns" the engines they build—from the beginning of the assembly process to getting them loaded onto a truck for delivery. As they begin each engine, these teams generally receive no instructions except for the date on which the engine is to be shipped from the plant. Getting the engine produced is the team goal, but that goal can be reached only if the teams effectively manage themselves. Besides producing an 8.5-ton jet engine out of 10,000 individual parts, team members order tools and parts; schedule their vacations, training, and overtime; make adjustments to the production process to improve their efficiency; monitor their product quality; and take responsibility for diagnosing and resolving problems that arise among members of a team.

Decisions about these and all other issues that the teams face are made by consensus, which was a founding principle for the plant. Each employee understands that living with ideas that they don't necessarily agree with is part of the job. They don't blame others when things go wrong, because they make the decisions. The process of reaching agreement on decisions is so much a way of life here that people routinely talk about "consensusing" on this or that.

The one boss in this plant—plant manager Paula Sims—keeps everyone's attention focused on the common goal: making perfect jet engines quickly, cheaply, and safely. Her job is to make sure that the efforts of all teams are coordinated so that together their decisions optimize the plant's performance, and then to free up resources for growth and improvement.

In her four years as the plant manager responsible for GE's jet engine production teams, Sims has learned that communicating your intentions properly isn't always easy. She describes her plant manager's job as "the most challenging four years of my life—and also the most rewarding. To do it well requires a different level of listening skills—

significantly different. More and more of what I do involves listening to people, to teams, to councils, to ideas, trying to find common themes."

In this culture of continuous feedback, one reason Sims has listened so carefully is to monitor her own effectiveness. She learned early that her actions can be easily misinterpreted. Recalling an incident from her early days, she explained, "An employee came to me and said, 'Paula, you realize that you don't need to follow up with us to make sure we're doing what we agreed to do. If we say we'll do something, we'll do it. You don't need to micro-manage us.'" At most plants, following up is just part of a manager's job, but here it was sending the wrong message. Because she always followed up, people concluded that she didn't trust them. The real problem was that she had not yet learned the plant's norms about decision making.

Sims also listens when the plant is trying to solve a problem. At other companies, the title of manager almost means "decision maker." At GE/Durham, however, the manager actually makes only about a dozen major decisions each year. All other decisions either rely heavily on input from, or are actually made by, the other plant employees. The plant manager is responsible for making sure plant employees know about problems, and for informing the GE managers that she reports to about the solutions. But to get the solutions, the plant manager is expected to listen, not decide. For major issues, such as reducing costs or improving safety, a task force is formed to decide how to address the problem. The plant manager educates the task force and everyone else about the problem and explains why it is important. Then the task force takes responsibility for finding solutions. When they have a plan for the future, the plant manager informs those above her about how the plant will proceed and makes sure the higher-ups are on-board with the plan.

As the HR manager for the plant, Sims has approached you with a request: She wants you to help her install 360-degree appraisals for everyone in the plant, including her. The 360-degree appraisals will not replace the other performance measures that already are being used. They will be simply be added on as a new element in the performance management system. You have expressed some concerns about the idea, but she is determined to move ahead with the plan. Describe how you will proceed.[66]

CASE QUESTIONS

Begin by analyzing the possible advantages and disadvantages of using 360-degree appraisals in this plant. Then indicate the decisions you would make regarding each of the following questions:

1. Will you use one set of performance dimensions for everyone, or will people in different jobs be evaluated on different dimensions? Explain your logic.

2. How will you determine the specific content of the 360-degree appraisal form?

3. What type of rating format will be used to make the appraisal ratings?

4. For members of the nine production teams, who will provide performance assessments: All members of the team? Members of other teams? Will Sims provide evaluations of all employees?

5. How will feedback be handled?

6. The plant is operating well right now. What steps will you take to ensure that this new activity doesn't reduce the plant's productivity?

ENDNOTES

1 D. B. Neary, "Creating a Company-wide, On-line Performance Management System: A Case Study at TRW, Inc.," *Human Resource Management Journal* 41 (2002): 491–498.

2 For a recent review, see R. D. Arvey and K. R. Murphy, "Performance Evaluation in Work Settings," *Annual Review of Psychology* 49 (1998): 141–168.

3 For a detailed discussion of factors that affect employees' reactions, see L. M. Keeping and P. E. Levy, "Performance Appraisal Reactions: Measurement, Modeling, and Method Bias," *Journal of Applied Psychology* 85(5) (2000): 708–723.

4 For detailed discussions of work motivation theory and research, see R. M. Steers, R. T. Mowday, and D. L. Shapiro, "The Future of Work Motivation Theory," *Academy of Management Review* 29 (2004): 379–387; E. A. Locke and G. P. Latham, "What Should We Do About Motivation Theory? Six Recommendations for the Twenty-First Century," *Academy of Management Review* 29 (2004): 388–403; H. M. Kehr, "Integrating Implicit Motives, Explicit Motives, and Perceived Abilities: The Compensatory Model of Work Motivation and Volition," *Academy of Management Review* 29 (2004): 479–499.

5 Staijkovic and F. Luthans, "Self-Efficacy and Work-Related Performance: A Meta-Analysis," *Psychological Bulletin* 124(2) (1998): 240–261; W. Van Erde and H. Thierry, "Vroom's Expectancy Models and Work-Related Criteria: A Meta-Analysis," *Journal of Applied Psychology* 81 (1996): 575–586.

6 D. Fenn, "Personnel Best," *Inc.* (February 2000): 75–83.

7 D. H. Lindsley, D. J. Brass, and J. B. Thomas, "Efficacy-Performance Spirals: A Multilevel Perspective," *Academy of Management Review* 20 (1995): 645–678.

8 P. Sellers, "Pepsi Opens a Second Front," *Fortune* (August 8, 1994): 71–76; J. R. Fulkerson and R. S. Schuler, "Managing Worldwide Diversity at Pepsi-Cola International," in S. E. Jackson (ed.), *Diversity in the Workplace: Human Resources Initiatives* (New York: Guilford Publications, 1992).

9 S. B. Malos, "Current Legal Issues in Performance Appraisal," in J. W. Smither (ed.), *Performance Appraisal: State of the Art in Practice* (San Francisco: Jossey-Bass, 1998): 49–94.

10 M. S. Taylor, M. K. Renard, and K.B. Tracy, "Managers' Reactions to Procedurally Just Performance Management Systems," *Academy of Management Journal* 41 (1998): 565–579.

11 G. Imperato, "How to Give Good Feedback," *Fast Company* (September 1998): 144–156.

12 D. Kiker and S. J. Motowdlo, "Main and Interaction Effects of Task and Contextual Performance on Supervisory Reward Decisions," *Journal of Applied Psychology* 84(4) (1999): 602–609; H. Findley, W. Giles, and K. M. Mossholder, "Performance Appraisal and System Facets: Relationships with Contextual Performance," *Journal of Applied Psychology* 85(4) (2000): 634–640; D. Grote, "The Secrets of Performance Appraisal," *Across the Board* (May 2000): 14–20.

13 S. Lam, C. Hui and K. Law, "Organizational Citizenship Behavior: Comparing Perspectives of Supervisors and Subordinates Across Four International Samples," *Journal of Applied Psychology* 84(4) (1999): 594–601; P. M. Podsakoff, M. Ahearne, and S. B. MacKenzie, "Organizational Citizenship Behavior and the Quantity and Quality of Work Group Performance," *Journal of Applied Psychology* 82 (1997): 262–270; T. D. Allen and M. C. Rush, "The Effects of Organizational Citizenship Behavior on Performance Judgments: A Field Study and a Laboratory Experiment," *Journal of Applied Psychology* 83 (1998): 247–260.

14 W. C. Borman and S. J. Motowidlo, "Expanding the Criterion Domain to Include Elements of Contextual Performance," in N. Schmitt et al. (eds.), *Personnel Selection in Organizations* (San Francisco: Jossey-Bass, 1993): 71–99.

15 H. S. Field and W. H. Holley, "The Relationship of Performance Appraisal System Characteristics to Verdicts in Selected Employment Discrimination Cases," *Academy of Management Journal* (1982): 392–406.

16 Based on J. P. Campbell et al., "A Theory of Performance," in N. Schmitt and W. C. Borman (eds.), *Personnel Selection in Organizations* (San Francisco: Jossey-Bass, 1993): 35–70; and E. D. Pulakos, S. Arad, M. A. Donovan, and K. E. Plamondon, "Adaptability in the Workplace: Development of a Taxonomy of Adaptive Performance," *Journal of Applied Psychology* 85 (2000): 612–624.

17 V. U. Druskat and S. Wolff, "Effects and Timing of Development Peer Appraisals in Self-Managing Work Groups," *Journal of Applied Psychology* 84(1) (1999): 38–74.

18 Note, however, that research on managers suggests that subordinates and peers often agree in the evaluations. See T. J. Maurer, N. S. Raju, and W. C. Collins, "Peer and Subordinate Performance Appraisal Measurement Equivalence," *Journal of Applied Psychology* 83 (1998): 693–702.

19 C. Viswesvaran, D. S. Ones, and F. L. Schmidt, "Comparative Analysis of the Reliability of Job Performance Ratings," *Journal of Applied Psychology* 81 (1996): 557–574.

20 S. J. Ashford, "Self-Assessments in Organizations: A Literature Review and Integrative Model," *Research in Organizational Behavior* 11 (1989): 133–374; T. H. Shore, L. M. Shore, and G. C. Thornton III, "Construct Validity of Self- and Peer Evaluations of Performance Dimensions in an Assessment Center," *Journal of Applied Psychology* 77 (1992): 42–54; J. L. Farh, G. H. Dobbins, and B. S. Cheng, "Cultural Relativity in Action: A Comparison of Self-Ratings Made by Chinese and U.S. Workers," *Personnel Psychology* 44 (1991): 129–147.

21 J. Dulebohn and G. Ferris, "The Role of Influence in Perceptions of Performance Evaluations' Fairness," *Academy of Management Journal* 42(3) (1999): 288–303; B. D. Cawley, L. M. Keeping, and P. E. Levy, "Participation in the Performance Appraisal Process and Employee Relations: A Meta-Analytic Review of Field Investigations," *Journal of Applied Psychology* 83 (1998): 615–633; M. A. Korsgaard, L. Roberson, and R. D. Rymph, "What Motivates Fairness? The Role of Subordinate Asssertive Behavior on Managers' Interactional Fairness," *Journal of Applied Psychology* 83 (1998): 731–744.

22 F. J. Yammarino and L. E. Atwater, "Do Managers See Themselves as Others See Them? Implications of Self-Other Rating Agreement for Human Resources Management," *Organizational Dynamics* (Spring 1997): 35–44; A. H. Church, "Managerial Self-Awareness in High-Performing Individuals in Organizations," *Journal of Applied Psychology* 82 (1997): 281–292; K. M. Nowack, "Congruence Between Self-Other Ratings and Assessment Center Performance," *Journal of Social Behavior and Personality* 12 (1997): 145–166.

23 S. Weisband and L. E. Atwater, "Evaluating Self and Others in Electronic and Face-to-Face Groups," *Journal of Applied Psychology* 84(4) (1999): 632–639; R. Jelley and R. Goffin, "Can Performance-Feedback Accuracy Be Improved? Effects of Rater Priming and Rating-Scale Format on Rating Accuracy," *Journal of Applied Psychology* 86(1) (2001): 134–144; J. E. Johnson and K. Ferstl, "The Effects of Interrater and Self-Other Agreement of Performance Improvement Following Upward Feedback," *Personnel Psychology* 52 (1999): 271–303; L. E. Atwater, C. Ostroff, F. J. Yammarino, and J. W. Fleenor, "Self-Other Agreement: Does It Really Matter?" *Personnel Psychology* 51 (1998): 577–598.

24 J. L. Farh, G. H. Dobbins, and C. S. Cheng, "Cultural Relativity in Action: A Comparison of Self-Ratings Made by Chinese and U.S. Workers," *Personnel Psychology* 44 (1991): 129–147.

25 Shore, Shore, and Thornton, "Construct Validity of Self- and Peer Evaluations"; R. Saavedra and S. K. Kwun, "Peer Evaluation in Self-Managing Work Groups," *Journal of Applied Psychology* 78 (1993): 450–462.

26 J. Maurere, N. S. Raju, and W. C. Collins, "Peer and Subordinate Performance Appraisal Measurement Equivalence," *Journal of Applied Psychology* 83 (1998): 693–702.

27 M. Goldsmith, "To Help Others, Start with Yourself," *Fast Company* (March 2004): 100.

28 D. Antonioni and H. Park, "The Relationship Between Rater Affect and Three Sources of 360-Degree Feedback Ratings," *Journal of Management* 27 (2001): 479–495; D. Antonioni, "The Effects of Feedback Accountability on Upward Appraisal Ratings," *Personnel Psychology* 47 (1994): 349–360.

29 A. J. Walker and J. Smither, "A Five-Year Study of Upward Feedback: What Managers Do with Their Results Matters," *Personnel Psychology* 52 (1999): 393–423.

30 P. A. Heslin and G. P. Latham, "The Effect of Upward Feedback on Managerial Behavior," *Applied Psychology: An International Review* 53 (2004): 23–37.

31 C. F. Seifer, G. Yukl, and R. A. McDonald, "Effects of Multisource Feedback and a Feedback Facilitator on the Influence Behaviors of Managers toward Subordinates," *Journal of Applied Psychology* 88 (2003): 561–569.

32 G. Huet-Cox, T. Nielsen, and E. Sundstrom, "Get the Most from 360-Degree Feedback: Put It on the Internet," *HR Magazine* (May 1999): 92–103; D. A. Waldman and L. E. Atwater, *The Power of 360 Feedback: How to Leverage Performance Evaluations for Top Productivity* (Houston, TX: Gulf Publishing, 1998); A. H. Church and D. W. Bracken (eds.), *360-Degree Feedback Systems* (Thousand Oaks, CA: Sage Publications, Special Issue of Group & Organization Management, June 1997); R. Lepsinger and A. D. Lucia, *The Art and Science of 360° Feedback* (San Francisco: Pfeiffer, 1997).

33 F. Luthans and S. J. Peterson, "360-Degree Feedback with Systematic Coaching: Empirical Analysis Suggests a Winning Combination," *Human Resource Management* 3(42) (Fall 2003): 243256; M. R. Edwards and A. J. Ewen, *Providing 360-Degree Feedback: An Approach to Enhancing Individual and Organizational Performance* (Scottsdale, AZ: American Compensation Association, 1996).

34 For a critique of 360-degree assessments, see G. Toegel and J. A. Conger, "360-Degree Assessment: Time for a Reinvention," *Academy of Management Learning and Education* 2 (2003): 297–311.

35 A. Meisler, "Dead Man's Curve," *Workforce Management* (July 2003): 44–49. See also S. Bates, "Forced Ranking," *HR Magazine* (June 2004): 63–68; D. Grote, "Forced Ranking: Behind the Scenes," *Across the Board* (November/December 2002): 40–45.

36 In some forms of BARS, the anchors are stated as expected behaviors (e.g., "Could be expected to develop loan documentation accurately"). When expected behaviors are included, the BARS is more appropriately labeled a BES—Behavioral Expectation Scale. For further discussion, see F. J. Landy and J. L. Farh, "Performance Rating," *Psychological Bulletin* (January 1980): 72–107; K. R. Murphy and J. I. Constans, "Behavioral Anchors as a Source of Bias in Rating," *Journal of Applied Psychology* (November 1987): 573.

37 Adapted from V. L. Huber, *Validation Study for Electronics Maintenance Technical Positions* (Washington, DC: Human Resource Development Institute, AFL-CIO, 1991).

38 "Busch's Performance Evaluations," *Workforce Management Archive* (July 30, 2003), at http://www.workforce.com/archive/article/23/42/03.php.

39 To learn more about how goal setting improves performance, see E. A. Locke and G. P. Latham, *A Theory of Goal Setting and Task Performance* (Englewood Cliffs, NJ: Prentice-Hall, 1990); R. E. Wood and E. A. Locke, "Goal Setting and Strategy Effects on Complex Tasks," *Research in Organizational Behavior* 12 (1990): 73–109; C. E. Shalley, "Effects of Productivity Goals, Creativity Goals, and Personal Discretion on Individual Creativity," *Journal of Applied Psychology* 76 (1991): 179–185; T. R. Mitchell and W. S. Silver, "Individual and Group Goals When Workers Are Interdependent: Effects on Task Strategies and Performance," *Journal of Applied Psychology* 75 (1990): 185–193; J. M. Phillips and S. M. Gully, "Role of Goal-Orientation, Ability, Need for Achievement, and Locus of Control in the Self-Efficacy and Goal-Setting Process," *Journal of Applied Psychology* 5 (1997): 792–802.

40 E. A. Locke, "Motivation, Cognition, and Action: An Analysis of Studies of Task Goals and Knowledge," *Applied Psychology: An International Review* 49 (2000): 408–429; E. A. Locke and G. P. Latham, *A Theory of Goal Setting and Task Performance* (Englewood Cliffs, NJ: Prentice-Hall, 1990).

41 P. J. Kiger, "How Performance Management Reversed NCCI's Fortunes," *Workforce* (May 2002): 48–51.

42 A. S. DeNisi and K. Williams, "Cognitive Approaches to Performance Appraisal," in G. R. Ferris and K. M. Rowland (eds.), *Research in Personnel and Human Resource Management* (Greenwich, CT: JAI Press, 1988): 109–156; A. S. DeNisi, T. P. Cafferty, and B. M. Meglino, "A Cognitive View of the Appraisal Process: A Model and Research Propositions," *Organizational Behavior and Human Performance* 33 (1984): 360–396.

43 J. Segal, "86 Your Appraisal Process?" *HR Magazine* (October 2000): 199–206; J. N. Cleveland and K. R. Murphy, "Analyzing Performance Appraisal as Goal-Directed Behavior," *Research in Personnel and Human Resource Management* 10 (1992): 121–185; T. A. Judge and G. R. Ferris, "Social Context of Performance Evaluation Decisions," *Academy of Management Journal* 36 (1993): 80–105.

44 DeNisi and Williams, "Cognitive Approaches to Performance Appraisal"; D. R. Ilgen and J. M. Feldman, "Performance Appraisal: A Process Focus," in B. Staw and L. Cummings (eds.), *Research in Organizational Behavior* (Greenwich, CT: JAI Press, 1983): 141–197.

45 A. L. Solomonson and C. E. Lance, "Examination of the Relationship Between True Halo and Halo Error in Performance Ratings," *Journal of Applied Psychology* 82 (1997): 665–674; M. Foschi, "Double Standards in the Evaluation of Men and Women," *Social Psychology Quarterly* 59 (1996): 237–254; S. J. Wayne and R. C. Liden, "Effects of Impression Management on Performance Ratings: A Longitudinal Study," *Academy of Management Journal* 38 (1995): 232–260; K. R. Murphy, R.A. Jako, and R. L. Anhalt, "Nature and Consequences of Halo Error: A Critical Analysis," *Journal of Applied Psychology* 78 (1993): 218–225; C. E. Lance, J. A. LaPointe, and A. M. Stewart, "A Test of the Context Dependency of Three Causal Models of Halo Rater Error," *Journal of Applied Psychology* 79 (1994): 332–340; W. K. Balzer and L. M. Sulsky, "Halo and Performance Appraisal Research: A Critical Examination," *Journal of Applied Psychology* 77 (1992): 975–985; I. M. Jawahar and C. R. Williams, "Where All The Children Are Above Average: The Performance Appraisal Purpose Effect," *Personnel Psychology* 50 (1997): 905–926; J. S. Kane, H. J. Bernardin, P. Villanova, and J. Peyrefitte, "Stability of Rater Leniency: Three Studies," *Academy of Management Journal* 38 (1995): 1036–1051.

46 R. L. Dipboye, "Some Neglected Variables in Research on Discrimination in Appraisals," *Academy of Management Review* (January 1985): 118–125; B. R. Nathan and R. A. Alexander, "The Role of Inferential Accuracy in Performance Rating," *Academy of Management Review* (January 1985): 109–117.

47 T. J. Maurer, J. K. Palmer, and D. K. Ashe, "Diaries, Checklists, Evaluations, and Contrast Effects in Measurement of Behavior," *Journal of Applied Psychology* 78 (1993): 226–231.

48 H. J. Bernadin, M. B. Buckley, C. Tyler, and D. S. Wiese, "A Reconsideration of Strategies in Rater Training," *Research in Personnel and Human Resource Management* 18 (2000): 221–274; N. M. A. Hauensstein, "Training Raters to Increase Accuracy of Appraisals and the Usefulness of Feedback," in J. W. Smither (ed.), *Performance Appraisal: State of the Art in Practice* (San Francisco: Jossey-Bass, 1998): 404–442.

49 D. T. Stamoulis and N. M. A. Hauenstein, "Rater Training and Rating Accuracy: Training for Dimensional Accuracy versus Training for Ratee Differentiation," *Journal of Applied Psychology* 78 (1993): 994–1003; D. V. Day and L. M. Sulsky, "Effects of Frame-of-Reference Training and Information Configuration on Memory Organization and Rating Accuracy," *Journal of Applied Psychology* 80 (1995): 158–167; L. M. Sulsky and D. V. Day, "Frame-of-Reference Training and Cognitive Categorization: An Empirical Investigation of Rater Memory Issues," *Journal of Applied Psychology* 77 (1992): 501–510.

50 K. R. Murphy and J. N. Cleveland, *Understanding Performance Appraisal: Social, Organizational, and Goal-Based Perspectives,* (Thousand Oaks, CA: Sage Publications, 1995); C. G. Banks and K. R. Murphy, "Toward Narrowing the Research-Practice Gap in Performance Appraisal," *Personnel Psychology* 38 (1985): 335–345.

51 M. K. Mount, M. R. Sytsma, J. Fisher Hazucha, and K. E. Holt, "Rater-Ratee Race Effects in Developmental Performance Ratings of Managers," *Personnel Psychology* 50 (1997): 51.

52 K. R. Murphy, "Difficulties in the Statistical Control of Halo," *Journal of Applied Psychology* 67 (1982): 161–164; L. Hirshhord, *Meaning in the New Team Environment* (Reading, MA: Addison-Wesley, 1991); Murphy and Cleveland, *Understanding Performance Appraisal.*

53 R. F. Martell and M. R. Borg, "A Comparison of the Behavioral Rating Accuracy of Groups and Individuals," *Journal of Applied Psychology* 78 (1993): 43–50.

54 R. Mayer and J. Davis, "The Effect of the Performance Appraisal System on Trust for Management: A Field Quasi-Experiment," *Journal of Applied Psychology* 84(1) (1999): 123–136; L. E. Atwater, P. Roush, and A. Fischthal, "The Influence of Upward Feedback on Self- and Follower Ratings of Leadership," *Personnel Psychology* 48 (1995): 35–59.

55 M. London, *Job Feedback: Giving, Seeking, and Using Feedback for Performance Improvement,* 2nd ed. (Mahwah, NJ: Lawrence Erlbaum Associates, 2003).

56 M. Ross and G. J. O. Fletcher, "Attribution and Social Perception," in G. Lindzey and E. Aronson (eds.), *Handbook of Social Psychology,* vol. II, 3rd ed. (New York: Random House, 1985): 73–122.

57 V. L. Huber, P. Podsakoff, and W. D. Todor, "An Investigation of Biasing Factors in the Attributions of Subordinates and Their Supervisors," *Journal of Business Research* 4 (1986): 83–97.

58 K. Renk, "I Want My TV," *Awards & Incentives* (2000): 158–162; K. Kirkland and S. Manoogian, *Ongoing Feedback: How to Get It, How to Use It* (Greensboro, NC: Center for Creative Leadership, 1998).

59 P. J. Kiger, "Frequent Employee Feedback Is Worth the Cost and Time," *Workforce* (March 2001): 62–65.

60 L. E. Atwater, D. A. Waldman, D. Atwater, and P. Cartier, "An Upward Feedback Field Experiment: Supervisors' Cynicism, Reactions, and Commitment to Subordinates," *Personnel Psychology* 53 (2000): 275–297.

61 M. M. Kennedy, "So How'm I Doing?" *Across the Board* (June 1997): 53–54.

62 A. Bandura, *Principles of Behavior Modification* (New York: Holt, Rinehart & Winston, 1969); R. W. Beatty and C. E. Schneier, "A Case for Positive Reinforcement," *Business Horizons* 2 (April 1975): 57–66.

63 B. P. Sunoo, "This Employee May Be Loafing, Can You Tell? Should You Tell?" *Personnel Journal* (December 1996): 54–62; "Jury Awards Manager Accused of Theft $25 Million," *Bulletin to Management* (March 27, 1997): 97; P. Carbonara, "Fire Me. I Dare You!" *Inc.* (March 1997): 58–64.

64 A. Park and P. Burrows, "What You Don't Know About Dell," *Business Week* (November 2003): 76–84.

65 B. Burlingham, "What's Your Culture Worth? *Inc.* (September 2001): 133; B. Burlingham, *A Stake in the Outcome* (New York: Doubleday, 2002).

66 The situation described is based on C. Fishman, "Engines of Democracy," *Fast Company* (October 1999): 175–202.

chapter 11

Using Performance-Based Pay to Enhance Motivation

When the telecommunications industry fell on hard times back in the 1990s, Corning Inc. was one of many companies that suffered. Due to huge declines in orders for fiber-optic cable, Corning's stock price dropped nearly 99% and forced it to cut 16,000 jobs. Motivating employees in this type of business climate is tough, but Corning found a way. For the past decade, Corning has used a performance-based pay plan that employees helped design. Instead of tying employees' bonuses to the company's profitability, Corning sets specific performance goals for employees in each business unit and then rewards employees when those goals are met. In setting the goals, managers are expected to establish a clear "line of sight" to the corporate goal for each employee. The expectation is that every employee can improve each year, and that everyone has an equal chance of success. The system emphasizes that the entire business unit must be successful in achieving its goals in order for each individual to be rewarded, which encourages employees to cooperate with each other. The system also helps buffer employees from uncontrollable swings in the firm's overall financial performance. When bonuses are tied to a company's overall financial performance, hard-working employees often feel discouraged when they receive no rewards because they feel the company's profitability is out of their control. Corning's approach recognizes that long-term success requires motivated employees who will help the company improve year after year, even when the company enters a downturn. At Corning, when employees meet the goals for their business unit, they're rewarded.[1]

THE STRATEGIC IMPORTANCE OF USING PERFORMANCE-BASED PAY TO ENHANCE MOTIVATION

Perhaps the most important reason for the increasing popularity of performance-based pay is the belief that it can improve an organization's ability to achieve its strategic objectives. At Corning, performance-based pay helped align the goals of employees with those of the company, which was essential to the firm's ability to execute a turnaround. At Lincoln Electric, the pay plan supports the strategic objective of producing low-cost, high-quality products. For start-up firms, performance-based pay helps attract outstanding talent. The strategic business objectives will be different at other companies, but the principle of using pay to drive performance against strategic objectives is equally applicable to many situations. Exhibit 11.1 illustrates this point.[2]

Commenting on the shift to performance-based pay:
"[It's] absolutely gut-wrenching. Some people hate it."

Lisa Weber
Executive Vice President of HR
Metlife

SUPPORTING STRATEGIC OBJECTIVES

Growing awareness that traditional pay plans often fail to align employee behavior with strategic objectives is probably the most important reason that more and more companies have introduced performance-based pay. To achieve their strategic objectives, organizations must find way to align the goals of individual employees with the goals of the organization. Performance-based pay helps create such alignment.

Ex 11.1   The Strategic Value of Three Types of Pay

	LONG-TERM INCENTIVES	SHORT-TERM BONUSES	BASE PAY
Controlling costs	53%	58%	52%
Attracting and retaining top performers	67	76	72
Achieving key strategic goals	57	76	35
Aligning participant behavior to desired culture	50	61	39
Aligning participant behavior to business goals	61	76	38
Improving financial performance	55	70	41

Note: Figures shown indicate the percentage of employers who ranked each type of pay as the most effective for achieving specific goals, in a survey conducted by Watson Wyatt Worldwide.

At Corning, the performance-based pay plan was developed to support a new company vision that emphasized customer satisfaction, employee dignity, and shareholder value. The new system makes it easy for Corning to maintain a consistent and transparent approach to performance-based pay while being flexible in setting specific business annual business targets. Those business targets change to reflect general economic conditions, changes in the industry, shareholder demands, and so on.

Avon, the direct sales cosmetics company, has a U.S. sales force of about 25,000 representatives (reps) who work as independent contractors and are paid on a commission basis. When Andrea Jung took over as CEO of Avon, the company had been growing well in several foreign markets, but U.S. sales were in a slump. To grow and motivate the U.S. sales force, Jung changed the design of pay to provide greater rewards to reps who signed up new reps to work for the company. The new multitiered commission system—called "Leadership"—rewards reps for their own sales and for the sales made by reps that they recruit and train. Jung believes the new pay plan is responsible for Avon's renewed growth. "Leadership is a gamechanger for Avon," she says.[3]

As industries change and new business opportunities arise, many firms continue to grow by entering new lines of business and gradually diversifying their businesses. For example, chemical companies invest in or acquire biotech firms, retail stores open e-commerce sites, and utilities pursue opportunities in deregulated markets. To align the behaviors and effort of employees, goals are set that fit the needs of the new business, and bonuses are offered for achieving those goals. Through carefully designed incentive programs, employers can direct the behavior of employees in different divisions of the company to fit the needs of each division. Some employees may be rewarded for innovation, while other are rewarded for cutting costs or providing reliable service.

MANAGING LABOR COSTS

Employers have always recognized the importance of rewarding employees for good performance. For the past several decades, most employers have relied on merit pay to achieve this objective. But in the long run, merit pay is costly. Suppose Rhonda Brown, an X-ray technician at Community General Hospital, is earning $20/hour. At her annual performance review, her supervisor gives her an overall performance rating of 6 on a 7-point scale. Subsequently, she receives a 10% pay raise. Rhonda will now always be paid at the higher rate, regardless of her performance in the future. For whatever reasons, Rhonda may not perform as well the next year or the year after that. Nevertheless, as long as Rhonda continues to perform satisfactorily and remains with the company, her prior merit raise has increased her employer's costs.

Cost considerations become more salient as more of the budget is spent on compensation. In service companies, compensation costs account for up to 80% of the operating budget. Thus, banks, hospitals, and other labor-intensive service providers place high priority on controlling compensation costs and using compensation wisely. Cost considerations also drive the design of executive compensation. Proportionately more of a company's total compensation dollars go to upper-level executives. Ideally, executive pay plans keep these costs in check by tying bonuses and other financial incentives to the company's financial performance.

ATTRACTING, RETAINING, AND MOTIVATING TALENT

Performance-based pay can influence whether applicants apply for a position and whether they accept an offer of employment. In start-up companies, risk is high, sales growth is slow, and earnings are low, so companies set their base pay rate at a level that is below the market average. To attract talent, they offer performance-based pay. Usually the rewards are based on companywide performance; it is assumed that the company's success will depend on the talents and efforts of each and every person. For employees who are willing to work hard and don't mind taking the risk, working for a start-up company like this is attractive because it is possible that they will become very wealthy as the company grows and succeeds. Employees who prefer more certainty, however, would not be attracted to this pay arrangement.

Performance-based pay can also influence employees' decisions to stay or leave. Recall that perceptions of equity are based on employees' comparisons of their inputs and outcomes relative to those of others. With traditional merit pay plans, differences in the compensation received by the best and worst performers are quite small. When high performers believe that they contribute more (inputs) but do not receive proportionately greater rewards (outcomes), they experience feelings of inequity and become dissatisfied (see Exhibit 9.2 on page 367).[4] Dissatisfaction, in turn, causes employees to look elsewhere for employment or to reduce their effort—in either case, the organization loses the potential benefit of those employees. **Performance-based pay** *recognizes that people working in the same job can differ greatly in terms of the value they contribute to the organization and seeks to provide employees with an incentive for maximizing the value they contribute.*

Effective performance-based pay plans create strong *instrumentality* perceptions among employees (see the discussion of expectancy theory in Chapter 10). Employees need to believe that their performance actually determines how much they earn. At Lincoln Electric and Avon, the instrumentality of performance is very clear. Employees know in advance what formula the company will use to translate their performance into dollar amounts in their paychecks.

Expectancy theory also states that the rewards attached to performance must have high *valence* in order for employees to be motivated by the rewards. At Lincoln Electric, the highest-performing factory workers often earn twice as much as the lowest performers, and the difference is due almost entirely to how people perform in their jobs. In dollar terms, the difference in earnings received by high versus low performers may be $50,000 or more. For factory workers at Lincoln Electric (and almost anyone else), the valence of $50,000 in earnings is quite high.

PERFORMANCE-BASED PAY WITHIN AN INTEGRATED HRM SYSTEM

No one HR practice accounts for the high levels of motivation and productivity found at companies like Corning, Avon, and Lincoln Electric. It is the HRM system as a whole that produces the desired results. To be effective, a performance-based pay plan must fit with other elements of the HRM system, and reflect conditions in the external and organizational environments. Exhibit 11.2 shows these linkages and the major choices employers make when designing performance-based pay plans.

OTHER HR ACTIVITIES

If you have read Chapters 9 and 10, some of the connections between performance-based pay and various other HR activities should be apparent to you. Here we discuss just three other HR activities—total compensation, performance measurement and feedback, and HR planning—to illustrate a few of the many possible interconnections.

Total Compensation. As Chapter 9 explained, performance-based pay is one form of monetary compensation that organizations can offer. It supplements the base pay of employees and the various benefits and services offered by the organization. When establishing base pay rates, organizations usually focus on the pay rates for *jobs*. Base pay reflects conditions in the external labor market and the relative value of jobs within a specific organization. Whereas base pay provides employees with predictable income, performance-based pay usually introduces some uncertainty—it isn't as easy

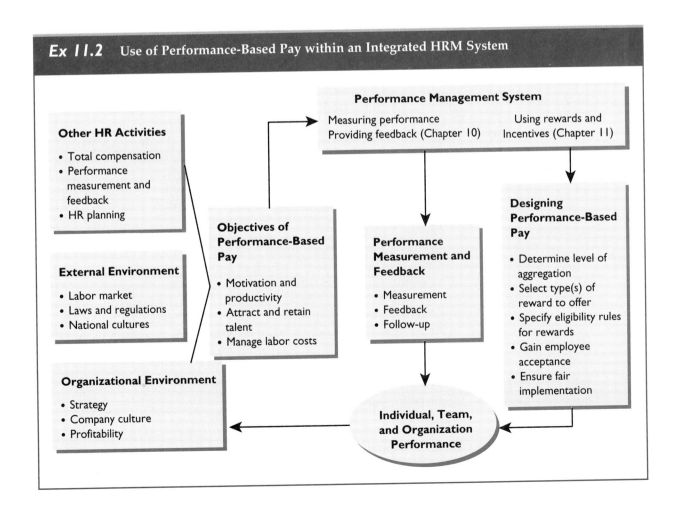

Ex 11.2 Use of Performance-Based Pay within an Integrated HRM System

for employees to predict how much performance-based pay they will receive over a period of several months or a year. When designing the total compensation system, a key decision is the proportion of total pay to guarantee employees in advance (base pay) versus the proportion to be paid based on performance. This point is discussed in more detail later in this chapter.

Performance Measurement and Feedback. For performance-based pay to be effective, it must motivate employees. As explained in Chapter 10, people are motivated when they believe that their efforts will influence their performance. Appropriate and valid performance measures help establish strong *expectancy* perceptions. When performance measures are deficient or contaminated, employees are less likely to feel that their efforts directly influence the performance measures used to determine performance-based pay.

Besides valid measures, performance-based pay works best when employees receive frequent feedback telling them how they are doing and how they can improve. At Lincoln Electric, for example, employees receive feedback about quality as soon as a customer notifies the company of a quality problem. When quality problems arise, the employee who produced a defective product is required to fix the problem. For Avon's sales reps, feedback about their performance is even more direct—employees know at the end of each day exactly how much they have sold.

HR Planning. The performance-based pay plan at Lincoln is also aligned well with the company's approach to HR planning regarding staffing levels. The Lincoln philosophy holds that employers should help employees achieve their personal goals by providing employment security. Employees are guaranteed employment security after three years of service. The company has not exercised the layoff options in the U.S. operations since 1948. At Lincoln, employment security is possible because employees agree to reduce their work schedules during slow times and work overtime during the busiest times. The performance-based pay plan is aligned with the philosophy of employment security. Employees understand that the company needs to sell the products employees produce in order to cover the costs of their performance-based pay. If orders decline, they understand that it would not be profitable to allow employees to produce at their highest capacity. Employment security is possible because the pay plan allows the company to cut production without laying off employees.

At Avon, the Leadership pay plan had some unexpected consequences for HR planning. After Leadership was introduced, the company found that many of the reps were taking on management responsibilities, such as recruiting and training new reps. Previously, these activities were the responsibility of the district managers, who are paid on a salary basis. When the reps began doing most of the recruiting and training, Avon was able to reduce the number of district sales managers by 20%.[5]

ORGANIZATIONAL ENVIRONMENT

With Corning, Avon, and Lincoln, you have already seen several examples of how companies can use performance-based pay to execute their business strategies. Perhaps less apparent is the importance of aligning the design of performance-based pay with the company's culture. According to Paul Beddia, who was vice president of human resources at Lincoln Electric for several years, the company's pay plan and its culture are completely entwined. "To explain why our workers are as motivated as they are requires an understanding of our basic philosophy, which is centered around the importance of people," he says. "Our main employment focus is to encourage growth by involvement, participation and teamwork. Thus, *we strive to create an environment where employees can achieve company goals and personal goals simultaneously.*" At Lincoln, involvement, participation, and teamwork are central to the performance-based pay plan. Since 1914, an elected Advisory Board has ensured that all employees have direct and open communication with senior managers. Through their participation and involvement in various aspects of the company's management activities, employees learn about the needs of the business and its implications for their pay. At the same time, the management team stays in touch with the concerns of employees.

Some companies are using performance-based pay to develop diversity-friendly company cultures. Examples of this use of performance-based pay are described in the feature "Managing Diversity: Rewarding Managers Who Achieve Diversity Goals."[6]

> *"Our famous incentive pay plan is just part of the story."*
>
> Paul J. Beddia
> Former Vice President of Human Resources
> Lincoln Electric

Managing Diversity

Rewarding Managers Who Achieve Diversity Goals

According to a study by the Society for Human Resource Management, most Fortune 500 companies either do not measure performance against diversity goals or they measure this performance but do not use compensation to reward success. Apparently, these organizations simply hope that the use of fair hiring methods and sending managers to diversity training programs will produce a truly multicultural organization. But about 30% of the Fortune 500 companies (and about 10% of firms in general) take a more controversial approach: They pay managers to achieve diversity objectives.

Tenneco, the oil company, was one of the mavericks. Back in the mid-1980s, Tenneco was among the first organizations to link a portion of managers' bonuses to how many women and people of color they hired and moved up the ladder. The number of professional women and people of color in the company soon doubled. At the same time, some managers lost out when it came time for bonuses: "We've all had some of our bonus subtracted because of this program," explained one human resource manager.

Deloitte, the big public accounting firm, also uses performance-based pay to achieve diversity goals.

Within two years of tying managers' bonuses to increasing the rate at which women were promoted, the company experienced a 50% increase in the number of women partners in the firm.

At Motorola, a belief in the strategic importance of managing diversity is reflected in the CEO's bonus formula, which includes goals for managing diversity, EEO, and affirmative action. Some experts think the practice is just another fad. Others predict it will eventually become a standard feature in the performance management systems of leading firms.

Managers who are perfectly comfortable using performance-based pay plans to achieve other types of strategic objectives—such as increasing ROI and improving customer satisfaction—often balk at this practice. For some critics, the practice seems misguided because it ties pay to something other than improved financial performance. Measuring the bottom-line consequences of diversity is difficult. Companies that link bonuses to effective diversity management are saying they value this objective even if the financial benefits of diversity can't be directly measured.

EXTERNAL ENVIRONMENT

Throughout this chapter, we emphasize the importance of designing performance-based pay that fits the organizational environment—especially its corporate culture and business strategy. It is worth noting, however, that the external environment also influences the use of performance-based pay.

Over the course of the past century, employers have preferred different performance-based pay approaches at different points in time. At the beginning of the 20th century, piece-rate pay plans were predominant. Following the Great Depression and a period of substantial labor unrest, employers started replacing these approaches and offering guaranteed wages. Labor-friendly legislation such as the Fair Labor Standards Act and successful union organizing efforts meant that the pay received by nonmanagerial employees was often based on negotiated union settlements. During the middle of the 20th century, merit pay plans became firmly established rates—so much so that they now are generally referred to as "traditional" pay.[7] Currently, the general trend in both the United States and Europe has been toward increasing use of incentive pay.[8] In other words, the pendulum has swung back to favor the more aggressive performance-based systems that were popular several decades ago.

Throughout the past century, the shifting popularity of different approaches to performance-based pay has reflected changes in economic conditions, fluctuations in union activity, and the enactment of various new laws and regulations. Of course, for global firms, national differences in culture and other external forces also influence the design of performance-based pay.

DESIGN CHOICES FOR PERFORMANCE-BASED PAY

Although external factors shape how employers use performance-based pay, employers have a great deal of latitude to design a system that fits their particular organization. Performance-based pay plans differ in the importance of monetary pay relative to nonmonetary rewards, the specific type of monetary pay offered, and the level of aggregation used to determine rewards (individuals, teams, or the business as a whole). Corning, Avon, and Lincoln Electric all use performance-based pay, but the details of their plans are quite different. Each company uses an approach that fits its specific situation.

Monetary and Nonmonetary Rewards. One key choice concerns the extent to which the company offers monetary rewards versus other rewards that employees may value. Organizations can choose to give employees no monetary rewards for performing well in their jobs and instead offer only nonmonetary rewards, such as recognition and praise. Among U.S. employers, however, this approach is extremely rare. Most employers provide some monetary reward for better performance in addition to praise and recognition for those who earn it.

Managers at Intuit understand that there are many ways besides a simple "thank you" to reward the efforts of their employees. Headquartered in Silicon Valley, Intuit's 16,000 employees work at 13 locations throughout the United States and Canada. Intuit is the maker of well-known software programs such as Quicken and Turbo-Tax. But one program you may not have heard about is the company's Thanks Program. At each site, giving out small awards is part of every manager's job. The company's philosophy is that awards should be given only to people who perform well above what is expected. Getting an award is special—it's a way to recognize excellence and communicate appreciation. Managers decide the criteria that will be used for giving awards, and they decide what awards to give. Examples of awards given include gift certificates to restaurants, movie tickets, written thank-you notes, and a Night-on-the-Town. Some employees get awards for going beyond the call of duty to help out their colleagues. Some get awards for making suggestions that reduce bureaucracy. Some get awards for technical programming achievements or even for outstanding service to the community. To make sure managers use good judgment when giving awards, Intuit developed a website that explains the importance of linking the awards they give to achieving business objectives. To monitor how employees feel about the Thanks Program, Intuit includes a question in the employee satisfaction survey that reads, "I am rewarded and recognized when I do a great job." As long as employees continue to agree with that statement, Intuit can be sure the Thanks Program is working.[9] When reading about the alternative approaches to performance-based pay described in this chapter, readers should keep in mind that monetary rewards are only one form of rewards valued by employees.

Forms of Performance-Based Pay. Assuming an employer decides that some monetary performance-based pay will be offered, another choice concerns which basic method to adopt for allocating monetary rewards. The major categories here are merit pay, incentive pay, and/or putting earnings at risk.

With **merit pay plans,** *base pay (the pay to be received regardless of performance) is set at a market rate and a small pool of money is allocated for distributing annual raises that reflect the past year's performance of each employee.* The differences in merit pay received by employees in the same job and with the same length of tenure in the job are usually quite small (e.g., 5%).

Like merit pay plans, **incentive pay plans** *peg base pay at the market rate. Additional compensation is available through bonuses or other forms of payment for peak performance.* The value of incentive pay that an excellent performer can earn in a given year is greater than the size of a merit increase (e.g., up to 20%). With incentive pay, there is no permanent adjustment made in an employee's base pay as a reward for past performance. Under this system, an employee whose performance has been "excellent" for the past five years will have received the same base pay as one whose performance has been average; however, the excellent employee will have received substantially more incentive pay during the previous five years. Thus, with incentive pay, there is little downside risk for employees and there is more upside potential.

With **earnings-at-risk plans,** *base pay is set below the market average and a larger portion of earnings are paid based on performance.* The lower base pay means that employees must earn their way back to the level that would have been guaranteed under a traditional or incentive pay plan. Offsetting this risk of a possible loss is an opportunity to earn much more than the market is paying. If designed appropriately, there is no economic reason to

FAST FACT

In 1929, E. Grace of Bethlehem Steel became the first millionaire CEO. His salary was $12,000 and his bonus was $1.6 million.

place a cap on the earnings of employees who work under these plans. Such plans may not be acceptable to employees who are used to more traditional reward structures that ensure earnings stability.[10] Yet, for salespeople who work on straight commission, placing their earnings at risk is just considered normal. By putting pay at risk, employers effectively buy insurance that protects the company from precipitous declines in performance.

The basic differences in these three forms of pay are illustrated in Exhibit 11.3. For employees, the differences in upside and downside risks are the most salient features of these three approaches. For employers, the implications for labor costs and productivity are most salient.

Aggregation. Independent of the degree to which pay depends on performance is the question of whether the performance measure reflects the performance of an individual, a work team, and/or the business as a whole. In merit plans and in most commission plans, individual performance is the basis for performance-based pay. At Corning and many other companies, team performance is the basis for performance-based pay. With profit-sharing plans, the rewards employees receive depend on the performance of the company as a whole.

The choice of whether to tie pay to individual, team, or companywide performance depends upon the strategic objectives of the company and the way work is structured. For employees working in jobs where individual efforts are the primary determinants of their performance, it is appropriate to base rewards on individual performance. Corning has learned that team

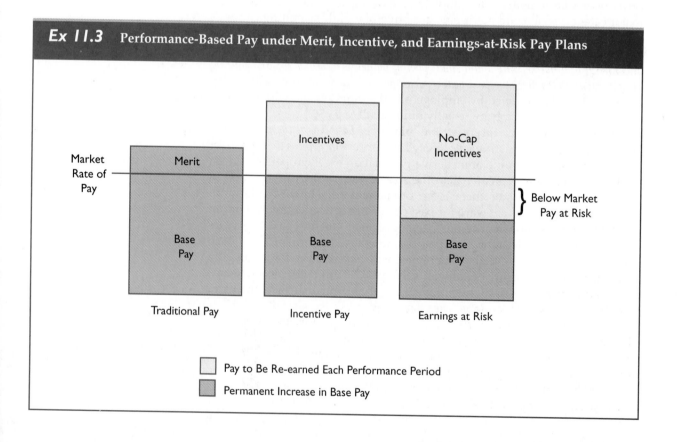

Ex 11.3   Performance-Based Pay under Merit, Incentive, and Earnings-at-Risk Pay Plans

rewards work well when they are tied to success in meeting team goals. For executives who are responsible for the performance of an entire business unit, companywide measures may be appropriate. In many companies a mix of individual, team, and companywide performance measures is used to allocate monetary rewards.

THE HR TRIAD

Designing and administering an effective performance-based pay plan requires close cooperation among all players in the HR Triad. In particular, line managers and HR professionals must work together to ensure that performance-based pay practices support the overall strategic objectives of the organization, as well as the specific strategic goals of smaller units and teams within the organization. Changes in strategic objectives often trigger organizations to scrutinize and redesign their compensations systems. In many organizations, such efforts represent major changes in the organization's culture. Thus, for many line managers and HR professionals, the roles and responsibilities associated with performance-based pay include those associated with managing organizational change, as described in Chapter 5.

As is true for any component of the HRM system, the ultimate effectiveness of performance-based pay depends on whether employees fully understand and accept the system. Seeking and using the input of the employees who will be affected by performance-based pay is an important responsibility of line managers and HR professionals. Even when employees participate in designing performance-based pay, however, the introduction of new performance-based pay plans often has unintended consequences. These can be quite disruptive if not detected quickly. Thus, continuous monitoring should be used to assess employee satisfaction, key behaviors, and performance results. These issues are summarized in the feature "The HR Triad: Roles and Responsibilities for Using Performance-Based Pay to Enhance Motivation."

DESIGNING PERFORMANCE-BASED PAY

Substantial research supports the conclusion that performance-based pay can improve productivity. For example, when a major retailer introduced an incentive plan into half its outlets, those outlets experienced increased sales, customer satisfaction, and profits. The positive effects of performance-based pay were especially great for outlets experiencing intense competition.[11] Numerous other studies have found similar results. However, research also shows that under some conditions, performance-based pay has no effects or even has detrimental effects.[12] Results from these latter studies serve as ammunition for critics of performance-based pay.

Compensation specialist Alfie Kohn has been a particularly vocal critic, stating that "any incentive or pay-for-performance system tends to make people less enthusiastic about their work and therefore less likely to approach it with a commitment to excellence."[13] Although it has been widely publicized, Kohn's assertion is not consistent with the findings of empirical research. While it's true that performance-based pay does not always improve performance, the research indicates that ineffective reward systems

The HR Triad

Roles and Responsibilities for Using Performance-Based Pay to Enhance Motivation

LINE MANAGERS	HR PROFESSIONALS	EMPLOYEES
• Work with HR professionals to establish the strategic objectives of performance-based pay (PBP).	• Work with line managers to establish the strategic objectives of PBP.	• Develop a comprehensive understanding of the strategic objectives of PBP.
• Work with HR professionals to establish the performance criteria to be linked to pay and the methods to assess performance.	• Work with line managers to establish the performance criteria to be linked to pay and the methods to assess performance.	• Make sure you accurately understand the performance criteria that will be used to determine your PBP.
• Assist with communicating the objectives and administrative procedures for PBP.	• Work with accounting and finance staff to assess the cost implications of PBP.	• Perhaps assist in administering PBP for team members.
• Assist HR in monitoring and revising PBP as needed.	• Monitor the effects of PBP on employee satisfaction, behavior, and results, and recommend revisions to the PBP system as needed.	• Be alert to dysfunctional attempts to "game" PBP systems, and work to improve PBP so it reduces dysfunctional behaviors.
• Understand the many forms of PBP pay available and their strengths and weaknesses. Learn the principles of how to use rewards effectively.	• Develop and deliver training and communications to ensure that line managers and other employees understand the PBP system's objectives and procedures.	• Adapt to needed changes in the PBP.

are due to poor design and implementation; their failure is not due to a widespread negative psychological effect of performance-based pay.[14]

To be effective, performance-based pay must successfully deal with six major issues: (1) specifying and measuring performance, (2) specifying the method for linking pay to performance, (3) specifying the level of aggregation for reward distribution, (4) specifying the type of reward, (5) specifying eligibility for rewards, and (6) gaining employee acceptance.[15] Of course, decisions about each of these issues also must be sensitive to legal considerations.

SPECIFYING AND MEASURING PERFORMANCE

A valid and transparent performance measurement system is central to any system that links pay to performance. The practice of linking pay to performance can quickly highlight and exacerbate any flaws in the performance measurement system.

"If you can't measure it, you can't manage it, and if you can't do either, you sure as heck shouldn't pay for it."

Steven J. Berman
Managing Director
PriceWaterhouseCoopers

What Gets Measured Gets Rewarded. A company may tell employees that speed, efficiency, quality, and customer satisfaction warrant equal attention, and they may really mean it. But if speed and efficiency are easier to measure than quality and customer satisfaction, the pay plan may weight them more heavily, leading employees to give them priority when situations force a trade-off.

If the performance measurement system focuses on one component of performance and rewards are given for a different component, employees will be confused and managers will wonder why the rewards do not work. In recent years, the use of the balanced scorecard approach to measuring organizational performance has put the spotlight on precisely this issue. Proponents of the balanced scorecard argue that organizations should monitor their performance using measures that reflect performance in four domains: finances, customers, operations, and employees (learning and development). But when it comes to offering incentives for performance in these four domains, financial performance is the most frequently used performance metric—by far! Exhibit 11.4 shows the results of a survey of 1,742 organizations conducted by Mercer HR Consulting.[16] What do *you* think explains the results of this survey?

When it comes to paying for performance, many companies have relied heavily on financial performance measures while ignoring other performance indicators that reflect the perspectives of employees, customers, and other strategic partners. The result is a mismatch between the incentive system and the company's full understanding of what it takes to be effective in the long run.[17]

Measuring Results versus Measuring Behaviors. When the Fibers Department of E.I. DuPont de Nemours initiated a major change in its pay plan, they intended to improve the relationship between pay and performance on tasks that were considered to be of strategic importance. The department shifted from straight base pay to an incentive plan that tied employees' compensation to their unit's overall performance. Managers expected the

> *"We use the scorecard system to ensure that our employees deliver customer satisfaction. For example, the incentive compensation of everyone in the company—the salespeople, the service people, the engineers, the product marketing people, everyone—is based on these same satisfaction scores."*
>
> Tom Siebel
> Former CEO
> Siebel Systems

Ex 11.4   **Metrics for Short-Term Incentives**

Metric	Percentage
Financial	92.0%
Operational (productivity)	43.6%
Customer satisfaction	19.8%
People (development and learning)	9.8%

Percentage of Employers Using Specific Metrics for Short-Term Incentives

incentive pay to build a greater sense of teamwork. One of the 20,000 employees covered by the plan described it as a shift from being paid for "coming to work" to being paid for how well a business unit succeeds. The plan sounded good in theory, but it was soon scrapped. To cope with a business slowdown, the company reduced the workforce 25%. The survivors worked harder than ever to turn things around. Despite their efforts, the company fell short of its profit goal. Rather than withhold the 6% pay-for-performance bonus it had designed, DuPont pulled the plug on the plan to avoid demoralizing its workforce.

As DuPont's experience illustrates, the strategic value of incentive pay depends on whether the pay plan supports the behaviors that are most important to the company's success. During an economic recession, Dupont needed employees who would put in their best effort, even if that effort didn't immediately translate into increased profitability. An incentive plan that defined the strategic objectives of smaller work groups and tied pay to outcomes that workers really could control may have worked more effectively for DuPont.

TRW ensures that employees can control the results on which their rewards depend by using behavior-based goals rather than results-based goals. In their Cleveland-based automotive plant, project teams start up and disband as project needs come and go. To support team efforts, team members establish specific behavioral goals that are tightly related to the team goals. Incentives ranging in size from 10 to 25% of base pay are tied to the team-driven individual goals.[18]

Short-Term versus Long-Term Perspective.　As more and more companies consider paying for knowledge or skill acquisition, they come face-to-face with the question of how much value they should place on performance in the current job versus behaviors that prepare employees for future jobs. Motorola discovered this conflict when it introduced pay for developing reading and math skills. Team members resented it when their colleagues disappeared to school for weeks, at full pay, leaving the teams weaker. The workers complained about the mixed message they were getting and the conflict between self-development and teamwork. They went to the compensation director and said, "Would you guys get a grip? Make up your minds what you really want from us."[19]

"It's the underlying philosophy which is the key thing. Three years ago we paid bonuses on sales. Then we moved to profit. Now we're looking for something which more accurately reflects the shareholder's position."

Andrew Higgins
Finance Director
Burton (a U.K. retailer)

Finding the appropriate balance between rewarding for current performance versus rewarding for long-term performance is a difficult balancing act. Many critics of performance-based incentive plans point to this as a common problem. Executive pay plans that focus attention on short-term movements in the company's stock price, for example, may lead managers to make decisions that protect the stock price in the short-term but with negative longer-term consequences. In sales jobs, balancing short-term and long-term performance objectives also poses a challenge. Traditional commissions focus the attention of a sales staff on the short-term objective of selling goods and services, and do nothing to ensure the customer is satisfied with the purchase. Yet building customer loyalty and repeat business is an important strategic objective for most organizations. Thus, performance-based pay plans for sales organizations increasingly include measures of customer satisfaction.[20]

METHODS FOR LINKING PAY TO PERFORMANCE

Compensation specialists use the terms *merit, incentive,* and *at-risk* to describe different philosophies about how much risk employees should be exposed to. In practice, however, the differences among pay plans are matters of degree. For example, to deal with the problem of escalating pay, some organizations have adopted merit pay plans that allocate zero raises to poor-performing employees, and they then force managers to identify a specific percentage of poorly performing employees; that is, they use the forced distribution format (described in Chapter 10) when measuring performance.[21] These merit pay plans function very much like an incentive plan. Similarly, it is sometimes difficult to tell the difference between incentive pay and plans that put earnings at risk. How far below the market must a company set its policy line before we say they have adopted an earnings-at-risk approach: 5%? 10%? 20%? And under what conditions do employees really feel that their pay is "at risk"?

Lincoln Electric employees clearly work under an earnings-at-risk plan (although it is usually referred to as an incentive system). Yet, year after year, most employees know that they can expect above-market compensation. From the employees' perspective, perceptions of risk reflect not only the formal plan but also their beliefs about whether they will perform at the level needed to be compensated at the market average.

LEVELS OF AGGREGATION FOR REWARD DISTRIBUTION

Performance can be measured at the individual, work team, department, plant, strategic business unit, or organizational level. Two factors that influence this choice are the objectivity of available measures and the types of behaviors needed from employees to achieve strategic objectives.

Objectivity. If individual performance can be measured only through subjective appraisals, it may not be appropriate to tie performance-based pay to individual performance. The more subjective the performance measure is, the less likely it is that employees who receive a low rating will accept the measure as valid. Tying pay to subjective measures exacerbates the problem because more is at stake.

Often, more objective performance measures can be obtained when performance is measured at a higher level of aggregation—for example, the team or strategic business unit. The trade-off is that the tie to individual performance is less direct; the gain is that the tie to achieving the company's business objectives is clearer.[22] Team-based pay plans are proving to be quite effective at Corning and many other companies. As Exhibit 11.5 reveals, team-based pay was consistently viewed as improving performance, while ratings of other approaches showed mixed results.[23]

Behaviors. Nordstrom's managers want their salespeople to be entrepreneurs, so they use individual incentive pay, which stimulates competition and increases performance pressures. When individual incentive pay plans pit employees against each other, they are likely to cut off information sharing and other forms of coworker support.[24] In some contexts, this may not be

"Individuals don't accomplish anything, teams do."

The late W. Edwards Deming
TQM Guru

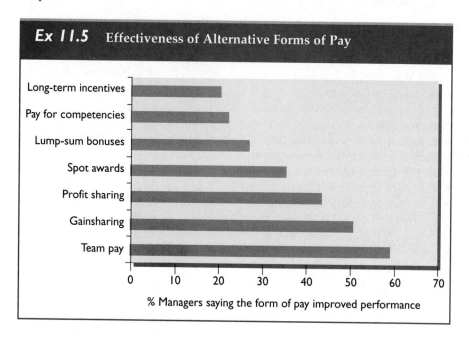

Ex 11.5   Effectiveness of Alternative Forms of Pay

a major problem, but usually cooperation among employees is beneficial and direct competition is somewhat dysfunctional.

One way to avoid the problem of competition among employees is by having employees compete against objective performance goals, rewarding everyone who achieves the goals. Often, this is more easily done when goals are set for teams, departments, or business units. As Corning has discovered, incentives that reward employees for the performance of a larger group reinforce behaviors that promote collective success. They encourage each team member to help the team attain its objectives.

Types of Rewards

Rewards for performance can be of many types, ranging from a feeling of personal satisfaction, to public recognition and small tokens, all the way to substantial monetary payments and stock ownership.

Form of Payment. Besides cash, a company may choose to give employees large prizes (e.g., all-expenses-paid vacations), direct stock awards, stock options, or any combination of these. All of these are considered monetary rewards. The terms *performance-based pay* and *incentive pay* are generally *not* used to refer to rewards that consist mostly of social recognition. In practice, however, no clear lines separate social rewards from those that are primarily monetary. Regardless of the specific form of the reward, employees must value it in order for it to be effective. Because the value of a reward is only partly a function of its monetary worth, judging "how much is enough" is mostly a matter of speculation and of trial and error. Perhaps the best advice is to intentionally use both recognition and monetary rewards. That's what Rackspace does, as described in the feature "Managing Teams: Rackspace Rewards Fanatical Customer Service."[25]

"I try to remember that people—good, intelligent, capable people—may actually need day-to-day praise and thanks for the job they do."

John Ball
Service Training Manager
Honda Motor Company, United States

Managing Teams

Rackspace Rewards Fanatical Customer Service

Located in San Antonio, Texas, Rackspace is a Web-hosting company that manages websites for clients such as e-tailers, on-line ad agencies, and game sites. In this business, technical tasks make up a large part of the staff member's jobs, but good customer relations are important too. When the company realized that employees were not as customer-friendly as they needed to be, they restructured the staff into customer-focused teams, introduced some simple new rules (e.g., you can be fired for criticizing a customer), and introduced new incentives. One new incentive is the Straightjacket Award. The Straightjacket Award recognizes the employee who is the best example of living the company's new motto of delivering "fanatical" customer support. Employees who win the award wow their customers by being friendly, reliable, and genuinely concerned about understanding the customer's perspective. Monthly bonuses also support fanatical customer service. Each month, teams can earn a bonus of up to 20%

of their base pay for excellent team performance, which is measured using both financial and customer-driven metrics. When companywide performance goals are reached, employees receive additional bonus pay. For teams and the company as a whole, customer-focused performance measures include speed in resolving customer problems, percent of customers who renew or expand their business with Rackspace, and customer referrals. By linking customer service behaviors to both the recognition employees receive and their monthly earnings, Rackspace has created a culture that respects customers and keeps them satisfied. Employees get the message. As Frederick Mendler, a leader of two teams that serve 1,200 medium-sized companies, puts it: "At most companies, these [customer-oriented] policies are just lip service, but that's our bonus you're talking about." Customers get the message too, and they repay Rackspace by giving it more business and referring it to others.

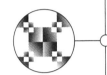

Eligibility for Rewards. The rules used to determine which employees are covered by the various components of a total pay plan are called **eligibility rules.** Many of the ongoing changes in the use of performance-based pay reflect changes in the eligibility rules used by employers rather than the introduction of truly new forms of pay. When companywide profit sharing is adopted, for example, the change usually involves going from a situation in which only a limited pool of employees share the profits (top-level executives) to making all employees eligible to receive this form of pay. The same is true for other forms of performance-based pay, such as bonuses and stock options.

FAST FACT

Nucor, the largest U.S. steel producer, has the lowest labor costs per ton among the American steel interests. It also pays the most, including bonuses of up to 60% of base pay.

Timing of Rewards. Generally speaking, the more quickly rewards follow desirable behavior, the more potent the rewards are in evoking subsequent desirable behavior.[27] In most companies, incentive pay is received from several weeks to a year after the performance being rewarded. Delayed rewards may decrease desired behavior because the employee doesn't see an immediate consequence. On the other hand, the longer the company delays paying the incentive, the longer it can use the money for its own purposes. Also, by delaying the payment of rewards, the company is less likely to reward employees who are about to leave.

Size of Rewards. Companies clearly make different choices in the sizes (or percentage of total pay coming from incentives) of the monetary rewards they offer.[26] The average for nonexecutives is about 7%, but for sales reps at Avon and other companies that use direct marketing, all earnings are paid as incentives. Even within the same company, employees in different jobs usually have different percentages of their total pay coming from incentive pay. The general pattern is that proportionately more of an employee's total pay is from incentive pay as you move up in the hierarchy. Exhibit 11.6 illustrates this pattern.

Combining Multiple Rewards. Companies that use rewards to support a performance-driven culture are likely to use several methods for rewarding excellent performance. As one of the nation's leading marketing services companies, Valassis Communications offers a variety of door-to-door marketing services for consumer package goods companies and franchise retailers. Valassis reaches nearly 60 million households each week via Sunday newspapers and distributes nearly 90% of all coupons in the United States. Free-standing inserts (FSIs) produce most of the company's revenues. These are full-color booklets containing coupons and other promotional offers from leading consumer package goods companies.

According to *Fortune* magazine, Valassis is also one of the "100 Best Companies" to work for in the United States. The achievement is due largely

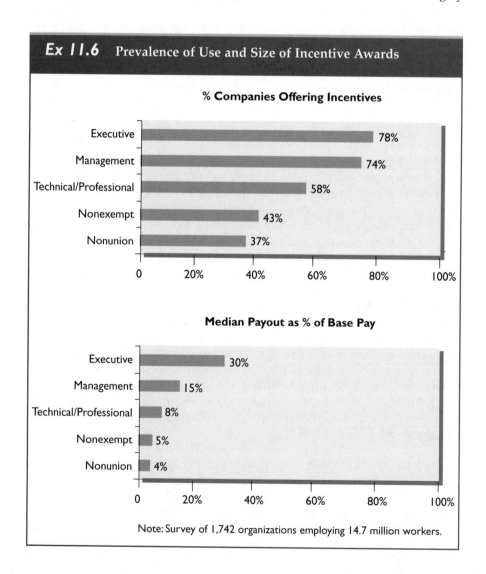

Ex 11.6 Prevalence of Use and Size of Incentive Awards

% Companies Offering Incentives

Executive	78%
Management	74%
Technical/Professional	58%
Nonexempt	43%
Nonunion	37%

Median Payout as % of Base Pay

Executive	30%
Management	15%
Technical/Professional	8%
Nonexempt	5%
Nonunion	4%

Note: Survey of 1,742 organizations employing 14.7 million workers.

to the company's highly motivating and enjoyable workplace. Valassis management views its key to success as having a culture that is fun and where goal-oriented individuals and teams are rewarded for achieving their goals. In this performance-driven company, executives want all employees to feel and behave like they are owners of the company and to believe that they will share in the rewards of the company. Supporting this culture is a total compensation plan that includes profit sharing, stock purchases, and "champion pay"—rewards for outstanding achievements. Festive occasions are used to celebrate past achievements, and recognition awards are given often and with fanfare. In these and many other ways, Valassis ensures that employees enjoy coming to work and brag about their employer in their community.

GAINING EMPLOYEE ACCEPTANCE

Employee opposition can be a major obstacle to the successful implementation of performance-based pay, especially plans that put earnings at risk. Several conditions that improve employee acceptance and thus the effectiveness of incentive pay are shown in Exhibit 11.7.[28] Particularly important for success is effective communication, which can dispel employees' fears, enhance their trust, and improve their understanding of how performance-based pay plans may affect their future earnings.

Fear. Employees may worry that performance-based pay plans will result in work speedups or will put some percentage of the workforce out of a job. Another legitimate concern may be that performance targets will be too difficult or out of the employees' control. When group performance serves as a criterion for incentive pay, individualistic U.S. employees may fear that their pay will be decreased because they have to depend on others for their rewards.

Distrust. Some approaches to performance-based pay tie the size of rewards employees receive to managerial decisions about what the company

"With better understanding comes better support." A good rule of thumb "is to communicate incentive plans two to three times as often as you pay them out."

Mark Stiffler
CEO and President
Synygy

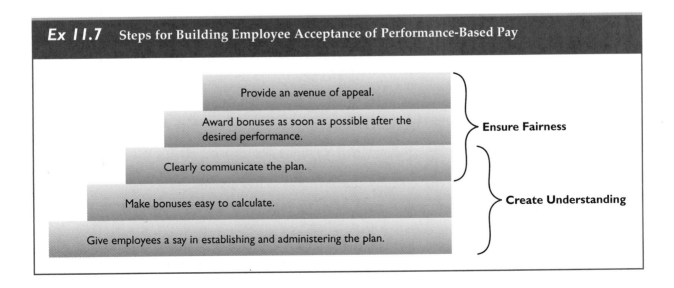

Ex 11.7   **Steps for Building Employee Acceptance of Performance-Based Pay**

Provide an avenue of appeal.

Award bonuses as soon as possible after the desired performance.

Clearly communicate the plan.

Ensure Fairness

Make bonuses easy to calculate.

Give employees a say in establishing and administering the plan.

Create Understanding

"The more the formula for payouts reads like the fine print in a contract, the more it seems as if management is trying to slip something by."

Don Barksdale
Communications Consultant
Knoxville, Tennessee

can afford to pay in a given year. For example, at Lincoln Electric, the size of the year-end bonus pool is set by the top management team. If trust in management is low, employees may not believe the figures when management tells them how the financial performance of their business unit translates into the size of the pool available for bonuses. Regularly providing detailed financial information about business performance is one way to deal with this concern. Another is to tie managers' rewards to the same pool of funds used to pay other employees. When separate pools of funds are set aside for managerial and nonmanagerial employees, distrust is likely to increase.[29]

Misunderstanding. For employers who use an intranet to communicate with employees about compensation and benefits, many convenient software tools can be used to improve employees' understanding of performance-based pay plans, and their consequences for an employee's income stream. Towers Perrin, a consulting firm with expertise in compensation systems, advocates setting up a system that allows employees to recalculate estimates of their likely annual income at least once per month. This can be especially useful for employees who (potentially) receive large annual bonuses that depend on both their own performance and the fluctuating performance of the firm. A sophisticated HRM system with the appropriate software makes it possible for employees to calculate their bonuses under various "what-if" scenarios. Scenarios can help employees see how changes in their performance would affect their earnings, as well as how changes in the firm's performance might affect their earnings.[30]

LEGAL CONSIDERATIONS

Legal considerations must also be taken into account when designing pay-for-performance systems. Issues of discrimination and tax laws are particularly important.

Discrimination. Under Title VII of the Civil Rights Act of 1964, the Civil Rights Act of 1991, and the Equal Pay Act of 1963, a supervisor may be charged with unlawful discrimination by an employee in a protected group who believes that a pay raise, bonus, or other monetary reward was denied on a basis not related to performance. Such problems are most likely to arise when performance measures are subjective and when the size of rewards given is left to managerial discretion rather than being driven by a fixed formula.[31] When awarding performance-based pay, applying the same decision rules to all employees is essential. Data showing persistent pay differences between men and women and among employees from differing ethnic backgrounds cause many people to believe that unfair pay discrimination persists in many organizations today. Although some of the pay differentials can be explained by years in the labor market, study after study has shown that human capital variables such as education, experience, and performance do not fully account for these pay differences.[32]

Taxes and Accounting Rules. Tax and accounting rules also are worthy of some comment here, although a discussion of these is beyond the scope of this chapter. Particularly in the specialized arena of executive compensation, changes in taxation and accounting rules can dramatically alter the methods companies use to administer performance-based pay. For example, when tax rates for long-term capital gains are low relative to tax rates for ordinary income, stock options become more popular. But when the differential is removed, cash becomes more popular than stock options. Likewise, laws that require taxes to be paid at the time a stock option is granted—as is true in Norway—discourage the use of stock as a form of reward; laws that defer taxation until the option is exercised have the opposite effect.

In the United States, the discussion about how to treat stock options has received input from a wide variety of tax and accounting officials, as well as senior managers, business owners, and compensation consultants.[33] In 2004, there was a raging debate over how publicly traded companies should treat stock options in their financial reports. Existing regulations didn't require companies to treat stock options as an expense on their income statements. Proposed new rules would require such reporting. For some companies, the change would have major implications. According to one estimate, the earnings of the S&P 500 in 2003 would have been reduced by 8% if the proposed rules had been in effect then. The earnings of the 100 largest companies traded on the Nasdaq stock exchange would have been reduced by 44%, because these are mostly start-ups and high-tech companies in which stock options are a major element of the pay package. For employees of many high-tech companies, the implications of the proposed rule were clear—eventually, companies would stop issuing stock options. Whether that prediction will eventually come true is not possible to predict at this time, however.

MERIT PAY PLANS

Merit pay plans have been the cornerstone of public and private compensation systems for many years.[34] In this section, we briefly explain how a typical merit plan works.

FAST FACT

About 40% of companies boost merit increases in a good financial year, while 45% reduce merit increases in a poor year.

THE PERFORMANCE-TO-PAY LINK

Performance measures are the foundation of all performance-based pay plans, including merit pay plans. Valid performance measures are essential to creating a strong link between performance and rewards (instrumentality). Merit pay plans usually link monetary rewards—pay raises—to subjective performance measures. As described in Chapter 10, many sources of error can influence subjective performance appraisals. The criteria may be contaminated or deficient. Supervisors all too frequently evaluate incumbents according to preconceived biases. Regardless of the appraisal form—whether it's based, for instance, on behavior, output, or traits—rating errors such as leniency and halo are rampant. Therefore, supervisors and employees often disagree on evaluation results.

MERIT INCREASE SIZE

Under merit pay plans, department heads usually recommend raises for the employees they supervise within the constraints of a merit pool budget. Typically, the budget allows for modest average pay increases. In order for truly outstanding employees to get meaningful raises, poor performers need to get no raise at all. Following is an example of a typical set of guidelines that managers use to assign merit raises:

Performance Level	Merit Increase
Performance consistently and significantly exceeds position requirements	Minimum of 6%
Performance consistently meets position requirements	0–4%
Performance requires improvement to meet position requirements	0%

Charles Peck, a compensation expert with the Conference Board, based in New York, explained some of the other problems often associated with such merit plans:

> *"Merit increases tend to be expensive and, contrary to their intent, not strongly related to performance. Usually everybody gets something. This so dilutes the salary increase budget that the top performer's increase isn't large enough to be significant (especially after it is prorated over the number of pay periods in the year and subjected to withholding). On the other hand, the poor performer is getting more than he or she should have, which is nothing. The result of all this is that the employees who are most dissatisfied are the ones the company wants satisfied—the top performers. If the concept of pay for performance is rigorously applied, there must be zero pay for zero performance."*[35]

Managerial Discretion. With merit pay, managers have considerable discretion. To help managers use their discretion wisely, Allstate provides them with a table that clearly lays out several different reward allocation scenarios. Using the table, managers can easily figure out how to fund larger merit raises for outstanding performers by allocating smaller increases for average and poor performers. Suppose the budget provides for an average merit increase of 4%. One option for the manager would be to distribute merit increases as follows:

	Exceeds	Meets	Requires Improvement
% of employees at the performance level	40%	55%	5%
Average % increase given to employees with this level of performance	6.0%	2.9%	0.0%

In this scenario, the best performers receive the minimum required increase of 6%. But suppose a manager feels this is too little. Can funds be allocated to give the best performers as much as an 8% increase? The answer is yes. Two possible ways to do it are as follows:

Option 1

	Exceeds	Meets	Requires Improvement
% of employees at the performance level	30%	70%	0%
Average % increase given to employees with this level of performance	8.0%	2.3%	0.0%

Option 2

	Exceeds	Meets	Requires Improvement
% of employees at the performance level	40%	55%	5%
Average % increase given to employees with this level of performance	8.0%	1.5%	0.0%

Employee's Position in Range. Exhibit 11.8 illustrates a more complex system, which allocates raises based on both performance and an individual's position in the salary range. At any performance rating higher than below average, employees with lower base pay will receive larger increases compared to employees at higher levels of base pay. Note, however, that although the percentage of merit increase is greater in the lower quartiles, the absolute size of the merit increase is often larger in the higher quartiles, provided the merit budget is large enough and the grid is designed correctly.

Employees may perceive this approach as unfair because equally performing employees do not get equal percentage increases in pay. Although employee education may help to minimize this problem, a more practical approach is to uncouple performance-based and range-based pay adjustments and award each type of increase separately.

Critics of merit pay contend that even the most well-designed merit pay plans are ineffective. According to Edward E. Lawler III, an expert on reward system design, merit increases don't work well because they're plugged into antiquated pay plans. He believes that the one thing shown by 40 years of researching reward systems is that merit pay isn't effective for increasing productivity—particularly for the service, information processing, and high-technology based industries of the 21st century. Still, many U.S. workers are paid under merit systems. Many others work in organizations that have abandoned the use of merit increases in favor of incentive pay plans.

INCENTIVE PAY PLANS

A major difference between merit pay and incentive pay is that merit pay is a permanent pay raise whereas incentive pay is a one-time award. Also, whereas merit pay plans typically rely on subjective performance appraisal

Ex 11.8 Merit Increase Based on Current Position in the Salary Range

	PERCENTAGE INCREASE IN ANNUAL SALARY			
Performance Rating	**First Quartile**	**Second Quartile**	**Third Quartile**	**Fourth Quartile**
1. Unacceptable	0%	0%	0%	0%
2. Below Average	2%	0%	0%	0%
3. Competent	8%	6%	4%	2%
4. Above Average	10%	8%	6%	4%
5. Superior	12%	10%	8%	6%

ratings, incentive pay is often based on more objective measures. Compared to merit pay plans, incentive plans often give managers more latitude to make large distinctions in the rewards received by employees. For the best performers, this provides opportunities to earn relatively large amounts of performance-based pay.

While recognizing that distinguishing incentive pay from earnings at risk is not straightforward, in this section we review the following: individual incentives, team incentives, special achievement awards, profit sharing, and gainsharing. Typically, these forms of incentives reward employees for performance that has occurred within the time frame of one year or less.

Individual Incentives

"Part of the appeal of incentive programs is the thrill of winning it."

Sandra Robinson
President
Incentive Travel House

Individual incentives are among the oldest and most popular form of incentive pay. With this type of plan, individual standards of performance are established and communicated in advance, and rewards are based on individual results. Fifth Third Bank is an aggressive user of individual incentives. Just about anyone can earn extra cash by persuading someone to apply for a credit card (up to $25), consumer loan ($25), or mortgage (up to $75). Branch managers can earn 20% above their base salary for meeting all of their goals. In addition, the 75 top-producing managers win all-expense-paid trips to luxury resorts.[36]

Piecework. In piecework plans, such as the one used at Lincoln Electric, employees are paid a certain rate for each unit of output. In a **straight piece-work plan,** *employees are guaranteed a standard pay rate for each unit.* The standard pay rate is based on the standard output and the base wage rate. For example, if the base pay of a job is $80 a day and the employee can produce at a normal rate 20 units a day, the standard rate may be established at $4 a unit. The normal rate is more than what time-and-motion studies indicate is typical because it is supposed to represent 100% efficiency. The standard rate that is agreed to may also reflect the bargaining power of the employees, the economic conditions of the organization and industry, and the amount the competition is paying.

With a **differential piece-rate plan,** *more than one rate of piecework pay is set for the same job.* This plan can be set up in several different ways. In Taylor plans, employees receive a higher rate of pay for work completed in a set period of time. For work that takes longer to complete, the rate of pay is lower. For example, employees may be paid $4 per piece if they complete five pieces per hour, but only $3.50 per piece if they complete only four pieces per hour.

When used appropriately, piecework increases individual performance, but there is no panacea. Consider what happened when a group of bank processing operators went to a per-item-processed reward system. The staff of 12 operators increased the items processed from an average of 980 items per hour to more than 3,000 items per hour. Their take-home pay increased an average of 50% over their former hourly pay. The program seemed to be a success—until the bank president made a visit to the unit. One operator cut off her conversation with the president after a brief time, telling him that he was costing her money. The president also could see that operators were unwilling to help each other out because it would reduce their own pay. As in this case, when piece-rate incentives reward individual employees without regard to the consequences for the larger organization, their disadvantages may outweigh any benefits.[37]

Standard Hour Plans. A **standard hour plan** *sets a standard time for each unit of production and uses this time unit to determine how much employees are paid.* Tasks are broken down by the amount of time it takes to complete them, which can be determined by historical records, time-and-motion studies, or both. The normal time to perform each task becomes a standard. Employees are paid for the normal time required to complete each task, not the actual time used.

If you go into an automobile repair shop, you will probably see a chart indicating the labor rates associated with various types of repair. These reflect the use of standard hour plans. Each rate includes the rate paid to the mechanic who does the work plus the premium charged by the owner of the shop. The rate is fixed regardless of how long it actually takes to do the repair. Thus, the mechanic and the shop owner both have incentives to ensure that the work is completed in a shorter amount of time than that used to set the standard rate. Consider a standard time of two hours and a rate of $30 an hour, of which the mechanic is paid $20 an hour. In this system, the mechanic receives $40 for each unit of work completed, regardless of the actual time spent. In an eight-hour day, the typical mechanic would earn $160 and complete four units. If the mechanic completes six units in an eight-hour day, he receives $6 \times \$40$, or $240.

On-the-Spot Awards. On-the-spot awards usually target performance in areas of particular strategic value, such as safety, customer service, productivity, quality, or attendance. Recipients typically are nominated by peers or supervisors to receive awards including gifts, savings bonds, dinner certificates, and cash incentives ranging from $150 to more than $1,000. When designed well, the activities associated with these bonuses effectively focus attention on core values and business objectives. One recent survey found that 55% of companies offer spot bonuses.[38]

Data I/O Corporation, an electronics manufacturing company in Redmond, Washington, makes extensive use of special achievement bonuses. For example, all members of a computer-aided electronics software development team—such as engineers, technical writers, shippers, and quality assurance personnel—garnered $60 dinner certificates when the product was released. Two high achievers in the groups also earned weekend trips for two to San Francisco, including $1,500 in airline and motel expenses. On other occasions, recognition plaques, mugs, T-shirts, and pen sets have been distributed. Monthly, an employee is recognized for her or his contribution to Data I/O. Recognition brings a parking place by the front door, an engraved plaque, and verbal acknowledgment in a company meeting.

The philosophy behind spot bonuses is to reward employees instantly, which strengthens the link between performance and rewards. While this can be an advantage, using spot bonuses can be risky. The biggest challenge goes to the foundation of performance-based pay—measuring performance. When giving spot bonuses, managers often are free to use their own idio-

"Recognition is the key."

Mary Kay Ash
Founder
Mary Kay Cosmetics

syncratic criteria. The challenge is to award these bonuses fairly and avoid the potential resentment that may arise among employees who don't receive these special awards.

Rewards for Suggestions. To encourage more innovative ideas, many companies have suggestion systems that involve some form of instant incentive. According to the National Association of Suggestion Systems, its 900 members received nearly 1 million suggestions from their employees, resulting in savings of over $2 billion annually. Crowley Maritime Corporation's "Ship Us an Idea" is typical of most suggestion plans. The shipping company receives an average of 20 suggestions a month from its 1,000 employees. Employees earn between $50 and $150 for most ideas and may earn up to 10% of the cost savings for significant ideas. A presidential award of $1,000 is given annually for the best idea. According to Moon Hui Kim, program developer, the benefits far outweigh the $6,000–$10,000 annual program administration costs.[39]

Rewards for Innovations and Patents. For some companies, new inventions and patents (i.e., "intellectual property") are essential to success. Motorola is one such company. It consistently ranks among the top ten companies awarded U.S. patents each year. To encourage inventors, Motorola pays bonuses to employees when a patent is filed and again when a patent is issued. For inventors receiving their tenth patent, another bonus is awarded. Depending on the company's estimate of the invention's value, these lump-sum awards may be in the range of $10,000 to $20,000.[40]

Executive Incentives. Executive incentive plans tie pay to the attainment of company goals. In addition to cash, performance-based pay for executives may include restricted stock grants (free shares given to the CEO for staying with the company), performance shares or units (free shares or cash for achieving multiyear goals), and stock options.

Debate over the effectiveness of executive incentives has raged for many years. Two issues fuel this debate—the size of incentive rewards received and the (small) role of performance in determining executive pay.

The pay of U.S. executives seems excessive relative to the pay of rank-and-file employees and of CEOs in other countries. Top-earning CEOs regularly make the news. Consider this: The average annual total compensation of the 25 highest-paid CEOs was $32.7 million for the years 2001–2003. That's 900 times the annual salary of the typical U.S. worker.[41] These are the types of figures that make the news, but "the relentless focus on how much CEOs are paid diverts public attention away from the real problem—how CEOs are paid," according to compensation experts Michael Jensen and Kevin J. Murphy. After studying the pay of CEOs in 1,400 companies over an eight-year period, the researchers contended that the "incentive" compensation of top executives is virtually independent of corporate performance and is no more variable than that of hourly workers. In fact, of the 25 highest earners in recent years, one-third headed companies that performed below the S&P 500 average. Another study found that company size, not performance, was the most important factor determining the total compensation received by CEOs.[42] To rectify the problem, the researchers recommended restructuring

> *"Intellectual property is a relatively new [business] concept, but it's as real and valuable as tangible assets."*
>
> Gary Hoshizaki
> Director of Intellectual Property
> Motorola

> *"The bottom line is that pay in corporate America is like manure in agriculture. Spread it around and it does a lot of good. But pile it up in one place and it stinks."*
>
> Nicolas D. Kristof
> Journalist
> New York Times

executive pay so that salaries, bonuses, and stock options provide big rewards for superior performance *and* big penalties for poor performance.[43]

TEAM INCENTIVES

Team incentives fall somewhere between individual plans and whole-organization plans such as gainsharing and profit sharing. Performance goals are tailored specifically to what the work team needs to accomplish. Strategically, they link the goals of individuals to those of the work group, which, in turn, are usually linked to financial goals.[44]

Exhibit 11.9 shows the performance measures used by a manufacturer for awarding incentives to employees working in its plants. In this plan, separate incentives exist for work teams within a plant (40% weight) and for the plant as a whole (60% weight).

When designed appropriately, team-based incentives offer four major advantages compared with individual incentive systems. First, the mere presence of team members who have some control over rewards evokes more vigorous and persistent behavior than is evidenced when individuals work alone. Second, the likelihood that conflicting contingencies (peer pressure) will evoke counterproductive control over behavior is reduced. Third, the strength of the rewards is increased, since they're now paired with group-administered rewards, such as praise and camaraderie. Fourth, the performance of another group member (usually the high performer) can serve as a model, encouraging other team members to imitate successful behavior.[45]

Types of Teams. As more and more companies restructure work around teams, new team structures are likely to proliferate. Different team structures may require different forms of pay. For example, three types of teams commonly found in today's organizations are:

- **Parallel Teams.** These teams operate in a structure that functions in parallel to the regular organizational chart. Often staffed by volunteers who serve the team on a temporary assignment, the

> *"Our experience has been that the group award alone does not do enough. Individuals want to be rewarded for group performance and for the individual contribution as well."*
>
> Judy H. Edge
> Compensation Manager
> FedEx

Ex 11.9 **Example of Incentives Used by a Manufacturer to Reward Team and Plant Performance**

Strategic Objective	How Measured (weight)	Level of Aggregation	Goals to Determine Payouts		
			Threshold	**Target**	**Maximum**
Improve productivity	Ratio of units produced over labor hours goal (40%)	Team	.75 against goal	.85 against goal	.95 against goal
Reduce defects	Percent units with quality defects (40%)	Plant	5%	3%	1%
Reduce waste	Cost of waste as a percentage of sales	Plant	3%	2%	1%

typical tasks of such teams include creating reports and making suggestions for improvements in the company. The team's work is usually a small portion of each member's full responsibility.

- **Project Teams.** Project teams may operate in a parallel structure or they may be integrated as part of the formal organizational structure. Such teams often have a somewhat stable core of members with diverse areas of specialized expertise. They often are self-managing and have a broad mandate to develop innovative products or services. The team's work may be a part- or full-time responsibility for each member.
- **Work Teams.** Work teams are fully integrated into the organizational structure. They have clear, narrow mandates, which usually focus on producing products or providing services. Membership in these teams is usually stable and the team's work is each member's full-time responsibility.

The very different natures of these team types mean that no single approach to rewarding the performance of team members would fit all three. Exhibit 11.10 shows how two leading experts recommend structuring the performance-based pay for these three types of teams.[46] In many organizations, multiple team types operate side-by-side. By implication, multiple forms of team pay should also be used.

At Children's Hospital Boston, the accounts receivable department is organized around work teams. The feature "Managing Teams: Performance-Based Pay at Children's Hospital Boston" describes how team pay helped improve both employee morale and customer service in that organization.

Team Pay Design Issues.   Although team-based incentives are promising, they involve administrative responsibilities that are as great as those associated with individual incentive plans. Job analysis is still necessary to identify how to structure the teams and to ensure that workloads are equivalent among teams.[47] Also, team incentives may produce unintended side effects, including competition between groups, which may or may not com-

---

Ex 11.10   **Pay Plans for Different Types of Teams**

	TYPE OF TEAM		
Pay Plan	**Parallel**	**Project**	**Work**
Pay for performance			
Individual	Merit pay for job performance	Possible if team assessed	Unusual but possible if team assessed
Team	Recognition or cash for suggestions	Possible at end of project	Possible if team independent
Unit	Possible gainsharing	Profit sharing or gainsharing	Profit sharing or gainsharing
Participation	Design of gainsharing plan	Assessment of individuals	All aspects of design and administration

Managing Teams

Performance-Based Pay at Children's Hospital Boston

Prior to introducing team-based pay, morale and productivity were low in the accounts receivable department at Children's Hospital Boston. Employees were struggling to learn how to use a new billing system, and it took more than 100 days to receive payment after bills were sent out. The hospital needed to shorten the billing cycle and improve cash flow. To motivate employees and establish a clear "line of sight" between their own work and the hospital's goals, hospital executives introduced team-based pay. Productivity goals were set for the department, and rewards were distributed based on the department's success in achieving the goals. To meet the goals, employees would have to work together to process each bill efficiently. Employees could earn quarterly bonuses for achieving preset goals. Achieving the "threshold" level paid $500 to each employee; achieving the "target" paid $1,000; and achieving "optimal" paid $1,500.

To explain the new pay plan to employees, the financial officer and several other managers from the Patient Financial Services Department held two meetings with employees. They described the plan, explained why it was being introduced, and showed how it would affect each employee. Employees learned how the length needed to collect bill payments affected cash flow, and how cash flow affected the hospital. They also learned that no one in the department would receive a bonus unless the department as a whole met its targets. To help employees see how they were doing, the department received a weekly progress report. Employees got the message. If someone wasn't carrying their weight, they felt the heat of peer pressure. Within a year, the average number of days a bill spent in accounts receivable fell from 100 to 75, and then it decreased to about 65. According to Steve Nicholl, director of Patient Financial Services, the new pay plan also helped recruitment and retention. "We had been losing our staff to local competitors," he explained. "Now we don't lose them. An HR director just down the street told me, 'I hire and train them, then you take them.'"

plement goal attainment. Exhibit 11.11 summarizes several issues to be addressed when designing performance-based pay for teams.[48]

To date, research on how to best design performance-based pay for work teams is scarce, so it's difficult to propose solutions to the challenges.[49] However, case studies of the experiences in two companies—Solectron California and XEL Communications—provide several insights. For example, one solution to the challenges of changing team membership, multiple team memberships, and interteam relationships is to fund the incentive pool at the business unit level. This reminds employees that, ultimately, their team should strive to enhance the organization's performance. Another lesson suggested by the experiences of these companies is that it's best to keep the pay system simple and plan to make adjustments to it as the team and company gain more experience with this approach to pay. Third, using 360-degree appraisals as the basis for developing or evaluating individuals should be resisted early in the life of the team. Until a team has matured and developed a level of trust in the team-based incentives, 360-degree appraisals may be threatening to employees, resulting in lack of candor and/or low team cohesiveness.[50]

PROFIT SHARING

Introduced first in the Gallatin glasswork factory in New Geneva, Pennsylvania, in 1794, **profit-sharing plans** *include any*

Procter and Gamble and 40 other companies began offering profit-sharing plans in 1890.

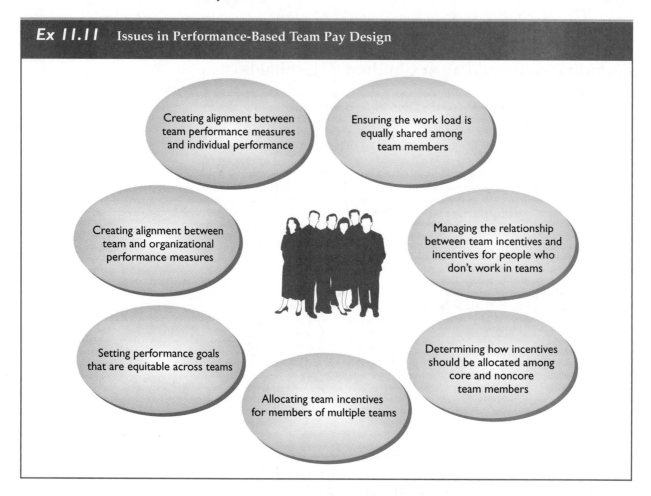

Ex 11.11   Issues in Performance-Based Team Pay Design

Creating alignment between team performance measures and individual performance

Ensuring the work load is equally shared among team members

Creating alignment between team and organizational performance measures

Managing the relationship between team incentives and incentives for people who don't work in teams

Setting performance goals that are equitable across teams

Allocating team incentives for members of multiple teams

Determining how incentives should be allocated among core and noncore team members

procedure under which an employer pays or makes available to regular employees, special current or deferred sums based on the profits of the business, in addition to their regular pay.

Timing. Profit-sharing plans are designed to pay out incentives when the organization is most able to afford them. The plans fall into three categories. **Current distribution plans** *provide a percentage of profits to be distributed quarterly or annually to employees.* **Deferred distribution plans** *place earnings in an escrow fund for distribution upon retirement, termination, death, or disability.* These are the fastest-growing type of plan owing to tax advantages. **Combined distribution plans** *distribute a portion of profits immediately to employees, setting the remaining amount aside in a designated account.*

Strategic Objectives. Other than sharing profits, these plans often do not have clear strategic objectives. Furthermore, the motivational potential of deferred plans is questionable because employees may not see the relationship between their performance and the profitability of the firm.

Critics of profit sharing argue that tying pay to achieving more specific strategic objectives is preferable to tying pay directly to profitability. For example, over a period of 14 years, Springfield Remanufacturing has selected 14 different goals based on their analysis of the key weaknesses that interfere with profitability. Each time a new goal is adopted, employees learn about why achieving the goal is important to long-term profitability and what they can do to help the company achieve the goal.[51]

FAST FACT

Since 1934, Lincoln Electric has paid more than $1 billion in year-end profit-sharing awards bonuses.

Rob Rodin, CEO of Marshall Industries, argues that it is exactly because so many different specific goals must be met that profit sharing is the way to go. "How do you design an incentive system robust enough to accommodate every change in every customer and every product and every market every day?" he asks. "You can't—you'd be designing it the rest of your life," he concludes. That's why Rodin eliminated all incentives, commissions, bonuses, and achievement awards and replaced them with a simple profit-sharing plan. He believes profit sharing helped rid the organization of all the gamesmanship he used to see—shipping early to meet quotas, pushing costs to the next quarter, and fighting over how to allocate computer system costs, just to name a few.[52]

Egon Zehnder, founder of an international executive recruiting firm, agrees that profit sharing is an effective pay strategy. In his view, it is an excellent way to attract employees who are willing to work for the good of the firm as a whole and screen out self-aggrandizing individuals. Zehnder needs employees who will share information, not hoard it. His firm's compensation plan is simple. In addition to base pay, employees receive equal shares of equity. In addition, they receive pay from two profit-sharing pools. The profit-sharing pools equal 90% of annual profits (10% of profits are put back into the firm). Of the total of the profit-sharing pools, 60% is distributed in equal portions to all employees. The remaining 40% is distributed to reward employees for the length of time they have been with the firm. Each year of service (up to a maximum of 15 years) results in a proportionately greater share of profits for the employee.[53]

GAINSHARING

Introduced in 1889, **gainsharing plans** *involve measuring a work unit's costs and productivity and then sharing future gains with employees.* Thus, gainsharing plans emphasize the need for continuous improvement. They are premised on the assumption that employees can help continuously reduce costs and improve productivity by eliminating wasted materials and labor, developing new or better products or services, or working smarter. Typically, gainsharing plans involve all employees in a work unit or firm. The median gainsharing payout is 3%.[54]

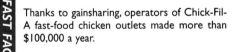

FAST FACT

Thanks to gainsharing, operators of Chick-Fil-A fast-food chicken outlets made more than $100,000 a year.

The introduction of gainsharing plans has improved productivity in a variety of settings. Presumably, this approach to performance-based pay is effective for two reasons: First, the rewards motivate employees to work harder, but second, and more importantly, the success of gainsharing may be due to the fact that employees become actively involved in suggesting new approaches for doing their work more efficiently.[55] Since they were first introduced more than a century ago, three generations of gainsharing plans have evolved.

First-Generation Plans. Two plans—Scanlon and Rucker—were developed in the Depression Era. Both focus on cost savings relative to historical standards. The **Scanlon and Rucker plans** are built around the following four principles:

- A management philosophy emphasizing employee participation
- A formula to share the benefits of productivity-generated savings among employees and the employer
- Employee committees to evaluate ideas
- A formal system for gathering and implementing employee suggestions on ways to increase productivity or reduce costs[56]

Even though the Scanlon and Rucker plans share a common philosophy, they differ in one important aspect: The Scanlon Plan focuses only on labor cost savings. Suppose that the historical costs of labor for your firm have been $1 million a year. If actual labor costs are less than anticipated costs ($800,000), a portion ($50,000) of the money saved is placed in a set-aside fund in case labor costs soar in subsequent quarters. The remaining savings ($150,000) is split among the company and the employees. In contrast, the Rucker Plan ties incentives to a wide variety of savings. A ratio is calculated that expresses the value of production required for each dollar of total wages.

Both plans are appropriate in small, mature firms employing fewer than 500 workers. Since standards are based on past performance, simple and accurate measures of performance are needed. Because of the heavy involvement of all employees, the culture must be open, trusting, and participative.[57]

Second-Generation Plans. Beginning in the 1960s, a second generation of gainsharing plans began to emerge. These differ from first-generation plans in several respects. First, they focus on labor *hours* saved, rather than labor *costs* saved. Detailed time-and-motion studies are conducted to develop engineered standards of physical production. Because of the depth of analysis required, employees typically aren't involved in the development of the plan. This may reduce perceptions of fairness.

Unlike first-generation plans, second-generation plans include nonproduction workers in the measurement of the organization's productivity and in the distribution of variable pay, realized from cost savings. ImproShare (which stands for improved production through sharing) is typical of second-generation plans. Developed by industrial engineer Mitchell Fein, ImproShare has been adopted in a wide array of firms, including service-sector firms such as hospitals and financial institutions. Exhibit 11.12 compares the details of the calculations of the Scanlon, Rucker, and ImproShare plans.

FAST FACT

Over 2,000 companies in the United States use gainsharing plans as a form of performance-based pay.

Third-Generation Plans. According to Marc Wallace, who studied new pay practices in 46 firms, a third generation of gainsharing plans emerged during the 1980s. These plans are "so different from first and second generation models that the term gainsharing may no longer be appropriate."[58] Third-generation plans encompass a much broader range of organizational goals and are more tailored to the specific needs of a company. The new plans have their roots in Scanlon, Rucker, and Improshare plans, but the variations that

---

Ex 11.12   Calculations for Selected Gainsharing Plans

Scanlon Plan Base Ratio
[(Sales Dollars − Returned Goods) + Inventory] ÷ [(Cost of Work and Nonwork Time Paid + Pension + Insurance)]

Rucker Plan Base Ratio
(Cost of All Wages and Benefits) ÷ (Sales Dollar Value of Product − Goods Returned − Supplies, Services, and Material)

Improshare Plan Base Formula
[(Standard Value Hours Earned, Current Period) x (Total Actual Hours Worked, Base Period ÷ Total Standard Value Hours Earned, Base Period)] ÷ [(Total Hours Worked, Current Period)]

---

have been introduced yield so many different approaches that customized plans are now almost idiosyncratic to each company.[59]

PAY THAT PUTS EARNINGS AT RISK

Merit-based and incentive-based pay systems apply to a large percentage of the workforce. However, sales personnel and high-level executives more frequently have their earnings placed at risk.

Some companies have pushed the notion of at-risk pay throughout the organization. Nucor, a steel mill, is a well-known pioneer of this approach. Factory workers at Nucor's steel mills earn wages set at less than half the typical union rate. At year's end, the company distributes 10% of pretax earnings to employees. Bonuses based on the number of tons of acceptable quality steel produced bump up total pay to about 10% more than that of comparable unionized workers. The bonuses reflect company productivity levels, but they also encourage individuals to behave responsibly. Workers who are late lose their bonus for the day; workers who are more than 30 minutes late lose their bonus for the week. Managers at Nucor earn bonuses also. The bonuses of department managers are based on return on plant assets and those of plant managers are based on return on equity. The system seems to work. Compared to many other steel companies, Nucor produces more than twice as much steel per employee.[60]

Arguably, Lincoln Electric's pay plan also puts employees' earnings at risk, as does any incentive plan that does not guarantee income that's near the market average. In other words, earnings at risk is a matter of degree. Usually, the degree of risk is most extreme for employees paid on commissions.

COMMISSIONS

Usually, the term **commission** *refers to pay based on a percentage of the sales price of the product.* About two-thirds of all salespeople receive commissions. In establishing a sales commission plan, the following questions need to be answered:

- What are the strategic objectives to be achieved?
- What criteria will be used to measure performance?
- Are territories equivalent in sales potential?

- Will commission rates vary by product or vary depending on sales level?
- Will earnings have a cap?
- What will be the timing of commission payments (e.g., monthly or quarterly)?

Straight Commission. Under straight commission plans, responsibility for generating an income rests directly on the salesperson. The more sales, the greater the earnings; no sales means no income. When employees accept these as legitimate pay plans, their effect on behavior is enormous. At Nordstrom, where salespeople work entirely on commission, the salespeople earn about twice what they would at a rival's store. Unfortunately, such incentives can be so powerful that they elicit unintended behaviors, as when Sears Auto Centers in California were caught for making unnecessary repairs on customers' cars.

As companies rethink their strategic objectives, they often evaluate their current pay plans for salespeople, who represent the company to their valued customers. When IBM's business declined in the 1990s, it needed its sales force to think about the implications for IBM of the deals they cut with customers. At the time, commissions were paid based mostly on sales revenue. But as the business came under pressure, improving IBM's profitability took on greater importance. To focus the attention of the sales force, IBM restructured its commission system. Instead of tying only 6% of commission pay to profits, the new system tied 60% of pay to profits. The other 40% was tied to customer satisfaction, in order to reduce the temptation to simply push fast-turnover, high-profit products. To support the new pay plan, IBM gives its salespeople access to the information they need to maximize their performance. For example, now they know the profit margins for each product they sell.

Combined Plans. Because of concerns about the negative effects of straight commission plans, more than half of all sales compensation plans combine base salary and commissions. In setting up a combined plan, the critical question is, "What percentage of total compensation should be salary and what percentage should be commission?" The answer depends on the availability of sales criteria (e.g., sales volume, units sold, product mix, retention of accounts, and number of new accounts) and the number of nonsales duties in the job. Commonly, these plans are based on an 80-to-20 salary-to-commission mix. However, organizations wishing to push sales over customer service functions may utilize different ratios: 60-to-40 or even 50-to-50.

The commission portion of the sales compensation can be established in two ways. The simplest is to combine the commission with a draw. The salesperson receives the draw, or specific salary, each payday. Quarterly or monthly, the total commission due the salesperson is calculated. The amount taken as a draw is deducted, with the salesperson receiving the remainder. Alternatively, bonuses can be given when sales reach a specific level.

Stock Ownership

Companies use many different approaches to encourage their employees to own company stock and so take part as an owner of the company. **Employee**

stock ownership plans (ESOPs) *grant shares of stock to employees as a means of long-term savings and retirement.* They usually do not link the amount of stocks that can be purchased or the purchase price to individual or group performance indicators. Stock ownership plans often give employees stock awards upon being hired, on their annual anniversary date, or at the end of the fiscal year. UPS has a stock ownership plan. Each year, 15% of the company's pretax profit is used to buy company stock and distribute it to employees in jobs at the supervisory level and above. Starbuck's, Whirlpool, Pepsi, and about 11,000 other companies also have ESOP plans in place, covering about 9 million U.S. employees.[61]

Another approach is to grant a **stock option,** *which gives the employee the right to buy stock during a specified time period or under other specified conditions.* When a company gives most of their employees the right to buy some amount of stock options, the plan is referred to as a broad-based stock option plan. Companies with broad-based stock option plans include Pfizer and Eli Lilly. Broad-based stock option plans—that is, those designed to distribute stock as a reward for all employees—seldom put earnings at risk.[62]

Many companies offer stock options only to executives. The awarding of stock options to executives is premised on the assumption that the plans encourage executives to "think like owners." After all, they profit only if the stock price goes up. During the rising stock market of the 1990s, the use of stock options exploded. For senior executives, the total value of stock awards often exceeds the combined value of their base salaries and all annual bonuses. The 1990s also saw companies offer stock options to more and more employees at lower levels in the organization. The popularity of stock options was fueled partly by accounting and tax rules and partly by the belief that stock options increase employee motivation.[63]

Exhibit 11.13 lists several forms of stock-based pay.[64] Note that the various plans differ with regard to the time frame for vesting, whether vesting is contingent on attaining performance goals, and pricing.

> "The most important thing I ever did was give our partners [employees] bean stock, meaning Starbuck's stock options. That's what sets us apart and gives a higher-quality employee, an employee that cares more."
>
> Howard Schultz
> Chair
> Starbucks

FAST FACT

A vesting schedule determines when employees may exercise their stock options.

Time-Restricted Stock Options. Companies may place a variety of restrictions to limit the conditions under which stocks become vested with employees. **Time-restricted stock options** *require some time to elapse after the stock is granted before vesting occurs, and during that time the employee must remain at the company.* In most cases, employees are required to work three to five years before they are vested in the plan. If the employee leaves the company before the required time of service elapses, the stock must be returned to the company. The intent of time restrictions is usually to deter turnover.

Performance-Based Stock Options. When stock option plans use performance measures to determine the distribution or vesting of stock options, they're using stock ownership as a form performance-based pay. Three common approaches to performance-based options are performance vesting, premium-priced options, and indexed options.

With **performance-vested stock options,** vesting occurs upon achieving specified goals. Often the goals are defined as changes in the price of the company's stock. Pegging the vesting schedule to growth in earnings per share is another method. For example, 1,000 options could be vested according to a schedule determined by increases in the price of the stock. The first

Ex 11.13   Explanation of Selected Stock-Based Pay Awards

Type of Plan	How It Works
Time-Restricted Stock Option	The basic "plain vanilla" plan: for a given period of time, employee may purchase a stock at a specified price.
Time-Based Restricted Stock	Award of shares with restrictions that require a predetermined length of service to elapse before vesting occurs. If employee leaves, stock is returned to the company.
Performance-Vested Stock Option	A stock option that vests upon the achievement of specified goals.
Performance-Vested Restricted Stock	Award of shares with restrictions that require the achievement of prespecified goals. Failure to attain goals in a specified time period may result in forfeiture.
Performance-Accelerated Stock Option	Award of shares that has a set vesting schedule but vesting may occur more rapidly if specified performance goals are met. If performance goals are not achieved, stock becomes vested with employee nevertheless.
Indexed Stock Option	Employee has the option to purchase stock at a price that fluctuates based on a specified standard index or a group of peer companies.
Premium-Priced Stock Option	Stock options with an exercise price that is above the market price at the time of the grant.

FAST FACT

At Bay State Gas Co., nobody gets any options unless the company's total return to shareholders beats that of at least half of 30 other comparable utility companies for at least three years.

200 shares might vest after a $5 increase in stock price, the next 200 might vest after a $10 increase, and so on. Though straightforward, the problem with this approach is that, under current accounting rules, performance-based vesting requires a charge to earnings, while time-based vesting does not. Nevertheless, about half of the firms in the Fortune 250 have adopted this approach. Dow Chemical is an example. Dow adopted performance-vested stock options for its top 100 executives in the mid-1990s to support its strategic objective of aggressive growth.[65]

With **premium-priced stock options,** *employees are granted options at an above-market price.* The principle behind premium-priced stock options is similar to performance vesting, but the mechanism is slightly different. With this method, employees won't want to exercise their option until the stock price advances to a level above the premium price. For example, if options are granted with an exercise price of $50, but the current market price is only $40, employees would not be able to realize any reward until shareholders realized a 25% gain. To further motivate employees, the company might place a time limit on the performance goal. For example, the option could expire in five years if the premium price hasn't been obtained. In 2003, German companies such as SAP and Siemans adopted premium-priced stock option plans in response to pressure from the German corporate governance council. In 2004, IBM became the first large American company to adopt such a plan for its senior management team (the CEO and top 300 executives). Stock awards were priced to become valuable only when the company's share price rose at least 10%.[66]

Indexed stock options *are designed to ensure that employees are not rewarded (or, in theory, punished) merely due to a robust or retreating economy.* They achieve this by indexing the exercise price to an external standard, such as the Russell 2000, the S&P 500, or the Dow Jones Industrial Average. This approach would seem to be the best method for motivating employees to ensure that shareholders receive the best possible return on their investment. But it is seldom used, presumably because it requires a charge to earnings and so does not enjoy the tax advantages associated with other approaches.

Underwater Stock Options. Stock options are attractive when a company's value is on the rise, but steep declines in stock prices create special problems. **Underwater stock options** *have an exercise price that is above the market value of a company's stocks.* Premium-priced stock options are "underwater" when they are first granted, and that is by design. In most situations, underwater stock options are the results of a decline in the value of shares that occurred after the options were awarded. When the market fell in the late 1990s, underwater stocks were especially problematic for employers who had used stock options as a means of retaining employees. Thinking that employees might leave when the paper value of their options declined in the market downturn, many companies responded by repricing their employees' options or making new grants priced at a much lower level.[67] Defenders of these tactics argued that employers had little choice if they wanted to hold on to their employees. Critics contended that repricing defeated the original purpose, which was to reward employees only if the company performed well. As one person put it, "It's a case of heads I win, tails I win." Furthermore, the practice appears to not be effective as a means for retaining key executives.[68]

The problem of underwater stocks, along with pending changes in financial reporting rules, recently led Microsoft to end the stock option plan that had made many Microsoft employees millionaires in the past. In 2002, Microsoft gave employees stock options worth $3.6 billion—nearly a third of its pretax income. Now it offers direct stock grants with restrictions. Steve Ballmer, CEO of Microsoft, said the change was necessary to prevent its best talent from leaving to join start-up companies. When Microsoft was thriving, its stock option plan was appealing to talented employees, but today the company is entering a stage of maturity. Growth will not be as rapid as in the past. As long as the company continues to perform well, the stocks employees receive should retain their value. In the current high-tech environment, that and a stimulating, secure job are enough to keep many people happy.[69]

Options and Ethics. Some critics of executive pay practices blame the use of stock options for the ethical problems at companies such as Enron, Tyco, and Worldcom. They point out that too often, stock options simply encourage executives to use accounting and other tricks to achieve short-term

About Microsoft's new stock grants: *"I think it's a very fair deal. I've heard no one who thinks it's a bad idea. The market and the environment have changed drastically, and you can't go out and recruit with stock options anymore."*

Project Manager
Microsoft

paper profits, which they can use to enrich themselves. They focus executives on achieving short-term increases in the stock price instead of long-term shareholder gains. Critics also point to the fact that corporate boards often develop stock option plans that tie executive pay to performance, but then release executives from the restrictions during tough economic times. The practice of reducing performance requirements for executives when goals aren't reached subverts the intentions of any performance-based pay plan. These and other criticisms have made regulators and shareholders alike skeptical of stock options, and it is likely that they will be less widely used in the future. We think it's doubtful, however, that eliminating the use of stock options will solve the problem of unethical behavior in business or achieve significant reform in corporate governance. Fixing these problems will require more than redesigning pay plans.[70]

INTERNATIONAL CONSIDERATIONS

FAST FACT

Until recently, Japanese companies were not permitted to issue their stock as compensation.

Predicting in advance how employees in different countries will react to different pay plans is seldom easy. When international management professor Chao Chen at Rutgers University compared the preferences of American and Chinese employees, he expected to find that the Americans would prefer unequal, performance-based distribution of rewards and the Chinese would prefer more equal distribution. Instead, his research showed that Chinese and American both preferred to have material rewards distributed unequally, based on performance. To his surprise, the Chinese also preferred to see socioemotional awards—such as parties and managerial friendliness—distributed unequally, whereas the Americans felt these socioemotional awards should be distributed to everyone equally.[71] Similarly, one might predict that Americans and Russians would have different preferences for how to allocate rewards, but recent research suggests that managers in both countries place primary emphasis on individual performance when allocating rewards, while showing less concern for treating everyone equally or worrying about how the reward allocations might affect coworker relations.[72]

FAST FACT

Surveys by the National Association of Stock Plan Professionals indicate that approximately 85% of U.S.-based multinational companies grant stock options internationally. Of those, 90% use the same eligibility rules for expatriates as for U.S.-based employees.

To date, there has been relatively little systematic research investigating cultural differences in how employees react to alternative forms of performance-based pay. Thus, companies are learning on their own. When HR professionals at Motorola conducted their own research on attitudes toward pay-at-risk plans, they found that such plans were acceptable to employees in many countries—and the pattern of findings was not always what they expected. Exhibit 11.14 summarizes the conclusions Motorola reached about which countries were most accepting of pay at risk.[73]

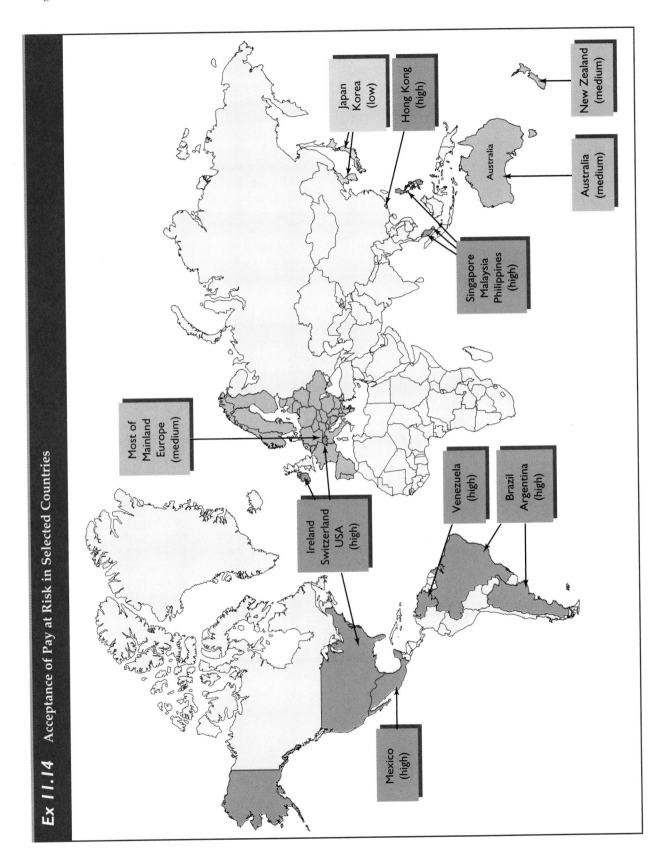

Ex 11.14 Acceptance of Pay at Risk in Selected Countries

Japan
Korea
(low)

Hong Kong
(high)

New Zealand
(medium)

Australia
(medium)

Australia

Singapore
Malaysia
Philippines
(high)

Most of
Mainland
Europe
(medium)

Venezuela
(high)

Brazil
Argentina
(high)

Ireland
Switzerland
USA
(high)

Mexico
(high)

SUMMARY

Performance-based pay plans continue to attract the attention of many human resource managers, and line managers continue to ask whether pay can be used to motivate their employees. The success of many incentive plans indicates that pay can motivate job performance. Nevertheless, many problems can arise due to the myriad issues associated with the design and implementation of performance-based pay. To be effective, performance-based pay must successfully address several challenges. Perhaps most importantly, valid and fair performance measurement and feedback serve as the foundation of performance-based pay. Other challenges include aligning employee behaviors and performance with the organization's strategic objectives, gaining employee acceptance and buy-in, and accurately predicting the cost implications of performance-based pay. If an organization has valid performance measures, and if everyone thinks the system is fair and tied to the objectives of the organization, paying for performance should increase profitability.

Performance-based pay can take many forms. Some forms link pay to the performance of individuals, while others link pay to the performance of teams or the entire organization. Some forms permanently affect the base pay of employees, while other forms have no implications for base pay. Some forms create opportunities for upside rewards without creating any downside risks, while others put substantial portions of an employee's expected pay at risk. Some forms emphasize short-term performance and offer employees immediate rewards, while others focus employees on longer-term results and defer rewards far into the future. Choosing the best methods of performance-based pay can be difficult.

The effects of any of the available methods of performance-based pay depend on many factors, including: the level at which job performance can accurately be measured (individual, department, or organization); the extent of cooperation needed between departments; the willingness of managers to take the time needed to design, implement, monitor, and continuously improve one or several systems; and the culture and degree of trust in the organization. Add to these the need to ensure alignment between performance-based pay plans and all other components of the HRM system, and the true magnitude of the challenge becomes apparent. Nevertheless, if the current trend continues, employees in many different industries can expect to see increasing use of performance-based pay.

TERMS TO REMEMBER

Combined distribution plans
Commission
Current distribution plans
Deferred distribution plans
Differential piece-rate plans
Earnings-at-risk plans
Eligibility rules
Employee stock ownership plans
  (ESOPs)
Gainsharing plans
Incentive pay plans
Indexed stock options

Merit pay plans
Performance-based pay
Performance-vested stock options
Premium-priced stock options
Profit-sharing plans
Scanlon and Rucker plans
Standard hour plan
Stock option
Straight piecework plan
Time-restricted stock options
Underwater stock options

DISCUSSION QUESTIONS

1. Describe the strategic importance of performance-based pay. Why do employers use it?

2. What are the major disadvantages of the three major forms of performance-based pay for employees (merit, incentives, earnings at risk)?

3. Debate the following assertion: If selection and placement decisions are made effectively, performance differences among employees should be relatively small; therefore, performance-based pay isn't needed and may even be disruptive.

4. What does it mean to put earnings at risk? List the potential costs and benefits of placing a substantial percentage of pay at risk for *all* employees in the following types of organizations: a hospital, a restaurant, a brokerage firm, and a fashion design house.

5. Describe the challenges associated with team-based pay. Do you think these challenges differ for team-based bonuses and team-based stock awards?

6. Do you think performance-based pay is more likely to cause employees to behave unethically than paying a straight salary or wage? Explain your reasoning.

PROJECTS TO EXTEND YOUR LEARNING

1. *Integration and Application.*

   a. Compare and contrast the components and use of performance-based pay plans at Lincoln Electric and Southwest. Overall, which plan do you think is more effective? Why?

   b. Anthony Massaro has said that Lincoln Electric may gradually move toward having a more traditional pay plan. What do you think he means by this? What strategic objectives would lead the company to conclude that a more traditional pay plan would be more effective? How do you think Lincoln Electric's employees would react to such a change? Why?

2. *Exploring the Internet.*

   c. The Bureau of Labor Statistics provides a wealth of information about economic conditions that affect pay policies. Learn more by visiting the BLS Editor's Desk, http://stats.bls.gov/.

   d. Find out more about the services offered by consulting groups who specialize in compensation, including:
Zigon Performance Group, http://www.zigonperf.com
William M. Mercer, http://www.mercer.com
Towers Perrin, http://www.towersperrin.com

   e. The issue of paying for performance is one that has been discussed at length in the field of education. Learn more about using merit pay and incentives to pay educators for excellent performance by visiting the home pages of
The American Federation of Teachers, http://www.aft.org
The National Education Association, http://www.nea.org

   f. Learn more about Scanlon Plans from Scanlon Leadership, http://www.scanlonleader.org. Learn about employee ownership from The National Council on Employee Ownership, http://www.nceo.org.
And learn more about stock options from http://myStockOptions.com.

3. *Experiential Activity.* Visit three different retail stores, such as Sears, Wal-Mart, and Macy's. Choose stores that are conveniently located, but try to choose stores that have different strategies (e.g., selling at the lowest price, providing excellent customer service, offering high-end luxury goods). Talk to at least two salespeople in each store to learn about how they are paid. Try to obtain answers to the following questions (be sure to keep notes about your conversations):

   a. Is the person paid a commission? If yes, is it a straight commission or a combined commission? What percentage of the person's average paycheck is a commission award?

   b. What other forms of performance-based pay, if any, does the person receive? Be sure to ask about achievement bonuses, merit pay, and stock ownership.

   c. Does the performance-based pay offered by the company focus on improving individual, team, or company performance?

   d. Does the person feel there are any drawbacks to the pay plan? If yes, what are the drawbacks?

After interviewing the salespeople, evaluate the pay plans at each of the three retail stores. Which store do you think has the most effective approach to paying their salespeople? Explain.

CASE STUDY

EVALUATING NONTRADITIONAL INCENTIVE SYSTEMS: HOWE 2 SKI STORES

The Howe 2 Ski Stores are a chain of three ski and windsurfing shops located in the suburbs of a large eastern city. Maria Howe, a ski enthusiast and business school major, opened a store 10 years ago after her college graduation with financial backing from her family and several friends. From its inception, the Howe 2 store was intended to provide state of the art equipment and clothing for skiers at all skill levels, from beginner to champion. It was to be staffed by employees who were themselves advanced skiers and could provide expert advice on the choice of clothing and equipment, and it was intended to have a quick response time that would permit the last-minute purchase of equipment and clothing prior to a ski trip.

Howe originally drew from a pool of skiing friends and fellow students to staff the stores and still prefers to hire part-time employees with skiing expertise who might leave in a year over more stable, full-time employees with less expertise and interest in the sport. Whether administrative staff, cashiers, clerks, or molders (employees who fit bindings to skis), employees were encouraged to keep up on the latest skiing equipment and trends, attend ski vendor shows, try out demo equipment, and give feedback on the store's inventory in order to help provide the highest-quality, state-of-the-art equipment and advice for the customer. Suggestion boxes were placed in the store and Howe herself regularly collected, read, and acted upon the suggestions made by the clerks and customers. She developed special advertising campaigns to build an image for the nearby slopes in order to increase the market. As the business grew, Howe even added a line of rental equipment in order to lower the costs and encourage people to try the sport.

Although profits grew irregularly due to weather effects and the faddish nature of the sport, Howe's efforts paid off in the long term, and within four years business had grown sufficiently to permit the opening of a second Howe 2 Ski Store in another suburb about 10 miles from the first. In order to even out sales across the year, about six years ago Howe took a chance on the growing windsurfing market and the East Coast location and added a line of equipment for this sport. The move turned out to be a very good one. The windsurfing market increased by more than 300% in four years and continues to experience a slower but stable pattern of growth as families and older adults attempt the sport. This market has enabled her to smooth out the number of sales occurring throughout the year.

Three years ago, Howe was able to open a third store, located within a 15-mile radius from the other two. Although managers have been hired to run each of the stores and the total number of employees has grown to 65, Howe's basic strategy has remained the same—high-quality, state-of-the-art products, a knowledgeable staff, and quick response time. Profits from the stores have continued to grow, although at a slower rate. Competition from other ski stores has also increased noticeably within the last two years.

The threat of increased competition has been exacerbated by signs that employee productivity has begun to slide. Last year, there were eight occasions where expensive ski orders were not delivered in time for the customer's ski vacation. Although Howe used a variety of maneuvers to retain the customers' patronage (e.g., paying for the customers to rent equipment of equivalent quality, expressing the equipment to the customer as soon as it was delivered, and lowering the price of the equipment), the costs of these late orders were high. She realizes that word of these kinds of incidents could significantly damage the store's reputation. Furthermore, at least 15% of all ski orders were more than two days late, even though customers did not miss a trip or vacation as a result.

In an attempt to respond to these difficulties, Howe instituted a merit performance system for the molders (employees who fit the binding to skis). Although productivity seemed to increase for awhile, waves of discontent popped out all over the stores. The molders felt that their merit ratings were inaccurate because the store managers could not observe them much of the time. Further, they argued that their performance would have been much higher had not other employees interrupted them with questions about appropriate bindings or failed to clearly identify the appropriate equipment on the sales tickets. Other employees also complained because they were not given the opportunity for merit pay. The buyers, who visit ski shows, examine catalogs, and talk with sales representatives in order to decide on the inventory, argued that their work was essential for high sales figures and quality equipment. Sales clerks claimed that their in-depth familiarity with an extensive inventory and their sales skills were essential to increasing sales. They also noted their important role in negotiating a delivery date that the molders could meet. Similar arguments were made by the people in the credit office who arranged for short-term financing if necessary, and by the cashiers who verified costs and checked credit card approvals. Even the stockers noted that the store would be in a bad way if they did not locate the correct equipment in a warehouse full of inventory and deliver it in a timely manner to the molders.

Howe had to concede that the employees were correct on many of these points, so she suspended the merit plan at the end of the ski season and promised to reevaluate its fairness. Even more convincing were several indications that productivity problems were not limited to molder employees. Complaints about customer service increased 20% during the year. Several customers noted that they were allowed to stand, merchandise in hand, waiting for a clerk to help them, while clerks engaged in deep conversations among themselves. Although Howe mentioned this to employees in the stores when she visited and asked the store managers to discuss it in staff meetings, the complaints continued. A record number of "as is" skis were sold at the end of the season sale because they were damaged in the warehouse, the store, or by the molders. The closing inventory revealed that 20% of the rental equipment had been lost or seriously damaged without resulting charges to the renters because records were poorly maintained. Regular checks of the suggestion boxes in the store revealed fewer and fewer comments. Although less extreme, similar problems occurred in windsurfing season. Employees just didn't seem to notice these problems or, worse, didn't seem to care.

Source: S. M. Nkomo, M. D. Fottler, and R. B. McAfee, *Applications in Human Resource Management: Cases, Exercises, and Skill Builders* (Mason, OH: South-Western, 2005). Reprinted with permission.

ENDNOTES

[1] S. Bates, "Top Pay for Best Performance," *HR Magazine* (January 2003): 32–36. For recent research on how the change orientation of a firm's strategy is related to the use of incentives, see B. K. Boyd and A. Salamin, "Strategic Reward Systems: A Contingency Model of Pay System Design," *Strategic Management Journal* 22 (2001): 777–792.

[2] Results of this survey as reported in "No Real Money on the Table," *Workforce Management* (December 2003): 115. For more details, visit http://www.watsonwyatt.com.

[3] N. Byrnes, "Avon Calling—Lots of New Reps," *Business Week* (June 2, 2003): 53–54.

[4] G. D. Jenkins Jr., A. Mitra, N. Gupta, and J. D. Shaw, "Are Financial Incentives Related to Performance? A Meta-Analytic Review of Empirical Research," *Journal of Applied Psychology* 83(5) (1998): 777–787; J. S. Kane and K. A. Freeman, "A Theory of Equitable Performance Standards," *Journal of Management* 23(1) (1997): 37–58.

[5] N. Byrnes, "Avon Calling—Lots of New Reps," *Business Week* (June 2, 2003): 53–54.

[6] P. Digh, "The Next Challenge: Holding People Accountable," *HR Magazine: Diversity Agenda* (October 1998): 63–69; S. N. Mehta, "Diversity Pays," *Wall Street Journal* (April 11, 1996): R12.

[7] Hay Group, *A Comparison of Top Executive Compensation Practices: Examining the Gaps and Similarities among European and US Companies* (New York: Hay Group, 2003); for an excellent brief historical summary, see G. T. Milkovich and J. Stevens, "From Pay to Rewards: 100 Years of Change," *ACA Journal* (First Quarter 2000): 6–18.

[8] E. Krell, "Getting a Grip on Executive Compensation," *Workforce* (February 2003): 30–34; "Executive Compensation: Recent Trends, Changes and Highlights," http://www.workforce.com/archive/article/23/45/11.php, June 24, 2003.

[9] J. Wiscombe, "Rewards Get Results," *Workforce* (April 2002): 42–48.

[10] K. A. Brown and V. L. Huber, "Lowering Floors and Raising Ceilings: A Longitudinal Assessment of the Effects of an Earnings-at-Risk Plan on Pay Satisfaction," *Personnel Psychology* 45 (June 1992): 279–311.

[11] R. D. Banker, S-Y Lee, G. Potter, and D. Srinivasan, "Contextual Analysis of Performance Impacts of Outcome-Based Incentive Compensation," *Academy of Management Journal* 39 (1996): 920–948.

[12] J. R. Deckop, R. Mangel, and C. Cirka, "Getting More than You Pay For: Organizational Citizenship Behavior and Pay-for-Performance Plans," *Academy of Management Journal* 41 (1999): 420–428; G. D. Jenkins, Jr., A. Mitra, N. Gupta, and J. D. Shaw, "Are Financial Incentives Related to

Performance? A Meta-analytic Review of Empirical Research," *Journal of Applied Psychology* 83 (1998): 777–787; N. Gupta and A. Mitra, "The Value of Financial Incentives," *ACA Journal* (Autumn 1998): 58–65.

13 For more discussion about these issues, see the entire issue of *Human Resource Management Journal,* Spring 2004.

14 For an excellent set of articles see the Spring 2004 issue of the *Human Resource Management Journal,* volume 43; E. Deci, R. Koestner, and R. Ryan, "A Meta-Analytic Review of Experiments Examining the Effects of Extrinsic Rewards on Intrinsic Motivation," *Psychological Bulletin* 125(6) (1999): 627–668; E. Deci, R. Koestner, and R. Ryan, "The Undermining Effect Is a Reality After All-Extrinsic Rewards, Task Interest, and Self-Determination: Reply to Eisenberger, Pierce, and Cameron (1999) and Lepper, Henderlong, and Gingras (1999)," *Psychological Bulletin* 125(6) (1999): 692–700; R. Eisenberger, W. Pierce, and J. Cameron, "Effects of Reward on Intrinsic Motivation-Negative, Neutral, and Positive: Comment on Deci, Koestner, and Ryan (1999)," *Psychological Bulletin* 125(6) (1999): 677–691; M. Lepper, J. Henderlong, and I. Gingras, "Understanding the Effects of Extrinsic Rewards on Intrinsic Motivation—Uses and Abuses of Meta-Analysis: Comment on Deci, Koestner, and Ryan (1999)," *Psychological Bulletin* 125(6) (1999): 669–676; R. Eisenberger and J. Cameron, "Detrimental Effects of Reward," *American Psychologist* 51 (November 1996): 1153–1166; see also W. Van Eerde and H. Thierry, "Vroom's Expectancy Models and Work-Related Criteria: A Meta-Analysis," *Journal of Applied Psychology* 81 (1996): 575–586.

15 J. Van Scotter, S. J. Motowidlo, and T. Cross, "Effects of Task Performance and Contextual Performance on Systemic Rewards," *Journal of Applied Psychology* 85(4) (2000): 526–535; P. R. J. Greene, "Effective Variable Compensation Plans," *ACA Journal* (Spring 1997): 32–39.

16 Results reported in "No Real Money on the Table," *Workforce Management* (December 2003): 115. For more details, go to http://www.mercerhr.com.

17 J. Kiska, "Customer Satisfaction Pays Off," *HR Magazine* (February 2004): 87–93; E. E. Lawler III, "Reward Practices and Performance Management System Effectiveness," *Organizational Dynamics* 32(4) (2003): 396404; S. J. Berman, "Using the Balance Scorecard in Strategic Compensation," *ACA News* (June 1998): 16–19.

18 P. Pascarella, "Compensating Teams," *Across the Board* (February 1997): 16–22; see also D. Knight, C. Durham, and E. E. Locke, "The Relationship of Team Goals, Incentives, and Efficacy to Strategic Risk, Tactical Implementation, and Performance," *Academy of Journal Management* 44(2) (2001): 326–338.

19 J. Fierman, "The Perilous New World of Fair Pay," *Fortune* (June 13, 1994): 58–59.

20 J. B. Wood, "Customer Satisfaction and Loyalty," *ACA Journal* (Summer 1998): 48–60.

21 R. J. Greene, "Improving Merit Pay Plan Effectiveness," *ACA News* (April 1998): 26–29.

22 B. Gerhart, "Designing Reward Systems: Balancing Result and Behaviors," in C. H. Fay, M. A. Thompson, and D. Knight, *The Executive Handbook on Compensation: Linking Strategic Rewards to Business Performance* (New York: Free Press, 2001): 214–237.

23 Hay Group, *The Hay Report: Compensation and Benefits for 1998 and Beyond* (New York: The Hay Group, 1998).

24 C. Gomez, B. Kirkman, and D. Shapiro, "The Impact of Collectivism and In-Group/Out-Group Membership on the Evaluation Generosity of Team Members," *Academy of Management Journal* 43(6) (2000): 1097–1106; F. Moussa, "Determinants, Process, and Consequences of Personal Goals and Performance," *Journal of Management* 26(6) (2000): 1259–1285; P. M. Wright et al., "Productivity and Extra-Role Behavior: The Effects of Goals and Incentives on Spontaneous Helping," *Journal of Applied Psychology* 78 (1993): 374–381.

25 A. L. Overhalt, "Cuckoo for Customers," *Fast Company* (June 2004): 86–87.

26 L. Lavelle, "The Gravy Train Is Slowing," *Business Week* (April 2, 2001): 44; B. Sosnin, "A Pat(ent) on the Back," *HR Magazine* (March 2000): 107–112; B. Gerhart and G. T. Milkovich, "Organizational Differences in Managerial Compensation and Financial Performance," *Academy of Management Review* 33 (1990): 663–691.

27 K. Bradsher, "Efficiency on Wheels," *New York Times* (June 16, 2000): C1, 8; B. Flannigan, "Turnaround from Feedback," *HR Focus* (October 1997): 3.

28 "Policy Guide: Incentive Pay Can Bring Many Rewards," *Bulletin to Management* (June 5, 1997): 184; "Policy Guide: Employers Use Pay to Lever Performance," *Bulletin to Management* (August 21, 1997): 272.

29 C. M. Ellis and C. L. Palus, "Blazing a Trail to Broad-Based Incentives: Lessons from Two Leading Manufacturing Companies," *World at Work Journal* (Fourth Quarter 2000): 33–41.

30 M. Frase-Blunt, "What Goes Up May Come Down," *HR Magazine* (August 2001): 85–90.

31 R. Gherson, "Getting the Pay Thing Right," *Workspan* (June 2000): 47–51; G. Flynn, "Your Grand Plan for Incentive Compensation May Yield a Grand Lawsuit," *Workforce* (July 1997): 89–92.

32 R. Sharpe, "As Leaders, Women Rule," *Business Week* (November 20, 2000): 75–84; T. Lewin, "Women Losing Ground to Men in Widening Income Difference," *New York Times* (September 15, 1997): A1, A6.

33 H. R. Varian, "Stock Options Are Still a Gamble but the Size of the Pot May Soon Be Clearer," *New York Times* (April 8, 2004): C2; "The Basics of Stock Options: 25 FAQs on Equity Compensation," http://www.workforce.com/archive/article/22/11/88_printer.php, June 24, 2003; N. Byrnes, "Beyond Options: However You Slice It, the New Mix Will Cost Companies More," *Business Week* (July 28, 2003): 3637; J. Greene, "Will Stock Options Lose Their Sex Appeal?" *Business Week* (July 21, 2003): 2324; J. D. Opdyke and M. Higgins, "What the New Options Rules Mean for Your Pay: Employees Will Bear the Brunt of Drive to Expense Them," *Wall Street Journal* (August 7, 2002): D1, D2.

34 R. L. Heneman, "Merit Pay," in C. H. Fay, M. A. Thompson, and D. Knight, *The Executive Handbook on Compensation: Linking Strategic Rewards to Business Performance* (New York: Free Press, 2001): 447–465; P. Burrows, "A Self-Inflicted Bonus Cut," *Business Week* (December 18, 2000): 12; R. Wood, P. Atkins, and J. Bright, "Bonuses, Goals, and Instrumentality Effects," *Journal of Applied Psychology* 84 (1999): 703–720.

35 C. Peck, *Variable Pay: New Performance Rewards* (New York: Conference Board, 1990).

36 P. D. Sweeney, "Counting the Till, Then Trolling for New Accounts," *New York Times* (June 14, 2000): B2.

37 W. B. Abernathy, "Linking Performance Scorecards to Profit-Indexed Performance Pay," *ACA News* (April 1998): 23–25.

38 C. Taylor, "On-the-Spot Incentives," *HR Magazine* (May 2004): 80–84.

39 J. Flaherty, "Suggestions Rise from the Floors of U.S. Factories," *New York Times* (April 18, 2001): C1,7; R. Rose, "Kentucky Plant Workers Are Cranking Out Good Ideas," *Wall Street Journal* (August 13, 1996): B1; J. Birnbaum, "Recognition Programs Are Widespread," *HR News* (November 1991): 2.

40 B. Sonsin, "A Pat(ent) on the Back," *HR Magazine* (March 2000): 107.

41 L. Lavelle, J. Hempel, and D. Brady, "Executive Pay," *Business Week* (April 19, 2004): 104–110.

42 P. Brandes, R. Dharwadkar, and G. V. Lemesis, "Effective Employee Stock Option Design: Reconciling Stakeholder, Strategic, and Motivational Factors," *Academy of Management Executive* 17(1) (2003): 7793; M. Jensen and K. Murphy, "Performance Pay and Top Management Incentives," *Journal of Political Economy* 98(2) (1990): 225264; M. Bloom and G. T. Milkovich, "Relationships Among Risks, Incentive Pay and

Organizational Performance," *Academy of Management Journal* 41 (1998): 283–297.

43 G. D. Ledford and E. Hawk, "Compensation Strategy: A Guide for Senior Managers," *ACA Journal* (First Quarter 2000): 28–38; J. Reingold, "Executive Pay: Tying Pay to Performance Is a Great Idea. But Stock-Option Deals Have Compensation Out of Control," *Business Week* (April 21, 1997): 58–66; T. A. Stewart, "CEO Pay: Mom Wouldn't Approve," *Fortune* (March 31, 1997): 119–120; J. Reingold, "Even Executives Are Wincing at Executive Pay," *Business Week* (May 12, 1997): 40–43; J. A. Byrne, "Smoke, Mirrors, and the Boss's Paycheck," *Business Week* (October 13, 1997): 63.

44 S. E. Gross and S. P. Leffler, "Team Pay," in C. H. Fay, M. A. Thompson, and D. Knight, *The Executive Handbook on Compensation: Linking Strategic Rewards to Business Performance* (New York: Free Press, 2001): 465–485; E. E. Lawler, III, and S. G. Cohen, "Designing Pay Systems for Teams," *ACA Journal* (Autumn 1992): 6–18; C. Meyer, "How the Right Measures Help Teams Excel," *Harvard Business Review* (May/June 1994): 95–103.

45 J. Davis, "Retaining Your Hot Skills Employees—Use Dollars AND Sense," *ACA Journal* (First Quarter 2000): 47–56; B. Nelson, "Does One Reward Fit All?" *Workforce* (February 1997): 67–70.

46 E. E. Lawler, III, and S. Cohen, "Designing Pay Systems for Teams," 6–16; E. E. Lawler, III, "Reward Practices and Performance Management System Effectiveness," *Organizational Dynamics* 32(4) (2003): 396–404.

47 E. Hollensbe and J. Guthrie, "Group Pay-for-Performance Plans: The Role of Spontaneous Goal Setting," *Academy of Management Review* 25(4) (2000): 854–872; J. S. DeMatteo, L. T. Eby, and E. Sundstrom, "Team-Based Rewards: Current Empirical Evidence and Directions for Future Research," *Research in Organizational Behavior* 20 (1998): 141–183; P. K. Zingheim and J. R. Schuster, "Best Practices for Small-Team Pay," *ACA Journal* (Spring 1997): 40–49; J. S. DeMatteo, M. C. Rush, E. Sundstrom, and L. T. Eby, "Factors Related to the Successful Implementation of Team-Based Rewards," *ACA Journal* (Winter 1997): 16–27.

48 R. K. Platt, "Driving Change—'Account Teams' Help Company to Fly into the Next Century," *ACA News* (January 1996): 17–21.

49 There have been hundreds of laboratory studies on the effects of team-based rewards, and these suggest that they can be effective. But studies in the field show mixed results, due perhaps to challenges in addressing all of the key design issues. For a complete review, see J. S. DeMatteo, L. T. Eby, and E. Sundstrom, "Team-Based Rewards: Current Empirical Evidence and Directions for Future Research," *Research in Organizational Behavior* 20 (1998): 141–183.

50 P. K. Zingheim and J. R. Schuster, "Best Practices for Small-Team Pay."

51 J. Stack, "The Problem with Profit Sharing," *Inc.* (November 1996): 67–69.

52 G. Colvin, "What Money Makes You Do," *Fortune* (August 17, 1998): 213–214.

53 E. Zehnder, "A Simple Way to Pay," *Harvard Business Review* (April 2001): 53–71.

54 A concise discussion is provided by B. Graham-Moore, "Gainsharing," in C. H. Fay, M. A. Thompson, and D. Knight, *The Executive Handbook on Compensation: Linking Strategic Rewards to Business Performance* (New York: Free Press, 2001): 527–538.

55 J. B. Arthur and L. Aidman-Smith, "Gainsharing and Organizational Learning: An Analysis of Employee Suggestions over Time," *Academy of Management Journal* 44 (2001): 737–754.

56 B. E. Moore and T. L. Ross, *The Scanlon Way to Improved Productivity: A Practical Guide* (New York: Wiley, 1978); R. J. Schulhof, "Five Years with a Scanlon Plan," *Personnel Administrator* (June 1979): 55–63.

57 B. Graham-Moore and T. Ross, *Productivity Gainsharing* (Englewood Cliffs, NJ: Prentice-Hall, 1983); R. J. Bullock and E. E. Lawler, III, "Gainsharing: A Few Questions and Fewer Answers," *Human Resource Management* 23 (1984): 23–40; D-O Kim, "Factors Influencing

Organizational Performance in Gainsharing Programs," *Industrial Relations* 35 (April 1996): 227.

58 M. J. Wallace, *Rewards and Renewal: America's Search for Competitive Advantage through Alternative Pay Strategies* (Scottsdale, AZ: American Compensation Association, 1990): 15. See also R. Balu, "Bonuses Aren't Just for the Bosses," *Fast Company* (December 2000): 74–76; K. Paulsen and D. Westman, "Using Gainsharing to Motivate," *ACA News* (July/August, 1999): 44–48.

59 K. Paulsen, D. Westman, McGladrey, and Pullen, "Using Gainsharing to Motivate Generation X," *ACA News* (July/August 1999): 44–48; T. M. Welbourne and L. R. Gomez Mejia, "Gainsharing: A Critical Review and a Future Research Agenda," *Journal of Management* 21 (1995): 559–609.

60 "A Tricky Business," *The Economist* (June 30, 2001): 55–56.

61 K. Bonamici, "Hot Starbucks to Go," *Fortune* (January 26, 2004): 6074; W. J. Duncan, "Stock Ownership and Work Motivation," *Organizational Dynamics* 30(1) (2001): 1–11; B. R. Ellig, "Broad-based Stock Ownership," in C. H. Fay, M. A. Thompson, and D. Knight, *The Executive Handbook on Compensation: Linking Strategic Rewards to Business Performance* (New York: Free Press, 2001): 580–595; National Center for Employee Ownership, "NCEO Releases Initial Results of Stock Survey," *Workspan* (January 2001): 13–14.

62 N. Byrnes, "Which Is Better—Stock or Options?" *Business Week* (July 21, 2003): 25; Bureau of Labor Statistics, "BLS Reports on Non-Executive Employee Stock Options," *Workspan* (January 2001): 13.

63 N. Byrnes, "Which Is Better—Stock or Options?" *Business Week* (July 21, 2003): 25; E. Ofek and D. Yemack, "Taking Stock: Equity-Based Compensation and the Evolution of Managerial Ownership," *Journal of Finance* 55 (2000): 1367–1384; P. Sparrow, "The Psychological Consequences of Employee Ownership: On the Role of Risk, Reward, Identity and Personality," *Trends in Organizational Behavior* 8 (2001): 79–90; J. Blasi, D. Kruse, and A. Bernstein, *In the Company of Owners: The Truth about Stock Options* (New York: Basic Books, 2003).

64 Based on D. G. Goodall, "Global Employee-Based Equity Plans—Can they Work for Your Company?" in C. Reynolds (ed.), *Guide to Global Compensation and Benefits* (San Diego: Harcourt, 2001): 121–158; G. Paulin, "Using Stock to Retain Key Employees," *World at Work Journal* (Third Quarter 2000): 45–51; P. L. Gilles, "Your Stock Price Dropped by 30%! Now What?" *ACA News* (April 2000).

65 R. Gotcher, "PBE Plans More Flavorful than Vanilla Equity," *Workspan* (January 2001): 46–48.

66 S. Lohr, "IBM to Alter How It Pays Stock Options to Executive," *New York Times* (February 25, 2004): C1, 4.

67 G. Koretz, "Why Options Are Repriced," *Business Week* (August 13, 2001): 24.

68 D. Delves, "Stock Options: Underused and Underwater," *Workforce* (January 2003): 50–54; L. Lavelle, "When Good Options Go Bad," *Business Week E.Biz* (December 11, 2000): 96–98; E. Schatzker, "What Tech Bust?" *Bloomberg Markets* (April 2001): 65–68; P. L. Gilles, "Your Stock Price Dropped by 30%! Now What?" *ACA News* (April 2000).

69 J. Markoff and D. Leonhardt, "Microsoft Will Award Stock, Not Options, to Employees," *New York Times* (July 9, 2003): 1, 4; S. Kershaw, "For Newer Microsoft Employees, a Sense of Redress," *New York Times* (July 10, 2003): 1, 4; P. J. Kiger, "Microsoft Leads the Way in Opting Out of Options," *Workforce Management* (August 2003): 74–76.

70 For some insights on this issue, see "Fat Cats Feeding," *The Economist* (October 11, 2003): 64–66.

71 D. R. Briscoe and R. S. Schuler, *International Human Resource Management*, 2nd ed. (London: Routledge, 2004); S. Gates, "Aligning Performance Measures and Incentives in European Companies," *World at Work Journal* (Third Quarter 2000): 19–26; C. C. Chen, "New Trends in Rewards Allocation Preferences: A Sino-U.S. Comparison," *Academy of Management Journal* 38 (1995): 408–428; see also Y. P. Hau and R. M. Steers, "Cultural Influences on the Design of Incentive Systems: The

Case of East Asia," *Asia Pacific Journal of Management* 10 (1996): 71–85; C. E. Rusbult, C. A. Insko, and Y-H W. Lin, "Seniority-based Reward Allocation in the United States and Taiwan," *Social Psychology Quarterly* 58 (1995): 13–30.

72 J. K. Giacobbe-Miller, D. J. Miller, and V. V. Victorov, "A Comparison of Russian and U.S. Pay Association Decisions, Distributive Justice Judgments, and Productivity under Different Pay Conditions," *Personnel Psychology* 51 (1998): 137–163.

73 D. G. Goodall, "Global Employee-Based Equity Plans—Can They Work for Your Company?" in C. Reynolds (ed.), *Guide to Global Compensation and Benefits,* 2nd ed. (2001): 121–158.

chapter 12

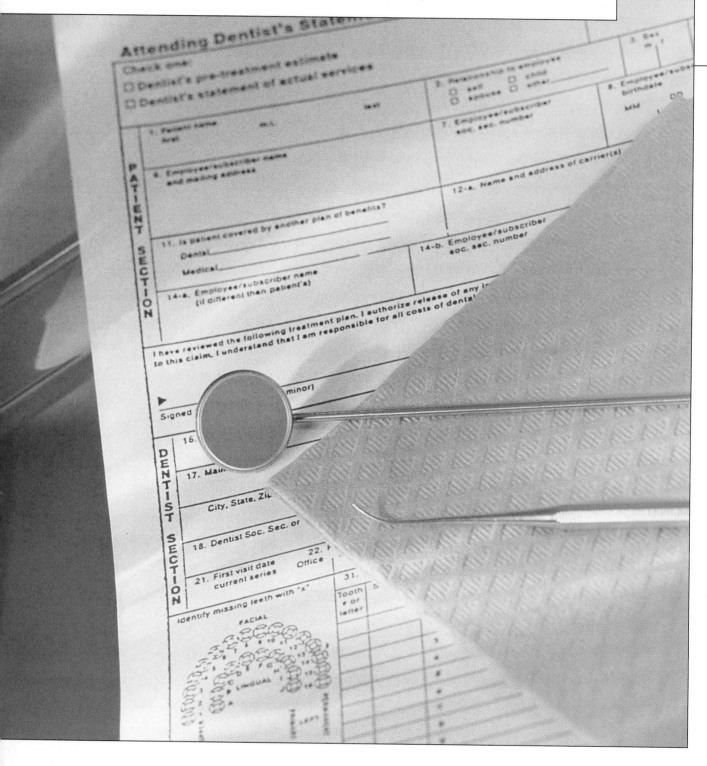

Providing Benefits and Services

Steelcase, headquartered in Grand Rapids, Michigan, for 90 years, is the world's leading provider of high-performance workplaces. It serves virtually every country of the world. Its workforce of almost 21,000 employees is also spread throughout the world. It has more than 50 manufacturing plants in the United States, 6 in France, 3 in the United Kingdom, and one each in seven other countries, including Mexico, Japan, and Germany.

To compete effectively, Steelcase must continually manage and reduce its costs. During the past decade, it has focused on reducing the costs of workers' compensation claims—essentially the costs associated with having people hurt, injured, and out of work. Under medical services and the safety director, Steelcase developed and implemented a "return-to-work" program that seeks to return injured employees to work as soon as they are able. The program has substantially reduced the average cost per claim, saving the company more than $50 million. Initiatives such as this one are among the reasons that Steelcase was recognized by Industry Week *as one of the 100 best-managed companies in the world.[1]*

Like many other companies, Steelcase is trying to address a mounting crisis. As international competition heats up, U.S. firms are struggling to contain their costs. For many firms, the costs of benefits and services are a significant part of the challenge. Steelcase's approach is an excellent example of what firms can do to reduce one part of these costs—workers' compensation claims. Other firms reduce costs by providing less health care coverage and cutting back on their pension plans and retirement plans.

Although the specific elements of plans vary, **employee benefits and services** *are generally defined as in-kind payments to employees for their membership or participation in the organization.* These payments provide protection against health and accident-related problems and ensure income at retirement. Benefits and services also include pay for time not at work—for instance, vacations, holidays, sick days and absences, breaks, and wash-up and cleanup. To attract and retain the best employees, some companies also offer discounts on company products, educational assistance, exercise and wellness centers, dry cleaning, and child and elder care. Benefits and services enable employees to enjoy a better lifestyle and maintain a reasonable work-life balance.

THE STRATEGIC IMPORTANCE OF EMPLOYEE BENEFITS AND SERVICES

Driving the desire to offer better employee benefits and services is the desire to attract and retain valued employees. Controlling costs, on the other hand, is a major counterbalancing force. The key strategic challenge is offering benefits and services that maximally leverage the employer's investments. Due to numerous laws and regulations that affect employee benefits and services, employers must carefully plan how to meet this challenge while also ensuring legal compliance. Exhibit 12.1 provides several examples of strategic business objectives and the ways in which benefits and services can be used to address them.

Ex 12.1   Business Objectives Addressed by Benefits and Services

BUSINESS OBJECTIVE	BENEFITS RESPONSE
1. To reduce total costs of doing business by 10% yearly.	1. Contain the rise in health care costs to 2% yearly and increase employee contributions by 2% yearly.
2. To develop a working environment that is founded on integrity, open communication, and individual growth.	2. Develop an employee career counseling system that provides employees with an opportunity to assess skills and develop competencies. Establish a tuition reimbursement program.
3. To establish the division as a recognized leader in support of its community.	3. Establish a corporate-giving matching fund.
4. To complete the downsizing of the company by the end of the third quarter.	4. Develop various termination subsidies such as severance pay, outplacement assistance, and early retirement benefits.
5. To cut accident rates 10% by year-end.	5. Establish an employee assistance program by year-end. Set up a free literacy training program to ensure that all employees can read job safety signs.

Unlike other elements of total compensation, employee benefits and services are not generally considered effective tools for improving employee motivation and productivity. This is because, generally, benefits and services are not tied to employee performance. Instead, most benefits and services are available on a noncontingent basis—as long as employees remain employed, they receive the same benefits and services regardless of job performance. Rather than appreciating the benefits and services offered, employees may view them simply as obligations that all employers are expected to meet.[2]

RECRUITING AND RETAINING TALENT

In their recruiting ads and literature, most companies describe their benefits and services packages as "competitive." Owing to increased competition, being competitive without spending more often means developing innovative packages to attract and retain employees. Wellness programs, health screenings, flexible benefits plans, and cash options offered in place of prepaid benefits packages are examples of relatively new benefits and services being offered by the leading firms.[3]

Communication. Many organizations pump so much money into benefits and services programs because they believe that it helps enhance the organization's image among employees and in the business community. Used wisely, this may be true. On the other hand, ample research demonstrates that these objectives are not always attained. Many, perhaps most, employees don't really know which benefits they receive or their worth. The benefits consulting firm, Towers Perrin, found that while more than 90% of companies think it is important that employees understand the value and cost of benefits, only 25% think that their companies are successful in achieving this objective.[4] Realizing this, Starbucks aggressively markets its benefits and services to employees. If employees don't know they receive a benefit, they won't stay with the company in order to retain that benefit.

Relative Value. Even when employee benefits and services succeed in attracting applicants, their importance relative to other job factors—for example, opportunity for advancement, salary, geographic location, responsibilities, and prestige—may be low. Furthermore, some of the potential value of a company's benefits and services plan may be lost on employees who value only some of the benefits and services offered, and may even resent the company's decision to spend money on benefits and services used only by other employees. For example, family-friendly benefits have been known to provoke nonfamily backlash.[5] Allowing employees to personalize their benefits and services is one solution to this problem. As firms reduce or even eliminate benefits and services and ask workers to share or even assume their costs, many employees are beginning to realize how expensive benefits and services can be.[6]

CONTROLLING COSTS

During the recent economic boom of the 1990s, employers were relatively generous—a growing economy meant that simply finding enough people to

"People come here for the benefits, and they stay for them. . . . Turnover is very expensive, and our benefits keep our rate down."

Bradley Honeycut
Director of Compensation and Benefits
Starbucks Coffee Company

"Balancing the benefit needs of both the company and employees can certainly be a challenge, but the rewards of sound, cost-effective benefits programs, and employee understanding and appreciation are certainly worth the effort."

Cherly Poulson
Management of Benefits Planning
GlaxoSmithKline

staff organizations required less focus on controlling costs. During the mid-1990s, the rate of growth for health care costs slowed, as employers found more economical ways to provide health insurance (e.g., managed care). But then, as we entered the 21st century, the tide shifted once more, and controlling costs again became a major concern.[7] In a recent survey of benefits specialists conducted by Deloitte & Touche, 86% said that controlling the costs of health and welfare benefits is a top priority.

In 1929, total benefits payments averaged 5% of total pay. By 2003, they had risen to an average of about 30% of total pay, or roughly $15,000 a year for each employee. Although these numbers vary across industries and by type of worker, the cost of benefits and services to organizations is, in general, enormous.[8] While wages and salaries have increased 40 times during the past 60 years, benefits and services have increased 500 times.[9] As will become soon become apparent, some of these costs cannot easily be avoided, due to governmental mandates. Many costs are due to voluntary benefits and services, however, and so are potential targets of cost-cutting efforts.

EMPLOYEE BENEFITS AND SERVICES WITHIN AN INTEGRATED HRM SYSTEM

Exhibit 12.2 shows the major elements of employee benefits and services, and the primary linkages between these and other HR practices. Also shown are the factors in the external and organizational environments that have the most impact on employee benefits and services. Included in this chapter are descriptions of mandatory public protection programs, voluntary private protection programs, and supplemental benefits and services aimed at improving the quality of employees' work and nonwork lives.

Protection programs required by the federal and state governments are referred to as **public protection programs.** In effect, public protection programs provide insurance for employees and their families when an employee's income (direct compensation) is terminated. Public protection programs grew rapidly during the Great Depression of the 1930s. In response to the hardships faced by millions of unemployed Americans, Congress enacted legislation that created a safety net to protect Americans from extreme poverty. Although the government manages public protection programs, both private and public employers help support the funding of these programs.

In addition to providing mandatory benefits, many employers also pay costs associated with providing additional insurance for health care and retirement. *Protection programs offered voluntarily by employers are called* **private protection programs.** Examples of each are listed in Exhibit 12.3.

Links with Other HR Practices

As described in Chapter 9, employee benefits and services are one element of a total compensation package. Indeed, as Exhibit 12.4 illustrates, approximately one-third of a company's total labor costs is due to the costs associated with the benefits and services offered to employees.[10] Base wages and performance-based incentive pay account for the remainder.

Especially when the labor market is tight, employers often provide generous benefits and services in an effort to attract and retain needed talent. An employer's choice of benefits and services to offer is usually shaped by other

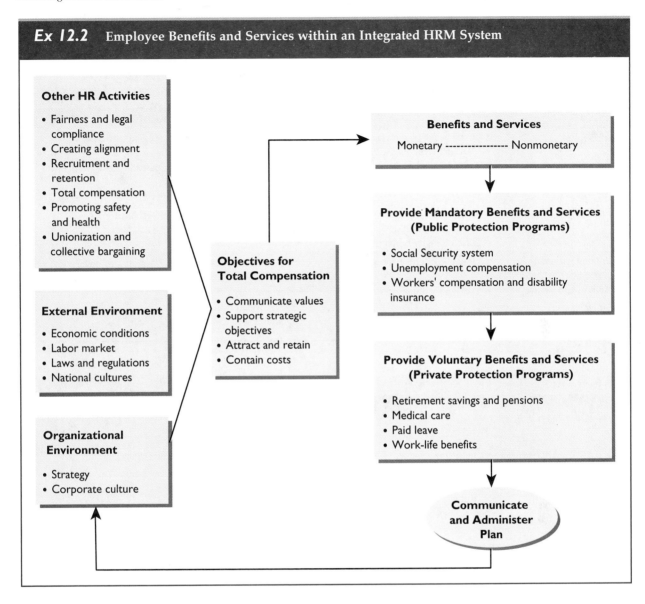

Ex 12.2 Employee Benefits and Services within an Integrated HRM System

Other HR Activities

- Fairness and legal compliance
- Creating alignment
- Recruitment and retention
- Total compensation
- Promoting safety and health
- Unionization and collective bargaining

External Environment

- Economic conditions
- Labor market
- Laws and regulations
- National cultures

Organizational Environment

- Strategy
- Corporate culture

Objectives for Total Compensation

- Communicate values
- Support strategic objectives
- Attract and retain
- Contain costs

Benefits and Services

Monetary ----------------- Nonmonetary

Provide Mandatory Benefits and Services (Public Protection Programs)

- Social Security system
- Unemployment compensation
- Workers' compensation and disability insurance

Provide Voluntary Benefits and Services (Private Protection Programs)

- Retirement savings and pensions
- Medical care
- Paid leave
- Work-life benefits

Communicate and Administer Plan

aspects of the organization, however. Choosing benefits and services that are aligned with other practices and with the strategy is important, given the significant costs involved. At Ernst & Young, flexible work arrangements are a service that many employees value. The firm considers their flex policy to be a strategic tool that enables this professional services firm to be more competitive.

Two other sets of HR practices that are intertwined with benefits and services are (a) safety and health and (b) unionization and collective bargaining. These linkages are described in more detail in subsequent chapters.

THE EXTERNAL ENVIRONMENT

Companies are trying to reduce the costs of benefits and services in part because they have grown so much over the years. The growth in the types

Ex 12.3   Public and Private Protection Programs

Issue	Public Programs	Private Programs
Retirement	• Social Security old-age benefits	• Defined benefit pensions • Defined contribution pensions • Money purchase and thrift plans [401(k)s and ESOPs]
Death	• Social Security survivors' benefits • Workers' compensation	• Group term life insurance including accidental death and travel insurance • Payouts from profit-sharing, pension, or thrift plans, or any combination of these • Dependent survivors' benefits
Disability	• Workers' compensation • Social Security disability benefits • State disability benefits	• Short-term accident and sickness insurance • Long-term disability insurance
Unemployment	• Unemployment benefits	• Supplemental unemployment benefits or severance pay, or both
Medical and dental expenses	• Workers' compensation	• Hospital surgical insurance • Other medical insurance • Dental insurance

Ex 12.4   Employer Costs for Benefits

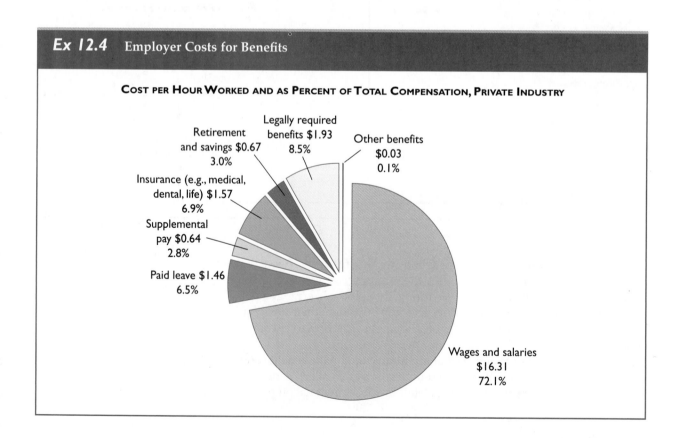

COST PER HOUR WORKED AND AS PERCENT OF TOTAL COMPENSATION, PRIVATE INDUSTRY

Retirement and savings $0.67 3.0%
Legally required benefits $1.93 8.5%
Other benefits $0.03 0.1%
Insurance (e.g., medical, dental, life) $1.57 6.9%
Supplemental pay $0.64 2.8%
Paid leave $1.46 6.5%
Wages and salaries $16.31 72.1%

and costs of employee benefits and services can be traced to several environmental trends.

Economic Conditions. Under normal business conditions, employers compete for labor primarily through the wages they offer. During times of major crises, such as World War II and the Korean War, the government curtailed such activity in order to prevent runaway inflation. Throughout the 20th century, the imposition of wage controls in times of war forced organizations to offer more and greater benefits and services in place of wage increases, to attract new employees. Recently the most important economic factor has been rising health care costs. In 1940, U.S. health care expenses were $4 billion, about 4% of the GDP. In 2002, they were more than $1.5 trillion, or almost 15% of the GDP. Regardless of their causes, these increases have major consequences for employee benefits and services.[11]

Inflation levels also come into play. Employee benefits and services managers, more so than compensation managers, must anticipate the long-term effects of inflation on medical service, education, and pension benefits. Also, employers' benefits and services packages often change because of tax code changes. Tax rules for benefits can substantially influence both their real cost for employers and their real value to employees.

Union Bargaining. From 1935 into the 1970s, unions were able to gain steady increases in wages and benefits for their members. Practically all benefits and services are now mandatory bargaining items, which means that employers must bargain in good faith on union proposals to add them. Companies without union representation may offer similar benefits and services in order to remain attractive to job applicants.

The effects of unions are greater for public employers than for private employers, for two reasons. The first reason is that 40% of all government employees are unionized, compared to less than 10% of employees in the private sector. The second reason is that government employers have been relatively generous in agreeing to pension plans that promise to reward employees in the future in exchange for employees agreeing to accept somewhat lower salaries and wages in the short term. Such agreements suited politicians because they allowed city and state governments to defer these costs well into the future. Unfortunately, as the Baby Boomer generation approaches retirement, it has become clear that state governments do not have the money needed to meet their obligations to employees.[12]

Laws and Regulations. A variety of laws significantly affect the administration and offering of monetary benefits, including the Family and Medical Leave Act of 1993 (FLMA), the Employee Retirement Income Security Act of 1974 (ERISA), and the Social Security Act of 1935. When Congress initiated the Social Security Act, it covered only 60% of all workers. Subsequently, the scope of these benefits and the percentage of eligible workers have increased substantially. Today 95% of all workers are eligible for Social Security benefits, including disability benefits, health benefits, and retirement pay. These laws and regulations are described more thoroughly later in this chapter.

THE ORGANIZATIONAL ENVIRONMENT

Initiatives such as major medical insurance, long-term disability plans, and child and elder care allowances reflect a general concern for employees. All were implemented by organizations in response to employee needs. Provisions such as educational assistance benefits, employee assistance programs, and wellness programs were inspired by pressures to improve productivity, enhance worker skills, and increase retention of key employees. More recently, benefits and services such as auto and home insurance, matching funds for charitable giving, and work-life balance programs have been prompted by private businesses' desire to be socially responsible and attract good workers.[13]

Traditionally, employers adopted a "father-knows-best" attitude toward benefits; the company assumed it knew what benefits and services were most appropriate for employees. As we begin the 21st century, this attitude is being replaced with one of higher employee involvement and choice. "Choice accounts" that provide various benefits and services options and allow employees, rather than the company, to allocate benefits dollars are increasingly popular.[14] Exhibit 12.5 shows how employees evaluate the importance of several benefits and services.[15]

Companies are also giving employees a choice in how they schedule their work. Ernst and Young employees are empowered to decide how, when, and where to get their jobs done. The company's flexible schedule options have been in place since the mid-1990s, when the initiative was launched to respond to employees' concerns about work-life balance. Those who use the flexible work arrangement (FWA) option value it greatly. According to a survey of those using FWA at the firm, 84% say this service is the primary reason they stay at Ernst and Young.

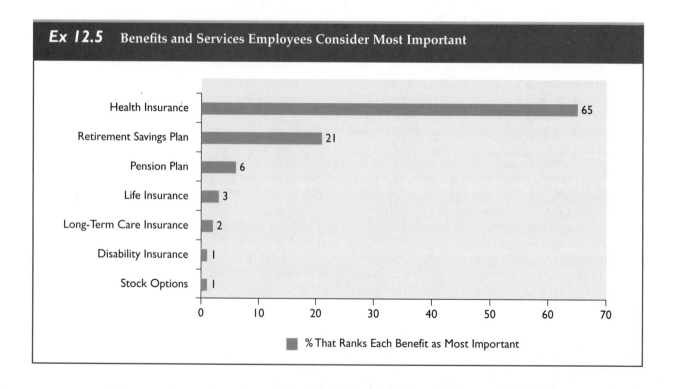

Ex 12.5   Benefits and Services Employees Consider Most Important

Benefit	% That Ranks Each Benefit as Most Important
Health Insurance	65
Retirement Savings Plan	21
Pension Plan	6
Life Insurance	3
Long-Term Care Insurance	2
Disability Insurance	1
Stock Options	1

One novel feature of the initiative is the FWA electronic site and database, which employees can use to learn more about the realities of such arrangements. From the electronic site, employees can access a database containing profiles of existing flextimers and quotes about their experiences. Employees also can use links to the firm's formal policies and participate in discussions with FWA experts. As an educational tool, the electronic site has proved useful for flextimers as well as their colleagues and supervisors. For those interested in pursuing FWA, a self-assessment tool is available to help employees evaluate whether they have the skills and personality needed to succeed on a flexible schedule.

Corporate Culture. An organization's fundamental values set the stage for developing an approach to managing employee benefits and services. The benefits and services manager must understand the underlying basis of the philosophy and the extent to which management supports human resources generally and benefits and services specifically. Some firms adopt an egalitarian approach to benefits and services by insisting that the same ones be provided to all employees. Other firms offer different benefits and services to employees at different levels or in different jobs within the organization. Lincoln Electric's approach is to offer essentially no voluntary benefits and services, and instead use the savings to fund the company's profit-sharing bonus pool. The company makes it easy for employees to participate in a group insurance plan, but doing so is completely voluntary on the part of employees.

The desire to create a more friendly corporate culture led Avon Products, Inc., in New York City, to develop a new retirement program. Most Avon employees are engaged in sales and marketing of beauty products; and about 75% of the workforce is female. In these jobs, Avon found, employees tend to move in and out of the workforce. As a result, they never qualified for the traditional defined benefit retirement plans. Recognizing that it was competing for labor in a tight "part-timers" market, Avon remodeled its retirement benefits to make them available and attractive to a broader range of employees.

For Avon's employees, the new retirement benefits were more attractive partly because they were more portable. **Portable benefits** *refer to those that employees can take with them when they leave the firm.* With the increasing mobility of workers, portability has become a major issue. Under Avon's new plan, retirement savings are immediately vested and the benefits are available to anyone chosen by the employee, not just the surviving spouse. The plan better serves the needs of Avon's workforce, and this in turn helps Avon better serve its customers and stockholders.

As these examples show, employers can choose to offer a broad array of benefits and services tailored to meet the needs of employees as well as employers. Next we describe some of the most widely offered benefits and services, beginning with those that are legally mandated.

PUBLIC PROTECTION PROGRAMS

Many public protection programs are outgrowths of the **Social Security Act of 1935,** *which provides retirement benefits, disability, and unemployment insurance.* Health insurance, particularly Medicare, was added in 1966 to provide hospital insurance to almost everyone age 65 and older.

Social Security Insurance

Social Security Insurance is intended to provide older Americans with a reliable source of income during the retirement years. Funding of the Social Security system is provided by equal contributions from the employer and employee under the terms of the Federal Insurance Contributions Act (FICA). Initially, employee and employer each paid into the Social Security system at the rate of 1% of the employee's annual income, up to a maximum income of $3,000. Today the employer and employee each pay the Social Security system 6.2% of the employee's annual income, up to a maximum income of $88,600 of the employee's income, for retirement and disability. In addition, each contributes 1.45% of the total income for hospital insurance through Medicare. Upon reaching a specified age (currently 62), employees may begin receiving the benefit of this forced savings plan. Currently, the average annual Social Security benefit paid out is about $9,100 for a single person and about $15,500 for a married couple, with adjustments routinely made for increases in the consumer price index.[16]

Unemployment Compensation Benefits

The Social Security Act also set up an unemployment compensation program that provides income to working-age employees who lose their employment. Unemployment compensation programs are jointly administered by the federal and state governments. The amount that employers contribute to unemployment compensation programs is determined by both the location of the employer and the employer's history of employee layoffs and dismissals. Unemployment compensation varies by state because income levels vary from state to state. Benefits paid to unemployed workers range from 50 to 70% of base salary up to a specified maximum weekly amount, which also varies by state. Since passage of the Tax Reform Act of 1986, unemployment compensation has been fully taxable, which reduces the net value of these benefits for employees.[17]

Another factor that determines how much an employer must pay for unemployment compensation is the employer's history. The required payments are higher for employers that have historically had higher proportions of employees drawing from the fund. Consequently, employers that dismiss many workers who later draw unemployment benefits pay higher taxes than employers with better employment records.

Workers' Compensation and Disability Insurance

Of the more than 6 million job-related injuries reported annually, about half are serious enough for the injured worker to lose work time or experience restricted work activity, or both. In addition, hundreds of thousands of new occupational injury cases are reported each year. More than 90% of these injuries are associated with repetitive motions such as vibration, repeated pressure, and carpal tunnel syndrome. Most require medical care and result in lost work time.[18]

When injuries or illnesses occur as a result of on-the-job events, workers may be eligible for workers' compensation benefits. Administered at the state level and fully financed by employers, these benefits cover medical costs and lost income due to temporary and permanent disability, disfigurement. Survivors' benefits are provided following fatal injuries.

Steelcase has been applying a variety of health care cost-containment strategies to reduce workers' compensation claims. Their "Return-to-Work" program, which resulted in a savings of more than $50 million, has been especially successful. As part of this program, a medical review board systematically examines the injured person and the injury situation to make the correct diagnosis of the claim. The intent here is to uncover all the facts and build an atmosphere of trust and understanding between worker and company. Then, a return-to-work component enables workers to get back to work as soon as possible: Once an injury is diagnosed, the biggest manageable expense is the time in getting the worker back to work. By setting up therapy centers and accommodating working conditions, Steelcase reduced time away from work for most injuries by 50% in six years.[19]

FAMILY AND MEDICAL LEAVE

The **Family and Medical Leave Act (FMLA)** *requires employers with 50 or more workers to grant an employee up to 12 weeks' unpaid leave annually "for the birth or adoption of a child, to care for a spouse or an immediate family member with a serious health condition, or when unable to work because of a serious health condition. Employers covered by the law are required to maintain any preexisting health coverage during the leave period."*[20] The employee taking leave must be allowed to return to the same job or a job of equivalent status and pay—with the exception of some highly paid executives. To be eligible for FMLA benefits, employees must have worked at a company for at least 12 months and have put in at least 1,250 hours in the year before the leave.[21]

PRIVATE PROTECTION PROGRAMS

Public protection programs are intended to ensure that employees and their families have a safety net that protects them from catastrophic poverty. In contrast, most private protection programs are designed to help employees achieve a greater level of comfort and security. For example, the benefits most people can expect to receive through Social Security are not enough to maintain their lifestyle at the time of retirement. Unless people have planned for their income needs during retirement, they will need to significantly reduce their spending after they stop working. Private protection programs encourage people to save and make it easy for them to do so. They include retirement income plans, capital accumulation plans, savings and thrift plans, and supplemental unemployment benefits and guaranteed pay.

FAST FACT

Only about 50% of workers have any idea how much they need to save for retirement.

LEGAL CONSIDERATIONS

To encourage Americans to save for retirement, the Economic Recovery Tax Act of 1981 allows employees to make tax deductible contributions to (a) an employer-sponsored pension, profit-sharing, or savings account; or (b) an individual retirement account (IRA). By providing tax relief for private retirement savings accounts, this tax law and its subsequent revisions stimulated the growth of private protection programs that give employees more control over their retirement investments. The act also made it possible for employers to provide company stock to employees and pay for it with tax credits or to establish a payroll-based plan that facilitates employee stock ownership (described in Chapter 11).[22]

Private protection plans are also governed by the Economic Growth and Tax Relief Reconciliation Act of 2001. In addition to enacting an across-the-board federal income tax rate cut, the Economic Growth and Tax Relief Reconciliation Act:

1. raised the contribution limits for IRAs and employer-sponsored retirement plans such as the 403(b) and 401(k) plans,
2. reduced from five years to three years the length of service required before employer contributions to employer-sponsored retirement programs must be available, and
3. shortened pension vesting waiting periods.

The law also contains a "sunset" provision, which means it will expire in 2010 and the previous laws will be reinstated unless Congress decides otherwise.

Qualified and Nonqualified Plans. The various retirement income plans can be classified in terms of whether they are qualified or nonqualified. A **qualified plan** *covers a broad class of employees (e.g., not just executives), meets Internal Revenue Code requirements, and consequently is qualified to receive favorable tax treatment.* For example, contributions to a qualified plan typically are tax deductible for employers for the current year, but contain provisions for the deferment of taxes for employees until retirement. A **nonqualified plan** *doesn't adhere to the strict tax regulations, covers only select groups of employees (e.g., senior management), and doesn't receive favorable tax treatment.*[23] Nonqualified plans are legal, but they are more costly for employers. By designing benefits that qualify for favorable tax treatment, employers can stretch the value of their investments considerably.

Pension Plans

The largest category of private protection plans is pensions. Four out of five employees in medium-sized and large firms are covered by some type of private pension or capital accumulation plan and rely on these plans to provide future security. A less-well-known fact is that the 20 largest pension funds, 13 of them for public employees, hold one-tenth of the equity capital of America's publicly owned companies. All told, pension funds also hold 40% or more of the medium- and long-term debt of the country's bigger companies. Thus, employees, through their pension funds, have become America's largest retirement bankers, lenders, and business owners.[24]

FAST FACT

Institutional investors (primarily pension funds) control almost 40% of the common stock of the country's largest businesses.

ERISA and Private Employers' Pensions. The **Employee Retirement Income Security Act of 1974 (ERISA)** *was designed to protect the interests of workers covered by private retirement plans by regulating the management of pension funds.* ERISA does not require an employer to offer a pension fund, and it does not specify how much money a participant must be paid as a benefit. It only requires that those who establish plans must meet certain minimum standards. However, for companies that do offer private pension plans, ERISA established several rules for how such funds are to be managed. For example, if an employer maintains a pension plan, ERISA specifies:

1. when an employee must be allowed to participate,
2. how long participants must work before they have a nonforfeitable interest in their pension funds,
3. how long an employee can be away from the job before it might affect the pension benefit,
4. the conditions under which a spouse has a right to part of the pension in the event of the participant's death,
5. the type of plan information the employer must provide to participants,
6. rules that employers must follow to ensure the plan is adequately funded, and
7. the fiduciary responsibilities of the employer and any other parties involved in managing the pension fund.[25]

Underfunded Pension Plans. In the past, some companies set up pension funds but then, when necessary, drew upon those funds to pay for operating expenses. This activity put employees' pensions at great risk. To protect employees against such risk, ERISA prohibits the use of unfunded pension programs that rely on the goodwill of the employer to pay retirement benefits out of current operating funds when needed. Money paid into a pension fund must be earmarked for retirees whether paid in part by the employee or paid solely by the employer (as in noncontributory programs).

Portability. Under ERISA, employers are not required to accommodate new or transferred employees who wish to deposit funds into their retirement plans. On a voluntary basis, employers can allow employees to transfer money to IRAs. When this occurs, the pension funds are said to be portable. Increasingly, employers are making it possible for employees to transfer their retirement funds to another firm.

FAST FACT

Half of employees still lack a company pension or savings plan.

Defined Benefit Plans. With a **defined benefit plan,** *the actual benefits received upon retirement are determined by the employee's age and length of service.* For example, an employee who retires at age 65 may receive $50 a month for each year of company service. Unions prefer defined benefit plans because they produce predictable, secure, and continuing income. To protect employees and prevent employers from using pension funds for other purposes, employers must adhere to stringent reporting rules, disclosure guidelines, fiduciary standards, plan participation rules, and vesting standards.

Defined benefit plans must adhere to specific funding-level requirements and be insured against termination due to economic hardship, misfunding, or corporate buyouts. The **Pension Benefit Guaranty Corporation (PBGC)** *administers the required insurance program and guarantees the payment of basic retirement benefits to participants if a plan is terminated.* The PBGC also can terminate seriously underfunded pension funds.

"The house isn't burning now, but we will have a crisis soon if some of these issues aren't fixed."

Steven A. Kandarian
Former Executive Director
PBGC

During the past decade, the number of insolvent pension funds has been rapidly increasing. In the airline industry, for example, the gap between pension benefits that have been promised and available funds to pay for these was $18 billion in 2004. Older companies such as Northwest and UAL have pension *deficits* of nearly $100,000 per employee. The struggling US Airways had an estimated $2 billion in pension obligations when it filed for bankruptcy protection in 2003. This unexpected situation has placed great pressure on the PBGC, which must cover the liabilities of insolvent pension funds. In fact, experts now worry that the PBGC itself is nearing the brink of insolvency.[26]

For employees nearing retirement age, pension fund insolvency is a major economic concern. Throughout much of their lifetime, employees covered by private pension funds have assumed they would receive pension income upon their retirement. For many of these employees, the amount of pension income expected during retirement was enough to cover their normal living expenses. A crane operator who retired at age 53 from Bethlehem Steel after working there for 30 years was receiving a pension of $1,887 per month. When Bethlehem Steel declared bankruptcy in 2002, its pension fund became insolvent. In 2003, the PBGC took it over, and now it is responsible for paying pensions to 95,000 Bethlehem Steel pensioners. Unfortunately for these pensioners, the PBGC is not obligated to pay the full pension amount promised by the company. Thus, the crane operator who had been receiving $1,887 per month suddenly found that his pension income had been reduced to $1,242 per month. At the same time, the crane operator lost his medical benefits, which were also part of Bethlehem's Steel's benefits package.

Traditional defined benefit plans helped retain employees because the value of these plans built up with age and tenure in the organization. At the same time, they discouraged or penalized employee mobility. Given the reality of employee mobility in the 21st century, such "benefits" are no longer as desirable as they were when employees enjoyed more job security. In addition, employers have learned that defined benefit plans can be expensive. And, unfortunately, many of the companies that once promised employees a continuing source of income now find that they cannot meet their obligations. For these and other reasons, many employers are phasing out defined benefits and replacing them with defined contribution plans.

Cash Balance Plans. Cash balance plans are another type of private pension plan offered by some employers. With a **cash balance plan,** *the employer pays a specified lump sum of cash to employees upon their departure from the company.* The IRS considers cash balance plans to be defined benefit plans because payouts are determined by a formula and are guaranteed by the PBGC.[27] However, for employees who work for several employers over the course of their careers, cash balance plans are more desirable than traditional defined benefit plans, which penalized people who did not stay with one employer throughout their careers. In July 2003, however, a federal court's landmark ruling said that IBM's cash balance plan violated age discrimination laws, throwing into question the legality of such plans. Nevertheless, cash balance plans cover about 7 million workers.[28]

Exhibit 12.6 uses a hypothetical example to illustrate the differing benefits that an employee would receive under a cash balance plan versus the traditional defined benefit plan. The example assumes that the employee entered

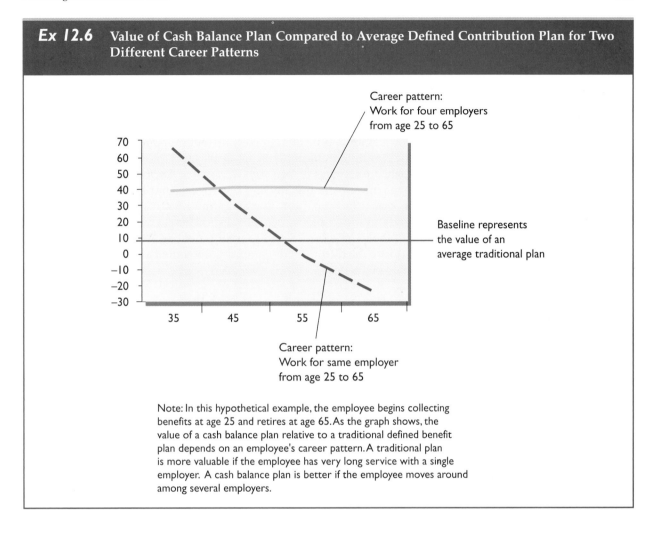

Ex 12.6 Value of Cash Balance Plan Compared to Average Defined Contribution Plan for Two Different Career Patterns

Note: In this hypothetical example, the employee begins collecting benefits at age 25 and retires at age 65. As the graph shows, the value of a cash balance plan relative to a traditional defined benefit plan depends on an employee's career pattern. A traditional plan is more valuable if the employee has very long service with a single employer. A cash balance plan is better if the employee moves around among several employers.

the organization at age 25 and retired from the same organization at age 65. The dashed line shows the relative (dis)advantage of a cash balance plan for the employee stays in the same organization for the full 40 years. Early in the employee's career, the retirement benefits that accrue under the cash balance plan would be large. However, by age 45, the advantages of a cash balance plan begin to erode. By age 65, the cash balance plan provides nearly 35% less benefit to the employee. However, the picture is very different if the employee changes jobs instead of staying with the same employer for 40 years. As the solid line shows, for the more mobile employee, a cash balance plan always results in greater accrued benefits. By age 65, a cash balance plan provides 40% greater benefit compared to an average defined benefit plan.[29]

Defined Contribution Plans. With a **defined contribution plan,** *each employee has an account to which contributions are added; the value of the account depends on how well the investment performs over time, so retirement payouts are not guaranteed.* The two major types of defined contribution plans are called noncontributory plans and contributory plans. *If only the employer contributes* to the retirement account, it's a **noncontributory plan.** *When both the employee and the employer contribute to the retirement account, it's a* **contributory plan.** Typically, the employee must activate a contributory plan by agreeing to contribute a set amount of money; the employer then matches the percentage contribution to a specific level. For example, the employee might choose to contribute 5% of each paycheck, and the employer might agree to match what the employee contributes up to 3%.

The most common type of defined contribution plan is a money purchase plan. With **money purchase plans,** *the employer makes fixed, regular contributions (usually a percentage of total pay) on behalf of participants.* Under current rules, the maximum amount any employee may contribute to such accounts is 25% of earned income, up to a maximum of $40,000. Monies are held in trust funds, and the employee is given several investment options that differ in terms of the degree of risk and growth potential. At retirement, accumulated funds are used to provide annuities. In some cases, lump-sum distributions may be made.

401(k) Plans

"People spend more time planning a vacation than planning for retirement."

Dallas Salisbury
CEO
Employee Benefit Research Institute

With a **401(k) plan,** *both the employer and the employee contribute to a fund, and the employee is responsible for investment decisions.* The total amount both can contribute is about $25,000. For public employees, a 403(b) plan functions in the same way, although slightly different rules apply. Invested successfully, an employee can have a sizeable retirement allowance.[30] As Exhibit 12.7 shows, employee participation in 401(k) plans rose steadily during the past 20 years. Today, three out of four employees participate in such plans.[31]

Prior to 2004, the telecommunications company Avaya offered a cash balance plan and a traditional defined benefit plan. But recently it switched to an enhanced 401(k) plan for all salaried employees. The two major reasons for making the switch were that Avaya's pension fund was running a deficit, and the company was uncertain about its legal liabilities related to the cash

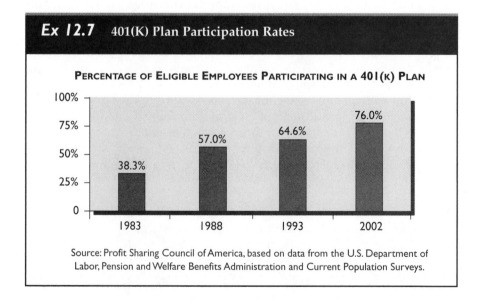

Ex 12.7   401(K) Plan Participation Rates

PERCENTAGE OF ELIGIBLE EMPLOYEES PARTICIPATING IN A 401(K) PLAN

Year	Participation Rate
1983	38.3%
1988	57.0%
1993	64.6%
2002	76.0%

Source: Profit Sharing Council of America, based on data from the U.S. Department of Labor, Pension and Welfare Benefits Administration and Current Population Surveys.

balance plan. With Avaya's new 401(k) plan, employees automatically receive 2% of their earned income and bonus plus a 100% company matching contribution of up to 2% of income and a 50% match for the next 4% that the employee contributes. Thus, employees who contribute at least 6% of their income to the 401(k) receive a matching contribution from the company of an additional 6%. Avaya's fund is managed by Fidelity Investments, and employees have 26 options for investing in mutual funds, bond funds, and company stock.[32]

Starbucks also offers a 401(k) plan. With the average employee being only 28 years old, Starbucks makes an extra effort to encourage employees to learn about and take advantage of this retirement savings account. It created a website called Futureroast.com to educate employees about the plan. The website features four computer games that teach concepts such as "company match" and illustrate how funds can grow in value over long periods of time. About 25% of Starbuck employees contribute to the company-sponsored 401(k) plan.[33]

EMPLOYEE STOCK AND STOCK OPTION PLANS

As described in Chapter 11, many corporations offer broad-based stock and stock option programs. Some companies view stock plans as an element of the company's incentive pay, and this is why we discussed them in Chapter 11. However, for many employees, plans that transfer stock to employees are considered a benefit because they improve their long-term earnings if the company performs well in the longer term.

HEALTH CARE BENEFITS AND SERVICES

Health care benefits generally are designed to help employees pay for medical expenses at a cost that is lower than they would have to pay as individual citizens. These benefits may help pay for hospital charges, home health care, physician charges, and a variety of other medical services. Health care benefits also include wellness programs, employee assistance programs, and short- and long-term disability insurance beyond what is legally mandated. Employees who receive health care benefits, particularly medical insurance, can expect to receive adequate health care at a cost that is far less than that paid by individuals who do not have such benefits. Although these benefits are very expensive for employers, most employees underestimate their employer's costs and view coverage as an entitlement rather than a discretionary benefit.[34]

FAST FACT

General Motors spends about $1,400 on retiree medical benefits for each automobile it makes in the United States.

Health care costs more than $1.5 trillion annually, and that figure continues to rise faster than inflation. Companies that buy health insurance for their employees spend, on average, about 15 cents of every dollar they make to pay for this coverage. This is 35 to 40% more than in other industrialized countries. As a consequence, U.S. companies have been very aggressive at reducing health care expenses. Reducing health care costs often means reducing the amount of choice employees have concerning which physicians they may use and increasing the amount that employees are required to pay to obtain health care coverage.[35]

FAST FACT

Of the total U.S. population that is without health insurance, about 60% of those who are uninsured are employed.

MEDICAL CARE

Employers usually finance and provide medical expense benefits to employees and their dependents through insurance companies or other third parties. Many employers offer employees a choice of plans. Healthier and younger employees who expect to have few medical needs may choose a low-cost plan with somewhat less desirable features, while older employees and those who expect to have more needs may opt for a more expensive plan. Employees who prefer the more expensive plan must then pay toward covering the additional cost of buying into that plan.

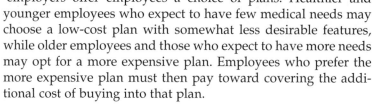

General Motors is the world's largest automaker. It provides medical benefits for 1.1 million Americans.

FAST FACT

Insurance Companies. Insurance carriers offer a broad range of health care services from which employers can select coverage. Premiums are set and adjusted depending on usage rates and increases in health care costs. The insurance company administers the plan, handling all the paperwork, approvals, and problems. Proponents of this approach argue that insurers protect the plan sponsor against wide fluctuations in claim exposure and costs and offer opportunities for participation in larger risk pools. Insurance companies also have administrative expertise related to certification reviews, claim audits, coordination of benefits, and other cost-containment services.

On the downside, the insurance company, not the employer, makes decisions regarding covered benefits. Its decisions may go against the corporation's ethics and sense of social responsibility. Companies that subscribe to a specific insurance plan don't have the luxury of ignoring the insurer's advice and doing what they feel is ethical. The insurance company makes all the tough calls.

Traditional Provider Organizations. Blue Cross and Blue Shield are the most well-known traditional providers. They are nonprofit organizations that operate within defined geographic areas. Blue Cross plans cover hospital expenses, and Blue Shield plans cover charges by physicians and other medical providers. Typically, these organizations negotiate arrangements with their member providers to reimburse the providers at a discounted rate when a subscriber incurs a charge. As originally established, the rate represented full payment for the service and no additional charge was levied. However, as a result of skyrocketing health care costs, employees may now be asked to pay deductibles ($500 to $2,500 a year) or a share of the cost of service (10 to 20%), or both.[36]

More employees with health insurance coverage have joined managed care programs: 48% in 1992 versus more than 90% in 2003.

FAST FACT

Health Maintenance Organizations. About 25% of all eligible employees participate in Health Maintenance Organization (HMO) plans.[37] The growth in HMOs was stimulated by the passage of the Health Maintenance Organization Act of 1973. This act requires companies with at least 25 employees living in an HMO service area to offer membership in that organization as an alternative to regular group health coverage, provided the HMO meets federal qualification requirements.

One successful HMO is operated by John Deere and Company, a farm machinery manufacturer. Realizing 20 years ago that its own health care costs were skyrocketing, Deere brought its health care operations in-house and established its own HMO, called John Deere Health. Deere has been so successful that it has attracted more than 300 other company clients.[38]

Preferred Provider Organizations. About 55% of U.S. employees with health care coverage are enrolled in preferred provider organizations (PPOs), making them the most popular form of health care benefit.[39] With these programs, employers contract directly or indirectly through an insurance company with health care providers (physicians, dentists, laboratories, hospitals, and so forth) to deliver discounted services to program participants. Because the rates and requirements for these plans are relatively unregulated, employers have a great deal of flexibility in structuring an arrangement.

Unlike HMO participants, employees in a PPO are not required to use the plan's providers exclusively. Thus, if they need to see a specialist who is not part of the PPO network, the plan will still cover those costs. However, incentives are often used to encourage employees to use providers from the PPO network. For example, the employer may cover all the costs of health care provided by a PPO but only 80% of the costs of health care provided by physicians outside the PPO network.[40]

Self-Funded Plans. Like Steelcase and the Camberley Hotel, a growing number of companies are opting for self-insured or self-funded plans as a way to control medical plan costs and gain relief from state insurance regulations. By eliminating or reducing insurance protection, the employer saves on carrier retention charges (the amount of money not utilized to pay claims), such as state premium taxes, administrative costs, risk and contingency expenses, and reserve requirements. Typically, the employer creates a voluntary employee beneficiary association and establishes a trust whose investment income is tax exempt as long as it's used to provide benefits to employees and their dependents.

FAST FACT The Camberley Hotel in Atlanta reduced health care costs and employee turnover when it became self-insured.

Cost-Containment Strategies. One popular method employers use to reduce their costs is shifting the burden for health care premium payments to employees. The impact of this strategy on employees can be seen in Exhibit 12.8. In 1998, employees paid on average about 25% of total annual health care costs. By 2004, they were paying nearly 35%—that represents a 44% increase in costs paid by employees over a period of just six years.[41]

FAST FACT DaimlerChrysler found 27,000 employees who had—by error, design, or oversight—ineligible family members on their policies.

To further control health care costs, firms employ a variety of other strategies such as the following:

- *Hospital utilization programs.* Employers set up a system to review the necessity and appropriateness of hospitalization prior to admission, during a stay, or both.
- *Coordination of benefits.* Employers coordinate their benefits with those of other providers to prevent duplicate payment for the same health care service.
- *Data analysis.* Employers analyze the available information to determine the most viable cost management approach. Simulations and experience-based utilization assumptions are used to develop models.

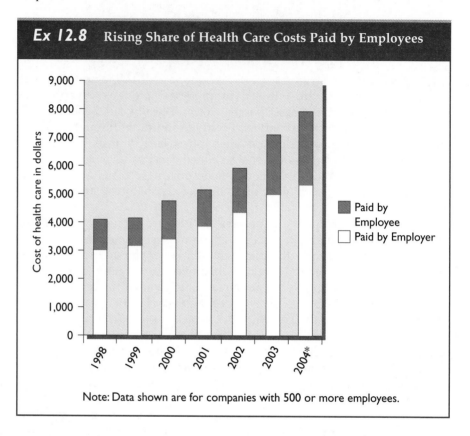

Ex 12.8 Rising Share of Health Care Costs Paid by Employees

Note: Data shown are for companies with 500 or more employees.

- *Case management.* Many employers are active participants in case management. Medical procedures may include requirements for second opinions and peer reviews.
- *Auditing employee policies.* Audits of policies are done to determine whether ineligible family members (e.g., children above the allowed age) are using the benefits.
- *Cost sharing with employees.* By raising deductibles and contribution levels, employers hold the line on overall expenses. Included here are copay arrangements and tiered cost sharing for prescription drugs.
- *Health promotion initiatives.* By offering initiatives, some firms hope to change employees' behaviors so they are healthier.[42] The types of initiatives and the percentage of companies offering them are shown in Exhibit 12.9.

WELLNESS PROGRAMS

FAST FACT

SAS employees have an opportunity to use a 77,000-square-foot fitness and recreation center at any time of the day.

Frustrated with efforts to manage health care costs for employees who already are sick, a growing number of employers are taking proactive steps to prevent health care problems. Wellness programs may include exercise classes held at on-site fitness facilities, training in stress management, assistance in quitting smoking, free health screening clinics, practices to promote healthy eating, and a variety of other programs. A handful of

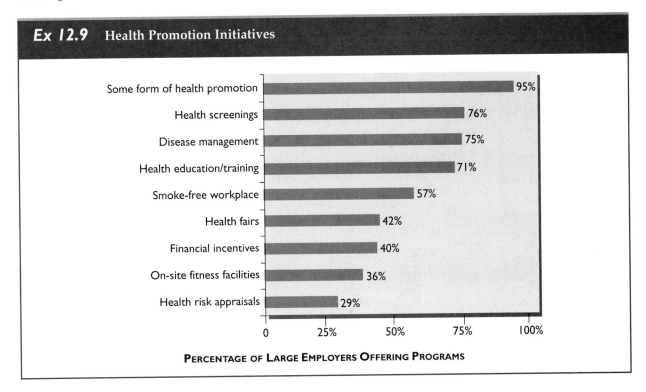

Ex 12.9 **Health Promotion Initiatives**

PERCENTAGE OF LARGE EMPLOYERS OFFERING PROGRAMS

firms implement well-designed wellness programs to produce significant savings on the bottom line.[43] Of course, such programs are good for employees, too. Dow's "Backs in Action" program encourages exercise, dieting, and ergonomics. Since it was implemented, on-the-job strains and sprains suffered by employees have decreased by about 90%.

Coors Brewing Company spent 10 years fine-tuning its wellness program. For every dollar spent on wellness, Coors sees a much greater return in the form of decreased medical costs, reduced sick leave, and increased productivity. According to William Coors, past chair and CEO, the secret to Coors's success is really no secret: "Wellness is an integral part of the corporate culture." Coors's commitment to wellness includes a health risk assessment, nutritional counseling, stress management, and programs for smoking cessation, weight loss, and orthopedic rehabilitation.[44]

EMPLOYEE ASSISTANCE PROGRAMS

Whereas wellness programs attempt to prevent the development of health problems, **Employee Assistance Programs (EAPs)** are designed to assist employees with chronic personal problems that hinder their job performance and attendance. EAPs often serve employees with alcohol or drug dependency, or both, or those with severe domestic problems. EAPs also help employees cope with mental disorders, financial problems, stress, eating disorders, smoking cessation, dependent care, bereavement, and AIDS. EAPs and wellness programs are described in more detail in Chapter 13.

PAID LEAVE

As Exhibit 12.4 showed, paid leave accounts for 6.5% of employers' total compensation costs, on average. The two major categories of paid leave are time not worked while off the job and time not worked while on the job.

Off the Job

The most common paid-off-the-job times are vacations, holidays, sick leaves, and personal days. The challenge in administering these benefits is to contain costs while seeking better ways to tailor the benefits and services to fit employees' needs and preferences.

Vacations and Holidays. Vacations give employees time to recuperate from the physical and mental demands of work. Vacation time is also viewed as an appropriate reward for service and commitment to the organization. More than 80% of all workers receive paid holidays and vacations; but of those in the bottom tenth of income earnings, only 10% received paid leave of any kind.

FAST FACT

Firms in the United States are not legally required to offer paid vacation days.

In setting up vacation programs, several issues need to be addressed: (1) Will vacation pay be based on scheduled hours or on hours actually worked? (2) Under what circumstances can an employee be paid in lieu of taking a vacation? (3) Can vacations be deferred, or will they be lost if not taken? (4) What pay rate applies if an employee works during a vacation? The trend is toward vacation banking, with employees being able to roll over a specified period of unused vacation days into a savings investment plan.

In some countries, the government mandates the minimum number of vacation days per year. International differences in vacation policies are described in the feature "Managing Globalization: Vacationing around the World."[45]

Paid Absences. On any given day, one million American employees will be absent from work. In the United States, the daily absenteeism rate ranges from 2 to 3% of total payroll, but some organizations report absenteeism in excess of 20%. Employees fail to show up for work for many reasons—health problems, family problems, bad weather, transportation difficulties, and so forth. Nevertheless, absences are greatly influenced by an organization's formal policies. As the number of paid days off increases, the number of days of actual absence increases proportionally. Because of lax policies, many organizations unwittingly not only tolerate or accept absenteeism but actually reward it. Their policies make it easier to be absent than to come to work.

Negative strategies to control absenteeism include disciplinary procedures against employees who are absent once a week or once every two weeks without a physician's excuse, before or after a holiday, after payday, without calling in, or for personal business. This discipline ranges from oral warnings for first offenses to discharge. Unfortunately, these policies appear to be generally ineffective in controlling absenteeism among habitual offenders.

Managing Globalization

Vacationing around the World

For employees who work in global firms, vacation policies and practices are among the most visible differences in benefits and services enjoyed by employees around the world. Countries differ substantially in terms of what the government mandates as well as whether and how employees actually use their vacation time. In the United States, in addition to national and local holidays, full-time employees typically receive a week's vacation after one year of service and two weeks after two years.

Countries also differ in terms of whether employees actually use their vacation days to take a vacation. Many Europeans would never consider not using all of their vacation time, while Americans often take fewer days than they are entitled to. The following chart indicates some of the differences in vacations taken by employees around the world.

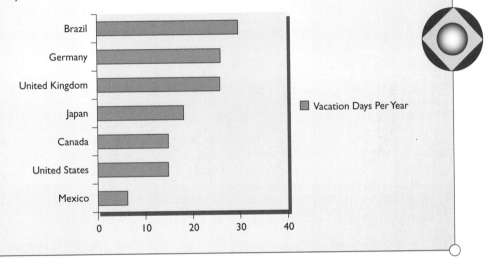

Programs that reward attendance—with, for instance, cash prizes, bonuses, or conversion of a proportion of unused absence days to vacation days—appear more promising. To prevent unscheduled absenteeism, many organizations grant personal days, or personal time off. The employees can use these days during the year for any reason, but to be eligible for pay, the employees must notify supervisors in advance that they will be absent. Self-management programs for habitual offenders also offer some hope for controlling excessive absenteeism.

FAST FACT

Companies that are on *Fortune's* "100 Best Companies to Work For" list have significantly lower absenteeism because of their culture, leadership, and HR practices.

On the Job

Time not worked on the job includes rest periods, lunch periods, wash-up times, and clothes-changing and getting-ready times. Together, these are the fifth most expensive benefit. Another benefit that's growing in popularity is paid time for use of on-site physical fitness facilities. This is clearly pay for time not worked, but organizations often offer it because of its on-the-job benefit: healthy workers.

WORK-LIFE BENEFITS

In response to a growing number of single-parent families, two-earner families, aging parents in need of care, and nontraditional families, employers are expanding their benefits and services packages to address new priorities.[46] Some of these benefits and services are offered by only a handful of firms. However, employers are realizing that a failure to address these needs in the future may restrict their ability to compete. Exhibit 12.10 shows the percentage of U.S. firms offering several types of work-life benefits.[47]

A recent survey of 600 U.S. companies found that the top reasons for offering work-life benefits were to:

1. improve morale (74%),
2. enhance recruitment (73%), and
3. remain competitive or improve the company's image in the industry (72%).[48]

CHILD CARE SERVICES

FAST FACT

At Johnson & Johnson, employees can bring their infants in for free tests and checkups six times annually. Illness prevention saves the company $13 million each year.

Recognizing that child care is a shared responsibility, more and more employers are providing some type of child care assistance to their employees. A survey of more than 10,000 firms employing 10 or more workers showed that more than 60% of those firms offered some type of assistance benefits, scheduling help, or services related to child care.[49] To be competitive in the labor market, firms should survey their employees to find out their preferences, and then work to offer options that meet employees' needs.[50] Options employers may offer include any or all of the following:

- Scholarships for dependents
- Summer employment for dependents

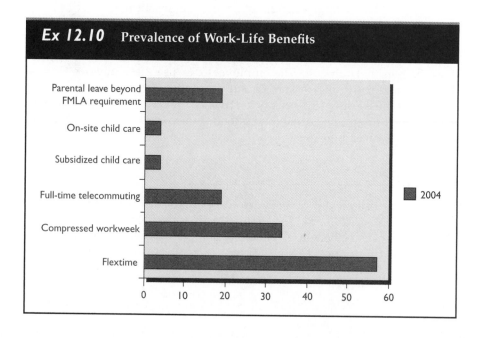

Ex 12.10   Prevalence of Work-Life Benefits

- Subsidized tutoring for dependents
- Sick-child care
- On-site or subsidized child care
- Laundry services
- Flexible scheduling
- Child care referrals
- Extended family care leave
- Adoption benefits
- Take-home meals from the company cafeteria[51]

Extended Family Leave. At KPMG, the accounting firm based in New York, the goal is to increase the number of female partners to 20% by 2007. To achieve their goal, KPMG needs to retain women by creating a family-friendly culture. One element of KPMG's retention strategy focuses on encouraging women to return to KPMG after they complete a maternity leave. To show their support for new mothers, KPMG offers 2 weeks of paid leave in addition to the 12 weeks of unpaid leave required by the FMLA. For employees who wish to stay home longer, KPMG offers 2 years of additional unpaid leave. For mothers who return to work, flexible schedules and part-time work are available. These practices seem to be working. Of women who take maternity leave, 88% return to KPMG.[52]

> *"Offering extended family leave is a retention program for us. We don't want to bring the talent into the company, invest in that talent, and have them leave."*
>
> Maria Ferris
> Manager of Work/Life Initiatives
> IBM

Resource and Referral Programs. Many companies firms offer child care information and referral assistance. These company-sponsored programs counsel employees about day care options and refer them to prescreened local providers. Prescreening helps to ensure that the centers in the network meet minimum care standards and are financially responsible.

On-Site Child Care Facilities. In San Francisco, office and hotel complexes with more than 50,000 square feet must either provide an on-site facility or pay into a city child care fund. But this city ordinance is not typical. Nationwide, only 5% of workers have access to employer-assisted on-site or off-site child care. Although the operation of child care centers is costly, a growing number of America's large employers view it as a social and business necessity.[53]

FAST FACT Cisco constructed a $16 million child care center for 432 children. Web cameras give parents a real-time window on their children.

Currently, an estimated 10% of large employers offer on-site or near-site child care. SAS, the software company, operates four on-site child care centers. Parents can visit their children during the day and even join them for lunch. When children's activities are held outside, parents often can watch their children from their office windows. Like other corporate child care centers, the one operated by SAS offers quality care that is far above the norm for this service. The teachers who work for SAS are paid above-average salaries, and many have been on the job for a decade or more. At Procter and Gamble's child care center, most staff members are college-educated, and many hold master's degrees.[54]

Backlash? Some employers fear that childless employees may resent progressive policies to assist families. In fact, the formation of The Childfree Network, which is an advocacy group that serves as a voice for childless workers, is one indication that there is good reason to be prepared for some possible backlash from employees who feel they are not able to benefit as much as their peers who can utilize these valuable services. A recent study of employee attitudes revealed some disparity in the reactions of employees with and without children. However, the study failed to find any evidence that the more negative attitudes of the childless employees translated into concrete behaviors.[55] Other research indicates that any backlash tends to be of limited scope and does not create generalized job dissatisfaction.[56]

Even if some backlash occurs, the benefits and services associated with child care initiatives may outweigh the disadvantages. Prudential Insurance Company estimates that its child care center saves the company $80,000 annually through reduced absenteeism.[57] Families and society as a whole reap even more valuable gains. A recent study of nine western European countries indicated that parental leave-taking is correlated with children's health and survival. In the countries studied, on average, eligible employees (men and women) used 32 weeks of parental leave benefits. Longer leaves significantly reduced deaths among infants and young children.[58]

ELDER CARE SERVICES

FAST FACT

One out of four households provides informal care to a relative or friend age 50 years or older.

Twenty-eight percent of employees over the age of 30 spend an average of 10 hours a week giving care to an older relative. For a significant faction, this commitment equals a second job. Some 12% of workers who care for aging parents are forced to quit their jobs to do so. With the aging of the Baby Boomers, more and more employers are considering ways to help workers who are caring for elderly relatives. Assistance ranges from information and referral programs to specialized care insurance. The Family and Medical Leave Act of 1993 supports employee time off for both child care and elder care.

Information and Referral Programs. In 1990, only 11% of employers offered information and referral programs for elder care; now the number exceeds 50%. Like dependent care referral programs, company-operated elder care referral programs are designed to help the caregiver identify appropriate community resources.[59]

Recent studies have shown that 60% of U.S. workers have child care or elder care responsibilities. Starbucks recognized, as many other companies have, that employees (their "partners") are more innovative and productive when less encumbered by personal stress and obligations. Starbucks implemented several programs that specifically address the life stages and personal needs of its workforce. To help employees deal with the fast-paced and demanding environment at Starbucks, the company provides referral services for partners and eligible dependents enrolled in the medical plan. It connects them with information that helps make extraordinary life issues more manageable. In one particular case, a partner needed emergency child care for his ill son. The Starbucks Working Solutions program made prompt arrangements for a certified in-home caretaker, no work was missed, and Starbucks covered half of the cost.[60]

Long-Term Care Insurance. One new and fast-growing option for elder care is long-term care insurance. Although fewer than 15% of firms offered this benefit in the mid-1990s, nearly 70% offer it now.[61] This type of insurance covers medical, social, custodial, and personal services for people who suffer from chronic physical or mental illnesses or disabling injury or disease over an extended period of time. Typically, coverage is offered to employees on an employee-pay-all basis. Nevertheless, employees gain by paying the lower rates that employers are able to negotiate with insurance companies. Premium rates are age-based, and some plans set a maximum age (typically 79) for participation. Benefit maximums are related to care site (e.g., nursing home versus day care center) and include lifetime limits.

OTHER BENEFITS AND SERVICES

With demographic and value shifts, a wider array of lifestyle choices is now available. As a consequence, a rising percentage of workers—such as unmarried couples, divorced people, and single parents—don't fit into conventional benefits and services packages. Recognizing that people are assets to the organization and that the world of work can never be fully separated from the rest of life, companies on the cutting edge are redesigning their benefits and services packages to address the needs of all employees.

BENEFITS FOR SPOUSAL EQUIVALENTS

In 1950, married couples made up 80% of all households. Today, married couples make up less than 50% of all households. Increasingly, adults are choosing to cohabitate instead of marrying.[62] In 1997, only about 10% of companies had extended "spousal" benefits to same-sex partners and to unmarried opposite-sex domestic partners. Today, an estimated 25% of companies offer benefits to domestic partners.[63] For example, at Prudential Securities, cohabitants can get health benefits for an opposite-sex or same-sex partner as long as they've lived together at least six months. The reasons firms provide domestic partner benefits include to:

1. attract and retain talent (80%),
2. comply with the company's nondiscrimination policy (30%), and
3. comply with local laws (18%).

Notice that one reason is complying with local government regulations. Federal laws do not require employers to provide domestic partner benefits, but some local ordinances do. At Shell, providing the full range of benefits to both same-sex and opposite-sex partners is just one element in an overall people strategy for supporting a diverse workforce. According to Ronnie Kurtin, Director of Corporate HR, domestic partner benefits are included as "part of the overall people strategy in order to create an inclusive environment so we can be sure folks are focusing on productive efforts." Of course, not all employers adopt this approach. Some employers consider domestic partnerships to be "morally reprehensible" and develop their policies accordingly.[64]

"Domestic partner benefits isn't a gay and lesbian issue. It's a business issue. We believe that by providing domestic partners access, we are enhancing our ability to recruit and retain the best employees."

Bill Shelley
Health and Welfare Supervisor
Pacific Gas & Electric

EDUCATIONAL EXPENSE ALLOWANCES.

Faced with skill obsolescence, downsizing, and retraining demands, many medium-sized and large firms provide some form of educational expense assistance. Most plans cover registration fees, and some assist with graduation, laboratory, entrance examination, professional certification, and activity fees. Typically, these programs require a relationship between the course and some phase of company operations. National Healthcorp, which is headquartered in Murfreesboro, Tennessee, offers tuition assistance to any aide who wishes to become a nurse. The company will pay for up to two years of school in exchange for the aide's promise to stay on staff that long after graduation.

Employers who provide educational benefits as a means of retaining talent are likely to be only partly successful in achieving their objective. A recent study of more than 8,000 salaried employees at a large manufacturing firm found that people who participated in a tuition reimbursement program were less like to leave the company while they were in school. But when employees earned their degrees, the likelihood of their leaving increased significantly unless they were subsequently promoted.[65]

ADMINISTRATIVE ISSUES

Effectively administering employee benefits and services is a complicated challenge. In addition to deciding which benefits and services to offer, employers must work to ensure that employees understand both the content of the plan and its economic cost/value.

DETERMINING THE BENEFITS AND SERVICES PACKAGE

The benefits and services package should be selected on the basis of what is good for the employees as well as for the employer. Knowing employee preferences can often help organizations determine what benefits and services to offer, but decisions about what to offer must also take into account the costs relative to the benefits for employers.

Employee Preferences. Individual differences play a large role in determining which benefits and services employees prefer. When it comes to benefits and services, one size does not fit all employees. The variation in employees' preferences was demonstrated in a study of more than 2,400 employees working in 60 different companies. Employees were presented with three alternative retirement plan options, including a traditional defined benefit plan, a cash balance plan, and a hybrid plan that had elements of both. The study found that it was difficult to predict which plan an employee would prefer based on demographic characteristics (e.g., age, gender, education). Instead, preferences for the different plans depended upon how much value an employee placed on various plan features. Some employees valued portability, others valued being in control of their investments, and some preferred to avoid risk.[66]

> **FAST FACT**
>
> The share of workers satisfied with company-provided benefits dropped from 41% in 2002 to 32% in 2003 as many U.S. companies raised the cost to employees, scaled back benefits, or both.

Employer's Ability to Pay. Even if employers know what employees prefer, they may not be able to offer it: A company's size may constrain the benefits and services it can provide.[67] Companies with fewer than 10 employees may have difficulty finding an insurance carrier. Dental and vision care insurance options aren't very good either. Disability plans for these small companies will be either very restrictive or very expensive. Only after a company has at least 25 employees can it begin to offer a choice of medical plans, according to some experts.

Companies having more than 50 employees, and certainly those with more than 100, have more options and can even participate in partial self-insurance programs. As companies grow, they encounter fewer limitations. A firm that has 300 to 400 employees can choose from among many options and carriers and can establish a large plan that can be modified easily. Unfortunately, like many other functions at young, fast-growing firms, benefits and services management tends to lag behind the more urgent line functions. As one consequence, fewer than 50% of employees who work in small companies (20 or fewer employees) are covered by an employer health insurance plan. By contrast, 98% of businesses with 200 or more employees provide coverage.[68]

Corporate Strategy and Culture. As is true for other HR practices, an organization's decisions about which benefits and services to offer are driven by many internal factors. For a labor-intensive organization pursuing a low-cost strategy, providing expensive benefits and services may not be an option. Conversely, when labor costs are a relatively minor portion of an organization's total costs, providing unusually good benefits may provide a competitive advantage that ensures the company gets the best possible employees. For knowledge-intensive companies that compete on the basis of innovation and intellectual capital, the importance of attracting and retaining the best talent may be of such high priority that cost considerations don't determine which benefits and services a company offers.

An organization's strategy and culture may also influence decisions about which benefits and services to offer. At Starbucks, customer service and a fun culture are critical. The benefits and services it offers to employees support these. With more than 75,000 partners (employees) working in more than 7,500 locations around the world, Starbucks seeks to create a spirit of camaraderie and fun. Supporting this effort, the company provides generous benefits to both full-time and part-time employees, including health and dental coverage, a pension plan, and disability and life insurance. At headquarters, employees enjoy on-site fitness services. And employees everywhere can access the company's Info-line to link up with other employees with shared interests and hobbies, or gather information about child care and elder care. Because of their relatively young workforce, Starbucks enjoys comparatively low health care costs—about 20% below the national average. And the costs of many of the other services it provides also are minimal. The payoff seems to justify the costs incurred. Their turnover rate of 60% annually is well below the industry average of 300%. Because people stay longer, recruiting and training costs also are relatively low compared to the industry.

To stay attuned to employees' concerns, Starbucks regularly conducts surveys and solicits employees' ideas. In response to what they were hearing, the company introduced flexible work schedules as a component of their work-life program and beefed up referral services for employees facing various life issues—which vary tremendously depending on age, family responsibilities, and other individual circumstances. Through all of these efforts, Starbucks communicates that it cares about employees and their needs and respects them as members of the company's team of key players.

PROVIDING FLEXIBILITY AND COMMUNICATING WITH EMPLOYEES

When employees can design their own benefits and services packages, both they and the company come out ahead. At some companies, all eligible employees elect their own benefits and services package over the standard no-choice plan. The options themselves may be developed by the employees, working in small discussion groups. This is happening in many companies today because workforces are becoming so diverse, and their needs for benefits and services are rather varied. Most companies now offer at least some variable benefits and services.

FAST FACT

Nearly 45% of workers feel they don't have enough information to make the right investment choices in their 401(k) plans.

Having benefits and services accessible through call centers or on an intranet makes it easier than ever to administer a flexible benefits program. At Oracle, Boeing, and Charles Schwab, workers can surf company intranets to learn about and self-manage 401(k) plans, health care benefits, and even tax withholding options. Hard Rock Café International makes information available through an interactive CD that can be played at publicly available monitors in the employee break room. As Exhibit 12.11 shows, many companies use web-based communication strategies.[69] In addition to providing information over the Web, many companies use the Web to involve employees in actively managing their benefits and services. By effectively communicating the benefits and services package and providing flexibility, companies can improve their image and increase employee satisfaction.

Ex 12.11 Web-Based Communications for Benefits and Services

TYPE OF INFORMATION OR SERVICE	FIRMS PROVIDING IT
General benefits information	81%
401(k) provider information	80%
Links to third-party vendors who manage 401(k) plan, prescriptions, savings plans, and so on	76%
Ability to make 401(k) plan changes	70%
Retirement planning information, tools, or links	69%
Links to other resources for financial planning, investment advice, travel, and so on	55%
Online health care enrollment	50%
Employee benefits transactions or self-service	41%

Note: Percentages of employers making information available through the organization's website, based on a survey of 676 companies conducted by World at Work and Buck Consultants.

SUMMARY

Due to the complexity of economic and legal issues surrounding the design and administration of benefits and services, organizations face significant challenges when attempting to design a benefits and services package that addresses the strategic concerns of attracting and retaining talent, maximizing productivity, reducing costs, and ensuring legal compliance. And they must do this at a time when health care costs are rising dramatically and employees' lifestyles are changing the types of benefits and services they value. In addition, U.S. firms often face stiff competition from global competitors who often have lower indirect compensation costs.

In the past several years, the costs of benefits and services have grown substantially more than the costs of direct compensation. The cost increases have occurred despite the lack of evidence that increased investment in benefits and services results in improved productivity. To help control these costs, employers are shifting more responsibility to employees, and also working to more closely align the benefits and services they offer with their employees' preferences. Thus, the trend has been to move away from the traditional paternalistic approach toward an increasing level of employee involvement, participation, and self-determination. Organizations also are becoming more concerned about communicating with their employees about their benefits programs. Employees' lack of awareness of the contents and value of their benefits programs may partially explain why these programs are not always perceived favorably.

Tax laws can greatly affect both the cost of some benefits and services, as well as their value to employees. By designing benefits and services that are eligible for favorable tax treatment, employers can more effectively leverage their investments in benefits and services. Legal considerations have also played a role in causing employers to shift away from offering traditional defined benefit pension plans toward increasing use of defined contribution plans.

TERMS TO REMEMBER

Cash balance plan
Contributory plan
Defined benefit plan
Defined contribution plan
Employee Assistance Programs
   (EAPs)
Employee benefits and services
Employee Retirement Income
   Security Act of 1974 (ERISA)
Family and Medical Leave Act
   (FMLA)

401(k) plan
Money purchase plans
Noncontributory plan
Nonqualified plan
Pension Benefit Guaranty
   Corporation (PBGC)
Portable benefits
Private protection programs
Public protection programs
Qualified plan
Social Security Act of 1935

DISCUSSION QUESTIONS

1. As a manager, how can you use benefits and services to improve an organization's productivity?

2. Do you think more companies should establish wellness programs? Why or why not?

3. As employers strive to offer benefits to an increasingly diverse workforce, they sometimes encounter backlash from employees who resent their policies. For example, some employees may not approve of

spending on child care facilities, given that they benefit some employees and not others. Or, some employees may not approve of policies that give equal treatment to spouses and domestic partners. Do you think employers should avoid offering a benefit if a substantial minority of its employees object to it? Explain your rationale.

4. Make a list of the advantages and disadvantages of providing a broad range of benefits and services and then letting employees choose a few that fit their needs. Compare this strategy to simply providing "bare-bones" benefits and services. Which approach would you recommend? Why?

PROJECTS TO EXTEND YOUR LEARNING

1. *Integration and Application.* After reviewing the Lincoln Electric and Southwest Airlines cases at the end of this book, answer the following questions.

   a. What are the objectives of the company's approach to benefits and services?
   b. How well are the benefits and services packages being offered serving the business objectives and the needs of employees? Which package would you prefer? Explain why.
   c. Could Southwest Airlines adopt the approach to benefits and services used at Lincoln Electric? What would be the advantages and disadvantages for Southwest Airlines of adopting the Lincoln Electric approach? Be sure to consider how various stakeholders would be affected by such a change.

2. *Exploring the Internet.*

   a. Find out what information employers can get on benefits and services from the following two sources:
      Employee Benefits Research Institute, http://www.ebri.org
      Bureau of Labor Statistics, http://www.bls.gov
   b. Learn about the assistance available to employers from several prominent consulting firms:
      Hay Group, http://www.haygroup.com
      Towers Perrin, http://www.towers.com
      Mercer, http://www.mercer.com
      Hewitt Associates, http://www.hewitt.com
   c. Find out about integrated disability management from the Integrated Benefits Institute at http://www.ibiweb.org.
   d. Learn more about the problem of underfunded pensions and the financial obligations of the Pension Benefit Guarantee Corporation at http://www.pbgc.gov.

3. *Experiential Learning Activity.* Choose medium- to large-sized companies within the same industry to focus on for this activity. For example, you might choose Coca Cola and Pepsi, or Colgate-Palmolive and Procter & Gamble, or Microsoft and IBM. Investigate the voluntary benefits and services offered by the two companies by exploring the companies' websites and, if possible, interviewing a few of the companies' employees. Try to fill in the following matrix:

Description of the Benefit or Service	How Important to You? 1 Not very 2 Somewhat 3 Extremely (Circle one number to indicate importance to you.)			Name of Company A: _____ Offered by A? (Circle Y for yes or N for no.)		Name of Company B: _____ Offered by B? (Circle Y for yes or N for no.)		If Offered by Both Companies, Which Approach Would Be Better for You? (Circle A or B for the company you prefer or circle NS if you are not sure.)		
Telecommuting	1	2	3	Y	N	Y	N	A	B	NS
Flextime	1	2	3	Y	N	Y	N	A	B	NS
Subsidized child care	1	2	3	Y	N	Y	N	A	B	NS
Extended parental leave beyond FMLA requirement	1	2	3	Y	N	Y	N	A	B	NS
Paid family leave	1	2	3	Y	N	Y	N	A	B	NS
Tuition reimbursement	1	2	3	Y	N	Y	N	A	B	NS
Educational loans	1	2	3	Y	N	Y	N	A	B	NS
Mortgage assistance	1	2	3	Y	N	Y	N	A	B	NS
Dental insurance	1	2	3	Y	N	Y	N	A	B	NS
Vision insurance	1	2	3	Y	N	Y	N	A	B	NS
Prescription drug coverage	1	2	3	Y	N	Y	N	A	B	NS
HMO	1	2	3	Y	N	Y	N	A	B	NS
PPO	1	2	3	Y	N	Y	N	A	B	NS
On-site fitness center	1	2	3	Y	N	Y	N	A	B	NS
Casual dress day(s)	1	2	3	Y	N	Y	N	A	B	NS
Defined contribution retirement plan	1	2	3	Y	N	Y	N	A	B	NS
Defined benefit retirement plan	1	2	3	Y	N	Y	N	A	B	NS
Stock purchase plan	1	2	3	Y	N	Y	N	A	B	NS
Paid holidays	1	2	3	Y	N	Y	N	A	B	NS
Paid release time for volunteering	1	2	3	Y	N	Y	N	A	B	NS
Discounts on company products/services	1	2	3	Y	N	Y	N	A	B	NS
Flexible benefits program	1	2	3	Y	N	Y	N	A	B	NS
Other benefits of interest to you: _____	1	2	3	Y	N	Y	N	A	B	NS
Other: _____	1	2	3	Y	N	Y	N	A	B	NS
Other: _____	1	2	3	Y	N	Y	N	A	B	NS
Other: _____	1	2	3	Y	N	Y	N	A	B	NS

Overall, which company offers the benefits and services that you most prefer? (circle one)   Company A   Company B

Turn to the next page to complete this activity.

a. Based on what you know about the benefits offered by these two companies, what conclusions can you draw about the corporate cultures of the companies? Does one company seem to be more employee-friendly than the other?

b. If you were offered similar jobs with similar salaries at these two companies, would the difference in benefits offered by the two companies influence which job offer you accepted? Why or why not?

c. Do you think the company with the less desirable benefits package is at a disadvantage strategically? Why or why not?

CASE STUDY

WHO'S BENEFITING?

Jack Parks is a benefits and services manager in the auto electronics division of USA Motors, a major manufacturer of audio systems and auto electronic ignition systems. After analyzing the impact of absenteeism on the division's staffing costs for the previous quarter, he is very concerned. What troubles Jack is an agreement negotiated 10 years ago between the national union and USA Motors that, in effect, pays workers for being absent.

The "paid absence" agreement was not supposed to work quite that way. The theory was that by giving workers one week of paid absence against which they could charge personal absences, the company would be encouraging workers to notify their supervisors when they would be gone, so that staffing arrangements could be made and production maintained. In practice, workers discovered that by not charging off any "paid absences," they could receive a full week's pay in June when the company paid off the balance of unused paid absences for the previous year. This cash bonus, as workers had come to think of it, often coincided with the summer vacations taken by many of the 8,000 hourly employees when USA Motors shuts down for inventory.

As Jack learned, employees with chronic absentee records had figured out how to charge off absences using the regular categories (sick days, and excused and unexcused absences), and then collect the cash for the week of "paid absenses." In Jack's mind, USA Motors might just as well have

negotiated a cash bonus for the hourly workers or given them another 10 to 15 cents per hour. After reviewing the division's absenteeism rates for controllable absences (i.e., those categories of absences believed to be of the employee's own choice), Jack concludes that the company could reduce this rate from the previous year's figure of 11%.

And then Jack has a brainstorm: What USA Motors needs to negotiate is an incentive plan for reducing absenteeism. The plan Jack has in mind entails a standard for the amount of controllable absence deemed acceptable. If a chronically absent employee exceeds the standard, then vacation, holiday, and sickness/accident pay would be cut by 10% during the next six months. If worker absence continues to exceed the allowable limits, then vacation, holiday, and sickness pay would be cut during the next six months by the actual percentage of absent days incurred by the chronic absentee. Hence, if a worker misses 15% of scheduled workdays during the first six-month period, vacation pay for the next six-month period would be reduced by 10%. If the employee continues to be absent at the 15% rate, then vacation pay would be reduced by 15% during the next six months.

Jack immediately drafted a memorandum outlining the program and submitted it to the corporate HR manager of USA Motors for inclusion in the upcoming bargaining session. To Jack's surprise and delight, the memorandum received strong corporate support and is scheduled as a high priority bargaining topic for the fall negotiations.

CASE QUESTIONS

1. Will the incentive plan to reduce absenteeism succeed?

2. How much absenteeism is really under the employee's control?

3. Why didn't the "paid absence" plan work?

4. What plan would you suggest to USA Motors?

ENDNOTES

1 Personal Communication with Libby Child, Manager, Managed Claims and Disability Management Services, Steelcase (October 1998 and April 2001). Also see http://www.steelcase.com.

2 J. Schu, "Even in Hard Times, SAS Keeps Its Culture Intact," *Workforce* (October 2001): 21; "Dr. Goodnight's Company Town," *Business Week* (June 19, 2000): 193–200; Society for Human Resource Management (SHRM), "The Labor Shortage," *Workplace Visions* 4 (2000): 1–8; L. Gaughan and J. Kasparek, "The Employee as Customer," *Workspan* (September 2000): 30–37; P. Kruger, "Jobs For Life," *Fast Company* (May 2000): 236–252; J. Pfeffer, "SAS Institute (B): The Decision to Go Public," Graduate School of Business Stanford University Case Number: HR-6B (July 2000): 1–12.

3 R. Levering and M. Moskowitz, "The 100 Best Companies to Work For," *Fortune* (January 12, 2004): 56–79; E. R. Demby, "Nothing Partial about These Benefits," *HR Magazine* (August 2003): 72–81; S. A. Feeney, "The Battle over Benefits," *Workforce Management* (November 2003): 28–34.

4 "The Changing Face of Health Care: Balancing Employer and Employee Needs," *TP Track* (New York: Towers Perrin, 2002).

5 M. Hammers, "'Family-Friendly'" Benefits Prompt Non-Parent Backlash," *Workforce Management* (August 2003): 77–79.

6 J. M. Border, R. Pear, and M. Freudenheim, "Problem of Lost Health Benefits Is Reaching into the Middle Class," *New York Times* (November 25, 2002): A1, A16.

7 "Benefits Costs Reach Crisis Stage," *Workforce Management* (December 2003): 119.

8 "Benefit Costs Reach Crisis Stage."

9 B. Beam and J. McFadden, *Employee Benefits* (Chicago: Real Estate Education Company, 2001); L. Johnson and J. Rich, "Dealing with Employee Benefit Issues in Mergers and Acquisitions," *Legal Report* (March–April 2000): 1–8; "Employee Benefits," *Workforce* (May 2000): 91–96.

10 "Employer Costs for Employee Compensation—September 2003," Bureau of Labor Statistics, U.S. Department of Labor; "Benefit Costs Reach Crisis Stage," *Workforce Management* (December 2003): 120–125; S. Esen, "Job Benefits Survey," *SHRM/CNN Job Satisfaction Series* (December 2003).

11 M. E. Burke, E. Esen, and J. Collison, *2003 Benefits Survey* (Alexandria, VA: SHRM/SHRM Foundation, 2003); R. Pear, "Health Spending at a Record Level," *New York Times* (January 9, 2004): A1–A16; M. Freudenheim, "Workers Feel Pinch of Rising Health Costs," *New York Times* (October 22, 2003): C1–C2; "Health Care Costs to Keep Rising at Double-Digits Rates," *HR Magazine* (2001): 32; J. Bruner, "Value of Health Coverage: As Costs Rise and Employee Satisfaction Slumps, Businesses Look for Better Returns," *ACA Journal* (First Quarter 2000): 57–65.

12 J. Revell, "The $366 Billion Outrage," *Fortune* (May 31, 2004): 130–141.

13 B. Leonard, "Employers' and Employees' Benefits Priorities Differ," *HR Magazine* (February 2001): 31; J. Cole, "Auto and Home Insurance: The New Employee Benefit," *HR Focus* (December 1997): 9; J. Landauer, "Bottom-Line Benefits of Work/Life Programs," *HR Focus* (July 1997): 3.

14 J. F. Burton, Jr., and D. J. B. Mitchell, "Employee Benefits and Social Insurance: The Welfare Side of Employee Relations," in B. E. Kaufman, R. A. Beaumont, and R. B. Helfgott (eds.), *Industrial Relations to Human Resources and Beyond: The Evolving Process of Employee Relations Management (Issues in Work and Human Resources* (New York: M. E. Sharpe, 2002); S. LoJacono, "Back-Up Care: The New Benefits Tie Breaker," *Workspan* (January 2001): 16–20; J. Stanger and T. Sawyer, "A Win/Win Addition to Employee Benefits," *ACA Journal* (First Quarter 2000): 19–27; "Benefits Values from the Employee's Perspective," *ACA News* (June 1998): 14–16; A. M. Rappaport, "The New Employment Contract and Employee Benefits: A Road Map for the Future," *ACA Journal* (Summer 1997): 6–15.

15 Based on responses to a survey by World at Work conducted in 2000, as reported in R. Platt, "Value of Benefits Remains Constant," *Workspan* (June 2000): 34–39.

16 R. Kuttner, "Social Security: Finally, An Honest Debate," *Business Week* (March 15, 2004): 24; see http://www.bls.gov; D. E. Rosenbaum, "Hard Truths Are Avoided on Social Security," *New York Times* (December 2002): 4; M. McNamee, "Yes: The Private Market Offers Better Returns," *Business Week* (March 23, 1998): 36; C. Farrell, "No: Why Let Wall Street Gamble with Our Nest Egg," *Business Week* (March 23, 1998): 37; G. Koretz, "How Not to Fix Social Security," *Business Week* (March 23, 1998): 24; R. J. Barro, "Don't Tinker with Social Security, Reinvent It," *Business Week* (June 8, 1998): 24.

17 P. Carroll, "Integrated Benefits Plans Offer Companies Key Advantages," *ACA News* (March 2000): 29–32; "State Unemployment Insurance Funds," *Bulletin to Management: Datagraph* (October 2, 1997): 316.

18 See statistics at http://www.osha.gov; T. Vander Neut, "Charting the Tides," *Human Resource Executive* (November 1997): 60–61; R. Kirsch, "Oh My Achin . . .," *Human Resource Executive* (June 6, 1997): 25; M. Weinstein, "Ably Assisted," *Human Resource Executive* (June 6, 1997): 27; J. A. Nixon, "Protected Plans," *Human Resource Executive* (June 6, 1997): 30–32.

19 Libby Child, personal conversation with authors April 7, 2001. See also T. Vander Neut, "Step by Step," *Human Resource Executive* (September 1998): 86–88; B. A. Morris, "Injury 101," *Human Resource Executive* (September 1998): 77.

20 M. M. Arthur, "Share Price Reactions to Work-Family Initiatives: An Institutional Perspective," *Academy of Management Journal* 46(4) (2003): 497–505; Burke et al., *2003 Benefits Survey;* Society for Human Resource Management (SHRM), "FMLA Still Poses Implementation Problems, Employers Say," *HR News* (February 2001): 3–12; B. P. Noble, "Interpreting the Family Leave Act," *New York Times* (August 1, 1993): F24. See also D. Gunsch, "The Family Leave Act: A Financial Burden?" *Personnel Journal* (September 1993): 48–57; "Companies Willing to Stretch Employees Still Further," *HR Reporter* (March 1993): 5–6.

21 G. M. Davis, "The Family and Medical Leave Act: 10 Years Later," *Legal Report* (July–August 2003): 1–8; J. W. Papa, "Sizing Up the FMLA," Workforce (August 1998): 38–43.

22 J. Blasi, D. Kruse, and A. Bernstein, *In the Company of Owners* (New York: Basic Books, 2003).

23 C. Hirschman, "Fiduciary Fitness," *HR Magazine* (September 2003): 6064; S. Bates, "More U.S. Firms offer Pension Investment Advice," http://www.shrm.org/hrnews_published/articles/CMS_005681.asp, October 7, 2003; J. Revell, "CEO Pensions: The Latest Way to Hide Millions," *Fortune* (April 28, 2003): 68–69.

24 E. Sylvers, "In Italy, a Way of Life Is Threatened: The Pension System Is Stretched to Limit," *International Herald Tribune* (August 20, 2003): 1, 8; R. Kuttner, "The Great American Pension-Fund Robbery," *Business Week* (September 8, 2003): 24; P. J. Kiger, "New Hope for Troubled Retirement Plans," *Workforce Management* (October 2003): 53–56; S. A. Feeney, "Participation in Pension Funds Falls: Employees Aren't Saving, Either," *Workforce Management* (December 2003): 26.

25 For more details about ERISA, visit the website of the U.S. Department of Labor, http://www.dol.gov/ebsa/faqs/faq_consumer_pension .html.

26 N. Byrnes, "The Benefits Trap," *Business Week* (July 19, 2004): 64–72; A. Borrus, M. McNamee, and D. Henry, "Will the Bough Break?" *Business Week* (April 14, 2003): 62–63; M. W. Walsh, "Pension Agency to Cut Its Stock Holdings," *New York Times* (January 30, 2004): C3; T. Nicholson, "Pension Safety Net Frays," *AARP Bulletin* (April 2003): 11.

27 "Cash Balance Plans Conversions Actually Increase Employer Costs, Study Reveals," *HR Magazine* (May 2004): 32, 38.

28 D. C. Johnston, "I.B.M. Employees Get $320 Million in Pension Suit," *New York Times* (September 30, 2004): A1, C4; M. V. Rafter, "The Insider: Pension Benefits," *Workforce Management* (June 2004): 81; U.S. Department of Labor, "Frequently Asked Questions about Cash Balance Plans," http://www.dol.gov/ebsa/faqs/faq_consumer_Cashbalanceplans.html, January 8, 2004; S. Bates, "Ruling Clouds Pension Plan Conversions," *HR Magazine* (September 2003): 26; E. R. Demby, "Cash Balance Makes a Comeback," *Workforce* (May 2003): 40–43; E. R. Demby, "Nothing Partial about These Benefits," *HR Magazine* (August 2003): 72–81.

29 J. VanDerhei, "The Controversy of Traditional vs. Cash Balance Plans," *ACA News* (Fourth Quarter 1999): 7–26.

30 P. J. Kiger, "New Hope for Troubled Retirement Plans," *Workforce Management* (October 2003): 53–56; E. R. Demby, "Changing the Recipe of 401(k) Plans," *HR Magazine* (September 2002): 59–68; "Benefit Costs Reach Crisis," *Workforce Management* (December 2003): 128; "Employee Attraction Retention Drive 401(k) Plans," *Workspan* (February 2001): 10–12.

31 "Benefit Costs Reach Crisis Stage," *Workforce Management* (December 2003): 128.

32 "The Insider: Pension Benefits," *Workforce Management* (June 2004): 81–82.

33 L. G. Kraft, "The Insider: Retirement," *Workforce Management* (July 2004): 57–58.

34 M. E. Burke et al., *2003 Benefits Survey.*

35 A. Tergesen, "The Hidden Bite of Retiree Health," *Business Week* (January 19, 2004): 86–87; W. C. Symonds, "Get Used to the Pain," *Business Week* (October 20, 2003): 42–43; H. Gleckman, "Old, Ill, and Uninsured," *Business Week* (April 7, 2003): 78–79; M. Freudenheim, "Workers Feel Pinch of Rising Health Costs," *New York Times* (October 22, 2003): C1, C2; J. Greene, "More Employees Declining Health Insurance Benefits," *HR Magazine* (December 2003): 31–32.

36 L. Walczak and R. S. Dunham, "Running on Middle-Class Relief," *Business Week* (February 9, 2004): 35–36; "Benefit Costs Reach Crisis Stage," *Workforce Management* (December 2003): 122.

37 Source: Family Kaiser Foundation, as reported in "Benefit Costs Reach Crisis Stage," *Workforce Management* (December 2003): 122.

38 B. O'Reilly, "Health Care: Taking on the HMOs," *Fortune* (February 16, 1998): 96–104; B. J. Feder, "Deere Sees a Future in Health Care," *New York Times* (July 1, 1994): D1; J. J. Laabs, "Deere's HMO Turns Crisis into Profit," *Personnel Journal* (October 1992): 82–89.

39 "Benefit Costs Reach Crisis Stage," *Workforce Management* (December 2003): 122.

40 "Benefit Costs Reach Crisis Stage," *Workforce Management* (December 2003): 122; T. Lieberman, "HMO or PPO: Are You in the Right Plan?" *Consumer Reports* (October 2001): 27–29; M. Freudenheim, "(Loosely) Managed Care Is in Demand," *New York Times* (September 29, 1998): C1, C4.

41 M. Freudenheim, "Workers Feel Pinch of Rising Health Costs," *New York Times* (October 22, 2003): C1, C2.

42 "Benefit Costs Reach Crisis Stage"; J. Weber, M. Arndt, and L. Cohen, "America, This Is Really Gonna Hurt," *Business Week* (September 17, 2001): 46–48.

43 H. Gleckman and J. Carey, "An Apple a Day—On the Boss," *Business Week* (October 14, 2002): 122–124; B. Kirsch, "Working Well," *Human Resource Executive* (May 5, 1998): 45–47; N. A. Jeffrey, "'Wellness Plans' Try to Target the Not-So-Well," *Wall Street Journal* (June 20, 1996): B1, B10; B. P. Sunoo and C. M. Solomon, "Wellness Begins with Compassion," *Personnel Journal* (April 1996): 79–89; "Policy Guide: Wellness Programs Offer Healthy Returns," *Bulletin to Management* (March 7, 1996): 80.

44 "Wellness Plans and the Disabilities Act," *Bulletin to Management* (May 27, 1993): 168.

45 J. Ewing, "Revolt of the Young," *Business Week* (September 22, 2003): 48; "Americans Work; Europeans Play," *Workforce* (July 2001): 19; "Less Rest Assured," *AAA World* (September/October 2001): 13; D. Briscoe and R. S. Schuler, *International Human Resource Management,* 2nd ed. (London: Routledge, 2004).

46 N. R. Lockwood, "Work/Life Balance: Challenges and Solutions," *SHRM Research Quarterly* 2 (2003): 1–10; D. Patel (ed.), "Work-Life Balance," *Workplace Visions* 4 (2002): 1–8.

47 *SHRM 2004 Benefits: Survey Report* (Alexandria, VA: SHRM, 2004); see also T. A. Kochan, *Regaining Control of Our Destinies: A Working Families' Agenda for America* (Cambridge, MA: MIT Workplace Center, 2004); M. Hammers, "Babies Deliver a Loyal Workforce," *Workforce* (April 2003): 52; S. Feeney, "Employees Find a Field of Family-Friendly Benefits in Des Moines," *Workforce Management* (July 2003): 81–83; S. Friedman and J. H. Greenhaus, *Work and Family—Allies or Enemies?* (London: Oxford University Press, 2000); E. E. Kossek, J. A. Colquitt, and R. A. Noe, "Caregiving Decisions, Well-Being, and Performance: The Effects of Place and Provider as a Function of Dependent Type and Work-Family Climates," *Academy of Management Journal* 44(1) (2001): 29–44; J. Perry-Smith and T. Blum, "Work-Family Human Resource Bundles and Perceived Organizational Performance," *Academy of Management Journal* 43(6) (2000): 1107–1117.

48 K. S. Robinson, "Employers Increase Work/Life Programs," *HR Magazine* (March 2004): 32.

49 "Benefit Costs Reach Crisis Stage"; Burke et al., *2003 Benefits Survey;* E. E. Kossek and V. Nichol, "The Effects of On-Site Child Care on Employee Attitudes and Performance," *Personnel Psychology* 45 (1992): 485–509.

50 "Family Friendly Benefits Have Spread Greatly," *Bulletin to Management* 47 (March 7, 1996): 73; A. Halcrow, "Optimas Reflects Changes in HR," *Personnel Journal* (January 1994): 50.

51 P. J. Kiger, "A Case for Child Care," *Workforce Management* (April 2004): 34–40; E. R. Demby, "Do Your Family-Friendly Programs Make Cents?" *HR Magazine* (January 2004): 75–78.

52 A. S. Wellner, "Welcoming Back Mom," *HR Magazine* (June 2004): 77–80.

53 "Benefits Reach Crisis Stage," *Workforce Management* (December 2003): 130, based on a survey of 2,984 private-industry organizations as reported by the Bureau of Labor Statistics.

54 P. J. Kiger, "A Case for Child Care," *Workforce Management* (April 2004): 34–40.

55 A. Hayashi, "Mommy-Track Backlash," *Harvard Business Review* (March 2001): 33–42; A. R. McIlvaine, "Drawing the Lines," *Human Resource Executive* (September 1997): 84.

56 M. Hammers, "'Family-Friendly'" Benefits Prompt Non-Parent Backlash," *Workforce Management* (August 2003): 77–79; T. J. Rothauser, J.A. Gonzalez, N. E. Clarke, and L. L. O'Dell, "Family-Friendly Backlash—Fact or Fiction? The Case of Organizations' On-Site Child Care Centers," *Personnel Psychology* 51 (1998): 685–706.

57 S. VanDerWall, "Survey Finds Unscheduled Absenteeism Hitting Seven-Year High," HR News (November 1998): 14.

58 "Parental Leave: Healthier Kids," Business Week (January 18, 1999): 30.

59 N. R. Lockwood, "The Aging Workforce," *2003 Research Quarterly* (Alexandria, VA: SHRM): 1–10.

60 D. Hellreigel, S. E. Jackson, and J. W. Slocum, *Management,* 10th ed. (Cincinnati, OH: South-Western, 2005).

61 C. Hirschman, "Long-Term Care Insurance Comes of Age," *HR Magazine* (July 2002): 65–70.

62 M. Conlin, "Unmarried America" *Business Week* (October 2003): 106–116.

63 *SHRM 2004 Benefits: Survey Report* (Alexandria, VA: SHRM, 2004).

64 R. W. Geisel, "Responding to Changing Ideas of Family," *HR Magazine* (August 2004): 89–98.

65 G. S. Benson, D. Finegold, and S.A. Mohrman, "You Paid for the Skills, Now Keep Them: Tuition Reimbursement and Voluntary Turnover," *Academy of Management Journal* 47 (2004): 315–331.

66 J. Ewing, "Revolt of the Young," *Business Week* (September 22, 2003): 48; J. Dulebohn, B. Murray, and M. Sun, "Selection Among Employer-Sponsored Pension Plans: The Role of Individual Differences," *Personnel Psychology* 53 (2000): 405–432.

67 K. Blanton, "Health Care Costs Dog Small Firms," *Boston Globe* (July 7, 2004): D1, D8.

68 E. L. Andrews, "Health Care Heights: Soaring Rates Leave Little Companies in a Bind," *New York Times* (February 24, 2004): G1, G8.

69 "Cost-Cutting Shifts the Terrain," *Workforce Management* (December 2003): 90.

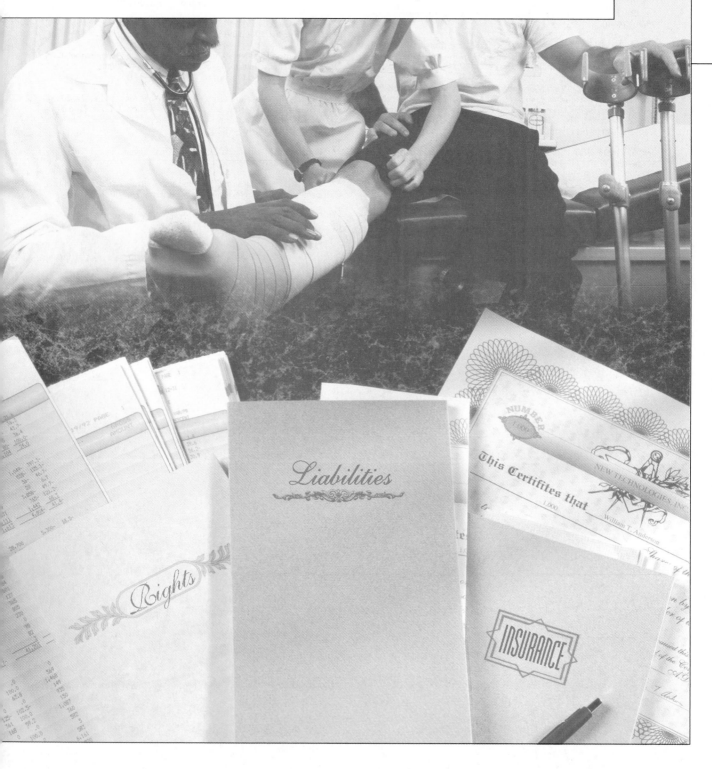

chapter 13

Promoting Workplace Safety and Health

Repetitive motion injuries were first recognized more than 200 years ago. In modern parlance, these are called cumulative trauma disorders. They result from motions that, although innocent in themselves, are chronically repeated, usually in an awkward or forceful manner, resulting in musculoskeletal disease, pain, or injury. You don't have to work in a factory to get them. Office workers are at risk, and so too are tennis players and runners. But at Ben and Jerry's, the former ice cream maker, work on the manufacturing line is the primary cause.

Injuries of this sort are the most common workplace injuries, and during the working years, between ages 18 and 64, they are the most common reason for lost work time. Ben and Jerry's had experienced a very high number of workers' compensation claims for these injuries, higher than those of Steelcase as described in Chapter 12.

These experiences encouraged Ben and Jerry's to institute a number of changes. The company discontinued its emphasis on the record of workdays without injuries and embarked on education, training, and meetings to encourage early reporting of potential injuries. Furthermore, the company hired a number of consultants who specialized in ergonomics to visit all the plants' operations and revise tools, posture, seating, and activities so as to prevent repetitive motion injuries. The

Waterbury, Vermont, production area was upgraded with new equipment and improved line layouts that bettered working conditions. Several material handling issues, such as palletizing, were also addressed via new equipment and/or improved procedures.[1]

THE STRATEGIC IMPORTANCE OF WORKPLACE SAFETY AND HEALTH

Virtually all employees in an organization are affected by workplace safety and health or the lack thereof.[2] Workers in factories are exposed to potentially dangerous machines. Construction workers may fall. Employees working in computer chip manufacturing plants are exposed to numerous chemicals and fumes. And while office workers may think they work in safe environments, five common sources of potential harm are:

1. injuries caused by poor ergonomic designs,
2. eyestrain caused by poor lighting,
3. accidents caused by poor adherence to safety codes and regulations,
4. respiratory problems caused by poor indoor air quality, and
5. stress induced by heat, cold, noise, and so on.[3]

White-collar workers also suffer. They are exposed to poor air quality, which is common in closed office buildings. Chemical components from sources such as carpeting and structural materials build up and are circulated through the ventilation system.[4] Infectious diseases can spread quickly through these environments, putting everyone at risk.

BENEFITS OF A SAFE AND HEALTHY WORK ENVIRONMENT

By reducing the rates and severity of occupational accidents, diseases, workplace violence, and stress-related illnesses, and improving the quality of work life for their employees, organizations can only become more effective.[5] Among the positive consequences of safe and healthy workplaces are (1) higher productivity owing to fewer lost workdays, (2) increased efficiency and quality from a more committed workforce, (3) reduced medical and insurance costs, (4) lower workers' compensation rates and direct payments because of fewer claims being filed, (5) and improved reputation as an employer of choice. Companies can thus increase their profits substantially and better serve the objectives of their multiple stakeholders.[6]

CONSEQUENCES OF AN UNSAFE AND UNHEALTHY WORK ENVIRONMENT

FAST FACT

NIOSH says there are 700,000 eye injuries yearly that cost employers about $4 billion in lost productivity.

The costs of poor safety and health are numerous. They include the human costs of injuries and death as well as economic costs.

Injuries. Back injuries are one of the most prevalent type of workplace injuries.[7] Every year an estimated 10 million employees in the United States encounter back pain that impairs their job performance. Approximately one million employees file workers' compensation claims for back injuries. Billions of dollars are spent each year to treat back pain—$50 billion in workers' compensation payments alone, and another $50 billion in finding and training substitute workers and running other programs to help recovery.[8]

For office workers, carpal tunnel syndrome has become an epidemic. It now causes more lost workdays than anything else. Half of all the people who suffer from carpal tunnel syndrome miss 30 days or more of work during the year. According to the Bureau of Labor Statistics, the record number of lost days is due to the fact that so many people undergo surgery to correct the problem. On average, the annual cost of each case of carpal tunnel syndrome is $13,000.[9]

As you might expect, some employees are more likely to be injured at work than others. Can you guess which types of workplaces have the highest rates of injuries? According to the Bureau of Labor Statistics, the industries with the highest numbers of worker injuries are:

1. Motor vehicles and equipment
2. Nursing and personal care facilities
3. Air transportation
4. Hospitals
5. Trucking and courier services
6. Department stores
7. Grocery stores
8. Eating and drinking places

Exposure to Chemicals. When employees suffer physical injuries or death, their pain is usually obvious, at least to them. But for workers exposed to dangerous chemicals, the effects often go undetected for many years. By the time a chemical is discovered to be dangerous, hundreds of employees may have been exposed to it for many years. Recently, some 250 former IBM workers sued that employer claiming they were poisoned while making computer components. IBM acknowledged that the "clean rooms" where employees work are filled with potentially dangerous chemicals, but they argued that the safety procedures they have in place prevent workers from experiencing any harm. Nevertheless, employees worry that they may develop cancer, and at least some of the available evidence shows that IBM programmers with 10 or more years of company experience had a threefold elevation in brain cancer. Some workers claimed that the chemicals had caused birth defects in their children. IBM has denied there is any evidence to prove the charges are true and has settled some of the claims out of court for undisclosed amounts. Other cases are still in the courts, and research is still underway to determine whether IBM employees actually suffer from various diseases at elevated rates. Unfortunately, the truth is that IBM workers and others in the industry routinely work with dozens of chemicals that have unknown health consequences.[10]

"It used to be a common joke here that once you leave you go outside and choke on the fresh air."

Lee Conrad
Fabrication lab employee
IBM

Mental Health. The physical injuries that employees suffer at work may be easier to count and quantify than psychological injuries, but mental health is just as important as physical health.[11] For some employees, the workplace is a source of substantial mental strain. As noted in Chapter 3, for example, employees who suffer harassment at work may suffer psychological symptoms that affect not only their productivity but also the quality of their lives away from work. Mental health may also suffer when employees' jobs subject them to heavy emotional workloads, or when there is simply too much work that needs to be done.

Death and Violence. Estimates of workplace deaths in the United States range from 2,800 to around 10,000 yearly. Workplace-related deaths now average about 7 per 100,000 employees. This is much better than in 1970, when the rate was about 18 per 100,000 employees.[12] The declining rate of death in U.S. workplaces reflects the changing nature of the U.S. economy. As manufacturing jobs have declined, and dangerous jobs have been replaced by automated technologies, fewer and fewer employees risk the most severe workplace hazards. Nevertheless, many employees worry about this potential risk. Some of their worry stems from news reports about workplace homicides. Each year, approximately 700 homicides occur in the workplace, and about one million employees are victims of nonfatal workplace violence.

> **FAST FACT**
>
> The International Labour Organization (ILO) estimates that about 220,000 workers die around the world every year in work accidents or from illnesses contracted at work.

Economic Costs. The National Center for Health Statistics estimates the annual cost of violence (mostly physical assaults) as $13.5 billion in medical costs and 1.75 million days of lost work.[13] Although deaths have declined, the economic cost to businesses of workplace deaths and injuries remains high at an estimated $50 billion annually. Similar costs are estimated for the more than 100,000 workers who annually succumb to occupational diseases. Enormous costs are also associated with psychological conditions. For example, alcoholism, which can result from attempts to cope with job pressures, costs organizations and society over $65 billion annually. Of this, $20 billion is attributed to lost productivity and the remainder to the direct costs of insurance, hospitalization, and other medical items. Perhaps more difficult to quantify, but just as symptomatic of stress and a poor quality of working life, are workers' feelings of lack of meaning and involvement in their work and loss of importance as individuals.[14]

> **FAST FACT**
>
> Of the 6 million workplace injuries in the United States, about half result in lost work time.

PROMOTING HEALTH AND SAFETY WITHIN AN INTEGRATED HRM SYSTEM

Workplace safety and health *refers to the physiological-physical and psychological conditions of a workforce that result from the work environment provided by the organization.* If an organization takes effective safety and health measures, fewer of its employees will have short- or long-term ill effects as a result of being employed at that organization.[15]

Physiological-physical conditions *include occupational diseases and accidents such as actual loss of life or limb, repetitive motion injuries, back pain, carpal tunnel syndrome, cardiovascular diseases, various forms of cancer such as lung cancer and leukemia, emphysema, and arthritis.* Other conditions that are known to result from an unhealthy work environment include white lung disease, brown lung disease, black lung disease, sterility, central nervous system damage, and chronic bronchitis.

Psychological conditions *result from organizational stress and a low quality of working life.* These encompass symptoms of poor mental health and job burnout, including apathy, emotional exhaustion, withdrawal, confusion about roles and duties, mistrust of others, inattentiveness, irritability, and a tendency to become distraught over trifles.

Links to Other HR Practices

As Exhibit 13.1 suggests, the linkages between other HR practices and workplace safety and health are many.[16]

Job Analysis. As described in Chapter 5, job analysis procedures can be used to identify aspects of a job that may contribute to workplace injuries, and ergonomic principles can be applied to redesign the work environment. At some companies, the selection process is designed to promote workplace safety and health. Research indicates that some personality characteristics predict workplace accidents, while others predict stress-related symptoms. Some employers use their selection procedures to screen out employees with tendencies that are contrary to a safe and healthy workplace.

Training. Training is another HR practice that can be effectively used to improve workplace safety and health. Employees participate in training in

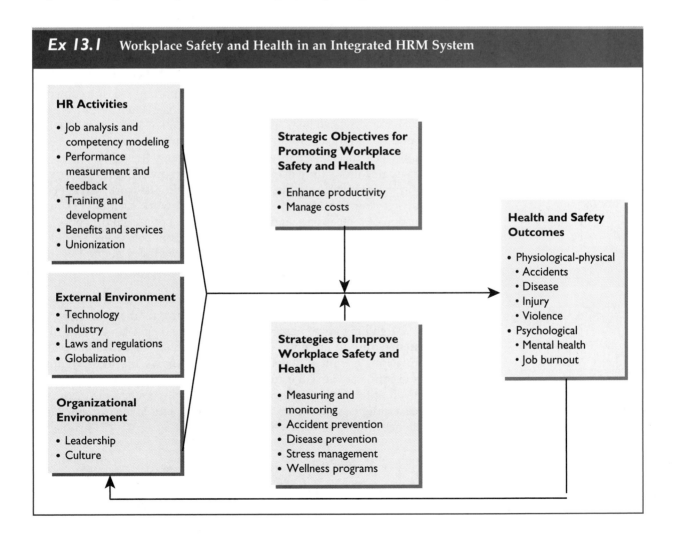

Ex 13.1   Workplace Safety and Health in an Integrated HRM System

HR Activities
- Job analysis and competency modeling
- Performance measurement and feedback
- Training and development
- Benefits and services
- Unionization

External Environment
- Technology
- Industry
- Laws and regulations
- Globalization

Organizational Environment
- Leadership
- Culture

Strategic Objectives for Promoting Workplace Safety and Health
- Enhance productivity
- Manage costs

Strategies to Improve Workplace Safety and Health
- Measuring and monitoring
- Accident prevention
- Disease prevention
- Stress management
- Wellness programs

Health and Safety Outcomes
- Physiological-physical
  - Accidents
  - Disease
  - Injury
  - Violence
- Psychological
  - Mental health
  - Job burnout

order to learn about safety policies and to learn behaviors that reduce the likelihood of accidents and injuries. Training may also be needed to teach employees how to use new equipment intended to protect them from workplace hazards. Training for managers may include detailed explanations of the relevant laws and regulations that govern workplace safety and health.

Performance Management. When safety and health are viewed as issues of strategic importance, they become central to the entire performance management process. Performance measures monitor how well managers are doing against their goals, and both managers and other employees may be offered monetary incentives for reducing accidents and improving safe behaviors on the job. Providing tangible incentives to employees for achieving health and safety goals appears to be effective. Incentives should be used cautiously, however. Critics of this approach worry that offering employees incentives may merely reduce their willingness to *report* accidents and injuries. Instead of offering incentives for safety outcomes, they suggest that managers use incentives to reward behaviors that are likely to affect safety and health outcomes.[17]

Benefits and Services. Because injured and unhealthy workers so often require medical care and must take time off from work while they recover, there is a close alignment between managing benefits and managing safety and health. For employers, improving safety and health is one way to reduce insurance claims and their related costs. It is also a way to reduce the number of days that employees must be paid for time not worked.[18]

At Dannon Yogurt, preventive measures are important, but the company recognizes that injuries are not completely avoidable. When employees are injured, Dannon strives to help employees return to work as quickly as possible. As part of an unusual return-to-work program, Dannon allows recovering employees to ease their way back by doing light-duty work for nonprofit organizations in the community. The program allows employees to build up their strength gradually before returning to work, while at the same time keeping them in the habit of going to work each day. Dannon pays a portion of their wages, and the community's nonprofit organizations reap the benefits. Dannon also wins: Since the program began, lost workdays have been reduced 30%, medical costs have been reduced about 35%, and recovery time has been reduced 27%.[19]

Unions. As described in Chapter 14, managing employee relationships in unionized environments often involves negotiating over issues of safety. Collective bargaining agreements typically include a clause that recognizes management's duty to provide safe work conditions.[20] In addition, specific safety provisions are often stated. Exhibit 13.2 shows the most common safety provisions stated in collective bargaining agreements in recent years.[21]

Despite all of these efforts, however, many employees become victims of workplace accidents, injuries, and illnesses. Thus, employers provide services and benefits to assist these employees.

THE ORGANIZATIONAL ENVIRONMENT

In organizations where safety is valued and embedded in the organization's culture, employees benefit by experiencing fewer injuries.[22] Developing such a culture requires the involvement of everyone in the organization.

"The people, they're nothing. You move them in and out. If they don't do the job, you fire them. If they get hurt or complain about safety, you put a bull's-eye on them."

Robert Rester
Former Plant Manager
McWane Inc.

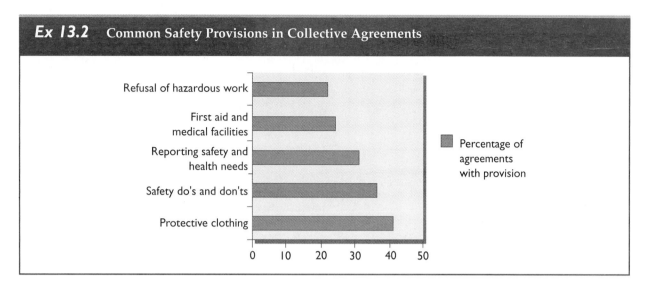

Ex 13.2 Common Safety Provisions in Collective Agreements

Organizational Culture. In industries where workplace hazards are an inevitable reality, attitudes toward issues of safety and health are reflected in the organizational culture.[23] Employee involvement can encourage employees to identify safety and health problems and develop solutions to address them.

John Deere has been involving workers in finding solutions to workplace injuries—especially those caused by repetitive motions—since 1993. When employees experience significant pain while working, they can summon the ergonomics team. Terry Hardy carries a beeper for this purpose. When it goes off, he rushes to the scene of the latest backache or painful wrist. Terry Hardy is a toolmaker at a John Deere tractor plant in Dubuque, Iowa. He's also a member of the plant's ergonomics team. In addition to all the normal tasks of a toolmaker, Terry is responsible for helping develop solutions that will reduce the incidents of workplace injuries in the plant. He and other members of the team may consult with the employee to find a quick fix for the problem, or the team may take days to come up with a feasible solution.[24] Having this type of procedure in place goes a long way toward creating an organizational environment conducive to safety and health.[25]

In an effort to understand the conditions needed to ensure workplace safety and health, the Conference Board conducted a study to identify "best practices." Exhibit 13.3 lists the eight core elements of an organizational culture that supports workplace safety and health.[26]

Leadership. During the strategic planning process, line managers can promote safety and health through the development of policies and goals. In order for such policies and goals to have an effect, everyone in the organization must direct their efforts toward creating a culture where safety is valued.

Creating a safety-driven culture requires visible leadership from top-level managers. Effective leaders do more than just talk about the importance of workplace safety—they explain why it is important, encourage safe behaviors, and reward safe performance. With leadership like this, employees get the message. They become more conscious of safety issues, and a climate that values safety is established.[27] A study of restaurant workers showed that

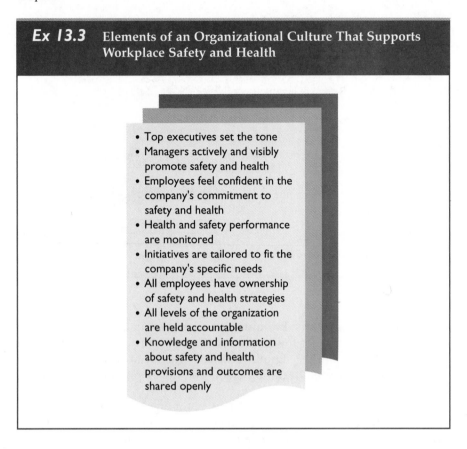

Ex 13.3   Elements of an Organizational Culture That Supports Workplace Safety and Health

- Top executives set the tone
- Managers actively and visibly promote safety and health
- Employees feel confident in the company's commitment to safety and health
- Health and safety performance are monitored
- Initiatives are tailored to fit the company's specific needs
- All employees have ownership of safety and health strategies
- All levels of the organization are held accountable
- Knowledge and information about safety and health provisions and outcomes are shared openly

these dynamics result in fewer safety incidents and fewer occupational injuries.[28]

Company leadership, of course, also can be blamed for creating a culture that puts profits ahead of employees' lives. That's the reputation of McWane's executive leadership. McWane is one of the world's largest makers of cast iron water and sewer pipes, and recently it had the highest injury rate in the nation for three out of four years. During the past decade, it has been cited 400 times for safety violations. That's four times more than the total number of safety violations received by all six of its competitors combined. Sadly, many workers have lost their lives. After one recent death, workers began displaying a bumper sticker that read, "Pray for me. I work at Kennedy Valve," the name of one of McWane's facilities.[29]

THE EXTERNAL ENVIRONMENT

External forces that are important to workplace safety and health include evolving technologies, industry conditions, and the laws and regulations that govern this aspect of work.[30]

Technology. In manufacturing environments, the introduction of new technologies often greatly improves workplace safety and health. By introducing the latest manufacturing equipment, including robotics, employers often can eliminate the need to expose employees to unsafe conditions.

On the other hand, some new technologies introduce new hazards into the workplace. For example, new buildings often do not allow employees to open their windows, making them completely dependent on ventilation systems for the provision of clean air. Office equipment that makes the workplace more efficient may emit fumes that induce illness.[31] As jobs of all types become increasingly dependent on computers, employees of all types are subjected to conditions that put them at greater risk of repetitive motion injuries, such as carpal tunnel syndrome.

FAST FACT Carpal tunnel syndrome accounts for one third of workplace injuries in the United States and costs more than $20 billion yearly.

Industry. For some industries, safety and health issues rise to the level of strategic importance, while in others these issues are of less concern. For example, the accident rate for 100,000 workers in the United States is 7, but for workers in Alaska's fishing industry, it's nearly 700. Another dangerous industry is construction, where workers face a constantly changing physical environment. Often, one misstep or forgetful moment can crush a limb or end a life. When pressure mounts to finish a job quickly to meet a deadline, supervisors may push their workers to take extra risks. Add to these pressures a "macho" culture that tends to belittle safety and romanticize danger, and the stage is set for accidents and injuries. Construction, mining, and agriculture are among the most dangerous industries nationwide, with yearly deaths for every 100,000 employees being around 32, 43, and 40, respectively. Meat packing and poultry processing are also dangerous. Some workers perform the same repetitive motion as many as 30,000 times per shift; knives are ever-present, too. When you consider their working environment, it's easy to understand why one of every seven poultry workers is injured on the job—double the national average.[32]

FAST FACT On September 11, 2001, more than 300 fire-fighters and police officers and more than 3,000 office workers lost their lives.

U.S. Laws and Regulations. As described in Chapter 3, the Occupational Safety and Health Act regulates workplace conditions and provides employees protection against workplace injuries and illness. It is the most important source of legal and regulatory oversight related to workplace safety and health. In addition, workplace safety and health are governed by workers' compensation regulations and state initiatives. In California, for example, employers are required to develop ergonomics programs that include work-site evaluation, hazard control, and employee training if two workers are medically diagnosed with injuries from identical tasks within the same 12-month period. Although California was the first state to adopt such a rigorous standard, other state legislatures have also begun to consider legislation designed to put more pressure on employers to ensure safe and healthy workplaces.[33]

Global Considerations. With globalization has come an increasing awareness of differences in national standards for workplace safety and health. Developing countries that attract foreign investment often have few government regulations regarding workplace safety and health. Unions in these countries often are weak, and their focus is more likely to be on issues of wages rather than safety and health.

During the 1990s, concerns about safety and health issues within Mexico became a stumbling block during congressional discussions of the North

American Free Trade Agreement (NAFTA). Many people were concerned that low standards for workplace safety and health would be yet another reason for U.S. companies to move operations across the border. Thus, besides losing jobs at home, Americans could potentially be guilty of unfairly exploiting Mexico's labor force. Subsequent to the enactment of NAFTA, a new concern arose. With more and more Mexican workers coming into the United States, people began to worry that U.S. employers would be lax in enforcing safety and health standards at facilities with large numbers of immigrant employees, who were unlikely to complain to the legal authorities. The Occupational Safety and Health Administration (OSHA) has sought to allay such concerns and assure concerned parties that they will actively enforce U.S. safety and health standards in plants that employ Mexican workers, as described in the feature "Managing Globalization: OSHA Signs Letter of Agreement with Mexico."[34]

FAST FACT

The ILO estimates that the HIV/AIDS epidemic will reduce the size of the available workforce in high prevalence by 10–30% by the year 2020.

Two global organizations that strive to improve workplace safety and health throughout the world are the International Labor Organization (ILO) and the World Health Organization (WHO). As described in Chapter 2, the ILO promotes internationally recognized labor rights. Toward this end, they formulate minimum standards that employers should meet in a variety of domains, including workplace safety and health. They also conduct research and provide technical assistance to employers.

Managing Globalization

OSHA Signs Letter of Agreement with Mexico

"Hispanics are an integral part of the American workforce, and Mexican workers comprise its largest segment," explained U.S. Secretary of Labor Elaine L. Chao. This is one reason why OSHA has been working with the Mexican Embassy to assure them that the Department of Labor will be vigorous in its efforts to ensure safe and healthful working conditions for workers from Mexico and other Latin American countries. "Working with the Mexican Consulates enables us to reach more workers and employers, and achieve greater success in ensuring the health and safety of Mexican workers, than would be possible if we addressed this issue alone," said John Henshaw, Assistant Secretary of Labor for Occupational Safety and Health.

The OSHA agreement outlines collaborative efforts regarding communication, outreach, and training for Mexican workers. The goal is to ensure that all workers understand their right to a safe and healthful workplace. Under the agreement, the Consulates will help Mexican workers and employers understand the role OSHA plays in worker protection, enforcement, and compliance assistance.

A specific example of how OSHA works to assure workplace safety and health is their alliance with the Hispanic-American Chamber of Commerce in Essex County, New Jersey, and the New Jersey Department of Labor. The alliance seeks to ensure that Hispanic employees come home safely at the end of the workday. According to Patricia Clark, the regional administrator of OSHA, these alliance partners "will reach out to build trust, raise awareness and educate both employers and workers in safety and health. We recognize the value of a collaborative relationship to achieve these goals." OSHA's specific role is to deliver a 10-hour construction course in both Spanish and English to Hispanic employers and employees; develop programs regarding hazards such as falls and electrical shocks; encourage bilingual individuals to take the OSHA 30-hour construction or general industry courses in order to qualify to teach Hispanic workers; and promote and encourage employers to participate in other OSHA-relevant programs.

The ILO's Code of Practice on HIV/AIDS is an example of how this organization seeks to improve workplace health. This manual contains practical advice to employers interested in HIV/AIDS prevention, training, and care. The ILO estimates that 25 million workers of prime working age are infected with HIV. Their belief is that employers have a social obligation and an economic self-interest in ridding the world's workforce of this and similar epidemics. At the same time, they seek to protect affected workers from unfair treatment by employers. Their stated policy is to "oppose discrimination and promote an environment of open and constructive discussion of HIV issues." To achieve their objectives, the ILO works cooperatively with employers to help them develop effective strategies for dealing with this monumental health crisis. For example, working with DaimlerChrysler, it showed that averting one new case of HIV infection saves the company the equivalent of three to four years' worth of an employee's annual salary. Data such as these prompted the company to offer free antiretroviral treatments to infected employees. In the future, it plans to extend its efforts to include community support.[35]

The World Health Organization also provides information on global occupational safety and health, and offers technical assistance to interested employers. The WHO's global strategy for workplace safety and health calls for it to:

1. Strengthen international and national policies,
2. Develop practices for improving health at work,
3. Promote health at work by providing technical assistance and support,
4. Develop human resources for the field of occupational health,
5. Establish relevant and useful registration and data systems,
6. Raise public awareness, and
7. Strengthen research on occupational health.

As this list of objectives reveals, the WHO is similar to the ILO in that it has no official regulatory power. It strives to improve workplace health around the world by educating employers and employees, developing knowledge about how to improve the health of workers, and establishing a shared view of the rights and responsibilities of employees and employers.

The federal government's primary response to the issue of safety and health in the workplace has been the **Occupational Safety and Health Act of 1970,** *which calls for safety and health inspections of organizations regardless of size, reporting by employers, and investigations of accidents and allegations of hazards.* The **Occupational Safety and Health Administration (OSHA)** *is the federal agency that's responsible for establishing and enforcing occupational safety and health standards and for inspecting and issuing citations to organizations that violate these standards.*

FAST FACT

OSHA's vision for 2003 through 2008 is: "Every employer and employee in the nation recognizes that occupational safety and health add value to American businesses, workplaces and workers' lives."

Two organizations that support the role of OSHA are the National Institute for Occupational Safety and Health (NIOSH) and the Occupational Safety and Health Review Commission (OSHRC). The **National Institute for Occupational Safety and Health (NIOSH)** *conducts research to reduce work-related illnesses and injuries and promotes safe and healthy workplaces by developing interventions and recommendations for employers.* The commission reviews appeals made by organizations that received citations from OSHA inspectors for alleged safety and health violations.[36]

Organizations are required to keep safety and health records so that OSHA can compile accurate statistics on work injuries and illnesses. These records should cover all disabling, serious, or significant injuries and illnesses, whether or not they involve loss of time from work. Excluded are minor injuries that require only first aid and don't involve medical treatment, loss of consciousness, restriction of work or motion, or transfer to another job. Falsification of records or failure to keep adequate records can result in substantial fines. However, the record-keeping requirements were revised effective 2002, changing some requirements (e.g., excluding organizations in low-hazard industries, such as education, from having to keep injury records).

FAST FACT

Since OSHA was established, an estimated 100,000 lives have been saved, and the workplace fatality rate has decreased 62%.

The employee's right to know about workplace hazards was strengthened by the Hazard Communication Standard, which went into effect in 1986. Under this standard, employers are required to provide workers with information and training on hazardous chemicals in their work area at the time of their initial assignment and whenever a new hazard is introduced. According to OSHA, effective communication is the real key and should include information for employees on:

- the standard's requirements and workplace operations that use hazardous chemicals,
- proper procedures for determining the presence of chemicals and detecting hazardous releases,
- protective measures and equipment that should be used,
- how to report accidents and near misses,
- the company's housekeeping and personal cleanup rules,
- the location of written hazard communication programs, and
- the location of emergency equipment, first-aid supplies, and designated smoking areas.[37]

Research on employees who work with hazardous waste materials suggests that training is most effective when employees develop a deep knowledge about safety issues and specific skills to address safety concerns. Training that merely provides a broad overview of the issues appears to be less effective in reducing unsafe behaviors.[38]

Whereas OSHA was established to provide protection against accidents and diseases for workers on the job, workers' compensation was established to provide financial aid for those unable to work because of accidents and diseases. For many years, workers' compensation awards were granted only to workers unable to work because of physical injury or damage. Since 1955, however, court decisions have either caused or enticed numerous states to allow workers' compensation awards in job-related cases of anxiety, depression, and mental disorders.

In 1955, the Texas Supreme Court charted this new direction in workers' compensation claims by stating that an employee who became terrified, highly anxious, and unable to work because of a job-related accident had a compensable claim even though he had no physical injury (*Bailey v. American General Insurance Company*, 1955). In another court ruling, *James v. State Accident Insurance Fund* (1980), an Oregon court ruled in favor of a worker's claim for compensation for inability to work due to job stress resulting from conflicting work assignments.

Determining responsibility is sometimes difficult because determining cause-and-effect relationships is difficult, especially since reactions such as asbestosis or hypertension take a long time to develop or occur only in some people working under the same conditions as others. Nevertheless, companies such as Steelcase, Dade Behring, and John Deere are very proactive in trying to make the workplace safer and help injured workers return to work as soon as possible.[39]

THE HR TRIAD

As is true of the critical HR policies and practices, promoting safety and health involves everyone in the organization. Even when they are not directly involved in the organization's operations themselves, managers play a key role by setting the tone and making safety and health a priority. As will become clear later in this chapter, HR professionals are responsible for monitoring and recording workplace incidents, as well as for developing HR practices that promote safety and health.

> **FAST FACT**
> Employers may be held liable for the violent action of an employee if they knew, or should have known, that the employee was at risk for committing violence.

Perhaps most importantly, employees must be actively committed to creating a safe and healthy workplace. Employees can spot problems and help to develop solutions. When solutions are found, employees often must be willing to adapt and change how they do their work. Unfortunately, some employees would rather suffer in silence than admit to experiencing physical symptoms. Another problem can be that employees may not recognize how their work habits affect their own health. Mike Rainville, owner of Maple Landmark Woodcraft in Vermont, was surprised when his wood workers resisted job changes designed to reduce repetitive motion injuries. Before the change, employees worked at the same tasks

> **FAST FACT**
> When Bottoms Up, a sportswear maker, replaced employee's stiff-back metal chairs with adjustable cushioned chairs, many workers refused to use the new chairs until they were forced to do so.

(e.g., hammering wheels onto a toy truck) all day, every day. An expert recommended changing the line so workers could rotate among tasks every hour, and buying new chairs that workers could more easily move around and adjust. At first, workers thought the changes would make their work more stressful. According to Rainville, "People just wanted to do one job every day and didn't want the stress of having to do something different." Eventually, with an education program that taught workers about ergonomics and constant preaching about the need for injury prevention, the workers accepted the change. For Rainville's small investment of about $7,000, he has reaped an annual return of about $8,000.[40] The roles and responsibilities of employees, HR professionals, and managers are summarized in "The HR Triad: Roles and Responsibilities in Promoting Workplace Safety and Health."

HAZARDS IN OCCUPATIONAL SAFETY AND HEALTH

As Exhibit 13.1 shows, workplace conditions and the strategies organizations use to manage safety and health have implications for both physiological-physical and psychological employee outcomes. Traditionally, physical hazards and disease have received the most attention. Increasingly, however,

The HR Triad

Roles and Responsibilities in Promoting Workplace Safety and Health

LINE MANAGERS	HR PROFESSIONALS	EMPLOYEES
• Recognize the strategic consequences of improved workplace safety and health.	• Educate managers to understand the long-term value of improved safety and health.	• Participate in the development and administration of safety and health programs (e.g., by serving on a Safety and Health Committee).
• Proactively promote workplace safety and health as core values of the organizational culture.	• Ensure that accidents and health-related incidents are accurately monitored, reported, and recorded.	• Perform in accordance with established safety and health guidelines.
• Encourage employees to report unsafe conditions and suggest how to improve workplace safety and health.	• Work with other professionals such as medical doctors and industrial engineers to develop new programs.	• Take an active role in promoting changes that will enhance workplace safety and health, including attending training programs.
• Avoid creating incentives for unsafe behaviors.	• Create HR programs that train employees for safe and healthy behaviors and reward them for their success.	• Promote work group norms that value safety and health.
• Help train employees in health and safety procedures.	• Develop selection programs that recognize individual characteristics for safety.	• Engage in safe and healthy behaviors.

employers and OSHA have come to recognize the importance of also attending to employees' psychological outcomes.[41]

OCCUPATIONAL ACCIDENTS

"At some of our plants, if there is one accident, everyone's bonus is cut by 25%; two accidents means a 50% cut; and three accidents means no bonus for anyone."

Dennis Bakke
Former CEO
AES Corporation

At AES, a global power company, top management is so concerned about safety that they hold everyone in the company accountable for reducing accidents. Under normal circumstances, the company may distribute as much as a 12% bonus for reaching safety-related goals. When the company experienced four fatalities worldwide, the bonus was reduced to 10%. By significantly penalizing poor safety performance, AES intends to motivate its employees to examine the causes of accidents and institute changes to prevent them in the future. At AES and elsewhere, the causes of organizational accidents are numerous, so eliminating them completely represents a major challenge.

Organizational Qualities. Accident rates vary substantially by industry. Firms in the construction and manufacturing industries have higher accident rates than do firms in services, finance, insurance, and real estate. But some high-risk firms are taking steps to beat the odds. Barden Bearings Corporation in Danbury, Connecticut, is one of them. Over the years, Barden employees assumed that because they work in a metal shop, people were going to get hurt. Then Barden created a Safety and Health Committee, which meets monthly to consider its safety and health performance. One of the major objectives is developing programs that strengthen safety awareness and performance. An example of one change made was to eliminate the safety engineering position and transfer its accountabilities to the Medical Department. The occupational health nurse in that department had shown considerable knowledge about safety matters, and she aggressively investigated accidents and near misses. The occupational health nurse was promoted to a new position entitled Manager of Employee Health and Safety.[42]

Small (those with fewer than 50 employees) and large organizations (those with more than 250 employees) have lower incidence rates than medium-sized organizations. This may be because supervisors in small organizations are better able to detect safety hazards and prevent accidents than those in medium-sized ones, while larger organizations have more resources to hire staff specialists who can devote all their efforts to safety and accident prevention.

Nationwide injury rates are higher for medium-sized companies employing 50 to 249 workers.

In general, the factors that most affect occupational accidents are: the working conditions and times (e.g., vehicle driving, desk work, shift work); the tools and technology available to do the job (e.g., heavy machinery, ladders, personal computers); and the availability of guns brought to work. Next in line are the workers themselves.

In 2001 more than 1,200 employees died from highway accidents and more than 600 employees died from falls.

The Unsafe Employee. Some experts point to the employee as the pivotal cause of accidents. Accidents depend on the behavior of the person, the degree of hazard in the work environment, and pure chance. The degree to which a person contributes to an accident can be an indication of the individual's proneness to accidents. No stable set of personal characteristics *always* contributes to accidents. Nevertheless, certain psychological and physical characteristics seem to make some people *more susceptible* to accidents. For example, employees who are emotionally "high" have fewer accidents than those who are emotionally "low," and employees who have fewer accidents are more optimistic, trusting, and concerned for others than those who have more accidents. Employees under greater stress are likely to have more accidents than those under less stress. Substance abusers also experience more job-related injuries, and this is true regardless of whether the substance abuse takes place at work or off the job. People who are quicker at recognizing visual patterns than at making muscular manipulations are less likely to have accidents than those who are just the opposite.

Older workers may be less likely to have accidents, but when they do they recover more slowly and are more likely to suffer fatalities.[43] As a consequence, the issue of older workers in the workplace is a significant one. This is described more in the feature "Managing Diversity: Safety Issues and the Aging Workforce."[44]

In addition to personal characteristics and age, many psychological conditions may be related to accident-proneness—for instance, hostility and emotional immaturity. Because these may be temporary, they are difficult to detect until at least one accident has occurred. Because these characteristics aren't related to accidents in all work environments and because they aren't

Managing Diversity

Safety Issues and the Aging Workforce

"I'm 51 years old, and I know for a fact that there's more risk for me to climb to the top of a rail car today than there was when I was younger and more agile," says Wayne Gordon, general manager of Farmers Cooperative Association in Jackson, Minnesota. Mr. Gordon indicates, however, that it's difficult to get other older workers to always agree with him: "Individuals have a tendency to think they can still do things they did 20 years ago." While he feels that it might be in the worker's interest to be prevented from performing a specific job, it might also violate age discrimination laws. The Age Discrimination in Employment Act of 1967 means that employers can't automatically exclude workers from jobs solely because of age. Older workers, in fact, are among the best performers many companies have.

Nevertheless, safety data give employers and society some concern. Federal studies show that older workers (above 54 years and particularly above 64 years of age) are 5.0 times more likely to die of a fatal transportation accident and 3.8 times as likely to be killed by objects and equipment than are younger workers. Significant medical differ-

ences also appear to exist between older and younger workers: As a group, older workers take nearly twice as long to mend and are more likely to die from injuries than younger workers; and the average-per-person cost of health claims per year for workers 65–69 years old is more than double that for workers 45–59 years old.

Especially given that the number of older workers is rising (3.0 to 3.8 million people became 65 each year during the past 10 years), the question remains, "What can be done about this?" Studies by the *American Journal of Industrial Medicine* suggest that only about 30% of those older workers injured in work accidents received safety training. Other studies suggest that relatively simple workplace modifications would be helpful, such as painting the steps of ladders with bright colors. Clearly, the answers aren't easily forthcoming. Older workers have better attendance and accident records, argues the American Association of Retired Persons (AARP), which encourages people to tread carefully in labeling older workers "those more likely to be more costly to employ."

always present in employees, selecting and screening job applicants on the basis of accident-proneness is difficult.[45]

VIOLENT EMPLOYEES

Each year, approximately 500 homicides occur in the workplace, accounting for about 10% of all workplace deaths.[46] About two-thirds of workplace homicides are committed during robberies (often in retail stores), but most others are committed by relatives, coworkers, or former coworkers.[47]

FAST FACT

Nationally, nearly 11% of all violent crimes are committed against people during work.

Homicide, as well as other less serious forms of violence, can be triggered by a number of forces, including being treated unfairly, an organizational culture that accepts aggressive behavior as normal, layoffs and downsizing, and even anger at being monitored too closely.[48] Although it may be difficult to identify the violent employee before the fact, employers are urged to be on the lookout for some common signs such as:

- *Verbal threats:* Individuals often talk about what they may do. An employee might say, "Bad things are going to happen to so-and-so," or "That propane tank in the back could blow up easily."
- *Physical actions:* Troubled employees may try to intimidate others, gain access to places they don't belong, or flash a concealed weapon in the workplace to test reactions.
- *Frustration:* Most cases of workplace violence don't involve a panicked individual who perceives the world as falling apart. A more

likely scenario involves an employee who has a frustrated sense of entitlement to a promotion, for example.

- *Obsession:* An employee may hold a grudge against a coworker or supervisor, which in some cases can stem from a romantic interest.

These may be early warning signals for acts of violence, including assault against coworkers and property damage. Like other forms of unacceptable performance on the job, the options for how to deal with violent employees include employee assistance programs, training in conflict management, and termination.[49]

For a period of several years during the 1980s and 1990s, the United States Postal Service (USPS) had "a culture that accepted a certain level of violence," according to Carl Augustinho. When employees fought with each other, they would simply be told to "shut up" and go back to work. After a dozen incidents in which coworkers were murdered, USPS decided it needed to do something to change its culture. Now supervisors are trained to handle violent situations. Employees who engage in violent behavior are immediately taken off the job while an investigation is conducted. Perhaps more importantly, USPS began efforts to ensure that supervisors treat their employees with respect. They learned the importance of providing for due process and taking employees' complaints seriously. HR professionals also improved the hiring procedures. Now applicants are interviewed more intensively to detect possible sources of problems, and background checks are more rigorous.[50]

> *"Nobody snaps. Violence is evolutionary; it builds up over time."*
>
> Eugene A. Rugala
> Federal Bureau of Investigation

OCCUPATIONAL DISEASES

Potential sources of work-related diseases are as distressingly varied as the symptoms of those diseases. Several federal agencies have systematically studied the workplace environment, and they have identified the following disease-causing hazards: arsenic, asbestos, benzene, bichloromethylether, coal dust, coke-oven emissions, cotton dust, lead, radiation, and vinyl chloride. Workers likely to be exposed to those hazards include chemical and oil refinery workers, miners, textile workers, steelworkers, lead smelters, medical technicians, painters, shoemakers, and plastics industry workers. Continued research will no doubt uncover additional hazards that firms will want to diagnose and remedy for the future well-being of their workforces.[51]

In the long term, environmental hazards in the workplace have been linked to occupational diseases such as thyroid, liver, lung, brain, and kidney cancer; white, brown, and black lung disease; leukemia; bronchitis; emphysema; lymphoma; aplastic anemia; central nervous system damage; and reproductive disorders (e.g., sterility, genetic damage, miscarriages, and birth defects). Chronic bronchitis and emphysema are among the fastest-growing diseases in the United States, doubling every five years since World War II; they account for the second highest number of disabilities under Social Security. Cancer tends to receive the most attention, however, since it's a leading cause of death in the United States (second after heart disease). Many of the known causes of cancer are physical and chemical agents in the environment. And because these agents are theoretically more controllable than human behavior, OSHA's emphasis is often on eliminating them from the workplace.[52]

OSHA is also concerned with the many categories of occupational diseases and illnesses including: occupation-related skin diseases and disorders, dust diseases of the lungs, respiratory conditions due to toxic agents, poisoning (the systematic effect of toxic materials), disorders due to physical agents, disorders associated with repeated trauma, and all other occupational illnesses. OSHA, therefore, requires employers to keep records on all these diseases.

Poorly Designed Jobs

For many workers, poorly designed jobs are a source of both psychological and physical stress. Job design quality, work pacing, and shift work are especially relevant to workplace safety and health.

Job Design Quality. Job characteristics theory is the most popular and extensively tested approach to designing jobs that employees enjoy and feel motivated to perform well. **Job characteristics theory** *states that employees are more satisfied and motivated when their jobs are meaningful, when jobs create a feeling of responsibility, and when jobs are designed to ensure that some feedback is available.* In essence, jobs should be designed to provide work that employees enjoy doing. People who enjoy doing their jobs may not need the extra motivation of high pay and impressive job titles. In fact, according to a recent survey of 1,200 U.S. employees, the nature of the work they did was the most important factor (ahead of direct and indirect financial rewards and career concerns) in determining how people felt about staying with their current employer and how motivated they were to work hard.[53]

FAST FACT

Combined workweek hours for dual-earning couples with children rose from 81 hours in 1977 to 91 hours in 2002.

When jobs are poorly designed, workers feel little sense of responsibility and self-worth; they experience little job involvement and are seldom challenged; their work often feels meaningless and their good deeds seem to go unnoticed. All of the conditions contribute to poor psychological health, and some also have been shown to increase accidents and injuries. For example, a large study of Australian workplaces found that workplace injuries were more likely to occur in organizations where employees received little training, worked at jobs that were highly repetitive, and had little autonomy over their work. Lower injury rates were found in organizations that offered more training and designed jobs to include both more variety and more employee control.[54] Other studies show that job design quality affects health outcomes such as cardiovascular disease and musculoskeletal problems.[55]

Work Pacing and Control. Work pacing, the speed at which work proceeds, may be controlled by machines or people. Machine pacing gives control over the speed of the operation and of the work output to something other than the individual. Employee pacing gives that control to the individual. The effects of machine pacing are severe, because the individual is unable to satisfy a crucial need for control of the situation. Employees who work at machine-paced jobs often feel exhausted at the end of their shifts and are unable to relax soon after work because of increased adrenaline secretion on the job. Giving more control over the pace of work reduces stress symptoms.[56]

Control over work also appears to be important in other types of jobs. Assembly-line workers are not the only ones who sometimes feel unable to control their work or their work life. In fact, some workers in almost all occupations report feeling that they have less control over their work environment than they would like. Workers with relatively low control are at greater risk of developing cardiovascular disease and gastrointestinal disorders. Thus, workplace practices that provide opportunities for employees to offer their input and participate in organizational decisions appear to also contribute to the development of a healthy workplace.[57]

Shift Work. During the past two decades, the demand for 24-hour consumer services, just-in-time delivery practices in manufacturing, and the globalization of business have all contributed to an increasing prevalence of shift work. **Shift work** *refers to any arrangements for daily work hours that differ significantly from the standard daylight hours.* Nonstandard shifts can be fixed or rotating, and of various lengths (e.g., 8, 10, or 12 hours), but usually they involve at least some night work. Shift workers often experience sleep disruptions, and they face extra challenges in meeting the normal demands of family life and pursuing personal leisure time. Many new shift workers find these disruptions so difficult that they quit soon after they are hired, but others may spend years working on nonstandard shifts—in part because shift workers typically receive higher pay than their daytime colleagues. In exchange for their higher pay, however, shift workers often accept higher rates of recurring gastrointestinal symptoms, such as constipation, gas, and appetite disturbances. Perhaps more frightening is research showing that shift workers have a 40% greater risk for cardiovascular disease. Accidents and injuries also are more common during shift work hours.[58]

Although shift work may be unavoidable, many studies have investigated the issue of how to design shift work to minimize its negative effects on employees. In general, this research shows that one of the most common shift arrangements—the weekly rotating shift, in which shift workers change their schedule every week—is one of the worst schedules. Research also shows that very few employees ever fully adapt to working the night shift, even when this is a permanent arrangement. The best shift arrangement appears to be a forward-rotating shift. With this schedule, an employee rotates from the day shift to the evening shift to the night shift. Furthermore, it appears that 12-hour shift systems (i.e., a compressed workweek) have fewer negative health consequences than traditional 8-hour shifts. Research findings such as these serve as the foundation for the ILO's standards for night work and for some of the laws that protect night workers in several European countries. In the United States, shift workers are not protected by special laws or regulations.[59]

Organizational Stressors

Poor-quality job designs often cause employees to feel disengaged from work and dissatisfied. Organizational stressors often result in employees becoming overly engaged and overly involved in work. In extreme cases, the result may be feelings of exhaustion and burnout. Organizational stressors that put employees at risk for severe strain include organizational change, the physical environment, and stress-prone employees.[60]

Organizational Change. Changes made by organizations usually involve something important and are accompanied by uncertainty (e.g., the devel-

"Being tired makes everything that much more stressful, but it's like having a baby. You get used to it. The kids sometimes ask, 'What's the deal with dad? Does he still live here?' It's kind of sad."

Codey Mooneyhan
Shift Worker
Germantown, Maryland

opment of new HR policies that are aligned with new strategic business objectives). Often when changes are made, there is too little communication about the need for change and the nature of changes to come. Rumors may circulate that a change is coming, but the exact nature of the change is left to speculation. People become concerned about whether the change will affect them—perhaps by displacing them, changing their job duties and pay level, or by causing them to be transferred. And they wonder how those remaining will do all the work! The result is that many employees suffer stress symptoms such as anxiety and depression at work as well as at home. To cope, employees who experience these symptoms are likely to be absent more frequently and for more total days.[61]

> **FAST FACT**
>
> According to NIOSH, health care expenditures are nearly 50% greater for workers who report high levels of stress.

Physical Environment. Although office technologies can improve productivity, they may also have stress-related drawbacks, as we have already noted. In addition to contributing to disease and injuries, exposure to hazardous chemicals and dangerous tools and machinery can cause employees to feel anxious or tense. Other aspects of the physical work environment associated with stress are crowding, noise, lack of privacy, and lack of control—for example, the inability to move a desk or chairs or even to hang pictures in a work area in an effort to personalize it.[62] Poor indoor air quality is another aspect of the work environment that employees report being a source of stress. According to one survey, about out of three managers believes that poor air quality is a significant cause of both illness among employees and lost productivity.[63]

> **FAST FACT**
>
> Working in hot environments promotes accidents because of sweaty palms, dizziness, and fogging of safety glasses.

Stress-Prone Employees. People differ in the ways they respond to organizational stressors. A classic difference is referred to as Type A versus Type B behavior. Type A people like to do things their way and are willing to exert a lot of effort to ensure that even trivial tasks are performed in the manner they prefer. They often fail to distinguish between important and unimportant situations. They are upset, for instance, when they have to wait 15 minutes to be seated in a restaurant, since this isn't in compliance with their idea of responsive service. In short, Type A people spend much of their time directing energy toward noncompliances in the environment. By comparison, Type B people are generally much more patient and accepting of current conditions. They aren't easily frustrated or easily angered, nor do they expend a lot of energy in response to noncompliance. Although Type A people are often "movers and shakers," some of their behaviors have the disadvantage of inducing stress, in themselves and others.[64]

JOB BURNOUT

Job burnout *is a particular type of stress that seems to be experienced by people who work in jobs in health care, education, police work, customer response centers, and in the airline industry.* This type of reaction to one's work includes attitudinal and emotional reactions that a person goes through as a result of job-related experiences.[65]

Emotional Exhaustion. Often the first sign of burnout is a feeling of being emotionally exhausted by one's work. Emotionally exhausted employees might express feelings of being drained, used-up, at the end of their rope, or physically fatigued. Waking up in the morning may be accompanied by a feeling of dread at the thought of having to put in another day on the job. For someone who was once enthusiastic about the job and idealistic about what could be accomplished, feelings of emotional exhaustion may come somewhat unexpectedly, though to an outsider looking at the situation, emotional exhaustion would be seen as a natural response to an extended period of intense interaction with people and their problems. Extreme emotional exhaustion can be very debilitating both on and off the job, so people who are experiencing it must find some way to cope. Even mild feelings of emotional exhaustion can affect how employees perform on the job, however. In a study of call center employees, for example, even the most conscientious workers completed fewer calls if they were emotionally exhausted.[66]

Depersonalization. One common coping reaction is to put psychological distance between one's self and one's clients and to decrease one's personal involvement with them. In moderation, this reaction may be an effective method for creating "detached concern," but when engaged in to excess, the employee may begin to dehumanize or depersonalize the clients. People who have reached the extreme end of the depersonalization continuum report feeling they have become callused by their jobs and that they have grown cynical about their *clients*.

Personal Accomplishment. In addition to emotional exhaustion and depersonalization, a third aspect of burnout is a feeling of low personal accomplishment. Many human service professionals begin their careers with great expectations that they will be able to improve the human condition through their work. After a year or two on the job, they begin to realize they aren't living up to these expectations. There are many systemic reasons for the gap that exists between the novice's goals and the veteran's accomplishments, including unrealistically high expectations due to a lack of exposure to the job during training, constraints placed on the worker through the rules and regulations of an immutable bureaucracy, inadequate resources for performing one's job, clients who are frequently uncooperative and occasionally rebellious, and a lack of feedback about one's successes. These and other characteristics of human service organizations almost guarantee that employees will be frustrated in their attempts to reach their goals, yet the workers may not recognize the role of the system in producing this frustration. Instead, workers may feel personally responsible and begin to think of themselves as failures. When combined with emotional exhaustion, feelings of low personal accomplishment may reduce motivation to a point where performance is in fact impaired, leading to further experienced failure.

Performance Deteriorates. Burned-out employees may perform more poorly on the job compared to their counterparts who are still "fired up." Consider as an example the job of an intake interviewer in a legal aid office. For the organization, the intake interview serves as a screening device through which all potential clients must pass. During the interview, specific information about the nature and details of a case must be assessed and an evaluation of the "appropriateness" of the case for the office must be made. Since as many as 40 intake interviews may be conducted per day, it's important that the interviewer work as efficiently as possible. Here the major index of efficiency is the number of forms accurately filled out for further processing. To the extent time is spent talking about problems not relevant for these forms, efficiency decreases.

Now consider the client's perspective. Upon arriving for an interview, the client is likely to be rehearsing the injustices done and planning for retaliation. The client does not consider the precise statutes encompassing the problem nor the essential details that make the case worthy of attention. Rather, the client is concerned with the problems faced as a result of the perceived injustices. The client's primary concern is to return emotional and physical life to normal—the law seems to offer a solution. The intake interview may be clients' first chance to explain the problems they are facing. From this perspective, an interviewer who lends a sympathetic ear displays good job performance.

How will the interviewer handle this situation? Typically, the person doing the interview will be a relatively recent graduate of law school with little or no clinical experience to rely on. Socialization has emphasized the supremacy of objectivity. But clearly, adoption of an objective, analytic attitude combined with the pressure to efficiently fill out forms does not add up to the sympathetic ear the client is looking for. The objective interviewer appears unconcerned and the client becomes frustrated. The emotionally involved client becomes an obstacle to detached efficiency, frustrating the interviewer. Whether or not open hostility erupts, both participants are aware of the antagonistic relationship they have formed.

Coworker Relations Deteriorate. Another unfortunate consequence of burnout is a deterioration of one's relationships with coworkers. A study of mental health workers found that people who were experiencing calloused feelings toward their clients also complained more about their clients to their coworkers, thereby generating a negative atmosphere within the work unit. These burned-out mental health workers were also absent from work more often and took more frequent work breaks. Thus, burnout can have a contagious effect, spreading throughout the organization.[67]

STRATEGIES FOR IMPROVING WORKPLACE SAFETY AND HEALTH

Once workplace hazards are identified, strategies can be developed for eliminating or reducing them. To determine whether a strategy is effective, organizations can compare the incidence, severity, and frequency of illnesses and accidents before and after the intervention. OSHA has approved methods for establishing these rates.

MONITORING SAFETY AND HEALTH RATES

OSHA requires organizations to maintain records of their injuries and illnesses. Organizations can record these by their incidence, severity, or frequency. Such records provide a basis for determining long-terms trends, including improvement in or deterioration of employee health and safety records.

Incidence Rate. The **incidence rate** *is a measure that takes into account the number of injuries and illnesses in a year.* It's calculated by the following formula:

Incidence Rate = *(Number of Injuries and Illnesses × 200,000) / Number of Employee Hours Worked*

The base for 100 full-time workers is 200,000 (40 hours a week times 50 weeks). Suppose an organization had 10 recorded injuries and illnesses and 500 employees. To calculate the number of employee hours worked, multiply the number of employees by 40 hours and by 50 weeks: $500 \times 40 \times 50 = 1,000,000$. Thus, the incidence rate is 2 for every 100 workers a year: $(10 \times 200,000) / 1,000,000 = 2$.

Frequency Rate. The **frequency rate** *is a measure of the number of injuries and illnesses for every million hours worked.* It's calculated as:

Frequency Rate = *(Number of Injuries and Illnesses × 1,000,000 hours) / Number of Employee Hours Worked*

Severity Rate. The **severity rate** *reflects the hours actually lost owing to injury or illness.* It recognizes that not all injuries and illnesses are equal. Four categories of injuries and illnesses have been established: deaths, permanent total disabilities, permanent partial disabilities, and temporary total disabilities. An organization with the same number of injuries and illnesses as another but with more deaths would have a higher severity rate. The severity rate is calculated by this formula:

Severity Rate = *(Total Hours Charged × 1,000,000 Hours) / Number of Employee Hours Worked*

ACCIDENT PREVENTION

Designing the work environment to make accidents unlikely is perhaps the best way to prevent accidents and increase safety. Among the safety features that can be designed into the physical environment are guards on machines, handrails in stairways, safety goggles and helmets, warning lights, self-correcting mechanisms, and automatic shutoffs. The extent to which these features will actually reduce accidents depends on employee acceptance, company policies, and company culture (e.g., that of Alcoa). For example, eye injuries will be reduced by the availability of safety goggles only if employees wear the goggles correctly.[68] This is more likely when employees accept the responsibility for safety, as is the trend in some firms. Alcoa employees understand that they bear responsibility for their safety. This responsibility has grown as the company has reduced its organizational levels, which means less supervision and a more participatory approach to management. With self-management and teamwork comes the burden on individuals to assume more responsibility. Teams are expected to work toward common objectives, and these objectives should include excellent safety performance.[69]

FAST FACT

By creating a culture of safety at Alcoa, CEO Paul O'Neill reduced the company's rate of lost time because of injuries from one-third the U.S. average to one-twentieth.

Ergonomics. One way to improve safety is to make the job itself more comfortable and less fatiguing, through ergonomics. **Ergonomics** *considers changes in the job environment in conjunction with the physical and physiological capabilities and limitations of the employees.*[70]

Possible ergonomic changes that companies can provide to employees for improving the health and comfort of their workplace include having employees:

1. Vary their tasks during the day, particularly the motions used to accomplish them
2. Take small, 10- to 30-second breaks every 30 minutes
3. Take longer breaks from the video display terminal (VDT) every 2 hours
4. Employ discretion in how they work—their posture, schedule, pace, work processes
5. Minimize the absolute number of key strokes whenever possible
6. Have opportunities to learn about their job performance, what they contribute to projects, their value
7. Become educated on the value of ergonomics
8. Reduce sources of environmental stress, such as heat, glare, noise
9. Discover the features and functions of their workspace that enable them to adjust their environment for safety and comfort[71]

In an effort to reduce the number of back injuries, the Ford Motor Company redesigned workstations and tasks that caused musculoskeletal problems for workers. For instance, lifting devices were introduced on the assembly line to reduce back strain, and walking and working surfaces were studied to determine how floor mats could be used to reduce body fatigue.[72]

Recently, OSHA has targeted injury-prone industries and offered to collaborate with them to develop voluntary guidelines to reduce specific types of injuries. With this new initiative, OSHA develops a set of guidelines and then asks for input from various experts, including physicians, industry representatives, and HR managers. The final guidelines are then made available to employers, who are encouraged to voluntarily adopt them as guides to improving workplace safety and health. The first industry to participate in this new program was the nursing home industry. Other industries that OSHA plans to work with include retail grocery, poultry processing, and shipyards.[73]

Health and Safety Committees. An estimated 75% of companies with 50 or more employees use health and safety committees to involve employees in improving workplace conditions, like Steelcase does. At least 16 states require certain businesses to establish permanent safety and health committees, but many businesses voluntarily establish safety committees in states where they are not required. Health and safety committees typically take responsibility for identifying issues that need to be addressed in the workplace and developing recommendations for how to make improvements. Often, organizations have several safety committees at the department level, for implementation and administration, and one larger committee at the organization level, for policy formulation. HR professionals often serve as coordinators for such committees, which typically include several employee representatives and several managers. In unionized settings, the committee should include union representatives as well. The available evidence indicates that such committees can be effective in reducing the frequency and severity of workplace injuries.[74]

Behavior Modification. Employers have known for a long time that a small percentage of their workforce is responsible for the majority of their health insurance claims. Originally, they tried to encourage their employees to be healthy by offering to subsidize health club memberships and building exercise facilities and jogging trails, but the results were disappointing. Now, many companies are implementing incentive-based health care programs.

Reinforcing behaviors through incentive systems that reduce the likelihood of accidents can be highly successful. Reinforcers can range from nonmonetary rewards (e.g., positive feedback) to activity rewards (e.g., time off) to material rewards (e.g., company-purchased doughnuts during a coffee break) to financial rewards (e.g., bonuses for attaining desired levels of safety). Caution, however, has to be exercised in the design of incentive systems.

One concern of OSHA is that poorly designed incentives can cause employees to hide injuries. Safety programs often include goals for reducing accidents and injuries, with rewards linked to goal achievement. When employees are injured, they may find themselves weighing the costs of reporting the injury and getting it treated quickly against the cost to themselves and their coworkers of not achieving their safety goals.

Jenny-O Foods Turkey Store shares OSHA's concerns. Jenny-O avoids that problem by setting goals and linking rewards to safety knowledge and behavior, not to reductions in injuries and accidents. Safety audits are used to check on dozens of workplace conditions that might cause accidents. Employees are randomly interviewed to check their knowledge of safety guidelines. Small rewards are given to employees who score well on these quizzes.

Assessing Intervention Effectiveness. Regardless of the specific interventions an organization chooses, the effectiveness of the interventions should be monitored.[75] When Maurice Myers became CEO of Waste Management, he soon realized the importance of measurement and training to improve safety. Early on, it became clear to Myers that Waste Management had problems. The company had never fully integrated the thousands of small-scale garbage operations it had acquired during the 1980s and 1990s into its system. Not only did Waste Management not know how many landfills it owned, it also didn't keep safety records. As a result, insurance costs and workers' compensation costs were high.

Waste Management had been claiming for years that it was the best in the industry and that it completely satisfied its customers, but Myers discovered this was just wishful thinking. Myers introduced rigorous measures to track all aspects of the company's performance—how long it took to answer a customer's call, how many customers reported billing problems, how many garbage pickups the company missed, and how many accidents company workers had. Executives were stunned by what they discovered. For instance, 68% of the company's accidents were being caused by 12% of its drivers. Those drivers had typically worked at Waste Management for less than a year and usually were repeat offenders. The answers were simple:

The company increased training and dismissed bad drivers. As a result, the driver accident rate fell 48%.[76]

Disease Prevention

Occupational diseases can be far more costly and harmful overall to organizations and employees than occupational accidents. Because the causal relationship between the physical environment and occupational diseases is often subtle, developing strategies to reduce their incidence is generally difficult.

OSHA requires organizations to:
- allow inspections
- keep records
- disclose medical records

FAST FACT

Record Keeping. At a minimum, OSHA requires that organizations measure the chemicals in the work environment and keep records on these measurements. The records must include precise information about ailments and exposures. Such information must be kept for as long as the incubation period of the specific disease—even as long as 40 years. If the organization is sold, the new owner must assume responsibility for storing the old records and continuing to gather the required data. If the company goes out of business, the administrative director of OSHA must be told where the records are. Guidelines for record keeping are given in Exhibit 13.4.

Monitoring Exposure. The obvious approach to controlling occupational illnesses is to rid the workplace of chemical agents or toxins; an alternative approach is to monitor and limit exposure to hazardous substances. Some organizations now monitor genetic changes due to exposure to carcinogens (e.g., arsenic, benzene, ether, and vinyl chloride). Samples of blood are obtained from employees at fixed intervals to determine whether the employees' chromosomes have been damaged. If damage has occurred, the affected employees are placed in different jobs, and, where feasible, conditions are modified.

Genetic Screening. Genetic screening is the most extreme, and consequently the most controversial, approach to controlling occupational disease. By using genetic testing to screen out individuals who are susceptible to certain ailments, organizations lower their vulnerability to workers' compensation claims and problems. As discussed in Chapters 3 and 7, opponents of genetic screening and many state laws contend that it measures predisposition to disease, not the actual presence of disease, and therefore violates an individual's rights.[77]

Stress Management

Increasingly, organizations are offering programs designed to help employees deal with work-related stress. For example, companies such as JPMorganChase offer stress management programs as part of a larger supervisory and management development curriculum. Available to supervisors, professional staff, and officers, these courses are designed to introduce supervisory and management material, information skills, and role definition. The emphasis is on providing concrete information to reduce the ambi-

Ex 13.4   OSHA Guidelines for Recording Cases

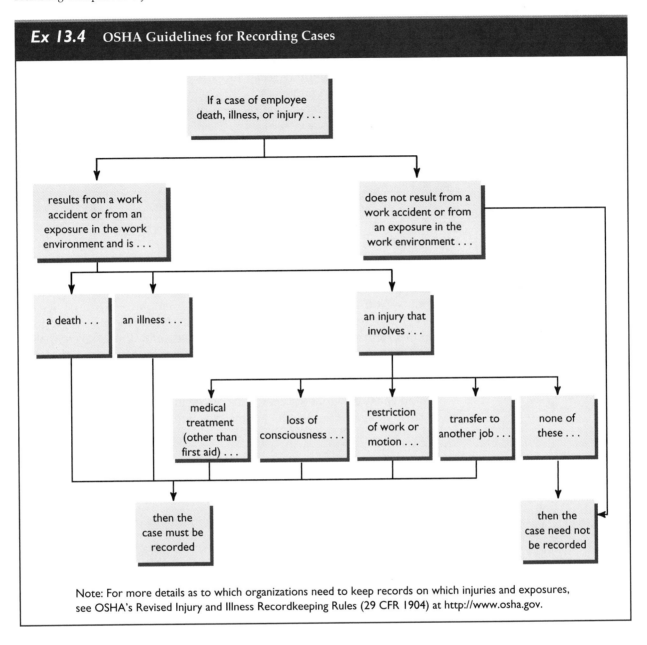

If a case of employee death, illness, or injury . . .

→ results from a work accident or from an exposure in the work environment and is . . .

→ does not result from a work accident or from an exposure in the work environment . . .

a death . . .

an illness . . .

an injury that involves . . .

medical treatment (other than first aid) . . .

loss of consciousness . . .

restriction of work or motion . . .

transfer to another job . . .

none of these . . .

then the case must be recorded

then the case need not be recorded

Note: For more details as to which organizations need to keep records on which injuries and exposures, see OSHA's Revised Injury and Illness Recordkeeping Rules (29 CFR 1904) at http://www.osha.gov.

guity associated with fast-paced, changing work roles. The hope is that these programs will reduce the stress experienced by employees.[78]

Besides attempting to reduce the sources of stress at work, many employers provide training and other programs intended to help employees cope more effectively with stress. Such programs recognize that workplace stressors will never be completely eliminated. By helping employees cope more effectively with stress, employers can reduce the negative health consequences of long-term exposure to it.

Developing time management skills is one effective strategy for employees to use in coping with organizational stress. It's based in large part on an

FAST FACT

St. Luke's Episcopal Hospital in Houston has seminars on topics from career management to dealing with stress. Despite a nurse shortage, St. Luke's staffed a new facility entirely from employee referrals.

initial identification of an individual's personal goals. Other strategies that should be part of an individual's stress management include following a good diet, getting regular exercise, getting a good night's sleep, monitoring physical health, and building social support groups.[79]

Besides educating employees in the benefits of such strategies, some employers make it easy for employees to follow these prescriptions by designing the workplace accordingly. For example, Coors encourages employees to enroll in regular exercise programs, where their fitness and health are carefully monitored. In addition, some employers offer training in muscle relaxation techniques, meditation, self-hypnosis, and imagery.[80] Finally, encouraging employees to use, not bank, their vacation time and regular days off is another effective strategy for managing stress and burnout.[81]

WELLNESS PROGRAMS

Corporations are increasingly focusing on keeping employees healthy and well. As Exhibit 13.5 shows, unhealthy workers increase employers' costs in several ways. By improving the health of their employees, companies can reduce these costs and increase their profitability. Often, the costs of wellness programs are small relative to the costs of disease and illness, so companies are investing in wellness programs at record rates. These investments appear to be paying off in terms of morale, performance, absentee rates, and health care costs.

Union Pacific Railroad estimates that its wellness program has saved the company about $53 million during the past decade. A key element of their program is a free and voluntary health-risk assessment. About two-thirds of the company's 47,000 employees have gone through this assessment, and up to half of those who were assessed subsequently enrolled in preventive health education and disease management programs. Union Pacific credits the program with reducing smoking, alcohol abuse, high blood pressure, and high cholesterol among employees.[82] These improvements reflect

Ex 13.5   How Unhealthy Employees Increase Costs

Costs for Individuals

- Lower productivity while at work due to illness
- Medical care
- Benefits payments
- Recruitment and training of replacement workers

Organizational Costs

- Production disruptions due to absence and turnover
- Increased insurance rates
- Increased accidents due to inexperienced replacement workers
- End-of-service costs associated with an employee's death, such as funeral expenses and depressed morale

behavioral changes employees have made in their eating, drinking, smoking, and exercise habits. That is, the benefits have accrued mostly because employees have changed their personal lifestyles outside of work—not because the company made changes in the work environment itself.

Weight Loss. In many companies today, weight-loss activities are an essential component of their wellness programs. Obesity costs U.S. companies nearly $13 billion annually, according to recent estimates. Health care costs for obese employees are about one-third higher than for normal-weight employees, and medication costs (often covered by prescription drug benefits) are 77% higher. Furthermore, obese workers are twice as likely to be absent more than 14 days per year.[83]

> **FAST FACT**
>
> At the new headquarters for Capital One outside Richmond, Virginia, the architects set the food court at the end of a string of buildings, rather than at the center of the complex.

At Union Pacific, 54% of the 48,000 employees are overweight. Looking at injury claims and illness records, the company estimated that reducing that percentage by one point would save $1.7 million; 5 points, $8.5 million; and 10 points, $16.9 million. As a consequence, Union Pacific Railroad has begun offering some employees the latest prescription weight-loss drugs as part of a study to determine how best to get its workers to slim down.[84] As employers become more sophisticated in their understanding of the bottom-line benefits of a healthy workforce, programs designed to actually improve employee health—not just prevent accidents and injuries—are likely to become more widespread.[85]

Smoking Cessation. Each year, an estimated 430,000 American adults die from smoking-related diseases, making smoking the largest preventable cause of premature mortality. For employers, the costs of smoking include lost productivity due to absenteeism and time spent on smoking breaks, increased health care costs and insurance premiums, and increased accidents and injuries. To reduce these costs, U.S. employers have adopted policies aimed at reducing smoking among employees. Banning smoking in the workplace and supporting employees in their efforts to quick smoking appear to be effective strategies. Research shows that banning smoking from the workplace is twice as effective in reducing tobacco consumption as permitting smoking in designated areas. Research also indicates that smokers are more likely to participate in smoking cessation programs when they receive financial incentives to do so. Thus, it appears that the workplace offers an important opportunity for improving the health of workers who wish to stop smoking but find it difficult to do so.[86]

HIV/AIDS. In sub-Saharan Africa, HIV/AIDS affects as many as one in four employees. Employers with operations in sub-Saharan Africa are finding that the costs of the HIV/AIDS epidemic are so great that it erodes the low cost advantage of operating there. AIDS drives up health care costs and reduces the productivity of affected employees for years during the prime of their productive work life. Increased absenteeism makes it more difficult to run operations efficiently, and higher turnover rates mean companies must invest more in training new workers. The devastating effects that this disease can have on the workforce also have implications for the consumer markets that they are part of. Money that might otherwise be spent on a variety of goods and services is spent caring for victims of the disease, slowing down national economic growth.

To cope with the HIV/AIDS epidemic, many companies are investing in AIDS prevention and treatment. Experts suggest that effective prevention programs have four components: (1) educating employees, their families, and the surrounding community about how to avoid HIV infection; (2) free and voluntary testing and counseling; (3) treatment for other sexually transmitted diseases that facilitate HIV transmission; and (4) distribution of free condoms. Such programs cost relatively little and appear to be quite effective in reducing infection rates. Treatment for HIV/AIDS generally involves providing daily supplies of required drugs and close monitoring by a medical professional. Some companies simply pay for these services through medical insurance benefits, while others contract with stand-alone providers of AIDS management programs. Employees who work for some of the largest mining and agricultural companies receive treatment at company-run clinics.[87]

To date, corporate investment in HIV/AIDS prevention and treatment is focused in Africa. But experts warn that this disease is spreading rapidly in China, India, Russia, and the Ukraine. Thus, companies with operations in any of these areas should be considering how this disease affects them and the role they should play in reducing their employees' risk.

SUMMARY

As the manufacturing sector of the U.S. economy shrinks and the services sector grows, the incidence of many accidents and injuries has declined. Nevertheless, employers are keenly aware of the cost of ill health and the benefits of having a healthy workforce. By improving workplace safety and health, they can reduce costs and improve productivity while also meeting the needs of their employees and fulfilling their obligations to the broader community. The federal government, through OSHA, monitors the performance of employers to protect workers from unnecessary harm and provides assistance to employers seeking to improve their work environments. The government's concern is primarily with occupational accidents and diseases, both aspects of the physical environment. However, organizations can choose to become involved in programs dealing with the psychological environment as well.

Safety and health committees provide a forum for employees to inform employers about unsafe and unhealthy conditions and make recommendations for improvement. Employers can also use their safety and health records to track changes in safety and health outcomes. Records on the rate and severity of accidents and injuries can alert employers to new dangers as they arise. These records also can provide data that can be used to determine whether interventions are having their desired effects.

Many types of interventions can be used to improve workplace safety and health. Among the most common are programs designed to reduce accidents and injuries, reduce disease, improve employees' ability to manage stress, and improve employees' overall health. While some of these interventions are intended to make the workplace safer and healthier, others are intended to change the lifestyles and nonwork behaviors of employees. All these interventions can reduce the many costs associated with employee injuries, illness, and death.

TERMS TO REMEMBER

Ergonomics
Frequency rate
Incidence rate
Job burnout
Job characteristics theory
National Institute for Occupational
  Safety and Health (NIOSH)
Occupational Safety and Health Act
  of 1970

Occupational Safety and Health
  Administration (OSHA)
Physiological-physical conditions
Psychological conditions
Severity rate
Shift work
Workplace safety and health

DISCUSSION QUESTIONS

1. Describe the legal responsibility of employers for providing safe workplaces. Do you think employers should invest more than is legally required in workplace safety and health? Why or why not?

2. Describe the responsibilities that employees have for improving workplace safety and health.

3. Explain how each of the following HR practices can be used to maintain safe and healthy workplaces: job analysis, selection, training, performance measurement and feedback, incentives.

4. Wellness prevention programs often target illnesses and diseases that are not caused by aspects of the workplace itself. Do you think it is appropriate for employers to intervene to improve their employees' personal health and wellness? Explain.

PROJECTS TO EXTEND YOUR LEARNING

1. *Integration and Application.* After reviewing the Lincoln Electric and Southwest Airlines cases at the end of the text, compare and contrast the threats to health and safety at these two companies. Choose one company and describe the safety and health programs that you believe should be in place. Be specific about the objectives of the programs, and make sure you state who should be responsible for them.

2. *Exploring the Internet.*

   a. Find out about safety and health statistics at the ILO (http://www.ilo.org); the Bureau of Labor Statistics (http://www.bls.gov); and OSHA (http://www.osha.gov).

   b. Learn about activities to promote safety and health at some of the firms discussed in this section by visiting their company home pages:
   John Deere, http://www.deere.com
   Steelcase, http://www.steelcase.com
   Union Pacific Railroad, http://www.unionpacific.com

   c. Learn more about OSHA's record-keeping requirements at http://www.osha.gov.

    d.   Investigate the safety issues that are most relevant to various industries on the National Safety Council website at http://www.nsc.org.

3.   *Experiential Activity.* To learn more about carpal tunnel syndrome, locate a worksite where employees seem to be at risk for this injury. Conduct interviews with three people: (1) a person who has suffered from carpal tunnel syndrome, (2) a coworker of someone who has suffered from carpal tunnel syndrome, and (3) a manager or supervisor of someone who has suffered from carpal tunnel syndrome. Based on your interviews and what you have learned in this chapter, write a memo that makes three recommendations for reducing the effects of carpal tunnel syndrome in the workplace you visited. Use the following questions to guide your interview.

For the person with carpal tunnel syndrome:
   a.   What symptoms did you experience?
   b.   For how long did you experience these symptoms before seeking medical advice?
   c.   How did the symptoms affect your productivity at work (e.g., making mistakes due to pain, working more slowly, taking days off to rest or get medical treatment)?
   d.   How did your symptoms affect your life outside of work?
   e.   Did you have surgery? If so, how many days were you absent while you recovered?
   f.   What did your employer do to reduce the risk of you experiencing these problems again in the future (e.g., new equipment, reassigned to different job duties, education or training)?
   g.   Do you feel any different about your employer as a result of how the organization responded to your problems? Explain.

For the coworker:
   a.   Did your coworker's experience with carpal tunnel syndrome have any consequences for you (e.g., disrupting your own work, creating more work for you, or causing you to worry about your own health)? If yes, for how long did you experience these consequences?
   b.   Do you feel your employer treated your coworker fairly when your coworker was dealing with the problems of carpal tunnel syndrome? Why or why not?
   c.   Did your employer make any changes in the workplace to reduce the risk of you and others developing carpal tunnel syndrome? If yes, describe these changes.
   d.   Do you have any suggestions for how the organization could improve the workplace to address this problem in the future? If yes, what are they?

For the supervisor or manager:
   a.   How many employees with carpal tunnel syndrome have you dealt with in the past five years?
   b.   Do you think the problem of injuries like this is increasing in importance? Staying the same? Becoming less important? Why?
   c.   Based on your experiences, what do you see as the most significant consequence of this injury for individual employees?

d. What are the consequences of this injury for the organization?

e. What is your estimate of the cost of this injury to the organization, taking into account medical expenses, lost productivity, and so on? [This estimate can be the cost for one individual or for the organization as a whole.]

f. Does the organization have a formal program for preventing the risk of carpal tunnel syndrome injuries? If yes, describe the program and explain your role in it.

CASE STUDY

WHO'S THERE ON THE LINE?

The telecommunications field is changing very rapidly. In perhaps no other field has technology had such a significant impact on the jobs of so many workers. Mitch Fields, for example, still remembers that tragic day in November 1963 when President Kennedy was assassinated while Mitch was pulling the afternoon shift as a switchman for Midwest Telephone Company (MTC). As Mitch described it, it sounded like 30 locomotives hammering their way through a large room filled with walls of mechanical switches putting phone calls through to their destination. Today, that room of switches has been replaced by a microchip. Mitch himself has undergone extensive training to operate a computer console used to monitor and diagnose switching problems.

The job of operator has changed from sitting in long rows of operating equipment attached to walls of jacks and cords to individual workstations that look like command centers out of a Star Trek spaceship. In addition, the competitive environment of telephone services has changed dramatically because of deregulation and competition from other phone companies offering similar services. The new thrust now is to shift operator performance from being not just fast and friendly but profitable as well, by marketing the company ("Thank you for using MTC") and selling high-profit-margin services ("Is there someone else you would like to talk to? The person-to-person rate is only additional for the first minute").

The operator's job at MTC remains unchanged in two respects: (1) Operators will talk to nearly 600 people in a typical day, some of whom are abusive; and (2) operator job performance is monitored. Technological innovation has enabled MTC to monitor each operator by computer to produce statistics on numbers of calls handled per shift, speed of the calls, and amount of revenue generated by the calls. In addition to computer monitoring, supervisors may also listen in on operators to ensure that proper operator protocol is being followed. For example, customers are never told they dialed the "wrong" number, obscene calls are routed to supervisors, and operators learn to say "hold the line" or "one moment please" instead of "hang on."

Meeting performance standards based on these criteria does not typically lead to large rewards. A beginning operator usually earns about $12,000 a year working swing shifts that may begin at 8:30 A.M., noon, 2:00 P.M., 4:30 P.M., 8:30 P.M., or 2:00 A.M. Only the highest-rated operators have opportunities to be transferred, promoted, or receive educational benefits.

Steve Buckley, training and development manager for MTC, knows that to change the fast and friendly MTC operator of the past to one who is fast and friendly but profitable as well is going to be a real challenge. Steve has not figured out yet how to get the operators to conclude each transaction by saying "Thank you for using MTC." A recent clandestine supervisor survey revealed that fewer than 20% of the operators were using the requested reply. Steve is also being pressured by the local union leaders who represent the telephone operators to reduce the job stress brought on by the high volume of people transactions and the constant, computer-assisted surveillance. One thing is for sure, however, Steve must implement a plan for improvement.

CASE QUESTIONS

1. Can Steve really change the behavior of the operators?

2. How can Steve succeed in getting the operators to say "Thank you for using MTC"?

3. Is computer monitoring the answer?

4. Should the operators really decide on the change?

ENDNOTES

[1] W. Atkinson, "The Carpal Tunnel Conundrum," *Workforce* (September 2002): 17; also from Ben and Jerry's *Annual Reports* 1992–2000; G. Smith, "A Famous Brand on the Rocky Road," *Business Week* (November 17, 2000): 54; "Ben & Jerry's Sacred Cow" (CNN: December 3, 1999); B. Cohen and J. Greenfield, *Ben & Jerry's Double Dip* (New York: Simon & Schuster, 1997).

[2] J. C. Quick and L. E. Tretrick (eds.), *Handbook of Occupational Health Psychology* (Washington, DC: American Psychological Association [APA], 2003).

[3] "New Health and Safety Issues," Steelcase, http://www.steelcase.com, January 15, 2004.

[4] R. J. Grossman, "Space: Another HR Frontier," *HR Magazine* (September 2002): 29–34; R. Grossman, "Back with a Vengeance," *HR Magazine* (August 2001): 36–46; S. Greenhouse, "Ergonomics Report Cites Job Injuries," *New York Times* (January 18, 2001): C6; R. Grossman, "Make Ergonomics," *HR Magazine* (April 2000): 36–42; M. Conlin, "Is Your Office Killing You?" *Business Week* (June 5, 2000): 114–124; M. Minehan, "OSHA Ergonomics Regs Draw Immediate Fire," *HR News* (January 2001): 1, 3; K. Tyler, "Sit Up Straight," *HR Magazine* (September 1998): 121–128.

[5] M. J. Burke, S. A. Sarpy, P. E. Tesluk, and K. Smith-Crowe, "General Safety Performance: A Test of a Grounded Theoretical Model," *Personnel Psychology* 55 (2002): 429–457; T. DeGroot and D. S. Kiker, "A Meta-Analysis of the Non-Monetary Effects of Employee Health Management Programs," *Human Resource Management* 42(1) (Spring 2003): 53–69.

[6] C. A. Heaney, "Worksite Health Interventions: Targets for Change and Strategies for Attaining Them," in J. C. Quick and L. E. Tetrick (eds.), *Handbook of Occupational Health Psychology* (Washington, DC: APA, 2003): 305–324; J. Lein, S. Markowitz, M. Fahs, and P. Landrigan, *Costs of Occupational Injuries and Illnesses* (Ann Arbor: University of Michigan Press, 2000); R. Shindledecker, "Health and the Bottom Line," *Workspan* (September 2000): 6–8; W. Altman, "Health and Safety Commission Chair Bill Callaghan on 'Good Health Is Good Business,'" *Academy of Management Executive* 14(2) (May 2000): 8–11; J. Quick, J. Gavin, C. L. Cooper, and J. D. Quick, "Executive Health: Building Strength, Managing Risks," *Academy of Management Executive* 14(2) (May 2000): 34–46; W. Atkinson, "Safety—at a Price," *HR Magazine* (November 1999): 52–59; M. Arndt, "It Pays to Tell the Truth," *Business Week* (June 5, 2000): 128–130; R. Grossman, "Out with the Bad Air . . .," *HR Magazine* (October 2000): 37–45; L. Grensing-Pophal, "Clearing the Air," *HR Magazine* (August 2000): 64–70; J. J. Laabs, "Cashing in on Safety," *Workforce* (August 1997): 53–57; E. Raimy, "Safety Pays," *Human Resource Executive* (November 1996): 1, 21–23; C. A. Bacon, "Is There a Nurse in the Office?" *Workforce* (June 1997): 107–113.

[7] R. J. Grossman, "Back with a Vengence," *HR Magazine* (August 2001): 36–46; W. Atkinson, "Is Workers Comp Changing?" *HR Magazine* (July 2000): 50–61; U. Lundberg, I. Dohns, B. Melin, L. Sandsjö, G. Palmerud, T. Kadefors, M. Elkström, and D. Parr, "Psychophysiological Stress Responses, Muscle Tension, and Neck and Shoulder Pain among Supermarket Cashiers," *Journal of Occupational Health Psychology* 4(3)

(1999): 245–255; V. Infante, "The Irony of Ergonomic Regulation," *Workforce* (January 2001): 26; P. Leigh, S. Markowitz, M. Fahs, and P. Landrigan, *Cost of Occupational Injuries and Illnesses* (Ann Arbor: University of Michigan Press, 2000).

[8] *Ibid.*

[9] W. Atkinson, "The Carpal Tunnel Conundrum," *Workforce* (September 2002): 17.

[10] N. Varchaver, "What Really Happened in IBM's Clean Room?" *Fortune* (December 8, 2004): 91–100; S. E. Ante, "Was IBM Hazardous to Workers Health?" *Business Week* (October 20, 2003): 46–48; L. J. Flynn, "Trial Against IBM Over Worker Safety Practices Is Nearing a Finish," *New York Times* (February 23, 2004): C4; L. J. Flynn, "IBM Settles Birth Defects Suit," *New York Times* (March 3, 2004): C5.

[11] D. L. Nelson and B. L. Simmons, "Health Psychology and Work Stress: A More Positive Approach," in J. C. Quick and L. E. Tetrick (eds.), *Handbook of Occupational Health Psychology* (Washington, DC: APA, 2003): 97–120.

[12] M. Clark, "DOL Agencies Report Record-Breaking Enforcement Totals, Rewards for 2003," *HR Magazine* (January 2004): 34; J. Adams, "Workplace Deaths Decline, Co-Worker Homicides Rise," *HR Magazine* (February 2001): 12.

[13] R. J. Grossman, "Bulletproof Practices," *HR Magazine* (November 2002): 34–42.

[14] J. B. Bennett, R. F. Cook, and K. R. Pelletier, "Toward an Integrated Framework for Comprehensive Organizational Wellness: Concepts, Practices, and Research in Workplace Health Promotion," in J. C. Quick and L. E. Tetrick (eds.), *Handbook of Occupational Health Psychology* (Washington, DC: APA, 2003): 69–96; M. J. Smith, B. T. Karsh, P. Carayon, and F. T. Conway, "Controlling Occupational Safety and Health Hazards," in J. C. Quick and L. E. Tetrick (eds.), *Handbook of Occupational Health Psychology* (Washington, DC: APA, 2003): 35–68; M. Budman, "Counting the Costs," *Across the Board* (March/April 2002): 38–40.

[15] For detailed discussions, see J. Barling and M. R. Frone (eds.), *The Psychology of Workplace Safety* (Washington, DC: APA, 2004), and D. A. Hofmann and L. E. Tetrick (eds.), *Health and Safety in Organizations* (San Francisco: Jossey-Bass, 2003). Also see P. J. Kiger, "Healthy, Wealthy and Wise," *Workforce Management* (July 2003): 40–42.

[16] C. Brotherton, "The Role of External Policies in Shaping Organizational Health and Safety," in D. A. Hofmann and L. E. Tetrick (eds.), *Health and Safety in Organizations: A Multilevel Perspective* (San Francisco: Jossey-Bass, 2003): 372–396; J. D. Shaw and J. E. Delery, "Strategic HRM and Organizational Health," in D. A. Hofmann and L. E. Tetrick (eds.), *Health and Safety in Organizations: A Multilevel Perspective* (San Francisco: Jossey-Bass, 2003): 233–260; D. A. Hofmann and L. E. Tetrick, "The Etiology of the Concept of Health: Implications for 'Organizing' Individual and Organizational Health," in D. A. Hofmann and

L. E. Tetrick (eds.), *Health and Safety in Organizations: A Multilevel Perspective* (San Francisco: Jossey-Bass, 2003): 128.

17 For a full discussion, see R. R. Sinclair and L. E. Tetrick, "Pay and Benefits: The Role of Compensation Systems in Workplace Safety," in J. Barling and M. R. Frone (eds.), *The Psychology of Workplace Safety* (Washington, DC: APA, 2004): 181–201.

18 K. Roberts, "Using Workers' Compensation to Promote a Healthy Workplace," in D. A. Hofmann and L. E. Tetrick (eds.), *Health and Safety in Organizations: A Multilevel Perspective* (San Francisco: Jossey-Bass, 2003): 341–371; A. G. Lipold, "The Soaring Costs of Workers' Comp," *Workforce* (February 2003): 42–48.

19 G. Kranz, "Transitional Duty Pays Off for Employers, Charities, and Injured Workers," *Workforce Management* (December 2003): 75–77.

20 E. K. Kelloway, "Labor Unions and Occupational Safety: Conflict and Cooperation," in J. Barling and M. R. Frone (eds.), *The Psychology of Workplace Safety* (Washington, DC: APA, 2004): 249–264.

21 G. R. Gray, D. W. Myers, and P. S. Myers, "Collective Bargaining Agreements: Safety and Health Provisions," *Monthly Labor Review* (May 1998): 13–35.

22 J. Barling and M.R. Frone (eds.), *The Psychology of Workplace Safety* (Washington, DC: APA, 2004); D. Zohar, "Safety Climate: Conceptual and Measurement Issues," in J. C. Quick and L. E. Tetrick (eds.), *Handbook of Occupational Health Psychology* (Washington, DC: APA, 2003): 123–142; P. Tesluk and N. R. Quigley, "Group and Normative Influences on Health and Safety: Perspectives from Taking a Broad View on Team Effectiveness," in D. A. Hofmann and L. E. Tetrick (eds.), *Health and Safety in Organizations: A Multilevel Perspective* (San Francisco: Jossey-Bass, 2003): 131–172; D. Zohar, "A Group-Level Model of Safety Climate: Testing the Effect of Group Climate on Microaccidents in Manufacturing Jobs," *Journal of Applied Psychology* 85(4) (2000): 587–596.

23 Research on organizational cultures and safety often focuses on the development of a positive "safety climate." For a detailed discussion, see A. Neal and M.A. Griffin, "Safety Climate and Safety at Work," in J. Barling and M. R. Frone (eds.), *The Psychology of Workplace Safety* (Washington, DC: APA, 2004): 15–34.

24 E. Tahmincioglu, "Battling Job-Related Aches and Pains," *New York Times* (January 3, 2001): G1.

25 M. J. Burke and S. A. Sarpy, "Improving Worker Safety and Health Through Interventions," in D. A. Hofmann and L. E. Tetrick (eds.), *Health and Safety in Organizations: A Multilevel Perspective* (San Francisco: Jossey-Bass, 2003): 56–90.

26 "Report Finds Safer Workplaces in U.S." *HR Magazine* (March 2004): 28.

27 D. A. Hofmann and F. P. Morgesen, "The Role of Leadership in Safety," in J. Barling and M. R. Frone (eds.), *The Psychology of Workplace Safety* (Washington, DC: APA, 2004): 159–180.

28 J. Barling, C. Loughlin, and E. K. Kelloway, "Development and Test of a Model Linking Safety-Specific Transformational Leadership and Occupational Safety," *Journal of Applied Psychology* 87(3) (2002): 488–496; see also D. Zohar, "The Influence of Leadership and Climate on Occupational Health and Safety," in D. A. Hofmann and L. E. Tetrick (eds.), *Health and Safety in Organizations: A Multilevel Perspective* (San Francisco: Jossey-Bass, 2003): 201–232.

29 D. Barstow and L. Bergman, "A Family's Fortune, a Legacy of Blood and Tears," *New York Times* (January 9, 2003): A1, A20, A21; D. Barstow and L. Bergman, "Deaths on the Job, Slaps on the Wrist," *New York Times* (January 10, 2003): A1, A16, A17; *FRONTLINE: A Dangerous Business* (PBS, 2003).

30 L. E. Tetrick and J. C. Quick, "Prevention at Work: Public Health in Occupational Settings," in J. C. Quick and L. E. Tetrick (eds.), *Handbook of Occupational Health Psychology* (Washington, DC: APA, 2003): 3–18; J. B. Bennett, R. F. Cook, and K. R. Pelletier, "Toward an Integrated Framework for Comprehensive Organizational Wellness: Concepts, Practices, and Research in Workplace Health Promotion," in J. C. Quick and L. E.

Tetrick (eds.), *Handbook of Occupational Health Psychology* (Washington, DC: APA, 2003): 69–96; M. J. Burke, S. A. Sarpy, P. E. Tesluk, and K. Smith-Crowe, "General Safety Performance: A Test of a Grounded Theoretical Model," *Personnel Psychology* 55 (2002): 429–457.

31 M. J. Smith, B. T. Karsh, P. Carayon, and F. T. Conway, "Controlling Occupational Safety and Health Hazards," in J. C. Quick and L. E. Tetrick (eds.), *Handbook of Occupational Health Psychology* (Washington, DC: APA, 2003): 35–68; K. S. Robinson, "Learn to Keep the Workplace Healthy: Toxic Mold Dangerous to Both Employees and Businesses," *Society for Human Management* (October 2002): 7, 11.

32 N. Stein, "Son of a Chicken Man," *Fortune* (May 13, 2002): 137–146.

33 D. Cadrain, "Workplace Safety's Ergonomic Twist," *HR Magazine* (October 2002): 43–47.

34 F. Meilinger, "OSHA Signs Letter of Agreement with Mexico," OSHA announcement published July 21, 2004, at http://www.osha.gov.

35 *Global Compact Policy Dialogue on HIV/AIDS* (Geneva, Switzerland: International Labour Organization [ILO], 2003).

36 OSHA 2003-2008 *Strategic Management Plan,* http://www.osha.gov, January 8, 2004.

37 "Six Need-to-Know Tips for a Safe Workplace," *Business and Legal Reports* (January 6, 2004): http://www2.hrnext.com.

38 M. J. Burke, S. A. Sarpy, P. E. Tesluk, and K. Smith-Crowe, "General Safety Performance: A Test of a Grounded Theoretical Model," *Personnel Psychology* 55 (2002): 429–457; see also M. J. Burke and S. A. Sarpy, "Improving Worker Safety and Health Through Interventions," in D. A. Hofmann and L. E. Tetrick (eds.), *Health and Safety in Organizations: A Multilevel Perspective* (San Francisco: Jossey-Bass, 2003): 56–90.

39 A. G. Lipold, "The Soaring Costs of Workers' Comp," *Workforce* (February 2003): 42–48.

40 E. Tahmincioglu, "Ergonomics Is Back on the Radar Screen for Both Business and Regulators," *Workforce Management* (July 2004): 59–61.

41 For a detailed discussion of safety and health hazards, see M. J. Smith, B.-T. Karsh, P. Carayon, and F. T. Conway, "Controlling Occupational Safety and Health Hazards," in J. C. Quick and L. E. Tetrick (eds.), *Handbook of Occupational Health Psychology* (Washington, DC: APA, 2003): 35–68; D. A. Hofmann and L. E. Tetrick, "The Etiology of the Concept of Health: Implications for 'Organizing' Individual and Organizational Health," in D. A. Hofmann and L. E. Tetrick (eds.), *Health and Safety in Organizations: A Multilevel Perspective* (San Francisco: Jossey-Bass, 2003): 1–28; K. Sparks, B. Faragher, and C. L. Cooper, "Well-Being and Occupational Health in the 21st Century Workplace," *Journal of Occupational and Organizational Psychology* 74 (2001): 489–509.

42 Personal correspondence with Donald Brush, President, Barden Bearings Corporation.

43 M. R. Frone, "Predictors of Work Injuries among Employed Adolescents," *Journal of Applied Psychology* 83 (1998): 565–576.

44 "Facing Middle-age Injuries," CNN (July 18, 2000): 1–3; M. Moss, "For Older Employees, On-the-Job Injuries Are More Often Deadly," *Wall Street Journal* (June 17, 1997): A1; "Workplace Deaths Unchanged; Homicides At Six-Year Low," *Bulletin to Management: Facts and Figures* (August 27, 1998): 269; "Occupational Injuries and Illnesses," *Bulletin to Management: Facts and Figures* (January 15, 1998): 13.

45 P. E. Spector, "Individual Differences in Health and Well-Being in Organizations," in D.A. Hofmann and L. E. Tetrick (eds.), *Health and Safety in Organizations: A Multilevel Perspective* (San Francisco: Jossey-Bass, 2003): 29–55.

46 U.S. Department of Labor and the Bureau of Labor Statistics, http://www.llstats.bls.gov, January 8, 2004; E. Esen, *SHRM Workplace Violence Survey* (Alexandria, VA: Society for Human Resource Management, 2004); S. A. Baron, S. Hoffman, and J. Merrill, *When Work Equals Life: The Next Stage of Workplace Violence* (San Francisco: Pathfinder,

2000); T. D. Schneid, *Occupational Health Guide to Violence in the Workplace* (Chelsea, MI: Lewis Publishers, 1998).

47 E. F. Sygnature and G. A. Toscano, "Work-Related Homicides: The Facts," *Compensation and Working Condition* (Spring 2000): 3–8.

48 M. M. LeBlanc and E. K. Kelloway, "Predictors and Outcomes of Workplace Violence and Aggression," *Journal of Applied Psychology* 87(3) (2002): 444–453; S. C. Douglas and M. J. Martinko, "Exploring the Role of Individual Differences in Predicting Workplace Aggression," *Journal of Applied Psychology* 86(4) (2001): 547–559; J. H. Neuman and R. A. Baron, "Workplace Violence and Workplace Aggression: Evidence Concerning Specific Forms, Potential Causes and Preferred Targets," *Journal of Management* 24(3) (1998): 391–419; G. R. VanderBos and E. Q. Bulatao (eds.), *Violence on the Job: Identifying Risks and Developing Solutions* (Washington, DC: American Psychological Association, 1996); A. M. O'Leary-Kelly, R. W. Griffin, and D. J. Glew, "Organization-Motivated Aggression: A Research Framework," *Academy of Management Review* 21 (1996): 225–253.

49 C. L. Cooper, P. Dewe, and M. O'Driscoll, "Employee Assistance Programs," in J. C. Quick and L. E. Tetrick (eds.), *Handbook of Occupational Health Psychology* (Washington, DC: APA, 2003): 289–304.

50 R. Valliere, "Spate of Murders Spurred Postal Service to Radically Change Handling Violence," *Occupational Safety and Health Reporter* 34(31) (July 29, 2004): 785–786.

51 Visit the websites of the U.S. Department of Labor and the Bureau of Labor Statistics, the National Safety Council, and the National Center for Health Statistics for the latest information.

52 See http://www.osha.gov for OSHA's 2003–2008 "Strategic Management Plan."

53 J. R. Hackman and G. R. Oldham, *Work Redesign* (Reading, MA: Addison-Wesley, 1980); G. Dodd and D. C. Ganster, "The Interactive Effects of Variety, Autonomy, and Feedback on Attitudes and Performance," *Journal of Organizational Behavior* 17 (1996): 329–347; R. W. Renn and R. J. Vandenberg, "The Critical Psychological States: An Underrepresented Component in Job Characteristics Model Research," *Journal of Management* 21 (1995): 279–303; S. P. Brown and T. W. Leigh, "A New Look at Psychological Climate and Its Relationship to Job Involvement, Effort, and Performance," *Journal of Applied Psychology* 81 (1996): 358–368.

54 J. Barling, E. K. Kelloway, and R. D. Iverson, "High-Quality Work, Job Satisfaction, and Occupational Injuries," *Journal of Applied Psychology* 88(2) (2003): 276–283.

55 S. K. Parker, N. Turner, and M. A. Griffin, "Designing Healthy Work," in D. A. Hofmann and L. E. Tetrick (eds.), *Health and Safety in Organizations: A Multilevel Perspective* (San Francisco: Jossey-Bass, 2003): 91–130.

56 D. H. Shapiro, Jr., C. E. Schwartz, and J. A. Astin, "Controlling Ourselves, Controlling Our World," *American Psychologist* 51 (December 1996): 1213–1230; Schaubroeck and D. E. Merritt, "Divergent Effects of Job Control on Coping with Work Stressors: The Key Role of Self-Efficacy," *Academy of Management Journal* 40 (1997): 738–754.

57 T. Thoerell, "To Be Able to Exert Control over One's Own Situation: A Necessary Condition for Coping with Stressors," in J. C. Quick and L. E. Tetrick (eds.), *Handbook of Occupational Health Psychology* (Washington, DC: APA, 2003): 201–219.

58 This summary is based on the excellent review provided by C. S. Smith, L. M. Sulsky, and W. E. Ormond, "Work Arrangements: The Effects of Shiftwork, Telework, and Other Arrangements," in D. A. Hofmann and L. E. Tetrick (eds.), *Health and Safety in Organizations: A Multilevel Perspective* (San Francisco: Jossey-Bass, 2003): 261–284; see also C. S. Smith, S. Folkard, and J. A. Fuller, "Shiftwork and Working Hours," in J. C. Quick and L. E. Tetrick (eds.), *Handbook of Occupational Health Psychology* (Washington, DC: APA, 2003): 163–220.

59 C. S. Smith, S. Folkard, and J. A. Fuller, "Shiftwork and Working Hours," in J. C. Quick and L. E. Tetrick (eds.), *Handbook of Occupational Health Psychology* (Washington, DC: APA, 2003): 163–183.

60 A useful booklet for employers interested in understanding job stress is NIOSH Working Group, *Stress at Work* (Cincinnati, OH: NIOSH, undated).

61 G. E. Hardy, D. Woods, and T. D. Wall, "The Impact of Psychological Distress on Absence from Work," *Journal of Applied Psychology* 88(2) (2003): 306–314.

62 For a review of research on the health consequences of modern office technology, see M. D. Coovert and L. F. Thompson, "Technology and Workplace Health," in J. C. Quick and L. E. Tetrick (eds.), *Handbook of Occupational Health Psychology* (Washington, DC: APA, 2003): 221–242.

63 A. Griffiths and F. Munir, "Workplace Health Promotion," in D. A. Hofmann and L. E. Tetrick (eds.), *Health and Safety in Organizations: A Multilevel Perspective* (San Francisco: Jossey-Bass, 2003): 316–340; "Please, Somebody! Open a Window!" *Business Week* (January 18, 1999): 8.

64 M. Friedman and R. Rosenman, *Type A Behavior and Your Heart* (New York: Alfred A. Knopf, 1974); for a review of more recent research on the relationship between personality and personal health and well-being, see P. E. Spector, "Individual Differences in Health and Well-Being in Organizations," in D. A. Hofmann and L. E. Tetrick (eds.), *Health and Safety in Organizations: A Multilevel Perspective* (San Francisco: Jossey-Bass, 2003): 29–55.

65 A. Shirom, "Job-Related Burnout: A Review," in J. C. Quick and L. E. Tetrick (eds.), *Handbook of Occupational Health Psychology* (Washington, DC: APA, 2003): 245–264.

66 L. A. Witt, M. C. Andrews, and D. S. Carlson, "When Conscientiousness Isn't Enough: Emotional Exhaustion and Performance among Call Center Customer Service Representatives," *Journal of Management* 30 (2004): 149–160.

67 M. Maslach and M. P. Leiter, *The Truth About Burnout: How Organizations Cause Personal Stress and What to Do About It* (San Francisco: Jossey-Bass, 1997); R. Cropanzano, D. E. Rupp, and Z. S. Byrne, "The Relationship of Emotional Exhaustion to Work Attitudes, Job Performance, and Organizational Citizenship Behaviors," *Journal of Applied Psychology* 88(1) (2003): 160–169; C. L. Cordes and T. W. Dougherty, "A Review and Integration of Research on Job Burnout," *Academy of Management Review* 18 (1993): 621–656.

68 M. W. Walsh, "Keeping Workers Safe, but at What Cost?" *New York Times* (December 20, 2000): G1; L. Miller, "People on the Move Are Going Back to Driving School," *Wall Street Journal* (May 20, 1997): A1; "Safety: A Quick Pay-Off, a Long-Term Commitment," *HR Reporter* (October 1990): 6; R. Pater, "Safety Leadership Cuts Costs," *HR Magazine* (November 1990): 46–47.

69 M. Arndt, "How O'Neill Got Alcoa Shining," *BusinessWeek* (February 5, 2001): 39.

70 T. Bland and P. Forment, "Navigating OSHA's Ergonomics Rule," *HR Magazine* (February 2001): 61–67; M. Moss, "For Older Employees, On-the-Job Injuries Are More Often Deadly," *Wall Street Journal* (June 17, 1997): A1; D. P. Levin, "The Graying Factor," *New York Times* (February 20, 1994): 3-1, 3-3.

71 "Some Ergonomic Tips Toward Healthy and Effective Offices," Steelcase website, January 15, 2004.

72 J. R. Hollenbeck, D. R. Ilgen, and S. M. Crampton, "Lower Back Disability in Occupational Settings: A Review of the Literature from a Human Resource Management View," *Personnel Psychology* 45 (1992): 247–278.

73 S. Bates, "Industry Ergonomic Guidelines 'Not Standards in Disguise,' OSHA Official Says," *HR Magazine* (September 2003): 34.

74 N. Turner and S. K. Parker, "The Effect of Teamwork on Safety Processes and Outcomes," in J. Barling and M. R. Frone (eds.), *The Psychology of Workplace Safety* (Washington, DC: APA, 2004): 35–62.

75 J. A. Adkins and H. M. Weiss, "Program Evaluation: The Bottom Line in Organizational Health," in J. C. Quick and L. E. Tetrick (eds.), *Handbook of Occupational Health Psychology* (Washington, DC: APA, 2003): 399–416;

K. DeRango and L. Franzini, "Economic Evaluations of Workplace Health Interventions: Theory and Literature Review," in J. C. Quick and L. E. Tetrick (eds.), *Handbook of Occupational Health Psychology* (Washington, DC: APA, 2003): 417–430; M. J. Burke and S. A. Sarpy, "Improving Worker Safety and Health Through Interventions," in D. A. Hofmann and L. E. Tetrick (eds.), *Health and Safety in Organizations: A Multilevel Perspective* (San Francisco: Jossey-Bass, 2003): 56–90.

76 D. Hellriegel, S. E. Jackson, and J. W. Slocum, Jr., *Management*, 10th ed. (Cincinnati, OH: South-Western, 2005).

77 T. Minton-Eversole, "Impact of Genetic Information in Workplace Explored," *HR News* (September 2000): 1, 15; K. Ridder, "Genetic Testing Raises Fears of Workplace Bias," *Dallas Morning News* (April 26, 1998): 8H; S. Greengard, "Genetic Testing: Should You Be Afraid? It's No Joke," *Workforce* (July 1997): 38–44.

78 L. Koss-Feder, "Slowing Down the Treadmill, with Help," *New York Times* (June 29, 2003): 10; J. D. Holloway, "Keeping Employees Healthy and Happy," *Monitor on Psychology* (December 2003): 32–33.

79 A. Weintraub, "I Can't Sleep," *Business Week* (January 26, 2004): 66–74; M. Frese, "Social Support as a Moderator of the Relationship Between Work Stressors and Psychological Dysfunctioning: A Longitudinal Study with Objective Measures," *Journal of Occupational Health Psychology* 4(3) (1999): 179–192; E. Diener, E. Suh, R. Lucas, and H. Smith, "Subjective Well-Being: Three Decades of Progress," *Psychological Bulletin* 125(2) (1999): 276–302.

80 R. E. Quillian-Wolever and M. Wolever, "Stress Management at Work," in J. C. Quick and L. E. Tetrick (eds.), *Handbook of Occupational Health Psychology* (Washington, DC: APA, 2003): 355–375.

81 K. Tyler, "Cut the Stress: With HR-Provided Training, Employees Can Learn How to Avoid What Makes Them Tense," *HR Magazine* (May 2003): 101–106; D. Etzion, D. Eden, and Y. Lapidot, "Relief from Job Stressors and Burnout: Reserve Service as a Respite," *Journal of Applied Psychology* 83 (1998): 577–585; M. Westman and D. Eden, "Effects of Vacation on Job Stress and Burnout: Relief and Fade Out," *Journal of Applied Psychology* 82 (1997): 516–527.

82 A. Meisler, "All Aboard," *Workforce Management* (July 2004): 30–32.

83 R. J. Grossman, "Countering a Weight Crisis," *HR Magazine* (March 2004): 42–50; J. C. Erfurt, A. Foote, and M. A. Heirich, "The Cost-Effectiveness of Worksite Wellness Programs for Hypertension Control, Weight Loss, Smoking Cessation and Exercise," *Personnel Psychology* 45 (1992): 5–27.

84 K. Zernike, "Fight Against Fat Shifting to the Workplace," *New York Times* (October 12, 2003): A1, A26.

85 For an illustration of how to estimate the ROI for active management of several diseases, see M. Hammers, "More Care, Less Cost," *Workforce Management* (March 2004): 55–58.

86 A. Griffiths and F. Munir, "Workplace Health Promotion," in D. A. Hofmann and L. E. Tetrick (eds.), *Health and Safety in Organizations: A Multilevel Perspective* (San Francisco: Jossey-Bass, 2003): 316–340.

87 S. Rosen, J. Simon, J. R. Vincent, W. MacLeod, M. Fox, and D. M. Thea, "AIDS Is Your Business," *Harvard Business Review* (February 2003): 81–87.

chapter 14

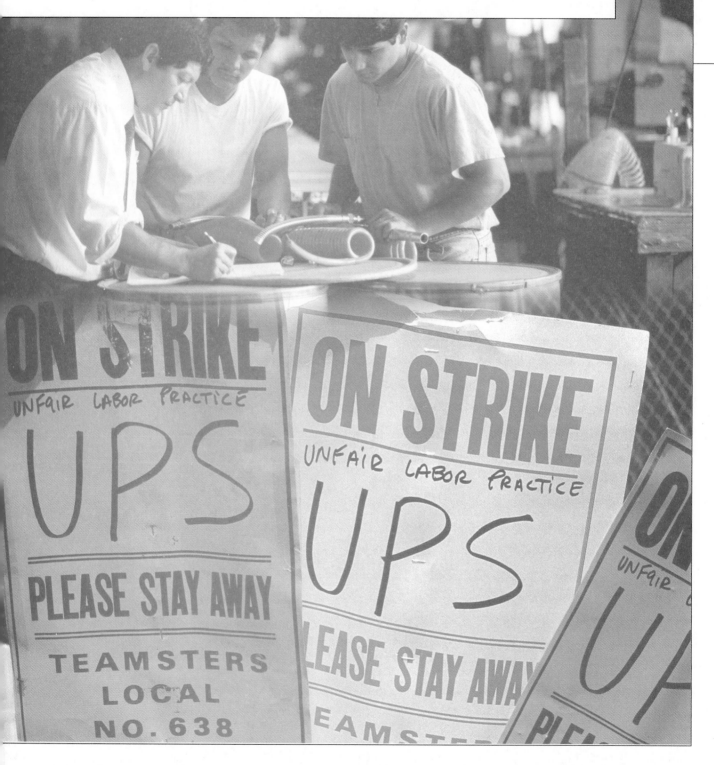

Understanding Unionization and Collective Bargaining

United Parcel Service (UPS) is known worldwide for package delivery service. Total revenues exceed $30 billion yearly, and it has been rated as the top in its industry in Fortune's "Most Admired Companies." Represented by the Teamsters union, the company's 350,000 employees (40,000 of whom are outside the United States) are some of the highest paid in the industry and have a relatively low turnover rate. UPS operates in over 200 countries. With the exception of when the union went on strike in August 1997, the Teamsters have worked collaboratively with the company for more than 80 years, guided by UPS founder Jim Casey's philosophy that "You can be a good Teamster and a good UPSer."

It appears that UPS learned from the strike experience of 1997. UPS, under the leadership of Mike Eskew, indicates that all parties need to work in partnership to make sure that all is well. Perhaps UPS had underestimated the union's resolve and the workers' belief in the importance of issues such as the use of part-timers and its desire to pull out of their multiemployer pension plan.[1]

FAST FACT

Unions are present in about 25% of *Fortune's* 100 Most Admired companies.

In retrospect, the events at UPS are a good reminder of how valuable union-management cooperation can be. For more than 80 years, UPS and the Teamsters union had worked together, producing an employment relationship that benefited both workers and the company. Over the years, service quality had been excellent, absenteeism was low, employees were relatively satisfied with their jobs, they enjoyed employment security and received continual training, and the result was (is) a profitable company.[2]

THE STRATEGIC IMPORTANCE OF UNIONIZATION AND COLLECTIVE BARGAINING

As economic conditions continue to change in the 21st century, the union-management relationship will likely also change. Changes are likely to occur both in unionization efforts and in the bargaining relationships between existing unions and management. For example, United Auto Workers (UAW) is extending its efforts to unionize nonteaching employees in universities. Changes are also occurring within unions as they consider offering alternative forms of membership such as an associate status.[3] To put into perspective these aspects of union-management relationships, this chapter describes the process of forming a union (unionization) and the characteristics of administering an agreement reached between the union and management (collective bargaining).

Unionization *is the effort by employees and outside agencies (unions or associations) to act as a single unit when dealing with management over issues relating to their work.* When recognized by the National Labor Relations Board (NLRB), a union has the legal authority to negotiate with the employer on behalf of employees—to improve wages, hours, and conditions of employment—and to administer the ensuing agreement.[4]

The core of union-management relations is collective bargaining. **Collective bargaining** *generally includes (a) the negotiation of work conditions that, when written up as the collective agreement, becomes the basis for employee-employer relationships on the job, and (b) activities related to interpreting and enforcing the collective agreement and resolving any conflicts arising from it.*[5]

The existence of, or possibility of, a union can significantly influence an employer's ability to manage its vital human resources. Unions can help employees get what they want—for example, high wages and job security—from their employers. For management, unionization may result in less flexibility in hiring new workers, making job assignments, and introducing new work methods such as automation; a loss of control; inefficient work practices; and an inflexible job structure. On the other hand, it may result in greater workforce cooperation and the development of new strategies to help the company be more competitive! This is exactly what the United Steelworkers of America (USWA) union did for the Goodyear Tire and Rubber Company in 2003.[6]

Unions obtain rights for their members that employees without unions don't legally have. This, of course, forces unionized companies to consider their employees' reactions to a wide variety of decisions. In nonunion companies, employers who want to remain that way may give more consideration and benefits to their employees.[7] Consequently, it may or may not be more expensive for a company to operate with unionized rather than nonunionized employees.[8]

When unions give wage concessions or cooperate in joint workplace efforts, such as teamwork programs, they can help employers remain profitable and competitive, and thus ensure their survival during especially difficult times.[9] This has happened particularly in the automobile, steel, and airline industries. Unions also can help identify workplace hazards and improve job security for their members.[10] Clearly, unions have important roles to play in the strategic issues of a company. These are described in more detail in the feature "Managing Change: Unions Get Involved."[11]

UNIONIZATION AND COLLECTIVE BARGAINING WITHIN THE INTEGRATED HRM SYSTEM

Exhibit 14.1 illustrates the general process of unionization and shows its relationship to other elements of the HRM system. As the story of UPS highlights and Exhibit 14.1 illustrates, unionizing and collective bargaining activities often involve other HR practices. In the UPS example, pensions and use of part-time workers were an important part of the strike between the Teamsters and UPS. While pension contributions are an important concern to both union leaders and members, so are traditional concerns like cost-of-living increases, working conditions, and health and safety.

Unions are increasingly concerned about training and educational benefits for their members.[12] They recognize the need for companies to remain competitive in this global market and the need to utilize the most current technologies available. Doing so often requires providing additional training and education.

 FAST FACT — In Seattle, the Communications Workers of America (CWA) teamed with Cisco to build a lab to house Web programming classes.

Managing Change

Unions Get Involved

Labor costs are critical to the success of many companies. Wage reductions reached between unions and management help to lower costs. During the 1980s, American Airlines, Boeing, and Ingersoll-Rand negotiated two-tier wage systems to help reduce total costs by reducing labor costs. In the 1990s, Southwest Airlines got concessions from its pilots and machinists to hold down wage costs. Without such jointly negotiated agreements, these companies may not have survived.

Survival still remains a concern of many unions and employers. Since 2000 Boeing has wrestled further concessions from the International Association of Machinists, resulting in a reduction of almost 20,000 members and an agreement to allow Boeing to outsource a large chunk of the

7E7 assembly work to Asia and Europe. In exchange Boeing said that it would build the new plane in Washington and offered to work hand-in-hand with the union to end decades of bitter labor relations that sank employee morale to an all-time low. Boeing sees this new relationship as vital to keeping costs down and being able to compete with rival Airbus. Still Boeing's commercial plane division makes only a 7% operating margin, while Airbus makes 16.7%.

Meanwhile, the United Steelworkers union is helping Goodyear Tire and Rubber to survive and remain. It agreed to wage concessions in exchange for a promise that the company would keep factories open in the United States.

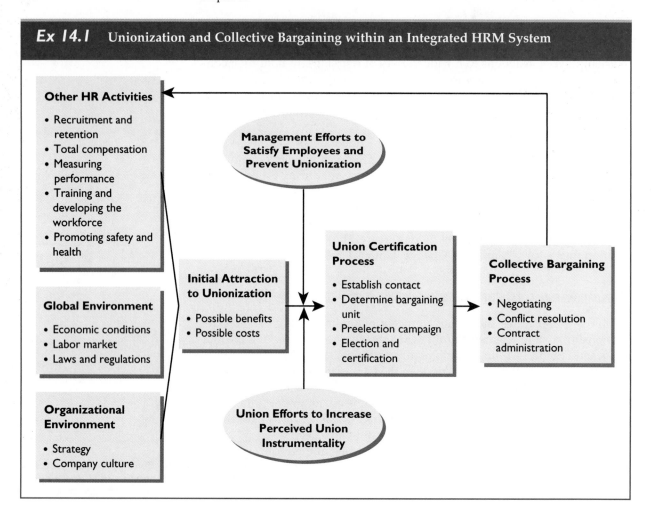

Ex 14.1   Unionization and Collective Bargaining within an Integrated HRM System

Unions also care about performance measurement and compensation plans that tie employee performance to pay. They want to ensure that these HR-designed activities are implemented with fairness and respect for each employee. Unions such as the Teamsters and the UAW have also worked with companies such as UPS to provide and implement programs in safety and health. Thus, unions often work with HR professionals as they design and help employers implement a variety of HR practices. But maintaining positive and cooperative relationships takes constant work from everyone involved. Among the roles and responsibilities to be fulfilled are those shown in the feature "The HR Triad—Extended: Roles and Responsibilities in Unionization and Collective Bargaining."

As formal organizations, unions also use all the HR practices described in this book to manage their own human resources. They need to plan for the union's long-term needs, recruit and retain their own employees, compensate those employees, and manage their performance. Unions are concerned about having a workforce that is diverse, well educated, and able to serve the needs of the membership.[13] Thus, a union's internal HR department plays a vital role in the success of the union and the attainment of its own strategic objectives (e.g., increasing union membership).

The HR Triad—Extended

Roles and Responsibilities in Unionization and Collective Bargaining

LINE MANAGERS	HR PROFESSIONALS	EMPLOYEES	UNIONS
• Know the laws and regulations that govern what can and can't be said to employees regarding unionization during an organizing campaign.	• Train line managers about the unionization rights of employees.	• Understand what unions do and how they function.	• Abide by laws and regulations governing legal union activities.
• Understand why employees are likely to join a union.	• Develop HR policies to provide good working conditions.	• Express views on workplace conditions, wages, and working hours.	• Strive to improve wages and working conditions for union members.
• Support the efforts of HR professionals in developing and implementing policies to support good working conditions.	• Continually survey employees' attitudes so that management knows employees' views and opinions.	• Bargain in good faith through union representatives with line managers and HR professionals.	• Offer to work with management to improve company profitability and survival.
• Manage employees with respect and equality.	• Work with line managers in dealing effectively with union representatives.	• Fulfill rights and responsibilities in the union contract.	• Bargain with line managers and HR professionals.
• Participate in grievance procedures to resolve complaints fairly.	• Develop mechanisms for effective grievance resolution and ensure managers and employees understand these procedures.	• Use mechanisms for grievances as appropriate.	• Participate in development of effective grievance procedures.
• Work with HR professionals to develop an effective relationship with union representatives.	• Be proactive in addressing employees' concerns before major conflicts erupt.	• Be aware of the issues management and labor leaders are discussing.	• Be willing to adapt to local conditions and changes in technology and economic conditions.

THE HISTORICAL CONTEXT AND UNIONS TODAY

A better understanding of the attitudes and behaviors of both unions and management can be gained through a knowledge of past union-management relations.

A BRIEF HISTORY

The beginning of the labor union movement in the United States can be traced back to the successful attempt of journeymen printers to win a wage increase in 1778. By the 1790s, unions of shoemakers, carpenters, and printers had appeared in Boston, Baltimore, New York, and other cities. The Federal Society of Journeymen Cordwainers, for example, was organized in Philadelphia in 1794, primarily to resist employers' attempts to reduce wages. Other issues of concern to these early unions were union shops (companies using only union members) and the regulation of apprenticeships to prevent the replacement of journeymen employees.

The early unions had methods and objectives that are still in evidence today. Although there was no collective bargaining, the unions did establish a price below which members would not work. Strikes were used to enforce this rate. These strikes were relatively peaceful and for the most part successful.

One negative characteristic of early unions was their susceptibility to depressions. Until the late 1800s, most unions thrived in times of prosperity but died off during depressions. Part of this problem may have been related to the insularity of the unions. Aside from sharing information on strikebreakers or scabs, the unions operated independently of each other. The work situation had undergone several important changes by the end of the 19th century. Transportation systems (canals, railroads, and turnpikes) expanded the markets for products and increased worker mobility. Increases in capital costs prevented journeymen from reaching the status of master craftworker (that is, from setting up their own businesses), thereby creating a class of skilled workers. Unionism found its start in these skilled occupations.

Unions continued to experience ups and downs that were largely tied to economic conditions. Employers took advantage of the depressions to combat unions: In "an all out frontal attack . . . they engaged in frequent lockouts, hired spies . . . summarily discharged labor 'agitators,' and [engaged] the services of strikebreakers on a widespread scale."[14] These actions, and the retaliations of unions, established a tenor of violence and lent a strong adversarial nature to union-management relations, the residual effects of which are still in evidence today.

Today, the adversarial nature of the union-management relationship has been replaced to a certain extent by a more cooperative one. This change toward relying on collective bargaining has been dictated in part by current trends in union membership, including the shifting distribution of the membership.

Decline in Membership

Union membership in the United States has declined steadily from its high of 35.5% of the workforce in 1945. In the mid-1950s, 35% of the workforce was unionized. In 1970, the percentage of unionized workers in the labor force was about 25%. In 2003, unions represented approximately 13% of all workers. The rates of unionization differ dramatically in the private and public sectors, however. Exhibit 14.2 shows the steady decline in union representation within the private sector.[15] Meanwhile, within the public sector, the rate of unionization has held fairly steady at about 35%. Thus, in mostly public occupations (e.g., law enforcement, firefighting, and education), rates of unionization are relatively high.

FAST FACT New York and Alaska have the highest percent of unionization at about 25%. North Carolina has the lowest at about 3%.

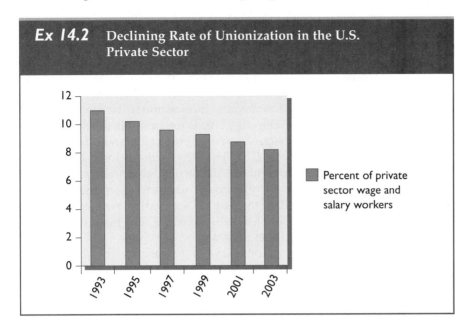

Ex 14.2 Declining Rate of Unionization in the U.S. Private Sector

One factor that contributed to these declines was the increase in service-sector employment, high-technology jobs, and white-collar jobs—all of which historically have had a low proportion of union members. Other contributing circumstances have included a decline in employment in industries that are highly unionized, increased decertification of unions, and management initiatives. To counter these trends, union leaders in the AFL-CIO and some of its member unions, including the Service Employees International Union, have increased their efforts to expand the membership base.[16]

When Linda Chavez-Thompson became the first executive vice-president of the AFL-CIO, a position critical to the future of the union movement, it signaled a change in the organization's strategic objectives. According to John J. Sweeney, president of the AFL-CIO, the election of Chavez-Thompson was very significant. It was an indication of just how much the union movement has changed. Traditionally dominated by (mostly white) men, today's unions must also be responsive to the concerns of women and minorities. These populations are increasingly present in the workforce, and they provide the best opportunities for growth in union membership.

In addition to including a greater variety of groups in the top management of the AFL-CIO, the union movement has sought to include more groups in the grassroots of labor. It has expanded its organizing efforts in the South, has increased efforts to organize construction and kitchen workers in Las Vegas, has signed up asbestos cleanup crews in New York, and has signed up more farm workers in California. It is doing this in part with a new crop of workers/organizers who are young, ambitious, college-educated people with a passion for the union movement. "They get to know every nuance of a company's operations and target the weak managers' departments as a way to appeal to employees who may be willing to organize." With the real wages of many workers remaining stagnant, or even falling, the voice of appeal may be heard by an increasing number of willing ears—especially those of white-collar workers.[17]

"I wanted someone who knew what it was like to go door-to-door organizing and to come home at night dead-tired and foot-sore."

John J. Sweeney
President
AFL-CIO

To gain organizational and financial strength, several unions have merged in recent years. For example, UNITE HERE was formed from a merger of the International Ladies' Garment Workers' Union (ILGWU), the Amalgamated Clothing Workers of America (ACWA), the Textile Workers Union of America (TWUA), and the Hotel Employees and Restaurant Employees International Union (HERE).[18] UNITE HERE (formerly UNITE) is the union that helped organize the widely publicized strike of blue-collar and office workers at Yale University in 2003. The strike closed down the student cafeteria and spurred about 100 faculty supporters of the strike to move their classes off campus to churches and government buildings. By the time the dispute was settled, workers had won a new contract that nearly doubled their pensions and guaranteed wage increases of 3 to 5% annually for eight years.[19]

Although mergers between unions may not increase membership directly, they generally improve the efficiency of union-organizing efforts and reduce costly jurisdictional disputes between unions. Increased organizational strength from mergers may also enable unions to cover industries and occupations previously underrepresented in union membership, such as health care and telecommunications workers.

FAST FACT

Rates of unionization around the world:

- Australia   35%
- Brazil   44%
- Denmark   80%
- France   9%
- Japan   24%
- Mexico   43%
- United Kingdom 33%

Distribution of Membership

Historically, membership has been concentrated in a small number of large unions. In 1976, 16 unions represented 60% of union membership, and 85 unions represented just 2.4%. Similarly, the National Education Association (NEA) accounted for 62% of all teaching association members. Many employee associations are small because they are state organizations; therefore, their membership potential is limited. Unions today are exhibiting a substantial and increasing amount of diversification of membership. The most pronounced diversification has occurred in manufacturing.[20]

As Exhibit 14.3 shows, unionization levels also vary by state.[21] States with relatively high levels of unionization include Alaska, Hawaii, Michigan, and New York; states with the lowest levels of unionization include Arizona, Arkansas, North Carolina, and South Carolina.

Structure of American Unions

The basic unit of labor unions in the United States is the national (or international) union, a body that organizes, charters, and controls member locals. National unions develop the general policies and procedures by which locals operate, and help locals in areas such as collective bargaining. National unions provide clout for locals because they control a large number of employees and can influence large organizations through national strikes or slowdown activities.

FAST FACT

The confederation of unions in Mexico is Concamin; in England, it is the Trade Union Congress (TUC).

The major umbrella organization for national unions is the American Federation of Labor and Congress of Industrial Organizations (**AFL-CIO**). With about 13 million members, it represents about 85% of the total union membership. The two largest unions in the AFL-CIO are the Teamsters and the American Federation of State, County and Municipal Employees.

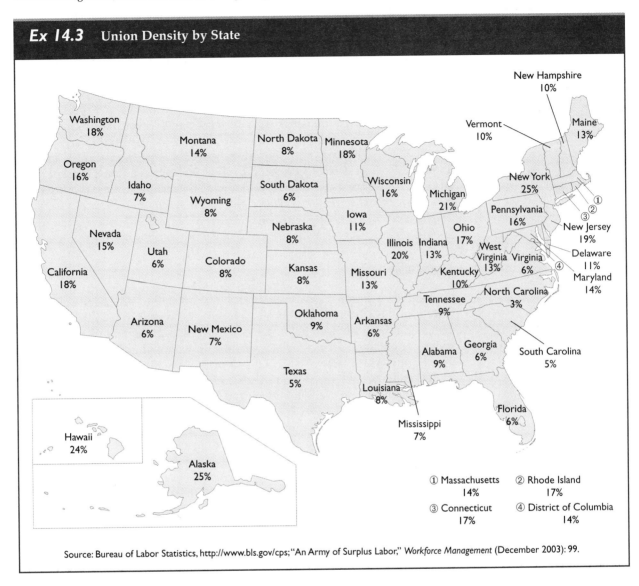

Ex 14.3 Union Density by State

New Hampshire 10%

Vermont 10%

Maine 13%

Washington 18%

Montana 14%

North Dakota 8%

Minnesota 18%

New York 25%

Oregon 16%

Idaho 7%

Wisconsin 16%

Pennsylvania 16%

Wyoming 8%

South Dakota 6%

Michigan 21%

New Jersey 19%

Nevada 15%

Utah 6%

Iowa 11%

Ohio 17%

West Virginia 13%

Delaware 11%

California 18%

Colorado 8%

Nebraska 8%

Illinois 20%

Indiana 13%

Virginia 6%

Maryland 14%

Kansas 8%

Missouri 13%

Kentucky 10%

North Carolina 3%

Arizona 6%

New Mexico 7%

Oklahoma 9%

Arkansas 6%

Tennessee 9%

Texas 5%

Alabama 9%

Georgia 6%

South Carolina 5%

Louisiana 8%

Florida 6%

Mississippi 7%

Hawaii 24%

Alaska 25%

① Massachusetts 14%   ② Rhode Island 17%

③ Connecticut 17%   ④ District of Columbia 14%

Source: Bureau of Labor Statistics, http://www.bls.gov/cps; "An Army of Surplus Labor," *Workforce Management* (December 2003): 99.

About 60 national unions, representing 4.5 million workers, operate independently of the AFL-CIO.

Every two years, the AFL-CIO holds a convention to develop policy and amend its constitution. Each national union is represented in proportion to its membership. Between conventions, an executive council (the governing body) and a general board direct the organization's affairs; a president is in charge of day-to-day operations.

The executive council's activities include evaluating legislation that affects labor and watching for corruption within the AFL-CIO. Standing committees are appointed to deal with executive, legislative, political, educational, organizing, and other activities. The department of organization and field services, for instance, focuses its attention on organizing activities. Three structures organize the local unions: Many of the craft unions are represented by the trade department and the industrial department, and the remaining locals are organized directly as part of the national unions, being affiliated with AFL-CIO headquarters but retaining independence in dealing with their own matters.

At the heart of the labor movement are the 70,000 or so local unions. The locals represent the workers at the workplace, where much of the day-to-day contact with management and the HR department takes place. Most locals elect a president, a secretary-treasurer, and perhaps one or two other officers from the membership.

The larger locals hire a **business representative,** *a full-time employee hired to handle employee grievances and contract negotiations.* Locals also have a **steward,** *an employee elected by the employee's work unit to act as the union representative at the workplace and to respond to company actions against employees that may violate the labor agreement.* The steward protects the rights of workers by filing grievances when the employer has acted improperly.

How Unions Operate

The activities of union locals revolve around collective bargaining and grievance handling. In addition, locals hold general meetings, publish newsletters, and otherwise keep their members informed. Unless a serious problem exists, attendance at meetings is usually low, and the election of officers often draws votes from less than one-fourth of the membership.

At headquarters, the AFL-CIO staff and committees work on a wide range of issues, including civil rights, job security, community service, economic policy, union-management cooperation, education, ethical practices, executive pay, housing, international affairs, legislation, public relations, health care, research, safety, Social Security, and veterans' affairs. A publications department produces literature for the membership and outsiders. National union headquarters also provides specialized services to regional and local bodies. People trained in organizing, strikes, legal matters, public relations, and negotiations are available to individual unions.[22]

National unions and the AFL-CIO are also active in the political arena. Labor maintains a strong lobbying force in Washington, DC, and is involved in political action committees at the state and local levels. Some large national unions have been active in international politics. The UAW lobbied in Washington, DC, to restrict car imports in an attempt to bolster U.S. automakers and increase jobs. They lobbied against the North American Free Trade Agreement (NAFTA) and for health care reform. To help their membership, unions are expanding their activities on all levels and, in some cases, working with other organizations to attain mutual goals. Unions are also trying to do a more effective job in their recruiting efforts and organizing campaigns. Descriptions of these activities in Mexico and Canada are offered in the feature "Managing Globalization: Unionization in Mexico and Canada."[23]

THE ORGANIZING CAMPAIGN

One major function of the NLRB is to conduct the process in which a union is chosen to represent employees. This is accomplished through a certification election to determine if the majority of employees want the union. The process by which a single union is selected to represent all employees in a particular unit is crucial to the American system of collective bargaining. If

Managing Globalization

Unionization in Mexico and Canada

In Mexico, unions have the right to organize workers at a business, but only one union represents a given location, covering all employees at that location. When a strike is called, the workplace is closed until the strike is settled—picket lines are unknown.

In case of a dispute, the burden of proof is always on the employer. Also, the labor law is part of Mexico's constitution, and workers aren't allowed to renounce these rights. Therefore, any individual employment contract or collective agreement that limits these rights is considered invalid.

Since the advent of NAFTA, union organizations in the United States have seen the development of positive relations with Mexico as a strategic opportunity and necessity. As firms like General Electric (GE) and General Motors increased operations in Mexico, the U.S. unions that were already active in these companies began providing support to the local unions in Mexico, which want to organize the workers of these companies. The U.S. union movement has also attempted to work through NAFTA to improve wages and working conditions in Mexico. NAFTA legislation empowers the secretaries of labor in Canada, the United States, and Mexico to impose fines on a country that fails to enforce its labor laws.

Approximately one-third of the Canadian labor force is unionized. About three-fourths of the union members are affiliated with the Canadian Labor Congress (CLC). As in the United States, the union local is the basic local unit. The CLC is the dominant labor group at the national level. Its political influence may be compared with that of the AFL-CIO.

The labor laws in Canada are similar to those in the United States, but with some noteworthy differences. For example, Canadian labor laws require frequent interventions by governmental bodies before a strike can take place. In the United States, such intervention is largely voluntary. For the Canadian union movement as a whole, the trend toward concessionary bargaining to avoid layoffs and plant closings appears to be less evident than it is in the United States. At the same time, Canadian labor organizations affiliated with unions dominated by labor organizations in the United States are becoming increasingly autonomous. This trend was highlighted when the UAW in Canada became independent from the same union in the United States.[24]

a majority of those voting opt for union representation, all employees are bound by that choice, and the employer is obligated to recognize and bargain with the chosen union.

Because unions may acquire significant power, employers may be anxious to keep them out. Adding to this potential union-management conflict is the possibility of competition and conflict between unions if more than one union is attempting to win certification by the same group of employees. The certification process has several stages, as outlined in Exhibit 14.4.[25]

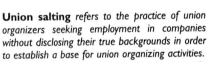

FAST FACT

Union salting *refers to the practice of union organizers seeking employment in companies without disclosing their true backgrounds in order to establish a base for union organizing activities.*

SOLICITING EMPLOYEE SUPPORT

In the campaign to solicit employee support, unions generally attempt to contact the employees, obtain a sufficient number of authorization cards, and request an election from the NLRB.

ESTABLISHING CONTACT BETWEEN THE UNION AND EMPLOYEES

Contact between the union and employees may be initiated by either party. National unions usually contact employees in industries or occupations in which they have an interest or are traditionally involved. The UAW, for example, has contacted nonunion employees in the new automobile plants that have been built in the South by German and Japanese auto companies.[26]

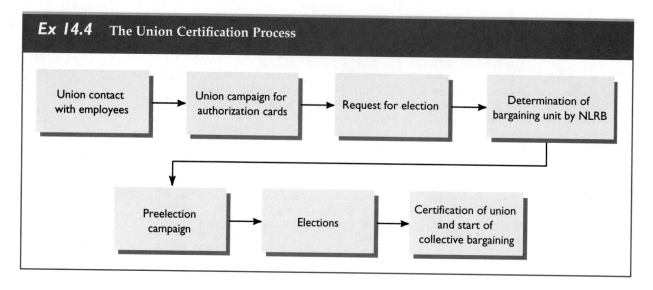

Ex 14.4   The Union Certification Process

In other cases, employees may approach the union, and the union is usually happy to oblige. Employees may or may not have strong reasons for desiring this affiliation—low pay, poor working conditions, and other issues relating to dissatisfaction. Because workers generally tend to be apathetic toward unions, however, their concern must become quite serious before they will take any action.

FAST FACT

In 2000, the meat-cutting department at one Wal-Mart voted to establish a union. Two weeks later, Wal-Mart disbanded its meat-cutting departments.

Prohibited Actions. At the point that contact occurs between the union and employees, the company must be careful to avoid engaging in unfair labor practices. Accordingly, *employers should not:*

- *Misrepresent the facts.* Any information management provides about a union or its officers must be factual and truthful.
- *Threaten employees.* It is unlawful to threaten employees with loss of their jobs or transfers to less desirable positions, income reductions, or loss or reductions of benefits and privileges. The use of intimidating language to dissuade employees from joining or supporting a union also is forbidden. In addition, supervisors may not blacklist, lay off, discipline, or discharge any employee because of union activity.
- *Promise benefits or rewards.* Supervisors may not promise a pay raise, additional overtime or time off, promotions, or other favorable considerations in exchange for an employee's agreement to refrain from joining a union or signing a union card, to vote against union representation, or to otherwise oppose union activity.
- *Make unscheduled changes in wages, hours, benefits, or working conditions.* Any such changes are unlawful unless the employer can prove they were initiated before union activity began.
- *Conduct surveillance activities.* Management is forbidden to spy on employees' union activities or to request antiunion workers to do so, or to make any statements that give workers the impression they are being watched. Supervisors also may not attend union meetings or

question employees about a union's internal affairs. They also may not ask employees for their opinions of a union or its officers.

- *Interrogate workers.* Managers may not require employees to tell them who has signed a union card, voted for union representation, attended a union meeting, or instigated an organization drive.
- *Prohibit solicitation.* Employees have the right to solicit members on company property during their nonworking hours, provided this activity does not interfere with work being performed, and to distribute union literature in nonwork areas during their free time.[27]

Employers can and perhaps should:

- Discuss the history of unions and make factual statements about strikes, violence, or the loss of jobs at plants that have unionized;
- Discuss their own experiences with unions;
- Advise workers about the costs of joining and belonging to unions;
- Remind employees of the company benefits and wages they receive without having to pay union dues;
- Explain that union representation won't protect workers against discharge for cause;
- Point out that the company prefers to deal directly with employees (not through a third party) in settling complaints about wages, hours, and other employment conditions;
- Tell workers that, in negotiating with the union, the company is not obligated to sign a contract or accept all the union's demands, especially those that aren't in its economic interests;
- Advise employees that unions often resort to work stoppages to press their demands and that such tactics can cost workers money; and
- Inform employees of the company's legal right to hire replacements for workers who go out on strike for economic reasons.[28]

Authorization Cards and the Request for Elections. Once contact has been made, the union begins the campaign to collect sufficient authorization cards, or signatures of employees interested in having union representation. This campaign must be carried out within the constraints set by law. If the union obtains cards from 30% of an organization's employees, it can petition the NLRB for an election. (Procedures in the public sector are similar.) If the NLRB determines there is indeed sufficient interest, it will schedule an election. If the union gets more than 50% of the employees to sign authorization cards, it may petition the employer as the bargaining representative. Usually employers refuse, whereupon the union petitions the NLRB for an election.

The employer usually resists the union's card-signing campaign. For instance, companies often prohibit solicitation on the premises. However, employers are legally constrained from interfering with an employee's freedom of choice. Union representatives have argued that employers ignore this law because the consequences are minimal—and by doing so, they can effectively discourage unionism.

During the union campaign and election process, it is important that the HR manager caution the company against engaging in unfair labor practices. Unfair labor practices, when identified, generally cause the election to be set aside. Severe violations by the employer can result in certification of the union as the bargaining representative, even if it has lost the election.

DETERMINATION OF THE BARGAINING UNIT

When a union gathers enough signatures to petition for an election, the NLRB identifies the **bargaining unit,** *which is the group of employees that will be represented by the union.* The bargaining unit must be truly appropriate and not contain a mix of antagonistic interests or submerge the legitimate interests of a small group of employees in the interests of a larger group.[29]

To ensure the fullest freedom of collective bargaining, legal constraints and guidelines have been established for specifying the bargaining unit. Professional and nonprofessional groups can't be included in the same unit, and a craft unit can't be placed in a larger unit unless both units agree to it. Other issues the NLRB considers when defining the bargaining unit include the physical location(s) of employees, skill levels, degree of company ownership, and collective bargaining history.

From the union's perspective, the most desirable bargaining unit is one whose members are pro-union and will help win certification. The unit also must have sufficient influence in the organization to give the union some power once it wins representation. Employers generally want a bargaining unit that's least beneficial to the union; they want to maximize the likelihood of union failure in the election and minimize the power of the unit.

PREELECTION CAMPAIGN

After the bargaining unit has been determined, both union and employer embark on a **preelection campaign.** Unions claim to provide a strong voice for employees, emphasizing improvement in wages and working conditions and the establishment of a grievance process to ensure fairness. Employers emphasize the costs of unionization—dues, strikes, and loss of jobs. Severe violations of the legal constraints on behavior, such as the use of threats or coercion, are prevented by the NLRB, which watches the preelection activity.

ELECTION, CERTIFICATION, AND DECERTIFICATION

Generally, elections are part of the process of determining if unions will win the right to represent workers. Elections can also determine if unions will retain the right to represent employees.

Election and Certification. The NLRB conducts the certification election. The **certification election** *determines whether the union is recognized as the legal representative of the employees in the organization.* To unionize a workplace, at least 30% of workers must sign cards calling for an election. Usually, however, unions won't call an election unless they are sure that at least 50% will vote favorably, in order to ensure a win.

Once a union has been certified, the employer is required to bargain with that union. If a majority of employees do not vote in favor of the union, another election won't be held for at least a year. Generally, about one-third to one-half of all certification elections result in a union being certified. The success rate of unions is lower in larger companies.

Card Checks. An alternative to the formal election is the card check approach to organizing a group of workers. With **card checks,** *workers gain* *the right to join a union if a majority of employees sign cards saying they wish to do so. The process is faster and less bureaucratic than holding elections."*[30] A contract settlement between Verizon and the International Brotherhood of Electrical Workers gave Verizon employees the right to be represented by the union if 55% signed up through the cards.

FAST FACT Companies organized by the card check process include Marriott, Rite-Aid, and Cingular.

Decertification Elections. The NLRB also conducts **decertification elections** *that can remove a union from representation.* If 30% or more of the employees in an organization request such an election, it will be held. Decertification elections most frequently occur in the first year of a union's representation when the union is negotiating its first contract. During this period, union strength has not yet been established, and employees are readily discouraged by union behavior.

Deciding to Join a Union

Unions were originally formed in response to the exploitation and abuse of employees by management. To understand the union movement today, we need to examine why employees decide to join unions and why they decide not to.

FAST FACT The largest unionized U.S. company is UPS. The largest nonunionized company in the United States is Wal-Mart.

Predicting whether or not employees will wish to join and will then actually sign up for union membership is difficult. Several factors influence employees in deciding whether to join a union. In general, however, three conditions strongly influence employees who decide to join a union: dissatisfaction, lack of power, and union instrumentality.[31]

Dissatisfaction. When an individual takes a job, certain conditions of employment (wages, hours, and type of work) are specified in the employment contract. In addition to the formal employment contract, an informal psychological contract also exists between employer and employee. The **psychological contract** *consists of an employee's unspecified expectations about reasonable working conditions, requirements of the work itself, the level of effort that should be expended on the job, and the nature of the authority the employer should have in directing the employee's work.*[32] These expectations are related to the employee's desire to satisfy certain personal preferences in the workplace. The degree to which the organization fulfills these preferences determines the employee's level of satisfaction. Dissatisfaction with the implicit terms and conditions of the employment will lead employees to attempt to improve the work situation, often through unionization. If management wants to make unionization less attractive to employees, it must make work conditions more satisfying.

Lack of Power. Unionization is seldom the first recourse of employees who are dissatisfied with some aspect of their jobs. The first attempt to improve the work situation is usually made by an individual acting alone. Someone who has enough power or influence can effect the necessary changes without collaborating with others. The amount of power the jobholder has in the organization is determined by how difficult it is to replace the person and how important or critical the job is to the overall success of the organization. An exclusive employee with an essential task may be able to force the employer to make a change. If, however, the employee can easily be replaced and the employee's task is not critical, other means, including collective action, must be considered in order to influence the organization.[33]

Union Instrumentality. When employees are dissatisfied with aspects of a work environment—such as pay, promotion opportunity, treatment by supervisor, the job itself, and work rules—they may perceive a union as being able to help improve the situation. If they believe that the union may be able to help, they then weigh the value of the benefits to be obtained through unionization against unionization's costs, such as a lengthy organizing campaign and bad feelings between supervisors, managers, and other employees who don't want a union. However, research suggests that employees' willingness to support a union is also affected by general attitudes about unions formed early in life.[34]

Beliefs about unions in general and about the particular union to be voted on shape employees' perceptions of union instrumentality. **Union instrumentality** *is the value an employee feels a union would have, after weighing the costs and benefits against the likelihood of a union's being able to obtain the benefits.*[35] The more that employees believe a union can obtain positive work aspects, the more instrumental employees perceive the union to be in removing the causes of dissatisfaction. When the benefits exceed the costs and union instrumentality is high, employees are more likely to be willing to support a union.[36] After joining a union, employee commitment to the union influences how much they participate in union activities.[37] Exhibit 14.5 summarizes the factors that influence whether employees unionize.

THE COLLECTIVE BARGAINING PROCESS

Collective bargaining is a complex process in which union and management negotiators maneuver to win the most advantageous contract.[38] How the issues involved are settled depends on

- the quality of the union-management relationship,
- the processes of bargaining used by labor and management,
- management's strategies in collective bargaining, and
- the union's strategies in collective bargaining.

The labor relations system is composed of three subunits—employees, management, and the union—with the government influencing interaction between the three. Employees may be managers or union members, and some union members are part of the union management system (local union leaders). Each of the three interrelationships in the system is regulated by specific federal statutes.

Each group in the labor relations model typically has different goals. Workers are interested in improved working conditions, wages, and opportunities. Unions also are interested in these, as well as their own survival, growth, and acquisition of power, which depend on their ability to maintain the support of the employees by providing for their needs. Management has overall organizational goals (e.g., increasing profits, market share, and growth rates) and also seeks to preserve managerial prerogatives to direct the workforce and to attain the personal goals of the managers (e.g., promo-

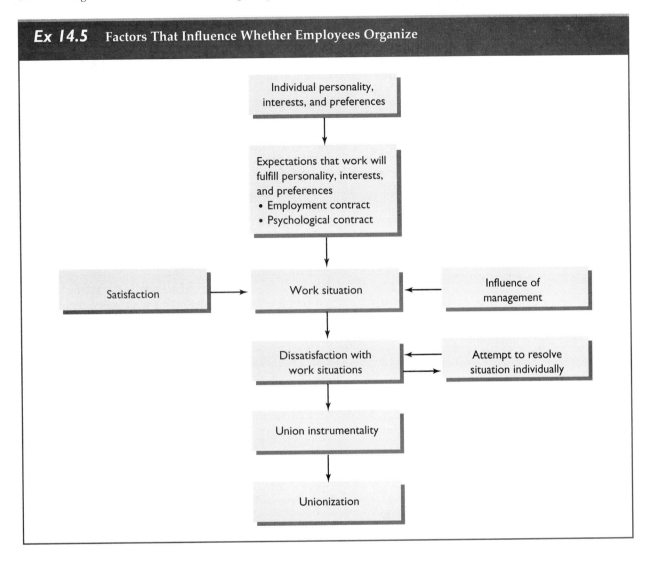

Ex 14.5   **Factors That Influence Whether Employees Organize**

tion or achievement). Government is interested in a stable and healthy economy, protection of individual rights, and safety and fairness in the workplace. All these factors influence the roles that these groups play.

ADVERSARIAL RELATIONSHIP

The goals of workers, unions, management, and governments were often seen as incompatible. Thus, an adversarial relationship emerged, with labor and management attempting to get a bigger cut of the pie, while government oversaw its own interests. In an **adversarial relationship** *between union and management, the union's role is to gain concessions from management during collective bargaining and to preserve those concessions through the grievance procedure.* The union is an outsider and critic.[39]

Historically, unions have adopted an adversarial role in their interactions with management. Their focus has been on wages, hours, and working conditions as they attempted to get "more and better" from management. This approach works well in economic boom times but encounters difficulties when the economy is not healthy. High unemployment and the threat of continued job losses induced unions to expand their role, especially since many of their traditional goals have already been achieved.

Cooperative Relationship

Some unions have begun to enter into new, collaborative efforts with employers.[40] For example, the USWA now works cooperatively with Bethlehem Steel, LTU, and National Steel. Together, labor and management are finding ways to restructure costs so the steel industry can survive and keep jobs in the United States.[41]

A **cooperative relationship** *requires that union and management solve problems, share information, and integrate outcomes.* Although cooperative approaches are not typical in the United States, they have been built into labor relations in other countries, including Sweden, Germany, and now throughout the European Union.[42] In a cooperative relationship, the union's role is that of a partner, not a critic. The union is jointly responsible with management for reaching a suitable solution to business challenges.

Cooperative agreements seem to be particularly fragile. One problem may be that neither partner—labor or management—has much experience with these relationships, which require that each side trust the other. Increasingly, managers recognize that the success of most of the programs they undertake to improve their organization depends on the acceptance of the unions present in the organization. Involving unions during the design of change initiatives is a good way to gain their acceptance.

Bargaining Processes

As we have noted, unions negotiate and implement agreements with management through the process of collective bargaining. In this section, we describe in more detail five types of bargaining that can occur during contract negotiations: distributive, integrative, concessionary, continuous, and intraorganizational.

Distributive Bargaining. Distributive bargaining takes place when the parties are in conflict over the issue, and the outcome represents a gain for one party and a loss for the other. With **distributive bargaining,** *each party tries to negotiate for the best possible outcome.* The process is outlined in Exhibit 14.6.[43]

On any particular issue, union and management negotiators each have three identifiable positions. The union has an *initial demand point,* which is generally more than it expects to get; a *target point,* which is its realistic assessment of what it may be able to get; and a *resistance point,* or the lowest acceptable level for the issue. Management has three similar points: an *initial offer point,* which is usually lower than the expected settlement; a *target point,* at which it would like to reach agreement; and a *resistance point,* or its upper acceptable limit.

If, as shown in Exhibit 14.6, management's resistance point is greater than the union's, a *positive settlement range* exists. If, however, management's resistance point is below the union's, a *negative settlement range,* or bargain-

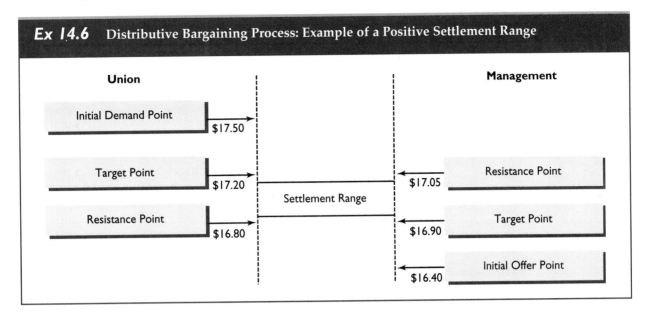

Ex 14.6 **Distributive Bargaining Process: Example of a Positive Settlement Range**

Union   Management

| Initial Demand Point | |
| $17.50 | |

| Target Point | | Resistance Point |
| $17.20 | $17.05 |

Settlement Range

| Resistance Point | | Target Point |
| $16.80 | $16.90 |

| | Initial Offer Point |
| | $16.40 |

ing impasse, exists, and there is no common ground for negotiation.[44] For example, on the issue of wages, the union may have a resistance point of $16.80 an hour, a target of $17.20, and an initial demand point of $17.50. Management may offer $16.40 but have a target of $16.90 and a resistance point of $17.05. The positive settlement range is between $16.80 and $17.05, and this is where the settlement will likely be. However, only the initial wage demand and offer are made public at the beginning of negotiations.

Because many issues are involved in a bargaining session, the actual process is complicated. Although the model shown describes the process of bargaining for each issue, in actual negotiations the issues are negotiated simultaneously, so the process is more complex than depicted. Union concessions on one issue may be traded for management concessions on another. Thus, the total process is dynamic.

Integrative Bargaining. When more than one issue needs to be resolved, integrative agreements may be pursued. **Integrative bargaining** *focuses on creative solutions that reconcile (integrate) the parties' interests and yield joint benefits.* It can occur only when negotiators have an "expanding-pie" perception—that is, when the two parties (union and management) have two or more issues and are willing to develop creative ways to satisfy both parties.[45]

Concessionary Bargaining. Distributive and integrative bargaining are the primary approaches to bargaining; concessionary bargaining often occurs within these two frameworks. With **concessionary bargaining,** *employers seek givebacks or concessions from the unions, promising job security in return.*

Concessionary bargaining may be prompted by severe economic conditions faced by employers. In the early 1990s, this type of bargaining was prevalent, especially in smokestack industries, such as automobiles, steel, and rubber, and to some extent in the transportation industry. Concessions sought by management from the unions included wage freezes, wage reductions, outsourcing, layoffs, work rule changes or elimination, fringe-benefit reductions, increased productivity, and more hours of work for the same pay.[46] Two-tier wage systems were tried in some industries, but problems of inequity and lower worker morale offset much of the savings from lower labor costs.[47] In addition, the available evidence suggests that agreements arrived at through concessionary bargaining erode union solidarity, leadership credibility, and control, as well as union power and effectiveness.[48]

Continuous Bargaining. Due to the rapid rate of change in the global and domestic environments, some labor and management negotiators are turning to continuous bargaining. With **continuous bargaining,** *joint committees with representatives from both labor and management meet on a regular basis to explore issues and solve problems of common interest.* Continuous bargaining committees have appeared in the retail food, over-the-road trucking, nuclear power, and men's garment industries.[49] Characteristics of continuous bargaining include

- frequent meetings during the life of the contract,
- a focus on external events and problem areas rather than on internal problems,
- use of the skills of outside experts in decision making, and
- use of a problem-solving (integrative) approach.[50]

The intention of continuous bargaining is to develop a union-management structure that's capable of adapting positively and productively to sudden changes in the environment. This approach is different from, but an extension of, the emergency negotiations that unions have insisted on when inflation or other circumstances have substantially changed the acceptability of the existing agreement. Continuous bargaining is a permanent arrangement intended to help avoid the crises that often occur under traditional collective bargaining systems.

Intraorganizational Bargaining. Regardless of how negotiations between management and labor proceed, the bargaining teams from each side usually must also engage in intraorganizational bargaining. During **intraorganizational bargaining,** *the representatives for labor and management confer with their respective constituents over changes in bargaining positions.* Management negotiators may have to convince management to change its position on an issue—for instance, to agree to a higher wage settlement. Union negotiators must eventually convince their members to accept the negotiated contract, so they must be sensitive to the demands of the membership, as well as realistic. When the membership votes on the proposed package, it will be strongly influenced by the opinions of the union negotiators.

NEGOTIATING THE AGREEMENT

Once a union is certified as the representative of a bargaining unit, it becomes the only party that can negotiate an agreement with the employer for all members of that work unit, whether they are union members or not. Technically, however, individuals within the unit can still negotiate with the employer personal deals that give them more than the other members receive, particularly if the agreement is silent on this issue.

The union serves as a critical link between employees and employer. It is responsible to its members to negotiate for what they want, and it has the duty to represent all employees fairly. The quality of its bargaining is an important measure of union effectiveness.

Negotiating Committees

The employer and the union select their own representatives for the negotiating committee. When choosing its representatives, neither party is required to consider the wishes of the other. For example, management negotiators can't refuse to bargain with representatives of the union because they dislike them or don't think they are appropriate.

Union negotiating teams typically include representatives of the union local—often the president and other executive staff members. In addition, the national union may send a negotiating specialist, who is likely to be a labor lawyer, to work with the team. The negotiators selected by the union don't have to be members of the union or employees of the company. The general goal is to balance skill and experience in bargaining with knowledge and information about the specific situation.

At the local level, when a single bargaining unit is negotiating a contract, the company is usually represented by the manager and members of the labor relations or HR staff. Finance and production managers also may be involved. When the negotiations are critical, either because the bargaining unit is large or because the effect on the company is great, specialists such as labor lawyers may be included on the team.

In national negotiations, top industrial relations or HR executives frequently head a team of specialists from corporate headquarters and perhaps managers from critical divisions or plants within the company. Again, the goal is to have expertise along with specific knowledge about critical situations.

The Negotiating Structure

Most contracts are negotiated by a single union and a single employer. In some situations, however, different arrangements can be agreed on. When a single union negotiates with several similar companies (e.g., firms in the construction industry), the employers may bargain as a group. At the local level, this is called multiemployer bargaining; at the national level, it is referred to as industrywide bargaining. Industrywide bargaining occurs in the railroad, coal, wallpaper, and men's suits industries. In 2003, the UAW engaged in multiemployer bargaining that led to the approval of similar new contracts for the big three automakers—General Motors (GM), Ford Motors, and Chrysler. After announcing that the union had reached the conclusion of its third deal in as many days, UAW President Ron Gettelfinger explained their objective, "Since the start of these negotiations, one of our goals has been to bring this industry together." GM's chair and CEO Rick Wagoner agreed that the deals moved the industry in that direction. Improved coordination within the industry is considered important as U.S. automakers struggle to compete against foreign competition.[51]

When several unions bargain jointly with a single employer, they engage in coordinated bargaining. Although not as common as the multiemployer and industrywide bargaining, coordinated bargaining appears to be increasing, especially in the public sector. One consequence of coordinated and industrywide bargaining is often pattern settlements, where similar wage rates are imposed on the companies whose employees are represented by the same union within a given industry.

In the construction industry, a wide-area and multicraft bargaining structure arose in response to the unionized employers' need to be more price-competitive and to have fewer strikes, and in response to the unions' desire to gain more control at the national level. Consequently, the bargaining is done on a regional (geographic) rather than local basis, and it covers several construction crafts simultaneously. The common contract negotiations that occur in wide-area and multicraft bargaining reduce the opportunity for unions to whipsaw the employer. **Whipsawing** *occurs when one contract settlement is used as a precedent for the next, which then forces the employer to get all contracts settled in order to have all the employees working.* As a result of whipsawing, an employer frequently agrees to more favorable settlements on all contracts, regardless of the conditions and merits of each one, just to keep all employees working.[52]

Preparation for Bargaining

Prior to the bargaining session, management and union negotiators need to develop the strategies and proposals they will use. These strategies reflect the objectives of the two sides.

Management Strategies. For negotiations with the union, management needs to complete four different tasks:

1. preparation of specific proposals for changes in contract language;
2. determination of the general size of the economic package that the company anticipates offering during the negotiations;
3. preparation of statistical displays and supportive data that the company will use during negotiations; and
4. preparation of a bargaining book for use by company negotiators that compiles the information on issues that will be discussed, giving an analysis of the effect of each clause, its use in other companies, and other facts.[53]

The relative cost of pension contributions, pay increases, health benefits, and other bargaining provisions should be determined prior to negotiations. Other costs should also be considered. For instance, management might ask itself, "What is the cost of union demands for changes in grievance and discipline procedures or transfer and promotion provisions?" Management should also ask, "What might be some of the benefits of agreeing to the demands of the union?" Besides avoiding a strike, benefits might include improved productivity and an improved reputation as an employer of choice. The goal is to be as well prepared as possible by considering the implications and ramifications of the issues that will be discussed and by being able to present a strong argument for the position taken.

Union Strategies. Like management, unions need to prepare for negotiations by collecting information. Because collective bargaining is the major means by which a union can convince its members of its effectiveness and value, this is a critical activity. Unions collect information on

- the financial situation of the company and its ability to pay;
- the attitude of management toward various issues, as reflected in past negotiations or inferred from negotiations in similar companies; and
- the attitudes and desires of the employees.

The first two areas give the union an idea of what demands management is likely to accept. The third area is sometimes overlooked. It involves awareness of the preferences of the union membership. For instance, the union might ask, "Is a pension increase preferred over increased vacation or holiday benefits?" Membership preferences will vary with the characteristics of the workers. Younger workers are more likely to prefer more holidays, shorter workweeks, and limited overtime, whereas older workers are more likely to be interested in pension plans, benefits, and overtime. The union can determine these preferences by using questionnaires and meetings to survey its members.

ISSUES FOR NEGOTIATION

The Labor Management Relations Act specifies the issues that can be discussed in collective bargaining sessions. This act established three categories of issues for negotiation: mandatory, permissive, and prohibited.

Mandatory issues *are those that employers and employee representatives (unions) are obligated to meet and discuss; these are "wages, hours, and other terms and conditions of employment."* These issues affect management's ability to run the company efficiently and are central to the union's desire to protect jobs and workers' standing in their jobs.

Permissive issues *are those that are not specifically related to the nature of the job but still of concern to both parties.* For example, decisions about price, product design, and new jobs may be subject to bargaining if the parties agree to it. Permissive issues usually develop when both parties see that mutual discussion and agreement will be beneficial, which may be more likely when a cooperative relationship exists between union and management. This is the case of the negotiation between the USWA union and Goodyear. Here the cooperative relationship enabled them to discuss the strategy of the company going forward. Management and union negotiators can't refuse to agree on a contract if they fail to settle a permissive issue.

Prohibited issues *concern illegal or outlawed activities, and these may not be discussed in collective bargaining sessions.* Examples of prohibited issues include the demand that an employer use only union-produced goods or, where it is illegal, that it employ only union members.

Total Compensation. Wage conflicts are a leading cause of strikes. Difficulties arise here because a wage increase is a direct cost to the employer, whereas a wage decrease is a direct cost to the employee. As discussed in Chapter 9, rates of pay are influenced by a variety of issues, including the going rate in an industry, the employer's ability to pay, the cost of living, and productivity. All these subjects are often debated and discussed in negotiations.

Benefits and Services. Because the cost of benefits and services can run as high as 40% of the total cost of wages, it is a major concern in collective bargaining. Benefit provisions are very difficult to remove once they are in place, so management tends to be cautious about agreeing to them. Some commonly negotiated forms of benefits and services are pensions, paid vacations, retraining, paid holidays, sick leave, job security, health care and life insurance, dismissal or severance pay, and supplemental unemployment benefits. As Exhibit 14.7 shows, unionized employees are much more likely to have defined benefit plans, medical care, dental care, and vision care.[54] For employees with families, these benefits can be worth several thousand dollars per year.

FAST FACT

Health care costs (for current workers and retirees), layoffs, outsourcing, and pension security are becoming more important bargaining issues than wages.

Because health care costs have continued to rise over the past several years, they have become one of the main issues in collective bargaining agreements. Often the negotiations address the issue of how much of the cost increases will be paid by the employer versus employees. GE recently was subjected to a nationwide strike over this issue, which closed down 48 GE facilities in 23 states. GE made a decision to raise health care copayments, which meant an increased cost to employees of about $300 per year. GE argued that it had the right to make this decision unilaterally, but union leaders argued that such health benefit issues have always been negotiated. For GE, increasing health care costs threatened to damage its competitiveness—its costs had increased more than 50% in the previous five years. It expected employees to pay for some of those increases. According to some union experts, disputes such as the one at GE are likely to be more common in the next few years. "Until the public policy crisis is resolved, we're going to have a much more chaotic labor relations process," predicted Tom Juravich, director of the Labor Relations and Research Center at the University of Massachusetts.[55]

Hours of Employment. Although organizations are already required by federal labor law to pay overtime for work beyond 40 hours a week, unions continually try to reduce the number of hours in the standard workweek.

Ex 14.7 Coverage for Major Benefits

	RETIREMENT BENEFITS			HEALTH CARE BENEFITS		
	DEFINED PLANS (ALL)	DEFINED BENEFIT PLANS	DEFINED CONTRIBUTION PLANS	MEDICAL CARE	DENTAL CARE	VISION CARE
All employees	49%	20%	40%	45%	32%	19%
Union	83%	72%	39%	60%	51%	37%
Nonunion	45%	15%	40%	44%	30%	17%

Note: Values indicate the percentage of workers participating in health care and retirement benefits, private industry, based on a 2003 survey of 2,984 private industry organizations.

Negotiations may focus on including the lunch hour in the 8-hour-day requirement, or on providing overtime for time spent working longer than an 8-hour shift.

Institutional Issues. Some issues are not directly related to jobs but are nevertheless important to both employees and management. Institutional issues that affect the security and success of both parties include:

- *Union security.* About two-thirds of the major labor contracts stipulate that employees must join the union after being hired into its bargaining unit. However, 20 states that traditionally have had low levels of unionization have passed right-to-work laws outlawing union membership as a condition of employment.
- *Check-off.* Unions have attempted to arrange for payment of dues through deductions from employees' paychecks. By law, employees must agree in writing to a dues check-off. A large majority of union contracts contain a provision for this agreement.
- *Strikes.* The employer may insist that the union agree not to strike during the life of the contract, typically when a cost-of-living clause has been included. The agreement may be unconditional, allowing no strikes at all, or it may limit strikes to specific circumstances.
- *Managerial prerogatives.* More than half the agreements today stipulate that certain activities are the right of management. In addition, management in most companies argues that it has "residual rights," meaning that rights not specifically limited by the agreement belong to management.

Administrative Issues. Administrative issues concern the treatment of employees at work. These issues include:

- *Breaks and cleanup time.* Some contracts specify the time and length of coffee breaks and meal breaks for employees. In addition, jobs requiring cleanup may have a portion of the work period set aside for this procedure.
- *Job security.* Job security is perhaps the issue of most concern to employees and unions. Employers are concerned with a restriction of their ability to lay off employees. Changes in technology or attempts to subcontract work impinge on job security. Today companies are outsourcing more work to other companies with lower wage costs. They are also offshoring work to their own employees in other countries. Both of these actions put pressure on jobs in the United States. Thus, job security continues to be a primary issue for most unions.
- *Seniority.* Length of service is used as a criterion for many HR decisions in most collective agreements. Layoffs are usually determined by seniority. "Last hired, first fired" is a common situation. Seniority is also important in transfer and promotion decisions. The method of calculating seniority is usually specified in order to clarify the relative seniority of employees.
- *Discharge and discipline.* Termination and discipline are tough issues, and even when an agreement addresses these problems, many grievances are filed concerning the way they are handled.

"A lot of people don't understand the union. They look at their wages and think they're doing as well as they would with the union. But when the hotel closes or they have no place to go, they get nothing. If you're in a union, you still have all the money that went into a pension. You have benefits. You have security."

Bernice Thomas
Las Vegas worker and
mother of eight children

- *Safety and health.* Although the Occupational Safety and Health Act specifically deals with worker safety and health, some contracts have provisions specifying that the company will provide safety equipment, first aid, physical examinations, accident investigations, and safety committees. Hazardous work may be covered by special provisions and pay rates. Often, the agreement will contain a general statement that the employer is responsible for the safety of the workers, so that the union can use the grievance process when any safety issues arise.
- *Production standards.* The level of productivity or performance of employees is a concern of both management and the union. Management is concerned with efficiency, and the union is concerned with the fairness and reasonableness of management's demands. Increasingly, both are concerned about total quality and quality of work life.
- *Grievance procedures.* The contract usually outlines a process for settling disputes that may arise during its administration.
- *Training.* The design and administration of training and development programs and the procedure for selecting employees for training may also be bargaining issues. This is particularly important when the company is attempting to introduce new technologies and needs people with new competencies to perform the new jobs.
- *Duration of the agreement.* Agreements can last for one year or longer, with the most common period being three years.

FACTORS AFFECTING BARGAINING

The preceding discussion suggests that negotiations proceed in a rational manner and end in resolution when a positive contract zone—a set of outcomes that is preferred over the imposition of a strike—exists. Unfortunately, negotiators often fail to reach agreement, even when a positive contract zone exists.

To fully understand the negotiation process, it is important to examine the decision processes of negotiators. If the biases of negotiators can be identified, then prescriptive approaches and training programs can be developed to improve negotiations. The following are common cognitive or mental limitations exhibited in negotiator judgments.[56]

The Mythical Fixed Pie. All too frequently, negotiators believe that their interests automatically conflict with the other party's interests. In other words, what one side wins, the other side loses. However, most conflicts have more than one issue at stake, with the parties placing different values on the different issues. Consequently, the potential usually exists for integrative agreements. A fundamental task in training negotiators lies in identifying and eliminating this false "fixed-pie" assumption and preparing them to look for trade-offs between issues of different value to each side.

Framing. Research on decision making shows that the perspective people take when deciding whether to accept a settlement is affected by whether they feel they are winning or losing. Consider the following bargaining situation. The union claims that its members need a raise to $12 an hour and that anything less will represent a loss due to inflation. Management argues that the company can't pay more than $10 an hour and that anything more would impose an unacceptable loss. In this situation, $11 an hour is seen as a loss by both sides. If each side had the choice between settling at $11 an hour or going to binding arbitration, they would be likely to take the risk and move toward arbitration rather than settlement. Changing the frame of the situation to a positive one, however, could result in a very different outcome. If the union viewed anything above $10 an hour as a gain, and if management viewed anything under $12 an hour as a gain, then a negotiated settlement at $11 an hour would be more likely.

As this example emphasizes, the frame (positive or negative) of negotiators can make the difference between settlement and impasse. One solution to impasses, then, is to train negotiators to alter their own frame of reference, and that of the other party as well, so both sides can recognize when gains are possible.[57]

CONFLICT RESOLUTION

Although the desired outcome of collective bargaining is agreement on the conditions of employment, on many occasions, negotiators are unable to reach such an agreement at the bargaining table. In these situations, several alternatives are used to break the deadlock. The most dramatic response is a strike or lockout; indirect responses are also used, and third-party interventions such as mediation and arbitration are common as well.

STRIKES AND LOCKOUTS

A **strike** *occurs when the union is unable to get management to agree to a demand it believes is critical and tells employees to refuse to work at the company.* When *management refuses to allow employees to work, the situation is called a* **lockout.** In 2003, a lockout by port operators and shipping lines was followed by an 11-day longshoremen's strike. When the longshoremen lockout occurred, the main issue was the introduction of computer technology to track cargo. Management wanted to introduce new technologies for scanning and tracking cargo, to modernize the ports and improve their efficiency. The International Longshore and Warehouse Union (ILWU) opposed the technology because they feared it would displace some of their members and create new jobs for nonunion workers. If they were going to agree to the new technology, the longshoremen wanted improved wages and benefits. Management ordered the lockout because, it said, the workers were engaging in a slowdown. A month later, an 11-day strike by the ILWU closed 29 ports around the country. The lockout and subsequent strike meant that ships were stranded at sea and unable to unload their cargo. Millions of dollars worth of agricultural cargo rotted, and many department stores were worried that they would not receive the merchandise they needed for the upcoming holiday season.[58]

FAST FACT The longshoremen lockout and strike caused a loss to the U.S. economy estimated at $1 billion.

Strong membership support for a strike strengthens the union negotiators' position. If the strike takes place, union members picket the employer, informing the public about the existence of a labor dispute and preferably, from the union's point of view, convincing it to avoid this company during the strike. Union members commonly refuse to cross the picket line of another striking union, which gives added support to the striking union.

Employers usually attempt to continue operations while a strike is in effect. They either run the company with supervisory personnel and people not in the bargaining unit or hire replacements for the striking employees. At the conclusion of the strike, employers will be expected to (1) reinstate strikers in all the positions that remain unfilled, unless they have substantial business reasons for doing otherwise; and (2) establish a preferential hiring list for displaced strikers to facilitate their recall as new openings occur.

The success of a strike depends on its ability to cause economic hardship to the employer. Severe hardship usually causes the employer to concede to the union's demands.[59] Thus, from the union's point of view, the cost of the company's lack of production must be high. The union, therefore, actively tries to prevent replacement employees from working. Although it appears that the company can legally hire replacements, the union reacts strongly to the employment of scabs, as these workers are called, and the replacement employees may be a cause of increasingly belligerent labor relations. The hiring of replacement workers has reached a level where companies are keeping them even after the strike is settled—if the strike is settled at all. This tactic has given employers even more power in a strike situation. Thus, the union movement seeks a law to prevent replacement workers from becoming permanent workers.

The timing of the strike is also often critical. The union attempts to hold negotiations just before the employer has a peak demand for its product or services, when a strike will have the maximum economic effect.

Although strikes have been on the decline, they are costly to both the employer, who loses revenue, and employees, who lose income. If a strike is prolonged, the cost to employers will likely never be fully recovered by the benefits gained. In part because of this, employers seek to avoid strikes. Moreover, the public interest is generally not served by strikes. They often are an inconvenience and can have serious consequences for the economy as a whole.

Slowdowns. Short of an actual strike, unions may invoke a work slowdown. At the Caterpillar plant, Lance Vaughan usually installed a set of small and large hoses on huge off-highway trucks—small hoses first, then the big hoses. But when a slowdown started, he began to install the big hoses first, and then reach awkwardly around them to attach the smaller hoses. The result was lost production time. Technically, Vaughan was just doing his job. The instructions furnished by Caterpillar's engineers described the inefficient procedure. Normally, Vaughan would have ignored such instructions and made a note to himself to tell the engineers to fix the mistake.

When the slowdown began, however, he stopped speaking up and began working according to the rules furnished by the company. "I used to give the engineers ideas," explained Vaughan, who had worked at Caterpillar for 20 years. "We showed them how to eliminate some hose clips and save money. And I recommended larger bolts that made assembly easier and faster, and were less likely to come loose."[60]

At Caterpillar, the slowdown was referred to as an "in-plant strategy." Regardless of the name, the result is the same: a reduction of work output, physically and mentally. Slowdowns can be more effective than actual strikes.

Primary Boycotts. Unions sometimes want to make the public more aware of their cause. As a consequence, they may engage in a primary boycott. For instance, a union that is striking a soda-bottling company may set up an informational picket line at grocery stores that sell the bottler's products. It has generally been ruled that as long as the picket line is directed at the target of the stike—in this case, the bottling company—it constitutes a primary boycott and is legal. The picket line becomes illegal, however, when it tries to prevent customers from shopping at the grocery store. Interfering with the grocery store's business would be called a secondary boycott. Secondary boycotts are illegal because they can harm innocent third parties.

Corporate Campaigns. In a corporate campaign, a union may ask the public and other unions to write letters to a company, requesting that it change the way it bargains with the union. Some unions are using their power as shareholders to influence companies' policies and practices (e.g., of reducing health care benefits of workers and outsourcing jobs to nonunion companies). Some unions manage the pension benefits of their members, contributions to which are made by their employees. The unions in turn invest this money in hopes of increasing the size of the pension funds. In Cincinnati, Ohio, the area's construction unions own 5 million shares of Kroger stock. (This grocery chain is also headquartered in Cincinnati.) Using this financial clout, the unions picketed Kroger in protest of its threat to cut health care benefits.[61]

MEDIATION

Mediation *is a procedure in which a neutral third party helps the union and management negotiators reach a voluntary agreement.*[62] Having no power to impose a solution, the mediator attempts to facilitate the negotiations between union and management. The mediator may make suggestions and recommendations and perhaps add objectivity to the often-emotional negotiations. To have any success at all, mediators must have the trust and respect of both parties and have sufficient expertise and neutrality to convince the union and employer that they will be fair and equitable. The U.S. government operates the Federal Mediation and Conciliation Service (FMCS) to make experienced mediators available to unions and companies. The core of the FMCS mission is: "Building Sound Labor-Management Relations through Mediation." They have been doing this for more than 50 years.

ARBITRATION

Arbitration *is a procedure in which a neutral third party studies the bargaining situation, listens to both parties and gathers information, and then makes a determination that is binding on the parties.* The arbitrator, in effect, determines the conditions of the agreement.

FAST FACT

The power of the arbitrator's decision was established by three Supreme Court decisions in 1960 referred to as the Trilogy cases, and all involved the United Steelworkers.

In final-offer arbitration, the arbitrator can choose between the final offer of the union and the final offer of the employer. The arbitrator can't alter these offers but must select one as it stands. Since the arbitrator chooses the offer that appears most fair, and since losing the arbitration decision means settling for the other's offer, each side is pressured to make as good an offer as possible. By contrast, in conventional arbitration, the arbitrator is free to fashion any award deemed appropriate.

Once the contract impasse is removed, union and management have an agreement. Abiding by it is the essence of contract administration; however, at times, arbitration will again be necessary—namely, when a grievance is filed. This type of arbitration is referred to as rights arbitration or grievance arbitration.

CONTRACT ADMINISTRATION

Once signed, the collective agreement becomes the contract that governs daily work life. That is, the daily operation and activities in the organization are subject to the conditions of the agreement. Because of the difficulty of writing an unambiguous agreement anticipating all the situations that will occur over its life, disputes will inevitably occur over the contract's interpretation and application. The most common method of resolving these disputes is a grievance procedure. Virtually all agreements negotiated today provide for a grievance process to handle employee complaints.

GRIEVANCE PROCEDURES

Basically, a grievance is a charge that the union-management contract has been violated.[63] A grievance may be filed by the union for employees, or by employers, although management rarely does so. The grievance process is designed to investigate the charges and to resolve the problem. Common sources of grievances are

- outright violation of the agreement,
- disagreement over facts,
- dispute over the meaning of the agreement,
- dispute over the method of applying the agreement, and
- argument over the fairness or reasonableness of actions.[64]

Grievance procedures typically involve several stages. The collective bargaining agreement specifies the maximum length of time that can elapse between the incident that is the subject of the dispute and the filing of a grievance on that incident. The most common grievance procedure, shown in Exhibit 14.8,[65] involves the following four steps:

Step 1. An employee who feels that the labor contract has been violated usually contacts the union steward, and together they discuss the problem with the supervisor involved. If the problem is simple and straightforward, it is often resolved at this level.

Step 2. If agreement cannot be reached at the supervisor level, or if the employee is not satisfied, the complaint can enter the second step of the grievance procedure. Typically, a human resource representative of the company now seeks to resolve the grievance.

Ex 14.8 Typical Union-Management Grievance Procedure

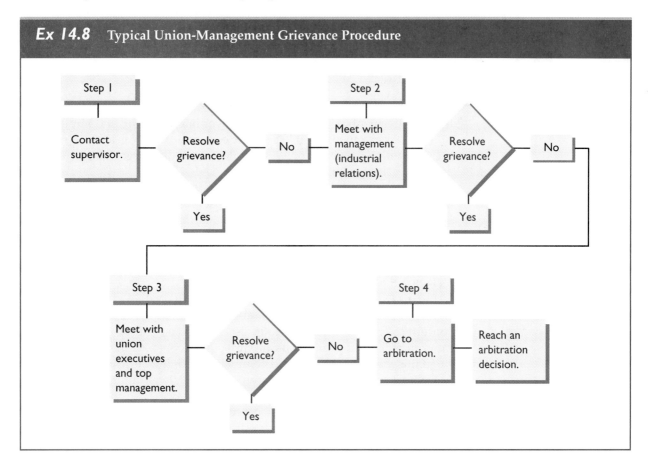

Step 3. If the grievance is sufficiently important or difficult to resolve, it may be taken to the third step. Although contracts vary, they usually specify that top-level management and union executives be involved at this stage. These people have the authority to make the major decisions that may be required to resolve the grievance.

Step 4. If a grievance cannot be resolved at the third step, an arbitrator will likely need to consider the case and reach a decision. The arbitrator is a neutral, mutually acceptable individual who may be appointed by the FMCS or some private agency. The arbitrator holds a hearing, reviews the evidence, and then rules on the grievance. The decision of the arbitrator is usually binding.

Because the cost of arbitration is shared by the union and employer, some incentive exists to settle the grievance before it goes to arbitration. An added incentive in some cases is the requirement that the loser pay for the arbitration. The expectation behind these incentives is that the parties will screen or evaluate grievances more carefully because pursuing a weak grievance to arbitration will be expensive.

Occasionally, the union will call a strike over a grievance in order to resolve it. This may happen when the issue at hand is so important that the union feels that it cannot wait for the slower arbitration process. Such an "employee rights" strike may be legal; however, if the contract specifically forbids strikes during the tenure of the agreement, it is not legal and is called a wildcat strike. Wildcat strikes are not common; most grievances are settled through arbitration.

Grievance Issues

Grievances can be filed over any workplace issue that is subject to the collective agreement, or they can be filed over interpretation and implementation of the agreement itself. The most common type of grievance reaching the arbitration stage involves discipline and discharge, although many grievances are filed over other issues.

Absenteeism can be grounds for discharge, and a grievance procedure may be used to determine whether the absenteeism in question is excessive. Insubordination is either failure to do what the supervisor requests or the outright refusal to do it. If the supervisor's orders are clear, explicit, and legal, and if the employee is warned of the consequences, discipline for refusal to respond is usually acceptable. The exception is when the employee feels that the work endangers health.

Because seniority is usually used to determine who is laid off, bumped from a job to make way for someone else, or rehired, its calculation is of great concern to employees. Seniority is also used as one of the criteria to determine eligibility for promotions and transfers, so management must be careful in this area in order to avoid complaints and grievances.

Compensation for time away from work, vacations, holidays, or sick leave is also a common source of grievances. Holidays cause problems because special pay arrangements often exist for people working on those days.

Wage and work schedules may also lead to grievances. Disagreements often arise over interpretation or application of the agreement relating to such issues as overtime pay, pay for reporting, and scheduling. Grievances have been filed over the exercise of such management rights as the right to introduce technological changes, use subcontractors (outsource), or change jobs in other ways. This type of behavior may also be the source of charges of unfair labor practices, since these activities may require collective bargaining.

The Taft-Hartley Act gives unions the right to file grievances on their own behalf if they feel their rights have been violated. It also gives unions access to information necessary to process the grievance or to make sure the agreement is not being violated. In addition, unions may file grievances for violations of union shop or check-off provisions. On the other hand, employees have the right to present their *own* grievances on an individual basis, and the employer can resolve such grievances without the union's presence. The only qualifying items are that adjustments cannot abrogate the collective agreement, and the union must be given an opportunity to participate in the grievance proceedings at some point prior to the adjustment.

Occasionally, other activities prompt grievances. Wildcat strikes or behavior that functions as a strike (e.g., mass absences from work) can result in a management grievance. Increasingly, outsourcing, offshoring, and the hiring of replacement workers are issues resulting in grievances.

Management Procedures

Management can significantly affect the grievance rate by adopting proper procedures for taking action against an employee. One of the most important procedures involves that of discipline and discharge. The issue of just cause and fairness is central to most discipline grievances. Employers must ensure that the employee is adequately warned of the consequences, that the rule involved is related to operation of the company, that a thorough investigation is undertaken, and that the penalty is reasonable. In areas outside of discipline and discharge, management can avoid grievance problems by educating supervisors and managers about labor relations and about the conditions of the collective agreement. It has been found that supervisors with labor knowledge are an important factor in the reduction of grievances.

Union Procedures

The union has an obligation to its members to provide them fair and adequate representation and to process and investigate grievances brought by its members speedily. Thus, it should have a grievance-handling procedure that aids in effectively processing grievances without being guilty of unfair representation. Unfair representation, according to the NLRB, is usually related to one of four types of union behavior:

1. *Improper motives.* The union cannot refuse to process a grievance because of the employee's race or gender or because of the employee's attitude toward the union.
2. *Arbitrary conduct.* Unions cannot dismiss a grievance without investigating its merits.
3. *Gross negligence.* The union cannot recklessly disregard the employee's interests.
4. *Union conduct after filing the grievance.* The union must process the grievance to a reasonable conclusion.[66]

Because the employer can also be cited for unfair representation, management should attempt to maintain a fair grievance process. Company labor relations managers should avoid taking advantage of union errors in handling grievances so that such actions do not affect fair representation.

Another important influence on the grievance process is the union steward. Since the union steward is generally the first person to hear about an employee's grievance, the steward has substantial influence on the grievance process. A steward can either encourage an employee to file a grievance, suggest that the problem is really not a grievance, or informally resolve the problem outside the grievance procedure. The personalities of stewards may, in fact, influence the number of grievances filed.[67] Because stewards are selected from the ranks of employees and may have little knowledge of labor relations, the union should train them to improve their effectiveness. The company can also be liable in a fair-representation suit and therefore should support such training.

Assessing the Collective Bargaining Process

The effectiveness of the entire collective bargaining process can be measured by the extent to which each party attains its goals, but this approach has its difficulties. Because goals are incompatible in many cases and can therefore lead to conflicting estimates of effectiveness, a more useful measure may be the quality of the system used to resolve conflict. Conflict is more apparent in the collective bargaining process, where failure to resolve the issues typically leads to strikes. Another measure of effectiveness is the success of the grievance process, or the ability to resolve issues developing from the bargaining agreement.

Effectiveness of Negotiations. Because the purpose of negotiations is to achieve an agreement, the agreement itself becomes an overall measure of bargaining effectiveness. A healthy and effective bargaining process encourages the discussion of issues and problems and their subsequent resolution at the bargaining table. In addition, the effort required to reach agreement is a measure of how well the process is working. Some indications of this effort are the duration of negotiations, the outcome of member ratification votes, the frequency and duration of strikes, the use of mediation and arbitration, the need for government intervention, and the quality of union-management relations (whether conflict or cooperation exists). Joint programs for productivity and quality-of-work-life improvements could be regarded as successes resulting from effective union-management relations.

Effectiveness of Grievance Procedures. The success of a grievance procedure may be assessed from different perspectives. Management may view the number of grievances filed and the number settled in its favor as measures of effectiveness, with a small number filed or a large number settled in its favor indicating success. Unions may also consider these numbers, but from their point of view, a large number filed and a large number settled in their favor may indicate success.

An overall set of measures to gauge grievance procedure effectiveness may be related to the disagreements between managers and employees. Measures that might be included are frequency of grievances; the level in the grievance procedure at which grievances are usually settled; the frequency of strikes or slowdowns during the term of labor agreements; the rates of absenteeism, turnover, and sabotage; and the necessity for government intervention.

The success of arbitration is often judged by the acceptability of the decisions, the satisfaction of the parties, the degree of innovation, and the absence of bias in either direction. The effectiveness of any third-party intervention rests in part on how successfully strikes are avoided, because the motivation for such intervention is precisely to avert this extreme form of conflict resolution.

SUMMARY

Line managers and HR professionals need to know as much as possible about unionization because the stakes are substantial. Unionization may be attractive to employees who are dissatisfied with their work conditions and feel powerless to change these conditions. By correcting unsatisfactory work conditions, or by not allowing them to occur in the first place, organizations reduce the likelihood of unionization. However, once a union-organizing campaign begins, a company cannot legally stop it without committing an unfair labor practice.

Historically, unions and management have operated as adversaries because many of their goals are in conflict. Because conflict is detrimental to both management and unions, effective labor relations have been established to reduce this conflict. Although cooperation is not widespread, it may become the dominant style of union-management relations in the future. Its effects are particularly apparent in collective bargaining, contract negotiation, and grievance processing.

The quality of the union-management relationship can have a strong influence on contract negotiations. Labor and management each select a bargaining committee to negotiate the new agreement. The negotiations may be between a single union and a single company or multiple companies, or between multiple unions and a single company. Bargaining issues are mandatory, permissive, or prohibited. Mandatory issues must be discussed, permissive issues can be discussed if both parties agree to do so, and prohibited issues can't be discussed. The issues can be grouped into wage, benefits and services, institutional, and administrative issues.

Almost all labor contracts outline procedures for handling employee complaints. The most common grievance is related to discipline and discharge, although wages, promotions, seniority, vacations, holidays, and management and union rights are also sources of complaints.

The effectiveness of the collective bargaining process is usually assessed by measures of how well the process is working. Bargaining can be evaluated using measures such as the duration of negotiations, the frequency of strikes, the use of third-party intervention, and the need for government intervention. The effectiveness of the grievance process can be assessed by the number of grievances; the level in the grievance process at which settlement occurs; the frequency of strikes or slowdowns; the rates of absenteeism, turnover, and sabotage; and the need for government intervention.

As economic conditions in the world have changed substantially, so have union-management relations. Increasingly, managers recognize that cooperative relationships can improve their company's competitiveness. Unions see cooperative relationships as instrumental in protecting the jobs and incomes of their members. And society as a whole sees cooperative relationships as necessary and appropriate in these times of intense global competition.

TERMS TO REMEMBER

Adversarial relationship
AFL-CIO
Arbitration
Bargaining unit
Business representative
Card checks
Certification election
Collective bargaining
Concessionary bargaining
Continuous bargaining
Cooperative relationship

Decertification election
Distributive bargaining
Integrative bargaining
Intraorganizational bargaining
Lockout
Mandatory issues
Mediation
Permissive issues
Preelection campaign
Prohibited issues
Psychological contract

Steward   Unionization
Strike   Union salting
Union instrumentality   Whipsawing

DISCUSSION QUESTIONS

1. Describe how a strike by the Teamsters against UPS would affect that company's various stakeholders. Would the timing of the strike make a difference? Explain.

2. Union membership has been declining in the United States for many years. What do you think are the major reasons for this?

3. Despite the fact that union membership is relatively low, many people believe that the fear of unionization serves to ensure that employers treat employees well. Do you agree or disagree with this view? Why?

4. Describe the actions that an employer may take when a union attempts to organize the workforce. What employer actions are prohibited?

5. Distinguish mediation from arbitration. How does a grievance procedure differ from interest arbitration? What is final-offer arbitration?

PROJECTS TO EXTEND YOUR LEARNING

1. *Integration and Application.* Using the cases at the end of the text, compare and contrast Lincoln Electric and Southwest Airlines with regard to the

   • views of management regarding union representation of their workers,
   • views of employees regarding union representation, and
   • consequences of these views for cooperation and conflict between employees and management.

   What changes in the environment or the company might lead Lincoln Electric's employees to become more interested in unionization? How likely do you think such changes are to occur?

2. *Exploring the Internet.*

   a. Learn about several union organizations by visiting their home pages, which contain a wealth of information:
      AFL-CIO, http://www.aflcio.org
      UAW, http://www.uaw.org
      CWA, http://www.cwa.org
      AFSCME, http://www.afscme.org
   b. Learn about labor union history and the development and structure of unions by visiting the website of the George Meany Center at http://www.georgemeany.org/resources.html.
   c. Learn more about patterns of union membership in the United States from the websites of the AFL-CIO (http://www.aflcio

.org) and the Bureau of Labor Statistics (http://www.bls.gov). For information about union rates around the world and to learn more about global unions, visit the International Labour Organization's website at http://www.ilo.org.

    d. Learn more about mediation from the Federal Mediation and Conciliation Service at http://www.fmcs.gov.

3. *Experiential Activity.* Learn more about union activities in your local area. Write a brief summary describing what you have learned, and if your instructor indicates it is appropriate, prepare a 5-minute report to present to your classmates. Begin by identifying one or two local organizations in which a union is present. Then find out the answers to the following questions. If possible, talk to the union steward, the business representative, and at least two union members.

    a. What are the names of the local unions in these organizations?

    b. Is the local affiliated with a larger national organization? If yes, how?

    c. Who is included the bargaining unit(s)?

    d. How long has the union been present in the organization? If the union was certified within the past two or three years, try to find someone who can tell you what it was like to go through the campaign and election process.

    e. Has the union held a strike in the past 5 years? If yes, find someone who can tell you what it was like to go on strike.

    f. What issues are of greatest concern to the members of this union?

CASE STUDY

THE UNION'S STRATEGIC CHOICE

Maria Dennis sits back and thoughtfully reads through the list of strategies that the union's committee gave her this morning. If her union is to rebuild the power it has lost over the past few years, it's time to take drastic action. If the union continues to decline as it has during the last few years, it won't be able to represent the members who voted for it to be their exclusive bargaining representative.

Maria was elected two years ago, at her union's convention, to be the international president of the Newspaper Workers International Union (NWIU). At the time, she knew it would not be an easy job, and she eagerly looked forward to taking on a new challenge. But she had no idea just how difficult it would be to get the union back on its feet again.

The NWIU was founded in the late 1890s and was made up of newspaper typographers who were responsible for such tasks as setting type on linotype machines, creating the layout of newspapers, proofing articles, and printing newspapers. Members of the union typically completed a six-year apprenticeship, learning all the different tasks involved in the printing process. Before 1960, printing professionals were considered the elite of the industrial workforce. The craft demanded that typographers be literate at a time when even the middle and upper classes were not. Furthermore, printing was a highly skilled, highly paid craft.

Since the 1980s, however, the union has declined. Literacy is no longer a unique characteristic, and automation has led to a deskilling of the craft. The introduction of video display terminals, optical character recognition scanners, and computerized typesetting has eliminated substantial composing room work, and the demand for skilled union workers has been reduced. The union experienced its peak membership of 120,000 in 1975. During the 1980s, membership began a substantial decline, and in 1998, the total membership was only 40,000. The reduced membership has resulted in other problems for the union. First, fewer members mean fewer dues, which are the union's main source of revenue. Consequently, the union is having some serious financial problems and is being forced to cut some of its services to members.

Second, the union is experiencing a significant loss in bargaining power with newspaper management. In the past, the printers were fairly secure in their jobs because there was a good demand in the labor market for individuals who could run the complicated printing equipment. But the recent switch to automation has eliminated many jobs and has also made it possible for employers to easily replace union employees. Anyone can be trained in a short time to use the new printing equipment. Therefore, if union members decide to strike for better wages, hours, and working conditions, management could easily, and legally, find replacements for them. In essence, the union is unable to fulfill its main mission, which is to collectively represent the employees who voted for it.

To solve the current crisis, Maria is considering five options:

1. Implement an associate member plan through which any individual can join the union for a fee of $50 a year. Although these members would not be fully represented on the job, they would get an attractive package of benefits, such as low-cost home, health, and auto insurance.

2. Attempt some cooperative labor-management relations programs, such as getting member representation on newspaper boards of directors or employee participation programs in the workplace.

3. Put more effort into political action. For example, lobby for labor law reform or for new laws more favorable to unions. Initiate action that would result in harsher penalties against employers that practice illegal union-avoidance activities, such as threatening to move the business if a union is voted in or firing pro-union employees.

4. Appeal to community leaders to speak out in favor of the union in order to improve public relations, to help recruit new members, and to encourage employers to bargain fairly when negotiating with the union.

5. Search for another union with which the printing professionals might merge, thus increasing their membership, strengthening their finances, increasing their bargaining power, and obtaining economies of scale.

Maria realizes that each of these options could have both positive and negative results, and is unsure which strategy, if any, she should recommend for the union to pursue. In less than three hours, however, she will have to present the list to the council with her recommendations.

CASE QUESTIONS

1. What are the strengths and weaknesses of each strategy?
2. What strategies could be employed to get new bargaining units?
3. What other types of services could the union offer to its members?
4. What would be your final recommendation? Justify your response.

Source: K. Stratton-Devine, University of Alberta.

ENDNOTES

1 R. J. Grossman, "Trying to Heal the Wounds," *HR Magazine* (September 1998): 85–92; D. A. Tosh, "After the UPS Strike," *ACA News* (October 1997): 11–14; M. Hammers, "Wanted: Part-Timers with Class," *Workforce* (January 2003): 27–29.

2 http://www.ups.com.

3 "GM Saturn Workers Weigh Innovative Labor Accord," *Wall Street Journal* (February 18, 1998): B6; A. R. McIlvaine, "The Comeback Trail," *Human Resource Executive* (November 1997): 55–58.

4 For a more extensive discussion of unionization and the entire union-management relationship, see W. H. Holley, Jr., K. M. Jennings, and

R. S. Wolters, *The Labor Relations Process*, 7th ed. (Fort Worth, TX: Harcourt, 2001); P. Clark, *Building More Effective Unions* (Ithaca, NY: ILR Press, 2000); J. A. Fossum, *Labor Relations: Development, Structure, Process*, 8th ed. (New York: Irwin McGraw-Hill, 2002); D. P. Twomey, *Labor Law and Legislation* (Cincinnati, OH: South-Western, 1998).

5 For an overview and in-depth discussion of collective bargaining, see H. C. Katz and T. A. Kochan, *An Introduction to Collective Bargaining and Industrial Relations* (New York: Irwin McGraw-Hill, 2003).

6 D. Welch, "What Goodyear Got from Its Union," *Business Week* (October 20, 2003): 148–149.

7 D. Welch, "Can the UAW Stay in the Game?" *Business Week* (June 10, 2002): 78–79.

8 Fossum, *Labor Relations*; Katz and Kochan, *An Introduction to Collective Bargaining and Industrial Relations*.

9 M. Arndt, "Salvation from the Shop Floor," *Business Week* (February 3, 2003): 100–101; D. Hakin, "Tough Times Force UAW to Employ New Strategy," *New York Times* (September 17, 2003): C1, C15; M. France, "After the Shooting Stops," *Business Week* (March 12, 2001): 98–99; J. Nee, P. Kennedy, and D. Langham, "Increasing Manufacturing Effectiveness Through Joint Union/Management Cooperation," *Human Resource Management* 38(1) (Spring 1999): 77–85; D. A. Tosh, "After the UPS Strike"; M. J. Koch and G. Hundley, "The Effects of Unionism on Recruitment and Selection Methods," *Industrial Relations* 36(3) (July 1997): 349.

10 D. Welch, "The UAW: Using Trade-Offs to Gain Traction," *Business Week* (September 8, 2003): 80–81.

11 D. Welch, "What Goodyear Got from Its Union"; S. Holmes, "Boeing Putting Out the Labor Fires," *Business Week* (December 29, 2003): 43; P. Elstrom, "Needed: A New Union for the New Economy," *Business Week* (September 4, 2000): 48; T. A. Kochan and P. Osterman, *The Mutual Gains Enterprise: Forging a Winning Partnership among Labor, Management, and Government* (Boston: Harvard Business School Press, 1994).

12 http://www.afl-cio.org.

13 *Ibid.*

14 A. A. Sloane and F. Witney, *Labor Relations* (Englewood Cliffs, NJ: Prentice-Hall, 1985) 62; see also R. O. Wright, *Chronology of Labor in the United States* (Jefferson, NC: McFarland, 2003).

15 U.S. Bureau of Labor Statistics, http://www.bls.gov.

16 *Ibid.*

17 http://www.afl-cio.org; C. Daniels, "Watch for Rallies in the Valley," *Fortune* (April 2, 2001): 36; M. B. Regan, "Shattering the AFL-CIO's Glass Ceiling," *Business Week* (November 13, 1998): 46; A. Bernstein, "Sweeney's Blitz," *Business Week* (February 17, 1997): 56–62.

18 A. Meisler, "Who Will Fold First?" *Workforce Management* (January 2004): 28–33; http://www.unitehere.org/about/ (October 21, 2004).

19 A. Meisler, "Unions Take Employers to School," *Workforce* (October 2003): 21–22.

20 C. D. Gifford, *Directory of U.S. Labor Organizations, 2001-2002 Edition* (Washington, DC: Bureau of National Affairs, 2002).

21 Source: Bureau of Labor Statistics.

22 For an interesting description of attempts that are being made to organize Wal-Mart, see C. Daniels, "Up Against the Wal-Mart," *Fortune* (May 17, 2004): 112–120.

23 For a detailed comparison of the United States and Canada, see S. M. Lipset and N. M. Meltz, *The Paradox of American Unionism: Why Americans Like Unions More than Canadians Do but Join Much Less* (Ithaca, NY: ILR Press, 2004); see also G. Gori, "Strike at VW Mexico Ends Unusually," *New York Times* (September 6, 2001): W1; S. Greenhouse, "In U.S. Unions, Mexico Finds Unlikely Ally on Immigration," *New York Times* (July 19, 2001): A1, A21; M. Maynard, "Canada Vote May Bring Union to Japan Carmaker," *New York Times* (July 6, 2001): C1, C11.

24 For a more detailed discussion of labor relations in other countries, see M. Morley, *Global Industrial Relations* (London: Routledge, in press).

25 Prepared for this chapter by William D. Todor, Professor of HRM, The Ohio State University.

26 D. Welch, "Can the UAW Stay in the Game?"

27 M. Bryant and R. Gilson, "Unions Can Organize Temporary Employees along with Regular Workforce," *Legal Report* (November–December 2000): 7–8; G. Flynn, "When the Unions Come Calling," *Workforce* (November 2000): 82–87; C. R. Fine, "Beware the Trojan Horse," *Workforce* (May 1998): 45–51.

28 J. Hoerr, "The Strange Bedfellows Backing Workplace Reform," *Business Week* (April 20, 1990): 57. See also R. Koenig, "Quality Circles Are Vulnerable to Union Tests," *Wall Street Journal* (March 28, 1990): B1; L. E. Hazzard, "A Union Says Yes to Attendance," *Personnel Journal* (November 1990): 47–49; Twomey, *Labor Law and Legislation,* 134.

29 J. R. Getman, J. B. Goldberg, and J. B. Herman, *Union Representation Elections: Law and Reality* (New York: Russell Sage, 1976): 72.

30 A. Meisler, "Who Will Fold First?" *Workforce Management* (January 2004): 28–33; S. Romero, "Accord Is Reached for Most Workers in Phone Walkout," *New York Times* (August 21, 2003): A1, A19.

31 H. H. Tan and S. Aryee, "Antecedents and Outcomes of Union Loyalty: A Constructive Replication and an Extension," *Journal of Applied Psychology* 87(4) (2002): 715–722; J. Barling, E. K. Kelloway, and E. H. Bremermann, "Preemployment Predictors of Union Attitudes: The Role of Family Socialization and Work Beliefs," *Journal of Applied Psychology* 75(5) (1991): 725–731; S. Mellor, "The Relationship between Membership Decline and Union Commitment: A Field Study of Local Unions in Crisis," *Journal of Applied Psychology* 75(3) (1990): 258–267; C. Fullagar and J. Barling, "A Longitudinal Test of a Model of the Antecedents and Consequences of Union Loyalty," *Journal of Applied Psychology* 74(2) (1989): 213–227.

32 A. Bernstein, "The Amalgamated Doctors of America?" *Business Week* (June 28, 1999): 36; S. Greenhouse, "The First Unionization Vote by Dot-Com Workers Is Set," *New York Times* (January 9, 2001): C4; C. Hirschman, "Overtime Overload," *HR Magazine* (December 2000): 84–92; M. Conlin, "Labor Laws Apply to Dot-Coms? Really?" *Business Week* (February 26, 2001): 96–98.

33 A. Ritter, "Are Unions Worth the Bargain?" *Personnel* (February 1990): 12–14.

34 P. Bamberger, A. Kluger, and R. Suchard, "The Antecedents and Consequences of Union Commitment: A Meta-Analysis," *Academy of Management Journal* 42(3) (1999): 304–318.

35 S. A. Youngblood et al., "The Impact of Work Attachment, Instrumentality Beliefs, Perceived Labor Union Image, and Subjective Norms on Union Voting Intentions and Union Membership," *Academy of Management Journal* (1984): 576–590.

36 H. Katz and T. A. Kochan, *An Introduction to Collective Bargaining and Industrial Relations* (New York: Irwin McGraw-Hill, 2003).

37 C. J. Fullagar, D. G. Gallagher, P. F. Clark, and A. E. Carroll, "Union Commitment and Participation: A 10-Year Longitudinal Study," *Journal of Applied Psychology* 89 (2004): 730-737.

38 For more details about collective bargaining, see P. F. Clark, J. Delaney, and A. Frost, *Collective Bargaining in the Private Sector* (Industrial Relations Research Association, 2003).

39 For a detailed discussion of grievance procedures, see BNA Editors, *Grievance Guide,* 11th ed. (Washington, DC: BNA Books, 2003); R. Peterson and D. Lewin, "Research on Unionized Grievance Procedures: Management Issues and Recommendations," *Human Resource Management* 39(4) (Winter 2000): 395–406; W. Zellner,

"Congestion at the Bargaining Table, Too," *Business Week* (March 19, 2001): 46; Brett, "Behavioral Research on Unions and Union-Management Systems," 200.

40   M. Arndt, "Salvation from the Shop Floor."

41   *Ibid.*

42   A. Fox, "To Consult and Inform," *HR Magazine* (October 2003): 87–91; C. Hirschman, "When Operating Abroad, Companies Must Adopt European-Style HR Plan," *HR News* (March 2001): 1, 6; R. Meredith, "Saturn Union Votes to Retain Its Cooperative Company Pact," *New York Times* (March 12, 1998): D1, D4.

43   Adapted from R. Walton and R. B. McKersie, *A Behavioral Theory of Labor Negotiations* (New York: McGraw-Hill, 1965): 43.

44   J. A. Fossum, *Labor Relations: Development, Structure, Processes,* 8th ed. (New York: McGraw-Hill, 2002).

45   L. L. Thompson, *The Mind and Heart of the Negotiator,* 2nd ed. (Upper Saddle River, NJ: Prentice-Hall, 2003); M. H. Bazerman, *Judgment in Managerial Decision Making* (New York: Wiley, 1986); M. H. Bazerman and J. S. Carroll, "Negotiator Cognition," in Cummings and Staw (eds.), *Research in Organizational Behavior,* vol. 9; M. H. Bazerman, T. Magliozzi, and M. A. Neale, "The Acquisition of an Integrative Response in a Competitive Market," *Organizational Behavior and Human Decision Processes* 34 (1985): 294–313.

46   S. Greenhouse, "Unions Finding That Employers Want More Concessions," *New York Times* (July 11, 2003): A12.

47   M. Winerip, "A Union Standing Fast Now Stands to Lose," *New York Times* (June 12, 1996): A16; K. Jennings and E. Traynman, "Two-Tier Plans," *Personnel Journal* (March 1988): 56–58.

48   *Ibid.;* W. Zellner, "What Was Don Carty Thinking?" *Business Week* (May 5, 2003): 32.

49   Sloane and Witney, *Labor Relations.*

50   Fossum, "Labor Relations," in Carroll and Schuler, *Human Resource Management in the 1980s,* 395–396.

51   G. M. Accord Finishes Talks for U.A.W.," *New York Times* (September 19, 2003): C1, C6.

52   P. Hartman and W. Franke, "The Changing Bargaining Structure in Construction: Wide-Area and Multicraft Bargaining," *Industrial and Labor Relations Review* (January 1980): 170–184.

53   Sloane and Witney, *Labor Relations,* 59.

54   "Benefit Costs Reach Crisis Stage," *Workforce Management* (December, 2003): 118–130.

55   D. Stires, "The Breaking Point," *Fortune* (March 3, 2003): 104–112.

56   M. H. Bazerman and M. A. Neale, "Heuristics in Negotiation: Limitations to Effective Dispute Resolution," in M. H. Bazerman and R. J. Lewick (eds.), *Negotiating in Organizations* (Beverly Hills, CA: Sage, 1983): 51–67; M. E. Gordon et al., "Laboratory Research in Bargaining and Negotiations: An Evaluation," *Industrial Relations* (Spring 1984): 218–223; R. E. Walton and R. B. McKersie, *A Behavioral Theory of Labor Negotiations* (New York: McGraw-Hill, 1965).

57   M. A. Neale, V. L. Huber, and G. Northcraft, "The Framing of Negotiations: Contextual versus Task Frame," *Organizational Behavior and Human Decision Processes* 39 (1987): 228–241.

58   S. Greenhouse, "Both Sides See Gains in Deal to End Port Labor Dispute," *New York Times* (November 25, 2003): A14.

59   C. Giambusso, "Delta's Labor Troubles: View from the Cockpit," *New York Times* (January 7, 2001): BU6; W. Zellner, "Up Against the Wal-Mart," *Business Week* (March 13, 2000): 76–78; E. Zimmerman, "HR Lessons from a Strike," *Workforce* (November 2000): 36–42; S. Greenhouse, "Unions, Growing Bolder, No Longer Shun Strikes," *New York Times* (September 7, 1998): A12; B. P. Sunoo, "Managing Strikes, Minimizing Loss," *Personnel Journal* (January 1995): 50–60.

60   D. Weimer, "A New Cat on the Hot Seat," *Business Week* (March 9, 1998): 56–61; A. Bernstein, "Why Workers Still Hold a Weak Hand," *Business Week* (March 2, 1998): 98; "Tentative Deal Reached by Caterpillar and the UAW," *Bulletin to Management* 49(7) (February 19, 1998): 49.

61   A. Bernstein, A. Borrus, and C. Palmeri, "Labor Sharpens Its Pension Sword," *Business Week* (November 24, 2003): 62–63; A. Meisler, "A High-Stakes Union Fight: Who Will Fold First?" *Workforce Management* (January 2004): 28–38.

62   S. Briggs, "Labor/Management Conflict and the Role of the Neutral," in R. S. Schuler, S. A. Youngblood, and V. L. Huber (eds.), *Personnel and Human Resource Management,* 3rd ed. (St. Paul, MN: West, 1988).

63   K. E. Boroff and D. Lewin, "Loyalty, Voice, and Intent to Exit a Union Firm: A Conceptual and Empirical Analysis," *Industrial and Labor Relations Review* 51(1) (October 1997): 50–63; S. Slichter, J. Healy, and E. Livernash, *The Impact of Collective Bargaining on Management* (Washington, DC: Brookings, 1960): 694.

64   B. Bemmels and J. R. Foley, "Grievance Procedure Research: A Review and Theoretical Recommendations," *Journal of Management* 22(3) (1996): 359–384.

65   Prepared by William D. Todor, Professor of HRM, The Ohio State University, for this chapter.

66   National Labor Relations Board, Memorandum 79–55 (July 7, 1979).

67   D. R. Dalton and W. D. Todor, "Manifest Needs of Stewards: Propensity to File a Grievance," *Journal of Applied Psychology* (December 1979): 654–659.

case

THE LINCOLN ELECTRIC COMPANY

People are our most valuable asset. They must feel secure, important, challenged, in control of their destiny, confident in their leadership, be responsive to common goals, believe they are being treated fairly, have easy access to authority and open lines of communication in all possible directions. Perhaps the most important task Lincoln employees face today is that of establishing an example for others in the Lincoln organization in other parts of the world. We need to maximize the benefits of cooperation and teamwork, fusing high technology with human talent, so that we here in the USA and all of our subsidiary and joint venture operations will be in a position to realize our full potential.

George Willis, former CEO,
The Lincoln Electric Company

INTRODUCTION

Today, the Lincoln Electric Company, under the leadership of John Stropki, is the world's largest manufacturer of arc-welding products and a leading producer of industrial electric motors. The firm employs almost 7,000 workers in factories near Cleveland and in 17 other countries, and a network of distributors and sales offices covers more than 160 countries. The company's U.S. market share (for arc-welding products) is estimated at more than 40%.[1]

The Lincoln incentive management plan has been well known for many years. Many college management texts make reference to the Lincoln plan as a model for achieving higher worker productivity. Certainly, the firm has been successful according to the usual measures.

James F. Lincoln died in 1965 and there was some concern, even among employees, that the management system would fall into disarray, that

profits would decline, and that year-end bonuses might be discontinued. Quite the contrary, since Lincoln's death, the company appears as strong as ever. Each year, except the recession years 1982 and 1983, has seen high profits and bonuses. In 1995, Lincoln Electric's centennial, sales for the first time surpassed $1 billion. While there was some employee discontent about relatively flat bonuses in 1995, employee morale and productivity remain very good.[2] Employee turnover is almost nonexistent except for retirements. Lincoln's market share is stable. The historically high stock dividends continue.

A HISTORICAL SKETCH

In 1895, after being "frozen out" of the depression-ravaged Elliott-Lincoln Company, a maker of Lincoln-designed electric motors, John C. Lincoln, took out his second patent and began to manufacture his improved motor. He opened his new business, unincorporated, with $200 he had earned redesigning a motor for young Herbert Henry Dow, who later founded the Dow Chemical Company.

Started during an economic depression and cursed by a major fire after only one year in business, the company grew, but hardly prospered, through its first quarter century. In 1906, John C. Lincoln incorporated the business and moved from his one-room, fourth-floor factory to a new three-story building he erected in east Cleveland. He expanded his workforce to 30 and sales grew to over $50,000 a year. John preferred being an engineer and inventor rather than a manager, though, and it was to be left to another Lincoln to manage the company through its years of success. In 1907, after a bout with typhoid fever forced him from Ohio State University in his senior year, James F. Lincoln, John's younger brother, joined the fledgling company. In 1914 he became the active head of the firm, with the titles of general manager and vice president. John remained president of the company for some years but became more involved in other business ventures and in his work as an inventor.

One of James Lincoln's early actions was to ask the employees to elect representatives to a committee that would advise him on company operations. This "Advisory Board" has met with the chief executive officer every two weeks since that time. This was only the first of a series of innovative personnel policies that have, over the years, distinguished Lincoln Electric from its competitors.

The first year the Advisory Board was in existence, working hours were reduced from 55 per week, then standard, to 50 hours a week. In 1915, the company gave each employee a paid-up life insurance policy. A welding school, which continues today, was begun in 1917. In 1918, an employee bonus plan was attempted. It was not continued, but the idea was to resurface later.

The Lincoln Electric Employees Association was formed in 1919 to provide health benefits and social activities. This organization continues today and has assumed several additional functions over the years. In 1923, a piecework pay system was in effect, employees got two weeks' paid vacation each year, and wages were adjusted for changes in the Consumer Price Index. Approximately 30% of the common stock was set aside for key employees in 1914. A stock purchase plan for all employees was begun in 1925.

The board of directors voted to start a suggestion system in 1929. The program is still in effect, but cash awards, a part of the early program, were discontinued several years ago. Now, suggestions are rewarded by "additional points" that affect year-end bonuses.

The legendary Lincoln bonus plan was proposed by the Advisory Board and accepted on a trial basis in 1934. The first annual bonus amounted to about 25% of wages. There has been a bonus every year since then. The bonus plan has been a cornerstone of the Lincoln management system and recent bonuses have approximated annual wages.

By 1944, Lincoln employees enjoyed a pension plan, a policy of promotion from within, and continuous employment. Base pay rates were determined by formal job evaluation and a merit rating system was in effect.

In the prologue of James F. Lincoln's last book, Charles G. Herbruck writes regarding the foregoing personnel innovations:

They were not to buy good behavior. They were not efforts to increase profits. They were not antidotes to labor difficulties. They did not constitute a "do-gooder" program. They were an expression of mutual respect for each person's importance to the job to be done. All of them reflect the leadership of James Lincoln, under whom they were nurtured and propagated.

During World War II, Lincoln prospered as never before. By the start of the war, the company was the world's largest manufacturer of arc-welding products. Sales of about $4,000,000 in 1934 grew to $24,000,000 by 1941. Productivity per employee more than doubled during the same period. The Navy's Price Review Board challenged the high profits. And the Internal Revenue Service questioned the tax deductibility of employee bonuses, arguing they were not "ordinary and necessary" costs of doing business. But the forceful and articulate James Lincoln was able to overcome the objections.

Certainly since 1935, and probably for several years before that, Lincoln's productivity has been well above the average for similar companies. The company claims levels of productivity more than twice those for other manufacturers from 1945 onward. Information available from outside sources tends to support these claims.

COMPANY PHILOSOPHY

James F. Lincoln was the son of a Congregational minister, and Christian principles were at the center of his business philosophy. The confidence that he had in the efficacy of Christ's teachings is illustrated by the following remark taken from one of his books:

The Christian ethic should control our acts. If it did control our acts, the savings in cost of distribution would be tremendous. Advertising would be a contact of the expert consultant with the customer, in order to give the customer the best product available when all of the customers' needs are considered. Competition then would be in improving the quality of products and increasing efficiency in producing and distributing them; not in deception, as is now too customary. Pricing would reflect efficiency of production; it would not be a selling dodge that the customer may be sorry he accepted. It would be proper for all concerned and rewarding for the ability used in producing the product.

There is no indication that Lincoln attempted to evangelize his employees or customers—or the general public for that matter. Neither the former chairman of the board and chief executive, George Willis, nor his predecessor, Donald F. Hastings, mentioned the Christian gospel in their speeches and interviews. The company motto, "The actual is limited, the possible is immense," is prominently displayed, but there is no display of religious slogans, and there is no company chapel.

Attitude Toward the Customer James Lincoln saw the customer's needs as the *raison d'etre* for every company. He wrote, "When any company has achieved success so that it is attractive as an investment, all money usually needed for expansion is supplied by the customer in retained earnings. It is obvious that the customer's interests, not the stockholder's, should come first." In 1947 he said, "Care should be taken . . . not to rivet attention on profit. Between 'How much do I get?' and 'How do I make this better, cheaper, more useful?' the difference is fundamental and decisive." Willis, too, ranked the customer as management's most important constituency. This is reflected in Lincoln's policy to "at all times price on the basis of cost and at all times keep pressure on our cost. . . ." Lincoln's goal, often stated, is "to build a better and better product at a lower and lower price." James Lincoln said, "It is obvious that the customer's interests should be the first goal of industry."

This priority, and the priority given to other groups, is reflected in the Vision, Missions, and Values Statements and the set of goals shown in Appendix LE.1.

Attitude Toward Stockholders Stockholders are given last priority at Lincoln. This is a continuation of James Lincoln's philosophy: "The last group to be considered is the stockholders who own stock because they think it will be more profitable than investing money in any other way." Concerning division of the largess produced by incentive management, he wrote, "The absentee stockholder also will get his share, even if undeserved, out of the greatly increased profit that the efficiency produces."

Attitude Toward Unionism There has never been a serious effort to organize Lincoln employees. While James Lincoln criticized the labor movement for "selfishly attempting to better its position at the expense of the people it must serve," he still had kind words for union members. He excused abuses of union power as "the natural reactions of human beings to the abuses to which management has subjected them." Lincoln's idea of the correct relationship between workers and managers is shown by this comment: "Labor and management are properly not warring camps; they are parts of one organization in which they must, and should, cooperate fully and happily."

Beliefs and Assumptions about Employees If fulfilling customer needs is the desired goal of business, then employee performance and productivity are the means by which this goal can best be achieved. It is the Lincoln attitude toward employees, reflected in the following comments by James Lincoln, that is credited by many with creating the success the company has experienced:

> *He is just as eager as any manager is to be part of a team that is properly organized and working for the advancement of our economy. He has no desire to make profits for those who do not hold up their end in production, as is true of absentee stockholders and inactive people in the company.*
>
> *If money is to be used as an incentive, the program must provide that what is paid to the worker is what he has earned. The earnings of each must be in accordance with accomplishment.*
>
> *Status is of great importance in all human relationships. The greatest incentive that money has, usually, is that it is a symbol of success. The resulting status is the real incentive. Money alone can be an incentive to the miser only.*
>
> *There must be complete honesty and understanding between the hourly worker and management if high efficiency is to be obtained.*

These beliefs and assumptions have helped shaped Lincoln's human resource objectives. These are shown in Appendix LE.2.

LINCOLN'S BUSINESS

Arc-welding has been the standard joining method in shipbuilding for decades. It is the predominant way of connecting steel in the construction industry. Most industrial plants have their own welding shops for maintenance and construction. Manufacturers of tractors and all kinds of heavy equipment use arc-welding extensively in the manufacturing process. Many hobbyists have their own welding machines and use them for making metal items such as patio furniture and barbecue pits. The popularity of welded sculpture as an art form is growing.

While advances in welding technology have been frequent, arc-welding products, in the main, have hardly changed. Lincoln's Innershield process is a notable exception. This process, described later, lowers welding cost and improves quality and speed in many applications. The most widely used Lincoln electrode, the Fleetweld 5P, has been virtually the same since the 1930s. The most popular engine-driven welder in the world, the Lincoln SA-200, has been a gray-colored assembly including a four-cylinder continental Red Seal engine and a 200-ampere direct-current generator with two current-control knobs for at least four decades. A 1989 model SA-200 even weighed almost the same as the 1950 model, and it certainly was little changed in appearance.

The company's share of the U.S. arc-welding products market appears to have been about 40% for many years. The welding products market has grown somewhat faster than the level of industry in general. The market is highly price-competitive, with variations in prices of standard items normally amounting to only a percent or two. Lincoln's products are sold directly by its engineering-oriented sales force and indirectly through its distributor organization. Advertising expenditures amount to less than three-fourths of a percent of sales. Research and development expenditures typically range from $10 million to $12 million, considerably more than competitors.

The other major welding process, flame-welding, has not been competitive with arc-welding since the 1930s. However, plasma-arc-welding, a relatively new process that uses a conducting stream of super heated gas (plasma) to confine the welding current to a small area, has made some inroads, especially in metal tubing manufacturing, in recent years. Major advances in technology that will produce an alternative superior to arc-welding within the next decade or so appear unlikely. Also, it seems likely that changes in the machines and

techniques used in arc-welding will be evolutionary rather than revolutionary.

It is also reasonable to observe that Lincoln Electric's business objectives, shown in Appendix LE.3, are likely to change in an evolutionary rather than a revolutionary way.

Products The company is primarily engaged in the manufacture and sale of arc-welding products–electric welding machines and metal electrodes. Lincoln also produces electric motors ranging from one-half horsepower to 200 horsepower. Motors constitute about 8–10% of total sales. Several million dollars have recently been invested in automated equipment that will double Lincoln's manufacturing capacity for one-half to 20-horsepower electric motors. The electric welding machines, some consisting of a transformer or motor and generator arrangement powered by commercial electricity and others consisting of an internal combustion engine and generator, are designed to produce 30 to 1,500 amperes of electrical power. This electrical current is used to melt a consumable metal electrode with the molten metal being transferred in super hot spray to the metal joint being welded. Very high temperatures and hot sparks are produced, and operators usually must wear special eye and face protection and leather gloves, often along with leather aprons and sleeves. Lincoln and its competitors now market a wide range of general purpose and specialty electrodes for welding mild steel, aluminum, cast iron, and stainless and special steels. Most of these electrodes are designed to meet the standards of the American Welding Society, a trade association. They are thus essentially the same as to size and composition from one manufacturer to another. Every electrode manufacturer has a limited number of unique products, but these typically constitute only a small percentage of total sales.

Welding electrodes are of two basic types: coated "stick" electrodes and coiled wire. Coated "stick" electrodes, usually 14 inches long and smaller than a pencil in diameter, are held in a special insulated holder by the operator, who must manipulate the electrode in order to maintain a proper arc-width and pattern of deposition of the metal being transferred. Stick electrodes are packaged in 6- to 50-pound boxes.

Thin coiled wire is designed to be fed continuously to the welding arc through a "gun" held by the operator or positioned by automatic positioning equipment. The wire is packaged in coils, reels, and drums weighing from 14 to 1,000 pounds and may be solid or flux-cored.

For more information on products visit the website at **http://www.lincolnelectric.com.**

Manufacturing Process The main plant is in Euclid, Ohio, a suburb on Cleveland's east side. There are no warehouses. Materials flow from the half-mile long dock on the north side of the plant through the production lines to a very limited storage and loading area on the south side.

Materials used on each workstation are stored as close as possible to the workstation. The administrative offices, near the center of the factory, are entirely functional. A corridor below the main level provides access to the factory floor from the main entrance near the center of the plant. *Fortune* declared the Euclid facility one of America's ten best-managed factories.

Another Lincoln plant in Mentor, Ohio, houses some of the electrode production operations, which were moved from the main plant. Electrode manufacturing is highly capital-intensive. Metal rods purchased from steel producers are drawn down to smaller diameters, cut to length, and coated with pressed-powder "flux" for stick electrodes or plated with copper (for conductivity) and put into coils or spools for wire. Lincoln's Innershield wire is hollow and filled with a material similar to that used to coat stick electrodes. As mentioned earlier, this represented a major innovation in welding technology when it was introduced. The company is highly secretive about its electrode production processes, and outsiders are not given access to the details of those processes.

Lincoln welding machines and electric motors are made on a series of assembly lines. Gasoline and diesel engines are purchased partially assembled, but practically all other components are made from basic industrial products, for example, steel bars and sheets and bar copper conductor wire.

Individual components, such as gasoline tanks for engine-driven welders and steel shafts for motors and generators, are made by numerous small "factories within a factory." The shaft for a certain generator, for example, is made from raw steel bar by one operator who uses five large machines, all running continuously. A saw cuts the bar to length, a digital lathe machines different sec-

tions to varying diameters, a special mining machine cuts a slot for the keyway, and so forth, until a finished shaft is produced. The operator moves the shafts from machine to machine and makes necessary adjustments. Another operator punches, shapes, and paints sheet metal cowling parts. One assembles steel laminations onto a rotor shaft, then winds, insulates, and tests the rotors. Finished components are moved by crane operators to the nearby assembly lines.

Worker Performance and Attitude

Exceptional worker performance at Lincoln is a matter of record. The typical Lincoln employee earns about twice as much as other factory workers in the Cleveland area. Yet the company's labor cost per sales dollar is well below industry averages. Worker turnover is practically nonexistent except for retirements and departures by new employees. Turnover is less than 4% for employees who have been on the jobs for at least 18 months.[3]

Sales per Lincoln factory employee currently exceed $150,000. An observer at the factory quickly sees why this figure is so high. Each worker is proceeding busily and thoughtfully about the task at hand. There is no idle chatter. Most workers take no coffee breaks. Many operate several machines and make a substantial component unaided. The supervisors are busy with planning and record-keeping duties and hardly glance at the people they "supervise." The manufacturing procedures appear efficient—no unnecessary steps, no wasted motions, no wasted materials. Finished components move smoothly to subsequent workstations. Appendix LE.4 includes summaries of interviews with employees.

Organizational Structure

Lincoln has never allowed development of a formal organization chart. The objective of this policy is to ensure maximum flexibility. An open-door policy is practiced throughout the company, and personnel are encouraged to take problems to the persons most capable of resolving them. Once, Harvard Business School researchers prepared an organization chart reflecting the implied relationships at Lincoln. The chart became available within the company, and present management feels that had a disruptive effect. Therefore, no organizational chart appears in this case.

Perhaps because of the quality and enthusiasm of the Lincoln workforce, routine supervision is almost nonexistent. A typical production foreman, for example, supervises as many as 100 workers, a span-of-control that does not allow more than infrequent worker-supervisor interaction.

Position titles and traditional flows of authority do imply something of an organizational structure, however. For example, the vice president of sales and the vice president of the Electrode Division report to the president, as do various staff assistants such as the personnel director and the director of purchasing.

Using such implied relationships, it has been determined that production workers have two or, at most, three levels of supervision between themselves and the president.

Human Resource Practices

As mentioned earlier, it is Lincoln's remarkable human resource practices that are credited by many with the company's success.

Recruitment and Selection Every job opening is advertised internally on company bulletin boards and any employee can apply for any job so advertised. External hiring is permitted only for entry-level positions. Selection for these jobs is done on the basis of personal interviews—there is no aptitude or psychological testing. A committee consisting of vice presidents and supervisors interviews candidates initially cleared by the personnel department. Final selection is made by the supervisor who has a job opening. Nonetheless, it is increasingly desirable that factory workers have some advanced math skills and understand the use of computers. Consequently, Lincoln's expansion is becoming increasingly dependent upon getting employees qualified to work in the Lincoln environment within the famous incentive system.[4]

Job Security In 1958 Lincoln formalized its guaranteed continuous employment policy, which had already been in effect for many years. There have been no layoffs since World War II. Since 1958, every worker with over two years' longevity has been guaranteed at least 30 hours per week, 49 weeks per year.

The policy has never been so severely tested as during the 1981 to 1983 recession. As a manufacturer of capital goods, Lincoln's business is highly cyclical. In previous recessions the company was able to avoid major sales declines. However, sales plummeted 32% in 1982 and another 16% the next year. Few companies could withstand such a revenue collapse and remain profitable. Yet, Lincoln not only earned profits, but no employee was laid off and year-end incentive bonuses continued. To weather the storm, management cut most of the nonsalaried workers back to 30 hours a week for varying periods of time. Many employees were reassigned, and the total workforce was slightly reduced through normal attrition and restricted hiring. Many employees grumbled at their unexpected misfortune, probably to the surprise and dismay of some Lincoln managers. However, sales and profits—and employee bonuses—soon rebounded.

Performance Evaluations Each supervisor formally evaluates subordinates twice a year using the cards shown in Exhibit LE.1. The employee (nonmanagement) performance criteria, "quality," "dependability," "ideas and cooperation," and "output," are considered to be independent of each other. Marks on the cards are converted to numerical scores that are forced to average 100 for each evaluating supervisor. Individual merit rating scores normally range from 80 to 110. Any score over 110 requires a special letter to top management. These scores (over 110) are not considered in computing the required 100-point average for each evaluating supervisor.

Suggestions for improvements often result in recommendations for exceptionally high performance scores. Supervisors discuss individual performance marks with the employees concerned. Each warranty claim is traced to the individual employee whose work caused the defect. The employee's performance score may be reduced, or the worker may be required to repay the cost of servicing the warranty claim by working without pay.

Performance evaluation for managerial and all salary employees is conducted using six criteria or competencies. These include: leadership/ownership; decision making and judgment; results orientation; teamwork/commitment; quality and customer focus; and creativity/innovation. The

Ex I Merit Rating Cards

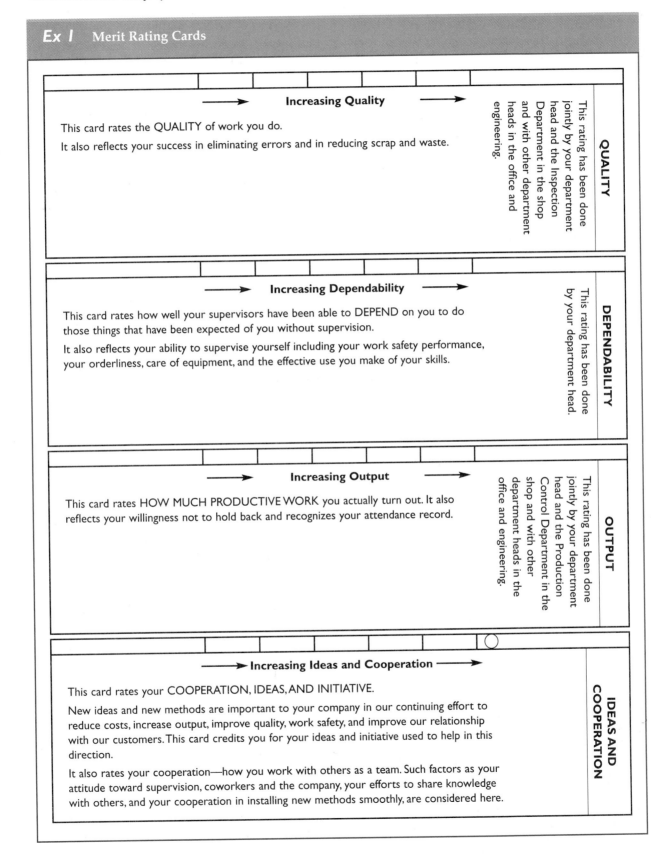

Increasing Quality

This card rates the QUALITY of work you do.

It also reflects your success in eliminating errors and in reducing scrap and waste.

This rating has been done jointly by your department head and the Inspection Department in the shop and with other department heads in the office and engineering.

QUALITY

Increasing Dependability

This card rates how well your supervisors have been able to DEPEND on you to do those things that have been expected of you without supervision.

It also reflects your ability to supervise yourself including your work safety performance, your orderliness, care of equipment, and the effective use you make of your skills.

This rating has been done by your department head.

DEPENDABILITY

Increasing Output

This card rates HOW MUCH PRODUCTIVE WORK you actually turn out. It also reflects your willingness not to hold back and recognizes your attendance record.

This rating has been done jointly by your department head and the Production Control Department in the shop and with other department heads in the office and engineering.

OUTPUT

Increasing Ideas and Cooperation

This card rates your COOPERATION, IDEAS, AND INITIATIVE.

New ideas and new methods are important to your company in our continuing effort to reduce costs, increase output, improve quality, work safety, and improve our relationship with our customers. This card credits you for your ideas and initiative used to help in this direction.

It also rates your cooperation—how you work with others as a team. Such factors as your attitude toward supervision, coworkers and the company, your efforts to share knowledge with others, and your cooperation in installing new methods smoothly, are considered here.

IDEAS AND COOPERATION

evaluation is conducted on a semiannual basis using a conventional graphic rating format. For each of these criteria, the employees must establish goals based on the strategic needs of the company. Employees are provided feedback and coaching at least once a year for performance improvement and development. Evaluation results influence merit pay and bonus decisions.

Compensation Basic wage levels for jobs at Lincoln are determined by a wage survey of similar jobs in the Cleveland area.[5] These rates are adjusted quarterly in accordance with changes in the Cleveland area wage index. Insofar as possible, base wage rates are translated into piece rates. Today the average Lincoln factory worker earns $16.54 an hour versus the average $14.25 manufacturing wage in the Cleveland area. Practically all production workers and many others—for example, some forklift operators—are paid by piece rate. Once established, piece rates are never changed unless a substantive change in the way a job is done results from a source other than the worker doing the job.

In December of each year, a portion of annual profits is distributed to employees as bonuses. Incentive bonuses since 1934 have averaged about 90% of annual wages. Individual bonuses are proportional to merit-rating scores. For example, assume the amount set aside for bonuses is 80% of total wages paid to eligible employees. A person whose performance score is 95 will receive a bonus of 76% of annual wages. While these percentages have often resulted in high total compensation, some employees believe that their bonuses are not rising fast enough, despite rising profits. This reflects the firm's decision to use profits to expand the operations rather than put them into higher bonuses. It also reflects the fact that there are more workers today sharing in a bonus pool that is only a little higher than in many years in the 1980s.[6]

Vacations The company is shut down for two weeks in August and two weeks during the Christmas season. Vacations are taken during these periods. For employees with over 25 years of service, a fifth week of vacation may be taken at a time acceptable to superiors.

Work Assignments Management has authority to transfer workers and to switch between over-time and short time as required. Supervisors have undisputed authority to assign specific parts to individual workers, who may have their own preferences due to variations in piece rates. During the 1982-1983 recession, 50 factory workers volunteered to join sales teams and fanned out across the country to sell a new welder designed for automobile body shops and small machine shops. The result: $10 million in sales and a hot new product.

Employee Participation in Decision Making Thinking of participative management usually evokes a vision of a relaxed, nonauthoritarian atmosphere. This is not the case at Lincoln. Formal authority is quite strong. "We're very authoritarian around here," says Willis. James F. Lincoln placed a good deal of stress on protecting management's authority. "Management in all successful departments of industry must have complete power," he said. "Management is the coach who must be obeyed. The men, however, are the Players who alone can win the game." Despite this attitude, there are several ways in which employees participate in management at Lincoln.

Richard Sabo, former assistant to the chief executive officer, relates job enlargement/enrichment to participation. He said, "The most important participative technique that we use is giving more responsibility to employees. We give a high school graduate more responsibility than other companies give their foremen." Management puts limits on the degree of participation that is allowed, however. In Sabo's words:

> When you use 'participation,' put quotes around it. Because we believe that each person should participate only in those decisions he is most knowledgeable about. I don't think production employees should control the decisions of the chairman. They don't know as much as he does about the decisions he is involved in.

The Advisory Board, elected by the workers, meets with the chairman and the president every two weeks to discuss ways of improving operations. As noted earlier, this board has been in existence since 1914 and has contributed to many innovations. The incentive bonuses, for example, were first recommended by this committee. Every employee has access to Advisory Board members, and answers to all Advisory Board suggestions are promised by the following meeting. Willis, Hastings, and Stropki are quick to point out, though, that the Advisory Board only recommends actions. "They do not have direct authority," Willis says, "and when they bring up something that management thinks is not to the benefit of the company, it will be rejected."

Under the early suggestion program, employees were awarded one-half of the first year's savings attributable to their suggestions. Now, however, the value of suggestions is reflected in performance evaluation scores, which determine individual incentive bonus amounts.

Training and Education Production workers are given a short period of on-the-job training and then placed on a piecework pay system. Lincoln does not pay for off-site education, unless very specific company needs are identified. The idea behind this latter policy, according to Sabo, is that everyone cannot take advantage of such a program, and it is unfair to expend company funds for an advantage to which there is unequal access. Recruits for sales jobs, already college graduates, are given on-the-job training in the plant followed by a period of work and training at one of the regional sales offices. Today, Lincoln Electric conducts a large number of training programs. Visit their website to review them all and you may be very impressed!

Fringe Benefits and Executive Perquisites A medical plan and a company-paid retirement program have been in effect for many years. A plant cafeteria, operated on a break-even basis, serves meals at about 60% of usual costs. The Employee Association, to which the company does not contribute, provides disability insurance and social and athletic activities. The employee stock ownership program has resulted in employee ownership of about 50% of the common stock. Under this program, each employee with more than two years of service may purchase stock in the corporation. The price of these shares is established at book value. Stock purchased through this plan may be held by employees only. Dividends and voting rights are the same as for stock that is owned outside the plan. Approximately 75% of the employees own Lincoln stock.

As to executive perquisites, there are none—crowded, austere offices, no executive washrooms or lunchrooms, and no reserved parking spaces.

Even the top executives pay for their own meals and eat in the employee cafeteria. If the CEO arrives late due to a breakfast speaking engagement, he has to park far away from the factory entrance.

FINANCIAL POLICIES

James F. Lincoln felt strongly that financing for company growth should come from within the company—through initial cash investment by the founders, through retention of earnings, and through stock purchases by those who work in the business. He saw the following advantages of this approach:

1. Ownership of stock by employees strengthens team spirit. "If they are mutually anxious to make it succeed, the future of the company is bright."
2. Ownership of stock provides individual incentive because employees feel that they will benefit from company profitability.
3. "Ownership is educational." Owner-employees "will know how profits are made and lost; how success is won and lost. There are few socialists in the list of stockholders of the nation's industries."
4. "Capital available from within controls expansion." Unwarranted expansion would not occur, Lincoln believed, under his financing plan.
5. "The greatest advantage would be the development of the individual worker. Under the incentive of ownership, he would become a greater man."
6. "Stock ownership is one of the steps that can be taken that will make the worker feel that there is less of a gulf between him and the boss. Stock ownership will help the worker to recognize his responsibility in the game and the importance of victory."

Until 1980, Lincoln Electric borrowed no money. Even now, the company's liabilities consist mainly of accounts payable and short-term accruals. The unusual pricing policy at Lincoln was succinctly stated by Willis: "At all times price on the basis of cost and at all times keep pressure on our cost." This policy resulted in the price for the most popular welding electrode then in use going from 16 cents a pound in 1929 to 4.7 cents in 1938. More recently, the SA-200 Welder, Lincoln's largest selling portable machine, decreased in price from 1958 through 1965. According to Dr. C. Jackson Grayson of the American Productivity Center in Houston, Texas, Lincoln's prices increased only one-fifth as fast as the Consumer Price Index from 1934 to about 1970. This resulted in a welding products market in which Lincoln became the undisputed price leader for the products it manufactures. Not even the major Japanese manufacturers, such as Nippon Steel for welding electrodes and Saka Transformer for welding machines, were able to penetrate this market.

Substantial cash balances accumulated each year preparatory to paying the year-end bonuses. Modest success with international expansion put some pressure on what was basically a conservative financial philosophy. However, the company borrowed money in 1992 to pay for employee bonuses in the United States. In 1995 Lincoln issued $119 million of new stock. This sale created greater public ownership. As a consequence, Don Hastings remarked that the company must now consider not only the employees but also its shareholders, customers, and suppliers.[7] For more current financial information, visit Lincoln's website.

How Well Does Lincoln Serve Its Stakeholders?

Lincoln Electric differs from most other companies in the importance it assigns to each of the groups it serves. Hastings identifies these groups, in the order of priority ascribed to them, as: (1) customers, (2) employees, and (3) stockholders. As suggested, the 1995 stock issue increased the salience of the stockholders.

Certainly the firm's customers have fared well over the years. Lincoln prices for welding machines and welding electrodes are acknowledged to be the lowest in the marketplace. Quality has consistently been high. The cost of field failures for Lincoln products was recently determined to be a remarkable 0.04% of revenues. The "Fleetweld" electrodes and the SA-200 welders have been the standard in the pipeline and refinery construction industry, where price is hardly a criterion, for decades. A Lincoln distributor in Monroe, Louisiana, says that he has sold several hundred of the popular AC-225 welders, which are warranted for one year, but has never handled a warranty claim.

Perhaps best-served of all management constituencies have been the employees. Not the least of their benefits, of course, are the year-end bonuses, which effectively double an already average compensation level. The foregoing description of the personnel program and the comments in Appendix LE.4 further illustrate the desirability of a Lincoln job.

While stockholders were relegated to an secondary status by James F. Lincoln, they have done very well indeed. Recent dividends exceeded $11 a share and earnings per share have approached $30. In January 1980, the price of restricted stock, committed to employees, was $117 a share. By 1989, the stated value, at which the company will repurchase the stock if tendered, was $201. A check with the New York office of Merrill Lynch at that time revealed an estimated price on Lincoln stock of $270 a share, with none being offered for sale. Technically, this price applies only to the unrestricted stock owned by the Lincoln family, a few other major holders, and employees who have purchased it on the open market. Risk associated with Lincoln stock, a major determinant of stock value, is minimal because of the small amount of debt in the capital structure, because of an extremely stable earnings record, and because of Lincoln's practice of purchasing the restricted stock whenever employees offer it for sale. The 1995 stock sale has changed this situation dramatically. The stock now trades freely on the NASDAQ stock exchange.

Management Quality

It is easy to believe that the reason for Lincoln's success is the excellent attitude of the employees and their willingness to work harder, faster, and more intelligently than other industrial workers. However, Sabo suggests that appropriate credit be given to Lincoln executives, whom he credits with carrying out the following policies:

1. Management has limited research, development, and manufacturing to a standard product line designed to meet the major needs of the welding industry.
2. New products must be reviewed by manufacturing and all producing costs verified before being approved by management.
3. Purchasing is challenged to not only procure materials at the lowest cost, but also to work

4. Manufacturing supervision and all personnel are held accountable for reduction of scrap, energy conservation, and maintenance of product quality.

5. Production control, material handling, and methods engineering are closely supervised by top management.

6. Management has made cost reduction a way of life at Lincoln, and definite programs are established in many areas, including traffic and shipping, where tremendous savings can result.

7. Management has established a sales department that is technically trained to reduce customer welding costs. This sales approach and other real customer services have eliminated nonessential frills and resulted in long-term benefits to all concerned.

8. Management has encouraged education, technical publishing, and long-range programs that have resulted in industry growth, thereby ensuring market potential for the Lincoln Electric Company.

closely with engineering and manufacturing to ensure that the latest innovations are implemented.

Sabo writes, "It is in a very real sense a personal and group experience in faith—a belief that together we can achieve results which alone would not be possible. It is not a perfect system and it is not easy. It requires tremendous dedication and hard work. However, it does work and the results are worth the effort."

GOING GLOBAL

As stated in the beginning of this case, Lincoln Electric has production sites in 17 other countries and distribution and sales offices in more than 160 countries. As Lincoln Electric has increased its global presence, it has learned just how much it can use the same philosophy of managing human resources. The company has learned that countries have important legal, cultural, and political conditions that can influence the effectiveness and applicability of some of their practices and that the company needs to either adapt to them or locate in places where the differences with the United States are more modest. This process of learning, however, was not necessarily easy or without some cost. During the late 1980s and early 1990s, Lincoln expanded rapidly, sometimes by acquiring existing companies, sometimes by joint ventures, and sometimes by establishing a new facility. Lincoln's top management assumed that there would be enough people around the world who would take to the Lincoln system as much as do the employees in Cleveland. They learned that this assumption was not always valid and as a consequence they had to close some facilities. As a result of top management's relatively limited international experience, the 1990s proved to be very challenging, costly, and humbling times. (See the letter from the CEO to the shareholders in Appendix LE.5.) Donald Hastings has described these times in great detail in his article entitled "Lincoln Electric's Harsh Lessons from International Expansion," in the *Harvard Business Review* (May–June 1999): 163–178. Their experiences are reflected today in the missions and values statements of the company shown in Appendix LE.1.

Credits: This case was written by Arthur Sharplin and appears in R. S. Schuler and P. D. Buller (eds.), *Cases in Management, Organizational Behavior and Human Resource Management,* 7th ed. (Cincinnati, OH: South-Western, 2006). It is adapted here by R. S. Schuler and used with the permission of the authors.

ENDNOTES

1   See the company's website for more current information on all issues and topics addressed in this case: http://www.lincolnelectric.com.

2   T. W. Gerdel, "Lincoln Electric Experiences Season of Worker Discontent," *Plain Dealer* [Cleveland] (December 10, 1995): 1-C.

3   Z. Schiller, "A Model Incentive Plan Gets Caught in a Vise," *Business Week* (January 22, 1996): 89, 92.

4   R. Narisetti, "Job Paradox Manufacturers Decry a Shortage of Workers While Rejecting Many," *Wall Street Journal* (September 8, 1995): A4.

5   Schiller, "A Model Incentive Plan Gets Caught in a Vise," 89, 92.

6   Gerdel, "Lincoln Electric Experiences Season of Worker Discontent."

7   *Ibid.*

8   R. M. Hodgetts, "A Conversation with Donald F. Hastings of the Lincoln Electric Company," *Organizational Dynamics* (Winter 1997): 68–74; M. Gleisser, "Lincoln CEO's Formula: Mutual Trust and Loyalty," *Plain Dealer* [Cleveland] (June 22, 1996): 2-C.

App LE.1   Vision, Missions, and Values Statements of the Lincoln Electric Company

VISION STATEMENT

Lincoln Electric will be the undisputed world leader in the arc-welding industry as measured by global sales volume, while simultaneously aiming to maximize shareholder value.

We will be the leader in supplying the finest quality welding and cutting products. In order to accomplish this, we will continue our emphasis on being the industry's lowest cost producer, on providing applications expertise and solutions for our customers, and on developing new and innovative technology that responds to customer needs with value-added products and services.

MISSION STATEMENT

- Total Solutions

We will be driven by customer satisfaction and become known as the supplier of choice in our industries. We will strive to exceed customer expectations. We will be a solutions company, not simply a supplier of equipment or consumables.

- Expertise

We will be differentiated from our competitors by technology, quality, applications engineering, sales and marketing expertise.

- Global

We will be global, with over 40% of our total sales coming from outside North America. We will have cost-competitive manufacturing facilities located worldwide, where appropriate, to best serve our customers' needs.

- Principles

We will base our human resources systems on our proven principles reflective of our core values and our commitment to attract, reward, develop, and motivate high-quality people. They will reflect the global scope of our business while demonstrating responsibility and flexibility with respect to cultural diversity and statutory and regional business realities.

- Stakeholders

Our emphasis on continuous improvement in all aspects of our business will enable us to reward our shareholders and employees.

- Responsibility

We will continually strive to be environmentally responsible and support the communities where we operate and the industries in which we participate.

VALUES STATEMENT

Our Core Values

As a responsible and successful company in partnership with our customers, distributors, employees, shareholders, suppliers, and our host communities, we pledge ourselves to conduct our business in accordance with these core values:

- Respond to our customers' needs and expectations with quality, integrity, and value.
- Recognize people as our most valuable asset.
- Maintain and expand the Lincoln Incentive Management philosophy.
- Practice prudent and responsible financial management.
- Strive continually to be environmentally responsible.
- Support communities where we operate and industries in which we participate.

TO REALIZE OUR MISSION AND SUPPORT OUR CORE VALUES, WE HAVE ESTABLISHED THE FOLLOWING GOALS:

Respond to Our Customers' Needs and Expectations with Quality, Integrity, and Value

- Assure value through innovative, functional, and reliable products and services in all the markets we serve around the world.
- Exceed global standards for products and service quality.
- Provide our customers with personalized technical support that helps them achieve improvements in cost reduction, productivity, and quality.
- Lead the industry in aggressive application of advanced technology to meet customer requirements.
- Invest constantly in creative research and development dedicated to maintaining our position of market leadership.
- Achieve and maintain the leading market share position in our major markets around the world.

App LE. I Vision, Missions, and Values Statements of the Lincoln Electric Company (*continued*)

Recognize People as Our Most Valuable Asset
- Maintain a safe, clean, and healthy environment for our employees.
- Promote employee training, education, and development, and broaden skills through multidepartmental and international assignments.
- Maintain an affirmative action program and provide all employees with opportunities for advancement commensurate with their abilities and performance regardless of race, religion, national origin, sex, age, or disability.
- Maintain an environment that fosters ethical behavior, mutual trust, equal opportunity, open communication, personal growth, and creativity.
- Demand integrity, discipline, and professional conduct from our employees in every aspect of our business and conduct our operations ethically and in accordance with the law.
- Reward employees through recognition, "pay for performance," and by sharing our profits with incentive bonus compensation based on extraordinary achievement.

Maintain and Expand the Lincoln Incentive Management Philosophy
Promote dynamic teamwork and innovation as the most profitable and cost-effective way of achieving:
- A committed work ethic and positive employee attitudes throughout the company.
- High-quality, low-cost manufacturing.
- Efficient and innovative engineering.
- Customer-oriented operation and administration.
- A dedicated and knowledgeable sales and service force.
- A total organization responsive to the needs of our worldwide customers.

Practice Prudent and Responsible Financial Management
- Establish attainable goals, strategic planning, and accountability for results that enhance shareholder value.
- Promote the process of employee involvement in cost reductions and quality improvements.
- Recognize profit as the resource that enables our Company to serve our customers.

Strive Continually to Be Environmentally Responsible
- Continue to pursue the most environmentally sound operating practices, processes, and products to protect the global environment.
- Maintain a clean and healthy environment in our host communities.

Support Communities Where We Operate and Industries in Which We Participate
- Invest prudently in social, cultural, educational, and charitable activities.
- Contribute to the industries we serve and society as a whole by continuing our leadership role in professional organizations and education.
- Encourage and support appropriate employee involvement in community activities.

App LE.2 Lincoln Electric's HR Objectives

What Are the HR Objectives of Lincoln Electric?
- To maintain and expand the Lincoln Incentive Management Philosophy
- To recognize people as [the company's] most valuable asset
- To promote training, education, and development that broaden employee skills
- To maintain an affirmative action program and provide all employees with opportunities for advancement commensurate with their abilities and performance regardless of race, religion, national origin, sex, age, or disability

App LE.3   Lincoln Electric's Business Objectives

Business Objectives of Lincoln Electric

To be a global leader in price and quality and serve the customers first

To achieve and retain global leadership as a total quality supplier of superior products and services

To respond to our customers with quality, integrity, and value

To practice prudent and responsible financial management

To strive continually to be environmentally responsible

To support communities where we operate and industries in which we participate

To maintain an environment that fosters ethical behavior, mutual trust, equal opportunity, open communication, personal growth, and creativity

To promote feedback

To demand integrity, discipline, and professional conduct from our employees in every aspect of our business and conduct operations ethically and in accordance with the law

To reward employees through recognition, pay for performance, and by sharing profits with incentive bonus compensation based on extraordinary achievement as a means of motivation

To promote dynamic teamwork and innovation

App LE.4   Employee Interviews

Following are typical questions and answers from employee interviews. In order to maintain each employee's personal privacy, fictitious names have been given to the interviewees.

Interview I

Betty Stewart, a 52-year-old high school graduate who had been with Lincoln 13 years, was working as a cost accounting clerk at the time of the interview.

Q: What jobs have you held here besides the one you have now?
A: I worked in payroll for awhile, and then this job came open and I took it.
Q: How much money did you make last year, including your bonus?
A: I would say roughly around $25,000, but I was off for back surgery for awhile.
Q: You weren't paid while you were off for back surgery?
A: No.
Q: Did the Employees Association help out?
A: Yes. The company doesn't furnish that, though. We pay $8 a month into the Employee Association. I think my check from them was $130 a week.
Q: How was your performance rating last year?
A: It was around 100 points, but I lost some points for attendance for my back problem.
Q: How did you get your job at Lincoln?
A: I was bored silly where I was working, and I had heard that Lincoln kept their people busy. So I applied and got the job the next day.
Q: Do you think you make more money than similar workers in Cleveland?
A: I know I do.
Q: What have you done with your money?
A: We have purchased a better home. Also, my son is going to the University of Chicago, which costs $13,000 a year. I buy the Lincoln stock which is offered each year, and I have a little bit of gold.
Q: Have you ever visited with any of the senior executives, like Mr. Willis or Mr. Hastings?
A: I have known Mr. Willis for a long time.
Q: Does he call you by name?

App LE.4   Employee Interviews *(continued)*

A: Yes. In fact, he was very instrumental in my going to the doctor that I am going to with my back. He knows the director of the clinic.

Q: Do you know Mr. Hastings?

A: I know him to speak to him, and he always speaks, always. But I have known Mr. Willis for a good many years. When I did Plant Two accounting I did not understand how the plant operated. Of course you are not allowed in Plant Two, because that's the Electrode Division. I told my boss about the problem one day, and the next thing I knew Mr. Willis came by and said, "Come on, Betty, we're going to Plant Two." He spent an hour and a half showing me the plant.

Q: Do you think Lincoln employees produce more than those in other companies?

A: I think with the incentive program the way that it is, if you want to work and achieve, then you will do it. If you don't want to work and achieve, you will not do it no matter where you are. Just because you are merit rated and have a bonus, if you really don't want to work hard, then you're not going to. You will accept your 90 points or 92 or 85 because even with that you make more money than people on the outside.

Q: Do you think Lincoln employees will ever join a union?

A: I don't know why they would.

Q: So you say that money is a very major advantage?

A: Money is a major advantage, but it's not just the money. It's the fact that having the incentive, you do wish to work a little harder. I'm sure that there are a lot of men here who, if they worked some other place, would not work as hard as they do here. Not that they are overworked—I don't mean that—but I'm sure they wouldn't push.

Q: Is there anything that you would like to add?

A: I do like working here. I am better off being pushed mentally. In another company if you pushed too hard you would feel a little bit of pressure, and someone might say, "Hey, slow down, don't try so hard." But here you are encouraged, not discouraged.

Interview 2

Ed Sanderson, a 23-year-old high school graduate who had been with Lincoln four years, was a machine operator in the Electrode Division at the time of the interview.

Q: How did you happen to get this job?

A: My wife was pregnant, and I was making three bucks an hour and one day I came here and applied. That was it. I kept calling to let them know I was still interested.

Q: Roughly, what were your earnings last year including your bonus?

A: $45,000.

Q: What have you done with your money since you have been here?

A: Well, we've lived pretty well and we bought a condominium.

Q: Have you paid for the condominium?

A: No, but I could.

Q: Have you bought your Lincoln stock this year?

A: No, I haven't bought any Lincoln stock yet.

Q: Do you get the feeling that the executives here are pretty well thought of?

A: I think they are. To get where they are today, they had to really work.

Q: Wouldn't that be true anywhere?

A: I think more so here because seniority really doesn't mean anything. If you work with a guy who has 20 years here, and you have two months and you're doing a better job, you will get advanced before he will.

Q: Are you paid on a piece-rate basis?

A: My gang does. There are nine of us who make the bare electrode, and the whole group gets paid based on how much electrode we make.

Q: Do you think you work harder than workers in other factories in the Cleveland area?

A: Yes, I would say I probably work harder.

Q: Do you think it hurts anybody?

A: No, a little hard work never hurts anybody.

Q: If you could choose, do you think you would be as happy earning a little less money and being able to slow down a little?

A: No, it doesn't bother me. If it bothered me, I wouldn't do it.

(continued)

App LE.4   Employee Interviews (*continued*)

Q: Why do you think Lincoln employees produce more than workers in other plants?

A: That's the way the company is set up. The more you put out, the more you're going to make.

Q: Do you think it's the piece rate and bonus together?

A: I don't think people would work here if they didn't know that they would be rewarded at the end of the year.

Q: Do you think Lincoln employees will ever join a union?

A: No.

Q: What are the major advantages of working for Lincoln?

A: Money.

Q: Are there any other advantages?

A: Yes, we don't have a union shop. I don't think I could work in a union shop.

Q: Do you think you are a career man with Lincoln at this time?

A: Yes.

Interview 3

Roger Lewis, a 23-year-old Purdue graduate in mechanical engineering who had been in the Lincoln sales program for 15 months, was working in the Cleveland sales office at the time of the interview.

Q: How did you get your job at Lincoln?

A: I saw that Lincoln was interviewing on campus at Purdue, and I went by. I later came to Cleveland for a plant tour and was offered a job.

Q: Do you know any of the senior executives? Would they know you by name?

A: Yes, I know all of them—Mr. Hastings, Mr. Willis, Mr. Sabo.

Q: Do you think Lincoln sales representatives work harder than those in other companies?

A: Yes. I don't think there are many sales reps for other companies who are putting in 50- to 60-hour weeks. Everybody here works harder. You can go out in the plant, or you can go upstairs, and there's nobody sitting around.

Q: Do you see any real disadvantage of working at Lincoln?

A: I don't know if it's a disadvantage, but Lincoln is a spartan company, a very thrifty company. I like that. The sales offices are functional, not fancy.

Q: Why do you think Lincoln employees have such high productivity?

A: Piecework has a lot to do with it. Lincoln is smaller than many plants, too; you can stand in one place and see the materials come in one side and the product go out the other. You feel a part of the company. The chance to get ahead is important, too. They have a strict policy of promoting from within, so you know you have a chance. I think in a lot of other places you may not get as fair a shake as you do here. The sales offices are on a smaller scale, too. I like that. I tell someone that we have two people in the Baltimore office, and they say, "You've got to be kidding." It's smaller and more personal. Pay is the most important thing. I have heard that this is the highest-paying factory in the world.

Interview 4

Jimmy Roberts, a 47-year-old high school graduate who had been with Lincoln 17 years, was working as a multiple-drill press operator at the time of the interview.

Q: What jobs have you had at Lincoln?

A: I started out cleaning the men's locker room in 1967. After about a year I got a job in the flux department, where we make the coating for welding rods. I worked there for seven or eight years and then got my present job.

Q: Do you make one particular part?

A: No, there are a variety of parts I make—at least 25.

Q: Each one has a different piece rate attached to it?

A: Yes.

Q: Are some piece rates better than others?

A: Yes.

Q: How do you determine which ones you are going to do?

A: You don't. Your supervisor assigns them.

Q: How much money did you make last year?

A: $53,000.

Q: Have you ever received any kind of award or citation?

A: No.

App LE.4 Employee Interviews (*continued*)

Q: Was your rating ever over 110?
A: Yes. For the past five years, probably, I made over 110 points.
Q: Is there any attempt to let the others know . . . ?
A: The kind of points I get? No.
Q: Do you know what they are making?
A: No. There are some who might not be too happy with their points and they might make it known. The majority, though, do not make it a point of telling other employees.
Q: Would you be just as happy earning a little less money and working a little slower?
A: I don't think I would, not at this point. I have done piecework all these years, and the fast pace doesn't really bother me.
Q: Why do you think Lincoln productivity is so high?
A: The incentive thing—the bonus distribution. I think that would be the main reason. The paycheck you get every two weeks is important too.
Q: Do you think Lincoln employees would ever join a union?
A: I don't think so. I have never heard anyone mention it.
Q: What is the most important advantage of working here?
A: Amount of money you make. I don't think I could make this type of money anywhere else, especially with only a high school education.
Q: As a black person, do you feel that Lincoln discriminates in any way against blacks?
A: No. I do not think any more so than any other job. Naturally, there is a certain amount of discrimination, regardless of where you are.

Interview 5

Joe Trahan, a 58-year-old high school graduate who had been with Lincoln 39 years, was employed as a working supervisor in the tool room at the time of the interview.

Q: Roughly what was your pay last year?
A: Over $56,000, salary, bonus, stock dividends.
Q: How much was your bonus?
A: About $26,000.
Q: Have you ever gotten a special award of any kind?
A: Not really.
Q: What have you done with your money?
A: My house is paid for, and my two cars. I also have some bonds and the Lincoln stock.
Q: What do you think of the executives at Lincoln?
A: They're really top-notch.
Q: What is the major disadvantage of working at Lincoln Electric?
A: I don't know of any disadvantage at all.
Q: Do you think you produce more than most people in similar jobs with other companies?
A: I do believe that.
Q: Why is that? Why do you believe that?
A: We are on the incentive system. Everything we do, we try to improve to make a better product with a minimum of outlay. We try to improve the bonus.
Q: Would you be just as happy making a little less money and not working quite so hard?
A: I don't think so.
Q: Do you think Lincoln employees would ever join a union?
A: I don't think they would ever consider it.
Q: What is the most important advantage of working at Lincoln?
A: Compensation.
Q: Tell me something about Mr. James Lincoln, who died in 1965.
A: You are talking about Jimmy Sr. He always strolled through the shop in his shirt sleeves. Big fellow. Always looked distinguished. Gray hair. Friendly sort of guy. I was a member of the Advisory Board one year. He was there each time.
Q: Did he strike you as really caring?
A: I think he always cared for people.

(*continued*)

App LE.4   Employee Interviews (continued)

Q: Did you get any sensation of a religious nature from him?
A: No, not really.
Q: And religion is not part of the program now?
A: No.
Q: Do you think Mr. Lincoln was a very intelligent man, or was he just a nice guy?
A: I would say he was pretty well educated. A great talker—always right off the top of his head. He knew what he was talking about all the time.
Q: When were bonuses for beneficial suggestions done away with?
A: About 18 years ago.
Q: Did that hurt very much?
A: I do not think so, because suggestions are still rewarded through the merit rating system.
Q: Is there anything you would like to add?
A: It's a good place to work. The union kind of ties other places down. At other places, electricians only do electrical work, carpenters only do carpentry work. At Lincoln Electric we all pitch in and do whatever needs to be done.
Q: So a major advantage is not having a union?
A: That's right.

App LE.5   Letter from the CEO

To Our Shareholders:

Each of you is aware that your company faced enormous challenges in 1993. Those challenges required a focused, creative and positive leadership approach on the part of your management team. As I write this, first quarter 1994 results indicate that the domestic economy is continuing its upward surge. Because of the many tough decisions we had to make in 1993, we are now poised to take advantage of an improved economic climate. Even though much of my personal time has been devoted to overseeing the situation in Europe, excellent results are being achieved in the U.S.A. and Canada.

During 1993, a thorough strategic assessment of our foreign operations led to the conclusion that Lincoln Electric lacked the necessary financial resources to continue to support 21 manufacturing sites. We did not have the luxury of time to keep those plants operating while working to increase our sales and profitability. As a result, with the endorsement of our financial community, the Board of Directors approved management's recommendation to restructure operations in Europe, Latin America, and Japan.

The restructuring included closing the Messer Lincoln operations in Germany; reducing employment throughout Lincoln Norweld, which operates plants in England, France, the Netherlands, Spain, and Norway; and closing manufacturing plants in Venezuela, Brazil, and Japan. The result was a workforce reduction totaling some 770 employees worldwide. We are not abandoning these markets by any means. Rather, the restructuring will allow us to retain and increase sales while relieving us of the high costs associated with excess manufacturing capacity. Now that the restructuring has been accomplished, we operate fifteen plants in ten countries. This capacity will be adequate to supply the inventory needed to support our customers and an increasingly aggressive marketing strategy. We are internationally recognized for outstanding products and service, and we have been certified to the international quality standard ISO-9002.

It was not easy for Lincoln Electric to eliminate manufacturing capacity and jobs. However, I must point out that the overseas companies were given repeated opportunities to turn their performance around. In all fairness, no one anticipated the depth of the recession that continues to devastate Europe, and particularly Germany. But we could not, in good conscience, risk both the continuous erosion of shareholder value and the jobs of our dedicated U.S. employees by remaining unprofitable in these manufacturing operations.

For the second year in the history of this company, it was necessary to take restructuring charges that resulted in a consolidated loss. The restructuring charge totaled $70,100,000 ($40,900,000 after tax), and contributed to a consolidated net loss for 1993 of $38,100,000, compared to a $45,800,000 consolidated loss in 1992.

App LE.5   Letter from the CEO *(continued)*

In 1993 our U.S. and Canadian operations achieved outstanding results with increased levels of sales and profitability and a significant gain in market share. We made a huge step forward by concentrating on the "Top Line" to meet one of our major goals—manufacturing and selling $2.1 million worth of product from our Ohio company each billing day from June 1 through the end of the year. Our Canadian company also made significant contributions with a 38% increase in sales. The bottom line automatically moved into greater profitability.

These impressive gains were not made without sacrifice. Lincoln manufacturing people voluntarily deferred 614 weeks of vacation, worked holidays, and many employees worked a seven-day-a-week schedule to fill the steady stream of orders brought in by the sales department as we capitalized on an emerging domestic economy that we felt was being largely ignored by our major competitors.

This remarkable achievement would never have been possible without the expert management of your President and Chief Operating Officer Frederick W. Mackenbach. His leadership consistently inspired our employees and management team alike. The U.S. company's extraordinary performance encouraged the Board of Directors to approve a gross bonus of $55 million, and to continue the regular quarterly dividend payment throughout the year. As you know, the usual course of action for a company reporting a consolidated loss is to cut or defer bonuses and dividends. That these were paid is a tribute to our Board and their steadfast belief in the long-range, proven benefits of the Incentive Management System.

Thinking in the long term is critical to our progress in a world that too often seems to demand instant solutions to complex problems. Your Chairman, your Board, and your management team are determined to resist that impulse. Currently, Lincoln people around the world are working diligently to formulate a Strategic Plan that will carry this company into the next century. An important element of this business plan will be our new state-of-the-art motor manufacturing facility, which is on schedule. Furthermore, we have strengthened our international leadership with the addition of executives experienced in global management to our Board and to key management posts.

While your company is indeed emerging from a very challenging period in its history, we project excellent results for 1994, with strong sales, increased profits, and the benefits of those developments accruing to shareholders, customers, and employees. As the year proceeds, we will be looking forward to our Centennial in 1995. I am confident that you and I will enjoy celebrating that event together.

Sincerely,

Donald E. Hastings

Chairman and Chief Executive Officer (Retired May 1997)

POSTSCRIPT: In Lincoln Electric's centennial year, 1995, sales topped $1 billion for the first time. It was also the year that Hastings eliminated the two-tier wage plan that was instituted in 1993. Under this plan, new hires started at 75% of the normal pay rate. This plan increased the turnover among the new hires and was regarded as unfair by senior workers.[8] According to one of them, "If an individual shows he can handle the workload, he should be rewarded."

case

SOUTHWEST AIRLINES

The tale of two men, one airline and cocktail napkin . . . "Let's start our own airline," Rollin W. King said to his friend Herb Kelleher in a bar years ago. "Convince me," Herb replied. Rolling drew a triangle connecting Texas's major cities on a cocktail napkin. He said, "We could offer fares so low people would fly instead of drive." Herb paused, placed his drink on the napkin, and then spoke, "Rollin, you're crazy. Let's do it."[1]

INTRODUCTION

Southwest Airlines is currently facing a multitude of challenges to its historically successful business strategy that has created concerns about its ability to grow in the future. These challenges are both external and internal. External challenges include competition and price pressures, current conditions in the airline industry stemming from deregulation, and competitors' continued access to short-haul markets that have long provided the company with significant profitability and competitive advantage. Internally the company faces challenges such as finding continued access to talent that is selected very carefully, and at the same time is compensated very competitively, resulting in relatively low labor costs for the company. The continued access to and availability of talent has direct impact on Southwest's operating strategy of being the cheapest and most efficient airline, which in turn depends upon highly motivated employees who deliver outstanding customer service.

Southwest's former CEO and current chairman, Herb Kelleher, has created a unique culture that has been sustained during the company's 30-year life. He is the figurehead that embodies the company's greatest strengths. The unique culture that has been created by Southwest and championed by its chairman has been able, thus far, to sustain its recruitment and retention goals for the types of employees it targets. Employee ownership

has been used extensively to tie the fortunes of the company with those responsible for it and to retain employees who might otherwise look to Southwest's competitors. Employee satisfaction and the recognition that Southwest is one of the best companies for attracting, developing, and retaining talented people makes it a well-oiled industry leader.

The question is whether Southwest can continue its profitability, outstanding level of customer service, and reputation for being low-cost, on time, and safe in the context of a limited pool of market talent, which is at the heart of its competitive advantage. Can the company maintain its relatively low turnover rate even though the demand for skilled labor has put significant pressures on recruitment and retention of employees? Can the firm continue to spend so much time and money on recruitment and training and remain competitive and equally profitable with all of the external conditions applying pressure on its business at the same time? Will the fact that Herb Kelleher is no longer Southwest's CEO and Gary Kelly has assumed the position hurt the company's reputation in the marketplace and cause it to lose its unique identity and cachet?

In addition to these questions, all of the external environmental issues, such as more direct competition, weakened labor relations, and the change from a short-haul airline to a longer-haul airline, will have an impact on the future growth and success of the company. The strategies that have been so successful in the past will have to be modified to allow the company to grow into other markets, and these modifications will come with all their accompanying challenges. The key to these challenges may be the company's understanding and appreciation of its people.

BACKGROUND

Few industries have experienced the turmoil faced by the U.S. domestic airline business during the past two decades. Once characterized by high wages, stable prices, and choreographed competition, the industry changed swiftly and dramatically when deregulation took effect in 1978. Several of the strongest and greatest airlines (e.g., Pan Am, Eastern) disappeared through mergers or bankruptcies. Strikes and disruptions interfered with companies' attempts to reduce costs. New competitors aggressively swooped into the marketplace; the majority failed.

The industry is again in a period of high demand and expanding profitability. Despite the volatile conditions and many organizational failures, one carrier grew and prospered throughout this entire period—Southwest Airlines.

Southwest was controversial from its inception. Although the Texas Aeronautics Commission approved Southwest's petition to fly on February 20, 1968, the nascent airline was locked in legal battles for three years because competing airlines—Braniff, TransTexas, and Continental—fought through political and legal means to keep it out of the market. Through the efforts of Herb Kelleher, a New York University law school graduate and the airline's former chief executive officer and current chairman of the board, Southwest finally secured the support of both the Texas Supreme Court and the U.S. Supreme Court.

Southwest emerged from these early legal battles with its now famous underdog fighting spirit. The company built its initial advertising campaigns around a prominent issue of the time as well as its airport location. Thus "Make Love, Not War" became the airline's theme, and the company became the "Love" airline. Fittingly, *LUV* was chosen as the company's stock ticker symbol. Southwest went on to see successful growth through three distinct periods. The "Proud Texan" period (1971–1978) saw the establishment of a large city-service network within its home state of Texas. Because it did not engage in interstate commerce, the fledgling carrier was not subject to many federal regulations, particularly those imposed by the Civil Aeronautics Board (CAB). The second phase, "Interstate Expansion" (1978–1986), was characterized by the opening of service to 14 other states. Interstate expansion was made possible by, and thus coincided with, the deregulation of the domestic airline industry. The most recent phase, "National Achievement" (1987–present), has been a time of considerable growth, distinguished recognition, and success.

THE AIRLINE INDUSTRY

The competitive environment in which Southwest operates can be subdivided into different value-added stages, customer and service segments, and competitor groups.

Airlines engage in several value-adding activities. These include aircraft procurement, aircraft maintenance, reservation systems, schedule and route planning, in-flight services, and after-flight services. Competitors may differ in their involvement in these activities. For example, Southwest performs some in-house maintenance but offers no postflight services. By contrast, American Airlines owns and markets its own reservation system, and Allegis, as United Airlines was known briefly in 1987, at one time operated a car rental agency (Hertz) and two hotel chains (Hilton and Westin).

Airlines compete for three primary types of customers: travel agents, corporate travel managers, and individual travelers. The two major categories of passengers are leisure travelers, who tend to be quite price-sensitive, and business travelers, who are more concerned with convenience. To satisfy the different needs of some or all of these groups, airlines present a wide variety of services, depending on their strategy.

Passenger service can be categorized along a number of dimensions. For example, airlines differ by geographical coverage; some specialize in short-haul service while others provide a vast network of interconnected long-haul and short-haul flights on a global basis through a network of strategic alliances. The U.S. airlines can be generally categorized into three major competitor groups based on geographical coverage. First are the national airlines such as American, Delta, United, America West, Southwest, JetBlue, AirTran, and Continental. Second are the regionals, which include Frontier Airlines, Spirit Airlines, and Alaska Airlines. Third is the commuter or "feeder" carriers, most of which operate as extensions of the "major" carriers. Some of these include Atlantic Coast Airlines that operates as United Express, Altantic Southeast Airlines that operates as Delta's Business Express, Ted, Song, and numerous others, some of which change quickly. These airlines can be further categorized into: (a) traditional carriers with business and coach classes and (b) low-fare/low-frills, single-class carriers.

They also differ in how their routes are structured within the territories they serve. The two extremes are point-to-point and hub-and-spoke. The former is characterized by direct service between two points. The latter is characterized by complex and coordinated routes and schedule structures that channel passengers from numerous far-flung airports (the spokes) through a central airport (the hub). The hub itself has many costly infrastructure requirements (baggage handling systems, large terminals, maintenance facilities, and parts inventories). To address the pricing complexity created by multiple traffic flows through a hub, hub-and-spoke carriers conduct complicated yield and inventory management calculations. The result of this complexity is that the hub-spoke pricing structure is systematically different from point-to-point pricing. These added complexities allow a carrier to offer flights between more "city-pairs" than it could under a point-to-point network. For a company that relies on a network, like an airline or telephone company, competitive advantage accrues from economies of scope (i.e., the geographic reach of that network). Economies of scope do not necessarily complement economies of scale, and in fact are often achieved at the expense of scale economies, and vice versa. Thus, although the hub-and-spoke system is driven by economies of scope, each strategy, hub-and-spoke or point-to-point, has its own inherent cost and organizational implications.[2]

Passenger service can also be characterized in terms of breadth. An airline may choose to provide a broad gamut of services including meals, advance seat assignments, and frequent flier programs (full service), or it can offer only Spartan services (no-frills). A further differentiation is the number of service classes offered. Most airlines have two classes of service, first-class and coach. Some offer three classes, first-class, business, and coach (United and American on select flights), while others offer only coach (Southwest) and a few offer only first-class (Midwest Express). In addition to the direct cost of providing differentiated service, amenities such as first-class seating and in-flight meals indirectly affect the cost structure of an airline by limiting the number of seats its aircraft can hold.

Competitive Environment The Airline Deregulation Act of 1978 redefined the industry by eliminating the ability of the CAB to set fares, allocate routes, and control entry into and exit from markets. Unfortunately, most airlines were hamstrung by high cost structures, including exorbitant labor costs, and highly inefficient planes and infrastructure facilities. After the complete removal of entry and price controls by 1980, competition intensified considerably as new entrants cherry-picked the large carriers' most profitable routes. This led to an extended period of severe industry shakeout and consolidation.

Structural Characteristics The industry's structural characteristics make it a tough place to be very profitable. The overall industry is not highly concentrated, although it has become more concentrated since deregulation. Nevertheless, most discrete markets are served by a limited number of carriers. In the oligopolistic markets in which most airlines compete, the pricing actions of one company affect the profits of all competitors. Intense price wars have been a frequent event in the industry. Because competition varies from route to route, a carrier can dominate one market, be dominated in another, and face intense rivalry in a third. As a result of the hub-and-spoke system, airlines face head-to-head competition with more carriers in more markets.

Suppliers tend to have relatively high bargaining power. Certain unions are in a position to shut down airlines. Airplane manufacturers (Boeing, Airbus) have considerable power in altering the terms of purchase for planes. Furthermore, the business is capital-intensive and requires very large expenditures for airplanes and other infrastructure.

Despite difficult economics, the industry is still attractive to new entrants. There are few substitutes for long-haul air travel. In addition, most of the incumbents have high cost structures that are exceedingly difficult to improve significantly. Carrier failures and downsizing have also created a large supply of relatively new "used" aircraft, and the cost of acquiring aircraft is reduced further by the practice of aircraft leasing. Given high debt levels and low profitability in comparison to other industries, most airlines, including Southwest, have begun to lease their planes rather than purchase them. In light of high debt and low profits, the depreciation tax shield is not as valuable to the airlines. By leasing, carriers can "sell" that tax shield to the leasing company, actually creating value for the carrier. As a result, entry barriers are not as high as one would expect in other capital-intensive industries.

Furthermore, new entrants generally gain significant cost advantage by securing lower labor costs because they are not burdened by the unfavorable union contracts that affect many older airlines. Many of the union contracts agreed to by the major airlines call for higher pay and contain work rule provisions that reduce labor productivity. In addition, new entrants are sometimes able to gain favorable terms by purchasing excess capacity of other airlines, such as training and maintenance.

Profitability In order to survive and profit in this tough environment, airlines attempt to manipulate three main variables: cost, calculated as total operating expenses divided by available seat miles (ASM); yield, calculated as total operating revenues divided by the number of revenue passenger miles (RPM); and load factor, calculated as the ratio between RPMs and ASMs, which measures capacity utilization. Thus, profitability, defined as income divided by ASM, is computed as:

$$\text{Profitability} = [\text{yield} \times \text{load factor}] - \text{cost}$$

The major airlines have faced intensive competition from low-priced airlines during the past 10–15 years. While these low-priced airlines expanded the market for air travel, they also placed great downward pressure on the prices of the majors, thereby reducing their yields. To compete, the majors engaged in great cost-cutting efforts.

Capacity JP Morgan analysts believe that the most important factor influencing pricing in the long-term will be the falling industry cost curve. They point out that low-cost airlines have already lowered and inverted the traditionally downward-sloping industry cost curve. "With it they have pressured fares industry-wide, but particularly in short-haul markets where their impact on costs have been most dramatic. . . . [T]he airlines that are increasing capacity are those lowest on the industry's cost curve."[3] This shift has occurred because of the growth in low-cost, short-haul travel.

Outlook Lehman Brothers analysts concluded that the U.S. airline industry was entering a mature and more stable phase, as the major restructuring it

required was largely accomplished. In their view, this restructuring was driven by two key developments. First was the retrenchment of the majors into their core hubs. Second was technology diffusion, which occurred when the weaker airlines upgraded their systems technology regarding pricing and yield management and eliminated many disparities among major carriers.

Arenas of competition have also shifted. This trend was heightened by the events of September 11, 2001, and the public's concern about flying. Low-cost carriers, including Southwest Airlines and Shuttle by United, dominate short-haul capacity in the West. Expansion of the low-cost carriers now seems to be increasing, and competition appears to be increasing. Meanwhile the East Coast is still dominated by higher-cost carriers such as Delta and Continental, although they are facing profitability issues. Consequently, it is not surprising that the low-cost airlines have targeted the East as a major arena for expansion. Southwest's invasion of Florida and Providence, Rhode Island, is a noteworthy example. In the Northeast, capacity reduction by high-cost competitors such as American and Continental has also enhanced the opportunities for low-cost airlines such at JetBlue which now has a hub at JFK and wants to add a plane a week to its fleet from now until 2008! Delta has recently entered this low-cost market with Song. As carriers learn to adapt the low-cost formula to the geographic, climatic, and market intricacies of the Northeast, low-cost operations will likely continue to expand.[4]

SOUTHWEST AIRLINES' MISSION AND OBJECTIVES

Southwest Airlines' mission focuses to an unusually large degree on customer service and employee commitment. According to its annual report, the mission of Southwest Airlines is "dedication to the highest quality of Customer Service delivered with a sense of warmth, friendliness, individual pride, and Company Spirit." Indeed, Southwest proudly proclaims, "We are a company of People, not planes. That is what distinguishes us from other airlines and other companies." In many respects, the vision that separates Southwest from many of its competitors is the degree to which it is defined by a unique partnership with, and pride in, its employees. As stated in its *Annual Report*:

At Southwest Airlines, People are our most important asset. Our People know that because that's the way we treat them. Our People, in turn, provide the best Customer Service in the airline industry. And that's what we are in business for— to provide Legendary Customer Service. We start by hiring only the best People, and we know how to find them. People want to work for a "winner," and because of our success and the genuine concern and respect we have for each of our Employees, we have earned an excellent reputation as a great place to work. As a result, we attract and hire the very best applicants. Once hired, we train, develop, nurture, and, most important of all, support our People! In other words, we empower our Employees to effectively make decisions and to perform their jobs in this very challenging industry.

The airline's goal is to deliver a basic service very efficiently and safely. This translates into a number of fundamental objectives. A central pillar of its approach is to provide safe, low-price transportation in conjunction with maximum customer convenience. The airline provides a high frequency of flights with consistent on-time departures and arrivals. Southwest's employees also aspire to make this commodity service a "fun" experience. Playing games is encouraged, such as "guess the weight of the gate agent." The fun spirit is tempered so that it is never in poor taste and does not alienate business travelers.

SOUTHWEST AIRLINES' STRATEGY

Southwest Airlines is categorized as a low-fare/no-frills airline. However, its size and importance have led most analysts to consider it to be one of the major airlines despite its fit in the low-fare segment. In a fundamental sense, Southwest's business-level strategy is to be the cheapest and most efficient operator in specific domestic regional markets, while continuing to provide its customers with a high level of convenience and service leveraged off its highly motivated employees. Essentially, Southwest's advantage is that it is low-cost and has a good safety reputation.

Cost Leadership   Southwest operates the lowest-cost major airline in the industry. The airline devised a number of clever stratagems to achieve this low-cost structure. For example, by serving smaller, less congested secondary airports in larger cities, which tend to have lower gate costs and landing fees, Southwest can maintain schedules cheaply and easily. Southwest's approach is also facilitated by its focus on the Southwest and other locations with generally excellent weather conditions, which leads to far fewer delays. Moreover, by following a point-to-point strategy, Southwest need not coordinate flight schedules into connecting hubs and spokes, which dramatically reduces scheduling complexity and costs.

Route Structure   Historically, Southwest has specialized in relatively short-haul flights and has experienced considerable threat from providers of ground transportation (cars, trains, and buses) because the buyers of these short-haul services tend to be quite price-sensitive. Southwest has widened the market for air travel by attracting large numbers of patrons who previously relied on ground transportation. For example, before it entered the Louisville to Chicago market, weekly traffic totaled 8,000 passengers. After Southwest entered the market, that number grew to over 26,000. This increase in traffic is now recognized as the "Southwest Effect." Emphasis on short-haul flights has also allowed them to pare costly services such as food, which passengers demand on longer flights. Passengers are provided with only an "extended snack"—cheese, crackers, and a Nutri-Grain bar.

Turnaround Time   Its route structure has helped Southwest to experience the most rapid aircraft turnaround time in the industry (15–20 minutes versus an industry average of 55 minutes). Interestingly, Southwest's "20 Minute Turnaround" can be traced directly to the carrier's first days of operation in Texas when financial pressures forced the company to sell one of the four Boeing 737s it had purchased for its initial service. Having only three planes to fly three routes necessitated very rapid turnaround.

Rapid turnaround time is essential for short-haul flights because airplanes are airborne for a smaller percentage of time than on long-haul flights. Faster turnaround also allows Southwest to fly more daily segments with each plane, which in turn increases its assets' turnover. Their ability to maintain this practice is being challenged by the increased security requirements, but so far they seem to be doing well. Only time will tell what the exact impact will be of the Airline Security Act signed into law by President Bush on November 19, 2001, but thus far it appears that the American traveling public has accepted the time required for increased security in exchange for feeling safer and having a greater peace of mind.

Fleet Composition Southwest has the simplest fleet composition among the major airlines. The company only flies Boeing 737 planes and has committed to fly the 737 exclusively through 2004.

In choosing the fuel-efficient 737, Southwest developed a close relationship with Boeing that enabled it to receive comparatively favorable purchase terms. Although Southwest flies a number of model variations of the 737, the cockpits of the entire fleet are standardized. Therefore, any pilot can fly any plane, and any plane can be deployed on any route. In addition to helping capture scale economies at a much smaller size than its larger competitors, the homogeneous fleet composition reduces the complexities of training, maintenance, and service. It is difficult to calculate the large savings associated with this approach, but they exist in almost all operating areas including scheduling, training, aircraft deployment and use, wages and salaries, maintenance, and spare parts inventories.

Travel Agency Exposure According to its *Annual Report,* Southwest sells over 80% of its seats directly through its own website rather than through travel agents (compared with the industry average of 20–25%), thereby saving the 10% commission paid to travel agents. This also alleviates the need to participate in many of the travel agent reservation systems.

Gates Access to gates is often a constraining factor in the ability of airlines to expand because major airports have limited numbers of gates and most are already taken by other airlines. An emphasis on less-crowded secondary airports has alleviated this problem for Southwest; the airline purchases or leases gates at airports, as opposed to renting the gates of other airlines, which enables it to use its own ground crews.

Connections Southwest does not offer connections to other airlines, which simplifies its ground operations. However, this also limits access for many passengers, particularly for international flights.

Fare Structure Southwest also controls costs through its simplified fare structure. While Southwest's major competitors have complex fare structures and use computers and artificial intelligence programs to maximize passenger revenues, Southwest offers no special business or first-class seating. Rather, they generally offer a regular coach fare and a limited number of discounted coach fares.

Labor Labor is the largest cost component of airlines despite the heavy capital investment demanded in the industry. Southwest's labor costs are roughly 30% of revenues and 40% of all expenses. This represents about 8 cents per seat mile.[5] About 82% of Southwest's employees are unionized. Given the ability of unions to bring carrier operations to a halt, it is not surprising that they wield considerable power. The International Association of Machinists and Aerospace Workers represents customer service and reservation employees; the Transportation Workers of America (TWU) represents flight attendants; the Southwest Airline Pilots' Association (SWAPA) represents pilots; and the International Brotherhood of Teamsters (IBT) represents aircraft cleaners and stock clerks. Mechanics and appearance technicians are represented by the Aircraft Mechanics Fraternal Association (AMFA), and the training instructors are represented by the Southwest Airlines Professional Instructors Association.

In an industry where unions and management have often been at war—and where unions have the power to resist essential changes—the quality of their relationship is a crucial issue. Perhaps one of the best examples of this is the 1994 agreement between Southwest Airlines and SWAPA. The pilots agreed to keep pay rates at existing levels for five years, with increases of 3% in three of the last five years of the ten-year deal (five-year base term, with an additional five years unless it is terminated by the union.). Pilots can earn additional pay based on company profits. The pilots also obtained options to acquire up to 1.4 million shares of company stock in each of the ten years, in accord with market prices on the date of the deal. Pilots hired between 1996 and 2003 obtain lesser amounts of options at 5% over the then market value of the stock. Maximum pilot salary at Southwest is $148,000 yearly while at United it is $290,000 yearly. At JetBlue it is $115,000. These, of course, are always subject to revision.

Customer Service Southwest's approach to customer service is one of its core strategies. Its "Positively Outrageous Service" (POS) is different from the customer service associated with other major airlines. Service is provided with friendliness, caring, warmth, and company spirit—staff go out of their way to be helpful. This approach to service leverages Southwest's outstanding relationship with its employees. However, this stellar customer service does not include costly amenities like reserved seats or food service, and only offers very limited automatic baggage rechecking. By emphasizing flight frequency and on-time performance, Southwest has redefined the concept of quality air service. This unusual approach has allowed Southwest to differentiate its service while maintaining its cost leadership strategy.

Marketing Marketing savvy also plays a key role in Southwest's strategy. Since Southwest's inception, the major elements of the product offering have been price, convenience, and service. As a Texas native serving mostly Texas markets, it has played the role of the hometown underdog, fighting against the majors. Now, when Southwest enters a new market, they use a sophisticated combination of advertising, public relations, and promotions in the belief that once people fly Southwest they will be hooked.

Growth Despite its remarkable growth in what had been until recently a relatively moribund industry, Southwest has not emphasized growth as an objective. In fact, Herb Kelleher has expressed a "go-slow" philosophy. For example, Southwest will not enter markets unless it perceives favorable conditions, which range from the wishes of the local community to the availability of an appropriate labor supply. Given its record of success and its reputation, it is not surprising that many communities want Southwest to serve their markets. After all, good air service is considered by most communities to be an essential aspect of economic development. However, Southwest's policy prohibits accepting monetary subsidies or other incentives that cities and airports offer to gain air service. Southwest has also demonstrated a remarkable ability to manage its growth, an essential commodity in an industry known for its complexity. The inability to manage rapid growth has been blamed for the failure of many carriers, including Braniff, PeopleExpress, and ValuJet.

ORGANIZATION

Structure Southwest, like most airlines, is a formal and centralized organization. Organizationally, Southwest is structured according to functions. The nature of operations in the airline business is quite mechanical. That is, airline operations naturally aim for efficiency and consistency. They are not spontaneous—they value clocklike behavior. Planes must be in certain places at certain times and must be operated safely and efficiently. Safety itself requires following very rigorous procedures to ensure proper maintenance and training. The reputation of an airline can be seriously damaged by only one or two serious accidents. Therefore, the organization of Southwest is characterized by a high degree of formalization and standardization.

Reporting to Chief Executive Officer (CEO) Gary C. Kelly are Colleen Barrett, president, and Laura Wright, chief financial officer. Colleen C. Barrett is in charge of such key functions as marketing, sales, advertising, human resources, customer relations, and governmental affairs. See the Southwest website (**http://www.southwest.com**) for a listing of all current directors and officers.

How has Southwest Airlines maintained high levels of customer and employee satisfaction in the context of a functional organization? The company uses a number of mechanisms to allow employee participation. The fundamental concept is the notion of a "loose-tight" design. Within the context of tight rules and procedures, employees are encouraged to take a wide degree of leeway. The company maintains rather informal job descriptions and decentralizes decision making regarding customer service. So while there is very high standardization regarding operations, it is low with respect to customer service. Employees are empowered to do what is necessary to satisfy customers. Flight attendants are allowed to improvise cabin instructions and use their judgment in addressing passengers' needs. The company management operates with an informal open-door policy that allows employees to circumvent the formal hierarchy. Employees are encouraged to try things, knowing they will not be punished.

Southwest's organization is considerably simpler than that of its major competitors. Most of its competitors must manage the spatial complexity of far-flung international operations and contend with the added intricacies of hub-and-spoke systems. These large international carriers are also involved in complex alliances with other airlines in foreign markets to augment the scope of their services. They manage code-sharing arrangements with small regional domestic carriers. In short, the large carriers are complex networks, with more complicated organizational management issues.

Size Southwest operates about 400 Boeing 737s in more than 58 cities and employs over 35,000 people. Nevertheless, Southwest is still a relatively small company compared to the other major airlines. It ranks eighth in revenues and fifth in passenger boardings. Southwest's Available Seat Miles (ASMs) total less than a quarter of American Airlines, and it operates a fleet of only 352 aircraft compared to about 700 aircraft for American. Nevertheless, Southwest is the largest carrier in a significant number of the markets in which it flies and the dominant airline in the short-haul niche of the airline business.

Adaptability Southwest has been a very nimble organization, quick to take advantage of market opportunities. For example, when American Airlines and USAir scaled back their California operations, Southwest quickly took over the abandoned gates, acquired more planes, and now has 50% of the California market. Another example is Southwest's expansion into the Chicago Midway market following the collapse of Midway Airlines. Much of this flexibility stems from the company's remarkable labor relations. In addition, although Southwest is still purely a domestic carrier, it is developing a strategic alliance with Icelandair, a small North European carrier.

HUMAN RESOURCE MANAGEMENT

At Southwest Airlines the human resource function is called the People Department. According to the department's mission statement: "[R]ecognizing that our people are the competitive advantage, we deliver the resources and services to prepare our people to be winners, to support the growth and profitability of the company, while preserving the values and special culture of Southwest Airlines." The crucial importance of human resources to the strategy of Southwest has made the People Department more organizationally central to the company than its counterparts are at its competitors. Given Southwest's reputation as a great place to work, it is no wonder that so many people apply for each job opening

Unique Approach Aligned with Culture Southwest Airlines distinguishes itself from its competitors by doing many things differently. One of the most striking differences is how it goes through the selection process. It begins with Chairman Herb Kelleher, who states, "We like mavericks—people who have a sense of humor. We look for attitude. We'll train you on whatever you need to do, but the one thing we can't do is change inherent attitudes."[6] Libby Sartain, former vice president of People, remarked that the company has had to become more and more creative in how it finds candidates.[7] In a typical year, she noted, the company hires 4,000 to 5,000 people. In the past, about one out of four applicants would be interviewed and less than 3% would actually be hired. In theory, the odds of getting into Harvard are higher.[8]

Hire Based on Attitude What does Southwest look for in the selection process? The approach places great emphasis on hiring based on attitude. During the interview process, there may not be a fixed set of skills or experiences that are examined. The search is for something that Southwest considers to be much more elusive and important—a blend of energy, humor, team spirit, and self-confidence. These key predictors are used by Southwest to indicate how well applicants will perform and fit in with its own unique culture.

The hiring process at Southwest also emphasizes the importance of hiring people who are inclined toward teamwork. Ann Rhodes, another former vice president of People, stated that one of the important unwritten rules at Southwest is that "you can't be an elitist." Southwest actually uses a personality test to rate candidates (on a scale from one to five) on seven separate traits.[9] The seven areas evaluated include cheerfulness, optimism, decision-making skills, team spirit, communication, self-confidence, and self-starter skills. Anything less than a three is considered cause for rejection. With this methodology, the airline has chosen to use a multiple-hurdles approach where an applicant must exceed fixed levels of proficiency on all of the predictors in order to be accepted. With this approach a higher rating in one area will not compensate for a lower score on one of the other predictors. Southwest believes in these seven predictors and that failing to make the grade in even one will guarantee that the person will be unsuccessful on the job.[10]

Interview Based on Strategy The process of selection based on the seven predictors applies to everyone from pilots to mechanics. In the words of Libby Sartain, "we would rather go short and work overtime than hire one bad apple." In addition to the evaluation of the seven predictors, Southwest uses other methods in the selection process. The process begins like most companies with an interview. The interviewer looks for team-oriented people with prior work experiences that match. A common theme in screening all candidates revolves around people skills. According to Gittell,[11] the easiest way to get in trouble at Southwest is to offend another employee. Even when pilots are interviewed, the airline goes out of its way to find candidates who lack an attitude of superiority and who seem likely to treat coworkers with respect. Southwest's system for selecting its people is time-intensive but based on a history of bringing in people who fit into the culture of the company.

Southwest publicly explains almost every detail of the practices it uses to select employees. In theory, any company could attempt to copy the process and claim it as their own, but it would probably fail for a number of reasons. First, Southwest expends much more energy and time than most companies do. In order to find the right people, they spend the money up front on the selection process in the belief that it becomes worthwhile over time. So, not every company would be willing or able to make that type of investment. Second, Southwest's selection process matches the culture of the company. They value people and "walk the talk" when it comes to finding the right employees. Some additional quotes from Herb Kelleher back this up:

Other companies don't value attitude. They don't pay all that much attention to it. They don't make it a priority. I've been with companies where they have an opening, and you know what they consider the function of the personnel department? To plug a hole as quickly as they possibly can. That's quite different from what we do in many cases. Some years ago our VP of the People Department told me they had interviewed 34 people for a ramp agent position in Amarillo, Texas, and she was a little embarrassed about the amount of time it was taking and the implied cost of it, and my answer was: if you have to interview 134 people to get the right attitude on the ramp in Amarillo, Texas, do it.

Developing the Process The People Department, which is the HR function at Southwest Airlines developed its interview process in collaboration with Development Dimensions International, a consulting firm that specializes in designing sound selection procedures. "The procedures at Southwest Airlines adhere to the basic principles of good interview design: structured questions, systematic scoring, multiple interviewers, and interviewer training."[12]

Benefits of Centralization and Role of the People Department The overall selection and placement process at Southwest is centralized like the rest of the organizational structure of the airline. The centralization of this process helps make the best candidate available for the right job (i.e., it makes the placement process successful and feasible). Having trained people involved in selection and placement decisions improves the efficiency of the process and also reduces the risk of bias or unfair judgements. It also helps the operating managers to concentrate on their job while remaining involved in selection and placement decisions without personally formulating the process. This, of course, is a huge benefit in terms of keeping decisions and policies consistent throughout the organization.

The People Department at Southwest enjoys an extremely important role in its selection and placement process. This kind of centralized process helps the organization, as the applicants have to go to one place to apply for any position, and specialists trained in selection techniques can assist in the process of deciding which candidates should be hired and where they ought to be placed. Southwest keeps the line managers and other employees involved in the process, which serves to its benefit for a number of reasons. Employees who get the opportunity to contribute in the selection of their team members become more committed to helping them succeed, and the process also gives them a sense of urgency. The involvement of all levels of management and employees along with the HR department in the selection and placement process helps Southwest build a strong network of employees, who can then successfully forward the organization's mission of providing the right attitude and service to its customers.

The Decision Making in Selection and Placement The People Department has sound procedures in place for any level of selection, be it in the form of interviews or written assessments. The selection and placement decisions, however, are finally made by a combined panel of line managers and specialized representatives from the People Department. Selection and placement decisions at Southwest seem to be made by line managers and senior management with full participation of present employees in the spirit of true partnership. The People Department is responsible for designing the process and is largely responsible for attracting, helping in the selection and placement of, and retaining a strong set of employees.

All applications go through the People Department, and prospective candidates are then interviewed and tested for *aptitude and attitude* by a panel of interviewers in keeping with a consistent process that is developed by the HR function. Once selection decisions are made, placement of the right individual in the right position is once again done with the involvement of all levels of employees from that department along with specialists.

The People Department has spent years analyzing the staff at Southwest and has calibrated its questions to the specific needs and requirements of each job, as well as attributes like judgment and decision-making skills. The process can take up to six weeks before anybody is hired. About 20% of recruits fail to make it through the training period at the University for People in Dallas.

The time and money spent on the recruitment process has resulted in a turnover rate of 9%, the lowest in the industry. Traditionally, an HR department in most companies does not do much to endear itself to finance. However, Southwest's CEO, Gary Kelly, is convinced that investing in hiring is vital. "If you are not going to work hard to get people who are a good fit, it will hurt you. For example, we have never had a strike. What airline is even close to being able to say that?"

The predictor most stringently used for selection and placement of employees is personality and values. A panel of representatives from the People Department and the Inflight Department first interviews the candidates for flight attendant jobs. Before the selection process is finished, the candidates will also have one-in-one interviews with a recruiter or supervisor from the hiring department and a peer. The selection is highly systematic and a multiple-hurdles approach combined with a good interview design: structured questions, systematic scoring, multiple interviews, and interviewer training imply that only the best candidates get selected. The selection of candidates who fit the organizational culture of Southwest is undoubtedly critical to the success of Southwest.

The selection process has enabled Southwest to maintain a strong, unified culture in the face of enormous growth and to groom management talent within it. This is reflected at the senior management level, where promotions within the ranks have led to all but five positions being occupied by insiders, some of them having started their careers in entry-level positions. Internal politics is not apparent from the sources available to us. We can, however, make the assumption that involvement of politics in decision making is always a possibility.

As Southwest grows, sustaining this zeal is likely to get harder. Previously, the question that was frequently asked was: After Kelleher, who? According to Bob Crandell, ex-CEO of American Airlines, "The kind of contribution Kelleher can make to Southwest is to select the next leader and help the next leader make a successful transition." Well, he did just that in 2001. James Parker, formerly the vice president, took over as the CEO until 2004. Despite a very challenging environment, Parker and his team continued the growth and success Southwest had enjoyed for the past three decades. Now Kelly is expected to continue this tradition as well.

Training In an organization where attitudes, culture, and fit are so important, it is natural that the company places such a great emphasis on socialization and training. Just as McDonald's has its Hamburger University, Southwest has its University for People. Everyone at Southwest has a responsibility for self-improvement and training. Once a year, all Southwest employees, including all senior management, are required to participate in training programs designed to reinforce shared values. Except for flight training, which is regulated and certified, all training is done on the employee's own time. Nonetheless, the training department operates at full capacity, seven days a week. The fun spirit of Southwest emerges in graduates very early.

Labor Relations The importance of labor relations cannot be underestimated in a company that is about 82% unionized. Here again Kelleher's unusual abilities emerged. Somehow he was able to convince union members and officials to identify with the company. Time will tell if Kelly can have the same success over the long term. This topic is discussed further in a later section entitled "Southwest Airlines Performance Indicators."

Compensation It is also noteworthy that in an era when chief executive pay has escalated to huge amounts, Kelleher was named one of the lowest-paid chief executive officers in Dallas on a performance-adjusted basis. Furthermore, company officers do not get the perks (e.g., cars or club memberships) often enjoyed by their counterparts in comparable organizations, and they even stay in the same hotels as flight crews. Southwest has refused to compete for executive talent based on salary.

Culture The most distinguishing feature of Southwest Airlines is its culture. When competitors and outside observers describe Southwest, they tend to focus on its cultural attributes. Herb Kelleher made the development and maintenance of culture one of his primary duties. The culture permeates the entire organization and sends clear signals about the behavior expected at Southwest. To promote employee awareness of the effects of their efforts on the company's bottom line, *LUV Lines* (the company newsletter) reports break-even volumes per plane. The newsletter informs employees not only of Southwest's issues, but of competitor news as well. The belief is that informed employees are better equipped to make decisions.

One of the shared values is the importance of having fun at work. Humor is a significant aspect of the work environment. Such attributes are believed by senior management to enhance a sense of community, trust, and spirit and to counterbalance the stress and pressures of the mechanistic demands of airline operations.

Another characteristic is the cooperative relationship among employee groups. This can be an advantage in functional structures, which are notorious for generating coordination problems. In other airlines, work procedures clearly demarcate job duties. However, at Southwest everyone pitches in regardless of the task. Stories abound of pilots helping with baggage and of employees going out of their way to help customers. In one particularly bizarre story, an agent baby-sat a passenger's dog for two weeks so that the customer could take a flight on which pets were not allowed. Employee cooperation affects the bottom line. When pilots help flight attendants clean the aircraft and check in passengers at the gate, turnaround time, a cornerstone of the low-cost structure, is expedited.

Because of its team-oriented culture, Southwest is not stifled by the rigid work rules that characterize most competitors. As a result, Southwest has tempered the stringent demands of a functional structure with the liberating force of an egalitarian culture. One excerpt from Southwest's "The Book on Service: What Positively Outrageous Service Looks Like at Southwest Airlines" is rather instructive:

> *"Attitude breeds attitude . . ." If we want our customers to have fun, we must create a fun-loving environment. That means we have to be self-confident enough to reach out and share our sense of humor and fun—with both our internal and external customers. We must want to play and be willing to expend the extra energy it takes to create a fun experience with our customers.*
>
> *Just as the words "it's not my job" can take away the source of life for a consumer-oriented business, the words "it's just a job" are equally as dangerous. Positively Outrageous Service cannot be learned from a book or manual; it cannot be artificially manufactured; and it is not required by*

law. It is born and bred in each individual according to his or her experiences, attitude, and genuine desire to succeed—both personally and professionally. Service does not start at the beginning of each work day, nor does it end when you go home. It is a very real part of you . . . it's your company; your success; your future.

This approach certainly contributes significantly to the lowest employee turnover rate in the industry (7%) and the highest level of consumer satisfaction.

Despite all of the freedom that the culture permits, in some areas the company also employs very stringent controls. Perhaps the best example is that Herb Kelleher himself had to approve all expenditures over $1,000!

Forged over 30 years, Southwest's culture has been a source of sustainable competitive advantage. A Bankers Trust analyst put it this way:

Southwest has an indefinably unique corporate culture and very special management/employee relationship that has taken years to cultivate. Employees have long had a significant stake in the company; employee ownership and employee contribution to wealth creation are not ideas that are alien to the workforce of Southwest Airlines since it is emphatically not 'just a job.' Then, too, the relationship is not merely spiritual—the employees have come to trust the only company that has a record of 23 consecutive years of earning stability combined with an impressive record of stock appreciation unmatched by virtually any company . . . within or beyond the airline industry. The pilots are well compensated relative to the industry average, and they understand that. The challenge was to find creative ways to tie together the fortunes of the company with those responsible for it without risk or destruction of shareholder value . . . and, unlike the employee groups at other major airlines, the Southwest pilots understand that.[13]

Management Until Parker and Kelly arrived as CEOs, there was no doubt about who was in charge at Southwest. In this respect, Southwest is like most of the other airlines—centralized with a very strong, if not dominating, CEO. What set Herb Kelleher apart was his charismatic nature. His friendly, participative, deeply involved, and caring approach was and is revered throughout the organization. A very large number of employees know the chairman, and he is reputed to know thousands of them by name. Nonetheless, it is also known that behind the scenes he can be extremely tough, implying that his public and private personae can be quite different.

Herb Kelleher started Southwest with a former client, Rollin King. King supposedly presented his idea for a low-cost Texas-only airline based on the success of Pacific Southwest Airlines in California to Kelleher over dinner at the St. Antony Club in San Antonio. The original "Love Triangle," the foundation of Southwest's strategy, was drawn on a cocktail napkin.

Kelleher's management style, which had been described as a combination of Sam Walton's thriftiness and Robin Williams's wackiness,[14] seems to have been consistent right from the beginning. Direct, visible, and, some would say, even bizarre, he has attended company parties dressed in drag and appeared in a company ad as Elvis. Known for constantly showing the flag in the field and interacting with large numbers of employees and customers, Kelleher is reputed to have engaged people in conversations for hours, at all hours, about company and industry issues, often with a drink in his hand. He almost always seems ready for a party, and this fun-oriented atmosphere pervades the organization. The company newspaper, *LUV Lines*, has a column entitled "So, What Was Herb Doing All This Time?" recounting the CEO's activities. Following his example, Southwest employees are well known for going the extra mile. Among the stories of such behavior is that of a customer service representative who stayed overnight at a hotel with an elderly woman who was afraid to stay alone when her flight was grounded due to fog. The agent "knew" that was what Herb would have done.[15]

Kelleher replaced formal strategic planning with "future scenario generation," arguing that "reality is chaotic, and planning is ordered and logical. The meticulous nit-picking that goes on in most strategic planning processes creates a mental straightjacket that becomes disabling in an industry where things change radically from one day to the next."[16] It seems likely that Kelly will continue these practices, as Parker did, but his style may be quite different.[17]

In the early 1990s Colleen Barrett set up a company culture committee, composed of people from all geographic areas and levels of the company. The committee, which meets four times a year, is charged with preserving and enhancing the company culture. One of the committee's successes is illustrated by the company organization. It is well known that functional structures such as Southwest's are designed to promote specialization and scale economies, but often at the expense of teamwork and coordination. As these organizations grow, they become even more difficult to operate in an integrated manner. The committee developed a number of initiatives to improve cross-functional cooperation. One example is that all company officers and directors have to spend one day every quarter in the field—working a real "line job."

Technology Like all airlines, Southwest is a very heavy user of computer-related technology. This technology supports all activities from scheduling to reservations to general operations support. The network is built on four superservers and a reservations subsystem that connects more than 5,000 PCs and terminals across the country. Remote locations communicate with the servers using TCP/IP across Novell LANs.

This network supports a reservation system that has enabled Southwest to be the first carrier to offer ticketless travel on all of its flights. Over 80% of Southwest's seats are now sold ticketless. The ticketless system offers significantly improved customer service by eliminating lines at ticket counters. The system also reduces costs; it is estimated that it costs an airline from $15 to $30 to produce and process a single paper ticket.

Customers using the Southwest ticketless system can purchase a seat on a Southwest flight by telephone or on the Internet. Customers receive a confirmation code, which is traded for a boarding pass at the airport. The concept of ticketless travel originated at Morris Air, a Salt Lake City airline acquired by Southwest in 1993. Although policy and operational differences prevented Southwest from adopting the Morris system, the company was able to accelerate the development of its own system with the assistance of Evan Airline Information Services, a consulting firm that helped to develop Morris Air's system. The first ticketless passenger boarded a Southwest plane only four months after development began.

Marketing activities explicitly build on the Internet as a primary marketing channel. Southwest was the first carrier to host a website (**http://www.southwest.com**), which was deemed "Best Airline Website" by Air Transport World. It recently launched a joint venture with Worldview Systems to enhance its Internet presence.

SOUTHWEST AIRLINES PERFORMANCE INDICATORS

Many different criteria can be used to evaluate Southwest's success in achieving its basic objectives. Certainly Southwest's different constituencies look at its performance in different ways. Southwest takes particular pride in the following accomplishments:

- 30 years of safe, reliable operations;
- number one in fewest customer complaints for the last nine consecutive years in the Department of Transportation's Air Travel Consumer Report;
- five consecutive years of Triple Crown Customer Service;
- nine consecutive years of increased profits and 30 years of profitability;
- top ranking in the Airline Quality Survey conducted by the National Institute for Aviation Research for two of the last three years;
- consistent financial success that provides thousands of jobs in the aerospace industry; and
- a route system that has grown to 58 airports in 29 states, carrying more than 60 million customers on 352 Boeing 737 aircraft.

Check magazine stories and the company's website regularly to update these performance figures.

No issue is more important than safety and security. One needs only to study the checkered history of ValuJet or Air Florida to see what one catastrophic crash can do to an airline when the airline is perceived to have been at fault. Meanwhile, Southwest maintains a 30-year safety record and is generally acknowledged to be one of the world's safest airlines.

Of course, Southwest's customers remain one of the company's main constituencies. Despite its no-frills orientation, Southwest consistently receives the highest rankings for customer satisfaction. This is achieved through the successful management of customer expectations. By emphasizing low price and consistency, Southwest has successfully redefined the concept of quality airline service. For example, the "Triple Crown Award" goes to the airline, if any, which has the best on-time record, best baggage handling, and fewest customer complaints according to statistics published in the Department of Transportation (DOT) Air Travel Consumer Reports. First won by Southwest in 1988, the airline has won the award every year since 1992. No other airline has ranked on top in all three categories for even a single month, although Continental Airlines is catching up fast!

Given its mission, employee satisfaction is another important indicator of company success. Personnel are a crucial determinant of organizational performance throughout the industry. Labor costs are about 40% of operating costs in the industry, while at Southwest they are considerably lower. Southwest's unit labor costs are about 40% less than American's and 20% less than Continental's. Average pay at Southwest is about $60,000 yearly while at American it is about $80,000.[18]

As noted, labor relations is an important determinant of company survival. With the emphasis today on cost containment, however, Southwest may find it more challenging, as time goes on, to maintain harmonious relations with the unions given that the most recent agreement (2004) with the flight attendants included a raise of 31% over the contract's six years and the 2002 contract with the pilots raised their pay a minimum of 20% over the past two years.[19] On the other hand, Southwest has had generally peaceful and cooperative labor relations throughout most of its history. One salient result of management-labor harmony is that Southwest employees are the most productive in the industry. A single agent usually staffs gates, where competitors commonly use two or three. Ground crews are composed of six or fewer employees, about half the number used by other carriers. Despite the lean staffing, planes are turned around in half the time of many rivals. Southwest pays its pilots wages that are comparable to the major carriers, but pilot productivity (e.g., number of flights per day, number of hours worked) is considerably higher. Southwest also has one of the lowest personnel turnover ratios in the industry.

Despite its low-cost structure, Southwest is not able to control all costs. One advantage that larger, broader-scope carriers can have is a more limited exposure to fuel price volatility. Broader scope can allow them to take advantage of geographic differences in fuel prices, but they do not always have the financial resources anymore to hedge against future price increases. So it is Southwest that does the better job at hedging against fuel price increases, and it (like JetBlue) also has the advantage of a younger and more fuel-efficient fleet than its larger competitors.

Market share is another indicator of an organization's performance. By this criterion, Southwest also ranks at the top of the industry. For example, it consistently ranks first in market share in 80–90 of its top 100 city-pair markets, and overall has 60–65% of total market share. Because of the "Southwest Effect," the carrier gains this share by growing the size of each of its markets—this is achieved by a fare structure that is on average $60 lower than the majors.

THE CHALLENGES AHEAD

Southwest Airlines is no Johnny-come-lately. Its basic strategy of consistent low-cost, no-frills, high-frequency, on-time air transportation with friendly service is a recipe that has been refined throughout the company's 30-year life. It has worked for the company in periods of catastrophic losses for the industry as well as in times of abundance. Southwest has been able to compete successfully with both the major airlines and those that have been formed to copy its formula.

Opportunities for Growth Southwest apparently recognizes the potential saturation of its historic markets and the limited number of attractive short-haul markets. Therefore, it has expanded into some longer-haul markets. Longer-haul markets not only provide avenues for future growth, but also provide potentially higher margins. On average, the company's cost per ASM is about 8 cents. However, on its longer routes, costs are as low as 4 cents per ASM. Furthermore, as mentioned, the 10% ticket tax has been replaced with a combination ticket tax and takeoff fee. This increases the attractiveness of longer-haul flights.

Limits to Growth As critics have noted, there are many challenges on the horizon. Southwest will eventually saturate its historic niche. The company currently flies into 58 airports with more than 2,700 flights per day. Its old strategy of focusing on good climates and smaller, less congested airports has contributed to Southwest's low costs. Many believe that poor weather conditions can affect Southwest's ability to maintain on-time performance and can significantly affect down-line operations. This is magnified by a schedule based on a rapid turnaround, which leaves little leeway for flight delays. Southwest entered and then left the Denver market when bad weather forced an unacceptable number of delays and canceled flights.

This puts a limit on growth because there are only a finite number of markets that can satisfy these criteria. Thus, Southwest has begun to enter markets in poorer climates and to introduce longer-haul flights. Providence, Rhode Island, and Philadelphia, Pennsylvania, two of the newer locations, are not good weather locations.[20] There are about 56 airports in good weather locations with populations of over 100,000. Southwest currently serves 36. It is unclear how much demand for point-to-point service exists in the remaining 20.

If Southwest decides to introduce food services as an amenity for longer-haul flights, it would require galleys and onboard services that would significantly boost the cost of operation of those airplanes. Longer flights also result in fewer flights per day and may serve to drive down yield. A mixture of galleyed and nongalleyed aircraft will also make fleet scheduling less flexible. Furthermore, there will be a greater need for functions in the organization responsible for new elements such as national marketing, the frequent flyer program, interline agreements, new geographic operations, and possibly food services.

People and culture also are major concerns to further expansion. Southwest is highly selective; it consequently needs a large pool of applicants in order to find a few people good enough for the culture. With labor shortages across the country, it may be difficult to attract large pools of applicants. Without the selectivity, Southwest may not be able to get the human resources it needs in order to differentiate itself from others. The unique culture of Southwest helps make the company really fly, but this is being called into question by such events as the 2004 contract negotiations with the flight attendants. As companies expand, particularly in size and geographic location, they often find that it becomes increasingly more difficult to maintain the same culture. No doubt, the new leadership will have its hands full in maintaining the culture and the costs that have been so critical to Southwest's success.

Competition During the last several years, the gap between Southwest and the rest of the majors has narrowed as other carriers have attempted to emulate Southwest's formula. Some of the larger traditional airlines have developed lower-cost short-haul divisions. For example, both United and Delta have introduced an "airline within an airline" to lower costs for short-haul flights. These separate divisions may hire their own pilots and ground support at much lower costs under separate contractual relations with unions. Under these arrangements, pilots can often be employed for less than half the cost of the parent airline.[21]

At the same time, Southwest has adopted many of the features that the majors use to support their large networks. As Southwest has grown in scope, it has introduced national advertising, including NFL sponsorship; a frequent flyer program, including a branded credit card; and interline and marketing agreements with international carriers. Southwest's operations at Nashville are developing into a hub. The carrier's average stage length has also increased over the last several years. Southwest has now expanded into geographic markets and climates that are not as compatible with its original fair-weather, low-congestion strategy. Its flights now compete head-to-head with some of the major carriers.

Recent successes of Continental Airlines under the leadership of Gordon Bethune and Larry Kellner have been most impressive. They virtually turned the airline around 180 degrees. In the near term, Continental, America West, United's Ted, and Delta's Song seem to be some of Southwest's strongest competitors, in addition to AirTran and JetBlue.[22] JetBlue, under the leadership of David Neeleman, the opposite in personality from Herb Kelleher, is fast becoming a no-frills airline for Southwest to take seriously. It has a philosophy similar to Southwest's, for example, it has just one type of plane, the Airbus A320, and doesn't serve meals. It does, however, let passengers pick their seats, and has leather upholstery, free satellite TV, and a frequent flyer program. Neeleman has big plans Southwest cannot afford to ignore. And now Virgin Airlines may be starting to enter the market in the United States.[23]

While Southwest and JetBlue are just thinking about going global, Ryanair and EasyJet based in Britain are expanding their networks out of Britain and setting up bases in Europe where low-fare airlines are few and far between. Debonair is now a player in this important market along with Virgin Express. These two carriers are in a regulatory environment that Southwest faced in 1978, that is, one that is becoming much more deregulated thanks to European Union (EU) legislation that took full effect in 1997 that allows any qualified airline to fly anywhere within the EU without government approval. Although both these low-fare airlines are copying much of the Southwest model, greater social costs and much more attractive high-speed rail alternatives make running a low-cost operation successfully in Europe a bit more challenging, as Virgin Express and Debonair have learned. Nonetheless, low-fare air travel is growing 25% yearly in Europe![24]

Credits: Ari Ginsberg and Richard Freedman prepared the original version of this case with the research assistance of Bill Smith. It is used here with their permission. They thank Myron Uretsky, Eric Greenleaf, and Bethany Gertzog for their valuable comments and suggestions. They also appreciate the careful review, corrections, and helpful recommendations made by Susan Yancey of Southwest Airlines on an earlier version. The case is intended to serve as the basis for class discussion rather than to illustrate either effective or ineffective handling of an administrative situation. A glossary of their key terms appears in Appendix SA.1.

The case was updated in 2005 by Randall S. Schuler and Susan E. Jackson. Materials to update this case were taken from Southwest's website, numerous articles, and the case materials (including Appendices SA.2 and SA.3) of a team composed of Megha Channa, Olympia Cicchino, Shirish Grover, Mohini Mukherjee, and Drew Von Tish, all students in the Rutgers University Master's of HRM program; the materials are used with their permission. Additional materials and insights were provided by Kristin Nordfors and the students at the GSBA Zürich.

App SA.1	**Glossary of Terms**
ARC	Airline Reporting Corporation. An organization owned by the airlines that serves as a clearinghouse for processing airline tickets.
ASM	Available Seat Mile. One ASM is one sellable seat, flown for one mile. For example, a 138-seat Boeing 737 traveling 749 miles from LGA to ORD (LaGuardia to O'Hare) represents 103,362 ASMs.
Class of Service	The fare level at which a ticket is sold. This does not refer to the cabin in which the passenger flies. For example, a United Airlines' availability display shows the following classes of service for coach: Y B M H Q V. By subdividing coach into classes, airlines can control inventory and manage yield.
Code Share	An interline agreement by which two carriers are able to apply their flight numbers to the same plane. This often includes an interline connection. For example, American Airlines and South African Airlines code share on SAA's flight to JHB (Johannesburg). The flight has an AA flight number and an SAA flight number. AA can sell it as an American Airlines flight.
CRS	Computer Reservation System. Allows airlines and travel agents to reserve and sell seats on airline flights. CRS companies include Apollo, Sabre, System One, and Worldspan.
Direct Flight	Any flight designated by a single flight number. Direct flights can include multiple stops and even changes of aircraft. For example, Pan Am Flight 1 at one time made 11 stops as it flew "round the world" direct from LAX to JFK.

App SA.1   Glossary of Terms (*continued*)

Full Fare	Designated as "Full Y." The undiscounted first, business, or coach fare. For domestic fares, this is used to calculate the level of discounted fares. Full Y is rarely paid for domestic flights, but is common on international flights when inventory is scarce.
Interline Agreement	Refers to various agreements between carriers. Common interline agreements concern the transfer of baggage, the endorsement and acceptance of tickets, and joint airfares (e.g., a passenger flies USAir from Albany to JFK and then SAS to Copenhagen).
Inventory	The number of seats available for each class of service for a given flight. For example, a USAir flight may have no K inventory available (seats to sell at K class fare levels), although higher-priced H seats may be available. Both seats are in coach.
Load Factor	The percentage of ASMs that are filled by paying passengers. Can be calculated by dividing RPMs by ASMs.
O&D	Origin and Destination. Refers to the originating and terminating airports of an itinerary segment. Connection points are not counted in O&Ds. This is different from city-pair, which refers to the origination and termination of a flight segment. For example, for a passenger traveling on NW from HPN (White Plains) to SMF (Sacramento), the O&D market is HPN-SMF. The city-pairs flown will be HPN-DTW and DTW-SMF (White Plains-Detroit, Detroit-Sacramento)
Restricted Fare	Any fare that has restrictive rules attached to it. Common restrictions include Saturday Night Stayover, Advance Purchase, Day/Time of Travel, Non-Refundability, and Class of Service. Generally, lower fares have greater restrictions.
RPM	Revenue Passenger Mile. One passenger paying to fly one mile. For example, a passenger who pays to fly from LGA to ORD represents 749 RPMs. The class of service and fare paid are not considered in calculating RPMs.
Stage Length	The length of a flight segment. The stage length between LGA and ORD is 749 miles.
Unrestricted Fare	A fare with no restrictions. Often, this is not the full fare. For example, American's Y26 fare is an unrestricted fare, but still lower than the full Y fare.
Yield	Measured as revenue per RPM.

App SA.2   Interview with an Employee in the Marketing Division

Interview of Joanna DePinto, employee in marketing division of Southwest Airlines, conducted by the team by telephone on March 23, 2001.

1. **When you got hired, what was the process?**
   I was an intern in Austin, when I applied. I got interviewed by a bunch of people many times. Group interviews are a big deal at Southwest. They see your ability to communicate well and get along with other people. You meet the group you will be working with and they see how you get on with them.

2. **Do you know of any other companies that have the same selection process?**
   No! Well, not exactly the same selection process. Some companies like Compac and Cisco are trying to emulate us. They are hiring people not just for technical skills but also for their people skills.

3. **Who do you think makes the final decision about selection?**
   The applicants work with a recruiter through all rounds of interviews, but I think the final decision is made by the manager of the department and the director.

4. **What affects the decision-making process most at Southwest?**
   Everyone works toward the good of the company. It all comes down to what is best for the company. Cost saving is very important. As far as hiring is concerned, it is definitely about the kind of person you are. They hire for personality and train for skill.

App SA.2 Interview with an Employee in the Marketing Division (*continued*)

5. So attitude and personality are the key drivers at Southwest?
Oh! Absolutely!

6. What about internal politics in hiring and selection?
There is no infighting or disagreement. People really try and do what is best for the company. I don't think there is any internal politics that affects decision making. People enjoy coming to work every day; there is no cut-throat competition or anything.

7. What is Herb like?
Oh! He is awesome! He is a wonderful man, very reachable. The first day I went to work, he got into the same elevator as me and kissed me! I got like quite excited, "Herb Kelleher kissed me." When I reached my office, I told my colleagues about it and they said, "Oh! But he kisses everyone!"

App SA.3 Interview with an Employee in the Marketing Division

Question 1A: Describe the Hiring Process at Southwest

Southwest Airlines tries to fill all vacancies from within the company if at all possible. The reason for this is because we are making the assumption that someone who is already employed by us has the "spirit" and attitude and work ethics we want, whereas we would be taking a chance by hiring from outside. The theory is that we will hire for attitude and train for skill. Obviously, there are times when we must hire from outside. First, of course, we do as close a match as possible for the job requirements—although if an internal doesn't meet all the requirements but does meet most of them and has a great attitude/spirit, we will give them a chance at interviewing for the position.

Our interview process can be quite strenuous. We do group interviews for some frontline positions such as Flight Attendant or Reservation Sales Agent. This would consist of a team of interviewers and each asks questions that the applicants respond to. Then each interviewer gets to cast a vote for or against bringing each applicant back for a second interview. From this point on the process is similar for all job applicants. The second interview (for those who participated in group interviews) and the first interview for other applicants usually consist of a smaller interview team. The questions are asked by all of the interviewers, but they are basically "behavior-based" questions. This means that applicants will be asked to describe a time in their past work life when they were faced with a certain situation. The response should include what the situation was, what the applicant did or how they handled it, and finally what was the result. For example, if the job required good conflict management skills, an interviewer might ask the applicant to describe a time when they were in a heated disagreement with a coworker—what was the situation, how did you handle it, and what was the result. The response from the applicant is a predictor of the behavior this potential employee would use in the future on this job if hired.

When the interview is over, all interview team members must come to a consensus as to whether to hire this individual or, as is frequently necessary, to bring the applicant back for a third interview. If there is a third interview, the next higher level of leadership will be involved. Sometimes, depending on the position being interviewed for, interviews can continue all the way through the vice president. An example of that is that anyone taking a position within our People Department (human resources) or even just moving from one position to another within the People Department will interview first with a recruiter and interview team consisting of peers and first-level leadership for that position, and continue all the way through our vice president of People (i.e., Colleen Barrett).

This is time-consuming; however, we are more confident of getting the right person in the right position. Also, you should be aware that we frequently start with a pool of applicants but end up reposting the job. The reasons this happens is that we do not take the best person in the pool; instead we are looking for the best person for the job and if we don't find him or her in the pool, then we start over. An empty desk for a period of time is sometimes a price we pay in order to find the best fit.

Question 1B: Can Any Company Duplicate What Southwest Does? Have Any Tried or Benchmarked and Then Launched Their Own?

Many companies have benchmarked Southwest for numerous reasons. In fact, SWA at one time hosted a "Culture Day" for outside companies because we had so many requests. We have stopped doing this because it got so big, it was taking

App SA.3 **Interview with an Employee in the Marketing Division (*continued*)**

us away from what we should be doing. I'm sure that some of those organizations have listened to what they were told and did try to implement some of what we do. However, I do not know who did not do it, nor do I have information on how successful they were. Obviously, there is a down side to the way we approach hiring. Lots of organizations probably decided not to put the extra burden on other employees by having a position vacant for very long and using resources in the hiring process for such a long interview process.

Question 2: Who Makes the Selection and Placement Decisions at Southwest?

I believe I answered this question in 1A above. To recap, the decision is a joint decision of the interview team if it is a frontline position. If not frontline, then not only does the interview team have to be in agreement, but so do all the leaders involved in the interview process. If any one of them kicks back on an application, it can take that applicant out of the running.

Question 3: What Affects the Decision-Making Process the Most at Southwest? Do Politics Affect the Process?

The hire/no hire decision is based on how well of a match the applicant is to the requirements of the job *plus* their attitude/spirit—it takes both! As far as politics are concerned, even Herb stays out of the hiring process. It is the least political, buddy-buddy system that it can be.

Question 4: How Important Is the Selection and Placement Process to Southwest's Success?

Southwest Airlines has a unique culture, and our financial success as an airline is founded on that culture; it is what makes us "different." We like to have fun, we love a challenge, we are made up of people who take accountability for their actions and for the success of our airline—we, therefore, believe in hard work/hard play. We like people who are willing to work outside the lines and are willing to step up to the plate and make a decision. We don't like people who take themselves too seriously, are complainers, or are not willing to "do whatever it takes." Not everyone is fit for this environment. If we do not continue to employ "the right stuff," our culture, overall, could fail. How important is the selection and placement process to Southwest's success? I don't know a word descriptive enough! Let's just say it is crucial!

—Pat Janson, Facilitator
University of People, Career Development Services
People Department, Southwest Airlines
March 27 and April 4, 2001

ENDNOTES

1 K. Brooker, "The Chairman of the Board Looks Back," *Fortune* (May 28, 2001): 63–76.

2 M. Maynard, "Get Out the Glue for a New Business Model," *New York Times* (July 11, 2004): Section 3: 1, 3; W. Zellner and M. Arndt, "Can Anything Fix the Airlines?" *Business Week* (April 7, 2003): 52–53; P. Coy, "The Airlines: Caught Between a Hub and a Hard Place," *Business Week* (August 5, 2002): 83.

3 ———, "Snip, Snip, Snip," *The Economist* (October 13, 2001): 59–60.

4 M. Maynard, "US Airways' Stock Hurt by Southwest's Route Plans," *New York Times* (December 12, 2003): C2; E. Wong, "Southwest to Fly into Philadelphia," *New York Times* (October 29, 2003): C2; E. Brown, "A Smokeless Herb," *Fortune* (May 28, 2001): 78–79; L. Zuckerman, "Airline Based at Kennedy Expands West," *New York Times* (May 23, 2001): C1, 6.

5 S. Tully, "The Airlines' New Deal: It's Not Enough," *Fortune* (April 28, 2003): 78–82; W. Zellner and M. Arndt, "It's Showtime for the Airlines," *Business Week* (September 2, 2002): 36–37.

6 CEO Profile of Herb Kelleher, *Chief Executive Magazine* (March 2000).

7 N. Wong, "Let Spirit Guide Leadership," *Workforce* (February 2000): 33–36; G. Donnelly, "Recruiting, Retention & Returns," *CFO* (March 1, 2000). Libby Sartain, most recent past VP for People, left in late 2001 to join Yahoo in a similar position.

8 J. H. Gittell, "Paradox of Coordination and Control," *California Management Review* (Spring 2000): 101–117.

9 P. Carbonara, "Hire for Attitude, Train for Skill," *Fast Company* (August 1996): 73–78.

10 *Ibid.*

11 J. H. Gittell, "Paradox of Coordination and Control."

12 S. E. Jackson and R. S. Schuler, *Managing Human Resources through Strategic Partnerships,* 9th ed. (Cincinnati, OH: South-Western, 2006).

13 K. Jones, "Herb's Flight Plan," *Texas Monthly* (March 1999); W. Zellner, "Southwest: After Kelleher, More Blue Skies," *Business Week* (April 2, 2001): 45.

14 K. Brooker, "Can Anyone Replace Herb?" *Fortune* (April 17, 2000): 186–192.

15 A. R. Myerson, "Air Herb," *New York Times Magazine* (November 9, 1997): 36.

16 L. Bean, "Why Is This Airline the Most Profitable? Ask the Industry's Only Woman President," *DiversityInc* (October/November 2003): 81–82; J. Freiberg and K. Freiberg, *NUTS! Southwest Airlines' Crazy Recipe for Business and Personal Success* (Austin, TX: Bard Books, 1996); R. Oppel, "Southwest Manages to Keep Its Balance," *New York Times* (September

25, 2001): C6; "Outlaw Flyboy CEOs," *Fortune* (November 13, 2000): 237–250.

17 M. Maynard, "Out of the Blue, Southwest Airlines Chief Resigns," *New York Times* (July 17, 2004): C2; A. Sewer, "Southwest Airlines: The Hottest Thing in the Sky," *Fortune* (March 8, 2004): 103; W. Zellner and M. Arndt, "Holding Steady," *Business Week* (February 3, 2003): 66–68.

18 E. Wong, "Low-Cost Airlines Become Big Spenders," *New York Times* (July 22, 2003): Section D: 8; W. Zellner, "Airline Stocks with Tailwind," *Business Week* (April 14, 2003): 90; W. Zellner, "It's Showtime for the Airlines," *Business Week* (September 2, 2002): 36–37; Tully, "The Airlines' New Deal: It's Not Enough"; W. Wells, "Lord of the Skies," *Forbes* (October 14, 2002): 130–137; E. Wong, "Airline's New Diet Has Rivals Watching," *New York Times* (January 12, 2003): Section 3: 1, 11; W. Zellner and M. Arndt, "Can Anything Fix the Airlines?" *Business Week* (April 7, 2003): 52–53.

19 J. Helyar, "Southwest Finds Trouble in the Air," *Fortune* (August 9, 2004): 38; M. Trottman, "Spirit of Fun and Hard Work Is Clouded by Picketing and Employee Complaints," *Wall Street Journal* (July 11, 2003): 1.

20 M. Maynard, "In Philadelphia, Southwest Is Trying the Front Door," *New York Times* (January 31, 2004): C1, 14.

21 W. Zellner, "Cute New Planes, Same Old Problems," *Business Week* (March 1, 2004): 42; M. Maynard, "The East Joins the Low-Fare Bazaar," *New York Times* (February 8, 2004): 1, 11; C. Haddad, "Getting Down and Dirty with the Discounters," *Business Week* (October 28, 2002): 76–78.

22 B. Grow, "Don't Discount This Discounter," *Business Week* (May 24, 2004): 84–85; W. Zellner, "Coffee, Tea, or Bile?: Resentful Airline Workers Could Hobble Turnaround Plans," *Business Week* (June 2, 2003): 56–58; W. Zellner, "Strafing the Big Boys Again," *Business Week* (June 23, 2003): 36; W. Wells, "Lord of the Skies," *Forbes* (October 14, 2002): 130–137; M. Arndt and W. Zellner, "American Draws a Bead on JetBlue," *Business Week* (June 24, 2002): 48; R. C. Ford, "David Neeleman, CEO of JetBlue Airways, on People = Strategy = Growth," *Academy of Management Executive* (May 2004): 139–143; L. Zuckerman, "JetBlue, Exception Among Airlines, Is Likely to Post a Profit," *New York Times* (November 7, 2001): C3; E. Wong, "Airline's New Diet Has Rivals Watching," *New York Times* (January 12, 2003): Section 3: 1, 11; E. Wong, "Delta Answer to JetBlue Is Set to Fly Next Week," *New York Times* (April 12, 2003): C1–2.

23 M. Maynard, "Virgin Plans to Build Its New Discount Air Carrier in U.S. from Scratch," *New York Times* (June 8, 2004): C2; W. Zellner, "Is JetBlue's Flight Plan Flawed?" *Business Week* (February 16, 2004): 72–75; M. Wells, "Lord of the Skies," *Forbes* (October 14, 2002): 130–138.

24 B. Lavery, "Price Competition Leads to Profit Warning from Ryanair," *New York Times* (January 29, 2004): W1, 7; K. Capell, "Ryanair Rising: Ireland's Discount Carrier Is Defying Gravity as the Industry Struggles," *Business Week* (June 2, 2003): 40–41; "The Squeeze on Europe's Air Fares," *The Economist* (May 26, 2001): 57–58; K. Done, "Ryanair Continues to Escape Turbulence," *Financial Times* (November 6, 2001): 23.

appendix a

HR Manager Position Description, Competencies, Certification, Test Specifications, and Salaries, Incentives, and Bonuses

A. SENIOR HR MANAGER POSITION DESCRIPTION AND CANDIDATE SPECIFICATIONS

POSITION: Vice President, Human Resources
COMPANY: Nationwide Clothing Retailer
LOCATION: Midwestern United States
REPORTS TO: President

COMPANY

Is an exciting, high-growth, publicly held specialty retailer of quality casual, classic American sportswear that appeals to customers of all ages yet specifically targets people in their 20s. As the "keeper of the culture," the ideal candidate must strongly embody and reinforce their unique brand image, which is casual, classic, and all-American.

Given the Company's distinctive culture and strong brand image, the Human Resource Department is critical to the continued success of the Company. The ideal candidate will bring a fresh and creative approach to the Human Resource Department to further the brand position through the recruitment, training, and motivation of all employees. The candidate must also be nonpolitical and able to diplomatically voice his/her opinions while operating in a team-oriented environment.

IDEAL CANDIDATE SPECIFICATIONS

- Build upon a premier recruiting program that reflects energy, vitality, and a team-oriented atmosphere.
- Establish a process to identify and recruit the very best brand representatives (sales associates) to ensure an ongoing flow of future talent for the business.
- Institute a program of design training and establish a reputation in programs that ensures that the Company becomes the number one choice of design graduates from the best schools in the country.

PROFESSIONAL CHARACTERISTICS

- Has built a strong career with either a "best of class" consumer or technology company that places a premium on attracting top talent or a premier organizational consulting firm that has a strong human resource focus.

- Quickly understands the critical organizational structure and unique culture to ensure the future growth of the business and its supporting mechanisms, i.e., recruiting, training, and succession planning and other key human resource aspects to accomplish this objective.
- Successfully tailors a new compensation program that reflects shareholder value, corporate profitability, and individual unit/group objectives.
- Able to partner with top management to bring a critical human resources perspective that complements the strategic, merchandising, business, and financial acumen of the Company.
- Has a passion for the Company's distinctive and powerful lifestyle brand.
- Has a "sixth sense" that allows them to grasp the inherent uniqueness of the Company's brand image and identify those same great qualities in prospective employees at all levels of the organization.
- Thrives in a team-oriented and creative atmosphere, yet also has the ability to bring a tough perspective to top management in human resources and other business issues.
- Takes a creative approach as a leader and partners with the Company's top management team.

B. DESIRED COMPETENCIES FOR HR PROFESSIONALS

Strategic management competencies regarding:
- Industry and environment knowledge
- Company understanding
- Financial understanding
- Global perspective/knowledge
- Strategic visioning
- Triad orientation
- Multiple stakeholder sensitivity
- e-business orientation and thinking

Leadership and managerial competencies relevant to:
- Strategic analysis
- Managing diversity
- Problem solving
- Creating a learning culture
- Decision making
- Planning skills
- Adaptability
- Resource allocation
- Shaping value

Change and knowledge management competencies for:
- Consulting and communicating
- Group process facilitation
- Organizational diagnosis
- Partnering and relationship building
- Designing and monitoring planned change efforts

- Assessing impact
- Managing learning transfer
- Negotiating

Professional and technical competencies in:
- Organization and job design
- Workforce planning, staffing, and workflow management
- Performance management
- Education/training/development
- Compensation/reward/recognition systems
- Employee communications and involvement
- Succession planning
- Employee and labor relations
- Safety/health/wellness
- Diversity management
- Technological awareness
- Strong personal and professional ethics

C. PROFESSIONAL CERTIFICATION

The Society for Human Resource Management (SHRM) has established the Human Resource Certification Institute to certify human resource professionals. The institute's purposes are to:

- recognize individuals who have demonstrated expertise in particular fields;
- raise and maintain professional standards;
- identify a body of knowledge as a guide to practitioners, consultants, educators, and researchers;
- help employers identify qualified applicants; and
- provide an overview of the field as a guide to self-development.

The certification institute has two levels of accreditation: (1) basic (PHR); and (2) senior (SPHR). The basic accreditation is the professional in human resources (PHR). The examinations for the PHR and SPHR focus on the same six major areas. The difference between the two examinations is the weight given to each area. The six major areas and the weights give to each area for the PHR and the SPHR are shown in section D of this appendix. Detailed contents of each area are also provided on the Institute's website. You will see that the contents are consistent with the materials covered in all the chapters of this textbook. The senior-level accreditation (SPHR) is designed for the senior professional in human resources and focuses more on the strategic/policy aspects of HR and the roles for the effective HR department shown earlier.

The Human Resources Certification Institute (http://www.hrci.org) recommends that HR professionals pursuing the SPHR designation have 6–8 years of professional work experience before taking the examination, but 2 years is the minimum requirement. All professionals receiving accreditation are listed in the *Register of Accredited Personnel and Human Resource Professionals*. In 2004 the institute began offering certification in Global HR. See their website for a description of these competences. For a further discussion of them, also see D. R. Briscoe and R. S. Schuler, *International Human Resource Management*, 2nd ed. (London: Routledge, 2004).

D. SHRM'S TEST SPECIFICATIONS FOR THE PHR AND SPHR CERTIFICATION EXAMINATIONS

CERTIFICATION EXAMINATION PROGRAMS		
AREA	**% PHR EXAM**	**% SPHR EXAM**
STRATEGIC MANAGEMENT	12%	26%

Responsibilities in Strategic Management
- Interpret information related to the organization's operations from internal sources, including financial/accounting, marketing, operations, information technology, and individual employees, in order to participate in strategic planning and policy making.
- Participate as a partner in the organization's strategic planning process.
- Provide direction and guidance during changes in organizational processes, operations, and culture that balances the expectations and needs of the organization, its employees, and other stakeholders (including customers).
- Cultivate leadership and ethical values in self and others through modeling and teaching.
- Monitor legislative environment for proposed changes in law and take appropriate action to support, modify, or stop the proposed action (e.g., write to a member of Congress, provide expert testimony at a public hearing, lobby legislators).

Knowledge in Strategic Management
- Knowledge of internal and external environmental scanning techniques.
- Knowledge of strategic planning process and implementation.
- Knowledge of techniques to sustain creativity and innovation.

WORKFORCE PLANNING AND EMPLOYMENT	26%	16%

Responsibilities in Workforce Planning and Employment
- Identify staffing requirements to meet the goals and objectives of the organization.
- Conduct job analyses to write job descriptions and develop job competencies.
- Develop a succession planning process.
- Establish hiring criteria based on the competencies needed.
- Assess internal workforce, labor market, and recruitment agencies to determine the availability of qualified applicants.

Knowledge in Workforce Planning and Employment
- Knowledge of immigration laws (e.g., visas, I-9).
- Knowledge of recruitment methods and sources.
- Knowledge of staffing alternatives (e.g., telecommuting, outsourcing).
- Knowledge of planning techniques (e.g., succession planning, forecasting).
- Knowledge of reliability and validity of selection tests/tools/methods.
- Knowledge of impact of compensation and benefits plans on recruitment and retention.
- Knowledge of international HR and implications of international workforce for workforce planning and employment.
- Knowledge of downsizing and outplacement.

AREA	% PHR EXAM	% SPHR EXAM
HUMAN RESOURCE DEVELOPMENT	15%	13%

Responsibilities in Human Resource Development
- Conduct needs analyses to identify and establish priorities regarding human resource development activities.
- Develop training programs.
- Implement training programs.
- Evaluate training programs.

Knowledge in Human Resource Development
- Knowledge of training methods, programs, and techniques.
- Knowledge of performance appraisal and performance management methods.

COMPENSATION AND BENEFITS	20%	16%

Responsibilities in Compensation and Benefits
- Analyze, select, implement, maintain, and administer executive compensation, stock purchase, stock options, and incentive and bonus programs.
- Analyze, develop, implement, and maintain compensation policies and a pay structure consistent with the organization's strategic objectives.

Knowledge in Compensation and Benefits
- Knowledge of federal, state, and local compensation and benefit laws (e.g., FLSA, ERISA, and COBRA).
- Knowledge of accounting practices related to compensation and benefits (e.g., excess group term life, compensatory time).
- Knowledge of job evaluation methods.
- Knowledge of benefit plans (e.g., health insurance, pension, education, health club).
- Knowledge of international compensation laws and practices (e.g., expatriate compensation, socialized medicine, mandated retirement).
- Knowledge of job pricing and pay structure.
- Knowledge of incentive and variable pay methods.

EMPLOYEE AND LABOR RELATIONS	21%	24%

Responsibilities in Employee and Labor Relations
- Promote, monitor, and measure the effectiveness of employee relations activities.
- Assist in establishing work rules and monitor their applications and enforcement to ensure fairness and consistency (for union and nonunion environments).
- Develop grievance and disciplinary policies and procedures to ensure fairness and consistency.

Knowledge in Employee and Labor Relations
- Knowledge of applicable federal, state, and local laws affecting employment in union and nonunion environments (e.g., antidiscrimination laws, sexual harassment, labor relations, privacy).
- Knowledge of individual employment rights issues and practices (e.g., employment-at-will, negligent hiring, defamation, employees' rights to bargain collectively).

AREA	% PHR EXAM	% SPHR EXAM
OCCUPATIONAL HEALTH, SAFETY, AND SECURITY	6%	5%

Responsibilities in Occupational Health, Safety, and Security
- Ensure compliance with all applicable federal, state, and local workplace health and safety laws and regulations.
- Implement injury/occupational illness prevention program.
- Implement workplace injury/occupational illness procedures (e.g., workers' compensation, OSHA).

Knowledge in Occupational Health, Safety, and Security
- Knowledge of potential violent behavior and workplace violence conditions.
- Knowledge of workplace injury and occupational illness compensation laws and programs (e.g., workers' compensation).
- Knowledge of employee assistance programs.

E. SALARIES, INCENTIVE PAY, AND VARIATION IN PAY

HR Professionals are making strides on the earnings front. According to the 2004 Mercer Benchmark Database Human Resource Management Survey of the most common HR positions in more than 1,900 companies, annual cash compensation ranged from the low of $51,000 (trainer) to a high of $220,200 (top HR executive with industrial relations experience).

SALARIES

Pay growth for many HR positions was stronger than the rate of inflation. In 2004 seven of the ten most common HR positions had pay increases of 4% or more and only one position (senior HR generalist) saw an increase that was less than the rate of inflation. Trainers received the largest pay increases at 9.0%, followed by the top HR executive (without industrial relations) at 7.5%. The median salary for the top HR executive (without industrial relations) was $220,200; the median salary for HR directors was $131,00; the median salary for compensation managers was $100,800. Other median salaries were as follows: Senior HR managers received $93,500. Employment and recruiting managers received $93,000. Benefits managers received $89,600. Payroll managers received $74,100. Senior compensation analysts received $69,000. And trainers received $46,900.

INCENTIVES AND BONUSES

Growth in HR compensation has come somewhat more from increases in incentive pay rather than increases in base pay. For example, the position of human resource director saw only 3.6% growth in median base pay from 2003 to 2004, but 5.6% growth in total cash compensation. This reflects a growing trend over the past few years of putting more pay at risk at lower levels in the organization. Companies more frequently are using variable pay to differentiate their strongest performers, and they are extending this pay philosophy to their HR professionals.

The 2004 Mercer Benchmark Database Human Resource Management Survey examined the use of both short-term and long-term incentives for all HR positions in the survey. Not surprisingly, senior-level executives are most likely to be eligible for both types of incentives. About two-thirds of HR executives are eligible for long-term incentives, which usually include non-qualified stock options, incentive stock options and restricted stock. Almost all HR executives are eligible for short-term incentives such as annual bonuses. Actual incentive awards ranged from 27% to 37% of media base pay for the top-level positions.

Variations by Industry, Size and Geography

Factors such as industry, company size, and geography also affect pay levels for HR professionals. Employers in the government, nonprofit and education sectors generally are on the low end of the pay scale for all HR positions, while the highest pay levels are found in banking/financial services and nondurable manufacturing. But even with these private sector firms, there is tremendous pay variation. For example, median total cash compensation for the top benefits executive was highest in banking/financial services ($186,000) compared to health care ($146,100). Similar pay variations were found for all HR positions in the survey.

Pay also varies by company size. Usually, larger firms pay more than smaller firms, although this general pattern is not perfect. For instance, median total cash compensation for HR managers in companies with fewer than 1,000 employees was $80,900, compared to $91,000 in companies with 1,000 to 9,999 employees and $97,200 in companies with 10,000 or more employees.

Geography also plays a role in determining pay for HR professionals. Regionally, the highest pay is found in the Northeast and the West Coast. A benefits manager, for example, would receive median total cash compensation of $94,700 in the Northeast, $99,400 on the West Coast, $82,900 in the Southeast, $87,700 in the South Central region of the U.S., and $83,400 in the North Central Region. These variations in pay are similar to those found for jobs in other specialty functions.

Credits: Compensation data were reported in J. Vocino, "HR Compensation Continues to Rise," (November 2004): 73–88. Annual compensation data for HR professionals in the U.S. can also be found at the Bureau of National Affairs in Washington, D.C. (http://hrlibrary.bna.com). Compensation data for HR positions around the world can be found in the Worldwide Total Remuneration study published by TowerPerrin and can be located at www.towersperrin.com.

appendix b

STATISTICS FOR MANAGING HUMAN RESOURCES

Throughout, this book refers to numerous research studies that provide documentation for its assertions. Readers who wish to learn more about the studies cited are encouraged to consult the original sources listed in the notes for each chapter. Much of this literature requires some basic familiarity with the statistics and research methods used in human resource management. This appendix describes some of the basic concepts needed to understand the original research reports. Although this appendix uses examples relevant to selection and placement (described in Chapter 7), the basic concepts described here also apply to research on most other topics.

Regardless of the method or site used to study human resource issues, researchers need to be concerned about the reliability and validity of measurement devices. *Reliability* refers to the consistency of measurement and *validity* relates to the truth or accuracy of measurement. Both are expressed by a *correlation coefficient* (denoted by the symbol r).

CORRELATION COEFFICIENT

A correlation coefficient expresses the degree of linear relationship between two sets of scores. A positive correlation exists when high values on one measure (e.g., a job knowledge test) are associated with high scores on another measure (e.g., overall ratings of job performance). A negative correlation exists when high scores on one measure are associated with low scores on another measure. The range of possible correlation coefficients is from +1 (a perfect positive correlation coefficient) to –1 (a perfect negative correlation coefficient). Several linear relationships represented by plotting actual data are shown in Exhibit B.1.

The correlation between scores on a predictor (x) and a criterion (y) is typically expressed for a sample as r_{xy}. If we did not have a sample but were able to compute our correlation on the population of interest, we would express the correlation as ρ_{xy} (ρ is the Greek letter *rho*). In almost all cases, researchers do not have access to the entire population. Therefore, they must estimate the population correlation coefficient based on data from a sample of the population. For instance, an organization may desire to know the correlation between a test for computer programming ability (scores on a predictor, x) and job performance (scores on a performance appraisal rating form, y) for all its computer programmers, but decides it cannot afford to test all computer programmers (i.e., the population of interest). Instead, the organization may select a sample of computer programmers and estimate the correlation coefficient in the population (ρ_{xy}) based on the observed correlation in the sample (r_{xy}).

For each scatterplot in Exhibit B.1, a solid line represents the pattern of data points. Each line is described by an equation, which takes the general form for a straight line: $y = a + bx$, where a is the point at which the line inter-

Ex B.1   **Scatterplots Indicating Possible Relationships between Selection Test Scores and Job Performance Scores**

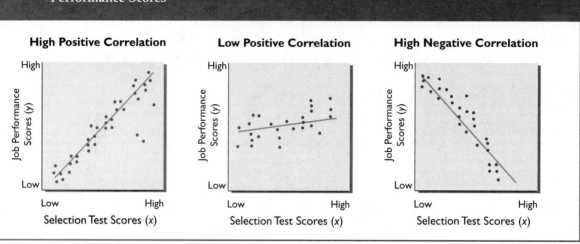

cepts the y-axis and b is the slope of the line. Such equations, called *prediction equations,* allow researchers to estimate values of y (the criterion) from their knowledge of x (the predictor). For example, we may conduct a study to determine the correlation between sales performance (i.e., dollar sales volume) and number of years of sales experience, for a group of salespeople. Once we have developed a prediction equation, we can then estimate how well a sales applicant might perform on the job. The equation might read,

Dollar Sales per Month = $50,290 + $2,000 × Years of Sales Experience

Using this equation, we would predict that a salesperson with 10 years of experience will generate $70,290 a month in sales, while a new salesperson with only one year of experience will be expected to generate only $52,290 a month in sales.

As you might expect, decision makers often employ more than one predictor in their equations. For example, organizations often use multiple predictors when making selection and placement decisions. Similar to that of the single-predictor approach, the purpose of multiple prediction is to estimate a criterion (y) from a linear combination of predictor variables: $y = a + b_1x_1 + b_2x_2 + \ldots + b_mx_m$). Such equations are called *multiple-prediction equations* or *multiple-regression equations.* The bs are the regression weights applied to the predictor measures. The relationship between the predictors and the criterion score is referred to as the *multiple-correlation coefficient* (denoted by the symbol R).

For example, suppose a manager believes that sales are a function of years of experience, education, and shyness (scored 0 for people who are not very shy to 7 for people who are very shy). To determine whether the manager's intuition is correct, we might conduct a research study. Information on each of these predictors could be collected, along with sales performance, or criterion, data. A multiple-regression equation such as the following could be generated:

Dollar Sales per Month = $25,000 + ($1,500 × Years of Experience) + ($500 × Years of Schooling) − ($25 × Score on Shyness)

This equation would indicate that a salesperson who scores low on shyness (1) and has 10 years of experience plus a college degree (16 years of schooling) will be expected to generate $47,975 in sales [$25,000 + ($1,500 × 10) + ($1,500 × 16) − (25 × 1)].

Multiple-regression analysis has been used to determine how to combine information from multiple selection devices. Multiple regression has also been used to assess such things as the effects of rater and ratee characteristics (e.g., sex, experience, prior performance rating, and rate of pay) on performance appraisal and pay decisions and to measure the effects of organizational characteristics (e.g., size, industry, and sales) on human resource planning and policies.

RELIABILITY

If a measure such as a selection test is to be useful, it must yield reliable results. The reliability of a measure can be defined and interpreted in several ways. Each of these methods is based on the notion that observed scores (x) comprise true scores (T) plus some error (E) or $x = T + E$ where T is the expected score if there were no error in measurement. To the extent that observed scores on a test are correlated with true scores, a test is said to be reliable. That is, if observed and true scores could be obtained for every individual who took a personnel selection test, the squared correlation between observed and true scores in the population is (ρ^2_x) would be called the reliability coefficient for that selection test.

One means of estimating reliability is *test-retest reliability* (ρ_{xx}). This method is based on testing a sample of individuals twice with the same measure and then correlating the results to produce a reliability estimate.

Another means of estimating the reliability of a measure is to correlate scores on alternate forms of the measure. *Alternate test forms* are any two test forms that have been constructed in an effort to make them parallel; their observed score means, variances (i.e., measures of the spread of scores about the means), and correlations with other measures may be equal or very similar.[4] They are also intended to be similar in content.

A problem with test-retest reliability and alternate forms reliability is the necessity of testing twice. In contrast, *internal consistency reliability* is estimated based on only one administration of a measure. The most common method, *coefficient* α (alpha), yields a *split-half reliability* estimate. That is, the measure (e.g., a test) is divided into two parts, which are considered alternate forms of each other, and the relationship between these two parts is an estimate of the measure's reliability.

Researchers are interested in assessing the reliability of measures based on one or more of these methods because reliability is a necessary condition for determining validity. The reliability of a measure sets a limit on how highly the measure can correlate with another measure, because it is very unlikely that a measure will correlate more strongly with a different measure than with itself.

ESTIMATING POPULATION COEFFICIENTS

If we were able to assess the relationship between a predictor and a criterion in a population of interest with no measurement error, then we would have computed the true correlation coefficient for the population, ρ_{xy}. Because we almost never have the population available and almost always have measurement error, our observed correlation coefficients underestimate the population coefficients. That is, predictor and criterion unreliability are statistical artifacts that lower predictor-criterion relationships.[5]

Two other statistical artifacts that obscure true relationships are sampling error and range restriction. A *sampling error* is an inaccuracy resulting from the use of a sample that is smaller than the population when computing the validity coefficient. A *range restriction* is a correlation or validity coefficient computed between the predictor and criterion scores for a restricted group of individuals. For example, suppose you were interested in determining the correlation between height and weight. If you had data that reflected the entire range of human variability, the correlation would be fairly substantial. However, if you studied only retired adult men, the correlation would be artificially low owing to the restricted range of heights and weights represented in your sample.

Formulas have been developed to remove the effects of predictor unreliability, criterion unreliability, and range restriction, and to determine sampling error variance. Researchers can use these correction formulas to remove the influence of statistical artifacts and, consequently, obtain a better idea of the predictor-criterion relationship in the relevant population. A number of studies have examined the effects of variations in sample size, range restriction, and reliability on the size and variability of observed validity coefficients. These studies have improved our understanding of how observed validity coefficients are affected by measurement error and statistical artifacts.

VALIDITY

As defined in the American Psychological Association's *Principles for the Validation and Use of Personnel Selection Procedures*, validity is the degree to which inferences from scores on tests or assessments are supported by evidence. This means that validity refers to the inferences made from the use of a measure, not to the measure itself. Two common strategies used to justify the inferences made from scores on measures are criterion-related validation and content-oriented validation.

CRITERION-RELATED VALIDATION

Criterion-related validation empirically assesses how well a predictor measure forecasts a criterion measure. Usually, predictor measures are scores on one or more selection "tests" (e.g., a score from an interview or a score to reflect the amount of experience), and criteria measures represent job performance (e.g., dollar sales per year or supervisory ratings of performance). Two types of criterion-related validation strategies are concurrent validation and predictive validation. These are shown in Exhibit B.2. *Concurrent validation* evaluates the relationship between a predictor and a criterion for all participants in the study at the same time. For example, the HR department could use this strategy to determine the correlation between years of experience and job performance. The department would collect from each person in the study information about years of experience and performance scores. All persons in the study would have to be working in similar jobs, generally in the same job family or classification. Then, a correlation would be computed between the predictor scores and criterion scores.

The steps in determining predictive validity are similar, except that the predictor is measured sometime before the criterion is measured. Thus, *predictive validity* is determined by measuring an existing group of employees on a predictor and then later gathering their criterion measures.

The classic example of a predictive validation analysis is AT&T's Management Progress Study.[1] In that study, researchers at AT&T administered an assessment center to 422 male employees. Then, they stored the scores from the assessment center and waited. After eight years, they correlated the assessment center scores with measures of how far the same individuals progressed in AT&T's management hierarchy. For a group of college graduates, the predictions were highly accurate; a correlation of .71 was obtained between the assessment center predictions and the level of management achieved.

CONTENT-ORIENTED VALIDATION

On many occasions, employers are not able to obtain sufficient empirical data for a criterion-related study. Consequently, other methods of validation are useful. One of the most viable is *content-oriented validation*. It differs from a criterion-related strategy in that it uses subjective judgments and logic as the basis for arguing that a predictor is likely to be effective in forecasting a criterion. To employ a content validation strategy, one must know the duties of the actual job. As discussed in Chapter 5, information about job tasks and duties can be obtained using one or more job analysis procedures. Once the duties are known, then logic is used to argue that a predictor is relevant to performance in the job. For example, if a job analysis showed that word processing duties were a substantial portion of a job, then you might logically

---

Ex B.2   Criterion-Related Validation Strategies

CONCURRENT VALIDATION		
Time I	**Time I**	**Time I**
Test (predictor) scores are gathered.	Criterion scores are gathered.	The correlation between scores on predictor measures (*x*) and criterion measures (*y*), r_{xy}, is calculated.
PREDICTIVE VALIDATION		
Time I	**Time 2**	**Time 2**
Test (predictor) scores are gathered.	Criterion scores are gathered.	The correlation between scores on predictor measures (*x*) and criterion measures (*y*), r_{xy}, is calculated.

conclude that a test of word processing skills would be a valid predictor of job performance. For this type of validation, the most important data are job analysis results.

VALIDITY GENERALIZATION

Since the mid-1900s, hundreds of criterion-related validation studies have been conducted in organizations to determine the predictive effectiveness of HR measures (e.g., ability tests) for selecting and placing individuals.[2] Often, the validity coefficients for the same or a similar predictor-criterion relationship differed substantially from one setting to another. Although researchers were aware that these differences were affected by range restriction, predictor unreliability, criterion unreliability, and sampling error, only recently were corrections for these statistical artifacts integrated into systematic procedures for estimating to what degree true validity estimates for the same predictor-criterion relationship generalize across settings.

A series of studies has applied validity generalization procedures to validity coefficient data for clerical jobs, computer programming jobs, petroleum industry jobs, and so on. In general, these investigations showed that the effects of range restriction, predictor unreliability, criterion unreliability, and sample size accounted for much of the observed variance in validity coefficients for the same or similar test-criterion relationship within an occupation (i.e., a job grouping or job family). Thus, the estimated true (corrected) validity coefficients were higher and less variable than the observed (uncorrected) validity coefficient.

The implication of these findings is that inferences (predictions) from scores on selection tests can be transported across situations for similar jobs. That is, if two similar jobs exist in two parts of an organization, a given selection test may have approximately the same validity coefficients for both jobs. If validity generalization can be successfully argued, an organization can save a great deal of time and money developing valid, job-related predictors when the inferences from a predictor for a job have already been established.

The concept of validity generalization, or *meta-analysis,* has also been applied to other areas of HR research.[3] Such research has led to a better understanding of the effectiveness of interventions such as training programs, goal-setting programs, and performance measurement (appraisal) programs.

CROSS-VALIDATION

HR researchers are also interested in how stable their prediction equations are across samples. Cross-validation studies address this concern. For the prediction equations developed by researchers to be of any practical use, they must produce consistent results. *Cross-validation* is a procedure for determining how much capitalization on chance has affected the prediction equation, (or *regression weights*). In the case of HR selection research, for example, one is interested in how well the regression weights estimated in a sample of job incumbents will predict the criterion value of new job applicants not tested in the sample.

Traditional or empirical cross-validation typically involves holding out some of the data from the initial sample and then applying the equation developed in the initial sample to the holdout sample to evaluate the equation's stability. In general, this procedure is less precise than one using a formula for estimating the stability of regression equations. The reason for this is that in formula-based estimates, all the available information (the total sample) is used at once in estimating the original weights.

Credits: The authors wish to express their thanks to Michael Burke, Tulane University, for his contributions, comments, and suggestions for the materials contained in this appendix.

ENDNOTES

1   A. Howard, "College Experience and Managerial Performance," *Journal of Applied Psychology* 53 (1968): 530–552. For a discussion of the AT&T Management Progress Study, as well as an overview of assessment centers, see A. Howard, "An Assessment of Assessment Centers," *Academy of Management Journal* 17(71) (1974): 115–134. See also A. Howard and D. W. Bray, *Managerial Lives in Transition: Advancing Age and Changing Times* (New York: Guilford, 1988).

2   For a review of validity generalization research, K. R. Murphy (ed.), *Validity Generalization: A Critical Review (Volume in the Applied Psychology Series)* (Mahwah, NJ: Lawrence Erlbaum 2002).

3   G. V. Glass coined the term *meta-analysis* to refer to the statistical analysis of the findings of many individual studies, in "Primary, Secondary, and Meta-Analysis of Research," *Educational Researcher* 5 (1976): 3–8. Numerous articles and books have been written on the subject of meta-analysis (of which validity generalization can be considered a subset); useful texts in this area are G. V. Glass, B. McGaw, and M. L. Smith, *Meta-Analysis in Social Research* (Beverly Hills, CA: Sage, 1981); F. M. Wolf, *Meta-Analysis: Quantitative Methods for Research Synthesis (Quantitative Applications in the Social Sciences)* (Newbury Park, CA: Sage, 1986); and J. E. Hunter and F. L. Schmidt, *Methods of Meta-Analysis: Correcting Error and Bias in Research Findings* (Newbury Park, CA: Sage, 1990).

name index

subject index

H

I